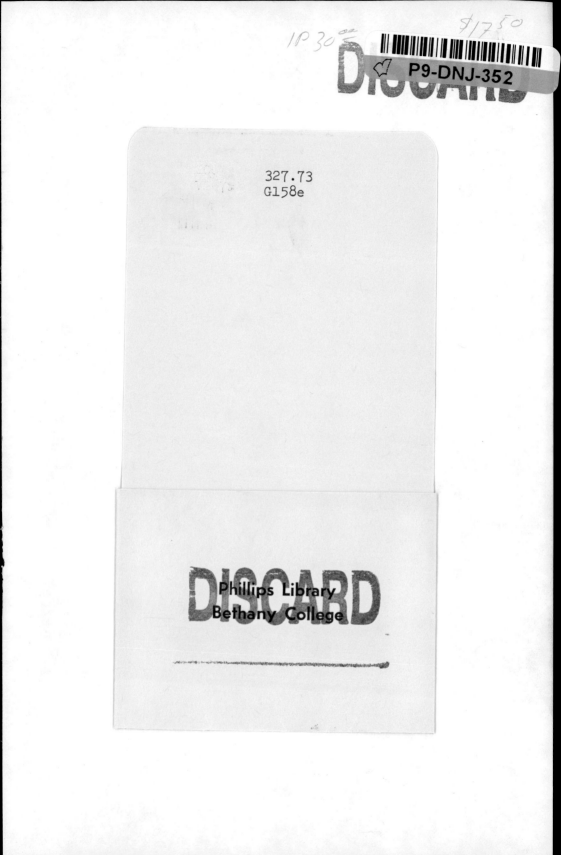

THE EVOLUTION OF OUR
Latin-American Policy

THE EVOLUTION OF OUR
Latin-American Policy

A Documentary Record

COMPILED AND EDITED BY

JAMES W. GANTENBEIN

1971
OCTAGON BOOKS
New York

Reprinted 1971

by special arrangement with Columbia University Press

OCTAGON BOOKS

A Division of Farrar, Straus & Giroux, Inc.

19 Union Square West

New York, N. Y. 10003

Library of Congress Catalog Card Number: 72-159187

ISBN 0-374-92987-4

Manufactured by Braun-Brumfield, Inc.
Ann Arbor, Michigan

Printed in the United States of America

To L.E.G.

WHO HAS ALWAYS BEEN
AN INSPIRATION TO HER MANY
NIECES AND NEPHEWS

Preface

IN COMPILING these papers I have endeavored to trace through official documents the principal lines of our foreign policy regarding Latin America. I have no theory or principle to prove or explain and have no purpose of presenting either propaganda or criticism with respect to any period.

In a comparatively short work of this kind, it has been necessary to omit a number of important chapters and many important pages of chapters in the history of our diplomatic relations with the other American Republics. No pretense is made as to completeness.

I should stress that the compilation is entirely nonofficial. Most of the work was performed at the Library of Congress during a leave of absence. For both the selection and presentation of the material, I bear entire responsibility personally.

With respect to sources, the greater part of the documents, as is indicated in the footnotes, have been taken directly from United States Government publications, more particularly, *American State Papers* and *Foreign Relations of the United States,* the *Lansing Papers,* and *Press Releases* and the *Bulletin* of the Department of State; various numbers of the Department's Latin American and Inter-American Series, Conference Series, Treaty Series, and Executive Agreement Series; John Bassett Moore's monumental *Digest of International Law;* William M. Malloy's *Treaties,* etc., 1776–1909, and sequel volumes; J. Reuben Clark's *Memorandum on the Monroe Doctrine;* James D. Richardson's *Messages and Papers of the Presidents* (the most recent edition of which is not a Government publication, being published by the Bureau of National Literature, Inc., New York); and certain other works on specific subjects, including *Diplomatic History of the Panama Canal* (63d Congress, 2d Session, Senate Document No. 474), *Inquiry into Occupation and Administration of Haiti and the Dominican Republic* (67th Congress, 2d Session, Senate Document No. 794), and the proceedings of various inter-American conferences before the beginning of the Department of State Conference Series. A number of papers have also been taken from the publications of the Carnegie Endowment for International Peace: *The International Conferences of American States, 1889–1928,* prepared by James Brown Scott (Oxford University Press, New York,

1931; a supplement covering the years 1933–1940 was published in 1940); *Diplomatic Correspondence of the United States Concerning the Independence of the Latin American Nations,* prepared by William R. Manning (in 3 volumes, Oxford University Press, New York, 1925); and Dr. Manning's *Diplomatic Correspondence of the United States, Inter-American Affairs, 1831–1860* (in 12 volumes, Carnegie Endowment for International Peace, Washington, 1932–1939). Several documents have been quoted from the New York *Times.* The Pan American Union has very kindly furnished the text of the Charter of the Organization of American States as adopted at the Bogotá Conference in 1948, together with the accompanying diagram.

I have also found of assistance Thomas A. Bailey, *A Diplomatic History of the American People* (F. S. Crofts and Co., New York, 1940); Robert Bacon and James Brown Scott, *Latin America and the United States, Addresses by Elihu Root* (Harvard University Press, Cambridge, 1917); Ray Stannard Baker and William E. Dodd, *The Public Papers of Woodrow Wilson* (Harper and Brothers, New York, 1925–1927); Samuel F. Bemis, *A Diplomatic History of the United States* (Henry Holt and Company, New York, 1943), *The Latin American Policy of the United States* (Harcourt, Brace and Company, New York, 1943), Samuel F. Bemis, ed., *The American Secretaries of State and Their Diplomacy* (Alfred A. Knopf, New York, 1927–1929), and the same author with Grace Gardner Griffin, *Guide to the Diplomatic History of the United States, 1775–1921* (United States Government Printing Office, Washington, 1935); Joseph B. Bishop, *Theodore Roosevelt and His Time* (Charles Scribner's Sons, New York, 1920); James G. Blaine, *Political Discussions* (The Henry Brill Publishing Company, Norwich, Conn., 1887) ; Philippe Bunau-Varilla, *Panama; the Creation, Destruction and Resurrection* (McBride, Nast and Company, New York, 1914); Charles E. Chapman, *A History of the Cuban Republic* (The Macmillan Company, New York, 1927); Henry Steele Commager, *Documents of American History,* 3d ed. (F. S. Crofts and Co., New York, 1944); Tyler Dennett, *John Hay* (Dodd, Mead and Company, New York, 1933) ; Carl Russell Fish, *American Diplomacy* (Henry Holt and Company, New York, 1929); Albert Bushnell Hart, *The Monroe Doctrine* (Duckworth and Co., London, 1916); Edward Hertslet, *Map of Europe by Treaty* (Butterworth's, London, 1875); Charles E. Hughes, *The Pathway of Peace* (Harper and Brothers, New York and London, 1925); Charles Cheney Hyde, *International Law, Chiefly as Interpreted and Applied by the United States* (Little, Brown and Company, Boston, 1945); S. Shepard Jones, Denys P. Myers, Leland M. Goodrich and Marie J. Carroll, *Docu-*

ments on American Foreign Relations (World Peace Foundation, Boston, annual volumes, 1939–); *International Conciliation,* published monthly by the Carnegie Endowment for International Peace, New York); Philip C. Jessup, *Elihu Root* (Dodd, Mead and Company, New York, 1938); Carl Kelsey, *The American Intervention in Haiti and the Dominican Republic* (reprinted from Vol. C of the Annals of the American Academy of Political and Social Science, Philadelphia, 1922); John H. Latané and David W. Wainhouse, *A History of American Foreign Policy* (The Odyssey Press, New York, 1940); John M. Mathews, *American Foreign Relations* (D. Appleton–Century Company, New York, 1938); Dana G. Munro, *The United States and the Caribbean Area* (World Peace Foundation, Boston, 1934); William Starr Myers, *The Foreign Policies of Herbert Hoover* (Charles Scribner's Sons, New York, 1940) and *The State Papers and Other Public Writings of Herbert Hoover* (Doubleday, Doran and Company, Garden City, New York, 1934); John Carl Parish, *The Emergence of the Idea of Manifest Destiny* (University of California Press, Los Angeles, 1932); Walter Alison Phillips, *The Confederation of Europe* (Longmans, Green and Company, London, 1920); Dexter Perkins, *The Monroe Doctrine, 1823–1826* (Harvard University Press, Cambridge, 1932), *The Monroe Doctrine, 1826–1867* (Johns Hopkins Press, Baltimore, 1933), *The Monroe Doctrine, 1867–1907* (Johns Hopkins Press, Baltimore, 1937), and *Hands Off, a History of the Monroe Doctrine* (Little, Brown and Company, Boston, 1941); Theodore Roosevelt, *Theodore Roosevelt, an Autobiography* (Charles Scribner's Sons, New York, 1925); Graham H. Stuart, *Latin America and the United States* (D. Appleton–Century Company, New York, 1943); Samuel I. Rosenman, *The Public Papers and Addresses of Franklin D. Roosevelt* (Random House, New York, 1938, and the Macmillan Company, New York, 1941); Charles Seymour, *The Intimate Papers of Colonel House* (Houghton-Mifflin Company, Boston and New York, 1926); Sumner Welles, *Naboth's Vineyard, the Dominican Republic, 1844–1924* (Payson and Clarke, New York, 1928); and Mary W. Williams, *Anglo-American Isthmian Policy, 1815–1915* (American Historical Association, Humphrey-Milford-Oxford University Press, London, 1916).

I feel grateful to those publishers and institutions mentioned above which have granted permission to reprint certain documents in this collection; and I wish to note here my sincere appreciation of the facilities and kind assistance extended by the Library of Congress, the National Archives, and the Library of the Department of State. Also I feel much indebted to Miss Matilda L. Berg, Assistant Editor of

Columbia University Press, for her generous and competent assistance in preparing the manuscript for printing.

Berlin, Germany   J.W.G.
June 10, 1949

Contents

Contents

Contents

Contents

THE ROOSEVELT-TRUMAN ADMINISTRATIONS

Contents

II: THE MONROE DOCTRINE

BACKGROUND

ENUNCIATON OF THE DOCTRINE

CERTAIN INTERPRETATIONS AND APPLICATIONS IN THE NINETEENTH CENTURY

PERIOD OF THE "ROOSEVELT COROLLARY"

SUBSEQUENT INTERPRETATIONS AND APPLICATIONS

III: INDEPENDENCE OF CUBA

INDEPENDENCE OF CUBA

Contents xix

IV: THE PANAMA CANAL CONCESSION

THE PANAMA CANAL CONCESSION

V: CERTAIN CONTROVERSIES WITH MEXICO

WAR OF 1846–1848

THE PERIOD OF 1911–1916

AGRARIAN AND PETROLEUM CLAIMS

VI: INTERVENTIONS IN NICARAGUA, HAITI, AND THE DOMINICAN REPUBLIC

Contents

The Dominican Republic

APPENDIX A: CERTAIN AGREEMENTS, RESOLUTIONS, AND CONVENTIONS OF VARIOUS INTER-AMERICAN CONFERENCES

First International Conference of American States, at Washington, October 2, 1889, to April 19, 1890

Contents

Contents

APPENDIX D: CERTAIN TREATIES AND AGREEMENTS WITH HAITI AND THE DOMINICAN REPUBLIC

HAITI

THE DOMINICAN REPUBLIC

I
General Principles

The Headwaters of Our
Latin-American Policy

FAREWELL ADDRESS of President George Washington to the People of the United States, September 17, 1796 (extract)

American State Papers, Foreign Relations, I, 34

OBSERVE GOOD FAITH and justice towards all nations; cultivate peace and harmony with all. Religion and morality enjoin this conduct; and can it be that good policy does not equally enjoin it? It will be worthy of a free, enlightened, and, at no distant period, a great nation, to give to mankind the magnanimous and too novel example of a people always guided by an exalted justice and benevolence. Who can doubt that, in the course of time and things, the fruits of such a plan would richly repay any temporary advantages which might be lost by a steady adherence to it? Can it be, that Providence has not connected the permanent felicity of a nation with its virtue? The experiment, at least, is recommended by every sentiment which ennobles human nature. Alas! is it rendered impossible by its vices?

In the execution of such a plan, nothing is more essential than that permanent inveterate antipathies against particular nations, and passionate attachments for others, should be excluded; and that, in place of them, just and amicable feelings towards all should be cultivated. The nation which indulges towards another an habitual hatred, or an habitual fondness, is, in some degree, a slave. It is a slave to its animosity or to its affection, either of which is sufficient to lead it astray from its duty and its interest. Antipathy in one nation against another, disposes each more readily to offer insult and injury, to lay hold of slight causes of umbrage, and to be haughty and intractable, when accidental or trifling occasions of dispute occur. Hence frequent collisions; obstinate, envenomed, and bloody contests. The nation, prompted by ill-will and resentment, sometimes impels to war the government, contrary to the best calculations of policy. The government sometimes participates in the national propensity, and adopts, through passion, what reason would reject; at other times, it makes the animosity of the nation subservient to projects of hostility, instigated by pride, ambition, and other sinister and pernicious motives. The peace, often, sometimes, perhaps, the liberty of nations has been the victim.

So, likewise, a passionate attachment of one nation to another produces a variety of evils. Sympathy for the favorite nation, facilitating the illusion of an imaginary common interest, in cases where no real common interest exists, and infusing into one the enmities of the other, betrays the former into a participation in the quarrels and wars of the latter, without adequate inducement or justification. It leads also to concessions to the favorite nation of privileges denied to others, which is apt doubly to injure the nation making the concessions; by unnecessarily parting with what ought to have been retained, and by exciting jealousy, ill-will, and a disposition to retaliate, in the parties from whom equal privileges are withheld: and it gives to ambitious, corrupted, or deluded citizens (who devote themselves to the favorite nation) facility to betray or sacrifice the interest of their own country, without odium, sometimes even with popularity; gilding with the appearances of a virtuous sense of obligation, a commendable deference for public opinion, or a laudable zeal for public good, the base or foolish compliances of ambition, corruption, or infatuation.

As avenues to foreign influence in innumerable ways, such attachments are particularly alarming to the truly enlightened and independent patriot. How many opportunities do they afford to tamper with domestic factions, to practice the art of seduction, to mislead public opinion, to influence or awe the public councils! Such an attachment of a small or weak, towards a great and powerful nation, dooms the former to be the satellite of the latter.

Against the insidious wiles of foreign influence (I conjure you to believe me fellow-citizens) the jealousy of a free people ought to be *constantly* awake; since history and experience prove that foreign influence is one of the most baneful foes of republican government. But that jealousy, to be useful, must be impartial; else it becomes the instrument of the very influence to be avoided, instead of a defence against it. Excessive partiality for one foreign nation, and excessive dislike for another, cause those whom they actuate to see danger only on one side, and serve to veil and even second the arts of influence on the other. Real patriots, who may resist the intrigues of the favorite, are liable to become suspected and odious; while its tools and dupes usurp the applause and confidence of the people, to surrender their interests.

The great rule of conduct for us, in regard to foreign nations, is, in extending our commercial relations, to have with them as little political connexion as possible. So far as we have already formed engagements, let them be fulfilled with perfect good faith. Here let us stop.

Europe has a set of primary interests, which to us have none, or a very remote relation. Hence she must be engaged in frequent controversies, the causes of which are essentially foreign to our concerns. Hence, therefore, it must be unwise in us to implicate ourselves, by artificial ties, in the ordinary vicissitudes of her politics, or the ordinary combinations and collisions of her friendships or enmities.

Our detached and distant situation invites, and ennables us to pursue, a different course. If we remain one people, under an efficient government, the period is not far off when we may defy material injury from external annoyance; when we may take such an attitude as will cause the neutrality we may at any time resolve upon, to be scrupulously respected; when belligerent nations, under the impossibility of making acquisitions upon us, will not lightly hazard the giving us provocation; when we may choose peace or war, as our interest, guided by justice, shall counsel.

Why forego the advantages of so peculiar a situation? Why quit our own, to stand upon foreign ground? Why, by interweaving our destiny with that of any part of Europe, entangle our peace and prosperity in the toils of European ambition, rivalship, interest, humor, or caprice?

'Tis our policy to steer clear of permanent alliances with any portion of the foreign world—so far, I mean, as we are now at liberty to do it: for let me not be understood as capable of patronising infidelity to existing engagements. I hold the maxim no less applicable to public than to private affairs, that honesty is always the best policy. I repeat it, therefore, let those engagements be observed in their genuine sense. But, in my opinion, it is unnecessary, and would be unwise, to extend them.

Taking care always to keep ourselves, by suitable establishments, on a respectable defensive posture, we may safely trust to temporary alliances for extraordinary emergencies.

Harmony, and a liberal intercourse with all nations, are recommended by policy, humanity, and interest. But even our commercial policy should hold an equal and impartial hand; neither seeking nor granting exclusive favors or preferences; consulting the natural course of things; diffusing and diversifying, by gentle means, the streams of commerce, but forcing nothing; establishing, with Powers so disposed, in order to give trade a stable course, to define the rights of our merchants, and to enable the Government to support them, conventional rules of intercourse, the best that present circumstances and mutual opinion will permit, but temporary, and liable to be, from time to time, abandoned or varied, as experience and circumstances shall dictate; constantly keeping in view, that 'tis folly in one nation to look for disinterested favors from another; that it must pay with a portion of its independence for whatever it may accept under that character; that by such acceptance it may place itself in the condition of having given equivalents for nominal favors, and yet with being reproached with ingratitude for not giving more. There can be no greater error than to expect or calculate upon real favors from nation to nation. 'Tis all illusion, which experience must cure—which a just pride ought to discard.

In offering to you, my countrymen, these counsels of an old and affectionate friend, I dare not hope they will make the strong and lasting impression I could wish; that they will control the usual current of the passions, or prevent our nation from running the course which has hitherto marked the destiny of nations: but if I may even flatter myself that they may be productive of some partial benefit, some occasional good; that they may now and then recur to moderate the fury of party spirit, to warn against the mischiefs of foreign intrigues, to guard against the impostures of pretended patriotism; this hope will be a full recompense for the solicitude for your welfare by which they have been dictated. . . .

INAUGURAL ADDRESS of President Thomas Jefferson, March 4, 1801 (extract)
American State Papers, Foreign Relations, I, 56

. . . ABOUT TO ENTER, fellow-citizens, on the exercise of duties which comprehend every thing dear and valuable to you, it is proper you should understand what I deem the essential principles of our Government, and consequently those which ought to shape its administration. I will compress them within the narrowest compass they will bear, stating the general principle, but not all its limitations. Equal and exact justice to all men, of whatever state or persuasion, religious or political; peace, commerce, and honest friendship, with all nations, entangling alliances with none . . .

Recognition of Independence

ROBERT SMITH, Secretary of State, to Joel Robert Poinsett, Appointed Special Agent of the United States to South America, June 28, 1810 (extract)

William R. Manning, *Diplomatic Correspondence of the United States Concerning the Independence of the Latin American Nations*, I, 6

SIR:

As a crisis is approaching which must produce great changes in the situation of Spanish America, and may dissolve altogether its colonial relations to Europe, and as the geographical position of the United States, and other obvious considerations, give them an intimate interest in whatever may effect the destiny of that part of the American continent, it is our duty to turn our attention to this important subject, and to take such steps, not incompatible with the neutral character and honest policy of the United States, as the occasion renders proper. With this view, you have been selected to proceed, without delay, to Buenos Ayres. You will make it your object, wherever it may be proper, to diffuse the impression that the United States cherish the sincerest good will towards the people of Spanish America as neighbors, as belonging to the same portion of the globe, and as having a mutual interest in cultivating friendly intercourse: that this disposition will exist, whatever may be their internal system or European relation with respect to which no interference of any sort is pretended: and that, in the event of a political separation from the parent country, and of the establishment of an independent system of National Government, it will coincide with the sentiments and policy of the United States to promote the most friendly relations, and the most liberal intercourse, between the inhabitants of this hemisphere, as having all a common interest, and as lying under a common obligation to maintain that system of peace, justice, and good will, which is the only source of happiness for nations.

Whilst you inculcate these as the principles and dispositions of the United States, it will be no less proper to ascertain those on the other side, not only towards the United States, but in reference to the great nations of Europe, and to the commercial and other connexions with them, respectively: and, generally, to inquire into the state, the characteristics, and the proportions, as to numbers, intelligence, and wealth, of the several parties, the amount of population, the extent and organization of the military force, and the pecuniary resources of the country.

The real as well as ostensible object of your mission is to explain the mutual advantages of commerce with the United States, to promote liberal and stable regulations, and to transmit seasonable information on the subject. In order that you may render the more service in this respect, and that you may, at the same time, enjoy the greater protection and respectability, you will be furnished with a credential letter, such as is held by sundry agents of the United States in the West Indies, and as was lately held by one at the Havana, and under the sanction of which you will give the requisite attention to commercial objects.

RICHARD RUSH, Secretary of State ad interim, to Caesar A. Rodney and John Graham, Special Commissioners of the United States to South America, July 18, 1817

William R. Manning, *Diplomatic Correspondence of the United States Concerning the Independence of the Latin American Nations*, I, 42

GENTLEMEN:

The contest between Spain and the Spanish colonies in the southern parts of this continent has been, from its commencement, highly interesting, under many views, to the United States. As inhabitants of the same hemisphere, it was natural that we should feel a solicitude for the welfare of the colonists. It was nevertheless our duty to maintain the neutral character with impartiality and allow of no privileges of any kind to one party, which were not extended to the other. The government of Spain viewing the colonies as in a state of rebellion, has endeavored to impose upon foreign powers in their intercourse with them, the conditions applicable to such a state. This pretension has not been acceded to by this government, which has considered the contest in the light of a civil war, in which the parties were equal. An entire conviction exists that the view taken on this point has been correct, and that the United States have fully satisfied every just claim of Spain.

In other respects we have been made to feel sensibly the progress of this contest. Our vessels have been seized and condemned, our citizens made captives and our lawful commerce, even at a distance from the theatre of the war, been interrupted. Acting with impartiality towards the parties, we have endeavored to secure from each a just return. In whatever quarter the authority of Spain was abrogated and an independent government erected, it was essential to the security of our rights that we should enjoy its friendship. Spain could not impose conditions on other powers incident to complete sovereignty in places where she did not maintain it. On this principle the United States have sent agents into the Spanish colonies, addressed to the existing authority, whether of Spain or of the colony, with instructions to cultivate its friendship and secure as far as practicable the faithful observance of our rights.

The contest, by the extension of the revolutionary movement and the greater stability which it appears to have acquired, becomes daily of more importance to the United States. It is by success that the colonists acquire new claims on other powers, which it may comport neither with their interest nor duty to disregard. Several of the colonies having declared their independence and enjoyed it for some years, and the authority of Spain being shaken in others, it seems probable that, if the parties be left to themselves, the most permanent political changes will be effected. It therefore seems incumbent on the United States to watch the movement in its subsequent steps with particular attention, with a view to pursue such course as a just regard for all those considerations which they are bound to respect may dictate.

Under these impressions, the President deems it a duty to obtain, in a manner more comprehensive than has heretofore been done, correct information of the actual state of affairs in those colonies. For this purpose he has appointed you commissioners, with authority to proceed, in a public ship, along the coast of South America, touching at the points where it is probable that the most precise and ample knowledge may be gained. The Ontario, Captain Biddle, is prepared to receive you on board at New York, and will have orders to sail as soon as you are ready to embark.

It is the President's desire that you go first to the River la Plate, visiting Buenos Ayres and Monte Video. On your way thither, you will call at Rio Janeiro delivering to our minister at that court the despatches which will be committed to your hands. On your return from Buenos Ayres, you will also touch, should circumstances allow it, at St. Salvador and Pernambuco. You will thence proceed to the Spanish Main, going to Margaretta, Cumana, Barcelona, Caracas and as far westward as Carthagena, looking in at any other convenient ports or places as you coast along.

In the different provinces or towns which you visit, your attention will be usefully, if not primarily, drawn to the following objects.

1. The form of government established, with the amount of population and pecuniary resources and the state and proportion as to numbers of intelligence and wealth of the contending parties, wherever a contest exists.

2. The extent and organization of the military force on each side, with the means open to each of keeping it up.

3. The names and characters of leading men, whether in civil life or as military chiefs, whose conduct and opinions shed an influence upon events.

4. The dispositions that prevail among the public authorities and people towards the United States and towards the great nations of Europe, with the probability of commercial or other connections being on foot, or desired, with either.

5. The principal articles of commerce, regarding the export and import trade. What articles from the United States find the best market? What prices do their productions, most useful in the United States, usually bear? The duties on exports and imports; are all nations charged the same?

6. The principal ports and harbors, with the works of defence.

7. The real prospect, so far as seems justly inferable from existing events and the operation of causes as well moral as physical in all the provinces where a struggle is going on, of the final and permanent issue.

8. The probable durability of the governments that have already been established with their credit, and the extent of their authority, in relation to adjoining provinces. This remark will be especially applicable to Buenos Ayres. If there be any reason to think, that the government established there is not likely to be permanent, as to which no opinion is here expressed, it will become desirable to ascertain the probable character and policy of that which is expected to succeed it.

9. In Caracas it is understood that there is, at present, no government, but that the forces are united under General Bolivar. It might be useful to know, whether any and what connection exists between this chief, and the chiefs or rulers at St. Domingo; also the number of negroes in arms.

Your stay at each place will not be longer than is necessary to a fair accomplishment of the objects held up. You will see the propriety, in all instances, of showing respect to the existing authority or government of whatever kind it may be, and of mingling a conciliatory demeanor with a strict observance of all established usages.

The track marked out for your voyage has been deemed the most eligible; but you will not consider yourselves as positively restricted to the limits or places specified. You will be free to deviate and touch at other places as your own judgments, acting upon circumstances and looking to the objects in view, may point out. In this respect the commander of the ship will have orders to conform to such directions as you may think fit to give him. You will however call first at Rio Janeiro, and not go further south than Buenos Ayres. At this point it is hoped that you may be able to command the means of obtaining useful information as respects Chili and Peru. You will also not fail to go to the Spanish Main, returning to the United States at as early a day as will comport with the nature and extent of your mission. Your observation and enquiries will not be exclusively confined to the heads indicated, but take other scope, keeping to the spirit of these instructions, as your own view of things upon the spot may suggest.

It only remains for me to add, that the President has great confidence in the ability and discretion with which you will execute, in all things, the trust committed to you, and that he anticipates from your report to this department such a statement of facts and views as may prove highly useful to the nation.

I have the honor [etc.]

JOHN QUINCY ADAMS, Secretary of State, to Richard Rush,
United States Minister to Great Britain, January 1, 1819
(extracts)

William R. Manning, *Diplomatic Correspondence of the United States Concerning the Independence of the Latin American Nations,* I, 85

IT IS MENTIONED in one of your despatches that Lord Castlereagh had made some enquiry of you, in what light the deputies from the South-American Revolutionary Governments were considered by that of the United-States? They have not been received or recognized in their official capacities, because that would have been equivalent to a formal recognition of the Governments from which they came, as Independent. But informal communications have been held with them, both verbal and written, freely and without disguise. We have considered the struggle between Spain and those Colonies, as a *Civil War,* the essential question of which was, their Independence of, or subjection to Spain. To this War, the avowed and real policy of the United-States has been to remain neutral; and the principles of Neutrality which we consider as applicable to the case are these. First; that the parties have, in respect to Foreign Nations, equal rights, and are entitled, as far as is practicable, to equal and the same treatment. Secondly; that while the contest is maintained, on both sides, with any reasonable prospect of eventual success, it would be a departure from Neutrality, to recognize, either the supremacy contended for by Spain, or the Independence contended for by the South-Americans. For to acknowledge either would be to take the side of that party, upon the very question at issue between them.

But while this state of things continues, an entire equality of treatment of the parties is not possible. There are circumstances arising from the nature of the contest itself, which produce unavoidable inequalities. Spain, for instance, is an acknowledged Sovereign Power, and as such, has Ministers and other accredited and priviledged agents to maintain her interests, and support her rights conformably to the usages of Nations. The South-Americans, not being acknowledged as Sovereign and Independent States, cannot have the benefit of such officers. We consider it, however, as among the obligations of Neutrality, to obviate this inequality, as far as may be practicable, without taking a side, as if the question of the War was decided. We listen therefore to the representations of their deputies or agents, and do them Justice as much as if they were formally accredited. By acknowledging the existence of a *Civil War,* the right of Spain, *as understood by* herself, is no doubt affected. She is no longer recognized as the Sovereign of the Provinces in Revolution against her. Thus far Neutrality itself operates against her, and not against the other party. This also is an inequality arising from the nature of the struggle: unavoidable, and therefore not incompatible with Neutrality.

But this state of things is temporary; and neither do the obligations of Neutrality require, nor do the rights, duties or interests of the neutral State permit that it should be unreasonably protracted. It naturally terminates with the preponderating success of either of the parties to the War.—If therefore we consider the Civil War, as no longer existing between Spain and Mexico, because there is no longer in that Province an organized Government, claiming to be Sovereign and Independent, and maintaining that claim by force of arms, upon the same principle, though differently applied, we think the period is fast approaching when it will be no longer a Civil War between Spain and Buenos-Ayres: because the Independence of the latter will be so firmly established, as to be beyond the reach of any reasonable pretension of Supremacy on the part of Spain. The mediation of the Allied European Powers, between Spain and her revolted Colonies, was solicited by Spain, with the professed object of obtaining

from the Allies a guarantee of the restoration of her Sovereign authority in South-America. But the very acceptance of the office of Mediators, upon such a basis, would have been a departure from Neutrality
by the Allies. This was clearly seen by Great-Britain, who very explicitly and repeatedly declared that her intention was in no event
whatever resulting from the mediation to employ force against the
South-Americans.

The Allies did, however, assent to become the mediators at the request of Spain alone, and upon the basis, that the object of the mediation should be, the restoration of the Spanish authority, though with
certain modifications favourable to the Colonies. As the United-
States were never invited to take a part in that mediation, so, as you
have been instructed, they neither desired, nor would have consented
to become parties to it, upon that basis. It appears, that in one of your
conversations with Lord Castlereagh, he expressed some regret that
the views of this Government, in relation to that question, were not
precisely the same as those of the British Cabinet, and that we disapprove of any interposition of third parties, upon any basis other
than that of the total emancipation of the Colonies.

The President wishes you to take an early and suitable occasion to
observe to Lord Castlereagh, that he hopes the difference between our
views and those of Great-Britain is more of form than of substance;
more founded in the degree of complacency respectively due by the
parties to the views of Spain, than to any inherent difference of
opinion upon the question to be solved;—that as Neutrals to the Civil
War, we think that no mediation between the parties ought to be
undertaken, without the assent of both parties to the War; and that
whether we consider the question of the conflict between Spanish
Colonial Dominion, and South-American Independence, upon principles, moral, or political, or upon those of the interest of either party
to the War, or of all other Nations as connected with them, whether
upon grounds of right or of fact, they all bring us to the same conclusion, that the contest cannot and ought not to terminate otherwise
than by the total Independence of South-America. Anxious, however,
to fulfil every obligation of good neighbourhood to Spain, notwithstanding our numerous and aggravated causes of complaint against
her, and especially desirous to preserve the friendship and good-will
of all the Allied European Powers, we have forborne, under circumstances of strong provocation, to take any decisive step which might
interfere with the course of their policy in relation to South-America.
We have waited patiently to see the effect of their mediation, without
an attempt to disconcert or defeat any measures upon which they
might agree for assuring its success. But convinced as we are that the

Spanish Authority never can be restored at Buenos-Ayres, in Chili, or in Venezuela, we wish the British Government and all the European Allies, to consider, how important it is to them as well as to us, that these newly formed States should be regularly recognized: not only because the right to such recognition cannot with Justice be long denied to them, but that they may be held to observe on their part the ordinary rules of the Law of Nations, in their intercourse with the civilized World. We particularly believe that the only effectual means of repressing the excessive irregularities and piratical depredations of armed vessels under their flags and bearing their Commissions, will be to require of them the observance of the principles, sanctioned by the practice of maritime Nations. It is not to be expected that they will feel themselves bound by the ordinary duties of Sovereign States, while they are denied the enjoyment of all their rights.

The Government of Buenos-Ayres have appointed a Consul General to reside in the United-States. He has applied as long since as last May, and again very recently for an *Exequatur,* which has not been issued; because that would be a formal recognition of his Government. You will in the most friendly manner mention to Lord Castlereagh, that the President has it in contemplation to grant this Exequatur, or otherwise to recognize the Government of Buenos-Ayres, at no remote period, should no event occur which will justify a further postponement of that intention. If it should suit the views of Great-Britain to adopt similar measures at the same time and in concert with us, it will be highly satisfactory to the President. When adopted, it will be a mere acknowledgment of the fact of Independence, and without deciding upon the extent of their Territory, or upon their claims to Sovereignty, in any part of the Province of La Plata, where it is not established and uncontested.

I am [etc.]

MESSAGE from President James Monroe to the United States House of Representatives, March 8, 1822

William R. Manning, *Diplomatic Correspondence of the United States Concerning the Independence of the Latin American Nations,* I, 146

To the House of Representatives of the United States:

In transmitting to the House of Representatives the documents called for by the resolution of that House of the 30th January, I consider it my duty to invite the attention of Congress to a very important subject, and to communicate the sentiments of the Executive on it, that, should Congress entertain similar sentiments, there may be such co-operation between the two departments of the Government as their respective rights and duties may require.

The revolutionary movement in the Spanish provinces in this hemisphere attracted the attention and excited the sympathy of our fellow-citizens from its commencement. This feeling was natural and honorable to them, from causes which need not be communicated to you. It has been gratifying to all to see the general acquiescence which has been manifested in the policy which the constituted authorities have deemed it proper to pursue in regard to this contest. As soon as the movement assumed such a steady and consistent form as to make the success of the provinces probable, the rights to which they were entitled by the law of nations, as equal parties to a civil war, were extended to them. Each party was permitted to enter our ports with its public and private ships, and to take from them every article which was the subject of commerce with other nations. Our citizens, also, have carried on commerce with both parties, and the Government has protected it with each in articles not contraband of war. Through the whole of this contest the United States have remained neutral, and have fulfilled with the utmost impartiality all the obligations incident to that character.

This contest has now reached such a stage, and been attended with such decisive success on the part of the provinces, that it merits the most profound consideration whether their right to the rank of independent nations, with all the advantages incident to it in their intercourse with the United States, is not complete. Buenos Ayres assumed that rank by a formal declaration in 1816, and has enjoyed it since 1810, free from invasion by the parent country. The provinces composing the republic of Colombia, after having separately declared their independence, were united by a fundamental law of the 17th of December, 1819. A strong Spanish force occupied at that time certain parts of the territory within their limits, and waged a destructive war: that force has since been repeatedly defeated, and the whole of it either made prisoners or destroyed, or expelled from the country, with the exception of an inconsiderable portion only, which is blockaded in two fortresses. The provinces on the Pacific have likewise been very successful. Chili declared independence in 1818, and has since enjoyed it undisturbed; and of late, by the assistance of Chili and Buenos Ayres, the revolution has extended to Peru. Of the movement in Mexico our information is less authentic, but it is, nevertheless, distinctly understood that the new Government has declared its independence, and that there is now no opposition to it there, nor a force to make any. For the last three years the Government of Spain has not sent a single corps of troops to any part of that country; nor is there any reason to believe it will send any in future. Thus, it is manifest that all those provinces are not only in the full enjoyment of their independence, but, considering the state of the war and other circumstances, that there is not the most remote prospect of their being deprived of it.

When the result of such a contest is manifestly settled, the new Governments have a claim to recognition by other Powers, which ought not to be resisted. Civil wars too often excite feelings which the parties cannot control. The opinion entertained by other Powers as to the result may assuage those feelings, and promote an accommodation between them useful and honorable to both. The delay which has been observed in making a decision on this important subject will, it is presumed, have afforded an unequivocal proof to Spain, as it must have done to other Powers, of the high respect entertained by the United States for her rights, and of their determination not to interfere with them. The provinces belonging to this hemisphere are our neighbors, and have, successively, as each portion of the country acquired its independence, pressed their recognition by an appeal to facts not to be contested, and which they thought gave them a just title to it. To motives of interest this Government has invariably disclaimed all pretension, being resolved to take no part in the controversy, or other measure in regard to it, which should not merit the sanction of the civilized world. To other claims a just sensibility has been always felt, and frankly acknowledged; but they, in themselves, could never become an adequate cause of action. It was incumbent on this Government to look to every important fact and circumstance on which a sound opinion could be formed, which has been done. When we regard, then, the great length of time which this war has been prosecuted, the complete success which has attended it in favor of the provinces, the present condition of the parties, and the utter inability of Spain to produce any change in it, we are compelled to conclude that its fate is settled, and that the provinces which have declared their independence, and are in the enjoyment of it, ought to be recognised.

Of the views of the Spanish Government on this subject, no particular information has been recently received. It may be presumed that the successful progress of the revolution through such a long series of years, gaining strength, and extending annually in every direction, and embracing, by the late important events, with little exception, all the dominions of Spain south of the United States on this continent, placing thereby the complete sovereignty over the whole in the hands of the people, will reconcile the parent country to an accommodation with them on the basis of their unqualified independence. Nor has any authentic information been recently received of the disposition of other Powers respecting it. A sincere desire has been cherished to act in concert with them in the proposed recognition, of which several were some time past duly apprized; but it was understood that they were not prepared for it. The immense space between those Powers, even those which border on the Atlantic and these provinces, makes the movement an affair of less interest and excitement to them than to us. It is probable, therefore, that they have been less attentive to its progress than we have been. It may be presumed, however, that the late events will dispel all doubt of the result.

In proposing this measure, it is not contemplated to change thereby, in the slightest manner, our friendly relations with either of the parties, but to observe, in all respects, as heretofore, should the war be continued, the most perfect neutrality between them. Of this friendly disposition an assurance will be given to the Government of Spain, to whom, it is presumed, it will be, as it ought to be, satisfactory. The measure is proposed under a thorough conviction that it is in strict accord with the law of nations; that it is just and right as to the parties; and that the United States owe it to their station and character in the world, as well as to their essential interests, to adopt it. Should Congress concur in the view herein presented, they will doubtless see the propriety of making the necessary appropriations for carrying it into effect.

REPORT *of the Committee on Foreign Affairs of the United States House of Representatives Regarding Recognition of the New American Nations, March 19, 1822 (extract)*

American State Papers, Foreign Relations, IV, 848, 850; William R. Manning, *Diplomatic Correspondence of the United States Concerning the Independence of the Latin American Nations,* I, 148

. . . YOUR COMMITTEE having thus considered the subject referred to them in all its aspects, are unanimously of opinion that it is *just and expedient* to acknowledge the independence of the several nations of Spanish America, without any reference to the diversity in the forms of their governments; and, in accordance with this opinion, they respectfully submit the following resolutions:

Resolved, That the House of Representatives concur in the opinion expressed by the President in his message of the 8th of March, 1822, that the American provinces of Spain which have declared their independence, and are in the enjoyment of it, ought to be recognised by the United States as independent nations.

Resolved, That the Committee of Ways and Means be instructed to report a bill appropriating a sum not exceeding one hundred thousand dollars, to enable the President of the United States to give due effect to such recognition.

JOHN QUINCY ADAMS, Secretary of State, to Joaquin de Anduaga, Spanish Minister to the United States, April 6, 1822

William R. Manning, *Diplomatic Correspondence of the United States Concerning the Independence of the Latin American Nations,* I, 156

SIR:

Your Letter of the 9th of March was, immediately after I had the honour of receiving it, laid before the President of the United States, by whom it has been deliberately considered, and by whose direction I am, in replying to it, to assure you of the earnestness and sincerity with which this Government desires to entertain and to cultivate the most friendly relations with that of Spain.

This disposition has been manifested, not only by the uniform course of the United States, in their direct political and commercial intercourse with Spain, but by the friendly interest which they have felt in the welfare of the Spanish Nation, and by the cordial sympathy with which they have witnessed their spirit and energy, exerted in maintaining their Independence of all foreign control, and their right of self-government.

In every question relating to the Independence of a Nation, two principles are involved; one of *right,* and the other of *fact;* the former exclusively depending upon the determination of the Nation itself, and the latter resulting from the successful execution of that determination—This right has been recently exercised as well by the Spanish Nation in Europe, as by several of those Countries in the American Hemisphere, which had for two or three Centuries been connected as Colonies with Spain—In the conflicts which have attended these Revolutions, the United States, have carefully abstained from taking any part, respecting the right of the nations concerned in them to maintain or now organize their own political Constitutions, and observing wherever it was a contest by arms, the most impartial neutrality—But the civil war, in which Spain was for some years involved with the inhabitants of her Colonies in America, has in substance, ceased to exist—Treaties equivalent to an acknowledgement of Independence, have been concluded by the Commanders and Viceroys of Spain herself, with the Republic of Colombia, with Mexico, and with Peru; while in the Provinces of La Plata, and in Chili, no Spanish force has for several years existed, to dispute the independence, which the Inhabitants of those Countries had declared.

Under these circumstances, the Government of the United States, far from consulting the dictates of a policy, questionable in its morality yielded to an obligation of duty of the highest order, by recognizing as Independent States, Nations which, after deliberately asserting their right to that character, have maintained and established it against all the resistance which had been or could be brought to oppose it. This recognition is neither intended to invalidate any right of Spain, nor to affect the employment of any means, which she may yet be disposed or enabled to use, with the view of re-uniting those Provinces to the rest of her dominions—It is the mere acknowledgement of existing facts, with the view to the regular establishment, with the Nations newly formed, of those relations, political and commercial, which it is the moral obligation of civilized and Christian Nations to entertain reciprocally with one another.

It will not be necessary to discuss with you a detail of facts, upon which your information appears to be materially different, from that which has been communicated to this Government, and is of public notoriety; nor the propriety of the denominations which you have attributed to the Inhabitants of the South American Provinces—It is not doubted that other and more correct views of the whole subject will very shortly be taken by your Government, and that it will, as well as the other European Governments, shew that deference to the example of the United States, which you urge it as the duty or the policy of the United States, to shew to theirs—The effect of the example of one Independent Nation upon the counsels and measures of another, can be just, only so far as it is voluntary: and as the United States desire that their example should be followed, so it is their intention to follow that of others, upon no other principle—They confidently reply that the time is at hand, when all the Governments of Europe friendly to Spain, and Spain herself, will not only concur in the acknowledgement of the Independence of the American Nations, but in the sentiment, that nothing will tend more effectually to the welfare and happiness of Spain, than the universal concurrence in that recognition.

I pray you, Sir, to accept [etc.]

Early Relations with the New American Nations

JOHN QUINCY ADAMS, Secretary of State, to Richard C. Anderson, Appointed United States Minister to Colombia, May 27, 1823

American State Papers, Foreign Relations, V, 888

THE REVOLUTION which has severed the colonies of Spanish America from European thraldom, and left them to form self-dependent Governments as members of the society of civilized nations, is among the most important events in modern history. As a general movement in human affairs it is perhaps no more than a development of principles first brought into action by the separation of these States from Great Britain, and by the practical illustration, given in the formation and establishment of our Union, to the doctrine that voluntary agreement is the only legitimate source of authority among men, and that all just Government is a compact. It was impossible that such a system as Spain had established over her colonies should stand before the progressive improvement of the understanding in this age, or that the light shed upon the whole earth by the results of our Revolution should leave in utter darkness the regions immediately adjoining upon ourselves. The independence of the Spanish colonies, however, has proceeded from other causes, and has been achieved upon principles in many respects different from ours. In our Revolution the principle of the social compact was, from the beginning, in immediate issue. It originated in a question of *right* between the Government in Europe and the subject in America. Our *independence* was declared in defence of our *liberties,* and the attempt to make the yoke a yoke of oppression was the cause and the justification for casting it off.

The revolution of the Spanish colonies was not caused by the oppression under which they had been held, however great it had been. Their independence was first forced upon them by the temporary subjugation of Spain herself to a foreign power. They were, by that event, cast upon themselves, and compelled to establish Governments of their own. Spain, through all the vicissitudes of her own revolutions, has clung to the desperate hope of retaining or reclaiming them to her own control, and has waged, to the extent of her power, a disastrous war to that intent. In the mind of every rational man it has been for years apparent that Spain can never succeed to recover her dominion where it has been abjured, nor is it probable that she can long retain the small remnant of her authority yet acknowledged in some spots of the South American continent.

The political course of the United States, from the first dawning of South American independence, has been such as was prescribed by their relative duties to all the parties. Being on terms of peace and amity with Spain through all the changes of her own Government, they have considered the struggles of the colonies for independence as a case of civil war, to which their national obligations prescribed to them to remain neutral. Their policy, their interest, and their feelings, all concurred to favor the cause of the colonies; and the principles upon which the right of independence has been maintained by the South American patriots have been approved, not only as identical with those upon which our own independence was asserted and achieved, but as involving the whole theory of Government on the emphatically American foundation of the sovereignty of the people and the unalienable rights of man. To a cause reposing upon this basis the people of this country never could be indifferent, and their sympathies have accordingly been, with great unanimity and constancy, enlisted in its favor. The sentiments of the Government of the United States have been in perfect harmony with those of their people, and while forbearing, as their duties of neutrality prescribed, from every measure which could justly be construed as hostile to Spain, they have exercised all the moral influence which they possessed to countenance and promote the cause of independence. So long as a contest of arms, with a rational or even remote prospect of eventual success, was maintained by Spain, the United States could not recognise the independence of the colonies as existing *de facto* without trespassing on their duties to Spain by assuming as decided that which was precisely the question of the war. In the history of South American independence there are two periods, clearly distinguishable from each other: the first, that of its origin, when it was rather a war of independence against France than against Spain; and the second, from the restoration of Ferdinand VII, in 1814. Since that period the territories now constituting the Republic of Colombia have been the only theatre upon which Spain has been able to maintain the conflict offensively, with even a probable color of ultimate success. But when, in 1815, she made her greatest effort, in the expedition from Cadiz.

commanded by Morillo, Mexico, Peru, and Chile were yet under her authority; and had she succeeded in reducing the coast of Terra Firma and New Granada, the provinces of La Plata, divided among themselves, and weakened by the Portuguese occupation of Montevideo, would probably not have held out against her long. This, at least, was the calculation of her policy; and from the geographical position of those countries, which may be termed the heart of South America, the conclusion might well be drawn that if the power of Spain could not be firmly reseated there, it must be, on her part, a fruitless struggle to maintain her supremacy in any part of the American continent. The expedition of Morillo, on its first arrival, was attended with signal success. Carthagena was taken, the whole coast of Terra Firma was occupied, and New Granada was entirely subdued. A remnant of Patriots in Venezuela, with their leader, Bolivar, returning from expulsion, revived the cause of independence; and after the campaign of 1819, in which they reconquered the whole of New Granada, the demonstration became complete, that every effort of Spain to recover the South American continent must thenceforward be a desperate waste of her own resources, and that the truest friendship of other nations to her would consist in making her sensible that her own interest would be best consulted by the acknowledgment of that independence which she could no longer effectually dispute.

To this conclusion the Government of the United States had at an earlier period arrived. But from that emergency, the President has considered the question of recognition, both in a moral and political view, as merely a question of the proper *time*. While Spain could entertain a reasonable hope of maintaining the war and of recovering her authority, the acknowledgment of the colonies as independent States would have been a wrong to her; but she had no right, upon the strength of this principle, to maintain the pretension after she was manifestly disabled from maintaining the contest, and, by unreasonably withholding her acknowledgment, to deprive the Independents of their right to demand the acknowledgment of others. To fix upon the precise *time* when the duty to respect the prior sovereign right of Spain should cease, and that of yielding to the claim of acknowledgment would commence, was a subject of great delicacy, and, to the President, of constant and anxious solicitude. It naturally became, in the first instance, a proper subject of consultation with other powers having relations of interest to themselves with the newly opened countries as well as influence in the general affairs of Europe. In August, 1818, a formal proposal was made to the British Government for a concerted and contemporary recognition of the independence of Buenos Ayres, then the only one of the South American States which, having declared independence, had no *Spanish* force contending against it within its borders; and where it therefore most unequivocally existed *in fact*. The British Government declined accepting the proposal themselves, without, however, expressing any disapprobation of it; without discussing it as a question of principle, and without assigning any reason for the refusal, other than that it did not then suit with their policy. It became a subject of consideration at the deliberations of the Congress of Aix-la-Chapelle, in October, 1818. There is reason to believe that it disconcerted projects which were there entertained of engaging the European Alliance in actual operations against the South Americans, as it is well known that a plan for their joint mediation between Spain and her colonies, for restoring them to her authority, was actually matured and finally failed at that place, only by the refusal of Great Britain to accede to the condition of employing *force* eventually against the South Americans for its accomplishment. Some dissatisfaction was manifested by several members of the Congress at Aix-la-Chapelle at this avowal on the part of the United States of their readiness to recognize the independence of Buenos Ayres.

The reconquest, in the campaign of 1819, of New Granada to the Patriot cause was immediately followed by the formation of the Republic of Colombia, consisting of three great divisions of the preceding Spanish Government: Venezuela, Cundinamarca, and Quito. It was soon succeeded by the dissolution of the Spanish authority in Mexico; by the revolution in Spain itself; and by the military operations which resulted in the declaration of independence in Peru. In November, 1820, was concluded the armistice between the Generals Morillo and Bolivar, together with a subsequent treaty, stipulating that, in case of the renewal of the war, the parties would abstain from all hostilities and practices not consistent with the modern law of nations and the humane maxims of civilization. In February, 1821, the partial independence of Mexico was proclaimed at Yguala; and in August of the same year was recognized by the Spanish Viceroy and Captain General O'Donoju, at Cordova.

The formation of the Republic of Colombia, by the fundamental law of the 17th of December, 1819, was notified to this Government by its agent, the late Don Manuel Torres, on the 20th of February, 1821, with a request that it might be recognized by the Government of the United States, and a proposal for the negotiation of treaties of commerce and navigation, *founded upon the bases of reciprocal utility and perfect equality,* as the most efficacious means of strengthening and increasing the relations of amity between the two Republics.

The request and proposal were renewed in a letter from Mr. Torres, of the 30th of November, 1821, and again repeated on the 2d of January, 1822. In the interval since the first demand, the General Congress of the new Republic had assembled, and formed a constitution, founded upon the principles of popular representation, and divided into legislative, executive, and judicial authorities. The Government under this constitution had been organized and was in full operation; while, during the same period, the principal remnant of the Spanish force had been destroyed by the battle of Carabobo, and its last fragments were confined to the two places of Porto Cabello and Panama.

Under these circumstances, a resolution of the House of Representatives of the United States, on the 30th of January, 1822, requested of the President to lay before the House the communications from the agents of the United States with the Governments south of the United States which had declared their independence, and those from the agents of such Governments here with the Secretary of State, tending to show the political condition of their Governments and the state of the war between them and Spain. In transmitting to the House the papers called for by this resolution, the President, by his message of the 8th of March, 1822, declared his own persuasion that the time had arrived when, in strict conformity to the law of nations and in the fulfilment of the duties of equal and impartial justice to all parties, the acknowledgment of the independence declared by the Spanish American colonies could no longer be withheld. Both Houses of Congress having almost unanimously concurred with these views of the President, an appropriation was made by law (4th of May, 1822), for such missions to the independent nations on the American continent as the President should deem proper.

On the day after the President's message of the 8th of March, the Spanish minister, Anduaga, addressed to this Department a remonstrance against the measure which it recommended, and a solemn protest against the recognition of the Governments mentioned of the insurgent Spanish provinces of America. He was answered on the 6th of April, by a letter recapitulating the circumstances under which the Government of the United States had "yielded to an obligation of duty of the highest order, by recognizing as independent States nations which, after deliberately asserting their right to that character, had maintained and established it against all the resistance which had been or could be brought to oppose it." On the 24th of April he gave information that the Spanish Government had disavowed the treaty of the 24th of August, 1821, between the Captain General O'Donoju and Colonel Iturbide, and had denied the authority of the former to conclude it.

On the 12th of February, 1822, the Spanish Extraordinary Cortes adopted the report of a committee proposing the appointment of Commissioners to proceed to South America to negotiate with the revolutionary Patriots concerning the relations to be established thereafter in regard to their connexion with Spain. They declared, at the same time, all treaties made with them before that time by Spanish commanders, implying any acknowledgment of their independence, null and void, as not having been authorized by the Cortes; and on the next day they passed three resolutions, the first annulling expressly the treaty between O'Donoju and Iturbide.

The second, "That the Spanish Government, by a declaration to all others with which it has friendly relations, make known to them that the Spanish nation will regard, *at any epoch,* as a violation of the treaties, the recognition, either partial or absolute, of the independence of the Spanish provinces of Ultramer, so long as the dissensions which exist between some of them and the Metropolis *are not terminated,* with whatever else may serve to convince foreign Governments that Spain has not yet renounced any of the rights belonging to it in those countries."

The third resolution recommended to the Government to take all necessary measures, and to apply to the Cortes for the needed resources to preserve and recover the authority of Spain in the ultramarine provinces.

These measures of the Cortes were not known to the President of the United States when he sent to Congress his message of the 8th of March; but information of them was received while the bill making an appropriation for the missions was before Congress, and on the 25th of April a resolution of the Senate requested of the President any information he might have, proper to be disclosed, from our minister at Madrid, or from the Spanish minister resident in this country, concerning the views of Spain relative to the recognition of the independence of the South American colonies and of the dictamen of the Spanish Cortes. In answer to this resolution, the letter from Mr. Anduaga, protesting against the recognition, and one from Mr. Forsyth, inclosing a translation of the dictamen, were transmitted to the Senate, which, with all these documents before them, gave their concurrent sanction, with that of the House of Representatives, to the passage of the bill of appropriation.

This review of the proceedings of the Government of the United States in relation to the independence of Spanish America has been taken to show the consistency of the principles by which they were uniformly dictated, and that they have been always eminently friendly to the new Republics, and disinterested. While Spain maintained a doubtful contest with arms to recover her dominion it was regarded as a civil war. When that contest became so manifestly desperate that Spanish Viceroys, Governors, and Captain Generals themselves, concluded treaties with the insurgents, virtually acknowledging their independence, the United States frankly and unreservedly recognized the fact, without making their acknowledgment the price of any favor to themselves, and although at the hazard of incurring the displeasure of Spain. In this measure they have taken the lead of the whole civilized world; for, although the Portuguese Brazilian Government had, a few months before, recognized the revolutionary Government of Buenos Ayres, it was at a moment when a projected declaration of their own independence made the question substantially their own cause, and it was presented as an equivalent for a reciprocal recognition of their own much more questionable right to the eastern shore of La Plata.

On the 17th day of June, 1822, Mr. Manuel Torres was received by the President of the United States as the chargé d'affaires from the Republic of Colombia, and the immediate consequence of our recognition was the admission of the vessels of the South American nations, under their own colors, into the ports of the principal maritime nations of Europe.

The European alliance of Emperors and Kings have assumed, as the foundation of human society, the doctrine of unalienable *allegiance*. Our doctrine is founded upon the principle of unalienable *right*. The European allies, therefore, have viewed the *cause* of the South Americans as rebellion against their lawful sovereign. We have considered it as the assertion of natural right. They have invariably shown their disapprobation of the revolution, and their wishes for the restoration of the Spanish power. We have as constantly favored the standard of independence and of America. In contrasting the principles and the motives of the European powers, as manifested in their policy towards South America, with those of the United States, it has not been my intention to boast of our superior purity, or to lay a claim of merit to any extraordinary favor from South America in return. Disinterestedness must be its own reward; but in the establishment of our future political and commercial intercourse with the new Republics it will be necessary to recur often to the principles in which it originated; they will serve to mark the boundaries of the rights which we may justly claim in our future relations with them, and to counteract the efforts which it cannot be doubted European negotiators will continue to make in the furtherance of their monarchical and monopolizing contemplations. . . .

Our commercial relations with the Colombian territory are of so recent origin, and have depended so much upon the revolutionary condition of that country, under which they have arisen, that our knowledge of their state and character is very imperfect, although we are certain that they are altogether different from those which may be expected to arise from permanent interests, when the independence of the Republic shall be universally recognized, and a free trade shall be opened to its inhabitants with all parts of the world. The only important point now to be settled, as the radical principle of all our future commercial intercourse, is the basis proposed by Mr. Torres, of *reciprocal utility and perfect equality.* As the necessary consequence of which, you will claim that, without waiting for the conclusion of a treaty, the commerce and navigation of the United States, in the ports of the Colombian Republic, should be received on the footing of equality with the most favored nation. . . .

The political systems of Europe are all founded upon partial rights and exclusive privileges. The colonial system had no other basis; and having no generous or liberal views of their own, it is not surprising that they should entertain and disseminate suspicions of the disinterestedness of others. The French Government sends an agent to Bogota, without daring to trust him with a credential or an avowed power; and he executes his commission by misrepresenting our motives, upon *suspicions* which those to whom he makes the misrepresentation know to be unfounded, and by testifying to those who were benefitted by our recognition that we had made it by the sacrifice of some part of our influence in Europe. It must be admitted that the address of the agent in the performance of his trust was upon a level with the candor and frankness in which it originated.

We are well aware that our recognition of South American independence was not palatable to the taste of any of the European Governments. But we felt that it was a subject upon which it became us to take the lead, and as we knew that the European Governments, sooner or later, must and would, whether with good or with bad grace, follow our example, we determined that both Europe and America should have the benefit of it. We hope, also, and this is the only return which we ask, and have a right to ask, from the South Americans for our forwardness in their favor, that Europe will be compelled to follow the whole of our example—that is, to recognize without condition and without equivalent. We claim no exclusive privilege for ourselves. We trust to the sense of justice, as well as to the interest of the South Americans, the denial of all exclusive privileges to others. The Colombian Government, at various times, have manifested a desire that the United States should take some further and active part in obtaining the recognition of their independence by the European Governments, and particularly by Great Britain. This has been done even before it was solicited. All the ministers of the United States in Europe have, for many years, been instructed to promote the cause, by any means consistent with propriety and adapted to their end, at the respective places of their residence. The formal proposal of a concerted recognition was made to Great Britain before the Congress of Aix-la-Chapelle. At the request of Mr. Torres, on his dying bed, and signified to us after his decease, Mr. Rush was instructed to give every aid in his power, without offence to the British Government, to obtain the admission of Mr. Ravenga; of which instruction we have recent assurances from Mr. Rush that he is constantly mindful. Our own recognition undoubtedly opened all the ports of Europe to the Colombian flag, and your mission to Colombia, as well as those to Buenos Ayres and Chile, cannot fail to stimulate the cabinets of maritime Europe, if not by the liberal motives which influenced us, at least by selfish impulses, to a direct, simple, and unconditional recognition. We shall pursue this policy steadily through all the changes to be foreseen of European affairs. There is every reason to believe that the preponderating tendency of the war in Spain will be to promote the universal recognition of all the South American Governments; and, at all events, our course will be to promote it by whatever influence we may possess. . . .

Our intercourse with the Republic of Colombia, and with the territories of which it is composed, is of recent origin, formed while their own condition was altogether revolutionary and continually changing its aspect. Our information concerning them is imperfect, and among the most important objects of your mission will be that of adding to its stores; of exploring the untrodden ground, and of collecting and transmitting to us the knowledge by which the friendly relations between the two countries may be extended and harmonized to promote the welfare of both, with due regard to the peace and good will of the whole family of civilized man. It is highly important that the first foundations of the permanent future intercourse between the two countries should be laid in principles benevolent and liberal in themselves, congenial to the spirit of our institutions, and consistent with the duties of universal philanthropy.

In all your consultations with the Government to which you will be accredited, bearing upon its political relations with this Union, your unvarying standard will be the spirit of independence and of freedom, as *equality* of rights and favors will be that of its commercial relations. The emancipation of the South American continent opens to the whole race of man prospects of futurity, in which this Union will be called, in the discharge of its duties to itself and to unnumbered ages of posterity, to take a conspicuous and leading part. It involves all that is precious in hope, and all that is desirable in existence, to the countless millions of our fellow creatures which, in the progressive revolution of time, this hemisphere is destined to rear and to maintain.

That the fabric of our social connexions with our southern neighbors may rise, in the lapse of years, with a grandeur and harmony of proportion corresponding with the magnificence of the means placed by Providence in our power, and in that of our descendants, its foundations must be laid in principles of politics and of morals new and distasteful to the thrones and dominations of the elder world, but co-extensive with the surface of the globe, and lasting as the changes of time.

HENRY CLAY, Secretary of State, to John M. Forbes, United States Chargé d'Affaires at Buenos Aires, April 14, 1825 (extracts)

William R. Manning, *Diplomatic Correspondence of the United States Concerning the Independence of the Latin American Nations*, I, 235

No ONE knows better than yourself what a deep interest has been taken by the people and Government of the United States in the success of the Patriot cause of Spanish America throughout all its fortunes and struggles. The recognition of the Independence of the new Governments was made as early as it was possible, consistently with all those considerations of policy and duty which this Government felt itself bound to entertain towards both parties. In point of fact, with the exception of the Act of the Portuguese Brazilian Government, to which it was prompted by self interest, and which preceded that of the United States only a few months, this Government was the first to assume the responsibility, and to risque the consequences of acknowledging the new Governments formed out of Spanish America. The United States have never claimed, and do not now desire, any particular favour or concession to their commerce or navigation, as the consideration of the liberal policy which they have observed towards those Governments. But the President does confidently expect that the priority of movement on our part, which disconcerted schemes meditated by the European Allies against the Independent Governments, and has tended to accelerate similar acts of recognition by the European Powers, and especially by Great Britain, will form a powerful motive with the Government of Buenos Ayres, for denying to the commerce and navigation of any of those European States any favours or privileges which shall not be equally extended to us. . . .

You will bring to the notice of the Government of Buenos Ayres, the message of the late President of the United States to their Congress, on the 2nd December, 1823, asserting certain important principles of intercontinental law in the relations of Europe and America. The first principle asserted in that message is that the American Continents are not, henceforth, to be considered as subjects for future Colonization by any European Powers. In the maintenance of that principle, all the Independent Governments of America have an interest, but that of the United States has probably the least. Whatever foundation may have existed three centuries ago, or even at a later period, when all this continent was under European subjection, for the establishment of a rule, founded on priority of discovery and occupation, for apportioning among the Powers of Europe, parts of this Continent, none can be now admitted as applicable to its present condition.

There is no disposition to disturb the Colonial possessions, as they may now exist, of any of the European Powers; but it is against the establishment of new European Colonies upon this continent, that the principle is directed. The countries in which any such new establishments might be attempted, are now open to the Enterprise and Commerce of all Americans. And the justice and propriety cannot be recognized, of arbitrarily limiting and circumscribing that enterprise and commerce, by the act of voluntarily planting a new Colony without the consent of America, under the auspices of foreign Powers belonging to another and a distant Continent. Europe would be indignant at any American attempt to plant a Colony on any part of her shores. And her justice must perceive, in the rule contended for, only a perfect reciprocity.

The other principle asserted in the message is, that whilst we do not desire to interfere, in Europe, with the political system of the allied Powers, we should regard as dangerous to our peace and safety, any attempt on their part, to extend their system to any portion of this hemisphere. The political systems of the two Continents are essentially different. Each has an exclusive right to judge for itself what is best suited to its own condition, and most likely to promote its happiness; but neither has a right to enforce upon the other, the establishment of its own peculiar system. This principle was declared in the face of the world, at a moment when there was reason to apprehend that the allied Powers were entertaining designs inimical to the freedom, if not the Independence, of the new Governments.

There is ground for believing that the declaration of it had considerable effect in preventing the maturity, if not in producing the abandonment, of all such designs. Both principles were laid down after much and anxious deliberation on the part of the late Administration. The President who then formed a part of it, continues entirely to coincide in both. And you will urge upon the Government of Buenos Ayres, the utility and expediency of asserting the same principles on all proper occasions.

The series of your despatches from No. 6. to No. 12, inclusive, has been received. The President has been gratified with the funeral honours awarded by the Government of Buenos Ayres, to the late Minister of the United States, Mr. Rodney, and the respectful attention subsequently shown to his memory. You will communicate to that Government the grateful sensibility which is entertained to their delicate and friendly testimonies on that melancholy occasion.

The Government of the United States is sincerely desirous to cultivate and maintain the most friendly relations with all the new States formed out of what was Spanish America. It is expected that every Representative of this Government near those States will constantly bear in mind, and seize every fit occasion to give effect to, this friendly policy. If amicable explanations are sought, of the nature of our institutions, and their social operation, they should be cheerfully and frankly rendered; whilst all improper interference in their public councils, all expressions of contempt for their habits, civil or religious, all intimations of incompetency on the part of their population, for self Government, should be sedulously avoided. Entertaining these views, the President saw with approbation, the discountenance you gave to the proposed meeting of Super-cargoes and Captains to remonstrate against the passage of the Law prohibiting the importation of flour, exceptionable as that Law is deemed. Such a meeting of foreigners would not have been tolerated in our own Country, and we could not expect that what we should be the first to condemn in respect to ourselves, would be agreeable to others. If our citizens have complaints to make, they must not take justice into their own hands, but prefer all such complaints through the regular and accredited organs.

You will communicate to the Government of Buenos Ayres the pleasure which the President derives from beholding the prospect of a speedy conclusion of the war between Spain and her late Colonies. The recent decisive events in Peru have terminated it on the Continent in fact; and there wants now only a Treaty which the interests of Spain would seem to recommend, that she should not longer delay negotiating, to put an end to it in form. If you should find that you can impart any strength to the dispositions for so happy an event in the Government of La Plata, you will not fail to impress upon it, how very agreeable it will be to the United States to see the People of La Plata in the full enjoyment of all the blessings of Peace, Independence, and Free Government.

MESSAGE *from President John Quincy Adams to the United States House of Representatives Regarding Participation in the Congress of Panama, March 15, 1826*
American State Papers, Foreign Relations, V, 882. See also *infra*, p. 497.

To the House of Representatives of the United States:

In compliance with the resolution of the House of the 5th ultimo, requesting me to cause to be laid before the House so much of the correspondence between the Government of the United States and the new States of America, or their ministers, respecting the proposed Congress or meeting of diplomatic agents at Panama, and such information respecting the general character of that expected Congress, as may be in my possession, and as may, in my opinion, be communicated without prejudice to the public interest, and also to inform the House, so far as in my opinion the public interest may allow, in regard to what objects the agents of the United States are expected to take part in the deliberations of that Congress, I now transmit to the House a report from the Secretary of State, with the correspondence and information requested by the resolution.

With regard to the objects in which the agents of the United States are expected to take part in the deliberations of that Congress, I deem it proper to premise that these objects did not form the only nor even the principal motive for my acceptance of the invitation. My first and greatest inducement was to meet in the spirit of kindness and friendship an overture made in that spirit by three sister Republics of this hemisphere.

The great revolution in human affairs which has brought into existence, nearly at the same time, eight sovereign and independent nations in our own quarter of the globe, has placed the United States in a situation not less novel, and scarcely less interesting, than that in which they had found themselves by their own transition from a cluster of colonies to a nation of sovereign States. The deliverance of the Southern American Republics from the oppression under which they had been so long afflicted was hailed, with great unanimity, by the people of this Union, as among the most auspicious events of the age. On the 4th of May, 1822, an act of Congress made an appropriation of one hundred thousand dollars "for such missions to the independent nations on the American continent as the President of the United States might deem proper."

In exercising the authority recognized by this act, my predecessor, by and with the advice and consent of the Senate, appointed, successively, ministers plenipotentiary to the Republics of Colombia, Buenos Ayres, Chile, and Mexico. Unwilling to raise among the fraternity of freedom questions of precedency and etiquette, which even the European monarchs had of late found it necessary in a great measure to discard, he despatched these ministers to Colombia, Buenos Ayres, and Chile, without exacting from those Republics, as by the ancient principals of political primogeniture he might have done, that the compliment of a plenipotentiary mission should have been paid *first* by them to the United States. The instructions, prepared under his direction, to Mr. Anderson, the first of our ministers to the southern continent, contain, at much length, the general principles upon which he thought it desirable that our relations, political and commercial, with these our new neighbors, should be established for their benefit and ours, and that of the future ages of our posterity. A copy of so much of these instructions as relates to these general subjects is among the papers now transmitted to the House. Similar instructions were furnished to the ministers appointed to Buenos Ayres, Chile, and Mexico, and the system of social intercourse which it was the purpose of those missions to establish, from the first opening of our diplomatic relations with those rising nations, is the most effective exposition of the principles upon which the invitation to the Congress at Panama has been accepted by me, as well as of the objects of negotiation at that meeting, in which it was expected that our plenipotentiaries should take part.

The House will perceive that, even at the date of these instructions, the first treaties between some of the southern Republics had been concluded, by which they had stipulated among themselves this diplomatic assembly at Panama. And it will be seen with what caution, so far as it might concern the policy of the United States, and at the same time with what frankness and good will towards those nations, he gave countenance to their design of inviting the United States to this high assembly for consultation upon *American interests*. It was not considered a conclusive reason for declining this invitation that the proposal for assembling such a Congress had not first been made by ourselves. It had sprung from the urgent, immediate, and momentous

common interests of the great communities struggling for independence, and, as it were, quickening into life. From them the proposition
to us appeared respectful and friendly; from us to them it could
scarcely have been made without exposing ourselves to suspicions of
purposes of ambition, if not of domination, more suited to rouse
resistance and excite distrust than to conciliate favor and friendship.
The first and paramount principle upon which it was deemed wise
and just to lay the corner-stone of all our future relations with them
was *disinterestedness;* the next was cordial good will to them; the
third was a claim of fair and equal reciprocity. Under these impressions, when the invitation was formally and earnestly given, had it
even been doubtful whether *any* of the objects proposed for consideration and discussion at the Congress were such as that immediate and
important interests of the United States would be affected by the
issue, I should, nevertheless, have determined, so far as it depended
upon me, to have accepted the invitation, and to have appointed
ministers to attend the meeting. The proposal itself implied that the
Republics by whom it was made *believed* that important interests
of ours or of theirs rendered our attendance there desirable. They
had given us notice that, in the novelty of their situation, and in the
spirit of deference to our experience, they would be pleased to have
the benefit of our friendly counsel. To meet the temper with which
this proposal was made with a cold repulse was not thought congenial
to that warm interest in their welfare with which the people and Government of the Union had hitherto gone hand in hand through the
whole progress of their revolution. To insult them by a refusal of
their overture, and then invite them to a similar assembly, to be
called by ourselves, was an expedient which never presented itself to
the mind. I would have sent ministers to the meeting had it been
merely to give them such advice as they might have desired, even with
reference to *their own* interests, not involving ours. I would have
sent them had it been merely to explain and set forth to them our
reasons for *declining* any proposal of specific measures to which they
might desire our concurrence, but which we might deem incompatible
with our interests or our duties. In the intercourse between nations
temper is a missionary perhaps more powerful than talent. Nothing
was ever lost by kind treatment. Nothing can be gained by sullen
repulses and aspiring pretensions.

But objects of the highest importance, not only to the future welfare of the whole human race, but bearing directly upon the special
interests of this Union, *will* engage the deliberations of the Congress
of Panama whether we are represented there or not. Others, if we
are represented, may be offered by our plenipotentiaries for considera-

tion, having in view both these great results—our own interests and the improvement of the condition of man upon earth. It may be that, in the lapse of many centuries, no other opportunity so favorable will be presented to the Government of the United States to subserve the benevolent purposes of Divine Providence, to dispense the promised blessings of the Redeemer of mankind, to promote the prevalence in future ages of peace on earth and good will to man, as will now be placed in their power by participating in the deliberations of this Congress.

Among the topics enumerated in official papers published by the Republic of Colombia, and adverted to in the correspondence now communicated to the House, as intended to be presented for discussion at Panama, there is scarcely one in which the *result* of the meeting will not deeply affect the interests of the United States. Even those in which the belligerent States alone will take an active part will have a powerful effect upon the state of our relations with the American, and probably with the principal European States. Were it merely that we might be correctly and speedily informed of the proceedings of the Congress, and of the progress and issue of their negotiations, I should hold it advisable that we should have an accredited agency with them, placed in such confidential relations with the other members as would insure the authenticity and the safe and early transmission of its reports. Of the same enumerated topics are the preparation of a manifesto setting forth to the world the justice of their cause and the relations they desire to hold with other Christian powers, and to form a convention of navigation and commerce applicable both to the confederated States and to their allies.

It will be within the recollection of the House that, immediately after the close of the war of our independence, a measure closely analogous to this Congress of Panama was adopted by the Congress of our confederation, and for purposes of precisely the same character. Three commissioners, with plenipotentiary powers, were appointed to negotiate treaties of amity, navigation, and commerce with all the principal powers of Europe. They met and resided for that purpose about one year at Paris, and the only result of their negotiations at that time was the first treaty between the United States and Prussia— memorable in the diplomatic annals of the world, and precious as a monument of the principles, in relation to commerce and maritime warfare, with which our country entered upon her career as a member of the great family of independent nations. This treaty, prepared in conformity with the instructions of the American plenipotentiaries, consecrated three fundamental principles of the foreign intercourse which the Congress of that period were desirous of establishing.

First, equal reciprocity and the mutual stipulation of the privileges of the most favored nation in the commercial exchanges of peace; secondly, the abolition of private war upon the ocean; and thirdly, restrictions favorable to neutral commerce upon belligerent practices with regard to contraband of war and blockades. A painful, it may be said a calamitous, experience of more than forty years has demonstrated the deep importance of these same principles to the peace and prosperity of this nation, and to the welfare of all maritime States, and has illustrated the profound wisdom with which they were assumed as cardinal points of the policy of the Union.

At that time, in the infancy of their political existence, under the influence of those principles of liberty and of right so congenial to the cause in which they had just fought and triumphed, they were able but to obtain the sanction of one great and philosophical, though absolute sovereign, in Europe to their liberal and enlightened principles. They could obtain no more. Since then a political hurricane has gone over three-fourths of the civilized portions of the earth, the desolation of which, it may with confidence be expected, is passing away, leaving at least the American atmosphere purified and refreshed. And now, at this propitious moment, the new-born nations of this hemisphere, assembling by their representatives at the isthmus between its two continents, to settle the principles of their future international intercourse with other nations and with us, ask, in this great exigency, for our advice upon those very fundamental maxims which we from our cradle at first proclaimed, and partially succeeded to introduce into the code of national law.

Without recurring to that total prostration of all neutral and commercial rights which marked the progress of the late European wars, and which finally involved the United States in them, and adverting only to our political relations with these American nations, it is observable that while, in all other respects, those relations have been uniformly, and without exception, of the most friendly and mutually satisfactory character, the only causes of difference and dissension between us and them which have ever arisen originated in those never-failing fountains of discord and irritation, discriminations of commercial favor to other nations, licentious privateers, and paper blockades. I cannot, without doing injustice to the Republics of Buenos Ayres and Colombia, forbear to acknowledge the candid and conciliatory spirit with which they have repeatedly yielded to our friendly representations and remonstrances on those subjects, in repealing discriminative laws which operated to our disadvantage, and in revoking the commissions of their privateers, to which Colombia has added the magnanimity of making reparation for unlawful captures by some of her cruisers, and of assenting, in the midst of war, to treaty stipulations favorable to neutral navigation. But the recurrence of these occasions of complaint has rendered the renewal of the discussions which result in the removal of them necessary, while in the mean time injuries are sustained by merchants and other individuals of the United States which cannot be repaired, and the remedy lingers in overtaking the pernicious operation of the mischief. The settlement of general principles, pervading with equal efficacy all the American States, can alone put an end to these evils, and can alone be accomplished at the proposed assembly.

If it be true that the noblest treaty of peace ever mentioned in history is that by which the Carthaginians were bound to abolish the practice of sacrificing their own children, *because it was stipulated in favor of human nature,* I cannot exaggerate to myself the unfading glory with which these United States will go forth in the memory of future ages if, by their friendly counsel, by their moral influence, by the power of argument and persuasion alone, they can prevail upon the American nations at Panama to stipulate, by general agreement among themselves, and so far as any of them may be concerned, the perpetual abolition of private war upon the ocean. And if we cannot yet flatter ourselves that this may be accomplished as advances towards it, the establishment of the principle that the friendly flag shall cover the cargo, the curtailment of contraband of war, and the proscription of fictitious paper blockades—engagements which we may reasonably hope will not prove impracticable—will, if successfully inculcated, redound proportionally to our honor, and drain the fountain of many a future sanguinary war.

The late President of the United States, in his message to Congress of December 2, 1823, while announcing the negotiation then pending with Russia, relating to the Northwest Coast of this Continent, observed that the occasion of the discussions to which that incident had given rise had been taken for asserting, as a principle, in which the rights and interests of the United States were involved, that the American continents, by the free and independent condition which they had assumed and maintained, were thenceforward not to be considered as subjects for future colonization by any European power. The principle had first been assumed in that negotiation with Russia. It rested upon a course of reasoning equally simple and conclusive. With the exception of the existing European colonies, which it was in no wise intended to disturb, the two continents consisted of several sovereign and independent nations, whose territories covered their whole surface. By this their independent condition the United States enjoyed the right of commercial intercourse with every part of their possessions. To attempt the establishment of a colony in those possessions would be to usurp, to the exclusion of others, a commercial intercourse, which was the common possession of all. It could not be done without encroaching upon existing rights of the United States. The Government of Russia has never disputed these positions, nor manifested the slightest dissatisfaction at their having been taken. Most of the new American Republics have declared their entire assent to them; and they now propose, among the subjects of consultation at Panama, to take into consideration the means of making effectual the assertion of that principle, as well as the means of resisting interference from abroad with the domestic concerns of the American Governments.

In alluding to these means it would obviously be premature at this time to anticipate that which is offered merely as matter for consultation, or to pronounce upon those measures which have been or may be suggested. The purpose of this Government is to concur in none which would import hostility to Europe, or justly excite resentment in any of her States. Should it be deemed advisable to contract any conventional engagement on this topic, our views would extend no further than to a mutual pledge of the parties to the compact to maintain the principle in application to its own territory, and to permit no colonial lodgments or establishments of European jurisdiction upon its own soil; and, with respect to the obtrusive interference from abroad, if its future character may be inferred from that which has been and perhaps still is exercised in more than one of the new States, a joint declaration of its character, and exposure of it to the world, may be probably all that the occasion would require. Whether the United States should or should not be parties to such a declaration may justly form a part of the deliberation. That there is an evil to be remedied needs little insight into the secret history of late years to know, and that this remedy may best be concerted at the Panama meeting deserves at least the experiment of consideration. A concert of measures, having reference to the more effectual abolition of the African slave trade, and the consideration of the light in which the political condition of the Island of Hayti is to be regarded, are also among the subjects mentioned by the minister from the Republic of Colombia, as believed to be suitable for deliberation at the Congress. The failure of the negotiations with that Republic, undertaken during the late administration, for the suppression of that trade, in compliance with a resolution of the House of Representatives, indicates the expediency of listening, with respectful attention, to propositions which may contribute to the accomplishment of the great end which was the purpose of that resolution, while the result of those negotiations will serve as admonition to abstain from pledging this Government to any arrangement which might be expected to fail of obtaining the advice and consent of the Senate by a constitutional majority to its ratification.

Whether the political condition of the island of Hayti shall be brought at all into discussion at the meeting may be a question for preliminary advisement. There are in the political constitution of Government of that people circumstances which have hitherto forbidden the acknowledgment of them by the Government of the United States as sovereign and independent. Additional reasons for withholding that acknowledgment have recently been seen in their acceptance of a nominal sovereign by the *grant* of a foreign prince, under conditions equivalent to the concession by them of exclusive commercial advantages to one nation, adapted altogether to the state of colonial vassalage, and retaining little of independence but the name. Our plenipotentiaries will be instructed to present these views to the assembly at Panama, and, should they not be concurred in, to decline acceding to any arrangement which may be proposed upon different principles.

The condition of the islands of Cuba and Porto Rico is of deeper import and more immediate bearing upon the present interests and future prospects of our Union. The correspondence herewith transmitted will show how earnestly it has engaged the attention of this Government. The invasion of both those islands by the united forces of Mexico and Colombia is avowedly among the objects to be matured by the belligerent States at Panama. The convulsions to which, from the peculiar composition of their population, they would be liable in the event of such an invasion, and the danger therefrom resulting of their falling ultimately into the hands of some European power other than Spain, will not admit of our looking at the consequences to which the Congress at Panama may lead with indifference. It is unnecessary to enlarge upon this topic, or to say more than that all our efforts in reference to this interest will be to preserve the existing state of things, the tranquillity of the islands, and the peace and security of their inhabitants.

And lastly, the Congress of Panama is believed to present a fair occasion for urging upon all the new nations of the South the just and liberal principles of religious liberty. Not by any interference whatever in their internal concerns, but by claiming for our citizens, whose occupations or interests may call them to occasional residence in their territories, the inestimable privilege of worshipping their Creator according to the dictates of their own consciences. This privilege, sanctioned by the customary law of nations, and secured by treaty stipulations in numerous national compacts—secured even to our own citizens in the treaties with Colombia and with the Federation of Central America—is yet to be obtained in the other South American States and Mexico. Existing prejudices are still struggling against it, which may, perhaps, be more successfully combatted at this general meeting than at the separate seats of Government of each Republic.

I can scarcely deem it otherwise than superfluous to observe that the assembly will be in its nature diplomatic and not legislative. That nothing can be transacted there obligatory upon any one of the States to be represented at the meeting, unless with the express concurrence of its own representatives; nor even then, but subject to the ratification of its constitutional authority at home. The faith of the United States to foreign powers cannot otherwise be pledged. I shall, indeed, in the first instance, consider the assembly as merely *consultative;* and although the plenipotentiaries of the United States will be empowered to receive and refer to the consideration of their Government any proposition from the other parties to the meeting, they will be authorized to conclude nothing unless subject to the definitive sanction of this Government in all its constitutional forms. It has, therefore, seemed to me unnecessary to insist that every object to be discussed at the meeting should be specified with the precision of a judicial sentence, or enumerated with the exactness of a mathematical demonstration. The purpose of the meeting itself is to deliberate upon the great and common *interests* of several new and neighboring nations. If the measure is new and without precedent, so is the situation of the parties to it. That the purposes of the meeting are somewhat indefinite, far from being an objection to it, is among the cogent reasons for its adoption. It is not the establishment of principles of intercourse with one, but with seven or eight nations at once. That, before they have had the means of exchanging ideas and communicating with one another in common upon these topics, they should have definitively settled and arranged them in concert is to require that the effect should precede the cause. It is to exact, as a preliminary to the meeting, that for the accomplishment of which the meeting itself is designed.

Among the inquiries which were thought entitled to consideration before the determination was taken to accept the invitation was that, whether the measure might not have a tendency to change the policy, hitherto invariably pursued by the United States, of avoiding all entangling alliances and all unnecessary foreign connexions.

Mindful of the advice given by the Father of our Country in his farewell address that the great rule of conduct for us in regard to foreign nations is, in extending our foreign relations, to have with them as little political connexion as possible, and faithfully adhering to the spirit of that admonition, I cannot overlook the reflection that the counsel of Washington, in that instance, like all the counsels of wisdom, was founded upon the circumstances in which our country and the world around us were situated at the time when it was given. That the reasons assigned by him for his advice were, that Europe had a set of primary interests which to us had none, or a very remote relation. That hence she must be engaged in frequent controversies, the cause of which were essentially foreign to our concerns. That our *detached* and *distant* situation invited and enabled us to pursue a different course. That by our union and rapid growth, with an efficient Government, the period was not far distant when we might defy material injury from external annoyance—when we might take such an attitude as would cause our neutrality to be respected, and, with reference to belligerent nations, might choose peace or war, as our interests, guided by justice, should counsel.

Compare our situation and the circumstances of that time with those of the present day, and what, from the very words of Washington then, would be his counsels to his countrymen now? Europe has still her set of primary interests with which we have little or a remote relation. Our distant and detached situation with reference to Europe remains the same. But we were then the only independent nation of this hemisphere; and we were surrounded by European colonies, with the greater part of which we had no more intercourse than with the inhabitants of another planet. Those colonies have now been transformed into eight independent nations, extending to our very borders. Seven of them Republics like ourselves; with whom we have an immensely growing commercial, and *must* have, and have, already important political connexions; with reference to whom our situation is neither distant nor detached; whose political principles and systems of Government, congenial with our own, must and will have an action and counteraction upon us and ours to which we cannot be indifferent if we would.

The rapidity of our growth and the consequent increase of our strength has more than realized the anticipations of this admirable political legacy. Thirty years have nearly elapsed since it was written, and in the interval our population, our wealth, our territorial extension, our power, physical and moral, have nearly trebled. Reasoning upon this state of things from the sound and judicious principles of Washington, and must we not say that the period which he predicted as then not far off has arrived? That *America* has a set of primary interests which have none or a remote relation to Europe. That the interference of Europe, therefore, in those concerns, should be spontaneously withheld by her upon the same principles that we have never interfered with hers; and that if she should interfere, as she may by measures which may have a great and dangerous recoil upon ourselves, we might be called, in defence of our own altars and firesides, to take an attitude which would cause our neutrality to be respected, and choose peace or war, as our interest, guided by justice, should counsel.

The acceptance of this invitation, therefore, far from conflicting with the counsel or the policy of Washington, is directly deducible from and conformable to it. Nor is it less conformable to the views of my immediate predecessor, as declared in his annual message to Congress of December 2, 1823, to which I have already adverted, and to an important passage of which I invite the attention of the House. "The citizens of the United States," said he, "cherish sentiments the most friendly in favor of the liberty and happiness of their fellow men on that (the European) side of the Atlantic. In the wars of the European Powers, in matters relating to themselves, we have never taken any part, nor does it comport with our policy so to do. It is only when our rights are invaded or seriously menaced that we resent injuries or make preparation for our defence. With the movements in this hemisphere we are of necessity more immediately connected, and by causes which must be obvious to all enlightened and impartial observers. The political system of the allied powers is essentially different in this respect from that of America. This difference proceeds from that which exists in their respective Governments. And to the defence of our own, which has been achieved by the loss of so much blood and treasure, and matured by the wisdom of their most enlightened citizens, and under which we have enjoyed unexampled felicity, this whole nation is devoted. We owe it, therefore, to candor and to the amicable relations subsisting between the United States and those powers, to declare that we should consider any attempt on their part to extend their system to any portion of this hemisphere as dangerous to our peace and safety. With the existing colonies or dependencies of any European power we have not interfered, and shall not interfere. But with the Governments who have declared their independence and maintained it, and whose independence we have, on great consideration and on just principles, acknowledged, we could not view any interposition, for the purposes of oppressing them or controlling in any other manner their destiny by any European power, in any other light than as the manifestation of an unfriendly disposition towards the United States. In the war between those new Governments and Spain we declared our neutrality at the time of their recognition, and to this we have adhered and shall continue to adhere, provided no change shall occur which, in the judgment of the competent authorities of this Government, shall make a corresponding change on the part of the United States indispensable to their security."

To the question which may be asked, whether this meeting and the principles which may be adjusted and settled by it as rules of intercourse between the American nations may not give umbrage to the Holy League of European powers or offence to Spain, it is deemed a sufficient answer that our attendance at Panama can give no *just cause* of umbrage or offence to either; and that the United States will stipulate nothing there which can give such cause. Here the right of inquiry into our purposes and measures must stop. The Holy League of Europe itself was formed without inquiring of the United States whether it would or would not give umbrage to them. The fear of giving umbrage to the Holy League of Europe was urged as a motive for denying to the American nations the acknowledgment of their independence. That it would be viewed by Spain as hostility to her was not only urged but directly declared by herself. The Congress and administration of that day consulted their rights and duties, and not their fears. Fully determined to give no needless displeasure to any foreign power, the United States can estimate the probability of their giving it only by the right which any foreign State could have to take it from their measures. Neither the representation of the United States at Panama, nor any measure to which their assent may be yielded there, will give to the Holy League, or any of its members, nor to Spain, the right to take offence. For the rest the United States must still, as heretofore, take counsel from their duties rather than their fears.

Such are the objects in which it is expected that the plenipotentiaries of the United States, when commissioned to attend the meeting at the Isthmus, will take part; and such are the motives and purposes with which the invitation of the three Republics was accepted. It was, however, as the House will perceive from the correspondence, accepted only upon condition that the nomination of Commissioners for the mission should receive the advice and consent of the Senate.

The concurrence of the House to the measure, by the appropriations necessary for carrying it into effect, is alike subject to its free determination and indispensable to the fulfilment of the intention.

That the Congress at Panama will accomplish all or even any of the transcendent benefits to the human race which warmed the conceptions of its first proposer, it were, perhaps, indulging too sanguine a forecast of events to promise. It is, in its nature, a measure speculative and experimental. The blessing of Heaven may turn it to the account of human improvement. Accidents unforseen and mischances not to be anticipated may baffle all its high purposes and disappoint its fairest expectations. But the design is great, is benevolent, is humane.

It looks to the melioration of the condition of man. It is congenial with that spirit which prompted the Declaration of our Independence; which inspired the preamble of our first treaty with France; which dictated our first treaty with Prussia, and the instructions under which it was negotiated; which filled the hearts and fired the souls of the immortal founders of our Revolution.

With this unrestricted exposition of the motives by which I have been governed in this transaction as well as of the objects to be discussed and of the ends, if possible, to be attained by our representation at the proposed Congress, I submit the propriety of an appropriation to the candid consideration and enlightened patriotism of the Legislature.

JOHN QUINCY ADAMS

Washington, March 15, 1826

[The United States subsequently sent delegates to the Congress, but they arrived too late to participate.]

JAMES BUCHANAN, Secretary of State, to William A. Harris, United States Chargé d'Affaires at Buenos Aires, March 30, 1846 (extract)

William R. Manning, Diplomatic Correspondence of the United States, Inter-American Affairs, 1831–1860, I, 29

. . . IN CONCLUSION, I would remark that much depends upon the personal deportment of foreign ministers in conciliating esteem and friendship in the countries where they are accredited. It is both the policy and the inclination of the United States to cultivate the most friendly relations with all nations and especially with our Sister Republics upon this continent. We are separated from Europe by a vast ocean and still more widely by our free Republican institutions. A spirit should be cherished among all the nations on this continent to resist European interference and maintain the freedom and independence of each of their Governments. The Government and people of the Argentine Republic have manifested to the world by their conduct that they feel the importance of asserting these principles and that they have the courage to maintain them against two of the greatest powers of Europe. It should, therefore, be your constant effort both in your public and private intercourse to impress upon that Government and people how deep an interest we feel in their success, and how anxious we are to cultivate with them the most friendly relations. Convince them by your conduct that we are truly their friends and they will continue to be ours. Your mission is one of great importance and responsibility and you have my best wishes for your success in accomplishing its important objects.

I am [etc.]

JAMES BUCHANAN, Secretary of State, to John Appleton, United States Chargé d'Affaires at Sucre, Bolivia, June 1, 1848

William R. Manning, *Diplomatic Correspondence of the United States, Inter-American Affairs*, V, 3

SIR:

The Republic of Bolivia to which you are accredited as chargé d'affaires is the only one of the independent States of the American Continent which has never been visited either by a diplomatic or consular agent of the United States. The important duty is, therefore, confided to you of opening diplomatic relations with that Republic.

You may assure the Bolivian Government that this delay (in accrediting a minister to them) has not been occasioned by any want of the most friendly feelings on our part.

The early and decided stand which the people of the United States and their Government took in recognizing the independence of the Spanish American Republics is known to the world. Ever since that period, we have felt the most lively interest in their prosperity and the strongest desire to see them elevated, under free, stable and Republican Governments, to a high rank among the nations of the earth. We entertain a cordial sympathy for all the Republics on this continent and desire nothing more than that their course should be prosperous and onward, securing the blessings of liberty and order to their people. This delay has on the contrary arisen solely from the fact that the territories of the Bolivian Republic lie chiefly in the interior of South America and that for want of good ports on the Pacific our commercial intercourse with them has been of a very limited character. It is believed that Cobeja [Cobija] is the only Bolivian port and this is but little frequented. It is understood that the Governments of Peru and Bolivia have been in Treaty for the cession of the Port of Arica from the former to the latter: and whilst this could not materially injure Peru it would be of essential advantage to Bolivia, as well as to the commerce of our country. Without attempting to interfere with the domestic concerns of either of these Republics, you might, should an opportunity offer, by your counsel and advice, promote this cession. Arica would seem naturally to belong to Bolivia; and of this that Republic cannot fail to be rendered more deeply sensible by the onerous transit duties which are now levied at Arica upon merchandise destined for consumption in Bolivia. The truth is that so long as Arica shall continue to be a Peruvian port it will be a perpetual cause of irritation between these Republics and will always endanger their friendly relations with each other.

The principal object of your mission is to cultivate the most friendly relations with Bolivia. The enemies of free Government throughout the world point with satisfaction to the perpetual revolutions and changes in the Spanish American Republics. They hence argue that man is not fit for self Government: and it is greatly to be deplored that the instability of these Republics and in many instances their disregard for private rights have afforded a pretext for such an unfounded assumption. Liberty cannot be preserved without order: and this can only spring from a sacred observance of law. So long as it shall be in the power of successive Military Chieftains to subvert the Governments of these Republics by the sword, their people cannot expect to enjoy the blessings of liberty. Anarchy, confusion and civil war must be the result. In your intercourse with the Bolivian authorities you will omit no opportunity of pressing these truths upon them, and of presenting to them the example of our own country where all controversies are decided at the ballot box. These truths you will endeavor to impress upon those whom you may meet in society, and you will avail yourself of all suitable opportunities, to strengthen, in a becoming manner, the opinions which must already exist in Bolivia, in favor of republican institutions.

You will bear in mind, also, the desire of your government for the mutual friendship and harmony of the South American Republics and will always encourage, when you can properly do so, every measure which may be fairly expected to tend towards such a result.

Instead of weakening themselves by domestic dissensions the Spanish race in these Republics have every motive for union and harmony. They nearly all have an enemy within their own bosoms burning for vengeance on account of the supposed wrongs of centuries, and ever ready, when a favorable opportunity may offer, to expel or exterminate the descendants of their conquerors. Already a war of races has arisen between the Indian and Spanish in Guatemala, and Yucatan, and the civil war now raging in Venezuela partakes largely of this character. In Bolivia it is understood that three fourths of the inhabitants belong to the Indian race. How unfortunate it is that, under these circumstances, the Spanish race there should be weakening themselves by warring with each other.

The nations on this Continent are placed in a peculiar position. Their interests and independence require that they should establish and maintain an American system of policy for their protection and security entirely distinct from that which has so long prevailed in Europe. To tolerate any interference on the part of European Governments with controversies in America and to suffer them to establish new colonies of their own intermingled with our free Republics, would be to make, to the same extent, a voluntary sacrifice of our independence. These truths ought every where throughout the continent of America to be impressed on the public mind.

The direct trade between the United States and Bolivia is believed to be insignificant but the inhabitants of that Republic are known to consume products of the United States to a considerable amount which they receive indirectly. These, they would probably use more largely if they were not circuitously conveyed and if the mutual wants of the two countries shall be better understood. One of the purposes of your mission will be to accomplish these results. . . .

ANNUAL MESSAGE from President Ulysses S. Grant to the United States Congress, December 5, 1870 (extract)
Foreign Relations of the United States, 1870, p. 3

. . . THE LONG DEFERRED peace conference between Spain and the allied South American republics has been inaugurated in Washington under the auspices of the United States. Pursuant to the recommendation contained in the resolution of the House of Representatives, of the 17th of December 1866, the Executive Department of the Government offered its friendly offices for the promotion of peace and harmony between Spain and the allied republics. Hesitations and obstacles occurred to the acceptance of the offer. Ultimately, however, a conference was arranged, and was opened in this city on the 29th of October last, at which I authorized the Secretary of State to preside. It was attended by the ministers of Spain, Peru, Chili, and Ecuador.

In consequence of the absence of a representative from Bolivia the conference was adjourned until the attendance of a plenipotentiary from that republic could be secured, or other measures could be adopted toward compassing its objects.

The allied and other republics of Spanish origin, on this continent, may see in this fact a new proof of our sincere interest in their welfare; of our desire to see them blessed with good governments, capable of maintaining order and of preserving their respective territorial integrity; and of our sincere wish to extend our own commercial and social relations with them. The time is not probably far distant when, in the natural course of events, the European political connection with this continent will cease. Our policy should be shaped, in view of this probability, so as to ally the commercial interests of the Spanish American States more closely to our own, and thus give the United States all the preëminence and all the advantages which Mr. Monroe, Mr. Adams, and Mr. Clay contemplated when they proposed to join in the Congress of Panama. . . .

Birth of the Pan-American Organization

JAMES G. BLAINE, Formerly Secretary of State, to President Chester A. Arthur, February 3, 1882
James G. Blaine, *Political Discussions*, p. 407

TO THE PRESIDENT OF THE UNITED STATES:

The suggestion that a Congress of all American nations should assemble in the city of Washington for the purpose of agreeing on such a basis of arbitration for International troubles as would remove all possibility of war in the Western Hemisphere, was warmly approved by your predecessor. His assassination on the 2d of last July necessarily suspended all action on the part of the Government. After your accession to the Presidency I acquainted you with the project, and submitted to you a draft for the invitation. You received the suggestion with appreciative consideration, and, after carefully examining the form of invitation, directed it to be sent. It was accordingly dispatched in November to the independent Governments of America, North and South, including all, from the Empire of Brazil to the smallest republic. In a communication, recently sent to the Senate, addressed by the present Secretary of State the 9th of last month to Mr. Trescott, now on a special mission to Peru and Chili, I was greatly surprised to find a proposition looking to the annulment of these invitations, and I was still more surprised when I read the reasons assigned. I quote Mr. Frelinghuysen's language:

The United States is at peace with all nations of the earth, and the President wishes hereafter to determine whether it will conduce to the general peace, which he would cherish and promote, for this Government to enter into negotiations and consultation for the promotion of peace with selected friendly nationalities without extending the line of confidence to other people with whom the United States is on equally friendly terms. If such partial confidence would create jealousy and ill will, peace, the object sought by such consultation, would not be promoted. The principles controlling the relations of the republics of this hemisphere with other nationalities may, on investigation, be found to be so well established that little would be gained at this time by re-opening the subject, which is not novel.

If I correctly apprehend the meaning of these words, it is that we might offend some European powers if we should hold in the United States a Congress of "selected nationalities" of America. This is certainly a new position for the United States and one which I earnestly beg you will not permit this Government to assume. European Powers assemble in Congress whenever an object seems to them of sufficient gravity to justify it. I have never heard of their consulting the Government of the United States in regard to the propriety of their so assembling, nor have I ever known of their inviting an American representative to be present, nor would there in my opinion be any good reason for their so doing. Two Presidents of the United States in the year 1881 adjudged it to be expedient that American Powers should meet in Congress for-the sole purpose of agreeing upon some basis for arbitration of differences that may arise between them, and for the prevention, as far as possible, of wars in the future. If that movement is now to be arrested for fear it may give offense in Europe, the voluntary humiliation of the United States could not be more complete, unless we should petition European Governments for the privilege of holding the Congress.

It is difficult to see how this country could be placed in a less enviable position than would be secured by sending in November a cordial invitation to all the Independent Nations in America to meet in Washington for the sole purpose of devising measures of peace, and in January recalling the invitation for fear it might create "jealousy and ill will" on the part of monarchical governments in Europe. It would be difficult to devise a more effective way for the United States to lose the friendship of its American neighbors, and it would certainly not add to our *prestige* in the European world. Nor can I see, Mr. President, how European Governments should feel "jealousy and ill will" toward the United States because of an effort on its part to assure lasting peace between the nations of America, unless indeed it be the interest of the European Powers that the American nations should at intervals fall into war, and bring reproach on Republican institutions. But from that very circumstance I see an additional and powerful motive for American Governments to be at peace among themselves. The United States is indeed at peace with all the world, as Mr. Frelinghuysen well says; but there are, and have been, serious troubles between other American republics. Peru, Chili and Bolivia have been for more than two years engaged in a desperate conflict. It was the fortunate intervention of the United States last spring that averted war between Chili and the Argentine Republic. Guatemala is at this moment asking the United States to interpose its good offices with Mexico to keep off war.

These important facts were all communicated in your late message to Congress. It was the existence or menace of these wars that influenced President Garfield, and, as I supposed, influenced yourself, to desire friendly conference of all the nations of America to devise methods of permanent peace and consequent prosperity for all. Shall the United States now turn back, hold aloof, and refuse to exert its great moral power for the advantage of its weaker neighbors? If you have not formally recalled the invitation to a Peace Congress, Mr. President, I beg you to consider well the effect of so doing. The invitation was not mine. It was yours. I performed only the part of Secretary of State to advise, and to draft. You spoke in the name of the United States to each of the independent nations of America. To revoke that invitation for any cause would be embarrassing; to revoke it for avowed fear of "jealousy and ill will" on the part of European Powers would appeal as little to American pride as to American hospitality. Those you have invited may decline, and, having now cause to doubt their welcome, will perhaps do so. This would break up the Congress, but it would not touch our dignity.

Beyond the philanthropic and Christian ends to be obtained by the American conference, devoted to peace and good will among men, we might well hope for material advantages as a result of a better understanding and closer friendship with the nations of America. At present the condition of trade between the United States and its American neighbors is unsatisfactory to us, and even deplorable. According to the official statistics of our own Treasury Department the balance against us in American trade last year was $120,000,000 in coin—a sum greater than the yearly product of the gold and silver mines in the United States. This large balance was paid by us in foreign exchange, and a very large proportion of it went to England, where shipments of cotton, provisions, and breadstuffs supplied the money. If any thing should change or check the balance in our favor in European trade, our commercial exchanges with Spanish America would drain us of our reserve of gold coin at a rate exceeding $100,000,000 per annum, and might precipitate the suspension of specie payment in this country. Such a result at home would be worse than a little "jealousy and ill will" abroad.

I do not say, Mr. President, that the holding of a Peace Congress will necessarily change the currents of trade, but it will bring us into kindly relations with all the American nations; it will promote the reign of law and order; it will increase production and consumption; it will stimulate the demand for articles which American manufacturers can furnish with profit. It will, at all events, be a friendly and auspicious beginning in the direction of American influence and American trade in a large field which we have hitherto neglected, and which has been practically monopolized by our commercial rivals in Europe.

As Mr. Frelinghuysen's dispatch foreshadowing an abandonment of a Peace Congress has been made public by your direction, I deem it a matter of propriety and justice to give this letter to the press.

I am, Mr. President, with great respect, your ever obedient servant,

JAMES G. BLAINE

THOMAS F. BAYARD, Secretary of State, to the United States Diplomatic Representatives in the Other American Republics and the Empire of Brazil, July 13, 1888

James Brown Scott, *The International Conferences of American States, 1889–1928*, p. 5

SIR:

At the present session of Congress an act was passed, to which the President's approval was given on the 24th of May last, by the terms of which the President is requested and authorized—

To invite the several Governments of the republics of Mexico, Central and South America, Hayti, San Domingo, and the Empire of Brazil to join the United States in a conference to be held at Washington, in the United States, at such time as he may deem proper in the year eighteen hundred and eighty-nine, for the purpose of discussing and recommending for adoption to their respective Governments some plan of arbitration for the settlement of disagreements and disputes that may hereafter arise between them, and for considering questions relating to the improvement of business intercourse and means of direct communication between said countries, and to encourage such reciprocal commercial relations as will be beneficial to all and secure more extensive markets for the products of each of said countries.

It is also provided in the act referred to that in forwarding the invitations to the said Governments the President of the United States shall set forth that the Conference is called to consider—

First. Measures that shall tend to preserve and promote the prosperity of the several American States.

Second. Measures toward the formation of an American customs union, under which the trade of the American nations with each other shall, so far as possible and profitable, be promoted.

Third. The establishment of regular and frequent communication between the ports of the several American States and the ports of each other.

Fourth. The establishment of a uniform system of customs regulations in each of the independent American States to govern the mode of importation and exportation of merchandise and port dues and charges, a uniform method of determining the classification and valuation of such merchandise in the ports of each country, and a uniform system of invoices, and the subject of the sanitation of ships and quarantine.

Fifth. The adoption of a uniform system of weights and measures, and laws to protect the patent-rights, copyrights, and trade-marks of citizens of either country in the other, and for the extradition of criminals.

Sixth. The adoption of a common silver coin, to be issued by each Government, the same to be legal tender in all commercial transactions between the citizens of all of the American States.

Seventh. An agreement upon and recommendation for adoption to their respective Governments of a definite plan of arbitration of all questions, disputes, and differences, that may now or hereafter exist between them, to the end that all difficulties and disputes between such nations may be peaceably settled and wars prevented.

Eighth. And to consider such other subjects relating to the welfare of the several States represented as may be presented by any of said States which are hereby invited to participate in said Conference.

I have to call your particular attention to the scope and object of the Conference suggested, which, as will be observed, is consultative and recommendatory only. The proposed Conference will be wholly without power to bind any of the parties thereto, and it is not designed to affect or impair in any degree the treaty relations now existing between any of the States which may be represented. The topics for discussion and deliberation are manifestly of profound importance, and it is believed that a friendly and frank exchange of views in relation to these subjects will be of practical use, and, by mutual enlightenment, will materially promote that expansion and intimacy of social and commercial relations which must be fruitful of blessings to all concerned.

Certain topics are suggested as proper subjects for a comparison of views, but the field is expressly left open to any participant State to bring before the Conference such other subjects as may appear important to the welfare of the several States represented.

By direction, therefore, of the President of the United States, and in his name, you will tender to the Government of ——— a cordial invitation to be represented by such number of Delegates as may seem to it convenient, at the International Conference to be convened as aforesaid in the city of Washington, on Wednesday, the 2d day of October, of the coming year, 1889, it being understood, however, that in the disposition of questions to come before such Conference no State shall be entitled to more than one vote, whatever be the number of Delegates it may send.

You will make this invitation known by reading this note to the Minister of Foreign Affairs of —— and by leaving with him a copy if he should express a desire to possess it. You will at the same time, and with the use of such suggestions and expression of views as in your judgment may be deemed appropriate, make known to his excellency the sincere desire and confident expectation of the President that this invitation will be received in the same spirit of friendship and deference by which it has been prompted.

I am sir, your obedient servant,

T. F. BAYARD
Secretary of State

ADDRESS by James G. Blaine, Secretary of State, at the Opening of the International American Conference, at Washington, October 2, 1889
International American Conference, I, 39

GENTLEMEN OF THE INTERNATIONAL AMERICAN CONFERENCE:

Speaking for the Government of the United States, I bid you welcome to this capital. Speaking for the people of the United States, I bid you welcome to every section and to every State of the Union. You come in response to an invitation extended by the President on the special authorization of Congress. Your presence here is no ordinary event. It signifies much to the people of all America to-day. It may signify far more in the days to come. No conference of nations has ever assembled to consider the welfare of territorial possessions so vast and to contemplate the possibilities of a future so great and so inspiring. Those now sitting within these walls are empowered to speak for nations whose borders are on both the great oceans, whose northern limits are touched by the Arctic waters for a thousand miles beyond the Straits of Behring and whose southern extension furnishes human habitations farther below the equator than is elsewhere possible on the globe.

The aggregate territorial extent of the nations here represented falls but little short of 12,000,000 of square miles—more than three times the area of all Europe, and but little less than one-fourth part of the globe; while in respect to the power of producing the articles which are essential to human life and those which minister to life's luxury, they constitute even a larger proportion of the entire world. These great possessions to-day have an aggregate population approaching 120,000,000, but if peopled as densely as the average of Europe, the total number would exceed 1,000,000,000. While considerations of this character must inspire Americans, both South and North, with the liveliest anticipations of future grandeur and power, they must also impress them with a sense of the gravest responsibility touching the character and development of their respective nationalities.

The Delegates I am addressing can do much to establish permanent relations of confidence, respect, and friendship between the nations which they represent. They can show to the world an honorable, peaceful conference of eighteen independent American Powers, in which all shall meet together on terms of absolute equality; a conference in which there can be no attempt to coerce a single Delegate against his own conception of the interests of his nation; a conference which will permit no secret understanding on any subject, but will frankly publish to the world all its conclusions; a conference which will tolerate no spirit of conquest, but will aim to cultivate an American sympathy as broad as both continents; a conference which will form no selfish alliance against the older nations from which we are proud to claim inheritance—a conference, in fine, which will seek nothing, propose nothing, endure nothing that is not, in the general sense of all the Delegates, timely and wise and peaceful.

And yet we can not be expected to forget that our common fate has made us inhabitants of the two continents which, at the close of four centuries, are still regarded beyond the seas as the New World. Like situations beget like sympathies and impose like duties. We meet in firm belief that the nations of America ought to be and can be more helpful, each to the other, than they now are, and that each will find advantage and profit from an enlarged intercourse with the others.

We believe that we should be drawn together more closely by the highways of the sea, and that at no distant day the railway systems of the north and south will meet upon the isthmus and connect by land routes the political and commercial capitals of all America.

We believe that hearty co-operation, based on hearty confidence, will save all American States from the burdens and evils which have long and cruelly afflicted the older nations of the world.

We believe that a spirit of justice, of common and equal interest between the American States, will leave no room for an artificial balance of power like unto that which has led to wars abroad and drenched Europe in blood.

We believe that friendship, avowed with candor and maintained with good faith, will remove from American States the necessity of guarding boundary lines between themselves with fortifications and military force.

We believe that standing armies, beyond those which are needful for public order and the safety of internal administration, should be unknown on both American continents.

We believe that friendship and not force, the spirit of just law and not the violence of the mob, should be the recognized rule of administration between American nations and in American nations.

To these subjects, and those which are cognate thereto, the attention of this Conference is earnestly and cordially invited by the Government of the United States. It will be a great gain when we shall acquire that common confidence on which all international friendship must rest. It will be a greater gain when we shall be able to draw the people of all American nations into close acquaintance with each other, an end to be facilitated by more frequent and more rapid intercommunication. It will be the greatest gain when the personal and commercial relations of the American States, south and north, shall be so developed and so regulated that each shall acquire the highest possible advantage from the enlightened and enlarged intercourse of all.

Before the Conference shall formally enter upon the discussion of the subjects to be submitted to it I am instructed by the President to invite all the Delegates to be the guests of the Government during a proposed visit to various sections of the country, with the double view of showing to our friends from abroad the condition of the United States, and of giving to our people in their homes the privilege and pleasure of extending the warm welcome of Americans to Americans.

ANNUAL MESSAGE from President Benjamin Harrison to the United States Congress, December 3, 1889 (extract)
Foreign Relations of the United States, 1889, p. iii

. . . IT IS A MATTER of high significance, and no less of congratulation, that the first year of the second century of our constitutional existence finds, as honored guests within our borders, the representatives of all the independent states of North and South America met together in earnest conference touching the best methods of perpetuating and expanding the relations of mutual interest and friendliness existing among them. That the opportunity thus afforded for promoting closer international relations and the increased prosperity of the states represented will be used for the mutual good of all, I can not permit myself to doubt. Our people will await with interest and confidence the results to flow from so auspicious a meeting of allied and, in large part, identical interests.

The recommendations of this international conference of enlightened statesmen will doubtless have the considerate attention of Congress, and its co-operation in the removal of unnecessary barriers to beneficial intercourse between the nations of America. But while the commercial results, which it is hoped will follow this conference, are worthy of pursuit and of the great interest they have excited, it is believed that the crowning benefit will be found in the better securities which may be devised for the maintenance of peace among all American nations and the settlement of all contentions by methods that a Christian civilization can approve. While viewing with interest our national resources and products, the delegates will, I am sure, find a higher satisfaction in the evidences of unselfish friendship which everywhere attend their intercourse with our people.

ADDRESS by James G. Blaine, Secretary of State, at the Close of the International American Conference, at Washington, April 19, 1890
International American Conference, I, 1166

GENTLEMEN:

I withhold for a moment the word of final adjournment, in order that I may express to you the profound satisfaction with which the Government of the United States regards the work that has been accomplished by the International American Conference. The importance of the subjects which have claimed your attention, the comprehensive intelligence and watchful patriotism which you have brought to their discussion, must challenge the confidence and secure the admiration of the Governments and peoples whom you represent; while that larger patriotism which constitutes the fraternity of nations has received from you an impulse such as the world has not before seen.

The extent and value of all that has been worthily achieved by your Conference can not be measured to-day. We stand too near it. Time will define and heighten the estimate of your work; experience will confirm our present faith; final results will be your vindication and your triumph.

If, in this closing hour, the Conference had but one deed to celebrate, we should dare call the world's attention to the deliberate, confident, solemn dedication of two great continents to peace, and to the prosperity which has peace for its foundation. We hold up this new *Magna Charta,* which abolishes war and substitutes arbitration between the American Republics, as the first and great fruit of the International American Conference. That noblest of Americans, the aged poet and philanthropist, Whittier, is the first to send his salutation and his benediction, declaring,

If in the spirit of peace the American Conference agrees upon a rule of arbitration which shall make war in this hemisphere well-nigh impossible, its sessions will prove one of the most important events in the history of the world.

I am instructed by the President to express the wish that before the members of the Conference shall leave for their distant homes, they will accept the hospitality of the United States in a visit to the Southern section of the Union, similar to the one they have already made to the Eastern and Western sections. The President trusts that the tour will not only be a pleasant incident of your farewell to the country, but that you will find advantage in a visit to so interesting and important a part of our Republic.

May I express to you, gentlemen, my deep appreciation of the honor you did me in calling me to preside over your deliberations. Your kindness has been unceasing, and for your formal words of approval I offer you my sincerest gratitude.

Invoking the blessing of Almighty God upon the patriotic and fraternal work which has been here begun for the good of mankind, I now declare the American International Conference adjourned without day.

Increasing Inter-American Relations

ADDRESS by Elihu Root, Secretary of State, at the Third International Conference of American States, at Rio de Janeiro, July 31, 1906

Robert Bacon and James Brown Scott, *Latin America and the United States, Addresses by Elihu Root*, p. 6

I BEG you to believe that I highly appreciate and thank you for the honor you do me.

I bring from my country a special greeting to her elder sisters in the civilization of America.

Unlike as we are in many respects, we are alike in this, that we are all engaged under new conditions, and free from the traditional forms and limitations of the Old World in working out the same problem of popular self-government.

It is a difficult and laborious task for each of us. Not in one generation nor in one century can the effective control of a superior sovereign, so long deemed necessary to government, be rejected, and effective self-control by the governed be perfected in its place. The first fruits of democracy are many of them crude and unlovely; its mistakes are many, its partial failures many, its sins not few. Capacity for self-government does not come to man by nature. It is an art to be learned, and it is also an expression of character to be developed among all the thousands of men who exercise popular sovereignty.

To reach the goal toward which we are pressing forward, the governing multitude must first acquire knowledge that comes from universal education; wisdom that follows practical experience; personal independence and self-respect befitting men who acknowledge no superior; self-control to replace that external control which a democracy rejects; respect for law; obedience to the lawful expressions of the public will; consideration for the opinions and interests of others equally entitled to a voice in the state; loyalty to that abstract conception—one's country—as inspiring as that loyalty to personal sovereigns which has so illumined the pages of history; subordination of personal interests to the public good; love of justice and mercy, of liberty and order. All these we must seek by slow and patient effort; and of how many shortcomings in his own land and among his own people each one of us is conscious!

Yet no student of our times can fail to see that not America alone but the whole civilized world is swinging away from its old governmental moorings and intrusting the fate of its civilization to the capacity of the popular mass to govern. By this pathway mankind is to travel, whithersoever it leads. Upon the success of this our great undertaking the hope of humanity depends.

Nor can we fail to see that the world makes substantial progress toward more perfect popular self-government.

I believe it to be true that, viewed against the background of conditions a century, a generation, a decade ago, government in my own country has advanced, in the intelligent participation of the great mass of the people, in the fidelity and honesty with which they are represented, in respect for law, in obedience to the dictates of a sound morality, and in effectiveness and purity of administration.

Nowhere in the world has this progress been more marked than in Latin America. Out of the wrack of Indian fighting and race conflicts and civil wars, strong and stable governments have arisen. Peaceful succession in accord with the people's will has replaced the forcible seizure of power permitted by the people's indifference. Loyalty to country, its peace, its dignity, its honor, has arisen above partisanship for individual leaders. The rule of law supersedes the rule of man. Property is protected and the fruits of enterprise are secure. Individual liberty is respected. Continuous public policies are followed; national faith is held sacred. Progress has not been equal everywhere, but there has been progress everywhere. The movement in the right direction is general. The right tendency is not exceptional; it is continental. The present affords just cause for satisfaction; the future is bright with hope.

It is not by national isolation that these results have been accomplished, or that this progress can be continued. No nation can live unto itself alone and continue to live. Each nation's growth is a part of the development of the race. There may be leaders and there may be laggards; but no nation can long continue very far in advance of the general progress of mankind, and no nation that is not doomed to extinction can remain very far behind. It is with nations as it is with individual men; intercourse, association, correction of egotism by the influence of others' judgment; broadening of views by the experience and thought of equals; acceptance of the moral standards of a community, the desire for whose good opinion lends a sanction to the rules of right conduct—these are the conditions of growth in civilization. A people whose minds are not open to the lessons of the world's progress, whose spirits are not stirred by the aspirations and the achievements of humanity struggling the world over for liberty and justice, must be left behind by civilization in its steady and beneficent advance.

To promote this mutual interchange and assistance between the American republics, engaged in the same great task, inspired by the same purpose, and professing the same principles, I understand to be the function of the American Conference now in session. There is not one of all our countries that cannot benefit the others; there is not one that cannot receive benefit from the others; there is not one that will not gain by the prosperity, the peace, the happiness of all.

According to your program, no great and impressive single thing is to be done by you; no political questions are to be discussed; no controversies are to be settled; no judgment is to be passed upon the conduct of any state, but many subjects are to be considered which afford the possibility of removing barriers to intercourse; of ascertaining for the common benefit what advances have been made by each nation in knowledge, in experience, in enterprise, in the solution of difficult questions of government, and in ethical standards; of perfecting our knowledge of each other; and of doing away with the misconceptions, the misunderstandings, and the resultant prejudices that are such fruitful sources of controversy.

And some subjects in the program invite discussion that may lead the American republics toward an agreement upon principles, the general practical application of which can come only in the future through long and patient effort. Some advances at least may be made here toward the complete rule of justice and peace among nations, in lieu of force and war.

The association of so many eminent men from all the republics, leaders of opinion in their own homes; the friendships that will arise among you; the habit of temperate and kindly discussion of matters of common interest; the ascertainment of common sympathies and aims; the dissipation of misunderstandings; the exhibition to all the American peoples of this peaceful and considerate method of conferring upon international questions—this alone, quite irrespective of the resolutions you may adopt and the conventions you may sign, will mark a substantial advance in the direction of international good understanding.

These beneficent results the Government and the people of the United States of America greatly desire.

We wish for no victories but those of peace; for no territory except our own; for no sovereignty except sovereignty over ourselves. We deem the independence and equal rights of the smallest and weakest member of the family of nations entitled to as much respect as those of the greatest empire; and we deem the observance of that respect the chief guaranty of the weak against the oppression of the strong. We neither claim nor desire any rights or privileges or powers that we do not freely concede to every American republic. We wish to increase our prosperity, to expand our trade, to grow in wealth, in wisdom, and in spirit; but our conception of the true way to accomplish this is not to pull down others and profit by their ruin, but to help all friends to a common prosperity and a common growth, that we may all become greater and stronger together.

Within a few months, for the first time, the recognized possessors of every foot of soil upon the American continents can be and I hope will be represented with the acknowledged rights of equal sovereign states in the great World Congress at The Hague. This will be the world's formal and final acceptance of the declaration that no part of the American continents is to be deemed subject to colonization. Let us pledge ourselves to aid each other in the full performance of the duty to humanity which that accepted declaration implies; so that in time the weakest and most unfortunate of our republics may come to march with equal step by the side of the stronger and more fortunate. Let us help each other to show that for all the races of men the liberty for which we have fought and labored is the twin sister of justice and peace. Let us unite in creating and maintaining and making effective an all-American public opinion, whose power shall influence international conduct and prevent international wrong, and narrow the causes of war, and forever preserve our free lands from the burden of such armaments as are massed behind the frontiers of Europe, and bring us ever nearer to the perfection of ordered liberty. So shall come security and prosperity, production and trade, wealth, learning, the arts, and happiness for us all.

Not in a single conference, nor by a single effort, can very much be done. You labor more for the future than for the present; but if the right impulse be given, if the right tendency be established, the work you do here will go on among all the millions of people in the American continents long after your final adjournment, long after your lives, with incalculable benefit to all our beloved countries, which may it please God to continue free and independent and happy for ages to come.

ADDRESS by Elihu Root, Secretary of State, at Kansas City, Missouri, November 20, 1906 (extract)

59th Congress, 2d Session, Senate Document No. 211. The address was delivered before the Trans-Mississippi Commercial Congress

MR. PRESIDENT AND GENTLEMEN OF THE CONGRESS:

A little less than three centuries of colonial and national life have brought the people inhabiting the United States, by a process of evolution, natural and with the existing forces inevitable, to a point of distinct and radical change in their economic relations to the rest of mankind.

During the period now past the energy of our people, directed by the formative power created in our early population by heredity, by environment, by the struggle for existence, by individual independence, and by free institutions, has been devoted to the internal development of our own country. The surplus wealth produced by our labors has been applied immediately to reproduction in our own land. We have been cutting down forests and breaking virgin soil and fencing prairies and opening mines of coal and iron and copper and silver and gold, and building roads and canals and railroads and telegraph lines and cars and locomotives and mills and furnaces and schoolhouses and colleges and libraries and hospitals and asylums and public buildings and storehouses and shops and homes. We have been drawing on the resources of the world in capital and in labor to aid us in our work. We have gathered strength from every rich and powerful nation and expended it upon these home undertakings; into them we have poured hundreds of millions of money attracted from the investors of Europe. We have been always a debtor nation, borrowing from the rest of the world, drawing all possible energy toward us and concentrating it with our own energy upon our own enterprises. The engrossing pursuit of our own opportunities has excluded from our consideration and interest the enterprises and the possibilities of the outside world. Invention, discovery, the progress of science, capacity for organization, the enormous increase in the productive power of mankind, have accelerated our progress and have brought us to a result of development in every branch of internal industrial activity marvelous and unprecedented in the history of the world.

Since the first election of President McKinley the people of the United States have for the first time accumulated a surplus of capital beyond the requirements of internal development. That surplus is increasing with extraordinary rapidity. We have paid our debts to Europe and have become a creditor instead of a debtor nation; we have faced about; we have left the ranks of the borrowing nations and have entered the ranks of the investing nations. Our surplus energy is beginning to look beyond our own borders, throughout the world, to find opportunity for the profitable use of our surplus capital, foreign markets for our manufactures, foreign mines to be developed, foreign bridges and railroads and public works to be built, foreign rivers to be turned into electric power and light. As in their several ways England and France and Germany have stood, so we in our own way are beginning to stand and must continue to stand toward the industrial enterprise of the world.

That we are not beginning our new rôle feebly is indicated by $1,518,561,666 of exports in the year 1905 as against $1,117,513,071 of imports, and by $1,743,864,500 exports in the year 1906 as against $1,226,563,843 of imports. Our first steps in the new field indeed are somewhat clumsy and unskilled. In our own vast country, with oceans on either side, we have had too little contact with foreign peoples readily to understand their customs or learn their languages; yet no one can doubt that we shall learn and shall understand and shall do our business abroad, as we have done it at home, with force and efficiency.

Coincident with this change in the United States the progress of political development has been carrying the neighboring continent of South America out of the stage of militarism into the stage of industrialism. Throughout the greater part of that vast continent revolutions have ceased to be looked upon with favor or submitted to with indifference; the revolutionary general and the dictator are no longer the objects of admiration and imitation; civic virtues command the highest respect; the people point with satisfaction and pride to the stability of their governments, to the safety of property and the certainty of justice; nearly everywhere the people are eager for foreign capital to develop their natural resources and for foreign immigration to occupy their vacant land. Immediately before us, at exactly the right time, just as we are ready for it, great opportunities for peaceful commercial and industrial expansion to the south are presented. Other investing nations are already in the field—England, France, Germany, Italy, Spain; but the field is so vast, the new demands are so great, the progress so rapid, that what other nations have done up to this time is but a slight advance in the race for the grand total. The opportunities are so large that figures fail to convey them. The area of this newly awakened continent is 7,502,848 square miles— more than two and one-half times as large as the United States without Alaska, and more than double the United States including Alaska. A large part of this area lies within the temperate zone, with an equable and invigorating climate, free from extremes of either heat or cold. Farther north in the Tropics are enormous expanses of high table-lands, stretching from the Atlantic to the foothills of the Andes, and lifted far above the tropical heats; the fertile valleys of the western cordilleras are cooled by perpetual snows even under the equator; vast forests grow untouched from a soil of incredible richness. The plains of Argentina, the great uplands of Brazil, the mountain valleys of Chile, Peru, Ecuador, Bolivia, and Colombia are suited to the habitation of any race, however far to the north its origin may have been; hundreds of millions of men can find healthful homes and abundant sustenance in this great territory.

The population in 1900 was only 42,461,381, less than six to the square mile. The density of population was less than one-eighth of that in the State of Missouri, less than one-sixtieth of that in the State of Massachusetts, less than one-seventieth of that in England, less than 1 per cent of that in Belgium.

With this sparse population the production of wealth is already enormous. The latest trade statistics show exports from South America to foreign countries of $745,530,000, and imports of $499,858,600. Of the five hundred millions of goods that South America buys we sell them but $63,246,525, or 12.6 per cent. Of the seven hundred and forty-five millions that South America sells we buy $152,092,000, or 20.4 per cent—nearly two and one-half times as much as we sell.

Their production is increasing by leaps and bounds. In eleven years the exports of Chile have increased 45 per cent, from $54,030,000 in 1894 to $78,840,000 in 1905. In eight years the exports of Peru have increased 100 per cent, from $13,899,000 in 1897 to $28,758,000 in 1905. In ten years the exports of Brazil have increased 66 per cent, from $134,062,000 in 1894 to $223,101,000 in 1905. In ten years the exports of Argentina have increased 168 per cent, from $115,868,000 in 1895 to $311,544,000 in 1905.

This is only the beginning; the coffee and rubber of Brazil, the wheat and beef and hides of Argentina and Uruguay, the copper and nitrates of Chile, the copper and tin of Bolivia, the silver and gold and cotton and sugar of Peru, are but samples of what the soil and mines of that wonderful continent are capable of yielding. Ninety-seven per cent of the territory of South America is occupied by ten independent Republics living under constitutions substantially copied or adapted from our own. Under the new conditions of tranquillity and security which prevail in most of them their eager invitation to immigrants from the Old World will not long pass unheeded.

The pressure of population abroad will inevitably turn its streams of life and labor toward those fertile fields and valleys. The streams have already begun to flow; more than two hundred thousand immigrants entered the Argentine Republic last year; they are coming this year at the rate of over three hundred thousand. Many thousands of Germans have already settled in southern Brazil. They are most welcome in Brazil; they are good and useful citizens there, as they are here; I hope that many more will come to Brazil and every other South American country, and add their vigorous industry and good citizenship to the upbuilding of their adopted home.

With the increase of population in such a field, under free institutions, with the fruits of labor and the rewards of enterprise secure, the production of wealth and the increase of purchasing power will afford a market for the commerce of the world worthy to rank even with the markets of the Orient as the goal of business enterprise. The material resources of South America are in some important respects complementary to our own; that continent is weakest where North America is strongest as a field for manufactures; it has comparatively little coal and iron. In many respects the people of the two continents are complementary to each other; the South American is polite, refined, cultivated, fond of literature and of expression, and of the graces and charms of life, while the North American is strenuous, intense, utilitarian. Where we accumulate, they spend. While we have less of the cheerful philosophy which finds sources of happiness in the existing conditions of life, they have less of the inventive faculty which strives continually to increase the productive power of man and lower the cost of manufacture. The chief merits of the peoples of the two continents are different; their chief defects are different. Mutual intercourse and knowledge can not fail to greatly benefit both. Each can learn from the other; each can teach much to the other, and each can contribute greatly to the development and prosperity of the other. A large part of their products find no domestic competition here; a large part of our products will find no domestic competition there. The typical conditions exist for that kind of trade which is profitable, honorable, and beneficial to both parties.

The relations between the United States and South America have been chiefly political rather than commercial or personal. In the early days of the South American struggle for independence the eloquence of Henry Clay awakened in the American people a generous sympathy for the patriots of the south as for brethren struggling in the common cause of liberty. The clear-eyed, judicious diplomacy of Richard Rush, the American minister at the Court of St. James, effected a complete understanding with Great Britain for concurrent action in opposition to the designs of the Holy Alliance, already contemplating the partition of the Southern Continent among the great powers of Continental Europe. The famous declaration of Monroe arrayed the organized and rapidly increasing power of the United States as an obstacle to European interference and made it forever plain that the cost of European aggression would be greater than any advantage which could be won even by successful aggression.

That great declaration was not the chance expression of the opinion or the feeling of the moment; it crystallized the sentiment for human liberty and human rights which has saved American idealism from the demoralization of narrow selfishness, and has given to American democracy its true world power in the virile potency of a great example. It responded to the instinct of self-preservation in an intensely practical people. It was the result of conference with Jefferson and Madison and John Quincy Adams and John C. Calhoun and William Wirt—a combination of political wisdom, experience, and skill not easily surpassed. The particular circumstances which led to the declaration no longer exists; no Holy Alliance now threatens to partition South America; no European colonization of the west coast threatens to exclude us from the Pacific. But those conditions were merely the occasion for the declaration of a principle of action. Other occasions for the application of the principle have arisen since; it needs no prophetic vision to see that other occasions for its application may arise hereafter. The principle declared by Monroe is as wise an expression of sound political judgment to-day, as truthful a representation of the sentiments and instincts of the American people to-day, as living in its force as an effective rule of conduct whenever occasion shall arise, as it was on the 2d of December, 1823.

These great political services to South American independence, however, did not and could not in the nature of things create any relation between the people of South America and the people of the United States except a relation of political sympathy.

Twenty-five years ago Mr. Blaine, sanguine, resourceful, and gifted with that imagination which enlarges the historian's understanding of the past into the statesman's comprehension of the future, undertook to inaugurate a new era of American relations which should supplement political sympathy by personal acquaintance, by the intercourse of expanding trade, and by mutual helpfulness. As Secretary of State under President Arthur he invited the American nations to a conference to be held on the 24th of November, 1882, for the purpose of considering and discussing the subject of preventing war between the nations of America. That invitation, abandoned by Mr. Frelinghuysen, was renewed under Mr. Cleveland, and on the 2d of October, 1889, Mr. Blaine, again Secretary of State under President Harrison, had the singular good fortune to execute his former design and to open the sessions of the First American Conference at Washington. In an address of wisdom and lofty spirit, which should ever give honor to his memory, he described the assembly as—

an honorable, peaceful conference of seventeen independent American powers, in which all shall meet together on terms of absolute equality; a conference in which there can be no attempt to coerce a single delegate against his own conception of the interests of his nation; a conference which will permit no secret understanding on any subject, but will frankly publish to the world all its conclusions; a conference which will tolerate no spirit of conquest, but will aim to cultivate an American sympathy as broad as both continents; a conference which will form no selfish alliance against the older nations from which we are proud to claim inheritance— a conference, in fine, which will seek nothing, propose nothing, endure nothing that is not, in the general sense of all the delegates, timely, wise, and peaceful.

The policy which Blaine inaugurated has been continued; the Congress of the United States has approved it; subsequent Presidents have followed it. The First Conference at Washington has been succeeded by a Second Conference in Mexico, and now by a Third Conference in Rio de Janeiro; and it is to be followed in years to come by further successive assemblies in which the representatives of all American States shall acquire better knowledge and more perfect understanding and be drawn together by the recognition of common interests and the kindly consideration and discussion of measures for mutual benefit.

Nevertheless, Mr. Blaine was in advance of his time. In 1881 and 1889 neither had the United States reached a point where it could turn its energies away from its own internal development and direct them outward toward the development of foreign enterprises and foreign trade, nor had the South American countries reached the stage of stability in government and security for property necessary to their industrial development.

Now, however, the time has come; both North and South America have grown up to Blaine's policy; the production, the trade, the capital, the enterprise of the United States have before them the opportunity to follow, and they are free to follow, the pathway marked out by the far-sighted statesmanship of Blaine for the growth of America, North and South, in the peaceful prosperity of a mighty commerce. . . .

*ANNUAL MESSAGE from President Theodore Roosevelt to the
United States Congress, December 3, 1906 (extract)*
Foreign Relations of the United States, 1906, I, vii, xlv

THE SECOND INTERNATIONAL CONFERENCE of American Republics,
held in Mexico in the years 1901–2, provided for the holding of the
third conference within five years, and committed the fixing of the
time and place and the arrangements for the conference to the governing board of the Bureau of American Republics, composed of the
representatives of all the American nations in Washington. That
board discharged the duty imposed upon it with marked fidelity and
painstaking care, and upon the courteous invitation of the United
States of Brazil, the conference was held at Rio de Janeiro, continuing
from the 23d of July to the 29th of August last. Many subjects of
common interest to all the American nations were discust by the conference, and the conclusions reached, embodied in a series of resolutions and proposed conventions, will be laid before you upon the
coming in of the final report of the American delegates. They contain
many matters of importance relating to the extension of trade, the
increase of communication, the smoothing away of barriers to free
intercourse, and the promotion of a better knowledge and good
understanding between the different countries represented. The
meetings of the conference were harmonious and the conclusions
were reached with substantial unanimity. It is interesting to observe
that in the successive conferences which have been held the representatives of the different American nations have been learning to work
together effectively, for, while the First Conference in Washington in
1889, and the Second Conference in Mexico in 1901–2, occupied many
months, with much time wasted in an unregulated and fruitless discussion, the Third Conference at Rio exhibited much of the facility
in the practical dispatch of business which characterizes permanent
deliberative bodies, and completed its labors within the period of six
weeks originally allotted for its sessions.

Quite apart from the specific value of the conclusions reached by
the conference, the example of the representatives of all the American
nations engaging in harmonious and kindly consideration and discussion of subjects of common interest is itself of great and substantial
value for the promotion of reasonable and considerate treatment of
all international questions. The thanks of this country are due to the

Government of Brazil and to the people of Rio de Janeiro for the generous hospitality with which our delegates, in common with the others, were received, entertained, and facilitated in their work.

Incidentally to the meeting of the conference, the Secretary of State visited the city of Rio de Janeiro and was cordially received by the conference, of which he was made an honorary president. The announcement of his intention to make this visit was followed by most courteous and urgent invitations from nearly all the countries of South America to visit them as the guest of their Governments. It was deemed that by the acceptance of these invitations we might appropriately express the real respect and friendship in which we hold our sister Republics of the southern continent, and the Secretary, accordingly, visited Brazil, Uruguay, Argentina, Chile, Peru, Panama, and Colombia. He refrained from visiting Paraguay, Bolivia, and Ecuador only because the distance of their capitals from the seaboard made it impracticable with the time at his disposal. He carried with him a message of peace and friendship, and of strong desire for good understanding and mutual helpfulness; and he was everywhere received in the spirit of his message. The members of government, the press, the learned professions, the men of business, and the great masses of the people united everywhere in emphatic response to his friendly expressions and in doing honor to the country and cause which he represented.

In many parts of South America there has been much misunderstanding of the attitude and purposes of the United States toward the other American Republics. An idea had become prevalent that our assertion of the Monroe Doctrine implied, or carried with it, an assumption of superiority, and of a right to exercise some kind of protectorate over the countries to whose territory that doctrine applies. Nothing could be farther from the truth. Yet that impression continued to be a serious barrier to good understanding, to friendly intercourse, to the introduction of American capital and the extension of American trade. The impression was so widespread that apparently it could not be reached by any ordinary means.

It was part of Secretary Root's mission to dispel this unfounded impression, and there is just cause to believe that he has succeeded. . . .

ADDRESS by Elihu Root, Secretary of State, at the Opening of the Central American Peace Conference, at Washington, December 13, 1907
Foreign Relations of the United States, 1907, II, 687

USAGE devolves upon me as the head of the Foreign Office of the country in which you are assembled to call this meeting together; to call it to order and to preside during the formation of your organization. I wish to express to you, at the outset, the high appreciation of the Government of the United States of the compliment you pay to us in selecting the city of Washington as the field of your labors in behalf of the rule of peace and order and brotherhood among the peoples of Central America. It is most gratifying to the people of the United States that you should feel that you will find here an atmosphere favorable to the development of the ideas of peace and unity, of progress and mutual helpfulness, in place of war and revolution and the retardation of the principles of liberty and justice.

So far as a sincere and friendly desire for success in your labors may furnish a favorable atmosphere, you certainly will have it here. The people of the United States are sincere believers in the principles that you are seeking to apply to the conduct of your international affairs in Central America. They sincerely desire the triumph and the control of the principles of liberty and order everywhere in the world. They especially desire that the blessings which follow the control of those principles may be enjoyed by all the people of our sister republics on the western hemisphere, and we further believe that it will be, from the most selfish point of view, for our interests to have peaceful, prosperous, and progressive republics in Central America.

The people of the United Mexican States and of the United States of America are now enjoying great benefits from the mutual interchange of commerce and friendly intercourse between the two countries of Mexico and the United States. Prosperity, the increase of wealth, the success of enterprise—all the results that come from the intelligent use of wealth—are being enjoyed by the people of both countries, through the friendly intercourse that utilizes for the people of each country the prosperity of the other. We in the United States should be most happy if the states of Central America might move with greater rapidity along the pathway of such prosperity, of such progress; to the end that we may share, through commerce and friendly intercourse, in your new prosperity, and aid you by our prosperity.

We cannot fail, gentlemen, to be admonished by the many failures which have been made by the people of Central America to establish agreement among themselves which would be lasting, that the task you have before you is no easy one. The trial has often been made and the agreements which have been elaborated, signed, ratified, seem to have been written in water. Yet I cannot resist the impression that we have at last come to the threshold of a happier day for Central America. Time is necessary to political development. I have great confidence in the judgment that in the long course of time, through successive steps of failure, through the accompanying education of your people, through the encouraging examples which now, more than ever before, surround you, success will be attained in securing unity and progress in other countries of the new hemisphere. Through the combination of all these, you are at a point in your history where it is possible for you to take a forward step that will remain.

It would ill become me to attempt to propose or suggest the steps which you should take; but I will venture to observe that the all-important thing for you to accomplish is that while you enter into agreements which will, I am sure, be framed in consonance with the most peaceful aspirations and the most rigid sense of justice, you shall devise also some practical methods under which it will be possible to secure the performance of those agreements. The mere declaration of general principles, the mere agreement upon lines of policy and of conduct, are of little value unless there be practical and definite methods provided by which the responsibility for failing to keep the agreement may be fixed upon some definite person, and the public sentiment of Central America brought to bear to prevent the violation. The declaration that a man is entitled to his liberty would be of little value with us in this country, were it not for the writ of habeas corpus that makes it the duty of a specific judge, when applied to, to inquire into the cause of a man's detention, and set him at liberty if he is unjustly detained. The provision which declares that a man should not be deprived of his property without due process of law would be of little value were it not for the practical provision which imposes on specific officers the duty of nullifying every attempt to take away a man's property without due process of law.

To find practical definite methods by which you shall make it somebody's duty to see that the great principles you declare are not violated, by which if an attempt be made to violate them the responsibility may be fixed upon the guilty individual—those, in my judgment, are the problems to which you should specifically and most earnestly address yourselves.

I have confidence in your success because I have confidence in your sincerity of purpose, and because I believe that your people have developed to the point where they are ready to receive and to utilize such results as you may work out. Why should you not live in peace and harmony? You are one people in fact; your citizenship is interchangeable—your race, your religion, your customs, your laws, your lineage, your consanguinity and relations, your social connections, your sympathies, your aspirations, and your hopes for the future are the same.

It can be nothing but the ambition of individuals who care more for their selfish purposes than for the good of their country, that can prevent the people of the Central American states from living together in peace and unity.

It is my most earnest hope, it is the hope of the American Government and people, that from this conference may come the specific and practical measures which will enable the people of Central America to march on with equal step abreast of the most progressive nations of modern civilization; to fulfill their great destinies in that brotherhood which nature has intended them to preserve; to exile forever from that land of beauty and of wealth incalculable the fraternal strife which has hitherto held you back in the development of your civilization.

STATEMENT by Philander C. Knox, Secretary of State, before the Committee on Foreign Relations of the United States Senate, Regarding a Convention between the United States and Honduras, May 24, 1911

Foreign Relations of the United States, 1912, p. 583. The Senate voted against ratification of the convention. See also *infra*, Part VI, Interventions in Nicaragua, Haiti, and the Dominican Republic

THE SITUATION

THE CENTRAL AMERICAN Republic of Honduras, which in area is about the size of the State of Pennsylvania, contains about 500,000 inhabitants. Its public improvements consist of about 57 miles of railroad and inadequate docks at Puerto Cortes on the Atlantic, and still more inadequate docks at Amapala on the Gulf of Fonseca on the Pacific side. The Gulf of Fonseca, by the way, is the best, if not the only harbor of value on the Pacific coast between Panama and San Diego if, indeed, it is not the only one between Valparaiso and San Diego. The only other public improvement in the Republic worth noting is the Sierra Road, a highway constructed by President Sierra, but so inadequately maintained that the carrying power of a mule cart on this highway is now less than one-half of what it was 15 years ago.

Honduras is bankrupt, famished, and discouraged. The condition of her people is well illustrated by the fact that it is estimated by a reputable writer that the average annual expenditures of its peasantry for clothing amounts to less than $1.50 a year.

"Señor," said an old Honduranean, "why should our people accumulate more than one shirt apiece, when a revolution may come along at any hour and rob them of everything?" (Central America and Its Problems—Palmer.)

A former President of Honduras, speaking of his country's condition and of its dependence upon the United States, is quoted as saying:

Will you not use your strong arm to give us peace—peace long enough to learn that continual revolution is not the natural order of a nation's existence? There is no act of yours guaranteeing good government which I would not welcome. How can we care for ourselves, how can we rule ourselves under such conditions? And you took away our principal source of income when you made Cuba so prosperous that she raises her own cattle and imports no more of ours.

Honduras has been the scene of seven bloody revolutions within the last 15 years. Within that time the United States has been compelled to intervene, in the interests of universal commerce and civilization, to close or to prevent sanguinary ruinous civil war within her borders.

The debt of Honduras with the interest thereon, which has not been paid for over 40 years, amounts now to about $125,000,000. Her revenue, according to the last available data, is a little more than $1,654,000 a year, of which $766,495 is customs receipts and $887,873 comes from liquor and other monopolies. Thirty-nine per cent of her revenue is absorbed by her military establishment.

In order to relieve the Republic from this crushing weight of debt, the burden of which has depressed her people to a pathetic helplessness, Honduras is endeavoring to borrow, upon the credit of her revenue, a sum of money that will enable her to compromise with her creditors and secure an amount adequate to undertake such internal improvements as will inspire her own people to new courage and establish such stability in her political and fiscal systems as will attract to her borders the enterprise and the capital of the type of immigration necessary to her regeneration.

THE REMEDY

Realizing the absolute inability to meet her obligations or even to pay the interest thereon, some of which runs at 10 per cent per annum, the Republic of Honduras has endeavored to reach some adjustment with her creditors, and in order to obtain reasonable terms sought the aid of the United States, and the convention which is now before the Senate has really been signed at the instance of Honduras. The reason why a convention has been entered into regarding this matter is that without materially upholding the now shattered public credit of Honduras it would be utterly impossible to obtain a loan sufficiently large to cancel outstanding obligations on terms anything like within the reach of Honduras. Honduras standing alone would have to borrow money at such exorbitant rates of interest, or obtain for its bonds such a low market price that a very much larger issue than that now proposed would have to be made.

The convention has been drawn for the purpose of giving security. That is, for the purpose of assuring the regular payment of interest and sinking fund upon the debt. Its provisions, briefly are:

1. Honduras engages to place the loan in the United States.

2. Honduras pledges her customs receipts for the payment of the interest and sinking fund.

3. Honduras agrees to appoint a receiver from a list of names prepared by the fiscal agent and approved by the President of the United States.

4. Honduras agrees to afford protection to the receiver and that if necessary the United States may give such protection.

5. The receiver is under obligation to report to the fiscal agent of the loan and to either Government regarding the discharge of his duties.

6. Honduras further agrees not to alter the customs receipts during the existence of the loan.

The convention applies to no specified contract, but any contract, to come within the scope of the convention, must receive the scrutiny of this Government.

That the collection of the customs should be honestly carried on and their receipts properly administered is an obvious necessity, and the provision in the convention as to the appointment of the receiver makes possible the selection of a competent, honest, bonded person. In this regard it will be noted that the Honduras convention differs in this respect somewhat from the Santo Domingo convention in not going quite so far. Under the terms of the latter the receiver general of customs is appointed by the President of the United States direct. That the Government of Honduras should promise to give this receiver adequate protection, and in the absence of which this Government should have the right to protect him in the discharge of his duties, is equally an obvious necessity. It is self-evident that as the customs duties are pledged for the service of the loan, they must be adequate to meet the interest and sinking fund, and that to prevent their being in any wise altered and thereby rendered insufficient, or to allow substituting for them any new duties different in name or collected from a different viewpoint, is likewise self-evident.

That Honduras should agree to permit its customs to be collected in the manner indicated and should further stipulate that such customs duties will not be altered will, from experience, in no wise decrease or interfere with the administration of these funds. When the Government of the United States entered into the agreement with the Dominican Republic, and subsequent to the appointment by the President of a receiver general of customs, the revenues of that Republic increased from about $1,800,000 to the sum of $3,300,000. The cost of the service of the loan negotiated for the Dominican Republic, interest and sinking fund, is $1,200,000 per annum. It will thus be seen that the Dominican Republic is now promptly meeting the payment of its obligations and that it also has more money than heretofore for the maintenance and conduct of the Government. Not only has the Dominican Republic had no difficulty regarding the alteration of its tariff laws, but the duties on staple articles have in almost all cases been subjected to a scaling down, so that goods are now delivered into that Republic at less cost than before the assistance of the United States was invoked. That this would be true in regard to Honduras may be confidently asserted.

Prior to the Dominican convention this Government was constantly having to interpose between clamorous foreign claimants and the Dominican Government and to use its naval forces for the protection of United States property. Since the Dominican convention no such necessity has arisen. The situation in the Dominican Republic prior to the convention is the situation in much of Central America and the Caribbean Republics of to-day.

Then several agreements between the Dominican Republic and foreign creditors existed which specifically pledged a portion of the customs duties of specified ports of the Republic. Some of these agreements, indeed, were protocols negotiated by the representatives of foreign governments with the Dominican Republic. Italy had several such protocols and the Spanish and German Governments also had a protocol assuring the payment of certain claims of their subjects. The Dominican Government was in default and was continuing in default, until finally the Italian Government sent a war vessel to Dominican waters, and had it not been for the action of the United States in extending a helping hand the Dominican customhouses would have been taken possession of by the Italians and the administration of the revenues of that Republic would have fallen into the hands of a European power. I am satisfied that if the present arrangement can not be carried out a similar situation may confront the Republic of Honduras.

In fact, at the time when the negotiations were begun for the purpose of refunding the Honduranean finances a proposition had been made by the representatives of Great Britain in Central America on behalf of the foreign bondholders, and was about to be consummated, which was highly objectionable. This plan contemplated the possible raising of the import duties in Honduras, and made absolutely no provision for the settlement of large American claims which were being asserted against the Government of Honduras and left the internal indebtedness of that Republic absolutely unsettled. It also contained provisions which might have placed the railroad running out of Puerto Cortes under the control of a foreign syndicate.

During the course of a year it is many times necessary for the United States to send forces to the ports of some of the Central American Republics in order to afford adequate protection to foreign life and property. This is done at an enormous expense, an informal estimate from some of the naval officers showing that the annual cost to this Government amounts to over $1,000,000. Twice in the past six months this Government has had to interfere in Honduras. Should the convention be put into operation, no such necessity will be likely to arise. The revolutions in Central America are in most instances unprincipled, the main—in fact, the only—object being to gain control of the collection of the customs duties. The removal of such a possibility from the revolutionary horizon would go far toward an effective dampening of the aspirations of adventurers.

The convention would have the effect of affording security to the bondholders; of assuring to Honduras the punctual and complete discharge of her obligations practically without cost to the Government; the enjoyment of continued peace, and the consequent internal development; and to the United States the saving in expense to this Government would alone seem to be a sufficient inducement.

Subsequently to the signing of the convention detailed negotiations were undertaken with a representative of four of the largest banking houses in this country, with a result that contracts, the text of which have already been submitted to the committee, have been drawn and signed. These contracts cover the details that have been worked out for the financial rehabilitation of Honduras. It may here be said that without such convention as has been negotiated none of the banking houses concerned would have been willing to loan Honduras money on anything like the same terms as have now been agreed to, if, indeed, they would have been willing to accept the obligations of that Republic at all. In this connection the benefit of the convention to Honduras is at once apparent. The details of the loan are, roughly, as follows:

The bankers have by previous agreement been able to obtain an option on about $20,000,000 principal of the outstanding foreign debt of Honduras and are confident that the balance will be surrendered upon terms as favorable as those offered to the bondholders now pledged.

Honduras agrees to issue $10,000,000 worth of bonds, $7,500,000 of which are to be issued now, the other $2,500,000 to be issued for the purpose of internal improvement and only when the revenues of the Republic justify it. These bonds the bankers agree to take at 88. The cash thus obtained will be sufficient to provide for the payment of all expenses, for the cancellation of the old outstanding bonds at the rate of 15 per cent of the principal and for the establishment of a cash fund of $2,100,000. This cash fund will be used for three purposes:

(a) Approximately $700,000 for the cancellation of the internal debt of Honduras, which amounts, roughly, to $1,700,000.

(b) To the provision for the payment, under direct settlement by approval by the State Department or impartial arbitration, of the claims of American citizens.

(c) The immediate investment of about $700,000 for the improvement of the Interoceanic Railway which runs from Puerto Cortes inland and which traverses one of the richest Central American banana zones.

Besides the customs revenues which are pledged for the payment of the interest and sinking fund of Honduras's debt on the new bonds, the Government of Honduras has further agreed with the bankers that the railroad at Puerto Cortes shall be extended as stated above, operated under expert management, and that after the proper expenditure of funds for the further development of the road any sums remaining over shall be paid to the fiscal agent for the service of the loan and shall thus partially relieve the customs receipts. The revenues for the road for the last year are calculated to have been about $140,000, and it is believed that with the expenditure above provided they will easily amount to $300,000. The interest cost of service of a loan of $7,500,000 at 5 per cent interest and 1 per cent sinking fund per annum is $450,000. War expenses in Honduras annually average not less than $600,000, and it must be assumed that these will be reduced by at least one-half. In other words, aside from the increase of the customs receipts under an honest and competent administration, sufficient funds would result from the earnings of the railway and decrease of the war expense to service the loan without cost to Honduras.

The price to be paid for the bonds by the bankers, that is, 88, in comparison with the price paid for the Dominican bonds, 98.5, both at 5 per cent interest, may perhaps cause surprise. Bearing in mind, however, that when the Dominican loan was taken there was already on deposit in New York the large sum of $3,800,000 collected under the modus vivendi, and the success of the loan was assured, besides the fact that the Dominican bonds were used to the extent of 80 per cent for the extinguishment of the claims outstanding against the Republic; and considering the woeful condition of Honduras's present financial status, her depleted credit, and the fact that the success of the loan has not yet been fiscally demonstrated, the price is not surprising. The price, comparatively speaking, is higher than any prices obtained for bonds by any Central American State. Salvador, which has the best credit of all, commands a price of 99 for 6 per cent bonds, thus paying $1 per annum for the use of $16.50. Nicaraguan bonds, also 6 per cent, have been quoted as high as 93. They were taken by the bankers at 75, so that Nicaragua paid $1 per annum for the use of $15.50. The Guatemalan 4 per cent bonds were sold in the neighborhood of 44, thus Guatemala pays $1 per annum for the use of $11. Costa Rican 5 per cent bonds have been averaging about 45, thus Costa Rica is paying $1 per annum for the use of $9. Honduras 5 per cent bonds will be taken at 88, thus Honduras will be compelled to pay $1 per annum for the use of $17.60.

From past experience of the United States in Central America it is manifest that either with or without a convention we must to some extent exert influence for peace and order. With the convention as it stands any intervention that may occur will be by virtue of a treaty right. Without the convention any intervention there may be must be of an armed and forcible character. Without the convention we must, when unfortunately necessary, intervene. With the convention intervention will probably be rendered unnecessary.

Whether rightfully or wrongfully, we are in the eyes of the world and because of the Monroe doctrine, held responsible for the order of Central America, and its proximity to the Canal Zone makes the preservation of peace in that neighborhood particularly necessary.

Aside from the purely altruistic motives which have been pointed out above, it must be borne in mind that there is another and a selfish motive which counsels the adoption of the present convention. The development and peace of all Central America must result in a direct and very substantial benefit to the southern ports of the United States—Galveston, New Orleans, Mobile, etc.—as they will all have more frequent intercourse and be able to cultivate a more extensive market for their products, while the Central American Republics, with their production increased, will find a ready market in these gateways of the United States. Railways leading to them must carry this freight for distribution throughout the Southern States.

For the fiscal year 1908–9 the total imports of the Republic of Honduras amounted to $2,581,553, of which the United States alone furnished $1,769,876, or over 68 per cent.

The amount of the export trade of Honduras for the same period was $1,990,601, of which the United States alone took $1,834,565, or more than 92 per cent.

As stated above, most of this trade is carried on with Honduras from the Gulf ports of the United States.

The principle involved, therefore, in this convention, which will enable the maintenance of peace in Central America, is in reality most important from a material standpoint to the South. In short, the matter may be summed up as follows:

Shall the Government of the United States make American capital an instrumentality to secure financial stability, and hence prosperity and peace, to the more backward Republics in the neighborhood of the Panama Canal? And in order to give that measure of security which alone would induce capital to be such instrumentality without imposing too great a burden upon the countries concerned, shall this Government assume toward the customs collections a relationship only great enough for this purpose—a relationship, however, the moral effect and potentialities of which result in preventing the customs revenues of such Republic from being seized as the means of carrying on devastating and unprincipled revolutions?

I here desire to invite the attention of the committee to this important feature of the policy so wisely adopted by the last administration, which it is now desired to extend to Honduras. This feature is that the more this plan of assistance to some of the more backward republics is extended, the less becomes the degree of intimacy established between the Government of the United States and that of the country to which the aid is given. I refer in particular to the fact that the provision in the Dominican convention made the general receiver of customs an appointee of the President of the United States, whereas the Honduras convention makes the collector of customs an appointee of the Government of the Republic of Honduras, the degree of intimacy in connection therefore being to that extent lessened. It may possibly be necessary to sign one more convention with provisions practically identical with this for the purpose of assisting the Government of Nicaragua, but in regard to the other Central American States it may be confidently stated that such a degree of intimacy will not be necessary. In the case of Costa Rica, which has just refunded its foreign debt, any possible relation on the part of this Government becomes effective only in case of default. In regard to Guatemala, which has recently indicated its desire to enlist the helpful support of this Government in rehabilitating its finances, the degree of intimacy will probably be even less. And in regard to Salvador no relation between this Government and the Government of that Republic concerning its foreign debt exists. In other words, the intimacy decreases in proportion as the ability and readiness of the country to meet its obligations increases. This, therefore, is not a policy of which the end can not be seen. The adoption of this convention is not setting such a precedent as might be desired to apply subsequently to all of the Caribbean Republics. This and the Nicaraguan convention will probably be the only two that it will be necessary for this Government to negotiate.

The contracts negotiated between the bankers and the Government of Honduras, in order to insure their fairness with regard to that Republic, have been subjected to the careful scrutiny of the Department of State, and have, further, been submitted to be examined from the standpoint of Honduras by financial and legal experts in New York, who have passed them as fair and equitable and probably the best that can be procured for Honduras under all the circumstances. . . .

ADDRESS by Philander C. Knox, Secretary of State, at Managua, Nicaragua, March 6, 1912

Foreign Relations of the United States, 1912, p. 1114. The address was made during a trip to the countries of Central America and the Caribbean

MR. PRESIDENT, LADIES, AND GENTLEMEN:
On behalf of the Government and people of the United States permit me to express my sincere appreciation and thanks for your

kindly greeting. I have come to Nicaragua to express to you the keen feeling of neighborly sympathy entertained by my Government for the Government and people of Nicaragua, and it is indeed a pleasure to meet you here and be privileged to speak to you face to face.

Thanks to the frank and most cordial relations which happily exist between our respective countries our people are rapidly becoming more deeply interested in the welfare and development and consequent prosperity of Nicaragua, and are more than ever before manifesting a desire to cultivate even closer and more intimate relations. Movements toward closer association and truer friendship between the peoples of different countries are not arbitrarily created by outward efforts; they spring from within. Their primary impulse is the growing conviction of neighboring countries that the development and prosperity of each is in harmony with the advancement of the welfare of all. Such movements are tremendously facilitated by the confidence and friendship that follows acquaintance, and that fact is the inspiration of my mission.

Although the interest of the people of the United States in the welfare of your country is keen there is not and never has been any desire either on the part of the American Government or people to mix unduly or unbidden in the internal affairs of Nicaragua, but to the request for assistance in the regeneration of Nicaragua my Government was happy promptly to respond.

The political and economic situation that had arisen, due to many years of misrule, rendered the task of reorganization of your Government exceedingly difficult, and your leaders, because of the frank friendship and good faith of the United States toward the Nicaraguan people as a whole, naturally turned to the American Government for council and assistance in the arduous task before them. My Government was glad to send to Managua a special commissioner to aid in making a fixed program which the leaders pledged themselves to carry out and in which was contemplated loyal cooperation in the rehabilitation of Nicaragua. The Government of the United States was glad to suggest, upon the invitation of Nicaragua, a competent financial adviser who should make a careful study of the economic conditions of the country and counsel the Government of Nicaragua as to the best methods to be pursued in dealing with this most difficult and important problem, and also to assist you in devising means to be adopted to deal with the claims against Nicaragua and to dispose in an adequate and just manner of the outstanding and legally or economically unsound and ruinous concessions.

The United States was likewise, upon your invitation, glad to conclude a convention with Nicaragua which will provide a sufficient measure of security for a new foreign loan, essential for your financial reorganization and internal public improvements. While this convention is still pending before the United States Senate it has become necessary for Nicaragua to make some provision for the immediate reformation of the local currency, and in order to accomplish this a short-time loan has been negotiated and my Government has gladly approved the name of an American collector general of customs, who has been appointed by the Government of Nicaragua.

The Nicaraguan people are to be congratulated that they have at the head of the nation a man quick to realize the necessities of the country and of courage sufficient to expeditiously set on foot the best and surest means of meeting the country's needs.

It must here be remembered that the progress already made and the continuance of Nicaragua along the path to national regeneration depend almost entirely upon the preservation of peace and contentment in the country, and that the surest means of reaching this end is the faithful observance of the pledges made by the leaders of all parties.

In the zone of the Caribbean the responsibilities of the United States are becoming increasingly great as the opening of the great waterway which is to change the trade routes of the world draws nearer and the desire of the United States to see order and prosperity becomes even more intensified. We are especially interested in the prosperity of all the people of Nicaragua. Their prosperity means contentment and contentment means repose. The United States have always cherished sentiments of the warmest regard and most cordial esteem for the people of Nicaragua, and from the very commencement of the independent existence of Nicaragua the Government of the United States has steadfastly adhered to the traditional policy that found expression in the words of President Monroe and which indicated a sympathetic interest in seeing this country develop and progress unrestricted and unfettered by the interference of foreign nations. Encouraged by that sympathy Nicaragua was able to add to its jurisdiction a strip of territory along the Atlantic coast which, with the establishment of better means of communication between the eastern and western portions of the country, will add greatly to the resources and the political prestige of the Republic. The people of the United States most earnestly desire that Nicaragua should steadily advance to that place in the family of nations to which its situation, its wealth, and the capacity of its people for self-government justly entitle it, and in that spirit of cordial good will and warm friendship the Government of the United States stands prepared to lend such counsel and assistance as may be requested and as may be proper in the establishment of a government calculated to maintain order, enforce law, discharge its international obligations, and promote peace, progress, and prosperity.

I was much impressed, sir, by the lofty standard Nicaragua has set for herself, so eloquently expressed by you in your gracious words of welcome to our Minister, whom you have so recently received. When you assured him that Nicaragua "had established as a firm base of government the respect for human life, the absolute right to property, the suppression of the odious system of forced contributions, the complete independence of the courts, the freedom of the press, and the observance of all individual guaranties," you justly concluded that these facts were "eloquent testimony of the unvarying purpose that animates the Government of Nicaragua to be faithful to its international obligations and to the promises of liberty and justice given to its citizens."

It has probably never happened that neighboring countries, which have been more or less afflicted with international and internal troubles of frequent recurrence arising from similar causes, have adopted such radical and effective means for their prevention as did the five Central American republics in the three treaties signed at Washington in 1907 under the friendly counsel and sympathy of the United States and Mexico.

By the convention for the establishment of a Central American Court of Justice they bound themselves to create and maintain a permanent tribunal and to submit to it all controversies and questions which may arise among them of whatever nature. By the general treaty of peace and amity they agreed to the maintenance of peace in their mutual relations, and to that end, taking into consideration the central geographical position of Honduras, they stipulated for its complete neutrality in event of conflict between the other republics, and, in order to remove one of the most frequent sources of trouble, provision was made calculated to suppress revolutionary activity on the part of the residents in adjacent republics. By the addition to that convention, and for the purpose of further discouraging and preventing internal disturbances in the five republics, they agreed to refuse to recognize revolutionary governments in each other's countries until first constitutionally recognized in the country where occurring; they agreed not to intervene in any country in case of civil war; and they agreed to constitutional reform. The mere fact that these high resolutions may not have been strictly observed in particular cases should by no means discourage the signatory parties, the important fact being that these five republics have indicated their sincere desire for international peace and domestic tranquility, and have devised complete and adequate means to that end, the faithful adherence to which will become more and more habitual as the excellent example of the more advanced republics continues to prompt it.

Mindful of the part the United States took in encouraging the making of these treaties and the moral obligations arising therefrom it is not the intention of our Government or our people to refrain from lending every possible proper aid and encouragement to the parties to these conventions to constantly carry into effect their wise and beneficient provisions.

If this or any other government is to endure in this or any other land it is necessary that wisdom, vigilance, patience, and loyalty should abide in its halls of legislation, its chambers of justice, in the centers of executive power, and with the dominating mass of its people.

The establishment and preservation of the institutions of free government, here as elsewhere, depend not upon those who think first of serving themselves and to that end would sacrifice their country; not upon those who think only of defeating the opposition and to that end would sacrifice the world; but upon those who think only of the welfare of their country and to that end would sacrifice themselves.

In Nicaragua there is to-day present the opportunity and the acute necessity for a display of the very highest and most enduring type of patriotism. There is now a call to her true sons to give the best that is within them to anxious and concerted effort for the public weal, to execute the compromises, adjustments, and concessions essential for the general welfare, and, by consistent and loyal adherence to the understandings and agreements that have been reached for the rehabilitation of their Government, to place their names first upon their country's enduring roll of fame.

ANNUAL MESSAGE from President William H. Taft to the United States Congress, December 3, 1912 (extracts)
Foreign Relations of the United States, 1912, pp. vii, xii, xxiv

SUCCESSFUL EFFORTS IN THE PROMOTION OF PEACE

IN THE FIELD of work toward the ideals óf peace this Government negotiated, but to my regret was unable to consummate, two arbitration treaties which set the highest mark of the aspiration of nations toward the substitution of arbitration and reason for war in the settlement of international disputes. Through the efforts of American diplomacy several wars have been prevented or ended. I refer to the successful tripartite mediation of the Argentine Republic, Brazil, and the United States between Peru and Ecuador; the bringing of the boundary dispute between Panama and Costa Rica to peaceful arbitration; the staying of warlike preparations when Haiti and the Dominican Republic were on the verge of hostilities; the stopping of a war in Nicaragua; the halting of internecine strife in Honduras. The Government of the United States was thanked for its influence toward the restoration of amicable relations between the Argentine Republic and Bolivia. The diplomacy of the United States is active in seeking to assuage the remaining ill-feeling between this country and the Republic of Colombia. In the recent civil war in China the United States successfully joined with the other interested powers in urging an early cessation of hostilities. An agreement has been reached between the Governments of Chile and Peru whereby the celebrated Tacna-Arica dispute, which has so long embittered international relations on the west coast of South America, has at last been adjusted. Simultaneously came the news that the boundary dispute between Peru and Ecuador had entered upon a stage of amicable settlement. The position of the United States in reference to the Tacna-Arica dispute between Chile and Peru has been one of non-intervention, but one of friendly influence and pacific counsel throughout the period during which the dispute in question has been the subject of interchange of views between this Government and the two Governments immediately concerned. In the general easing of international tension on the west coast of South America the tripartite mediation, to which I have referred, has been a most potent and beneficent factor.

CENTRAL AMERICA NEEDS OUR HELP IN DEBT ADJUSTMENT

In Central America the aim has been to help such countries as Nicaragua and Honduras to help themselves. They are the immediate beneficiaries. The national benefit to the United States is twofold. First, it is obvious that the Monroe doctrine is more vital in the neighborhood of the Panama Canal and the zone of the Caribbean than anywhere else. There, too, the maintenance of that doctrine falls most heavily upon the United States. It is therefore essential that the countries within that sphere shall be removed from the jeopardy involved by heavy foreign debt and chaotic national finances and from the ever-present danger of international complications due to disorder at home. Hence the United States has been glad to encourage and support American bankers who were willing to lend a helping hand to the financial rehabilitation of such countries because this financial rehabilitation and the protection of their customhouses from being the prey of would-be dictators would remove at one stroke the menace of foreign creditors and the menace of revolutionary disorder.

The second advantage to the United States is one affecting chiefly all the southern and Gulf ports and the business and industry of the South. The Republics of Central America and the Caribbean possess great natural wealth. They need only a measure of stability and the means of financial regeneration to enter upon an era of peace and prosperity, bringing profit and happiness to themselves and at the same time creating conditions sure to lead to a flourishing interchange of trade with this country.

I wish to call your especial attention to the recent occurrences in Nicaragua, for I believe the terrible events recorded there during the revolution of the past summer—the useless loss of life, the devastation of property, the bombardment of defenseless cities, the killing and wounding of women and children, the torturing of noncombatants to exact contributions, and the suffering of thousands of human beings—might have been averted had the Department of State, through approval of the loan convention by the Senate, been permitted to carry out its now well-developed policy of encouraging the extending of financial aid to weak Central American States with the primary objects of avoiding just such revolutions by assisting those Republics to rehabilitate their finances, to establish their currency on a stable basis, to remove the customhouses from the danger of revolutions by arranging for their secure administration, and to establish reliable banks.

During this last revolution in Nicaragua, the Government of that Republic having admitted its inability to protect American life and property against acts of sheer lawlessness on the part of the malcontents, and having requested this Government to assume that office, it became necessary to land over 2,000 marines and bluejackets in Nicaragua. Owing to their presence the constituted Government of Nicaragua was free to devote its attention wholly to its internal troubles, and was thus enabled to stamp out the rebellion in a short space of time. When the Red Cross supplies sent to Granada had been exhausted, 8,000 persons having been given food in one day upon the arrival of the American forces, our men supplied other unfortunate, needy Nicaraguans from their own haversacks. I wish to congratulate the officers and men of the United States Navy and Marine Corps who took part in reestablishing order in Nicaragua upon their splendid conduct, and to record with sorrow the death of seven

American marines and bluejackets. Since the reestablishment of peace and order, elections have been held amid conditions of quiet and tranquillity. Nearly all the American marines have now been withdrawn. The country should soon be on the road to recovery. The only apparent danger now threatening Nicaragua arises from the shortage of funds. Although American bankers have already rendered assistance, they may naturally be loath to advance a loan adequate to set the country upon its feet without the support of some such convention as that of June, 1911, upon which the Senate has not yet acted.

ENFORCEMENT OF NEUTRALITY LAWS

In the general effort to contribute to the enjoyment of peace by those Republics which are near neighbors of the United States, the administration has enforced the so-called neutrality statutes with a new vigor, and those statutes were greatly strengthened in restricting the exportation of arms and munitions by the joint resolution of last March. It is still a regrettable fact that certain American ports are made the rendezvous of professional revolutionists and others engaged in intrigue against the peace of those Republics. It must be admitted that occasionally a revolution in this region is justified as a real popular movement to throw off the shackles of a vicious and tyrannical government. Such was the Nicaraguan revolution against the Zelaya régime. A nation enjoying our liberal institutions can not escape sympathy with a true popular movement, and one so well justified. In very many cases, however, revolutions in the Republics in question have no basis in principle, but are due merely to the machinations of conscienceless and ambitious men, and have no effect but to bring new suffering and fresh burdens to an already oppressed people. The question whether the use of American ports as *foci* of revolutionary intrigue can be best dealt with by a further amendment to the neutrality statutes or whether it would be safer to deal with special cases by special laws is one worthy of the careful consideration of the Congress.

VISIT OF SECRETARY KNOX TO CENTRAL AMERICA AND THE CARIBBEAN

Impressed with the particular importance of the relations between the United States and the Republics of Central America and the Caribbean region, which of necessity must become still more intimate by reason of the mutual advantages which will be presented by the opening of the Panama Canal, I directed the Secretary of State last February to visit these Republics for the purpose of giving evidence of the sincere friendship and good will which the Government and people of the United States bear toward them. Ten Republics were visited. Everywhere he was received with a cordiality of welcome and a generosity of hospitality such as to impress me deeply and to merit our warmest thanks. The appreciation of the Governments and peoples of the countries visited, which has been appropriately shown in various ways, leaves me no doubt that his visit will conduce to that closer union and better understanding between the United States and those Republics which I have had it much at heart to promote.

OUR MEXICAN POLICY

For two years revolution and counter-revolution have distraught the neighboring Republic of Mexico. Brigandage has involved a great deal of depredation upon foreign interests. There have constantly recurred questions of extreme delicacy. On several occasions very difficult situations have arisen on our frontier. Throughout this trying period, the policy of the United States has been one of patient nonintervention, steadfast recognition of constituted authority in the neighboring nation, and the exertion of every effort to care for American interests. I profoundly hope that the Mexican nation may soon resume the path of order, prosperity, and progress. To that nation in its sore troubles, the sympathetic friendship of the United States has been demonstrated to a high degree. There were in Mexico at the beginning of the revolution some thirty or forty thousand American citizens engaged in enterprises contributing greatly to the prosperity of the Republic and also benefiting the important trade between the two countries. The investment of American capital in Mexico has been estimated at $1,000,000,000. The responsibility of endeavoring to safeguard those interests and the dangers inseparable from propinquity to so turbulent a situation have been great, but I am happy to have been able to adhere to the policy above outlined—a policy which I hope may be soon justified by the complete success of the Mexican people in regaining the blessings of peace and good order. . . .

SOUTH AMERICA

Our relations with the Argentine Republic are most friendly and cordial. So, also, are our relations with Brazil, whose Government has accepted the invitation of the United States to send two army officers to study at the Coast Artillery School at Fort Monroe. The longstanding Alsop claim, which had been the only hindrance to the healthy growth of the most friendly relations between the United States and Chile, having been eliminated through the submission of the question to His Britannic Majesty King George V as "amiable compositeur," it is a cause of much gratification to me that our relations with Chile are now established upon a firm basis of growing friendship. The Chilean Government has placed an officer of the United States Coast Artillery in charge of the Chilean Coast Artillery School, and has shown appreciation of American methods by confiding to an American firm important work for the Chilean coast defenses.

Last year a revolution against the established Government of Ecuador broke out at the principal port of that Republic. Previous to this occurrence the chief American interest in Ecuador, represented by the Guayaquil & Quito Railway Co., incorporated in the United States, had rendered extensive transportation and other services on account to the Ecuadorian Government, the amount of which ran into a sum which was steadily increasing and which the Ecuadorian Government had made no provision to pay, thereby threatening to crush out the very existence of this American enterprise. When tranquillity had been restored to Ecuador as a result of the triumphant progress of the Government forces from Quito, this Government interposed its good offices to the end that the American interests in Ecuador might be saved from complete extinction. As a part of the arrangement which was reached between the parties, and at the request of the Government of Ecuador, I have consented to name an arbitrator, who, acting under the terms of the railroad contract, with an arbitrator named by the Ecuadorian Government, will pass upon the claims that have arisen since the arrangement reached through the action of a similar arbitral tribunal in 1908.

In pursuance of a request made some time ago by the Ecuadorian Government, the Department of State has given much attention to the problem of the proper sanitation of Guayaquil. As a result a detail of officers of the Canal Zone will be sent to Guayaquil to recommend measures that will lead to the complete permanent sanitation of this plague and fever infected region of that Republic, which has for so long constituted a menace to health conditions on the Canal Zone. It is hoped that the report which this mission will furnish will point out a way whereby the modicum of assistance which the United States may properly lend the Ecuadorian Government may be made effective in ridding the west coast of South America of a focus of contagion to the future commercial current passing through the Panama Canal.

In the matter of the claim of John Celestine Landreau against the Government of Peru, which claim arises out of certain contracts and transactions in connection with the discovery and exploitation of guano, and which has been under discussion between the two Governments since 1874, I am glad to report that as the result of prolonged negotiations, which have been characterized by the utmost friendliness and good will on both sides, the Department of State has succeeded in securing the consent of Peru to the arbitration of the claim, and that the negotiations attending the drafting and signature of a protocol submitting the claim to an arbitral tribunal are proceeding with due celerity.

An officer of the American Public Health Service and an American sanitary engineer are now on the way to Iquitos, in the employ of the Peruvian Government, to take charge of the sanitation of that river port. Peru is building a number of submarines in this country, and continues to show every desire to have American capital invested in the Republic.

In July the United States sent undergraduate delegates to the Third International Students Congress held at Lima, American students having been for the first time invited to one of these meetings.

The Republic of Uruguay has shown its appreciation of American agricultural and other methods by sending a large commission to this country and by employing many American experts to assist in building up agricultural and allied industries in Uruguay.

Venezuela is paying off the last of the claims the settlement of which was provided for by the Washington protocols, including those of American citizens. Our relations with Venezuela are most cordial, and the trade of that Republic with the United States is now greater than with any other country.

CENTRAL AMERICA AND THE CARIBBEAN

During the past summer the revolution against the administration which followed the assassination of President Cáceres a year ago last November brought the Dominican Republic to the verge of administrative chaos, without offering any guaranties of eventual stability in the ultimate success of either party. In pursuance of the treaty relations of the United States with the Dominican Republic, which were threatened by the necessity of suspending the operation under American administration of the customhouses on the Haitian frontier, it was found necessary to dispatch special commissioners to the island to reestablish the customhouses and with a guard sufficient to insure needed protection to the customs administration. The efforts which have been made appear to have resulted in the restoration of normal conditions throughout the Republic. The good offices which the commissioners were able to exercise were instrumental in bringing the contending parties together and in furnishing a basis of adjustment which it is hoped will result in permanent benefit to the Dominican people.

Mindful of its treaty relations, and owing to the position of the Government of the United States as mediator between the Dominican Republic and Haiti in their boundary dispute, and because of the further fact that the revolutionary activities on the Haitian-Dominican frontier had become so active as practically to obliterate the line of demarcation that had been heretofore recognized pending the definitive settlement of the boundary in controversy, it was found necessary to indicate to the two island Governments a provisional *de facto* boundary line. This was done without prejudice to the rights or obligations of either country in a final settlement to be reached by arbitration. The tentative line chosen was one which, under the circumstances brought to the knowledge of this Government, seemed to conform to the best interests of the disputants. The border patrol which it had been found necessary to reestablish for customs purposes between the two countries was instructed provisionally to observe this line.

The Republic of Cuba last May was in the throes of a lawless uprising that for a time threatened the destruction of a great deal of valuable property—much of it owned by Americans and other foreigners—as well as the existence of the Government itself. The armed forces of Cuba being inadequate to guard property from attack and at the same time properly to operate against the rebels, a force of American marines was dispatched from our naval station at Guantánamo into the Province of Oriente for the protection of American and other foreign life and property. The Cuban Government was thus able to use all its forces in putting down the outbreak, which it succeeded in doing in a period of six weeks. The presence of two American warships in the harbor of Habana during the most critical period of this disturbance contributed in great measure to allay the fears of the inhabitants, including a large foreign colony.

There has been under discussion with the Government of Cuba for some time the question of the release by this Government of its lease-hold rights at Bahia Honda, on the northern coast of Cuba, and the enlargement, in exchange therefor, of the naval station which has been established at Guantánamo Bay, on the south. As the result of the negotiations then carried on an agreement has been reached between the two Governments providing for the suitable enlargement of the Guantánamo Bay station upon terms which are entirely fair and equitable to all parties concerned.

At the request alike of the Government and both political parties in Panama, an American commission undertook supervision of the recent presidential election in that Republic, where our treaty relations, and, indeed, every geographical consideration, make the maintenance of order and satisfactory conditions of peculiar interest to the Government of the United States. The elections passed without disorder, and the new administration has entered upon its functions.

The Government of Great Britain has asked the support of the United States for the protection of the interests of British holders of the foreign bonded debt of Guatemala. While this Government is hopeful of an arrangement equitable to the British bondholders, it is naturally unable to view the question apart from its relation to the broad subject of financial stability in Central America, in which the policy of the United States does not permit it to escape a vital interest. Through a renewal of negotiations between the Government of Guatemala and American bankers, the aim of which is a loan for the rehabilitation of Guatemalan finances, a way appears to be open by which the Government of Guatemala could promptly satisfy any equitable and just British claims, and at the same time so improve its whole financial position as to contribute greatly to the increased prosperity of the Republic and to redound to the benefit of foreign investments and foreign trade with that country. Failing such an arrangement, it may become impossible for the Government of the United States to escape its obligations in connection with such measures as may become necessary to exact justice to legitimate foreign claims.

In the recent revolution in Nicaragua, which, it was generally admitted, might well have resulted in a general Central American conflict but for the intervention of the United States, the Government of Honduras was especially menaced; but fortunately peaceful conditions were maintained within the borders of that Republic. The financial condition of that country remains unchanged, no means having been found for the final adjustment of pressing outstanding foreign claims. This makes it the more regrettable that the financial convention between the United States and Honduras has thus far failed of ratification. The Government of the United States continues to hold itself ready to cooperate with the Government of Honduras, which, it is believed, can not much longer delay the meeting of its foreign obligations, and it is hoped at the proper time American bankers will be willing to cooperate for this purpose. . . .

STATEMENT by President Woodrow Wilson on Policy with Regard to Latin America, March 11, 1913
Foreign Relations of the United States, 1913, p. 7

ONE OF the chief objects of my administration will be to cultivate the friendship and deserve the confidence of our sister republics of Central and South America, and to promote in every proper and honorable way the interests which are common to the peoples of the two continents. I earnestly desire the most cordial understanding and cooperation between the peoples and leaders of America and, therefore, deem it my duty to make this brief statement.

Cooperation is possible only when supported at every turn by the orderly processes of just government based upon law, not upon arbitrary or irregular force. We hold, as I am sure all thoughtful leaders of republican government everywhere hold, that just government rests always upon the consent of the governed, and that there can be no freedom without order based upon law and upon the public conscience and approval. We shall look to make these principles the basis of mutual intercourse, respect, and helpfulness between our sister republics and ourselves. We shall lend our influence of every kind to the realization of these principles in fact and practice, knowing that disorder, personal intrigues, and defiance of constitutional rights weaken and discredit government and injure none so much as the people who are unfortunate enough to have their common life and their common affairs so tainted and disturbed. We can have no sympathy with those who seek to seize the power of government to advance their own personal interests or ambition. We are the friends of peace, but we know that there can be no lasting or stable peace in such circumstances. As friends, therefore, we shall prefer those who act in the interest of peace and honor, who protect private rights and respect the restraints of constitutional provision. Mutual respect seems to us the indispensable foundation of friendship between states, as between individuals.

The United States has nothing to seek in Central and South America except the lasting interests of the peoples of the two continents, the security of governments intended for the people and for no special group or interest, and the development of personal and trade relationships between the two continents which shall redound to the profit and advantage of both and interfere with the rights and liberties of neither.

From these principles may be read so much of the future policy of this Government as it is necessary now to forecast, and in the spirit of these principles I may, I hope, be permitted with as much confidence as earnestness to extend to the Governments of all the Republics of America the hand of genuine disinterested friendship, and to pledge my own honor and the honor of my colleagues to every enterprise of peace and amity that a fortunate future may disclose.

WILLIAM J. BRYAN, Secretary of State, to United States Diplomatic Officers in Various Countries, July 7, 1913
Foreign Relations of the United States, 1913, p. 9

SIR:

The following nations: Argentina, Austria-Hungary, Belgium, Bolivia, Brazil, China, Denmark, France, Germany, Great Britain, Haiti, Italy, Netherlands, Norway, Peru, Portugal, Russia, Santo Domingo, Spain and Sweden, have announced their acceptance of the principle embodied in the President's peace plan, a copy of which I herewith enclose.

I have submitted to the Washington representatives of those countries a copy of a memorandum, which I also enclose, covering the suggested details. It occurs to me that it might be well for you to supplement the work that is being done through the representatives here by bringing these details to the attention of the Foreign Office and explaining them. They are offered merely by way of suggestion and we are prepared to consider anything that the other countries may suggest as a means of perfecting the plan.

It is very gratifying to the President and to myself that the plan has been so quickly and so widely accepted. We believe that it will go forward toward the prevention of war, and I think that by fall we will have reached an understanding with all the nations in regard to both the principle and the details and thus be able to complete the treaties during the present year.

I am [etc.]   W. J. BRYAN.

PRESIDENT WILSON'S PEACE PROPOSAL

The parties hereto agree that all questions of whatever character and nature, in dispute between them, shall, when diplomatic efforts fail, be submitted for investigation and report to an international commission (the composition to be agreed upon); and the contracting parties agree not to declare war or begin hostilities until such investigation is made and report submitted.

The investigation shall be conducted as a matter of course upon the initiative of the commission, without the formality of a request from either party; the report shall be submitted within (time to be agreed upon) from the date of the submission of the dispute, but the parties hereto reserve the right to act independently on the subject matter in dispute after the report is submitted.

SUPPLEMENTARY MEMORANDUM BY THE SECRETARY OF STATE

In the peace plan proposed by the President to all the nations, the composition of the International Commission is left to agreement between the parties, and I am authorized to suggest for the consideration of those who are willing to enter into this agreement:

1. That the International Commission be of five members, to be composed as follows: one member from each of the contracting countries, to be chosen by the Government; one member to be chosen by each of the contracting countries from some other country, and the fifth member of the Commission to be agreed upon by the two Governments, the Commission to be appointed as soon as convenient after the making of the treaty, vacancies to be filled according to the original appointment.

2. The time also is to be agreed upon, and it is suggested that that time be one year. If a year is considered too long or too short, this Government will consider either a greater or a less period.

3. This Government is prepared to consider the question of maintaining the status quo as to military and naval preparation during the period of investigation, if the contracting nation desires to include this, and this Government suggests tentatively that the parties agree that there shall be no change in the military and naval program during the period of investigation unless danger to one of the contracting parties from a third power compels a change in said program, in which case the party feeling itself menaced by a third power, shall confidentially communicate the matter in writing to the other contracting party and it shall thereupon be released from the obligation not to change its military or naval program, and this release will at the same time operate as a release of the other contracting party. This protects each party from the other in ordinary cases, and yet provides freedom of action in emergencies.

All of these suggestions, however, are presented for consideration, and not with the intention of imposing any fixed conditions. The principle of investigation being accepted, the details are matters for conference and consideration.

ADDRESS by President Woodrow Wilson at Mobile, Alabama, October 27, 1913 (extracts)

Henry Steele Commager, *Documents of American History,* 3d ed., p. 269, citing U.S. 63d Congress, 1st Session, *Senate Doc.* 226. The address was delivered before the Southern Commercial Congress

. . . THE FUTURE, ladies and gentlemen, is going to be very different for this hemisphere from the past. These States lying to the south of us, which have always been our neighbors, will now be drawn closer to us by innumerable ties, and, I hope, chief of all, by the tie of a common understanding of each other. Interest does not tie nations together; it sometimes separates them. But sympathy and understanding does unite them, and I believe that by the new route that is just about to be opened, while we physically cut two continents asunder, we spiritually unite them. It is a spiritual union which we seek. . . .

There is one peculiarity about the history of the Latin American States which I am sure they are keenly aware of. You hear of "concessions" to foreign capitalists in Latin America. You do not hear of concessions to foreign capitalists in the United States. They are not granted concessions. They are invited to make investments. The work is ours, though they are welcome to invest in it. We do not ask them to supply the capital and do the work. It is an invitation, not a privilege; and States that are obliged, because their territory does not lie within the main field of modern enterprise and action, to grant concessions are in this condition, that foreign interests are apt to dominate their domestic affairs, a condition of affairs always dangerous and apt to become intolerable. What these States are going to see, therefore, is an emancipation from the subordination, which has been inevitable, to foreign enterprise and an assertion of the splendid character which, in spite of these difficulties, they have again and again been able to demonstrate. The dignity, the courage, the self-possession, the self-respect of the Latin American States, their achievements in the face of all these adverse circumstances, deserve nothing but the admiration and applause of the world. They have had harder bargains driven with them in the matter of loans than any other peoples in the world. Interest has been exacted of them that was not exacted of anybody else, because the risk was said to be greater; and then securities were taken that destroyed the risk—an admirable arrangement for those who were forcing the terms! I rejoice in nothing so much as in the prospect that they will now be emancipated from these conditions, and we ought to be the first to take part in assisting in that emancipation. I think some of these gentlemen have already had occasion to bear witness that the Department of State in recent months has tried to serve them in that wise. In the future they will draw closer and closer to us because of circumstances of which I wish to speak with moderation and, I hope, without indiscretion.

We must prove ourselves their friends, and champions upon terms of equality and honor. You cannot be friends upon any other terms than upon the terms of equality. You cannot be friends at all except upon the terms of honor. We must show ourselves friends by comprehending their interest whether it squares with our own interest or not. It is a very perilous thing to determine the foreign policy of a nation in the terms of material interest. It not only is unfair to those with whom you are dealing, but it is degrading as regards your own actions.

Comprehension must be the soil in which shall grow all the fruits of friendship, and there is a reason and a compulsion lying behind all this which is dearer than anything else to the thoughtful men of America. I mean the development of constitutional liberty in the world. Human rights, national integrity, and opportunity as against material interests—that, ladies and gentlemen, is the issue which we now have to face. I want to take this occasion to say that the United States will never again seek one additional foot of territory by conquest. She will devote herself to showing that she knows how to make honorable and fruitful use of the territory she has, and she must regard it as one of the duties of friendship to see that from no quarter are material interests made superior to human liberty and national opportunity. I say this, not with a single thought that anyone will gainsay it, but merely to fix in our consciousness what our real relationship with the rest of America is. It is the relationship of a family of mankind devoted to the development of true constitutional liberty. We know that that is the soil out of which the best enterprise springs. We know that this is a cause which we are making in common with our neighbors, because we have had to make it for ourselves. . . .

In emphasizing the points which must unite us in sympathy and in spiritual interest with the Latin American peoples, we are only emphasizing the points of our own life, and we should prove ourselves untrue to our own traditions if we proved ourselves untrue friends to them. . . .

ANNUAL MESSAGE from President Woodrow Wilson to the United States Congress, December 2, 1913 (extract)
Foreign Relations of the United States, 1913, p. ix

. . . THE COUNTRY, I am thankful to say, is at peace with all the world, and many happy manifestations multiply about us of a growing cordiality and sense of community of interest among the nations, foreshadowing an age of settled peace and good will. More and more readily each decade do the nations manifest their willingness to bind themselves by solemn treaty to the processes of peace, the processes of frankness and fair concession. So far the United States has stood at the front of such negotiations. She will, I earnestly hope and confidently believe, give fresh proof of her sincere adherence to the cause of international friendship by ratifying the several treaties of arbitration awaiting renewal by the Senate. In addition to these, it has been the privilege of the Department of State to gain the assent, in principle, of no less than 31 nations, representing four-fifths of the population of the world, to the negotiations of treaties by which it shall be agreed that whenever differences of interest or of policy arise which can not be resolved by the ordinary processes of diplomacy they shall be publicly analyzed, discussed, and reported upon by a tribunal chosen by the parties before either nation determines its course of action.

There is only one possible standard by which to determine controversies between the United States and other nations, and that is compounded of these two elements: our own honor and our obligations to the peace of the world. A test so compounded ought easily to be made to govern both the establishment of new treaty obligations and the interpretation of those already assumed. . . .

Plan of a Pan-American Treaty
1915–1917

PRESIDENT WOODROW WILSON to William J. Bryan,
Secretary of State, January 29, 1915
Department of State, *The Lansing Papers*, II, 472

Dear Mr. Secretary:

Here are the four articles of agreement complete. I am sorry not to have had time to send them before.

Faithfully Yours,

W.W.

[ENCLOSURE]

Draft Articles for Proposed Pan-American Treaty

I

That the contracting parties to this solemn covenant and agreement hereby join in a common and mutual guarantee to one another of undisturbed and indisputed territorial integrity and of complete political independence under republican forms of government.

II

That, to this end, and as a condition precedent to the foregoing guarantee of territorial integrity, it is covenanted and agreed between them that all disputes now pending and unconcluded between any two or more of them with regard to their boundaries or territories shall be brought to an early and final settlement in the following manner, unless some equally prompt and satisfactory method of settlement can be agreed upon and put into operation in each or any case within three months after the signing of this convention and brought to a decision within one year after its inception.

Each of the parties to the dispute shall select two arbiters and those thus selected and commissioned shall select an additional arbiter or umpire; to the tribunal thus constituted the question or questions at issue shall be submitted without reservation; and the decisions and findings of this tribunal shall be final and conclusive as between the parties to the dispute and under the terms of this convention as to the whole subject-matter submitted. The findings of such tribunal or tribunals shall be arrived at and officially announced and accepted within not more than one year after the formal constitution of the tribunal; and the tribunal shall be constituted not more than three months after the signing and ratification of the convention.

III

That the high contracting parties severally pledge themselves to obtain and establish by law such control of the manufacture and sale of munitions of war within their respective jurisdictions as will enable them absolutely to control and make them responsible for the sale and shipment of such munitions to any other of the nations who are parties to this convention.

IV

That the high contracting parties further agree, First, that all questions, of whatever character, arising between any two or more of them which cannot be settled by the ordinary means of diplomatic correspondence shall, before any declaration of war or beginning of hostilities, be first submitted to a permanent international commission for investigation, one year being allowed for such investigation; and, Second, that, if the dispute is not settled by investigation, to submit the same to arbitration, provided the question in dispute does not affect the honour, independence, or vital interests of the nations concerned or the interests of third parties; and the high contracting parties hereby agree, where this has not already been done, to enter into treaty, each with all of the others severally, to carry out the provisions of this Article.

EDWARD M. HOUSE to Robert Lansing, Secretary of State, October 12, 1915

Department of State, The Lansing Papers, II, 486. A notation attached to this paper reads: "This is for a record which you told me you desired. E.M.H. I shall hope to see you tomorrow"

DEAR MR. SECRETARY:

Sometime early in January of this year the President requested me to see the Ambassadors of the A.B.C. Powers and ascertain from them whether or not they would be willing to join the United States in a convention which would guarantee the political and territorial integrity of the North, Central and South American Republics under republican forms of government.

Also if they would be willing to agree that all manufacture of munitions of war should be owned by the governments of the respective countries.

The President wrote these two articles himself and I took them first to the Argentine Ambassador whom we thought would perhaps be most sympathetic. The Ambassador received the proposal cordially, after I had outlined to him just what the President had in mind. I called his attention to the fact that there was a military party in the United States just as there was in other countries, and after President Wilson relinquished office, there was a possibility of a military policy being adopted. I said if this happened it was quite probable that instead of following the path laid down by President Wilson there might be a sentiment for expansion. I told him there was sure to be a large part of the people who would want to try out the military and naval machine. If this should happen, no one could tell the final outcome.

I told him, too, that the President thought the time had come when this nation should cease to assume a guardianship over its sister republics and to ask them to come into partnership. I explained it was the President's intention to approach the A.B.C. Powers first and later to approach the smaller republics, either directly or through the A.B.C.

The Ambassador was very much in favor of permitting the A.B.C. Powers [to] deal with the smaller republics, and it was tacitly agreed that this should be done. He spoke of writing to his government in regard to the proposal, to which I objected and asked him to cable it so we might hear in a few days.

He was filled with enthusiasm and declared that the proposal was almost epoch making, and that he was sure it would be cordially received by his people. He doubted, however, whether Chile would be agreeable because of her territorial aspirations. . . .

The Ambassador begged me to give him the original draft which the President had written, saying he believed it would be an historic document of enormous interest. I gave it to him and he wrote with his own hand a copy for me to use with the other Ambassadors.

I had a similar reception by the Brazilian Ambassador, and I gave him practically the same argument. The discussion followed largely along the lines I have mentioned with Naón.

The Chilian Ambassador was somewhat less receptive and showed a disposition to delay. He brought up at once the question of their boundary conflict with Peru—a subject about which I had informed myself in advance so as to be able to discuss the matter with intelligence.

I told him the President had in mind that there should be an article in the convention which would permit a reasonable time for the settlement of such disputes and a mode of procedure. This seemed to satisfy him.

All three ambassadors promised an answer within a few days. The one came first from Argentine and was entirely favorable. Then Brazil was heard from to the same effect. Chile, later gave an equivocal consent. This was a few days before my departure for Europe, and the President requested me to acquaint Mr. Bryan with what had been done and ask him to carry it to a conclusion.

Mr. Bryan was receptive, but suggested that his peace treaties should be also concluded between them. He wanted to know if there was any objection to this. The President said there was not.

I heard nothing from the matter while abroad until sometime in April when the President cabled me that the Chilian Ambassador had said he was under the impression that I had agreed in my conversation with him that the covenant should not be binding unless all the A.B.C. Powers concurred. I cabled the President that there was no such understanding, and that probably the Ambassador had in mind the tacit consent that the smaller republics should be approached by the A.B.C. Powers rather than by us directly.

This, Mr. Secretary, is a record of what occurred through me. I do not know what Mr. Bryan did.

Of course you understand that the President's purpose is to broaden the Monroe Doctrine so that it may be upheld by all the American Republics instead of by the United States alone as now.

Sincerely yours,

E. M. HOUSE

New York, October 12, 1915

ROBERT LANSING, Secretary of State, to President Woodrow Wilson, December 30, 1915
Department of State, *The Lansing Papers,* II, 492

MY DEAR MR. PRESIDENT:

In regard to the Pan American Treaty—I have seen, in addition to the Ambassadors, nine of the ministers, and given them copies of the four articles. They all express personal delight at the Treaty and feel sure that their governments will be glad to enter into such a convention. I have still the representatives of three other countries to see, and hope to do so tomorrow.

The number of persons who know of this plan makes the possibility of secrecy very difficult, in fact, some of the papers have already got hold of the fact that there is some plan on foot for a Pan American Agreement, or conference in line with the address which I made on

Monday. I have, since being questioned by one of the reporters on the subject, notified all the Ambassadors and Ministers to be kind enough to keep the matter secret. I had already told them that the matter was confidential when I gave them the memorandum, but I am afraid that they have showed it to some of their fellow-countrymen who are here attending the Scientific Congress and so a considerable number are undoubtedly in possession of the fact that we are attempting to unite the Americas in an agreement of some sort. I thought I would tell you this so that you will understand if you see anything in the papers on the subject.

Yesterday Ambassador Suárez said to me that he was in hopes of receiving from his Government an acceptance of the plan and that he was most desirous to obtain it and felt sure if a little time was given he could do so. His change of attitude is certainly interesting.

Faithfully yours,

ROBERT LANSING

HENRY P. FLETCHER, United States Ambassador to Mexico, to Robert Lansing, Secretary of State, August 9, 1916
Department of State, *The Lansing Papers*, II, 496

MY DEAR MR. LANSING:

No progress has been made in the negotiation of the Pan-American treaty during your absence. On the 27th of June Naón informed me that he was not willing to proceed to the signature of the treaty without consulting his Government, on account of the tense United States–Mexican situation. He promised to let me know as soon as he was in a position to proceed. He has not done so. Lauro Müller [Brazilian Minister of Foreign Affairs] arrived in New York on the 18th.

Mr. Wright [J. B. Wright, Acting Chief of the Division of Latin American Affairs, Department of State] had two interviews with him, but got nothing definite from him on the subject of the treaty. Ambassador da Gama seems to think that it would be unfortunate to go ahead with the treaty without Chile, and that we would lose all the ground we have lately gained along the lines of true Pan-Americanism. Mr. Lauro Müller is expected to return from French Lick in about a week.

In view of the check put on the negotiation by Mr. Naón's unwillingness to agree to sign, I could not open out the treaty to the other Republics. So the matter rests *in statu quo*.

Chile is definitely and decidedly opposed to the treaty. The *Mercurio*—speaking for the Government—characterizes it, in its 4th of July editorial, as a "convention which involves vague and indeterminate powers of intervention in the entire continent" and goes on to say that Chile does not desire to remain isolated; that she understands her continental duties and has lent her assistance or has taken important initiatives tending to establish that policy. But Chile sustains that the Pan-Americanism of concord and equality is a measure of union, but that Pan-Americanism of predominance is a serious obstacle to guaranteeing that cordiality which is indispensable in foreign affairs. A treaty which would give *de facto* preponderance to one part of the continent over the other would tend to destroy true Pan-American confraternity. It is becoming generally known among the diplomats in Washington that Chile objects to the treaty, and the British Ambassador insinuated to me that the negotiations which Chile is said to be carrying on now with representatives of the Deutsche Bank in New York for a loan might be attributed to the lack of agreement between Chile and the United States over this treaty. I do not believe this is the case, but on the other hand I feel sure that if we go on without Chile, that is, isolating her from the American concert, she will turn naturally elsewhere in finance and trade, and that gradually a spirit of hostility against the United States will be engendered.

My advices from Chile show that they believe we are going ahead with the treaty, and they feel that we are placing them unnecessarily in a false position. If, therefore, neither Argentina nor Brazil really means to go ahead, I think we should know it and act accordingly; otherwise we are uselessly and needlessly alienating the goodwill of Chile.

H. P. F[LETCHER]

ROBERT LANSING, Secretary of State, to President Woodrow Wilson, April 17, 1917
Department of State, The Lansing Papers, II, 498

MY DEAR MR. PRESIDENT:

Ambassador da Gama has been absent from the city and also ill so that I have not taken up with him the Pan American Treaty. This enforced delay has given me time to think the matter over carefully, and there are some difficulties which seem involved if a general invitation is issued to all the countries to the south of us.

For example, it might be that a signatory to the Treaty would become an ally of Germany against her European enemies (I am thinking particularly of Mexico where the oil wells at Tampico may cause trouble). In that event would we be bound under the Treaty to maintain the guarantee of territorial integrity with force of arms? Or it might be that a signatory might permit its territory to become the base of German military or naval operations (as might be the case of Ecuador in regard to the Galapagos Islands, or of Colombia in regard to her coasts). Could we observe the territorial integrity of the nation permitting this? Or could we do so if a Latin American country permitted its territory to become a refuge for Germans where they could conspire and carry on their propaganda in this country and other countries?

Possibly this difficulty could be cured by limiting at present the signatories to such governments as declare war against Germany, sever relations with that Government, or declare a benevolent neutrality with the assurance that they will only enter the war on our side or as our ally.

Furthermore under the guarantee of territorial integrity and political independence would the other signatories be bound to declare war against Germany? If it could be so interpreted, what I have said above has no weight. But could it be, unless our territory or waters were actually invaded by the Germans?

These are the questions which have been running through my mind and I would like your opinion upon them

Faithfully yours,

ROBERT LANSING

PRESIDENT WOODROW WILSON to Robert Lansing, Secretary of State, April 19, 1917
Department of State, *The Lansing Papers*, II, 499

MY DEAR MR. SECRETARY:

The answers to the important questions you here raise are reasonably clear to me. (By the way, I do not find among my papers here the Brazilian proposals you spoke of the other day.)

If any one of the signatories to our proposed Pan-American treaty should become an ally of Germany against her European enemies, we would undoubtedly be bound to protect her against any loss of territory or any curtailment of her political independence that any of the Entente group might attempt; but we would be obliged to do that in any case, under the Monroe Doctrine.

Should any one of the signatories permit its territory to be used as a base of military or naval operations against us, it would manifestly be acting in contravention of the patent meaning of the pact and we would be free to act as if there were no pact.

As for "influences" and propaganda, we could not prevent them, any more than Great Britain has been able to prevent them in the United States, where they were very formidable, though they of course did not have the countenance of the Government.

I do not see that the other signatories would in the present circumstances be obligated to declare war on Germany. They would be obligated to come to our assistance with arms only when our political independence or territorial integrity were evidently and immediately threatened.

These questions do not seem to me to constitute difficulties of practical importance. If we can meet Brazil's wishes sufficiently to get her adherence to the pact, I shall feel warranted in pressing on. It seems to me that this is the very time when such a league would make the deepest impression and have the greatest moral effect on both sides of the water.

Faithfully Yours,

W.W.

ROBERT LANSING, Secretary of State, to Edwin V. Morgan, United States Ambassador to Brazil, May 24, 1917

Department of State, *The Lansing Papers*, II, 500

DEPARTMENT is not sending to you the text of the Pan American treaty which you were informed prior to your departure from the United States would be cabled to you, as it does not desire you to take up this question with the Government of Brazil at this time.

LANSING

The Harding-Coolidge-Hoover Administrations

ADDRESS by Charles E. Hughes, Secretary of State, at Cleveland, November 4, 1922
The Bulletin of the Pan American Union, December, 1922, p. 13

THE PRINCIPLES of American foreign policy are simple and readily stated. We do not covet any territory anywhere on God's broad earth. We are not seeking a sphere of special economic influence and endeavoring to control others for our aggrandizement. We are not seeking special privileges anywhere at the expense of others. We wish to protect the just and equal rights of Americans everywhere in the world. We wish to maintain the equality of commercial opportunity; as we call it, the open door. That is not in derogation of anybody else; the door is just as open to others as it is to us. Equality means equality. It doesn't mean privilege. We desire to see peaceful settlements. We are most desirous to see the world starting again on a sound economic basis, with every people inspired by hope and girded to the highest achievements in the interest of their prosperity. Wherever we have had a chance to promote peaceful settlements in this troubled world we have taken it.

We found Panama and Costa Rica about to engage in war, and we established peace on the basis of the arbitral award of the Chief Justice of the United States which both Governments had agreed to accept. The treaty with Colombia has been ratified. There was an old controversy between Chile and Peru which had disturbed their relations for upward of 40 years and, indeed, in its indirect consequences had seriously affected the relations between the other countries of Latin America. I am happy to say, that recognizing our desire to promote peaceful dispositions and to aid in every practicable way with the consent of the Governments concerned, both Chile and Peru signified their willingness to accept an invitation from the President of the United States to send their representatives to Washington to endeavor to compose this old and serious difference. In the friendly atmosphere of Washington these representatives met and were able to reach an agreement for the peaceful settlement of the controversy.

We have constantly testified to our deep interest in the prosperity, the independence, the unimpaired sovereignty, and the prosperity of the countries of Latin America. We are now arranging for a conference at Washington between the representatives of the five Central American Republics, Costa Rica, Guatemala, Honduras, Nicaragua, and Salvador, in order that a way may be found to establish better relations in the interest of peace, order, and stability. We rejoice in the fact that throughout this hemisphere we have peace.

ADDRESS by Charles E. Hughes, Secretary of State, at the Opening of the Conference on Central American Affairs, at Washington, December 4, 1922
The Bulletin of the Pan American Union, January, 1923, p. 2

GENTLEMEN:

It is a high privilege to extend to you, on behalf of the President of the United States, a most cordial welcome.

Solicitous as you must be of the dignity, rights and interest of your respective nations, your presence here attests your appreciation of a community of interest and your sincere purpose to promote a common welfare by assurances of mutual esteem and the establishment of the essential conditions of tranquility and security.

You will find here the most friendly atmosphere, the helpful spirit of cooperation, and an intense desire to aid you in the furtherance of your own wishes for an abiding peace and a constantly increasing prosperity. The Government of the United States has no ambition to gratify at your expense, no policy which runs counter to your national aspirations, and no purpose save to promote the interests of peace and to assist you, in such manner as you may welcome, to solve your problems to your own proper advantage. The interest of the United States is found in the peace of this hemisphere and in the conservation of your interests.

The same desire which now animated you prompted the Central American Peace Conference of the year 1907. The passing of the years, the important changes recently wrought, the spectacle of the devastating results of war, have heightened your determination to consider the fundamental requisites of stability and development.

Your purpose, manifested in your cordial acceptance of the invitation of the Government of the United States, is to build on foundations already laid; to take account of changed conditions in order that you may apply the wisdom of experience in devising improved methods.

I shall not attempt to review the conference of 1907. Because all that was hoped for was not attained in practice; because all stipulations then agreed upon have not been found to be effective, its results should not be depreciated. It was a decisive, forward step. The spirit of cooperation which it fostered is still dominant despite all difficulties. The goal is still the same and you are here to-day, more deeply conscious than ever of opportunity and of the advantage of mutually helpful relations, to give new form and substance to a united effort for Central American progress.

In August last a meeting of great promise and importance was held by the Presidents of Nicaragua, Salvador, and Honduras on board the U.S.S. *Tacoma* in order to concert measures looking to the establishment of more peaceful relations in Central America. The Government of the United States was deeply gratified at the action of those countries in acknowledging the validity of the general treaty of peace and friendship signed at Washington on December 20, 1907, and in the subsequent action of the Governments of Costa Rica and Guatemala in definitely declaring that this treaty, so far as they are concerned, is still in force. Believing that a great advance had been made toward peace and stability and that the friendly relations and the prosperity of their peoples could still further be assured by a frank exchange of views and recommendations, the Government of the United States invited the Governments of the Central American Republics to send their plenipotentiaries to Washington for this conference. In this invitation it was proposed that the following subjects should be discussed:

1. The negotiation of a treaty or treaties to make effective those provisions of the treaties signed at Washington on December 20, 1907, which experience has shown to be effective in maintaining friendly relations and cooperation among the Central American States.

2. Measures whereby, in view of the achievements accomplished with regard to the limitation of armaments by the powers participating in the conference at Washington in 1921, the Central American States may carry on the endeavor and set an example to the world and above all to the powers of this hemisphere, by adopting effective measures for the limitation of armaments in Central America.

3. The working out of a plan for setting up tribunals of inquiry whenever any disputes or questions regarding the proposed treaty or treaties, which can not be settled by diplomatic means, shall unfortunately arise between any two or more of the countries.

4. Any other questions which the countries represented at the conference unanimously desire to consider.

The subjects to which attention has thus been directed are now before you.

With your permission, I desire to emphasize the fact that, as the separate treaty establishing the Central American Court of Justice was terminated in 1917, it is most important that adequate provision now be made for appropriate arbitral disposition of controversies and that suitable methods be devised for carrying out the fundamental purpose of existing treaties in securing a basis for a lasting and just accord.

It is also earnestly hoped that means may be found at least to curtail, and if possible to end, unnecessary and unproductive outlays, as there can be no stability or progress in the absence of a sound economic basis.

You are blessed with the riches of natural resources; you command the conditions of orderly development and widespread contentment; you have the opportunity of fostering mutual relations which will promote the security of each of your Republics without depriving it of any of its natural advantages; you have the good will and friend-ship of all powers. It is our earnest hope that this conference may register your high and effective resolve to put an end to strife which impoverishes and to bring to naught all attempts to foment mutual distrust; and thus that it may afford that sense of national security and repose and of true fellowship between peoples by which you may each realize to the fullest extent the blessings of your national heritage.

In all that you may endeavor to this end you have the assurance of the interest and cooperation of the Government of the United States.

RADIO ADDRESS by Charles E. Hughes, Secretary of State, January 20, 1925
Charles E. Hughes, *The Pathway of Peace*, p. 164

I SHALL SPEAK to you briefly upon the subject of our relations with Latin America.

Our historic friendship with our sister republics of this hemi-sphere was born of the sympathy and satisfaction with which we witnessed the struggle of their peoples for independence—a struggle which culminated in the battle on the heights of Ayacucho one hun-

dred years ago. The patriots of our own Revolution and the statesmen who fashioned our institutions were the exemplars of the leaders
in South America, and in the ardor, sacrifices, and persistence of
Bolivar and San Martin, of Miranda and O'Higgins, of Marino, Sucre,
and other heroes, we saw the devotion to the cause of liberty which
had consecrated the name of Washington. This generous sentiment
found eloquent expression in the impassioned speeches of Henry
Clay, which were as familiar to the men in arms in the southern
continent as in our own land. Clay was fascinated by what he called
"the glorious spectacle of eighteen millions of people struggling to
burst their chains and be free." Impatient of a cautious diplomacy,
he demanded early recognition of the new states. Our interest in the
progress and prosperity of these republics has never abated. And in
recent years that interest has been crowned most happily by the
efforts at systematic co-operation which we describe as Pan Americanism.

This Pan-American co-operation rests upon the conviction that
there are primary and mutual interests which are peculiar to the
republics of this hemisphere and that these can best be conserved by
taking counsel together and by devising appropriate means of collaboration. This implies no antagonism to any other people, or part
of the world, no menace to the prosperity of others, but in itself
constitutes a most important contribution to world peace. Some of our
people may think of Pan-American endeavor as of especial concern
to the interests of the Latin-American republics rather than to our
own. But this is a serious mistake. We have the inescapable relations
created by propinquity. We have the privileges and obligations of
neighborhood; our activities are destined to be more and more in-
terlaced; resistless economic forces draw us together. What could be
more shortsighted than to ignore our mutual interests?

The essential basis of Pan-American co-operation is peace, and
hence we lose no opportunity to promote the amicable settlement of
all differences that could be the cause of strife. One of the happiest
auguries of the future is that there are now no controversies between
the nations in Latin America which cannot be peacefully adjusted or
which in fact are not in course of peaceful adjustment. The difficulties which our sister republics face are caused by internal dissensions
rather than by any external aggression.

At the last Pan-American Conference at Santiago a treaty was signed
by the representatives of sixteen American States providing that all
controversies which may arise between two or more of the contracting
powers and which it has been impossible to settle through diplomatic
channels, or to submit to arbitration in accordance with existing

treaties, shall be submitted for investigation and report to a commission of inquiry. The contracting parties undertake not to begin mobilization or to engage in any hostile acts or preparation for hostilities until the commission has rendered its report. Any one of the governments directly interested in the investigation of the facts giving rise to the controversy may apply for the convocation of the commission. The representatives of the American republics have thus sought in an entirely practicable way by a general agreement to assure the maintenance of peace in this hemisphere. And to this important treaty the Senate of the United States gave prompt approval. Apart from the specific application of this treaty, it is our high privilege through our good offices to aid in the amicable disposition of such disputes as may still exist in Latin America and it is manifest that our contribution to this end must depend upon the confidence of other peoples in our sense of justice and integrity of purpose.

There are those among us who constantly assail our motives in relation to the countries of Latin America. What a pity it is that among our fellow citizens are those who cannot be fair to their own government! And, of course, there are those in other countries who ever seek to create a feeling of animosity toward us. But I am happy to say that these efforts, however persistent, are of diminishing effect. The number is constantly increasing of those who know the truth. Our Latin-American friends who live among us, who know our purposes and ideals, who intelligently observe our activities, taking into account both preponderant sentiment and governmental action, are our best friends.

What a hopeless twist there is in the minds of those who accuse us of cherishing an imperialistic policy! Anyone who really understands our people must realize that the last thing in the world we desire is to assume responsibility as to other peoples. We wish to have prosperous and independent neighbors with whom we can deal in peace to our mutual advantage. We harbor no thought of aggression upon anyone. Instead of encouraging the exploitation of other peoples we are constantly by word and deed diminishing the opportunities for it and throwing the weight of governmental influence against it.

Our historic policy which we call the Monroe Doctrine is itself designed to thwart measures of aggression. While this doctrine, which I have elsewhere summarized, was set forth and must be maintained as the policy of the United States, there is no reason whatever why every one of our sister republics should not have and formulate a similar principle as a part of its own foreign policy. We have always welcomed declarations by other American States to that effect. In this way without sacrifice by any American State of its particular interests, the doctrine would have the support of all the American republics.

I have pointed out that the chief danger of strife among our neighbors to the south lies in internal dissensions and in the tendency to have revolutions instead of fair elections. The influence of our government is directed to the support of peaceful and constitutional methods. Recurrent revolutions are a poor sort of educational process; the greatest menace to progress and prosperity lies in political instability.

We have no desire to take advantage of this regrettable condition in neighboring countries, either to acquire territory or to assume political control. Nothing could demonstrate this attitude more completely than our recent withdrawal from Santo Domingo. Of course we could have remained in control had we desired, but instead of doing so we have been solicitous to aid in the establishment of an independent government so that we could withdraw and, such a government having been established through our efforts, we have withdrawn. We had made our plans to withdraw our small contingent from Nicaragua at the end of this month, but the newly elected President has besought us in the interest of peace and order to permit it to remain until a constabulary or local police can be provided, and we have agreed to do so, but with the distinct understanding that this local police must be established and that we shall withdraw entirely before next September. In Haiti we are only waiting to see a reasonable promise of internal peace and stability to effect our withdrawal. And meanwhile we are doing our utmost to promote the interests of the people of Haiti without selfish considerations. Nowhere else in Latin America have we any forces, and everywhere we are seeking to encourage constitutional government, to use our friendly offices in the interest of peace, and to assure our neighbors of our respect for them as independent States.

The Pan American Union is based on the principle of the equality of the American States. In Pan-American co-operation the idea of force and of economic pressure is eliminated. It is thought to obtain results through the processes of reason, by discussion and mutual accommodation. Cultural contacts are therefore of the greatest value and fortunately are increasing. They are multiplied by the ever-developing facilities of communication. They are aided by the formal methods of conference. We have not only the general Pan-American Conferences which meet at intervals of five years, but also special conferences which deal with specific and often technical problems and as a result of which each of the republics of this hemisphere is able to profit by the experiences of others. Thus I may refer to the

Pan American Conference on Electrical Communications, held at Mexico City in May last; the Pan American Child Welfare Congress, held at Santiago in October last; the Pan American Sanitary Conference which has recently closed its sessions at Havana; the Pan American Scientific Conference, which has just finished its labors at Lima; the Pan American Highway Conference which is to be held in Buenos Aires in May next; and the Pan American Educational Conference which is to be held at Santiago, Chile, next September. Through these conferences the positive results which have been achieved in one part of this hemisphere are made available to all, and through them a spirit of Pan American helpfulness in the solution of educational, social, and industrial problems is fostered.

Our economic relations are of constantly increasing importance. I am advised that, taking the South American countries and leaving out our enormous trade with Cuba and Mexico, and after making deductions corresponding to the change in the general level of prices, the increase in our exports to South America in 1923 over 1913 was thirty-five per cent and in our imports forty-one per cent. The economic opportunities which lie at our door are almost boundless, and the advantages are mutual, but of chief consequence is the realization that we are all co-workers, each struggling to attain the democratic ideal. Each has much to learn from the others but all have a permanent interest in a friendly co-operation, the fundamental principle of which should be the international application of the Golden Rule. If anywhere in the world men can dwell together in peace and secure the benefits of peace it is in the western hemisphere and here the United States has its greatest opportunity to exhibit a wise practicality without departure from the liberal ideals upon which its prestige and moral influence must ultimately depend.

ADDRESS by President Calvin Coolidge, at New York City, April 25, 1927 (extracts)

The New York *Times*, April 26, 1927. The address was delivered before the United Press

. . . THERE ARE TWO attitudes that the press may take which distinctly endanger our friendly relations. If they do not bring us to the verge of conflict, they are injurious to our trade. One is the constant criticism and misrepresentation of foreign people. Human nature provides sufficient distrust of all that is alien, so that there is no need of any artificial supply. The world is in far more danger from nations not trusting each other enough than from their trusting each other too much. A press which is given over to a narrow and bigoted nationalism, accompanied by misrepresentations of other countries, not only misinforms and misleads the people at home but produces the reaction of a rankling bitterness abroad. An almost equally harmful attitude is the other extreme. It usually consists of malicious and misleading partisan attacks on the conduct of our own Government in its efforts to defend American rights when they are threatened or invaded in foreign countries. Our Government has usually been too remiss, rather than too active, in supporting the lawful rights of its citizens abroad. That has been so long our established policy that it is rather difficult to conceive it assuming a truculent and arrogant attitude. But when it is proceeding with moderation, attempting by peaceful negotiation to adjust differences, defending the rights of its citizens and maintaining national dignity, great care is necessary to give the public the exact facts and avoid the appearance of seeming to support the position of foreign Governments. When such an attitude becomes known in the offending country, it is widely quoted there and, when all other arguments have been answered, becomes their chief reliance for maintaining their position. It not only furnishes ammunition for our adversaries, but attacks our own forces in the rear. An American press which has all the privileges which it enjoys under our institutions, and which derives its support from the progress and well-being of our people, ought to be first of all thoroughly American.

Progress and civilization have always depended upon effort and sacrifice. We have set up our institutions, established our ideals and adopted our social standards. We believe that they are consistent with right and truth and justice. We live under a system that guarantees the sanctity of life and liberty through public order and protects the rights of private property under the principle of due process of law. We have thrown every possible safeguard around the individual in order to protect him from any invasion of his rights even by the Government itself. It is peculiarly an American doctrine, now usually accepted in principle if not adopted in practice by all civilized countries, that these are inalienable rights, that they ought to belong to all persons everywhere, and that it is the chief function of Government to provide instrumentalities by which these rights can be secured and protected. We have adopted these ideals because we believe that they are of universal application and square with the eternal principles of right. But we may as well realize that they will not continue to prevail unless we are prepared constantly to put forth great efforts and make large sacrifices for their support.

While we have not been willing to assume any general attitude of crusading toward other nations, and realizing that institutions cannot be bestowed but must be adopted, have left them for the most part secure in their right to work out their own destiny, yet we have always been willing to encourage and assist, in so far as we could in harmony with international law and custom, other people in securing for themselves the benefit of these principles and ideals. In that conflict between freedom and despotism, which is as old as humanity, and which constantly recurs in one form or another, both among ourselves and among other people, it has always been the policy of this Government to extend its sympathy and, in so far as it lawfully could, its support to the side of freedom.

These are some of the standards which it has been the policy of our Government to support among its people at home and in its dealings with other nations. While it is well-established international law that we have no right to interfere in the purely domestic affairs of other nations in their dealings with their own citizens, it is equally well established that our Government has certain rights over and certain duties toward our own citizens and their property, wherever they may be located. The person and property of a citizen are a part of the general domain of the nation, even when abroad. On the other hand, there is a distinct and binding obligation on the part of self-respecting Governments to afford protection to the persons and property of their citizens, wherever they may be. This is both because it has an interest in them and because it has an obligation toward them. It would seem to be perfectly obvious that if it is wrong to murder and pillage within the confines of the United States, it is equally wrong outside our borders. The fundamental laws of justice are universal in their application. These rights go with the citizen. Wherever he goes, these duties of our Government must follow him.

It is all right to say that when our citizens enter a foreign country they should do so with the understanding that they are to abide by the laws of that country. They should, and they do, and our Government would be the last to interfere in the just application of the law of his domicile to our citizens. But this is only a partial statement of the case. The admission of our citizens within their territory is a voluntary act of foreign Governments. It is a tacit invitation. When we permit foreigners to come here, and when other countries admit our citizens, we know and they know that such aliens come and go not only under the rights and duties imposed by domestic law, but also under the rights and duties imposed by international law. There is nothing unfair, nothing imperialistic, in this principle. It has been universally adopted and recognized as right and just, and is the only reasonable method by which enlightened humanity can safeguard friendly intercourse among the citizens of different nations. This policy has been adopted in furtherance of the humanitarian desire for a universal reign of law.

These principles are involved in some of the difficulties that we have recently been trying to work out with foreign nations, especially with Mexico. We have had claims against that country running over a long series of years, growing out of the death of many of our citizens and the loss of their property running into hundreds of millions of dollars. A very considerable portion of these cases has been due to revolutionary activities and other forms of public violence. Public order has never been entirely complete in that country. But lately our difficulties have been increased by the enactment of laws by the Government itself which we feel threaten the virtual confiscation of the property of our citizens, even where their holdings are under titles which have been established for scores of years.

In 1857 Mexico adopted a constitution. In its relation to the protection of acquired property it provided ample security. Under its terms many of our people acquired holdings both through individual and corporate ownership. During the more than thirty years of President Diaz we were especially encouraged to make investments, to promote all kinds of development of the natural resources, transportation and industries. After he was driven from office by revolution, much disorder existed, with Presidents following one another in rapid succession.

In 1917 a new Constitution was adopted, with provisions affecting agricultural, mining and oil lands, which we thought threatened the holdings of our nationals with confiscation. Their Constitution is not self-enforcing, but requires the promulgation of laws to put it into effect. While this was in process of being brought about, a Government was established which we did not recognize. In 1920 General Obregon was chosen President and sought recognition. In negotiating for that purpose it was repeatedly pointed out that we feared that the new Constitution, although one of its provisions expressly prohibited the enactment of retroactive laws, might be interpreted as retroactive in its effect upon the holdings of real estate which our people had secured prior to its adoption. We sought assurances from the Mexican Government that such was not the case. In order to prevent misunderstanding we sent two Commissioners to Mexico City in 1923 to confer upon this subject, and also on the question of our claims, with two Mexican Commissioners. Charles Beecher Warren and John Barton Payne represented our Government. They had a series of conferences and kept written records of their proceedings, in which are set out the recommendation for the appointment of two claims commissions and the understanding that the Constitution of 1917 was not to be given retroactive or confiscatory application. These records were duly signed and attested by the Commissioners and were submitted to the President of Mexico and the President of the United States for their mutual approval, which was given. It was solely because of our understanding secured in this formal way that our property rights would be respected that recognition of the Government of President Obregon was granted on Sept. 3, 1923.

During the Winter of 1924 revolutionary activities started in Mexico which it seems probable would have succeeded in displacing President Obregon had not our Government furnished him with arms and ammunition largely on credit and given him the advantage of our moral support. Our help maintained his position. Soon after President Calles came into power he and the Mexican Congress proposed laws and regulations which we deemed threatened confiscation of American property. To prevent the appearance of acquiescence we so notified Mexico prior to the passage of such laws. Nevertheless, they were passed. We have made further protest against their being put into effect, as they are contrary to our understanding of the conference as a result of which we granted recognition. In the notes which have been received the Government of President Calles refuses to be bound by what we thought was the understanding arrived at with President Obregon. We closed the correspondence by notifying the Mexican Government that we stood squarely on the understanding made with President Obregon, and we expected it not to take any action that would deprive American citizens of their property or their property rights.

Agricultural lands have apparently been seized from time to time for which no compensation has yet been made. While there have been threats to seize oil property, no such seizures have lately been made, and suits are now pending in Mexican courts to restrain such seizures. Former decisions of their courts are relied on to support these suits.

Stripped of all technicalities and involved legal discussion, this is the main difference which our Government has with the Mexican Government. We do not question their right to take any property, provided they pay fair compensation. With their efforts to secure a division of great estates, so that more of their people may be landowners, we have every sympathy. We have even agreed that our Government would accept the bonds of the Mexican Government in payment for damages awarded by the commission for land taken for this purpose. Of course, we do not want any controversy with Mexico. We feel every sympathy with her people in their distress and have every desire to assist them. That they welcome conditions under which life and property are secure is shown by the hundreds of thousands of them who are coming to the United States, where, through their industry, they thrive and prosper. Under these conditions small land holdings would develop in Mexico as they have developed here. Those of her citizens who preferred to seek employment in industry, like many of our own people, would have an abundant opportunity in their own country. Instead of desiring to pursue any aggression or to take part in any oppression, we are endeavoring through the most friendly offices to demonstrate to their Government that their attitude in relation to property will not only result in the economic disadvantage of their own people, by preventing the investment of outside capital so necessary for their development, but will greatly impair their friendly relations with other interested nations.

It is a cardinal principle of law that private property should not be taken without fair compensation. This principal is declared in our national Constitution and in those of all our States. I know of no written Constitution that does not contain a similar provision. Under the Constitution of 1917, and by-laws and regulations for carrying it into effect, we feel that Mexico is threatening to disregard this great elementary principle by undertaking a retroactive application of their Constitution to property of our citizens acquired long before their Constitution was adopted.

The Senate recently passed a resolution supporting the protection of American life and property and suggesting resort to arbitration. We have at present two commissions of arbitration with Mexico, and the principle of arbitration has always been strongly advocated by our Government. Everybody favors arbitration when the question at issue is arbitrable. Under the present circumstances I can see grave difficulties in formulating a question which the two Governments would agree to submit to such a tribunal. The principle that property is not to be confiscated and the duty of our Government to protect it are so well established that it is doubtful if they should be permitted to be questioned. Very likely Mexico would feel that the right to make a Constitution and pass laws is a privilege of her sovereignty which she could not permit to be brought into question. It has therefore seemed that we are more likely to secure an adjustment through negotiation. I am glad to report that the Mexican Ambassador has recently declared to me that she does not intend to confiscate our property, that she has shown diligence in capturing and punishing those who have murdered our citizens, and expressed the wish, which we so thoroughly entertain, of keeping cordial and friendly relations. With a strong sentiment of this nature, which, I am convinced, animates the people of both countries, it will surely be possible to reach an amicable adjustment. Our two peoples ought so to conduct themselves that there will never be any interference with our ancient ties of friendship.

Our relationship to Nicaragua I have set out in detail in a message to the Congress. For a dozen years we kept a force of marines in that country at the earnest solicitation of its Government. During this time the people were peaceful, orderly and prosperous, and their national debt was greatly reduced. Almost at once after I withdrew the marines revolution was started. Finally a President was designated by the Congress which appeared to us and to other Central American countries to have a constitutional title, and we therefore recognized him. As the disorders continued, on his representation that he was unable to protect American lives and property, I sent a force of marines for that purpose. Their presence has undoubtedly prevented the larger towns from being pillaged and confined the fighting for the most part to uninhabited areas. We have sold arms and ammunition, as we did in the case of Mexico, to the Nicaraguan Government. The revolutionary forces appear to have received arms and ammunition from some source in Mexico. With a hope that we might be furnished with information which would better enable us to deal with the situation, I have sent Henry L. Stimson, former Secretary of War, to that country. Meantime, it is reported that the Government forces have been apparently successful in driving the revolutionists from the field.

In addition to the private property of our citizens which is employed in lumber and agricultural operations, our Government has secured the right to construct a canal and establish a naval base, for which it paid $3,000,000. Contrary to the general impression, there are no oil properties in this country. Nevertheless, I have seen cartoons that pictured it as filled with oil derricks. Our country consumes vast quantities of oil and gasoline in its use of automobiles, gas engines and oil-burning furnaces. If these products are to be kept within a reasonable price, which is very important to a great body of our citizens, our people who go abroad to develop new fields and to increase the supply ought to have the encouragement and support of our Government. We are not making war on Nicaragua any more than a policeman on the street is making war on passers-by. We are there to protect our citizens and their property from being destroyed by war and to lend every encouragement we can to the restoration of peace. While the destruction of life and property has been serious enough, had it not been for the presence of our forces it would undoubtedly have been much worse.

Toward the Governments of countries which we have recognized this side of the Panama Canal we feel a moral responsibility that does not attach to other nations. We wish them to feel that our recognition is of real value to them and that they can count on such support as we can lawfully give when they are beset with difficulties. We have undertaken to discourage revolutions within that area and to encourage settlement of political differences by the peaceful method of elections. This policy is bound to meet with some discouragements, but it is our hope and belief that ultimately it will prevail. This territory is rich in natural resources, and under orderly Governments is capable of a development that will give to its inhabitants all the advantages of modern civilization. It is a curious circumstance that some of those who have been willing to have us take mandates over far-off countries in Asia, where we have no interest that does not attach to all humanity, are most critical when we are attempting to encourage the maintenance of order, the continuity of duly established government, and the protection of lives and property of our own citizens under a general reign of law in these countries that are near at hand and where we have large and peculiar interests. . . .

The recent period has brought America into a new position in the world. We shall have to bear the inevitable criticisms and try to discharge the inevitable obligations which arise from this condition. Because some others have pursued that course, it may be feared that we shall embark upon a program of military aggrandizement. Such, however, is not the spirit of the American people. If, even where our national interests and the protection of the rights of our citizens are involved, we attempt to assist in composing difficulties and supporting international law, we must expect to be charged with imperialistic motives. In our international intercourse we must hold ourselves up to high standards of justice and equity. We should be slow to take offense and quick to grant redress. The world knows that the whole genius of America always calls it to the support of the universal rights of humanity.

The civilization of the world has been accomplished by the acceptance and general observance of definite rules of human conduct. Our duty demands that it be clearly understood at home and abroad, that we are unwavering in our faith in those principles. Those who violate them cannot hope for our approbation. Our attitude toward all nations is one of friendship and good will. Toward those who are yet struggling to improve the conditions of their people and achieve a larger liberty it is especially one of forbearance. We support the demands of right and justice, but we are equally solicitous to observe the requirements of mercy and compassion. In the attempt of your

Government to meet these great obligations by which alone an enlightened civilized society can be maintained a united America must constantly respond with service and sacrifice.

INAUGURAL ADDRESS by President Herbert Hoover, March 4, 1929 (extract)

71st Congress, Special Session, Senate Document No. 1

. . . THE UNITED STATES fully accepts the profound truth that our own progress, prosperity and peace are interlocked with the progress, prosperity and peace of all humanity. The whole world is at peace. The dangers to a continuation of this peace to-day are largely the fear and 'suspicion which still haunt the world. No suspicion or fear can be rightly directed toward our country.

Those who have a true understanding of America know that we have no desire for territorial expansion, for economic or other domination of other peoples. Such purposes are repugnant to our ideals of human freedom. Our form of government is ill adapted to the responsibilities which inevitably follow permanent limitation of the independence of other peoples. Superficial observers seem to find no destiny for our abounding increase in population, in wealth and power except that of imperialism. They fail to see that the American people are engrossed in the building for themselves of a new economic system, a new social system, a new political system—all of which are characterized by aspirations of freedom of opportunity and thereby are the negation of imperialism. They fail to realize that because of our abounding prosperity our youth are pressing more and more into our institutions of learning; that our people are seeking a larger vision through art, literature, science, and travel; that they are moving toward stronger moral and spiritual life—that from these things our sympathies are broadening beyond the bounds of our Nation and race toward their true expression in a real brotherhood of man. They fail to see that the idealism of America will lead it to no narrow or selfish channel, but inspire it to do its full share as a nation toward the advancement of civilization. It will do that not by mere declaration but by taking a practical part in supporting all useful international undertakings. We not only desire peace with the world, but to see peace maintained throughout the world. We wish to advance the reign of justice and reason toward the extinction of force.

The recent treaty for the renunciation of war as an instrument of national policy sets an advanced standard in our conception of the relations of nations. Its acceptance should pave the way to greater limitation of armament, the offer of which we sincerely extend to the world. But its full realization also implies a greater and greater perfection in the instrumentalities for pacific settlement of controversies between nations. In the creation and use of these instrumentalities we should support every sound method of conciliation, arbitration, and judicial settlement. American statesmen were among the first to propose and they have constantly urged upon the world, the establishment of a tribunal for the settlement of controversies of a justiciable character. The Permanent Court of International Justice in its major purpose is thus peculiarly identified with American ideals and with American statesmanship. No more potent instrumentality for this purpose has ever been conceived and no other is practicable of establishment. The reservations placed upon our adherence should not be misinterpreted. The United States seeks by these reservations no special privilege or advantage but only to clarify our relation to advisory opinions and other matters which are subsidiary to the major purpose of the court. The way should, and I believe will, be found by which we may take our proper place in a movement so fundamental to the progress of peace.

Our people have determined that we should make no political engagements such as membership in the League of Nations, which may commit us in advance as a nation to become involved in the settlements of controversies between other countries. They adhere to the belief that the independence of America from such obligations increases its ability and availability for service in all fields of human progress.

I have lately returned from a journey among our sister Republics of the Western Hemisphere. I have received unbounded hospitality and courtesy as their expression of friendliness to our country. We are held by particular bonds of sympathy and common interest with them. They are each of them building a racial character and a culture which is an impressive contribution to human progress. We wish only for the maintenance of their independence, the growth of their stability, and their prosperity. While we have had wars in the Western Hemisphere, yet on the whole the record is in encouraging contrast with that of other parts of the world. Fortunately the New World is largely free from the inheritances of fear and distrust which have so troubled the Old World. We should keep it so.

It is impossible, my countrymen, to speak of peace without profound emotion. In thousands of homes in America, in millions of homes around the world, there are vacant chairs. It would be a shameful confession of our unworthiness if it should develop that we have abandoned the hope for which all these men died. Surely civilization is old enough, surely mankind is mature enough so that we ought in our own lifetime to find a way to permanent peace. Abroad, to west and east, are nations whose sons mingled their blood with the blood of our sons on the battle fields. Most of these nations have contributed to our race, to our culture, our knowledge, and our progress. From one of them we derive our very language and from many of them much of the genius of our institutions. Their desire for peace is as deep and sincere as our own.

Peace can be contributed to by respect for our ability in defense. Peace can be promoted by the limitation of arms and by the creation of the instrumentalities for peaceful settlement of controversies. But it will become a reality only through self-restraint and active effort in friendliness and helpfulness. I covet for this administration a record of having further contributed to advance the cause of peace.

In our form of democracy the expression of the popular will can be effected only through the instrumentality of political parties. We maintain party government not to promote intolerant partisanship but because opportunity must be given for expression of the popular will, and organization provided for the execution of its mandates and for accountability of government to the people. It follows that the government both in the executive and the legislative branches must carry out in good faith the platforms upon which the party was intrusted with power. But the government is that of the whole people; the party is the instrument through which policies are determined and men chosen to bring them into being. The animosities of elections should have no place in our Government, for government must concern itself alone with the common weal. . . .

ANNUAL MESSAGE from President Herbert Hoover to the United States Congress, December 3, 1929 (extract)
Foreign Relations of the United States, 1929, I, v

. . . AT THE beginning of the present administration the neighboring State of Mexico was beset with domestic insurrection. We maintained the embargo upon the shipment of arms to Mexico but permitted the duly constituted Government to procure supplies from our surplus war stocks. Fortunately, the Mexican Government by its own strength successfully withstood the insurrection with but slight damage. Opportunity of further peaceful developments is given to that country. At the request of the Mexican Government, we have since lifted the embargo on shipment of arms altogether. The two governments have taken further steps to promote friendly relationships and so solve our differences. Conventions prolonging for a period of two years the life of the general and special claims commissions have been concluded.

In South America we are proud to have had part in the settlement of the long-standing dispute between Chile and Peru in the disposal of the question of Tacna-Arica.

The work of the commission of inquiry and conciliation between Bolivia and Paraguay, in which a representative of this Government participated, has successfully terminated an incident which seemed to threaten war. The proposed plan for final settlement as suggested by the neutral governments is still under consideration.

This Government has continued its efforts to act as a mediator in boundary difficulties between Guatemala and Honduras.

A further instance of profound importance in establishing good will was the inauguration of regular air mail service between the United States and Caribbean, Central American, and South American countries.

We still have marines on foreign soil—in Nicaragua, Haiti, and China. In the large sense we do not wish to be represented abroad in such manner. About 1,600 marines remain in Nicaragua at the urgent request of that government and the leaders of all parties pending the training of a domestic constabulary capable of insuring tranquility. We have already reduced these forces materially and we are anxious to withdraw them further as the situation warrants. In Haiti we have about 700 marines, but it is a much more difficult problem, the solution of which is still obscure. If Congress approves, I shall dispatch a commission to Haiti to review and study the matter in an endeavor to arrive at some more definite policy than at present. Our forces in China constitute 2,605 men, which we hope also further to reduce to the normal legation guard.

It is my desire to establish more firmly our understanding and relationships with the Latin American countries by strengthening the diplomatic missions to those countries. It is my hope to secure men long experienced in our Diplomatic Service, who speak the languages of the peoples to whom they are accredited, as chiefs of our diplomatic missions in these States. I shall send to the Senate at an early date the nominations of several such men. . . .

ADDRESS by Henry L. Stimson, Secretary of State, "The United States and the Other American Republics," at New York City, February 6, 1931

Department of State, Latin American Series, No. 4. The address was delivered before the Council on Foreign Relations. The U.S. non-recognition policy in Central America terminated when the 1923 treaty expired, January, 1934

DURING the past two years widespread economic depression and consequent unemployment have brought instability and unrest to many of the countries of the Western Hemisphere. Since March, 1929, there have been revolutions in no less than seven Latin American republics, resulting in the forcible overthrow in six of them of the existing governments. These changes, and the armed contests by which some of them have been accompanied, have presented to the State Department of this country a rapid succession of critical problems for decision. It was inevitable in such a situation that criticism of our decisions should be excited, and it has been.

Therefore, this evening, I shall place before you from the standpoint of the State Department a brief statement of the facts as well as of the underlying principles and reasons upon which some of these recent decisions have been based. In particular, I shall discuss the principles by which we have been guided in the recognition of the new governments which have arisen and also the principles which have underlain our action in the regulation of the sale and transportation of arms and munitions to the countries which have been involved in strife.

As a background for this discussion a brief review of the general policy of the United States towards the other republics of this hemisphere during the past century is pertinent. That policy, in its general conception, has been a noble one. From the beginning we have made the preservation of individual independence of these nations correspond with our own interest. This was announced in the Monroe Doctrine and has been maintained ever since. That doctrine, far from being an assertion of suzerainty over our sister republics, was an assertion of their individual rights as independent nations. It declared to the world that this independence was so vital to our own safety that we would be willing to fight for it against an aggressive Europe. The Monroe Doctrine was a declaration of the United States versus Europe—not of the United States versus Latin America.

In taking this position in the Western Hemisphere, our policy has coincided with the basic conception of international law, namely, the equal rights of each nation in the family of nations. The law justly regards this conception as the chief protection of weak nations against oppression. Our people led in the recognition of the independence of those countries with an instinctive readiness which was based upon their sympathy with the doctrine upon which that independence rested. In the language of John Quincy Adams, Secretary of State at the time:

the principles upon which the right of independence has been maintained by the South American patriots have been proved not only as identical with those upon which our own independence was asserted and achieved, but as involving the whole theory of government on the emphatically American foundation of the sovereignty of the people and the unalienable rights of men. To a cause reposing upon this basis the people of this country never could be indifferent, and their sympathies have accordingly been, with great unanimity and constancy, enlisted in its favor. (*J. Q. Adams, May 27, 1823, American State Papers, Foreign Relations, V, 888.*)

I am not forgetful of the fact that the foreign policy of every nation is devoted primarily to its own interest. It also rises and falls with the character and wisdom of the individuals or groups who from time to time are in power. I do not close my eyes to the occasional dark spots which have been charged to that record, particularly seventy-five or eighty years ago. But the actions which were the foundation for the most serious of these charges were directly attributable to the influence of slavery in this country, then at the height of its political power, and that influence has long since been wiped out in the blood of a great Civil War. They have no more reflected the democratic idealism which has generally characterized our foreign policy at its best than the Fugitive Slave Act has fairly reflected our domestic social policy.

In spite of these and all other aberrations, it is a very conservative statement to say that the general foreign policy of the United States during the past century towards the republics of Latin America has been characterized by a regard for their rights as independent nations which, when compared with current international morality in other hemispheres, has been as unusual as it has been praiseworthy.

People are sometimes prone to forget our long and honorable fulfillment of this policy towards our younger sister nations. It was our action which obtained the withdrawal of French imperialism from Mexico. It was our influence which provided for the return from Great Britain of the Bay Islands to Honduras, and the Mosquito Coast, including Greytown, to Nicaragua. It was our pressure which secured the arbitration of the boundary dispute between Great Britain and Venezuela and which later secured by arbitration the solution of serious disputes between Venezuela, Germany, and Italy. Between the republics themselves, our influence has constantly been exerted for a friendly solution of controversies which might otherwise mar their independent and peaceful intercourse. To speak only of recent matters, I may refer to the long-standing Tacna-Arica dispute between Chile and Peru, and the open clash between Bolivia and Paraguay. During the past seven years our good offices have resulted in the settlement of eight boundary disputes between eleven countries of this hemisphere.

In our successive Pan American conferences, as well as in the Pan American Union, the fundamental rule of equality, which is the mainstay of independence, has been unbroken. Action is taken only by unanimous consent. No majority of states can conclude a minority, even of the smallest and weakest. This is in sharp contrast to the practice which prevailed in the former Concert of Europe, where only the great powers were admitted on a basis of equality. It was also at variance with the original organization of the Covenant of the League of Nations, where it was proposed that a majority of the seats in the Council should be permanently occupied by the Great Powers.

While such recognition of their equal rights and national independence has always been the basic foundation upon which our policy toward these republics has rested, there is another side of the picture which must be borne in mind. This basic principle of equality in international law is an ideal resting upon postulates which are not always and consistently accurate. For independence imposes duties as well as rights. It presupposes ability in the independent nation to fulfill the obligations towards other nations and their nationals which are prescribed and expected to exist in the family of nations. The hundred years which have ensued since the announcement of our policy towards these republics have contained recurring evidence of how slow is the progress of mankind along that difficult highway which leads to national maturity and how difficult is the art of popular self-government. Years and decades of alternations between arbitrary power at one time and outbreaks of violence at another have pointed out again and again how different a matter it is in human affairs to have the vision and to achieve the reality.

Furthermore, the difficulties which have beset the foreign policy of the United States in carrying out these principles cannot be understood without the comprehension of a geographical fact. The very locality where the progress of these republics has been most slow; where the difficulties of race and climate have been greatest; where the recurrence of domestic violence has most frequently resulted in the failure of duty on the part of the republics themselves and the violation of the rights of life and property accorded by international law to foreigners within their territory, has been in Central America, the narrow isthmus which joins the two Americas, and among the islands which intersperse the Caribbean Sea adjacent to that isthmus. That locality has been the one spot external to our shores which nature has decreed to be most vital to our national safety, not to mention our prosperity. It commands the line of the great trade route which joins our eastern and western coasts. Even before human hands had pierced the isthmus with a seagoing canal, that route was vital to our national interest. Since the Panama Canal has become an accomplished fact, it has been not only the vital artery of our coastwise commerce but, as well, the link in our national defense which protects the defensive power of our fleet. One cannot fairly appraise American policy toward Latin America or fully appreciate the standard which it has maintained without taking into consideration all of the elements of which it is the resultant.

Like the rocks which mark the surface of a steady river current, all of the facts and circumstances which I have outlined have produced ripples in the current of our steady policy towards the Latin American republics. Some of them have resulted in temporary intrusions into the domestic affairs of some of those countries, which our hostile critics have not hesitated to characterize as the manifestation of a selfish American imperialism. I am clear that a calm historical perspective will refute that criticism and will demonstrate that the international practice of this Government in the Western Hemisphere has been asserted with a much readier recognition of the legal rights of all the countries with which we have been in contact than has been the prevalent practice in any other part of the world. The discussion of the particular topics which I am bringing before you this evening, will, I hope, help to develop the character, trend, and uniformity of our country's policy.

RECOGNITION

The recognition of a new state has been described as the assurance given to it that it will be permitted to hold its place and rank in the character of an independent political organism in the society of nations. The recognition of a new government within a state arises in practice only when a government has been changed or established by revolution or by a *coup d'état*. No question of recognition normally arises, for example, when a king dies and his heir succeeds to the throne, or where as the result of an election in a republic a new chief executive constitutionally assumes office. The practice of this country as to the recognition of new governments has been substantially uniform from the days of the administration of Secretary of State Jefferson in 1792 to the days of Secretary of State Bryan in 1913. There were certain slight departures from this policy during the Civil War, but they were manifestly due to the exigencies of warfare and were abandoned immediately afterwards. This general policy, as thus observed, was to base the act of recognition not upon the question of the constitutional legitimacy of the new government but upon its *de facto* capacity to fulfill its obligations as a member of the family of nations. This country recognized the right of other nations to regulate their own internal affairs of government and disclaimed any attempt to base its recognition upon the correctness of their constitutional action.

Said Mr. Jefferson in 1792:

We certainly cannot deny to other nations that principle whereon our own Government is founded, that every nation has a right to govern itself internally under what forms it pleases, and to change these forms at its own will; and externally to transact business with other nations through whatever organ it chooses, whether that be a king, convention, assembly, committee, president, or whatever it be. (*Jefferson to Pinckney, Works, Vol. III, p. 500.*)

In these essentials our practice corresponded with the practice of the other nations of the world.

The particular considerations upon which our action was regularly based were well stated by Mr. Adee, long the trusted Assistant Secretary of State of this Government, as follows:

Ever since the American Revolution entrance upon diplomatic intercourse with foreign states has been *de facto*, dependent upon the existence of three conditions of fact: the control of the administrative machinery of the state; the general acquiescence of its people; and the ability and willingness of their government to discharge international and conventional obligations. The form of government has not been a conditional factor in such recognition; in other words, the *de jure* element of legitimacy of title has been left aside. (*Foreign Relations of the United States, 1913, p. 100.*)

With the advent of President Wilson's administration this policy of over a century was radically departed from in respect to the Republic of Mexico, and, by a public declaration on March 11, 1913, it was announced that—

Cooperation (with our sister republics of Central and South America) is possible only when supported at every turn by the orderly processes of just government based upon law, not upon arbitrary or irregular force. We hold, as I am sure that all thoughtful leaders of republican government everywhere hold, that just government rests always upon the consent of the governed, and that there can be no freedom without order based upon law and upon the public conscience and approval. We shall look to make these principles the basis of mutual intercourse, respect, and helpfulness between our sister republics and ourselves. (*Foreign Relations of the United States, 1913, p. 7.*)

Mr. Wilson's government sought to put this new policy into effect in respect to the recognition of the then Government of Mexico held by President Victoriano Huerta. Although Huerta's government was in *de facto* possession, Mr. Wilson refused to recognize it, and he sought through the influence and pressure of his great office to force it from power. Armed conflict followed with the forces of Mexico, and disturbed relations between us and that republic lasted until a comparatively few years ago.

In his sympathy for the development of free constitutional institutions among the people of our Latin American neighbors, Mr. Wilson did not differ from the feelings of the great mass of his countrymen in the United States, including Mr. Jefferson and Mr. Adams, whose statements I have quoted; but he differed from the practice of his predecessors in seeking actively to propagate these institutions in a foreign country by the direct influence of this Government and to do this against the desire of the authorities and people of Mexico.

The present administration has refused to follow the policy of Mr. Wilson and has followed consistently the former practice of this Government since the days of Jefferson. As soon as it was reported to us, through our diplomatic representatives, that the new governments in Bolivia, Peru, Argentina, Brazil, and Panama were in control of the administrative machinery of the state, with the apparent general acquiescence of their people, and that they were willing and apparently able to discharge their international and conventional obligations, they were recognized by our Government. And, in view of the economic depression, with the consequent need for prompt measures of financial stabilization, we did this with as little delay as possible in order to give those sorely pressed countries the quickest possible opportunities for recovering their economic poise.

Such has been our policy in all cases where international practice was not affected or controlled by preexisting treaty. In the five republics of Central America, Guatemala, Honduras, Salvador, Nicaragua, and Costa Rica, however, we have found an entirely different situation existing from that normally presented under international law and practice. As I have already pointed out, those countries geographically have for a century been the focus of the greatest difficulties and the most frequent disturbances in their earnest course towards competent maturity in the discharge of their international obligations.

Until some two decades ago, war within and without was their almost yearly portion. No administration of their government was long safe from revolutionary attack instigated either by factions of its own citizens or by the machinations of another one of the five republics. Free elections, the cornerstone upon which our own democracy rests, had been practically unknown during the entire period. In 1907 a period of strife, involving four of the five republics, had lasted almost without interruption for several years. In that year, on the joint suggestion and mediation of the Governments of the United States and Mexico, the five republics met for the purpose of considering methods intended to mitigate and, if possible, terminate the intolerable situation. By one of the conventions which they then adopted, the five republics agreed with one another as follows:

The Governments of the high contracting parties shall not recognize any other government which may come into power in any of the five republics as a consequence of a *coup d'état,* or of a revolution against the recognized government, so long as the freely elected representatives of the people thereof, have not constitutionally reorganized the country.

Sixteen years later, in 1923, the same five republics, evidentally satisfied with the principle they had thus adopted and desiring to reinforce it and prevent any future evasions of that principle, met again, reenacted the same covenant, and further promised each other that even after a revolutionary government had been constitutionally reorganized by the representatives of the people, they would not recognize it if its president should have been a leader in the preceding revolution or related to such a leader by blood or marriage, or if he should have been a cabinet officer or held some high military command during the accomplishment of the revolution. Some four months thereafter, our own Government, on the invitation of these republics, who had conducted their meeting in Washington, announced, through Secretary Hughes, that the United States would in its future dealings with those republics follow out the same principle which they had thus established in their treaty. Since that time we have consistently adhered to this policy in respect to those five republics.

We followed that policy in Guatemala in the case of a recent revolution in which some fifty-seven people were killed. General Orellano, the leader of the revolt, set himself up as the provisional president of that republic on December 16, 1930. On December 22, 1930, we notified him that in accordance with the policy established by the 1923 treaty he would not be recognized by us. No recognition was granted him by any of the other four republics. Following this, he tendered his resignation and retired from office; and on January 2,

1931, through the constitutional forms provided in the Guatemalan Constitution, Señor Reina Andrade was chosen provisional president by the Guatemalan Congress and immediately called a new election for a permanent president. Thereupon this country and the other four republics recognized the government of Señor Reina Andrade.

Since the adoption by Secretary Hughes, in 1923, of the policy of recognition agreed upon by the five republics in their convention, not one single revolutionary government has been able to maintain itself in those five republics. Twice, once in Nicaragua and once in the case of Guatemala, just described, a revolutionary leader has succeeded in grasping the reins of government for a brief period. But in each case the failure to obtain recognition has resulted in his prompt resignation, on account of his inability to borrow money in the international markets. Several times within the same period a contemplated revolution has been abandoned by its conspirators on the simple reminder by a minister from this country or one of the other republics that, even if they were successful, their government would not be recognized; and undoubtedly in many more cases has the knowledge of the existence of the policy prevented even the preparation for a revolution or *coup d'état*. In every one of these cases the other four republics have made common cause in the efforts of the United States to carry out their policy and maintain stability. When one compares this record with the bloodstained history of Central America before the adoption of the treaty of 1923, I think that no impartial student can avoid the conclusion that the treaty and the policy which it has established in that locality has been productive of very great good.

Of course it is a departure from the regular international practice of our Government, and it undoubtedly contains possible difficulties and dangers of application which we in the State Department are the last to minimize and in case of which, should they arise, this Government must reserve its freedom of action. But the distinction between this departure, which was suggested by the five republics themselves and in which we have acted at their earnest desire and in cooperation with them, and the departure taken by President Wilson in an attempt to force upon Mexico a policy which she resented must be apparent to the most thoughtless student. A few weeks ago Judge John Bassett Moore, who as Counselor of the State Department was a member of Mr. Wilson's administration, criticized Mr. Wilson's departure from the former practice of this country, and he included within his criticism the departure initiated by the treaty of 1923. He did not, however, point out the foregoing radical difference of principle between the two policies, nor the entirely different results which have followed each, and which thus far seem quite to justify the policy of 1923.

Furthermore, it may be noted that one of the dangers which might be apprehended from this policy of recognition adopted by the five Central American republics under the treaty of 1923 has not materialized. One of the most serious evils in Central America has been the fact that throughout the history of those republics, until recently, it has been the habitual practice of the president who held the machinery of government to influence and control the election of his successor. This has tended to stimulate revolution as the only means by which a change of government could be accomplished. The danger was therefore manifest that this treaty of 1923 might result in perpetuating the autocratic power of the governments which were for the time in possession. As a matter of fact this has not happened. On the contrary, significant improvement has taken place in election practice. The Government of Nicaragua of its own motion has sought and obtained the assistance of the United States in securing free and uncontrolled elections in 1928 and 1930. The Government of Honduras, in 1928, without any such assistance, conducted an election which was so free that the party in power was dispossessed by the opposition party; and a similar free election has apparently occurred in 1930. For nearly one hundred years before 1923 free elections have been so rare in Central America as to be almost unique. Of course, it is too early to make safe generalizations, but it would seem that the stability created by the treaty of 1923 apparently has not tended to perpetuate existing autocracies but, on the contrary, to stimulate a greater sense of responsibility in elections.

TRAFFIC IN ARMS

I will now pass to the subject of the policy of this Government in respect to the export of arms and munitions to countries which are engaged in civil strife. Twice during the present Administration we have had to make important decisions and take important action in respect to this subject. The first of these occasions was in March, 1929, when a military insurrection broke out in the Republic of Mèxico. This insurrection was of serious nature and extent. It involved disturbances in many of the Mexican provinces and much fighting and bloodshed. Acting under a joint resolution of our Congress, adopted in 1922, this Government maintained an embargo upon the exportation of all arms and munitions which might reach the rebels. At the same time, it permitted the sale and itself sold arms and ammunition to the established government of Mexico, with which we were then and had been for a number of years in diplomatic relations. In about three months the insurrection was suppressed, and I think it can be fairly said that it is due in no slight degree to our action in this matter that the feelings of hostility on the part of Mexico to the United States which had existed ever since the intervention of President Wilson against Huerta in 1913 were finally ended and the relations of the two countries became friendly and cordial.

The second occasion was in October, 1930, when armed insurrection had broken out against the Government of Brazil. In the same way in which we had acted towards Mexico, we permitted that government to purchase arms both from our Government and from our nationals in this country; and, when the Ambassador of Brazil brought to our attention the fact that arms were being purchased in this country for export to the rebel forces fighting against the recognized government, we placed an embargo against the exportation of such arms. Two days later the Government of Brazil suddenly fell, the immediate cause being the revolt of its own garrison in Rio de Janeiro.

In placing the embargo upon the exportation of arms to the Brazilian rebel forces, our Government acted under the same joint resolution of our Congress of 1922 and with the same purpose and upon the same policy as had guided our action in the case of Mexico and in other cases where action has been taken under that resolution. That purpose was "to prevent arms and munitions procured from the United States being used to promote conditions of domestic violence" in countries whose governments we had recognized and with which we were in friendly intercourse. This was the purpose and policy as stated by our Congress in the language of the resolution itself.

In the case of Brazil there also was in effect a treaty between the United States and Brazil which made it compulsory for us to act as we did in placing this embargo. With Mexico that treaty had not yet gone into effect. This treaty was the convention executed at Habana on February 20, 1928, between the United States and the twenty Latin American republics, providing for the rights and duties of states in the event of civil strife. Between its signatories it rendered compulsory the policy of protecting our Latin American sister republics against the traffic in arms and war material carried on by our nationals, which previously the joint resolution of 1922 had left within the discretion of the Executive. The language of the treaty of 1928 is as follows:

ARTICLE 1. The contracting states bind themselves to observe the following rules with regard to civil strife in another one of them: . . .

    3. To forbid the traffic in arms and war material, except when intended for the government, while the belligerency of the rebels has not been recognized, in which latter case the rules of neutrality shall be applied.

Our action in regard to Brazil has been criticized by gentlemen who have confused the legal situation which existed in Brazil with an entirely different situation. We have been criticized for "taking sides in that civil strife," as if we had been under the duty to maintain neutrality between the Brazilian Government and the rebels who were seeking to overthrow it.

Under the law of nations the duty of neutrality does not arise until the insurgents have assumed the status of a belligerent power between whom and the mother country other governments must maintain impartiality. This occurs when a condition of belligerency is recognized either by the parent state itself or by the governments of other nations. Such a situation arose in our Civil War when the Confederate States, having occupied exclusively a portion of the territory of the United States and having set up their own capital at Richmond, were recognized as belligerents by the nations of Europe. It has not arisen in any of the recent revolutions of Latin America, whether successful or unsuccessful. The revolutionists in Brazil had not been recognized as belligerents either by the Brazilian Government, by the United States, or by any other nation. Until that happens, under the law and practice of nations, no duty of impartiality arises either on the part of our Government or our citizens. Until that time there is only one side towards which, under international law, other nations owe any duty. This is so well established as to be elementary. It was recognized in the clause of the treaty of 1928 which I have just quoted. It is recognized in the standard legal treatises, including that of Mr. John Bassett Moore, who cites among other precedents an opinion of one of our Attorney Generals and says that—

It (the United States Neutrality Act of 1818) would extend to the fitting out and arming of vessels for a revolted colony, whose belligerency had not been recognized, but it should not be applied to the fitting out, etc., of vessels for the parent state for use against a revolted colony whose independence has not in any manner been recognized by our Government. (*Hoar, Attorney General, 1869, 13 Op. 177. Cited in Judge Moore's International Law Digest, Vol. VII, p. 1079.*)

Until belligerency is recognized and the duty of neutrality arises, all the humane predispositions towards stability of government, the preservation of international amity, and the protection of established intercourse between nations are in favor of the existing government. This is particularly the case in countries where civil strife has been as frequent, as personal, and as disastrous as it has been in some sections of Central and South America during the past century. The law of nations is not static. It grows and develops with the experience

of mankind, and its development follows the line of human predispositions and experiences such as those to which I have referred.

The domestic legislation of the United States prescribing the duties
of its citizens towards nations suffering from civil strife is following
the line of these predispositions and is blazing the way for the subsequent growth of the law of nations. I am not one who regards this
development of American domestic legislation, exemplified by the
joint resolution of 1922, as a departure from the principles of international law or as a reactionary or backward step. The reverse is true.
Although I have had little occasion to deal with the subject of international law from an academic viewpoint, it has happened that at
different times during my life I have occupied public offices where
I came in official contact with international conditions before they
were remedied by the beneficent effect of the joint resolution of 1922
and its predecessor, the joint resolution of 1912.

Twenty-five years ago, as United States Attorney in the Southern
District of New York, much of my time and energy was devoted to
the enforcement of the so-called neutrality acts of the United States.
Our laws were then insufficient to control the shipment of arms from
this country, even when the purpose of stirring up strife, sedition, and
revolutions in the republics to the south of us was manifest. I can
remember the time when a single concern in the State of New York
used to make it known that they were fully prepared to outfit on short
notice, for war service, expeditions of any size up to several thousand
men. I personally witnessed the activities by which some of our munitions manufacturers for sordid gain became a veritable curse to
the stability of our neighboring republics. Later, as Secretary of War,
I became a witness to the fact that our own citizens were sometimes
the innocent victims of domestic strife in adjacent countries stirred
up by this disgraceful traffic. When an insurrection broke out in
Mexico the first effort of the rebels was usually to try to seize a
customhouse on one of the important railroad crossings between our
two countries, in order that they might freely receive arms and
ammunition from this country. And I myself have seen the bullet
marks on the houses in El Paso, Texas, caused by a conflict of this
kind in Juarez, across the river, in which over a score of innocent
citizens of El Paso, going about their accustomed duties on American
soil, were killed or injured.

With these personal experiences in mind, I had little difficulty in
reaching the conclusion that those who argued for the liberty of our
munitions manufacturers to continue for profit a traffic which was
staining with blood the soil of the Central American republics were
not the progressives in international law or practice. I am glad that

I had a share in the drafting of the joint resolution of 1912, and I have studied closely the progress of its remedial effect upon the conditions which it was designed to cure. I am glad to find that that effect has been beneficial. By our own Government it has been found so beneficent that in 1922 its scope was extended from civil strife in America to civil strife in certain other portions of the world. By 1928 its beneficent influence was so generally recognized that at the great Pan American Conference which was held in Habana in that year, all of the nations of this hemisphere embodied in the treaty of 1928 as a definite and compulsory legal obligation the same policy which we had been able in 1912 to initiate as a discretionary power of the American President. I believe that this marks the line which the law of nations will eventually follow throughout the world. When it does so, I believe that international law and practice will have achieved another step forward towards the ultimate peace of mankind. It is my hope that the decisions of the State Department during the past two years will be found to have assisted in this beneficent progress.

ADDRESS by President Herbert Hoover before the Governing Board of the Pan American Union, at Washington, April 14, 1931
Bulletin of the Pan American Union, May, 1931, p. 460

GENTLEMEN OF THE GOVERNING BOARD:

I am glad to be your guest at this special session of the Governing Board of the Pan American Union which you are holding in honor of Pan American Day. I recently issued a proclamation, calling upon our people to give this day due observance, and this proclamation has received general approval throughout the country. Exercises are being held at this time in public schools and universities and by civic organizations in every section of the Union. Pan American Day will become an outward symbol of the constantly strengthening unity of purpose and unity of ideals of the republics of this hemisphere.

In the latter part of 1928, I had the privilege of visiting eleven of the countries of Latin America. This visit made a deep and lasting impression upon me. It was inspiring to observe, at first hand, not only the progress that Latin America is making along social, economic and cultural lines, but also the important part which the countries you represent are destined to play in world affairs. It was clear, too, that the nations of America have everything to gain by keeping in close touch with one another and by developing that spirit of mutual confidence which has its roots in a reciprocal understanding of national aims and aspirations.

Although each of the republics of this hemisphere possesses problems peculiar to itself, there are certain basic questions relating to democratic progress and social betterment common to us all and in the solution of which we can be most helpful to one another. This spirit of mutual helpfulness is the cornerstone of true Pan Americanism. The Pan American Union not only symbolizes this spirit, but gives to it concrete expression in many practical and constructive ways.

It is of the greatest importance that the people of the United States become better acquainted with the history, the traditions, the culture and the ideals of the other republics of America. To an increasing extent, courses on the languages, literature and history of the nations of Latin America are being offered in the educational institutions of the United States. A similar realization of the importance of becoming better acquainted with the history and development of the United States exists in the countries of Latin America. Increasing numbers of students from the countries to the south are being enrolled in the colleges and universities of the United States. I cannot emphasize too strongly this important aspect of inter-American relations. These cultural currents not only contribute to better international understanding, but also emphasize the essential unity of interest of the American republics.

Through the Pan American *Society* and its branches established in different sections of the country, the importance and significance of the culture of the Latin American nations are being brought home to our people. We owe much to the unselfish men who have devoted so much time and energy to this work. The activities of the Pan American *Society* admirably supplement the important work that is being done by the Pan American *Union*.

A peculiarly heavy responsibility rests upon the nations of the Western Hemisphere; a responsibility which, at the same time, is a high privilege. Richly endowed by nature, we enjoy the great advantage of inhabiting a hemisphere free from the jealousies and antagonisms which have proved such obstacles to progress and prosperity in other sections of the world. We have developed an international system based on the principle of equality, combined with a full recognition of the obligations as well as the rights of States.

The American republics are today rapidly approaching the time when every major difference existing between them will be settled by the orderly processes of conciliation and arbitration. In this respect, the Western Hemisphere has placed an enviable record before the nations of the world. From the earliest period of their history, the governments of the republics of this hemisphere have been earnest advocates of the peaceful settlement of international disputes. They have demonstrated their willingness and even eagerness to adopt and apply mediation, conciliation and arbitration. The common purpose to eliminate war and the determination to achieve peace and security represent a major contribution of the Americas to modern civilization.

The full significance of this achievement is not always realized, for it carries with it heavy obligations to posterity. Future progress along these lines can only be assured through constant vigilance and by an unswerving determination to make the Union of the American Republics, as, now expressed in the Pan American Union, an example to the world. We are not attempting in any way to develop a superstate, or to interfere with the freedom of action of any of the States, members of the Union, but rather to develop an atmosphere of good will—a spirit of cooperation and mutual understanding—in which any difference that may arise, no matter how important, will find a ready solution.

I cordially congratulate you, gentlemen of the Governing Board, on your happy initiative in establishing Pan American Day and, at the same time, I send a message of fraternal greeting, in the name of the people of the United States, to all the inhabitants of our sister republics.

ADDRESS by Walter C. Thurston, Chief of the Division of Latin American Affairs, Department of State, "Our Future Relations with Latin America," at Philadelphia, April 18, 1931

Department of State, *Press Releases*, April 18, 1931, p. 293. The address was delivered at the Annual Meeting of the American Academy of Political and Social Science

IN CONFORMITY with one of the characteristics of our time, present day international relations are complex. To the economic, political, and other familiar factors in the dealings of nations many newer interrelated elements have been added, and modern statecraft is concerned with such varied problems as those arising from the reciprocal implications of commerce, and domestic measures designed to prevent the introduction of animal and plant diseases, and the tendency of radio communication and aerial transportation to obliterate frontiers.

Moreover, this is indeed the New World. Two republics have been created and three states have been added to our own Union within the present century, while areas measurable only by hundreds of thousands of square miles remain virtually unexplored. The accident of geographical isolation and imposed self-reliance in the early days of colonization and the later wars of independence have profoundly influenced the social and political theories of the American nations, and in consequence our mutual problems, our relationships, and our devices are often unlike those of any comparable group of states.

Nevertheless, although an attempt to descry the future relations of the United States and its 20 fellow-American republics must necessarily involve consideration of many circumstances, it is both convenient and customary to confine attention to three major categories—commercial, cultural, and political.

I. COMMERCIAL RELATIONS

The predominant attribute of America is its dynamic energy. There is nothing static about it. The processes by which it has been successively explored, subjugated, populated, and brought into productivity are all at work to-day. If our frontier has vanished, Brazil's has not; if the torrent of immigration no longer pours into the United States, it has but been deflected, though in lesser volume, to South America; and if we are no longer borrowing vast sums for the development of this country, we are lending them for the development of our neighbors.

While the munificence of Providence has made of the United States both an agricultural and an industrial nation, in its economic relationship to Latin America it may be regarded as preponderantly a producer of manufactured articles. The Latin American republics, in contrast, are principally producers of agricultural and mineral commodities. Proximity and adequate communications make effective this complementary relationship, and commerce between the northern and southern republics has assumed important proportions.

Nor is this trade merely a war and post-war development, as seems so often to be assumed, and consequently one which having been captured may be recaptured. Statistics compiled by the United States Department of Commerce show that in 1900 we sold to Latin America over $135,000,000 worth of goods, and bought almost $200,000,000 worth of its products. Ten years later, our sales to Latin America had increased to over $300,000,000 and our purchases to nearly $450,-

000,000—a combined increase of over 100 per cent in the decade immediately preceding the war. Since the war, our trade with Latin America has assumed vastly greater proportions, amounting during several recent years to more than $2,000,000,000, and to nearly $1,500,-000,000 in 1930, a period of depression. The ratio of expansion has not greatly altered, and it may reasonably be assumed that the fortuitous element in this great interchange is negligible, and that on the contrary it obeys the usual laws of economics and commerce.

In 1910 the population of the Latin American republics was perhaps 75,000,000, and that of the United States about 92,000,000. Today, their respective populations are approximately 110,000,000 and 122,000,000, an increase of some 65,000,000. Concurrently with this increase of population—the equivalent of a Germany—the mechanics and forces of modern social advancement have been active. Public education, public health measures, improved communications, and similar causes have combined to better the general standard of living, to widen the individual horizon, and thereby to bring about the awakening to new needs. The demands which are thus created by the physical expansion of the reciprocal markets and by the improving standards of living and resultant increasing *per capita* consumption constitute, of course, the basic stimulus and sustaining element of our trade.

The major commodities making up inter-American trade are so well known that reference need only be made to a few, such as coffee, sugar, nitrate, and copper on the one side, and on the other, to automobiles, electrical appliances, and agricultural machinery. In this connection our Department of Commerce has expressed the opinion that approximately 80 per cent of Latin American imports from the United States are mass-produced commodities, without a rival as to price and quality. It has not generally been remarked, however, that some of the major imports into the United States from Latin America likewise are the result of mass production. Brazilian coffee, Chilean nitrate, and Cuban sugar may be cited.

However, in addition to the tendency of commodities to seek their markets, there are other influences of major importance to the commercial relationship between the United States and Latin America, such as the vast investments of American capital in tangible property. To quote again from statistics compiled by our Department of Commerce, out of some $7,500,000,000 of direct foreign investments of American corporations and business men at the end of 1929, some $3,500,000,000 represented investments in manufacturing, selling, petroleum, mining and smelting, agricultural, communication, and transportation activities in Latin America. Other influences are the

Panama Canal, our splendid and improving merchant marine, American direct and efficient cable, radiotelegraph, and more recently, radiotelephone services to Latin America, and equally recent, our American airways—which now circumnavigate the entire South American continent.

The period of depression which announced its presence with such destructive suddenness near the close of 1929 is now perceived to have been universal. It was accompanied by drastic declines in commodity prices. Coffee, sugar, tin, copper, and other major sources of Latin American prosperity were seriously affected. The influence of this economic depression, and in some instances the added influence of domestic political disturbances (and perhaps the two react upon one another where they are not related) have, of course, profoundly affected the general financial condition of several of the countries, some of which, but thus far surprisingly few, are finding it difficult to maintain full service upon their foreign indebtedness. It is but reasonable to assume, however, in the light of past crises, that the present depression is but transitory and that eventual improvement is inevitable.

To summarize then, it may be anticipated that the future commercial relations of the United States with Latin America will continue to respond to the usual motive forces, and that the United States, desiring coffee, bananas, sugar, and similar products, will continue to buy them from the most convenient producing country, and that its own industrial products will continue to be purchased by its neighbors who do not make them. The periods of unusual prosperity and of extreme depression presumably will be of varying but not of extraordinary duration. Future trade, briefly, should be increasingly important and reciprocally beneficial.

II. CULTURAL RELATIONS

Historical influences of great force long retarded the development of inter-American cultural fellowship. The differing racial and linguistic heritages of the American colonies were accentuated, as obstacles to cultural interchange, by their respective isolation and the difficulties of communication, and each in consequence turned to Europe rather than to the other for the intellectual and cultural nurture which its developing civilization demanded. It is only in comparatively recent times that these barriers have been surmounted and there has been effective cultural association between the United States, with its English language, literature, common law, and customs, and the southern republics, with their Romance languages, Napoleonic Code, and Latin traditions.

International cultural relations are maintained through two groups of agencies. In one are those which may be called the automatic activities, existing or engaged in spontaneously and with no particular, or at most only incidental, thought to the actual function they perform in this respect, such as art, literature, and music; and commerce, the press, travel, radio, and the motion picture. The second group, of course, comprises the voluntary agencies—deliberately established for the purpose of fostering international cultural relationships.

The importance of the so-called automatic agencies and the manner in which they operate require but little comment. They have contributed to inter-American cultural relations in varying degrees, according to their nature. Works of pictorial or plastic art, for example, do not ordinarily migrate and remigrate singly, and assembled exhibitions abroad were hazardous and costly. Their exchange, however, has been stimulated by improved communications, which now make it possible for valuable collections to be transported safely and conveniently; and several important exhibitions of Latin American paintings and other works of art have in consequence recently been held in the United States. The influence of communication upon cultural interchanges has just been demonstrated in an unusual and charming fashion at the International Tropical Flower Show of the Garden Club of Miami, Fla., in connection with which exhibits of tropical flowers, many of the most delicate nature, were transported to Miami by air from South America, Central America, and the West Indies. Music, on the other hand, by virtue of its mobility and universal intelligibility has long been a most active and effective factor in this field, and has of course, among all the cultural achievements of man, been the one most utilized by radio. In this connection it may be mentioned that one of the innumerable services being rendered by the Pan American Union is its annual series of concerts at which the inspiring contributions of Latin American composers are interpreted and broadcast.

One of the most striking and effective of this group of agencies, however, is the press, for news is a commodity supplying a universal demand. The ascending scale of literacy and the almost incredible modern developments in the field of communications now make it possible for this commodity to be exchanged in volumes and with a rapidity never before achieved or even imagined. One of the great American press associations, for example, sends by cable more than 16,000,000 words annually to Latin America, and receives by cable from that region approximately 2,000,000 words.

The influence which this exchange of news between the United

States and Latin America exercises is great. Despite the advances in convenient and economic transportation facilities and the impressive statistics of tourist movements, only a minute portion of the inhabitants of one country—even of so rich and travel-disposed a nation as the United States—can be expected personally to visit the other. It is therefore left to other agencies, and especially to the press, to perform the function of making the nations better known to one another. Our own great dailies have established a high standard in this respect, for most of them devote particular attention to foreign news.

But the greatest promise for the future of inter-American cultural relations lies, it is believed, in the second group—the voluntary agencies. Their several activities are perhaps best described as intellectual cooperation. In surveying this group one is impressed by the number of agencies which it comprises, by their importance, and by the extraordinary success which they have already achieved. The following may be mentioned:

The Institute of International Education. This institute has fostered the development of the exchange of students with foreign countries, the circuiting of foreign professors, statesmen, and publicists among our colleges and universities, the publication of books having to do with various aspects of international education, the holding of conferences on critical problems of international education, and the issuance of letters of introduction to American scholars going abroad and foreign scholars visiting our institutions, as well as many other activities of the kind.

Through its agency, a commission of scholars and teachers from Argentina visited our colleges, museums, newspaper plants, industrial establishments, social service organizations, and distinguished individuals two years ago, in consequence of which classes for the study of English were established by the Argentine–North American Cultural Institute at Buenos Aires which to-day has over 800 students. These activities likewise resulted in fellowships being granted in the United States to Argentine students in engineering, agriculture, journalism, business administration, and similar courses.

The importance which the Institute of International Education attaches to the Latin American field is indicated by the fact that it is sending its very able Director, Dr. Stephen P. Duggan, to South America this summer for an extended visit, with the express purpose of endeavoring to strengthen our cultural and educational cooperation with that region.

The Guggenheim Foundation. With the additional $1,000,000 endowment from former United States Senator Simon Guggenheim and Mrs. Guggenheim for the establishment of Latin American exchange fellowships, the foundation has made fellowships available to Mexico, Argentina, and Chile, and is planning to extend these fellowships to still other parts of the hemisphere.

The Inter-American Institute of Intellectual Cooperation. This organization, initiated by a resolution of the last Pan American Conference, will, through national councils established in each of the 21 American republics, collect and exchange information relative to education, science, arts, and letters, and will promote the interchange of professors, students, and research workers between the American republics, and perform other similar measures of actual and useful intellectual cooperation.

The Pan American Institute of Geography and History. This institute also was initiated at the last Pan American Conference. It is now established in Mexico City, in splendid quarters furnished by the Mexican Government. The Government of the United States is not, however, as yet definitively associated with this organization, although careful and sympathetic consideration is being given to the question of adherence.

The Carnegie Endowment for International Peace. In addition to subsidizing and distributing pertinent publications, the endowment for some years past has dispatched to Latin America an American able to lecture in Spanish for the purpose of visiting the great universities. We are indebted to it for the presence in the United States at this time of the great Chilean poetess, Gabriela Mistral, who is lecturing at Barnard and at Vassar.

The Carnegie Institution of Washington. This institution is devoting great sums of money and the services of the foremost scientists in that field to archeological research in Latin America. The importance of the advanced civilization which flourished in this hemisphere prior to the advent of the Europeans is receiving increasing recognition, and efforts to reveal and restore its culture undoubtedly will be amply repaid not only by the contribution it will make to our present-day civilization, but by the stimulus it may give to those nations still possessing in great numbers the splendid racial stock descended from those who created it.

The Rockefeller Foundation. Extraordinary feats have been performed by this agency in many places in Latin America in eradicating some of the more destructive and disabling afflictions common to the tropics. By its efforts vast areas have been freed from malaria, hookworm, and yellow fever, and through its example and cooperation sanitary measures of the utmost importance have been organized and are being sustained.

While limitations on the time allotted preclude further detailed comments, this enumeration can not omit mention of the activities of the American Association of University Professors, the Committee on Library Cooperation with the Hispanic peoples of the American Library Association, the American Federation of Art, the International Congress of Americanists, the Association of American Museums, and the Pan American Society; nor fail to refer to the summer schools established in several Latin American states, primarily for United States students and teachers, such as that at Mexico City, which is attended, it is stated, by more than 300 American teachers and students of Spanish at each session, nor to the School for Teachers of Spanish at Middlebury College. You are, of course, familiar with the Institute of Politics at Williamstown, and similar organizations, such as the Institute of International Relations, Riverside, Calif., the Institutes of Public Affairs of the Universities of Georgia and Virginia, the Institute of Inter-American Affairs of the University of Florida, and that of MacMurray College, Illinois, and others.

The activities of other enterprises likewise demand inclusion in this category. It is believed, as an illustration, that the American Academy of Political and Social Science is rendering a real service by including in its program topics which should stimulate interest in Latin America. Similarly, the work of the Council on Foreign Relations should be cited, which, through its splendid quarterly, *Foreign Affairs,* affords a medium through which the opinions of authoritative writers on this subject may be disseminated. Incidentally, there are many other publications of this character, such as the *Bulletin of the Pan American Union,* published monthly in Spanish, English, Portuguese, and French, and the *Pan American Magazine.*

Perhaps the greatest organization in this group of voluntary agencies, however, is the Pan American Union, which is, as you know, the permanent secretariat, the tangible and visible evidence, of the union of the 21 American republics. Under the wise guidance of its present Director General, the Honorable Dr. Leo S. Rowe, almost every activity tending to promote the cultural welfare of the member governments is in some way strengthened and promoted by it. Among its many departments is a special division of intellectual cooperation.

It is too early to evaluate the results of the combined influences of all the so-called automatic and voluntary agencies. One has but to compare the conditions, however, which prevailed at the time the great Argentine statesman and educator, Sarmiento, after his residence in the United States, brought about what probably was the first voluntary transportation of teachers from one American nation to another some 60 years ago, with the present; and to recall that whereas less than a dozen colleges and universities in the United States offered classes in Latin American history, literature, art, and institutions at the close of the World War, more than 200 do so to-day, and that there are now more than 1,200 students from Latin American republics enrolled in our schools. The accomplishments which already have rewarded the activities of these agencies amply warrant the conviction that the cultural ties between the United States and Latin America will become increasingly numerous and strengthened, and that the good understanding which they will bring about will constitute the greatest monument to Pan Americanism.

III. POLITICAL RELATIONS

It has frequently been remarked that our official dealings with the Governments of the other republics of this hemisphere are not described with accuracy by the usual caption "Political Relations between the United States and Latin America," inasmuch as the convenient term "Latin America" applies in fact to a region, not a political entity. Such dealings, of course, vary according to the distinctive personality and individual problems of each of the 20 nations which share that region.

Understanding of the relations between the United States and the Latin American republics likewise may be confused by failure to differentiate settled policies and occasional or special acts. The convictions of a government regarding questions affecting the general conduct of its international relations, its institutions, its welfare, or its safety, as repeatedly expressed by its statesmen or as made apparent by consistent practice, may be said to constitute its policies; whereas many of its international proceedings are the direct sequence of earlier causes or are mandatory as the result of treaty engagements. Some respond to the obligations of international comity, and others to emergencies that must be met as they arise. The Government of the United States, of course, cherishes several well-defined policies. They are largely defensive, they entail no aggression or threat to any other people, and in some instances they serve the general welfare. Among them may be cited the avoidance of entangling alliances in Europe, the Monroe doctrine, and the "open door" policy.

The Secretary of State has very recently commented on the Monroe doctrine in an address before the Council on Foreign Relations, with which most of you undoubtedly are familiar. Such pronouncements by authoritative speakers must be made from time to time to correct erroneous interpretations, since what the doctrine is and what it is not furnish subjects for apparently endless speculation. I know of no more able and lucid general exposition of the Monroe doctrine than that which appears in the current edition of the *Encyclopedia*

Britannica, and which is the work of that great statesman and jurist, Chief Justice Charles Evans Hughes. From the viewpoint of the practical conduct of our international relations it need only be added that the Monroe doctrine does not imply tutelage, that it is not a shield against honest redress, nor one in the shelter of which aggression may be committed.

Among the occasional emergency measures to which allusion has been made is that which is loosely referred to as "intervention." It is a measure which provokes widespread criticism, founded in part upon popular misapprehension of the immediate compelling facts, but most of which is the sincere expression of the instinctive repugnance to such action entertained by the American people—both in the United States and in Latin America. Again from the viewpoint of the practical conduct of our foreign relations, it may be said that while "intervention" or "interposition" enjoys the full sanction of international law, and under certain conditions is inescapable, it is both undesirable and undesired. It is resorted to by this Government with reluctance and terminated at the earliest opportunity. You are reminded, in this connection, of President Hoover's reiterated public statement that the Government of the United States has no desire for representation abroad through its military forces.

Despite racial and other divergent influences, disparity of power, and even mutual ignorance, a basic doctrine—Pan Americanism— is shared by the American republics. The ceremonies held throughout this hemisphere four days ago in connection with the observance of "Pan American Day," and the unanimity of the statements of public men on that occasion, amply testify to its existence. Its essence is equality, as is recognized in its fundamental charter, the Convention on the Pan American Union, which affirms that the moral union of the American republics rests upon their juridic equality and mutual respect of the rights inherent in complete independence. No "balance of power" problem besets inter-American relations—nor, in fact, does any major political problem. Such difficulties as do exist between American republics, and they are fortunately very few, are with but one or two exceptions those arising from unsettled boundary questions. The impressive record of the American nations in the amicable adjustment of such questions in the past lends encouragement to the belief that the states concerned will bring about the solution of these difficulties within the reasonably near future. It should be a source of gratification to every citizen of the United States that its relations with the republics of Latin America are those of friendship, and that in consequence it often has the privilege of contributing to the settlement of such **problems.**

With respect to the special relationships which exist between the Government of the United States and certain republics of the Caribbean area, the origins and general circumstances of which are well known, the following observations are submitted:

Cuba.—The basic fact of the relationship between the United States and Cuba is the Platt Amendment. Cross currents of opinion concerning the domestic political affairs of that Republic have recently created some confusion as to the implications of the amendment. With respect to this, it will perhaps suffice to quote the views of this Government as conveyed in 1901 to the Cuban Constitutional Assembly:

. . . In the view of the President the intervention described in the third clause of the Platt Amendment is not synonymous with intermeddling or interference with the affairs of the Cuban Government, but the formal action of the Government of the United States, based upon just and substantial grounds, for the preservation of Cuban independence, and the maintenance of a government adequate for the protection of life, property, and individual liberty, and adequate for discharging the obligations with respect to Cuba imposed by the Treaty of Paris on the United States.

Haiti.—The special relationship of the United States to the Republic of Haiti rests upon the treaty of 1915. With a view to timely preparation for its expiration in 1936, President Hoover dispatched a special commission to Haiti last year to undertake a study of conditions there. Arrangements brought about by the President's Commission and recommendations submitted by it are being carried into effect. Elections for the establishment of the National Assembly of the Republic were held; a President was elected by that body and inaugurated; and a civilian Minister Plenipotentiary has been appointed and has assumed the duties formerly entrusted to the High Commissioner, who has been withdrawn. The two Governments are now engaged in the preparation of a program of "Haitianization"— the restoration to Haitian control of administrative functions heretofore under the treaty largely entrusted to American officials—which it is to be hoped will expedite our withdrawal from Haiti, thus satisfying the eminently natural desire of the Haitian people for self-government.

Dominican Republic.—American military intervention in the Dominican Republic terminated seven years ago, in midyear 1924. Our present relationship to that Republic is restricted to a convention, signed in December, 1924 (quite similar to an earlier one signed in 1907), whereunder the assistance of the Government of the United States is extended in the collection and application of Dominican customs revenues, and the Republic is inhibited from increasing its public debt except by previous agreement with the United States, so long as it shall not have discharged its bonded obligations.

Panama.—A unique relationship has been established between the United States and the Republic of Panama by their collaboration in the construction of the great isthmian canal. The generous contribution by Panama of the very core of its territory for that purpose and the titanic labor of the Americans who made the vision a reality form an enduring bond of common interest. The formal basis of the relationship is the treaty of 1903.

Nicaragua.—The treaty basis of the special relationship between the United States and the Republic of Nicaragua is the treaty of 1914, whereunder the United States is granted exclusive proprietary rights for the construction and operation of an interoceanic canal, the lease of certain islands, and the right to establish a naval base on the Gulf of Fonseca. The actual special relationship, however, antedates that treaty by several years, and falls rather within the group of occasional or special dealings, to which earlier reference was made in this paper.

Plans recently agreed to by both Governments provided for the increase of the Nicaraguan National Guard in the bandit area, thus making possible the withdrawal, probably by June of this year, of the United States Marines now on combat duty, leaving in Nicaragua only the Marines engaged in instruction in the Nicaraguan National Guard and an instruction battalion to support such instruction and an aviation section which is being used to carry supplies in the bandit provinces which are entirely without roads. By June next the total force of Marines in Nicaragua will have been reduced from over 5,000 men in January, 1929, to probably not over 500 men. Nicaraguan officers are being trained to completely replace the Marines now officering the National Guard. The Nicaraguan Government has obtained further funds which it has agreed to spend in the construction of long-needed roads and trails in the bandit provinces. The foregoing steps will greatly expedite the completion of the task of this Government in instructing the National Guard of Nicaragua and pave the way for the ultimate removal of all Marine forces from Nicaragua immediately after the election of 1932.

It is as yet too soon to estimate the consequences of the disaster that recently visited Nicaragua, resulting in the virtually complete destruction of its capital city, Managua. Unless unforeseen developments occur, however, the general program of withdrawal will be carried out.

At no previous time have the agencies through which this Government conducts its foreign relations been brought to such a degree of effectiveness as at present, nor has such earnest attention been bestowed upon the field of its Latin American relations. President Hoover, you will recall, preceded the assumption of his high office with a tour of Latin America, which was regarded there with the utmost gratification as heralding a new era of conscious effort toward better understanding.

After his inauguration, the President announced to Congress his desire to establish more firmly our understanding and relations with the Latin American countries by strengthening our diplomatic missions, and his hope to secure men long experienced in our diplomatic service, speaking the languages of the peoples to whom they would be accredited, as chiefs of our diplomatic missions in those states. This aspiration was speedily realized, and we have to-day as chiefs of mission in the capitals of Latin America 16 career officers, and at the four remaining posts, one chief of mission having nearly 10 years' successful service in Latin America, one having long held high office in the Department of State, and two whose command of Spanish and understanding of the peoples of Latin America eminently qualify them for the positions they hold.

CONCLUSION

To the degree that it is given to us to view the future, it seems quite clear that all the circumstances which enter into the relations between the United States and its fellow-American republics, and which only imperfectly have been presented in this paper, are tending to make those relations more profitable through commercial intercourse, to foster good fellowship through cultural interchanges, and to remove misunderstanding and strengthen friendship through reasoned and reasonable dealings.

ADDRESS by President Herbert Hoover at the Fourth Pan American Commercial Conference, at Washington, October 8, 1931

Department of State, *Press Releases*, October 10, 1931, p. 279

GENTLEMEN OF THE CONFERENCE:

I am most happy to extend to you the warmest possible welcome on behalf of the Government and people of the United States. We are grateful to you for coming to Washington at this time to discuss the commercial problems of common interest to the nations of America. You are meeting during a period of widespread economic depression, but this fact emphasizes rather than diminishes the necessity for the nations of this continent to take counsel with one another.

We recognize that the prosperity of each and every nation contributes to the prosperity of all. It is important that at conferences such as this the experience of each and every nation should be placed at the disposal of all in order that we may profit by our successes as well as learn the lessons of our failures.

There is one lesson from this depression to which I wish to refer, and I can present it no more forcibly than by repeating a statement which I made to this Conference just four years ago, when we were in the heyday of foreign loans. I stated, in respect to such loans, that they are helpful in world development,

provided always one essential principle dominates the character of these transactions. That is, that no nation as a government should borrow or no government lend and nations should discourage their citizens from borrowing or lending unless this money is to be devoted to productive enterprise.

Out of the wealth and the higher standards of living created from enterprise itself must come the ability to repay the capital to the borrowing country. Any other course of action creates obligations impossible of repayment except by a direct subtraction from the standards of living of the borrowing country and the impoverishment of its people.

In fact, if this principle could be adopted between nations of the world —that is, if nations would do away with the lending of money for the balancing of budgets for purposes of military equipment or war purposes, or even that type of public works which does not bring some direct or indirect productive return—a great number of blessings would follow to the entire world.

There could be no question as to the ability to repay; with this increasing security, capital would become steadily cheaper, the dangers to national and individual independence in attempts of the lender to collect his defaulted debts would be avoided; there would be definite increase in the standard of living and the comfort and prosperity of the borrower.

There could be no greater step taken in the prevention of war itself. This is perhaps a little further toward the millennium than our practical world has reached, and I do not propose that these are matters that can be regulated by law or treaty. They are matters that can be regulated solely by the commercial and financial sentiment of each of our countries; and if this body may be able to develop the firm conviction, develop the understanding that the financial transactions between nations must be built upon the primary foundation that money transferred is for reproductive purposes, it will have contributed to the future of the Western Hemisphere in a degree seldom open to a conference of this character.

I repeat this to-day, because had it been followed during these past five years our problems throughout the world would be far different, our difficulties infinitely less.

I have learned with particular interest and gratification that by far the greater number of those in attendance at this Conference are not governmental delegates, but representatives of the commercial and financial establishments of the several American Republics. Particularly do we in the United States hold to the theory that commercial enterprise, except as rare emergency action, is essentially a private undertaking, and that the sole function of government is to bring about a condition of affairs favorable to the beneficial development of private enterprise. It is the failure to comprehend this conception of the relation between the function of government and the function of private enterprise that sometimes leads the thoughtless to assume the existence of an international indifference which does not in fact exist.

The larger significance of your meeting is attested by the fact that at stated intervals the accredited representatives of the Governments and of the commercial organizations of this continent come together with a view to interchange of experience and fostering that mutual confidence without which the development of international commerce is impossible. Your work possesses a significance far beyond the concrete problems with which you will have to deal.

Permit me in closing to combine with my welcome the confident expectation that your deliberations will redound to the benefit of all the nations of this continent.

ADDRESS by Francis White, Assistant Secretary of State, at the Pan American Union, November 11, 1931

Department of State, *Press Releases*, November 14, 1931, p. 457

IT IS A GREAT honor and privilege for me to open this inaugural meeting between the delegates of Bolivia and Paraguay to discuss a non-aggression pact. This is one more demonstration of the desire of the countries of this hemisphere to settle in an amicable way all differences that exist between them. This is the American way of settling disputes. For nearly 50 years now there have been no wars between American countries. This does not mean to say that there have not been many differences which have caused tension and strained relations, but they have always been settled by good offices, mediation, conciliation, or arbitration.

It was a most fortunate circumstance that the Pan American Conference of Arbitration and Conciliation was in session here in this room when the difficulties between Bolivia and Paraguay in December, 1928, broke out. That Conference at once offered its good offices to the two countries to conciliate that difference. A subcommittee, consisting of delegates from five of the American countries, was appointed to this end, and with their assistance an agreement was drawn up between the delegates of Bolivia and Paraguay referring their difficulty to a Commission of Inquiry and Conciliation. This latter Commission succeeded in conciliating the two parties, and an agreement to this effect was signed on September 12, 1929.

The fundamental question at issue between the two parties still exists, however, and the diplomatic representatives of the five Governments represented on the Commission of Inquiry and Conciliation have since been endeavoring to be of assistance to the two countries in bringing about a complete understanding between them. This meeting to-day is the result thereof.

While there may be minor differences in point of view and outlook in dealing with many questions, no one, I think, will dispute the fact that the principal questions which can seriously disturb relations between two or more countries of this hemisphere are boundary ones. These questions are the ones which cause the most bitterness and ill feeling between nations, and hence, superficially, may at first be considered the most difficult of solution. The history of America, however, shows that quite the contrary is in fact the case. We are meeting here to-day in the presence of the representatives of all the 21 countries of America, and there is not one of them that can not point with pride to the settlement of some boundary question by peaceful methods.

It has been my privilege to help in some small way in the settlement of eight such boundary questions. Some of them, at the outset, appeared complicated and difficult, but when the matter was discussed dispassionately and fully, as is the custom between American nations, it was found that a common ground of agreement could eventually be found. Next month, in this small hall, will be held the opening meeting of an arbitral tribunal to settle the boundary between two of our sister nations. These examples, given to us by the history of all the countries present, point the way to what can be done. Good will, moderation, restraint, consideration of the opponent's point of view, and a desire not to win points in a debate but to bring about a settlement truly beneficial to one's country, can not fail to result in a settlement satisfactory to all concerned. That is the spirit, I am convinced, in which the delegates of Bolivia and Paraguay have come to this meeting, and the result, therefore, is bound to be success for all concerned. A settlement which is considered a victory by one and a defeat by the other is only a sham victory. That is not what we are seeking here. The victory that we are seeking is an equitable settlement giving justice to all and respecting the rights of both; an agreement that both parties will be pleased with. I feel confident that this end will be attained.

RADIO ADDRESS by William R. Castle, Jr., Under Secretary of State, January 5, 1932 (extract)
Department of State, *Press Releases*, January 9, 1932, p. 33

. . . LATIN AMERICA, like the rest of the world, has been going through difficult experiences. The hard times have brought, in some countries, revolutions, but taken all in all we can congratulate our Latin American neighbors for the courage and the energy with which they have grappled with their problems. And from our point of view one of the most encouraging and heartening features of it all is that the old suspicion of the United States seems to be fading away. All we ask is to be understood, and the wise forbearance with which the President has treated all the problems between this country and those to the south of us is bringing rapidly that greatly needed understanding. In accord with the recommendations of the President's Commission, we are rapidly withdrawing from Haiti, leaving that Republic better able to care for itself in the future. Of the marines in Nicaragua, only those are left who are necessary to train the National Guard. We have at their request, assisted Nicaragua in conducting fair and free elections; and after the next election, which we have promised to supervise, all our armed forces will be withdrawn. These proofs, among others, that our interests are only friendly and in no sense imperialistic, are proving to all Latin America that its old idea that the Monroe Doctrine, which had no purpose except to preserve this continent from foreign aggression and colonization, gave us the right to interfere in the internal affairs of other countries, is wholly false. We are only the older brother in the family of independent American nations. The time has come when the younger members of the family can look after themselves.

It is true, of course, that governments vary in their ability to look after foreigners within their borders, in their sense of obligations, perhaps, to do this. When our traders go out into the world to carry

on honest trade, when our citizens build up in other countries enterprises which are necessarily of value to the countries where they
operate, as well as to themselves, it is our duty to give them protection
if they fail to get it in the courts of the countries where they are at
work. I do not for a moment mean that we should use the Army or
the Navy, but that we have the right and duty diplomatically to insist
on fair play. That is all we have the right to ask, just as it is all that
other governments whose nationals are in the United States have
the right to ask us. And we ask no more in Latin America than in any
other part of the world. I hope that the coming year may give to all
governments a greater sense of responsibility toward the stranger
within their gates so that no protests of unfairness may be made either
to us or by us. . . .

The Roosevelt-Truman
Administrations

*INAUGURAL ADDRESS by President Franklin D. Roosevelt,
March 4, 1933 (extract)*
Congressional Record, 77.1, 73d Congress, Special Session p. 5

. . . IN THE FIELD of world policy I would dedicate this Nation to the
policy of the good neighbor—the neighbor who resolutely respects
himself and, because he does so, respects the rights of others—the
neighbor who respects his obligations and respects the sanctity of his
agreements in and with a world of neighbors. We now realize as we
have never realized before our interdependence on each other; that
we cannot merely take, but must give as well. . . .

*ADDRESS by President Franklin D. Roosevelt, Delivered before
the Governing Board of the Pan American Union, at Washington, April 12, 1933*
Department of State, *Press Releases*, April 15, 1933, p. 243

I REJOICE in this opportunity to participate in the celebration of "Pan
American Day" and to extend on behalf of the people of the United
States a fraternal greeting to our sister American republics. The
celebration of "Pan American Day" in this building, dedicated to international good will and cooperation exemplifies a unity of thought
and purpose among the peoples of this hemisphere. It is a manifestation of the common ideal of mutual helpfulness, sympathetic understanding, and spiritual solidarity.

There is inspiration in the thought that on this day the attention
of the citizens of the 21 republics of America is focused on the common
ties—historical, cultural, economic, and social—which bind them to
one another. Common ideals and a community of interest, together

with a spirit of cooperation, have led to the realization that the well-being of one nation depends in large measure upon the well-being of its neighbors. It is upon these foundations that Pan Americanism has been built.

This celebration commemorates a movement based upon the policy of fraternal cooperation. In my inaugural address I stated that I would "dedicate this nation to the policy of the good neighbor—the neighbor who resolutely respects himself and, because he does so, respects the rights of others—the neighbor who respects his obligations and respects the sanctity of his agreements in and with a world of neighbors." Never before has the significance of the word "good neighbor" been so manifest in international relations. Never have the need and benefit of neighborly cooperation in every form of human activity been so evident as they are today.

Friendship among nations, as among individuals, calls for constructive efforts to muster the forces of humanity in order that an atmosphere of close understanding and cooperation may be cultivated. It involves mutual obligations and responsibilities, for it is only by sympathetic respect for the rights of others and a scrupulous fulfillment of the corresponding obligations by each member of the community that a true fraternity can be maintained.

The essential qualities of a true Pan Americanism must be the same as those which constitute a good neighbor, namely, mutual understanding and, through such understanding, a sympathetic appreciation of the other's point of view. It is only in this manner that we can hope to build up a system of which confidence, friendship, and good will are the cornerstones.

In this spirit the people of every republic on our continent are coming to a deep understanding of the fact that the Monroe Doctrine, of which so much has been written and spoken for more than a century, was and is directed at the maintenance of independence by the peoples of the continent. It was aimed and is aimed against the acquisition in any manner of the control of additional territory in this hemisphere by any non-American power.

Hand in hand with this Pan American doctrine of continental self-defense, the peoples of the American republics understand more clearly, with the passing years, that the independence of each republic must recognize the independence of every other republic. Each one of us must grow by an advancement of civilization and social well-being and not by the acquisition of territory at the expense of any neighbor.

In this spirit of mutual understanding and of cooperation on this continent you and I cannot fail to be disturbed by any armed strife between neighbors. I do not hesitate to say to you, the distinguished members of the Governing Board of the Pan American Union, that I regard existing conflicts between four of our sister republics as a backward step.

Your Americanism and mine must be a structure built of confidence, cemented by a sympathy which recognizes only equality and fraternity. It finds its source and being in the hearts of men and dwells in the temple of the intellect.

We all of us have peculiar problems, and, to speak frankly, the interest of our own citizens must, in each instance, come first. But it is equally true that it is of vital importance to every nation of this continent that the American governments, individually, take, without further delay, such action as may be possible to abolish all unnecessary and artificial barriers and restrictions which now hamper the healthy flow of trade between the peoples of the American republics.

I am glad to deliver this message to you, gentlemen of the Governing Board of the Pan American Union, for I look upon the Union as the outward expression of the spiritual unity of the Americas. It is to this unity which must be courageous and vital in its element that humanity must look for one of the great stabilizing influences in world affairs.

In closing, may I refer to the ceremony which is to take place a little later in the morning at which the Government of Venezuela will present to the Pan American Union the bust of a great American leader and patriot, Francisco de Miranda. I join with you in this tribute.

ADDRESS by Cordell Hull, Secretary of State, at the Seventh International Conference of American States, at Montevideo, December 15, 1933

Report of the Delegates of the United States of America to the Seventh International Conference of American States, p. 114

MR. CHAIRMAN AND MEMBERS OF THE COMMITTEE:

I arise to say that the Delegation of the United States of America is in the heartiest accord with the very timely and vitally important resolution offered by the able Minister of Foreign Affairs of Argentina, Dr. Saavedra Lamas. The beneficial effects of this proposal on peace will be far-reaching. Their stimulating influence will extend beyond this hemisphere and to the uttermost parts of the earth. They will bring cheer and hope to the struggling and discouraged forces of peace everywhere.

May I express what is in the mind of every delegate, that our grateful appreciation of this outstanding service of Dr. Saavedra Lamas will most appropriately climax a series of splendid services to the cause of peace which he has rendered. Let me also thank the heads of each delegation with whom I have conferred during the past days for their prompt and most valuable cooperation in support of this proposal.

The passage of this resolution and the agreement to attach from twelve to twenty signatures of governments to the five peace pacts or agencies thus far unsigned by them is not a mere mechanical operation. The real significance is the deep and solemn spirit of peace which pervades the minds and hearts of every delegate here and moves each to undertake a wise and effective step to promote conditions of peace at this critical stage. The adoption of this resolution and the agreement to sign these five splendid peace instruments will thoroughly strengthen the peace agencies of the 21 American states and make peace permanently secure in this hemisphere. This wholesale affixing of signatures to five treaties through conference action within itself thoroughly vindicates the policy of international conference.

I desire most heartily to second the motion to report this resolution favorably. I desire also to say that in harmony with its purpose, the Government of the United States is ready to affix its signature to the Argentine Anti-War Pact, and I venture at the same time to express the earnest hope that representatives of all other governments present will aid in a great service to peace by signifying at this time their willingness to affix on behalf of their governments their signatures on any of these five treaties which they have not yet signed.

Universal peace has been the chief aim of civilization. Nations fail or succeed according to their failure or success in this supreme undertaking. I profoundly believe that the American nations during the coming years will write a chapter of achievement in the advancement of peace that will stand out in world history.

It is in these inspiring circumstances that I and my associates have come to the conference here in Montevideo. We come, too, for the reason that the people and the Government of the United States feel the keenest interest in this Conference and have the strongest desire to contribute to its success. We come because we share in common the things that are vital to the entire material, moral, and spiritual welfare of the people of this hemisphere, and because the satisfactory development of civilization itself in this Western World depends on cooperative efforts by all the Americas. No other common aspiration could so closely draw peoples together. We can have no other objective than these. Our common hopes and responsibilities, chaperoned by common sense and initiative, beckon to all of us. We sense a yearning here for a spirit of fine cooperative endeavor. We know, too, that in this great region, the future possibilities of which no man dare calculate, the world is being given another chance to right itself. With you, pooling all our resources in an unselfish spirit, we shall undertake to meet the test of service to ourselves and to humanity, and make the most of the spacious opportunities that lie ahead. We know when we survey our assets that we have the foundations laid in this part of the world for the greatest civilization of all the past—a civilization built upon the highest moral, intellectual, and spiritual ideals.

Indeed, while older nations totter under the burden of outworn ideas, cling to the decayed and cruel institution of war, and use precious resources to feed cannon rather than hungry mouths, we stand ready to carry on in the spirit of that application of the Golden Rule by which we mean the true good will of the true good neighbor.

It is really a very old and universal, though sometimes neglected, rule of conduct, this revitalized policy. It is, however, the real basis of that political liberty for which your own great heroes fought and which is our greatest common heritage. It is high time for the world to take new heed of it and to restore its ancient and potent meaning.

I am gratified to say that I have already found much of this spirit among the distinguished leaders with whom I have talked here in Montevideo. They all keenly realize the crisis that has been thrust upon the New World. The Old World looks hopefully in this direction and we must not disappoint that hope. Today Europe staggers under the load of bristling armaments, paid for out of treasuries depleted by the clogging of trade channels. Our common ties with them redouble our desire to offer our best in the molding of a new world order. We have the opportunity and the duty to carry on. We have a belt of sanity on this part of the globe. We are as one as to the objective we seek. We agree that it is a forward-looking enterprise which brings us here and we must make it a forward-moving enterprise.

Peace and economic rehabilitation must be our objectives. The avoidance of war must be our supreme purpose. Most gratifying is the practical appeal which your leaders are making to bring about an end to the bloody conflict between two of our sister republics, the one small and remaining exception to our hopes and ideals for enduring peace in this hemisphere. This is a blot on our civilization which we must erase. I pray with all my heart that, with the end of that conflict, war as an instrument for settling international disputes will have lost its last foothold in this hemisphere.

In its own forward-looking policy, the administration at Washington has pledged itself, as I have said, to the policy of the good neighbor. As President Roosevelt has defined the good neighbor, he "resolutely respects himself and, because he does so, respects the rights of others." We must think, we must speak, we must act this part.

I am safe in the statement that each of the American nations wholeheartedly supports this doctrine—that every nation alike earnestly favors the absolute independence, the unimpaired sovereignty, the perfect equality, and the political integrity of each nation large or small, as they similarly oppose aggression in every sense of the word.

May I for a moment direct attention to the significance of this broad policy as my country is steadily carrying it into effect under the Roosevelt administration, the extent and nature of which should be familiar to each of the nations here represented. My Government is doing its utmost, with due regard to commitments made in the past, to end with all possible speed engagements which have been set up by previous circumstances. There are some engagements which can be removed more speedily than others. In some instances disentanglement from obligations of another era can only be brought about through the exercise of some patience. The United States is determined that its new policy of the New Deal—of enlightened liberalism—shall have full effect and shall be recognized in its fullest import by its neighbors. The people of my country strongly feel that the so-called right of conquest must forever be banished from this hemisphere and, most of all, they shun and reject that so-called right for themselves. The New Deal indeed would be an empty boast if it did not mean that.

Let us in the broad spirit of this revitalized policy make this the beginning of a great new era of a great renaissance in American cooperative effort to promote our entire material, moral, and spiritual affairs and to erect an edifice of peace that will forever endure. Let each American nation vie with the other in the practice of the policy of the good neighbor. Let suspicion, misunderstanding, and prejudice be banished from every mind, and genuine friendship for and trust in each other and a singleness of purpose to promote the welfare of all be substituted. Let each nation welcome the closest scrutiny by the others of the spirit and manner in which it carries out the policy of the good neighbor. Let actions rather than mere words be the acid test of the conduct and motives of each nation. Let each country demonstrate by its every act and practice the sincerity of its purposes and the unselfishness of its relationships as a neighbor.

It is in this spirit that the Government and the people of the United States express their recognition of the common interests and common aspirations of the American nations and join with them in a renewed spirit of broad cooperation for the promotion of liberty under law, of peace, of justice, and of righteousness.

ADDRESS by President Franklin D. Roosevelt at Washington, December 28, 1933 (extracts)

Department of State, *Press Releases,* December 30, 1933, p. 380. The address was delivered before the Woodrow Wilson Foundation

"COMPREHENSION must be the soil in which shall grow all the fruits of friendship." Those words, used by President Wilson in the Mobile speech in 1913, can well serve as a statement of policy by the Government of the United States. That policy applies equally to a comprehension of our internal problems and our international relations. . . .

In that speech in Mobile, President Wilson first enunciated the definite statement "that the United States will never again seek one additional foot of territory by conquest." The United States accepted that declaration of policy. President Wilson went further pointing out with special reference to our Latin American neighbors that material interests must never be made superior to human liberty.

Nevertheless, and largely as a result of the convulsion of the World War and its after effects, the complete fruition of that policy of unselfishness has not in every case been obtained. And in this we, all of us, have to share the responsibility.

I do not hesitate to say that if I had been engaged in a political campaign as a citizen of some other American republic, I might have been strongly tempted to play upon the fears of my compatriots of that republic by charging the United States of North America with some form of imperialistic desire for selfish aggrandizement. As a citizen of some other republic, I might have found it difficult to believe fully in the altruism of the richest American republic. In particular, as a citizen of some other republic, I might have found it hard to approve of the occupation of the territory of other republics, even as a temporary measure.

It therefore has seemed clear to me as President that the time has come to supplement and to implement the declaration of President

Wilson by the further declaration that the definite policy of the United States from now on is one opposed to armed intervention.

The maintenance of constitutional government in other nations is not a sacred obligation devolving upon the United States alone. The maintenance of law and the orderly processes of government in this hemisphere is the concern of each individual nation within its own borders first of all. It is only if and when the failure of orderly processes affects the other nations of the continent that it becomes their concern; and the point to stress is that in such an event it becomes the joint concern of a whole continent in which we are all neighbors.

It is the comprehension of that doctrine—a comprehension not by the leaders alone but by the peoples' of all the American republics, that has made the conference now concluding its labors in Montevideo such a fine success. A better state of feeling among the neighbor nations of North and Central and South America exists today than at any time within a generation. For participation in the bringing about of that result we can feel proud that so much credit belongs to the Secretary of State of the United States, Cordell Hull. . . .

ADDRESS by Sumner Welles, Assistant Secretary of State, "The Trade-Agreements Program in Our Inter-American Relations," at Baltimore, February 4, 1936

Department of State, Publication No. 841. The address was delivered before the Bar Association of Baltimore City

THERE HAS BEEN, I believe, during these past three years, more than ever before, an interest in, and an appreciation of the value of, our inter-American relationships; there exists a greater realization on the part of the people of the United States of the value to themselves of a sure political and commercial understanding with the other republics of this hemisphere. Perhaps we have also, as a people, a belated but nevertheless salutary grasp of the fact that during the preceding decades there had existed on the part of our American neighbors a latent, and at times a vocal, mistrust of the ulterior objectives of the United States; a justifiable resentment of the high-handed or patronizing attitude of this Government, and an equally definite resentment of the tariff policy pursued by the United States, which made it impossible for any free flow of goods between their countries and ours. This general atmosphere of mistrust had been enhanced by open acts of armed intervention by the United States in many of the smaller republics. There existed likewise a general misconception of the Monroe Doctrine, due in no small part to the erroneous interpretation of that doctrine advanced by many of our citizens occupying high official positions.

My purpose tonight, however, is to touch but briefly on these phases of the past and to speak, as I can, hopefully of the present and, I believe, of the future, but it is essential that at least a summary reference should be made to the conditions which obtained in 1932. Further, it must not be overlooked that as a people we had in general ignored the fact that in the hundred and more years since the other American republics declared their own independence, these republics had in many cases grown into powerful nations, like ourselves, rightly proud of their history and of their traditions, and very naturally resentful of any attempt on our part either to dictate the course they should follow or to intervene in their domestic concerns, whether such intervention was undertaken in flagrant disregard of the basic principles of international law or whether it was carried out in accordance with contractual rights which we had obtained through negotiated treaties.

The past three years have seen a far-reaching and decidedly healthy change in the whole nature of our inter-American policy. Our new policy of the "good neighbor" has been predicated upon the belief of this Government that there should exist an inter-American political relationship based on a recognition of actual and not theoretical equality between the American republics; on a complete forbearance from interference by any one republic in the domestic concerns of any other; on economic cooperation; and, finally, on the common realization that in the world at large all of the American republics confront the same international problems, and that in their relations with non-American powers, the welfare and security of any one of them cannot be a matter of indifference to the others.

To attain those objectives, acts and not words were required. I should list as the significant achievements of your Government during these past three years the following practical accomplishments:

(1) The formal declaration by the President of the United States that armed intervention by the United States in any other American republic was a thing of the past, and the adherence by the United States Government to the Convention on the Rights and Duties of States formulated at the Inter-American Conference at Montevideo in 1933, which contains the provision that no state has the right to intervene in the internal or external affairs of another.

(2) The abolition of the Platt Amendment in our treaty with Cuba

so that our contractual rights of intervention in that Republic have been abolished.

(3) The effective economic cooperation which we have been enabled to offer the Cuban Government and people at a time when our previous tariff policy had driven the Republic of Cuba to the brink of ruin and chaos, and which cooperation has resulted in the economic and social rehabilitation of Cuba.

(4) The complete evacuation from Haiti of the American military forces which had been in occupation of that Republic since 1915.

(5) Our negotiations with Panama, now concluding, whereby I believe all of those questions which have created friction and misunderstanding between our two peoples will receive a settlement fair and equitable to the vital interests of both nations.

(6) Our cooperation with other American governments in furthering a pacific solution of the tragic war of the Chaco, which had continued for so many years. This joint mediation has resulted only a short time ago in the signing of agreements between Bolivia and Paraguay which provide for a cessation of the state of belligerency existing between them, and pave the way for permanent peace.

(7) The program proposed by the Secretary of State at the Inter-American Conference at Montevideo providing for a return to sound principles of international trade, emphasizing the decided value of the most-favored-nation policy and the need to work toward lower tariffs and toward the elimination of artificial restrictions upon trade, which program was adopted unanimously by all of the American republics.

(8) Finally, the realization by our neighbors of this continent that the day of "dollar diplomacy," with all of its many vicious implications, is a thing of the past.

All of that which I have said above relates primarily to our general political relationship with the American republics. Let me now turn to the more strictly economic and commercial pages of the ledger; and it is particularly appropriate to discuss this phase of our program—and by that I mean in particular our trade-agreements program—in one of the great ports of this Nation which has a really important stake in foreign trade.

During 1934 I have been interested to learn from the annual report of the Chief of Engineers that imports into the port of Baltimore were valued at $52,000,000, while exports aggregated $41,000,000. This type of commerce forms a substantial part of the activity in this thriving modern port.

I have also been interested to learn from the same source of the great variety of articles which are transported through Baltimore. Of the imports, I note that among the most important are bananas, coffee, molasses, sugar, copra, rubber, wood pulp, iron ore, and tin. On the other hand, the exports cover a wide range of typical American products and specialties. I observe that lard is exported in considerable quantities, as well as apples, canned vegetables and fruits, oatmeal, oil cake, tobacco, lumber, coal, refined copper, tin plate, wire, automotive vehicles, and chemicals. The variety and extent of the foreign trade which clears through Baltimore make it an easy matter for me to describe what we have been endeavoring to do by means of the trade-agreements program. As a community you know at first hand how important it is to keep the seaways filled with ships loaded with cargoes. You know what it means to have your harbor filled with empty ships, while warehouses are bulging with merchandise which cannot be moved, due to stoppages or disruption of trade channels. Foreign trade means a great deal, of course, to everyone concerned in it, both directly and indirectly, not only to the people who grow or produce the products which clear through your port, but also to the transportation companies, and so on down the line. The important thing is that you, so to speak, have a ringside seat, while the producer far inland is often seated far from the stage.

The foreign trade of the United States suffered, as you are well aware, a tremendous shrinkage during the depression years. The Administration had been impressed from the start with the necessity of evolving and executing a well-balanced program for the revival of our foreign trade. The result was the passage of the Trade Agreements Act of June 12, 1934, authorizing the President to enter into foreign trade agreements under the conditions and with the objectives therein defined. The two chief objectives of this act are to permit the removal or prevention of discriminations against American commerce and to stimulate advantageous foreign trade through the mutual and reciprocal reduction of trade barriers. These objectives are simple and understandable enough. They become perhaps even more significant if I should say that the basic underlying purpose of the trade-agreements program is to create employment. This it does by permitting trade to take place which at one time took place but which has in the last few years often been throttled out of existence by the many destructive trade controls and devices which nations have resorted to in their mistaken belief that it is all right to sell their goods abroad but that it is iniquitous to accept imports from foreign countries. I sometimes think that this factor—of increased employment—has not been sufficiently emphasized in considering the Trade Agreements Act, and in stating that foreign trade creates employment I am not limiting my statement to exports. I might add that imports are considered often to furnish as much employment as exports. According to one study, of every dollar spent in this country for imported manufactured goods, only 20 to 40 cents are remitted abroad, while from 60 to 80 cents go for duty, dock labor, trucking, rail transport, importing organization, wholesaler, advertising, retailer, salesmen, etc. This is perfectly understandable, particularly here in Baltimore, where millions of dollars in imported merchandise pass through your port every year. This merchandise creates business for your shipping companies, brings wages to dock labor in connection with its discharge from ship to shore, and furnishes employment to many other persons before it is finally sold to the ultimate consumer.

As soon as authority was received, the administration undertook at once to make the trade-agreements program a genuine factor in restoring world trade to something like the levels which prevailed prior to the depression. Progress has been slow for several reasons, but principally because the difficulty and importance of the task require a most painstaking and conscientious approach. For another thing, the negotiation of a trade agreement is a two-way proposition. Each government has its own ideas and its own objectives; to reconcile these often requires months of tedious negotiation. Despite these factors, I believe that we have thus far made a very satisfactory showing. In the approximately one year and a half since the Trade Agreements Act was enacted, agreements have been concluded with Cuba, Belgium, Haiti, Sweden, Brazil, Colombia, Canada, Honduras, the Netherlands, and Switzerland, while limited agreements have been made with Czechoslovakia and the Union of Soviet Socialist Republics.

I desire, of course, this evening, to talk to you particularly regarding the trade-agreements program insofar as it concerns our relations with Latin America. You will have observed that of the agreements thus far concluded, five, namely, those with Cuba, Haiti, Brazil, Colombia, and Honduras, are with Latin American republics. Negotiations are now pending with Costa Rica, El Salvador, Guatemala, and Nicaragua, and it is hoped that agreements may be signed during the coming months with these countries.

While several of the agreements have not yet run for a long enough period to evaluate their effects on trade, I believe you will be interested in a few figures showing the results of our agreement with Cuba, which was the first agreement concluded under authority of the Trade Agreements Act. Our exports to Cuba over a 15-month basic period in 1932–33 totaled $33,200,000; over a 15-month period in 1934–35 they totaled $71,395,000. Our purchases from Cuba increased in about the same degree: during the period of 1932–33 above mentioned, they totaled $68,273,000, while in the 1934–35 period they were $162,-000,000. In other words, our trade with Cuba has increased substantially in both directions, which is, of course, as it should be.

The only other agreement which has been in effect long enough to allow statistical comparisons to be made is that with Haiti, which took effect on June 3, 1935. According to figures just compiled by the Department of Commerce, the value of our exports to Haiti during the last 7 months of 1935, or the period immediately following the entry into effect of the trade agreement, was $2,136,000, an increase of 25 percent over the comparable total of $1,714,000 for the corresponding period of 1934.

While detailed figures for the calendar year 1935 are not yet available, you will doubtless be interested to learn that our trade with Latin America has increased in a very gratifying way. During the 11 months ending November 1935, our exports to Central and South America totaled $196,000,000, as compared with $182,000,000 for the same period in 1934. Imports increased from $234,000,000 to $283,000,000 during the same period. These figures show that a healthy revival is under way.

We hope in the months to come to stimulate the recovery which is already taking place by the negotiation of mutually advantageous trade agreements with the other countries of Latin America and thus to aline all of the countries of this hemisphere with us in the program. There are difficulties in the way, of course, but I feel certain that they can be solved by loyally cooperative efforts. One of the most gratifying features of the trade-agreements program is the response it has elicited from the countries of this hemisphere, which are earnestly desirous of helping this Government in its task of furthering the rebuilding of world trade on sound foundations.

There is probably no other section of the world more dependent on foreign trade for prosperity and well-being than our neighbors to the south of us. With most of them we have a trade that reposes on complementary bases. We supply finished manufactures and certain foodstuffs, while they supply us in turn with raw materials, tropical products, and foodstuffs on a seasonal schedule. The trade between the Americas is susceptible of tremendous expansion. Increasing national recovery, aided by the trade-agreements program, I am sure, will gradually develop this trade and bring it to new high levels. This process will not only be beneficial to our neighbors but also to ourselves, in the form of increased employment and business activity, and from this improvement our port of Baltimore should profit very substantially.

I have thus had the opportunity of indicating to you briefly the forward strides which we have made during this short period in promoting a sound relationship, both political and commercial, with our neighbors. May I, in conclusion, present you with a brief study in contrasts. Four years ago the antagonism of the Government and people of that great Republic of the south, Argentina, toward the Government and people of the United States was hardly concealed. The Argentine press and economic publications were filled with denouncements of the commercial policy pursued by this Government and with pleas to the Argentine people that they buy only from those who bought from them, and that purchases from the United States be restricted if not eliminated. The misunderstandings between the two Governments were hardly less apparent. Today, notwithstanding the practical difficulties which we both recognize, both Governments are cooperating in the closest manner to improve the flow of commerce between them, to remove such barriers to trade as can be removed without injury to the interests of either one, and the two Governments have further cooperated in the most cordial and effective manner for some time past in the great peace work undertaken by the Chaco Conference. Finally, perhaps I may be permitted to quote a statement made by the Foreign Minister of Argentina, who has distinguished himself in that office for the past four years. In an exclusive interview which Dr. Saavedra Lamas, the Foreign Minister, gave to our United Press on January 23, he said:

President Roosevelt's policy of the "good neighbor," the most wise, the most prudent, and the most sagacious that the great Republic of the north has ever followed, has assisted in converting the American Continent into one sole moral and spiritual state. This policy has gained the confidence of the American republics. Pan-Americanism today is a bilateral link between the Anglo-Saxon and the Latin worlds. For the first time, perhaps, there exists a current of community of ideas and sentiments flowing between Washington and Buenos Aires, Rio de Janeiro, Santiago, and Montevideo, without suspicions and without ill will. This birth of the united Americas, coherent and coordinated, not as a formal association, but as a definite entity of objectives, conscience, and tendencies, is called upon to influence the economic, international, and social destinies of the entire world.

ADDRESS by Sumner Welles, Assistant Secretary of State, "Our Foreign Policy and Peace," at New York City, October 19, 1936 (extract)

Department of State, *Press Releases*, October 20, 1936. The address was delivered before the Foreign Policy Association

. . . No MORE HEARTENING statement, insofar as our relations with the rest of the republics of this continent are concerned, has ever been made by a President of the United States than that made by President Roosevelt on December 28, 1933, when he announced that "the definite policy of the United States from now on is one opposed to armed intervention." This showed our neighbors that we intended to practice what we preached, and that declaration of policy, together with the formal ratification of the nonintervention convention adopted at the Montevideo conference in 1933, has been more conducive to good understanding than any one other feature of this administration's so-called "good neighbor" policy.

Before passing from this general topic, may I add one further consideration for your reflection. It should be borne in mind that as a general matter when the American citizen invests his capital in some other republic of this continent, he does so because of his belief that the profits he will derive from such investment will be larger than they would have been if that investment had been made here within our own borders. He makes that investment, generally, fully aware of the risks involved, fully cognizant of the fact that in some of the younger nations of the western world the maintenance of law and order has not reached the same degree which we like to feel exists in our own country. It would seem that when one of our nationals, individual or corporate, invests his money in a foreign land and trouble ensues, that individual, that corporation, should not expect his Government to adopt any policy in that foreign country which runs counter to the very basis of international law, which jeopardizes the vital interests of all of the American people, and which the American people themselves would be the first to oppose if it were resorted to within the United States by some foreign power.

What is really the crux of the problem is this. The majority of the other American republics, in order to develop profitably and with reasonable expedition the natural resources of their respective territories, require and desire the investment of foreign capital, just as we ourselves did in the earlier stages of our development as a nation. The peoples and the governments of those countries are today fully aware of the fact that foreign capital will not be invested within their borders except at usurious rates, unless that foreign investment is given both a reasonable measure of security and an equitable, nondiscriminatory treatment. It is not the intervention nor the interference of governments which will promote profitable commercial and financial interchange between the American republics—it is rather the establishment of a relationship of confidence between the borrower and the lender, and the existence of stable political conditions where individual industry and initiative can thrive. . . .

ADDRESS by President Franklin D. Roosevelt at the Inter-American Conference for the Maintenance of Peace, at Buenos Aires, December 1, 1936

Report of the Delegation of the United States of America to the Inter-American Conference for the Maintenance of Peace, p. 77

MEMBERS OF THE AMERICAN FAMILY OF NATIONS:

On the happy occasion of the convening of this Conference, I address you thus, because members of a family need no introduction or formalities when, in pursuance of excellent custom, they meet together for their common good.

As a family we appreciate the hospitality of our host, President Justo, and the Government and people of Argentina; and all of us are happy that to our friend Dr. Saavedra Lamas has come the well-deserved award of the Nobel Prize for great service in the cause of world peace.

Three years ago the American family met in nearby Montevideo, the great capital of the Republic of Uruguay. They were dark days. A shattering depression, unparalleled in its intensity, held us, with the rest of the world, in its grip. And in our own hemisphere a tragic war was raging between two of our sister Republics.

Yet, at that conference there was born not only hope for our common future but a greater measure of mutual trust between the American democracies than had ever existed before. In this Western Hemisphere the night of fear has been dispelled. Many of the intolerable burdens of economic depression have been lightened and, due in no small part to our common efforts, every nation of this hemisphere is today at peace with its neighbors.

This is no conference to form alliances, to divide the spoils of war, to partition countries, to deal with human beings as though they were pawns in a game of chance. Our purpose, under happy auspices, is to assure the continuance of the blessings of peace.

Three years ago, recognizing that a crisis was being thrust upon the New World, with splendid unanimity our twenty-one Republics set an example to the whole world by proclaiming a new spirit, a new day, in the affairs of this hemisphere.

While the succeeding period has justified in full measure all that was said and done at Montevideo, it has unfortunately emphasized the seriousness of threats to peace among other nations. Events elsewhere have served only to strengthen our horror of war and all that

war means. The men, women, and children of the Americas know
that warfare in this day and age means more than the mere clash of
armies: they see the destruction of cities and of farms; they foresee
that children and grandchildren, if they survive, will stagger for
long years not only under the burden of poverty but also amid the
threat of broken society and the destruction of constitutional government.

I am profoundly convinced that the plain people everywhere in the
civilized world today wish to live in peace one with another. And still
leaders and governments resort to war. Truly, if the genius of mankind that has invented the weapons of death cannot discover the
means of preserving peace, civilization as we know it lives in an evil
day.

But we cannot now, especially in view of our common purpose, accept any defeatist attitude. We have learned by hard experience that
peace is not to be had for the mere asking; that peace, like other
great privileges, can be obtained only by hard and painstaking effort.
We are here to dedicate ourselves and our countries to that work.

You who assemble today carry with you in your deliberations the
hopes of millions of human beings in other less-fortunate lands. Beyond the ocean we see continents rent asunder by old hatreds and
new fanaticisms. We hear the demand that injustice and inequality
be corrected by resorting to the sword and not by resorting to reason
and peaceful justice. We hear the cry that new markets can be achieved
only through conquest. We read that the sanctity of treaties between
nations is disregarded.

We know, too, that vast armaments are rising on every side and that
the work of creating them employs men and women by the millions.
It is natural, however, for us to conclude that such employment is
false employment, that it builds no permanent structures and creates
no consumers' goods for the maintenance of a lasting prosperity. We
know that nations guilty of these follies inevitably face the day either
when their weapons of destruction must be used against their neighbors or when an unsound economy, like a house of cards, will fall
apart.

In either case, even though the Americans become involved in no
war, we must suffer too. The madness of a great war in other parts
of the world would affect us and threaten our good in a hundred ways.
And the economic collapse of any nation or nations must of necessity
harm our own prosperity.

Can we, the Republics of the New World, help the Old World to
avert the catastrophe which impends? Yes; I am confident that we can.

First, it is our duty by every honorable means to prevent any future war among ourselves. This can best be done through the strengthening of the processes of constitutional democratic government—to make these processes conform to the modern need for unity and efficiency and, at the same time, preserve the individual liberties of our citizens. By so doing, the people of our nations, unlike the people of many nations who live under other forms of government, can and will insist on their intention to live in peace. Thus will democratic government be justified throughout the world.

In this determination to live at peace among ourselves we in the Americas make it at the same time clear that we stand shoulder to shoulder in our final determination that others who, driven by war madness or land hunger, might seek to commit acts of aggression against us, will find a hemisphere wholly prepared to consult together for our mutual safety and our mutual good. I repeat what I said in speaking before the Congress and the Supreme Court of Brazil: "Each one of us has learned the glories of independence. Let each one of us learn the glories of interdependence."

Secondly, and in addition to the perfecting of the mechanisms of peace, we can strive even more strongly than in the past to prevent the creation of those conditions which give rise to war. Lack of social or political justice within the borders of any nation is always cause for concern. Through democratic processes we can strive to achieve for the Americas the highest possible standard of living conditions for all our people. Men and women blessed with political freedom, willing to work and able to find work, rich enough to maintain their families and to educate their children, contented with their lot in life and on terms of friendship with their neighbors will defend themselves to the utmost but will never consent to take up arms for a war of conquest.

Interwoven with these problems is the further self-evident fact that the welfare and prosperity of each of our nations depend in large part on the benefits derived from commerce among ourselves and with other nations, for our present civilization rests on the basis of an international exchange of commodities. Every nation of the world has felt the evil effects of recent efforts to erect trade barriers of every known kind. Every individual citizen has suffered from them. It is no accident that the nations which have carried this process farthest are those which proclaim most loudly that they require war as an instrument of their policy. It is no accident that attempts to be self-sufficient have led to falling standards for their people and to ever-increasing loss of the democratic ideals in a mad race to pile armament on armament. It is no accident that because of these suicidal policies and the suffering attending them many of their people have come to believe with despair that the price of war seems less than the price of peace.

This state of affairs we must refuse to accept with every instinct of defense, with every exhortation of enthusiastic hope, with every use of mind and skill.

I cannot refrain here from reiterating my gratification that in this, as in so many other achievements, the American Republics have given a salutary example to the world. The resolution adopted at the Inter-American Conference at Montevideo endorsing the principles of liberal trade policies has shown forth like a beacon in the storm of economic madness which has been sweeping over the entire world during these later years. Truly, if the principles there embodied find still wider application in your deliberations, it will be a notable contribution to the cause of peace. For my own part I have done all in my power to sustain the consistent efforts of my Secretary of State in negotiating agreements for reciprocal trade, and even though the individual results may seem small, the total of them is significant. These policies in recent weeks have received the approval of the people of the United States, and they have, I am sure, the sympathy of the other nations here assembled.

There are many other causes for war—among them, long-festering feuds, unsettled frontiers, territorial rivalries. But these sources of danger which still exist in the Americas, I am thankful to say, are not only few in number but already on the way to peaceful adjudication. While the settlement of such controversies may necessarily involve adjustments at home or in our relations with our neighbors which may appear to involve material sacrifice, let no man or woman forget that there is no profit in war. Sacrifices in the cause of peace are infinitesimal compared with the holocaust of war.

Peace comes from the spirit and must be grounded in faith. In seeking peace, perhaps we can best begin by proudly affirming the faith of the Americas: the faith in freedom and its fulfillment, which has proved a mighty fortress beyond reach of successful attack in half the world.

That faith arises from a common hope and a common design given us by our fathers in differing form but with a single aim: freedom and security of the individual, which has become the foundation of our peace.

If, then, by making war in our midst impossible, and if within ourselves and among ourselves we can give greater freedom and fulfillment to the individual lives of our citizens, the democratic form of representative government will have justified the high hopes of the liberating fathers. Democracy is still the hope of the world. If we in our generation can continue its successful applications in the Americas, it will spread and supersede other methods by which men are governed and which seem to most of us to run counter to our ideals of human liberty and human progress.

Three centuries of history sowed the seeds which grew into our nations; the fourth century saw those nations become equal and free and brought us to a common system of constitutional government; the fifth century is giving to us a common meeting ground of mutual help and understanding. Our hemisphere has at last come of age. We are here assembled to show its unity to the world. We took from our ancestors a great dream. We here offer it back as a great unified reality.

Finally, in expressing our faith of the Western World, let us affirm:

That we maintain and defend the democratic form of constitutional representative government.

That through such government we can more greatly provide a wider distribution of culture, of education, of thought, and of free expression.

That through it we can obtain a greater security of life for our citizens and a more equal opportunity for them to prosper.

That through it we can best foster commerce and the exchange of art and science between nations.

That through it we can avoid the rivalry of armaments, avert hatreds, and encourage good will and true justice.

That through it we offer hope for peace and a more abundant life to the peoples of the whole world.

But this faith of the Western World will not be complete if we fail to affirm our faith in God. In the whole history of mankind, far back into the dim past before man knew how to record thoughts or events, the human race has been distinguished from other forms of life by the existence, the fact, of religion. Periodic attempts to deny God have always come and will always come to naught.

In the constitution and in the practice of our nations is the right of freedom of religion. But this ideal, these words, presuppose a belief and a trust in God.

The faith of the Americas, therefore, lies in the spirit. The system, the sisterhood, of the Americas, is impregnable so long as her nations maintain that spirit.

In that faith and spirit we will have peace over the Western World. In that faith and spirit we will all watch and guard our hemisphere. In that faith and spirit may we also, with God's help, offer hope to our brethren overseas.

ADDRESS by Cordell Hull, Secretary of State, at the Inter-American Conference for the Maintenance of Peace, at Buenos Aires, December 5, 1936
Department of State, Conference Series, No. 25

THE PRIMARY PURPOSE of this Conference is to banish war from the Western Hemisphere. In its earnest pursuit of this great undertaking, it is necessary at the outset to visualize numerous dangerous conditions and practices in general international affairs to the extent that they bear upon and affect the work of this Conference. It is manifest that every country today is faced with a supreme alternative. Each must play its part in determining whether the world will slip backward toward war and savagery, or whether it can maintain and will advance the level of civilization and peace. None can escape its responsibility.

The 21 American republics cannot remain unconcerned by the grave and threatening conditions in many parts of the world. Our convocation here in Buenos Aires utters this hemisphere's common voice of its interest, nay, its intense concern, over the determination of this momentous question. The repercussions of wars and preparations for wars have been so universally disastrous that it is now as plain as mathematical truth that each nation in any part of the world is concerned in peace in every part of the world. The nations of all the Americas, through their chosen delegates, have assembled to make careful survey and analysis of all aspects of their responsibilities; to take account of their common duties; and to plan accordingly for the safety and welfare of their peoples.

The Western Hemisphere must now face squarely certain hard realities. For the purpose of our undertaking, we must frankly recognize that for some time the forces of militarism have been in the ascendant in a large part of the world; those of peace have been correspondingly on the decline. We should be lacking in common sense if we ignored the plain fact that the effects of these forces will unavoidably have direct impact upon all of us. We should be lacking in ordinary caution if we fail to counsel together for our common safety and welfare.

It is bad enough when many statesmen and peoples close their minds and memories to the awful lesson taught by the millions of soldiers sacrificed in the World War; the shattered cities, the desolated fields, and all the other material, moral, and spiritual ravages of that conflict. Still worse, that war has• brought in its train wounds to man's heart and spirit, national hatreds and fears, the dislocation or destruction of indispensable political and governmental structures, and the collapse or cool abandonment of former high standards of national conduct. The supreme tragedy is completed by the breakdown of the commerce of mind and culture, the attempt to isolate the nations of the earth into sealed compartments, all of which have made war a burden not to be endured by mankind.

The delegates of the American nations, meeting here in the face of these grave and threatening world conditions, must realize that mere words will not suffice. From every wise and practical viewpoint, concrete peace planning, peace views, and peace objectives are imperative. We must quicken our words and our hopes into a specific, embracing program to maintain peace. Such a program, adequately implemented, should constitute an armory of peace. It should comprise a structure affording all practical means for safeguarding peace. At a time when many other governments or peoples fail or fear to proclaim and embrace a broad or definite peace plan or movement, while their statesmen are shouting threats of war, it is all the more necessary that we of the Americas must cry out for peace, keep alive the spirit of peace, live by the rules of peace, and forthwith perfect the machinery for its maintenance. Should we fail to make this outstanding contribution, it would be a practical desertion of the cause of peace and a tragic blow to the hopes of humanity.

In meeting this problem, the American republics are in a peculiarly advantageous situation. There are among us no radical differences, no profound mistrusts or deep hatreds. On the contrary we are inspired by the impulse to be constant friends and the determination to be peaceful neighbors.

We recognize the right of all nations to handle their affairs in any way they choose, and this quite irrespective of the fact that their way may be different from our way or even repugnant to our ideas. But we cannot fail to take cognizance of the international aspect of their policies when and to the extent that they may react upon us. I, myself, am unalterably of the view that a policy leading to war may react upon us. In the face of any situation• directly leading to war, can we therefore be other than apprehensive?

In sustaining the firm determination that peace must be maintained and that any country whose policies make war likely is threatening injury to all, I believe that the nations of this hemisphere would find themselves in accord with governments elsewhere. I strongly entertain the hope that a united group of American nations may take common action at this Conference further to assure peace among themselves and define their attitude toward war; and that this action may not only demonstrate the happy position of the New World, but, though designed primarily for our own benefit, embody policies of world application and correspond to the views and interests of nations outside this hemisphere.

There is no need for war. There is a practical alternative policy at hand, complete and adequate. It is no exclusive policy aimed at the safety or supremacy of a few, leaving others to struggle with distressful situations. It demands no sacrifices comparable to the advantages which will result to each nation and to each individual.

In these circumstances the representatives of the 21 American republics should frankly call the attention of the people of this hemisphere to the possibilities of danger to their future peace and progress and at the same time set forth the numerous steps that can well be undertaken as the most effective means of improving and safeguarding the conditions of permanent peace.

While carefully avoiding any political entanglements, my Government strives at all times to cooperate with other nations to every practical extent in support of peace objectives, including reduction or limitation of armaments, the control of traffic in arms, taking the profits out of war, and the restoration of fair and friendly economic relationships. We reject war as a method of settling international disputes and favor such methods as conference, conciliation, and arbitration.

Peace can be partially safeguarded through international agreements. Such agreements, however, must reflect the utmost good faith; this alone can be the guaranty of their significance and usefulness. Contemporary events clearly show that, where mutual trust, good will, and sincerity of purpose are lacking, pacts or agreements fail; and the world is seized by fear and left to the mercy of the wreckers.

The Conference has the duty of considering all peace proposals of merit. Let me enumerate and briefly discuss eight separate and vitally important principles and proposals for a comprehensive peace program and peace structure. They are not designed to be all-inclusive. In considering them, we should be guided by the knowledge that other forces and agencies of peace exist besides those made and to be made on our continents; what we do contemplates no conflict with sincere efforts the world over.

First. I would emphasize the local and unilateral responsibility of each nation carefully to educate and organize its people in opposition to war and its underlying causes. Support must be given to peace, to the most effective policies for its preservation; and, finally, each nation must maintain conditions within its own borders which will permit it to adopt national policies that can be peacefully pursued. More than any other factor, a thoroughly informed and alert public opinion in each country as to the suitable and desirable relationships with other nations and the principles underlying them, enables a government in time of crisis to act promptly and effectively for peace.

The forces of peace everywhere are entitled to function both through governments and through public opinion. The peoples of the world would be far wiser if they expended more of their hard-earned money in organizing the forces of peace and fewer of the present 5 billion dollars in educating and training their military forces.

Since the time when Thomas Jefferson insisted upon a "decent respect to the opinions of mankind," public opinion has controlled foreign policy in all democracies. It is, therefore, all important that every platform, every pulpit, and every forum should become constant and active agencies in the great work of education and organization. The limited extent of such highly organized and intelligent public opinion in support of peace is by far the largest drawback to any plan to prevent war. Truly the first step is that each nation must thus make itself safe for peace. This, too, develops a common will for freedom, the soil from which peace springs.

People everywhere should be made to know of the peace mechanisms. Even more, there should be brought home to them the knowledge that trade, commerce, finance, debts, communications, have a bearing on peace. The workman at his bench, the farmer on his land, the shopkeeper by his shelves, the clerk at his books, the laborer in factory, plantation, mine, or construction camp, must realize that his work is the work of peace; that to interrupt it for ends of national or personal rapacity is to drive him toward quick death by bayonets, or to slower, but not less grievous suffering, through economic distress.

In all our countries we have scholars who can demonstrate these facts; let them not be silent. Our churches have direct contact with all groups; may they remember that the peacemakers are the children of God. We have artists and poets who can distill their needed knowledge into trenchant phrase and line; they have work to do. Our great journals on both continents cover the world. Our women are awake; our youth sentient; our clubs and organizations make opinion everywhere. There is a strength here available greater than that of armies. We have but to ask its aid; it will be swift to answer, not only here, but in continents beyond the seas.

Second. Indispensable in their influence for peace and well-being are frequent conferences between representatives of the nations and intercourse between their peoples. Collaboration and the exchange of views, ideas, and information are the most effective means of establishing understanding, friendship, and trust. I would again emphasize that any written pacts or agreements not based upon such relationships as these too often exist on paper only. Development of the atmosphere of peace, understanding, and good will during our sessions here will alone constitute a vast accomplishment.

Third. Any complete program would include safeguarding the nations of this hemisphere from using force, one against the other, through the consummation of all of the five well-known peace agreements, produced in chief part by previous conferences, as well as through the Draft Convention Coordinating the Existing Treaties between the American States and Extending Them in Certain Respects, which the Delegation of the United States is presenting for the consideration of this Conference.

In these, virtually all of the essentials of adequate machinery are present. If their operation is somewhat implemented by provisions in the draft proposal I have just mentioned to be considered by this Conference, such machinery would be complete.

The first of these is the Treaty to Avoid and Prevent Conflicts between the American States, which was signed in Santiago in 1923.

The second is the Treaty for the Renunciation of War, known as the Kellogg-Briand Pact, or the Pact of Paris, signed at Paris in 1928.

The third is the General Convention of Inter-American Conciliation, signed at Washington in 1929.

The fourth is the General Treaty of Inter-American Arbitration, signed at Washington in 1929.

The fifth is the Anti-War Treaty of Nonaggression and Conciliation, signed at Rio de Janeiro in 1933.

While the Montevideo Conference in 1933 went on record in favor of the valid execution of these five agreements by each of the 21 governments represented, several have not yet completed this ratification. These agreements provide a many-sided and flexible functioning machinery for the adjustment of difficulties that may arise in this hemisphere. A government could not give more tangible proof of its readiness to translate into practicable form its desire to promote and to maintain peace. Swift action by all of us to ratify these agreements should be the natural assertion of our intentions.

Fourth. If war should occur, any peace program must provide for the problem then presented. For the belligerent, there is the ruin and suffering of war. For the neutrals, there is the task of remaining neutral, of not being too disturbed in their own affairs, of not having their own peace imperiled, of working in common to restrict the war and bring it to an end. Can we in this Conference work out for ourselves a common line of policy that might be pursued during a period of neutrality? Some first broad approaches toward that end are, I think, possible. If these are to be sound they must be inspired by the determination to stay at peace. When interests are challenged, when minds are stirred, when entry into war in some particular juncture may appear to offer to some country the chance of national advantage, then determination is needed to retain neutrality. The maintenance of neutrality is an achievement to be attained more readily if undertaken jointly. Such agreement would be a tremendous safeguard for each of us. It might be a powerful means of ending war.

When we have done all that seems to be possible in extending and perfecting an integrated and permanent mechanism for preserving peaceful relations among ourselves, and when we have placed in operation these various instruments, the 21 republics of this hemisphere will have given overt expression to the most determined will for peace to be found in the world today. In the face of a weakening elsewhere in the world of reliance on and observance of international agreements, we shall have proclaimed our firm intention that these peaceful instruments shall be the foundation of relations between nations throughout this whole region.

If we can endow peace with certainty, if we can make it glow in our part of the world, then we may indulge the hope that our example will not be in vain.

Fifth. The peoples of this region have a further opportunity. They must make headway with a liberal policy of commerce, which would lower excessive barriers to trade and lessen injurious discriminations as between the trade of different countries. This means the substitution of a policy of economic benefit, good will, and fair dealing for one stimulated by greedy and short-sighted calculations of momentary advantage in an impractical isolation. It would have most beneficial effects, both direct and indirect, upon political difficulties and antagonisms.

A thriving international commerce, well adjusted to the resources and talents of each country, brings benefit to all. It keeps men employed, active, and usefully supplying the wants of others. It leads each country to look upon others as helpful counterparts to itself rather than as antagonists. It opens up to each country, to the extent mutually profitable and desirable, the resources and the organized productive power of other countries; by its benefits small nations with limited territory or resources can have a varied, secure, and prosperous life; it can bring improvement to those who feel their toil too hard and their reward too meager.

Prosperity and peace are not separate entities. To promote one is to promote the other. The economic well-being of peoples is the greatest single protection against civil strife, large armaments, war. Economic isolation and military force go hand in hand; when nations cannot get what they need by the normal processes of trade, they will continue to resort to the use of force. A people employed and in a state of reasonable comfort is not a people among whom class struggles, militarism, and war can thrive. But a people driven to desperation by want and misery is at all times a threat to peace, their conditions an invitation to disorder and chaos, both internal and external.

The intervening years have given added significance to the economic program adopted at the Conference at Montevideo 3 years ago. That program is today the greatest potential force both for peace and prosperity. Our present Conference should reaffirm and secure action upon this program of economic intelligence.

One feature of the resolutions adopted at Montevideo was the support for the principle of equality of treatment as the basis of acceptable commercial policy. This rule has been followed in a number of commercial agreements that have already been concluded between American nations. Their benefits are already becoming manifest and will continue to grow. We cannot blind ourselves to the fact, however, that at the same time there has taken place even among the American nations a growth in the restrictions upon trade and an extension of discriminatory practices; these have tended to counteract the advantages resulting from the liberalizing terms embodied in other agreements.

I would urge again the wisdom of avoiding discrimination in our commercial policy. The practice of discrimination prevents trade from following the lines which would produce the greatest economic benefits—it inevitably in the long run must provoke retaliation from those who suffer from discrimination; makes it more difficult for countries eager to pursue a liberal trade policy to secure the fair gains from this policy, and thereby checks the lowering of restrictions. It will not serve our broad and deep aims; on the contrary, if steadily extended, will lead us into new controversies and difficulties. The Montevideo program offers the only alternative to the present shortsighted, war-breeding bilateral bargaining method of trade, to the exclusion of triangular and multilateral trade, which is being employed in many parts of the world with sterile results.

The ends we seek can best be achieved by the concurrent or concerted action of many countries. Each can exert itself steadfastly amidst the particular circumstances of its economic situation to make its contribution toward the rebuilding of trade. Each can grant new opportunities to others as it receives new opportunities for itself. All are called upon to share in the concurrent or concerted action which is required. Any country which seeks the benefits of the program while avoiding its responsibilities, will in time shut itself off from the benefits. Any country which is tempted or forced by some special calculation to depart from these lines of action and which conveys and seeks special advantage jeopardizes the progress, and perhaps the very existence, of the program. Faithful dealing, without favor, between equal partners will be required to readjust trade along the lines of growth, which is our goal.

Sixth. The Conference must recognize the all-important principle of practical international cooperation to restore many indispensable relationships between nations; for international relationships, in many vital respects, are at a low ebb. The entire international order is severely dislocated. Chaotic conditions in the relations between nations have appeared. Human progress already has slowed down.

Nations in recent years have sought to live a hermit existence by isolating themselves from each other in suspicion and fear. The inevitable result is not unlike that experienced by a community where individuals undertake to live a hermit existence, with the resultant decline and decay of the spiritual, the moral, the educational, and the material benefits and blessings which spring from community organization and effort. The difference, when nations live apart, is that the entire human race in countless instances suffers irreparable injury—political, moral, material, spiritual, and social. Today, for illustration, through lack of comprehension, understanding, and confidence, we see many nations exhausting their material substance and the vitality of their people by piling up huge armaments. We behold others, in their attempted isolation, becoming more indifferent and less considerate toward the rights, privileges, and honest opinions of others. National character and conduct are threatened with utter demoralization. At no distant time we shall see a state of moral and spiritual isolation, bringing with it the condemnation of the world, covering great parts of the earth, unless peoples halt and turn toward a sane course.

Seventh. International law has been in large measure flouted. It should be reestablished, revitalized, and strengthened by general demand. International law protects the peace and security of nations and so safeguards them against maintaining great armaments and wasting their substance in continual readiness for war. Founded upon justice and humanity, the great principles of international law are the source and fountain of the equality, the security, and the very existence of nations. Armies and navies are no permanent substitute. Abandonment of the rule of law would not only leave small or unarmed states at the mercy of the reckless and powerful but would hopelessly undermine all international order. It is inconceivable that the civilized nations would long delay a supreme effort to reestablish that rule of law.

Eighth. Observance of understandings, agreements, and treaties between nations constitutes the foundation of international order. May I say here that this is not a time for crimination or recrimination, nor is such in my mind during this discussion. There must be the fullest patience and forbearance, one country with another, as the nations endeavor to climb back to that high ground of wholesome and elevating relationship of loyalty to the given word and faithful fair dealing.

International agreements have lost their force and reliability as a basis of relations between nations. This extremely ominous and fateful development constitutes the most dangerous single phenomenon in the world of today; not international law merely, but that which is higher—moral law—and the whole integrity and honor of governments are in danger of being ruthlessly trampled upon. There has been a failure of the spirit. There is no task more urgent than that of remaking the basis of trusted agreement between nations. They must ardently seek the terms of new agreements and stand behind them with unfailing will. The vitality of international agreements must be restored.

If the solemn rights and obligations between nations are to be treated lightly or brushed aside, the nations of the world will head straight toward international anarchy and chaos. And soon, too, the citizen begins to lower his individual standards of personal, moral, and business conduct to those of his government. Trust in each nation's honor and faith in its given word must be restored by the concerted resolve of all governments.

It is to the interest of everyone that there be an end of treaties broken by arbitrary unilateral action. Peaceful procedure, agreements between the signatories, and mutual understanding must be restored as the means of modifying or ending international agreements.

In the accomplishment of the high aims and purposes of this eightfold program, the people of every nation have an equal interest. We of this hemisphere have reason to hope that these great objectives may receive the support of all peoples. If peace and progress are to be either maintained or advanced, the time is overripe for renewed effort on each nation's part. There can be no delay. Through past centuries, the human race fought its way up from the low level of barbarism and war to that of civilization and peace. This accomplishment has only been partial, and it may well be but temporary.

It would be a frightful commentary on the human race if, with the awful lesson of its disastrous experience, responsible and civilized governments should now fail.

The nations of this continent should omit no word or act in their attempt to meet the dangerous conditions which endanger peace. Let our actions here at Buenos Aires constitute the most potent possible appeal to peacemakers and warmakers throughout the world.

So only does civilization become real. So only can we rightly ask that universal support which entitles governments to speak for their peoples to the world not with the voice of propaganda but with that of truth. Having affirmed our faith, we should be remiss if we were to leave anything undone which will tend to assure our peace here and make us powerful for peace elsewhere. In a very real sense, let this continent set the high example of championing the forces of peace, democracy, and civilization.

ADDRESS by Laurence Duggan, Chief of the Division of the American Republics, at Philadelphia, April 2, 1938 (extract)

Department of State, *Press Releases*, April 2, 1938, p. 439. The address was delivered before the American Academy of Political and Social Science

. . . IN EXTERNAL AFFAIRS, the first century and a quarter of our independent existence was characterized primarily by "expansionism." From 13 States along the Atlantic seaboard, our country grew to 48, touching upon two oceans and including many territorial and island possessions. This growth in the national domain was justified by a curious philosophy which may be termed "manifest destiny." In his *Farewell Address,* George Washington laid down certain precepts for the guidance of our foreign relations. He said: "Observe good faith and justice toward all nations. Cultivate peace and harmony with all." Nevertheless, within a very short time, in extenuation of the growth in territory and power of the United States, the other American republics heard such statements as these:

In explaining the argument of natural law, Representative Wilde of Georgia declared with respect to the lands held by the Cherokee Nation:

And if it were possible to perpetuate the race of Indians, what would be the consequence? Why, that a hundred or a thousand fold the number of white men would not be born, because the Indians would roam over and possess, without enjoying, the land which must afford the future whites subsistence.

Or Representative Duncan, in extolling the extension-of-freedom doctrine, which was employed to cover the annexation of Texas, Oregon, and California:

If ours is to be the home of the oppressed, we must extend our territory in latitude and longitude to the demand of the millions who are to follow us, as well of our own posterity as those who are invited to our peaceful shores to partake in our republican institutions.

It was only natural that generations of territorial expansion should give rise to deep distrust and fear on the part of our immediate neighbors. Only as recently as a generation ago, the United States purchased the Virgin Islands, 1 year after President Wilson had stated "America does not want any additional territory."

As the era of territorial aggrandizement drew toward an end, the United States assumed a new role equally objectionable to our southern neighbors, that of international police power. In this connection Dr. Ricardo Alfaro, former President of Panama, recently placed in juxtaposition two statements of President Theodore Roosevelt. Dr. Alfaro said:

In 1906 President Theodore Roosevelt in a message to Congress stated:
"In many parts of South America there has been much misunderstanding of the attitude of the United States toward the other American republics. An idea has become prevalent that our assertion of the Monroe Doctrine implied or carried with it the assumption of superiority and of a right to exercise some kind of protectorate over the countries to whose territory that doctrine applies. Nothing could be farther from the truth."

Yet, Colonel Roosevelt throughout his two terms of office maintained and enforced the famous Corollary to the Monroe Doctrine which he formulated as follows:
"Chronic wrongdoing, or an impotence which results in a general loosening of the ties of civilized society, may in America, as elsewhere, ultimately require intervention by some civilized nation, and in the Western Hemisphere the adherence of the United States to the Monroe Doctrine may force the United States, however reluctantly, in flagrant cases of such wrongdoing or impotence, to the exercise of an international police power."

The exercise of this assumed police power, which resulted in the infringement of sovereignty of many nearby nations, met with a growing hue and cry throughout the other republics of this hemisphere. The wave of nationalism which swept the world after the war brought them fortitude and determination. Their opposition to the philanthropies of intervention on the part of the United States became open, direct, and acrid. At the Inter-American Conference in

1928, the Argentine delegation withdrew from the Conference because of the opposition of the United States delegation to discussion of the question of intervention, then very alive because of the presence of United States marines in Nicaragua. In the United States people began to ask themselves in what way the national welfare which cost the lives of many marines and the expenditure of considerable money was advanced by a policy of intimidation and intervention.

Although the first indications that the United States Government likewise entertained doubts occurred under the tenure of Secretary Stimson, it was left to the present administration to give tangible proofs by a series of definite visible steps of a determination to conduct its relations with the other American republics on a different plane. In general, the "good neighbor" policy does not enunciate any new concepts for the conduct of our relations with the other American republics. The principles of understanding, confidence, friendship, and respect have been proclaimed by every President. What is new is a new and more far-reaching application of these principles. As the references earlier given show, in the past there has been no lack of willingness to employ specious moral principles to justify actions contrary to the basic principles enunciated in the first days of our independent existence as the bases of our foreign relations, or to pervert or distort those basic principles to explain deeds of a totally irreconcilable nature. However, it is my belief that a careful examination will disclose no period in our relations with the other American republics when there has been as close a correlation between declared purpose and fulfillment, between theory and fact, as during the past 5 years.

It might be interesting to consider the reasons for the change in popular attitude which was given form by the present administration.

First of all it had become apparent that the antagonisms fired by our past activities had resulted in the erection of a barrier of distrust more efficacious in its insulating quality than any physical barrier of distance or topography. At international gatherings the United States delegations instead of being welcomed as friends and associates were eyed askance and with misgivings. This suspicion extended beyond the confines of the Government to include our citizens, regardless of walk of life. They were distinctly handicapped because they discovered that outside the confines of the United States they were considered to possess to a greater or lesser degree the same qualities that their country was considered to have exhibited in its international dealings. They found that the influence of the United States was related directly to that flowing from the might of material strength. They came to realize that the United States had few real friends on this hemisphere, friends who shared a similar outlook, friends whose sympathy and aid could be counted upon in case of need. And as storm clouds arose in other parts of the world, and the depression deepened, our people wondered whether this was a healthy situation.

Moreover, the antagonisms were adversely affecting our commercial interests. During the period of the second intervention in Nicaragua (1926–1933) and of the acute period of our intervention in Haiti (1920–1930), groups in many countries boycotted United States goods. While for a variety of reasons the trade statistics are poor indices of the force of those boycotts, our businessmen were well aware of the business actually lost because of the ill feeling toward the United States. Their concern was not alleviated by the passage of the Smoot-Hawley tariff of 1930, which, because of its very substantial increases on many important export products of the other American countries, caused deep resentment. Retaliatory tariffs were erected, and the new far-reaching trade controls instituted during the depression were sometimes availed of to our disadvantage. Some of the more enlightened and far-sighted American businessmen even took steps of their own to endeavor to correct some of the misconceptions regarding the United States—for there were many of these. For instance the Inter-American Committee, composed of several of the important business interests, took several useful steps in the early thirties along this line.

Finally, considering that the other American countries have known us by our interventions and dollars, it was not surprising that the United States should have been regarded as a great culture desert, void of art, music, literature—in short, of a soul. Oases here and there were admitted, but they were not considered typical and were generally believed to be nourished by subterranean foreign springs. Of course there were persons in every one of the American countries who knew that the United States was not a cultural vacuum. They have stood out like lighthouses. To them, this country owes a deep debt of gratitude for their efforts to interest their countrymen in the cultural activity of the United States. If they have not been successful, the fault is not theirs. It lies with the antagonisms created by our past policies, and with the indifference of our scholars and scientists and foundations to the almost uncharted sea of cultural cooperation in the Americas. With a steadfastness reminiscent of the captain's daughter lashed to the mast of the *Hesperus,* they have kept their attentions and activities riveted on the Old World.

These then are the principal, if not all, of the motives that led directly to a reorientation of policy. This picture may omit the overtones and shadings that give perspective and body to the central theme. But in its essentials it is my belief that it is accurate.

Let us now briefly consider the bases upon which the "good neighbor" policy rests.

First of all, the President declared in December 1933 that "the definite policy of the United States from now on is one opposed to armed intervention." The Government has ratified two inter-American treaties, one adopted at Montevideo, the other at Buenos Aires, that contain the provision that no country has the right to intervene directly or indirectly in the internal or external affairs of another. Thus the peril of intervention by the United States which has hung over some countries like a sword of Damocles has been removed.

The question may be raised as to what attitude this country would take if confronted with a break-down of law and order in any country of this hemisphere. Contemplating that contingency, the President has said: "It is only if and when the failure of orderly processes affects the other nations of the continent that it becomes their joint concern; and the point to stress is that in such an event it becomes the joint concern of a whole continent in which we are all neighbors."

Secondly, the Government is endeavoring to improve and extend the trade relations, principally through the medium of the trade-agreements program, which has been fully discussed by others at this conference. The United States has negotiated agreements with 9 of the 20 countries.

Thirdly, the United States has ratified every one of the 10 inter-American peace treaties. This machinery has been constructed little by little as experience and need have shown desirable. The prestige and influence which this body of international law is acquiring is revealed by the rapidity with which a direct settlement was arrived at between the Dominican Republic and Haiti after the latter had invoked one of the important peace instruments. While doubtlessly there are imperfections in this machinery, it would seem advisable to give prolonged and careful consideration before scrapping it for a completely new mechanism. For instance if it is generally believed desirable to provide for regular meetings of foreign ministers during the intervals between the formal conferences, the objective might be attained by amendment to the existing treaties that provide for consultation.

Fourthly, the United States has ratified the convention for the maintenance, preservation, and reestablishment of peace adopted at the Buenos Aires Conference which provides for consultation "in the event that the peace of the American Republics is menaced." Moreover, in the declaration of principles of inter-American solidarity and cooperation the American republics stated: "That every act susceptible of disturbing the peace of America affected each and every one of them, and justifies the initiation of the procedure of consultation" provided for in the convention just mentioned. This Government stands ready to consult at the moment that any country on this hemisphere requests consultation in the belief that there exists a threat to the peace of the Americas. The convention and the declaration of necessity could not precisely define what constitutes a threat to the peace of the Americas. A threat probably would include the attempt at the use of armed force against any country of this hemisphere by any foreign power. However, a threat might also be considered to include many other actions, however veiled they may be, and in this connection there comes to mind another pertinent quotation from Washington's *Farewell Address:* "Against the insidious wiles of foreign influence . . . the jealousy of a free people ought to be *constantly* awake, since history and experience prove that foreign influence is one of the most harmful foes of republican government."

Fifthly, if there is to be real understanding between this country and the other American countries, it is essential that our people through education come to an appreciation of the many aspects of life and culture in the other American republics, and in turn that these countries develop an appreciation of the nonmaterial aspects of the civilization that is in process of dynamic development in the United States. The Department of State is now giving careful study to the ways in which it can interest and cooperate with private organizations in this important work.

In the "good neighbor" policy this Government believes that it is contributing its share toward the improvement of international relationships on this hemisphere. The general acceptance and support of this policy by the nations of the New World is the most convincing testimony of the soundness and broad applicability of its principles that could be adduced. Indeed no higher plane of international relationships can be conceived than one of fair play, equity, mutual accommodation, and mutual trust. It is superfluous to mention that departure from this plane by any country at any time presents large difficulties for the other countries who recognize not only that their own particular advantage but the welfare of all is advanced by conducting their relations on that plane. There may have existed a day when a country could go its own way without greatly affecting the destinies of other countries, but, if that day ever existed, it has now passed. Our present civilization is characterized by the interdependence of peoples and nations, and it is therefore more than ever desirable that some common and satisfactory basis for the conduct of international relationships be found. It is my belief that the "good neighbor" policy provides that basis.

ADDRESS by Cordell Hull, Secretary of State, at the Eighth International Conference of American States, at Lima, December 10, 1938
Report of the Delegation of the United States of America to the Eighth International Conference of American States, p. 93

MR. PRESIDENT, MEMBERS OF THE CONFERENCE, LADIES AND GENTLEMEN:

It is a matter of unusual satisfaction to me and my associates to meet and greet the members of the other American delegations, with many of whom I have had the good fortune of being associated at previous inter-American conferences.

This being one of our regular inter-American conferences, it is well to survey briefly the course of events since we last assembled in this capacity. These events are today of profound significance to our nations and to the whole world.

I

Five years have elapsed since the Seventh International Conference of the American States met at Montevideo. That conference faced a somber prospect of continuing deterioration in the field of international relations in several parts of the world.

The years of profound and world-wide economic dislocation had taken a heavy toll of material losses and human suffering everywhere. International commercial, financial, and monetary relations were in a state of disorder and confusion. Unprecedented trade barriers of every description had arisen and continued to rise in all countries. Exchange of goods among nations had fallen precipitately, both in value and in physical volume. These developments were serving to intensify economic depression in all countries, to disrupt and reduce prices, especially of primary products, to destroy values, to discourage enterprise, to create wide-spread unemployment and general distress, and to undermine the foundations of social and political stability.

Side by side with these mounting difficulties—and, in large measure, as their result—there appeared ominous signs of a disastrous lowering of standards in international political relations. Respect for the pledged word and willingness to fulfil treaty obligations were rapidly weakening. An effort to reach agreement on a broad program of limitation and progressive reduction of armaments was swiftly moving to the point of tragic failure.

On our continent, too, the relationships among the American nations were not altogether happy. Misunderstanding, prejudice, and aloofness characterized many phases of relations between some of the American nations.

The Seventh International Conference of American States performed a task of historic importance. The representatives of the sister republics brought to the work of the Conference a deep sense of responsibility, a firm determination to find a better way of international life than that toward which mankind seemed to be drifting. The Conference laid a solid foundation for future accomplishments on the broadest scale and outlined definite and concrete programs to promote peace, progress, and prosperity in the Western Hemisphere.

The twenty-one American republics, represented at Montevideo, affirmed their devotion to peace and their condemnation of resort to armed force as an instrument of accomplishing national aims. They proclaimed their belief in fair play, fair dealing, and mutual respect for the independence, the sovereignty, and the rights of nations as the indispensable bases of a civilized world-order under law. They took important steps toward making effective a concrete machinery for the maintenance of peace on the American Continent.

The Montevideo Conference laid greater emphasis than had ever been done before in inter-American relations on the imperative need of expanding economic relationships, among the American nations and among all nations, upon a sound and healthy basis of fair dealing and equal treatment. In the discussions and formal pronouncements of the Conference, there was fuller recognition than ever before of the indispensability of such economic relationships for the prosperity and social stability within nations, as well as for peaceful and orderly relations between nations. In its resolutions, the Conference urged vigorously a comprehensive program of rehabilitation and improvement of international economic and financial relations.

During the years that followed the Montevideo Conference, the influence of the work accomplished there bore fruit in the form of steadily and rapidly improving relations among the American nations. But at the same time, elsewhere in the world international relationships continued to deteriorate. Solemn treaty obligations were being increasingly brushed aside or breached. A gigantic program of rearmament was being rendered inevitable for the entire world by the announced determination on the part of a number of large countries to use armed force as an instrument of attaining their national aims and by their intensive activity in armament construction.

New world problems, affecting the vital interests of all American nations, were arising with startling rapidity. Accordingly, the representatives of our twenty-one republics met, two years ago at Buenos

Aires, in an Inter-American Conference for the Maintenance of Peace.

Building on the foundations laid down at Montevideo, the Buenos Aires Conference carried far forward the work of strengthening and perfecting the structure of peace in the Western Hemisphere. By the signing at that Conference of several far-reaching conventions, treaties, and protocols and by the adoption of a declaration of principles of inter-American solidarity and cooperation, powerful instruments of peace were forged at Buenos Aires. A system was thus created under which the American nations undertook to maintain peace among themselves and pledged themselves to consult with each other in the event that the peace of any one of them might be threatened— whether on the American continent or from outside.

The creation of this American system was the outstanding accomplishment of the Buenos Aires Conference. In addition, our nations reaffirmed their determination, already clearly and vigorously expressed at Montevideo, to work in the direction of improved economic relations and of closer cultural relationships as necessary foundations of order under law. Under this system and as a result of this determination, peace and friendly cooperation prevail today in the Western Hemisphere.

The treaty of peace between the Republics of Bolivia and Paraguay concluded last July is one of the most significant and encouraging developments in inter-American relations during recent years. By this peace the two countries gave an undeniable example to the faithless and the reckless who think that questions can be settled only by force or frightfulness.

Finally, may I add that it should be a matter of profound gratification to all of us that our nations can point to an impressive record of accomplishment during the past five years. To be sure, stock-taking alone, even as satisfying as this, is not sufficient. We are faced today with world problems and world conditions which are even more difficult and fraught with more danger for all of us than those with which we were confronted at Montevideo and at Buenos Aires. Our present Conference has before it tasks of utmost gravity and responsibility. But a clear visualization of what we have already accomplished and a realization, therefore, of what we are capable of accomplishing should aid us enormously in applying ourselves to the tasks which are before us.

II

There is no mystery about the reasons why developments in the Western Hemisphere during recent years have been so markedly different from those which have occurred in many other parts of the world. In large measure, the explanation lies in the fact that the

American nations have in common certain important and fundamental characteristics.

Each of our nations arose out of a revolution which had for its objective national independence, the assertion of human rights and of popular government. The men and women of the particular generation in each of our countries which achieved for its people independent nationhood staked their all on a passionate conviction that forms of government can be created under which human rights will be secure. They gladly fought for the vindication of their conviction. They bequeathed to us of today not only the forms of such government but also the spirit on the basis of which alone institutions of this character can endure.

Throughout its national existence, each of our nations has sought to perfect within its frontiers a system of representative government and of liberty for the individual. In this supreme endeavor, some of us have encountered greater internal difficulties than have others. Some of us have remained free from interference of outside forces; some have had to combat such forces. But in each and every one of our nations there has been no flagging in the determination of the people to preserve national independence and freedom for the individual.

Our nations have drawn into their populations men of many races, creeds, and languages. This fact has not operated as an element of weakness. The occasion for the adjustment of race to race and of creed to creed has been in large measure instrumental in teaching us how to develop adjustment of individual to individual and of group to group without which civilized society and democratic forms of social and political organization cannot function satisfactorily.

A spirit of tolerance, mutual respect, and understanding is as important in the relations of our nations with each other as in our internal relations. Happily, this spirit has been present, although it has not always developed uninterruptedly along an upward trend. Like all things human, it has had its fluctuations. Disagreements and controversies have arisen among us. But they have remarkably seldom been settled by the arbitrament of violent conflict, in the form of either military or other types of coercion.

International relations in the Western Hemisphere have not been free from the paralyzing and disruptive forces of narrow nationalism. But the operation of these forces has been paralleled—and, happily, increasingly overcome—by the growth of solidarity, of common concern for peace and progress in our relations with each other, by a strengthening of determination to adjust by pacific means alone whatever differences may arise among us.

It is not an accident that American nations have been peculiarly interested in the development of international law. Relationships such as those which have been steadily growing up among us are impossible unless rules of international conduct are carefully defined and unless such rules are fully accepted and become governing. That is the essence of civilized order in the international life of the world.

Historically speaking, the developments which I have briefly described have not been peculiar to the Western Hemisphere. For a century and a half, the progress of human enlightenment and human freedom continued throughout the world, overturning the bulwarks of tyranny and opening the way for the establishment of democratic institutions and the assertion of human rights. Nor has the earnest search for world-order under law been confined to any one portion of the globe. The developments which have taken place in the Western Hemisphere have been a part of a mighty stream of new ideas, new concepts, new attitudes of mind and spirit, which has coursed and ramified, with differing degrees of vigor and success, throughout the world. We have made important contributions to that stream, and have, in turn, been nourished by it.

III

Unfortunately, in recent years, powerful forces in some parts of the world have challenged the validity of the primary and basic principles upon the foundation of which we and the rest of mankind have been building the edifice of our social organization and of our international life. Whatever outer garments they may wear today, these forces are not new in the experience of mankind. Fundamentally, they are the same forces that had for centuries held men in bodily slavery and spiritual degradation and had impressed upon the relations among nations a state of anarchy, of reliance upon armed force, of complete absence of any kind of safety and security.

Mankind is tragically confronted once more by the alternatives of freedom or serfdom, of order or anarchy, of progress or retrogression, of civilization or barbarism.

Let there be no illusion. The alternatives are real and concrete not only in the portions of the world lying in the immediate vicinity of the countries in which these resurgent forces find their organized expression, but they loom threateningly throughout the world. Their ominous shadow falls athwart our own hemisphere.

In the face of this threat, it is our most important duty to ourselves and to humanity to maintain and preserve inviolate our own institutions and the beliefs on which they rest. It is imperative that the twenty-one Republics of the Western Hemisphere proclaim, unequivocally and unmistakably, their profound belief that only the type of national organization and of international relationships which we and the rest of mankind have been persistently and laboriously building up in the course of recent generations can make it possible for nations to advance materially and culturally, and for man to be free. It is imperative that our peoples rededicate themselves to the ideals which actuated the founders of our respective nations. It is imperative that our generation should find again that clarity of vision, that tenacity of purpose, and that heroic determination which led our forefathers to stake their all—to make every sacrifice, if need should be—for the assertion of human rights and the creation and maintenance of free popular government.

The characteristics which our nations have in common and which have already rendered possible in the Western Hemisphere a recent course of developments different from those which have occurred in many other parts of the world, are powerful factors in enabling us to perform this duty. Toward that end we must work unremittingly.

Each and all of us desire passionately to live at peace with every nation of the world. But there must not be a shadow of a doubt anywhere as to the determination of the American nations not to permit the invasion of this hemisphere by the armed forces of any power or any possible combination of powers. Each of our nations obviously must decide for itself what measures it should take in order to meet its share of our common interest and responsibility in this respect. So far as my country is concerned, let no one doubt for a moment that, so long as the possibility of armed challenge exists, the United States will maintain adequate defensive military, naval, and air establishments.

At the same time, we all know that armed force is not the only instrumentality by which nations can be conquered. Equally, the dissemination by nations of doctrines and the carrying on of other types of activity can be utilized for the purpose of undermining and destroying in other nations established institutions of government and basic social order. Such activities are based on the fallacious theories of class or racial superiority, or claims to national dominance, which are being revived again in some parts of the world. Those who fail to see their ominous signs all about us must have both their eyes and minds closed. There is no place in the Western Hemisphere for a revival of such doctrines and theories, which our nations, in common with an overwhelming majority of civilized mankind, rejected long ago. Each and all of us desire to maintain friendly relations with every nation of the world—resting upon the basis of mutual respect for national independence, upon non-interference in the internal affairs of others, upon fair dealing in every phase of international relationships. But there should not be a shadow of a doubt anywhere as to the determination of the American nations not to permit the invasion of this hemisphere from any quarter by activities contrary or inimical to this basis of relations among nations. Here again, with a full consciousness of our common interest and responsibility, each of our nations must decide for itself what measures it should take in order to meet these insidious dangers.

All this is of surpassing importance. And yet, adequate defense against actual or potential danger is not enough as the objective of responsible statesmanship. There is equal or even greater need for unstinted effort in the direction of removing the causes of danger and of opening the way for the constructive processes of human progress. The conditions which confront us require also a vigorous program of positive action.

In an important measure, such a program already exists. It is the fruitful result of inter-American conferences held in the past and of the influence exerted upon the life of our hemisphere by these periodic exchanges of views and by the agreements which we reach on vital problems. The conference in which we are again assembled now as representatives of the American nations offers a timely and precious opportunity for advancing and perfecting this indispensable program of assuring the solidarity, security, independence, prosperity, and progress of the Americas and of making our individual and joint contribution to the peace and well-being of the world.

IV

Our Conference must carry forward the work of building an enduring structure of peace. It is within the power of the American nations to furnish a conclusive demonstration that peace, based on justice, law, and cooperative effort, is unquestionably feasible. To that end, we must examine anew the existing instruments of peace, by which we are all bound to a system of pacific settlement, and give our best thought to every possible method of perfecting further the inter-American machinery of peace.

Our Conference must devote sincere effort to discovering the means of strengthening the foundations of international law. At a time when the structure of world-order under law is being undermined and impaired in many parts of the globe, the very highest responsibility rests upon us to keep alive those fundamental principles of relations among nations upon which alone such order can be maintained. The right of each nation to manage its own affairs free from outside interference; recognition of the sovereignty and equality of states irrespective of size and strength; respect for the pledged word and the sanctity of treaty obligations—these and numerous other basic principles must be the governing rules of international conduct if peace rather than anarchy is to prevail, and civilization is to advance.

Our Conference must extend and make more secure the bases of sound and healthy economic relations among nations. Excessive trade barriers and other obstacles to the flow of mutually profitable international commerce still weigh heavily upon the economic life of the world—on our continent, as well as elsewhere. Nations cannot prosper and provide for their populations a full measure of stable employment and a rising standard of living if international trade is destroyed by suicidal attempts at autarchy or is impaired by being forced into the artificial channels of narrow bilateralism or exclusive regionalism. And just as production cannot be expanded and improved by a return to hand operation, so trade cannot be fostered by a reversion to the primitive forms of physical barter. Only through a liberalization of trade relations, through a reduction of excessive trade barriers, through a firm establishment of equality of commercial treatment, can the exchange of goods among nations play its vital and indispensable role of enhancing the prosperity and stability of national economics.

The removal of excessive trade barriers and the restoration of the trade process to a basis of equality of commercial treatment and commercial opportunity is today a task of the utmost importance. Unless the nations of the world can achieve this task, the prospect for economic and social improvement and stability within nations, and for peace and friendly cooperation among nations, must remain dark indeed. Our Conference should examine every feasible method of aiding in the successful performance of this task—among ourselves, as well as between each of us and the rest of the world. We seek to restore mutually profitable trade to the fullest practical extent, both among the American nations and among all the nations of the world.

Our Conference must carry forward the work of providing wider and stronger foundations for international cultural relations and better understanding among nations—again, among ourselves, as well as between each of us and the rest of the world. This work of moral disarmament, already far advanced on the American Continent, is indispensable for the creation and maintenance of a civilized world-order under law. It is an important vehicle for strengthening and developing those innumerable international relationships in every phase of human activity through which the lives of nations have already been vastly enriched.

The American nations, with the cooperation of some of the nations of the other hemisphere, are faithfully carrying forward the program of principles underlying world-order, peace, and economic restoration, which I have fully summarized. The success of this program is indispensable to the welfare and progress and civilization of the human race. For each and every nation the establishment of these principles throughout the world would bring immense benefit, as any alternative policy resting on force must bring each and every one disaster. Each nation has a sincere standing invitation to join in approval and support of this program of principles. It would be an unspeakable calamity if any nation at this crucial and critical time in the affairs of men should further pursue the opposing course of force and military aggression. Here is presented the greatest single issue confronting all peaceful nations. We shall not lose sight of it for a moment as we grapple with the vital questions peculiar to this hemisphere.

The world's greatest need today is that there be created and maintained conditions which will give to nations and to individuals peace of mind and of spirit. Toward producing those conditions, we must strive with all our strength in every field—political, social, economic, and moral. Only as favorable conditions develop in all these fields, will the way be open for a reversal of the present-day trend in military armaments, which impose so crushing a burden upon the lives of nations and individuals and open before mankind the horrible vista of a marvelous civilization crashing into ruin under the impact of a period of all-destroying warfare.

We of the Americas are fortunate beyond words in being so situated that we can make our example and our influence a potent factor in promotion of conditions in which there may be peace with justice and with security. Nor do we stand alone. There are in other parts of the world powerful forces, actual or latent, working toward the same end.

We must not bring the labors of this Conference to a conclusion without providing a renewed basis of hope and a renewed determination—not only for our own nations, but for all other nations or groups within nations, which, at times against great odds and in the face of heartbreaking difficulties, are working for a better world.

PAN AMERICAN DAY ADDRESS by President Franklin D. Roosevelt, before the Governing Board of the Pan American Union, at Washington, April 15, 1940
Department of State Bulletin, Vol. II, No. 43, p. 403

IN THE YEAR 1890, on April fourteenth, and without fanfare of trumpets, an inter-American conference unanimously adopted a resolution providing that "there shall be formed by the countries represented in this Conference an association under the title of the International Union of American Republics."

The tasks of the new organization were simple. They were to collect and distribute commercial information, to publish a bulletin, to provide trade information, and to carry forward the work of promoting sound business relations.

But behind these prosaic words there was the driving force of a great American conception which had been gathering headway for 60 years.

The ideal originated in the mind of Simon Bolívar; and a kindly history has preserved for us the draft he had written in 1825, sketching his purpose and objective.

His aim was peace for the Americas. His hope was that the American example might eventually give peace to the entire world. His plan was stated in a single, brilliant sentence: "The New World takes shape in the form of independent nations, all joined by a common law which would control their foreign relations and would offer them the stabilizing force of a general and permanent Congress." The result, as you know, was the calling of the Conference of Panamá in 1826.

At that time, it took bold minds even to dream of universal peace. And yet, the Congress of Panamá gave clear expression to precisely that aspiration. Before that time, there had been but two systems of peace known to the world. One of them had been the peace of universal conquest, which Rome had achieved and lost and which Napoleon had vainly endeavored to imitate. The other was the dangerous and temporary peace of balance of power—which even in 1826 was plainly no permanent solution.

At the Congress of Panamá, the American nations proclaimed the ideal of a Cooperative Peace: the peace of free equals, freely agreeing to settle whatever differences might arise among them by none but pacific means—determined to cooperate with each other for the greater good of all.

Never before had any group of nations been asked to renounce the splendors of indefinite conquest and to achieve their true grandeur by peaceful cooperation. Yet that was precisely what the Americas were considering.

The dream of Bolívar was not realized at the Congress of Panamá. But it did remain a hope, an inspiration. To the writers, the poets, the dreamers, who kept the ideal of Cooperative Peace alive through the imperialist nineteenth century we owe an everlasting debt of gratitude.

In spite of several attempts to bring to a realization the ideal of inter-American unity, more than 6 decades went by before the seed began to grow. I am proud of the fact that on that occasion the initiative came from the United States. In 1888, President Cleveland approved an act of Congress authorizing him to call a conference of the American countries in order that there might be worked out a peaceful plan for the settling of disagreements and disputes and a means of encouraging such reciprocal relations as would benefit all.

It was that inter-American conference, 50 years ago, that set up the International Union of the American Republics, the anniversary of which we are observing today. In opening the conference, James G. Blaine expressed its high purpose in the following words: "We believe that a spirit of justice, of common and equal interest between the American states, will leave no room for an artificial balance of power like unto that which has led to wars abroad and drenched Europe in blood."

Fifty years of unremitting effort have brought our republics far along the road that leads to this goal. Today, as never before, our nations have reason to appreciate the fruits of that progress. For today we are again face to face with the old problem.

Universal and stable peace remains a dream. War, more horrible and destructive than ever, has laid its blighting hand on many parts of the earth. Peace among our American nations remains secure because of the instruments we have succeeded in creating. They embody, in great measure at least, the principles upon which, I believe, enduring peace must be based throughout the world.

Peace reigns today in the Western Hemisphere because our nations have liberated themselves from fear. No nation is truly at peace if it lives under the shadow of coercion or invasion. By the simple process of agreeing that each nation shall respect the integrity and independence of the others, the New World has freed itself of the greatest and simplest cause of war. Self-restraint and the acceptance of the equal rights of our neighbors as an act of effective will has given us the peace we have had and will preserve that peace so long as we abide by this ultimate moral law.

Peace reigns among us today because we have agreed, as neighbors should, to mind our own businesses. We have renounced, each and all of us, any right to intervene in each other's domestic affairs, recognizing that free and independent nations must shape their own destinies and find their own ways of life.

Peace reigns among us today because we have resolved to settle any dispute that should arise among us by friendly negotiation in accordance with justice and equity, rather than by force. We have created effective machinery for this purpose and we have demonstrated our willingness to have full recourse to that method.

Peace reigns among us because we have recognized the principle that only through vigorous and mutually beneficial international economic relations can each of us have adequate access to materials and opportunities necessary to a rising level of economic well-being for our peoples. In every practicable way we are seeking to bring this vital principle to its realization.

We of this hemisphere have no need to seek a new international order; we have already found it. This was not won by hysterical outcries or violent movements of troops. We did not stamp out nations, capture governments, or uproot innocent people from the homes they had built. We did not invent absurd doctrines of race supremacy or claim dictatorship through universal revolution.

The inter-American order was not built by hatred and terror. It has been paved by the endless and effective work of men of good will. We have built a foundation for the lives of hundreds of millions. We have unified these lives by a common devotion to a moral order.

The Coöperative Peace in the Western Hemisphere was not created by wishing; and it will require more than words to maintain it. In this association of nations, whoever touches any one of us touches all of us. We have only asked that the world go with us in the path of peace. But we shall be able to keep that way open only if we are prepared to meet force with force if challenge is ever made.

Today we can have no illusions. Old dreams of universal empire are again rampant. We hear of races which claim the right of mastery. We learn of groups which insist they have the right to impose their way of life on other nations. We encounter economic compulsions shrewdly devised to force great areas into political spheres of influence.

All of this is not of mere academic interest. We know that what happens in the Old World directly and powerfully affects the peace and well-being of the New. It was for this very reason that we have adopted procedures that enable us to meet any eventuality. At Buenos Aires we agreed that we would consult should our peace be threatened. At Lima we agreed to stand together to defend and maintain the absolute integrity of every American nation from any attack, direct or indirect, from beyond the seas. At Panamá we worked out ways and means for keeping war away from this hemisphere. I pray God that we shall not have to do more than that; but should it be necessary, I am convinced that we should be wholly successful. The inner strength of a group of free people is irresistible when they are prepared to act.

In my conception, the whole world now is struggling to find the basis of its life in coming centuries.

I affirm that that life must be based on positive values.

The value of love will always be stronger than the value of hate, since any nation or group of nations which employs hatred eventually is torn to pieces by hatred within itself.

The value of a belief in humanity and justice is always stronger than the value of belief in force, because force at last turns inward, and if that occurs each man or group of men is finally compelled to measure his strength against his own brother.

The value of truth and sincerity is always stronger than the value of lies and cynicism. No process has yet been invented which can permanently separate men from their hearts and consciences or can prevent them from seeing the results of their ideas as time rolls by. You cannot make men believe that a way of life is good when it spreads poverty, misery, disease, and death. Men cannot be everlastingly loyal unless they are free.

We acclaim today the symbol of 50 years of the American way. We are determined to continue on that way in friendship. We are determined that our mutual relations be built upon honor and good faith. We are determined to live in peace and to make that peace secure. We are determined to follow the path of free peoples to a civilization worthy of free men.

ADDRESS by Cordell Hull, Secretary of State, at the Second Meeting of the Ministers of Foreign Affairs of the American Republics, at Habana, July 22, 1940

Second Meeting of the Ministers of Foreign Affairs of the American Republics, Report of the Secretary of State, p. 46

MR. CHAIRMAN, FELLOW REPRESENTATIVES OF THE AMERICAN RE-PUBLICS:

Permit me, first of all, to express my deep personal pleasure in setting foot once more on the soil of the great nation whose guests we are at this time. Forty years have passed since my first visit to these shores, when I had the honor to serve with my regiment in the cause of Cuba's liberation. I doubly welcome the present opportunity to re-visit this country—both because of the personal gratification which it affords me and because of the vital importance of the purpose which has brought us together in this beautiful city of Habana.

We are here as representatives of the 21 free and independent American republics. We meet when world conditions are perhaps graver than they have ever been before. Our purpose is to devise concrete measures by which a number of pressing problems may be met. Our objective is to safeguard the independence, the peace, and the well-being of the American republics.

For nearly a year now, a new major war has raged, with increasing fury, over important areas of the earth. It came as a culmination of a process of deterioration of international conduct and international morality, extending over a period of years, during which forces of ruthless conquest were gathering strength in several parts of the world.

These forces, now at work in the world, shrink from no means of attaining their ends. In their contempt for all moral and ethical values, they are bent on uprooting the very foundations of orderly relations among nations and on subverting, undermining, and destroying existing social and political institutions within nations. They have already left in their wake formerly sovereign nations with their independence trampled into dust and millions of proud men and women with their liberties destroyed.

Our American republics had no part in kindling the tragic conflagration which has thus been sweeping across the world. On the contrary, severally and jointly, we did everything in our power to stay its outburst. Once the conflict had begun, we did everything we could to limit its spreading. But it has been increasingly clear that in the vast tragedy which has befallen large portions of the earth there are dangers to the American nations as well, which it would be suicidal not to recognize in time and not to prepare to meet fully and decisively.

It has been increasingly clear that our nations must not bind themselves into fatal complacency—as so many nations have done to their mortal sorrow—regarding the possibility of attack against them from without or of externally directed attempts from within to undermine their national strength and to subvert their cherished social and political institutions, or both. Too many nations have only recently paid a tragic price for confidently placing reliance for their safety and security solely upon a clearly expressed desire to remain at peace, upon unequivocally proclaimed neutrality, upon scrupulous avoidance of provocation. Conquerors, invaders, and destroyers ignore or brush aside reasons such as these.

Looming ominously on our horizon is the danger that attempts may be made to employ against our nations, too, the same means of subordinating their destinies to control and dictation from abroad that have already been notoriously employed elsewhere against numerous other countries. We must recognize the serious possibility that no effort or method may be spared to achieve, with respect to some of us, economic domination and political penetration, and to sow, among our nations, the seeds of suspicion, dissension, and discord—the frequent prelude to even more menacing action.

Lest our nations, too, suffer the fate that has already befallen so many other peace-loving and peace-seeking nations, wisdom and prudence require that we have in our hands adequate means of defense. To that end, in the face of common danger, our nations are already working together, in accordance with their firmly established practice of free consultation among equals and of voluntary cooperation with regard to problems which are of common concern to all of us. It is to examine such of these problems as are immediately pressing and to seek for them most effective solutions that the representatives of the 21 American republics have come together at this time.

I

I should like to consider first the situation which confronts us in the economic sphere.

The war now in progress has brought with it a disruption in the channels of international commerce and a curtailment of foreign markets for the products of the Western Hemisphere. This has meant to many American nations a diminution of foreign-exchange resources and a loss of purchasing power sufficiently serious to place severe strains on their national economies. In some cases, stagnant surpluses of commodities, the exportation of which is essential to the economic life of the countries concerned, have accumulated and continue to accumulate. Their existence is a matter of present and future concern to farmers, workers, businessmen, and governments throughout the continental area.

We must assume that these difficulties will continue, certainly as long as the war exists. We must anticipate that these problems, and possibly others, will continue for some time after the war ends.

If the standards of living of the American peoples are to be maintained at levels already achieved, and particularly if they are to be raised in accordance with the legitimate aspirations of these peoples, production and distribution must expand, not only in this hemisphere but throughout the world. This same condition is essential to the well-being of all other areas. For no nation or group of nations can hope to become or to remain prosperous when growing poverty stalks the rest of the earth.

Under existing conditions, the problem is singularly pressing. Though war now is in progress, we must contemplate its eventual end. At that time, perhaps 80 millions of people in Europe, and many millions in other parts of the world, who have been entirely engaged in war work, must find a place for themselves in the economics of peace. At the same time, it is to be assumed that, once the pressures of war are ended, there will be a general demand that reasonable conditions of life may be restored. To effect this transition, and to supply the world with what it then needs, will necessitate a great increase in production, distribution, and exchange of goods. Failure to achieve this can only mean that the tragedy of war would be followed by the still greater horror of disintegration in great areas.

It is plain that international commerce is indispensable if economic rehabilitation is to be achieved. It is also plain that the only available means of doing this is to resume, as soon as circumstances permit, the normal currents of world trade. I have no doubt that the American republics are ready and indeed anxious to do their part in bringing this about; though the extent to which we can thus play our part must depend materially on the economic methods and policies pursued by other countries.

We are confronted with two opposite trading methods. Open trade, freed as rapidly as may be practicable from the obstruction and regimentation of excessive restrictions, can accomplish the necessary task. Prosperity for the American republics or for any part of the world cannot be achieved—even the necessities of the war-torn areas of the earth cannot be met—by regimented or restricted trade, especially directed under a policy of national or regional autarchy. We recognize the need for a transition period; but we are convinced that there can be only one satisfactory permanent policy.

We have long known from experience that international trade inevitably declines in volume and usefulness when it is conducted on a basis of exclusive bilateralism, or is pressed to unfair advantage, or is used to attempt economic domination. Eventually, such methods destroy the trade and the trader alike. In the present situation, they are totally unable to provide that volume and distribution of goods which alone can save great areas from intense distress. Only where equal treatment, fair practices, non-discrimination, and peaceful motives lie beneath trade, can it develop to the degree needed to rehabilitate a shattered world and to provide a foundation for further economic progress.

Today, in spite of what has occurred in other parts of the world, the American nations continue to adhere to liberal trade principles and are applying them in their relations with each other as fully as the present state of affairs permits. They should be prepared to resume the conduct of trade with the entire world on this basis as rapidly as other nations are willing to do likewise.

In the meantime, the American nations must and should do everything in their power to strengthen their own economic position, to improve further the trade and other economic relations between and among themselves, and to devise and apply appropriate means of effective action to cope with the difficulties, disadvantages, and dangers of the present disturbed and dislocated world conditions. To accomplish these purposes, the nations of the Western Hemisphere should undertake the fullest measure of economic cooperation, so designed and so conducted as to serve the best interests of each nation and to bring injury to none.

Progress has already been made toward the forging of new tools to carry out certain phases of economic cooperation on an inter-American basis. The Inter-American Financial and Economic Advisory Committee, which was established last November pursuant to a resolution of the Panamá Meeting, has proven itself to be an efficient body for considering and working out such mechanisms. It has recently created the Inter-American Development Commission to carry out the work of planning and promoting the development of new productive facilities in the American republics. In addition, it prepared the framework for the establishment of an Inter-American Bank to foster cooperation in the spheres of long-term development and of money and foreign exchange. The Government of the United States is taking steps to implement the inter-American bank convention and urges that the governments of the other American republics give their cooperation so that this important institution may be placed in operation as rapidly as possible.

Useful as these organizations can be in the long run, there remains the immediately pressing situation confronting the American republics as a result of the curtailment and changed character of important foreign markets. Fully realizing that under present disturbed conditions no nation can expect to maintain a normal economic situation, and in order to meet the emergencies which confront their nations, the governments of the American republics, it is believed, should give consideration to the following program of immediate cooperative action:

1. Strengthening and expansion of the activities of the Inter-American Financial and Economic Advisory Committee as an instrument for continuing consultation with respect to trade matters, including especially the situation immediately confronting the American republics as a result of the curtailment and changed character of important foreign markets.

2. Creation of facilities for the temporary handling and orderly marketing of accumulated surpluses of those commodities which are

of primary importance to the maintenance of the economic life of the American republics, whenever such action becomes necessary.

3. Development of commodity agreements with a view to assuring equitable terms of trade for both producers and consumers of the commodities concerned.

4. Consideration of methods for improving the standard of living of the peoples of the Americas, including public-health measures, nutrition studies, and suitable organizations for the relief distribution of some part of any surplus commodities.

The Government of the United States of America has already utilized its existing agencies to enter into mutually advantageous cooperative arrangements with a number of American republics in connection with programs for the development of their national economies and by way of assistance to their central banks in monetary and foreign-exchange matters.

It is now taking steps which will make possible the extension of both the volume and character of the operations of such agencies. When these steps have been completed, the Government of the United States of America will be in a position to expand its cooperative efforts with other American nations in the fields of long-term development and of monetary and exchange matters.

It will also be able to participate in immediate joint action with other nations of this hemisphere to meet pressing trade situations which may arise before the program outlined has come into operation.

Finally, it will be enabled to enter effectively into the cooperative program as it proceeds, assisting in the temporary handling and orderly marketing of the important commodities of the hemisphere; implementing, on its part, the commodity agreements which are developed; and carrying out other operations involving such export products.

While the proposed measures are being developed, consideration should be given to the desirability of a broader system of inter-American cooperative organization in trade matters to complement inter-American cooperative organizations in the field of long-term economic development and of money and foreign exchange.

By helping each other, by carrying out with vigor, determination, and loyalty whatever decisions are reached, the American nations can build a system of economic defense that will enable each of them to safeguard itself from the dangers of economic subordination from abroad and of economic distress at home. It is no part of our thought to obstruct in any way logical and natural trade with Europe or with any other portion of the world, but rather to promote such trade with nations willing to meet us, in good faith, in a spirit of friendly and peaceful purpose, and on a plane of frank and fair dealing. Against any other kind of dealing, we naturally will protect ourselves.

II

The solution of our economic problems alone is not enough to preserve the peace and security of this hemisphere. There exist also other problems, which are of an altogether different character but the solution of which is of no less importance to our freedom and independence.

I refer to the threat to our security arising from activities directed from without the hemisphere but which operate within our respective borders. A new and evil technique has been invented which seeks by devious methods to corrupt the body politic in order to subject it to alien purposes. With cynical effrontery, sanctuary within the generous citadels of free speech and freedom of assembly is demanded by agents whose masters would obliterate those institutions and foment instead dissension, prejudice, fear, and hatred.

Make no mistake concerning the purposes of this sinister campaign. It is an attempt to acquire domination of the American republics by foreign governments in their own interest. Already we have seen the tragic results abroad when government structures have been undermined and the fabric of established institutions riddled by the termites of alien propaganda.

We long ago recognized the sources and extent of this infection and have already taken some steps to eradicate it. At Lima we declared that it was incompatible with the sovereignty of any American republic that persons or groups within our countries should be controlled by any outside government for its own purposes. It is now urgently incumbent upon us to take decisive remedial action to the end that the independence and political integrity of each of the American republics may be fully safeguarded.

To this no friendly government can legitimately object. The inter-American system carries no implication of aggression and no threat to any nation. It is based solely on a policy of self-defense, designed to preserve the independence and the integrity of each of the American nations. It implies no hegemony on the part of any member of the inter-American group; but it equally rejects the thesis of hegemony by anyone else. It resembles in no way regional policies, recently pursued in other parts of the world, which pretend to invoke our inter-American system as precedent. The difference is that our sole purpose is self-defense, while these other policies seem instead to be pretexts for conquest by the sword, for military occupation, and for complete economic and political domination of other free and independent peoples.

There are other pressing political problems arising out of the vast changes which have taken place on the Continent of Europe. The principles on which we act with respect to these problems have been forged by the American republics through years of discussion and practice. They are applied entirely without discrimination, solely for the purpose of assuring that the security of the American Hemisphere shall not be impaired by the repercussions of warfare elsewhere.

Specifically, there is before us the problem of the status of European possessions in this hemisphere. These geographic regions have not heretofore constituted a menace to the peace of the Americas; their administrations were established, for the most part, many generations ago and, in our time, have acted as congenial neighbors. We have no desire to absorb these possessions or to extend our sovereignty over them, or to include them in any form of sphere of influence.

We could not, however, permit these regions to become a subject of barter in the settlement of European differences, or a battleground for the adjustment of such differences. Either situation could only be regarded as a threat to the peace and safety of this hemisphere, as would any indication that they might be used to promote systems alien to the inter-American system. Any effort, therefore, to modify the existing status of these areas—whether by cession, by transfer, or by any impairment whatsoever in the control heretofore exercised— would be of profound and immediate concern to all the American republics.

It is accordingly essential that we consider a joint approach to this common problem. We must be in a position to move rapidly and without hesitation.

It has been suggested that our action take the form of the establishment of a collective trusteeship, to be exercised in the name of all of the American republics. The Government of the United States endorses this suggestion and is prepared to cooperate, should occasion arise, in its execution.

The establishment of a collective trusteeship for any region must not carry with it any thought of the creation of a special interest by any American republic. The purpose of a collective trusteeship must be to further the interests and security of all the American nations, as well as the interest of the region in question. Moreover, as soon as conditions permit, the region should be restored to its original sovereign or be declared independent when able to establish and maintain stable self-government.

IV

Seldom has a meeting of friendly nations opened in an atmosphere of more wide-spread misconception and more flagrant misrepresentation as to its aims and purposes than have emanated in recent weeks, from responsible and irresponsible quarters, in connection with this meeting.

We have met to consult together regarding our own pressing problems. We covet nothing anywhere in the world. We are free from the spirit of enmity toward any nation. But we cannot fail to be acutely conscious of the dangers which confront us as a result of present world conditions and against which we are taking and intend to take fully adequate measures of defense.

National life itself today imposes, as an absolute obligation, the will to national defense, should national institutions or integrity ever be threatened. Achievement of this requires that we call out anew the endless energy, the complete spirit of sacrifice, the iron will, which characterized the pioneers, the liberators, and the defenders, to whom we owe our present freedom. Let no man say that in the world of today any nation not willing to defend itself is safe. The fortitude and resolution of our forefathers won for us our free institutions. We proudly have inherited them, and proudly are prepared to maintain them.

At the same time, while meeting the imperative needs of emergency conditions, we must—and, I am certain, we will—continue our abiding faith that what is happening today is but a temporary interruption in the progress of civilization. Mankind can advance only when human freedom is secure; when the right of self-government is safeguarded; when all nations recognize each other's right to conduct its internal affairs free from outside interference; when there exist among nations respect for the pledged word, determination to abstain from the use of armed force in pursuit of policy, and willingness to settle controversies by none but peaceful means; when international economic relations are based upon mutual benefit, equality of treatment, and fair dealing.

In 1937, in an attempt to prevent the impending catastrophe of a new war, the Government of the United States addressed a communication to all nations, reciting these basic principles of orderly international relations under the rule of law as the foundation of its foreign policy and inviting comment thereon. More than fifty nations expressed on that occasion their belief in the validity of these principles. At Montevideo, at Buenos Aires, at Lima, at Panamá, the 21 American republics proclaimed their acceptance.

I am confident that, sooner or later, the entire world must return to a system of international relations based on those principles. They are the only possible foundation stones of an organized society assured of enduring peace and of sustained prosperity. The price of their abandonment is the chaos of international anarchy and the inexorable impoverishment of nations and individuals, such as we witness today in Europe and in Asia.

In a system of cooperative peace such as we envisage there is no exclusion. Its underlying principles are universal in their applicability; they can be accepted by all nations to the benefit of each and all; they must be accepted by all, if the light of modern civilization is not to be extinguished. Any nation which in good faith accepts and practices them automatically shares in the vast benefits they confer.

At this time, when these principles and these ideals are being widely challenged, when institutions based on them are being crushed by force over large areas of the world, it is doubly essential that our nations keep them alive and re-dedicate themselves to the cause of their preservation.

It is in this spirit, and in this spirit alone, that the Government which I have the honor to represent approaches the tasks that are before our present meeting—in complete confidence that in this vital respect all the American nations stand today as united as ever.

RADIO ADDRESS by President Franklin D. Roosevelt, to the Western Hemisphere, October 12, 1940
Department of State Bulletin, Vol. III, No. 68, p. 291

MY FRIENDS OF THE AMERICAS:

It is no mere coincidence that this radio broadcast to the entire Western Hemisphere—North America, Central America and South America—should take place on the anniversary of Christopher Columbus' discovery of the New World. No day could be more appropriate than this day on which we celebrate the exploits of the bold discoverer.

Today, all of us Americans of North and Central and South America join with our fellow citizens of Italian descent to do honor to the name of Columbus.

Many and numerous have been the groups of Italians who have come in welcome waves of immigration to this hemisphere. They have been an essential element in the civilization and make-up of all of the 21 republics. During these centuries Italian names have been high in the list of statesmen in the United States and in the other republics—and in addition, those who have helped to create the scientific, commercial, professional, and artistic life of the New World.

The Americas have excelled in the adventure of many races living together in harmony. In the wake of the discoverers came the first settlers, the first refugees from Europe. They came to plough new fields, build new homes, establish a new society in a new world. Later, they fought for liberty. Men and women of courage, of enterprise, of vision, they knew what they were fighting for; they gained it— and thereby "gave hope to all the world for all future time."

They formed, here in the Western Hemisphere, a new human reservoir, and into it has poured the blood, the culture, the traditions of all the races and peoples of the earth. To the Americas they came— the "masses yearning to be free"—"the multitudes brought hither out of many kindreds and tongues," cherishing common aspirations, not for economic betterment alone, but for the personal freedoms and liberties which had been denied to them in the Old World.

They came not to conquer one another but to live with one another. They proudly carried with them their inheritance of culture, but they cheerfully left behind the burden of prejudice and hatred.

In this New World were transplanted the great cultures of Spain and Portugal. In our own day the fact is that a great part of the Spanish and Portuguese culture of the entire world now comes from the Americas.

It is natural that all American citizens from the many nations of the Old World should kindly remember the lands where their ancestors lived and the great attributes of the old civilization in those lands. But in every single one of the American republics, the first and final allegiance and loyalty of these citizens, almost without exception, is to the republic in which they live and move and have their being.

For when our forefathers came to these shores, they came with a determination to stay and to become citizens of the New World. As it established its independence, they wanted to become citizens of America—not an Anglo-Saxon America, nor an Italian, nor a German, nor a Spanish, nor a Portuguese—but just citizens of an independent nation of America.

Here, we do not have any dual citizenship. Here, the descendants of the very same races who had always been forced to fear or hate each other in lands across the ocean have learned to live in peace and in friendship.

No one group or race in the New World has any desire to subjugate the others. No one nation in this hemisphere has any desire to dominate the others. In the Western Hemisphere no nation is considered a second-class nation. And that is something worth remembering.

We know that attempts have been made—we know that they will continue to be made—to divide these groups within a nation and to divide these nations among themselves.

There are those in the Old World who persist in believing that here in this new hemisphere the Americas can be torn by the hatreds and fears which have drenched the battlegrounds of Europe for so many centuries. Americans as individuals, American republics as nations, remain on guard against those who seek to break up our unity by preaching ancient race hatreds, by working on old fears, or by holding out glittering promises which they know to be false.

"Divide and conquer" has been the battle-cry of the totalitarian powers in their war against the democracies. It has succeeded on the continent of Europe for the moment. On our continents it will fail.

We are determined to use our energies and our resources to counteract and repel the foreign plots and propaganda—the whole technique of underground warfare originating in Europe and now clearly directed against all the republics on this side of the ocean.

That propaganda repeats and repeats that democracy is a decadent form of government. They tell us that our old democratic ideal, our old traditions of civil liberties, are things of the past.

We reject this thought. We say that *we are* the future. We say that the direction in which they would lead us is backward, not forward—backward to the bondage of the Pharaohs, backward to the slavery of the Middle Ages.

The command of the democratic faith has been ever onward and upward. Never have free men been satisfied with the mere maintenance of any *status quo,* however comfortable or secure it may have seemed at the moment.

We have always held to the hope, the belief, the conviction that there is a better life, a better world, beyond the horizon.

That fire of freedom was in the eyes of Washington, and Bolívar, and San Martín, and Artigas, and Juárez, and Bernardo O'Higgins, and all the brave, rugged, ragged men who followed them in the wars of independence.

That fire burns now in the eyes of those who are fighting for freedom in lands across the sea.

On this side of the ocean there is no desire, there will be no effort, on the part of any one race, or people, or nation, to control any other. The only encirclement sought is the encircling bond of good old-fashioned neighborly friendship. So bound together, we are able to withstand any attack from the east or from the west. Together we are able to ward off any infiltration of alien political and economic ideas which would destroy our freedom and democracy.

When we speak of defending this Western Hemisphere, we are speaking not only of the territory of North, Central, and South America and the immediately adjacent islands. We include the right to the peaceful use of the Atlantic and Pacific Oceans. That has been our traditional policy.

It is a fact, for example, that as far back as 1798 the United States found that its peaceful trade and commerce with other parts of the Americas were threatened by armed privateers sent to the West Indies by nations then at war in Europe. Because of this threat to peace in this hemisphere of ours, the United States Ships *Constellation, Constitution, United States,* and many others were fitted out; and they drove the armed vessels of Europe out of the waters to the south of us, and made commerce between the Americas once more peaceable and possible.

We of the Americas still consider that this defense of these oceans of the Western Hemisphere against acts of aggression is the first factor in the defense and protection of our own territorial integrity. We reaffirm that policy, lest there be any doubt of our intention to maintain it.

There are some in every single one of the 21 American republics who suggest that the course the Americas are following is slowly drawing one or all of us into war with some nation or nations beyond the seas.

The clear facts have been stated over and over again. This country wants no war with any nation. This hemisphere wants no war with any nation. The American republics are determined to work in unity for peace, just as we work in unity to defend ourselves from attack.

For many long years every ounce of energy I have had has been devoted to keeping this nation and the other republics at peace with the rest of the world. That is what continues uppermost in my mind today—the objective for which I hope and work and pray.

We arm to defend ourselves. The strongest reason for that is that it is the strongest guarantee for peace.

The United States of America is mustering its men and resources, arming not only to defend itself, but, in cooperation with the other American republics, to help defend the whole hemisphere.

We are building a total defense on land and sea and in the air, sufficient to repel total attack from any part of the world. Forewarned by the deliberate attacks of the dictators upon free peoples, the United States, for the first time in its history, has undertaken the mustering of its men in peacetime. Unprecedented dangers have caused the United States to undertake the building of a navy and an air force sufficient to defend all the coasts of the Americas from any combination of hostile powers.

We have asked for, and we have received, the fullest cooperation and assistance of industry and labor. All of us are speeding the preparation of adequate defense.

And we are keeping the nations of this hemisphere fully advised of our defense preparations. We have welcomed the military missions from neighboring republics; and in turn our own military experts have been welcomed by them. We intend to encourage this frank interchange of information and plans.

We shall be all for one and one for all.

This idea of a defense strong enough and wide enough to cover this half of the world had its beginnings when the Government of the United States announced its policy with respect to South America. It was the policy of the good neighbor, the neighbor who knew how to mind his own business, but was always willing to lend a friendly hand to a friendly nation which sought it, the neighbor who was willing to discuss in all friendship the problems which will always arise between neighbors.

From the day on which that policy was announced, the American republics have consulted with each other; they have peacefully settled their old problems and disputes; they have grown closer and closer to each other; until at last in 1938 at Lima, their unity and friendship were sealed.

There was then adopted a declaration that the New World proposed to maintain collectively the freedom upon which its strength had been built. It was the culmination of the good-neighbor policy, the proof of what was said by that famous Argentinian of Italian birth, Alberdi—"The Americas are a great political system: the parts draw life from the whole; and the whole draws life from its parts."

Through the acquisition of eight naval bases in territories of the British Empire lying within the sphere of the New World, from Newfoundland to Guiana, we have increased the immediate effectiveness of the great Navy which we now have and of the greater Navy we have under construction. These bases were acquired by the United States; but not for the protection of the United States alone. They were acquired for the protection of the whole Western Hemisphere.

The unity of the American republics was proven to the world when these naval bases were promptly opened by the United States to the other republics for cooperative use. In that act was typified the good-neighbor conception of hemispheric defense through cooperation by and for all of us.

American radio stations will play their part in the new unity which has been built so solidly between the American nations during the past eight years. They must be effective instruments for the honest exchange and communication of ideas. They must never be used as stations in other lands are used, to send out on the same day one false story to one country, and a different false story to another.

The core of our defense is the faith we have in the institutions we defend. The Americas will not be scared or threatened into the ways the dictators want us to follow.

No combination of dictator countries of Europe and Asia will halt us in the path we see ahead for ourselves and for democracy.

No combination of dictator countries of Europe and Asia will stop the help we are giving to almost the last free people fighting to hold them at bay.

Our course is clear. Our decision is made. We will continue to pile up our defense and our armaments. We will continue to help those who resist aggression, and who now hold the aggressors far from our shores. Let no American in any part of the Americas question the possibility of danger from overseas. Why should we accept assurances that we are immune? History records that not long ago those same assurances were given to the people of Holland and Belgium and Norway.

It can no longer be disputed that forces of evil which are bent on conquest of the world will destroy whomever and whenever they can destroy. We have learned the lessons of recent years. We know now that if we seek to appease them by withholding aid from those who stand in their way, we only hasten the day of their attack upon us.

The people of the United States, the people of all the Americas, reject the doctrine of appeasement. They recognize it for what it is— a major weapon of the aggressor nations.

I speak bluntly. I speak the love the American people have for freedom and liberty and decency and humanity.

That is why we arm. Because, I repeat, this nation wants to keep war away from these two continents. Because we all of us are determined to do everything possible to maintain peace on this hemisphere. Because great strength of arms is the practical way of fulfilling our hopes for peace and for staying out of this war or any other war.

Because we are determined to muster all our strength so that we may remain free.

The men and women of Britain have shown how free people defend what they know to be right. Their heroic defense will be recorded for all time. It will be perpetual proof that democracy, when put to the test, can show the stuff of which it is made.

I well recall during my recent visit to three great capital cities in South America, the vast throngs which came to express by their cheers their friendship for the United States. I especially remember that above all the cheers I heard one constant cry again and again— one shout above all others: "¡Viva la democracia!"—"Long live democracy!"

Those three stirring words cry out the abiding conviction of people in all the democracies that freedom shall rule in the land.

As I salute the peoples of all the nations in the western world, I echo that greeting from our good neighbors of the Americas: "¡Viva la democracia!"—"Long live democracy!"

ADDRESS by President Franklin D. Roosevelt, before the Governing Board of the Pan American Union, at Washington, May 27, 1941
Department of State Bulletin, May 31, 1941, p. 647

I AM SPEAKING tonight from the White House in the presence of the Governing Board of the Pan American Union, the Canadian Minister, and their families. The members of this Board are the ambassadors and ministers of the American republics in Washington. It is appropriate that I do this. Now, as never before, the unity of the American republics is of supreme importance to each and every one of us and to the cause of freedom throughout the world. Our future independence is bound up with the future independence of all our sister republics.

The pressing problems that confront us are military problems. We cannot afford to approach them from the point of view of wishful thinkers or sentimentalists. What we face is cold, hard fact.

The first and fundamental fact is that what started as a European war has developed, as the Nazis always intended it should develop, into a world war for world-domination.

Adolf Hitler never considered the domination of Europe as an end in itself. European conquest was but a step toward ultimate goals in all the other continents. It is unmistakably apparent to all of us that, unless the advance of Hitlerism is forcibly checked now, the Western Hemisphere will be within range of the Nazi weapons of destruction.

For our own defense we have accordingly undertaken certain obviously necessary measures.

First, we joined in concluding a series of agreements with all the other American republics. This further solidified our hemisphere against the common danger.

And then, a year ago, we launched, and are successfully carrying out, the largest armament-production program we have ever undertaken.

We have added substantially to our splendid Navy, and we have mustered our manpower to build up a new Army which is already worthy of the highest traditions of our military service.

We instituted a policy of aid for the democracies—the nations which have fought for the continuation of human liberties.

This policy had its origin in the first month of the war, when I urged upon the Congress repeal of the arms-embargo provisions in the Neutrality Law. In that message of September 1939, I said, "I should like to be able to offer the hope that the shadow over the world might swiftly pass. I cannot. The facts compel my stating, with candor, that darker periods may lie ahead."

In the subsequent months, the shadows deepened and lengthened. And the night spread over Poland, Denmark, Norway, Holland, Belgium, Luxemburg, and France.

In June 1940, Britain stood alone, faced by the same machine of terror which had overwhelmed her allies. Our Government rushed arms to meet her desperate needs.

In September 1940, an agreement was completed with Great Britain for the trade of 50 destroyers for 8 important off-shore bases.

In March 1941, the Congress passed the Lend-Lease Bill and an appropriation of seven billion dollars to implement it. This law realistically provided for material aid "for the government of any country whose defense the President deems vital to the defense of the United States."

Our whole program of aid for the democracies has been based on hard-headed concern for our own security and for the kind of safe and civilized world in which we wish to live. Every dollar of material we send helps to keep the dictators away from our own hemisphere. Every day that they are held off gives us time to build more guns and tanks and planes and ships.

We have made no pretense about our own self-interest in this aid. Great Britain understands it—and so does Nazi Germany.

And now—after a year—Britain still fights gallantly, on a "far-flung battle line." We have doubled and redoubled our vast production, increasing, month by month, our material supply of tools of war for ourselves and Britain and China—and eventually for all the democracies.

The supply of these tools will not fail—it will increase.

With greatly augmented strength, the United States and the other American republics now chart their course in the situation of today.

Your Government knows what terms Hitler, if victorious, would impose. They are, indeed, the only terms on which he would accept a so-called "negotiated" peace.

Under those terms, Germany would literally parcel out the world—hoisting the swastika itself over vast territories and populations and setting up puppet governments of its own choosing, wholly subject to the will and the policy of a conqueror.

To the people of the Americas, a triumphant Hitler would say, as he said after the seizure of Austria, and after Munich, and after the seizure of Czechoslovakia: "I am now completely satisfied. This is the last territorial readjustment I will seek." And he would of course add: "All we want is peace, friendship, and profitable trade relations with you in the New World."

And were any of us in the Americas so incredibly simple and forgetful as to accept those honeyed words, what would then happen?

Those in the New World who were seeking profits would be urging that all that the dictatorships desired was "peace." They would oppose toil and taxes for more American armament. Meanwhile, the dictatorships would be forcing the enslaved peoples of their Old-World conquests into a system they are even now organizing—to build a naval and air force intended to gain and hold and be master of the Atlantic and the Pacific as well.

They would fasten an economic stranglehold upon our several nations. Quislings would be found to subvert the governments in our republics; and the Nazis would back their fifth columns with invasion, if necessary.

I am not speculating about all this. I merely repeat what is already in the Nazi book of world-conquest. They plan to treat the Latin American nations as they are now treating the Balkans. They plan then to strangle the United States of America and the Dominion of Canada.

The American laborer would have to compete with slave labor in the rest of the world. Minimum wages, maximum hours? Nonsense!

Wages and hours would be fixed by Hitler. The dignity and power and standard of living of the American worker and farmer would be gone. Trade unions would become historical relics and collective bargaining a joke.

Farm income? What happens to all farm surpluses without any foreign trade? The American farmer would get for his products exactly what Hitler wanted to give. He would face obvious disaster and complete regimentation.

Tariff walls—Chinese walls of isolation—would be futile. Freedom to trade is essential to our economic life. We do not eat all the food we can produce; we do not burn all the oil we can pump; we do not use all the goods we can manufacture. It would not be an American wall to keep Nazi goods out; it would be a Nazi wall to keep us in.

The whole fabric of working life as we know it—business, manufacturing, mining, agriculture—all would be mangled and crippled under such a system. Yet to maintain even that crippled independence would require permanent conscription of our manpower; it would curtail the funds we could spend on education, on housing, on public works, on flood control, on health. Instead, we should be permanently pouring our resources into armaments; and, year in and year out, standing day and night watch against the destruction of our cities.

Even our right of worship would be threatened. The Nazi world does not recognize any God except Hitler; for the Nazis are as ruthless as the Communists in the denial of God. What place has religion which preaches the dignity of the human being, of the majesty of the human soul, in a world where moral standards are measured by treachery and bribery and fifth columnists? Will our children, too, wander off, goose-stepping in search of new gods?

We do not accept, and will not permit, this Nazi "shape of things to come." It will never be forced upon us if we act in this present crisis with the wisdom and the courage which have distinguished our country in all the crises of the past.

The Nazis have taken military possession of the greater part of Europe. In Africa they have occupied Tripoli and Libya, and they are threatening Egypt, the Suez Canal, and the Near East. But their plans do not stop there, for the Indian Ocean is the gateway to the East.

They also have the armed power at any moment to occupy Spain and Portugal; and that threat extends not only to French North Africa and the western end of the Mediterranean, but also to the Atlantic fortress of Dakar, and to the island outposts of the New World—the Azores and Cape Verde Islands.

The Cape Verde Islands are only seven hours' distance from Brazil by bomber or troop-carrying planes. They dominate shipping routes to and from the South Atlantic.

The war is approaching the brink of the Western Hemisphere itself. It is coming very close to home.

Control or occupation by Nazi forces of any of the islands of the Atlantic would jeopardize the immediate safety of portions of North and South America and of the island possessions of the United States and of the ultimate safety of the continental United States itself.

Hitler's plan of world-domination would be near its accomplishment today, were it not for two factors: One is the epic resistance of Britain, her Colonies, and the great Dominions, fighting not only to maintain the existence of the Island of Britain, but also to hold the Near East and Africa. The other is the magnificent defense of China, which will, I have reason to believe, increase in strength. All of these, together, prevent the Axis from winning control of the seas by ships and aircraft.

The Axis powers can never achieve their objective of world-domination unless they first obtain control of the seas. This is their supreme purpose today; and to achieve it, they must capture Great Britain.

They could then have the power to dictate to the Western Hemisphere. No spurious argument, no appeal to sentiment, and no false pledges like those given by Hitler at Munich, can deceive the American people into believing that he and his Axis partners would not, with Britain defeated, close in relentlessly on this hemisphere.

But if the Axis powers fail to gain control of the seas, they are certainly defeated. Their dreams of world-domination will then go by the board; and the criminal leaders who started this war will suffer inevitable disaster.

Both they and their people know this—and they are afraid. That is why they are risking everything they have, conducting desperate attempts to break through to the command of the ocean. Once they are limited to a continuing land war, their cruel forces of occupation will be unable to keep their heel on the necks of the millions of innocent, oppressed peoples on the continent of Europe; and in the end, their whole structure will break into little pieces. And the wider the Nazi land effort, the greater the danger.

We do not forget the silenced peoples. The masters of Germany—those, at least, who have not been assassinated or escaped to free soil—have marked these peoples and their children's children for slavery. But those people, spiritually unconquered: Austrians, Czechs, Poles,

Norwegians, Dutch, Belgians, Frenchmen, Greeks, Southern Slavs—yes, even those Italians and Germans who themselves have been enslaved—will prove to be a powerful force in disrupting the Nazi system.

Yes, all freedom—meaning freedom to live, and not freedom to conquer and subjugate other peoples—depends on freedom of the seas. All of American history—North, Central, and South American history—has been inevitably tied up with those words "freedom of the seas."

Since 1799, when our infant Navy made the West Indies and the Caribbean and the Gulf of Mexico safe for American ships; since 1804 and 1805 when we made all peaceful commerce safe from the depredations of the Barbary pirates; since the War of 1812, which was fought for the preservation of sailors' rights; since 1867, when our sea power made it possible for the Mexicans to expel the French Army of Louis Napoleon, we have striven and fought in defense of freedom of the seas—for our own shipping, for the commerce of our sister republics, for the right of all nations to use the highways of world trade—and for our own safety.

During the first World War we were able to escort merchant ships by the use of small cruisers, gunboats, and destroyers; and this type of convoy was effective against submarines. In this second World War, however, the problem is greater, because the attack on the freedom of the seas is now fourfold: first, the improved submarine; second, the much greater use of the heavily armed raiding cruiser or hit-and-run battleship; third, the bombing airplane, which is capable of destroying merchant ships seven or eight hundred miles from its nearest base; and fourth, the destruction of merchant ships in those ports of the world which are accessible to bombing attack.

The battle of the Atlantic now extends from the icy waters of the North Pole to the frozen continent of the Antarctic. Throughout this huge area, there have been sinkings of merchant ships in alarming and increasing numbers by Nazi raiders or submarines. There have been sinkings even of ships carrying neutral flags. There have been sinkings in the South Atlantic, off West Africa and the Cape Verde Islands; between the Azores and the islands off the American coast; and between Greenland and Iceland. Great numbers of these sinkings have been actually within the waters of the Western Hemisphere.

The blunt truth is this—and I reveal this with the full knowledge of the British Government: the present rate of Nazi sinkings of merchant ships is more than three times as high as the capacity of British shipyards to replace them; it is more than twice the combined British and American output of merchant ships today.

We can answer this peril by two simultaneous measures: First, by speeding up and increasing our great ship-building program; and second, by helping to cut down the losses on the high seas.

Attacks on shipping off the very shores of land which we are determined to protect, present an actual military danger to the Americas. And that danger has recently been heavily underlined by the presence in Western Hemisphere waters of Nazi battleships of great striking-power.

Most of the supplies for Britain go by a northerly route, which comes close to Greenland and the nearby island of Iceland. Germany's heaviest attack is on that route. Nazi occupation of Iceland or bases in Greenland would bring the war close to our continental shores because they are stepping-stones to Labrador, Newfoundland, Nova Scotia, and the northern United States, including the great industrial centers of the North, East, and the Middle West.

Equally, the Azores and the Cape Verde Islands, if occupied or controlled by Germany, would directly endanger the freedom of the Atlantic and our own physical safety. Under German domination they would become bases for submarines, warships, and airplanes raiding the waters which lie immediately off our own coasts and attacking the shipping in the South Atlantic. They would provide a springboard for actual attack against the integrity and independence of Brazil and her neighboring republics.

I have said on many occasions that the United States is mustering its men and its resources only for purposes of defense—only to repel attack. I repeat that statement now. But we must be realistic when we use the word "attack"; we have to relate it to the lightning speed of modern warfare.

Some people seem to think that we are not attacked until bombs actually drop on New York or San Francisco or New Orleans or Chicago. But they are simply shutting their eyes to the lesson we must learn from the fate of every nation that the Nazis have conquered.

The attack on Czechoslovakia began with the conquest of Austria. The attack on Norway began with the occupation of Denmark. The attack on Greece began with occupation of Albania and Bulgaria. The attack on the Suez Canal began with the invasion of the Balkans and North Africa. The attack on the United States can begin with the domination of any base which menaces our security—north or south.

Nobody can foretell tonight just when the acts of the dictators will ripen into attack on this hemisphere and us. But we know enough by now to realize that it would be suicide to wait until they are in our front yard.

When your enemy comes at you in a tank or a bombing plane, if you hold your fire until you see the whites of his eyes, you will never know what hit you. Our Bunker Hill of tomorrow may be several thousand miles from Boston.

Anyone with an atlas and a reasonable knowledge of the sudden striking-force of modern war, knows that it is stupid to wait until a probable enemy has gained a foothold from which to attack. Old-fashioned common sense calls for the use of a strategy which will prevent such an enemy from gaining a foothold in the first place.

We have, accordingly, extended our patrol in north and south Atlantic waters. We are steadily adding more and more ships and planes to that patrol. It is well known that the strength of the Atlantic Fleet has been greatly increased during the past year, and is constantly being built up.

These ships and planes warn of the presence of attacking raiders, on the sea, under the sea, and above the sea. The danger from these raiders is greatly lessened if their location is definitely known. We are thus being forewarned; and we shall be on our guard against efforts to establish Nazi bases closer to our hemisphere.

The deadly facts of war compel nations, for simple self-preservation, to make stern choices. It does not make sense, for instance, to say, "I believe in the defense of all the Western Hemisphere," and in the next breath to say, "I will not fight for that defense until the enemy has landed on our shores." And if we believe in the independence and integrity of the Americas, we must be willing to fight to defend them just as much as we would to fight for the safety of our own homes.

It is time for us to realize that the safety of American homes even in the center of our country has a definite relationship to the continued safety of homes in Nova Scotia or Trinidad or Brazil.

Our national policy today, therefore, is this:

First, we shall actively resist wherever necessary, and with all our resources, every attempt by Hitler to extend his Nazi domination to the Western Hemisphere, or to threaten it. We shall actively resist his every attempt to gain control of the seas. We insist upon the vital importance of keeping Hitlerism away from any point in the world which could be used and would be used as a base of attack against the Americas.

Second, from the point of view of strict naval and military necessity, we shall give every possible assistance to Britain and to all who, with Britain, are resisting Hitlerism or its equivalent with force of arms. Our patrols are helping now to insure delivery of the needed supplies to Britain. All additional measures necessary to deliver the goods will be taken. Any and all further methods or combination of methods, which can or should be utilized, are being devised by our military and naval technicians, who, with me, will work out and put into effect such new and additional safeguards as may be needed.

The delivery of needed supplies to Britain is imperative. This can be done; it must be done; it will be done.

To the other American nations—20 republics and the Dominion of Canada—I say this: The United States does not merely propose these purposes, but is actively engaged today in carrying them out.

I say to them further: You may disregard those few citizens of the United States who content that we are disunited and cannot act.

There are some timid ones among us who say that we must preserve peace at any price—lest we lose our liberties forever. To them I say: Never in the history of the world has a nation lost its democracy by a successful struggle to defend its democracy. We must not be defeated by the fear of the very danger which we are preparing to resist. Our freedom has shown its ability to survive war, but it would never survive surrender. "The only thing we have to fear is fear itself."

There, is, of course, a small group of sincere, patriotic men and women whose real passion for peace has shut their eyes to the ugly realities of international banditry and to the need to resist it at all costs. I am sure they are embarrassed by the sinister support they are receiving from the enemies of democracy in our midst—the Bundists and Fascists and Communists and every group devoted to bigotry and racial and religious intolerance. It is no mere coincidence that all the arguments put forward by these enemies of democracy—all their attempts to confuse and divide our people and to destroy public confidence in our Government—all their defeatist forebodings that Britain and democracy are already beaten—all their selfish promises that we can "do business" with Hitler—all of these are but echoes of the words that have been poured out from the Axis bureaus of propaganda. Those same words have been used before in other countries—to scare them, to divide them, to soften them up. Invariably, those same words have formed the advance guard of physical attack.

Your Government has the right to expect of all citizens that they take loyal part in the common work of our common defense—take loyal part from this moment forward.

I have recently set up the machinery for civilian defense. It will rapidly organize, locality by locality. It will depend on the organized effort of men and women everywhere. All will have responsibilities to fulfil.

Defense today means more than merely fighting. It means morale, civilian as well as military; it means using every available resource; it means enlarging every useful plant. It means the use of a greater American common sense in discarding rumor and distorted statement. It means recognizing, for what they are, racketeers and fifth columnists, who are the incendiary bombs of the moment.

All of us know that we have made very great social progress in recent years. We propose to maintain that progress and strengthen it. When the Nation is threatened from without, however, as it is today, the actual production and transportation of the machinery of defense must not be interrupted by disputes between capital and capital, labor and labor, or capital and labor. The future of all free enterprise—of capital and labor alike—is at stake.

This is no time for capital to make, or be allowed to retain, excess profits. Articles of defense must have undisputed right-of-way in every industrial plant in the country.

A nation-wide machinery for conciliation and mediation of industrial disputes has been set up. That machinery must be used promptly—and without stoppage of work. Collective bargaining will be retained, but the American people expect that impartial recommendations of our Government services will be followed both by capital and by labor.

The overwhelming majority of our citizens expect their Government to see that the tools of defense are built; and for the very purpose of preserving the democratic safeguards of both labor and management, this Government is determined to use all of its power to express the will of its people and to prevent interference with the production of materials essential to our Nation's security.

Today the whole world is divided between human slavery and human freedom—between pagan brutality and the Christian ideal.

We choose human freedom—which is the Christian ideal.

No one of us can waver for a moment in his courage or his faith.

We will not accept a Hitler-dominated world. And we will not accept a world, like the post-war world of the 1920's, in which the seeds of Hitlerism can again be planted and allowed to grow.

We will accept only a world consecrated to freedom of speech and expression—freedom of every person to worship God in his own way—freedom from want—and freedom from terrorism.

Is such a world impossible of attainment?

Magna Charta, the Declaration of Independence, the Constitution of the United States, the Emancipation Proclamation, and every other milestone in human progress—all were ideals which seemed impossible of attainment, yet they were attained.

As a military force, we were weak when we established our independence, but we successfully stood off tyrants, powerful in their day, who are now lost in the dust of history.

Odds meant nothing to us then. Shall we now, with all our potential strength, hesitate to take every single measure necessary to maintain our American liberties?

Our people and our Government will not hesitate to meet that challenge.

As the President of a united and determined people, I say solemnly:

We reassert the ancient American doctrine of freedom of the seas.

We reassert the solidarity of the 21 American republics and the Dominion of Canada in the preservation of the independence of the hemisphere.

We have pledged material support to the other democracies of the world—and we will fulfil that pledge.

We in the Americas will decide for ourselves whether and when and where our American interests are attacked or our security threatened.

We are placing our armed forces in strategic military position.

We will not hesitate to use our armed forces to repel attack.

We reassert our abiding faith in the vitality of our constitutional republic as a perpetual home of freedom, of tolerance, and of devotion to the Word of God.

Therefore, with profound consciousness of my responsibilities to my countrymen and to my country's cause, I have tonight issued a proclamation that an unlimited national emergency exists and requires the strengthening of our defense to the extreme limit of our national power and authority.

The Nation will expect all individuals and all groups to play their full parts without stint and without selfishness and without doubt that our democracy will triumphantly survive.

I repeat the words of the Signers of the Declaration of Independence—that little band of patriots, fighting long ago against overwhelming odds, but certain, as are we, of ultimate victory: "With a firm reliance on the protection of Divine Providence, we mutually pledge to each other our lives, our fortunes, and our sacred honor."

ADDRESS by Sumner Welles, Under Secretary of State, at the Opening Session of the Third Meeting of Foreign Ministers of the American Republics, at Rio de Janeiro, January 15, 1942

Department of State Bulletin, January 17, 1942, p. 55. Mr. Welles was the United States representative at the meeting

THE PEOPLES of the Americas face today the greatest danger which they have ever confronted since they won their independence.

We are meeting together under the terms, and in the spirit, of inter-American agreements to take counsel as to the course which our governments should take under the shadow of this dire threat to our continued existence as free peoples.

We meet as the representatives of nations which in former times have had their differences and controversies. But I believe that I may speak for all of us, and not least in the name of my own Government, when I say that we all of us have learned by our past errors of omission and of commission. We are assembled as representatives of the 21 sovereign and independent republics of the American Continent, now welded together as no continent has ever before been united in history, by our faith in the ties of mutual trust and of reciprocal interdependence which bind us and, most of all, by our common devotion to the great cause of democracy and of human liberty to which our New World is dedicated.

The calamity which has now engulfed humanity was not unforeseen by any of us.

Just five years ago, at the Inter-American Conference for the Maintenance of Peace, of Buenos Aires, we met because of the clear signs that the earth would be engulfed by the tidal wave of a worldwide war. By common accord we determined upon measures indispensable to our common security. At the Inter-American Conference at Lima further measures were taken. After the war broke out, at the meetings of the Foreign Ministers at Panamá and Habana, the American republics adopted additional far-reaching measures of protection and of cooperation for their common safety.

We were thus in many ways prepared for that eventuality from which we then still hoped we might be spared—the involvement of the Americas in the war which has been forced upon mankind by Hitlerism.

I regard it as my obligation here on behalf of my Government to inform you with complete frankness of the course which it had pursued up to the time when, on Sunday, December 7, my country was suddenly attacked by means of an act of treachery that will never be forgotten by the people of the United States, nor, I believe, by the people of any of the other American republics.

My Government was never blind to the ultimate purposes and objectives of Hitlerism. It long since realized that Hitler had formulated his plans to conquer the entire world. These plans, the plans of a criminal paranoiac, were conceived before he had even seized power in Germany. They have been carried out step by step, first through guile and deceit, later by fire and sword. No evil has been too monstrous for him. No infamy has been too vile for him to perpetrate.

Time and again, as you all know, the President of the United States, with your knowledge and with your approval, made every effort in earlier years by fervent appeal and by constructive and just proposal to avert the final holocaust.

All of us learned a bitter lesson in those years between 1936 and 1941.

We learned by the tragic experience of others, that all of those standards of international decency and of international law, upon which the hopes of a law-abiding and a peaceful world were based, were utterly disregarded by Hitler and by his ignominious satellites.

Those free nations who sought ingenuously, by the very innocence of their conduct and by the very completeness of their neutrality, to maintain at least the shadow of their independence were occupied more promptly and ravaged more cruelly than those who resisted the attack of Hitler's armies.

We have been taught this lesson, which it took all of us a long time to learn, that in the world of today, confronted by Hitlerism and all of the black reversion to barbarism which that evil word implies, no nation can hope to maintain its own independence and no people can hope to maintain its liberty, except through the power of armed might and through the courage and devotion of men and women in many lands and of many races, but who all of them love liberty more than life itself.

The people of the United States learned that lesson.

And for that reason, because of their determination to defend their country and to safeguard the security of our common continent, they determined to lend every form of assistance to that gallant band of nations who against great odds continued nevertheless to defend their own liberties.

We had learned our lesson so clearly that we saw that the defense by these peoples of their independence constituted likewise the defense of our own independence and of that of the Western Hemisphere.

Then suddenly, last June, Hitler, distraught by the realization that he could no longer attempt successfully to invade Great Britain, but intoxicated by the easy victories which he had achieved in other parts of Europe, perfidiously attacked the Soviet Union with which he had only recently entered into a pact of non-aggression.

"Whom the gods would destroy, they first make mad."

Many months ago Japan entered into the Tripartite Pact with Germany and Italy. My Government learned that this arrangement, which made of Japan the submissive tool of Hitler, for the primary purpose of preventing the United States from continuing to give assistance to Great Britain, was not supported by certain elements in Japan. These elements clearly foresaw the ultimate destruction of Japan if the Japanese Government dared to embark upon an adventure which would ultimately bring Japan into conflict with all of the other powers which had direct interests in the western Pacific.

These elements in Japan also realized that, while Hitler had been able to inveigle the war lords in control of the Japanese Government into believing that should Japan carry out German orders, and were the Western democracies defeated, Germany would permit Japan to control the Far East, Hitler would of course take her spoils from Japan whenever he saw fit.

My Government sought over a period of more than ten months to negotiate with Japan a peaceful and equitable adjustment of differences between the two countries so as to prevent the outbreak of war in the Pacific.

The United States, however, utterly refused to agree to any settlement which would infringe upon the independence or the legitimate rights of the people of China, who for four and a half years had been bravely and successfully resisting every effort on the part of Japan to conquer their ancient land. Nor would the United States agree to any proposal offered by the Japanese Government which would controvene those basic principles of right and justice for which, I am proud to say, my country stands.

We now know that at the very time that the present Japanese Government was carrying on, at its own urgent request, the pretense of conducting peaceful negotiations with the United States for the purpose of reaching a settlement which would have averted war, every plan in its uttermost detail had already been made to attack my country's territory.

During those last two weeks before December 7, when Japan's notorious peace emissary was protesting to my Government that his country desired nothing except peace and profitable commercial relations with the United States, the airplane carriers were already on their way to Pearl Harbor to launch their dastardly attack upon the United States Navy.

The Japanese war lords, under the orders of their German masters, adopting the same methods of deceit and treachery which Hitler has made a stench in the nostrils of civilized mankind, while peace negotiations were actually still in progress in Washington, suddenly attacked a country which had been Japan's friend and which had made every honorable effort to find a basis for a just and lasting peace in the Pacific.

A few days later Germany and her satellites declared war upon the United States.

And so war has been forced upon some of us in the American Continent.

The greatest assurance that our great association of sovereign and independent peoples, the American family of nations, can survive this world upheaval safely lies in the unity with which we face the common peril.

Some of us by our own power, by our own resources, by the extent of our population, are able successfully beyond the shadow of a doubt to defend ourselves. Others of us who do not possess these material advantages, equal though they be in their courage and in their determination to resist aggression, must depend for their continued security upon the cooperation which other members of the American family may give them. The only assured safety which this continent possesses lies in full cooperation between us all in the common defense; equal and sovereign partners in times of aggression as in times of peace.

The record of the past two years is ever before us. You and I know that had there existed during the past decade an international order based upon law, and with the capacity to enforce such law, the earth today would not be subjected to the cruel scourge which is now ravaging the entire globe. Had the law-abiding and peaceful nations of Europe been willing to stand together when the menace of Hitlerism first began to become manifest, Hitler would never have dared to embark upon his evil course. It was solely because of the fact that these nations, instead of standing together, permitted themselves to hold aloof one from the other and placed their hope of salvation in their own neutrality, that Hitler was enabled to overrun them one by one as time and circumstances made it expedient for him.

The security of the three hundred millions of people who inhabit the Western Hemisphere and the independence of each of the countries here represented will be determined by whether the American nations stand together in this hour of peril, or whether they stand apart one from the other.

I am fully aware of what the representatives of the Axis Powers have been stating to some of you, day in and day out during the past months. I know that Hitler's representatives have said to some of you that Germany has not the slightest thought of dominating the Western Hemisphere. All that Germany wants, they have told you, is complete domination over every part of Europe, of Africa, and of the Near

East, the destruction of the British Empire, the enslavement of the Russian people, the overlordship of the Far East, and when this is accomplished, only friendship and peaceful trade with the Americas.

But Hitler's representatives have omitted to mention that in such a fateful contingency we would all of us then also be living in a Hitler-dominated world.

You may remember that a few days ago Hitler publicly denounced President Roosevelt as the greatest war-monger of all times, because the President had declared that the people of the United States "did not want to live in the type of world" that Hitler wished for.

In a Hitler-dominated universe not one of us could trade except on Hitler's terms. Not one of us could live except under a *gauleiter* appointed for us by Hitler. Not one of us could educate our children except as Hitler dictated. Not one of us could enjoy our God-given rights to think and to speak freely and to worship the Deity as our conscience may dictate.

Can even Hitler wonder that we are not willing to live in such a world as that?

I know what representatives of Japan have been saying to some of you. They are telling you that the Japanese Government is sure that the governments and peoples of the American republics will certainly not be influenced by any thought that Japan may harbor ulterior motives towards them. They are telling you that Japan desires nothing but peace with you and the maintenance of profitable commercial relations.

You will remember that they told us that also!

The Japanese Government is even telling you that they are soon going to send ships to the Pacific ports of South America to take cargoes of your goods.

But they did not add that were some Japanese ship to be foolhardy enough to attempt to make such a trip, it would not be able to travel many miles after leaving the port of the Americas to which it had gone, except under the naval custody of Japan's adversaries.

But there is no useful purpose to be served by our dwelling on the lies with which the Axis Governments still attempt to deceive us. We all of us know that no sane man can place the slightest shred of credence in any solemn or sworn assurance which the Axis Governments give.

We likewise know full well that the sole aim, the ultimate objective of these partners in crime, is conquest of the surface of the entire earth, the loot of the possessions of every one of us, and the subjugation of free men and women everywhere to the level of serfs.

Twelve months ago Hitler solemnly assured the German people

that before the end of the year 1941, Germany would complete the defeat of all her enemies in the greatest victory of all time.

On October third last Hitler swore to his people that before the first of the New Year of 1942 Russia would be crushed, "never to rise again."

What are the facts? Today the German armies are retreating from Russian territory, routed and dispersed by the magnificent offensive of the Russian armies. Hitler has lost over one third of his air force, over one half of his tank force, and more than three million men. But more than that, the German people now see for themselves the utter falsity of the promises held out to them by the evil charlatan who rules them. Their morale is running low.

In North Africa the British armies have utterly destroyed the Axis forces in Libya and are clearing the Southern Mediterranean littoral of Axis threats.

In the Atlantic the British and United States convoys are moving ever more safely to their destinations, and the loss of merchant shipping through German submarine action has steadily diminished during the past six months.

In the Far East the United States and Great Britain have met with initial reverses.

We all remember that as a result of the Washington Limitation of Armaments Conference of 1922 the powers directly interested in the Far East, in order to assure the basis for peaceful relations between them, pledged themselves not to increase the fortifications of their possessions in that area. During all of the years that the treaties agreed upon at that Conference remained in effect the United States consequently took no steps to fortify the Philippines. But we also now know that, counter to her sworn obligations, Japan during these same years was creating naval bases and feverishly constructing fortifications throughout the islands of the South Seas which she had received as a mandate from the League of Nations.

Furthermore, at the request of the Philippine people the Government of the United States had pledged itself to grant full independence to them in the year 1946.

The infamous attack by Japan upon the United States consequently found the Philippine Islands largely unfortified, and protected solely by a modest army of brave Filipino soldiers, supported by only two divisions of United States troops, with a small air force utterly inadequate to withstand the concentrated strength of the Japanese.

But the control of the Pacific Ocean itself rests with the Allied fleets. Japan, after suffering disastrously in her four-year-long war with China, is surrounded on all sides. She possesses no resources. Once the *matériel* which she is now using is destroyed it can only be replaced by what Japan herself can produce. And that replacement will be inferior in quality, and small in quantity without the raw materials which Japan will now be largely unable to secure.

The commencement of the year 1942 has marked the turn of the tide.

The United States is now in the war. Our industrial production, the greatest in the world, is fast mounting towards the maximum. During the coming year we will produce some 60,000 airplanes, including 45,000 military airplanes, some 45,000 tanks, some 300 new combatant ships, from the mightiest battleships to coastal patrol craft, and some 600 new merchant ships. We will attain a rate of 70,000 per year in the training of combat airplane pilots. We have drafted for military service all of our men between the ages of 20 and 44 years, and of this great total we will soon have an initial army of three million men fully trained and fully equipped. We will spend 50 billions of dollars, or half of our total national income, in the year thereafter in order to secure the use of every ounce of our national resources in our war effort. Every weapon that we produce will be used wherever it is determined that it may be of the most service in the common cause, whether that be here in the Western Hemisphere, on the deserts of Libya, on the steppes of Russia, or in the territory of the brave people of China.

Those of us who have joined in this holy war face a ruthless and barbarous foe. The road before us will be hard and perhaps long. We will meet unquestionably with serious reverses from time to time. But the tide has turned and will run swiftly and ever more swiftly until it ends in the flood of victory.

As each one of you knows, my Government has made no suggestion, and no request, as to the course which any of the governments of the other American republics should pursue subsequent to the Japanese attack upon the United States, and the declaration of war upon it by the other Axis Powers.

We do not function in that way in the American family of nations.

But may I assure you from my heart today that the spontaneous declaration of war upon the enemies of mankind of nine of the other American republics; the severance of all relations with Germany, Italy, and Japan by Mexico, Colombia, and Venezuela; and the official declarations of solidarity and support by all of the other American republics, including our traditional and unfailing friend, in evil days as well as good, the great Republic of Brazil, whose guests we all are today, represents to my Government and to my fellow citizens a measure of support, of strength, and of spiritual encouragement which no words of mine would be adequate to express.

May I merely say that these acts of faith in our common destiny, so generously realized, will never be forgotten by the people of the United States. They have heartened us all. They have made us all, all the more anxious to be worthy, not in words but in deeds, of your confidence. They have made us all the more desirous of showing our gratitude through the extent of the cooperative strength which we can furnish to insure the ultimate triumph of the cause to which we are dedicated.

Each one of the American governments has determined, and will continue to determine, in its own wisdom, the course which it will pursue to the best interest of its people in this world struggle. But of one thing I feel sure we are all convinced. In accordance with the obligations we have all undertaken under the provisions of our inter-American agreements and in accordance with the spirit of that continental solidarity unanimously proclaimed, those nations of the Americas which are not engaged in war will never permit their territory to be used by agents of the Axis Powers in order that these may conspire against, or prepare attacks upon, those republics which are fighting for their own liberties and for those of the entire continent.

We all of us are fully aware of the record of the activities of Axis agents in our several countries which the past two years have brought to light. We know how the Axis diplomatic representatives, taking advantage of the immunity which international custom has granted them for their legitimate functions, have been doing their utmost to poison inter-American relations; to create internal discord; and to engender domestic strife, so as to try and pave the way for subversive movements financed with funds obtained through extortion from residents in our midst, or transferred from the loot they have procured in the occupied countries of Europe. We know that their so-called consular officials have in reality been the directing heads of espionage rings in every part of this hemisphere. The full history of this record will some day be published in full detail, when the divulging of this information will no longer be of assistance to the enemy.

So long as this hemisphere remained out of the war all of our governments dealt with this ever-increasing danger in the manner which they believed most effective, exchanging intelligence one with the other, as existing agreements between them provide, whenever such exchange was mutually helpful.

But today the situation has changed. Ten of the American republics are at war and three others have severed all relations with the Axis

Powers. The continued presence of these Axis agents within the Western Hemisphere constitutes a direct danger to the national defense of the republics engaged in war. There is not a Japanese nor a German consul, nor a consul of Hitler's satellite countries, in the New World at this moment who is not reporting to his superiors every time a ship leaves the ports of the country where he is stationed, for the purpose of having that ship sunk by an Axis submarine. There is not a diplomatic representative of the Axis Powers anywhere in the Americas who is not seeking to get for his masters information regarding the defense preparations of the American nations now at war; who is not conspiring against the internal security of every one of us; who is not doing his utmost, through every means available to him, to hinder our capacity to insure the integrity of our freedom and our independence.

Surely this danger must be of paramount concern to all of us. The preeminent issue presented is solely that those republics engaged in war shall not be dealt a deadly thrust by the agents of the Axis ensconced upon the soil and enjoying the hospitality of others of the American republics.

The shibboleth of classic neutrality in its narrow sense can, in this tragic modern world, no longer be the ideal of any freedom-loving people of the Americas.

There can no longer be any real neutrality as between the powers of evil and the forces that are struggling to preserve the rights and the independence of free peoples.

It is far better for any people to strive gloriously to safeguard its independence; it is far better for any people to die, if need be, in the battle to save its liberties, than by clinging to the tattered fiction of an illusory neutrality, to succeed only by so doing in committing suicide.

Our devotion to the common cause of defending the New World against aggression does not imply necessarily engagement in war. But it does imply, I confidently believe, the taking of all measures of cooperation between us which redound to the great objective of keeping the Americas free.

Of equal importance with measures of political solidarity, defense cooperation, and the repression of subversive activity are economic measures related to the conduct of war against the aggressor nations and the defense of the Western Hemisphere.

All of the American republics have already taken some form of measures breaking off financial and commercial intercourse between them and the non-American aggressor states and to eliminate other alien economic activities prejudicial to the welfare of the American republics.

It is of the utmost importance that these measures be expanded in order that they may prevent all business, financial, and trade transactions between the Western Hemisphere and the aggressor states, and all transactions within the Western Hemisphere which directly or indirectly redound to the benefit of the aggressor nations or are in any way inimical to the defense of the hemisphere.

The conduct of war and the defense of the hemisphere will require an ever-increasing production of the implements of war and an ever-increasing supply of the basic and strategic materials necessary for their production. The spread of the war has cut off many of the most important sources of strategic materials, and it is essential that the American republics conserve their stocks of such commodities and, by every possible means, encourage the production and the free flow within the hemisphere of the greatest possible quantity of these materials.

The universal character of the war is placing increasing demands upon the merchant-shipping facilities of all of us. The increased production of strategic materials will be of no avail unless adequate transportation can be provided, and it is consequently of vital importance that all of the shipping facilities of the Americas be mobilized to this essential end.

The Government of the United States is prepared to cooperate whole-heartedly with the other American republics in handling the problems arising out of these economic warfare measures. It stands prepared to render financial and technical assistance, where needed, to alleviate injury to the domestic economy of any of the American republics which results from the control and curbing of alien economic activities inimical to our common defense.

It is ready to enter into broad arrangements for the acquisition of supplies of basic and strategic materials, and to cooperate with each of the other American republics in order to increase rapidly and efficiently their production for emergency needs. Finally, it stands ready through the United States Maritime Commission to render every assistance in the efficient operation of merchant vessels in accordance with the plan of August 28, 1941 of the Inter-American Financial and Economic Advisory Committee.

My Government is also fully aware of the important role which imported materials and articles play in the maintenance of the economies of your nations. On December 5, 1941 I advised the Inter-American Financial and Economic Advisory Committee in Washington that the United States was making every effort consistent with the defense program to maintain a flow to the other American republics of materials to satisfy the minimum essential import requirements of your economies. I added that the policy of my Government was being interpreted by all of the appropriate agencies as calling for recognition of and provision for the essential needs of the American republics equal to the treatment accorded United States civilian needs.

The attack by Japan and the declarations of war by the other members of the Tripartite Pact have resulted in greater and unprecedented demands upon our production facilities. But I am able to state today, as I did on the fifth of December, that the policy of the United States toward the satisfaction of your essential requirements remains firm.

On December 26, 1941 after the outbreak of war, the Board of Economic Warfare of my Government resolved unanimously:

"It is the policy of the Government of the United States to aid in maintaining the economic stability of the other American Republics by recognizing and providing for their essential civilian needs on the basis of equal and proportionate consideration with our own."

Pursuant to this declaration of policy our allocation of 218,600 tons of tin-plate for your needs during this year has been followed by further allocations, which I am privileged to announce today. The Office of Production Management has advised me that allocations have been made to you for the next quarter in amounts adequate to meet your needs for rayon; for twenty essential agricultural and industrial chemicals, including copper sulphate, ammonium sulphate, soda ash, and caustic soda; for farm equipment; and for iron and steel products.

In addition, I am able to announce that a special mechanism has been organized within the Office of Production Management which is now facilitating the clearance of your individual priority applications.

In the light of this action, it seems appropriate to recognize that the arsenal of democracy continues mindful of its hemisphere responsibilities.

I am confident that your people will join the people of the United States, who are sharing their civilian supplies with you, in recognizing that military and other defense needs must continue to be given precedence over civilian demands.

All of these economic measures relate directly to the conduct of war, the defense of the hemisphere, and the maintenance of the economies of our several nations during the war emergency. Obviously our greatest efforts must be extended towards victory. Nevertheless, the full consummation of victory must include the building of an economic and social order in which all of our citizens may subsequently enjoy the blessings of peace.

My Government believes that we must begin now to execute plans, vital to the human defense of the hemisphere, for the improvement of health and sanitary conditions, the provision and maintenance of adequate supplies of food, milk, and water, and the effective control of insect-borne and other communicable diseases. The United States is prepared to participate in and to encourage complementary agreements among the American republics for dealing with these problems of health and sanitation by provision, according to the abilities of the countries involved, of funds, raw materials, and services.

The responsibility with which we are all charged requires that we plan for broad economic and social development, for increased production of the necessities of the world, and for their equitable distribution among the people.

If this economic rehabilitation of the world is to take place it is indispensable that there be a resurgence of international trade—international trade, as was declared by the Second Meeting of Ministers of Foreign Affairs at Habana, "conducted with peaceful motives and based upon equality of treatment and fair and equitable practices."

I urge upon you all the imperative need for unity between us, not only in the measures which must presently be taken in the defense of our Western World, but also in order that the American republics, joined as one, may prove to be the potent factor which they should be of right in the determination of the nature of the world of the future, after the victory is won.

We, the American nations, are trustees for Christian civilization. In our own relationships we have wished to show scrupulous respect for the sovereign rights of all states; we have sought to undertake only peaceful processes in the solution of controversies which may have arisen between us; and we have wished to follow the course of decency and of justice in our dealings with others.

When peace is restored it is to the interest of the whole world that the American republics present a united front and be able to speak and act with the moral authority to which, by reason of their own enlightened standards as much as by reason of their number and their power, they are entitled.

The prayer of peoples throughout the world is that when the task of peacemaking is once more undertaken it will be better done than it was in 1919. And we cannot forget that the task this time will be infinitely more difficult than it was the last time.

In the determination of how these stupendous problems may best be solved, the united voice of the free peoples of the Americas must be heard.

The ideals which men have cherished have always throughout the course of history proved themselves to be more potent than any other factor. Nor conquest, nor migrations; nor economic pressure, nor pestilence; nor revolt, nor assassinations have ever yet been able to triumph over the ideals which have sprung from men's hearts and men's minds.

Notwithstanding the hideous blunders of the past generation; notwithstanding the holocaust of the present moment, that great ideal of "a universal dominion of right by such a concert of free peoples as shall bring peace and safety to all nations and make the world itself at last free" still stands untarnished as the supreme objective of a suffering humanity.

That ideal will yet triumph.

We, the free peoples of the Americas, must play our full part in its realization so that we may hasten the day when we can thus insure the maintenance of a peaceful world in which we, and our children, and our children's children, can safely live.

At this time the issue is clearly drawn. There can be no peace until Hitlerism and its monstrous parasites are utterly obliterated, and until the Prussian and Japanese militarists have been taught in the only language they can understand that they will never again be afforded the opportunity of wrecking the lives of generation upon generation of men and women in every quarter of the globe.

When that time comes men of good-will must be prepared and ready to build with vision afresh upon new and lasting foundations of liberty, of morality, of justice, and, by no means least perhaps, of intelligence.

In the attainment of that great achievement the measure of our devotion will be the measure of the world's regeneration.

PAN AMERICAN DAY ADDRESS by Cordell Hull, Secretary of State, before the Governing Board of the Pan American Union, at Washington, April 14, 1944
Department of State Bulletin, April 15, 1944, p. 349

PAN AMERICAN DAY is an important anniversary to the nations of the Americas. We meet today to honor those whose vision and energy established and for more than 50 years have carried forward the Pan

American Union and all that it signifies. It is well to ask ourselves why it is that we can meet in the midst of the greatest war of history and why it is that we have so great an achievement to commemorate. For in doing so we may more clearly see the guideposts which point the true direction in which we may go forward to new cooperation among ourselves and new cooperation with other nations of the earth.

Inter-American unity was not brought about by force and is not based upon the conception of a master race whose mission is to rule. It was not produced by nations with a homogeneous racial origin. It does not depend upon the bonds of a common language or a culture based on a common literature or common customs and habits.

Were these the only sources of international unity and common action, the future for the world would be dark indeed. But inter-American unity proves that there are other sources more subtle and even stronger—sources which offer hope to a world which can find no hope in the factors which I have mentioned. Our unity comes from a passionate devotion to human liberty and national independence which is so strong that it does not stop with the effort of each people to secure liberty for itself but goes on to respect as no less valid the desire of other peoples to achieve the same liberty in accordance with their own traditions and historic institutions. Although the language of Bolivar and San Martín was different from that of Washington and Jefferson, they were expressing the same purposes and principles, and they led their countrymen along the same paths. These are the paths along which inter-American unity has developed, growing ever stronger as the American nations have come to understand one an- -other and to have trust and confidence in one another's purposes and to work together for purposes so identic that they produced, not division and jealousy, but unity of thought and action.

As the years have gone on, the true principles underlying inter-American unity have been made more specific as one inter-American conference has followed another. In the years between the world wars the trust and confidence between the American nations grew ever stronger while elsewhere the growth of ambitions of conquest by force brought division and fear. It is the common pride of the American republics and the good fortune of all mankind that the torch of international cooperation has burned at its brightest in the affairs of this hemisphere precisely at a time when it was being blacked out elsewhere. It is natural that the history of an international association which has endured longer than any other should provide encouraging guidance for the future.

At the Montevideo Conference in 1933 the American republics affirmed their belief in certain essential principles upon which cooperation between nations and international order must be based. Among them was the principle that every nation, large and small, was equal before the law of nations. Another was the right of every nation to develop its own institutions, free from intervention by others. We already see the beginning of a wider application of these basic principles. They were stated in the Atlantic Charter, the United Nations Declaration, and the declarations made at Moscow. Specifically, it was agreed at Moscow that membership in the world security organization must be upon the basis of the sovereign equality of all nations, weak as well as strong, and the right of every nation to a government of its own choice.

The American nations spoke with a united voice at Buenos Aires as early as 1936 and Lima in 1938 of the dangers to world peace which impended, and took united action to defend the hemisphere against them. When the attack came many of the American republics immediately sprang to the defense of the hemisphere. Shortly after the conference at Rio de Janeiro others took the same course. This chapter in our American history will ever be a gallant and glorious one. It teaches that unity of purpose, a common and passionate devotion to the maintenance of freedom, and mutual trust and confidence are the essential elements without which no amount of international organization and machinery can succeed. But it also teaches us and other nations that international organization and machinery are necessary. Successful as our common action has been, it has not been complete. And it took time, which may not always be available. Therefore, we learn that an international organization, whether in the field of inter-American cooperation or in the broader field of world peace, must have two main supports. It must gather its greatest strength from the rightness and justness of the principles upon which it is founded and the mutual trust of its members. It must also have such an essential framework and machinery and such an acceptance of their obligations on the part of its members as will enable it to act promptly and effectively in times of crisis.

Another guidepost for the future which our common experience before and during this war has raised is in the economic field. With the outbreak of the war the continent mobilized economically. The extent to which the products of the hemisphere have contributed to the growing success of the war against Germany and Japan cannot be overestimated. Millions of men and women throughout the hemisphere are devoting themselves unsparingly to the production of essential materials and to the forging of the weapons of our common victory. All this has been done under the great handicaps of the dislocations produced by the war.

At the end of the war all of our countries will be faced by problems of immense gravity. Out of the experience of our association in peace and in war we have learned that the expansion of material well-being can only come with an expansion of production and trade and hence an increase in consumption. We have learned too that no one nation can solve its problems by itself. An increase in production requires financing, a wise selection of the goods to be produced, and wise and fair commercial policies to enable goods to flow to their markets and necessary purchases to be made in return. All of this requires cooperative effort and the creation of international arrangements through which that effort may have concrete expression. But it requires something more than this. It requires the respect by each nation for each other nation, of which I have spoken, in the field of political relations. International cooperation in the economic field is the opposite of economic imperialism, by which one country seeks to exploit another. It is also the opposite of economic nationalism, by which each nation seeks to live unto itself.

We citizens of this hemisphere have great opportunities before us. The community of action among the American nations, already highly developed, will at the end of the war be indispensable in the advancement of our economic well-being and in the establishment of an international organization to prevent the recurrence of world wars. Together, as I have said, we foresaw, pointed out, and prepared against the dangers of war. Together we must foresee and prepare for the ever-greater common task of the peace. I believe that as in future years men of the Americas meet to commemorate this day they will see unfolded before their eyes ever-increasing evidence that the path along which inter-American cooperation has led is the path to human liberty and human welfare.

ADDRESS by James F. Byrnes, Secretary of State, "Neighboring Nations in One World," at New York City, October 31, 1945

Department of State Bulletin, November 4, 1945, p. 709. The address was delivered before the New York Herald Tribune Forum

THE SUBJECT about which I wish to speak briefly this evening is "Neighboring Nations in One World."

It was no accident that President Roosevelt, who did so much to develop our inter-American system, did even more to develop the world community of the United Nations. For today all nations are neighbors, and although we may have special relations with our nearer neighbors in the Americas, we must remember that we and they are parts of a single, interdependent world.

When we consider the principles which govern our inter-American system as it has been worked out in recent years, it is well to remember that these principles were not always recognized by us in our relations with our neighbors. There were times, not so far distant, when we tried "dollar diplomacy" and intervention and were accused of "Yankee imperialism."

But we have learned by experience that to have good neighbors we must be a good neighbor.

We have discovered that understanding and good-will cannot be bought and cannot be forced. They must spring spontaneously from the people. We have learned also that there can be no lasting friendship between governments unless there is understanding and good-will between their peoples.

In the inter-American system the members do not interfere in the internal affairs of their neighbors nor do they brook interference in those internal affairs by others. Freedom means more than freedom to act as we would like them to act.

But we do want other people to know what our people are thinking and doing. And we want to know what other people are thinking and doing. Only with such knowledge can each people determine for itself its way of life.

We believe other nations have a right to know of our own deep attachment to the principles of democracy and human rights; our profound belief that governments must rest upon the free consent of the governed; and our firm conviction that peace and understanding among nations can best be furthered by the free exchange of ideas.

While we adhere to the policy of non-intervention, we assert that knowledge of what other people are thinking and doing brings understanding; and understanding brings tolerance and a willingness to cooperate in the adjustment of differences.

Censorship and blackouts, on the other hand, breed suspicion and distrust. And all too often this suspicion and distrust are justified. For censorship and blackouts are the handmaidens of oppression.

The policy of non-intervention in internal affairs does not mean the approval of local tyranny. Our policy is intended to protect the right of our neighbors to develop their own freedom in their own way. It is not intended to give them free rein to plot against the freedom of others.

We have learned by bitter experience in the past ten years that Nazi and Fascist plans for external aggression started with tyrannies at home which were falsely defended as matters of purely local concern. We have learned that tyranny anywhere must be watched, for it may come to threaten the security of neighboring nations and soon become the concern of all nations.

If, therefore, there are developments in any country within the inter-American system which, realistically viewed, threaten our security, we consult with other members in an effort to agree upon common policies for our mutual protection.

We Americans can take genuine pride in the evolution of the good-neighbor policy from what, in a way, were its beginnings in the Monroe Doctrine. We surely cannot and will not deny to other nations the right to develop such a policy.

Far from opposing, we have sympathized with, for example, the effort of the Soviet Union to draw into closer and more friendly association with her central and eastern European neighbors. We are fully aware of her special security interests in those countries, and we have recognized those interests in the arrangements made for the occupation and control of the former enemy states.

We can appreciate the determination of the people of the Soviet Union that never again will they tolerate the pursuit of policies in those countries deliberately directed against the Soviet Union's security and way of life. And America will never join any groups in those countries in hostile intrigue against the Soviet Union. We are also confident that the Soviet Union would not join in hostile intrigue against us in this hemisphere.

We are concerned to promote friendship, not strife, among neighbors everywhere. For twice in our generation strife among neighbors has led to world conflict. Lasting peace among neighbors has its roots in spontaneous and genuine friendship. And that kind of friendship among nations depends upon mutual respect for one another.

It is our belief that all peoples should be free to choose their own form of government, a government based upon the consent of the governed and adapted to their way of life.

We have put that belief into practice in our relations with our neighbors. The Soviet Union has also declared that it does not wish to force the Soviet system on its neighbors. The whole-hearted acceptance of this principle by all the United Nations will greatly strengthen the bonds of friendship among nations everywhere.

But the point I wish to emphasize is that the policy of the good neighbor, unlike the institution of marriage, is not an exclusive arrangement. The best neighbors do not deny their neighbors the right to be friends with others.

We have learned that our security interests in this hemisphere do not require its isolation from economic and cultural relations with the rest of the world.

We have freely accepted the Charter of the United Nations, and we recognize the paramount authority of the world community. The Charter, while reserving to us and other nations the inherent right of individual and collective self-defense in case of armed attack, requires that enforcement action taken under regional arrangements be sanctioned by the Security Council of the United Nations Organization.

Moreover, we adhere strictly to the policy that cooperation among the American republics does not justify discrimination against non-American states. The American republics have practiced the policy of equal treatment for all states which respect the sovereignty and integrity of their fellow states.

Inter-American cooperation is not inconsistent with world-wide cooperation among the nations. Regional arrangements, like the inter-American system, which respect the rights and interests of other states and fit into the world system can become strong pillars in the structure of world peace.

But we cannot recognize regional arrangements as a substitute for a world system. To do so would not promote the common and paramount interests of all nations, large and small, in world peace.

We live in one world; and in this atomic age regional isolationism is even more dangerous than is national isolationism.

We cannot have the kind of cooperation necessary for peace in a world divided into spheres of exclusive influence and special privilege.

This was the great significance of the Moscow Declaration of 1943. That joint statement of policy pledged the world's most powerful nations to mutual cooperation in winning the war and maintaining the peace. It was a landmark in our efforts to create a world community of nations and to abandon the discredited system of international relations based upon exclusive spheres of influence.

Out of the Moscow Declaration have come the Dumbarton Oaks, Tehran, Crimea, San Francisco, and Potsdam conferences. And the United Nations Organization and the London Council of Foreign Ministers were created in the spirit of that Declaration.

International cooperation must—as I emphasized in my recent report on the London Council—depend upon intelligent compromise. It does not require us or any other nation to neglect its special relations with its nearer neighbors. But it does require that all neighborly relations be fitted into an organized system of international relations world-wide in scope.

The world system which we seek to create must be based on the principle of the sovereign equality of nations.

That does not mean that all nations are equal in power and influence any more than all men are equal in power and influence. But it does mean equal respect for the individuality and sovereignty of nations, large and small. Nations, like individuals, should be equal before the law.

That principle is the cornerstone of our inter-American system as it is the cornerstone of the United Nations.

Adherence to that principle in the making of the peace is necessary if we are to achieve enduring peace. For enduring peace is indivisible. It is not the exclusive concern of a few large states or a few large groups of states. It is the concern of all peoples.

Believing this, the position of the United States will continue to be that the nations, large and small, which have borne the burdens of the war must participate in making the peace.

In centuries past powerful nations have for various purposes tried to divide the world among themselves. They failed, and in failing left a trail of blood through the centuries. Such efforts have even less chance of success in the modern world where all nations have become neighbors.

Today the world must make its choice. There must be one world for all of us or there will be no world for any of us.

RADIO BROADCAST by Spruille Braden, Assistant Secretary of State, and Ellis O. Briggs, Director of the Office of American Republic Affairs, Department of State, "Our Inter-American Policy," January 4, 1946

Department of State, Inter-American Series, No. 28

ANNOUNCER: Here are *Headlines From Washington:*
   Assistant Secretary of State Braden Says Axis Forces in Argentina Still Constitute a Danger to the Americas; Reaffirms United States Support of Uruguayan Proposal for Collective Security in Western Hemisphere.
   Ellis Briggs of State Department Says United States Policy Is to Avoid Unilateral Action, but That We Reserve the Right to Speak Out and Work for Collective Action for Peace in the Americas.

This is the fourth in a group of State Department programs broadcast by the NBC University of the Air as part of a larger series entitled "Our Foreign Policy." This time the question "What Is Our Inter-American Policy?" will be discussed by Mr. Spruille Braden, Assistant Secretary of State for American republic affairs, and Mr. Ellis O. Briggs, Director of the Office of American Republic Affairs. Sterling Fisher, Director of the NBC University of the Air, will serve as chairman of the discussion. Mr. Fisher—

FISHER: Mr. Braden, I'd like to say right here that a good many of us have followed your forthright career, as Ambassador to Argentina and as Assistant Secretary of State, with interest and more than a little admiration. Because we admired your actions down in Buenos Aires, we're especially delighted to have you as our guest on this program.

BRADEN: Thanks, Mr. Fisher. But you must realize that I acted in Buenos Aires as the official representative of my Government.

FISHER: Granted. But I still think you interpreted United States policy with a unique vigor. Mr. Briggs, you've worked with Mr. Braden a good deal—don't you agree?

BRIGGS: Yes, I think he added his own touch.

FISHER: Now, if you don't object, Mr. Braden, I'd like to ask you a personal question.

BRADEN: Go right ahead.

FISHER: Many of us would be interested in knowing how a former mining engineer like yourself became a diplomat. When did you first start working with the State Department?

BRADEN: Well, in 1933—12 years ago—the President appointed me as a delegate to the Seventh International Conference of American States at Montevideo. A little over a year later I was named a delegate to the Pan American Commercial Conference. But for years before that I had been in business in various parts of the hemisphere.

BRIGGS: You also had a lengthy assignment as our representative at the Chaco Peace Conference in the thirties.

BRADEN: Yes, that kept me down there from 1935 until the end of 1938. In the early part of that period it looked as if the negotiations between Bolivia and Paraguay might break down. If they had, the whole peace structure in the Americas might have gone down too.

FISHER: And after that was settled you went to the Republic of Colombia.

BRADEN: That's right. That was a very interesting period. I was Ambassador to Colombia when the Axis airlines down there were closed out in 1940.

FISHER: And in 1942 you went to Cuba as our Ambassador. That assignment lasted until early in 1945, didn't it?

BRADEN: Yes, until last April, when I was transferred to Argentina. Mr. Briggs here was with me in Habana for over two years, as Counselor of Embassy. He put in a total of eight years in Cuba, at different times. And he has served in Peru, Chile, and as Ambassador to the Dominican Republic—and for three years as Assistant Chief of the Office of American Republic Affairs.

FISHER: That's quite a background for your present work, Mr. Briggs. I understand that you were one of the youngest ambassadors in our history when you were accredited to the Dominican Republic.

BRIGGS: I may have been, Mr. Fisher.

FISHER: Now, to get down to the main business at hand—Mr. Braden, as you know, there has been a good deal of discussion of our inter-American policy. Before you became Assistant Secretary for American republic affairs, it was sometimes charged that we were appeasing the Argentine dictatorship. Since you came to Washington that sort of criticism has stopped, but some commentators have claimed that we were *intervening* too actively in our dealings with the other American republics. What about that, Mr. Secretary?

BRADEN: Our policy of non-intervention in the affairs of the other American nations is fundamental and will continue. We have no intention of taking that kind of unilateral action. Neither do we intend to stand idly by while the Nazi-Fascist ideology against which we fought a war endeavors to entrench itself in this hemisphere. But our policy is one of *joint* action with the other republics—*group* action for our mutual security.

FISHER: If we can be more specific, Mr. Braden—what is the situation with regard to Argentina today?

BRADEN: There is one basic fact about Argentina, Mr. Fisher. The majority of the Argentine people have always been pro-democratic and opposed to totalitarian dictatorship. That's truer today than ever.

FISHER: I should think that would be difficult to prove.

BRADEN: A good example of the opposition to the Fascist regime was the magnificent "March of the Constitution and of Freedom" last September. An estimated half-million Argentines paraded through the streets of Buenos Aires that day. Society women and men in overalls marched side by side. It was an impressive demonstration for democracy, carried out despite every possible obstacle put in its path. Over 500,000 people, and they were not divided up in groups of businessmen, labor-union members, or students—they all marched together. They alternated in singing their own national anthem and "God Bless America." You can't say that people like that are not our friends.

BRIGGS: Shortly after that the Government clamped down a "state of siege" again.

FISHER: Just what is a "state of siege," Mr. Briggs?

BRIGGS: Well, it means the establishment of martial law. Here it would involve the setting aside of the Bill of Rights.

BRADEN: It means that hoodlums with brass knuckles can strike girls in the face for shouting, "Long live democracy." It means that the saber-wielding mounted police can ride down men, women, and children and beat, slug, or arrest anyone at will, without fear of reprisal.

FISHER: I understand that Dictator Juan Perón got his training in the Fascist School in Milan, Italy.

BRADEN: I'm not concerned as much with personalities, Mr. Fisher, as I am with *ideologies*. All through the war, the Axis forces in this hemisphere used Argentina as a base of operations. These Axis forces still constitute a danger to the Americas.

FISHER: You mean that Axis business firms in Argentina are still untouched, despite all the promises that were made?

BRADEN: No, I wouldn't say that. I *would* say that nothing has been done against the most powerful and therefore most dangerous Axis elements.

FISHER: How does the present Argentine regime manage to keep enough popular support to stay in power, Mr. Briggs?

BRIGGS: They have the police, an important segment of the Army, armed "action groups," and a typically National Socialist program, not excluding the old formula of bread and circuses for the millions. Following recognized Nazi tactics, they secured control of certain strategic labor unions. If you take over the transport, utilities, and a few other important unions, with the help of the police, you can control a nation.

BRADEN: It follows the German pattern of 1933 to 1938. The object is to convert a military revolution into a National Socialist revolution.

FISHER: The question is, what can be done to stop this sort of thing before it spreads to other countries? The New York *Herald Tribune* pointed out the other day that here you have the same dilemma that faced the democracies in 1939 and before. To intervene would be to violate the principles of international law; and "not to intervene"—to quote the *Herald Tribune*—"is to see Fascism . . . take hold and fester in Latin America, until it ultimately threatens to wreck the continent if not the larger world." Mr. Braden, how can you escape from that dilemma?

BRADEN: You are perfectly right, Mr. Fisher. We are pledged not to intervene in the internal affairs of any American republic by taking unilateral action, and we shall not do so. On the contrary we intend to consult with other countries in this hemisphere and to follow this by such joint action as may be agreed upon.

FISHER: Which brings up a second major question in our Latin American relations—what about the Uruguayan proposal? But first, Mr. Briggs, you might tell us just what it is.

BRIGGS: What the Uruguayan Foreign Minister proposed was that the notorious and repeated violation of human rights by any country endangers the peace and is a matter of concern to other countries. The Foreign Minister pointed out the close connection between democracy and peace, and also visualized the necessity of harmonizing the doctrine of no unilateral intervention with the need for action to be taken with respect to a regime violating human rights.

FISHER: But what is new about the Uruguayan plan?

BRIGGS: First, it clearly recognizes that democracy and peace are parallel, and that the close connection between them constitutes a legitimate basis for inter-American action. Second, Uruguay stressed that "non-intervention" should not be a shield behind which crimes may be committed, Axis forces sheltered, and obligations disregarded. Dr. Rodríguez Larreta put forward this proposal and suggested that it be the subject of consultation looking toward its adoption.

BRADEN: When Secretary Byrnes gave the message of the Uruguayan Foreign Minister his whole-hearted approval, he put the issue very clearly: "Violation of the elementary rights of man by a government of force and the non-fulfillment of obligations by such a government is a matter of common concern to all the republics. As such," said Mr. Byrnes, "it justifies collective multilateral action after full consultation among the republics in accordance with established procedures."

FISHER: And Secretary Byrnes' endorsement still stands?

BRADEN: It does. We are convinced that the Uruguayan proposal is sound and moreover fully in accordance with the development of the inter-American system. We believe that it merits full public examination and discussion. Furthermore, the replies sent to the Uruguayan Minister which have thus far come to our attention show a broad area of agreement with respect to the principle involved.

FISHER: I remember Sumner Welles said that our endorsement of the Uruguayan proposal made it look as though the proposal announced in Montevideo had in reality been made through prior agreement in Washington. Would you care to comment on that, Mr. Braden?

BRADEN: The proposal was entirely the idea of the Foreign Minister of Uruguay. It was drafted by him and was submitted simultaneously to this Government and to the others. We were prompt to approve the general principles involved, because they are consistent with our whole inter-American policy. The proposal recognizes that the American republics have the same right of discussion and consultation which they themselves have already granted to the United Nations Organization, in empowering the Assembly to discuss any matter affecting the peace. Furthermore, the United Nations Organization will have the power to take collective action to meet threats to the peace. That's what Uruguay proposes for this hemisphere. It may of course take time to implement the proposal. That can only be done if after thorough consultation the other American republics of their own volition are convinced of its wisdom. That's the inter-American way.

FISHER: There have been some charges, Mr. Braden, that this plan would mean the scrapping of the doctrine of non-intervention in the internal affairs of other countries, on which the good-neighbor policy is based.

BRADEN: There's no basis for such charges. When we take a stand for democracy in the Balkans, no one cries "intervention." That's a complaint that seems to be reserved for the Americas. Our approval of the Uruguayan proposal doesn't mean that we're going to attempt to impose our will or send the Marines anywhere. What we need first of all is frank and friendly discussion of our problems, in the same sort of town-meeting atmosphere as in the United Nations Assembly. The spotlight of public opinion can do a lot.

FISHER: What would you add to that, Mr. Briggs?

BRIGGS: Just this: We don't intend to intervene to impose democracy on anyone. We do feel most friendly toward those governments that rest on the freely and periodically expressed approval of those who are governed. We are just as friendly to the people living under regimes where they must struggle for such expression.

FISHER: Then, Mr. Briggs, the Uruguayan proposal doesn't mean intervention—certainly not unilateral intervention. But doesn't it imply that something less than unanimity should be required for action, in case fundamental human rights are threatened in any country?

BRIGGS: It definitely implies that, Mr. Fisher, though certainly no steps would be undertaken by this nation or the others unless there was general agreement. The idea that we must have *unanimity* before we can act together, however, is not in accord with practical reality. If we want to implement our international ideals, we'll have to be content with the reasonable and attainable objective of a substantial majority of nations, while seeing to it that the rights of the minority are fully protected. But these are all questions that remain to be worked out with our sister republics.

BRADEN: I'd like to add, Mr. Fisher, that a nation as powerful as ours must be particularly scrupulous in any matter involving collective action. No one fears the intervention of small countries, but the possession of great military and economic power is bound to arouse suspicion unless we are extremely careful in the use of that power. But we also have to recognize this fact: *Not* to use our power in the interests of peace and freedom may be *mis*using that power just as much as if we brought our influence to bear on the wrong side of an issue. We must lean over backwards to avoid intervention by action or inaction alike.

FISHER: That's a little complicated, I'm afraid, Mr. Braden; perhaps you'd better explain what you mean by "intervention by inaction."

BRADEN: Well, let me put it this way: Suppose a totalitarian regime comes to power in some country. If we withhold recognition, that regime may claim we're intervening. If we recognize it, then its opponents may claim that we are intervening on its behalf.

FISHER: In other words, you're damned if you do and damned if you don't.

BRADEN: Sometimes that's the way it seems. But the only course we can follow is to consider all the possibilities and then throw our weight on the side of the principles of justice and freedom—the principles for which this country was born and for which we have just fought a tragically costly war. In that war alone we sustained a million casualties and increased our national debt by 300 billion dollars, in defending these principles. We shall continue to defend them. In so doing we shall act in concert with the great majority of other American nations.

BRIGGS: What we're really trying to say is that the doctrine of non-intervention means no intervention by any *one* nation. It's my own belief that the necessity for intervention by the use of force would rarely occur. You wouldn't have to go this far in a majority of cases. The airing of the facts should in itself do much to correct the condition.

BRADEN: I'd like to quote something at this point from one of the greatest legal figures this hemisphere has produced—the Brazilian jurist, Ruy Barbosa.

FISHER: Go right ahead, Mr. Secretary.

BRADEN: Ruy Barbosa said, on July 14, 1916:

"When violence arrogantly tramples the written law underfoot, to cross one's arms is to serve it. . . . In the face of armed insurrection against established law, neutrality cannot take the form of abstention, it cannot take the form of indifference, it cannot take the form of silence."

FISHER: That's an eloquent statement—don't you think, Mr. Briggs?

BRIGGS: Yes; and that reference to silence is particularly appropriate. Any nation certainly has a right to speak its mind on issues it considers important. We endorse the right to speak freely, to offer sympathy to oppressed peoples, and to try to persuade other·nations to join us in group action, where action is required.

BRADEN: Any other interpretation of non-intervention is grotesque. People who argue that any action or any statement on our part constitutes intervention are really asking us to go isolationist; they are asking us to see no evil and hear no evil, even if evil is there under our very noses.

BRIGGS: No international association could prosper if its member nations were denied the right to express their opinions, or to seek agreement among themselves on necessary action to be taken. And I'd like to emphasize again that such action need not be *unanimous*. The fact is, very few treaties and conventions are unanimously ratified.

FISHER: Haven't a good many Pan-American treaties been adopted unanimously, Mr. Briggs?

BRIGGS: On the contrary; out of a hundred or more treaties and conventions signed in this hemisphere since 1890, only one of any importance—the Pan American Sanitary Convention—was ratified by all 21 American republics. You can't expect to get unanimity on all major issues. If you stick for unanimity, what you'll often get is the lowest common denominator—something watered down and tasteless rather than useful and inspiring.

FISHER: I am sorry if I keep returning to this question of intervention, or rather unilateral action, Mr. Briggs, but I seem to remember that the same charges were made when the conference scheduled for Rio de Janeiro was postponed late last year. What was behind that?

BRIGGS: Well, Mr. Fisher, the Rio conference was called for just one purpose: to write the Act of Chapultepec into the form of a permanent treaty, whereby the countries of this hemisphere would come to the aid of any American republic whose security might be threatened. But Argentine developments were such that we felt it would be meaningless to conclude such a treaty with the present Argentine Government as a cosignatory. So we suggested to Brazil, the host country, that the conference be postponed.

FISHER: There was some talk at the time to the effect that we didn't consult the other countries before taking that step.

BRIGGS: That talk was totally unfounded. We proceeded in a perfectly proper way. We took the matter up with the host government first, and then discussed it informally with the other governments. That discussion was carried on through two channels—we talked with their ambassadors in Washington, and our ambassadors abroad consulted with their Ministers of Foreign Affairs. Finally, at the October meeting of the Pan American Union's Governing Board, the representatives of the other republics indicated that postponement was satisfactory to them.

BRADEN: As a matter of fact, some of the governments indicated they had desired postponement for weeks prior to our taking initiative, and for the same reason.

FISHER: Then, Mr. Braden, the reports of unilateral action were completely false?

BRADEN: Yes, the other American republics were all consulted prior to the meeting of the Pan American Union where the decision was made.

FISHER: And where does the matter stand now? When will the conference be held?

BRADEN: It is scheduled for some time between March 15 and April 15 of this year. Our own suggestions have been drafted with the collaboration of members of the Congress and of the War and Navy Departments. Other nations have been invited to send in their suggestions to the host government. The treaty, when it is drawn up, will be in full harmony with the United Nations Organization.

FISHER: Now, what about our economic policy for the Americas, Mr. Briggs? The end of the war must have brought some severe problems south of the border.

BRIGGS: Yes, that's true. The war put a severe strain on the economy of many of the American republics, at the same time that their various industries were greatly expanded. Just as we are now going through a process of reconversion, the other American republics are in process of changing many lines of trade from wartime to peace time demands. Fortunately most of our neighbors have substantial dollar balances because of our purchases of strategic war goods, and the possession of these balances will help them in making the transition.

FISHER: Isn't the problem of maintaining employment highly important to them?

BRIGGS: It is indeed. At the Mexico City conference early last year this problem was recognized by all of us, and our Government agreed to a policy of easing the transition as much as we could by tapering off our purchases of strategic materials and giving them as much notice as possible before curtailing or terminating our purchases.

FISHER: And have we kept our word?

BRIGGS: Yes. Of course "tapering off" is subject to various interpretations. We are still buying some strategic materials. How long we can continue that, even for stockpiling purposes, is a question. .

FISHER: Mr. Braden, what about our long-range economic policy in the Americas?

BRADEN: We believe first of all, Mr. Fisher, that we should do everything in our power to help our American neighbors to increase industrialization along sound lines and to achieve higher standards of living.

FISHER: I've heard the argument that that policy will operate to reduce the market for American goods.

BRADEN: That argument was exploded by Adam Smith 200 years ago, but it dies hard. When our industrial revolution got under way, there were some Englishmen who said that, if English capital were sent over here, in time we would stop buying English goods. What happened? Within two generations we were buying six times as much English goods as before. No. If you want to sell goods, you have to find people with money or goods to trade for them.

FISHER: And what about the political results of industrialization, Mr. Braden? Do you feel that democracy goes with higher living standards, almost automatically?

BRADEN: Rising standards of living help to make free institutions possible. But higher living standards don't necessarily produce democracy. The Germans had higher living standards—and for that matter, a higher rate of literacy—than most of their neighbors, but they weren't democratic. Nor were they peaceful. And we should keep this in mind in encouraging industrialization in the Americas. I should be guilty of a lack of candor if I failed to point this out: We have no interest in promoting increased industry and productivity in nations which intend to build self-contained, nationalistic economies and aggressive military machines. That would be against our own interests and against the interests of the inter-American society of nations.

FISHER: You are thinking in terms of an inter-American economic system, then?

BRADEN: Quite the contrary, Mr. Fisher! We want to see this hemisphere an integral part of a freely trading world. The best way we know to protect this hemisphere—and ourselves—is to help to promote prosperity and stability and mutual trust not only throughout the Americas but throughout the world.

BRIGGS: And that means the lowering of commercial barriers, here as in the rest of the world.

BRADEN: Yes. I hope that every American republic will be represented at the United Nations Trade and Employment Conference this year. That conference can and should do a lot to break the shackles limiting world trade.

FISHER: And what about cultural cooperation, Mr. Briggs?

BRIGGS: That's highly important also, Mr. Fisher, in the long run. We need to build up more and more travel, more exchanges of teachers and students, within this hemisphere. Too many North Americans are ignorant of South America, and too many of our southern friends are ignorant of the United States. It's just as important for them to understand us as it is for us to understand them.

BRADEN: Yes, our history books are notoriously shy on facts about Latin American history and culture. Every schoolboy in the United States should learn that Bolívar and San Martín, as well as George Washington, were fathers of American freedom. And as they go on in school they should learn about the contributions of the other republics to our literature, art, music, law, and government. If this were done—if we learned more about our neighbors and they learned more about us—we would gradually come to think of ourselves not only as citizens of a single country but as citizens of the inter-American system as well, and of the world.

BRIGGS: That would also help undermine the exaggerated nationalism from which nearly every country is suffering. Perhaps we all do too much thinking about our own country's sovereignty and not enough about the responsibility that goes with sovereignty—the responsibility of each individual nation to the community of nations.

FISHER: Now, gentlemen, we've dealt with political, economic, and cultural questions. In the time that's left, I'd like to ask Mr. Braden to summarize our over-all policy for the Americas.

BRADEN: In the first place, Mr. Fisher, it's no different from our foreign policy generally. It springs from the same basic principles. We have a special interest in the security of the Western Hemisphere, it's true, because we live in this hemisphere. But we know that we can only have regional security in a secure and peaceful world. Further, we recognize that international peace and individual freedom are intertwined, so it is to our interest to encourage representative government and oppose irresponsible tyranny.

BRIGGS: It's a matter of bringing political development up to date with modern science and technology. That's a world problem, and a tough one. But unless we can develop the science of living together it's apparent that the achievements of the industrial era aren't going to be enjoyed by anyone very long.

BRADEN: As a practical matter we appreciate that this can't be done overnight, even though we recognize how urgent it is to bring our political thinking up to a par with our scientific achievements. Actually it may be more important to determine the direction in which a country is developing than it is to estimate the position which it may be in at any given moment. The main thing is to know whether a country is moving in the direction of dictatorship and disregard for the rights of man, or whether it is moving toward government "of the people, by the people, and for the people."

FISHER: But coming down to our *specific* policies, Mr. Braden—how would you summarize them?

BRADEN: We believe in the inter-American system as a practical operating arrangement among the 21 American republics. We want to see our inter-American system developed, to the benefit of all of the people of the hemisphere. We believe that the inter-American system can be and should be a strong supporting pillar of the United Nations Organization. We stand for collaboration for mutual benefit. We think that cooperation should be reciprocal—a two-way street.

FISHER: Collaboration for mutual benefit? Can you give us a more concrete example of what you mean?

BRADEN: Suppose country *A* wants to expand its public-health program and comes to our Government with a request for our cooperation. Country *A* asks, for example, if we can furnish technical assistance, trained personnel, and scientific equipment. If after consideration the project appears sound, we would offer to participate in a *joint* program—not necessarily 50–50, but one in which along with our contribution the other country would contribute according to its resources additional personnel, local material, or funds. The program would become a genuine reciprocal undertaking. It would benefit the country concerned by raising the standard of health and hence of living, and that would be of benefit to all of us.

BRIGGS: I should like to call attention, Mr. Fisher, to Mr. Braden's reference to the fact the country concerned had come to us with its project. That is, that country would have taken the initiative and thereby demonstrated its desire to have the project carried out. We don't believe in extravagance or paternalism. We do believe in reciprocal cooperation on a sound basis.

BRADEN: Let me add this, Mr. Fisher: We firmly believe in the original good-neighbor policy, as President Roosevelt stated it many years ago. You remember he said that the good neighbor was "he who resolutely respects himself, and because he does so, respects others and their rights . . . the neighbor who respects his obligations and the sanctity of his agreements in and with a world of neighbors." That means a policy of respect—first self-respect, and then mutual respect among nations. That's the fundamental policy that we have had, and still have, in the Americas. We offer our friendship and cooperation on a reciprocal basis, each country giving in proportion of its abilities—economic, intellectual, and in other fields. Through such cooperation we can all benefit, from the raising of standards of living and the growth of democracy in each country.

FISHER: That's a very clear statement of a very sound credo, Mr. Braden. And I want to thank you and Mr. Briggs for giving us this review of our foreign policy for the Americas.

ADDRESS by President Harry S. Truman at the Inter-American Conference for the Maintenance of Continental Peace and Security, at Quitandinha, Brazil, September 2, 1947
The New York *Times,* September 3, 1947

MR. PRESIDENT, Delegates to the Inter-American Conference for the Maintenance of Continental Peace and Security, Ladies and Gentlemen:

It is a distinguished privilege to address the final session of this historic conference. You are assembled here as the representatives of the nations of this hemisphere which have been banded together for over half a century in the inter-American System. You have successfully accomplished the task of putting into permanent form the commitments made in the Act of Chapultepec. You have made it clear to any possible aggressor that the American Republics are determined to support one another against attacks. Our nations have provided an example of good neighborliness and international amity to the rest of the world, and in our association together we have strengthened the fabric of the United Nations. You can be justly proud of the achievements of this conference and I commend the noble spirit which has inspired your efforts.

The cordial and gracious invitation of President Dutra to visit this beautiful land has allowed me to fulfill a desire I have long cherished. I consider it most fortunate that I am enabled also to meet with the foreign ministers and other leaders of the American Republics. Thus, in a sense, I am visiting not only Brazil, but I am visiting all your countries, since each of you carries his country in his heart.

While we are assembled here together, I wish to discuss with you the responsibilities which our nations share as a result of the recent war. For our part, the United States is deeply conscious of its position in world affairs. We recognize that we have an obligation and that we share this obligation with the other nations of the Western Hemisphere. Therefore, I take this occasion to give you a frank picture of our view of our responsibility and how we are trying to meet it.

The people of the United States engaged in the recent war in the deep faith that we were opening the way to a free world, and that out of the terrible suffering caused by the war something better would emerge than the world had known before.

The post-war era, however, has brought us bitter disappointment and deep concern.

We find that a number of nations are still subjected to a type of foreign domination which we fought to overcome. Many of the remaining peoples of Europe and Asia live under the shadow of armed aggression.

No agreement has been reached among the Allies on the main outlines of a peace settlement. In consequence, we are obliged to contemplate a prolonged military occupation of enemy territories. This is profoundly distasteful to our people.

Almost everywhere in Europe, economic recovery has lagged. Great urban and industrial areas have been left in a state of dependence on our economy, which is as painful to us as it is to them. Much of this economic distress is due to the paralysis of political fear and uncertainty in addition to the devastation caused by war.

This situation has impeded the return to normal economic conditions everywhere in the world and has hampered seriously our efforts to develop useful forms of economic collaboration with our friends in other areas.

We did not fully anticipate these developments. Our people did not conceive, when we were fighting the war, that we would be faced with a situation of this nature when hostilities ceased. Our planning for peace pre-supposed a community of nations sobered and brought together by frightful suffering and staggering losses, more than ever appreciative of the need for mutual tolerance and consideration, and dedicated to the task of peaceful reconstruction.

In view of the unfortunate conditions which now prevail, we have faced some difficult problems of adjustment in our foreign policy. I would not say that we have made no mistakes. But I think that the elements of the policy we have evolved thus far are sound and justifiable.

The fundamental basis of the policy of the United States is the desire for permanent world peace.

We are determined that, in the company of our friends, we shall achieve that peace.

We are determined because of the belief of our people in the principle that there are basic human rights which all men everywhere should enjoy. Men can enjoy these rights—the right to life itself, and the right to share fully in the bounties of modern civilization—only when the threat of war has been ended forever.

The attainment of world-wide respect for essential human rights is synonymous with the attainment of world peace. The peoples of the earth want a peaceful world, a prosperous world, and a free world, and when the basic rights of men everywhere are observed and respected, there will be such a world.

We know that in the hearts of the common people everywhere there is a deep longing for stability and for settled conditions in which men can attain personal security and a decent livelihood for themselves and their children. We know that there are aspirations for a better and a finer life which are common to all humanity. We know—and the world knows—that these aspirations have never been promoted by policies of aggression.

We shall pursue the quest for peace with no less persistence and no less determination than we applied to the quest for military victory.

There are certain important elements in our policy which are vital in our search for permanent peace.

We intend to do our best to provide economic help to those who are prepared to help themselves and each other. But our resources are not unlimited. We must apply them where they can serve most effectively to bring production, freedom and confidence back to the world. We undertook to do this on an individual basis in the case of Greece and Turkey, where we were confronted with specific problems of limited scope and of peculiar urgency. But it was evident, at the time that the decision was made early this year, that this precedent could not be applied generally to the problems of other European countries. The demands elsewhere were of far greater dimensions. It was clear that we would not be able to meet them all. It was equally clear that the peoples of Europe would have to get together and work out a solution of their common economic problems. In this way they would be able to make the most of their own resources and of such help as they might receive from others.

The representatives of 16 nations are now meeting in Paris in an effort to get to the root of Europe's continued economic difficulties and to chart a program of European recovery based on helping themselves and each other. They will then make known their needs in carrying this program to completion. Unquestionably it is in the interest of our country and of the Western Hemisphere in general that we should receive this appeal with sympathy and good will, prepared to do everything we can, within safe limits, that will be helpful and effective.

Our own troubles—and we have many—are small in contrast with the struggle for life itself that engrosses the peoples of Europe. The nations of free Europe will soon make known their needs. I hope that the nations of free America will be prepared, each according to its ability and in its own manner, to contribute to lasting peace for the benefit of mankind.

Another important element of our policy vital to our search for peace, is fidelity to the United Nations. We recognize that the United Nations has been subjected to a strain which it was never designed to bear. Its role is to maintain the peace and not to make the peace. It has been embroiled in its infancy in almost continual conflict. We must be careful not to prejudge it by this unfair test. We must cherish the seedling in the hope of a mighty oak. We shall not forget our obligations under the Charter, nor shall we permit others to forget theirs.

In carrying out our policy we are determined to remain strong. This is in no way a threat. The record of the past speaks for us. No great nation has been more reluctant than ours to use armed force. We do not believe that the present international differences will have to be resolved by armed conflict. The world may depend upon it that we shall continue to go far out of our way to avoid anything that would increase the tensions of international life.

But we are determined that there shall be no misunderstanding in these matters. Our aversion to violence must not be misread as a lack of determination on our part to live up to the obligations of the United Nations Charter or as an invitation to others to take liberties with the foundations of international peace. Our military strength will be retained as evidence of the seriousness with which we view our obligations.

This is the course which our country is endeavoring to follow. I need not tell you how important it is to our success that we have your understanding, support and counsel. The problem is in the deepest sense a common one for this hemisphere. There is no important aspect of it which does not affect all of us. No solution of it can be fully successful in which we do not all cooperate.

I have already mentioned our collective responsibility for economic assistance. By the grace of God and by our united armed efforts our countries have been saved from the destruction of war. Our economies are intact, our productive powers undiminished, our resources not even yet fully explored. In consequence, our collective importance in the affairs of a distressed world has become immense.

The Western Hemisphere cannot alone assure world peace, but without the Western Hemisphere no peace is possible. The Western Hemisphere cannot alone provide world prosperity, but without the Western Hemisphere no world prosperity is possible.

Insofar as the economic problems common to the nations of North and South America are concerned, we have long been aware that much remains to be done. In reaching a solution there are many subjects which will have to be discussed among us. We have been obliged, in considering these questions, to differentiate between the urgent need for rehabilitation of war-shattered areas and the problems of development elsewhere. The problems of countries in this hemisphere are different in nature and cannot be relieved by the same means and the same approaches which are in contemplation for Europe. Here the need is for long-term economic collaboration. This is a type of collaboration in which a much greater role falls to private citizens and groups than is the case in a program designed to aid European countries to recover from the destruction of war. You have my solemn assurance that we in Washington are not oblivious to the needs of increased economic collaboration within the family of American nations and that these problems will be approached by us with the utmost good faith and with increased vigor in the coming period.

If acceptable solutions of these economic problems can be found, and if we can continue to work with mutual confidence and courage at the building of that great edifice of political security to which this Conference has made so signal a contribution, then I believe that we can look with high hopes on the further development of our community life in this hemisphere.

I have no desire to overlook the difficulties that have been encountered in the past and will continue to be encountered in the future. All of us are young and vigorous nations. At times we have been impetuous in our relations with one another. There has been a natural tendency for us to exhibit the same exuberance in our differences and our criticisms as in our friendships. Wide differences of background and tradition have had to be overcome.

But I believe that we may view with sober satisfaction the general history of our hemisphere. There has been steady progress in the development of mutual respect and of understanding among us. As the United States acquires greater maturity, as its experience becomes deeper and richer, our people gain in appreciation of the distinguished cultural traditions which flourish among our neighbors in the western world. I hope that as your acquaintance with us broadens, you will appreciate our fundamental good will and will understand that we are trying to bear with dignity and decency the responsibility of an economic power unique in human history.

There are many concrete problems ahead of us on the path of inter-American relations. They will not be solved with generalities or with sentimentality. They will call for the utmost we can give in practical ingenuity, in patience, and good will. But their solution will be easier if we are able to set our sights above the troubles of the moment and to bear in mind the great truths upon which our common prosperity and our common destiny must rest.

This Western Hemisphere of ours is usually referred to as the New World. That it is the New World is clearer today than ever before. The Old World is exhausted, its civilization imperilled. Its people are suffering. They are confused and filled with fears for the future. Their hope must lie in this new world of ours.

The sick and the hungry cannot build a peaceful world. They must have the support of the strong and the free. We cannot depend upon those who are weaker than we to achieve a peace for us to enjoy.

The benefits of peace, like the crops in the field, come to those who have sown the seeds of peace.

It is for us, the young and the strong, to erect the bulwarks which will protect mankind from the horrors of war—forever.

The United States seeks world peace—the peace of free men. I know that you stand with us. United, we can constitute the greatest single force in the world for the good of humanity.

We approach our task with resolution and courage, firm in the faith of our Lord, whose will it is that there shall be peace on earth.

We cannot be dissuaded, and we shall not be diverted, from our efforts to achieve His will.

ADDRESS by Norman Armour, Assistant Secretary of State, "Economic Aspects of the Bogota Conference," at New York City, December 9, 1947

Department of State press release, December 9, 1947 (No. 957). The address was delivered at a dinner given by the Pan American Society at the University Club

IT IS ALWAYS a pleasure to meet with a group in which are many old friends, and it is a privilege to discuss with the distinguished membership which makes up the Board of Directors of the Pan American Society, certain of our hemisphere problems and particularly some of the economic questions which may be expected to come before the

Ninth International Conference of American States at Bogota. These questions are highly important to the future of inter-American relations, and it is essential that our Delegation to the Conference be fully aware of the views of groups of citizens such as the Society, whose members have for so long played an outstanding role in advising and assisting in our economic relations with the other American nations. I have therefore looked forward particularly to this opportunity to speak to you tonight.

Economic cooperation among the American Republics was given extensive consideration at the Inter-American Conference on Problems of War and Peace, which was held in Mexico City in 1945. Subsequently, the subject was raised at the Conference for the Maintenance of Continental Peace and Security at Rio de Janeiro last August. You all know how successful the Rio Conference was. The treaty which it produced was described yesterday by Senator Vandenberg as "sunlight in a dark world." He characterized it as "a supplement and not a substitute for the United Nations" and called it "cheerful, encouraging and happy news in a war-weary world which is groping, amid constant and multiple alarms, toward the hopes by which men live." Certainly the acclamation with which the treaty has been received both in the New World and the Old has marked it as one of the few encouraging international agreements in these trying times. The United States was fortunate in having at Rio de Janeiro a delegation of broad vision, the members of which left all Party politics on our own shores when they set forth for Brazil. Rarely we have sent abroad a more distinguished delegation. You will recall that it consisted of the Secretary of State, the Chairman of the Senate Foreign Relations Committee, Senator Vandenberg, the former Chairman of that Committee, Senator Connally, our representative to the United Nations, ex-Senator Austin, the former Chairman of the Foreign Affairs Committee of the House, Congressman Bloom, and our Ambassador to Brazil. The result of their work was worthy of their ability, and the Treaty of Reciprocal Assistance which, as you know, was ratified yesterday by the Senate by an unprecedented vote of 72 to 1, is an example of community action by the countries of the New World which we trust will be the means of forever banishing war from this Hemisphere.

The question has been asked, "If it is desirable to conclude an agreement for hemisphere cooperation in the field of defense, is it not equally desirable to conclude a parallel agreement in the economic field?" The answer at Rio was emphatically "yes," with the result that the Inter-American Economic and Social Council was requested to prepare a draft of a basic agreement for inter-American economic cooperation, for consideration at the Bogota meeting. The Council is now engaged in that work, and will present a draft for study by the American Governments prior to the Conference. I should like to go over with you some of the problems as they are developing, and to indicate our hopes as to the kind of agreement which may finally result.

Close economic cooperation among the American nations has a growing tradition—in fact, it has become of great importance in contributing to improved economic conditions in the Americas. What we must seek in the agreement to be signed at Bogota is the basis for making that economic cooperation even more effective in the future.

The Bogota Conference, as you know, has now been set for March 30 instead of January 17 as originally planned. While we did not initiate the proposal to postpone the Conference we were glad to go along with the majority in this decision, particularly as we hope by the end of March that plans for economic aid to Europe should have been decided and the United Nations Trade Conference at Habana will have been concluded. The Bogota Conference will meet at a time when serious economic problems concern all of the American Republics, including our own country. At the present period, unfortunately, instead of being well on our way out of the transition period and into full post-war development, we are still faced with many difficulties and it is evident that this situation will continue for some time to come. The plans for the future which will be discussed at Bogota must therefore be based on the economic facts as they exist today. I think we will all agree that we should not attempt too much too rapidly, but preferably build upon the lines which have in the past proven most successful. In any case, the agreement which we look forward to signing at Bogota will be a basic agreement, detailed development of which we may expect at the technical economic conference which is scheduled to follow in the latter part of 1948.

From the viewpoint of both our neighboring nations and ourselves, the matter of economic development and the means by which it can go forward will certainly be one of the most important elements in the Bogota agreement. When we say that the sound economic development of Latin America is in our own interest, we are not merely paying lip service to a popular idea. Unfortunately, however, one still hears the criticism that this Government and the people of the United States do not favor economic development in Latin America since such development would compete with our own production. This opinion is definitely in error. Our Government holds the view that fuller utilization should be made of the resources of underdeveloped countries in such a way that a better balance of economic activity results between primary and secondary industries. Careful consideration should be given both to the improvement and the extension of primary industries and to the proportion in which soundly based manufacturing industries should be developed.

How economic development programs can best be carried out is a serious problem. Proposals have been discussed in the press to the effect that our Government should make available tremendous sums, running into billions of dollars. I should be less than frank if I were to fail to state that such proposals are not possible of attainment. The International Bank for Reconstruction and Development has large funds at its disposal for development loans to supplement private investments, and, if the Bank has not up to now adequately met Latin American requests for financing, I am sure that the matter is being given careful study at the present time, and I am confident that solutions will be found to the problems which have in the past delayed operations of this character.

Aside from the International Bank, the Export-Import Bank is an important factor in Latin American development programs. In past years actual loans in excess of four hundred million dollars have been made and additional amounts totalling nearly two hundred and fifty million dollars are committed. Further proposals submitted by various American Governments and nationals are now under consideration by the Export-Import Bank.

In this connection, I may say that, in our view, the use of Government funds for development operations should not displace or discourage private investments. There is no question of the existence of numberless opportunities for sound investment in Latin America. Many of these should be and will be developed by private capital if a favorable climate is created and if other factors, such as the growth of technical skills, can keep pace—for the development of new industries requires the simultaneous expansion of all the necessary economic factors essential to production and not merely the investment of capital.

Another factor of great importance if real progress is to be made in development programs is the treatment to be accorded foreign capital and skills and this will doubtless have a place in the basic economic agreement at Bogota. The economic development of Latin America is a long-range and continuing operation—requiring as much as twenty or thirty years, not merely four or five. We should, therefore, plan for the long pull, and we must recognize that, if development programs are to be carried out by means of cooperative action between this country and the Latin American countries individually, the arrangements must be beneficial to both parties. There needs to be a restatement of the rights and obligations entailed in international investments, and then a full and continued observance of them, so that both sides may come to know and respect the rules of the game.

Moreover, the Government of the United States, through the Institute of Inter-American Affairs, is today actively engaged in carrying out large-scale and long-range programs for working with the other American governments to improve the standard of living in their countries. These programs, which are in the fields of health and sanitation, agriculture and education, have for their objective the raising of standards to a point where the other American Republics may more fully realize the opportunities of a democratic way of life. We fully realize that the attainment of this objective will also result in economic benefits to our own country, since prosperous, healthy and literate peoples are not only better neighbors but also better customers. Also, in the field of technical cooperation we have had another program which will show increasing results as time goes on. For nearly ten years the Congress has been appropriating funds, through the Interdepartmental Committee on Scientific and Cultural Cooperation for such cooperative purposes as the study of mineral resources and development of mining and metallurgical methods; surveys of fishery and wildlife resources; maintenance of weather stations; studies of methods of insect pest elimination and disease control; and agricultural experiment stations for research in the development and uses of various products. In no field of activity has the Good Neighbor Policy been demonstrated in such a concrete and constructive fashion as in these programs.

The measures which I have mentioned as contributing to the economic development of Latin America are largely of a cooperative nature. Equally important are the steps which can be taken by each country individually. The fact is sometimes overlooked that national measures can be taken which will do much to advance economic development; in fact, in many cases these should precede rather than follow efforts to obtain external cooperation in development programs. I think this is particularly true in the field of fiscal policy, but it applies elsewhere as well. To recognize this, and to state it, is not to be unsympathetic to the need of various countries for economic assistance—it is simply to keep things in proper perspective. There is a large field for inter-American economic cooperation, and there is likewise a large field for national action to make that cooperation effective.

The questions being discussed at the moment at the Habana Conference bear an important relationship to the economic matters to be considered at Bogota. While it might not seem wise to bring into the inter-American economic agreement at this stage the same issues which the American nations and others are debating at Habana, the results of the Habana Conference—the degree to which it succeeds— will contribute to the success and effectiveness of the agreement to be drafted at Bogota.

For inter-American economic cooperation to be fully effective, it must include an understanding on both principles and practices in the broad field covered by the ITO Charter, including undertakings to reduce trade barriers to mutual advantage and to place trade on a non-discriminatory and multilateral basis, the conditions under which new industries are to be protected, the joint action which should be taken to meet surplus commodity problems when they arise, and the measures to handle the problems caused by restrictive trading practices by private business organizations. At the Geneva Conference during the past spring and summer, which produced the draft ITO Charter now under study at Habana, there was concluded, as you know, the General Agreement on Tariffs and Trade, the most comprehensive undertaking ever attempted in this field. Of the other American Republics, Brazil, Chile, and Cuba were represented at Geneva and contributed their full share to the final success of the Agreement, and during the months ahead we look forward to having all of the other American Republics become parties through the negotiation of further tariff agreements. The gradual widening of the scope of the General Agreement among the American nations and others will of course contribute in a specific and important manner to strengthening the bases for effective inter-American and international economic cooperation. It may be that the American Republics, without entering into any preferential undertakings, can reach an even more comprehensive agreement at Bogota than may be possible at Habana in the fields covered by the ITO Charter; this remains to be determined.

One problem which causes considerable concern on the part of our neighbors in the Western Hemisphere is that relating to the availability of materials which are still in short supply in this country and which may become even more difficult to obtain in future months. While our industries are converted fully to peace-time activities, production of many items is still inadequate to meet our own and world requirements, and it has therefore been necessary to retain export controls on certain commodities. Through these controls our Government has attempted to protect the interests of all and to ensure a fair and equitable distribution of available supplies. This will continue to be our policy even though our efforts on behalf of the European Recovery Program make some products more scarce and difficult to obtain than they have been in the past.

The European Recovery Program presents another problem bearing directly on our economic relations with Latin America. As you know, the question is frequently asked: "Is there to be a program for Latin America similar to the European Recovery Program?" The answer must be "no," if one is thinking of a comparable short term program. However, the European Recovery Program will very definitely affect Latin America.

The purpose of the European Recovery Program is to enable Western Europe to continue to eat and work until they can get back into production and export enough to maintain their trade balance. The largest requirements are food and fuel, and raw materials.

Some Latin American countries have balance of payments problems but they are more readily manageable because they do not arise from the necessary heavy importations of food and raw materials as is the case with Western Europe. What Latin America needs is capital goods such as equipment, machinery, tools, engineering services, for the development of their resources and industrialization. The Export-Import Bank has already made some sizeable loans to Latin America for this purpose. Latin American countries can also expect assistance from the International Bank for which Congress has already provided a share of capital.

There are actually two aspects of the European Recovery Program. The first relates to food and raw materials. As I have said, Europe must be enabled to continue to eat and work until production can be well started. The second aspect of the Recovery Program involves capital goods items, a considerable part of which will be produced by Europe itself. The fact that many types of machinery and equipment for reconstruction are similar to those needed for development and replacement purposes in Latin America—and in our own country as well—will undoubtedly contribute to accentuate the shortages to which I have previously referred. We shall endeavor to minimize the inconveniences that may result and, as I said, we shall endeavor to administer whatever export controls may be necessary with fair and equitable treatment for all.

Of particular interest to the other American Republics is a statement made by Secretary Marshall to the effect that the specific proposals to be made to the Congress contemplate the use of substantial funds for purchases outside the United States of commodities not readily available in sufficient quantities in this country. In all probability, the United States will operate a very large part of its own supply program on a grant basis—that is, the commodities will be sent to Europe free of charge. While the procurement program will provide a large amount of dollars for part of the supplies from the other countries in the Western Hemisphere, they will certainly not be sufficient to cover the total sum. Obviously these dollar expenditures will directly benefit the countries concerned, at a time when European markets—or at least payment in convertible currencies— might otherwise be lacking. The availability of dollar exchange will thus help to relieve difficult foreign exchange situations.

Thus we see that though the European Recovery Program does not apply directly to Latin America, the whole economic fabric of the world is today so closely interwoven that such a program is bound to affect vitally the people of the Western Hemisphere. From a humanitarian point of view I am sure that the countries of this Hemisphere want to support the program. Moreover, if the world is to be preserved from Communism their assistance is needed. And, finally, the program will restore their former markets in Europe. It is safe to say that without the restoration of these former markets there can be no permanent solution to the economic difficulties which now beset the American Republics.

In addition to the economic problems on which I have touched here this evening, many other important subjects will be considered at the Conference at Bogota. These include reorganization and strengthening of the Inter-American System, the general question of recognition of *de facto* governments, and the development and improvement of inter-American social services. The American Republics will, with their traditional spirit of friendship, which was so well exemplified last summer at the Conference of Rio de Janeiro, discuss these subjects with respect for one another's opinions and with appreciation of the local problems out of which arise whatever differences of opinion as may exist. Together, in mutual sympathy and understanding, they will undoubtedly reach agreement on the subjects considered by them. I anticipate that the Bogota Conference will represent another major step forward in the march of this Hemisphere toward international good will and cooperative assistance to one another and to all countries. It is thus that a region, acting within the United Nations, can contribute immeasurably to the future well-being and peace of the entire world.

ADDRESS by George C. Marshall, Secretary of State, at the Ninth International Conference of American States at Bogotá, April 1, 1948

Department of State, Publication 3139, "International Organization and Conference II, American Republics 2," reprinted from *Department of State Bulletin*, April 11, 1948

IT IS A GENUINE pleasure for me to meet again with the distinguished delegates of the American republics, and especially so under the hospitable auspices of the Republic of Colombia. I wish to express through His Excellency Doctor (Laureano) Gómez, Foreign Minister of Colombia, our distinguished presiding officer, the very sincere appreciation we feel for the Government of Colombia as our host, our respectful admiration for His Excellency President Ospina Pérez, and our strong feeling of friendship and regard for the people of Colombia.

It is my privilege and duty to convey to the conference warm greetings from President Truman with his earnest wish that our efforts here will be successful in behalf of all the peoples of the Americas.

Ten years have passed since the Eighth International Conference of American States was held in Lima. The momentous events of that period delayed this Ninth Conference but did not halt progress in inter-American cooperation.

The emergency meetings of the Foreign Ministers, which enabled us to coordinate our wartime efforts, were followed by the all-important conference at Mexico City in 1945 which resulted in the Act of Chapultepec, and the Conference on the Maintenance of Continental Peace and Security so successfully concluded last August at Rio de Janeiro with the treaty of reciprocal assistance.

We are here to consolidate and to carry forward the decisions of these previous conferences. We have to consider a lengthy agenda to give effect to the provisions of the ninth resolution of the Mexico City conference, pertaining to the reorganization, consolidation, and strengthening of the inter-American system. This is no small undertaking, for what we do in this respect will have an important bearing on the future of all our joint undertakings. The proposed organic pact will be the very heart of our hemispheric organization.

Cooperation among our countries has been greatly broadened and intensified during recent years. We need for this cooperation an organizational structure which will on the one hand be adequate to the increased responsibilities placed upon it, and on the other hand, efficiently administered so that duplication of effort may be avoided. The inter-American conferences and meetings of Foreign Ministers are the instruments through which the inter-American system formulates policy and reaches decisions on questions of major importance. The drafters of the organic pact have wisely concluded that to insure that these policies and decisions are effectively carried out, the Pan American Union, as the central permanent agency of the inter-American system, must be given a greater responsibility and commensurate staff. Under the direction of the inter-American conferences and meetings of Foreign Ministers the Pan American Union should play an increasingly significant role in the effective functioning of the inter-American system.

I am sure we all are agreed that the development of the inter-American system is within the concept of the United Nations and contributes to the attainment of its objectives.

The urgent need of effective methods of economic cooperation presents us with problems that call for the utmost good will and understanding in order to accommodate complex interests.

Agreement on a convention setting forth the procedures for the pacific settlement of disputes is one of the necessary aims of this conference. By this means we will establish a broad juridical basis for the peaceful adjudication of any differences that may arise among the American states. At the same time we will set an example to a distracted world in the maintenance of peace among neighbor states under an accepted system of law that assures justice and equity to all nations, large and small.

Significant questions related to social progress and the rights of the individual man are to receive full consideration in the deliberations of the conference. These are matters in which all our peoples are deeply concerned. They rightfully expect us to take positive action for their protection and welfare. That, in reality, is the purpose of our endeavors.

The overwhelming desire of the people of the world is for peace and security, freedom to speak their thoughts, freedom to earn a decent living in their own way. It is the earnest, the very genuine desire of the people of my country to continue to assist, so far as they are able to do so, the other people of the world to attain these objectives.

We have encountered, as you are aware, the determined and open opposition of one group of states. If the genuine cooperation of the Soviet Union could be secured, world recovery and peace would be assured. Until such cooperation is secured, we must proceed with our own efforts.

My Government has assumed heavy responsibilities in this undertaking, but we cannot do the job alone. We need the understanding and the cooperation of other nations whose objectives are the same as ours.

We must face reality. Allow me to talk to you frankly regarding the tremendous problems the United States is facing. After four years of supreme effort and a million casualties, we had looked forward to a state of tranquillity which would permit us to reorganize our economy, having made vast expenditures in natural resources and money. Instead my people find themselves today faced with the urgent necessity of meeting staggering and inescapable responsibilities—humanitarian, political, financial, and military—all over the world, in western Europe, in Germany and Austria, in Greece and Turkey, in the Middle East, in China, Japan, and Korea. Meeting these unprecedented responsibilities has demanded tremendous drafts on our resources and imposed burdensome taxes on our people. These are heavy exactions—far heavier than seems to be realized.

The basic economic trouble has been the collapse of European economy. Europe was formerly the most important center of international trade, and the disastrous impact of the war on the European economy has been felt everywhere in the world. The Western Hemisphere, for example, formerly enjoyed a substantial business with Europe and the virtual breakdown of that commerce has adversely and directly affected the American republics. The recovery of Europe is therefore a prerequisite to the resumption of trade relationships.

In the planning of the European Recovery Program, the United States gave and will continue to give careful consideration to the interests of the countries represented at this conference, both as to the procurement of materials to be purchased and the need of goods in short supply.

The difficulties you have experienced in obtaining certain materials from the United States to meet the needs of your industrial and agricultural development are understood. The problem of shortages is not yours alone. I am constantly under the necessity of explaining and defending this situation to manufacturers at home and particularly to farmers in the United States, who are themselves short of tools of production, of fertilizers, of steel, and other vital elements of our economy. The pressure on our production comes from every direction.

The Recovery Program provides the economic means of achieving a purpose essentially moral in nature. We propose to provide the free nations of Europe with that additional marginal material strength they require to defend the free way of life and to preserve the institutions of self-government. If human rights and liberties are blotted out in Europe, they will become increasingly insecure in the new world as well. This is a matter of as much concern to your countries as it is to mine.

But the United States cannot continue to bear alone the burdens on its own economy now necessary to initiate a restoration of prosperity. We have to look to other nations whose interests correspond with ours for active cooperation. All that are able should contribute. All will share the benefits. We have poured out our substance to secure the victory and prevent suffering and chaos in the first years of peace, but we cannot continue this process to the danger of exhaustion.

The rewards of freedom are economic as well as political. Only in such freedom can opportunity and incentive give full rein to individual initiative.

We have already agreed to certain principles that are stated in the Economic Charter of the Americas, signed in Mexico City in 1945. In that document the American republics proclaimed their common purpose to promote the sound development of national economies. The charter pointed the way toward realization of this aim through the encouragement of private enterprise and the fair treatment of foreign capital.

Our specific task here is to find workable methods by which our principles may be effectively applied in practical affairs. In a few moments I shall discuss the proposals of the United States Delegation for achieving this objective. But first I wish to draw attention to the general background from which they proceed. I do so because I believe that the experience of my country in its economic development offers some useful precedents.

One of the principal needs of the United States after it achieved independence was private capital for development of its resources and for western expansion. From overseas, and this is the point I wish to emphasize, at first cautiously and often with misunderstanding on both sides, the venture capital of Europe was invested in the new United States of America.

The great benefits accruing to the people of the United States from its material development were attributable in an important degree to this assistance received from abroad which together with the economic and political freedom of action enabled our people to capitalize rapidly upon the great natural resources of the country, and thus develop the production which has enabled us to bear today the heaviest responsibilities ever placed upon a single nation.

By 1900 the people of the United States themselves were becoming large investors in enterprises abroad. But internal development continued unabated. Despite the transformation from debtor to creditor nation and the accumulation of capital for foreign investments of its own, the United States continues to welcome money and technical assistance from other countries.

The point I wish to make is that even after the United States had achieved economic maturity and had become a major source of venture capital foreign investors continued to participate in the industrial and commercial growth of the nation without discrimination.

This policy has enabled the United States to prosper. The large-scale exchange of capital, goods, and services; the system of free enterprise; the confidence of other people in our future and the protection afforded foreign investments; the contributions made by skilled, energetic immigrants—all these helped immeasurably in making our nation not only productive and vigorous, but free. I repeat, this policy has enabled the United States to prosper, and I wish here to stress that it has enabled the United States to do a great deal for other countries, including the protection of their freedoms along with our own.

May I at this time invite your attention to a fact of particular significance related to the broad benefits to which I have just referred? That is, the fact that these benefits have been transferred into human values through the elevation of the real wages of labor to a point higher than has been achieved under any other system of enterprise in the history of mankind. These benefits automatically transfer themselves into the cultural and physical advancement of all of the people.

The United States is qualified, I submit, by its own historical experience to respond understandingly to the purpose of other American republics to improve their economic status. We understand the wish to achieve balanced economies through development of industries, mechanization of agriculture, and modernization of transportation.

My Government is prepared to increase the scale of assistance it has been giving to the economic development of the American republics. But it is beyond the capacity of the United States Government itself to finance more than a small portion of the vast development needed. The capital required through the years must come from private sources, both domestic and foreign.

As the experience of the United States has shown, progress can be achieved best through individual effort and the use of private resources. Encouragement should therefore be given to the increase of investment capital from internal as well as external sources. It is obvious that foreign capital will naturally gravitate most readily to countries where it is accorded fair and equitable treatment.

For its part, the United States fully supports the promotion of economic development in the American republics. We advocate the prompt preparation of sound development programs, which will set specific and realistic goals to be accomplished in the next few years.

The United States supports the International Bank of Reconstruction and Development as an important source of long-term capital for developing the economies of the American republics. My Government confidently expects the role of this institution to be one of increasing usefulness.

The President of the United States is submitting to Congress a request for an increase in the lending authority of the Export-Import Bank which will be available for sound projects in the American republics. These Government funds will be in addition to the private financing which will be needed for a much greater number of development projects.

The United States has studied the proposals regarding the taxation of foreign investments, with a view to avoiding double taxation and to encouraging the flow of private capital into other countries desiring it. I am glad to report that the President has under consideration measures to liberalize taxes on capital invested in foreign countries. These measures are designed to encourage not only initial investment but also the retention and reinvestment abroad of earnings derived from such capital. These measures also would liberalize the tax treatment of United States citizens residing abroad, and should therefore encourage technical experts to accept employment in other countries.

My Government attaches special importance to efforts to improve health, sanitation, education, and agricultural and industrial processes throughout the Hemisphere. We look forward to an expansion of the cooperative efforts of the American republics in these fields. We are surveying the availability of technical experts who may collaborate in the progress and development of the American republics, as recently authorized by the Congress, on a more flexible basis.

The economic advancement and security of this Hemisphere are supremely important to all countries, large and small, and to every citizen of our countries. Through joint endeavor, with each country accepting its share of responsibility and seeking faithfully to carry out its obligations, I am confident that the American republics will consistently move forward and attain the objectives which we all so earnestly desire.

Before concluding I wish to call attention to the close relationship between the solemn pacts we are here to conclude at Bogotá and the treaty of reciprocal assistance signed at Rio de Janeiro last September. Together, these pacts, when ratified, will form a harmonious whole guaranteeing the social, cultural, and economic progress of the Americas and at the same time the preservation of their independence, security, and sovereignty. I am informed that ten countries have already ratified the treaty of reciprocal assistance and that several other nations plan to take positive action along this line. It is to be hoped that during our labors here we may receive the gratifying word that the required number of ratifications have been deposited to enable the treaty to enter into effect. Such action is particularly important in the present world situation. We need the other vital measures we are to consider here as indispensable contributions to the welfare of the Americas. The peoples for whom we speak are impatient to launch this promising cooperative endeavor, for they see in it their greatest hope for achieving a better life for themselves, their children, and their children's children. They look to this conference to set in motion the concerted effort that will make their constant dream of peace and plenty a living, satisfying reality. We must not fail them.

[*Following the conclusion of his formal address to the conference, Secretary Marshall spoke extemporaneously substantially as follows*]

As has been the case with my predecessors here, it has been necessary for me to speak formally from a prepared statement. Much of what is said here goes far beyond this table to ears other than ours. Now my friends, I wish to speak to you personally and directly. I feel that in the discussions, particularly of economic matters, so much of detail necessarily becomes involved that the great purpose for which we are assembled and the situation in which we find ourselves becomes somewhat submerged, if not at least partially lost sight of.

I feel that what has already been said and, I suppose, much of what has yet to be said refers directly or indirectly, but specifically in many instances, to my country, to its international actions and present undertakings. I also have the feeling that there is a very limited understanding of the tremendous responsibilities and the equally tremendous burdens that the Government of the United States has been compelled to assume and which is very pertinent to our discussions here in this conference. For example, at the present moment our Legislature is under the necessity of considering at the request of the President the strengthening of our armed forces which would involve the expenditure of additional billions. Now you have a direct interest in that, because we hope that through such a process we can terminate this subversion of democratic governments in western Europe, and we can reach an understanding to maintain the peace and security, the tranquillity, and the future trade developments of the entire Western Hemisphere and not alone the United States. But the great burden of such action has rested on the people of the United States, and it is a very heavy burden.

I think that I can to a reasonable degree understand your reactions and your views because I had a considerable experience along very similar lines immediately preceding and during the war years. As Chief of Staff of the United States Army from the fall of 1939 up until almost the end of the war, I was under continual and the heaviest possible pressure from almost every part of the world, from rulers of countries, from our own military commanders in those regions, and from groups or sections at home or their representatives in Congress who felt very deeply regarding a particular situation. Now if we had not resisted those multitudes of pressures, all of which were based on the logical belief to a reasonable extent of the people concerned of the importance, the necessity, and urgency of their situation, the duration of the war and the situation at the end of the war would probably have been quite different.

The United States today with its tremendous responsibility, which involves us all over the world, has to proceed with great wisdom in all it does and what it feels it must do in the future. I ask you to have this in mind and to realize what a tremendous burden the people of my country have undertaken. You profit by it as much as we do.

I was sitting here yesterday and regarding this very decorative and impressive mural painting (the mural of Liberator Simón Bolívar) which illuminates this room. It suddenly occurred to me that it had a peculiar significance in relation to an event far distant from us here— in the far Pacific, as a matter of fact. The last territory that we wrested from the hands of the Japanese was a small island called Okinawa, between Formosa and Japan. That was the last big fight. One hundred and ten thousand Japanese were killed. The only captured were those wounded to the extent that they could not commit suicide. We had very heavy casualties. That operation was carried out by the 10th United States Army. But the point that occurred to me yesterday was this: the Commander of that Army was Simon Bolivar Buckner. He died in the last days of the fight—on the front line. Surely, that has some significance here in this room dominated by this painting in the rear of me; that out in the Pacific that man who made a great contribution and finally gave his life for the peace and security of the Pacific, that it would no longer carry a threat to your western shores, should have borne the name of your great liberator. Certainly that indicates something of our common purpose and much more of our common bonds.

ADDRESS by Willard F. Barber, Chief of the Division of Central America and Panama Affairs, Department of State, at Chicago, December 29, 1948 (extract)

Department of State press release No. 1025, December 27, 1948. The address was delivered at the Inter-American Panel Meeting of the American Political Science Association

. . . SENATOR VANDENBERG said that the Inter-American Treaty of Reciprocal Assistance signed at Rio de Janeiro on September 2, 1947 is "sunlight in a dark world."

The Treaty has a triple aspect:

A. It is under the United Nations a regional arrangement for the maintenance of peace and security under articles 52 through 54 of the Charter. It invokes the right (in article 51) of individual and collective self-defense against armed attack, pending action by the Security Council.

B. It states that an armed attack by any state against one American State is an attack against all. An armed attack from any source made upon the area described in article 4 of the treaty or upon the territory of an American State outside the area, obliges the signatories to assist in meeting the attack, as well as to consult. The nature of the help which they are pledged to render individually will be determined by each state pending a consultation to decide upon the collective measures required of all. Thus the *right* of collective self-defense in article 51 of the Charter becomes an *obligation* under the Rio Treaty. Decisions taken by a two-thirds vote are binding on all parties, including those not concurring. However, no state is required to use armed force without its consent.

C. It provides for consultation in the event of an act or threat of aggression against an American State or of any fact or situation which might endanger the peace of the Americas.

YEARS OF DEVELOPMENT

These forthright treaty obligations were not signed at Rio in an outburst of hemispheric sentimentality. On the contrary. The Treaty was not an outburst, but an *outgrowth* which has been steady and cumulative in the more than fifty years of development of the Inter-American System. Furthermore, it is based on the trial-and-error method, hammered out through years of actual practical experience. It is an *outgrowth*, not an *outburst*. It does indeed offer sunlight in a dark world.

From our own national point of view, if I may be permitted a reminder, the bi-partisan foreign policy of the United States, which is now widely accepted, has prevailed for some time in the Inter-American area.

THE PRACTICE OF CONSULTATION

It was at the Inter-American Conference of Buenos Aires in 1936 that the principle of *consultation* was agreed to in the event that the peace of the Americas was threatened. This was, therefore, an important milestone in establishing the *machinery* for implementing the basic policy of hemispheric solidarity.

The consultative procedure originating in 1936, confirmed at Lima in 1938, and manifested during the war years by meetings in 1939 at Panama, in 1940 at Habana and in 1942 at Rio de Janeiro, contributed substantially to Inter-American security.

The Act of Chapultepec, adopted at Mexico in 1945, reaffirmed the pronouncements of Buenos Aires and Lima. It restated the justifications for continental consultation.

Consultation, indeed, is provided for in the Rio Treaty in articles 3, 6, 7, 8, 9, 11, 12, 13, 17, and 21. It also appears in the Charter of the Organization of American States and in the Treaty on Pacific Settlement signed at Bogota in 1948. Thus the principle of consultation is now firmly imbedded in the constitutional law of the Inter-American System.

THE DOCTRINE OF ALL FOR ONE AND ONE FOR ALL

At Habana in 1940, the consultative procedure produced a resolution that an attack upon one American state by a non-American state would be considered as an attack upon all of them. This was none too early as a security measure, for it was in the very next year that Pearl Harbor was bombed.

Before the war was concluded, however, further steps to improve hemispheric security were taken. These include the work of the Montevideo Committee for Political Defense, the Inter-American Juridical Committee, and the Defense Board, which I have insufficient time to discuss. These steps reached a culmination with statements in the "Declaration of Mexico" and The Act of Chapultepec of 1945 that an attack upon an American State by any state constitutes an aggression against all the American States. The Act went on to provide for consultation (more consultation!) to decide upon the measures to meet such aggression, including the possible use of armed force.

It will be recalled that at the time of Chapultepec the Charter of the United Nations did not yet exist. Nonetheless that Act provided that the treaty which might grow out of it should be consistent with the UN Charter.

It was, then, at Rio that in 1947 the next logical and orderly steps were taken to put in treaty form the "all for one" doctrine. That treaty we will examine in a moment.

In the Charter of the Organization of American States signed at Bogota on May 2, 1948 a number of the principles adopted in the Rio Treaty were unanimously confirmed. Article 5(f) reaffirms the "all for one" principle. Articles 24 and 25 reiterate the collective security provisions of the Rio Treaty in precise languages, and article 43 states again that consultations shall be held without delay in case of armed attack.

Thus we see that the resolutions on consultation, accepted in 1936, and the doctrine of "all for one," agreed upon since 1940, were brought together and considerably advanced by their incorporation into treaty form at Rio in 1947. That it was not an isolated peak of inter-American solidarity is proven by the categoric repetitions of the same two concepts in the Charter of Bogota signed in 1948.

THE RIO TREATY

To return to the Rio Treaty. It consists of twenty-six articles, most of them short.

The all-for-one doctrine appears in articles 3 and 6. The Treaty establishes a clear obligation on the parties to take action in meeting armed attack; it requires consultation respecting other acts of aggression and any other situations endangering the peace of America. It specifies the procedure and organs through which the community of states will act and lists measures which may be taken against an aggressor. There is no veto. Each party is committed in advance to carry out decisions of the Organ of Consultations, although it may have voted against that decision. The sole exception is that its armed forces may not be used without a state's consent.

The Rio Treaty is open for signature by any American state. This includes Canada. Of the twenty-one American republics, representatives of twenty have already signed. The life of the Treaty is indefinite.

The United States Senate approved the Treaty on December 8, 1947, 72 to 1. Our ratification, deposited on December 30, was the second. On December 3, 1948 the Pan American Union received the ratification of Costa Rica, the fourteenth, bringing the Treaty into effect with respect to the ratifying states. It was a pleasure and an honor to attend in person that epochal event.

Cuba has since deposited her ratification.

Regarding the relationship of the Rio Treaty to the UN, Secretary Marshall stated on September 4, 1947 that "the successful formulation of this regional treaty affords the United Nations a significant example—an example, I feel, of which it is in great need at the present time."

The example, in summary, arises out of the following points:

1. There is no veto.

2. The implementation of sanctions are binding even upon States not concurring.

3. It provides for immediate action.

4. It is technically sound, applying to relations between States, within a regional group, and to the world organization.

5. It is a culmination of nearly 60 years of inter-American effort. . . .

ADDRESS by Paul C. Daniels, Director of the Office of American Republic Affairs, Department of State, at the University of Wisconsin, March 30, 1949 (extracts)
Department of State press release No. 194, March 28, 1949

. . . YOU ARE ALL familiar with the history of relations between the United States and its good neighbors in the other American republics. These relations are of long standing. There have been ups and downs, to be sure, but the outstanding feature through many decades has been the determination of the American nations to get along together for the benefit of all.

At the root of this historic cooperation is the factor of geography which binds us together. Deeper still is the strong psychological factor of love of liberty and freedom, and the aspirations of democracy which we share. Nearly all the American republics, like our own country, obtained their freedom by fighting for it. They have carefully guarded their hard-won independence ever since. . . .

Only recently we saw the effectiveness of the Rio de Janeiro Treaty positively demonstrated. Since I have first hand knowledge of the circumstances, I would like to review them in some detail.

Eight days after the treaty became effective, the Council of the Organization of American States, the permanent executive agency of the Organization, received from Costa Rica a request that the treaty be invoked against Nicaragua. It is a striking coincidence that Costa Rica should be the first to call the treaty into operation, since it was Costa Rica's ratification, deposited on the 3rd of last December, that made the treaty a binding instrument.

Costa Rica charged that it had been invaded by forces organized within Nicaragua, and contended that this constituted a threat to the peace within the meaning of Article 6 of the Rio Treaty.

The next day, Sunday, the 12th of December, the Council met but found it had insufficient information on which to invoke the Pact and thereby to establish far-reaching precedents. Under the able chairmanship of Ambassador Corominas of Argentina, the Council requested by telegram more information from the governments concerned and from other American governments as well. On December 14, 48 hours later, it met again and on the basis of the information that had been supplied, the treaty was invoked and the council set itself up as the provisional organ of consultation, pending the convocation of a Meeting of Foreign Ministers.

A five member commission was named on December 15 and left the following day by special airplane for San José and Managua to investigate on the spot. Appointed to this group were the Ambassadors of Mexico, Brazil and Colombia, and myself as representative of the United States. The Commission was able to carry out its instructions in an atmosphere of willing cooperation of the two nations involved in the dispute. The job was done expeditiously and the commission returned to Washington on December 23 to report its findings.

On the 24th the Council met again and after hearing the Commission's report, agreed on a resolution which called on both parties to cease all hostile acts and urged them to come to an amicable agreement. This was accomplished without the Council having to call a Meeting of Foreign Ministers for consultation on further action. Negotiations went on between the two countries, while at the same time compliance with the resolution was observed by a military commission appointed by the Council. On the 21st of February, a little more than a month ago, Nicaragua and Costa Rica signed a friendship pact which not only ended the entire incident peacefully, but also constitutes an added guarantee of tranquility for years to come.

I have given you this quick review of these developments in order to impress upon you the speed with which this Rio Treaty mechanism worked. It merits special mention because it proves that a group of representatives of many countries, animated by good will, is able to move with speed and decisiveness. On the other hand, thoroughness and justice were not sacrificed for the sake of speed. The Council took great care to obtain reliable information which made it possible to take intelligent, well-founded decisions. Solid precedents were set on which to base future procedure and decisions.

Other tried and proved features of United States relations with Latin America are being elaborated and extended in our current international programs. You will recall that President Truman at his inauguration called for a "bold new program for making the benefits of our scientific advances and industrial progress available for the improvement and growth of underdeveloped areas." This program is, indeed, both new and bold, if only by virtue of the vast scope it embraces. In its principal elements, however, its prototype may be found in the technical and scientific programs of cooperation which we have been conducting with Latin America for many years.

The experience we have gained in the last ten years of coordinated effort in this field will prove to be of untold value in the formulation and execution of the new Point Four program. Indeed, in its early phases, this program will consist largely of a continuation and extension of our work in this field with the other American Republics. As it takes shape it will undoubtedly rely heavily on the wealth of experience and "know-how" that we already possess.

Let me review, for a moment, some of the basic considerations that have been guiding our technical cooperation efforts. First of all, we enter into projects only at the request of the individual governments and when we are convinced that a project is desirable for its effects on national and international welfare. There must also be real evidence that the other government is eager to pursue the project to a successful finish. Our cooperation is intended to help the other countries to help themselves. Their self-help is expressed in different ways: by dollar reimbursements or advance of funds for services rendered; by providing land, buildings and other facilities and equipment within the foreign country; by making available the best qualified nationals of the recipient country or other countries to work with American technicians; by providing maintenance personnel, and in other constructive ways.

The important thing that has stood out in some of these ventures is that as the programs became larger and more effective, a correspondingly larger percentage of the total costs was borne by the other governments, and less and less by the United States. At the outset most of the programs of the Institute of Inter-American Affairs were almost wholly financed by the United States. Today, the United States contributions to those same programs are down to below 10% in one instance and in every case below 50%. The cooperative approach to these projects has already served as a pattern for comparable activities in other parts of the world and undoubtedly will provide valuable experience in further development of the President's program.

Another characteristic of our technical and scientific programs is that they are flexible. Not only do they vary in form and method from country to country, but they are actually sponsored and carried out by many different agencies.

In addition to the Institute of Inter-American Affairs, the United States Government cooperates with other governments through the Interdepartmental Committee on Scientific and Cultural Cooperation. This committee coordinates the technical operations abroad of some twenty-five bureaus with ten Federal departments. The government also participates in constructive cooperative programs through such Inter-American agencies as the Pan American Sanitary Bureau. Other operations have long been conducted by private nonprofit organizations such as the Rockefeller Institute, the Institute of International Education, to name but two.

A considerable amount of technical assistance, on the other hand, is directly related to and dependent upon private business enterprises. Private investments through contracts with foreign governments or with private foreign firms are frequently accompanied by American technology. American business firms not only furnish detailed technical information with the capital goods they send abroad, but they frequently send along technicians to supervise installations and operations and, at the same time, to train local national personnel. In addition many firms bring personnel to this country for intensive training in their plants and laboratories. There are also many private engineering consultant firms engaged in making available to the Latin Americans our technical know-how and services.

This sort of private enterprise is welcomed wholeheartedly by the State Department. The Department attempts to encourage private agencies to the greatest extent possible, to supplement the limited government-sponsored programs. It recognizes the importance of the role of private activities in contributing to our common objectives of economic and social advancement. In attempting to avoid past errors which came to be known as "dollar diplomacy," we expect that American citizens and enterprises will interfere in no way with the political affairs of the country in which they are engaged.

The specific projects, both official and private, now being carried on in Latin America are far too numerous to enumerate here. Suffice it to say they have dealt with public health, education, industry, agriculture, aviation, geologic investigations, and many other subjects.

Economic cooperation with Latin America has long since gone beyond the basic and essential considerations of trade for private gain.

It has taken the shape of sincere attempts to develop and bolster the economies of the respective countries for the betterment of all concerned. This is a lofty goal; it is difficult to realize. Nevertheless it is constantly before us. It is a basic objective sought in the technical and scientific cooperation programs I have mentioned. We also seek that goal through other means.

I will not attempt a discussion of all the various factors and conditions which enter into the economic relationship of the Americas. What we are seeking is a healthy economy, based on the fullest possible development, increased trade, and a higher standard of living for all the people, with its obvious influence on political stability.

At Rio, when the politico-military cooperative agreement was reached, it was proposed that similar cooperation be sought in the economic field. This would be a continuation of other long standing cooperative efforts, and would put them on a well-defined and firmer basis. The Inter-American Economic and Social Council prepared a basic draft to be considered at the Bogota Conference. The basic draft was formalized at Bogota as an agreement among the states "to cooperate individually and collectively and with other nations to carry out the principles of facilitating access, on equal terms, to the trade, products, and means of production, including scientific and technical advances, that are needed for their industrial and general economic development."

The Economic Agreement of Bogota is important because it sets forth a detailed set of principles for economic cooperation and development. We have not yet been able to see it through to ratification because of numerous reservations that were made at Bogota. However, we are now exerting every effort to reduce these reservations, in order to make the document comprehensible when it is presented for ratification. To this end the United States took the initiative in having it referred to the Inter-American Economic and Social Council, which is now attempting to eliminate duplications and consolidate the others into a draft protocol form. According to present plans it will be restudied at the economic conference which is scheduled to be held in Buenos Aires the latter part of this year.

Meanwhile, various economic programs of the United States are contributing to the alleviation of the economic difficulties of Latin America. These are fully in keeping with our history of cooperation, as well as with the objectives of the Bogota Agreement.

Moreover, the great economic momentum which has gathered in this country under our system of individual enterprise could easily expand into Latin America to an extent never before visualized. There is an abundance of business and private capital which could be poured into the countries to the south of us. The economic and social betterment in those countries that would derive from this capital is almost boundless. The obstacles that stand in the way of this development are not insurmountable. Guaranties against expropriation and other hazards would open the way to thousands of prospective investors bringing in a short time results that it will otherwise require a great span of years to accomplish.

It is unfortunate that the conditions in Europe that followed in the wake of the last war were so severe that we have had to concentrate our efforts upon them. The war, as you know, left the economy of Europe in virtual chaos. It was obvious that no recovery would be possible without outside assistance and we were the only nation in a position to help the European countries get back on their feet.

It has been our confident hope and belief that the urgent assistance we are now providing under the European Recovery Program will have a beneficial effect on Latin America. This effect will be felt in the availability in Europe of materials and capital goods that are needed for the further development of the other American Republics. At the same time it will serve to restore to their former extent and even to widen traditional European markets for Latin American exports.

This is not to say that these benefits are the solution to the economic problems of Latin America. Far from it. We, in this country, are acutely aware of the existence of those problems. However, it is apparent that while there is no limit to the political cooperation we can give to Latin America at the present time, and while we have an abundance of technical and scientific skill to export, we cannot stretch the burden on our taxpayers or the limited resources of the United States Treasury to fill all of the world's needs at once. We must be guided, primarily, by considerations of security and our own available resources.

From the security aspect, alone, the logic of the great effort we are placing on the recovery of the European democracies is readily apparent. Security and a sound economy go hand in hand.

Naturally, European recovery will have effects that go well beyond the limited spheres of Europe, or of the United States. The American community of interests will be served at the same time, since, in the Western Hemisphere, the security of one country is the security of all, and Western Hemisphere security is dependent upon world security.

We hope to be able to increase the degree of cooperation between ourselves and our immediate neighbors. We will continue to respect the sovereignty and juridical equality of all the American nations.

We will continue to abide by the solemn Inter-American commitments of non-intervention in the internal and external affairs of those countries. We will continue to give tangible evidence of our good neighborliness and of our faith in the Americas. Our history, our traditions and our international goals stand as guarantees to that effect. These same objectives represent, I am confident, the deep conviction of every individual American citizen.

ADDRESS by Dean Acheson, Secretary of State, at the Pan American Union, Washington, D.C., April 14, 1949

Department of State press release No. 255, April 14, 1949. The address was delivered at the special session of the Council of the Organization of American States on the occasion of Pan American Day

I APPRECIATE the invitation of the Council to join with you in observing Pan American Day. Although this occasion is the first opportunity I have had since my return to the State Department, to meet with the representatives of the American Republics in the Pan American Union, I feel at home here, in the same way that all of us feel at home together in the inter-American community of good neighbors.

Wholehearted support of the inter-American system has been a foundation stone of the foreign relations of my country for many years. None of the momentous international developments that have taken place during these years has lessened the importance of this policy for my country—some have increased it. This policy is not the policy of any one man or any one political party, nor is it the policy of any one moment. It is an established national policy, strongly and actively supported by the will of the people of my country.

The Pan American Union, with its important place in the inter-American system, symbolizes a spirit, increasingly important to international affairs—a disposition on the part of governments to sit down together and work out their common problems in an atmosphere of concord and mutual trust. This habit of cooperation is firmly established and deeply rooted in the Western Hemisphere. Perhaps to some extent we take it for granted and forget that many other nations have not accepted this principle so thoroughly or practiced it so long as we have. But many states have now come to realize the great value of the example and pattern of friendship and cooperation set by the American republics in this Hemisphere.

It is apparent that two opposing forces are at work in the world of today. One is disruptive. It divides nations and peoples. It turns individuals against each other even in the same country and the same community. The other force draws peoples and nations together in common endeavor. It harmonizes the interests of individuals.

Observation of the operation of these contrasting influences reveals a paradox. Free people are willing to share their privileges and prerogatives with others—to entrust their vital interests to the decision of the community of which they are a part. Repressed people hold aloof, suspect the motives of those who offer friendship and aid, and shrink from or oppose cooperative action.

We can see clearly which of these attitudes is normal and healthy, and which is abnormal and morbid. It is my conviction that the cohesive forces at work for unity and cooperation will prevail in time over the divisive forces working for disruption and disaster. I believe this because the desire for cohesion and cooperation is rooted in man's long search for security, peace and spiritual advancement in a social order devised to further the realization of those aims.

It is understandable that leadership for the attainment of those ends through cooperative action comes largely from the western world which believes so firmly that the objective of individual liberty and well-being can best be realized through the exercise of tolerance and restraint by individuals toward the other members of the community. Fortunately, these principles are steadily gaining welcome support as the basis of the peaceful and orderly world community now being built by collective endeavor devoted to the common purpose of a better life for all peoples.

Cooperation among nations on a *world-wide* scale is a comparatively recent development. A start was made scarcely three decades ago with the League of Nations. In the vision of Woodrow Wilson, the people of the world caught a glimpse of the family of nations moving forward in unison. But my country faltered and held back. It had not fully learned that its security was bound up in the security of a free world. Hindered by other adverse factors, the League proved unable to check the resurgent militarism that forced the world, including my own country, again into war.

But war only confirmed that the compulsion toward international cooperation is too great to be ignored or defeated. Even while World War II was being fought, the Allied powers began organizing the United Nations. These efforts achieved success at San Francisco, where the American republics exerted a strong and constructive influence in the drafting of the Charter.

Once more men possessed an instrument for consultation and collective action. And once more they learned that form and organization are not enough, that the spirit which animates the members is all important. The attitude of one member can keep the United Nations—or any international organization—from working as it is intended to work and can seriously hamper the sincere efforts of the majority to achieve security and progress through collective action.

But the *will* to attain the objectives of the United Nations through joint action in keeping with the spirit and principles of the Charter is as strong as ever. The nations and peoples dedicated to peace and security through international cooperation have refused to be defeated or dismayed by obstruction and threats. They have sought and found ways to carry forward their purpose and, at the same time, to strengthen the United Nations as their primary choice of the means of collective action.

Some of the means that have been developed within the spirit of the Charter are aid to free countries whose integrity and independence are threatened; the European Recovery Program; the Treaty of Rio de Janeiro; the Brussels Pact; and the North Atlantic Treaty. All of these measures are of major importance to the American republics. Some originated in the community of American nations and directly concern the security of this hemisphere and relationships within the inter-American system. Others have been strongly influenced by principles evolved and institutions developed by the American republics.

The nations represented here today actively supported the inclusion in the United Nations Charter of the concept of regional arrangements—a need foreseen by the conference of American states held in Mexico City prior to the San Francisco conference on organization of the United Nations.

The mutual defense treaty for the Western Hemisphere concluded at Rio de Janeiro in 1947 was based on the principle, recognized by Article 51 of the Charter, that an attack on one of the American nations would be considered an attack on all, and would be dealt with accordingly, by joint action. An immediate result of the conclusion of this Treaty was the wide-spread recognition of the fact that the purposes of the Charter were strengthened and furthered by ancillary arrangements in accordance with the principles of the Charter.

The principle of the inherent right of individual and collective self-defense, embodied in Article 51 of the United Nations Charter, became the heart of the North Atlantic Treaty, which is designed to assure the maintenance of international peace and security for the North Atlantic community, just as the Treaty of Rio de Janeiro is designed to provide the same assurance for the American community. The American family of nations can justifiably take pride in the way their pioneering for peace has borne fruit for others who earnestly desire to achieve the same purpose. The principles of consultation on matters of mutual concern and of close cooperation in the economic as well as the security field likewise are incorporated in the North Atlantic Treaty, as they are in the formal agreements of the American republics.

Another important element common to both treaties is that they are explicitly designed to fit into the universal system of the United Nations. Both are reinforcements and developments of the United Nations concept, not alternatives to it.

The Organization of American States is an element of strength for the United Nations, and conversely, the United Nations is an element of strength for the Organization of American States. All of us belong to and are active in both. There are no divided loyalties here. We can honestly and sincerely serve the same cause in both the regional and the universal system.

In dealing with the instrumentalities and mechanisms for international cooperation, may I mention an additional development upon which intensive work is now proceeding. This is President Truman's plan of technical cooperation among the peoples of the earth in improving their living conditions and strengthening their national economies. This effort also will be a practical demonstration in international cooperation, with many nations participating.

The great hopes for this program are shared, I believe, by the peoples of the Western Hemisphere as well as the peoples of other areas. The program will be unique in many respects. It will require full and continuing cooperation not only among governments, but also among the people who carry on the great work of producing for the needs of the world. Real understanding can develop out of the mingling, on a practical workaday basis, of the technicians of many countries with the peoples of other lands. They cannot deal with each other at arm's length, but must work shoulder to shoulder, demonstrating and learning new ways of sowing and harvesting crops, controlling and eliminating disease, producing more goods with less effort and at less cost. When international cooperation takes place on a wide enough scale on the farms and in the factories of the world, the tasks of statesmen will be easier.

One reason I have such great hopes for this program is that already, in the republics of the Western Hemisphere, there is proof of how much can be accomplished by this method. The pioneering done by the members of the inter-American system will prove invaluable in the wider application of the processes arrived at by trial and error. The prototype of almost every kind of project contemplated in the world wide program envisioned by President Truman has been developed and tested in cooperative programs carried on in recent years between the United States and its sister American countries. Present plans include a substantial expansion of these joint activities in this hemisphere even as they are extended to new areas.

The experience of our countries in technical cooperation will also serve as a caution to other peoples that, promising as this technique is, too much cannot be expected too soon. Raising the living standards of large groups of people, over large areas, is a complex problem involving many diverse factors. It cannot be accomplished without intensive, continuous effort.

Modern technology can make the earning of one's daily bread less exhausting. It can relieve man of much back-breaking drudgery and release his creative powers for things of the spirit. It is in this sense that President Truman's "Point Four" opens up almost limitless vistas in the long future.

The effective inter-American system which exists today is the work of many men. As representatives of the American Republics we can be justly proud of those who contributed to this success. We can best pay tribute to them by maintaining and perfecting the system they initiated in the full knowledge that the welfare of the Western Hemisphere requires mutual trust and cooperation.

II
The Monroe Doctrine

Background

MESSAGE from President John Adams to the United States Congress, May 16, 1797 (extract)

American State Papers, Foreign Relations, I, 40. See also Washington's Farewell Address, *supra*, p. 3. For various other references to the Monroe Doctrine, see *supra*, I. General Principles, and *infra*, III. Independence of Cuba, and VI. Interventions in Nicaragua, Haiti, and the Dominican Republic

. . . ALTHOUGH it is very true that we ought not to involve ourselves in the political system of Europe, but to keep ourselves always distinct and separate from it, if we can; yet, to effect this separation, early, punctual, and continual, information of the current chain of events, and of the political projects in contemplation, is no less necessary than if we were directly concerned in them: it is necessary, in . . . the discovery of the efforts made to draw us into the vortex, in season to make preparation against them. However we may consider ourselves, the maritime and commercial Powers of the world will consider the United States of America as forming a weight in that balance of power in Europe, which never can be forgotten or neglected. It would not only be against our interest, but it would be doing wrong to one half of Europe at least, if we should voluntarily throw ourselves into either scale. It is a natural policy for a nation that studies to be neutral, to consult with other nations, engaged in the same studies and pursuits at the same time; that measures might be pursued with this view, our treaties with Prussia and Sweden, one of which is expired, and the other near expiring, might be renewed. . . .

TREATY between Austria, Prussia, and Russia (the "Holy Alliance"), Signed at Paris, September 26, 1815

Edward Hertslet, *Map of Europe by Treaty* (1875), p. 317

IN THE NAME of the Most Holy and Indivisible Trinity, Their Majesties the Emperor of Austria, the King of Prussia, and the Emperor of Russia, having, in consequence of the great events which have marked the course of the three last years in Europe, and especially of the blessings which it has pleased Divine Providence to shower down upon those States which place their confidence and their hope on it alone, acquired the intimate conviction of the necessity of settling the steps to be observed by the Powers, in their reciprocal relations, upon the sublime truths which the Holy Religion of our Saviour teaches;

They solemnly declare that the present Act has no other object than to publish, in the face of the whole world, their fixed resolution, both in the administration of their respective States, and in their political relations with every other Government, to take for their sole guide the precepts of that Holy Religion, namely, the precepts of Justice, Christian Charity, and Peace, which, far from being applicable only to private concerns, must have an immediate influence on the councils of Princes, and guide all their steps, as being the only means of consolidating human institutions and remedying their imperfections. In consequence, their Majesties have agreed on the following Articles:

ARTICLE I

Conformably to the words of the Holy Scriptures, which command all men to consider each other as brethren, the Three contracting Monarchs will remain united by the bonds of a true and indissoluble fraternity, and considering each other as fellow countrymen, they will, on all occasions and in all places, lend each other aid and assistance; and, regarding themselves towards their subjects and armies as fathers of families, they will lead them, in the same spirit of fraternity with which they are animated, to protect Religion, Peace, and Justice.

ARTICLE II

In consequence, the sole principle of force, whether between the said Governments or between their Subjects, shall be that of doing each other reciprocal service, and of testifying by unalterable good will the mutual affection with which they ought to be animated, to consider themselves all as members of one and the same Christian nation; the three allied Princes looking on themselves as merely delegated by Providence to govern three branches of the One family, namely, Austria, Prussia, and Russia, thus confessing that the Christian world, of which they and their people form a part, has in reality no other Sovereign than Him to whom alone power really belongs, because in Him alone are found all the treasures of love, science, and infinite wisdom, that is to say, God, our Divine Saviour, the Word of the Most High, the Word of Life. Their Majesties consequently recommend to their people, with the most tender solicitude, as the sole means of enjoying that Peace which arises from a good conscience, and which alone is durable, to strengthen themselves every day more and more in the principles and exercise of the duties which the Divine Saviour has taught to mankind.

ARTICLE III

All the Powers who shall choose solemnly to avow the sacred principles which have dictated the present Act, and shall acknowledge how important it is for the happiness of nations, too long agitated, that these truths should henceforth exercise over the destinies of mankind all the influence which belongs to them, will be received with equal ardour and affection into this Holy Alliance.

Done in triplicate, and signed at Paris, the year of Grace 1815, $\frac{14}{26}$th September.

(L.S.) FRANCIS
(L.S.) FREDERICK WILLIAM
(L.S.) ALEXANDER

JOHN QUINCY ADAMS, Secretary of State, to Henry Middleton, United States Minister to Russia, July 5, 1820
John Bassett Moore, *A Digest of International Law*, VI, 376

THE PRESENT political system of Europe is founded upon the overthrow of that which had grown out of the French Revolution, and has assumed its shape from the body of treaties concluded at Vienna in 1814 and 1815, at Paris towards the close of the same year, 1815, and in Aix-la-Chapelle in the autumn of 1818. Its general character is that of a compact between the five principal European powers—Austria, France, Great Britain, Prussia, and Russia—for the preservation of universal peace. These powers having then just emerged victorious from a long, portentous and sanguinary struggle against the oppressive predominancy of one of them, under revolutionary sway, appear to have bent all their faculties to the substitution of a system which should preserve them from that evil—the preponderancy of one power by the subjugation, virtual if not nominal, of the rest. Whether they perceived in its full extent, considered in its true colours, or provided by judicious arrangements for the revolutionary temper of the weapons by which they had so long been assailed and from which they had so severely suffered, is a question now in a course of solution. Their great anxiety appears to have been to guard themselves each against the other.

The League of Peace, so far as it was a covenant of organized governments, has proved effectual to its purposes by an experience of five years. Its only interruption has been in this hemisphere, though between nations strictly European; by the invasion of the Portuguese on the territory claimed by Spain, but already lost to her, on the eastern shore of the Rio de la Plata. This aggression, too, the European alliance have undertaken to control; and in connection with it they have formed projects hitherto abortive of interposing in the revolutionary struggle between Spain and her South American colonies.

As a compact between governments it is not improbable that the European alliance will last as long as some of the states who are parties to it. The warlike passions and propensities of the present age find their principal aliment, not in the enmities between nation and nation, but in the internal dissensions between the component parts of all. The war is between nations and their rulers.

The Emperor Alexander may be considered as the principal patron and founder of the League of Peace. His interest is the more unequivocal in support of it. His empire is the only party to the compact free from that internal fermentation which threatens the existence of all the rest. His territories are the most extensive, his military establishment the most stupendous, his country the most improvable and thriving of them all. He is therefore naturally the most obnoxious to the jealousy and fears of his associates, and his circumstances point his policy to a faithful adhesion to the general system, with a strong reprobation of those who would resort to special and partial alliances, from which any one member of the league should be excluded. This general tendency of his policy is corroborated by the mild and religious turn of his individual character. He finds a happy coincidence between the dictates of his conscience and the interest of his Empire. And as from the very circumstance of his preponderancy, partial alliances might be most easily contracted by him, from the natural resort of the weak for succour to the strong, by discountenancing all such partial combinations he has the appearance of discarding advantages entirely within his command, and reaps the glory of disinterestedness, while most efficaciously providing for his own security.

Such is accordingly the constant indication of the Russian policy since the peace of Paris in 1815. The neighbors of Russia which have the most to dread from her overshadowing and encroaching power are Persia, Turkey, Austria, and Prussia; the two latter of which are members of the European and even of the Holy Alliance, while the two former are not only extra-European in their general policy, but of religions which excluded them from ever becoming parties, if not from ever deriving benefit from that singular compact.

The political system of the United States is also essentially extra-European. To stand in firm and cautious independence of all entanglement in the European system, has been a cardinal point of their policy under every administration of their Government, from the peace of 1783 to this day. If at the original adoption of their system there could have been any doubt of its justice or its wisdom, there can be none at this time. Every year's experience rivets it more deeply in the principles and opinions of the nation. Yet in proportion as the importance of the United States as one of the members of the general society of civilized nations increases in the eyes of the others, the difficulties of maintaining this system and the temptations to depart from it increase and multiply with it. The Russian Government has not only manifested an inclination that the United States should concur in the general principles of the European league, but a direct though unofficial application has been made by the present Russian minister here that the United States should become formal party to the Holy Alliance. It has been suggested, as inducement to obtain their compliance, that this compact bound the parties to no specific engagement of anything. That it was a pledge of mere principles—that its real as well as its professed purpose was merely the general preservation of peace—and it was intimated that if any question should arise between the United States and other governments of Europe, the Emperor Alexander, desirous of using his influence in their favour, would have a substantial motive and justification for interposing if he could regard them as *his allies,* which, as parties to the Holy Alliance, he would.

It is possible that overtures of a similar character may be made to you; but whether they should be or not it is proper to apprize you of the light in which they have been viewed by the President. No direct refusal has been signified to Mr. Poletica. It is presumed that none will be necessary. His instructions are not to make the proposal in form unless with a prospect that it will be successful. It might, perhaps, be sufficient to answer that the organization of our Government is such as not to admit of our acceding formally to that compact. But it may be added that the President, approving its general principles and thoroughly convinced of the benevolent and virtuous motives which led to the conception and presided at the formation of this system by the Emperor Alexander, believes that the United States will more effectually contribute to the great and sublime objects for which it was concluded by abstaining from a formal participation in it than they could as stipulated members of it. As a general declaration of principles, disclaiming the impulses of vulgar ambition and unprincipled aggrandizement and openly proclaiming the peculiarly Christian maxims of mutual benevolence and brotherly love to be binding upon the intercourse between nations no less than upon that of individuals, the United States not only give their hearty assent to the articles of the Holy Alliance, but will be among the most earnest and conscientious in observing them. But independent of the prejudices which have been excited against this instrument in the public opinion, which time and an experience of its good effects will gradually wear away, it may be observed that for the repose of Europe as well as of America, the European and American political system should be kept as separate and distinct from each other as possible. If the United States as members of the Holy Alliance could acquire a right to ask the influence of its most powerful member in their controversies with other states, the other members must be entitled in return to ask the influence of the United States, for themselves or against their opponents, in the deliberations of the league they would be entitled to a voice, and in exercising their right must occasionally appeal to principles, which might not harmonize with those of any European member of the bond. This consideration alone would be decisive for declining a participation in that league, which is the President's absolute and irrevocable determination, although he trusts that no occasion will present itself rendering it necessary to make that determination known by an explicit refusal.

JOHN QUINCY ADAMS, Secretary of State, to Henry Middleton, United States Minister to Russia, July 22, 1823
John Bassett Moore, *A Digest of International Law*, VI, 414

THERE CAN, perhaps, be no better time for saying, frankly and explicitly, to the Russian Government, that the future peace of the world, and the interest of Russia herself, can not be promoted by Russian settlements upon any part of the American continent. With the exception of the British establishments north of the United States, the remainder of both the American continents must henceforth be left to the management of American hands.

It can not possibly be the purpose of Russia to form extensive *colonial* establishments in America. The new American republics will be as impatient of a Russian neighbor as the United States; and the claim of Russia to territorial possessions extending to the fifty-first degree of north latitude is equally compatible with the British pretensions.

RICHARD RUSH, United States Minister to Great Britain, to John Quincy Adams, Secretary of State, August 19, 1823

John Bassett Moore, *A Digest of International Law,* VI, 386. The communication was received October 9, 1823

WHEN MY INTERVIEW with Mr. Canning, on Saturday, was about to close, I transiently asked him whether, notwithstanding the late news from Spain, we might not still hope that the Spaniards would get the better of all their difficulties. I had allusion to the defection of Ballasteros in Andalusia, an event seeming to threaten with new dangers the constitutional cause. His reply was general, importing nothing more than his opinion of the increased difficulties and dangers with which, undoubtedly, this event was calculated to surround the Spanish cause.

Pursuing the topic of Spanish affairs, I remarked that should France ultimately effect her purposes in Spain, there was at least the consolation left that Great Britain would not allow her to go further and lay her hands upon the Spanish colonies, bringing them, too, under her grasp. I here had in my mind the sentiments promulgated upon this subject in Mr. Canning's note to the British ambassador at Paris of the 31st of March, during the negotiations that preceded the invasion of Spain. It will be recollected that the British Government say in this note that time and the course of events appeared to have substantially decided the question of the separation of these colonies from the mother country, although their formal recognization as independent states by Great Britain might be hastened or retarded by external circumstances, as well as by the internal condition of those new states themselves; and that as His Britannic Majesty disclaimed all intention of appropriating to himself the smallest portion of the late Spanish possessions in America, he was also satisfied that no attempt would be made by France to bring any of them under *her* dominion, either by conquest or by cession from Spain.

By this we are to understand, in terms sufficiently distinct, that Great Britain would not be passive under such an attempt by France, and Mr. Canning, on my having referred to this note, asked me what

I thought my Government would say to going hand in hand with this, in the same sentiment; not, as he added, that any concert in action under it could become necessary between the two countries, but that the simple fact of our being known to hold the same sentiment would, he had no doubt, by its moral effect, put down the intention on the part of France, admitting that she should ever entertain it. This belief was founded, he said, upon the large share of the maritime power of the world which Great Britain and the United States shared between them, and the consequent influence which the knowledge that they held a common opinion upon a question on which such large maritime interests, present and future, hung, could not fail to produce upon the rest of the world.

I replied that in what manner my Government would look upon such a suggestion I was unable to say, but that I would communicate it in the same informal manner in which he threw it out. I said, however, that I did not think I should do so with full advantage, unless he would at the same time enlighten me as to the precise situation in which His Majesty's Government stood at this moment in relation to those new states, and especially on the material point of their own independence.

He replied that Great Britain certainly never again intended to lend her instrumentality or aid, whether by mediation or otherwise, towards making up the dispute between Spain and her colonies, but that if this result could still be brought about she would not interfere to *prevent* it. Upon my intimating that I had supposed that all idea of Spain ever recovering her authority over the colonies had long since gone by, he explained by saying that he did not mean to controvert that opinion, for he, too, believed that the day had arrived when all America might be considered as lost to Europe so far as the tie of political dependence was concerned. All that he meant was, that if Spain and the colonies should still be able to bring the dispute, not yet totally extinct between them, to a close upon terms satisfactory to both sides, and which should at the same time secure to Spain commercial or other advantages not extended to other nations, that Great Britain would not object to a compromise in this spirit of preference to Spain. All that she would ask would be to stand upon as favored a footing as any other nation after Spain. Upon my again alluding to the improbability of the dispute ever settling down now even upon this basis, he said that it was not his intention to maintain such a position, and that he had expressed himself as above rather for the purpose of indicating the feeling which this cabinet still had towards Spain in relation to the controversy than of predicting results

Wishing, however, to be still more specifically informed, I asked whether Great Britain was at this moment taking any step, or contemplating any, which had reference to the recognition of these States, this being the point in which we felt the chief interest.

He replied that she had taken none whatever, as yet, but was upon the eve of taking one, not final, but preparatory, and which would still leave her at large to recognize or not, according to the position of events at a future period. The measure in question was to send out one or more individuals under authority from this Government to South America, not strictly diplomatic, but clothed with powers in the nature of a commission of inquiry, and which in short he described as analogous to those exercised by our own commissioners in 1817, and that upon the result of this commission much might depend as to the ulterior conduct of Great Britain. I asked whether I was to understand that it would comprehend all the new States, or which of them. To which he replied that for the present it would be limited to Mexico.

Reverting to his first idea, he again said that he hoped that France would not, should even events in the Peninsula be favorable to her, extend her views to South America for the purpose of reducing the colonies, nominally, perhaps, for Spain, but in effect to subserve ends of her own; but that, in case she should meditate such a policy, he was satisfied that the knowledge of the United States being opposed to it, as well as Great Britain, could not fail to have its influence in checking her steps. In this way he thought good might be done by prevention, and peaceful prospects all around increased. As to the form in which such knowledge might be made to reach France, and even the other powers of Europe, he said, in conclusion, that that might probably be arranged in a manner that would be free from objection.

I again told him that I would convey his suggestions to you for the information of the President, and impart to him whatever reply I might receive. My own inference rather is that his proposition was a fortuitous one; yet he entered into it, I thought, with some interest, and appeared to receive with a corresponding satisfaction the assurance I gave him that it should be made known to the President. I did not feel myself at liberty to express any opinion unfavorable to it, and was as careful to give none in its favor.

Mr. Canning mentioned to me, at this same interview, that a late confidential dispatch which he had seen from Count Nesselrode to Count Lieven, dated, I think, in June, contained declarations respecting the Russian ukase, relative to the northwest coast, that were satisfactory; that they went to show that it would probably not be executed in a manner to give cause of complaint to other nations, and that, in particular, it had not yet been executed in any instance under orders issued by Russia subsequently to its first promulgation.

*GEORGE CANNING, British Secretary of State for Foreign
Affairs, to Richard Rush, United States Minister to Great
Britain, August 20, 1823*

John Bassett Moore, *A Digest of International Law*, VI, 389. The communication
was marked "private and confidential"

MY DEAR SIR:

Before leaving town I am desirous of bringing before you in a more
distinct, but still in an unofficial and confidential shape, the question
which we shortly discussed the last time that I had the pleasure of
seeing you.

Is not the moment come when our Governments might understand
each other as to the Spanish-American colonies? And if we can arrive
at such an understanding, would it not be expedient for ourselves, and
beneficial for all the world, that the principles of it should be clearly
settled and plainly avowed?

For ourselves we have no disguise.

1. We conceive the recovery of the colonies by Spain to be hopeless.

2. We conceive the question of the recognition of them, as independent states, to be one of time and circumstances.

3. We are, however, by no means disposed to throw any impediment
in the way of an arrangement between them and the mother country
by amicable negotiation.

4. We aim not at the possession of any portion of them ourselves.

5. We could not see any portion of them transferred to any other
power with indifference.

If these opinions and feelings are, as I firmly believe them to be,
common to your Government with ours, why should we hesitate
mutually to confide them to each other, and to declare them in the
face of the world?

If there be any European power which cherishes other projects,
which looks to a forcible enterprise for reducing the colonies to
subjugation, on the behalf or in the name of Spain, or which meditates
the acquisition of any part of them to itself, by cession or by conquest,
such a declaration on the part of your Government and ours would
be at once the most effectual and the least offensive mode of intimating
our joint disapprobation of such projects.

It would at the same time put an end to all the jealousies of Spain
with respect to her remaining colonies, and to the agitation which prevails in those colonies, an agitation which it would be but humane
to allay, being determined (as we are) not to profit by encouraging it.

Do you conceive that, under the power which you have recently received, you are authorized to enter into negotiation, and to sign any convention upon this subject? Do you conceive, if that be not within your competence, you could exchange with me ministerial notes upon it?

Nothing could be more gratifying to me than to join with you in such a work, and I am persuaded there has seldom, in the history of the world, occurred an opportunity when so small an effort of two friendly Governments might produce so unequivocal a good, and prevent such extensive calamities.

I shall be absent from London but three weeks at the utmost, but never so far distant but that I can receive and reply to any communication within three or four days.

RICHARD RUSH, United States Minister to Great Britain, to George Canning, British Secretary of State for Foreign Affairs, August 23, 1823
John Bassett Moore, *A Digest of International Law*, VI, 390

MY DEAR SIR:

Your unofficial and confidential note of the 20th instant reached me yesterday, and has commanded from me all the reflection due to the interests of its subject and to the friendly spirit of confidence upon which it is so emphatically founded.

The Government of the United States having, in the most formal manner, acknowledged the independence of the late Spanish provinces in America, desires nothing more anxiously than to see this independence maintained with stability, and under auspices that may promise prosperity and happiness to these new states themselves, as well as advantage to the rest of the world. As conducing to these great ends, my Government has always desired, and still desires, to see them received into the family of nations by the powers of Europe, and especially, I may add, by Great Britain.

My Government is also under a sincere conviction that the epoch has arrived when the interests of humanity and justice, as well as all other interests, would be essentially subserved by the general recognition of these states.

Making these remarks, I believe I may confidently say, that the sentiments unfolded in your note are fully those which belong also to my Government.

It conceives the recovery of the colonies by Spain to be hopeless.

It would throw no impediment in the way of an arrangement between them and the mother country, by amicable negotiation, supposing an arrangement of this nature to be possible.

It does not aim at the possession of any portion of those communities for or on behalf of the United States.

It would regard as highly unjust and fruitful of disastrous consequences any attempt on the part of any European power to take possession of them by conquest, or by cession, or on any ground or pretext whatever.

But in what manner my Government might deem it expedient to avow these principles and feelings, or express its disapprobation of such projects as the last, are points which none of my instructions, or the power which I have recently received, embrace; and they involve, I am forced to add, considerations of too much delicacy for me to act upon them in advance.

It will yield me particular pleasure to be the organ of promptly causing to be brought under the notice of the President the opinions and views of which you have made me the depositary upon this subject, and I am of nothing more sure than that he will fully appreciate their intrinsic interest, and not less the frank and friendly feelings towards the United States in which they have been conceived and communicated to me on your part.

Nor do I take too much upon myself when I anticipate the peculiar satisfaction the President will also derive from the intimation which you have not scrupled to afford me as to the just and liberal determinations of His Majesty's Government in regard to the colonies which still remain to Spain.

With a full reciprocation of the personal cordiality which your note also breathes, and begging you to accept the assurances of my great respect,

I have [etc.]

GEORGE CANNING, *British Secretary of State for Foreign Affairs, to Richard Rush, United States Minister to Great Britain, August 23, 1823*

John Bassett Moore, *A Digest of International Law,* VI, 392. The communication was marked "private and confidential"

MY DEAR SIR:

Since I wrote to you on the 20th, an additional motive has oc-

curred for wishing that we might be able to come to some understanding on the part of our respective Governments on the subject
of my letter; to come to it soon, and to be at liberty to announce it
to the world.

It is this. I have received notice, but not such a notice as imposes
upon me the necessity of any immediate answer or proceeding—that
so soon as the military objects in Spain are achieved (of which the
French expect, how justly I know not, a very speedy achievement) a
proposal will be made for a Congress, or some less formal concert and
consultation, specially upon the affairs of Spanish America.

I need not point out to you all the complications to which this
proposal, however dealt with by us, may lead.

Pray receive this communication in the same confidence with the
former; and believe me with great truth, [etc.]

*RICHARD RUSH, United States Minister to Great Britain, to
John Quincy Adams, Secretary of State, August 23, 1823*
John Bassett Moore, *A Digest of International Law*, VI, 391

I YESTERDAY received from Mr. Canning a note, headed "private and
confidential," setting before me, in a more distinct form, the proposition respecting South American affairs which he communicated to
me in conversation on the 16th, as already reported in my number
323. Of his note I lose no time in transmitting a copy for your information, as well as a copy of my answer to it, written and sent this day.

In shaping the answer on my own judgment alone, I feel that I
have had a task of some embarrassment to perform, and shall be happy
if it receives the President's approbation.

I believe that this Government has the subject of Mr. Canning's
proposition much at heart, and certainly his note bears, upon the face
of it, a character of cordiality towards the Government of the United
States which can not escape notice.

I have therefore thought it proper to impart to my note a like character and to meet the points laid down in his, as far as I could, consistently with other and paramount considerations.

These I conceived to be chiefly twofold: First, the danger of pledging my Government to any measure or course of policy which might in
any degree, now or hereafter, implicate it in the federative system of
Europe; and, secondly, I have felt myself alike without warrant to
take a step which might prove exceptional in the eyes of France, with
whom our pacific and friendly relations remain, I presume, undis-

turbed, whatever may be our speculative abhorrence of her attack upon the liberties of Spain.

In framing my answer, I had also to consider what was due to Spain herself, and I hope that I have not overlooked what was due to the colonies.

The whole subject is open to views on which my mind has deliberated anxiously. If the matter of my answer shall be thought to bear properly upon the motives and considerations which belong most materially to the occasion, it will be a source of great satisfaction to me.

The tone of earnestness in Mr. Canning's note, and the force of some of his expressions, naturally start the inference that the British cabinet can not be without its serious apprehensions that ambitious enterprises are meditated against the independence of the South American states. Whether by France alone I can not now say on any authentic grounds.

PRESIDENT JAMES MONROE to Former-President Thomas Jefferson, October 17, 1823
John Bassett Moore, *A Digest of International Law*, VI, 393

I TRANSMIT to you two despatches, which were receiv'd from Mr. Rush, while I was lately in Washington, which involve interests of the highest importance. They contain two letters from Mr. Canning, suggesting designs of the holy alliance against the Independence of So. America, & proposing a cooperation, between G. Britain & the U. States, in support of it, against the members of that alliance. The project aims in the first instance, at a mere expression of opinion, somewhat in the abstract, but which it is expected by Mr. Canning, will have a great political effect, by defeating the combination. By Mr. Rush's answers, which are also inclosed, you will see the light in which he views the subject, & the extent to which he may have gone. Many important considerations are involved in this proposition. 1st. Shall we entangle ourselves, at all, in European politicks, & wars, on the side of any power, against others, presuming that a concert by agreement, of the kind proposed, may lead to that result? 2d. If a case can exist, in which a sound maxim may, & ought to be departed from, is not the present instance, precisely that case? 3d. Has not the epoch arriv'd when G. Britain must take her stand, either on the side of the monarchs of Europe, or of the U. States, & in consequence, either in favor of Despotism or of liberty & may it not be presum'd, that aware of that necessity, her government, has seiz'd on the present occurrence, as that, which it deems, the most suitable, to announce & mark the commenc'ment of that career.

My own impression is that we ought to meet the proposal of the British govt., & to make it known, that we would view an interference on the part of the European powers, and especially an attack on the Colonies, by them, as an attack on ourselves, presuming that if they succeeded with them, they would extend it to us. I am sensible however of the extent, & difficulty of the question, & shall be happy to have yours, & Mr. Madison's opinions on it. I do not wish to trouble either of you with small objects, but the present one is vital, involving the high interests, for which we have so long & so faithfully, & harmoniously, contended together. Be so kind as to enclose to him the despatches, with an intimation of the motive.

FORMER-PRESIDENT THOMAS JEFFERSON to President James Monroe, October 24, 1823
John Bassett Moore, *A Digest of International Law,* VI, 394

THE QUESTION presented by the letters you have sent me, is the most momentous which has ever been offered to my contemplation since that of independence. That made us a nation, this sets our compass and points the course which we are to steer through the ocean of time opening on us. And never could we embark upon it under circumstances more auspicious. Our first and fundamental maxim should be, never to entangle ourselves in the broils of Europe; our second, never to suffer Europe to intermeddle with cis-Atlantic affairs. America, North and South, has a set of interests distinct from those of Europe, and particularly her own. She should therefore have a system of her own, separate and apart from that of Europe. While the last is laboring to become the domicile of despotism, our endeavor should surely be, to make our hemisphere that of freedom.

One nation, most of all, could disturb us in this pursuit; she now offers to lead, aid, and accompany us in it. By acceding to her proposition, we detach her from the bands, bring her mighty weight into the scale of free government, and emancipate a continent at one stroke, which might otherwise linger long in doubt and difficulty, Great Britain is the nation which can do us the most harm of any one, or all on earth; and with her on our side we need not fear the whole world. With her, then, we should most sedulously cherish a cordial friendship; and nothing would tend more to knit our affections than to be fighting once more, side by side, in the same cause. Not that I would purchase even her amity at the price of taking part in her wars.

But the war in which the present proposition might engage us, should that be its consequence, is not her war, but ours. Its object is to introduce and establish the American system, of keeping out of our land all foreign powers—of never permitting those of Europe to intermeddle with the affairs of our nations. It is to maintain our own principle, not to depart from it. And if, to facilitate this, we can effect a division in the body of the European powers, and draw over to our side its most powerful member, surely we should do it. But I am clearly of Mr. Canning's opinion, that it will prevent instead of provoking war. With Great Britain withdrawn from their scale and shifted into that of our two continents, all Europe combined would not undertake such a war, for how would they propose to get at either enemy without superior fleets? Nor is the occasion to be slighted which this proposition offers of declaring our protest against the atrocious violations of the rights of nations by the interference of any one in the internal affairs of another, so flagitiously begun by Bonaparte, and now continued by the equally lawless Alliance calling itself Holy.

But we have first to ask ourselves a question. Do we wish to acquire to our own confederacy any one or more of the Spanish provinces? I candidly confess that I have ever looked on Cuba as the most interesting addition which could ever be made to our system of States. The control which, with Florida Point, this island would give us over the Gulf of Mexico, and the countries and isthmus bordering on it, as well as all those whose waters flow into it, would fill up the measure of our political well-being. Yet, as I am sensible that this can never be obtained, even with her own consent, but by war, and its independence, which is our second interest (and especially its independence of England), can be secured without it, I have no hesitation in abandoning my first wish to future chances, and accepting its independence, with peace and the friendship of England, rather than its association, at the expense of war and her enmity.

I could honestly, therefore, join in the declaration proposed, that we aim not at the acquisition of any of those possessions, that we will not stand in the way of any amicable arrangement between them and the mother country; but that we will oppose, with all our means, the forcible interposition of any other power, as auxiliary, stipendiary, or under any other form or pretext, and most especially their transfer to any power by conquest, cession or acquisition in any other way. I should think it, therefore, advisable, that the Executives should encourage the British Government to a continuance in the dispositions expressed in these letters by an assurance of his concurrence with them as far as his authority goes; and that as it may lead to war, the declaration of which requires an act of Congress, the case shall be laid before them for consideration at their first meeting, and under the reasonable aspect in which it is seen by himself.

I have been so long weaned from political subjects, and have so long ceased to take any interest in them, that I am sensible I am not qualified to offer opinions on them worthy of any attention; but the question now proposed involves consequences so lasting, and effects so decisive of our future destinies, as to rekindle all the interest I have heretofore felt on such occasions, and to induce me to the hazard of opinions which will prove only my wish to contribute still my mite toward anything which may be useful to our country. And, praying you to accept it at only what it is worth, I add the assurance of my constant and affectionate friendship and respect.

FORMER-PRESIDENT JAMES MADISON to President James Monroe, October 30, 1823
John Bassett Moore, *A Digest of International Law*, VI, 396

I HAVE JUST received from Mr. Jefferson your letter to him, with the correspondence between Mr. Canning and Mr. Rush, sent for his and my perusal, and our opinions on the subject of it.

From the disclosures of Mr. Canning it appears, as was otherwise to be inferred, that the success of France against Spain would be followed by an attempt of the holy allies to reduce the revolutionized colonies of the latter to their former dependence.

The professions we have made to these neighbours, our sympathies with their liberties and independence, the deep interest we have in the most friendly relations with them, and the consequences threatened by a command of their resources by the great powers, confederated against the rights and reforms of which we have given so conspicuous and persuasive an example, all unite in calling for our efforts to defeat the meditated crusade. It is particularly fortunate that the policy of Great Britain, though guided by calculations different from ours, has presented a co-operation for an object the same with ours. With that co-operation we have nothing to fear from the rest of Europe, and with it the best assurance of success to our laudable views. There ought not, therefore, to be any backwardness, I think, in meeting her in the way she has proposed, keeping in view, of course, the spirit and forms of the Constitution in every step taken in the road to war, which must be the last step if those short of war should be without avail.

It can not be doubted that Mr. Canning's proposal, though made with the air of *consultation*, as well as concert, was founded on a pre-determination to take the course marked out, whatever might be the reception given here to his invitation. But this consideration ought not to divert us from what is just and proper in itself. Our co-operation is due to ourselves and to the world; and whilst it must ensure success in the event of an appeal to force, it doubles the chance of success without that appeal. It is not improbable that Great Britain would like best to have the merit of being the sole champion of her new friends, notwithstanding the greater difficulty to be encountered, but for the dilemma in which she would be placed. She must, in that case, either leave us, as neutrals, to extend our commerce and navigation at the expense of hers, or make us enemies, by renewing her paper blockades and other arbitrary proceedings on the ocean. It may be hoped that such a dilemma will not be without a permanent tendency to check her proneness to unnecessary wars.

Why the British Cabinet should have scrupled to arrest the calamity it now apprehends, by applying to the threats of France against Spain the small effort which it scruples not to employ in behalf of Spanish America, is best known to itself. It is difficult to find any other ex-planation than that interest in the one case has more weight in its casuistry than principle had in the other.

Will it not be honorable to our country, and possibly not altogether in vain, to invite the British Government to extend the "avowed dis-approbation" of the project against the Spanish colonies to the enter-prise of France against Spain herself, and even to join in some de-claratory act in behalf of the Greeks? On the supposition that no form could be given to the act clearing it of a pledge to follow it up by war, we ought to compare the good to be done with the little injury to be apprehended to the United States, shielded as their interests would be by the power and the fleets of Great Britain united with their own. These are questions, however, which may require more information than I possess, and more reflection than I can now give them.

What is the extent of Mr. Canning's disclaimer as to "the remain-ing possessions of Spain in America?" Does it exclude future views of acquiring Porto Rico, &c., as well as Cuba? It leaves Great Britain free, as I understand it, in relation to other quarters of the globe.

FORMER-PRESIDENT JAMES MADISON to Former-President Thomas Jefferson, November 1, 1823

John Bassett Moore, *A Digest of International Law*, VI, 397

I RETURN the letter of the President. The correspondence from abroad has gone back to him, as you desired. I have expressed to him my concurrence in the policy of meeting the advances of the British Government, having an eye to the forms of our Constitution in every step in the road to war. With the British power and navy combined with our own, we have nothing to fear from the rest of the world; and in the great struggle of the epoch between liberty and despotism, we owe it to ourselves to sustain the former, in this hemisphere at least. I have even suggested an invitation to the British Government to join in applying the "small effort for so much good" to the French invasion of Spain, and to make Greece an object of some such favorable attention. Why Mr. Canning and his colleague did not sooner interpose against the calamity, which could not have escaped foresight, can not be otherwise explained but by the different aspect of the question when it related to liberty in Spain, and to the extension of British commerce to her former colonies.

JOHN QUINCY ADAMS, Secretary of State, to Richard Rush, United States Minister to Great Britain, November 29, 1823

William R. Manning, *Diplomatic Correspondence of the United States Concerning the Independence of the Latin American Nations*, I, 210

SIR:

Your despatches numbered 323–325–326–330–331–332–334 and 336 have been received; containing the reports of your conferences, and copies of your confidential correspondence, with Mr. Secretary Canning, in relation to certain proposals made by him, tending to a concert of principles, with reference to the affairs of South America, between the United States and Great Britain, and a combined manifestation of them to the world.

The whole subject has received the deliberate consideration of the President, under a deep impression of its genial importance, a full conviction of the high interests and sacred principles involved in it, and an anxious solicitude for the cultivation of that harmony of opinions and unity of object, between the British and American Nations, upon which so much of the peace and happiness and liberty of the world obviously depend.

I am directed to express to you the President's entire approbation of the course which you have pursued in referring to your Government the proposals contained in Mr. Canning's private and confidential letter to you, of 20 August; and I am now to signify the determination of the President concerning them:—a determination which he wishes to be at once candid, explicit and conciliatory; and which being formed by referring each of the proposals to the single and unvarying standard of right and wrong, as understood and maintained by us, will present to the British Góvernment the whole system of opinions and of purposes of the American Government with regard to South America.

The first of the *principles* of the British Government, as set forth by Mr. Canning, is—

"1. We conceive the recovery of the colonies by Spain, to be hopeless."

In this we concur.

The second is—

"2. We conceive the question of the recognition of them, as independent States, to be one of time and circumstances."

We *did* so conceive it, until with a due regard to all the rights of Spain, and with a due sense of our responsibility to the judgment of mankind, and of posterity, we had come to the conclusion that the recovery of them by Spain *was hopeless.* Having arrived at that conclusion, we considered that the people of these emancipated Colonies, were, *of right* independent of all other nations, and that it was our duty so to acknowledge them. We did so acknowledge them, in March, 1822; from which time the recognition has no longer been a question *to us.* We are aware of considerations, just and proper in themselves, which might deter Great Britain from fixing upon the same *time* for this recognition, with us; but we wish to press it earnestly upon her consideration, whether, after having settled the point that the recovery of the colonies by Spain was *hopeless,* and after maintaining, at the cannon's mouth, commercial relations with them, incompatible with their colonial condition, while subject to Spain, the *moral* obligation does not necessarily result of recognizing them as independent States.

"3. We are however, by no means disposed to throw any impediment in the way of an arrangement between them and the mother country by *amiable negociation.*"

Nor are we—Recognizing them as independent States, we acknowledge them as possessing full power to levy war, conclude peace, contract alliances, establish commerce, and do all other acts and things which independent States may of right do.—Among these, an arrangement between them and Spain, by amicable negociation is one which far from being disposed to impede, we would earnestly desire, and, by every proper means in our power, endeavour to promote, provided it should be founded on the basis of independence. But recognizing them as independent States, we do, and shall justly and necessarily, claim in our relations political and commercial, to be placed upon a footing of equal favour, with the most favoured nation.

"4. We aim not at the possession of any portion of them transferred to any other Power, with indifference."

In both these positions we concur,—and we add—

That we could not see with indifference, any attempt by one or more powers of Europe to restore those new states to the crown of Spain, or to deprive them, in any manner, whatever of the freedom and independence which they have acquired.

With a view to this object, it is indispensable that the British Government take like ground with that which is now held by the United States, and that it recognize the independence of the new Governments. That measure being taken, we may then harmonize in all the arrangements and acts which may be necessary for its accomplishment. It is upon this ground alone, as we conceive that a firm and determined stand could now be jointly taken by Great-Britain and the United States, in behalf of the *Independence of Nations:* and never, in the history of mankind, was there a period when a stand so taken and maintained, would exhibit to present and future ages, a more glorious example of power, animated by justice, and devoted to the ends of beneficence. On this basis this Government is willing to move in concert with Great-Britain for the purposes specified.

We believe, however, that for the most effectual accomplishment of the object, common to both Governments, a perfect understanding with regard to it being established between them, it will be most advisable that they should act separately, each making such representations to the Continental European Allies, or either of them, as circumstances may render proper, and mutually communicating to each other, the purport of such representations, and all information respecting the measures and purposes of the Allies, the knowledge of which may enlighten the councils of Great Britain and of the United

States, in the course of policy, and towards the honourable end, which will be common to them both. Should an emergency occur, in which a *joint* manifestation of opinion, by the two Governments may tend to influence the Councils of the European Allies, either in the aspect of persuasion or of admonition, you will make it known to us without delay, and we shall according to the principles of our Government, and in the forms prescribed by our Constitution, cheerfully join in any act by which we may contribute to support the cause of human freedom, and the Independence of the South American Nations.

I am [etc.]

Enunciation of the Doctrine

ANNUAL MESSAGE from President James Monroe to the United States Congress, Containing the "Monroe Doctrine," December 2, 1823 (extract)
John Bassett Moore, *A Digest of International Law*, VI, 401

AT THE PROPOSAL of the Russian Imperial Government, made through the minister of the Emperor residing here, a full power and instructions have been transmitted to the minister of the United States at St. Petersburg, to arrange, by amicable negotiation, the respective rights and interests of the two nations on the northwest coast of this continent. A similar proposal has been made by his Imperial Majesty to the Government of Great Britain, which has likewise been acceded to. The Government of the United States has been desirous, by this friendly proceeding, of manifesting the great value which they have invariably attached to the friendship of the Emperor, and their solicitude to cultivate the best understanding with his Government. In the discussions to which this interest has given rise, and in the arrangements by which they may terminate, the occasion has been judged proper for asserting as a principle in which the rights and interests of the United States are involved, that the American continents, by the free and independent condition which they have assumed and maintain, are henceforth not to be considered as subjects for future colonization by any European powers. [Paragraph 7, message of December 2, 1823.]

It was stated at the commencement of the last session that a great effort was then making in Spain and Portugal to improve the condition of the people of those countries, and that it appeared to be conducted with extraordinary moderation. It need scarcely be remarked that the result has been, so far, very different from what was then anticipated. Of events in that quarter of the globe with which we have so much intercourse, and from which we derive our origin, we have always been anxious and interested spectators. The citizens of the United States cherish sentiments the most friendly in favor of the liberty and happiness of their fellow-men on that side of the Atlantic. In the wars of the European powers in matters relating to themselves we have never taken any part, nor does it comport with our policy so to do. It is only when our rights are invaded or seriously menaced that we resent injuries or make preparation for our defense. With the movements in this hemisphere we are, of necessity, more immediately connected, and by causes which must be obvious to all enlightened and impartial observers. The political system of the allied powers is essentially different in this respect from that of America. This difference proceeds from that which exists in their respective Governments. And to the defense of our own, which has been achieved by the loss of so much blood and treasure, and matured by the wisdom of their most enlightened citizens, and under which we have enjoyed unexampled felicity, this whole nation is devoted. We owe it, therefore, to candor, and to the amicable relations existing between the United States and those powers, to declare that we should consider any attempt on their part to extend their system to any portion of this hemisphere as dangerous to our peace and safety. With the existing colonies or dependencies of any European power we have not interfered and shall not interfere. But with the governments who have declared their independence and maintained it, and whose independence we have, on great consideration and on just principles, acknowledged, we could not view any interposition for the purpose of oppressing them, or controlling in any other manner their destiny, by any European power, in any other light than as the manifestation of an unfriendly disposition toward the United States. In the war between these new governments and Spain we declared our neutrality at the time of their recognition, and to this we have adhered and shall continue to adhere, provided no change shall occur which, in the judgment of the competent authorities of this Government, shall make a corresponding change on the part of the United States indispensable to their security.

The late events in Spain and Portugal show that Europe is still unsettled. Of this important fact no stronger proof can be adduced than that the allied powers should have thought it proper, on any principle satisfactory to themselves, to have interposed, by force, in the internal concerns of Spain. To what extent such interposition may be carried, on the same principle, is a question in which all independent powers whose governments differ from theirs are interested, even those most remote, and surely none more so than the United States. Our policy in regard to Europe, which was adopted at an early stage of the wars which have so long agitated that quarter of the globe, nevertheless remains the same, which is, not to interfere in the internal concerns of any of its powers; to consider the government de facto as the legitimate government for us; to cultivate friendly relations with it, and to preserve those relations by a frank, firm, and manly policy, meeting, in all instances, the just claims of every power, submitting to injuries from none. But in regard to these continents, circumstances are eminently and conspicuously different. It is impossible that the allied powers should extend their political system to any portion of either continent without endangering our peace and happiness; nor can anyone believe that our southern brethren, if left to themselves, would adopt it of their own accord. It is equally impossible, therefore, that we should behold such interposition, in any form, with indifference. If we look to the comparative strength and resources of Spain and those new governments, and their distance from each other, it must be obvious that she can never subdue them. It is still the true policy of the United States to leave the parties to themselves, in the hope that other powers will pursue the same course. [Paragraphs 48 and 49, message of December 2, 1823.]

Certain Interpretations and Applications in the Nineteenth Century

HENRY CLAY, Secretary of State, to John M. Forbes, United States Chargé d'Affaires at Buenos Aires, January 3, 1828

William R. Manning, *Diplomatic Correspondence of the United States Concerning the Independence of the Latin American Nations*, I, 292

SIR:

I should have, long since, noticed the subject which formed the principal topic of your conference with the President of the Argentine Republic, in August of the year before last (a minute of which, together with your correspondence on the same subject, with the Minister of Foreign Affairs of that Republic is transmitted with your despatch No. 40) if the arrival of a Minister from Buenos Ayres had not been expected. In both the minute and the correspondence above referred to, it is stated that such a minister was about to be sent to the United States; but as he has not arrived, and as we have heard nothing, of late, about him, I will not longer delay communicating to you the views which are entertained by the President of the United States, on the two enquiries with which Mr. de la Cruz concludes his note to you. Those enquiries relate to the declaration of the late President of the United States, contained in his message to Congress, of the 2d. December 1823, against the interference of Europe with the affairs of America. At the period of that declaration, apprehensions were entertained of designs, on the part of the Allied Powers of Europe to interfere, in behalf of Spain, to reduce again to subjection, those parts of the Continent of America which had thrown off the Spanish yoke. The declaration of the late President was that of the head of the Executive Government of the United States. Although there is every reason to believe that the policy which it announced was in conformity with the opinion both of the nation and of Congress, the declaration must be regarded as having been voluntarily made, and not as conveying any pledge or obligation, the performance of which foreign nations have a right to demand. When the case shall arrive, if it should ever occur, of such an European interference as the message supposes, and it becomes consequently necessary to decide whether this country will or will not engage in war, Congress alone, you well know, is competent, by our Constitution, to decide that question. In the event of such an interference, there can be but little doubt that the sentiment contained in President Monroe's message, would be still that of the People and Government of the United States.

We have much reason to believe that the declaration of Mr. Monroe had great, if not decisive, influence, in preventing all interference, on the part of the Allied Powers of Europe to the prejudice of the new Republics of America. From that period down to the present time, the efforts of the Government of the United States have been unremitted to accomplish the same object. It was one of the first acts of the present administration to engage the head of the European Alliance, the late Emperor Alexander, to employ his good offices to put a stop to the further effusion of human blood, by the establishment of a peace between Spain and those new Republics. Entering fully into the views of the United States, he did give his advice, to that effect, to the Spanish Government. His successor, the Emperor Nicholas, is known to march in the same line of policy which was marked out by his illustrious brother.

Not long after President Monroe's declaration, Great Britain took the decided step of acknowledging the independence of several of the new Republics. More recently France, and other European Powers, have given indications of their intention to follow the example of the United States.

It may then be confidently affirmed that there is no longer any danger whatever of the contingency happening, which is supposed by Mr. Monroe's message, of such an interference, on the part of Europe, with the concerns of America, as would make it expedient for the Government of the United States to interpose.

In respect to the war which has unhappily been raging between the Argentine Republic, and the Emperor of Brazil, the President has seen it with great regret, and would be very glad to hear of its honorable conclusion. But that war cannot be conceived as presenting a state of things bearing the remotest analogy to the case which President Monroe's message deprecates. It is a war strictly American in its origin and its object. It is a war in which the Allies of Europe have taken no part. Even if Portugal and the Brazils had remained united, and the war had been carried on by their joint arms, against the Argentine

Republic, that would have been far from presenting the case which the message contemplated. But, by the death of the late King of Portugal, there has been a virtual separation between the Brazils and Portugal, and during the greater part, if not the whole, of the period of the war, the condition of Portugal has been such as to need succor, rather than be capable of affording it to the Brazils.

The general policy of the United States is that of strict and impartial neutrality in reference to all wars of other Powers. It would be only in an extreme case that they would deviate from that policy. Such a case is not presented by the present war.

You will communicate in the most friendly manner, the substance of this despatch to the Government near which you reside.

I am [etc.]

ANNUAL MESSAGE from President James K. Polk to the United States Congress, December 2, 1845 (extract)
John Bassett Moore, *A Digest of International Law*, VI, 420

IT IS WELL KNOWN to the American people and to all nations, that this Government has never interfered with the relations subsisting between other governments. We have never made ourselves parties to their wars or their alliances; we have not sought their territories by conquest; we have not mingled with parties in their domestic struggles; and, believing our own form of government to be the best, we have never attempted to propagate it by intrigues, by diplomacy, or by force. We may claim on this continent a like exemption from European interference. The nations of America are equally sovereign and independent with those of Europe. They possess the same rights, independent of all foreign interposition, to make war, to conclude peace, and to regulate their internal affairs. The people of the United States can not, therefore, view with indifference attempts of European powers to interfere with the independent action of the nations on this continent. The American system of government is entirely different from that of Europe. Jealousy among the different sovereigns of Europe, lest any one of them might become too powerful for the rest, has caused them anxiously to desire the establishment of what they term the "balance of power." It can not be permitted to have any application on the North American continent, and especially to the United States. We must ever maintain the principle, that the people of this continent alone have the right to decide their own destiny.

Should any portion of them, constituting an independent state, propose to unite themselves with our confederacy, this will be a question for them and us to determine, without any foreign interposition. We can never consent that European powers shall interfere to prevent such a union, because it might disturb the "balance of power" which they may desire to maintain upon this continent. Near a quarter of a century ago the principle was distinctly announced to the world, in the annual message of one of my predecessors, that "the American continents, by the free and independent condition which they have assumed and maintain, are henceforth not to be considered as subjects for future colonization by any European power." This principle will apply with greatly increased force, should any European power attempt to establish any new colony in North America. In the existing circumstances of the world, the present is deemed a proper occasion to reiterate and reaffirm the principle avowed by Mr. Monroe, and to state my cordial concurrence in its wisdom and sound policy. The reassertion of this principle, especially in reference to North America, is, at this day, but the promulgation of a policy which no European power should cherish the disposition to resist. Existing rights of every European nation should be respected; but it is due alike to our safety and our interests, that the efficient protection of our laws should be extended over our whole territorial limits, and that it should be distinctly announced to the world as our settled policy, that no future European colony or dominion shall, with our consent, be planted or established on any part of the North American continent.

JAMES BUCHANAN, Secretary of State, to William A. Harris,
United States Minister to Argentina, March 30, 1846
John Bassett Moore, *A Digest of International Law,* VI, 422

THE LATE annual message of the President to Congress has so clearly presented the great American doctrine in opposition to the interference of European Governments in the internal concerns of the nations of this continent, that it is deemed unnecessary to add another word upon this subject. That Great Britain and France have flagrantly violated this principle by their armed intervention on the La Plata is manifest to the whole world. Whilst existing circumstances render it impossible for the United States to take a part in the present war; yet the President desires that the whole moral influence of this Republic should be cast into the scale of the injured party. We cordially wish the Argentine Republic success in its struggle against foreign interference. It is for these reasons, that although the Government of the United States never did authorise your predecessor Mr. Brent to offer his mediation in the affairs of Great Britain, France and the Argentine Republic, this act has not been publicly disavowed. His example, however, is not to be followed by you without express instructions. An offer of mediation by one nation in the disputes of other nations is an act of too much importance and may involve consequences too serious to be undertaken by a diplomatic agent on his own responsibility.

Mr. Pakenham on the 7th November, last, placed in my hands the copy of a despatch from Lord Aberdeen to himself under date the 3d of October, last, with which you shall be furnished. From this it would appear that Great Britain and France in their armed intervention have no view to territorial aggrandisement on the La Plata. It will be your duty closely to watch the movements of these two Powers in that region; and should either of them in violation of this declaration attempt to make territorial acquisitions, you will immediately communicate the fact to this Government.

SPECIAL MESSAGE from President James K. Polk to the United States Congress, April 29, 1848 (extract)
John Bassett Moore, *A Digest of International Law*, VI, 423

WHILST IT IS NOT my purpose to recommend the adoption of any measure, with a view to the acquisition of the "dominion and sovereignty" over Yucatan, yet, according to our established policy, we could not consent to a transfer of this "dominion and sovereignty" to either Spain, Great Britain, or any other European power. In the language of President Monroe, in his message of December, 1823, "we should consider any attempt on their part to extend their system to any portion of this hemisphere as dangerous to our peace and safety." In my annual message of December, 1845, I declared that "near a quarter of a century ago, the principle was distinctly announced to the world, in the annual message of one of my predecessors, that the 'American continents, by the free and independent condition which they have assumed and maintain, are henceforth not to be considered as subjects for future colonization by any European power.' This principle will apply with greatly increased force, should any European power attempt to establish any new colony in North America. In the existing circumstances of the world, the present is deemed a proper occasion to reiterate and reaffirm the principle avowed by Mr. Monroe, and to state my cordial concurrence in its wisdom and sound policy."

EDWARD EVERETT, Secretary of State, to William C. Rives,
United States Minister to France, December 17, 1852
John Bassett Moore, *A Digest of International Law,* VI, 514

I TRANSMIT you a document printed by order of the House of Representatives which will acquaint you with the steps taken by France, England, and the United States to preserve the tranquillity and integrity of the eastern portion of the island of San Domingo. The policy pursued by the United States in this respect has been wholly disinterested. It has been, no dóubt, in our power to obtain a permanent foothold in Dominica; and we have as much need of a naval station at Samaná as any European power could possibly have. It has, however, been the steady rule of our policy to avoid, as far as possible, all disturbance of the existing political relations of the West Indies. We have felt that any attempts on the part of any one of the great maritime powers to obtain exclusive advantages in any of the islands, where such an attempt was likely to be made, would be apt to be followed by others, and end in converting the archipelago into a great theater of national competition for exclusive advantages and territorial acquisitions which might become fatal to the peace of the world.

WILLIAM H. SEWARD, Secretary of State, to Carl Schurz,
United States Minister to Spain, April 27, 1861
John Bassett Moore, *A Digest of International Law,* VI, 515

WE ARE INFORMED by what seems reliable authority, that the Dominican Republic on the island of San Domingo has been overthrown by a force introduced there by subjects of Spain who proceeded thither from the island of Cuba. And on authority equally probable we are informed that the Government of Her Catholic Majesty has been speedily proclaimed on the subversion of the Republic, and that this proclamation is maintained by a very large detachment of the Spanish army stationed in the West Indies.

By direction of the President, I have called the attention of the minister plenipotentiary of Her Catholic Majesty at this place to these very extraordinary facts and asked for an explanation thereof. You are furnished with a copy of that communication and also with a copy of Mr. Tassara's reply. He having promised to communicate further after consulting his Government, the President awaits that communication before taking any decisive measure concerning the transaction. You are authorized and instructed to call the attention of the Spanish Government to the subject, and in such manner as you can adopt without impropriety, urge the necessity of a prompt and satisfactory explanation. For this purpose you are authorized to say that the President will regard any attempt of Her Catholic Majesty's Government to retain the territory of the late Dominican Republic as a matter claiming very serious attention on the part of the Government of the United States.

WILLIAM H. SEWARD, Secretary of State, to Charles Francis Adams, United States Minister to Great Britain, March 3, 1862

Henry Steele Commager, *Documents of American History,* 3d ed., p. 424, citing U.S. 37th Congress, 2d Session, House Doc. No. 100, p. 207

SIR:

We observe indications of a growing opinion in Europe that the demonstrations which are being made by Spanish, French, and British forces against Mexico are likely to be attended with a revolution in that country which will bring in a monarchical government there, in which the crown will be assumed by some foreign prince.

This country is deeply concerned in the peace of nations, and aims to be loyal at the same time in all its relations, as well to the allies as to Mexico. The President has therefore instructed me to submit his views on the new aspect of affairs to the parties concerned. He has relied upon the assurances given to this government by the allies that they were seeking no political objects and only a redress of grievances. He does not doubt the sincerity of the allies, and his confidence in their good faith, if it could be shapen, would be reinspired by explanations apparently made in their behalf that the governments of Spain, France and Great Britain are not intending to intervene and will not intervene to effect a change of the constitutional form of government now existing in Mexico, or to produce any political change there in opposition to the will of the Mexican people. Indeed, he understands the allies to be unanimous in declaring that the proposed revolution in Mexico is moved only by Mexican citizens now in Europe.

The President, however, deems it his duty to express to the allies, in all candor and frankness, the opinion that no monarchical government which could be founded in Mexico, in the presence of foreign navies and armies in the waters and upon the soil of Mexico, would have any prospect of security or permanency. Secondly, that the instability of such a monarchy there would be enhanced if the throne should be assigned to any person not of Mexican nativity. That under such circumstances the new government must speedily fall unless it could draw into its support European alliances, which, relating back to the present invasion, would, in fact, make it the beginning of a permanent policy of armed European monarchical intervention injurious and practically hostile to the most general system of government on the continent of America, and this would be the beginning rather than the ending of revolution in Mexico.

These views are grounded upon some knowledge of the political sentiments and habits of society in America.

In such a case it is not to be doubted that the permanent interests and sympathies of this country would be with the other American republics. It is not intended on this occasion to predict the course of events which might happen as a consequence of the proceeding contemplated, either on this continent or in Europe. It is sufficient to say that, in the President's opinion, the emancipation of this continent from European control has been the principal feature in its history during the last century. It is not probable that a revolution in the contrary direction would be successful in an immediately succeeding century, while population in America is so rapidly developing, resources so rapidly developing, and society so steadily forming itself upon principles of democratic American government. Nor is it necessary to suggest to the allies the improbability that European nations could steadily agree upon a policy favorable to such a counter-revolution as one conducive to their own interests, or to suggest that, however studiously the allies may act to avoid lending the aid of their land and naval forces to domestic revolutions in Mexico, the result would nevertheless be traceable to the presence of those forces there, although for a different purpose, since it may be deemed certain that but for their presence there no such revolution could probably have been attempted or even conceived.

The Senate of the United States has not, indeed, given its official sanction to the precise measures which the President has proposed for lending our aid to the existing government in Mexico, with the approval of the allies, to relieve it from its present embarrassments. This, however, is only a question of domestic administration. It would be very erroneous to regard such a disagreement as indicating any serious difference of opinion in this government or among the American people in their cordial good wishes for the safety, welfare, and stability of the republic system of government in that country.

I am [etc.]

WILLIAM H. SEWARD, Secretary of State, to John L. Motley, United States Minister to Austria, April 16, 1866

Henry Steele Commager, *Documents of American History*, 3d ed., p. 426, citing U.S. 39th Congress, 1st Session, House Doc. No. 93, p. 46

SIR:

I have had the honor to receive your despatch of the 27th of March, No. 155, which brings the important announcement that a treaty, called a "miltary supplementary convention," was ratified on the 15th of that month between the Emperor of Austria and the Prince Maximilian, who claims to be an emperor in Mexico.

You inform me that it is expected that about one thousand volunteers will be shipped (under this treaty) from Trieste to Vera Cruz very soon, and that at least as many more will be shipped in autumn.

I have heretofore given you the President's instructions to ask for explanations, and, conditionally, to inform the government of Austria that the despatch of military expeditions by Austria under such an arrangement as the one which seems now to have been consummated would be regarded with serious concern by the United States.

The subject has now been further considered in connexion with the official information thus recently received. The time seems to have arrived when the attitude of this government in relation to Mexican affairs should be once again frankly and distinctly made known to the Emperor of Austria, and all other powers whom it may directly concern. The United States, for reasons which seem to them to be just, and to have their foundation in the laws of nations, maintain that the domestic republican government with which they are in relations of friendly communication is the only legitimate government existing in Mexico; that a war has for a period of several years been waged against that republic by the government of France; which war began with a disclaim of all political or dynastic designs that that war has subsequently taken upon itself, and now distinctly wears the character of an European intervention to overthrow that domestic republican government, and to erect in its stead a European, imperial, military despotism by military force. The United States, in view of the character of their own political institutions, their proximity and intimate relations towards Mexico, and their just influence in the political affairs of the American continent, cannot consent to the accomplishment of that purpose by the means described. The United States have therefore addressed themselves, as they think, seasonably to the government of France, and have asked that its military forces, engaged in that objectionable political invasion, may desist from further intervention and be withdrawn from Mexico.

A copy of the last communication upon this subject, which was addressed by us to the government of France, is herewith transmitted for your special information. This paper will give you the true situation of the question. It will also enable you to satisfy the government of Vienna that the United States must be no less opposed to military intervention for political objects hereafter in Mexico by the government of Austria, than they are opposed to any further intervention of the same character in that country by France.

You will, therefore, at as early a day as may be convenient, bring the whole case, in a becoming manner, to the attention of the imperial royal government. You are authorized to state that the United States sincerely desire that Austria may find it just and expedient to come upon the same ground of non-intervention in Mexico which is maintained by the United States, and to which they have invited France.

You will communicate to us the answer of the Austrian government to this proposition.

This government could not but regard as a matter of serious concern the despatch of any troops from Austria while the subject which you are directed to present to the Austrian government remains under consideration.

I am [etc.]

HAMILTON FISH, Secretary of State, to President Ulysses S. Grant, July 14, 1870 (extracts)

John Bassett Moore, *A Digest of International Law*, VI, 429

. . . THE AVOIDANCE of entangling alliances, the characteristic feature of the foreign policy of Washington, sprang from this condition of things. But the entangling alliances which then existed were engagements made with France as a part of the general contract under which aid was furnished to us for the achievement of our independence. France was willing to waive the letter of the obligation as to her West India possessions, but demanded, in its stead, privileges in our ports which the Administration was unwilling to concede. To make its refusal acceptable to a public which sympathized with France, the Cabinet of General Washington exaggerated the principle into a theory tending to national isolation. . . .

The foreign policy of these early days was not a narrow one. During this period we secured the evacuation by Great Britain of the country wrongfully occupied by her on the lake; we acquired Louisiana; we measured forces on the sea with France, and on the land and sea with England; we set the example of resisting and chastising the piracies of the Barbary States; we initiated in negotiations with Prussia the long line of treaties for the liberalization of war and the promotion of international intercourse; and we steadily demanded, and at length obtained, indemnification from various governments for the losses we had suffered by foreign spoliations in the wars of Europe.

To this point in our foreign policy we had arrived when the revolutionary movements in Spanish and Portuguese America compelled a modification of our relations with Europe, in consequence of the rise of new and independent states in America. . . .

The new states were, like ourselves, revolted colonies. They continued the precedent we had set, of separating from Europe. Their assumption of independence was stimulated by our example. They professedly imitated us, and copied our national Constitution, sometimes even to their inconvenience. . . .

The formation of these new sovereignties in America was important to us, not only because of the cessation of colonial monopolies to that extent, but because of the geographical relations to us, held by so many new nations, all, like ourselves, created from European stock, and interested in excluding European politics, dynastic questions, and balances of power from further influence in the New World.

Thus the United States were forced into new lines of action, which, though apparently in some respects conflicting, were really in harmony with the line marked out by Washington. The avoidance of entangling political alliances and the maintenance of our own independent neutrality became doubly important from the fact that they became applicable to the new republics as well as to the mother country. The duty of noninterference had been admitted by every President. The question came up in the time of the first Adams, on the occasion of the enlistment projects of Miranda. It appeared again under Jefferson (anterior to the revolt of the Spanish colonies) in the schemes of Aaron Burr. It was an ever present question in the administrations of Madison, Monroe, and the younger Adams, in reference to the questions of foreign enlistment or equipment in the United States, and when these new Republics entered the family of nations, many of them very feeble, and all too much subject to internal revolution and civil war, a strict adherence to our previous policy and a strict enforcement of our laws became essential to the preservation of friendly relations with them. . . .

A vast field was thus opened to the statesmen of the United States for the peaceful introduction, the spread, and the permanent establishment of the American ideas of republican government, of modification of the laws of war, of liberalization of commerce, of religious freedom and toleration, and of the emancipation of the New World from the dynastic and balance of power controversies of Europe.

Mr. John Quincy Adams, beyond any other statesman of the time in this country, had the knowledge and experience, both European and American, the comprehension of thought and purpose, and the moral convictions which peculiarly fitted him to introduce our country into this new field, and to lay the foundation of an American policy. The declaration known as the Monroe doctrine, and the objects and purposes of the congress of Panama, both supposed to have been largely inspired by Mr. Adams, have influenced public events from that day to this, as a principle of government for this continent and its adjacent islands. . . .

This declaration resolved the solution of the immediate question of the independence of the Spanish American colonies, and is supposed to have exercised some influence upon the course of the British cabinet in regard to the absolutist schemes in Europe as well as in America.

It has also exercised a permanent influence on this continent. It was at once invoked in consequence of the supposed peril of Cuba on the side of Europe; it was applied to a similar danger threatening Yucatan; it was embodied in the treaty of the United States and Great Britain as to Central America; it produced the successful opposition of the United States to the attempt of Great Britain to exercise dominion in Nicaragua under the cover of the Mosquito Indians; and it operated in like manner to prevent the establishment of a European dynasty in Mexico.

The United States stand solemnly committed by repeated declarations and repeated acts to this doctrine, and its application to the affairs of this continent. In his message to the two Houses of Congress at the commencement of the present session, the President, following the teachings of all our history, said that the existing "dependencies are no longer regarded as subject to transfer from one European power to another. When the present relation of colonies ceases, they are to become independent powers, exercising the right of choice and of self-control in the determination of their future condition and relations with other powers."

This policy is not a policy of aggression; but it opposes the creation of European dominion on American soil, or its transfer to other European powers, and it looks hopefully to the time when, by the voluntary departure of European governments from this continent and the adjacent islands, America shall be wholly American.

It does not contemplate forcible intervention in any legitimate contest; but it protests against permitting such a contest to result in the increase of European power or influence; and it ever impels this Government, as in the late contest between the South American Republics and Spain, to interpose its good offices to secure an honorable peace.

HAMILTON FISH, Secretary of State, to General Robert Schenck, United States Minister to Great Britain, June 2, 1871

John Bassett Moore, *A Digest of International Law*, VI, 531

BARON GEROLT (the German envoy and minister plenipotentiary) yesterday enquired how the Government of the United States would receive the proposal contained in what he said was a circular addressed by his Government to their Representatives at London, Madrid, Florence, and Copenhagen, proposing a joint and concerted movement to urge on Venezuela a more orderly government, better observance of her engagements, &c., &c. I failed to obtain from the baron any definition of the precise nature of the proposed movement, or of the precise objects to be attained, or of the extent to which it was in contemplation either to advise or to coerce Venezuela, nor whether coercion was really in contemplation, although he made once an illusion to a "combined fleet" and "guns."

The United States is among the creditors of Venezuela, so are France, Holland, Great Britain, Italy, Denmark, and Spain.

We are not aware that Germany is among the creditors of Venezuela, or that she has any special cause of complaint against that Government for any injuries to her people or commerce.

Her movement, therefore, in this direction excites some surprise.

Baron Gerolt stated that he was directed to make the inquiry "confidentially," and that he was not to make the proposal to the United States unless it would be favorably received.

He was told that we had a vivid recollection of a combined European movement against Mexico a few years since, and that we would wish to know the causes of Germany's complaint, and the precise object and means which they proposed and the limits which they intended to prescribe to their operations. That the United States could not look with indifference upon any combination of European powers against an American state; that if Germany or any other power had just cause of war against Venezuela, this Government could interpose no objection to her resorting thereto.

If the object of Germany be a united remonstrance to Venezuela against the anarchy and chronic revolutionary condition of that state, or an appeal to honesty in the observance of her engagements, this Government would not object, but would, of itself, make a similar remonstrance and appeal. If, however, the object be a forcible demonstration of coercion by a combination of European states, the United States could not regard it with indifference.

You will inquire confidentially of Her Majesty's Secretary of State for Foreign Affairs whether any proposal has been made in behalf of the German Government to that of Great Britain on this subject, and ask whether the Government of Her Majesty has it in contemplation to unite therein. You will at the same time, delicately but decidedly, express the anxiety which the suggestion of the proposition has excited in this Government, and may say that the President hopes that the suggested proposal may not be carried to the extent of disturbing the sensibilities which would be aroused by a combination of European powers against one of the Republics of this Continent.

THOMAS F. BAYARD, Secretary of State, to Robert M. Mc-Lane, United States Minister to France, December 21, 1888 (extract)

John Bassett Moore, *A Digest of International Law*, VI, 433

THAT GOVERNMENT [the French] is perfectly aware of the well-settled policy of the United States which would lead us to oppose any attempt on the part of a European government to extend its influence in any portion of America. In view of events which are currently reported to be taking place in France at this time arising out of the pecuniary embarrassments of the Panama Canal Company, and of the possibility of the French Government being asked to undertake the construction of that work as a national measure, it may be well for you, without referring especially to affairs in Panama, to take this opportunity also to call the attention of the minister of foreign affairs in somewhat explicit language to the consistent attitude maintained by the United States in regard to this subject. The wish of the United States has always been that the independent countries to the south of us should be left free to develop their own resources in such manner as they might deem most advisable for their own interests free from foreign dictation or interference of any kind. The United States has no interest other than that of the well being and prosperity of its neighbors. It has never attempted colonization, but it has consistently maintained that no part of America is to be considered as a subject for future colonization of any European power. The views of this Government in this regard have heretofore been fully explained to the Government of France, not only on the occasion above referred to, when some acquisition by it of Haytian territory was reported to be in contemplation, but also on the occasion of the expedition to Mexico, undertaken upwards of 25 years ago, and at the time of the commencement of work by the French company upon the Panama Canal.

RICHARD OLNEY, Secretary of State, to Thomas F. Bayard, United States Ambassador to Great Britain, July 20, 1895 (extracts)

John Bassett Moore, *A Digest of International Law*, VI, 535

I AM DIRECTED by the President to communicate to you his views upon a subject to which he has given much anxious thought and respecting which he has not reached a conclusion without a lively sense of its great importance as well as of the serious responsibility involved in any action now to be taken. . . .

The important features of the existing situation, as shown by the foregoing recital, may be briefly stated.

1. The title to territory of indefinite but confessedly very large extent is in dispute between Great Britain on the one hand and the South American Republic of Venezuela on the other.

2. The disparity in the strength of the claimants is such that Venezuela can hope to establish her claim only through peaceful methods—through an agreement with her adversary either upon the subject itself or upon an arbitration.

3. The controversy, with varying claims on the part of Great Britain, has existed for more than half a century, during which period many earnest and persistent efforts of Venezuela to establish a boundary by agreement have proved unsuccessful.

4. The futility of the endeavor to obtain a conventional line being recognized, Venezuela for a quarter of a century has asked and striven for arbitration.

5. Great Britain, however, has always and continuously refused to arbitrate, except upon the condition of a renunciation of a large part of the Venezuelan claim and of a concession to herself of a large share of the territory in controversy.

6. By the frequent interposition of its good offices at the instance of Venezuela, by constantly urging and promoting the restoration of diplomatic relations between the two countries, by pressing for arbitration of the disputed boundary, by offering to act as arbitrator, by expressing its grave concern whenever new alleged instances of British aggression upon Venezuelan territory have been brought to its notice, the Government of the United States has made it clear to Great Britain and to the world that the controversy is one in which both its honor and its interests are involved and the continuance of which it can not regard with indifference.

The accuracy of the foregoing analysis of the existing status can not, it is believed, be challenged. It shows that status to be such that those charged with the interests of the United States are now forced to determine exactly what those interests are and what course of action they require. It compels them to decide to what extent, if any, the United States may and should intervene in a controversy between and primarily concerning only Great Britain and Venezuela and to decide how far it is bound to see that the integrity of Venezuelan territory is not impaired by the pretensions of its powerful antagonist. Are any such right and duty devolved upon the United States? If not, the United States has already done all, if not more than all, that a purely sentimental interest in the affairs of the two countries justifies, and to push its interposition further would be unbecoming and undignified and might well subject it to the charge of impertinent intermeddling with affairs with which it has no rightful concern. On the other hand, if any such right and duty exist, their due exercise and discharge will not permit of any action that shall not be efficient and that, if the power of the United States is adequate, shall not result in the accomplishment of the end in view. The question thus presented, as matter of principle and regard being had to the settled national policy, does not seem difficult of solution. Yet the momentous practical consequences dependent upon its determination require that it should be carefully considered and that the grounds of the conclusion arrived at should be fully and frankly stated.

That there are circumstances under which a nation may justly interpose in a controversy to which two or more other nations are the direct and immediate parties is an admitted canon of international law. The doctrine is ordinarily expressed in terms of the most general character and is perhaps incapable of more specific statement. It is declared in substance that a nation may avail itself of this right whenever what is done or proposed by any of the parties primarily concerned is a serious and direct menace to its own integrity, tranquillity, or welfare. The propriety of the rule when applied in good faith will not be questioned in any quarter. On the other hand, it is an inevitable though unfortunate consequence of the wide scope of the rule that it has only too often been made a cloak for schemes of wanton spoliation and aggrandizement. We are concerned at this time, however, not so much with the general rule as with a form of it which is peculiarly and distinctively American. Washington, in the solemn admonitions of the Farewell Address, explicitly warned his countrymen against entanglements with the politics or the controversies of European powers.

"Europe [he said] has a set of primary interests which to us have none or a very remote relation. Hence she must be engaged in frequent controversies the causes of which are essentially foreign to our concerns. Hence, therefore, it must be unwise in us to implicate ourselves by artificial ties in the ordinary vicissitudes of her politics or the ordinary combinations and collisions of her friendships or enmities. Our detached and distant situation invites and enables us to pursue a different course."

During the Administration of President Monroe this doctrine of the Farewell Address was first considered in all its aspects and with a view to all its practical consequences. The Farewell Address, while it took America out of the field of European politics, was silent as to the part Europe might be permitted to play in America. Doubtless it was thought the latest addition to the family of nations should not make haste to prescribe rules for the guidance of its older members, and the expediency and propriety of serving the powers of Europe with notice of a complete and distinctive American policy excluding them from interference with American political affairs might well seem dubious to a generation to whom the French alliance, with its manifold advantages to the cause of American independence, was fresh in mind.

Twenty years later, however, the situation had changed. The lately born nation had greatly increased in power and resources, had demonstrated its strength on land and sea and as well in the conflicts of arms as in the pursuits of peace, and had begun to realize the commanding position on this continent which the character of its people, their free institutions, and their remoteness from the chief scene of European contentions combined to give to it. The Monroe Administration therefore did not hesitate to accept and apply the logic of the Farewell Address by declaring in effect that American nonintervention in European affairs necessarily implied and meant European nonintervention in American affairs. Conceiving unquestionably that complete European noninterference in American concerns would be cheaply purchased by complete American noninterference in European concerns, President Monroe, in the celebrated message of December 2, 1823, used the following language: . . .

The Monroe Administration, however, did not content itself with formulating a correct rule for the regulation of the relations between Europe and America. It aimed at also securing the practical benefits to result from the application of the rule. Hence the message just quoted declared that the American continents were fully occupied and were not the subjects for future colonization by European powers. To this spirit and this purpose, also, are to be attributed the passages of the same message which treat any infringement of the rule against interference in American affairs on the part of the powers of Europe as an act of unfriendliness to the United States. It was realized that it was futile to lay down such a rule unless its observance could be enforced. It was manifest that the United States was the only power in this hemisphere capable of enforcing it. It was therefore courageously declared not merely that Europe ought not to interfere in American affairs, but that any European power doing so would be regarded as antagonizing the interests and inviting the opposition of the United States.

That America is in no part open to colonization, though the proposition was not universally admitted at the time of its first enunciation, has long been universally conceded. We are now concerned, therefore, only with that other practical application of the Monroe doctrine the disregard of which by an European power is to be deemed an act of unfriendliness towards the United States. The precise scope and limitations of this rule can not be too clearly apprehended. It does not establish any general protectorate by the United States over other American states. It does not relieve any American state from its obligations as fixed by international law nor prevent any European power directly interested from enforcing such obligations or from inflicting merited punishment for the breach of them. It does not contemplate any interference in the internal affairs of any American state or in the relations between it and other American states. It does not justify any attempt on our part to change the established form of government of any American state or to prevent the people of such state from altering that form according to their own will and pleasure. The rule in question has but a single purpose and object. It is that no European power or combination of European powers shall forcibly deprive an American state of the right and power of self-government and of shaping for itself its own political fortunes and destinies.

That the rule thus defined has been the accepted public law of this country ever since its promulgation can not fairly be denied. Its pronouncement by the Monroe Administration at that particular time was unquestionably due to the inspiration of Great Britain, who at once gave to it an open and unqualified adhesion which has never been withdrawn. But the rule was decided upon and formulated by the Monroe Administration as a distinctly American doctrine of great import to the safety and welfare of the United States after the most careful consideration by a Cabinet which numbered among its members John Quincy Adams, Calhoun, Crawford, and Wirt, and which before acting took both Jefferson and Madison into its counsels. Its promulgation was received with acclaim by the entire people of the country irrespective of party. Three years after, Webster declared that the doctrine involved the honor of the country. "I look upon it," he said, "as part of its treasures of reputation, and for one I intend to guard it," and he added,

I look on the message of December, 1823, as forming a bright page in our history. I will help neither to erase it nor to tear it out; nor shall it be by any act of mine blurred or blotted. It did honor to the sagacity of the Government, and I will not diminish that honor.

Though the rule thus highly eulogized by Webster has never been formally affirmed by Congress, the House in 1864 declared against the Mexican monarchy sought to be set up by the French as not in accord with the policy of the United States, and in 1889 the Senate expressed its disapproval of the connection of any European power with a canal across the Isthmus of Darien or Central America. It is manifest that, if a rule has been openly and uniformly declared and acted upon by the executive branch of the Government for more than seventy years without express repudiation by Congress, it must be conclusively presumed to have its sanction. Yet it is certainly no more than the exact truth to say that every administration since President Monroe's has had occasion, and sometimes more occasions than one, to examine and consider the Monroe doctrine and has in each instance given it emphatic endorsement. Presidents have dwelt upon it in messages to Congress and Secretaries of State have time after time made it the theme of diplomatic representation. Nor, if the practical results of the rule be sought for, is the record either meager or obscure. Its first and immediate effect was indeed most momentous and far-reaching. It was the controlling factor in the emancipation of South America and to it the independent states which now divide that region between them are largely indebted for their very existence. Since then the most striking single achievement to be credited to the rule is the evacuation of Mexico by the French upon the termination of the civil war. But we are also indebted to it for the provisions of the Clayton-Bulwer treaty, which both neutralized any interoceanic canal across Central America and expressly excluded Great Britain from occupying or exercising any dominion over any part of Central America. It has been used in the case of Cuba as if justifying the position that, while the sovereignty of Spain will be respected, the island will not be permitted to become the possession of any other European power. It has been influential in bringing about the definite relinquishment of any supposed protectorate by Great Britain over the Mosquito coast.

President Polk, in the case of Yucatan and the proposed voluntary transfer of that country to Great Britain or Spain, relied upon the Monroe doctrine, though perhaps erroneously, when he declared in a special message to Congress on the subject that the United States could not consent to any such transfer. Yet, in somewhat the same spirit, Secretary Fish affirmed in 1870 that President Grant had but followed "the teachings of all our history" in declaring in his annual message of that year that existing dependencies were no longer regarded as subject to transfer from one European power to another, and that when the present relation of colonies ceases they are to become independent powers. Another development of the rule, though apparently not necessarily required by either its letter or its spirit, is found in the objection to arbitration of South American controversies by an European power. American questions, it is said, are for American decision, and on that ground the United States went so far as to refuse to mediate in the war between Chili and Peru jointly with Great Britain and France. Finally, on the ground, among others, that the authority of the Monroe doctrine and the prestige of the United States as its exponent and sponsor would be seriously impaired, Secretary Bayard strenuously resisted the enforcement of the Pelletier claim against Hayti.

"The United States [he said] has proclaimed herself the protector of this western world, in which she is by far the stronger power, from the intrusion of European sovereignties. She can point with proud satisfaction to the fact that over and over again has she declared effectively, that serious indeed would be the consequences if European hostile foot should, without just cause, tread those states in the New World which have emancipated themselves from European control. She has announced that she would cherish as it becomes her the territorial rights of the feeblest of those states, regarding them not merely as in the eye of the law equal to even the greatest of nationalities, but in view of her distinctive policy as entitled to be regarded by her as the objects of a peculiarly gracious care. I feel bound to say that if we should sanction by reprisals in Hayti the ruthless invasion of her territory and insult to her sovereignty which the facts now before us disclose, if we approve by solemn Executive action and Congressional assent that invasion, it will be difficult for us hereafter to assert that in the New World, of whose rights we are the peculiar guardians, these rights have never been invaded by ourselves."

The foregoing enumeration not only shows the many instances wherein the rule in question has been affirmed and applied, but also demonstrates that the Venezuelan boundary controversy is in any view far within the scope and spirit of the rule as uniformly accepted and acted upon. A doctrine of American public law thus long and firmly established and supported could not easily be ignored in a proper case for its application, even were the considerations upon which it is founded obscure or questionable. No such objection can be made, however, to the Monroe doctrine understood and defined in the manner already stated. It rests, on the contrary, upon facts and principles that are both intelligible and incontrovertible. That distance and three thousand miles of intervening ocean make any permanent political union between an European and an American state unnatural and inexpedient will hardly be denied. But physical and geographical considerations are the least of the objections to such a union. Europe, as Washington observed, has a set of primary interests which are peculiar to herself. America is not interested in them and ought not to be vexed or complicated with them. Each great European power, for instance, to-day maintains enormous armies and fleets in self-defense and for protection against any other European power or powers. What have the states of America to do with that condition of things, or why should they be impoverished by wars or preparations for wars with whose causes or results they can have no direct concern? If all Europe were to suddenly fly to arms over the fate of Turkey, would it not be preposterous that any American state should find itself inextricably involved in the miseries and burdens of the contest? If it were, it would prove to be a partnership in the cost and losses of the struggle but not in any ensuing benefits.

What is true of the material, is no less true of what may be termed the moral interests involved. Those pertaining to Europe are peculiar to her and are entirely diverse from those pertaining and peculiar to America. Europe as a whole is monarchical, and, with the single important exception of the Republic of France, is committed to the monarchical principle. America, on the other hand, is devoted to the exactly opposite principle—to the idea that every people has an inalienable right of self-government—and, in the United States of America, has furnished to the world the most conspicuous and conclusive example and proof of the excellence of free institutions, whether from the standpoint of national greatness or of individual happiness. It can not be necessary, however, to enlarge upon this phase of the subject—whether moral or material interests be considered, it can not but be universally conceded that those of Europe are irreconcilably diverse from those of America, and that any European control of the latter is necessarily both incongruous and injurious. If, however, for the reasons stated the forcible intrusion of European powers into American politics is to be deprecated—if, as it is to be deprecated, it should be resisted and prevented—such resistance and prevention must come from the United States. They would come from it, of course, were it made the point of attack. But, if they come at all, they must also come from it when any other American state is attacked, since only the United States has the strength adequate to the exigency.

Is it true, then, that the safety and welfare of the United States are so concerned with the maintenance of the independence of every American state as against any European power as to justify and require the interposition of the United States whenever that independence is endangered? The question can be candidly answered in but one way. The States of America, South as well as North, by geographical proximity, by natural sympathy, by similarity of governmental constitutions, are friends and allies, commercially and politically of the United States. To allow the subjugation of any of them by an European power is, of course, to completely reverse that situation and signifies the loss of all the advantages incident to their natural relations to us. But that is not all. The people of the United States have a vital interest in the cause of popular self-government. They have secured the right for themselves and their posterity at the cost of infinite blood and treasure. They have realized and exemplified its beneficent operation by a career unexampled in point of natural greatness or individual felicity. They believe it to be for the healing of all nations, and that civilization must either advance or retrograde accordingly as its supremacy is extended or curtailed. Imbued with these sentiments, the people of the United States might not impossibly be wrought up to an active propaganda in favor of a cause so highly valued both for themselves and for mankind. But the age of the Crusades has passed, and they are content with such assertion and defense of the right of popular self-government as their own security and welfare demand. It is in that view more than in any other that they believe it not to be tolerated that the political control of an American state shall be forcibly assumed by an European power.

The mischiefs apprehended from such a source are none the less real because not immediately imminent in any specific case, and are none the less to be guarded against because the combination of circumstances that will bring them upon us can not be predicted. The civilized states of Christendom deal with each other on substantially the same principles that regulate the conduct of individuals. The greater its enlightenment, the more surely every state perceives that its permanent interests require it to be governed by the immutable principles of right and justice. Each, nevertheless, is only too liable to succumb to the temptations offered by seeming special opportunities for its own aggrandizement, and each would rashly imperil its own safety were it not to remember that for the regard and respect of other states it must be largely dependent upon its own strength and power. To-day the United States is practically sovereign on this continent, and its fiat is law upon the subjects to which it confines its interposition. Why? It is not because of the pure friendship or good will felt for it. It is not simply by reason of its high character as a civilized state, nor because wisdom and justice and equity are the invariable characteristics of the dealings of the United States. It is because, in addition to all other grounds, its infinite resources combined with its isolated position render it master of the situation and practically invulnerable as against any or all other powers.

All the advantages of this superiority are at once imperiled if the principle be admitted that European powers may convert American states into colonies or provinces of their own. The principle would be eagerly availed of, and every power doing so would immediately acquire a base of military operations against us. What one power was permitted to do could not be denied to another, and it is not inconceivable that the struggle now going on for the acquisition of Africa might be transferred to South America. If it were, the weaker countries would unquestionably be soon absorbed, while the ultimate result might be the partition of all South America between the various European powers. The disastrous consequences to the United States of such a condition of things are obvious. The loss of prestige, of authority, and of weight in the councils of the family of nations, would be among the least of them. Our only real rivals in peace as well as enemies in war would be found located at our very doors. Thus far in our history we have been spared the burdens and evils of immense standing armies and all the other accessories of huge warlike establishments, and the exemption has largely contributed to our national greatness and wealth as well as to the happiness of every citizen. But, with the powers of Europe permanently encamped on American soil, the ideal conditions we have thus far enjoyed can not be expected to continue. We too must be armed to the teeth; we too must convert the flower of our male population into soldiers and sailors, and by withdrawing them from the various pursuits of peaceful industry, we too must practically annihilate a large share of the productive energy of the nation.

How a greater calamity than this could overtake us it is difficult to see. Nor are our apprehensions to be allayed by suggestions of the friendliness of European powers—of their good will toward us— of their disposition, should they be our neighbors, to dwell with us in peace and harmony. The people of the United States have learned in the school of experience to what extent the relations of states to each other depend not upon sentiment nor principle, but upon selfish interest. They will not soon forget that, in their hour of distress, all their anxieties and burdens were aggravated by the possibility of demonstrations against their national life on the part of powers with whom they had long maintained the most harmonious relations. They have yet in mind that France seized upon the apparent opportunity of our civil war to set up a monarchy in the adjoining state of Mexico. They realize that had France and Great Britain held important South American possessions to work from and to benefit, the temptation to destroy the predominance of the Great Republic in this hemisphere by furthering its dismemberment might have been irresistible. From that grave peril they have been saved in the past and may be saved again in the future through the operation of the sure but silent force of the doctrine proclaimed by President Monroe. To abandon it, on the other hand, disregarding both the logic of the situation and the facts of our past experience, would be to renounce a policy which has proved both an easy defense against foreign aggression and a prolific source of internal progress and prosperity.

There is, then, a doctrine of American public law, well founded in principle and abundantly sanctioned by precedent, which entitles and requires the United States to treat as an injury to itself the forcible assumption by an European power of political control over an American state. The application of the doctrine to the boundary dispute between Great Britain and Venezuela remains to be made and presents no real difficulty. Though the dispute relates to a boundary line, yet, as it is between states, it necessarily imports political control to be lost by one party and gained by the other. The political control at stake, too, is of no mean importance, but concerns a domain of great extent— the British claim, it will be remembered, apparently expanded in two years some 33,000 square miles—and, if it also directly involves the command of the mouth of the Orinoco, is of immense consequence in connection with the whole river navigation of the interior of South America. It has been intimated, indeed, that in respect of South American possessions Great Britain is herself an American state like any other, so that a controversy between her and Venezuela is to be settled between themselves as if it were between Venezuela and Brazil or between Venezuela and Colombia, and does not call for or justify United States intervention. If this view be tenable at all, the logical sequence is plain.

Great Britain as a South American state is to be entirely differentiated from Great Britain generally, and if the boundary question can not be settled otherwise than by force, British Guiana, with her own independent resources and not those of the British Empire, should be left to settle the matter with Venezuela—an arrangement which very possibly Venezuela might not object to. But the proposition that an European power with an American dependency is for the purposes of the Monroe doctrine to be classed not as an European but as an American state will not admit of serious discussion. If it were to be adopted, the Monroe doctrine would be too valueless to be worth asserting. Not only would every European power now having a South American colony be enabled to extend its possessions on this continent indefinitely, but any other European power might also do the same by first taking pains to procure a fraction of South American soil by voluntary cession.

The declaration of the Monroe message—that existing colonies or dependencies of an European power would not be interfered with by the United States—means colonies or dependencies then existing, with their limits as then existing. So it has been invariably construed, and so it must continue to be construed unless it is to be deprived of all vital force. Great Britain can not be deemed a South American state within the purview of the Monroe doctrine, nor, if she is appropriating Venezuelan territory, is it material that she does so by advancing the frontier of an old colony instead of by the planting of a new colony. The difference is matter of form and not of substance, and the doctrine if pertinent in the one case must be in the other also. It is not admitted, however, and therefore can not be assumed, that Great Britain is in fact usurping dominion over Venezuelan territory. While Venezuela charges such usurpation, Great Britain denies it, and the United States, until the merits are authoritatively ascertained, can take sides with neither. But while this is so—while the United States may not, under existing circumstances at least, take upon itself to say which of the two parties is right and which wrong—it is certainly within its right to demand that the truth shall be ascertained. Being entitled to resent and resist any sequestration of Venezuelan soil by Great Britain, it is necessarily entitled to know whether such sequestration has occurred or is now going on. Otherwise, if the United States is without the right to know and have it determined whether there is or is not British aggression upon Venezuelan territory, its right to protest against or repel such aggression may be dismissed from consideration.

The right to act upon a fact, the existence of which there is no right to have ascertained, is simply illusory. It being clear, therefore, that the United States may legitimately insist upon the merits of the boundary question being determined, it is equally clear that there is but one feasible mode of determining them, viz, peaceful arbitration. The impracticability of any conventional adjustment has been often and thoroughly demonstrated. Even more impossible of consideration is an appeal to arms—a mode of settling national pretensions unhappily not yet wholly obsolete. If, however, it were not condemnable as a relic of barbarism and a crime in itself, so one-sided a contest could not be invited nor even accepted by Great Britain without distinct disparagement to her character as a civilized state. Great Britain, however, assumes no such attitude. On the contrary, she both admits that there is a controversy and that arbitration should be resorted to for its adjustment. But, while up to that point her attitude leaves nothing to be desired, its practical effect is completely nullified by her insistence that the submission shall cover but a part of the controversy—that, as a condition of arbitrating her right to a part of the disputed territory, the remainder shall be turned over to her. If it were possible to point to a boundary which both parties had ever agreed or assumed to be such, either expressly or tacitly, the demand that territory conceded by such line to British Guiana should be held not to be in dispute might rest upon a reasonable basis. But there is no such line. The territory which Great Britain insists shall be ceded to her as a condition of arbitrating her claim to other territory has never been admitted to belong to her. It has always and consistently been claimed by Venezuela.

Upon what principle—except her feebleness as a nation—is she to be denied the right of having the claim heard and passed upon by an impartial tribunal? No reason nor shadow of reason appears in all the voluminous literature of the subject. "It is to be so because I will it to be so" seems to be the only justification Great Britain offers. It is, indeed, intimated that the British claim to this particular territory rests upon an occupation, which, whether acquiesced in or not, has ripened into a perfect title by long continuance. But what prescription affecting territorial rights can be said to exist as between sovereign states? Or, if there is any, what is the legitimate consequence? It is not that all arbitration should be denied, but only that the submission should embrace an additional topic, namely, the validity of the asserted prescriptive title either in point of law or in point of fact. No different result follows from the contention that as matter of principle Great Britain can not be asked to submit and ought not to submit to arbitration her political and sovereign rights over territory. This contention, if applied to the whole or to a vital part of the possessions of a sovereign state, need not be controverted. To hold otherwise might be equivalent to holding that a sovereign state was bound to arbitrate its very existence.

But Great Britain has herself shown in various instances that the principle has no pertinency when either the interests or the territorial area involved are not of controlling magnitude and her loss of them as the result of an arbitration can not appreciably affect her honor or her power. Thus, she has arbitrated the extent of her colonial possessions twice with the United States, twice with Portugal, and once with Germany, and perhaps in other instances. The Northwest Water Boundary arbitration of 1872 between her and this country is an example in point and well illustrates both the effect to be given to long-continued use and enjoyment and the fact that a truly great power sacrifices neither prestige nor dignity by reconsidering the most emphatic rejection of a proposition when satisfied of the obvious and intrinsic justice of the case. By the award of the Emperor of Germany, the arbitrator in that case, the United States acquired San Juan and a number of smaller islands near the coast of Vancouver as a consequence of the decision that the term "the channel which separates the continent from Vancouver's Island," as used in the treaty of Washington of 1846, meant the Haro channel and not the Rosario channel. Yet a leading contention of Great Britain before the arbitrator was that equity required a judgment in her favor because a decision in favor of the United States would deprive British subjects of rights of navigation of which they had had the habitual enjoyment from the time when the Rosario Strait was first explored and surveyed in 1798. So, though by virtue of the award, the United States acquired San Juan and the other islands of the group to which it belongs, the British foreign secretary had in 1859 instructed the British minister at Washington as follows:

> Her Majesty's Government must, therefore, under any circumstances, maintain the right of the British Crown to the island of San Juan. The interests at stake in connection with the retention of that island are too important to admit of compromise, and your lordship will consequently bear in mind that, whatever arrangement as to the boundary line is finally arrived at, no settlement of the question will be accepted by Her Majesty's Government which does not provide for the island of San Juan being reserved to the British Crown.

Thus, as already intimated, the British demand that her right to a portion of the disputed territory shall be acknowledged before she will consent to an arbitration as to the rest seems to stand upon nothing but her own *ipse dixit*. She says to Venezuela, in substance: "You can get none of the debatable land by force, because you are not strong enough; you can get none by treaty, because I will not agree; and you can take your chance of getting a portion by arbitration, only if you first agree to abandon to me such other portion as I may designate." It is not perceived how such an attitude can be defended nor how it is reconcilable with that love of justice and fair play so eminently characteristic of the English race. It in effect deprives Venezuela of her free agency and puts her under virtual duress. Territory acquired by reason of it will be as much wrested from her by the strong hand as if occupied by British troops or covered by British fleets. It seems therefore quite impossible that this position of Great Britain should be assented to by the United States, or that, if such position be adhered to with the result of enlarging the bounds of British Guiana, it should not be regarded as amounting, in substance, to an invasion and conquest of Venezuelan territory.

In these circumstances, the duty of the President appears to him unmistakable and imperative. Great Britain's assertion of title to the disputed territory combined with her refusal to have that title investigated being a substantial appropriation of the territory to her own use, not to protest and give warning that the transaction will be regarded as injurious to the interests of the people of the United States as well as oppressive in itself would be to ignore an established policy with which the honor and welfare of this country are closely identified. While the measures necessary or proper for the vindication of that policy are to be determined by another branch of the Government, it is clearly for the Executive to leave nothing undone which may tend to render such determination unnecessary.

You are instructed, therefore, to present the foregoing views to Lord Salisbury by reading to him this communication (leaving with him a copy should he so desire), and to reinforce them by such pertinent considerations as will doubtless occur to you. They call for a definite decision upon the point whether Great Britain will consent or will decline to submit the Venezuelan boundary question in its entirety to impartial arbitration. It is the earnest hope of the President that the conclusion will be on the side of arbitration, and that Great Britain will add one more to the conspicuous precedents she has already furnished in favor of that wise and just mode of adjusting international disputes. If he is to be disappointed in that hope, however—a result not to be anticipated and in his judgment calculated to greatly embarrass the future relations between this country and Great Britain— it is his wish to be made acquainted with the fact at such early date as will enable him to lay the whole subject before Congress in his next annual message.

ANNUAL MESSAGE from President Grover Cleveland to the United States Congress, December 2, 1895 (extract)

Foreign Relations of the United States, 1895, I, xxi, xxviii; John Bassett Moore, A Digest of International Law, VI, 575

IT BEING APPARENT that the boundary dispute between Great Britain and the Republic of Venezuela concerning the limits of British Guiana was approaching an acute stage, a definite statement of the interest and policy of the United States as regards the controversy seemed to be required both on its own account and in view of its relations with the friendly powers directly concerned. In July last, therefore, a dispatch was addressed to our ambassador at London for communication to the British Government, in which the attitude of the United States was fully and distinctly set forth. The general conclusions therein reached and formulated are in substance that the traditional and established policy of this Government is firmly opposed to a forcible increase by any European power of its territorial possessions on this continent;

that this policy is as well founded in principle as it is strongly supported by numerous precedents; that as a consequence the United States is bound to protest against the enlargement of the area of British Guiana in derogation of the rights and against the will of Venezuela; that, considering the disparity in strength of Great Britain and Venezuela, the territorial dispute between them can be reasonably settled only by friendly and impartial arbitration, and that the resort to such arbitration should include the whole controversy, and is not satisfied if one of the powers concerned is permitted to draw an arbitrary line through the territory in debate and to declare that it will submit to arbitration only the portion lying on one side of it. In view of these conclusions, the dispatch in question called upon the British Government for a definite answer to the question whether it would or would not submit the territorial controversy between itself and Venezuela in its entirety to impartial arbitration. The answer of the British Government 'has not yet been received, but it is expected shortly, when further communication on the subject will probably be made to the Congress.

SPECIAL MESSAGE from President Grover Cleveland to the United States Congress, December 17, 1895
John Bassett Moore, *A Digest of International Law*, VI, 576

IN MY ANNUAL MESSAGE addressed to the Congress on the third instant I called attention to the pending boundary controversy between Great Britain and the Republic of Venezuela and recited the substance of a representation made by this Government to her Britannic Majesty's Government suggesting reasons why such dispute should be submitted to arbitration for settlement, and inquiring whether it would be so submitted.

The answer of the British Government, which was then awaited, has since been received and, together with the dispatch to which it is a reply, is hereto appended.

Such reply is embodied in two communications addressed by the British Prime Minister to Sir Julian Pauncefote, the British Ambassador at this Capital. It will be seen that one of these communications is devoted exclusively to observations upon the Monroe doctrine, and claims that in the present instance a new and strange extension and development of this doctrine is insisted on by the United States, that the reasons justifying an appeal to the doctrine enunciated by President Monroe are generally inapplicable"to the state of things in which we live at the present day," and especially inapplicable to a controversy involving the boundary line between Great Britain and Venezuela.

Without attempting extended argument in reply to these positions, it may not be amiss to suggest that the doctrine upon which we stand is strong and sound because its enforcement is important to our peace and safety as a nation, and is essential to the integrity of our free institutions and the tranquil maintenance of our distinctive form of government. It was intended to apply to every stage of our national life, and can not become obsolete while our Republic endures. If the balance of power is justly a cause for jealous anxiety among the governments of the Old World, and a subject for our absolute noninterference, none the less is an observance of the Monroe doctrine of vital concern to our people and their Government.

Assuming, therefore, that we may properly insist upon this doctrine without regard to "the state of things in which we live," or any changed conditions here or elsewhere, it is not apparent why its application may not be invoked in the present controversy.

If a European power, by an extension of its boundaries, takes possession of the territory of one of our neighboring republics against its will and in derogation of its rights, it is difficult to see why to that extent such European power does not thereby attempt to extend its system of government to that portion of this continent which is thus taken. This is the precise action which President Monroe declared to be "dangerous to our peace and safety," and it can make no difference whether the European system is extended by an advance of frontier or otherwise.

It is also suggested in the British reply that we should not seek to apply the Monroe doctrine to the pending dispute because it does not embody any principle of international law which "is founded on the general consent of nations," and that "no statesman, however eminent, and no nation, however powerful, are competent to insert into the code of international law a novel principle which was never recognized before, and which has not since been accepted by the government of any other country."

Practically the principle for which we contend has peculiar if not exclusive relation to the United States. It may not have been admitted in so many words to the code of international law, but since in international councils every nation is entitled to the rights belonging to it, if the enforcement of the Monroe doctrine is something we may justly claim it has its place in the code of international law as certainly and as securely as if it were specifically mentioned, and where the United States is a suitor before the high tribunal and that administers international law the question to be determined is whether or not we present claims which the justice of that code of law can find to be right and valid.

The Monroe doctrine finds its recognition in those principles of international law which are based upon the theory that every nation shall have its rights protected and its just claims enforced.

Of course this Government is entirely confident that under the sanction of this doctrine we have clear rights and undoubted claims. Nor is this ignored in the British reply. The prime minister, while not admitting that the Monroe doctrine is applicable to present conditions, states: "In declaring that the United States would resist any such enterprise if it was contemplated, President Monroe adopted a policy which received the entire sympathy of the English Government of that date." He further declares: "Though the language of President Monroe is directed to the attainment of objects which most Englishmen would agree to be salutary, it is impossible to admit that they have been inscribed by any adequate authority in the code of international law." Again he says: "They (Her Majesty's Government) fully concur with the view which President Monroe apparently entertained, that any disturbance of the existing territorial distribution in the hemisphere by any fresh acquisitions on the part of any European state, would be a highly inexpedient change."

In the belief that the doctrine for which we contend was clear and definite, that it was founded upon substantial considerations and involved our safety and welfare, that it was fully applicable to our present conditions and to the state of the world's progress and that it was directly related to the pending controversy and without any conviction as to the final merits of the dispute, but anxious to learn in a satisfactory and conclusive manner whether Great Britain sought, under a claim of boundary, to extend her possessions on this continent without right, or whether she merely sought possession of territory fairly included within her lines of ownership, this Government proposed to the Government of Great Britain a resort to arbitration as the proper means of settling the question to the end that a vexatious boundary dispute between the two contestants might be determined and our exact standing and relation in respect to the controversy might be made clear.

It will be seen from the correspondence herewith submitted that this proposition has been declined by the British Government, upon grounds which in the circumstances seem to me to be far from satisfactory. It is deeply disappointing that such an appeal actuated by the most friendly feelings towards both nations directly concerned, addressed to the sense of justice and to the magnanimity of one of the

great powers of the world and touching its relations to one comparatively weak and small, should have produced no better results.

The course to be pursued by this Government in view of the present
condition does not appear to admit of serious doubt. Having labored
faithfully for many years to induce Great Britain to submit this dispute to impartial arbitration, and having been now finally apprized of
her refusal to do so, nothing remains but to accept the situation, to
recognize its plain requirements and deal with it accordingly. Great
Britain's present proposition has never thus far been regarded as ad-
missible by Venezuela, though any adjustment of the boundary which
that country may deem for her advantage and may enter into of her
own free will can not of course be objected to by the United States.

Assuming, however, that the attitude of Venezuela will remain unchanged, the dispute has reached such a stage as to make it now incumbent upon the United States to take measures to determine with sufficient certainty for its justification what is the true divisional line between the Republic of Venezuela and British Guiana. The inquiry to
that end should of course be conducted carefully and judicially and
due weight should be given to all available evidence records and facts
in support of the claims of both parties.

In order that such an examination should be prosecuted in a thorough and satisfactory manner I suggest that the Congress make an adequate appropriation for the expenses of a commission, to be appointed
by the Executive, who shall make the necessary investigation and report upon the matter with the least possible delay. When such report
is made and accepted it will in my opinion be the duty of the United
States to resist by every means in its power as a willful aggression upon
its rights and interests the appropriation by Great Britain of any lands
or the exercise of governmental jurisdiction over any territory which
after investigation we have determined of right belongs to Venezuela.

In making these recommendations I am fully alive to the responsibility incurred, and keenly realize all the consequences that may
follow.

I am nevertheless firm in my conviction that while it is a grievous
thing to contemplate the two great English-speaking peoples of the
world as being otherwise than friendly competitors in the onward
march of civilization, and strenuous and worthy rivals in all the arts of
peace, there is no calamity which a great nation can invite which equals
that which follows a supine submission to wrong and injustice and the
consequent loss of national self-respect and honor beneath which are
shielded and defended a people's safety and greatness.

Period of the
"Roosevelt Corollary"

*ANNUAL MESSAGE from President Theodore Roosevelt to the
United States Congress, December 3, 1901 (extracts)*
Foreign Relations of the United States, 1901, pp. ix, xxxvi. See also *infra*, VI. In-
terventions in Nicaragua, Haiti, and the Dominican Republic

. . . MORE AND MORE the civilized peoples are realizing the wicked
folly of war and are attaining that condition of just and intelligent
regard for the rights of others which will in the end, as we hope and
believe, make world-wide peace possible. The peace conference at
The Hague gave definite expression to this hope and belief and
marked a stride toward their attainment.

This same peace conference acquiesced in our statement of the Monroe doctrine as compatible with the purposes and aims of the conference.

The Monroe doctrine should be the cardinal feature of the foreign
policy of all the nations of the two Americas, as it is of the United
States. Just seventy-eight years have passed since President Monroe in
his Annual Message announced that "The American continents are
henceforth not to be considered as subjects for future colonization by
any European power." In other words, the Monroe doctrine is a
declaration that there must be no territorial aggrandizement by any
non-American power at the expense of any American power or American soil. It is in no wise intended as hostile to any nation in the Old
World. Still less is it intended to give cover to any aggression by one
New World power at the expense of any other. It is simply a step, and
a long step, toward assuring the universal peace of the world by securing the possibility of permanent peace on this hemisphere.

During the past century other influences have established the permanence and independence of the smaller states of Europe. Through
the Monroe doctrine we hope to be able to safeguard like independence and secure like permanence for the lesser among the New World
nations.

This doctrine has nothing to do with the commercial relations of any American power, save that it in truth allows each of them to form such as it desires. In other words, it is really a guaranty of the commercial independence of the Americans. We do not ask under this doctrine for any exclusive commercial dealings with any other American state. We do not guarantee any state against punishment if it misconducts itself, provided that punishment does not take the form of the acquisition of territory by any non-American power.

Our attitude in Cuba is a sufficient guaranty of our own good faith. We have not the slightest desire to secure any territory at the expense of any of our neighbors. We wish to work with them hand in hand, so that all of us may be uplifted together, and we rejoice over the good fortune of any of them, we gladly hail their material prosperity and political stability, and are concerned and alarmed if any of them fall into industrial or political chaos. We do not wish to see any Old World military power grow up on this continent, or to be compelled to become a military power ourselves. The peoples of the Americas can prosper best if left to work out their own salvation in their own way. . . .

Our people intend to abide by the Monroe doctrine and to insist upon it as the one sure means of securing peace of the Western Hemisphere. The Navy offers us the only means of making our insistence upon the Monroe doctrine anything but a subject of derision to whatever nation chooses to disregard it. We desire the peace which comes as of right to the just man armed; not the peace granted on terms of ignominy to the craven and the weakling. . . .

ANNUAL MESSAGE *from President Theodore Roosevelt to the United States Congress, December 2, 1902 (extract)*
Foreign Relations of the United States, 1902, pp. xi, xxi

. . . THE CANAL will be of great benefit to America, and of importance to all the world. It will be of advantage to us industrially and also as improving our military position. It will be of advantage to the countries of tropical America. It is earnestly to be hoped that all of these countries will do as some of them have already done with signal success, and will invite to their shores commerce and improve their material conditions by recognizing that stability and order are the prerequisites of successful development. No independent nation in America need have the slightest fear of aggression from the United States. It behooves each one to maintain order within its own borders and to discharge its just obligations to foreigners. When this is done, they can rest assured that, be they strong or weak, they have nothing to dread from outside interference. More and more the increasing interdependence and complexity of international political and economic relations render it incumbent on all civilized and orderly powers to insist on the proper policing of the world. . . .

ADDRESS by President Theodore Roosevelt at Chicago, April 2, 1903 (extract)

Joseph B. Bishop, *Theodore Roosevelt and His Time*, I, 239

I BELIEVE in the Monroe Doctrine with all my heart and soul; I am convinced that the immense majority of our fellow-countrymen so believe in it; but I would infinitely prefer to see us abandon it than to see us put it forward and bluster about it, and yet fail to build up the efficient fighting strength which in the last resort can alone make it respected by any strong foreign power whose interest it may ever happen to be to violate it.

There is a homely old adage which runs: "Speak softly and carry a big stick; you will go far." If the American nation will speak softly and yet build and keep at a pitch of the highest training a thoroughly efficient navy the Monroe Doctrine will go far.

ANNUAL MESSAGE from President Theodore Roosevelt to the United States Congress, December 6, 1904 (extract)

J. Reuben Clark, *Memorandum on the Monroe Doctrine*, p. 174

IT IS NOT TRUE that the United States feels any land hunger or entertains any projects as regards the other nations of the Western Hemisphere save such as are for their welfare. All that this country desires is to see the neighboring countries stable, orderly, and prosperous. Any country whose people conduct themselves well can count upon our hearty friendship. If a nation shows that it knows how to act with reasonable efficiency and decency in social and political matters, if it keeps order and pays its obligations, it need fear no interference from the United States. Chronic wrongdoing, or an impotence which results in a general loosening of the ties of civilized society, may in America, as elsewhere, ultimately require intervention by some civilized nation, and in the Western Hemisphere the adherence of the United States to the Monroe Doctrine may force the United States, however reluctantly, in flagrant cases of such wrongdoing or impotence, to the exercise of an international police power. If every country washed by the Caribbean Sea would show the progress in stable and just civilization which with the aid of the Platt amendment Cuba has shown since our troops left the island, and which so many of the republics in both Americas are constantly and brilliantly showing, all question of interference by this Nation with their affairs would be at an end. Our interests and those of our southern neighbors are in reality identical. They have great natural riches, and if within their borders the reign of law and justice obtains, prosperity is sure to come to them. While they thus obey the primary laws of civilized society they may rest assured that they will be treated by us in a spirit of cordial and helpful sympathy. We would interfere with them only in the last resort, and then only if it became evident that their inability or unwillingness to do justice at home and abroad had violated the rights of the United States or had invited foreign aggression to the detriment of the entire body of American nations. It is a mere truism to say that every nation, whether in America or anywhere else, which desires to maintain its freedom, its independence, must ultimately realize that the right of such independence can not be separated from the responsibility of making good use of it.

In asserting the Monroe Doctrine, in taking such steps as we have taken in regard to Cuba, Venezuela, and Panama, and in endeavoring to circumscribe the theater of war in the Far East, and to secure the open door in China, we have acted in our own interest as well as in the interest of humanity at large.

ANNUAL MESSAGE from President Theodore Roosevelt to the United States Congress, December 5, 1905 (extract)
Foreign Relations of the United States, 1905, pp. ix, xxxiii

ONE OF THE MOST effective instruments for peace is the Monroe Doctrine as it has been and is being gradually developed by this Nation and accepted by other nations. No other policy could have been as efficient in promoting peace in the Western Hemisphere and in giving to each nation thereon the chance to develop along its own lines. If we had refused to apply the Doctrine to changing conditions it would now be completely outworn, would not meet any of the needs of the present day, and indeed would probably by this time have sunk into complete oblivion. It is useful at home, and is meeting with recognition abroad because we have adapted our application of it to meet the growing and changing needs of the Hemisphere. When we announce a policy, such as the Monroe Doctrine, we thereby commit ourselves to the consequences of the policy, and those consequences from time to time alter. It is out of the question to claim a right and yet shirk the responsibility for its exercise. Not only we, but all American Republics who are benefited by the existence of the Doctrine, must recognize the obligations each nation is under as regards foreign peoples no less than its duty to insist upon its own rights.

That our rights and interests are deeply concerned in the maintenance of the Doctrine is so clear as hardly to need argument. This is especially true in view of the construction of the Panama Canal. As a mere matter of self-defense we must exercise a close watch over the approaches to this canal; and this means that we must be thoroughly alive to our interests in the Caribbean Sea.

There are certain essential points which must never be forgotten as regards the Monroe Doctrine. In the first place we must as a nation make it evident that we do not intend to treat it in any shape or way as an excuse for aggrandizement on our part at the expense of the republics to the south. We must recognize the fact that in some South American countries there has been much suspicion lest we should interpret the Monroe Doctrine as in some way inimical to their interests, and we must try to convince all the other nations of this continent once and for all that no just and orderly government has anything to fear from us. There are certain republics to the south of us which have already reached such a point of stability, order, and prosperity that they themselves, though as yet hardly consciously, are among the guarantors of this Doctrine. These republics we now meet not only on a basis of entire equality, but in a spirit of frank and respectful friendship, which we hope is mutual. If all of the republics to the south of us will only grow as those to which I allude have already grown, all need for us to be the especial champions of the Doctrine will disappear, for no stable and growing American Republic wishes to see some great non-American military power acquire territory in its neighborhood. All that this country desires is that the other republics on this Continent shall be happy and prosperous; and they can not be happy and prosperous unless they maintain order within their boundaries and behave with a just regard for their obligations toward outsiders. It must be understood that under no circumstances will the United States use the Monroe Doctrine as a cloak for territorial aggression. We desire peace with all the world, but perhaps most of all with the other peoples of the American Continent. There are of course limits to the wrongs which any self-respecting nation can endure. It is always possible that wrong actions toward this Nation, or toward citizens of this Nation, in some State unable to keep order among its own people, unable to secure justice from outsiders, and unwilling to do justice to those outsiders who treat it well, may result in our having to take action to protect our rights; but such action will not be taken with a view to territorial aggression, and it will be taken at all only with extreme reluctance and when it has become evident that every other resource has been exhausted.

Moreover, we must make it evident that we do not intend to permit the Monroe Doctrine to be used by any nation on this Continent as a shield to protect it from the consequences of its own misdeeds against foreign nations. If a republic to the south of us commits a tort against a foreign nation, such as an outrage against a citizen of that nation, then the Monroe Doctrine does not force us to interfere to prevent punishment of the tort, save to see that the punishment does not assume the form of territorial occupation in any shape. The case is more difficult when it refers to a contractual obligation. Our own Government has always refused to enforce such contractual obligations on behalf of its citizens by an appeal to arms. It is much to be wished that all foreign governments would take the same view. But they do not; and in consequence we are liable at any time to be brought face to face with disagreeable alternatives. On the one hand, this country would certainly decline to go to war to prevent a foreign government from collecting a just debt; on the other hand, it is very inadvisable to permit any foreign power to take possession, even temporarily, of the customhouses of an American Republic in order to enforce the payment of its obligations; for such temporary occupation might turn into a permanent occupation. The only escape from these alternatives may at any time be that we must ourselves undertake to bring about some arrangement by which so much as possible of a just obligation shall be paid. It is far better that this country should put through such an arrangement, rather than allow any foreign country to undertake it. To do so insures the defaulting republic from having to pay debts of an improper character under duress, while it also insures honest creditors of the republic from being passed by in the interest of dishonest or grasping creditors. Moreover, for the United States to take such a position offers the only possible way of insuring us against a clash with some foreign power. The position is, therefore, in the interest of peace as well as in the interest of justice. It is of benefit to our people; it is of benefit to foreign peoples; and most of all it is really of benefit to the people of the country concerned.

This brings me to what should be one of the fundamental objects of the Monroe Doctrine. We must ourselves in good faith try to help upward toward peace and order those of our sister republics which need such help. Just as there has been a gradual growth of the ethical element in the relations of one individual to another, so we are, even though slowly, more and more coming to recognize the duty of bearing one another's burdens, not only as among individuals, but also as among nations.

INSTRUCTIONS *from Elihu Root, Secretary of State, to the United States Delegates to the Second International Peace Conference at The Hague, May 31, 1907 (extract)*
Foreign Relations of the United States, 1907, II, 1128, 1133

. . . 4. The other subject which the United States specifically reserved the right to propose for consideration is the attainment of an agreement to observe some limitation upon the use of force for the collection of ordinary public debts arising out of contract.

It has long been the established policy of the United States not to use its army and navy for the collection of ordinary contract debts due to its citizens by other governments. This Government has not considered the use of force for such a purpose consistent with that respect for the independent sovereignty of other members of the family of nations which is the most important principle of international law and the chief protection of weak nations against the oppression of the strong. It seems to us that the practice is injurious in its general effect upon the relation of nations and upon the welfare of weak and disordered States, whose development ought to be encouraged in the interests of civilization; that it offers frequent temptation to bullying and oppression and to unnecessary and unjustifiable warfare. It is doubtless true that the nonpayment of such debts may be accompanied by such circumstances of fraud and wrongdoing or violation of treaties as to justify the use of force; but we should be glad to see an international consideration of this subject which would discriminate between such cases and the simple nonperformance of a contract with a private person, and a resolution in favor of reliance upon peaceful means in cases of the latter class.

The Third International Conference of the American States, held at Rio de Janeiro in August, 1906, resolved:

To recommend to the Governments therein that they consider the point of inviting the Second Peace Conference at The Hague to examine the question of the compulsory collection of public debts, and, in general, means tending to diminish between nations conflicts having a peculiarly pecuniary origin.

You will ask for the consideration of this subject by the conference. It is not probable that in the first instance all the nations represented at the conference will be willing to go as far in the establishment of limitations upon the use of force in the collection of this class of debts as the United States would like to have them go, and there may be serious objection to the consideration of the subject as a separate and independent topic. If you find such objections insurmountable, you will urge the adoption of provisions under the head of arbitration looking to the establishment of such limitations. The adoption of some such provision as the following may be suggested, and, if no better solution seems practicable, should be urged:

The use of force for the collection of a contract debt alleged to be due by the Government of any country to a citizen of any other country is not permissible until after—

1. The justice and amount of the debt shall have been determined by arbitration, if demanded by the alleged debtor.

2. The time and manner of payment, and the security, if any, to be given pending payment, shall have been fixed by arbitration, if demanded by the alleged debtor . . .

[Article I of the Convention on Recovery of Contract Debts, signed at the conference on October 18, 1907, reads as follows: "The contracting Powers agree not to have recourse to armed force for the recovery of contract debts claimed from the government of one country by the government of another country as being due to its nationals.

"This undertaking is, however, not applicable when the debtor State refuses or neglects to reply to an offer of arbitration, or, after accepting the offer, prevents any 'compromis' from being agreed on, or after the arbitration, fails to submit to the award" (ibid., p. 1199).]

REPORT of the United States Delegates to the Second International Peace Conference at The Hague, June 15 to October 18, 1907 (extract)
Foreign Relations of the United States, 1907, II, 1144, 1152

ARTICLE 48 of the revision of the convention of 1899 reads as follows:

The signatory powers consider it their duty, if a serious dispute threatens to break out between two or more of them, to remind these latter that the permanent court is open to them.

Consequently, they declare that the fact of reminding the conflicting parties of the provisions of the present convention, and the advice given to them, in the highest interests of peace, to have recourse to the permanent court, can only be regarded as friendly actions.

To these two paragraphs was added the following provision:

In case of a controversy between two powers, one of them may always address to the International Bureau a note containing its declaration that it is willing to submit the difference to arbitration.

The bureau shall immediately make the declaration known to the other power.

The American delegation of 1899 made the following reserve regarding this article, and the American delegation of 1907 repeated the reserve in the exact language of 1899:

Nothing contained in this convention shall be so construed as to require the United States of America to depart from its traditional policy of not entering upon, interfering with, or entangling itself in the political questions or internal administration of any foreign state, nor shall anything contained in the said convention be so construed as to require the relinquishment, by the United States of America, of its traditional attitude toward purely American questions.

Subsequent Interpretations
and Applications

RESOLUTION Adopted by the United States Senate, August 2.
1912
Congressional Record, Vol. 48. 10, p. 10046

RESOLVED, That when any harbor or other place in the American continents is so situated that the occupation thereof for naval or military purposes might threaten the communications or the safety of the United States, the Government of the United States could not see without grave concern the possession of such harbor or other place by any corporation or association which has such a relation to another Government, not American, as to give that Government practical power of control for naval or military purposes.

[The resolution was approved by a vote of 51 to 4. In supporting the resolution, which he had submitted on July 31, 1912, Senator Henry Cabot Lodge stated:

Mr. President, . . . this resolution rests on a generally accepted principle of the law of nations, older than the Monroe doctrine. It rests on the principle that every nation has a right to protect its own safety, and that if it feels that the possession by a foreign power, for military or naval purposes, of any given harbor or place is prejudicial to its safety, it is its duty as well as its right to interfere.

I will instance as an example of what I mean the protest that was made successfully against the occupation of the port of Agadir, in Morocco, by Germany. England objected on the ground thàt it threatened her communication through the Mediterranean. That view was shared largely by the European powers, and the occupation of that port was prevented in that way. That is the principle upon which the resolution rests.

It has been made necessary by a change of modern conditions, under which, while a Government takes no action itself, the possession of an important place of the character I have described may be taken by a corporation or association which would be under the control of the foreign Government.

The Monroe doctrine was, of course, an extension in our own interests of this underlying principle—the right of every nation to provide for its own safety. The Monroe doctrine, as we all know, was applied, so far as the taking possession of territory was concerned, to its being open to further colonization, and naturally did not touch upon the precise point involved here. But without any Monroe doctrine the possession of a harbor such as that of Magdalena Bay, which has led to this resolution, would render it necessary, I think, to make some declaration covering a case where a corporation or association was involved.

In this particular case it became apparent from the inquiries made by the committee and by the administration that no Government was concerned in taking possession of Magdalena Bay; but it also became apparent that those persons who held control of the Mexican concession, which included the land about Magdalena Bay, were engaged in negotiations which have not yet been completed certainly but which have only been tentative, looking to the sale of that bay and the land about it to a corporation either created or authorized by a foreign Government, or in which the stock was largely held or controlled by foreigners.

The passage of this resolution has seemed to the committee, without division, I think, to be in the interest of peace. It is always desirable to make the position of a country in regard to a question of this kind known beforehand, not to allow a situation to arise in which it might be necessary to urge a friendly power to withdraw when that withdrawal could not be made, perhaps, without some humiliation.

The resolution is merely a statement of policy, allied to the Monroe doctrine, of course, but not necessarily dependent upon it or growing out of it. . . . It seemed to the committee that it was very wise to make this statement of policy at this time, when it can give offense to no one and makes the position of the United States clear.

Of course I need not say to the Senate that the opening of the Panama Canal gives to the question of Magdalena Bay and to that of the Galapagos Islands . . . an importance such as they have never possessed, and I think it eminently desirable in every interest that this resolution should receive the assent of the Senate.]

ROBERT LANSING, Counselor for the Department of State, to
William J. Bryan, Secretary of State, June 16, 1914
Department of State, *The Lansing Papers,* II, 459

MY DEAR MR. SECRETARY:

I am submitting to you a memorandum upon the "Present Nature and Extent of the Monroe Doctrine and Its Need of Restatement," since the questions, with which it deals, appear to me to require consideration and decision at the present time.

In all frankness I should say that my personal inclination has been against expanding our traditional policy in dealing with Latin America, and that I have been concerned over certain actions of this Government which seemed to be beyond the purposes of that policy. I approached the subject with this prejudice against any radical departure from established policy, but after taking into consideration the scope of the Monroe Doctrine, the present problems in Latin America, and the motives which to-day inspire our conduct in the international affairs of this hemisphere, I have been compelled to change my views.

It seems to me that the logic of the situation is irresistible, and that we must modify our present declared policy.

Whether this is to be done by a wider application of the Monroe Doctrine so as to include new methods of obtaining political control by European powers; or whether it is to be done by announcing a new doctrine, which will include the present standard of international duty, are questions which I am not prepared to answer without a more careful study of the subject. But that something should be done I am convinced, if this Government is to avoid the charge of insincerity and inconsistency in its relations with Latin America, of which suggestions are already too frequent and not without apparent justification.

When you have had opportunity to examine the annexed memorandum I would like very much to discuss the subject with you.

Very sincerely yours,

ROBERT LANSING

[ENCLOSURE]

MEMORANDUM BY THE COUNSELOR FOR THE DEPARTMENT OF STATE

[WASHINGTON,] *June 11, 1914*

PRESENT NATURE AND EXTENT OF THE MONROE DOCTRINE, AND ITS NEED
OF RESTATEMENT

The Monroe Doctrine is in substance that the United States considers an extension of political control by a European power over any territory in this hemisphere, not already occupied by it, to be a menace to the national safety of the United States.

In 1823, when the doctrine was enunciated, the dangers of the extension of European political power on this continent lay in the possible occupation of unsettled regions and in the conquest of the territory of an independent American state.

Later, during the Polk Administration, another danger was recognized in the possibility of a voluntary cession of territory by an American state to a European power, and the Monroe Doctrine was shown to be broad enough to include this means of acquiring political dominion.

While the primary idea of the Monroe Doctrine is opposition by the United States to any extension of European control over American territory or institutions, the idea is subject to the modification that the control must possess the element of *permanency*.

When the hostile occupation of the territory of an American state or the coercion by force of its government by a European power is intended to be temporary, and is employed solely as a means to compel the government of the state to meet a particular international obligation, which it has wilfully neglected or refused to perform, the territorial occupation or coercion would not appear to be in violation of the Monroe Doctrine. Nevertheless the intention of temporary control must be beyond question, and any indication of converting temporary control for a particular purpose into permanent control for general purposes would bring the case within the scope of the Doctrine and create a situation, in which the United States might be compelled to intervene.

Just how far a European government should be permitted to exercise control over American territory or over an American government as a means of obtaining redress for an international wrong is a question which must be decided in each case upon the facts. If it may be reasonably presumed from the circumstances surrounding the assumption of control or from the length of time it continues that the intention is to make it permanent, denial of such intention by the controlling power should in no way interfere with the assertion by the United States of its established policy or with its insistence that the European aggressor immediately withdraw from the territory or surrender its control.

In dealing with the cases as they arise the two essential elements of the Monroe Doctrine must be constantly borne in mind; first, that the doctrine is exclusively a *national* policy of the United States and relates to its national safety and vital interests; and second, that the European control, against which it is directed, must possess the element of *permanency,* or a reasonable possibility of permanency.

While occupation and conquest, as means of obtaining political control over American territory by a European power, are acts of that power alone, voluntary cession, as a means, is the mutual act of the two governments which are parties to the transfer. As a consequence the inclusion of voluntary cession among the acts of acquisition, against which the Monroe Doctrine is directed, introduces the necessary corollary that it may be invoked against an American government as well as against a European government. It is manifest from this that the Monroe Doctrine is, as has been said, a national policy of the United States and also that it is not a Pan-American policy. The opposition to European control over American territory is not primarily to preserve the integrity of any American state— that may be a result but not a purpose of the Doctrine. The essential idea is to prevent a condition which would menace the national interests of the United States.

In case it should become necessary to enforce the Monroe Doctrine against another American republic, which has ceded or apparently intends to cede any of its territorial rights to a European power, the preventive action of the United States would appear to be a direct interference with the sovereign authority of the American republic over its own territory. Logically such action, in case a cession is made or intended, amounts to an assertion of the primacy of the United States in the Western Hemisphere. The primacy of one nation, though possessing the superior physical might to maintain it, is out of harmony with the principle of the equality of nations which underlies Pan-Americanism, however just or altruistic the primate may be.

While, therefore, the Monroe Doctrine and Pan-Americanism may come into conflict, the Monroe Doctrine will in case of conflict prevail so long as the United States maintains the Doctrine and is the dominant power among the American nations. The equality of American republics and, in a measure, their independence are legal rather than actual, but it is necessary to acknowledge their legal existence, if the theory of Pan-Americanism is accepted. The Monroe Doctrine, on the contrary, is founded upon no assumptions of this character but upon a fact, namely, the superior power of the United States to compel submission to its will whenever a condition arises involving European control over American territory, which, because of the permanent nature of the control, is considered to be a menace to the national safety of the United States.

The Monroe Doctrine, therefore, should not be confused with Pan-Americanism. It is purely a national policy of the United States, while Pan-Americanism is the joint policy of the American group of nations. The Pan-American policy may support and may probably be considered as invariably supporting the idea of the Monroe Doctrine in opposing the extension of European political control over any portion of this continent. The reason, however, for such support will not be the national safety of the United States, but the mutual protection of American nations from European attempts upon their independence. In its advocacy of the Monroe Doctrine the United States considers its own interests. The integrity of other American nations is an incident, not an end. While this may seem based on selfishness alone, the author of the Doctrine had no higher or more generous motive in its declaration. To assert for it a nobler purpose is to proclaim a new doctrine.

As stated, this traditional policy, as originally declared and subsequently defined, relates to European acquisition of political power in America by means of occupation, conquest or cession of territory. There is, nevertheless, another method by which such power may be acquired, a method, which to-day can be more easily and more successfully employed than those to which the Monroe Doctrine has been in the past applied. It is a mode of extending political power, which, in my opinion, has caused much of the confusion and uncertainty as to the scope of the Monroe Doctrine because of its gradual development and the failure to recognize it as in practical conflict with that policy.

Within the past quarter of a century the rapid increase of wealth in the United States and the great nations of Europe has caused their people, in constantly increasing numbers, to seek investments in foreign lands. No richer field has been presented than the vast undeveloped resources of the republics south of the United States. Hundreds of millions of dollars have been expended in these lands by the capitalists of this country, Great Britain, France, Germany, and other European nations in the construction of railways, the establishment of steamship lines, the development of mines, the cultivation of cotton, fruits, and other agricultural products, and the operation of various industrial enterprises.

In the opening up of these countries and the development of their resources their governments require financial aid, or seize the opportunity to replenish their treasuries. Eager investors, appreciating the natural riches of these regions and the possibilities of reward to those who obtain the right to exploit them, lend their money readily in exchange for special privileges, concessions and large rates of interest.

The governments of many of these republics, impoverished and improvident and frequently in the hands of unscrupulous and greedy men, careless of the future and heedless of their country's welfare, borrow beyond the limit of their capacity to repay, hypothecating every possible source of national revenue for years to come. As a result some of the smaller American republics, ruled by military dictators or oligarchies, who have enriched themselves at the expense of their countries, have become hopelessly bankrupt. In some cases the United States, in others a European power, is the chief creditor, to whose favor the insolvent nation must look for the means to continue its political existence.

With the present industrial activity, the scramble for markets, and the incessant search for new opportunities to produce wealth, commercial expansion and success are closely interwoven with political domination over the territory which is being exploited.

The European power, whose subjects supply the capital to install and operate the principal industries of a small American republic and furnish the funds upon which its government is dependent, may, if it so wishes, dominate the political action of the American government. To state it in another way, a European power whose subjects own the public debt of an American state and have invested there large amounts of capital, may control the government of the state as completely as if it had acquired sovereign rights over the territory through occupation, conquest or cession.

The question, which is unavoidable, but which can only be answered after mature thought for it is pregnant with difficulties and with seeming departures from the time-honored policy of the United States, is this—

When by reason of commercial and financial domination a European power becomes undoubted master of the political conduct of an American republic, is a condition presented which may justify the United States in applying to it the Monroe Doctrine with the same vigor, with which it would have applied the Doctrine if the European power had by force or treaty established a protectorate over the American republic?

If the conditions are compared, it is evident that in both cases a European nation has extended political control over American territory; and in both cases the element of permanency is present. They are to all intents identical in their results, though they differ in the means by which the results were obtained.

The United States would certainly oppose the surrender by an American republic of all or a portion of its sovereignty to one of the great powers of Europe. It would be a voluntary and peaceable act of the republic, but it would be manifestly contrary to the Monroe Doctrine. If voluntarily and peaceably an American republic becomes so financially dependent upon a European power that the latter controls the government of the former, is not that also contrary to the Monroe Doctrine? Is not one case as great a menace to the national safety of the United States as the other? If there is a practical distinction between the two cases, what is that distinction? If there is no practical distinction, why should the Monroe Doctrine not be applied to both?

These questions suggest the following:

Has the time arrived, as a result of modern economic conditions in Central and South America, when the Monroe Doctrine, if it is to continue effective, should be restated so as to include European acquisition of political control through the agency of financial supremacy over an American republic?

If a more radical change of policy than the one suggested by the foregoing query seems necessary and advisable under present conditions the question to be answered may be stated thus:

Should a new doctrine be formulated declaring that the United States is opposed to the extension of European control over American territory and institutions through financial as well as other means, and having for its object, not only the national safety and interests of this country, but also the establishment and maintenance of republican constitutional government in all American states, the free exercise by their people of their public and private rights, the administration of impartial justice, and the prevention of political authority from becoming the tool of personal ambition and greed, the chief enemies of liberal institutions, of economic development, and of domestic peace?

Stated in a more general way the question is this:

Do not the modern ideals and aims of government in the United States require us to abandon the purely selfish principle, which has so long controlled our policies in dealing with other American nations, and to adopt more altruistic and humanitarian principles, which will be in harmony with the sense of fraternal responsibility, which is increasingly dominant in all our international relations?

In the presentation of these questions there is no intention to advocate a particular policy in dealing with the international affairs of the Western Hemisphere. They are submitted solely for the purpose of suggesting possible changes in the Monroe Doctrine, either conservative or radical, which will be more in accord with modern ideals and conditions. It appears to me to be necessary, in order to avoid confusion and contradiction in the future conduct of affairs of the Department, to determine definitely whether the Monroe Doctrine should remain unchanged, should be restated, or should be superseded. Uncertainty as to the policy, which this Government intends to pursue, will undoubtedly cause embarrassment when special cases are presented for action. The subject, in my judgment, should receive prompt and careful consideration.

ROBERT LANSING

WILLIAM J. BRYAN, Secretary of State, to Count von Bernstorff, German Ambassador to the United States, September 16, 1914 (extract)

Manuscript in National Archives (State Department files, 838.51/354); also 67th Congress, 2d Session, Senate Report No. 794, p. 31. See *infra*, p. 639

REPLYING to the note of Your Government's Chargé, dated July 25th, 1914, regarding the matter of customs control in Haiti, I beg to say that the Government of the United States recognizes the large part which German merchants and German bankers have played in the development of the trade and enterprise of Haiti and wishes to make this correspondence the occasion for expressing the pleasure with which it witnesses the employment of German capital and the activity of German men of affairs in this hemisphere; but represents to the Government of his Imperial Majesty that German interests are not the only interests which have played a conspicuous and highly influential part in the development of the Haitian Republic and that the Government of the United States is well known to have taken for many years and without variation of policy the position that neither foreign mercantile influences and interests, nor any other foreign influence or interest proceeding from outside the American hemisphere, could with the consent of the United States be so broadened or extended as to constitute a control, either wholly or in part, of the government or administration of any independent American state.

The Government of the United States cannot depart from that policy and feels confident that the Government of His Imperial Majesty will not expect it to do so.

Probably a participation of the Government of His Imperial Majesty in any method which might be agreed upon by which the Government of the Republic of Haiti should be assisted in the orderly, efficient and economical administration of its customs revenues did not present itself to His Imperial Majesty's Government as a departure from the traditional policy of the Government of the United States when its note of July 25th was drafted. But this Government would regard such participation as a very serious departure from that policy alike in principle and in practice. The Government of the United States regards it as one of the grave possibilities of certain sorts of concessions granted by governments in America to European financiers and contractors and of certain sorts of contracts entered into by those governments with European banking houses and financiers that the legitimate and natural course of enforcing claims might lead to measures which would imperil the political independence, or at least, the complete political autonomy of the American states involved, and might issue in results which the Government of the United States has always regarded as its duty to guard against as the nearest friend and natural champion of those states whenever they should need a friend and champion.

[An examination of the Department of State file copy of this document in the National Archives, indicates that it was written by President Wilson. Attached to the file copy is a typed memorandum, headed "Haiti," which is undated, unsigned and not addressed to anyone, but presumably written by the President. The note to the German Ambassador is, with the exception of a few introductory words, identical with this memorandum. In a letter to the President dated February 25, 1915, Secretary of State Bryan inquired, with reference to replying to a note from the French Ambassador on the same subject, "as you wrote the note to the German Ambassador do you desire to write this one . . . ?"]

ROBERT LANSING, *Secretary of State, to President Woodrow Wilson, November 24, 1915*
Department of State, *The Lansing Papers*, II, 466

MY DEAR MR. PRESIDENT:

I enclose a memorandum covering the subject of the Monroe Doctrine, its application, and the possible extension of the principle in a way to constitute a policy which may be termed a "Caribbean Policy," since it is limited in application to the territory in and about the Caribbean Sea.

Briefly, the memorandum is this:

The Monroe Doctrine is based on the theory that any extension by a European power of political control, beyond that which exists over any territory in this hemisphere, is a menace to the national safety of the United States. The means of extending political control, thus far recognized, has been by occupation of unattached territory, by conquest and by cession.

Recently the financing of revolutions and corruption of governments of the smaller republics by European capitalists have frequently thrown the control of these governments into the hands of a European power.

To avoid this danger of European political control by this means which may be as great a menace to the national safety of this country as occupation or cession, the only method seems to be to establish a stable and honest government and to prevent the revenues of the republic from becoming the prize of revolution and of the foreigners who finance it.

Stability and honesty of government depend on sufficient force to resist revolutions and on sufficient control over the revenues and over the development of the resources to prevent official graft and dishonest grants of privileges.

The possession of the Panama Canal and its defense have in a measure given to the territories in and about the Caribbean Sea a new importance from the standpoint of our national safety. It is vital to the interests of this country that European political domination should in no way be extended over these regions. As it happens within this area lie the small republics of America which have been and to an extent still are the prey of revolutionists, of corrupt governments, and of predatory foreigners.

Because of this state of affairs our national safety, in my opinion, requires that the United States should intervene and aid in the establishment and maintenance of a stable and honest government, if no other way seems possible to attain that end.

I make no argument on the ground of the benefit which would result to the peoples of these republics by the adoption of this policy. That they would be the chief beneficiaries in that their public and private rights would be respected, and their prosperity and intellectual development insured, is manifest. Nevertheless the argument based on humanitarian purpose does not appeal to me, even though it might be justly urged, because too many international crimes have been committed in the name of Humanity.

It seems to me that the ground of national safety, the conservation of national interests, is the one which should be advanced in support of this policy. It is reasonable, practical, and in full accord with the principle of the Monroe Doctrine.

In considering this policy it should be borne in mind what has been done already in Cuba, Panama, Nicaragua, the Dominican Republic and Haiti, and what may have to be done in the small neighboring republics. The Danish West Indies and the colonial possessions of other European nations in the Caribbean should not be forgotten

in considering this policy as through a change of their sovereignty they might become a serious menace to the interests of the United States.
Faithfully yours,

ROBERT LANSING

[ENCLOSURE—MEMORANDUM—EXTRACT]

The omitted portion of this memorandum is substantially the same as the first 15 paragraphs of the memorandum of June 11, 1914, *supra*, p. 370

PRESENT NATURE AND EXTENT OF THE MONROE DOCTRINE

. . . In a large proportion of the instances to which the United States has felt called upon to apply the Monroe Doctrine the acts complained of have been direct political acts of a European Government, as, for example, the invasion of Mexico by France during the Civil War; British interposition in the boundary question of Venezuela; the offer of Italy to purchase the Island of St. Bartholomew in 1870; the attempts of Spain to reannex Santo Domingo and other former Spanish possessions in America. There have however been some instances of interference for the purpose of satisfying claims of foreign subjects, as, for example, the French claims based on Mexican bonds; and Spanish claims against Mexico of various sorts; and the French, German, British and Italian claims, including claims based on war damage and on Government contracts, but it does not appear that the United States protested against drastic action by these Governments on the ground of the Monroe doctrine, but, on the contrary, used its good offices to effect an amicable settlement. As a protest against the forcible collection of contract debts, Drago advanced the doctrine bearing his name. Now it is to political action growing out of investments in the Carribean countries that I make particular reference. The purchase of Government securities upon which payments of interest and sinking funds are defaulted, and the development of a concession, perhaps obtained in return for financing a revolution, which is infringed or annulled, open the offending Government to claims to the foreign bond holders or concessionaires who enlist the aid of their Governments.

Thus the European power, whose subjects supply the capital to install and operate the principal industries of a small American republic and furnish the funds upon which its government is dependent, may, if it finds it expedient to do so, dominate the political action of the weak and bankrupt government. To state it in another way, a European power whose subjects own the public debt of an American state and have invested large amounts of capital, would be able to control the government of the state almost as completely as if it had acquired sovereign rights over the territory through occupation, conquest or cession.

The method of obtaining political mastery by means of financial control has been an increasing menace to the independence of the republics situated in or about the Carribean Sea. Revolutions have been frequent, due in the majority of cases to the desire of a factional leader by becoming master of the nation's revenues to amass wealth for himself and his immediate friends. A revolutionary chief finds little difficulty in financing his venture among foreign speculators in exchange for concessions or other privileges and the chance of large profits which will be theirs if the revolution is successful. As a result the people of these countries are the victims of constant strife between rival leaders, and their condition is little improved by the governments, which exist only a short time and which are used to enrich their rulers and those who have financed them.

The corrupt character of the rulers, and the powerful influence of foreign financiers who have aided the rulers in obtaining and will aid them in maintaining control, tends toward instability of Government in these same republics and not only threaten their national independence but prevents the people from developing intellectually or from attaining any degree of prosperity.

The United States in any circumstances would be desirous as a friend of an American republic, which is suffering from this state of affairs, to aid it in removing the cause. But in the case of the Carribean republics self-interest as well as friendship appeals. Since the construction of the Panama Canal it is essential for its safety that the neighboring nations should not come under the political domination of any European power either directly by force or by cession or indirectly through the agency of financial control by its subjects. While force and cession are not impossible means if the government of a republic is corrupt or weak, the greater danger lies in the subtlety of financial control.

To meet this danger the surest if not the only means, is the establishment of a stable and honest government which will devote the revenues of the state to defraying its just obligations, to developing its resources, and to educating its people, and which will protect individuals in their rights of life, liberty and property, and in the enjoyment of their political rights.

In order to accomplish this the first thing to be done is to remove the prize of revolution, namely, the control of the public revenues. If this can be done there will be few revolutions about the Carribean. In the second place the government must not be dependent on foreign financiers for its continuance in power. In the third place it must possess a reliable and efficient military force sufficient to suppress insurrection against the established authority.

If there could arise in all the Carribean republics men of strong character, patriotic and honest, as there have in some, who are able to carry out such a policy, it would be well for all concerned. Unfortunately this is not the case, and the United States is of necessity forced to choose between permitting these republics to continue to be the prey of unscrupulous adventurers native and foreign, or to undertake the task of aiding in the establishment of a stable and honest government, upon principles which will insure political independence and prevent any possibility of European control.

It would seem, therefore, that in the case of the republics about the Carribean Sea the United States should expand the application of the Monroe Doctrine, and declare as a definite Carribean policy that, while it does not seek dominion over the territory of any of these republics, it is necessary for the national safety of the United States, and particularly in view of its interests on the Isthmus of Panama, that it aid the people of those republics in establishing and maintaining responsible and honest governments to such extent as may be necessary in each particular case, and that it will not tolerate control over or interference with the political or financial affairs of these republics by any European power or its nationals or permit the occupation, even temporarily, by a European power, of any territory of such republics.

November 24, 1915

PRESIDENT WOODROW WILSON to Robert Lansing, Secretary of State, November 29, 1915
Department of State, *The Lansing Papers*, II, 470

MY DEAR MR. SECRETARY:

The argument of this paper seems to be unanswerable, and I thank you for setting it out so explicitly and fully.

This will serve us as a memorandum when the time comes, and the proper occasion, for making a public declaration of policy in this important particular. Just now, I take it for granted, it is only for the guidance and clarification of our own thought, and for informal discussion with our Latin American friends from time to time, semiconfidentially and for the sake of a frank understanding.

Faithfully Yours,

W.W.

ADDRESS by President Woodrow Wilson before the United States Senate, January 22, 1917 (extract)
James D. Richardson, *Messages and Papers of the Presidents*, p. 8199

. . . IN HOLDING out the expectation that the people and Government of the United States will join the other civilized nations of the world in guaranteeing the permanence of peace upon such terms as I have named I speak with the greater boldness and confidence because it is clear to every man who can think that there is in this promise no breach in either our traditions or our policy as a nation, but a fulfilment, rather, of all that we have professed or striven for.

I am proposing, as it were, that the nations should with one accord adopt the doctrine of President Monroe as the doctrine of the world: that no nation should seek to extend its policy over any other nation or people, but that every people should be left free to determine its own polity, its own way of development, unhindered, unthreatened, unafraid, the little along with the great and powerful.

I am proposing that all nations henceforth avoid entangling alliances which would draw them into competitions of power; catch them in a net of intrigue and selfish rivalry, and disturb their own affairs with influences intruded from without. There is no entangling alliance in a concert of power. When all unite to act in the same sense and with the same purpose all act in the common interest and are free to live their own lives under a common protection.

ADDRESS by President Woodrow Wilson at San Francisco, September 17, 1919 (extract)

Ray Stannard Baker and William E. Dodd, *The Public Papers of Woodrow Wilson*, Vol. III (*War and Peace*), Part II, pp. 217, 227

. . . I WANT TO SAY again that Article X is the very heart of the Covenant of the League, because all the great wrongs of the world have had their root in the seizure of territory or the control of the political independence of other peoples. I believe that I speak the feeling of the people of the United States when I say that, having seen one great wrong like that attempted and having prevented it, we are ready to prevent it again.

Those are the two principal criticisms, that we did not do the impossible with regard to Shantung and that we may be advised to go to war. That is all there is in either of those. But they say, "We want the Monroe Doctrine more distinctly acknowledged." Well, if I could have found language that was more distinct than that used, I should have been very happy to suggest it, but it says in so many words that nothing in that document shall be construed as affecting the validity of the Monroe Doctrine. I do not see what more it could say, but, as I say, if the clear can be clarified, I have no objection to its being clarified. The meaning is too obvious to admit of discussion, and

I want you to realize how extraordinary that provision is. Every nation in the world had been jealous of the Monroe Doctrine, had studiously avoided doing or saying anything that would admit its validity, and here all the great nations of the world sign a document which admits its validity. That constitutes nothing less than a moral revolution in the attitude of the rest of the world toward America.

What does the Monroe Doctrine mean in that Covenant? It means that with regard to aggressions upon the Western Hemisphere we are at liberty to act without waiting for other nations to act. That is the Monroe Doctrine. The Monroe Doctrine says that if anybody tries to interfere with affairs in the Western Hemisphere it will be regarded as an unfriendly act to the United States—not to the rest of the world—and that means that the United States will look after it, and will not ask anybody's permission to look after it. The document says that nothing in this document must be construed as interfering with that. . . .

ADDRESS by Charles E. Hughes, Secretary of State, "Observations on the Monroe Doctrine," at Minneapolis, August 30, 1923 (extracts)
Charles E. Hughes, *The Pathway of Peace*, p. 113

THE POSTULATES of our foreign policy were determined by the ideals of liberty. The dominant motive was the security of the Republic; it was a policy with no imperialistic designs or thought of aggression. There was a deep-seated conviction that the opportunities of a hard-won freedom would be threatened by the ambitions of European powers constantly seeking their own aggrandizement by the forcible imposition of their will upon weaker peoples, and that the peaceful aims of the new Nation could be achieved only by keeping clear of the toils of European politics and strife. It was this conviction of the necessity of maintaining an independent position which led to the declaration of neutrality in 1793 despite .the treaty of alliance with France which had sprung from the exigencies of the Revolutionary struggle. The words of the Farewell Address were more than a solemn admonition of the foremost American patriot—they set forth principles which those who established our foreign policy held to be its cornerstone.

It is interesting to recall that the conduct of our foreign affairs was directed for many years by a few men, the most enlightened of our statesmen, and, considering the perplexities which vexed the new Nation, exhibited a remarkable continuity and definiteness of purpose. Jefferson had been Secretary of State for about four years under Washington, and Hamilton had been a constant adviser. During the eight years of Jefferson's Presidency, Madison was Secretary of State; and, during Madison's two terms as President, James Monroe was Secretary of State for six years. Monroe had served as United States Senator and Governor of Virginia; had been minister to France, to Spain, and to England; had been engaged in the most important diplomatic negotiations; and in the midst of the War of 1812 had also served as Secretary of War *ad interim*. When he became President, in 1817, Monroe appointed John Quincy Adams as Secretary of State. Adams had been minister to The Hague and to Portugal under Washington; had been transferred to Prussia by his father, President John Adams, and, under Madison, had been minister to Russia; and, after representing the United States throughout the difficult negotiations which resulted in the treaty of Ghent, had been made minister to England. Adams served as Secretary of State until the end of Monroe's second term, in 1825, when he succeeded Monroe as President. In these close relations and continuity of service there was rare opportunity for the early development of a distinctively American policy reflecting the ripe wisdom of our ablest men.

The Monroe doctrine had its dramatic setting as a striking and carefully formulated announcement, but it was in no sense a departure or something novel or strange engrafted upon American policy. It was the fruition of that policy, and the new definition was in complete accord with principles long cherished and made almost sacred by the lessons of experience. The people of the United States had watched with deep sympathy the long struggle of our southern neighbors for independence. "In contemplating the scenes which distinguish this momentous epoch," said President Madison to the Congress, in 1811, "an enlarged philanthropy and enlightened forecast concur in imposing upon the national councils an obligation to take a deep interest in their destinies, to cherish reciprocal sentiments of good will." But, notwithstanding our natural sympathies, we remained neutral in the contest. "All Europe must expect," said President Monroe, in 1820, "that the citizens of the United States wish success to the colonies, and all that they can claim, even Spain herself, is that we will maintain an impartial neutrality between the parties. By taking this ground openly and frankly we acquit ourselves to our own consciences, we accommodate with the feelings of our constituents, we render to the colonies all the aid that we can render them, for I am satisfied that had we even joined them in the war we should have done them more harm than good, as we might have drawn all Europe on them, not to speak of the injury we should have done to ourselves."

While Spain maintained a doubtful contest, it was regarded as a civil war, but when that contest became so desperate that Spanish viceroys, governors, and captains-general concluded treaties with the insurgents virtually acknowledging their independence, the United States frankly and unreservedly recognized the fact without, as Secretary Adams said, "making their acknowledgment the price of any favor to themselves, and although at the hazard of incurring the displeasure of Spain." And in this measure, he added with pride, the United States "have taken the lead of the whole civilized world." The Republic of Colombia was recognized in 1822, the Government of Buenos Aires and the State of Mexico and Chile early in 1823. Deeply interested as we were in the development of republican institutions, the United States did not hesitate because of the political form of government and was the first to recognize the independent Empire of Brazil in May, 1824, and this was followed by the recognition of the Federation of Central American States in August of the same year.

Meanwhile, the Holy Alliance formed by the sovereigns of Austria, Russia, and Prussia had sought to enforce the divine right of kings against the progress of liberal principles. Joined by France, they undertook "to put an end to the system of representative government" and after France had proceeded accordingly to restore the rule of Ferdinand the Seventh in Spain, it was proposed to direct their efforts to the overthrowing of the new governments erected out of the old colonies of Spain in the Western Hemisphere. This was the situation 100 years ago—in August, 1823—when George Canning, British foreign secretary, wrote his celebrated letter to Richard Rush, American minister in London, suggesting a joint declaration, in substance, that the recovery of the colonies by Spain was hopeless; that neither Great Britain nor the United States was aiming at the possession of any portion of these colonies; and that they could not see with indifference any portion of them transferred to any other power. Great Britain, however, had not at that time recognized the new States in Spanish America, and this made a point of distinction. You doubtless have in mind these familiar facts and will remember the correspondence which followed between President Monroe and Jefferson and Madison, whose advice he sought. It was after mature deliberation by the President and his Cabinet, which contained not only John Quincy Adams, Secretary of State, but John C. Calhoun and William Wirt, that the American position was formally stated. It was deemed advisable to make a separate declaration of policy and this was formulated in President Monroe's message of December 2, 1823.

The doctrine is set forth in two paragraphs of this message. . . .

That these statements not only constituted a separate announcement but incorporated a distinctively American policy is manifest. Canning himself, in his letter to Bagot, of January 9, 1824, pointed out that the general agreement between the sentiments of the governments of Great Britain and the United States as to the Spanish colonies was qualified, as I have said, by the most important difference that the United States had acknowledged their independence and the British Government had not. And with the portion of President Monroe's message relating to future colonization, which lay entirely outside the purview of Canning's suggestion, Canning was not at all in sympathy. This proposal, he said, was as new to the British government as to that of France. The basis of the objection on the part of this government to future colonization by European powers was found in the fact, as Mr. Adams said later, when President, that "with the exception of the existing European colonies, which it was in nowise intended to disturb, the two continents consisted of several sovereign and independent nations, whose territories covered their whole surface. By this, their independent condition, the United States enjoyed the right of commercial intercourse with every part of their possessions. To attempt the establishment of a colony in those possessions would be to usurp, to the exclusion of others, a commercial intercourse which was the common possession of all."

Not only did American statesmen fear the extension of European colonization but they viewed with deep concern the possibility of the transfer of American territory from one European power to another. In 1811 Congress passed a resolution as to East Florida, stating that "considering the influence which the destiny of the territory adjoining the southern border of the United States may have upon their security, tranquillity, and commerce" the United States could not, "without serious inquietude, see any part of the said territory pass into the hands of any foreign power." The declarations in the messages of President Polk, in 1845 and 1848, were so closely associated with the doctrine announced by Monroe as to be deemed to fall within the same governing principle. President Polk's reference to "the transfer of dominion and sovereignty" clearly stated opposition to the acquisition of territorial control by any means. And this position has frequently been reiterated by the government of the United States.

It is not my purpose to review the historical applications of what is called the Monroe doctrine or to attempt to harmonize the various redactions of it. Properly understood, it is opposed (1) to any non-American action encroaching upon the political independence of American States under any guise and (2) to the acquisition in any manner of the control of additional territory in this hemisphere by any non-American power.

The Monroe doctrine is not a legislative pronouncement; it has been approved by action of Congress, but it does not rest upon any congressional sanction. It has had the implied indorsement of the treaty-making power in the reservations to the two Hague conventions of 1899 and 1907, but it is not defined by treaty and does not draw its force from any international agreement. It is not like a constitutional provision deriving its authority from the fact that it is a part of the organic law transcending and limiting executive and legislative power. It is not a part of international law, maintained by the consent of the civilized powers and alterable only at their will. It is a policy declared by the Executive of the United States and repeated in one form and another by Presidents and Secretaries of State in the conduct of our foreign relations. Its significance lies in the fact that in its essentials, as set forth by President Monroe and as forcibly and repeatedly asserted by our responsible statesmen, it has been for 100 years, and continues to be, an integral part of our national thought and purpose, expressing a profound conviction which even the upheaval caused by the Great War, and our participation in that struggle upon European soil, has not uprooted or fundamentally changed.

Taking the doctrine as it has been, and as it is believed to remain, I desire to comment upon certain points which, as I believe, deserve special emphasis at this time.

First, the Monroe doctrine is not a policy of aggression; it is a policy of self-defense. It was asserted at a time when the danger of foreign aggression in this hemisphere was very real, when the new American States had not yet established a firm basis of independent national life, and we were menaced by threats of Old World powers directed against republican institutions. But the achievements of the century have not altered the scope of the doctrine or changed its basis. It still remains an assertion of the principle of national security. As such, it is obviously not exclusive. Much time has been wasted in the endeavor to find in the Monroe doctrine either justification, or the lack of it, for every governmental declaration or action in relation to other American States. Appropriate action for our defense may always be taken, and our proper influence to promote peace and good will may always be exerted, with the use of good offices to that end, whether or not the particular exigency comes within the range of the specific declarations which constitute the doctrine.

In 1912, the Senate of the United States adopted a resolution apparently having immediate reference to Magdalena Bay "that when any harbor or other place in the American Continent is so situated that the occupation thereof for naval or military purposes might threaten the communications or the safety of the United States, the government of the United States could not see without grave concern possession of such harbor or other place by any corporation or association which has such a relation to another government, not American, as to give that government practical power or control for naval or military purposes." It was explained in debate that this resolution, while allied to the Monroe doctrine, was "not necessarily dependent upon it, or growing out of it." It was said to rest "on the principle that every nation has a right to protect its own safety, and that if it feels that the possession by a foreign power for military or naval purposes of any given harbor or place is prejudicial to its safety, it is its duty as well as its right to interfere."

The decision of the question as to what action the United States should take in any exigency arising in this hemisphere is not controlled by the content of the Monroe doctrine, but may always be determined on grounds of international right and national security as freely as if the Monroe doctrine did not exist. The essential character of that doctrine is found in its particularization, in the definite and limited application of the general principle relating to national safety to a particular set of circumstances; that is, in the assertion and maintenance of opposition to the encroachment by non-American powers upon the political independence of American States and to the extension by non-American powers of their control over American territory. And in this pronouncement, as a phase of our exercise of the right of self-defense, there is no hint, much less threat, of aggression on our part. Said President Roosevelt: "It is in no wise intended as hostile to any nation in the Old World. Still less is it intended to give cover to any aggression by any New World power at the expense of any other."

Second, as the policy embodied in the Monroe doctrine is distinctively the policy of the United States, the government of the United States reserves to itself its definition, interpretation, and application. This government has welcomed the recognition by other governments of the fact and soundness of this policy and of the appropriateness of its application from time to time. Great powers have signified their acquiescence in it. But the United States has not been disposed to enter into engagements which would have the effect of submitting to any other power or to any concert of powers the determination either of the occasions upon which the principles of the Monroe doctrine shall be invoked or of the measures that shall be taken in giving it effect. This government has not been willing to make the doctrine or the regulation of its enforcement the subject of treaties with European powers; and, while the United States has been gratified at expressions on the part of other American States of their accord with our government in its declarations with respect to their independence and at their determination to maintain it, this government in asserting and pursuing its policy has commonly avoided concerted action to maintain the doctrine, even with the American Republics. As President Wilson observed: "The Monroe doctrine was proclaimed by the United States on her own authority. It always has been maintained and always will be maintained upon her own responsibility."

This implies neither suspicion nor estrangement. It simply means that the United States is asserting a separate national right of self-defense, and that in the exercise of this right it must have an unhampered discretion. As Mr. Root has pithily said: "Since the Monroe doctrine is a declaration based upon the nation's right of self-protection, it can not be transmuted into a joint or common declaration by American States or any number of them." They have, of course, corresponding rights of self-defense, but the right is individual to each.

Further, in its own declarations the United States has never bound itself to any particular course of conduct in case of action by other powers contrary to the principles announced. In any such event it is free to act according to its conception of the emergency and of its duty. Dana, commenting upon this point in 1866 (in his edition of Wheaton), said: "The declarations do not intimate any course of conduct to be pursued in case of such interpositions, but merely say that they would be 'considered as dangerous to our peace and safety' and as 'the manifestation of an unfriendly disposition toward the United States,' which it would be impossible for us to 'behold with indifference,' thus leaving the nation to act at all times as its opinion of its policy or duty might require." This is equally true today; but it may be added that this carefully preserved freedom does not detract from the tenacity with which the doctrine is held but, like the doctrine itself, has been maintained as essential to our independence and security.

Third, the policy of the Monroe doctrine does not infringe upon the independence and sovereignty of other American States. Misconception upon this point is the only disturbing influence in our relations with Latin American States. Great Republics, whose independent sovereignty has been safeguarded by the historic doctrine no longer fear the danger of encroachments and control by European powers, but look with apprehension at the expansion, vast resources, rapidly growing population, and formidable strength of the Republic of the North. They do not feel the need of protection against European powers, and the Monroe doctrine is apt to be conceived, and criticized, as a suggestion of a policy of interference in their internal affairs.

This notion springs from a misunderstanding of the doctrine itself and of our national sentiment and purpose. We have frequently sought to remove it, and we must continue our efforts to render futile the aspersions of the few, here and abroad, misapprehending or distorting American opinion. In speaking last year at Rio de Janeiro on the occasion of the dedication of the site for the American Centennial Monument, I sought to reassert what I believed to be the actual sentiment of the American people in these words: "We shall also be glad to have this monument associated in the thought of our friends with a true appraisement of our North American ideals and aspirations. You, my fellow countrymen of the United States, know full well how sincerely we desire the independence, the unimpaired sovereignty and political integrity, and the constantly increasing prosperity of the peoples of Latin America. We have our domestic problems incident to the expanding life of a free people, but there is no imperialistic sentiment among us to cast even a shadow across the pathway of our progress. We covet no territory; we seek no conquest; the liberty we cherish for ourselves we desire for others; and we assert no rights for ourselves that we do not accord to others. We sincerely desire to see throughout this hemisphere an abiding peace, the reign of justice, and the diffusion of the blessings of a beneficent co-operation. It is this desire which forms the basis of the Pan American sentiment."

The Monroe doctrine does not attempt to establish a protectorate over Latin American States. Certainly, the declaration that intervention by non-American powers encroaching upon the independence of American States will be regarded as dangerous to our own safety, gives no justification for such intervention on our part. If such foreign interposition is deemed menacing to us, and our vigorous determination to oppose it serves to safeguard the independence of American States, they can have no just objection on that score, being the more secure to develop their own life without hindrance. The declaration against acquisition by non-American powers of American territory even by transfer might seem, at first glance, to furnish some basis for objection (although plainly in the interest of the integrity of American States) as an interference with the right of cession—but even this theoretical objection disappears when we consider the ground of the declaration upon this point by the government of the United States. That ground is found in the recognized right which every State enjoys, and the United States no less than any other, to object to acts done by other powers which threaten its own safety. The United States has all the rights of sovereignty, as well as any other power; we have lost none of our essential rights because we are strong, and other American States have gained none either because of increasing strength or relative weakness. The maxim of the civil law—*"sic utere tuo, ut alienum non laedas"*—may be applied to States where their action threatens the safety of another State.

Mr. Charles Cheney Hyde, in his recent work on international law—a work which will be of lasting credit to the American bar—sums up the matter in saying: "It is subversive of justice among nations that any state should, in the exercise of its own freedom of action, directly endanger the peace and safety of any other which has done no wrong. Upon such an occurrence the state which is menaced is free to act. For the moment it is justified in disregarding the political independence of the aggressor and in so doing it may be guided by the requirements of its own defense. . . . It is not, therefore, the broad ground of self-preservation, but the narrower yet firmer basis of one form of self-preservation, that of self-defense, on which justification rests." Of the immediate application of this sound principle to the Monroe doctrine Mr. Root has given a complete exposition. Speaking of the right of self-protection, as recognized by international law and as a necessary corollary of independent sovereignty, he says: "It is well understood that the exercise of the right of self-protection may, and frequently does, extend in its effect beyond the limits of the territorial jurisdiction of the state exercising it. The strongest example probably would be the mobilization of an army by another power immediately across the frontier. Every act done by the other power may be within its own territory. Yet the country threatened by this state of facts is justified in protecting itself by immediate war. The most common exercise of the right of self-protection outside a state's own territory and in time of peace is the interposition of objection to the occupation of territory of points of strategic military or maritime advantage or to indirect accomplishment of this effect by dynastic arrangement." The Monroe doctrine rests "upon the right of every sovereign state to protect itself by preventing a condition of affairs in which it will be too late to protect itself." This right we recognize in our sister republics of this hemisphere as we claim it for ourselves. American sentiment, it is believed, despite changes of circumstances, still regards the acquisition of additional control of American territory by non-American powers as a menace to our safety, and in asserting and maintaining this view in the interest of our peace and security in the future we not only do not interfere practically with the independence of our sister republics of the South but we simply assert a right which corresponds to rights which they themselves enjoy, and hence even in theory this assertion does not infringe upon their sovereignty.

The declaration of our purpose to oppose what is inimical to our safety does not imply an attempt to establish a protectorate any more than a similar assertion by any one of the great southern republics of opposition to conduct on the part of any of the others endangering its security would aim at the establishment of a protectorate. I utterly disclaim, as unwarranted, the observations which occasionally have been made implying a claim on our part to superintend the affairs of our sister republics, to assert an overlordship, to consider the spread of our authority beyond our own domain as the aim of our policy, and to make our power the test of right in this hemisphere. I oppose all such misconceived and unsound assertions or intimations. They do not express our national purpose; they belie our sincere friendship; they are false to the fundamental principles of our institutions and of our foreign policy which has sought to reflect, with rare exceptions, the ideals of liberty; they menace us by stimulating a distrust which has no real foundation. They find no sanction whatever in the Monroe doctrine. There is room in this hemisphere, without danger of collision, for the complete recognition of that doctrine and the independent sovereignty of the Latin American republics.

Fourth, there are, indeed, modern conditions and recent events which can not fail to engage our attention. We have grown rich and powerful, but we have not outgrown the necessity, in justice to ourselves and without injustice to others, of safeguarding our future peace and security. By building the Panama Canal we have not only established a new and convenient highway of commerce but we have created new exigencies and new conditions of strategy and defense. It is for us to protect that highway. It may also be necessary for us at some time to build another canal between the Atlantic and the Pacific oceans and to protect that. I believe that the sentiment of the American people is practically unanimous that in the interest of our national safety we could not yield to any foreign power the control of the Panama Canal, or the approaches to it, or the obtaining of any position which would interfere with our right of protection or would menace the freedom of our communications.

So far as the region of the Caribbean Sea is concerned, it may be said that if we had no Monroe doctrine we should have to create one. And this is not to imply any limitation on the scope of the doctrine, as originally proclaimed and as still maintained, but simply to indicate that new occasions require new applications of an old principle which remains completely effective. What has taken place of late years in the region of the Caribbean has given rise to much confusion of thought and misapprehension of purpose. As I have said, the Monroe doctrine as a particular declaration in no way exhausts American right or policy; the United States has rights and obligations which that doctrine does not define. And in the unsettled condition of certain countries in the region of the Caribbean it has been necessary to assert these rights and obligations as well as the limited principles of the Monroe doctrine.

In 1898, the United States intervened in Cuba in the cause of humanity and because of a condition of affairs at our very door so injurious to our interests that it had become intolerable. In view of the distress, miseries, and barbarities that existed, our action, as John Bassett Moore has said, "was analogous to what is known in private law as the abatement of a nuisance." In the settlement that followed the establishment of Cuban independence Cuba agreed "that the United States may exercise the right to intervene for the preservation of Cuban independence, the maintenance of a government adequate for the protection of life, property, and individual liberty, and for discharging the obligations with respect to Cuba imposed by the treaty of Paris on the United States, now to be assumed and undertaken by the government of Cuba." Cuba also agreed not to enter into any treaty with any foreign power which would tend to impair her independence, "nor in any manner authorize or permit any foreign power or powers to obtain by colonization or for military or naval purposes or otherwise lodgment in or control of any portion of said island." There were also restrictive provisions as to the contracting of debts. The United States thus holds a special position in relation to Cuba, but it should be pointed out and clearly understood that, while in view of this position we have acted as the friendly adviser of the Cuban government, our action has been solely for the purpose of aiding in maintaining the independence and stability of Cuba and thus not to create but to preclude the necessity of intervention under the treaty by encouraging the Cuban people to eliminate waste and corruption, to reduce public expenses to the normal requirements of government, and to secure the just and efficient administration which will safeguard the desired independence of Cuba and promote the prosperity which, with their abundant natural resources, the Cuban people are entitled to enjoy.

It is impossible for me to review in any detail the events which led to the occupation of Santo Domingo and Haiti. In Santo Domingo, during the forty years prior to 1907, there had been sixteen revolu-

tionary movements, and complete political and economic demoralization had resulted. The total debts of the Dominican Republic
amounted to about $20,000,000, and in 1907 a convention was con-
cluded between the governments of the United States and Santo
Domingo for the issue of bonds to that amount and providing for
the appointment by the President of the United States of a general
receiver of customs. The government of the United States agreed to
give to the general receiver and his assistants such protection as it
might find to be requisite for the performance of their duties. While
this arrangement was most advantageous to Santo Domingo and for a
time there was an improvement in conditions, there was a recurrence
of revolutionary disturbances and the Dominican government failed
to observe the terms of the convention. When civil war was imminent
the United States landed naval forces to prevent further bloodshed
and to protect the lives of foreigners. A military government was established in 1916 and until recent months was continued in the interest of public order.

This occupation was due to the demonstration, to use the phrase
of President Roosevelt, of an impotence resulting in the lessening
of the ties of civilized society and thus requiring intervention. But
the point that I desire to make is that instead of using this opportunity, as has falsely been charged, to establish a permanent control
of Santo Domingo, the government of the United States has been
solicitous to arrange for the termination of the occupation and the
withdrawal of its forces and has devoted its endeavors, earnestly and
effectively, to the assistance of the Dominican people in establishing
a sound basis for an independent government. Accordingly, as a result
of conversations with prominent Dominican representatives, a formal
agreement was reached on June 30, 1922, upon a plan of evacuation.
The plan provided for a provisional government which was to take
over the executive departments from the American military government, the American officials remaining in Santo Domingo only for
the purpose of lending their assistance to the respective secretaries of
the provisional government. The military forces of the United States
were to be concentrated at not more than three places, and order was
to be maintained during the tenure of office of the provisional government by the Dominican national police under the orders of the
provisional government.

The provisional President was to promulgate legislation regarding
the holding of elections and the reorganization of the government of
the provinces and communes; he was also to convene the primary
assemblies in accordance with the provision of the new election laws.
Electoral colleges were to be elected and were in turn to elect the

members of the Senate and of the Chamber of Deputies and to present the lists of the members of the judiciary to be submitted to the Senate. Provision was made for amendments to the constitution, the negotiation of an appropriate convention of ratification, and the establishment of a permanent government, whereupon the military forces of the United States would be withdrawn. On October 21, 1922, the provisional President was accordingly inaugurated. Last March the new electoral law was promulgated. The provisional government has also promulgated legislation providing for the reorganization of the provincial and municipal governments of the Republic. It is expected that elections in which the authorities of the United States will not intervene will be held about the middle of September and in due course the permanent government will be established. The United States intervened in the interest of peace and order and when these are assured it is not only willing but glad to withdraw.

In order to understand conditions in Haiti it should be recalled that since the Republic of Haiti gained its independence it has been the scene of almost continuous revolution. This is true of its recent history as well as of the earlier years. From 1886, when General Salomon completed his full presidential term, until 1915 every President except one had been overthrown by revolution, some escaping to near-by islands, others being assassinated. As the result of these successive revolutions, the Republic, by the summer of 1915, had reached a stage of exhaustion and devastation more complete than at any prior period of its existence. It is unnecessary to review the causes of these revolutions; it is sufficient for the present purpose to state the fact. Between the years 1910 and 1915 the foreign relations of the Haitian government became seriously involved because of the pressure brought to bear by the governments of France, Great Britain, Germany, Italy, and the United States to obtain a settlement of the claims of their nationals. Because of the unwillingness or inability of the Haitian people to settle these claims in a satisfactory manner there were armed demonstrations; armed forces of foreign powers had been landed at various points in Haiti on the ground that lives and property of their nationals were in danger.

In 1914 and 1915 there were continuous disturbances, which culminated in the latter year in the murder by armed mobs of ex-President Oreste Zamor and President Sam, the latter having been dragged by a mob from the French Legation, where he had taken refuge, and torn to pieces in the street. Following this the members of the cabinet took refuge in foreign legations or escaped from the country, so that there was no executive to assume direction of affairs. It was in this situation that on July 28, 1915, the U.S.S. *Washington* arrived and it was deemed necessary to land American forces. Within a short time the legislative chamber assembled and, under the protection of the United States marines, elected Sudre Dartiguenave, president of the former Senate, President of the Republic. In connection with the immediate exigency of preserving peace, it appeared essential from a humanitarian standpoint to aid the Haitian people to free themselves from the hopeless conditions which continued revolutions and a policy of despotic militarism had produced. In a large part of the island agriculture had practically been abandoned and in the theater of the revolutionary disturbances the country was devastated. A treaty was negotiated by our government with President Dartiguenave shortly after his election to "aid the Haitian people in the proper and efficient development of its agricultural, mineral, and commercial resources and in the establishment of the finances of Haiti on a firm and solid basis." Provision was made for the appointment by the President of Haiti, upon the nomination of the President of the United States, of a general receiver and the necessary aids for the collection of customs dues, and of a financial adviser, who was to devise an adequate system of public accounting, aid in increasing the revenues and adjusting them to the expenses, and otherwise make recommendations in relation to economic requirements.

Conditions in Haiti have not yet permitted the withdrawal of American forces, as there is general agreement that such a withdrawal would be the occasion for revolution and bloodshed. The government of the United States desires to effect a withdrawal as soon as this can be done consistently with the obligations it has assumed. The government is endeavoring to improve administration and to aid in establishing the basis for a sound and stable local government. Brig. Gen. John H. Russell, who was sent to Haiti in the early part of 1922 as American High Commissioner, has steadily sought to bring about improved political and financial conditions, and his endeavors have already met with almost unhoped-for success. General Russell has worked in the closest co-operation with the local government. Peace and order have been established and there is safety of lives and property. The great mass of Haitians, who formerly had been completely at the mercy of a rapacious military oligarchy, which had exploited it to such an extent that there was no incentive, but rather a real danger, in producing or in owning anything beyond the merest necessities, are now free to engage in profitable activities. Graft and embezzlement have been eliminated by the customs service and the currency has been stabilized. The public debt has been appreciably reduced. Last October this government was instrumental in obtaining a loan of $16,000,000 to Haiti upon favorable terms, and this has permitted the undertaking of numerous constructive works. A claims commission has been set up in Port au Prince, which is disposing of foreign and internal claims for debts.

The practice of financing the government by private and public loans at ruinous terms has been discontinued and expenses have been kept within the bounds of the revenue of the country. Although the public debt has been decreased, large sums have been expended on constructive public works. Telegraph and telephone systems have been repaired and new construction has been extended to all the principal towns of the interior. Roads have been reconstructed and new construction has been undertaken so far as the financial resources of the country permit. A modern efficient sanitation system has been installed in the seaboard cities and in some of the large interior towns. I can not attempt to enumerate all the improvements that have been undertaken. They are gratifying, but they are not yet adequate and much remains to be done. An American legal adviser in Haiti is now endeavoring to establish a basis for a sound judicial system. Agricultural surveys are being undertaken in order that all practicable assistance may be given for the development of the resources of the island. The government of the United States is seeking to make its relation to Haiti beneficial to the Haitian people; it has no other aim but to establish peace and stability. It does not seek to acquire or to control the territory of Haiti and it will welcome the day when it can leave Haiti with the reasonable assurance that the Haitians will be able to maintain an independent government competent to keep order and discharge its international obligations.

The disturbed conditions and revolutionary tendencies in some of the Central American Republics have given great solicitude to the government of the United States, and its efforts have been directed to the promotion of tranquillity and stability. This is in the interest of the maintenance of the unimpaired integrity and sovereignty of these republics. The conference of 1907 and the treaties which were then concluded constituted an important forward step, but the objects sought were not attained, and it recently became advisable to call another conference. Accordingly the government of the United States tendered an invitation to the governments of the Central American Republics, which they accepted, and the conference met in Washington last December. Delegates of our government participated. The result was the conclusion of a general treaty of peace and amity and a series of conventions, among them being conventions for the establishment of an international Central American tribunal, for the limitation of armaments, for permanent Central American commissions, for extradition, for the preparation of projects of electoral legislation, for the unification of protective laws for workmen, and laborers, for the establishment of stations for agricultural experiments and animal industries, and for the reciprocal exchange of Central American students. The treaty of peace and amity contained those provisions of a similar treaty of 1907 which have been found to be of practical value and additional provisions which the conference believed would promote the objects in view.

Reiterating the desire to maintain free institutions and to promote stability, the treaty provides that the governments of the Central American Republics will not recognize any other government which may come into power in any of the Republics through a *coup d'état* or a revolution against a recognized government so long as the freely elected representatives of the people have not constitutionally reorganized the country. This treaty and the conventions endeavor not only to assure amity but to build upon this foundation in each of the Republics an improved civic structure. In opening the conference it was my privilege to assure the delegates of the helpful spirit of cooperation which they would find in Washington. "The government of the United States," I said, "has no ambition to gratify at your expense, no policy which runs counter to your national aspirations, and no purpose save to promote the interests of peace and to assist you, in such manner as you may welcome, to solve your problems to your own proper advantage. The interest of the United States is found in the peace of this hemisphere and in the conservation of your interests."

The difficulties of these republics, and of other countries in a similar condition, are due in no small measure to the lack of the development of their resources and to the absence of needed facilities of intercourse, such as highways and railroads. It is idle to expect stability unless it has a basis in education, in improved methods of agriculture and industry, and in the provision of instrumentalities of communication which give opportunities for reasonable economic satisfactions. Progress in these directions, however, can not be achieved without the investment of capital, and this must be supplied from the outside until sufficient available wealth has been produced within these countries to permit their people to meet their own exigencies. It is not the policy of our government to make loans to other governments and the needed capital, if it is to be supplied at all, must be furnished by private organizations. This has given rise to much misunderstanding and baseless criticism. We have no desire to exploit other peoples; on the other hand, it is surely not the policy of this government to stand in the way of the improvement of their condition. It is an inescapable fact, however, that private capital is not obtainable unless investment is reasonably secure and returns are commensurate with risks. There are always abundant opportunities for financial enterprise in our own country and in other parts of the world on these terms. We thus have the difficulty that the instability of governments creates a hazard which private capital refuses to ignore, while that very instability can be cured only by the economic betterment which private capital alone can make possible.

It must also be remembered that the government of the United States has no power to compel its citizens to lend money or to fix the terms of their investment. Nor is it in a position to control the action of other governments who desire to borrow. In this situation our government endeavors by friendly advice to throw its influence against unfairness and imposition, and it has at times, with the consent of the parties—indeed, at their instance—agreed to a measure of supervision in the maintenance of security for loans which otherwise would have been denied or would have been made only at oppressive rates. But anyone who supposes that this helpful contact and friendly relation are either sought or used by the government of the United States for purposes of aggression or with the intention of dominating the affairs of these countries or their governments has slight knowledge of the aims and actual endeavors of the Department of State. We are not seeking to extend this relation but to limit it; we are aiming not to exploit but to aid; not to subvert, but to help in laying the foundations for sound, stable and independent government. Our interest does not lie in controlling foreign peoples; that would be a policy of mischief and disaster. Our interest is in having prosperous, peaceful, and law-abiding neighbors with whom we can co-operate to mutual advantage.

Fifth, it is apparent that the Monroe doctrine does not stand in the way of Pan American co-operation; rather it affords the necessary foundation for that co-operation in the independence and security of American States. The basis of Pan Americanism is found in the principles of the Farewell Address. There was striking prophecy in the hope expressed by Jefferson that we would recognize "the advantages of a cordial fraternalization among all the American nations" and in what he described as "the importance of their coalescing in an American system of policy." That system is not hostile to Europe; it simply conserves the opportunity for the cultivation of the interests which are distinctively American.

With the aim of furthering this Pan American co-operation there have been five Pan American conferences, the last of which was recently held in Santiago. The best results of these conferences are not to be found in any formal acts or statements but in the generation of helpful and friendly influences which draw peoples together through a better mutual understanding. There is always a tendency in connection with this co-operation to emphasize plans and purposes of a political nature, and if these are not successfully developed there is a disposition to minimize achievement. The most fruitful work, however, is generally found along less sensational lines where there is real progress in facilitating the interchanges of commerce and culture. Important as are these general Pan American conferences, I should give large place to the utility of special conferences to meet specific needs. Thus, one of the most promising results of the recent Santiago conference was in the provision for special conferences on the standardization of specifications of raw materials, tools, machinery, supplies, and other merchandise in order to promote economy in production and distribution; on public health; on eugenics and homoculture; on the codification of international law; on education; on electrical communications; on the uniformity of communications statistics; on automobile highways; and, last, but not least, on the dissemination of news.

The essential condition of co-operation is peace, and this government is constant in its endeavors to promote peace in this hemisphere by using its good offices, whenever they are welcome, in eliminating the causes of strife, and in making provision for the settlement of disputes that can not be adjusted by diplomacy. Almost all the boundary disputes in Latin America have been settled, and those that remain are in process of adjustment. Especially gratifying was the enlightened action of the governments of Chile and Peru in their recent agreement concluded at Washington for the arbitration by the President of the United States of certain questions growing out of the treaty of Ancon with respect to the territory of Tacna-Arica. Such efforts are not in strictness an application of the Monroe doctrine, but they are facilitated by its recognition.

Finally, it should be observed that the Monroe doctrine is not an obstacle to a wider international co-operation, beyond the limits of Pan American aims and interests, whenever that co-operation is congenial to American institutions. From the foundation of the government we have sought to promote the peaceful settlement of international controversies. Prior to the first peace conference at The Hague in 1899 the United States had participated in fifty-seven arbitrations. The United States became a party to the two Hague conventions for establishment of the Permanent Court of Arbitration, at the same time safeguarding its historic position by stating, as a part of the ratification, that nothing contained in these conventions should "be so construed as to require the United States of America to depart from its traditional policy of not entering upon, interfering with, or entangling itself in the political questions or internal administration of any foreign States" or "be construed to imply relinquishment by the United States of its traditional attitude toward purely American questions."

It should further be observed that the establishment of a permanent court of international justice, which might make available the facilities of a permanent tribunal (instead of the less satisfactory provision of temporary tribunals of arbitration) to governments desiring to submit their controversies to it, has been a distinct feature of the policy of the government of the United States for many years. We are also interested in measures of conciliation and in the facilities of conference. Our desire to co-operate in maintaining peaceful relations, in removing the misapprehensions and suspicion which are the most fruitful causes of conflict, in relieving the burdens of injurious and unnecessary competition in armament, in maintaining the declared principles of fair and equal opportunity, is sufficiently attested by the treaties which were concluded at the recent Washington conference. Moreover, aside from that obvious field of international co-operation in which we have postal conventions, rules of navigation, protection of submarine cables, regulation of fisheries, preservation of rights of property, copyrights and trade-marks, etc., our people have always and earnestly desired to join in the humanitarian endeavor of the nations for the elimination of common ills, the prevention of the spread of disease, and the restriction or prevention of abuses with which it is impracticable to deal effectively by the separate action of governments. This was shown many years ago when we joined in international conventions for the purpose of putting an end to the African slave trade, and it has had very definite illustration of late in our endeavor to make international action effective in controlling the pernicious distribution of narcotic drugs.

Our attitude is one of independence, not of isolation. Our people are still intent upon abstaining from participation in the political strife of Europe. They are not disposed to commit this government in advance to the use of its power in unknown contingencies, preferring to reserve freedom of action in the confidence of our ability and readiness to respond to every future call of duty. They have no desire to put their power in pledge, but they do not shirk co-operation with other nations whenever there is a sound basis for it and a consciousness of community of interest and aim. Co-operation is not dictation, and it is not partisanship. On our part it must be the co-operation of a free people drawing their strength from many racial stocks, and a co-operation that is made possible by a preponderent sentiment permitting governmental action under a system which denies all exercise of autocratic power. It will be the co-operation of a people of liberal ideals, deeply concerned with the maintenance of peace and interested in all measures which find support in the common sense of the country as being practicable and well designed to foster common interests.

To such aims the Monroe doctrine is not opposed, and with the passing of 100 years it remains a cherished policy, inimical to no just interest and deemed to be vitally related to our own safety and to the peaceful progress of the peoples of this hemisphere.

J. REUBEN CLARK, Under Secretary of State, to Frank B. Kellogg, Secretary of State, December 17, 1928 (extracts)

Department of State, *Memorandum on the Monroe Doctrine*, Publication No. 37, p. xix. The memorandum and communication of transmittal, from which these extracts are taken, were published by the Department in 1930

THE SECRETARY:

Herewith I transmit a Memorandum on the Monroe Doctrine, prepared by your direction, given a little over two months ago.

Voluminous as it is, the Memorandum makes no pretense at being either a treatise or a commentary on the Doctrine; the shortness of time available for the work and the urgency for its completion coupled with the performance of regular Departmental duties assigned to me, forbade such an undertaking.

Obviously the views set out, both herein and in the Memorandum, are not authoritative statements, but merely personal expressions of the writer. . . .

. . . It is of first importance to have in mind that Monroe's declaration in its terms, relates solely to the relationships between European states on the one side, and, on the other side, the American continents, the Western Hemisphere, and the Latin American Governments which on December 2, 1823, had declared and maintained their independence which we had acknowledged.

It is of equal importance to note, on the other hand, that the declaration does not apply to purely inter-American relations.

Nor does the declaration purport to lay down any principles that are to govern the interrelationship of the states of this Western Hemisphere as among themselves.

The Doctrine states a case of United States *vs.* Europe, not of United States *vs.* Latin America.

Such arrangements as the United States has made, for example, with Cuba, Santo Domingo, Haiti, and Nicaragua, are not within the Doctrine as it was announced by Monroe. They may be accounted for as the expression of a national policy which, like the Doctrine itself, originates in the necessities of security or self-preservation—a policy which was foreshadowed by Buchanan (1860) and by Salisbury (1895), and was outlined in what is known as the "Roosevelt corollary" to the Monroe Doctrine (1905) in connection with the Dominican debt protocol of 1904; but such arrangements are not covered by the terms of the Doctrine itself.

Should it become necessary to apply a sanction for a violation of the Doctrine as declared by Monroe, that sanction would run against the European power offending the policy, and not against the Latin American country which was the object of the European aggression, unless a conspiracy existed between the European and the American states involved.

In the normal case, the Latin American state against which aggression was aimed by a European power, would be the beneficiary of the Doctrine not its victim. This has been the history of its application. The Doctrine makes the United States a guarantor, in effect, of the independence of Latin American states, though without the obligations of a guarantor to those states, for the United States itself determines by its sovereign will when, where, and concerning what aggressions it will invoke the Doctrine, and by what measures, if any, it will apply a sanction. In none of these things has any other state any voice whatever.

Furthermore while the Monroe Doctrine as declared, has no relation in its terms to an aggression by any other state than a European state, yet the principle "self-preservation" which underlies the Doctrine—which principle, as we shall see, is as fully operative without the Doctrine as with it—would apply to any non-American state in whatever quarter of the globe it lay, or even to an American state, if the aggressions of such state against other Latin American states were "dangerous to our peace and safety," or were a "manifestation of an unfriendly disposition towards the United States," or were "endangering our peace and happiness"; that is, if such aggressions challenged our existence.

In other words, there is a broad domain occupied by self-preservation which is incapable of definite boundary as to its extent, or of definition as to the kind of act which lies within it, because new conditions, new advances in the arts and sciences, new instrumentalities of international contact and communication, new political theories and combinations, vary from age to age and can not be certainly foretold. As the law stands, whatever falls within the necessities of self-preservation, under existing or future conditions, lies within the boundaries of the domain of the principle.

By his declaration President Monroe occupied and bounded but a narrow portion of this whole domain—that portion which contained situations immediately threatening. But that can hardly be said to have changed under the rules and principles of international law the fundamental character of the acts defined and bounded. These acts still remained within the domain of self-preservation, for, obviously, if they would constitute a menace to our existence, such menace would not disappear by virtue of their being listed.

In this view, the Monroe Doctrine as such might be wiped out and the United States would lose nothing of its broad, international right; it would still possess, in common with every other member of the family of nations, the internationally recognized right of self-preservation, and this right would fully attach to the matters specified by the Doctrine if and whenever they threatened our existence, just as the right would attach in relation to any other act carrying a like menace.

The Doctrine has been useful, and such indeed was the real motive of its announcement, and it will remain of such use that it should never be abandoned, as a forewarning to European powers as to what this country would regard, in a restricted field, as inimical to its safety. It has been equally useful to the Americas as forecasting our attitude towards certain international problems and relations in which they might be involved.

But, recalling that the Doctrine is based upon the recognized right of self-preservation, it follows (it is submitted) that by the specification of a few matters in the Doctrine, the United States has not surrendered its right to deal, as it may be compelled, and under the rules and principles of international law, with the many others which are unspecified as these may arise, which others might, indeed, have been included in the declaration with as much propriety, legally, as those which were mentioned. By naming either one act or a series of acts which challenges our self-preservation, we do not estop ourselves from naming others as they may arise; otherwise the mention of one such act would foreclose all others. The custom of nations shows that invoking the right as to one menace does not foreclose a power from invoking it as to others.

Moreover, by specifying a few of the world powers which, if they performed the prohibited acts, would bring themselves within the inhibitions of the Doctrine, the United States has not estopped itself from asserting the same principles against other and unnamed powers making the same sort of aggression. That against these other powers, the United States might, in its intervention, speak of the right of self-preservation and not of the Monroe Doctrine, would neither enlarge nor diminish its rights under international law as to the Monroe Doctrine or otherwise.

It is evident from the foregoing that the Monroe Doctrine is not an equivalent for "self-preservation"; and therefore the Monroe Doctrine need not, indeed should not, be invoked in order to cover situations challenging our self-preservation but not within the terms defined by Monroe's declaration. These other situations may be handled, and more wisely so, as matters affecting the national security and self-preservation of the United States as a great power.

It has been sometimes contended (see particularly the speech in the Senate by Senator Calhoun in 1848 regarding the situation in Yucatan) that the Doctrine was announced merely to meet the threatened aggressions of the European Alliance in 1823, and that the Doctrine became obsolete with the passing of this immediate threat. But this view is not supported by the language of the declaration which as to action *"by any European power"* (both as to colonization and interposition) is unlimited in time; nor by that part of the declaration which specifically mentions the *"allied powers"* for here the declaration is couched in such general terms as to be, with sound reason, applied to any power or powers whatsoever who should, at any time, commit the aggressions against which the announced policy was aimed.

During the period since the Doctrine was announced there have been assertions at various times as to situations which were not objectionable to the Doctrine or to the principles underlying the same. In few of these instances has it been categorically asserted that the Monroe Doctrine did not cover the specific matter in question, the ruling or declaration having usually come in the form of a statement to the effect that some particular situation was not inimical to the interests of the United States.

The statement of the Doctrine itself that "with the existing colonies or dependencies of any European power we have not interfered and shall not interfere," has been more than once reiterated.

It has also been announced that the Monroe Doctrine is not a pledge by the United States to other American states requiring the United States to protect such states, at their behest, against real or fancied wrongs inflicted by European powers, nor does it create an obligation running from the United States to any American state to intervene for its protection.

Mr. Clay in 1828 asserted that the Monroe Doctrine was not applicable to wars as between American states, and it was likewise very early declared by Mr. Clay (1825) "that whilst the war is confined to the parent country and its former colony, the United States remain neutral, extending their friendship and doing equal justice to both parties."

Beginning in the second half of the last century (1861) the United States took the position that it would consider that Spain was "manifesting an unfriendly spirit toward the United States" if it should undertake the resubjection of certain of her former colonies, and this position was reiterated at later dates.

Commencing with 1825 and running on down through the whole of the last century it was repeatedly asserted that the Monroe Doctrine did not require the United States to prevent Europe from waging war against Latin American countries, and from almost as early a period down to the close of the century the principle was followed (as announced by Secretary Sherman in 1898) that it was not the duty of the United States "to protect its American neighbors from the responsibilities which attend the exercise of independent sovereignty."

The United States has at times jointly intervened with European countries in internal situations existing in the Latin Americas; at other times it has declined to participate in such intervention.

A popular feeling exists that the Monroe Doctrine is hostile to monarchial government as such, but this is not the fact. Monarchies have been set up in Brazil, Haiti, and Mexico without objection by the United States, and for many years we dealt with the Brazilian monarchy on terms and in language of sincere friendship. Even the establishment of the Maximilian Empire in Mexico was objected to not so much from the point of view of its being a monarchy as from the point of view that this monarchy was established and maintained by European troops.

One of the interesting suggestions that have been made by European powers is that the possession of colonies by that power upon this hemisphere makes of that possessing power an American state. This suggestion has, of course, not been acceptable to the United States.

The Monroe Doctrine has always been considered as covering a possession—either "temporary or permanent" (Forsyth, 1840) —of American territory by European powers, and in line with that principle, we have declared that the Monroe Doctrine forbade the occupation of American territory by such powers. President Roosevelt in his message of February 15, 1905, in relation to the situation in Santo Domingo, declared:

An aggrieved nation can without interfering with the Monroe Doctrine take what action it sees fit in adjustment of its disputes with American States, provided that action does not take the shape of interference with their form of government or of the despoilment of their territory under any disguise.

At various times proposals have been made that the United States should join with Europe in neutralizing certain areas (notably Cuba) on this continent, but the United States has steadily declined to join in such an action. One of the classic notes that have been written regarding the relationship between the United States and the other Americas was penned by Secretary Everett on December 1, 1852, regarding a proposal to neutralize Cuba.'

The so-called "Roosevelt corollary" was to the effect, as generally understood, that in case of financial or other difficulties in weak Latin American countries, the United States should attempt an adjustment thereof lest European Governments should intervene, and intervening should occupy territory—an act which would be contrary to the principles of the Monroe Doctrine. This view seems to have had its inception in some observations of President Buchanan in his message to Congress of December 3, 1860, and was somewhat amplified by Lord Salisbury in his note to Mr. Olney of November 6, 1895, regarding the Venezuelan boundary dispute.

As has already been indicated above, it is not believed that this corollary is justified by the terms of the Monroe Doctrine, however much it may be justified by the application of the doctrine of self-preservation.

These various expressions and statements, as made in connection with the situations which gave rise to them, detract not a little from the scope popularly attached to the Monroe Doctrine, and they relieve that Doctrine of many of the criticisms which have been aimed against it.

Finally, it should not be overlooked that the United States declined the overtures of Great Britain in 1823 to make a joint declaration regarding the principles covered by the Monroe Doctrine, or to enter into a conventional arrangement regarding them. Instead this Government determined to make the declaration of high national policy on its own responsibility and in its own behalf. The Doctrine is thus purely unilateral. The United States determines when and if the principles of the Doctrine are violated, and when and if violation is threatened. We alone determine what measures if any, shall be taken to vindicate the principles of the Doctrine, and we of necessity determine when the principles have been vindicated. No other power of the world has any relationship to, or voice in, the implementing of the principles which the Doctrine contains. It is our Doctrine, to be by us invoked and sustained, held in abeyance, or abandoned as our high international policy or vital national interests shall seem to us, and to us alone, to demand.

It may, in conclusion, be repeated: The Doctrine does not concern itself with purely inter-American relations; it has nothing to do with the relationship between the United States and other American nations, except where other American nations shall become involved with European governments in arrangements which threaten the security of the United States, and even in such cases, the Doctrine runs against the European country, not the American nation, and the United States would primarily deal thereunder with the European country and not with the American nation concerned. The Doctrine states a case of the United States *vs.* Europe, and not of the United States *vs.* Latin America. Furthermore, the fact should never be lost to view that in applying this Doctrine during the period of one hundred years since it was announced, our Government has over and over again driven it in as a shield between Europe and the Americas to protect Latin America from the political and territorial thrusts of Europe; and this was done at times when the American nations were weak and struggling for the establishment of stable, permanent governments; when the political morality of Europe sanctioned, indeed encouraged, the acquisition of territory by force; and when many of the great powers of Europe looked with eager, covetous eyes to the rich, undeveloped areas of the American hemisphere. Nor should another equally vital fact be lost sight of, that the United States has only been able to give this protection against designing European powers because of its known willingness and determination, if and whenever necessary, to expend its treasure and to sacrifice American life to maintain the principles of the Doctrine. So far as Latin America is concerned, the Doctrine is now, and always has been, not an instrument of violence and oppression, but an unbought, freely bestowed, and wholly effective guaranty of their freedom, independence, and territorial integrity against the imperialistic designs of Europe.

December 17, 1928   J. REUBEN CLARK

FRANK B. KELLOGG, Secretary of State, to the United States
Diplomatic Representatives in the Other American Re-
publics, February 28, 1929 (extracts)
Foreign Relations of the United States, 1929, I, 698

SIRS:

The discussions in the United States Senate incident to its consideration of the Multilateral Peace Pact, and the report of the Senate Committee on Foreign Affairs which dealt briefly but specifically with the
Monroe Doctrine, have given rise to questions regarding the true
meaning given by the United States to that Doctrine. The present
seems a propitious opportunity to prepare for communication to the
countries of Latin America when the occasion shall be thought by
the Department to be opportune, the views of the Government of the
United States on the scope and purpose of that Doctrine.

The Monroe Doctrine is sometimes conceived as a policy formulated by President Monroe and his Cabinet solely as a result of the
formation in Europe of the Holy Alliance, and the operations, through
France, of that Alliance against Spain. This is not a true appraisal
of the Doctrine. The formation of the Holy Alliance and its subsequent activities constituted the occasion for casting into definite
formula the principles behind the Doctrine, and for announcing such
formula when made; but the principles of the Doctrine are as old
as the nation itself. They were understood and, from time to time,
announced, as occasion required, by the Revolutionary Fathers themselves.

The fundamental concept of the Doctrine is the peace and safety of
the Western Hemisphere through the absolute political separation
of Europe from the countries of this Western World, subject to this
exception that the principle was not to be operative as against those
American possessions which were held by European powers at the
time the Doctrine was announced. A mere statement of this principle
shows that while announced by the United States, in 1823, and by it
since maintained for the primary purpose of protecting the interests,
integrity, and political life of itself, yet all the other independent
republics of the Western Hemisphere have, for a century, been equal
beneficiaries with the United States in the advantages which have
flowed from the complete political separation of Europe from the
Republics on the Western Hemisphere. . . .

As I have already said, the Doctrine laid down principles which were to be operative as between the United States and Europe, not as between the United States and the Latin American Republics save in the most unlikely event of a Latin American Republic being involved in a conspiracy with a European power to run counter to the principles of the Doctrine. The Doctrine did not lay down any principles that should govern the relationships between the United States and Latin American Republics, nor between and among the Latin American Republics themselves, nor between the Latin American Republics and European countries save only in those matters specifically inhibited by the terms of the Doctrine.

As President Roosevelt said:—

. . . The Monroe Doctrine is a declaration that there must be no territorial aggrandizement by any non-American power at the expense of any American power on American soil. It is in no wise intended as hostile to any nation in the Old World. Still less is it intended to give cover to any aggression by one New World power at the expense of any other.

In accordance with this conception, it was very early declared that the principles of the Doctrine had no application to wars between American States themselves; nor were the principles considered to apply (at least immediately after their promulgation) to a war confined to a parent country and its former colony, though later (by the middle of the last century) it was specifically declared that the United States would deny the rightfulness of Spain's re-annexation of certain territory which, though once a Spanish colonial possession, had established and maintained its independence from the time of the announcement of the Doctrine.

It has been many times affirmed by the appropriate authorities of the United States that the principles of the Doctrine are challenged by wars between American States and European powers, only when such wars threaten the subversion or exclusion of the self-determined government of a free American State, or the acquisition by a non-American power of the territory of one of these States.

As Mr. Roosevelt said:

We do not guarantee any state against punishment if it misconducts itself, provided that punishment does not take the form of the acquisition of territory by any non-American power.

An analogous rule was stated by Mr. Sherman, who instructed Mr. Powell, the Minister of the United States to Haiti in 1898, that

You certainly should not proceed on the hypothesis that it is the duty of the United States to protect its American neighbors from the responsibilities which attend the exercise of independent sovereignty;

or as the general principle had been earlier stated by Secretary Cass—

It is the established policy of this country not to interfere with the relations of foreign nations to each other and that it would be both improper and impossible for the United States to decide upon the course of conduct towards Venezuela which Spain may think required by her honor or her interests.

Nor is the Monroe Doctrine to be understood, nor has it ever been so interpreted by the United States, as inhibiting any form of government which any American Republic might desire to establish for itself. The United States has willingly yielded to the peoples of this hemisphere the right to set up any form of government they wished; it has recognized and dealt equally and freely with the monarchies in Haiti, Santo Domingo, Mexico, and Brazil, and with the Republics in those and other Latin American countries. Its attitude toward Emperor Maximilian in Mexico was, as expressed by Secretary Seward to Mr. Adams, the Minister of the United States to Great Britain (March 3, 1862) that the United States owed a

. . . duty to express to the allies, in all candor and frankness, the opinion that no monarchical government which could be founded in Mexico, in the presence of foreign navies and armies in the waters, and upon the soil of Mexico, would have any prospect of security or permanence.

Later Mr. Seward, in reply to a communication from the French Minister of November 29, 1865, said:

The real cause of our national discontent is, that the French army which is now in Mexico is invading a domestic republican government there which was established by her people, and with whom the United States sympathize most profoundly, for the avowed purpose of suppressing it and establishing upon its ruins a foreign monarchical government, whose presence there, so long as it should endure, could not but be regarded by the people of the United States as injurious and menacing to their own chosen and endeared republican institutions.

Thus the Monroe Doctrine has nothing whatever to do with the domestic concerns or policies or the form of government or the international conduct of the peoples of this hemisphere as among themselves. Each of the Republics of this half of the world is left free to conduct its own sovereign affairs as to it seems fit and proper. The principles of the Monroe Doctrine become operative only when some European power (either by its own motion or in complicity with an American state) undertakes to subvert or exclude the self-determined form of government of one of these Republics or acquire from them all or a part of their territory; and the principles of the Doctrine are then vitalized solely because the aggression of the European power constitutes a threat against the United States, not because of its effect upon the other American state.

It has sometimes been said that the treaty and conventional relations which have been created between the United States and certain Caribbean powers are the fruition of the application of the principles of the Monroe Doctrine. Nothing could be farther from the truth. These relations have been built between the United States and those powers by the free and voluntary act of the parties concerned; they have in each case been created either for the protection of these powers from foreign aggression which, had it taken place, might have been violative of the Monroe Doctrine, or to insure a domestic tranquillity which was to make for the peace, prosperity, and happiness of the people concerned. But the treaty and conventional obligations incurred, the treaty and conventional rights created, being wholly between and relating solely to American powers, have nothing whatever to do with the Monroe Doctrine which, by definition, is concerned only when a European power is involved in some aggression upon this hemisphere.

At times effort has been put forth to make it appear that on the rare occasions when the United States has been forced to land forces in areas of this hemisphere for the protection of American life, it has done so pursuant to the principles of the Monroe Doctrine. This is not true. The United States has landed troops for the same purpose in other parts of the world with perhaps at least equal frequency, and no one has suggested or would suggest that such landing was pursuant to the presumed mandates of the Monroe Doctrine. The historical fact is that, under principles universally recognized as justifying such an act, troops have been landed by all the great powers in temporarily disturbed areas in which local governments were not able, for the moment, to protect foreign life. These occupations are always temporary and terminate so soon as the local sovereign becomes able to maintain peace and order and to protect the lives of foreigners within the disturbed areas. Such landings do not constitute intervention in the domestic affairs of nations. They are merely interpositions, police measures taken to assist the local sovereign where his own power is, for the time being, inadequate to afford necessary protection.

As I have repeatedly affirmed, the Monroe Doctrine is a unilateral Doctrine; the principle of self-defense on the part of the United States was implicit in the Doctrine, and has been repeatedly declared by American statesmen from the time of its announcement until the present time. It would be superfluous for me to list here the expressions to this effect of statesmen of the earlier days of the Republic, but I may call your attention to the expressions of American statesmen during this century,—a period during which there have been voiced some false interpretations of the Doctrine to the effect that instead of being a Doctrine of self-defense, it was a Doctrine of excuse and justification for armed aggression.

Secretary Knox, speaking in 1912 [*1911*], affirmed:

The maintenance of the Monroe Doctrine is considered by us essential to our peace, prosperity, and national safety.

Senator Lodge, speaking of a Resolution which he had introduced into the Senate of the United States (July 31, 1912), stated:

. . . It rests on the principle that every nation has a right to protect its own safety. . . . The Monroe Doctrine was, of course, an extension in our own interests of this underlying principle—the right of every nation to provide for its own safety.

Mr. Root, speaking in 1914 on the subject of the Monroe Doctrine, affirmed:

It is a declaration of the United States that certain acts would be injurious to the peace and safety of the United States and that the United States would regard them as unfriendly. . . .

The Doctrine is not international law, but it rests upon the right of self-protection and that right is recognized by international law. . . .

We frequently see statements that the Doctrine has been changed or enlarged; that there is a new or different doctrine since Monroe's time. They are mistaken. There has been no change. . . .

Since the Monroe Doctrine is a declaration based upon this nation's right of self-protection, it can not be transmuted into a joint or common declaration by American States or any number of them.

On January 9 [*6*], 1915 [*1916*], President Wilson declared:

The Monroe Doctrine was proclaimed by the United States on her own authority. It has always been maintained, and always will be maintained, upon her own responsibility. But the Monroe Doctrine demanded merely that European governments should not attempt to extend their political systems to this side of the Atlantic.

Mr. Hughes, writing in 1923, declared:

The Monroe Doctrine is not a policy of aggression; it is a policy of self-defense. . . . It still remains an assertion of the principle of national security. . . .

The decision of the question as to what action the United States should take in any exigency arising in this hemisphere is not controlled by the content of the Monroe Doctrine, but may always be determined on grounds of international right and national security as freely as if the Monroe Doctrine did not exist. . . .

The Monroe Doctrine rests "upon the right of every sovereign state to protect itself by preventing a condition of affairs in which it will be too late to protect itself."

Speaking to the American Academy of Political and Social Science on November 30, 1923, Mr. Hughes declared:

It should be recognized that the doctrine is only a phase of American policy in this hemisphere and the other phases of that policy should be made clear. . . . The principle of exclusion embodies a policy of self-defense on the part of the United States; it is a policy set up and applied by the United States. While the Monroe Doctrine is thus distinctively a policy of the United States maintained for its own security, it is a policy which has rendered an inestimable service to the American Republics by keeping them free from the intrigues and rivalries of European powers.

It is high time that misunderstanding as to the meaning of the Monroe Doctrine shall cease; that international trouble makers shall find so clear a conception of the Doctrine in the minds of the people of this hemisphere that false representations concerning it shall no longer find lodgment in the prejudices upon which such misrepresentations have heretofore lived; that irresponsible exploiters of great economic resources shall not be able hereafter to invoke an untrue concept of the Doctrine to justify and induce unwarranted international attitudes and actions; that poorly visioned, grandiose schemes of the dreamers of unrighteous dominion shall no longer be built upon erroneous principles unknown to the Doctrine.

The Monroe Doctrine is not now and never was an instrument of aggression; it is and always has been a cloak of protection. The Doctrine is not a lance; it is a shield.

I submit the foregoing to you as an official statement of and commentary upon the Monroe Doctrine which it is hoped may tend to clear up past uncertainties, remove hitherto existing apprehensions, if any, and so open the way for such a mutual understanding and appreciation of the Doctrine as shall serve to augment between the United States and Latin American countries that existing good will which already binds us together as members of the great sisterhood of Republics which, as time goes on, constantly embraces new peoples of the world.

You will be prepared to communicate the foregoing to the Minister of Foreign Affairs at such time and in such manner as the Secretary of State shall direct; in the meanwhile you will hold this instruction strictly confidential.

I am [etc.]

FRANK B. KELLOGG

ADDRESS by William R. Castle, Jr., Acting Secretary of State,
"Aspects of the Monroe Doctrine," at Charlottesville, July 4,
1931 (extract)

Department of State, *Press Releases,* July 4, 1931, p. 24. The address was read at the University of Virginia by James O. Murdock, Assistant to the Legal Adviser, Department of State

FROM THESE early interpretations we can deduce the following clear definitions, both of what the doctrine was and what it was not. It had no application to the then existing possessions on this continent held by European powers. It was not a pledge of alliance nor a guarantee against war by a European power against Latin America. It does not relieve the Latin American republics from their responsibilities as independent sovereignties. It was not directed against the monarchial form of government on this hemisphere; nor did it apply to wars between American states; nor to wars between a parent country and its former colony. Asserting the intention of the United States to prevent a non-American power from establishing itself on this continent, it does not give our Republic any warrant to interfere in the internal affairs of an American state. It has no taint of imperialism. In a speech before the American Society of International Law in 1914, Mr. Elihu Root explained vividly to what matters the Monroe Doctrine does not apply. He said:

A false conception of what the Monroe Doctrine is, of what it demands and what it justifies, of its scope and of its limits, has invaded the public press and affected public opinion within the past few years. Grandiose schemes of national expansion invoke the Monroe Doctrine. Interested motives to compel Central or South American countries to do or refrain from doing something by which individual Americans may profit invoke the Monroe Doctrine. Clamors for national glory for minds too shallow to grasp at the same time a sense of national duty invoke the Monroe Doctrine. The intolerance which demands that control over the conduct and the opinions of other peoples which is the essence of tyranny invoke the Monroe Doctrine. Thoughtless people who see no difference between lawful right and physical power assume that the Monroe Doctrine is a warrant for interference in the internal affairs of all weaker nations in the New World. Against this supposititious doctrine, many protests both in the United States and in South America have been made, and justly made. To the real Monroe Doctrine these protests have no application.

The doctrine is to-day, I believe, as sound a policy as it ever was and, although at the present time one can not see the remotest possibility that we shall have to invoke it again, since it runs only against foreign aggression, that is no reason to strike it from the roll of American responsibilities. Your maps give you an idea of what it has accomplished, in conjunction with the capacity for self-government and the progressive spirit of our neighbors to the south.

There has been in the past and there still remains in Latin America a certain irritation toward the Monroe Doctrine. First of all this is because the doctrine is unilateral. As President Wilson said, "The Monroe Doctrine was proclaimed by the United States on her own authority. It always has been maintained and always will be maintained, upon her own responsibility." It had to be unilateral at first because at the time of Monroe the United States was the only nation of the Western Hemisphere whose independence was recognized by Europe and whose potential power was grudgingly admitted. As I have already said, it was under the protection against foreign invasion given by this country that the genius of self-government developed in Latin America resulting finally in those powerful nations which are no longer our wards but our friends. If this be true, many people say, why should we not give up the unilateral aspect of the Monroe Doctrine and invite them to join with us in making it an American doctrine. The answer seems to me very clear. This would constitute a treaty of alliance which is contrary to our traditions and our institutions. On the other hand, if the Latin American nations do not themselves individually proclaim similar doctrines, it is because they know they would act in accord with the spirit of the doctrine whether or not it had been proclaimed as a policy. Not one of our friends in South America would be more willing than we to see one of their independent neighbors absorbed into the political system of a non-American nation. All these nations are instinctively as surely supporters of the policy of America for Americans as we are. The fact that we happen publicly to have declared the policy makes our interest no greater. The Monroe Doctrine confers no superior position on the United States. It was originally intended to help; it accomplished its task; in the changed circumstances of the 20th century it offers no threat, but remains as an assurance of our unswerving friendship toward our sister nations of this Western Hemisphere.

Another reason that the Monroe Doctrine has been disliked by Latin America is that it has been wrongly credited with giving us a right—in our own minds at least—to interfere in the internal affairs of other nations. In the protection of American interests in Latin

American countries, the Monroe Doctrine has no more place than in the protection of those interests in the Orient. Perhaps diplomatic intervention has sometimes been unwise, even unfair. One hears of "dollar diplomacy." If this ever existed it has, thank God, gone the way of all bad policies. Every nation has the right and the duty to demand justice for its citizens engaged in legitimate business abroad. No nation has a right to demand more than justice. It is only in case of miscarriage of justice that diplomatic protests have any part. I can assure you that no one in the American Government asks for our citizens engaged in business in Latin America more than we ask for them in other parts of the world. But everywhere, at all times, we expect that the governments of the nations where they reside and work shall give them protection, shall treat them fairly as we treat foreigners in our own country; that, subservient to the laws of the land where they live, they shall receive a full measure of justice and consideration in their legitimate pursuits. In Latin America this does not flow from anything contained or implied in the Monroe Doctrine, but rather from international law and from the custom of nations.

The building and operation of the Panama Canal have imposed on the American Government duties in connection with the defense of this great work which we hold as trustees for the world quite as much as for our own benefit. We must protect this international waterway because it is of the highest benefit to both North and South America. This responsibility entails duties in the whole Caribbean region, which, of necessity, become a part of the foreign policy of the United States; but the present is no time to discuss our Caribbean policy, although I should be glad of the opportunity to explain and defend the actions of the American Government in the Caribbean. They have often been sadly misunderstood, and I am sorry to say that false explanations of this policy have frequently disturbed the tenor of our relations with Latin America. I feel sure that complete understanding would do away with suspicion and bad feeling. All this, however, is not for to-day, because we are here to pay tribute to the memory of President Monroe, to explain once more the purpose and results of the great policy which he enunciated in 1823.

Our relations with Latin America are, above all, not in any way partisan. It is the United States which has duties and responsibilities, not the party. To be sure the party in power has to carry out those duties and responsibilities, but no Government would dare to stray far from the national policy. That is, and must always be a policy of frank and friendly cooperation with our friends in Latin America. As Americans we must hold together. All through his trip, Mr. Hoover stressed our common interests. In his address in Costa Rica he said:

Good will between nations is not a policy—it is a deduction arising from a series of actions. It is not a diplomatic formula; it is an aspiration which flows from the ideals of a people. So generous a recognition by you that the spirit of the people of the United States has ever been steadfast in resolution to act not only with justice to its neighbors, but that they do aspire to cooperate with them for the making of good will, will find a deep response from the very hearts of my countrymen.

It is in this spirit that the United States carries on and will continue to carry on its relations with South America.

STATEMENT by the Department of State Regarding European Possessions in the Western Hemisphere, June 19, 1940
Department of State Bulletin, June 22, 1940, p. 681

THE SECRETARY OF STATE, Mr. Cordell Hull, on June 17 instructed the American Chargé at Berlin and the American Ambassador at Rome to send in writing to the Minister for Foreign Affairs of Germany and to the Minister for Foreign Affairs of Italy, respectively, the following communication in the name of the Government of the United States:

"The Government of the United States is informed that the Government of France has requested of the German Government the terms of an armistice.

"The Government of the United States feels it desirable, in order to avoid any possible misunderstanding, to inform Your Excellency that in accordance with its traditional policy relating to the Western Hemisphere, the United States would not recognize any transfer, and would not acquiesce in any attempt to transfer, any geographic region of the Western Hemisphere from one non-American power to another non-American power.

"I avail myself [etc.]"

The Governments of France, Great Britain, and the Netherlands have been informed in the same sense.

STATEMENT by Cordell Hull, Secretary of State, Regarding European Possessions in the Western Hemisphere, July 5, 1940

Department of State Bulletin, Vol. III, No. 54, p. 3

THE AMERICAN Chargé d'Affaires in Berlin has communicated to the Department the text of a note dated July 1, which he has received from the German Minister of Foreign Affairs.

The note in question refers to the note delivered by the American Chargé d'Affaires under instructions of the Government of the United States on June 18, in which this Government informed the Government of the German Reich that it would not recognize any transfer of a geographical region of the Western Hemisphere from one non-American power to another non-American power, and that it would not acquiesce in any attempt to undertake such transfer.

The German Minister of Foreign Affairs states that the Government of the German Reich is unable to perceive for what reason the Government of the United States of America has addressed this communication to the Reich Government. He states that in contrast with other countries, especially in contrast with England and France, Germany has no territorial possessions in the American Continent, and has given no occasion whatever for the assumption that it intends to acquire such possessions, and he asserts that thus insofar as Germany is concerned, the communication addressed to the Reich Government is without object.

The German Minister of Foreign Affairs continues by remarking that in this case the interpretation of the Monroe Doctrine implicit in the communication of the Government of the United States would amount to conferring upon some European countries the right to possess territories in the Western Hemisphere and not to other European countries. He states that it is obvious that such an interpretation would be untenable. He concludes by remarking that apart from this, the Reich Government would like to point out again on this occasion that the nonintervention in the affairs of the American Continent by European nations which is demanded by the Monroe Doctrine can in principle be legally valid only on condition that the American nations for their part do not interfere in the affairs of the European Continent.

The foregoing is the substance of the German note.

I feel that no useful purpose will be served at this time for this Government to undertake to make any further communication to the Government of the German Reich on the subject matter of the communication above quoted.

The fundamental questions involved are entirely clear to all of the peoples of the American republics, and undoubtedly as well to the majority of the governments and peoples in the rest of the world.

The Monroe Doctrine is solely a policy of self-defense, which is intended to preserve the independence and integrity of the Americas. It was, and is, designed to prevent aggression in this hemisphere on the part of any non-American power, and likewise to make impossible any further extension to this hemisphere of any non-American system of government imposed from without. It contains within it not the slightest vestige of any implication, much less assumption, of hegemony on the part of the United States. It never has resembled, and it does not today resemble, policies which appear to be arising in other geographical areas of the world, which are alleged to be similar to the Monroe Doctrine, but which, instead of resting on the sole policies of self-defense and of respect for existing sovereignties, as does the Monroe Doctrine, would in reality seem to be only the pretext for the carrying out of conquest by the sword, of military occupation, and of complete economic and political domination by certain powers of other free and independent peoples.

The Monroe Doctrine has, of course, not the remotest connection with the fact that certain European nations exercise sovereignty over colonies in the Western Hemisphere and that certain other European nations do not. This situation existed before the Monroe Doctrine was proclaimed. The Doctrine did not undertake to interfere with the existing situation, but did announce that further incursions would not be tolerated. It made clear that the future transfer of existing possessions to another non-American state would be regarded as inimical to the interests of this hemisphere. This has become a basic policy of the Government of the United States. As already stated in the communication addressed to the German Government by this Government under date of June 18, the Government of the United States will neither recognize nor acquiesce in the transfer to a non-American power of geographical regions in this hemisphere now possessed by some other non-American power.

The Government of the United States pursues a policy of nonparticipation and of noninvolvement in the purely political affairs of Europe. It will, however, continue to cooperate, as it has cooperated in the past, with all other nations, whenever the policies of such nations make it possible, and whenever it believes that such efforts are practicable and in its own best interests, for the purpose of promoting economic, commercial, and social rehabilitation, and of advancing the cause of international law and order, of which the entire world stands so tragically in need today.

REPORT of Cordell Hull, Secretary of State, Regarding the Second Meeting of the Ministers of Foreign Affairs of the American Republics, at Habana, July 21–30, 1940 (extract)

Second Meeting of the Ministers of Foreign Affairs of the American Republics, Report of the Secretary of State, p. 20. For the text of the Act of Habana, see *infra,* p. 799

. . . THE MINISTERS of Foreign Affairs also adopted the Act of Habana, which is designed to give immediate effect to the main provisions of the convention regarding the setting up of a collective trusteeship over any of the possessions now under the jurisdiction of a non-American government if an attempt shall be made to transfer control or sovereignty thereof to another non-American government before the convention has been ratified by the required two thirds of the American republics. The Act of Habana puts into immediate effect the principle of solidarity with regard to European colonies and possessions in the Western Hemisphere as an emergency measure.

The Act of Habana consists of a declaration and a resolution. The declaration states that when islands or regions now in the possession of non-American nations are in danger of becoming the subject of barter of territory or change of sovereignty, the American nations, taking into account the imperative need of continental security and the desires of the inhabitants of the islands or possessions, may set up a regime of provisional administration under the conditions (a) that as soon as the reasons requiring this measure shall cease to exist, and in the event that it would not be prejudicial to the safety of the American republics, such territories shall be organized as autonomous states if it shall appear that they are able to constitute and maintain themselves or be restored to their previous status, whichever of these alternatives shall appear the more practicable and just, and (b) that the regions shall be placed temporarily under the provisional administration of the American republics, which shall have a twofold purpose of contributing to the security and defense of the continent, and to the economic, political, and social progress of such regions. These provisions are both general and permanent in character.

The resolution provides for the establishment of an emergency committee composed of a representative of each of the American republics and will be constituted as soon as two thirds of the American republics shall have appointed their members. The committee shall assume the administration of any region in the Western Hemisphere now controlled by a European power whenever it becomes necessary as an imperative emergency measure to apply the provisions of the convention in order to safeguard the peace of the continent. The emergency committee is to function only until the convention on the provisional administration of European colonies and possessions in the Americas shall come into effect, at which time it will be superseded by the Inter-American Commission for Territorial Administration.

The resolution also contains the important provision that, should the need for emergency action be so urgent that action by the committee cannot be awaited, any of the American republics may, individually or jointly with others, act in the manner which its own defense or that of the continent requires. The American republic or republics taking action under these circumstances must place the matter before the emergency committee immediately in order that it may adopt appropriate measures.

The general provisions of the declaration and resolution are permanent in character. They authorize action by the American states, individually or collectively, at any time, whether before or after the convention comes into operation. The fundamental principles of the Monroe Doctrine are recognized by all the American republics as an essential means of protecting individual states as well as the continent. The provisions constitute a recognition of our right and the right of any other American government to enforce such principles by giving complete expression to the principle of solidarity in both the convention and the Act of Habana. . . .

III

Independence of Cuba

Independence of Cuba

JOHN QUINCY ADAMS, Secretary of State, to Hugh Nelson,
United States Minister to Spain, April 28, 1823 (extracts)
John Bassett Moore, *A Digest of International Law*, VI, 380

IN THE WAR between France and Spain, now commencing, other interests, peculiarly ours, will, in all probability, be deeply involved. Whatever may be the issue of this war as between those two European powers, it may be taken for granted that the dominion of Spain upon the American continents, north and south, is irrevocably gone. But the islands of Cuba and Porto Rico still remain nominally, and so far really, dependent upon her, that she yet possesses the power of transferring her own dominion over them, together with the possession of them, to others. These islands, from their local position are natural appendages to the North American continent, and one of them (Cuba) almost in sight of our shores, from a multitude of considerations has become an object of transcendent importance to the commercial and political interests of our Union. Its commanding position, with reference to the Gulf of Mexico and the West India seas; the character of its population; its situation midway between our southern coast and the island of St. Domingo; its safe and capacious harbor of the Havana, fronting a long line of our shores destitute of the same advantage; the nature of its productions and of its wants, furnishing the supplies and needing the returns of a commerce immensely profitable and mutually beneficial, give it an importance in the sum of our national interests with which that of no other foreign territory can be compared, and little inferior to that which binds the different members of this Union together. Such, indeed, are, between the interests of that island and of this country, the geographical, commercial, moral, and political relations, formed by nature, gathering, in the process of time, and even now verging to maturity, that, in looking forward to the probable course of events, for the short period of half a century, it is scarcely possible to resist the conviction that the annexation of Cuba to our Federal Republic will be indispensable to the continuance and integrity of the Union itself.

It is obvious, however, that for this event we are not yet prepared.

Numerous and formidable objections to the extension of our territorial dominions beyond sea present themselves to the first contemplation of the subject; obstacles to the system of policy by which alone that result can be compassed and maintained are to be foreseen and surmounted, both from at home and abroad; but there are laws of political as well as of physical gravitation; and if an apple, severed by the tempest from its native tree, can not choose but fall to the ground, Cuba, forcibly disjoined from its own unnatural connection with Spain, and incapable of self-support, can gravitate only towards the North American Union, which, by the same law of nature, can not cast her off from its bosom. . . .

[After this exordium Mr. Adams went on to say that, if the constitution of Spain should be demolished by the Armies of the Holy Alliance, represented by France, and the people of Cuba should as a result be shorn of the liberties with which they had been invested under that constitution, it was not to be presumed that they would be willing to surrender them to foreign violence committed upon the parent country. In that case France might attempt the invasion of Cuba, unless restrained by maritime weakness and the probability of resistance by Great Britain. Meanwhile the condition of the island was one of great, imminent, and complicated danger. If the people were homogeneous the invasion of Spain by France would be the signal for their declaration of independence, but in reality they were not competent to a system of permanent self-dependence; and if, in the event of the overthrow of the Spanish constitution, they were obliged to rely for protection on some force outside, their only alternative of dependence must be upon Great Britain or upon the United States. The United States had wished that the connection between Cuba and Spain as it has existed for several years should continue. Of this Mr. Forsyth, the American minister at Madrid, had been authorized in a suitable manner to advise the Spanish Government. But if a government was to be imposed by violence on the Spanish nation it was neither to be expected nor desired that the people of Cuba should submit to be governed by the oppressors of Spain. Great Britain had formally withdrawn from the councils of the European alliance in regard to Spain, and had avowed her determination to defend Portugal against the application of the principles on which the invasion of Spain was based; and unless the conflict between France and Spain should be as short and decisive as that of which Italy had lately been the scene, she might not be able to maintain her neutrality. If she made common cause with Spain, the two remaining islands of the latter in the West Indies might be considered the proper price of the alliance. The Government of the United States had been confidently told more than two years before, by indirect communication from the French Government, that Great Britain was negotiating with Spain for the cession of Cuba, and was so eager as to have offered Gibraltar in exchange. There was reason to believe that the French Government was misinformed. Recently the Government of the United States had been confidentially informed that the present British secretary for foreign affairs (Canning) had declared to the French Government that Great Britain would hold it disgraceful to avail herself of the distressed situation of Spain to obtain any portion of her American colonies. But this assurance was given with reference to a state of peace then existing, and the condition of the parties had since changed, and Great Britain had not forborne to take advantage of Spain's situation by order of reprisals given to two successive squadrons dispatched to the West Indies and stationed in immediate proximity to the island of Cuba. By this means she had obtained the revocation of the blockade which the Spanish generals had proclaimed on the coast of Terra Firma and pledges of reparation for all the captures of British vessels made under cover of that military fiction. She had also secured from Spain the promise to pay many long-standing claims of British subjects upon the Spanish Government. In satisfaction of all these demands the island of Cuba might be the only indemnity in the power of Spain to grant, as it would undoubtedly be to Great Britain the most satisfactory indemnity which she could receive.] Continuing, Mr. Adams said:

The war between France and Spain changes so totally the circumstances under which the declaration above mentioned of Mr. Canning was made, that it may, at its very outset, produce events, under which the possession of Cuba may be obtained by Great Britain, without even raising a reproach of intended deception against the British Government for making it. An alliance between Great Britain and Spain may be one of the first fruits of this war. A guaranty of the island to Spain may be among the stipulations of that alliance; and, in the event either of a threatened attack upon the island by France, or of attempts on the part of the islanders to assume their independence, a resort to the temporary occupation of the Havana by British forces may be among the probable expedients through which it may be obtained, by concert, between Great Britain and Spain herself. It is not necessary to point out the numerous contingencies by which the transition from a temporary and fiduciary occupation to a permanent and proprietary possession may be effected.

The transfer of Cuba to Great Britain would be an event unpropitious to the interests of this Union. This opinion is so generally entertained, that even the groundless rumors that it was about to be accomplished, which have spread abroad, and are still teeming, may be traced to the deep and almost universal feeling of aversion to it, and to the alarm which the mere probability of its occurrence has stimulated. The question both of our right and of our power to prevent it, if necessary by force, already obtrudes itself upon our councils, and the Administration is called upon, in the performance of its duties to the nation, at least to use all the means within its competency to guard against and forefend it.

It will be among the primary objects requiring your most earnest and unremitting attention, to ascertain and report to us every movement of negotiation between Spain and Great Britain upon this subject. We can not, indeed, prescribe any special instructions in relation to it. We scarcely know where you will find the Government of Spain upon your arrival in the country, nor can we foresee, with certainty, by whom it will be administered. Your credentials are addressed to Ferdinand, the King of Spain, under the constitution. You may find him under the guardianship of a Cortes, in the custody of an army of faith, or under the protection of the invaders of his country. So long as the *constitutional* government may continue to be administered in his name, your official intercourse will be with his ministers, and to them you will repeat, what Mr. Forsyth has been instructed to say, that the wishes of your Government are that Cuba and Porto Rico may continue in connection with independent and constitutional Spain.

You will add that no countenance has been given by us to any projected plan of separation from Spain, which may have been formed in the island. This assurance becomes proper, as by a late despatch received from Mr. Forsyth, he intimates that the Spanish Government have been informed that a revolution in Cuba was secretly preparing, fomented by communications between a society of Freemasons there and another of the same fraternity in Philadelphia. Of this we have no other knowledge; and the societies of Freemasons in this country are so little in the practice of using agency of a political nature on any occasion, that we think it most probable the information of the Spanish Government, in that respect, is unfounded. It is true that the Freemasons at the Havana have taken part of late in the politics of Cuba, and so far as it is known to us, it has been an earnest and active part in favor of the continuance of their connexion with Spain. While disclaiming all disposition on our part either to obtain possession of Cuba or Porto Rico ourselves, you will declare that the American Government had no knowledge of the lawless expedition undertaken against the latter of those islands last summer.

*JAMES BUCHANAN, Secretary of State, to Romulus M.
Saunders, United States Minister to Spain, June 17, 1848*
John Bassett Moore, *A Digest of International Law,* VI, 451

By DIRECTION of the President, I now call your attention to the
present condition and future prospects of Cuba. The fate of this
island must ever be deeply interesting to the people of the United
States. We are content that it shall continue to be a colony of Spain.
Whilst in her possession we have nothing to apprehend. Besides, we
are bound to her by the ties of ancient friendship, and we sincerely
desire to render these perpetual.

But we can never consent that this island shall become a colony
of any other European power. In the possession of Great Britain or
any strong naval power it might prove ruinous both to our domestic
and foreign commerce, and even endanger the Union of the States.
The highest and first duty of every independent nation is to provide
for its own safety; and acting upon this principle, we should be compelled to resist the acquisition of Cuba by any powerful maritime
State, with all the means which Providence has placed at our command.

Cuba is almost within sight of the coast of Florida, situated between
that State and the peninsula of Yucatan, and possessing the deep,
capacious and impregnably fortified harbor of the Havana. If this
island were under the dominion of Great Britain she could command
both the inlets to the Gulf of Mexico. She would thus be enabled, in
time of war, effectively to blockade the mouth of the Mississippi, and
to deprive all the Western States of this Union, as well as those within
the Gulf, teeming as they are with an industrious and enterprising
population, of a foreign market for their immense productions. But
this is not the worst. She could also destroy the commerce by sea
between our ports on the Gulf and our Atlantic ports, a commerce
of nearly as great a value as the whole of our foreign trade.

Is there any reason to believe that Great Britain desires to acquire
the island of Cuba?

We know that it has been her uniform policy, throughout her past
history, to seize upon every valuable commercial point throughout the
world, whenever circumstances have placed this in her power. And
what point so valuable as the island of Cuba? The United States are
the chief commercial rival of Great Britain; our tonnage at the pres-

ent moment is nearly equal to hers, and it will be greater, within a brief period, if nothing should occur to arrest our progress. Of what vast importance would it, then, be to her to obtain the possession of an island from which she could at any time destroy a very large portion both of our foreign and coasting trade? Besides, she well knows that if Cuba were in our possession, her West India Islands would be rendered comparatively valueless. From the extent and fertility of this island, and from the energy and industry of our people, we should soon be able to supply the markets of the world with tropical productions, at a cheaper rate than these could be raised in any of her possessions.

EDWARD EVERETT, Secretary of State, to Count Sartiges, French Minister to the United States, December 1, 1852
John Bassett Moore, *A Digest of International Law*, VI, 460

You ARE well acquainted with the melancholy circumstances which have hitherto prevented a reply to the note which you addressed to my predecessor on the 8th of July.

That note, and the instruction of M. de Turgot of the 31st March, with a similar communication from the English minister, and the *projet* of a convention between the three powers relative to Cuba, have been among the first subjects to which my attention has been called by the President.

The substantial portion of the proposed convention is expressed in a single article in the following terms:

"The high contracting parties hereby, severally and collectively, disclaim, now and for hereafter, all intention to obtain possession of the island of Cuba, and they respectively bind themselves to discountenance all attempt to that effect on the part of any power or individuals whatever.

"The high contracting parties declare, severally and collectively, that they will not obtain or maintain for themselves, or for any one of themselves, any exclusive control over the said island, nor assume nor exercise any dominion over the same."

The President has given the most serious attention to this proposal, to the notes of the French and British ministers accompanying it, and to the instructions of M. de Turgot and the Earl of Malmesbury, transmitted with the project of the convention, and he directs me to make known to you the view which he takes of this important and delicate subject.

The President fully concurs with his predecessors, who have on more than one occasion authorized the declaration referred to by M. de Turgot and Lord Malmesbury, that the United States could not see with indifference the island of Cuba fall into the possession of any other European Government than Spain; not, however, because we should be dissatisfied with any natural increase of territory and power on the part of France or England. France has, within twenty years, acquired a vast domain on the northern coast of Africa, with a fair prospect of indefinite extension. England, within half a century, has added very extensively to her Empire. These acquisitions have created no uneasiness on the part of the United States.

In like manner, the United States have, within the same period, greatly increased their territory. The largest addition was that of Louisiana, which was purchased from France. These accessions of territory have probably caused no uneasiness to the great European powers, as they have been brought about by the operation of natural causes, and without any disturbance of the international relations of the principal states. They have been followed, also, by a great increase of mutually beneficial commercial intercourse between the United States and Europe.

But the case would be different in reference to the transfer of Cuba from Spain to any other European power. That event could not take place without a serious derangement of the international system now existing, and it would indicate designs in reference to this hemisphere which could not but awaken alarm in the United States.

We should view it in somewhat the same light in which France and England would view the acquisition of some important island in the Mediterranean by the United States, with this difference, it is true; that the attempt of the United States to establish themselves in Europe would be a novelty, while the appearance of a European power in this part of the world is a familiar fact. But this difference in the two cases is merely historical, and would not diminish the anxiety which, on political grounds, would be caused by any great demonstration of European power in a new direction in America.

M. de Turgot states that France could never see with indifference the possession of Cuba by *any* power but Spain, and explicitly declares that she has no wish or intention of appropriating the island to herself; and the English minister makes the same avowal on behalf of his Government. M. de Turgot and Lord Malmesbury do the Government of the United States no more than justice in remarking that they have often pronounced themselves substantially in the same sense. The President does not covet the acquisition of Cuba for the United States; at the same time, he considers the condition of Cuba as mainly an American question. The proposed convention proceeds on a different principle. It assumes that the United States have no other or greater interest in the question than France or England; whereas it is necessary only to cast one's eye on the map to see how remote are the relations of Europe, and how intimate those of the United States, with this island.

The President, doing full justice to the friendly spirit in which his concurrence is invited by France and England, and not insensible to the advantages of a good understanding between the three powers in reference to Cuba, feels himself, nevertheless, unable to become a party to the proposed compact, for the following reasons:

It is, in the first place, in his judgment, clear (as far as the respect due from the Executive to a coordinate branch of the Government will permit him to anticipate its decision) that no such convention would be viewed with favor by the Senate. Its certain rejection by that body would leave the question of Cuba in a more unsettled position than it is now. This objection would not require the President to withhold his concurrence from the convention if no other objection existed, and if a strong sense of the utility of the measure rendered it his duty, as far as the executive action is concerned, to give his consent to the arrangement. Such, however, is not the case.

The convention would be of no value unless it were lasting: accordingly its terms express a perpetuity of purpose and obligation. Now, it may well be doubted whether the Constitution of the United States would allow the treaty-making power to impose a permanent disability on the American Government for all coming time, and prevent it, under any future change of circumstances, from doing what has been so often done in times past. In 1803 the United States purchased Louisiana of France; and in 1819 they purchased Florida of Spain. It is not within the competence of the treaty-making power in 1852 effectually to bind the Government in all its branches; and, for all coming time, not to make a similar purchase of Cuba. A like remark, I imagine, may be made even in reference both to France and England, where the treaty-making power is less subject than it is with us to the control of other branches of the Government.

There is another strong objection to the proposed agreement. Among the oldest traditions of the Federal Government is an aversion to political alliances with European powers. In his memorable farewell address, President Washington says: "The great rule of conduct for us in regard to foreign nations is, in extending our commercial relations, to have with them as little political connexion as possible. So far as we have already formed engagements, let them be fulfilled with perfect good faith. Here let us stop." President Jefferson, in his inaugural address in 1801, warned the country against "entangling alliances." This expression, now become proverbial, was unquestionably used by Mr. Jefferson in reference to the alliance with France of 1778—an alliance, at the time, of incalculable benefit to the United States; but which, in less than twenty years, came near involving us in the wars of the French revolution, and laid the foundation of heavy claims upon Congress, not extinguished to the present day. It is a significant coincidence, that the particular provision of the alliance which occasioned these evils was that, under which France called upon us to aid her in defending her West Indian possessions against England. Nothing less than the unbounded influence of Washington rescued the Union from the perils of that crisis, and preserved our neutrality.

But the President has a graver objection to entering into the proposed convention. He has no wish to disguise the feeling that the compact, although equal in its terms, would be very unequal in substance. France and England, by entering into it, would disable themselves from obtaining possession of an island remote from their seats of government, belonging to another European power, whose natural right to possess it must always be as good as their own—a distant island in another hemisphere, and one which by no ordinary or peaceful course of things could ever belong to either of them. If the present balance of power in Europe should be broken up, if Spain should become unable to maintain the island in her possession, and France and England should be engaged in a death struggle with each other, Cuba might then be the prize of the victor. Till these events all take place, the President does not see how Cuba can belong to any European power but Spain.

The United States, on the other hand, would, by the proposed convention, disable themselves from making an acquisition which might take place without any disturbance of existing foreign relations, and in the natural order of things. The island of Cuba lies at our doors. It commands the approach to the Gulf of Mexico, which washes the shores of five of our States. It bars the entrance of that great river which drains half the North American continent, and with its tributaries forms the largest system of internal water-communication in the world. It keeps watch at the door-way of our intercourse with California by the Isthmus route. If an island like Cuba, belonging to the Spanish Crown, guarded the entrance of the Thames and the Seine, and the United States should propose a convention like this to France and England, those powers would assuredly feel that the disability assumed by ourselves was far less serious than that which we asked them to assume.

The opinions of American statesmen, at different times, and under varying circumstances, have differed as to the desirableness of the acquisition of Cuba by the United States. Territorially and commercially it would, in our hands, be an extremely valuable possession. Under certain contingencies it might be almost essential to our safety. Still, for domestic reasons, on which, in a communication of this kind, it might not be proper to dwell, the President thinks that the incorporation of the island into the Union at the present time, although effected with the consent of Spain, would be a hazardous measure; and he would consider its acquisition by force, except in a just war with Spain (should an event so greatly to be deprecated take place) as a disgrace to the civilization of the age.

The President has given ample proof of the sincerity with which he holds these views. He has thrown the whole force of his constitutional power against all illegal attacks upon the island. It would have been perfectly easy for him, without any seeming neglect of duty, to allow projects of a formidable character to gather strength by connivance. No amount of obloquy at home, no embarrassments caused by the indiscretions of the colonial government of Cuba, have moved him from the path of duty in this respect. The captain-general of that island, an officer apparently of upright and conciliatory character, but probably more used to military command than the management of civil affairs, has, on a punctilio in reference to the purser of a private steamship (who seems to have been entirely innocent of the matters laid to his charge) refused to allow passengers and the mails of the United States to be landed from a vessel having him on board. This certainly is a very extraordinary mode of animadverting upon a supposed abuse of the liberty of the press by the subject of a foreign Government in his native country. The captain-general is not permitted by his Government, 3,000 miles off, to hold any diplomatic intercourse with the United States. He is subject in no degree to the direction of the Spanish minister at Washington; and the President has to choose between a resort to force, to compel the abandonment of this gratuitous interruption of commercial intercourse (which would result in war) and a delay of weeks and months, necessary for a negotiation with Madrid, with all the chances of the most deplorable occurrences in the interval—and all for a trifle, that ought to have admitted a settlement by an exchange of notes between Washington and the Havana. The President has, however, patiently submitted to these evils, and has continued faithfully to give to Cuba the advantages of those principles of the public law under the shelter of which she has departed, in this case, from the comity of nations. But the incidents to which I allude, and which are still in train, are among many others which point decisively to the expediency of some change in the relations of Cuba; and the President thinks that the influence of France and England with Spain would be well employed in inducing her so to modify the administration of the Government of Cuba as to afford the means of some prompt remedy for evils of the kind alluded to, which have done much to increase the spirit of unlawful enterprise against the island.

That a convention such as is proposed would be a transitory arrangement, sure to be swept away by the irresistible tide of affairs in a new country, is, to the apprehension of the President, too obvious to require a labored argument. The project rests on principles applicable, if at all, to Europe, where international relations are, in their basis, of great antiquity, slowly modified, for the most part, in the progress of time and events; and not applicable to America, which, but lately a waste, is filling up with intense rapidity, and adjusting on natural principles those territorial relations which, on the first discovery of the continent, were in a good degree fortuitous.

The comparative history of Europe and America, even for a single century, shows this. In 1752 France, England, and Spain were not materially different in their political position in Europe from what they are now. They were ancient, mature, consolidated states, established in their relations with each other and the rest of the world— the leading powers of western and southern Europe. Totally different was the state of things in America. The United States had no existence as a people; a line of English colonies, not numbering much over a million of inhabitants, stretched along the coast. France extended from the Bay of Saint Lawrence to the Gulf of Mexico, and from the Alleghanies to the Mississippi; beyond which, westward, the continent was a wilderness, occupied by wandering savages, and subject to a conflicting and nominal claim on the part of France and Spain. Everything in Europe was comparatively fixed; everything in America provisional, incipient, and temporary, except the law of progress, which is as organic and vital in the youth of states as of individual men. A struggle between the provincial authorities of France and England for the possession of a petty stockade at the confluence of the Monongahela and Alleghany, kindled the seven years' war; at the close of which, the great European powers, not materially affected in their relations at home, had undergone astonishing changes on this continent. France had disappeared from the map of America, whose inmost recesses had been penetrated by her zealous missionaries and her resolute and gallant adventurers; England had added the Canadas to her transatlantic dominions; Spain had become the mistress of Louisiana, so that, in the language of the archbishop of Mexico, in 1770, she claimed Siberia as the northern boundary of New Spain.

Twelve years only from the treaty of Paris elapsed, and another great change took place, fruitful of still greater changes to come. The American Revolution broke out. It involved France, England, and Spain in a tremendous struggle, and at its close the United States of America had taken their place in the family of nations. In Europe the ancient states were restored substantially to their former equilibrium; but a new element, of incalculable importance in reference to territorial arrangements, is henceforth to be recognized in America.

Just twenty years from the close of the war of the American Revolution, France, by a treaty with Spain—of which the provisions have never been disclosed—possessed herself of Louisiana, but did so only to cede it to the United States; and in the same year Lewis and Clark started on their expedition to plant the flag of the United States on the shores of the Pacific. In 1819 Florida was sold by Spain to the United States, whose territorial possessions in this way had been increased threefold in half a century. This last acquisition was so much a matter of course that it had been distinctly foreseen by the Count Aranda, then prime minister of Spain, as long ago as 1783.

But even these momentous events are but the forerunners of new territorial revolutions still more stupendous. A dynastic struggle between the Emperor Napoleon and Spain, commencing in 1808, convulsed the peninsula. The vast possessions of the Spanish Crown on this continent—vice-royalties and captain-generalships, filling the space between California and Cape Horn—one after another, asserted their independence. No friendly power in Europe, at that time, was able, or, if able, was willing, to succor Spain, or aid her to prop the crumbling buttresses of her colonial empire. So far from it, when France, in 1823, threw an army of one hundred thousand men into Spain to control her domestic policies, England thought it necessary to counteract the movement by recognizing the independence of the Spanish provinces in America. In the remarkable language of the distinguished minister of the day, in order to redress the balance of power in Europe, he called into existence a New World in the West— somewhat overrating, perhaps, the extent of the derangement in the Old World, and not doing full justice to the position of the United States in America, or their influence on the fortunes of their sister republics on this continent.

Thus, in sixty years from the close of the seven years' war, Spain, like France, had lost the last remains of her once imperial possessions on this continent. The United States, meantime, were by the arts of peace and the healthful progress of things, rapidly enlarging their dimensions and consolidating their power.

The great march of events still went on. Some of the new republics, from the effect of a mixture of races, or the want of training in liberal institutions, showed themselves incapable of self-government. The province of Texas revolted from Mexico by the same right by which Mexico revolted from Spain. At the memorable battle of San Jacinto, in 1836, she passed the great ordeal of nascent states, and her independence was recognized by this Government, by France, by England, and other European powers. Mainly peopled from the United States, she sought naturally to be incorporated into the Union. The offer was repeatedly rejected by Presidents Jackson and Van Buren, to avoid a collision with Mexico. At last the annexation took place. As a domestic question, it is no fit subject for comment in a communication to a foreign minister; as a question of public law, there never was an extension of territory more naturally or justifiably made.

It produced a disturbed relation with the Government of Mexico; war ensued, and in its results other extensive territories were for a large pecuniary compensation on the part of the United States, added to the Union. Without adverting to the divisions of opinion which arose in reference to this war, as must always happen in free countries in reference to great measures, no person surveying these events with the eye of a comprehensive statesmanship can fail to trace in the main result the undoubted operation of the law of our political existence. The consequences are before the world. Vast provinces, which had languished for three centuries under the leaden sway of a stationary system, are coming under the influences of an active civilization. Freedom of speech and the press, the trial by jury, religious equality, and representative government, have been carried by the Constitution of the United States into extensive regions in which they were unknown before. By the settlement of California, the great circuit of intelligence round the globe is completed. The discovery of the gold of that region—leading, as it did, to the same discovery in Australia—has touched the nerves of industry throughout the world. Every addition to the territory of the American Union has given homes to European destitution and gardens to European want. From every part of the United Kingdom, from France, from Switzerland and Germany, and from the extremest north of Europe, a march of immigration has been taken up, such as the world has never seen before. Into the United States—grown to their present extent in the manner described—but little less than half a million of the population of the Old World is annually pouring, to be immediately incorporated into an industrous and prosperous community, in the bosom of which they find political and religious liberty, social position, employment, and bread. It is a fact which would defy belief, were it not the result of official inquiry, that the immigrants to the United States from Ireland alone, besides having subsisted themselves, have sent back to their kindred, for the three last years, nearly five million of dollars annually; thus doubling in three years the purchase money of Louisiana.

Such is the territorial development of the United States in the past century. Is it possible that Europe can contemplate it with an unfriendly or jealous eye? What would have been her condition in these trying years but for the outlet we have furnished for her starving millions?

Spain, meantime, has retained of her extensive dominions in this hemisphere but the two islands of Cuba and Porto Rico. A respectful sympathy with the fortunes of an ancient ally and a gallant people, with whom the United States have ever maintained the most friendly relations, would, if no other reason existed, make it our duty to leave her in the undisturbed possession of this little remnant of her mighty trans-Atlantic empire. The President desires to do so; no word or deed of his will ever question her title or shake her possession. But can it be expected to last very long? Can it resist this mighty current in the fortunes of the world? Is it desirable that it should do so? Can it be for the interest of Spain to cling to a possession that can only be maintained by a garrison of twenty-five or thirty thousand troops, a powerful naval force, and an annual expenditure for both arms of the service of at least twelve millions of dollars? Cuba, at this moment, costs more to Spain than the entire naval and military establishment of the United States costs the Federal Government. So far from being really injured by the loss of this island, there is no doubt that, were it peacefully transferred to the United States, a prosperous commerce between Cuba and Spain, resulting from ancient associations and common language and tastes, would be far more productive than the best contrived system of colonial taxation. Such, notoriously, has been the result to Great Britain of the establishment of the independence of the United States. The decline of Spain from the position which she held in the time of Charles the Fifth is coeval with the foundation of her colonial system; while within twenty-five years, and since the loss of most of her colonies, she has entered upon a course of rapid improvement unknown since the abdication of that Emperor.

I will but allude to an evil of the first magnitude: I mean the African slave-trade, in the suppression of which France and England take a lively interest—an evil which still forms a great reproach upon the civilization of Christendom, and perpetuates the barbarism of Africa, but for which it is to be feared there is no hope of a complete remedy while Cuba remains a Spanish colony.

But, whatever may be thought of these last suggestions, it would seem impossible for anyone who reflects upon the events glanced at in this note to mistake the law of American growth and progress, or think it can be ultimately arrested by a convention like that proposed. In the judgment of the President, it would be as easy to throw a dam from Cape Florida to Cuba, in the hope of stopping the flow of the Gulf Stream, as to attempt, by a compact like this, to fix the fortunes of Cuba "now and for hereafter"; or, as expressed in the French text of the convention, "for the present as for the future" (*pour le present comme pour l'avenir*), that is, for all coming time. The history of the past—of the recent past—affords no assurance that twenty years hence France or England will even wish that Spain should retain Cuba; and a century hence, judging of what will be from what has been, the pages which record this proposition will, like the record of the family compact between France and Spain, have no interest but for the antiquary.

Even now the President can not doubt that both France and England would prefer any change in the condition of Cuba to that which is most to be apprehended, viz: An internal convulsion which should renew the horrors and the fate of San Domingo.

I will intimate a final objection to the proposed convention. M. de Turgot and Lord Malmesbury put forward, as the reason for entering into such a compact, "the attacks which have lately been made on the island of Cuba by lawless bands of adventurers from the United States, with the avowed design of taking possession of that island." The President is convinced that the conclusion of such a treaty, instead of putting a stop to these lawless proceedings, would give a new and powerful impulse to them. It would strike a death-blow to the conservative policy hitherto pursued in this country toward Cuba. No administration of this Government, however strong in the public confidence in other respects, could stand a day under the odium of having stipulated with the great powers of Europe, that in no future time, under no change of circumstances, by no amicable arrangement with Spain, by no act of lawful war (should that calamity unfortunately occur), by no consent of the inhabitants of the island, should they, like the possessions of Spain on the American continent, succeed in rendering themselves independent: in fine, by no over-ruling necessity of self-preservation should the United States ever make the acquisition of Cuba.

For these reasons, which the President has thought it advisable, considering the importance of the subject, to direct me to unfold at some length, he feels constrained to decline respectfully the invitation of France and England to become a party to the proposed convention. He is persuaded that these friendly powers will not attribute this refusal to any insensibility on his part to the advantages of the utmost harmony between the great maritime states on a subject of such importance. As little will Spain draw any unfavorable inference from this refusal; the rather, as the emphatic disclaimer of any designs against Cuba on the part of this Government, contained in the present note, affords all the assurance which the President can constitutionally, or to any useful purpose, give of a practical concurrence with France and England in the wish not to disturb the possession of that island by Spain.

WILLIAM H. SEWARD, Secretary of State, to Carl Schurz, United States Minister to Spain, April 27, 1861
John Bassett Moore, *A Digest of International Law*, VI, 516

THE UNITED STATES have a traditional policy in regard to the islands of Cuba and Porto Rico, which are dependencies of Spain. In view of the propinquity of those islands to our own coast, the United States have felt it their right and duty to watch them and prevent their falling into the hands of an inimical power. They have constantly indulged the belief that they might hope at some day to acquire those islands by just and lawful means, with the consent of their sovereign. In the meantime the United States have believed it to be most conducive to their present and ulterior safety and interests that Cuba and Porto Rico remain in the possession and ownership of Spain.

Although there have been times when a disposition to deviate from this policy has been manifested by some parties, yet it has neverthe-less been persevered in with great fidelity on the part of the Government. The President is satisfied of the wisdom of this course and is well inclined to adhere to it as steadily as any of his predecessors.

But it must be borne in mind that this forbearance on our part has always proceeded on the ground that Spain is not an aggressive power, and that she is content to leave the Spanish-American independent states free from her intervention, and at liberty to regulate their own affairs and work out their own destiny.

ANNUAL MESSAGE from President Ulysses S. Grant to the United States Congress, December 6, 1869 (extract)
John Bassett Moore, *A Digest of International Law*, VI, 429

As THE UNITED STATES is the freest of all nations, so, too, its people sympathize with all people struggling for liberty and self-government; but while so sympathizing it is due to our honor that we should abstain from enforcing our views upon unwilling nations and from taking an interested part, *without invitation,* in the quarrels between different nations or between governments and their subjects. Our course should always be in conformity with strict justice and law, international and local. Such has been the policy of the Administration in dealing with these questions. For more than a year a valuable province of Spain, and a near neighbor of ours, in whom all our people can not but feel a deep interest, has been struggling for independence and freedom. The people and Government of the United States entertain the same warm feelings and sympathies for the people of Cuba in their pending struggle that they manifested throughout the previous struggles between Spain and her former colonies in behalf of the latter. But the contest has at no time assumed the conditions which amount to a war in the sense of international law, or which would show the existence of a *de facto* political organization of the insurgents sufficient to justify a recognition of belligerency.

The principle is maintained, however, that this nation is its own judge when to accord the rights of belligerency, either to a people struggling to free themselves from a government they believe to be oppressive or to independent nations at war with each other.

The United States have no disposition to interfere with the existing relations of Spain to her colonial possessions on this continent. They believe that in due time Spain and other European powers will find their interest in terminating those relations and establishing their present dependencies as independent powers—members of the family of nations. These dependencies are no longer regarded as subject to transfer from one European power to another. When the present relation of colonies ceases, they are to become independent powers, exercising the right of choice and of self-control in the determination of their future condition and relations with other powers.

HAMILTON FISH, Secretary of State, to Caleb Cushing, United States Minister to Spain, February 6, 1874

John Bassett Moore, *A Digest of International Law*, VI, 78

WHATEVER general instructions you may need at the present time for your guidance in representing this government at Madrid have reference entirely to the actual state of the island of Cuba and its relation to the United States as well as to Spain.

It is now more than five years since an organized body of the inhabitants of that island assembled at Yara, issued a declaration of independence, and took up arms to maintain the declaration. The movement rapidly spread, so as to occupy extensive regions of the eastern and central portions of the island, and all the resources of the Spanish government have been exerted ineffectually to suppress the revolution and reclaim the districts in insurrection to the authority of Spain. The prosecution of the war on both sides has given rise to many questions, seriously affecting the interests and the honor of the United States, which have become the subject of diplomatic discussion between this government and that of Spain.

You will receive herewith a selection, in chronological order, of the numerous dispatches in this relation which have passed between the two governments. From these documents you will derive ample information, not only respecting special questions, which have arisen from time to time, but also respecting the general purposes and policy of the President in the premises.

Those purposes and that policy, as indicated in the accompanying documents, have continued to be substantially the same during the whole period of these events, except in so far as they may have been modified by special circumstances, seeming to impart greater or less prominence to the various aspects of the general question, and thus, without producing any change of principle, yet, according to the particular emergency, to direct the action of the United States.

It will suffice, therefore, on the present occasion, first, briefly to state these general views of the President; and, secondly, to show their application to the several incidents of this desperate struggle on the part of the Cubans to acquire independence, and of Spain to maintain her sovereignty, in so far as those incidents have immediately affected the United States.

Cuba is the largest insular possession still retained by any European power in America. It is almost contiguous to the United States. It is pre-eminently fertile in the production of objects of commerce which are of constant demand in this country, and, with just regulations for reciprocal interchange of commodities, it would afford a large and lucrative market for the productions of this country. Commercially, as well as geographically, it is by nature more closely connected with the United States than with Spain.

Civil dissensions in Cuba, and especially sanguinary hostilities, such as are now raging there, produce effects in the United States second in gravity only to those which they produce in Spain.

Meanwhile our political relation to Cuba is altogether anomalous, seeing that for any injury done to the United States or their citizens in Cuba we have no direct means of redress there, and can obtain it only by slow and circuitous action by way of Madrid. The captain-general of Cuba has, in effect, by the laws of Spain, supreme and absolute authority there for all purposes of wrong to our citizens; but this government has no adequate means of demanding immediate reparation of such wrongs on the spot, except through a consul, who does not possess diplomatic character, and to whose representations, therefore, the captain-general may, if he choose, absolutely refuse to listen. And, grievous as this inconvenience is to the United States in ordinary times, it is more intolerable now, seeing that, as abundantly appears, the contest in Cuba is between peninsular Spaniards on the one hand and native-born Spanish-Americans on the other; the former being the real representatives of Spanish force in Cuba, and exerting that force when they choose, with little, if any, respect for the metropolitan power of Spain. The captain-general is efficient to injure, but not to redress, and if disposed to redress, he may be hampered, if not prevented, by resolute opposition on the part of the Spaniards around him, disobedient alike to him and to the supreme government.

In fine, Cuba, like the former continental colonies of Spain in America, ought to belong to the great family of American republics, with political forms and public policy of their own, and attached to Europe by no ties save those of international amity, and of intellectual, commercial, and social intercourse. The desire of independence on the part of the Cubans is a natural and legitimate aspiration of theirs, because they are Americans. And while such independence is the manifest exigency of the political interests of the Cubans themselves, it is equally so that of the rest of America, including the United States.

That the ultimate issue of events in Cuba will be its independence, however that issue may be produced, whether by means of negotiation, or as the result of military operations or of one of those unexpected incidents which so frequently determine the fate of nations, it is impossible to doubt. If there be one lesson in history more cogent in its teachings than any other, it is that no part of America large enough to constitute a self-sustaining state can be permanently held in forced colonial subjection to Europe. Complete separation between the metropolis and its colony may be postponed by the former conceding to the latter a greater or less degree of local autonomy, nearly approaching to independence. But in all cases where a positive antagonism has come to exist between the mother country and its colonial subjects, where the sense of oppression is strongly felt by the latter, and especially where years of relentless warfare have alienated the parties, one from another, more widely than they are sundered by the ocean itself, their political separation is inevitable. It is one of those conclusions which have been aptly called the inexorable logic of events.

Entertaining these views, the President at an early day tendered to the Spanish government the good offices of the United States for the purpose of effecting, by negotiation, the peaceful separation of Cuba from Spain, and thus putting a stop to the further effusion of blood in the island, and relieving both Cuba and Spain from the calamities and charges of a protracted civil war, and of delivering the United States from the constant hazard of inconvenient complications on the side either of Spain or of Cuba. But the well-intended proffers of the United States on that occasion were unwisely rejected by Spain, and, as it was then already foreseen, the struggle has continued in Cuba, with incidents of desperate tenacity on the part of the Cubans, and of angry fierceness on the part of the Spaniards, unparalleled in the annals of modern warfare.

True it is that now, when the war has raged for more than five years, there is no material change in the military situation. The Cubans continue to occupy, unsubdued, the eastern and central parts of the island, with exception of the larger cities or towns, and of fortified points held by the government, but their capacity of resistance appears to be undiminished, and with no abatement of their resolution to persevere to the end in repelling the domination of Spain.

Meanwhile this condition of things grows, day by day, more and more insupportable to the United States. The government is compelled to exert constantly the utmost vigilance to prevent infringement of our law on the part of Cubans purchasing munitions or materials of war, or laboring to fit our military expeditions in our ports; we are constrained to maintain a large naval force to prevent violations of our sovereignty, either by the Cubans or the Spaniards; our people are horrified and agitated by the spectacle, at our very doors, of war, not only with all its ordinary attendants of devastation and carnage, but with accompaniments of barbarous shooting of prisoners of war, or their summary execution by military commissions, to the scandal and disgrace of the age; we are under the necessity of interposing continually for the protection of our citizens against wrongful acts of the local authorities of Spain in Cuba; and the public peace is every moment subject to be interrupted by some unforeseen event, like that which recently occurred, to drive us at once to the brink of war with Spain. In short, the state of Cuba is the one great cause of perpetual solicitude in the foreign relations of the United States.

While the attention of this government is fixed on Cuba, in the interest of humanity, by the horrors of civil war prevailing there, we can not forbear to reflect, as well in the interest of humanity as in other relations, that the existence of slave labor in Cuba, and its influence over the feelings and interests of the peninsular Spaniards, lie at the foundation of all the calamities which now afflict the island. Except in Brazil and in Cuba, servitude has almost disappeared from the world. Not in the Spanish-American republics alone, nor in the British possessions, nor in the United States, nor in Russia, not in those countries alone, but even in Asia, and in Africa herself, the bonds of the slave have been struck off, and personal freedom is the all but universal rule and public law, at least to the nations of Christendom. It can not long continue in Cuba, environed as that island is by communities of emancipated slaves in the other West India Islands and in the United States.

Whether it shall be put an end to by the voluntary act of the Spanish government, by domestic violence, or by the success of the revolution of Yara, or by what other possible means, is one of the grave problems of the situation, of hardly less interest to the United States than the independence of Cuba.

The President has not been without hope that all these questions might be settled by the spontaneous act of Spain herself, she being more deeply interested in that settlement than all the rest of the world. It seemed for awhile that such a solution was at hand, during the time when the government of Spain was administered by one of the greatest and wisest of the statesmen of that country, or indeed of Europe, President Castelar. Before attaining power he had announced a line of policy applicable to Cuba, which, though falling short of the concession of absolute independence, yet was of a nature to command the approbation of the United States.

"Let us," he declared, on a memorable occasion, "let us reduce to formulas our policy in America.

"First, *the immediate abolition of slavery.*

"Secondly, autonomy of the islands of Puerto Rico and Cuba, which shall have a parliamentary assembly of their own, their own administration, their own government, and a federal tie to unite them with Spain, as Canada is united with England, in order that we may found the liberty of those states and at the same time conserve the national integrity. I desire that the islands of Cuba and Puerto Rico shall be our sisters, and I do not desire that they shall be trans-Atlantic Polands."

I repeat, that to such a line of policy as this, especially as it relates to Cuba, the United States would make no objection; nay, they could accord to it hearty co-operation and support, as the next best thing to the absolute independence of Cuba.

Of course, the United States would prefer to see all that remains of colonial America pass from that condition to the condition of absolute independence of Europe.

But we might well accept such a solution of present questions as, while terminating the cruel war which now desolates the island and disturbs our political intercourse, should primarily and at the outset abolish the iniquitous institution of slavery, and, in the second place, should place Cuba practically in the possession of herself by means of political institutions of self-government, and enable her, while nominally subject to Spain, yet to cease to be the victim of Spanish colonial interests, and to be capable of direct and immediate relations of interests and intercourse with the other states of America. . . .

In these circumstances, the question what decision the United States shall take is a serious and difficult one, not to be determined without careful consideration of its complex elements of domestic and foreign policy, but the determination of which may at any moment be forced upon us by occurrences either in Spain or in Cuba.

Withal the President can not but regard *independence,* and emancipation, of course, as the only certain, and even the necessary, solution of the question of Cuba. And, in his mind, all incidental questions are quite subordinate to those, the larger objects of the United States in this respect.

It requires to be borne in mind that, in so far as we may contribute to the solution of these questions, this government is not actuated by any selfish or interested motive. The President does not meditate or desire the annexation of Cuba to the United States, but its elevation into an independent republic of freemen, in harmony with ourselves and with the other republics of America.

You will understand, therefore, that the policy of the United States in reference to Cuba at the present time is one of expectancy, but with positive and fixed convictions as to the duty of the United States when the time or emergency of action shall arrive. When it shall arrive you will receive specific instructions what to do. Meantime, instructed as you now are as to the intimate purposes of the government, you are to act in conformity therewith in the absence of any specific instructions, and to comport yourself accordingly in all your communications and intercourse, official or unofficial, with persons or public men in Spain.

In conclusion, it remains to be said that, in accordance with the established policy of the United States in such cases, as exemplified in the many changes of government in France during the last eighty years, and in the Mexican Republic since the time of its first recognition by us, and in other cases which have occurred in Europe and America, you will present your credentials to the persons or authorities whom you may find in the actual exercise of the executive power of Spain.

The President has not, as yet, received any official notice of the termination of the authority of President Castelar and the accession of President Serrano, and, of course, we have no precise information as to the intention or views of the new executive of the Spanish Republic.

While we can not expect from him any more hearty friendship for the United States than his predecessor entertained, it is to be hoped that he may not be moved by any unfriendly sentiments toward us. If, however, such should, unhappily, prove to be the case, it would be all the more necessary that you should be vigilantly watchful to detect and report any signs of possible action in Spain to the prejudice of the United States.

HAMILTON FISH, Secretary of State, to Caleb Cushing, United States Minister to Spain, November 5, 1875 (extract)
John Bassett Moore, *A Digest of International Law*, VI, 85

. . . WHILE REMEMBERING and observing the duties which this government, as one of the family of nations, owes to another member, by public law, treaties or the particular statutes of the United States, it would be idle to attempt to conceal the interest and sympathy with which Americans in the United States regard any attempt of a numerous people on this continent to be relieved of ties which hold them in the position of colonial subjection to a distant power, and to assume the independence and right of self-control which natural rights and the spirit of the age accord to them.

When, moreover, this struggle, in progress on our very borders, from its commencement has involved the property and interests of citizens of the United States; has disturbed our tranquillity and commerce; has called upon us not infrequently to witness barbarous violations of the rules of civilized warfare, and compelled us for the sake of humanity to raise our voice by way of protest, and when more than all we see in the contest the final struggle in this hemisphere between slavery and freedom, it would be strange indeed if the Government and people of this country failed at any time to take peculiar interest in the determination of such contest.

In this early instruction was expressed the sincere and unselfish hope of the President that the government of Spain would seek some honorable and satisfactory adjustment, based upon emancipation and self-government, which would restore peace and afford a prospect of a return of prosperity to Cuba.

Almost two years have passed since those instructions were issued and those strong hopes expressed, and it would appear that the situation has in no respect improved.

The horrors of war have in no perceptible measure abated; the inconvenience and injuries which we then suffered have remained, and others have been added; the ravages of war have touched new parts of the island and well-nigh ruined its financial and agricultural system and its relations to the commerce of the world. No effective steps have been taken to establish reforms or remedy abuses, and the effort to suppress the insurrection, by force alone, has been a complete failure.

In the meantime the material interests of trade and of commerce are impaired to a degree which calls for remonstrance, if not for another line of conduct, on the part of all commercial nations.

Whether it be from the severity and inhumanity with which the effort has been made to suppress the insurrection and from a supposed justification of retaliation for violations of the rules of civilized warfare by other violations and by acts of barbarism, of incendiarism and outrage, the world is witnessing on the part of the insurgents, whom Spain still claims as subjects, and for whose acts, if subjects, Spain must be held accountable in the judgment of the world, a warfare, not of the legitimate strife of relative force and strength, but of pillage and incendiarism, the burning of estates and of sugar mills, the destruction of the means of production and of the wealth of the island.

The United States purchases more largely than any other people of the productions of the island of Cuba and therefore, more than any other for this reason, and still more by reason of its immediate neighborhood, is interested in the arrest of a system of wanton destruction which disgraces the age and affects every commercial people on the face of the globe.

Under these circumstances, and in view of the fact that Spain has rejected all suggestions of reform or offers of mediation made by this government, and has refused all measures looking to a reconciliation, except on terms which make reconciliation an impossibility, the difficulty of the situation becomes increased.

When, however, in addition to these general causes of difficulty, we find the Spanish government neglectful also of the obligations of treaties and solemn compacts, and unwilling to afford any redress for long-continued and well-founded wrongs suffered by our citizens, it becomes a serious question how long such a condition of things can or should be allowed to exist, and compels us to enquire whether the point has not been reached where longer endurance ceases to be possible.

During all this time, and under these aggravated circumstances, this government has not failed to perform her obligations to Spain as scrupulously as toward other nations.

In fact, it might be said that we have not only been long suffering because of the embarrassments surrounding the Spanish government, but particularly careful to give no occasion for complaint for the same reason.

I regret to say that the authorities of Spain have not at all times appreciated our intentions or our purposes in these respects, and while insisting that a state of war does not exist in Cuba, and that no rights as belligerents should be accorded to the insurrectionists, have at the same time demanded for themselves all the rights and privileges which flow from actual and acknowledged war.

It will be apparent that such a state of things can not continue. It is absolutely necessary to the maintenance of our relations with Spain, even on their present footing, that our just demands for the return to citizens of the United States of their estates in Cuba, unincumbered, and for securing to them a trial for offenses according to treaty provisions, and all other rights guaranteed by treaty and by public law, should be complied with.

Whether the Spanish government, appreciating the forebearance of this country, will speedily and satisfactorily adjust the pending questions—not by the issue of empty orders or decrees without force or effect in Cuba, but by comprehensive and firm measures which shall everywhere be respected—I anxiously await further intelligence.

Moreover, apart from these particular questions, in the opinion of the President, the time has arrived when the interests of this country, the preservation of its commerce and the instincts of humanity alike demand that some speedy and satisfactory ending be made of the strife that is devastating Cuba.

A disastrous conflict of more than seven years' duration has demonstrated the inability of Spain to maintain peace and order in an island lying at our door. Desolation and destruction of life and property have been the only results of this conflict.

The United States sympathize in the fact that this inability results in a large degree from the unhappy condition of Spain at home, and to some extent from the distractions which are dividing her people. But the fact remains. Added to this are the large expanse of ocean separating the peninsula from the island, and the want of harmony and of personal sympathy between the inhabitants of the territory of the home government and those of the colony—the distinction of classes in the latter, between rulers and subjects—the want of adaptation of the ancient colonial system of Spain to the present times, and to the ideas which the events of the past age have impressed upon the peoples of every reading and thinking country.

Great Britain, wisely, has relaxed the old system of colonial dependence, and is reaping the benefits in the contentedness and peaceful prosecution of the arts of peace, and in the channels of commerce and of industry, in colonies which under restraint might have questioned and resisted the power of control from a distant government, and might have exhibited, as does Cuba, a chronic condition of insurrection, turbulence, and rebellion.

In addition to all this, it can not be questioned, that the continued maintenance, in the face of decrees and enactments to the contrary, of a compulsory system of slave labor, is a cause of disquiet and of excitement to a large class in the island, as also in the United States, which the government of Spain has led us, by very distinct assurances, to expect should be removed, and which the enlightened Christianity of the age condemns.

The contest and disorder in Cuba affect the United States directly and injuriously by the presence in this country of partisans of the revolt who have fled hither (in consequence of the proximity of territory) as to a political asylum, and who, by their plottings, are disturbers of the public peace.

The United States has exerted itself to the utmost, for seven years, to repress unlawful acts, on the part of these self-exiled subjects of Spain, relying on the promise of Spain to pacify the island. Seven years of strain on the powers of this government to fulfill all that the most exacting demands of one government can make, under any doctrine or claim of international obligation, upon another, have not witnessed the much hoped for pacification. The United States feels itself entitled to be relieved of this strain.

The severe measures, injurious to the United States and often in conflict with public law, which the colonial officers have taken to subdue the insurrection—the indifference, and ofttimes the offensive assaults upon the just susceptibilities of the people of the United States and their government which have characterized that portion of the peninsular population of Havana which has sustained and upheld, if it has not controlled, successive governors-general, and which have led to the disregard of orders and decrees which the more enlarged wisdom and the more friendly councils of the home government had enacted, the cruelty and inhumanity which have characterized the contest, both on the part of the colonial government and of the revolt, for seven years—and the destruction of valuable properties and industries by arson and pillage, which Spain appears unable, however desirous to prevent and stop, in an island three thousand miles distant from her shores but lying within sight of our coast, with which trade and constant intercourse are unavoidable, are causes of annoyance and of injury to the United States which a people can not be expected to tolerate without the assured prospect of their termination.

The United States has more than once been solicited by the insurgents to extend to them its aid, but has for years hitherto resisted such solicitation, and has endeavored by the tender of their good offices in the way of mediation, advice and remonstrance, to bring to an end a great evil, which has pressed sorely upon the interests both of the government and of the people of the United States, as also upon the commercial interests of other nations.

A sincere friendship for Spain, and for her people, whether peninsular or insular, and an equally sincere reluctance to adopt any measures which might injure or humble this ancient ally of the United States, has characterized the conduct of this government in every step during these sad and distressing years, and the President is still animated by the same feelings, and desires above all things to aid her and her people to enter once more upon the path of safety and repose.

It will be remembered that the President, in the year 1869, tendered the good offices of the United States for the purpose of bringing to a close the civil war in Cuba. This offer was made delicately, in good faith and in friendship, to both parties to the contest.

General Prim, as the representative of the Spanish government, while recognizing the good faith and friendship with which this offer was made, replied: "We can better proceed in the present situation of things without even this friendly intervention. A time will come when the good offices of the United States will be not only useful, but indispensable, in the final arrangements between Spain and Cuba. We will ascertain the form in which they can be employed and confidently count upon your assistance."

The United States replied that its good offices for that object would be at any time at the service of the parties to the conflict. This government has ever since been ready thus to aid in restoring peace and quiet.

The government of the United States has heretofore given expression to no policy in reference to the insurrection in Cuba, because it has honestly and sincerely hoped that no declaration of policy on its part would be required.

The President feels that longer reticence would be inconsistent with the interests of both governments.

Our relations with Spain are in that critical position that another seizure similar to that of the "Virginius"; other executions of citizens of the United States in Cuba; other wrongs of a less objectionable character even than many which have been already suffered by our citizens with simple remonstrance, or possibly even some new act of exceptional severity in Cuba, may suddenly produce a feeling and excitement which might force events which this Government anxiously desires to avoid.

The President hopes that Spain may spontaneously adopt measures looking to a reconciliation, and to the speedy restoration of peace and the organization of a stable and satisfactory system of government in the island of Cuba.

In the absence of any prospect of a a termination of the war, or of any change in the manner in which it has been conducted on either side, he feels that the time is at hand when it may be the duty of other governments to intervene, solely with the view of bringing to an end a disastrous and destructive conflict and of restoring peace in the island of Cuba. No government is more deeply interested in the order and peaceful administration of this island than is that of the United States, and none has suffered as has the United States from the condition which has obtained there during the past six or seven years. He will therefore feel it his duty at an early day to submit the subject in this light, and accompanied by an expression of the views above presented, for the consideration of Congress.

This conclusion is reached with reluctance and regret.

It is reached after every other expedient has been attempted and proved a failure, and in the firm conviction that the period has at last arrived when no other course remains for this government.

It is believed to be a just and friendly act to frankly communicate this conclusion to the Spanish government.

You will therefore take an early occasion thus to inform that government.

In making the communication it is the earnest desire of the President to impress upon the authorities of Spain the continued friendly disposition of this government, and that it has no ulterior or selfish objects in view, and no desire to become a party in the conflict, but is moved solely by the imperative necessities of a proper regard to its own protection and its own interests and the interests of humanity, and, as we firmly believe, in the ultimate interest of Spain itself.

In informing the Spanish government of these conclusions pursuant hereto, you are authorized to read this instruction to the minister of state, or to state the substance and purport thereof, as you may deem most advisable.

You will, of course, keep me advised, by telegraph and by post, of your proceedings pursuant to this instruction.

RICHARD OLNEY, Secretary of State, to Enrique Dupuy de Lôme, Spanish Minister to the United States, April 4, 1896
John Bassett Moore, *A Digest of International Law*, VI, 105

IT MIGHT WELL be deemed a dereliction of duty to the government of the United States, as well as a censurable want of candor to that of Spain, if I were longer to defer official expression as well of the anxiety with which the President regards the existing situation in Cuba as of his earnest desire for the prompt and permanent pacification of that island. Any plan giving reasonable assurance of that result and not inconsistent with the just rights and reasonable demands of all concerned would be earnestly promoted by him by all means which the Constitution and laws of this country place at his disposal.

It is now some nine or ten months since the nature and prospects of the insurrection were first discussed between us. In explanation of its rapid and, up to that time, quite unopposed growth and progress, you called attention to the rainy season which from May or June until November renders regular military operations impracticable. Spain was pouring such numbers of troops into Cuba that your theory and opinion that, when they could be used in an active campaign, the insurrection would be almost instantly suppressed, seemed reasonable and probable. In this particular you believed, and sincerely believed, that the present insurrection would offer a most marked contrast to that which began in 1868, and which, being feebly encountered with comparatively small forces, prolonged its life for upward of ten years.

It is impossible to deny that the expectations thus entertained by you in the summer and fall of 1895, and shared not merely by all Spaniards but by most disinterested observers as well, have been completely disappointed. The insurgents seem to-day to command a larger part of the island than ever before. Their men under arms, estimated a year ago at from ten to twenty thousand, are now conceded to be at least two or three times as many. Meanwhile, their discipline has been improved and their supply of modern weapons and equipment has been greatly enlarged, while the mere fact that they have held out to this time has given them confidence in their own eyes and prestige with the world at large. In short, it can hardly be questioned that the insurrection, instead of being quelled, is to-day more formidable than ever, and enters upon the second year of its existence with decidedly improved prospects of successful results.

Whether a condition of things entitling the insurgents to recognition as belligerents has yet been brought about may, for the purposes of the present communication, be regarded as immaterial. If it has not been, it is because they are still without an established and organized civil government, having an ascertained situs, presiding over a defined territory, controlling the armed forces in the field, and not only fulfilling the functions of a regular government within its own frontiers, but capable internationally of exercising those powers and discharging those obligations which necessarily devolve upon every member of the family of nations. It is immaterial for present purposes that such is the present political status of the insurgents, because their defiance of the authority of Spain remains none the less pronounced and successful, and their displacement of that authority throughout a very large portion of the island is none the less obvious and real.

When, in 1877, the President of the so-called Cuban Republic was captured, its legislative chamber surprised in the mountains and dispersed, and its presiding officer and other principal functionaries killed, it was asserted in some quarters that the insurrection had received its deathblow and might well be deemed to be extinct. The leading organ of the insurrectionists, however, made this response:

"The organization of the liberating army is such that a brigade, a regiment, a battalion, a company, or a party of twenty-five men can operate independently against the enemy in any department without requiring any instructions save those of their immediate military officers, because their purpose is but one, and that is known by heart as well by the general as the soldier, by the negro as well as the white man or the Chinese, viz., to make war on the enemy at all times, in all places, and by all means, with the gun, the machete, and the firebrand. In order to do this, which is the duty of every Cuban soldier, the direction of a government or a legislative chamber is not needed; the order of a subaltern officer, serving under the general in chief, is sufficient. Thus it is that the government and chamber have in reality been a superfluous luxury for the revolution."

The situation thus vividly described in 1877 is reproduced to-day. Even if it be granted that a condition of insurgency prevails and nothing more, it is on so large a scale and diffused over so extensive a region, and is so favored by the physical features and the climate of the country, that the authority of Spain is subverted and the functions of its government are in abeyance or practically suspended throughout a great part of the island. Spain still holds the seaports and most, if not all, of the large towns in the interior. Nevertheless, a vast area of the territory of the island is in effect under the control of roving bands of insurgents, which, if driven from one place to-day by an exhibition of superior force, abandon it only to return tomorrow when that force has moved on for their dislodgment in other quarters.

The consequences of this state of things can not be disguised. Outside of the towns still under Spanish rule, anarchy, lawlessness, and terrorism are rampant. The insurgents realize that the wholesale destruction of crops, factories, and machinery advances their cause in two ways. It cripples the resources of Spain on the one hand. On the other, it drives into their ranks the laborers who are thus thrown out of employment. The result is a systematic war upon the industries of the island and upon all the means by which they are carried on, and whereas the normal annual product of the island is valued at something like eighty or a hundred millions, its value for the present year is estimated by competent authority as not exceeding twenty millions.

Bad as is this showing for the present year, it must be even worse for the next year and for every succeeding year during which the rebellion continues to live. Some planters have made their crops this year who will not be allowed to make them again. Some have worked their fields and operated their mills this year in the face of a certain loss who have neither the heart nor the means to do so again under the present even more depressing conditions. Not only is it certain that no fresh money is being invested on the island, but it is no secret that capital is fast withdrawing from it, frightened away by the utter hopelessness of the outlook. Why should it not be? What can a prudent man foresee as the outcome of existing conditions except the complete devastation of the island, the entire annihilation of its industries, and the absolute impoverishment of such of its inhabitants as are unwise or unfortunate enough not to seasonably escape from it?

The last preceding insurrection lasted for ten years and then was not subdued, but only succumbed to the influence of certain promised reforms. Where is found the promise that the present rebellion will have a shorter lease of life, unless the end is sooner reached through the exhaustion of Spain herself? Taught by experience, Spain wisely undertook to make its struggle with the present insurrection short, sharp, and decisive, to stamp it out in its very beginnings by concentrating upon its large and well-organized armies, armies infinitely superior in numbers, in discipline, and in equipment to any the insurgents could oppose to them.

Those armies were put under the command of its ablest general, as well as its most renowned statesman—of one whose very name was an assurance to the insurgents both of the skillful generalship with which they would be fought and of the reasonable and liberal temper in which just demands for redress of grievances would be received. Yet the efforts of Campos seem to have utterly failed, and his successor, a man who, rightfully or wrongfully, seems to have intensified all the acerbities of the struggle, is now being reenforced with additional troops. It may well be feared, therefore, that if the present is to be of shorter duration than the last insurrection, it will be because the end is to come sooner or later through the inability of Spain to prolong the conflict, and through her abandonment of the island to the heterogeneous combination of elements and of races now in arms against her.

Such a conclusion of the struggle can not be viewed even by the most devoted friend of Cuba and the most enthusiastic advocate of popular government except with the gravest apprehension. There are only too strong reasons to fear that, once Spain were withdrawn from the island, the sole bond of union between the different factions of the insurgents would disappear; that a war of races would be precipitated, all the more sanguinary for the discipline and experience acquired during the insurrection, and that, even if there were to be temporary peace, it could only be through the establishment of a white and a black republic, which, even if agreeing at the outset upon a division of the island between them, would be enemies from the start, and would never rest until the one had been completely vanquished and subdued by the other.

The situation thus described is of great interest to the people of the United States. They are interested in any struggle anywhere for freer political institutions, but necessarily and in special measure in a struggle that is raging almost in sight of our shores. They are interested, as a civilized and Christian nation, in the speedy termination of a civil strife characterized by exceptional bitterness and exceptional excesses on the part of both combatants. They are interested in the noninterruption of extensive trade relations which have been and should continue to be of great advantage to both countries. They are interested in the prevention of that wholesale destruction of property on the island which, making no discrimination between enemies and neutrals, is utterly destroying American investments that should be of immense value, and is utterly impoverishing great numbers of American citizens.

On all these grounds and in all these ways the interest of the United States in the existing situation in Cuba yields in extent only to that of Spain herself, and has led many good and honest persons to insist that intervention to terminate the conflict is the immediate and imperative duty of the United States. It is not proposed now to consider whether existing conditions would justify such intervention at the present time, or how much longer those conditions should be endured before such intervention would be justified. That the United States can not contemplate with complacency another ten years of Cuban insurrection, with all its injurious and distressing incidents, may certainly be taken for granted.

The object of the present communication, however, is not to discuss intervention, nor to propose intervention, nor to pave the way for intervention. The purpose is exactly the reverse—to suggest whether a solution of present troubles can not be found which will prevent all thought of intervention by rendering it unnecessary. What the United States desires to do, if the way can be pointed out, is to cooperate with Spain in the immediate pacification of the island on such a plan as, leaving Spain her rights of sovereignty, shall yet secure to the people of the island all such rights and powers of local self-government as they can reasonably ask. To that end the United States offers and will use her good offices at such time and in such manner as may be deemed most advisable. Its mediation, it is believed, should not be rejected in any quarter, since none could misconceive or mistrust its purpose.

Spain could not, because our respect for her sovereignty and our determination to do nothing to impair it have been maintained for many years at great cost and in spite of many temptations. The insurgents could not, because anything assented to by this government which did not satisfy the reasonable demands and aspirations of Cuba would arouse the indignation of our whole people. It only remains to suggest that, if anything can be done in the direction indicated, it should be done at once and on the initiative of Spain.

The more the contest is prolonged, the more bitter and more irreconcilable is the antagonism created, while there is danger that concessions may be so delayed as to be chargeable to weakness and fear of the issue of the contest, and thus be infinitely less acceptable and persuasive than if made while the result still hangs in the balance, and they could be properly credited in some degree at least to a sense of right and justice. Thus far Spain has faced the insurrection sword in hand, and has made no sign to show that surrender and submission would be followed by anything but a return to the old order of things. Would it not be wise to modify that policy and to accompany the application of military force with an authentic declaration of the organic changes that are meditated in the administration of the island with a view to remove all just grounds of complaint?

It is for Spain to consider and determine what those changes would be. But should they be such that the United States could urge their adoption, as substantially removing well-founded grievances, its influence would be exerted for their acceptance, and it can hardly be doubted, would be most potential for the termination of hostilities and the restoration of peace and order to the island. One result of the course of proceeding outlined, if no other, would be sure to follow, namely, that the rebellion would lose largely if not altogether, the moral countenance and support it now enjoys from the people of the United States.

In closing this communication it is hardly necessary to repeat that it is prompted by the friendliest feelings toward Spain and the Spanish people. To attribute to the United States any hostile or hidden purposes would be a grave and most lamentable error. The United States has no designs upon Cuba and no designs against the sovereignty of Spain. Neither is it actuated by any spirit of meddlesomeness nor by any desire to force its will upon another nation. Its geographical proximity and all the considerations above detailed compel it to be interested in the solution of the Cuban problem whether it will or no. Its only anxiety is that that solution should be speedy, and, by being founded on truth and justice, should also be permanent.

To aid in that solution it offers the suggestions herein contained. They will be totally misapprehended unless the United States be credited with entertaining no other purpose toward Spain than that of lending its assistance to such termination of a fratricidal contest as will leave her honor and dignity unimpaired at the same time that it promotes and conserves the true interests of all parties concerned.

ANNUAL MESSAGE from President Grover Cleveland to the United States Congress, December 7, 1896 (extract)
John Bassett Moore, *A Digest of International Law*, VI, 124

THE INSURRECTION in Cuba still continues with all its perplexities. It is difficult to perceive that any progress has thus far been made towards the pacification of the island or that the situation of affairs as depicted in my last annual message has in the least improved. If Spain still holds Havana and the seaports and all the considerable towns, the insurgents still roam at will over at least two-thirds of the inland country. If the determination of Spain to put down the insurrection seems but to strengthen with the lapse of time, and is evinced by her unhesitating devotion of largely increased military and naval forces to the task, there is much reason to believe that the insurgents have gained in point of numbers, and character, and resources, and are none the less inflexible in their resolve not to succumb, without practically securing the great objects for which they took up arms. If Spain has not yet reestablished her authority, neither have the insurgents yet made good their title to be regarded as an independent state. Indeed, as the contest has gone on, the pretense that civil government exists on the island, except so far as Spain is able to maintain it, has been practically abandoned. Spain does keep on foot such a government, more or less imperfectly, in the large towns and their immediate suburbs. But, that exception being made, the entire country is either given over to anarchy or is subject to the military occupation of one or the other party. It is reported, indeed, on reliable authority that, at the demand of the commander in chief of the insurgent army, the putative Cuban government has now given up all attempt to exercise its functions, leaving that government confessedly (what there is the best reason for supposing it always to have been in fact) a government merely on paper.

Were the Spanish armies able to meet their antagonists in the open, or in pitched battle, prompt and decisive results might be looked for, and the immense superiority of the Spanish forces in numbers, discipline, and equipment, could hardly fail to tell greatly to their advantage. But they are called upon to face a foe that shuns general engagements, that can choose and does choose its own ground, that from the nature of the country is visible or invisible at pleasure, and that fights only from ambuscade and when all the advantages of position and numbers are on its side. In a country where all that is indispensable to life in the way of food, clothing, and shelter is so easily obtainable, especially by those born and bred on the soil, it is obvious that there is hardly a limit to the time during which hostilities of this sort may be prolonged. Meanwhile, as in all cases of protracted civil strife, the passions of the combatants grow more and more inflamed and excesses on both sides become more frequent and more deplorable. They are also participated in by bands of marauders, who, now in the name of one party and now in the name of the other, as may best suit the occasion, harry the country at will and plunder its wretched inhabitants for their own advantage. Such a condition of things would inevitably entail immense destruction of property even if it were the policy of both parties to prevent it as far as practicable. But while such seemed to be the original policy of the Spanish government, it has now apparently abandoned it and is acting upon the same theory as the insurgents, namely, that the exigencies of the contest require the wholesale annihilation of property, that it may not prove of use and advantage to the enemy.

It is to the same end that in pursuance of general orders, Spanish garrisons are now being withdrawn from plantations and the rural population required to concentrate itself in the towns. The sure result would seem to be that the industrial value of the island is fast diminishing, and that unless there is a speedy and radical change in existing conditions, it will soon disappear altogether. That value consists very largely, of course, in its capacity to produce sugar—a capacity already much reduced by the interruptions to tillage, which have taken place during the last two years. It is reliably asserted that should these interruptions continue during the current year and practically extend, as is now threatened, to the entire sugar-producing territory of the island, so much time and so much money will be required to restore the land to its normal productiveness that it is extremely doubtful if capital can be induced to even make the attempt.

The spectacle of the utter ruin of an adjoining country, by nature one of the most fertile and charming on the globe, would engage the serious attention of the government and people of the United States in any circumstances. In point of fact, they have a concern with it which is by no means of a wholly sentimental or philanthropic character. It lies so near to us as to be hardly separated from our territory. Our actual pecuniary interest in it is second only to that of the people and government of Spain. It is reasonably estimated that at least from $30,000,000 to $50,000,000 of American capital are invested in plantations and in railroad, mining, and other business enterprises on the island. The volume of trade between the United States and Cuba, which in 1889 amounted to about $64,000,000, rose in 1893 to about $103,000,000, and in 1894, the year before the present insurrection broke out, amounted to nearly $96,000,000. Besides this large pecuniary stake in the fortunes of Cuba, the United States finds itself inextricably involved in the present contest in other ways both vexatious and costly.

Many Cubans reside in this country and indirectly promote the insurrection through the press, by public meetings, by the purchase and shipment of arms, by the raising of funds, and by other means, which the spirit of our institutions and the tenor of our laws do not permit to be made the subject of criminal prosecutions. Some of them, though Cubans at heart and in all their feelings and interests, have taken out papers as naturalized citizens of the United States, a proceeding resorted to with a view to possible protection by this government, and not unnaturally regarded with much indignation by the country of their origin. The insurgents are undoubtedly encouraged and supported by the widespread sympathy the people of this country always and instinctively feel for every struggle for better and freer government, and which, in the case of the more adventurous and restless elements of our population, leads in only too many instances to active and personal participation in the contest. The result is that this government is constantly called upon to protect American citizens, to claim damages for injuries to persons and property, now estimated at many millions of dollars, and to ask explanations and apologies for the acts of Spanish officials, whose zeal for the repression of rebellion sometimes blinds them to the immunities belonging to the unoffending citizens of a friendly power. It follows from the same causes that the United States is compelled to actively police a long line of seacoast against unlawful expeditions, the escape of which the utmost vigilance will not always suffice to prevent.

These inevitable entanglements of the United States with the rebellion in Cuba, the large American property interests affected, and considerations of philanthropy and humanity in general, have led to a vehement demand in various quarters, for some sort of positive intervention on the part of the United States. It was at first proposed that belligerent rights should be accorded to the insurgents—a proposition no longer urged because untimely and in practical operation clearly perilous and injurious to our own interests. It has since been and is now sometimes contended that the independence of the insurgents should be recognized. But imperfect and restricted as the Spanish government of the island may be, no other exists there— unless the will of the military officer in temporary command of a particular district can be dignified as a species of government. It is now also suggested that the United States should buy the island— a suggestion possibly worthy of consideration if there were any evidence of a desire or willingness on the part of Spain to entertain such a proposal. It is urged, finally, that, all other methods failing, the existing internecine strife in Cuba should be terminated by our intervention, even at the cost of a war between the United States and Spain—a war which its advocates confidently prophesy could be neither large in its proportions nor doubtful in its issue.

The correctness of this forecast need be neither affirmed nor denied. The United States has nevertheless a character to maintain as a nation, which plainly dictates that right and not might should be the rule of its conduct. Further, though the United States is not a nation to which peace is a necessity, it is in truth the most pacific of powers, and desires nothing so much as to live in amity with all the world. Its own ample and diversified domains satisfy all possible longings for territory, preclude all dreams of conquest, and prevent any casting of covetous eyes upon neighboring regions, however attractive. That our conduct towards Spain and her dominions has constituted no exception to this national disposition is made manifest by the course of our government, not only thus far during the present insurrection, but during the ten years that followed the rising at Yara in 1868. No other great power, it may safely be said, under circumstances of similar perplexity, would have manifested the same restraint and the same patient endurance. It may also be said that this persistent attitude of the United States towards Spain in connection with Cuba unquestionably evinces no slight respect and regard for Spain on the part of the American people. They in truth do not forget her connection with the discovery of the Western Hemisphere, nor do they underestimate the great qualities of the Spanish people, nor fail to fully recognize their splendid patriotism and their chivalrous devotion to the national honor.

They view with wonder and admiration the cheerful resolution with which vast bodies of men are sent across thousands of miles of ocean, and an enormous debt accumulated, that the costly possession of the Gem of the Antilles may still hold its place in the Spanish Crown. And yet neither the government nor the people of the United States have shut their eyes to the course of events in Cuba, or have failed to realize the existence of conceded grievances, which have led to the present revolt from the authority of Spain—grievances recognized by the Queen Regent and by the Cortes, voiced by the most patriotic and enlightened of Spanish statesmen, without regard to party, and demonstrated by reforms proposed by the executive and approved by the legislative branch of the Spanish government. It is in the assumed temper and disposition of the Spanish government to remedy these grievances, fortified by indications of influential public opinion in Spain, that this government has hoped to discover the most promising and effective means of composing the present strife, with honor and advantage to Spain and with the achievement of all the reasonable objects of the insurrection.

It would seem that if Spain should offer to Cuba genuine autonomy—a measure of home rule which, while preserving the sovereignty of Spain, would satisfy all rational requirements of her Spanish subjects—there should be no just reason why the pacification of the island might not be effected on that basis. Such a result would appear to be in the true interest of all concerned. It would at once stop the conflict which is now consuming the resources of the island and making it worthless for whichever party may ultimately prevail. It would keep intact the possessions of Spain without touching her honor, which will be consulted rather than impugned by the adequate redress of admitted grievances. It would put the prosperity of the island and the fortunes of its inhabitants within their own control, without severing the natural and ancient ties which bind them to the mother country, and would yet enable them to test their capacity for self-government under the most favorable conditions. It has been objected on the one side that Spain should not promise autonomy until her insurgent subjects lay down their arms; on the other side, that promised autonomy, however liberal, is insufficient, because without assurance of the promise being fulfilled.

But the reasonableness of a requirement by Spain, of unconditional surrender on the part of the insurgent Cubans before their autonomy is conceded, is not altogether apparent. It ignores important features of the situation—the stability two years' duration has given to the insurrection; the feasibility of its indefinite prolongation in the nature of things, and as shown by past experience; the utter and imminent ruin of the island, unless the present strife is speedily composed; above all, the rank abuses which all parties in Spain, all branches of her government, and all her leading public men concede to exist and profess a desire to remove. Facing such circumstances, to withhold the proffer of needed reforms until the parties demanding them put themselves at mercy by throwing down their arms has the appearance of neglecting the gravest of perils and inviting suspicion as to the sincerity of any professed willingness to grant reforms. The objection on behalf of the insurgents—that promised reforms can not be relied upon—must of course be considered, though we have no right to assume, and no reason for assuming, that anything Spain undertakes to do for the relief of Cuba will not be done according to both the spirit and the letter of the undertaking.

Nevertheless, realizing that suspicions and precautions on the part of the weaker of two combatants are always natural and not always unjustifiable—being sincerely desirous in the interest of both as well as on its own account that the Cuban problem should be solved with the least possible delay—it was intimated by this government to the government of Spain some months ago that, if a satisfactory measure of home rule were tendered the Cuban insurgents, and would be accepted by them upon a guaranty of its execution, the United States would endeavor to find a way not objectionable to Spain of furnishing such guaranty. While no definite response to this intimation has yet been received from the Spanish government, it is believed to be not altogether unwelcome, while, as already suggested, no reason is perceived why it should not be approved by the insurgents. Neither party can fail to see the importance of early action and both must realize that to prolong the present state of things for even a short period will add enormously to the time and labor and expenditure necessary to bring about the industrial recuperation of the island. It is therefore fervently hoped on all grounds that earnest efforts for healing the breach between Spain and the insurgent Cubans, upon the lines above indicated, may be at once inaugurated and pushed to an immediate and successful issue. The friendly offices of the United States, either in the manner above outlined or in any other way consistent with our Constitution and laws, will always be at the disposal of either party.

Whatever circumstances may arise, our policy and our interests would constrain us to object to the acquisition of the island or an interference with its control by any other power.

It should be added that it can not be reasonably assumed that the hitherto expectant attitude of the United States will be indefinitely maintained. While we are anxious to accord all due respect to the sovereignty of Spain, we can not view the pending conflict in all its features, and properly apprehend our inevitably close relations to it, and its possible results, without considering that by the course of events we may be drawn into such an unusual and unprecedented condition, as will fix a limit to our patient waiting for Spain to end the contest, either alone and in her own way, or with our friendly cooperation.

When the inability of Spain to deal successfully with the insurrection has become manifest, and it is demonstrated that her sovereignty is extinct in Cuba for all purposes of its rightful existence, and when a hopeless struggle for its reestablishment has degenerated into a strife which means nothing more than the useless sacrifice of human life and the utter destruction of the very subject-matter of the conflict, a situation will be presented in which our obligations to the sovereignty of Spain will be superseded by higher obligations, which we can hardly hesitate to recognize and discharge. Deferring the choice of ways and methods until the time for action arrives, we should make them depend upon the precise conditions then existing; and they should not be determined upon without giving careful heed to every consideration involving our honor and interest, or the international duty we owe to Spain. Until we face the contingencies suggested, or the situation is by other incidents imperatively changed, we should continue in the line of conduct heretofore pursued, thus in all circumstances exhibiting our obedience to the requirements of public law and our regard for the duty enjoined upon us by the position we occupy in the family of nations.

A contemplation of emergencies that may arise should plainly lead us to avoid their creation either through a careless disregard of present duty or even an undue stimulation and ill-timed expression of feeling. But I have deemed it not amiss to remind the Congress that a time may arrive when a correct policy and care for our interests, as well as a regard for the interests of other nations and their citizens, joined by considerations of humanity and a desire to see a rich and fertile country, intimately related to us, saved from complete devastation, will constrain our government to such action as will subserve the interests thus involved and at the same time promise to Cuba and its inhabitants an opportunity to enjoy the blessings of peace.

SPECIAL MESSAGE from President William McKinley to the United States Congress, April 11, 1898
John Bassett Moore, *A Digest of International Law,* VI, 211

OBEDIENT to that precept of the Constitution which commands the President to give from time to time to the Congress information of the state of the Union and to recommend to their consideration such measures as he shall judge necessary and expedient, it becomes my duty now to address your body with regard to the grave crisis that has arisen in the relations of the United States to Spain by reason of the warfare that for more than three years has raged in the neighboring island of Cuba.

I do so because of the intimate connection of the Cuban question with the state of our own Union and the grave relation the course which it is now incumbent upon the nation to adopt must needs bear to the traditional policy of our government if it is to accord with the precepts laid down by the founders of the Republic and religiously observed by succeeding Administrations to the present day.

The present revolution is but the successor of other similar insurrections which have occurred in Cuba against the dominion of Spain, extending over a period of nearly half a century, each of which, during its progress, has subjected the United States to great effort and expense in enforcing its neutrality laws, caused enormous losses to American trade and commerce, caused irritation, annoyance, and disturbance among our citizens, and, by the exercise of cruel, barbarous, and uncivilized practices of warfare, shocked the sensibilities and offended the humane sympathies of our people.

Since the present revolution began, in February, 1895, this country has seen the fertile domain at our threshold ravaged by fire and sword in the course of a struggle unequaled in the history of the island and rarely paralleled as to the numbers of the combatants and the bitterness of the contest by any revolution of modern times where a dependent people striving to be free have been opposed by the power of the sovereign state.

Our people have beheld a once prosperous community reduced to comparative want, its lucrative commerce virtually paralyzed, its exceptional productiveness diminished, its fields laid waste, its mills in ruins, and its people perishing by tens of thousands from hunger and destitution. We have found ourselves constrained, in the observance of that strict neutrality which our laws enjoin, and which the law of nations commands, to police our own waters and watch our own seaports in prevention of any unlawful act in aid of the Cubans.

Our trade has suffered; the capital invested by our citizens in Cuba has been largely lost, and the temper and forbearance of our people have been so sorely tried as to beget a perilous unrest among our own citizens which has inevitably found its expression from time to time in the national legislature, so that issues wholly external to our own body politic engross attention and stand in the way of that close devotion to domestic advancement that becomes a self-contained commonwealth whose primal maxim has been the avoidance of all foreign entanglements. All this must needs awaken, and has, indeed, aroused the utmost concern on the part of this government, as well during my predecessor's term as in my own.

In April, 1896, the evils from which our country suffered through the Cuban war became so onerous that my predecessor made an effort to bring about a peace through the mediation of this Government in any way that might tend to an honorable adjustment of the contest between Spain and her revolted colony, on the basis of some effective scheme of self-government for Cuba under the flag and sovereignty of Spain. It failed through the refusal of the Spanish government then in power to consider any form of mediation or, indeed, any plan of settlement which did not begin with the actual submission of the insurgents to the mother country, and then only on such terms as Spain herself might see fit to grant. The war continued unabated. The resistance of the insurgents was in no wise diminished.

The efforts of Spain were increased, both by the dispatch of fresh levies to Cuba and by the addition to the horrors of the strife of a new and inhuman phase happily unprecedented in the modern history of civilized Christian peoples. The policy of devastation and concentration, inaugurated by the captain-general's bando of October 21, 1896, in the Province of Pinar del Rio was thence extended to embrace all of the island to which the power of the Spanish arms was able to reach by occupation or by military operations. The peasantry, including all dwelling in the open agricultural interior, were driven into the garrison towns or isolated places held by the troops.

The raising and movement of provisions of all kinds were interdicted. The fields were laid waste, dwellings unroofed and fired, mills destroyed, and, in short, everything that could desolate the land and render it unfit for human habitation or support was commanded by one or the other of the contending parties and executed by all the powers at their disposal.

By the time the present administration took office a year ago, reconcentration—so called—had been made effective over the better part of the four central and western provinces, Santa Clara, Matanzas, Habana, and Pinar del Rio.

The agricultural population to the estimated number of 300,000 or more was herded within the towns and their immediate vicinage, deprived of the means of support, rendered destitute of shelter, left poorly clad, and exposed to the most unsanitary conditions. As the scarcity of food increased with the devastation of the depopulated areas of production, destitution and want became misery and starvation. Month by month the death rate increased in an alarming ratio. By March, 1897, according to conservative estimates from official Spanish sources, the mortality among the reconcentrados, from starvation and the diseases thereto incident, exceeded 50 per centum of their total number.

No practical relief was accorded to the destitute. The overburdened towns, already suffering from the general dearth, could give no aid. So called "zones of cultivation" established within the immediate areas of effective military control about the cities and fortified camps proved illusory as a remedy for the suffering. The unfortunates, being for the most part women and children, with aged and helpless men, enfeebled by disease and hunger, could not have tilled the soil without tools, seed, or shelter for their own support or for the supply of the cities. Reconcentration, adopted avowedly as a war measure in order to cut off the resources of the insurgents, worked its predestined result. As I said in my message of last December, it was not civilized warfare; it was extermination. The only peace it could beget was that of the wilderness and the grave.

Meanwhile the military situation in the island had undergone a noticeable change. The extraordinary activity that characterized the second year of the war, when the insurgents invaded even the thitherto unharmed fields of Pinar del Rio and carried havoc and destruction up to the walls of the city of Habana itself, had relapsed into a dogged struggle in the central and eastern provinces. The Spanish arms regained a measure of control in Pinar del Rio and parts of Habana, but, under the existing conditions of the rural country, without immediate improvement of their productive situation. Even thus partially restricted, the revolutionists held their own, and their conquest and submission, put forward by Spain as the essential and sole basis of peace, seemed as far distant as at the outset.

In this state of affairs my administration found itself confronted with the grave problem of its duty. My message of last December reviewed the situation and narrated the steps taken with a view to relieving the acuteness and opening the way to some form of honorable settlement. The assassination of the prime minister, Canovas, led to a change of government in Spain. The former administration, pledged to subjugation without concession, gave place to that of a more liberal party, committed long in advance to a policy of reform involving the wider principle of home rule for Cuba and Puerto Rico.

The overtures of this government, made through its new envoy, General Woodford, and looking to an immediate and effective amelioration of the condition of the island, although not accepted to the extent of admitted mediation in any shape, were met by assurances that home rule, in an advanced phase, would be forthwith offered to Cuba, without waiting for the war to end, and that more humane methods should thenceforth prevail in the conduct of hostilities. Coincidentally with these declarations, the new government of Spain continued and completed the policy already begun by its predecessor, of testifying friendly regard for this nation by releasing American citizens held under one charge or another connected with the insurrection, so that, by the end of November, not a single person entitled in any way to our national protection remained in a Spanish prison.

While these negotiations were in progress the increasing destitution of the unfortunate reconcentrados and the alarming mortality among them claimed earnest attention. The success which had attended the limited measure of relief extended to the suffering American citizens among them by the judicious expenditure through the consular agencies of the money appropriated expressly for their succor by the joint resolution approved May 24, 1897, prompted the humane extension of a similar scheme of aid to the great body of sufferers. A suggestion to this end was acquiesced in by the Spanish authorities. On the 24th of December last, I caused to be issued an appeal to the American people, inviting contributions in money or in kind for the succor of the starving sufferers in Cuba, following this on the 8th of January by a similar public announcement of the formation of a central Cuban relief committee, with headquarters in New York City, composed of three members representing the American National Red Cross and the religious and business elements of the community.

The efforts of that committee have been untiring and have accomplished much. Arrangements for free transportation to Cuba have greatly aided the charitable work. The president of the American Red Cross and representatives of other contributory organizations have generously visited Cuba and cooperated with the consul-general and the local authorities to make effective distribution of the relief collected through the efforts of the central committee. Nearly $200,-000 in money and supplies has already reached the sufferers and more is forthcoming. The supplies are admitted duty free, and transportation to the interior has been arranged so that the relief, at first necessarily confined to Havana and the larger cities, is now extended through most if not all of the towns where suffering exists.

Thousands of lives have already been saved. The necessity for a change in the condition of the reconcentrados is recognized by the Spanish government. Within a few days past the orders of General Weyler have been revoked; the reconcentrados, it is said, are to be permitted to return to their homes and aided to resume the self-supporting pursuits of peace. Public works have been ordered to give them employment, and a sum of $600,000 has been appropriated for their relief.

The war in Cuba is of such a nature that short of subjugation or extermination a final military victory for either side seems impracticable. The alternative lies in the physical exhaustion of the one or the other party, or perhaps of both—a condition which in effect ended the ten years' war by the truce of Zanjon. The prospect of such a protraction and conclusion of the present strife is a contingency hardly to be contemplated with equanimity by the civilized world, and least of all by the United States, affected and injured as we are, deeply and intimately, by its very existence.

Realizing that, it appeared to be my duty, in a spirit of true friendliness, no less to Spain than to the Cubans, who have so much to lose by the prolongation of the struggle, to seek to bring about an immediate termination of the war. To this end I submitted, on the 27th ultimo, as a result of much representation and correspondence, through the United States minister at Madrid, propositions to the Spanish government looking to an armistice until October 1 for the negotiation of peace with the good offices of the President.

In addition, I asked the immediate revocation of the order of reconcentration, so as to permit the people to return to their farms and the needy to be relieved with provisions and supplies from the United States, cooperating with the Spanish authorities, so as to afford full relief.

The reply of the Spanish cabinet was received on the night of the 31st ultimo. It offered, as the means to bring about peace in Cuba, to confide the preparation thereof to the insular parliament, inasmuch as the concurrence of that body would be necessary to reach a final result, it being, however, understood that the powers reserved by the constitution of the central government are not lessened or diminished. As the Cuban parliament does not meet until the 4th of May next, the Spanish Government would not object, for its part, to accept at once a suspension of hostilities if asked for by the insurgents from the general in chief, to whom it would pertain, in such case, to determine the duration and conditions of the armistice.

The propositions submitted by General Woodford and the reply of the Spanish government were both in the form of brief memoranda, the texts of which are before me, and are substantially in the language above given. The function of the Cuban parliament in the matter of "preparing" peace and the manner of its doing so are not expressed in the Spanish memorandum; but from General Woodford's explanatory reports of preliminary discussions preceding the final conference it is understood that the Spanish government stands ready to give the insular congress full powers to settle the terms of peace with the insurgents—whether by direct negotiation or indirectly by means of legislation does not appear.

With this last overture in the direction of immediate peace, and its disappointing reception by Spain, the Executive is brought to the end of his effort.

In my annual message of December last I said:

Of the untried measures there remain only: Recognition of the insurgents as belligerents; recognition of the independence of Cuba; neutral intervention to end the war by imposing a rational compromise between the contestants, and intervention in favor of one or the other party. I speak not of forcible annexation, for that can not be thought of. That, by our code of morality, would be criminal aggression.

Thereupon I reviewed these alternatives, in the light of President Grant's measured words, uttered in 1875, when after seven years of sanguinary, destructive, and cruel hostilities in Cuba he reached the conclusion that the recognition of the independence of Cuba was impracticable and indefensible, and that the recognition of belligerence was not warranted by the facts according to the tests of public law. I commented especially upon the latter aspect of the question, pointing out the inconveniences and positive dangers of a recognition of belligerence which, while adding to the already onerous burdens of neutrality within our own jurisdiction, could not in any way extend our influence or effective offices in the territory of hostilities.

Nothing has since occurred to change my view in this regard; and I recognize as fully now as then that the issuance of a proclamation of neutrality, by which process the so-called recognition of belligerents is published, could, of itself and unattended by other action, accomplish nothing toward the one end for which we labor—the instant pacification of Cuba and the cessation of the misery that afflicts the island.

Turning to the question of recognizing at this time the independence of the present insurgent government in Cuba, we find safe precedents in our history from an early day. They are well summed up in President Jackson's message to Congress, December 21, 1836, on the subject of the recognition of the independence of Texas. He said:

In all the contests that have arisen out of the revolution of France, out of the disputes relating to the Crowns of Portugal and Spain, out of the separation of the American possessions of both from the European governments, and out of the numerous and constantly occurring struggles for dominion in Spanish America, so wisely consistent with our just principles has been the action of our Government, that we have, under the most critical circumstances, avoided all censure, and encountered no other evil than that produced by a transient estrangement of good will in those against whom we have been by force of evidence compelled to decide.

It has thus made known to the world that the uniform policy and practice of the United States is to avoid all interference in disputes which merely relate to the internal government of other nations, and eventually to recognize the authority of the prevailing party without reference to our particular interests and views or to the merits of the original controversy.

. . . But on this, as on every other trying occasion, safety is to be found in a rigid adherence to principle.

In the contest between Spain and the revolted colonies we stood aloof, and waited not only until the ability of the new states to protect themselves was fully established, but until the danger of their being again subjugated had entirely passed away. Then, and not until then, were they recognized.

Such was our course in regard to Mexico herself. . . . It is true that with regard to Texas the civil authority of Mexico has been expelled, its invading army defeated, the chief of the Republic himself captured, and all present power to control the newly organized government of Texas annihilated within its confines; but, on the other hand, there is, in appearance, at least, an immense disparity of physical force on the side of Texas. The Mexican Republic, under another executive, is rallying its forces under a new leader and menacing a fresh invasion to recover its lost dominion.

Upon the issue of this threatened invasion the independence of Texas may be considered as suspended; and were there nothing peculiar in the relative situation of the United States and Texas, our acknowledgment of its independence at such a crisis could scarcely be regarded as consistent with that prudent reserve with which we have hitherto held ourselves bound to treat all similar questions.

Thereupon Andrew Jackson proceeded to consider the risk that there might be imputed to the United States motives of selfish interest in view of the former claim on our part to the territory of Texas, and of the avowed purpose of the Texans in seeking recognition of independence as an incident to the incorporation of Texas into the Union, concluding thus:

Prudence, therefore, seems to dictate that we should still stand aloof and maintain our present attitude, if not until Mexico itself or one of the great foreign powers shall recognize the independence of the new government, at least until the lapse of time or the course of events shall have proved beyond cavil or dispute the ability of the people of that country to maintain their separate sovereignty and to uphold the government constituted by them. Neither of the contending parties can justly complain of this course. By pursuing it we are but carrying out the long-established policy of our Government, a policy which has secured to us respect and influence abroad and inspired confidence at home.

These are the words of the resolute and patriotic Jackson. They are evidence that the United States, in addition to the test imposed by public law as the condition of the recognition of independence by a neutral state (to wit, that the revolted state shall "constitute in fact a body politic, having a government in substance as well as in name, possessed of the elements of stability," and forming de facto, "if left to itself, a state among the nations, reasonably capable of discharging the duties of a state"), has imposed for its own governance in dealing with cases like these the further condition that recognition of independent statehood is not due to a revolted dependency until the danger of its being again subjugated by the parent state has entirely passed away.

This extreme test was, in fact, applied in the case of Texas. The Congress to whom President Jackson referred the question as one "probably leading to war," and therefore a proper subject for "a previous understanding with that body by whom war can alone be declared and by whom all the provisions for sustaining its perils must be furnished," left the matter of the recognition of Texas to the discretion of the Executive, providing merely for the sending of a diplomatic agent when the President should be satisfied that the Republic of Texas had become "an independent state." It was so recognized by President Van Buren, who commissioned a chargé d'affaires March 7, 1837, after Mexico had abandoned an attempt to reconquer the Texan territory, and when there was at the time no bona fide contest going on between the insurgent province and its former sovereign.

I said in my message of December last, "It is to be seriously considered whether the Cuban insurrection possesses beyond dispute the attributes of statehood which alone can demand the recognition of belligerency in its favor." The same requirement must certainly be no less seriously considered when the graver issue of recognizing independence is in question, for no less positive test can be applied to the greater act than to the lesser; while, on the other hand, the influences and consequences of the struggle upon the internal policy of the recognizing state, which form important factors when the recognition of belligerency is concerned, are secondary, if not rightly eliminable, factors when the real question is whether the community claiming recognition is or is not independent beyond peradventure.

Nor from the standpoint of expediency do I think it would be wise or prudent for this government to recognize at the present time the independence of the so-called Cuban republic. Such recognition is not necessary in order to enable the United States to intervene and pacify the island. To commit this country now to the recognition of any particular government in Cuba might subject us to embarrassing conditions of international obligation toward the organization so recognized. In case of intervention our conduct would be subject to the approval or disapproval of such government. We would be required to submit to its direction and to assume to it the mere relation of a friendly ally.

When it shall appear hereafter that there is within the island a government capable of performing the duties and discharging the functions of a separate nation, and having, as a matter of fact, the proper forms and attributes of nationality, such government can be promptly and readily recognized and the relations and interests of the United States with such nation adjusted.

There remain the alternative forms of intervention to end the war, either as an impartial neutral by imposing a rational compromise between the contestants, or as the active ally of the one party or the other.

As to the first, it is not to be forgotten that during the last few months the relation of the United States has virtually been one of friendly intervention in many ways, each not of itself conclusive, but all tending to the exertion of a potential influence toward an ultimate pacific result, just and honorable to all interests concerned. The spirit of all our acts hitherto has been an earnest, unselfish desire for peace and prosperity in Cuba, untarnished by differences between us and Spain, and unstained by the blood of American citizens.

The forcible intervention of the United States as a neutral to stop the war, according to the large dictates of humanity and following many historical precedents where neighboring states have interfered to check the hopeless sacrifices of life by internecine conflicts beyond their borders, is justifiable on rational grounds. It involves, however, hostile constraint upon both the parties to the contest as well to enforce a truce as to guide the eventual settlement.

The grounds for such intervention may be briefly summarized as follows:

First. In the cause of humanity and to put an end to the barbarities, bloodshed, starvation, and horrible miseries now existing there, and which the parties to the conflict are either unable or unwilling to stop or mitigate. It is no answer to say this is all in another country, belonging to another nation, and is therefore none of our business. It is specially our duty, for it is right at our door.

Second. We owe it to our citizens in Cuba to afford them that protection and indemnity for life and property which no government there can or will afford, and to that end to terminate the conditions that deprive them of legal protection.

Third. The right to intervene may be justified by the very serious injury to the commerce, trade, and business of our people, and by the wanton destruction of property and devastation of the island.

Fourth, and which is of the utmost importance. The present condition of affairs in Cuba is a constant menace to our peace, and entails upon this government an enormous expense. With such a conflict waged for years in an island so near us and with which our people have such trade and business relations; when the lives and liberty of our citizens are in constant danger and their property destroyed and themselves ruined; where our trading vessels are liable to seizure and are seized at our very door by war ships of a foreign nation, the expeditions of filibustering that we are powerless to prevent altogether, and the irritating questions and entanglements thus arising—all these and others that I need not mention, with the resulting strained relations, are a constant menace to our peace, and compel us to keep on a semiwar footing with a nation with which we are at peace.

These elements of danger and disorder already pointed out have been strikingly illustrated by a tragic event which has deeply and justly moved the American people. I have already transmitted to Congress the report of the naval court of inquiry on the destruction of the battle ship *Maine* in the harbor of Havana during the night of the 15th of February. The destruction of that noble vessel has filled the national heart with inexpressible horror. Two hundred and fifty-eight brave sailors and marines and two officers of our Navy, reposing in the fancied security of a friendly harbor, have been hurled to death, grief and want brought to their homes and sorrow to the nation.

The naval court of inquiry, which, it is needless to say, commands the unqualified confidence of the government, was unanimous in its conclusion that the destruction of the *Maine* was caused by an exterior explosion, that of a submarine mine. It did not assume to place the responsibility. That remains to be fixed.

In any event the destruction of the *Maine,* by whatever exterior cause, is a patent and impressive proof of a state of things in Cuba that is intolerable. That condition is thus shown to be such that the Spanish government can not assure safety and security to a vessel of the American Navy in the harbor of Havana on a mission of peace, and rightfully there.

Further referring in this connection to recent diplomatic correspondence, a dispatch from our minister to Spain, of the 26th ultimo, contained the statement that the Spanish minister for foreign affairs assured him positively that Spain will do all that the highest honor and justice require in the matter of the *Maine*. The reply above referred to of the 31st ultimo also contained an expression of the readiness of Spain to submit to an arbitration all the differences which can arise in this matter, which is subsequently explained by the note of the Spanish minister at Washington of the 10th instant, as follows:

As to the question of fact which springs from the diversity of views between the reports of the American and Spanish boards, Spain proposes that the facts be ascertained by an impartial investigation by experts, whose decision Spain accepts in advance.

To this I have made no reply.

President Grant, in 1875, after discussing the phases of the contest as it then appeared, and its hopeless and apparent indefinite prolongation, said:

In such event, I am of opinion that other nations will be compelled to assume the responsibility which devolves upon them, and to seriously consider the only remaining measures possible—mediation and intervention. Owing, perhaps, to the large expanse of water separating the island from the Peninsula, . . . the contending parties appear to have within themselves no depository of common confidence, to suggest wisdom when passion and excitement have their sway, and to assume the part of peacemaker.

In this view in the earlier days of the contest the good offices of the United States as a mediator were tendered in good faith, without any selfish purpose, in the interest of humanity and in sincere friendship for both parties, but were at the time declined by Spain, with the declaration, nevertheless, that at a future time they would be indispensable. No intimation has been received that in the opinion of Spain that time has been reached. And yet the strife continues with all its dread horrors and all its injuries to the interests of the United States and of other nations.

Each party seems quite capable of working great injury and damage to the other, as well as to all the relations and interests dependent on the existence of peace in the island; but they seem incapable of reaching any adjustment, and both have thus far failed of achieving any success whereby one party shall possess and control the island to the exclusion of the other. Under these circumstances, the agency of others, either by mediation or by intervention, seems to be the only alternative which must sooner or later be invoked for the termination of the strife.

In the last annual message of my immediate predecessor during the pending struggle, it was said:

When the inability of Spain to deal successfully with the insurrection has become manifest, and it is demonstrated that her sovereignty is extinct in Cuba for all purposes of its rightful existence, and when a hopeless struggle for its reestablishment has degenerated into a strife which means nothing more than the useless sacrifice of human life and the utter destruction of the very subject-matter of the conflict, a situation will be presented in which our obligations to the sovereignty of Spain will be superseded by higher obligations, which we can hardly hesitate to recognize and discharge.

In my annual message to Congress, December last, speaking to this question, I said:

The near future will demonstrate whether the indispensable condition of a righteous peace, just alike to the Cubans and to Spain, as well as equitable to all our interests so intimately involved in the welfare of Cuba, is likely to be attained. If not, the exigency of further and other action by the United States will remain to be taken. When that time comes that action will be determined in the line of indisputable right and duty. It will be faced, without misgiving or hesitancy, in the light of the obligation this government owes to itself, to the people who have confided to it the protection of their interests and honor, and to humanity.

Sure of the right, keeping free from all offense ourselves, actuated only by upright and patriotic considerations, moved neither by passion nor selfishness, the government will continue its watchful care over the rights and property of American citizens and will abate none of its efforts to bring about by peaceful agencies a peace which shall be honorable and enduring. If it shall hereafter appear to be a duty imposed by our obligations to ourselves, to civilization and humanity to intervene with force, it shall be without fault on our part and only because the necessity for such action will be so clear as to command the support and approval of the civilized world.

The long trial has proved that the object for which Spain has waged the war can not be attained. The fire of insurrection may flame or may smolder with varying seasons, but it has not been and it is plain that it can not be extinguished by present methods. The only hope of relief and repose from a condition which can no longer be endured is the enforced pacification of Cuba. In the name of humanity, in the name of civilization, in behalf of endangered American interests which give us the right and the duty to speak and to act, the war in Cuba must stop.

In view of these facts and of these considerations, I ask the Congress to authorize and empower the President to take measures to secure a full and final termination of hostilities between the Government of Spain and the people of Cuba, and to secure in the island the establishment of a stable government, capable of maintaining order and observing its international obligations, insuring peace and tranquillity and the security of its citizens as well as our own, and to use the military and naval forces of the United States as may be necessary for these purposes.

And in the interest of humanity and to aid in preserving the lives of the starving people of the island I recommend that the distribution of food and supplies be continued, and that an appropriation be made out of the public Treasury to supplement the charity of our citizens.

The issue is now with the Congress. It is a solemn responsibility. I have exhausted every effort to relieve the intolerable condition of affairs which is at our doors. Prepared to execute every obligation imposed upon me by the Constitution and the law, I await your action.

Yesterday, and since the preparation of the foregoing message, official information was received by me that the latest decree of the Queen Regent of Spain directs General Blanco, in order to prepare and facilitate peace, to proclaim a suspension of hostilities, the duration and details of which have not yet been communicated to me.

This fact with every other pertinent consideration will, I am sure, have your just and careful attention in the solemn deliberations upon which you are about to enter. If this measure attains a successful result, then our aspirations as a Christian, peace-loving people will be realized. If it fails, it will be only another justification for our contemplated action.

JOINT RESOLUTION of the United States Congress for Recognition of the Independence of Cuba, April 20, 1898
John Bassett Moore, *A Digest of International Law*, VI, 226

PUBLIC RESOLUTION

JOINT RESOLUTION for the recognition of the independence of the people of Cuba, demanding that the Government of Spain relinquish its authority and government in the island of Cuba, and to withdraw its land and naval forces from Cuba and Cuban waters, and directing the President of the United States to use the land and naval forces of the United States to carry these resolutions into effect.

WHEREAS the abhorrent conditions which have existed for more than three years in the Island of Cuba, so near our own borders, have shocked the moral sense of the people of the United States, have been a disgrace to Christian civilization, culminating, as they have, in the destruction of a United States battle ship, with two hundred and sixty-five of its officers and crew, while on a friendly visit in the harbor of Havana, and can not longer be endured, as has been set forth by the President of the United States in his message to Congress of April eleventh, eighteen hundred and ninety-eight, upon which the action of Congress was invited: Therefore,

Resolved by the Senate and House of Representatives of the United

States of America in Congress assembled, First. That the people of the Island of Cuba are, and of right ought to be, free and independent:

Second. That it is the duty of the United States to demand, and the Government of the United States does hereby demand, that the Government of Spain at once relinquish its authority and government in the Island of Cuba, and withdraw its land and naval forces from Cuba and Cuban waters.

Third. That the President of the United States be, and he hereby is, directed and empowered to use the entire land and naval forces of the United States, and to call into the actual service of the United States the militia of the several States, to such extent as may be necessary to carry these resolutions into effect.

Fourth. That the United States hereby disclaims any disposition or intention to exercise sovereignty, jurisdiction, or control over said Island, except for the pacification thereof, and asserts its determination, when that is accomplished, to leave the government and control of the Island to its people.

Approved, April 20, 1898

JOHN SHERMAN, Secretary of State, to W. L. Woodford, United States Minister to Spain, April 20, 1898
John Bassett Moore, *A Digest of International Law,* VI, 225

YOU HAVE BEEN furnished with the text of a joint resolution voted by the Congress of the United States on the 19th instant (approved today) in relation to the pacification of the island of Cuba. In obedience to that act, the President directs you to immediately communicate to the government of Spain said resolution, with the formal demand . . . [of] the government of the United States that the government of Spain at once relinquish its authority and government in the island of Cuba and withdraw its land and naval forces from Cuba and Cuban waters. In taking this step the United States hereby disclaims any disposition or intention to exercise sovereignty, jurisdiction, or control over said island except for the pacification thereof, and asserts its determination when that is accomplished to leave the government and control of the island to its people under such free and independent government as they may establish.

If by the hour of noon on Saturday next, the 23d day of April, instant, there be not communicated to this government by that of Spain a full and satisfactory response to this demand and resolution whereby the ends of peace in Cuba shall be assured, the President will proceed without further notice to use the power and authority enjoined and conferred upon him by the said joint resolution to such extent as may be necessary to carry the same into effect.

ANNUAL MESSAGE from President William McKinley to the United States Congress, December 5, 1898 (extract)

John Bassett Moore, *A Digest of International Law*, VI, 230

IN MY LAST annual message very full consideration was given to the question of the duty of the government of the United States toward Spain and the Cuban insurrection as being by far the most important problem with which we were then called upon to deal. The considerations then advanced, and the exposition of the views therein expressed, disclosed my sense of the extreme gravity of the situation. Setting aside, as logically unfounded or practically inadmissible, the recognition of the Cuban insurgents as belligerents, the recognition of the independence of Cuba, neutral intervention to end the war by imposing a rational compromise between the contestants, intervention in favor of one or the other party, and forcible annexation of the island, I concluded it was honestly due to our friendly relations with Spain that she should be given a reasonable chance to realize her expectations of reform to which she had become irrevocably committed. Within a few weeks previously she had announced comprehensive plans which it was confidently asserted would be efficacious to remedy the evils so deeply affecting our own country, so injurious to the true interests of the mother country as well as to those of Cuba, and so repugnant to the universal sentiment of humanity.

The ensuing month brought little sign of real progress toward the pacification of Cuba. The autonomous administrations set up in the capital and some of the principal cities appeared not to gain the favor of the inhabitants nor to be able to extend their influence to the large extent of territory held by the insurgents, while the military arm, obviously unable to cope with the still active rebellion, continued many of the most objectionable and offensive policies of the government that had preceded it. No tangible relief was afforded the vast numbers of unhappy reconcentrados despite the reiterated professions made in that regard and the amount appropriated by Spain to that end. The proffered expedient of zones of cultivation proved illusory; indeed no less practical nor more delusive promises of succor could well have been tendered to the exhausted and destitute people, stripped of all that made life and home dear and herded in a strange region among unsympathetic strangers hardly less necessitous than themselves.

By the end of December the mortality among them had frightfully increased. Conservative estimates from Spanish sources placed the deaths among these distressed people at over forty per cent from the time General Weyler's decree of reconcentration was enforced. With the acquiescence of the Spanish authorities a scheme was adopted for relief by charitable contributions raised in this country and distributed, under the direction of the consul-general and the several consuls, by noble and earnest individual effort through the organized agencies of the American Red Cross. Thousands of lives were thus saved, but many thousands more were inaccessible to such forms of aid.

The war continued on the old footing without comprehensive plan, developing only the same spasmodic encounters, barren of strategic result, that had marked the course of the earlier ten years' rebellion as well as the present insurrection from its start. No alternative save physical exhaustion of either combatant, and therewithal the practical ruin of the island, lay in sight, but how far distant no one could venture to conjecture.

At this juncture, on the 15th of February last, occurred the destruction of the battle ship *Maine* while rightfully lying in the harbor of Havana on a mission of international courtesy and good will— a catastrophe the suspicious nature and horror of which stirred the nation's heart profoundly. It is a striking evidence of the poise and sturdy good sense distinguishing our national character that this shocking blow, falling upon a generous people, already deeply touched by preceding events in Cuba, did not move them to an instant, desperate resolve to tolerate no longer the existence of a condition of danger and disorder at our doors that made possible such a deed, by whomsoever wrought. Yet the instinct of justice prevailed and the nation anxiously awaited the result of the searching investigation at once set on foot. The finding of the naval board of inquiry established that the origin of the explosion was external by a submarine mine, and only halted, through lack of positive testimony, to fix the responsibility of its authorship.

All these things carried conviction to the most thoughtful, even before the finding of the naval court, that a crisis in our relations with Spain and toward Cuba was at hand. So strong was this belief that it needed but a brief executive suggestion to the Congress to receive immediate answer to the duty of making instant provision for the possible and perhaps speedily probable emergency of war, and the remarkable, almost unique, spectacle was presented of a unanimous vote of both Houses, on the 9th of March, appropriating fifty million dollars "for the national defense and for each and every purpose connected therewith, to be expended at the discretion of the President." That this act of prevision came none too soon was disclosed when the application of the fund was undertaken. Our coasts were practically undefended. Our Navy needed large provision for increased ammunition and supplies, and even numbers to cope with any sudden attack from the navy of Spain, which comprised modern vessels of the highest type of continental perfection. Our Army also required enlargement of men and munitions. The details of the hurried preparation for the dreaded contingency is told in the reports of the Secretaries of War and of the Navy, and need not be repeated here. It is sufficient to say that the outbreak of war, when it did come, found our nation not unprepared to meet the conflict.

Nor was the apprehension of coming strife confined to our own country. It was felt by the continental powers, which, on April 6th, through their ambassadors and envoys, addressed to the Executive an expression of hope that humanity and moderation might mark the course of this government and people, and that further negotiations would lead to an agreement which, while securing the maintenance of peace, would afford all necessary guarantees for the reestablishment of order in Cuba. In responding to that representation, I said I shared the hope the envoys had expressed that peace might be preserved in a manner to terminate the chronic condition of disturbance in Cuba so injurious and menacing to our interests and tranquillity, as well as shocking to our sentiments of humanity; and, while appreciating the humanitarian and disinterested character of the communication they had made on behalf of the powers, I stated the confidence of this government, for its part, that equal appreciation would be shown for its own earnest and unselfish endeavors to fulfill a duty to humanity by ending a situation the indefinite prolongation of which had become insufferable.

Still animated by the hope of a peaceful solution and obeying the dictates of duty, no effort was relaxed to bring about a speedy ending of the Cuban struggle. Negotiations to this object continued activity with the government of Spain, looking to the immediate conclusion of a six months' armistice in Cuba, with a view to effect the recognition of her people's right to independence. Besides this, the instant revocation of the order of reconcentration was asked, so that the sufferers, returning to their homes and aided by united American and Spanish effort, might be put in a way to support themselves, and, by orderly resumption of the well-nigh destroyed productive energies of the island, contribute to the restoration of its tranquillity and well-being. Negotiations continued for some little time at Madrid, resulting in offers by the Spanish government which could not but be regarded as inadequate. It was proposed to confide the preparation of peace to the insular parliament, yet to be convened under the autonomous decrees of November, 1897, but without impairment in anywise of the constitutional powers of the Madrid government, which, to that end, would grant an armistice, if solicited by the insurgents, for such time as the general-in-chief might see fit to fix. How and with what scope of discretionary powers the insular parliament was expected to set about the "preparation" of peace did not appear. If it were to be by negotiation with the insurgents, the issue seemed to rest on the one side with a body chosen by a fraction of the electors in the districts under Spanish control, and on the other with the insurgent population holding the interior country, unrepresented in the so-called parliament, and defiant at the suggestion of suing for peace.

Grieved and disappointed at this barren outcome of my sincere endeavors to reach a practicable solution, I felt it my duty to remit the whole question to the Congress. In the message of April 11, 1898, I announced that with this last overture in the direction of immediate peace in Cuba, and its disappointing reception by Spain, the effort of the Executive was brought to an end. I again reviewed the alternative courses of action which had been proposed, concluding that the only one consonant with international policy and compatible with our firm-set historical traditions was intervention as a neutral to stop the war and check the hopeless sacrifice of life, even though that resort involved "hostile constraint upon both the parties to the contest, as well to enforce a truce as to guide the eventual settlement." The grounds justifying that step were, the interests of humanity; the duty to protect the life and property of our citizens in Cuba; the right to check injury to our commerce and people through the devastation of the island, and, most important, the need of removing at once and forever the constant menace and the burdens entailed upon our government by the uncertainties and perils of the situation caused by the unendurable disturbance in Cuba. I said:

The long trial has proved that the object for which Spain has waged the war can not be attained. The fire of insurrection may flame or may smolder with varying seasons, but it has not been, and it is plain that it can not be, extinguished by present methods. The only hope of relief and repose from a condition which can no longer be endured is the enforced pacification of

Cuba. In the name of humanity, in the name of civilization, in behalf of endangered American interests which give us the right and the duty to speak and to act, the war in Cuba must stop.

In view of all this, the Congress was asked to authorize and empower the President to take measures to secure a full and final termination of hostilities between Spain and the people of Cuba and to secure in the island the establishment of a stable government, capable of maintaining order and observing its international obligations, insuring peace and tranquillity, and the security of its citizens as well as our own, and for the accomplishment of those ends to use the military and naval forces of the United States as might be necessary; with added authority to continue generous relief to the starving people of Cuba.

The response of the Congress, after nine days of earnest deliberation, during which the almost unanimous sentiment of your body was developed on every point save as to the expediency of coupling the proposed action with a formal recognition of the Republic of Cuba as the true and lawful government of that island—a proposition which failed of adoption—the Congress, after conference, on the 19th of April, by a vote of 42 to 35 in the Senate and 311 to 6 in the House of Representatives, passed the memorable joint resolution declaring—

First. That the people of the island of Cuba are, and of right ought to be, free and independent.

Second. That it is the duty of the United States to demand, and the Government of the United States does hereby demand, that the Government of Spain at once relinquish its authority and government in the island of Cuba and withdraw its land and naval forces from Cuba and Cuban waters.

Third. That the President of the United States be, and he hereby is, directed and empowered to use the entire land and naval forces of the United States, and to call into the actual service of the United States the militia of the several States, to such extent as may be necessary to carry these resolutions into effect.

Fourth. That the United States hereby disclaims any disposition or intention to exercise sovereignty, jurisdiction, or control over said island except for the pacification thereof, and asserts its determination when that is accomplished to leave the government and control of the island to its people.

This resolution was approved by the Executive on the next day, April 20th. A copy was at once communicated to the Spanish minister at this capital, who forthwith announced that his continuance in Washington had thereby become impossible, and asked for his passports, which were given him. He thereupon withdrew from Washington, leaving the protection of Spanish interests in the United

States to the French ambassador and the Austro-Hungarian minister. Simultaneously with its communication to the Spanish minister here, General Woodford, the American minister at Madrid, was telegraphed confirmation of the text of the joint resolution and directed to communicate it to the Government of Spain with the formal demand that it at once relinquish its authority and government in the island of Cuba and withdraw its forces therefrom, coupling this demand with announcement of the intentions of this Government as to the future of the island, in conformity with the fourth clause of the resolution, and giving Spain until noon of April 23d to reply.

That demand, although, as above shown, officially made known to the Spanish envoy here, was not delivered at Madrid. After the instruction reached General Woodford on the morning of April 21st, but before he could present it, the Spanish minister of state notified him that upon the President's approval of the joint resolution the Madrid government, regarding the act as "equivalent to an evident declaration of war," had ordered its minister in Washington to withdraw, thereby breaking off diplomatic relations between the two countries and ceasing all official communication between their respective representatives. General Woodford thereupon demanded his passports and quitted Madrid the same day.

Spain having thus denied the demand of the United States and initiated that complete form of rupture of relations which attends a state of war, the Executive powers authorized by the resolution were at once used by me to meet the enlarged contingency of actual war between sovereign states. On April 22d I proclaimed a blockade of the north coast of Cuba, including ports on said coast between Cardenas and Bahia Honda and the port of Cienfuegos on the south coast of Cuba; and on the 23d I called for volunteers to execute the purpose of the resolution. By my message of April 25th the Congress was informed of the situation, and I recommended formal declaration of the existence of a state of war between the United States and Spain. The Congress accordingly voted on the same day the act approved April 25, 1898, declaring the existence of such war from and including the 21st day of April, and reenacted the provision of the resolution of April 20th, directing the President to use all the armed forces of the nation to carry that act into effect. Due notification of the existence of war as aforesaid was given April 25th by telegraph to all the governments with which the United States maintain relations, in order that their neutrality might be assured during the war. The various governments responded with proclamations of neutrality, each after its own methods. It is not among the least gratifying incidents of the struggle that the obligations of neutrality were impartially discharged by all, often under delicate and difficult circumstances.

In further fulfillment of international duty I issued, April 26, 1898, a proclamation announcing the treatment proposed to be accorded to vessels and their cargoes as to blockade, contraband, the exercise of the right of search, and the immunity of neutral flags and neutral goods under enemy's flag. A similar proclamation was made by the Spanish government. In the conduct of hostilities the rules of the Declaration of Paris, including abstention from resort to privateering have accordingly been observed by both belligerents, although neither was a party to that declaration.

ANNUAL MESSAGE from President William McKinley to the United States Congress, December 5, 1899 (extract)

John Bassett Moore, *A Digest of International Law*, VI, 471

THE WITHDRAWAL of the authority of Spain from the island of Cuba was affected by the 1st of January, so that the full reestablishment of peace found the relinquished territory held by us in trust for the inhabitants, maintaining, under the direction of the Executive, such government and control therein as should conserve public order, restore the productive conditions of peace so long disturbed by the instability and disorder which prevailed for the greater part of the preceding three decades, and build up that tranquil development of the domestic state whereby alone can be realized the high purpose, as proclaimed in the joint resolution adopted by the Congress on the 19th of April, 1898, by which the United States disclaimed any disposition or intention to exercise sovereignty, jurisdiction, or control over Cuba, except for the pacification thereof, and asserted its determination when that was accomplished to leave the government and control of the island to its people. The pledge contained in this resolution is of the highest honorable obligation and must be sacredly kept.

I believe that substantial progress has been made in this direction. All the administrative measures adopted in Cuba have aimed to fit it for a regenerated existence by enforcing the supremacy of law and justice; by placing wherever practicable the machinery of administration in the hands of the inhabitants; by instituting needed sanitary reforms; by spreading education; by fostering industry and trade; by inculcating public morality, and, in short, by taking every rational step to aid the Cuban people to attain to that plane of self-conscious respect and self-reliant unity which fits an enlightened community for self-government within its own sphere, while enabling it to fulfill all outward obligations.

This nation has assumed before the world a grave responsibility for the future good government of Cuba. We have accepted a trust the fulfillment of which calls for the sternest integrity of purpose and the exercise of the highest wisdom. The new Cuba yet to arise from the ashes of the past must needs be bound to us by ties of singular intimacy and strength if its enduring welfare is to be assured. Whether those ties shall be organic or conventional, the destinies of Cuba are in some rightful form and manner irrevocably linked with our own, but how and how far is for the future to determine in the ripeness of events. Whatever be the outcome, we must see to it that free Cuba be a reality, not a name, a perfect entity, not a hasty experiment bearing within itself the elements of failure. Our mission, to accomplish which we took up the wager of battle, is not to be fulfilled by turning adrift any loosely framed commonwealth to face the vicissitudes which too often attend weaker states whose natural wealth and abundant resources are offset by the incongruities of their political organization and the recurring occasions for internal rivalries to sap their strength and dissipate their energies.

ANNUAL MESSAGE from President Theodore Roosevelt to the United States Congress, December 3, 1901 (extract)
John Bassett Moore, *A Digest of International Law*, VI, 472

IN CUBA such progress has been made toward putting the independent government of the island upon a firm footing that before the present session of the Congress closes this will be an accomplished fact. Cuba will then start as her own mistress; and to the beautiful Queen of the Antilles, as she unfolds this new page of her destiny, we extend our heartiest greetings and good wishes. Elsewhere I have discussed the question of reciprocity. In the case of Cuba, however, there are weighty reasons of morality and of national interest why the policy should be held to have a peculiar application, and I most earnestly ask your attention to the wisdom, indeed to the vital need, of providing for a substantial reduction in the tariff duties on Cuban imports into the United States. Cuba has in her constitution affirmed what we desired, that she should stand, in international matters, in closer and more friendly relations with us than with any other power; and we are bound by every consideration of honor and expediency to pass commercial measures in the interest of her material well-being.

TREATY of Relations between the United States and Cuba, Signed at Habana, May 22, 1903

William M. Malloy, *Treaties, Conventions, International Acts,* I, 362. The treaty embodies the so-called "Platt Amendment"

WHEREAS the Congress of the United States of America, by an Act approved March 2, 1901, provided as follows:

Provided further, That in fulfillment of the declaration contained in the joint resolution approved April twentieth, eighteen hundred and ninety-eight, entitled, "For the recognition of the independence of the people of Cuba, demanding that the Government of Spain relinquish its authority and government in the island of Cuba, and to withdraw its land and naval forces from Cuba and Cuban waters, and directing the President of the United States to use the land and naval forces of the United States to carry these resolutions into effect," the President is hereby authorized to "leave the government and control of the island of Cuba to its people" so soon as a government shall have been established in said island under a constitution which, either as a part thereof or in an ordinance appended thereto, shall define the future relations of the United States with Cuba, substantially as follows:

I. That the government of Cuba shall never enter into any treaty or other compact with any foreign power or powers which will impair or tend to impair the independence of Cuba, nor in any manner authorize or permit any foreign power or powers to obtain by colonization or for military or naval purposes or otherwise, lodgment in or control over any portion of said island.

II. That said government shall not assume or contract any public debt, to pay the interest upon which, and to make reasonable sinking fund provision for the ultimate discharge of which, the ordinary revenues of the island, after defraying the current expenses of government shall be inadequate.

III. That the government of Cuba consents that the United States may exercise the right to intervene for the preservation of Cuban independence, the maintenance of a government adequate for the protection of life, property, and individual liberty, and for discharging the obligations with respect to Cuba imposed by the treaty of Paris on the United States, now to be assumed and undertaken by the government of Cuba.

IV. That all Acts of the United States in Cuba during its military occupancy thereof are ratified and validated, and all lawful rights acquired thereunder shall be maintained and protected.

V. That the government of Cuba will execute, and as far as necessary extend, the plans already devised or other plans to be mutually agreed upon, for the sanitation of the cities of the island, to the end that a recurrence of epidemic and infectious diseases may be prevented thereby assuring protection to the people and commerce of Cuba, as well as to the commerce of the southern ports of the United States and the people residing therein.

VI. That the Isle of Pines shall be omitted from the proposed constitutional boundaries of Cuba, the title thereto being left to future adjustment by treaty.

VII. That to enable the United States to maintain the independence of Cuba, and to protect the people thereof, as well as for its own defense, the government of Cuba will sell or lease to the United States lands necessary for coaling or naval stations at certain specified points to be agreed upon with the President of the United States.

VIII. That by way of further assurance the government of Cuba will embody the foregoing provisions in a permanent treaty with the United States.

WHEREAS the Constitutional Convention of Cuba, on June twelfth, 1901, adopted a Resolution adding to the Constitution of the Republic of Cuba which was adopted on the twenty-first of February 1901, an appendix in the words and letters of the eight enumerated articles of the above cited act of the Congress of the United States;

And WHEREAS, by the establishment of the independent and sovereign government of the Republic of Cuba, under the constitution promulgated on the 20th of May, 1902, which embraced the foregoing conditions, and by the withdrawal of the Government of the United States as an intervening power, on the same date, it becomes necessary to embody the above cited provisions in a permanent treaty between the United States of America and the Republic of Cuba;

The United States of America and the Republic of Cuba, being desirous to carry out the foregoing conditions, have for that purpose appointed as their plenipotentiaries to conclude a treaty to that end,

The President of the United States of America, Herbert G. Squiers, Envoy Extraordinary and Minister Plenipotentiary at Havana,

And the President of the Republic of Cuba, Carlos de Zaldo y Beurmann, Secretary of State and Justice,—who after communicating to each other their full powers found in good and due form, have agreed upon the following articles:

ARTICLE I

The Government of Cuba shall never enter into any treaty or other compact with any foreign power or powers which will impair or tend to impair the independence of Cuba, nor in any manner authorize or permit any foreign power or powers to obtain by colonization or for military or naval purposes, or otherwise, lodgment in or control over any portion of said island.

ARTICLE II

The Government of Cuba shall not assume or contract any public debt to pay the interest upon which, and to make reasonable sinking-fund provision for the ultimate discharge of which, the ordinary revenues of the Island of Cuba, after defraying the current expenses of the Government, shall be inadequate.

ARTICLE III

The Government of Cuba consents that the United States may exercise the right to intervene for the preservation of Cuban independence, the maintenance of a government adequate for the protection of life, property, and individual liberty, and for discharging the obligations with respect to Cuba imposed by the Treaty of Paris on the United States, now to be assumed and undertaken by the Government of Cuba.

ARTICLE IV

All acts of the United States in Cuba during its military occupancy thereof are ratified and validated, and all lawful rights acquired thereunder shall be maintained and protected.

ARTICLE V

The Government of Cuba will execute, and, as far as necessary, extend the plans already devised, or other plans to be mutually agreed upon, for the sanitation of the cities of the island, to the end that a recurrence of epidemic and infectious diseases may be prevented, thereby assuring protection to the people and commerce of Cuba, as well as to the commerce of the Southern ports of the United States and the people residing therein.

ARTICLE VI

The Island of Pines shall be omitted from the boundaries of Cuba specified in the Constitution, the title thereto being left to future adjustment by treaty.

ARTICLE VII

To enable the United States to maintain the independence of Cuba, and to protect the people thereof, as well as for its own defense, the Government of Cuba will sell or lease to the United States lands necessary for coaling or naval stations, at certain specified points, to be agreed upon with the President of the United States.

ARTICLE VIII

The present Convention shall be ratified by each party in conformity with the respective Constitutions of the two countries, and the ratifications shall be exchanged in the City of Washington within eight months from this date.

In witness whereof, we the respective Plenipotentiaries, have signed the same in duplicate, in English and Spanish, and have affixed our respective seals at Havana, Cuba, this twenty-second day of May, in the year nineteen hundred and three.

H. G. SQUIERS [*seal*]

CARLOS DE ZALDO [*seal*]

ANNUAL MESSAGE from President Theodore Roosevelt to the United States Congress, December 3, 1906 (extract)
Foreign Relations of the United States, 1906, I, vii, xliv

. . . LAST AUGUST an insurrection broke out in Cuba which it speedily grew evident that the existing Cuban Government was powerless to quell. This Government was repeatedly asked by the then Cuban Government to intervene, and finally was notified by the President of Cuba that he intended to resign; that his decision was irrevocable; that none of the other constitutional officers would consent to carry on the Government, and that he was powerless to maintain order. It was evident that chaos was impending, and there was every probability that if steps were not immediately taken by this Government to try to restore order, the representatives of various European nations in the island would apply to their respective governments for armed intervention in order to protect the lives and property of their citizens. Thanks to the preparedness of our Navy, I was able immediately of War and the Assistant Secretary of State, in order that they becoming hopeless; and I furthermore dispatched to Cuba the Secretary to send enough ships to Cuba to prevent the situation from might grapple with the situation on the ground. All efforts to secure an agreement between the contending factions, by which they should themselves come to an amicable understanding and settle upon some modus vivendi—some provisional government of their own—failed. Finally the President of the Republic resigned. The quorum of Congress assembled failed by deliberate purpose of its members, so that there was no power to act on his resignation, and the Government came to a halt. In accordance with the so-called Platt amendment, which was embodied in the constitution of Cuba, I thereupon proclaimed a provisional government for the island, the Secretary of War acting as provisional governor until he could be replaced by Mr. Magoon, the late minister to Panama and governor of the Canal Zone on the Isthmus; troops were sent to support them and to relieve the Navy, the expedition being handled with most satisfactory speed and efficiency. The insurgent chiefs immediately agreed that their troops should lay down their arms and disband; and the agreement was carried out. The provisional government has left the personnel of the old government and the old laws, so far as might be, unchanged, and will thus administer the island for a few months until tranquillity can be restored, a new election properly held, and a new government inaugurated. Peace has come in the island; and the harvesting of the sugar-cane crop, the great crop of the Island, is about to proceed.

When the election has been held and the new government inaugurated in peaceful and orderly fashion the provisional government will come to an end. I take this opportunity of expressing upon behalf of the American people, with all possible solemnity, our most earnest hope that the people of Cuba will realize the imperative need of preserving justice and keeping order in the Island. The United States wishes nothing of Cuba except that it shall prosper morally and materially, and wishes nothing of the Cubans save that they shall be able to preserve order among themselves and therefore to preserve their independence. If the elections become a farce, and if the insurrectionary habit becomes confirmed in the Island, it is absolutely out of the question that the Island should continue independent; and the United States, which has assumed the sponsorship before the civilized world for Cuba's career as a nation, would again have to intervene and to see that the government was managed in such orderly fashion as to secure the safety of life and property. The path to be trodden by those who exercise self-government is always hard, and we should have every charity and patience with the Cubans as they tread this difficult path. I have the utmost sympathy with, and regard for, them; but I most earnestly adjure them solemnly to weigh their responsibilities and to see that when their new government is started it shall run smoothly, and with freedom from flagrant denial of right on the one hand, and from insurrectionary disturbances on the other. . . .

TREATY of Relations between the United States and Cuba, Signed at Washington, May 29, 1934

Department of State, Treaty Series, No. 866. The treaty was ratified by the President of the United States, June 5, 1934

THE UNITED STATES of America and the Republic of Cuba, being animated by the desire to fortify the relations of friendship between the two countries and to modify, with this purpose, the relations established between them by the Treaty of Relations signed at Habana, May 22, 1903, have appointed, with this intention, as their Plenipotentiaries:

[*Names of Plenipotentiaries*]

Who, after having communicated to each other their full powers which were found to be in good and due form, have agreed upon the following articles:

ARTICLE I

The Treaty of Relations which was concluded between the two contracting parties on May 22, 1903, shall cease to be in force, and is abrogated, from the date on which the present Treaty goes into effect.

ARTICLE II

All the acts effected in Cuba by the United States of America during its military occupation of the island, up to May 20, 1902, the date on which the Republic of Cuba was established, have been ratified and held as valid; and all the rights legally acquired by virtue of those acts shall be maintained and protected.

ARTICLE III

Until the two contracting parties agree to the modification or abrogation of the stipulations of the agreement in regard to the lease to the United States of America of lands in Cuba for coaling and naval stations signed by the President of the Republic of Cuba on February 16, 1903, and by the President of the United States of America on the 23d day of the same month and year, the stipulations of that agreement with regard to the naval station of Guantánamo shall continue in effect. The supplementary agreement in regard to naval or coaling stations signed between the two Governments on July 2, 1903, also shall continue in effect in the same form and on the same conditions with respect to the naval station at Guantánamo. So long as the United States of America shall not abandon the said naval station of Guantánamo or the two Governments shall not agree to a modification of its present limits, the station shall continue to have the territorial area that it now has, with the limits that it has on the date of the signature of the present Treaty.

ARTICLE IV

If at any time in the future a situation should arise that appears to point to an outbreak of contagious disease in the territory of either of the contracting parties, either of the two Governments shall, for its own protection, and without its act being considered unfriendly, exercise freely and at its discretion the right to suspend communications between those of its ports that it may designate and all or part of the territory of the other party, and for the period that it may consider to be advisable.

ARTICLE V

The present Treaty shall be ratified by the contracting parties in accordance with their respective constitutional methods; and shall go into effect on the date of the exchange of their ratifications, which shall take place in the city of Washington as soon as possible.

In faith whereof, the respective Plenipotentiaries have signed the present Treaty and have affixed their seals hereto.

Done in duplicate, in the English and Spanish languages, at Washington on the twenty-ninth day of May, one thousand nine hundred and thirty-four.

[SEAL]	CORDELL HULL
[SEAL]	SUMNER WELLES
[SEAL]	M. MÁRQUEZ STERLING

IV

The Panama Canal Concession

The Panama Canal Concession

INSTRUCTIONS from Henry Clay, Secretary of State, to the United States Delegates to the Congress of Panama, May 18, 1826 (extract)

International American Conference, IV, 113, 143. See also *supra*, p. 32. For various treaties relating to the concession, see *Appendix* C, *infra*, p. 879; and for documents on United States policy regarding Central America, *infra*, pp. 607 ff. and 916 ff.

. . . A CUT OR CANAL for purposes of navigation somewhere through the isthmus that connects the two Americas, to unite the Pacific and Atlantic Oceans, will form a proper subject of consideration at the congress. That vast object, if it should be ever accomplished, will be interesting, in a greater or less degree, to all parts of the world. But to this continent will probably accrue the largest amount of benefit from its execution; and to Colombia, Mexico, the Central Republic, Peru, and the United States, more than to any other of the American nations. What is to redound to the advantage of all America should be effected by common means and united exertions, and should not be left to the separate and unassisted efforts of any one power.

In the present limited state of our information as to the practicability and the probable expense of the object, it would not be wise to do more than to make some preliminary arrangements. The best routes will be most likely found in the territory of Mexico or that of the Central Republic. The latter Republic made to this Government, on the 8th day of February of last year, in a note to which Mr. Canaz, its minister here, addressed to this Department (a copy of which is now furnished), a liberal offer, manifesting high and honorable confidence in the United States. The answer which the President instructed me to give (of which a copy is also now placed in your hands) could go no farther than to make suitable acknowledgments for the friendly overture and to assure the Central Republic that measures would be adopted to place the United States in the possession of the information necessary to enlighten their judgment. If the work should ever be executed so as to admit of the passage of sea vessels from ocean to ocean, the benefits of it ought not to be exclusively appropriated to any one nation, but should be extended to all parts of the globe upon the payment of a just compensation or reasonable tolls. What is most desirable at present is to possess the data necessary to form a correct judgment of the practicability and the probable expense of the undertaking on the routes which offer the greatest facilities.

Measures may have been already executed or be in progress to acquire the requisite knowledge. You will inquire particularly as to what has been done or may have been designed by Spain or by either of the new States, and obtain all other information that may be within your reach, to solve this interesting problem. You will state to the ministers of the other American powers that the Government of the United States takes a lively interest in the execution of the work, and will see, with peculiar satisfaction, that it lies within the compass of reasonable human efforts. Their proximity and local information render them more competent than the United States are at this time to estimate the difficulties to be overcome. You will receive and transmit to this Government any proposals that may be made or plans that may be suggested for its joint execution, with assurances that they will be attentively examined, with an earnest desire to reconcile the interests and views of all the American nations.

DANIEL WEBSTER, Secretary of State, to William Radcliff, Designated Special Agent of the State of the Isthmus to the United States, January 28, 1842

William R. Manning, *Diplomatic Correspondence of the United States, Inter-American Affairs, 1831–1860*, V, 352

SIR:

Your interesting communication of the 31st of December, last, setting forth the causes which have led the States of Panama and Veragua to declare their independence of the Republic of New Granada and to form for themselves a separate government under the title 'of the State of the Isthmus,' was laid before the President, who has directed me to acquaint you in reply, that it has been read with the respectful consideration due to the source from which it emanated and with a just sensibility in regard to the invitation which it offers. But although the President does not doubt that the facts mentioned in it are substantially correct, the shortness of the time which has elapsed since the declaration of independence referred to was made, the duty of this government to avoid doing any thing which might give just cause of offence to the Republic of New Granada, with which it has hitherto maintained pacific and friendly relations, and that wise yet generous caution which have heretofore marked its steps in similar cases, all admonish that there is no occasion in this instance to deviate from the usual course by acknowledging the State of the Isthmus upon information less authentic and satisfactory than in other cases. Measures will consequently be taken without delay to inquire as to the ability of the States of Panama and Veragua to maintain their independence under their new form of government and to assume the obligations and discharge the duties of an independent power. If the result of such inquiry should be favorable, the application which has been made through you will, it is presumed, be disposed of accordingly. The document which accompanied your note is now returned, a copy of it having been taken.

I have the honor [etc.]

FLETCHER WEBSTER, Acting Secretary of State, to William M. Blackford, United States Chargé d'Affaires at Bogotá, May 20, 1842 (extracts)

William R. Manning, *Diplomatic Correspondence of the United States, Inter-American Affairs,* V, 353

SIR:

You have received your commission as Chargé d'Affaires of the United States to the Republic of New Granada. I now transmit the following papers which will be useful or necessary in the transaction of the business of your mission. . . .

6. A copy of the principal letters of instruction which have from time to time been addressed by this department to your predecessor.

His dispatches to the department and his correspondence with the Minister for Foreign Affairs of that Republic with which the records and files of the Legation will, it is presumed, enable you to acquaint Yourself, will show the pending business of the mission. This may be described in general terms as of a three-fold character: 1. The commercial relations between the two countries. 2. The unadjusted claims of our citizens upon the late Republic of Colombia. 3. Similar claims upon the Government of New Granada.

The anarchy and civil war which had until very recently prevailed for some time in that country, interrupted Mr. Semple's negotiations upon these subjects. There is reason to believe, however, that order and quiet are restored there and it is hoped that they may be permanent enough to allow you to attend continuously to the affairs which have now devolved upon you, and to prosecute them to a successful result. Still, it is apprehended that an auspicious period for negotiating upon the subject of our commerce with that country may not present itself at least immediately upon your arrival at Bogotá. The full power, therefore, with which you are provided, it is intended you shall use only when a favorable conjuncture for that purpose may arise, and when the Department shall be in possession of sufficient information to form an opinion as to the terms which it may be expedient to offer that government. Consequently, you will communicate the best intelligence which may be within your reach respecting the disposition of the Government of New Granada on this point, and any facts which may tend to show the propriety of modifying the terms which your predecessors were authorized to offer. Such further instructions as may then be thought necessary will be transmitted to you.

The projects for facilitating the communication between the Atlantic and Pacific oceans by means of a canal or railroad across the Isthmus of Panama, are connected with this topic. The states of Panama and Veragua, which comprise that Isthmus, were for some time separated from the other States of New Granada, and in the course of last year applied to this Government to be acknowledged as an independent power with the title of the State of the Isthmus. The application, though not granted, was respectfully received and considered, and a special agent on the part of this government was about to proceed to that quarter for the purpose of inquiring into the ability of the people of the Isthmus to maintain their independence, when intelligence arrived that Panama and Veragua had reunited themselves to New Granada. A treaty of commerce with this Republic, placing our citizens on a footing of equality with other foreigners within its confines, might serve to prevent a grant by the New Granadian Government to any other foreign government, company or individuals of a special privilege in regard to the communication above referred to or, if such privilege should be accorded, might give us a right to claim the same, or indemnification if it should be refused. It is of great importance to the United States that the railroad or canal referred to should be constructed, and that we should have the free use of it upon the same terms as the citizens or subjects of other commercial nations. You will consequently be diligent in your inquiries in relation to this matter. . . .

I am, Sir [etc.]

JAMES BUCHANAN, Secretary of State, to Benjamin A. Bidlack, United States Chargé d'Affaires at Bogotá, June 23, 1845 (extracts)

William R. Manning, *Diplomatic Correspondence of the United States, Inter-American Affairs*, V, 357

SIR:

The claims of citizens of the United States on the late Republic of Colombia and on the Republic of New Granada, constitute the principal pending business of the mission to which you are appointed. . . .

The United States have strong motives for viewing with interest any project which may be designed to facilitate the intercourse between the Atlantic and Pacific oceans. Within a few years past the scheme of a railroad or a canal across the Isthmus of Panama, has been much agitated and it is understood that surveys have been made for the purpose of testing its practicability, but we are not aware that they have been authorized or countenanced by any foreign government. As it is important to us that no other nation should obtain either an exclusive privilege or an advantage in regard to such a communication between the two oceans, you will lose no time in transmitting to the department any information upon the subject which you may be able to collect. You will also use your influence, should this become necessary, with the government of New Granada, to prevent it from granting privileges to any other nation which might prove injurious to the United States.

Mr. Acosta addressed several communications to Mr. Blackford for the purpose of exposing the encroachments of the British authorities upon that part of the territory of New Granada commonly called the Mosquito Shore. The communications contained no application from that government to the United States, but you may avail yourself of a proper opportunity to assure its Minister for Foreign Affairs, orally, that the information was highly interesting to this government, which can never be indifferent to any thing that concerns the interest and prosperity of New Granada.

I am, Sir, [etc.]

BENJAMIN A. BIDLACK, United States Chargé d'Affaires at Bogotá, to James Buchanan, Secretary of State, December 14, 1846 (extract)

William R. Manning, *Diplomatic Correspondence of the United States, Inter-American Affairs*, V, 634

. . . IT WILL BE REMEMBERED that in my dispatches in the early part of September last, I intimated my hopes of being able to make a Treaty, and that I solicited powers and instructions.—

As the Senate of the United States adjourns on the 4th March next, and as it was advisable that, whatever Project should be agreed upon should be presented at its present session, in case the President should deem it of sufficient importance. The Granadian government under these circumstances proposed to consider me as having full powers and, as will be seen has negociated with me accordingly, and I now, send you the result. It would be useless to speak of the terms of this Treaty, you will have it before you and it must explain itself.—

I will only say that so far as it relates to commerce and navigation it conceeds to the United States the *abolition of all differential* duties concession which has heretofore been urged in vain for the last 20 years, and in all other respects it is as liberal as any Treaty we have with any other nation. You will observe that the 14th Article in relation to the right of worship & the liberty of conscience, grants the most entire freedom, and that it is much, more tollerant than the Treaty with Colombia in that respect.—

With regard to the right, of transit, & free passage over the Isthmus, (which appeard to me to be becoming of more and *more importance every day*), I have only to remark that I have procured the "largest liberty" and *the very best terms, that could be obtained.*

I could not obtain these terms, without consenting to guarantee the integrity and neutrality of the Teritory, and in fact, it seemed to me upon reflection, that in order to preserve the rights & priveleges thus ceeded it would be both, the policy, the interest and the duty of the United States thus to enter into an obligation to protect them.— The guarantee extends *only to the Isthmus,* and anything like a general alliance is carefully avoided—with these hasty observations, I refer you to the "Exposition of motives," presented by Mr. Mallarino, the Secretary of State in answer to my objection to including, this question in the commercial Treaty. . . .

CHARLES M. CONRAD, Acting Secretary of State, to Victoriano de Diego Paredes, Colombian Chargé d'Affaires at Washington, October 5, 1852

William R. Manning, *Diplomatic Correspondence of the United States, Inter-American Affairs,* V, 366

THE UNDERSIGNED, Acting Secretary of State of the United States, has the honor to acknowledge the receipt of the note addressed to this Department on the 20th. June last by Mr. Paredes, Chargé d'Affaires of the Republic of New Grenada [Granada], and to express his regret that it should have remained so long unanswered. The Undersigned begs leave to assure Mr. Paredes that this delay has not arisen from any indifference to the subject to which his note refers, but is solely attributable to the numerous calls upon this Department and to the indisposition and subsequent absence of its permanent Head.

Mr. Paredes informs this government that he "has just received definite instructions from his government, directing him to address himself to the Honorable Secretary of State of the United States informing His Excellency that, inasmuch as there is cause for the fears which are entertained that the expedition of Ex-General Juan José Flores against Ecuador is a continuation of that which he undertook in 1846, and that said expedition is countenanced not only by the Government of Peru, but by that of Spain, and may be by other European Governments, that it would be of great importance to the present and future welfare of New Granada, and the rest of the American Republics, for the Government of the United States to make a demonstration condemnatory of said expedition, and of the plans more or less disguised or concealed of which it may be the precursor or the first instrument, besides adopting all such other measures which its wisdom and foresight may suggest, in order to frustrate the views of the traitor and of his instigators," &c. &c. &c.

The President directs the Undersigned to say in reply to Mr. Paredes that, he has not been an unconcerned spectator of the events to which his letter refers. On the contrary he has seen with regret the peace of Ecuador disturbed and her territory invaded by a private individual who appears to be acting under no national flag or recognised authority. That he would be slow to believe, however, that any enlightened Government would countenance an enterprize at war with those principles of national law which all civilized nations are bound to respect, because they are essential to the peace and security of all—and therefore ventures to express the hope that Mr. Paredes is mistaken when he supposes that this lawless enterprise was countenanced by Peru, and by Spain and other European nations.

But, at all events, the circumstances detailed in the communication of Mr. Paredes are not such as call for the interposition of this Government. The principle by which its policy has always been guided is that of non-interference in the disputes of foreign nations; and it cannot, consistently with this principle, interfere to defeat or counteract the secret plots and intrigues of one foreign Government against another. In the present case particularly it would hardly be warranted in assuming, even as the ground of a friendly remonstrance, that either of the governments alluded to had sanctioned a proceeding in violation of the laws and usages of nations.

The President, however, directs the Undersigned to assure Mr. Paredes that this government has always endeavored to prevent its own citizens from engaging in any unlawful enterprize against the peace of other nations, and that it will do all that it can do consistently with its well-established policy to discountenance such conduct in the citizens or subjects of other governments.

The Undersigned avails himself of this occasion [etc.]

GENERAL REYES, Colombian Special Minister to the United States, to John Hay, Secretary of State of the United States, December 23, 1903
John Bassett Moore, *A Digest of International Law*, III, 78

THE GOVERNMENT and people of Colombia consider themselves aggrieved by that of the United States in that they are convinced that the course followed by its administration, in relation to the events that have developed and recently been accomplished at Panama, have worked deep injury to their interests.

If the matter were one of little importance, even though right were wholly on its side, my Government would not hesitate in yielding some of its advantages out of regard for the friendly relations which have happily existed without interruption between the two countries. But as the facts that have taken place affect not only valuable and valued interests, but also the independence and sovereignty of Colombia, my Government deems it its duty to remind that of the United States of the stipulation contained in section 5 of article 35 of the treaty of 1846, in force between the two countries, which reads word for word as follows:

If, unfortunately, any of the articles contained in this treaty should be violated or infringed in any way whatever, it is expressly stipulated that neither of the two contracting parties shall ordain or authorize any acts of reprisal, nor shall declare war against the other in complaints of injuries or damages, until the said party considering itself offended shall have laid before the other a statement of such injuries or damages, verified by competent proofs, demanding justice and satisfaction, and the same shall have been denied, in violation of the laws and of international right.

On formulating the statement of "injuries and damages," referred to in the quoted abstract, there is nothing as natural or just as to recall to mind that in the treaty concluded on the 22d of January of this year between your excellency and the chargé d'affaires of Colombia, Señor Doctor Tomás Herran, there appears the following stipulation:

The convention when signed by the contracting parties shall be ratified in conformity with the laws of the respective countries, etc.

This condition, which rests at once on a correct conception of the doctrine accepted in such matters by nearly all the constitutional countries in the world, could not be foregone by Mr. Herran, since under our constitution and laws it is for the Congress to approve or disapprove the treaties signed by the Government, so that the said treaties are not valid unless the requirement has been observed, and as it likewise happens that under the law of nations covenants entered into with any authority that may not be competent are null, it is evident that no Colombian representative in the absence of a pre-existing law conferring such authority could have signed the said convention without the above-quoted reservation. Furthermore, this formality was at the outset admitted by the American Government in the course of the negotiations that preceded the Hay-Herran convention, as shown in articles 25, 26, and 28 of the "Draft of convention" submitted by the American Administration and dated November 28, 1902. Article 25 says, textually, that the convention will be exchanged "after approval by the legislative bodies of both countries."

The Hay-Herran convention did not take in Washington a course different from that it took at Bogotá. The parliamentary debate that took place in the Senate was so full and earnest that it was not approved until the following extraordinary sessions. And if it had been rejected the disapproval would have involved no grievance for Colombia, for if the mere entering upon negotiations for a convention implied the obligatory approval of the legislative body it would be superfluous to submit it to its decision. Among the precedents of international usage that could be mentioned in this respect there may be cited the case that occurred between the same United States of America and Her Britannic Majesty, when, after the signing of the treaty intended to abrogate the convention known as the Clayton-Bulwer treaty, England, as I understand it, declined to accept the amendment introduced by the Senate, and her refusal delayed for some time the approval and ratification of the treaty.

It follows that the Congress of Colombia, which is vested, according to our laws, with the faculty or power to approve or disapprove the treaties concluded by the Government, exercised a perfect right when it disapproved the Hay-Herran convention. This course did not disqualify the Government for the conclusion of another treaty with the Government of your excellency; and it indeed resolved to make a proposition to that effect, and Mr. Herran, whom our minister for foreign affairs intrusted with that duty by cable, had the honor of bringing this purpose to your excellency's knowledge. Neither did that course imply any slight toward the Government of the United States, and, on the contrary, the Senate, observant of the existing friendly relations, relied on the sentiments of American fraternity, by which it is animated, for the introduction in the new agreement that was to be made of stipulations more consonant with the notion of sovereignty entertained by the people of Colombia.

It is proper to observe that under our constitution the Congress is the principal guardian, defender, and interpreter of our laws. And it can not be denied by any one, I take it, that the Hay-Herran convention provides for the execution of public works on a vast scale and for the occupancy in perpetuity of a portion of the territory of Colombia, the occupant being not a juridical person whose acts were to be governed by the civil law and the Colombian code, but rather a sovereign political entity, all of which would have given occasion for frequent conflicts, since there would have been a coexistence in Panama of two public powers, the one national, the other foreign.

Hence the earnest efforts evinced by the Senate in ascertaining whether the American Government would agree to accept certain amendments tending especially to avoid as far as practicable any restriction in the treaty of the jurisdiction of the nation within its own territory. There is abundant evidence of the efforts of the Senate in that direction, and I firmly believe that it would have approved the convention with amendments that would probably have been acceptable to the United States had not the American minister at Bogotá repeatedly declared in the most positive manner that his Government would reject any amendment that might be offered.

In a note dated April 24 last he made the following statement to the minister of foreign relations:

With reference to the interview I had with your excellency at which were discussed the negotiations for the annulment of the present concessions of the Panama Canal and railroad companies and other matters I have the honor to inform your excellency that I have received instructions from my Government in that respect.

I am directed to inform your excellency, if the point should be raised, that everything relative to this matter is included in the convention recently signed between Colombia and the United States on 22d of January last, and that, furthermore, any modification would be violative of the Spooner Act, and therefore inadmissible.

The memorandum handed by the same minister to the minister of foreign relations on the 13th of June of this year reads as follows:

I have received instructions from my Government by cable in the sense that the Government of Colombia to all appearances does not appreciate the gravity of the situation. The Panama Canal negotiations were initiated by Colombia and were earnestly solicited of my Government for several years. The propositions presented by Colombia with slight alterations were finally accepted by us. By virtue of this agreement our Congress reconsidered its previous decision and decided in favor of the Panama route. If Colombia now rejects the treaty or unduly delays its ratification the friendly relations between the two countries would be so seriously compromised that our Congress might next winter take steps that every friend of Colombia would regret with sorrow.

In his note of the 5th of August of this year he says this, among other things:

It seems to me that the commission (referring to the Senate commission) has not been sufficiently informed of the contents of my notes of April 24 and June 10, [sic] 1903, or that it has not given them the importance they merit, as being the final expression of the opinion or intentions of my Government. They clearly show that the amendment the commission proposes to introduce in article 1 is, by itself, equivalent to an absolute rejection of the treaty. I deem it my duty to repeat the opinion I already expressed to your excellency that my Government will not consider or discuss such an amendment in any way. There is another important amendment that the commission believes should be introduced in article 3, consisting in the suppression of the tribunals therein dealt with. I consider it my duty again to state my opinion that this will also in no wise be accepted by my Government.

And further, in the same note, he adds:

I avail myself of this opportunity respectfully to repeat that which I already stated to your excellency, that if Colombia truly desires to maintain the friendly relations that at present exist between two countries, and at the same time secure for herself the extraordinary advantages that are to be produced for her by the construction of the canal in her territory, in case of its being backed by so intimate an alliance of national interests as that which would supervene with the United States, the present treaty will have to be ratified exactly in its present form without amendment whatsoever. I say this because I am profoundly convinced that my Government will not in any case accept amendments.

The Congress being unable to accept in its actual wording at least one of the stipulations contained in the treaty, because inhibited from doing so by the constitution, no one will wonder that under the pressure of threats so serious and irritating and in presence of a formal notification from the party which had authority to serve it that no amendment would be accepted, preference was given to disapproval.

The integrity of any nation [said Mr. William H. Seward] is lost, and its fate becomes doubtful, whenever strange hands, and instruments unknown to the constitution, are employed to perform the proper functions of the people, established by the organic law of the state.

Before dismissing this point, it is proper to observe, in accordance with article 4 of the Spooner Act:

SEC. 4. That should the President be unable to obtain for the United States a satisfactory title to the property of the New Panama Canal Company and the control of the necessary territory of the Republic of Colombia and the rights mentioned in sections 1 and 2 of this act, within a reasonable time and upon reasonable terms, then the President, having first obtained for the United States perpetual control by treaty of the necessary territory from Costa Rica and Nicaragua, upon terms which he may consider reasonable, for the construction, perpetual maintenance, operation, and protection of a canal connecting the Caribbean Sea with the Pacific Ocean by what is commonly known as the Nicaragua route, shall, through the said Isthmian Canal Commission, cause to be excavated and constructed a ship canal and waterway from a point on the shore of the Caribbean Sea, near Greytown, by way of Lake Nicaragua, to a point near Brito, on the Pacific Ocean.

This act, on account of its having served as the basis of the treaty draft on the part of the United States, as stated in the preamble, which adds that it is accompanied by a copy of the act, had for Colombia exceptional importance. For it is so imperative that it seems to leave no faculty other than that of selecting one of the two routes, Panama or Nicaragua, and therefore it was to be presumed that the action of the American Government could not overstep the limits therein fixed. Whence it follows that the sole evil that could befall Colombia if her Congress should disapprove the treaty was that the route eventually selected would be that of Nicaragua. It may be that we fell into error when we entertained that belief, but it was sincere, and we were led into it by the profound respect with which the American laws inspire us.

All governments being, as is well known, bound to respect the rights born of the independence and sovereignty of nations, the premature recognition by the United States of the province of Panama, rising in arms to detach itself from the country of which it is a part, while it is a matter of public knowledge that the mother country commands sufficient forces to subdue it, constitutes, according to the most ancient and modern authorities on international law, not only a grave offense to Colombia, but also a formal attack upon her wealth.

For, as the territory forms the most important part of the national wealth, its dismemberment impairs the revenues applied to the discharge of corporate obligations, among which are foreign debts and those enterprises entailed on the insurgent province, from which Colombia derives a considerable income.

If there be an end and eternal and immutable principles in right, that right of Colombia has been injured by the United States by an incredible transgression of the limits set by equity and justice.

Before the *coup de main* which proclaimed the independence of the Isthmus took place at Panama, there were in this very city agents of the authors of that *coup* in conference with high personages clothed with official character, as is asserted by reputable American newspapers. I have received information to the effect that a bank in New York opened a considerable credit in their favor, with a knowledge of the general use for which it was intended, even though unaware that it was to be applied in part to the bribery of a large part of the garrison at Panama.

Intercourse of any kind [said Mr. Seward] with the so-called "commissioners" is liable to be construed as a recognition of the authority which appointed them. Such intercourse would be none the less hurtful to us for being called unofficial, and it might be even more injurious, because we should have no means of knowing what points might be resolved by it. Moreover, unofficial intercourse is useless and meaningless if it is not expected to ripen into official intercourse and direct recognition.

It will be well to say that before the news was divulged that a revolution was about to break out on the Isthmus, American cruisers which reached their destination precisely on the eve of the movement were plowing the waters of the Atlantic and Pacific oceans. Cablegrams that are given public circulation in an official document show that two days before the movement the Secretary of the Navy issued orders to those cruisers not to permit the landing of troops of the Government of Colombia on Panama's territory.

A military officer of the Government of the United States stopped the railway from carrying to Panama, as it was under obligations to do, a battalion that had just arrived at Colón from Bogotá at the very time when its arrival in that city would have impeded or suppressed any revolutionary attempt. A few days thereafter, when my Government intrusted me with the duty of leading the army that was to embark at Puerto Colombia to go and restore order on the Isthmus, being unacquainted except in an imperfect manner with the attitude assumed by the American war ships, I had the honor to address a note on the subject to Vice-Admiral Coghlan, and in his reply, which was not delayed, he tells me that—

his present orders are to prevent the landing of soldiers with hostile intent within the boundary of the State of Panama.

The Republic of Colombia, with a population of 5,000,000 souls, is divided into nine departments, of which Panama is one of the least populous, as the number of its inhabitants does not exceed 250,000, while there are others in each of which they number over 900,000. The Colombian army at the time consisted of 10,000 men, a force more than sufficient to suppress the Panaman revolution if Your Excellency's Government had not prevented the landing of the troops under my command that were to embark at Puerto Colombia under Generals Ospina, Holguín, and Calballero, who soon thereafter accompanied me to that city, and at Buenaventura, on the Pacific, under Generals Velazco, Dominguez, and others. It is known that there is no overland way to reach Panama with troops from the interior of Colombia.

The gravity of the facts contained in this recital increases as they draw closer to the end.

In the midst of profound peace between the two countries, the United States prevented by force the landing of troops where they were necessary to reestablish order, in a few hours, in the insurgent province. Because of this circumstance, and as a *coup de main,* certain citizens of Panama, without taking into account the consent of the other towns of the department, proclaimed the independence of the Isthmus and organized a government. Two days after effecting that movement they were recognized by the American Government as a sovereign and independent republic, and fourteen days later the American Government signed a treaty with the Republic of Panama which not only recognized and guaranteed its independence, but agreed to open a canal for the purpose of uniting the waters of the Atlantic with those of the Pacific.

It is well known that the contract which Colombia made with the French company, in the exercise of its perfect right, for the construction of this canal, is in force and will remain in full force and vigor, legally at least, so long as Colombia does not give her consent for its transfer to a foreign government; since in the aforesaid contract it is expressly stipulated that a transfer to any foreign government, or any attempt whatever to make a transfer, would be cause for absolute nullification.

The same is true with regard to the Panama Railroad Company; so that, without the express consent of Colombia, no transfer can have legal effect, because it can not cancel the legal bonds which exist between the Republic of Colombia and those companies—bonds growing out of perfect contracts, which, according to the precepts of universal jurisprudence, can not be disregarded because one of the parties may consider that the strip of land in which the enterprise radicated has been conquered by a foreign country. The lapse of many years is necessary in order that the facts may establish the right, and even without the need of such time elapsing the Colombians feel sure that the justice and equity which control the acts of Your Excellency's Government in its relations with all nations are a sure pledge that our complaints and claims will be heeded.

Nor is it just to expect anything else in view of the constant practice which the United States has established in similar cases. Among many others, are set forth in its diplomatic annals the antecedent history relative to the independence of South American States, proclaimed in 1810; that of the new state of Hungary, in the middle of the last century; and that of Ireland, later, in 1866; not to make mention of the practice systematically observed by the powers, of which their procedure when the Netherlands proclaimed independence in the time of the Philips of Spain is an example. In this relation the precedent of Texas, when the United States Senate disapproved the treaty signed by the Washington Cabinet with the secessionists of that Mexican province, has an especial significance.

In the note of Mr. Seward, Secretary of State, to Mr. Adams, United States minister, in 1861, this doctrine is found:

We freely admit that a nation may, and even ought, to recognize a new state which has absolutely and beyond question effected its independence, and permanently established its sovereignty; and that a recognition in such a case affords no just cause of offense to the government of the country from which the new state has so detached itself. On the other hand, we insist that a nation that recognizes a revolutionary state, with a view to aid its effecting its sovereignty and independence, commits a great wrong against the nation whose integrity is thus invaded, and makes itself responsible for a just and ample redress. (Foreign Relations, 1861, pp. 76–77.)

At another point, in the same note, the Secretary says to the minister:

To recognize the independence of a new state, and so favor, possibly determine, its admission into the family of nations, is the highest possible exercise of sovereign power, because it affects in any case the welfare of two nations, and often the peace of the world. In the European system this power is now seldom attempted to be exercised without invoking a consultation or congress of nations. That system has not been extended to this continent. But there is even a greater necessity for prudence in such cases in regard to American states than in regard to the nations of Europe. (Foreign Relations, 1861, p. 79, Mr. Seward to Mr. Adams, No. 2, April 10, 1861.)

Referring to the consideration which nations should mutually observe, he adds:

Seen in the light of this principle, the several nations of the earth constitute one great federal republic. When one of them casts its suffrages for the admission of a new member into that republic, it ought to act under a profound sense of moral obligation, and be governed by considerations as pure, disinterested, and elevated as the general interest of society and the advancement of human nature. (Foreign Relations, 1861, p. 79, Mr. Seward to Mr. Adams, No. 2, April 10, 1861.)

It would seem that nothing could be added to the benevolence of these noble and humanitarian doctrines, written by the great man, who, unhappily for his country and for Colombia, is not living to-day.

If the sovereignty of a nation gives to it especially the power to govern itself; if the right to look after its own interests is an attribute of sovereignty; if, upon such right, rests the stability and security of international relations, respect for such sovereignty should be the more heeded by one who is obligated, as is the United States, not only by international precepts, but also by an existing public treaty from which it has derived indisputable advantages. The pertinent part of the thirty-fifth article of the treaty in force between the United States and Colombia reads as follows:

And, in order to secure to themselves the tranquil and constant enjoyment of these advantages, and as an especial compensation for the said advantages and for the favors they have acquired by the fourth, fifth, and sixth articles of this treaty, the United States guarantees, positively and efficaciously, to New Granada, by the present stipulation, the perfect neutrality of the before-mentioned Isthmus, with the view that the free transit from the one to the other sea may not be interrupted or embarrassed in any future time while this treaty exists; and, in consequence, the United States also guarantees, in the same manner, the rights of sovereignty and property which New Granada has and possesses over the said territory.

It may be said that the power of the United States is for the time being limitless, not only by reason of its laws and its resources of every kind, but also on account of the respect with which its greatness inspires the world. But in order to deal justly with a weak country this circumstance should be taken into account—that, in stipulating to guarantee "the perfect neutrality and property of the Isthmus" it could not be supposed that the words "neutrality" and "property" could be given any other interpretation than the technical one they have. If, by a *coup de main*, the revolutionists have snatched from Colombia the property of the Isthmus, it seems natural that the United States, in view of the aforesaid stipulation, should return the property to its legitimate owner. It does not seem right to give the word "neutrality" the interpretation that, by its application, the acts of the revolutionists shall be left free, because, among other reasons, the stipulation contained in the thirty-fifth article above quoted excepts no case; nor did it foresee, as it could not have foreseen, that the United States would prevent Colombia from landing her forces in Panama territory in case of secession.

If Colombia had not sufficient force to compel Panama to remain a part of the national unit, it would, without doubt, have asked the mediation of some friendly country in order to reach an understanding with the de facto government which has been established there.

But for it to have been able to subdue it by force it was necessary that Your Excellency's Government should remain neutral in the dispute; in not having done so, your Government itself violated "the rights of sovereignty and the property which Colombia has and possesses over the said territory," not complying, consequently, with the obligation it contracted to guarantee those rights as set forth in the above-cited part of the thirty-fifth article of the treaty. And it may be observed that the United States continues deriving the advantages granted under the treaty, while we lose those which we gave in order to obtain such guaranties.

The true character of the new state of Panama is revealed in the fact that it came into existence by a *coup de main*, effected by the winning over of troops, valorous without doubt, but who have fought against no one, assaulted no intrenchment, captured no fort—contenting themselves with putting in prison the constituted authorities.

If conserving our national integrity, with a few years of peace, we could recover the powers we have lost through unfortunate civil wars, and could hope, by reason of the moral and physical capacity of our race, to take a distinguished position in the American Continent; but if the Government of the United States, by preventing the military action of Colombia to subject the rebels to loyal obedience, should, in a way, make itself the ally of the Panama revolutionists, that Government will be responsible for any new secession movement that may occur, and also, before history at least, for any anarchy, license, and dissolution which a further dismemberment might occasion. Sad indeed is the fate of my country, condemned at times to suffer calamities from its own revolutions and at others to witness the unexpected attacks of a powerful but friendly state, which for the first time breaks its honored traditions of respect for right—especially the right of the weak—to deliver us pitilessly to the unhappy hazards of fortune.

There shall be a perfect, firm, and inviolable peace [says the first article of the aforesaid treaty] and sincere friendship between the United States of America and the Republic of New Granada (now Colombia) in all the extent of their possessions and territories, and between their citizens, respectively, without distinction of persons or places.

If the United States repels by force the action of our armies in Panama, is not this a clear violation of this article, since peace in one of the Colombian territorial possessions is broken?

The Panama revolutionists, counseled by speculators from several countries, who had assumed the direction of affairs, did not consult the opinion of the inhabitants of their own territory, for there are good reasons for the belief that there are in that territory thousands of persons who, respecting order and authority, have condemned the separatist movement with a determined will and in most energetic and severe terms.

Colombia, in its internal law, has never recognized the principle of secession, because, among other reasons, the obligations contracted with foreign nations by treaty, or with private parties by contract, rest upon the mass of the assets which the State possessed at the moment when the common authority contracted such obligations.

If the people of Panama, animated by the noble sentiments which induced men of action to seek quicker and more rapid progress, had proclaimed their independence and, without foreign aid, been victorious in battle waged against the armies of the mother country, had organized a government, drawn up laws, and proved to the world that it could govern itself by itself and be responsible to other nations for its conduct, without doubt it would have become entitled to recognition by all the powers.

But none of these things having occurred, and judging by the practice which in similar cases has guided the conduct of the American Government, the belief is warrantable that the recognition that has been given would probably not have been made if there had not existed in Panama the best route for the isthmian canal.

In the former case Colombia would have had no right to complain of the failure to fulfill the existing treaty, nor would it have shunned any legitimate means for seeking an arrangement that should dissolve the civil bonds which unite it with those enterprises radicated on Panama territory by contracts made in the exercise of a perfect right.

But Panama has become independent, has organized a Government, has induced a few powers prematurely to recognize her sovereignty, has usurped rights which do not belong to her in any case, and has ignored the debts which weigh upon Colombia (debts contracted, many of them, to reestablish order which her sons have often disturbed), because the Government of the United States has desired it; because, with its incomparably superior force, the United States has prevented the landing of Colombian troops destined to reestablish order after our having exhausted every possible means of friendly understanding; because the United States, even before the separatist movement was known in Bogotá, had its powerful war vessels at the entrances of our ports, preventing the departure of our battalions; because, without regarding the precedents established by statesmen who have dealt with this matter, the United States has not respected our rights in that strip of land which Colombia considers as a divine bequest for the innocent use of the American family of states; and, finally, because the Government of the United States, invoking and putting into practice the right of might, has taken from us by bloodless conquest—but by conquest, nevertheless—the most important part of the national territory.

Every nation is responsible to other nations for its conduct, whence it follows that all have among themselves rights and obligations, but these rights and obligations are limited by the right of property. The owner of an estate can not oppose the passage through his land— for example, of a railroad which the community needs—but he may demand that he be indemnified for the damage done him. In the same manner a state should certainly not obstruct the passage through its territory of a canal which the progress of the age and the needs of humanity have made necessary, but it has the right to impose conditions which shall save its sovereignty and to demand indemnification for the use thereof. Reasons based on the needs of humanity are undoubtedly very powerful, but they do not convincingly prove that the legitimate owner shall be deprived of a large part of his territory to satisfy such needs.

It might be said to me that exaggerated demands or obstacles which are intentionally raised are equivalent to a refusal. But this is not our case. Colombia has made divers treaties and contracts with foreign countries for the construction of a Panama Canal, and if they have not been carried into effect, as was the case with the treaty with the United States in 1870 and the contract with the French company later, it was not the fault of Colombia. Our demands have not been exaggerated, inasmuch as the terms of the treaty negotiated with the American representative were more advantageous than those stipulated with the French representative, and the conditions set forth in the Hay-Herran convention were much more disadvantageous than those made with the French company. The fact that the United States demands from us, in order to carry out the enterprise, a part of our sovereignty, which, under our laws, we can not legally concede so long as the constitution is not modified, because the powers that did it would be responsible before the judicial branch, does not mean that we have been opposed nor that we are opposed to the realization of the greatest undertaking of the kind which the past and future centuries have seen or will see.

Civil wars are a calamity from which no nation has ever been able to free itself. This being true, to hold responsible the Government which suffers revolutions because it can not prevent them or because it hastens to remedy them when danger menaces seems a notorious injustice, because, if the principle of foreign intervention in civil conflicts were accepted, there would be few cases that would not be converted in the end into international wars. To refrain from dealing or treating with a state for fear of civil wars might be deemed equivalent to refraining from "constructing ships for fear of shipwrecks or building houses for fear of fire." Nor is it understood what power there would be that would assume the unhappy task of imposing peace upon the rest, nor under what conditions it would do so, since to take away portions of their territory would be a punishment greater than the fault.

In this crisis of the life of my country, as unlooked for as it is terrible, Colombia rests its most comforting hopes in the sentiments of justice which animate the Government of your excellency, and confidently trusts that that Government, which has so many times surprised the world by its wisdom, will, on this occasion, astonish it by its example.

In any event, Colombia complies with the duty imposed upon her by the treaty of 1846 in that part of the 35th article which says:

. . . neither of the two contracting parties shall ordain or authorize any acts of reprisal, nor shall declare war against the other on complaints of injuries or damages, until the said party considering itself offended shall have laid before the other a statement of such injuries or damages, verified by competent proofs, demanding justice and satisfaction, and the same shall have been denied, in violation of the laws and of international right.

Since the aforesaid treaty is the law which governs between the two countries, and now that the weakness and ruin of my country, after three years of civil war scarcely at an end, and in which her bravest sons were lost by thousands, place her in the unhappy position of asking justice of the Government of your excellency, I propose that the claims which I make in the present note on account of the violation of the aforesaid treaty, and all other claims which may hereafter be made in connection with the events of Panama, be submitted to the Arbitration Tribunal of The Hague.

JOHN HAY, Secretary of State, to General Reyes, Colombian Special Minister to the United States, January 5, 1904
John Bassett Moore, *A Digest of International Law*, III, 90

THE GOVERNMENT of the United States has carefully considered the grave complaints so ably set forth in the "statement of grievances" presented on behalf of the Government and people of Colombia, with your note of the 23d ultimo.

The Government and people of the United States have ever entertained toward the Government and people of Colombia the most friendly sentiments, and it is their earnest wish and hope that the bonds of amity that unite the two peoples may forever remain unbroken. In this spirit the Government of the United States, mindful that between the most friendly nations differences sometimes unhappily arise, has given to your representations the most deliberate and earnest attention, and in the same spirit it will employ every effort consistent with justice and with its duty to itself and to other nations not only to maintain but also to strengthen the good relations between the two countries.

At the present moment the questions which you submit can be viewed only in the light of accomplished facts. The Republic of

Panama has become a member of the family of nations. Its independence has been recognized by the Governments of the United States, France, China, Austria-Hungary, Germany, Denmark, Russia, Sweden and Norway, Belgium, Nicaragua, Peru, Cuba, Great Britain, Italy, Japan, Costa Rica, and Switzerland. These solemn acts of recognition carry with them international obligations which, in peace as in war, are fixed by the law of nations and which can not be disregarded. A due appreciation of this circumstance is shown in your admission, made with a frankness and fairness honorable alike to your Government and to yourself, that "Panama has become independent—has organized a government."

The action not merely, as you observe, of a "few powers," but of all the so-called "great powers" and many of the lesser ones, in recognizing the independence of Panama, leaves no doubt as to the public opinion of the world concerning the propriety of that measure. The law of nations does not undertake to fix the precise time at which recognition shall or may be extended to a new state. This is a question to be determined by each state upon its own just sense of international rights and obligations; and it has rarely happened, where a new state has been formed and recognized within the limits of an existing state, that the parent state has not complained that the recognition was premature. And if in the present instance the powers of the world gave their recognition with unwonted promptitude, it is only because they entertained the common conviction that interests of vast importance to the whole civilized world were at stake, which would by any other course be put in peril.

The independence of the Republic of Panama being an admitted fact, the Department will proceed to consider the complaints presented by you on behalf of your Government as to the manner in which that independence was established. In performing this task I desire to avoid all appearance of recrimination; and if I shall not be wholly successful in so doing, it is only because I am under the necessity of vindicating the conduct of this Government against reproaches of the most grave and unusual character. The Department is in duty bound to deal with these charges in a spirit of the utmost candor; but in performing this duty it will not seek in unofficial sources material for unjust and groundless aspersions. It is greatly to be regretted that your duty to your Government could not, in your estimation, have been discharged within similar limitations.

With every disposition to advance the purpose of your mission, the Department has read with surprise your repetition of gross imputations upon the conduct and motives of this Government, which are said to have appeared in "reputable American newspapers." The press in this country is entirely free, and as a necessary consequence represents substantially every phase of human activity, interest, and disposition. Not only is the course of the Government in all matters subject to daily comment, but the motives of public men are as freely discussed as their acts; and if, as sometimes happens, criticism proceeds to the point of calumny, the evil is left to work its own cure. Diplomatic representatives, however, are not supposed to seek in such sources material for arguments, much less for grave accusations. Any charge that this Government or any responsible member of it held intercourse, whether official or unofficial, with agents of revolution in Colombia is utterly without justification.

Equally so is the insinuation that any action of this Government prior to the revolution in Panama was the result of complicity with the plans of the revolutionists. The Department sees fit to make these denials, and it makes them finally.

The origin of the Republic of Panama and the reasons for its independent existence may be traced in certain acts of the Government of Colombia, which are matters of official record.

It is a matter of common knowledge that the quest of a way to the westward, across the sea, from Europe to Asia led to the discovery and settlement of the American continents. The process of colonization had, however, scarcely begun when the adventurous spirits of that age, not to be balked in their undertaking by an obstacle that seemed to be removable, began to form projects for a canal to connect the Atlantic and Pacific oceans. As early as 1528 a proposal was laid before the Emperor Charles V. for the opening of such a way across the Isthmus of Panama. From that day to the present the project has continued to occupy a place among the great enterprises yet to be accomplished. It remains unfulfilled only because the experience of four hundred years has demonstrated that private effort is wholly inadequate to the purpose, and that the work must be performed, if at all, under the auspices of a government of the largest resources. There was only one such government in a position to undertake it. By a well-settled policy, in which all American nations are understood to concur, the assumption of the task by any of the great governments of Europe was pronounced to be inadmissible. Among American governments there was only one that seemed to be able to assume the burden, and that was the Government of the United States.

Such was the precise situation when the United States manifested its determination to construct the great highway across the American isthmus. Its purpose was universally applauded. The circumstance that this Government possibly might, in return for the great expenditures which it was about to hazard, derive from the construction of the canal some special advantage was not thought to be a reason for opposing what was to be of such vast benefit to all mankind. The Clayton-Bulwer treaty was conceived to form an obstacle, and the British Government therefore agreed to abrogate it, the United States only promising in return to protect the canal and keep it open on equal terms to all nations, in accordance with our traditional policy. Nor were indications wanting of appreciation on the part of the American Republics. On January 22, 1902, the second Pan-American conference, sitting at the City of Mexico, adopted the following resolution:

The Republics assembled at the International Conference of Mexico applaud the purpose of the United States Government to construct an interoceanic canal, and acknowledge that this work will not only be worthy of the greatness of the American people, but also in the highest sense a work of civilization and to the greatest degree beneficial to the development of commerce between the American States and the other countries of the world.

Among the delegates who signed this resolution, which was adopted without dissent, was the delegate of Colombia.

At that time the Government of the United States had not formally decided upon the route for the canal, whether by way of Panama or of Nicaragua. Owing to the lack of correct information there had long existed a strong tendency toward the latter route, but, as the result of more thorough investigations, a decided change in opinion had begun to appear. To Colombia this change was understood to be very gratifying. As early as May 15, 1897, the Colombian. chargé d'affaires at Washington, speaking in the name of his Government, represented in a "friendly spirit" that any official assistance extended by the United States to the Nicaraguan Canal Company would work serious injury to Colombia.

In a similar sense Señor Martinez Silva, then Colombian minister at this capital, in a note of December 7, 1901, referring to a press report that the Isthmian Canal Commission had, by reason of the excessive price fixed by the Panama Canal Company, reported in favor of the Nicaraguan route, assured the Department that the price was not final, and after declaring that the matter was one that affected "the interests of the Colombian Government, which is well disposed to facilitate the construction of the proposed interoceanic canal through its territory," said:

It would indeed be unfortunate if, through misunderstandings arising from the absence of timely explanations, the Government of the United States should be forced to select a route for the proposed canal which would be longer, more expensive, both in construction and maintenance, and less adapted to the commerce of the world than the short and half-finished canal available at Panama.

On June 28, 1902, the President of the United States gave his approval to the act now commonly referred to as the Spooner Act, to provide for the construction of the interoceanic canal. Following the report of the Isthmian Canal Commission, which confirmed the opinion expressed by the Colombian Government, it embodied the formal decision of the United States in favor of the Panama route. It accordingly authorized the President to acquire, at a cost not exceeding $40,000,000, "the rights, privileges, franchises, concessions," and other property of the New Panama Canal Company, including its interests in the Panama Railroad Company, and to obtain from Colombia on such terms as he might deem reasonable, perpetual control for the purposes of the canal of a strip of land not less than six miles wide, such control to include jurisdiction to make and, through such tribunals as might be agreed on, to enforce such police and sanitary rules and regulations as should be necessary to the preservation of order and of the public health.

The act also provided, in a clause to which your statement adverts, that, in case the President should "be unable to obtain for the United States a satisfactory title to the property of the New Panama Canal Company and the control of the necessary territory of the Republic of Colombia," together with the "rights" mentioned in connection therewith, "within a reasonable time and upon reasonable terms," he should turn to Nicaragua. But this provision, while it indicated that the construction of the canal was not wholly to depend upon the success or failure to make reasonable terms with Colombia and the canal company, by no means implied that the question of routes was a matter of indifference.

In the nature of things it could not be so. Not only was the work to endure for all time, but its prompt construction was felt to be of vast importance; and it could not be a matter of less concern to the United States than to Colombia that this Government might possibly be forced to adopt a route which would, as the Colombian minister had observed—

be longer, more expensive, both in construction and maintenance, and less adapted to the commerce of the world than the short and half-finished canal available at Panama.

Nevertheless, even if the route by Panama had been found to be the only feasible one, it would have been highly imprudent for this Government to expose itself to exorbitant demands.

It possessed, indeed, the gratifying assurance that the Colombian

Government was "well disposed to facilitate the construction of the proposed interoceanic canal through its territory," and the Department is pleased to add to this your present assurance that Colombia considers the canal strip "as a Divine bequest for the innocent use of the American family;" but it was fully understood that, before the canal was begun, arrangements of a very substantial kind would have to be made; and it was felt that, no matter how generous the views of the Colombian Government might be, the canal company might be indisposed to act in the same liberal spirit.

The Spooner Act, in providing for the acquisition by the United States of a limited control over the canal strip, merely followed the lines of previous negotiations with Nicaragua and Costa Rica. Under any circumstances, the exercise of such control could not have been considered unreasonable, but it was deemed to be altogether essential, in view of the unsettled political and social conditions which had for many years prevailed, and which unhappily still continued to exist, along the canal routes, both in Nicaragua and in Panama. Its necessity was clearly recognized in the Hay-Pauncefote treaty, and it was on all sides fully understood to form a requisite part of any plan for the construction of the canal by the United States. Neither while the Spooner Act was pending before Congress nor at any previous time was it intimated from any quarter that it would form a bar to the carrying out of the great project for which the local sovereigns of the canal routes were then such ardent competitors.

After the Spooner Act was approved, negotiations were duly initiated by Colombia. They resulted on January 22, 1903, in the conclusion of the Hay-Herran convention. By this convention every reasonable desire of the Colombian Government was believed to be gratified. Although the concession to the United States of the right to construct, operate, and protect the canal was understood to be in its nature perpetual, yet, in order that no technical objection might be raised, it was limited to a term of one hundred years, renewable at the option of this Government for periods of a similar duration. The limited control desired by the United States of the canal strip for purposes of sanitation and police, not only in its own interest but also in that of Colombia and all other governments, was duly acquired. But in order that neither this, nor any other right or privilege, granted to the United States, might give rise to misconception as to the purposes of this Government, there was inserted in the convention this explicit declaration:

The United States freely acknowledges and recognizes this sovereignty [of Colombia] and disavows any intention to impair it in any way whatever or to increase its territory at the expense of Colombia or of any of the sister republics in Central or South America; but, on the contrary, it desires to strengthen the power of the republics on this continent, and to promote, develop, and maintain their prosperity and independence.

This declaration was, besides, confirmed by the reaffirmation of article 35 of the treaty of 1846, as well as by the stipulations made with reference to the protection of the canal; for it was expressly provided that only in exceptional circumstances, on account of unforeseen or imminent danger to the canal, railways, or other works, or to the lives and property of the persons employed upon them, should the United States employ its armed forces without obtaining the previous consent of the Government of Colombia, and that as soon as sufficient Colombian forces should arrive for the purpose those of the United States should retire.

Moreover, in view of the great and to some extent necessarily unforeseen expenses and responsibilities to be incurred by the United States, the pecuniary compensation agreed to be made to Colombia was exceedingly liberal. Upon the exchange of the ratifications of the convention, $10,000,000 in gold were to be paid, a sum equivalent to two-thirds of what is reputed to be the total amount of the Colombian public debt; and, in addition to this, beginning nine years after the same date, an annual payment of $250,000 in gold was to be made, a sum equivalent to the interest on $15,000,000 at the rate at which loans can be obtained by this Government.

Such was the convention. The Department will now consider the manner in which it was dealt with.

In the "statement of grievances," to which I have now the honor to reply, a prominent place is given to the stipulation that the convention when signed should be "ratified according to the laws of the respective countries," and it is said that the course taken in Washington was not different from that at Bogotá. In a narrow, technical sense this is true, but in a broader sense no supposition could be more misleading. The convention was submitted to the Senate of the United States on the day following its signature. From first to last it was cordially supported by the Administration, and on the 17th of March it was approved without amendment.

The course taken at Bogotá affords a complete antithesis. The Department is not disposed to controvert the principle that treaties are not definitively binding till they are ratified; but it is also a familiar rule that treaties, except where they operate on private rights, are, unless it is otherwise provided, binding on the contracting parties from the date of their signature, and that in such case the exchange of ratifications confirms the treaty from that date. This rule necessarily implies that the two Governments, in agreeing to the treaty through their duly authorized representatives, bind themselves, pending its ratification, not only not to oppose its consummation, but also to do nothing in contravention of its terms.

We have seen that by the Spooner Act, with reference to which the convention was negotiated, the President was authorized to acquire, at a cost not to exceed $40,000,000, "the rights, privileges, franchises, concessions," and other property of the New Panama Canal Company. It was, of course, well known to both Governments that the company under the terms of the concession of 1878 could not transfer to the United States "its rights, privileges, franchises, and concessions" without the consent of Colombia. Therefore the Government of the United States before entering upon any dealings with the New Panama Canal Company negotiated and concluded the convention with Colombia. The first article of this convention provides:

The Government of Colombia authorizes the New Panama Canal Company to sell and transfer to the United States its rights, privileges, properties, and concessions, as well as the Panama Railroad and all the shares or part of the shares of that company.

The authorization thus given, in clear and unequivocal terms, covers expressly the "rights, privileges, . . . and concessions" of the company, as well as its other property.

Some time after the convention was signed the Government of the United States learned, to its utter surprise, that the Government of Colombia was taking with the canal company the position that a further permission, in addition to that contained in the convention, was necessary to the transfer of its concessions and those of the Panama Railroad Company, respectively, to the United States, and that, as a preliminary to this permission, the companies must enter into agreements with Colombia for the cancellation of all her obligations to either of them under the concession. This proceeding seemed all the more singular in the light of the negotiations between the two Governments. The terms in which the convention authorized the New Panama Canal Company to sell and transfer its "rights, privileges, properties, and concessions" to the United States were the same as those embodied in the original draft of a treaty presented to this Government by the Colombian minister on March 31, 1902.

No change in this particular was every suggested by Colombia, in all the discussions that followed, until November 11, 1902. On that day the Colombian minister presented a memorandum in which it was proposed that the authorization should be so modified that "the permission accorded by Colombia to the canal and the railroad companies to transfer their rights to the United States" should "be regulated by a previous special arrangement entered into by Colombia." To this proposal this Department answered that "the United States considers this suggestion wholly inadmissible." The proposition was then abandoned by Colombia, and the convention was nearly three months later signed without any modification of the absolute authorization to sell.

The notices actually sent to the companies went, however, even further than the rejected and abandoned proposal presented by the Colombian minister, since they required the companies to cancel all obligations of Colombia to them, and thus to destroy the rights, privileges, and concessions which she had by the convention solemnly authorized the canal company to sell and transfer to the United States. The whole superstructure so laboriously reared was thus threatened with destruction by the removal of one of its foundation stones.

It was against this act of the Colombian Government itself that the remonstrance made by the American minister, Mr. Beaupré, by instruction' of his Government, on the 24th of April last, was presented. Great stress is laid upon this remonstrance in Colombia's "statement of grievances," as the first of a series of three diplomatic representations which, by assuming to deny to the Colombian Congress the exercise of its constitutional functions, affronted that body and led the Colombian Senate to reject the convention. Unfortunately for this supposition, the Colombian Congress was not in session. It had not then been convoked; nor did it meet until the 20th of June. The representation was made solely with a view to recall to the Colombian Government the terms of the agreement which it had itself concluded, but of which it seemed to have become oblivious. The second representation was made, as you state, on the 18th of June, two days before Congress met, but the cabled instruction under which it was made was sent by this Government on the 9th of June. The third was made on the 5th of August, while the Congress was in session. Its obvious purpose was, if possible, to exhibit the situation in its true light.

The Department would here gladly end its recital of the course of the Colombian Government with what has already been exhibited, but the circumstances do not permit it to do so. As the "statement of grievances" presented on behalf of Colombia is founded upon the tacit assumption that her present plight is due solely to wrongs committed by this Government, it is necessary that the facts should be disclosed.

The violation by the Colombian Government, long before the Congress assembled, of its agreement to the sale and transfer to the United States of the rights and concessions of the canal and railway companies was not the only act by which it manifested its purpose to repudiate its own engagements. For some time after the convention was signed, its terms appeared to be as satisfactory to the people of Colombia as they seemingly had been to the Colombian Government.

This state of affairs continued until General Fernandez, in charge of the ministry of finance, issued more than a month before the Congress was convoked and more than two months before it met, a circular to the Bogotá press, which, as Mr. Beaupré reported, "had suddenly sprung into existence," inviting discussion of the convention. The circular in substance stated, according to Mr. Beaupré's report, that the Government "had no preconceived wishes for or against the measure;" that it was "for Congress to decide," and that Congress would be largely guided by "public opinion." In view of what the Government had already done, it is not strange that this invitation to discussion was followed by violent attacks upon the convention, accompanied by the most extravagant speculations as to the gains which Colombia might possibly derive from its rejection. No thought whatever seems to have been taken of the incalculable benefits that would accrue to Colombia as the direct and necessary result of the construction of the canal. Only the immediate possibilities, which the resources of this Government and the situation of the canal company served to suggest, seem to have been taken into account.

It is entirely impossible [said Mr. Beaupré, writing on May 4, 1903] to convince these people that the Nicaragua route was ever seriously considered by the United States; that the negotiations concerning it had any other motive than the squeezing of an advantageous bargain out of Colombia; nor that any other than the Panama route will be selected. . . . Therefore, it is contended, and generally believed, that there is no immediate necessity of confirming the Hay-Herran convention; that the negotiations can be safely prolonged, in the end securing very much better terms for Colombia. The public discussion is largely along the lines of the loss of national honor by the surrender of sovereignty; . . . private discussion, which perhaps more clearly reflects the real situation, is to the effect that the price is inadequate.

That Mr. Beaupré's summary of the situation—a situation which seems logically to have followed from the Government's own measures—was correct is amply demonstrated in the sequel. The Department deems it unnecessary to enter into any argument upon the question raised at Bogotá as to Colombia's "sovereignty." The convention speaks for itself, and its provisions for the acknowledgment and assurance of Colombia's sovereignty have already been set forth. The explanations put forward in Colombia's "statement of grievances" merely repeat the pleas devised at the Colombian capital. The sudden discovery that the terms of the convention, as proposed and signed by the Colombian Government, involved a violation of the Colombian constitution, because it required a cession to the United States of the "sovereignty" which it expressly recognized and confirmed, could be received by this Government only with the utmost surprise. Nevertheless, the Colombian Senate unanimously rejected the convention.

This fact was communicated to the Department by Doctor Herran on the 22d of August last, by means of a copy of a cablegram from his Government. In that telegram the "impairment" of Colombian "sovereignty" was mentioned as one of the "reasons advanced in debate" for the Senate's action; but joined with it there was another reason, with which the Department had long been familiar, namely, the "absence" of a "previous agreement" of the companies with the Colombian Government for the transfer of their privileges. To these reasons there was added a reference to the representations made by Mr. Beaupré; but it was said to be "probable" that the Colombian Congress would "provide bases" for "reopening negotiations."

No such action, however, was taken by the Colombian Congress. On the contrary, by a report of the majority of the Panama canal committee, read in the Colombian Senate on the 14th of October last, it was recommended that a bill which had been introduced to authorize the Government to enter upon new negotiations should be "indefinitely postponed." The reason for this recommendation is disclosed in the same report. By a treaty concluded April 4, 1893, the original concession granted to the Panama Canal Company was extended until December 31, 1904.

By a legislative act in 1900 a new extension was made till October 31, 1910; but the report, adopting a suggestion which had been put forward in the press, raises a question as to whether this legislative extension was valid, and adds that if it was not valid the aspect of the question would be entirely changed in consequence of the fact that when a year later the Colombian Congress should meet in ordinary session the extension of 1893 would have "expired and every privilege with it." In that case, the report goes on to say, the Republic would become the "possessor and owner, without any need of a previous judicial decision and without any indemnity, of the canal itself and of the adjuncts that belong to it," and would not only be able to "contract . . . without any impediments," but would be in more clear, more definite, and more advantageous possession, both legally and materially.

This programme, if not expressly, was at least tacitly adopted by the Colombian Congress, which adjourned on the 31st of October without providing any bases for the reopening of negotiations. It was a scheme to which this Government could not possibly have become a party. Of this fact the Colombian Government was duly notified when the first intimation of its purpose was, long anterior to the assembling of the Congress, first disclosed. The Colombian Government was expressly informed that such action on its part, or on that of the companies, would be inconsistent with the agreements already made between the United States and the canal company, with the act of June 28, 1902, under the authority of which the convention was made, and with the express terms of the convention itself. It was, under the circumstances, equivalent to a refusal of all negotiation with this Government.

Under these circumstances it was the intention of the President before further action to submit the matter to Congress, which was then soon to assemble. The situation, however, was presently changed. If the Government at Bogotá, as the "statement of grievances" assures us, "fell into error" in supposing that the only consequence of its rejection of the convention would be the abandonment of the Panama route by this Government, its blindness to a situation at home that was attracting the attention of the world can only be imputed to itself. Reports of impending trouble, as the result of what was going on at Bogotá, were rife.

Advices came to this Government, not only through the press but also through its own officials, of the existence of dangerous conditions on the Isthmus, as well as in the adjacent States whose interests were menaced. Disorders in that quarter were not new. In the summer of 1902, as well as in that of 1901, this Government had been obliged by its forces to maintain order on the transit route, and it took steps, as it had done on previous occasions, to perform a similar duty should the necessity arise. The form the trouble might take could not be foreseen, but it was important to guard against any destructive effects.

The reasonableness of these precautions soon became evident. The people of Panama rose against an act of the Government at Bogotá that threatened their most vital interests with destruction and the interests of the whole world with grave injury. The movement assumed the form of a declaration of independence. The avowed object of this momentous step was to secure the construction of the interoceanic canal. It was inspired by the desire of the people at once to safeguard their own interests and at the same time to assure the dedication of the Isthmus to the use for which Providence seemed to have designed it.

The situation thus suddenly created, as the direct and immediate consequence of the act of the Government at Bogotá, was, as has already been observed, one that deeply concerned not only this Government but the whole civilized world; but the interests of the United States were especially implicated by reason of the treaty of 1846 with New Granada. This treaty is frequently cited in Colombia's "statement of grievances," and the United States is repeatedly charged with having violated it. But, while its terms are employed as the basis of every accusation against this Government that they can with any plausibility be made to support, its great and fundamental design, the disregard of which by Colombia produced the revolution on the Isthmus, is wholly passed over and neglected. The Department is obliged to remedy this defect.

In speaking of the treaty of 1846 both Governments have in mind the thirty-fifth article, which forms in itself a special and distinctive international engagement. By this article—

the Government of New Granada guarantees to the Government of the United States that the right of way or transit across the Isthmus of Panama upon any modes of communication that now exist, or that may be hereafter constructed, shall be free and open to the Government and citizens of the United States.

In return—

the United States guarantees positively and efficaciously to New Granada . . . the perfect neutrality of the before-mentioned Isthmus, with the view that the free transit from the one to the other sea may not be interrupted or embarrassed,

and—

in consequence the United States also guarantee, in the same manner, the rights of sovereignty and property which New Granada has and possesses over the said territory.

The circumstances in which these engagements originated are matters of history. For some years exceptional efforts had been put forth to secure the construction of an interoceanic canal, and it was commonly believed that certain European governments, and particularly that of Great Britain, were seeking to obtain control of the transit routes. That no capitalist could be found to engage in the construction of a canal without some greater security for their investments than the feeble and irregular local governments could afford was universally admitted. But, on the other hand, it was apprehended that the introduction of European monarchical interests would prove to be but the beginning of a process of colonization that would in the end be fatal to the cause of republican government.

In this predicament all eyes were turned to the United States. The first result was the conclusion of the treaty of 1846 with New Granada. Its primary object was to assure the dedication of the Isthmus to purposes of interoceanic transits, and above all to the construction of an interoceanic canal. President Polk, in submitting it to the Senate, assigned as the chief reason for its ratification that a passage through the Isthmus—

would relieve us from a long and dangerous navigation of more than nine thousand miles around Cape Horn, and render our communication with our own possessions on the northwest coast of America comparatively easy and speedy.

It is true that the treaty did not require Colombia to permit such a passage to be constructed; but such an obligation was so obviously implied that it was unnecessary to express it.

Apart from the adaptation of the Isthmus to interoceanic transit, and its use for that purpose, there existed, as between the United States and New Granada, no common reason for the treaty's existence. This has always been well understood by both Governments. In a note of the Colombian chargé d'affaires at Washington, of January 3, 1899, commending the Panama enterprise to the good will of this Government, reference is made to the advantages which the United States "would derive from the Panama Canal, when studied in the light of that international agreement," the treaty of 1846. The same treaty was expressly incorporated into and perpetuated in the Hay-Herran convention. And it may be added that the Panama Canal, so far as it has progressed, was built under the protection of the same engagement.

The guaranty by the United States of the neutrality of the Isthmus, and of the sovereignty and property of New Granada thereover, was given for the conservation of precisely this purpose. To this end the United States undertook to protect the sovereign of the Isthmus from attacks by foreign powers. The powers primarily in view were those of Europe, but the treaty made no discriminations. The theory on which the "statement of grievances" proceeds, that the treaty obliged the Government of the United States to protect the Government of New Granada against domestic insurrection or its consequences, finds no support in the record, and is in its nature inadmissible.

Only a few years before the treaty was made the original Republic of Colombia was dissolved into the States of Venezuela, Ecuador, and

New Granada, and since the treaty was made the Republic of New Granada has been successively transformed into the United States of Colombia and the present Republic of Colombia. With these internal changes the Government of the United States was not permitted to concern itself, so far as they did not affect its treaty rights and obligations. Indeed, it is not to be imagined that New Granada desired or that the United States would have been willing to take part in the former's internal revolutions.

That the United States has faithfully borne, during the long period since the treaty was concluded, the full burden of its responsibilities does not admit of question.

A principal object of New Granada [said Mr. Fish, in a note to the Colombian minister of May 27, 1871] in entering into the treaty is understood to have been to maintain her sovereignty over the Isthmus of Panama against any attack from abroad. That object has been fully accomplished. No such attack has taken place, though this Department has reason to believe that one has upon several occasions been threatened, but has been averted by warning from this Government as to its obligations under the treaty.

In January, 1885, when Colombia appealed to the United States in the hope of averting the hostilities with which she was believed to be threatened on account of the Italian subject, Cerruti, this Government caused an intimation to be made of the serious concern which it—

could not but feel were a European power to resort to force against a sister republic of this hemisphere as to the sovereign and uninterrupted use of a part of whose territory we are guarantors, under the solemn faith of a treaty.

Such is the spirit in which the United States has on various occasions discharged its obligations.

The United States has done more than this. It has assumed and discharged, as if primarily responsible, duties which in the first instance rested on Colombia. According to the language of the treaty, the right of the Government and people of the United States to a free and open transit across the Isthmus was guaranteed by New Granada; but the United States has been able to secure the benefits of it only by its own exertions; and in only one instance, and that as far back as 1857, has it been able to obtain from Colombia any compensation for the injuries and losses resulting from her failure to perform her obligation. The Department deems it unnecessary now to enter into particulars, but is abundantly able to furnish them.

Meanwhile, the great design of the treaty of 1846 remained unful-filled; and in the end it became apparent, as has heretofore been shown, that it could be fulfilled only by the construction of a canal by the Government of the United States. By reason of the action of the Government at Bogotá in repudiating the Hay-Herran convention, and of the views and intentions disclosed in connection with that re-pudiation, the Government was confronted, when the revolution at Panama took place, with the alternative of either abandoning the chief benefit which it expected and was entitled to derive from the treaty of 1846, or of resorting to measures the necessity of which it could contemplate only with regret.

By the declaration of independence of the Republic of Panama a new situation was created. On the one hand stood the Government of Colombia invoking in the name of the treaty of 1846 the aid of this Government in its efforts to suppress the revolution; on the other hand stood the Republic of Panama that had come into being in order that the great design of that treaty might not be forever frus-trated, but might be fulfilled. The Isthmus was threatened with desolation by another civil war; nor were the rights and interests of the United States alone at stake—the interests of the whole civilized world were involved. The Republic of Panama stood for those inter-ests; the Government of Colombia opposed them. Compelled to choose between these two alternatives, the Government of the United States, in no wise responsible for the situation that had arisen, did not hesitate. It recognized the independence of the Republic of Pan-ama, and upon its judgment and action in the emergency the powers of the world have set the seal of their approval.

In recognizing the independence of the Republic of Panama the United States necessarily assumed toward that Republic the obliga-tions of the treaty of 1846. Intended, as the treaty was, to assure the protection of the sovereign of the Isthmus, whether the government of that sovereign ruled from Bogotá or from Panama, the Republic of Panama, as the successor in sovereignty of Colombia, became en-titled to the rights and subject to the obligations of the treaty.

The treaty was one which in its nature survived the separation of Panama from Colombia. "Treaties of alliance, of guaranty, or of com-merce are not," says Hall, "binding upon a new state formed by separation;" but the new state "is saddled with local obligations, such as that to regulate the channel of a river, or to levy no more than certain dues along its course." (International Law, 4th edition, p. 98.) To the same effect it is laid down by Rivier "that treaties relating to boundaries, to water courses, and to ways of communication," constitute obligations which are connected with the territory and follow it through the mutations of national ownership. (Principes du Droit des Gens, I, 72–73.) This Government, therefore, does not perceive that, in discharging in favor of the present sovereign of the Isthmus its duties under the treaty of 1846, it is in any way violating or failing in the performance of its legal duties.

Under all the circumstances the Department is unable to regard the complaints of Colombia against this Government, set forth in the "Statement of grievances," as having any valid foundation. The responsibility lies at Colombia's own door rather than at that of the United States. This Government, however, recognizes the fact that Colombia has, as she affirms, suffered an appreciable loss. This Government has no desire to increase or accentuate her misfortunes, but is willing to do all that lies in its power to ameliorate her lot. The Government of the United States, in common with the whole civilized world, shares in a sentiment of sorrow over the unfortunate conditions which have long existed in the Republic of Colombia by reason of the factional and fratricidal wars which have desolated her fields, ruined her industries, and impoverished her people.

Entertaining these feelings, the Government of the United States would gladly exercise its good offices with the Republic of Panama, with a view to bring about some arrangement on a fair and equitable basis. For the acceptance of your proposal of a resort to The Hague tribunal, this Government perceives no occasion. Indeed, the questions presented in your "Statement of grievances" are of a political nature, such as nations of even the most advanced ideas as to international arbitration have not proposed to deal with by that process. Questions of foreign policy and of the recognition or nonrecognition of foreign states are of a purely political nature, and do not fall within the domain of judicial decision; and upon these questions this Government has in the present paper defined its position.

But there may be, no doubt, other questions which may form a proper subject of negotiation; among them, for instance, the establishment of diplomatic relations between the Republics of Colombia and Panama, the delimitation of their respective boundaries, the possible apportionment of their mutual pecuniary liabilities. If the Government of Colombia will take these matters up, with any others which they think may require discussion, and will put their suggestions in regard to them in a definite and concrete form, they will receive at the hands of this Government the most careful consideration, with a view to bringing them, in the exercise of good offices, to the attention of the Government of Panama.

STATEMENT on the Panama Canal by Theodore Roosevelt, Formerly President of the United States
From *The Autobiography of Theodore Roosevelt* (1913), p. 590

BY FAR the most important action I took in foreign affairs during the time I was President related to the Panama Canal. Here again there was much accusation about my having acted in an "unconstitutional" manner—a position which can be upheld only if Jefferson's action in acquiring Louisiana be also treated as unconstitutional; and at different stages of the affair believers in a do-nothing policy denounced me as having "usurped authority"—which meant, that when nobody else could or would exercise efficient authority, I exercised it. . . .

. . . Colombia was under a dictatorship. In 1898 M. A. Sanclamente was elected president, and J. M. Maroquin vice-president, of the Republic of Colombia. On July 31, 1900, the vice-president, Maroquin, executed a *coup d'état* by seizing the person of the president, Sanclamente, and imprisoning him at a place a few miles out of Bogota. Maroquin thereupon declared himself possessed of the executive power because of "the absence of the president"—a delightful touch of unconscious humor. He then issued a decree that public order was disturbed, and, upon that ground, assumed to himself legislative power under another provision of the constitution; that is, having himself disturbed the public order, he alleged the disturbance as a justification for seizing absolute power. Thenceforth Maroquin, without the aid of any legislative body, ruled as a dictator, combining the supreme executive, legislative, civil, and military authorities, in the so-called Republic of Colombia. The "absence" of Sanclamente from the capital became permanent by his death in prison in the year 1902. When the people of Panama declared their independence in November, 1903, no congress had sat in Colombia since the year 1898, except the special congress called by Maroquin to reject the canal treaty, and which did reject it by a unanimous vote, and adjourned without legislating on any other subject. The constitution of 1886 had taken away from Panama the power of self-government and vested it in Colombia. The *coup d'état* of Maroquin took away from Colombia herself the power of government and vested it in an irresponsible dictator.

Consideration of the above facts ought to be enough to show any human being that we were not dealing with normal conditions on the Isthmus and in Colombia. We were dealing with the government of an irresponsible alien dictator, and with a condition of affairs on the Isthmus itself which was marked by one uninterrupted series of outbreaks and revolutions. As for the "consent-of-the-governed" theory, that absolutely justified our action; the people on the Isthmus were the "governed"; they were governed by Colombia, without their consent, and they unanimously repudiated the Colombian Government, and demanded that the United States build the canal.

I had done everything possible, personally and through Secretary Hay, to persuade the Colombian Government to keep faith. Under the Hay-Pauncefote Treaty, it was explicitly provided that the United States should build the canal, should control, police, and protect it, and keep it open to the vessels of all nations on equal terms. We had assumed the position of guarantor of the canal, including, of course, the building of the canal, and of its peaceful use by all the world. The enterprise was recognized everywhere as responding to an international need. It was a mere travesty on justice to treat the government in possession of the Isthmus as having the right—which Secretary Cass forty-five years before had so emphatically repudiated—to close the gates of intercourse on one of the great highways of the world. When we submitted to Colombia the Hay-Herran Treaty, it had been settled that the time for delay, the time for permitting any government of antisocial character, or of imperfect development, to bar the work, had passed. The United States had assumed in connection with the canal certain responsibilities not only to its own people, but to the civilized world which imperatively demanded that there should be no further delay in beginning the work. The Hay-Herran Treaty, if it erred at all, erred in being overgenerous toward Colombia. The people of Panama were delighted with the treaty, and the president of Colombia, who embodied in his own person the entire government of Colombia, had authorized the treaty to be made. But after the treaty had been made the Colombia Government thought it had the matter in its own hands; and the further thought, equally wicked and foolish, came into the heads of the people in control at Bogota that they would seize the French Company at the end of another year and take for themselves the forty million dollars which the United States had agreed to pay the Panama Canal Company.

President Maroquin, through his minister, had agreed to the Hay-Herran Treaty in January, 1903. He had the absolute power of an unconstitutional dictator to keep his promise or break it. He determined to break it. To furnish himself an excuse for breaking it he devised the plan of summoning a congress especially called to reject the canal treaty. This the congress—a congress of mere puppets—

did, without a dissenting vote; and the puppets adjourned forthwith without legislating on any other subject. The fact that this was a mere sham, and that the president had entire power to confirm his own treaty and act on it if he desired, was shown as soon as the revolution took place, for on November 6 General Reyes, of Colombia, addressed the American minister at Bogota, on behalf of President Maroquin, saying that "if the government of the United States would land troops and restore the Colombian sovereignty" the Colombian president would "declare martial law; and, by virtue of vested constitutional authority, when public order is disturbed, would approve by decree the ratification of the canal treaty as signed; or, if the government of the United States prefers, would call an extra session of the congress—with new and friendly members—next May to approve the treaty." This, of course, is proof positive that the Colombian dictator had used his congress as a mere shield, and a sham shield at that, and it shows how utterly useless it would have been further to trust his good faith in the matter.

When, in August, 1903, I became convinced that Colombia intended to repudiate the treaty made the preceding January, under cover of securing its rejection by the Colombian legislature, I began carefully to consider what should be done. By my direction, Secretary Hay, personally and through the minister at Bogota, repeatedly warned Colombia that grave consequences might follow her rejection of the treaty. The possibility of ratification did not wholly pass away until the close of the session of the Colombian congress on the last day of October. There would then be two possibilities. One was that Panama would remain quiet. In that case I was prepared to recommend to Congress that we should at once occupy the Isthmus anyhow, and proceed to dig the canal; and I had drawn out a draft of my message to this effect. But from the information I received, I deemed it likely that there would be a revolution in Panama as soon as the Colombian congress adjourned without ratifying the treaty, for the entire population of Panama felt that the immediate building of the canal was of vital concern to their well-being. Correspondents of the different newspapers on the Isthmus had sent to their respective papers widely published forecasts indicating that there would be a revolution in such event.

Moreover, on October 16, at the request of Lieutenant-General Young, Captain Humphrey, and Lieutenant Murphy, two army officers who had returned from the Isthmus, saw me and told me that there would unquestionably be a revolution on the Isthmus, that the people were unanimous in their criticism of the Bogota Government and their disgust over the failure of that government to ratify the treaty; and that the revolution would probably take place immediately after the adjournment of the Colombian congress. They did not believe that it would be before October 20, but they were confident that it would certainly come at the end of October or immediately afterward, when the Colombian congress had adjourned. Accordingly I directed the Navy Department to station various ships within easy reach of the Isthmus, to be ready to act in the event of need arising.

These ships were barely in time. On November 3 the revolution occurred. Practically everybody on the Isthmus, including all the Colombian troops that were already stationed there, joined in the revolution, and there was no bloodshed. But on that same day four hundred new Colombian troops were landed at Colon. Fortunately, the gunboat *Nashville*, under Commander Hubbard, reached Colon almost immediately afterward, and when the commander of the Colombian forces threatened the lives and property of the American citizens, including women and children, in Colon, Commander Hubbard landed a few score sailors and marines to protect them. By a mixture of firmness and tact he not only prevented any assault on our citizens, but persuaded the Colombian commander to re-embark his troops for Cartagena. On the Pacific side a Colombian gunboat shelled the city of Panama, with the result of killing one Chinaman— the only life lost in the whole affair.

No one connected with the American Government had any part in preparing, inciting, or encouraging the revolution, and except for the reports of our military and naval officers, which I forwarded to Congress, no one connected with the government had any previous knowledge concerning the proposed revolution, except such as was accessible to any person who read the newspapers and kept abreast of current questions and current affairs. By the unanimous action of its people, and without the firing of a shot, the state of Panama declared themselves an independent republic. The time for hesitation on our part had passed.

My belief then was, and the events that have occurred since have more than justified it, that from the standpoint of the United States it was imperative, not only for civil but for military reasons, that there should be the immediate establishment of easy and speedy communication by sea between the Atlantic and the Pacific. These reasons were not of convenience only, but of vital necessity, and did not admit of indefinite delay. The action of Colombia had shown not only that the delay would be indefinite, but that she intended to confiscate the property and rights of the French Panama Canal Company. The report of the Panama Canal Committee of the Colombian senate on October 14, 1903, on the proposed treaty with the United States, proposed that all consideration of the matter should be postponed until October 31, 1904, when the next Colombian congress would have convened, because by that time the new Congress would be in condition to determine whether through lapse of time the French Company had not forfeited its property and rights. "When that time arrives," the report significantly declared, "the Republic, without any impediment, will be able to contract and will be in more clear, more definite and more advantageous possession, both legally and materially." The naked meaning of this was that Colombia proposed to wait a year, and then enforce a forfeiture of the rights and property of the French Panama Company, so as to secure the forty million dollars our government had authorized as payment to this company. If we had sat supine, this would doubtless have meant that France would have interfered to protect the company, and we should then have had on the Isthmus, not the company, but France; and the gravest international complications might have ensued. Every consideration of international morality and expediency, of duty to the Panama people, and of satisfaction of our own national interests and honor, bade us take immediate action. I recognized Panama forthwith on behalf of the United States, and practically all the countries of the world immediately followed suit. The State Department immediately negotiated a canal treaty with the new republic. One of the foremost men in securing the independence of Panama, and the treaty which authorized the United States forthwith to build the canal, was M. Philippe Bunau-Varilla, an eminent French engineer formerly associated with De Lesseps and then living on the Isthmus; his services to civilization were notable, and deserve the fullest recognition.

From the beginning to the end our course was straightforward and in absolute accord with the highest of standards of international morality. Criticism of it can come only from misinformation, or else from a sentimentality which represents both mental weakness and a moral twist. To have acted otherwise than I did would have been on my part betrayal of the interests of the United States, indifference to the interests of Panama, and recreancy to the interests of the world at large. Colombia had forfeited every claim to consideration; indeed, this is not stating the case strongly enough: she had so acted that yielding to her would have meant on our part that culpable form of weakness which stands on a level with wickedness. As for me personally, if I had hesitated to act, and had not in advance discounted the clamor of those Americans who have made a fetich of disloyalty to their country, I should have esteemed myself as deserving a place in Dante's inferno beside the faint-hearted cleric who was guilty of *il gran rifiuto*. The facts I have given above are mere bald statements from the record. They show that from the beginning there had been acceptance of our right to insist on free transit, in whatever form was best, across the Isthmus; and that toward the end there had been a no less universal feeling that it was our duty to the world to provide this transit in the shape of a canal—the resolution of the Pan-American Congress was practically a mandate to this effect. Colombia was then under a one-man government, a dictatorship, founded on usurpation of absolute and irresponsible power. She eagerly pressed us to enter into an agreement with her, as long as there was any chance of our going to the alternative route through Nicaragua. When she thought we were committed, she refused to fulfil the agreement, with the avowed hope of seizing the French company's property for nothing and thereby holding us up. This was a bit of pure bandit morality. It would have achieved its purpose had I possessed as weak moral fibre as those of my critics who announced that I ought to have confined my action to feeble scolding and temporizing until the opportunity for action passed. I did not lift my finger to incite the revolutionists. The right simile to use is totally different. I simply ceased to stamp out the different revolutionary fuses that were already burning. When Colombia committed flagrant wrong against us, I considered it no part of my duty to aid and abet her in her wrong-doing at our expense, and also at the expense of Panama, of the French company, and of the world generally. There had been fifty years of continuous bloodshed and civil strife in Panama; because of my action Panama has now known ten years of such peace and prosperity as she never before saw during the four centuries of her existence—for in Panama, as in Cuba and Santo Domingo, it was the action of the American people, against the outcries of the professed apostles of peace, which alone brought peace. We gave to the people of Panama self-government, and freed them from subjection to alien oppressors. We did our best to get Colombia to let us treat her with a more than generous justice; we exercised patience to beyond the verge of proper forbearance. When we did act and recognize Panama, Colombia at once acknowledged her own guilt by promptly offering to do what we had demanded, and what she had protested it was not in her power to do. But the offer came too late. What we would gladly have done before, it had by that time become impossible for us honorably to do; for it would have necessitated our abandoning the people of Panama, our friends, and turning them over to their and our foes, who would have wreaked vengeance on them precisely because they had shown friendship to us. Colombia was solely responsible for her own humiliation; and she had not then, and has not now, one shadow of claim upon us, moral or legal; all the wrong that was done was done by her. If, as representing the American people, I had not acted precisely as I did, I would have been an unfaithful or incompetent representative; and inaction at that crisis would have meant not only indefinite delay in building the canal, but also practical admission on our part that we were not fit to play the part on the Isthmus which we had arrogated to ourselves. I acted on my own responsibility in the Panama matter. John Hay spoke of this action as follows: "The action of the President in the Panama matter is not only in the strictest accordance with the principles of justice and equity, and in line with all the best precedents of our public policy, but it was the only course he could have taken in compliance with our treaty rights and obligations."

I deeply regretted, and now deeply regret, the fact that the Colombian Government rendered it imperative for me to take the action I took; but I had no alternative, consistent with the full performance of my duty to my own people, and to the nations of mankind. (For, be it remembered, that certain other nations, Chile for example, will probably benefit even more by our action than will the United States itself.) I am well aware that the Colombian people have many fine traits; that there is among them a circle of high-bred men and women which would reflect honor on the social life of any country; and that there has been an intellectual and literary development within this small circle which partially atones for the stagnation and illiteracy of the mass of the people; and I also know that even the illiterate mass possesses many sterling qualities. But unfortunately in international matters every nation must be judged by the action of its government. The good people in Colombia apparently made no effort, certainly no successful effort, to cause the government to act with reasonable good faith toward the United States; and Colombia had to take the consequences. If Brazil, or the Argentine, or Chile, had been in possession of the Isthmus, doubtless the canal would have been built under the governmental control of the nation thus controlling the Isthmus, with the hearty acquiescence of the United States and of all other powers. But in the actual fact the canal would not have been built at all save for the action I took. If men choose to say that it would have been better not to build it, than to build it as the result of such action, their position, although foolish, is compatible with belief in their wrong-headed sincerity. But it is hypocrisy, alike odious and contemptible, for any man to say both that we ought to have built the canal and that we ought not to have acted in the way we did act. . . .

MESSAGE from President Warren G. Harding to the United States Senate, March 9, 1921

James D. Richardson, *Messages and Papers of the Presidents*, p. 8930. For the text of the treaty signed April 6, 1914, see *infra*, pp. 910 ff.

I VERY RESPECTFULLY invite the attention of the Senate to the pending treaty which has been negotiated between the United States and the Republic of Colombia which is in the hands of your honorable body, with full information relating to its negotiation and its later modification and revision.

The early and favorable consideration of this treaty would be very helpful at the present time in promoting our friendly relationships. There have been many and long delays in dealing with this treaty until we have been made to seem unmindful, when in truth we have had no thought but to deal with this sister Republic in a most cordial consideration. I believe the revised treaty to be a fair expression of our just and friendly relationship with the Republic of Colombia, and I would rejoice to have our example in dealing with the Republic of Colombia to be made an assurance of that promptness and firmness and justice which shall invite added confidence in our Government and a new regard for our own Republic.

V

Certain Controversies
with Mexico

War of 1846–1848

ANNUAL MESSAGE from President James K. Polk to the United States Congress, December 2, 1845 (extract)
James D. Richardson, *Messages and Papers of the Presidents*, p. 2235

IN CALLING THE ATTENTION of Congress to our relations with foreign powers, I am gratified to be able to state that though with some of them there have existed since your last session serious causes of irritation and misunderstanding, yet no actual hostilities have taken place. Adopting the maxim in the conduct of our foreign affairs "to ask nothing that is not right and submit to nothing that is wrong," it has been my anxious desire to preserve peace with all nations, but at the same time to be prepared to resist aggression and maintain all our just rights.

In pursuance of the joint resolution of Congress "for annexing Texas to the United States," my predecessor, on the 3d day of March, 1845, elected to submit the first and second sections of that resolution to the Republic of Texas as an overture on the part of the United States for her admission as a State into our Union. This election I approved, and accordingly the chargé d'affaires of the United States in Texas, under instructions of the 10th of March, 1845, presented these sections of the resolution for the acceptance of that Republic. The executive government, the Congress, and the people of Texas in convention have successively complied with all the terms and conditions of the joint resolution. A constitution for the government of the State of Texas, formed by a convention of deputies, is herewith laid before Congress. It is well known, also, that the people of Texas at the polls have accepted the terms of annexation and ratified the constitution. I communicate to Congress the correspondence between the Secretary of State and our chargé d'affaires in Texas, and also the correspondence of the latter with the authorities of Texas, together with the official documents transmitted by him to his own Government. The terms of annexation which were offered by the United States having been accepted by Texas, the public faith of both parties is solemnly pledged to the compact of their union. Nothing remains to consummate the event but the passage of an act by Congress to admit the State of Texas into the Union upon an equal footing with the original States. Strong reasons exist why this should be done at an early period of the session. It will be observed that by the constitution of Texas the existing government is only continued temporarily till Congress can act, and that the third Monday of the present month is the day appointed for holding the first general election. On that day a governor, a lieutenant-governor, and both branches of the legislature will be chosen by the people. The President of Texas is required, immediately after the receipt of official information that the new State has been admitted into our Union by Congress, to convene the legislature, and upon its meeting the existing government will be superseded and the State government organized. Questions deeply interesting to Texas, in common with the other States, the extension of our revenue laws and judicial system over her people and territory, as well as measures of a local character, will claim the early attention of Congress, and therefore upon every principle of republican government she ought to be represented in that body without unnecessary delay. I can not too earnestly recommend prompt action on this important subject. As soon as the act to admit Texas as a State shall be passed the union of the two Republics will be consummated by their own voluntary consent.

This accession to our territory has been a bloodless achievement. No arm of force has been raised to produce the result. The sword has had no part in the victory. We have not sought to extend our territorial possessions by conquest, or our republican institutions over a reluctant people. It was the deliberate homage of each people to the great principle of our federative union. If we consider the extent of territory involved in the annexation, its prospective influence on America, the means by which it has been accomplished, springing purely from the choice of the people themselves to share the blessings of our Union, the history of the world may be challenged to furnish a parallel. The jurisdiction of the United States, which at the formation of the Federal Constitution was bounded by the St. Marys on the Atlantic, has passed the capes of Florida and been peacefully extended to the Del Norte. In contemplating the grandeur of this event it is not to be forgotten that the result was achieved in despite of the diplomatic interference of European monarchies. Even France, the country which had been our ancient ally, the country which has a common interest with us in maintaining the freedom of the seas, the country which, by the cession of Louisiana, first opened to us access to the Gulf of Mexico, the country with which we have been every year drawing more and more closely the bonds of successful commerce, most unexpectedly, and to our unfeigned regret, took part in an effort to prevent annexation and to impose on Texas, as a condition of the recognition of her independence by Mexico, that she would never join herself to the United States. We may rejoice that the tranquil and pervading influence of the American principle of self-government was sufficient to defeat the purposes of British and French interference, and that the almost unanimous voice of the people of Texas has given to that interference a peaceful and effective rebuke. From this example European Governments may learn how vain diplomatic arts and intrigues must ever prove upon this continent against that system of self-government which seems natural to our soil, and which will ever resist foreign interference.

Toward Texas I do not doubt that a liberal and generous spirit will actuate Congress in all that concerns her interests and prosperity, and that she will never have cause to regret that she has united her "lone star" to our glorious constellation.

I regret to inform you that our relations with Mexico since your last session have not been of the amicable character which it is our desire to cultivate with all foreign nations. On the 6th day of March last the Mexican envoy extraordinary and minister plenipotentiary to the United States made a formal protest in the name of his Government against the joint resolution passed by Congress "for the annexation of Texas to the United States," which he chose to regard as a violation of the rights of Mexico, and in consequence of it he demanded his passports. He was informed that the Government of the United States did not consider this joint resolution as a violation of any of the rights of Mexico, or that it afforded any just cause of offense to his Government; that the Republic of Texas was an independent power, owing no allegiance to Mexico and constituting no part of her territory or rightful sovereignty and jurisdiction. He was also assured that it was the sincere desire of this Government to maintain with that of Mexico relations of peace and good understanding. That functionary, however, notwithstanding these representations and assurances, abruptly terminated his mission and shortly afterwards left the country. Our envoy extraordinary and minister plenipotentiary to Mexico was refused all official intercourse with that Government, and, after remaining several months, by the permission of his own Government he returned to the United States. Thus, by the acts of Mexico, all diplomatic intercourse between the two countries was suspended.

Since that time Mexico has until recently occupied an attitude of hostility toward the United States—has been marshaling and organizing armies, issuing proclamations, and avowing the intention to make war on the United States, either by an open declaration or by invading Texas. Both the Congress and convention of the people of

Texas invited this Government to send an army into that territory to protect and defend them against the menaced attack. The moment the terms of annexation offered by the United States were accepted by Texas the latter became so far a part of our own country as to make it our duty to afford such protection and defense. I therefore deemed it proper, as a precautionary measure, to order a strong squadron to the coasts of Mexico and to concentrate an efficient military force on the western frontier of Texas. Our Army was ordered to take position in the country between the Nueces and the Del Norte, and to repel any invasion of the Texan territory which might be attempted by the Mexican forces. Our squadron in the Gulf was ordered to co-operate with the Army. But though our Army and Navy were placed in a position to defend our own and the rights of Texas, they were ordered to commit no act of hostility against Mexico unless she declared war or was herself the aggressor by striking the first blow. The result has been that Mexico has made no aggressive movement, and our military and naval commanders have executed their orders with such discretion that the peace of the two Republics has not been disturbed. Texas had declared her independence and maintained it by her arms for more than nine years. She has had an organized government in successful operation during that period. Her separate existence as an independent state had been recognized by the United States and the principal powers of Europe. Treaties of commerce and navigation had been concluded with her by different nations, and it had become manifest to the whole world that any further attempt on the part of Mexico to conquer her or overthrow her Government would be vain. Even Mexico herself had become satisfied of this fact, and whilst the question of annexation was pending before the people of Texas during the past summer the Government of Mexico, by a formal act, agreed to recognize the independence of Texas on condition that she would not annex herself to any other power. The agreement to acknowledge the independence of Texas, whether with or without this condition, is conclusive against Mexico. The independence of Texas is a fact conceded by Mexico herself, and she had no right or authority to prescribe restrictions as to the form of government which Texas might afterwards choose to assume. But though Mexico can not complain of the United States on account of the annexation of Texas, it is to be regretted that serious causes of misunderstanding between the two countries continue to exist, growing out of unredressed injuries inflicted by the Mexican authorities and people on the persons and property of citizens of the United States through a long series of years. Mexico has admitted these injuries, but has neglected and refused to repair them. Such was the character of the wrongs and such the insults repeatedly offered to American citizens and the American flag by Mexico, in palpable violation of the laws of nations and the treaty between the two countries of the 5th of April, 1831, that they have been repeatedly brought to the notice of Congress by my predecessors. As early as the 6th of February, 1837, the President of the United States declared in a message to Congress that—

The length of time since some of the injuries have been committed, the repeated and unavailing applications for redress, the wanton character of some of the outrages upon the property and persons of our citizens, upon the officers and flag of the United States, independent of recent insults to this Government and people by the late extraordinary Mexican minister, would justify in the eyes of all nations immediate war.

He did not, however, recommend an immediate resort to this extreme measure, which, he declared, "should not be used by just and generous nations, confiding in their strength for injuries committed, if it can be honorably avoided," but, in a spirit of forbearance, proposed that another demand be made on Mexico for that redress which had been so long and unjustly withheld. In these views committees of the two Houses of Congress, in reports made to their respective bodies, concurred. Since these proceedings more than eight years have elapsed, during which, in addition to the wrongs then complained of, others of an aggravated character have been committed on the persons and property of our citizens. A special agent was sent to Mexico in the summer of 1838 with full authority to make another and final demand for redress. The demand was made; the Mexican Government promised to repair the wrongs of which we complained, and after much delay a treaty of indemnity with that view was concluded between the two powers on the 11th of April, 1839, and was duly ratified by both Governments. By this treaty a joint commission was created to adjudicate and decide on the claims of American citizens on the Government of Mexico. The commission was organized at Washington on the 25th day of August, 1840. Their time was limited to eighteen months, at the expiration of which they had adjudicated and decided claims amounting to $2,026,139.68 in favor of citizens of the United States against the Mexican Government, leaving a large amount of claims undecided. Of the latter the American commissioners had decided in favor of our citizens claims amounting to $928,-627.88, which were left unacted on by the umpire authorized by the treaty. Still further claims, amounting to between three and four millions of dollars, were submitted to the board too late to be considered, and were left undisposed of. The sum of $2,026,139.68, decided by the board, was a liquidated and ascertained debt due by Mexico to the claimants, and there was no justifiable reason for delaying its payment according to the terms of the treaty. It was not, however, paid. Mexico applied for further indulgence, and, in that spirit of liberality and forbearance which has ever marked the policy of the United States toward that Republic, the request was granted, and on the 30th of January, 1843, a new treaty was concluded. By this treaty it was provided that the interest due on the awards in favor of claimants under the convention of the 11th of April, 1839, should be paid on the 30th of April, 1843, and that—

The principal of the said awards and the interest accruing thereon shall be paid in five years, in equal installments every three months, the said term of five years to commence on the 30th day of April, 1843, aforesaid.

The interest due on the 30th day of April, 1843, and the three first of the twenty installments have been paid. Seventeen of these installments remain unpaid, seven of which are now due.

The claims which were left undecided by the joint commission, amounting to more than $3,000,000, together with other claims for spoliations on the property of our citizens, were subsequently presented to the Mexican Government for payment, and were so far recognized that a treaty providing for their examination and settlement by a joint commission was concluded and signed at Mexico on the 20th day of November, 1843. This treaty was ratified by the United States with certain amendments to which no just exception could have been taken, but it has not yet received the ratification of the Mexican Government. In the meantime our citizens, who suffered great losses— and some of whom have been reduced from affluence to bankruptcy— are without remedy unless their rights be enforced by their Government. Such a continued and unprovoked series of wrongs could never have been tolerated by the United States had they been committed by one of the principal nations of Europe. Mexico was, however, a neighboring sister republic, which, following our example, had achieved her independence, and for whose success and prosperity all our sympathies were early enlisted. The United States were the first to recognize her independence and to receive her into the family of nations, and have ever been desirous of cultivating with her a good understanding. We have therefore borne the repeated wrongs she has committed with great patience, in the hope that a returning sense of justice would ultimately guide her councils and that we might, if possible, honorably avoid any hostile collision with her. Without the previous authority of Congress the Executive possessed no power to adopt or enforce adequate remedies for the injuries we had suffered, or to do more than to be prepared to repel the threatened aggression on the part of Mexico. After our Army and Navy had remained on the frontier and coasts of Mexico for many weeks without any hostile movement on her part, though her menaces were continued, I deemed it important to put an end, if possible, to this state of things. With this view I caused steps to be taken in the month of September last to ascertain distinctly and in an authentic form what the designs of the Mexican Government were—whether it was their intention to declare war, or invade Texas, or whether they were disposed to adjust and settle in an amicable manner the pending differences between the two countries. On the 9th of November an official answer was received that the Mexican Government consented to renew the diplomatic relations which had been suspendid in March last, and for that purpose were willing to accredit a minister from the United States. With a sincere desire to preserve peace and restore relations of good understanding between the two Republics, I waived all ceremony as to the manner of renewing diplomatic intercourse between them, and, assuming the initiative, on the 10th of November a distinguished citizen of Louisiana was appointed envoy extraordinary and minister plenipotentiary to Mexico, clothed with full powers to adjust and definitely settle all pending differences between the two countries, including those of boundary between Mexico and the State of Texas. The minister appointed has set out on his mission and is probably by this time near the Mexican capital. . . .

MESSAGE from President James K. Polk to the United States Congress, May 11, 1846
James D. Richardson, *Messages and Papers of the Presidents,* 2287

TO THE SENATE AND HOUSE OF REPRESENTATIVES:
The existing state of the relations between the United States and Mexico renders it proper that I should bring the subject to the consideration of Congress. In my message at the commencement of your present session the state of these relations, the causes which led to the suspension of diplomatic intercourse between the two countries in March, 1845, and the long-continued and unredressed wrongs and injuries committed by the Mexican Government on citizens of the United States in their persons and property were briefly set forth.
As the facts and opinion which were then laid before you were

carefully considered, I can not better express my present convictions of the condition of affairs up to that time than by referring you to that communication.

The strong desire to establish peace with Mexico on liberal and honorable terms, and the readiness of this Government to regulate and adjust our boundary and other causes of difference with that power on such fair and equitable principles as would lead to permanent relations of the most friendly nature, induced me in September last to seek the reopening of diplomatic relations between the two countries. Every measure adopted on our part had for its object the furtherance of these desired results. In communicating to Congress a succinct statement of the injuries which we had suffered from Mexico, and which have been accumulating during a period of more than twenty years, every expression that could tend to inflame the people of Mexico or defeat or delay a pacific result was carefully avoided. An envoy of the United States repaired to Mexico with full powers to adjust every existing difference. But though present on the Mexican soil by agreement between the two Governments, invested with full powers, and bearing evidence of the most friendly dispositions, his mission has been unavailing. The Mexican Government not only refused to receive him or listen to his propositions, but after a long-continued series of menaces have at last invaded our territory and shed the blood of our fellow-citizens on our own soil.

It now becomes my duty to state more in detail the origin, progress, and failure of that mission. In pursuance of the instructions given in September last, an inquiry was made on the 13th of October, 1845, in the most friendly terms, through our consul in Mexico, of the minister for foreign affairs, whether the Mexican Government "would receive an envoy from the United States intrusted with full powers to adjust all the questions in dispute between the two Governments," with the assurance that "should the answer be in the affirmative such an envoy would be immediately dispatched to Mexico." The Mexican minister on the 15th of October gave an affirmative answer to this inquiry, requesting at the same time that our naval force at Vera Cruz might be withdrawn, lest its continued presence might assume the appearance of menace and coercion pending the negotiations. This force was immediately withdrawn. On the 10th of November, 1845, Mr. John Slidell, of Louisiana, was commissioned by me as envoy extraordinary and minister plenipotentiary of the United States to Mexico, and was intrusted with full powers to adjust both the questions of the Texas boundary and of indemnification to our citizens. The redress of the wrongs of our citizens naturally and inseparably blended itself with the question of boundary. The settlement of the one question in any correct view of the subject involves that of the other. I could not for a moment entertain the idea that the claims of our much-injured and long-suffering citizens, many of which had existed for more than twenty years, should be postponed or separated from the settlement of the boundary question.

Mr. Slidell arrived at Vera Cruz on the 30th of November, and was courteously received by the authorities of that city. But the Government of General Herrera was then tottering to its fall. The revolutionary party had seized upon the Texas question to effect or hasten its overthrow. Its determination to restore friendly relations with the United States, and to receive our minister to negotiate for the settlement of this question, was violently assailed, and was made the great theme of denunciation against it. The Government of General Herrera, there is good reason to believe, was sincerely desirous to receive our minister; but it yielded to the storm raised by its enemies, and on the 21st of December refused to accredit Mr. Slidell upon the most frivolous pretexts. These are so fully and ably exposed in the note of Mr. Slidell of the 24th of December last to the Mexican minister of foreign relations, herewith transmitted, that I deem it unnecessary to enter into further detail on this portion of the subject.

Five days after the date of Mr. Slidell's note General Herrera yielded the Government to General Paredes without a struggle, and on the 30th of December resigned the Presidency. This revolution was accomplished solely by the army, the people having taken little part in the contest; and thus the supreme power in Mexico passed into the hands of a military leader.

Determined to leave no effort untried to effect an amicable adjustment with Mexico, I directed Mr. Slidell to present his credentials to the Government of General Paredes and ask to be officially received by him. There would have been less ground for taking this step had General Paredes come into power by a regular constitutional succession. In that event his administration would have been considered but a mere constitutional continuance of the Government of General Herrera, and the refusal of the latter to receive our minister would have been deemed conclusive unless an intimation had been given by General Paredes of his desire to reverse the decision of his predecessor. But the Government of General Paredes owes its existence to a military revolution, by which the subsisting constitutional authorities had been subverted. The form of government was entirely changed, as well as all the high functionaries by whom it was administered.

Under these circumstances, Mr. Slidell, in obedience to my direction, addressed a note to the Mexican minister of foreign relations, under date of the 1st of March last, asking to be received by that Government in the diplomatic character to which he had been appointed. This minister in his reply, under date of the 12th of March, reiterated the arguments of his predecessor, and in terms that may be considered as giving just grounds of offense to the Government and people of the United States denied the application of Mr. Slidell. Nothing therefore remained for our envoy but to demand his passports and return to his own country.

Thus the Government of Mexico, though solemnly pledged by official acts in October last to receive and accredit an American envoy, violated their plighted faith and refused the offer of a peaceful adjustment of our difficulties. Not only was the offer rejected, but the indignity of its rejection was enhanced by the manifest breach of faith in refusing to admit the envoy who came because they had bound themselves to receive him. Nor can it be said that the offer was fruitless from the want of opportunity of discussing it; our envoy was present on their own soil. Nor can it be ascribed to a want of sufficient powers; our envoy had full powers to adjust every question of difference. Nor was there room for complaint that our propositions for settlement were unreasonable; permission was not even given our envoy to make any proposition whatever. Nor can it be objected that we, on our part, would not listen to any reasonable terms of their suggestion; the Mexican Government refused all negotiation, and have made no proposition of any kind.

In my message at the commencement of the present session I informed you that upon the earnest appeal both of the Congress and convention of Texas I had ordered an efficient military force to take a position "between the Nueces and the Del Norte." This had become necessary to meet a threatened invasion of Texas by the Mexican forces, for which extensive military preparations had been made. The invasion was threatened solely because Texas had determined, in accordance with a solemn resolution of the Congress of the United States, to annex herself to our Union, and under these circumstances it was plainly our duty to extend our protection over her citizens and soil.

This force was concentrated at Corpus Christi, and remained there until after I had received such information from Mexico as rendered it probable, if not certain, that the Mexican Government would refuse to receive our envoy.

Meantime Texas, by the final action of our Congress, had become an integral part of our Union. The Congress of Texas, by its act of December 19, 1836, had declared the Rio del Norte to be the boundary of that Republic. Its jurisdiction had been extended and exercised beyond the Nueces. The country between that river and the Del Norte had been represented in the Congress and in the convention of Texas, had thus taken part in the act of annexation itself, and is now included within one of our Congressional districts. Our own Congress, had, moreover, with great unanimity, by the act approved December 31, 1845, recognized the country beyond the Nueces as a part of our territory by including it within our own revenue system, and a revenue officer to reside within that district has been appointed by and with the advice and consent of the Senate. It became, therefore, of urgent necessity to provide for the defense of that portion of our country. Accordingly, on the 13th of January last instructions were issued to the general in command of these troops to occupy the left bank of the Del Norte. This river, which is the southwestern boundary of the State of Texas, is an exposed frontier. From this quarter invasion was threatened; upon it and in its immediate vicinity, in the judgment of high military experience, are the proper stations for the protecting forces of the Government. In addition to this important consideration, several others occurred to induce this movement. Among these are the facilities afforded by the ports at Brazos Santiago and the mouth of the Del Norte for the reception of supplies by sea, the stronger and more healthful military positions, the convenience for obtaining a ready and a more abundant supply of provisions, water, fuel, and forage, and the advantages which are afforded by the Del Norte in forwarding supplies to such posts as may be established in the interior and upon the Indian frontier.

The movement of the troops to the Del Norte was made by the commanding general under positive instructions to abstain from all aggressive acts toward Mexico or Mexican citizens and to regard the relations between that Republic and the United States as peaceful unless she should declare war or commit acts of hostility indicative of a state of war. He was specially directed to protect private property and respect personal rights.

The Army moved from Corpus Christi on the 11th of March, and on the 28th of that month arrived on the left bank of the Del Norte opposite to Matamoras, where it encamped on a commanding position, which has since been strengthened by the erection of fieldworks. A depot has also been established at Point Isabel, near the Brazos Santiago, 30 miles in rear of the encampment. The selection of his position was necessarily confided to the judgment of the general in command.

The Mexican forces at Matamoras assumed a belligerent attitude, and on the 12th of April General Ampudia, then in command, notified General Taylor to break up his camp within twenty-four hours and to retire beyond the Nueces River, and in the event of his failure to comply with these demands announced that arms, and arms alone, must decide the question. But no open act of hostility was committed until the 24th of April. On that day General Arista, who had succeeded to the command of the Mexican forces, communicated to General Taylor that "he considered hostilities commenced and should prosecute them." A party of dragoons of 63 men and officers were on the same day dispatched from the American camp up the Rio del Norte, on its left bank, to ascertain whether the Mexican troops had crossed or were preparing to cross the river, "became engaged with a large body of these troops, and after a short affair, in which some 16 were killed and wounded, appear to have been surrounded and compelled to surrender."

The grievous wrongs perpetrated by Mexico upon our citizens throughout a long period of years remain unredressed, and solemn treaties pledging her public faith for this redress have been disregarded. A government either unable or unwilling to enforce the execution of such treaties fails to perform one of its plainest duties.

Our commerce with Mexico has been almost annihilated. It was formerly highly beneficial to both nations, but our merchants have been deterred from prosecuting it by the system of outrage and extortion which the Mexican authorities have pursued against them, whilst their appeals through their own Government for indemnity have been made in vain. Our forbearance has gone to such an extreme as to be mistaken in its character. Had we acted with vigor in repelling the insults and redressing the injuries inflicted by Mexico at the commencement, we should doubtless have escaped all the difficulties in which we are now involved.

Instead of this, however, we have been exerting our best efforts to propitiate her good will. Upon the pretext that Texas, a nation as independent as herself, thought proper to unite its destinies with our own, she has affected to believe that we have severed her rightful territory, and in official proclamations and manifestoes has repeatedly threatened to make war upon us for the purpose of reconquering Texas. In the meantime we have tried every effort at reconciliation. The cup of forbearance had been exhausted even before the recent information from the frontier of the Del Norte. But now, after reiterated menaces, Mexico has passed the boundary of the United States, has invaded our territory and shed American blood upon the American soil. She has proclaimed that hostilities have commenced, and that the two nations are now at war.

As war exists, and, notwithstanding all our efforts to avoid it, exists by the act of Mexico herself, we are called upon by every consideration of duty and patriotism to vindicate with decision the honor, the rights, and the interests of our country.

Anticipating the possibility of a crisis like that which has arrived, instructions were given in August last, "as a precautionary measure" against invasion or threatened invasion, authorizing General Taylor, if the emergency required, to accept volunteers, not from Texas only, but from the States of Louisiana, Alabama, Mississippi, Tennessee, and Kentucky, and corresponding letters were addressed to the respective governors of those States. These instructions were repeated, and in January last, soon after the incorporation of "Texas into our Union of States," General Taylor was further "authorized by the President to make a requisition upon the executive of that State for such of its militia force as may be needed to repel invasion or to secure the country against apprehended invasion." On the 2d day of March he was again reminded, "in the event of the approach of any considerable Mexican force, promptly and efficiently to use the authority with which he was clothed to call to him such auxiliary force as he might need." War actually existing and our territory having been invaded, General Taylor, pursuant to authority vested in him by my direction, has called on the governor of Texas for four regiments of State troops, two to be mounted and two to serve on foot, and on the governor of Louisiana for four regiments of infantry to be sent to him as soon as practicable.

In further vindication of our rights and defense of our territory, I invoke the prompt action of Congress to recognize the existence of the war, and to place at the disposition of the Executive the means of prosecuting the war with vigor, and thus hastening the restoration of peace. To this end I recommend that authority should be given to call into the public service a large body of volunteers to serve for not less than six or twelve months unless sooner discharged. A volunteer force is beyond question more efficient than any other description of citizen soldiers, and it is not to be doubted that a number far beyond that required would readily rush to the field upon the call of their country. I further recommend that a liberal provision be made for sustaining our entire military force and furnishing it with supplies and munitions of war.

The most energetic and prompt measures and the immediate appearance in arms of a large and overpowering force are recommended to Congress as the most certain and efficient means of bringing the existing collision with Mexico to a speedy and successful termination.

In making these recommendations I deem it proper to declare that it is my anxious desire not only to terminate hostilities speedily, but to bring all matters in dispute between this Government and Mexico to an early and amicable adjustment; and in this view I shall be prepared to renew negotiations whenever Mexico shall be ready to receive propositions or to make propositions of her own.

I transmit herewith a copy of the correspondence between our envoy to Mexico and the Mexican minister for foreign affairs and so much of the correspondence between that envoy and the Secretary of State and between the Secretary of War and the general in command on the Del Norte as is necessary to a full understanding of the subject.

JAMES K. POLK

MESSAGE from President James K. Polk to the United States Congress, July 6, 1848 (extract)

James D. Richardson, *Messages and Papers of the Presidents*, p. 2437

TO THE SENATE AND HOUSE OF REPRESENTATIVES OF THE UNITED STATES:

I lay before Congress copies of a treaty of peace, friendship, limits, and settlement between the United States and the Mexican Republic, the ratifications of which were duly exchanged at the city of Queretaro, in Mexico, on the 30th day of May, 1848.

The war in which our country was reluctantly involved, in the necessary vindication of the national rights and honor, has been thus terminated, and I congratulate Congress and our common constituents upon the restoration of an honorable peace.

The extensive and valuable territories ceded by Mexico to the United States constitute indemnity for the past, and the brilliant achievements and signal successes of our arms will be a guaranty of security for the future, by convincing all nations that our rights must be respected. The results of the war with Mexico have given to the United States a national character abroad which our country never before enjoyed. Our power and our resources have become known and are respected throughout the world, and we shall probably be saved from the necessity of engaging in another foreign war for a long series of years. It is a subject of congratulation that we have passed through a war of more than two years' duration with the business of the country uninterrupted, with our resources unexhausted, and the public credit unimpaired.

I communicate for the information of Congress the accompanying documents and correspondence, relating to the negotiation and ratification of the treaty.

Before the treaty can be fully executed on the part of the United States legislation will be required.

It will be proper to make the necessary appropriations for the payment of the $12,000,000 stipulated by the twelfth article to be paid to Mexico in four equal annual installments. Three million dollars were appropriated by the act of March 3, 1847, and that sum was paid to the Mexican Government after the exchange of the ratifications of the treaty.

The fifth article of the treaty provides that—

In order to designate the boundary line with due precision upon authoritative maps, and to establish upon the ground landmarks which shall show the limits of both Republics as described in the present article, the two Governments shall each appoint a commissioner and a surveyor, who, before the expiration of one year from the date of the exchange of ratifications of this treaty, shall meet at the port of San Diego and proceed to run and mark the said boundary in its whole course to the mouth of the Rio Bravo del Norte.

It will be necessary that provision should be made by law for the appointment of a commissioner and surveyor on the part of the United States to act in conjunction with a commissioner and surveyor appointed by Mexico in executing the stipulations of this article.

It will be proper also to provide by law for the appointment of a "board of commissioners" to adjudicate and decide upon all claims of our citizens against the Mexican Government, which by the treaty have been assumed by the United States.

New Mexico and Upper California have been ceded by Mexico to the United States, and now constitute a part of our country. Embracing nearly ten degrees of latitude, lying adjacent to the Oregon Territory, and extending from the Pacific Ocean to the Rio Grande, a mean distance of nearly 1,000 miles, it would be difficult to estimate the value of these possessions to the United States. They constitute of themselves a country large enough for a great empire, and their acquisition is second only in importance to that of Louisiana in 1803. Rich in mineral and agricultural resources, with a climate of great salubrity, they embrace the most important ports on the whole Pacific coast of the continent of North America. The possession of the ports of San Diego and Monterey and the Bay of San Francisco will enable the United States to command the already valuable and rapidly increasing commerce of the Pacific. The number of our whale ships alone now employed in that sea exceeds 700, requiring more than 20,000 seamen to navigate them, while the capital invested in this particular branch of commerce is estimated at not less than $40,000,-000. The excellent harbors of Upper California will under our flag afford security and repose to our commercial marine, and American mechanics will soon furnish ready means of shipbuilding and repair, which are now so much wanted in that distant sea.

By the acquisition of these possessions we are brought into immediate proximity with the west coast of America, from Cape Horn to the Russian possessions north of Oregon, with the islands of the Pacific Ocean, and by a direct voyage in steamers we will be in less than thirty days of Canton and other ports of China.

In this vast region, whose rich resources are soon to be developed by American energy and enterprise, great must be the augmentation of our commerce, and with it new and profitable demands for mechanic labor in all its branches and new and valuable markets for our manufactures and agricultural products.

While the war has been conducted with great humanity and forbearance and with complete success on our part, the peace has been concluded on terms the most liberal and magnanimous to Mexico. In her hands the territories now ceded had remained, and, it is believed, would have continued to remain, almost unoccupied, and of little value to her or to any other nation, whilst as a part of our Union they will be productive of vast benefits to the United States, to the commercial world, and the general interests of mankind. . . .

The Period of 1911–1916

ANNUAL MESSAGE from President William H. Taft to the United States Congress, December 7, 1911 (extracts)
Foreign Relations of the United States, 1911, pp. ix, xi

. . . THE RECENT POLITICAL events in Mexico received attention from this Government because of the exceedingly delicate and difficult situation created along our southern border and the necessity for taking measures properly to safeguard American interests. The Government of the United States, in its desire to secure a proper observance and enforcement of the so-called neutrality statutes of the Federal Government, issued directions to the appropriate officers to exercise a diligent and vigilant regard for the requirements of such rules and laws. Although a condition of actual armed conflict existed, there was no official recognition of belligerency involving the technical neutrality obligations of international law.

On the 6th of March last, in the absence of the Secretary of State, I had a personal interview with Mr. Wilson, the ambassador of the United States to Mexico, in which he reported to me that the conditions in Mexico were much more critical than the press dispatches disclosed; that President Diaz was on a volcano of popular uprising; that the small outbreaks which had occurred were only symptomatic of the whole condition; that a very large per cent of the people were in sympathy with the insurrection; that a general explosion was probable at any time, in which case he feared that the 40,000 or more American residents in Mexico might be assailed, and that the very large American investments might be injured or destroyed.

After a conference with the Secretary of War and the Secretary of the Navy, I thought it wise to assemble an Army division of full strength at San Antonio, Tex., a brigade of three regiments at Galveston, a brigade of Infantry in the Los Angeles district of southern California, together with a squadron of battleships and cruisers and transports at Galveston, and a small squadron of ships at San Diego. At the same time, through our representative at the City of Mexico, I expressed to President Diaz the hope that no apprehensions might result from unfounded conjectures as to these military maneuvers, and assured him that they had no significance which should cause concern to his Government.

The mobilization was effected with great promptness, and on the 15th of March, through the Secretary of War and the Secretary of the Navy, in a letter addressed to the Chief of Staff, I issued the following instructions:

> It seems my duty as Commander in Chief to place troops in sufficient number where, if Congress shall direct that they enter Mexico to save American lives and property, an effective movement may be made. Meantime the movement of the troops to Texas and elsewhere near the boundary, accompanied with sincere assurances of the utmost good-will toward the present Mexican Government and with larger and more frequent patrols along the border to prevent insurrectionary expeditions from American soil, will hold up the hands of the existing Government and will have a healthy moral effect to prevent attacks upon Americans and their property in any subsequent general internecine strife. Again, the sudden mobilization of a division of troops has been a great test of our Army and full of useful instruction, while the maneuvers that are thus made possible can occupy the troops and their officers to great advantage.
>
> The assumption by the press that I contemplate intervention on Mexican soil to protect American lives or property is, of course, gratuitous, because I seriously doubt whether I have such authority under any circumstances; and if I had, I would not exercise it without express congressional approval. Indeed, as you know, I have already declined, without Mexican consent, to order a troop of Cavalry to protect the breakwater we are constructing just across the border in Mexico at the mouth of the Colorado River to save the Imperial Valley, although the insurrectos had scattered the Mexican troops and were taking our horses and supplies and frightening our workmen away. My determined purpose, however, is to be in a position so that when danger to American lives and property in Mexico threatens and the existing Government is rendered helpless by the insurrection I can promptly execute congressional orders to protect them, with effect.
>
> Meantime I send you this letter, through the Secretary, to call your attention to some things in connection with the presence of the division in the Southwest which have doubtless occurred to you, but which I wish to emphasize.
>
> In the first place, I want to make the mobilization a first-class training for the Army, and I wish you would give your time and that of the War College to advising and carrying out maneuvers of a useful character and plan to continue to do this during the next three months. By that time we may expect that either Ambassador Wilson's fears will have been realized and chaos and its consequence have ensued or that the present Government of Mexico will have so readjusted matters as to secure tranquillity

—a result devoutly to be wished. The troops can then be returned to their posts. I understood from you in Washington that Gen. Aleshire said that you could probably meet all the additional expense of this whole movement out of the present appropriations if the troops continue in Texas for three months. I sincerely hope this is so. I observe from the newspapers that you have no blank cartridges, but I presume that this is an error or that it will be easy to procure those for use as soon as your maneuvers begin.

Second. Texas is a State ordinarily peaceful; but you can not put 20,000 troops into it without running some risk of a collision between the people of that State, and especially the Mexicans who live in Texas near the border and who sympathize with the insurrectos, and the Federal soldiers. For that reason I beg you to be as careful as you can to prevent friction of any kind. We were able in Cuba, with the army of pacification there of something more than 5,000 troops, to maintain them for a year without any trouble, and I hope you can do the same thing in Texas. Please give your attention to this, and advise all the officers in command of the necessity for very great circumspection in this regard.

Third. One of the great troubles in the concentration of troops is the danger of disease; and I suppose that you have adopted the most modern methods for the preventing and, if necessary, for stamping out epidemics. That is so much a part of a campaign that it hardly seems necessary for me to call attention to it.

Finally, I wish you to examine the question of the patrol of the border and put as many troops on that work as is practicable, and more than are now engaged in it, in order to prevent the use of our borderland for the carrying on of the insurrection. I have given assurances to the Mexican ambassador on this point.

I sincerely hope that this experience will always be remembered by the Army and Navy as a useful means of education, and I should be greatly disappointed if it resulted in any injury or disaster to our forces from any cause. I have taken a good deal of responsibility in ordering this mobilization, but I am ready to answer for it if only you and those under you use the utmost care to avoid the difficulties which I have pointed out.

You may have a copy of this letter made and left with Gen. Carter and such other generals in command as you may think wise and necessary to guide them in their course, but to be regarded as confidential.

I am more than happy to here record the fact that all apprehensions as to the effect of the presence of so large a military force in Texas proved groundless; no disturbances occurred; the conduct of the troops was exemplary, and the public reception and treatment of them was all that could have been desired, and this notwithstanding the presence of a large number of Mexican refugees in the border territory.

From time to time communications were received from Ambassador

Wilson, who had returned to Mexico, confirming the view that the massing of American troops in the neighborhood had had good effect. By dispatch of April 3, 1911, the ambassador said:

The continuing gravity of the situation here and the chaos that would ensue should the constitutional authorities be eventually overthrown, thus greatly increasing the danger to which American lives and property are already subject, confirm the wisdom of the President in taking those military precautions which, making every allowance for the dignity and the sovereignty of a friendly state, are due to our nationals abroad.

Charged as I am with the responsibility of safeguarding these lives and property, I am bound to say to the department that our military dispositions on the frontier have produced an effective impression on the Mexican mind and may, at any moment, prove to be the only guaranties for the safety of our nationals and their property. If it should eventuate that conditions here require more active measures by the President and Congress, sporadic attacks might be made upon the lives and property of our nationals, but the ultimate result would be order and adequate protection.

The insurrection continued and resulted in engagements between the regular Mexican troops and the insurgents, and this along the border, so that in several instances bullets from the contending forces struck American citizens engaged in their lawful occupations on American soil.

Proper protests were made against these invasions of American rights to the Mexican authorities. On April 17, 1911, I received the following telegram from the governor of Arizona:

As a result of to-day's fighting across the international line, but within gunshot range of the heart of Douglas, five Americans wounded on this side of the line. Everything points to repetition of these casualties on to-morrow, and while the Federals seem disposed to keep their agreement not to fire into Douglas, the position of the insurrectionists is such that when fighting occurs on the east and southeast of the intrenchments people living in Douglas are put in danger of their lives. In my judgment radical measures are needed to protect our innocent people, and if anything can be done to stop the fighting at Agua Prieta the situation calls for such action. It is impossible to safeguard the people of Douglas unless the town be vacated. Can anything be done to relieve situation, now acute?

After a conference with the Secretary of State, the following telegram was sent to Governor Sloan, on April 18, 1911, and made public:

Your dispatch received. Have made urgent demand upon Mexican Government to issue instructions to prevent firing across border by Mexican federal troops, and am awaiting reply. Meantime I have sent direct warning to the Mexican and insurgent forces near Douglas. I infer from your dispatch that both parties attempt to heed the warning, but that in the strain and exigency of the contest wild bullets still find their way into Douglas. The situation might justify me in ordering our troops to cross the border and attempt to stop the fighting, or to fire upon both combatants from the American side. But if I take this step, I must face the possibility of resistance and greater bloodshed, and also the danger of having our motives misconstrued and misrepresented, and of thus inflaming Mexican popular indignation against many thousand Americans now in Mexico and jeopardizing their lives and property. The pressure for general inter-vention under such conditions it might not be practicable to resist. It is impossible to foresee or reckon the consequences of such a course, and we must use the greatest self-restraint to avoid it. Pending my urgent repre-sentation to the Mexican Government, I can not therefore order the troops at Douglas to cross the border, but I must ask you and the local authorities, in case the same danger recurs, to direct the people of Douglas to place themselves where bullets can not reach them and thus avoid casualty. I am loath to endanger Americans in Mexico, where they are necessarily exposed, by taking a radical step to prevent injury to Americans on our side of the border who can avoid it by a temporary inconvenience.

I am glad to say that no further invasion of American rights of any substantial character occurred.

The presence of a large military and naval force available for prompt action, near the Mexican border, proved to be most fortu-nate under the somewhat trying conditions presented by this invasion of American rights. Had no movement theretofore taken place, and because of these events it had been necessary then to bring about the mobilization, it must have had sinister significance. On the other hand, the presence of the troops before and at the time of the un-fortunate killing and wounding of American citizens at Douglas, made clear that the restraint exercised by our Government in regard to this occurrence was not due to a lack of force or power to deal with it promptly and aggressively, but was due to a real desire to use every means possible to avoid direct intervention in the affairs of our neighbor, whose friendship we valued and were most anxious to retain.

The policy and action of this Government were based upon an earnest friendliness for the Mexican people as a whole, and it is a matter of gratification to note that this attitude of strict impartiality as to all factions in Mexico and of sincere friendship for the neigh-boring nation, without regard for party allegiance, has been generally recognized and has resulted in an even closer and more sympathetic understanding between the two Republics and a warmer regard one for the other. Action to suppress violence and restore tranquillity throughout the Mexican Republic was of peculiar interest to this Government, in that it concerned the safeguarding of American life and property in that country. The Government of the United States had occasion to accord permission for the passage of a body of Mexican rurales through Douglas, Ariz., to Tia Juana, Mexico, for the suppression of general lawlessness which had for some time existed in the region of northern Lower California. On May 25, 1911, President Diaz resigned, Señor de la Barra was chosen provisional President. Elections for President and Vice President were thereafter held throughout the Republic, and Señor Francisco I. Madero was formally declared elected on October 15 to the chief magistracy. On November 6 President Madero entered upon the duties of his office.

Since the inauguration of President Madero a plot has been unearthed against the present Government, to begin a new insurrection. Pursuing the same consistent policy which this administration has adopted from the beginning, it directed an investigation into the conspiracy charged, and this investigation has resulted in the indictment of Gen. Bernardo Reyes and others and the seizure of a number of officers and men and horses and accoutrements assembled upon the soil of Texas for the purpose of invading Mexico. . . .

ANNUAL MESSAGE from President Woodrow Wilson to the United States Congress, December 2, 1913 (extract)

Foreign Relations of the United States, 1913, p. ix

. . . THERE IS BUT ONE cloud upon our horizon. That has shown itself to the south of us, and hangs over Mexico. There can be no certain prospect of peace in America until Gen. Huerta has surrendered his usurped authority in Mexico; until it is understood on all hands, indeed, that such pretended governments will not be countenanced or dealt with by the Government of the United States. We are the friends of constitutional government in America; we are more than its friends, we are its champions; because in no other way can our neighbors, to whom we would wish in every way to make proof of our friendship, work out their own development in peace and liberty. Mexico has no Government. The attempt to maintain one at the City of Mexico has broken down, and a mere military despotism has been set up which has hardly more than the semblance of national authority. It originated in the usurpation of Victoriano Huerta, who, after a brief attempt to play the part of constitutional President, has at last cast aside even the pretense of legal right and declared himself dictator. As a consequence, a condition of affairs now exists in Mexico which had made it doubtful whether even the most elementary and fundamental rights either of her own people or of the citizens of other countries resident within her territory can long be successfully safeguarded, and which threatens, if long continued, to imperil the interests of peace, order, and tolerable life in the lands immediately to the south of us. Even if the usurper had succeeded in his purposes, in despite of the constitution of the Republic and the rights of its people, he would have set up nothing but a precarious and hateful power, which could have lasted but a little while, and whose eventual downfall would have left the country in a more deplorable condition than ever. But he has not succeeded. He has forfeited the respect and the moral support even of those who were at one time willing to see him succeed. Little by little he has been completely isolated. By a little every day his power and prestige are crumbling and the collapse is not far away. We shall not, I believe, be obliged to alter our policy of watchful waiting. And then, when the end comes, we shall hope to see constitutional order restored in distressed Mexico by the concert and energy of such of her leaders as prefer the liberty of their people to their own ambitions. . . .

ADDRESS by President Woodrow Wilson before the United States Congress, on "The Situation in Our Dealings with General Victoriano Huerta," April 20, 1914
Foreign Relations of the United States, 1914, p. 474

GENTLEMEN OF THE CONGRESS:

It is my duty to call your attention to a situation which has arisen in our dealings with General Victoriano Huerta at Mexico City which calls for action, and to ask your advice and cooperation in acting upon it. On the 9th of April a paymaster of the U.S.S. *Dolphin* landed at the Iturbide Bridge landing at Tampico with a whaleboat and boat's crew to take off certain supplies needed by his ship, and while engaged in loading the boat was arrested by an officer and squad of men of the army of General Huerta. Neither the paymaster nor anyone of the boat's crew was armed. Two of the men were in the boat when the arrest took place and were obliged to leave it and submit to be taken into custody, notwithstanding the fact that the boat carried, both at her bow and at her stern, the flag of the United States. The officer who made the arrest was proceeding up one of the streets

of the town with his prisoners when met by an officer of higher authority, who ordered him to return to the landing and await orders; and
within an hour and a half from the time of the arrest orders were received from the commander of the Huertista forces at Tampico for
the release of the paymaster and his men. The release was followed by
apologies from the commander and later by an expression of regret
by General Huerta himself. General Huerta urged that martial law
obtained at the time at Tampico; that orders had been issued that no
one should be allowed to land at the Iturbide Bridge; and that our
sailors had no right to land there. Our naval commanders at the port
had not been notified of any such prohibition; and, even if they had
been, the only justifiable course open to the local authorities would
have been to request the paymaster and his crew to withdraw and to
lodge a protest with the commanding officer of the fleet. Admiral
Mayo regarded the arrest as so serious an affront that he was not satisfied with the apologies offered, but demanded that the flag of the
United States be saluted with special ceremony by the military commander of the port.

The incident can not be regarded as a trivial one, especially as two
of the men arrested were taken from the boat itself—that is to say,
from the territory of the United States—but had it stood by itself it
might have been attributed to the ignorance or arrogance of a single
officer. Unfortunately, it was not an isolated case. A series of incidents have recently occurred which can not but create the impression
that the representatives of General Huerta were willing to go out of
their way to show disregard for the dignity and rights of this Government and felt perfectly safe in doing what they pleased, making free
to show in many ways their irritation and contempt. A few days after
the incident at Tampico an orderly from the U.S.S. *Minnesota* was
arrested at Vera Cruz while ashore in uniform to obtain the ship's
mail, and was for a time thrown into jail. An official dispatch from this
Government to its Embassy at Mexico City was withheld by the
authorities of the telegraphic service until peremptorily demanded
by our Chargé d'Affaires in person. So far as I can learn, such wrongs
and annoyances have been suffered to occur only against representatives of the United States. I have heard of no complaints from other
Governments of similar treatment. Subsequent explanations and
formal apologies did not and could not alter the popular impression,
which it is possible it had been the object of the Huertista authorities
to create, that the Government of the United States was being singled
out, and might be singled out with impunity, for slights and affronts
in retaliation for its refusal to recognize the pretensions of General

Huerta to be regarded as the constitutional provisional President of the Republic of Mexico.

The manifest danger of such a situation was that such offenses might grow from bad to worse until something happened of so gross and intolerable a sort as to lead directly and inevitably to armed conflict. It was necessary that the apologies of General Huerta and his representatives should go much further, that they should be such as to attract the attention of the whole population to their significance, and such as to impress upon General Huerta himself the necessity of seeing to it that no further occasion for explanations and professed regrets should arise. I, therefore, felt it my duty to sustain Admiral Mayo in the whole of his demand and to insist that the flag of the United States should be saluted in such a way as to indicate a new spirit and attitude on the part of the Huertistas.

Such a salute General Huerta has refused, and I have come to ask your approval and support in the course I now purpose to pursue.

This Government can, I earnestly hope, in no circumstances be forced into war with the people of Mexico. Mexico is torn by civil strife. If we are to accept the tests of its own constitution, it has no government. General Huerta has set his power up in the City of Mexico, such as it is, without right and by methods for which there can be no justification. Only part of the country is under his control. If armed conflict should unhappily come as a result of his attitude of personal resentment toward this Government, we should be fighting only General Huerta and those who adhere to him and give him their support, and our object would be only to restore to the people of the distracted Republic the opportunity to set up again their own laws and their own government.

But I earnestly hope that war is not now in question. I believe that I speak for the American people when I say that we do not desire to control in any degree the affairs of our sister Republic. Our feeling for the people of Mexico is one of deep and genuine friendship, and everything that we have so far done or refrained from doing has proceeded from our desire to help them, not to hinder or embarrass them. We would not wish even to exercise the good offices of friendship without their welcome and consent. The people of Mexico are entitled to settle their own domestic affairs in their own way, and we sincerely desire to respect their right. The present situation need have none of the grave implications of interference if we deal with it promptly, firmly, and wisely.

No doubt I could do what is necessary in the circumstances to enforce respect for our Government without recourse to the Congress, and yet not exceed my constitutional powers as President; but I do not wish to act in a matter possibly of so grave consequence except in close conference and cooperation with both the Senate and House. I, therefore, come to ask your approval that I should use the armed forces of the United States in such ways and to such an extent as may be necessary to obtain from General Huerta and his adherents the fullest recognition of the rights and dignity of the United States, even amidst the distressing conditions now unhappily obtaining in Mexico.

There can in what we do be no thought of aggression or of selfish aggrandizement. We seek to maintain the dignity and authority of the United States only because we wish always to keep our great influence unimpaired for the uses of liberty, both in the United States and wherever else it may be employed for the benefit of mankind.

WILLIAM W. CANADA, United States Consul at Vera Cruz, to William J. Bryan, Secretary of State, April 21, 1914
Foreign Relations of the United States, 1914, p. 479

MARINES AND BLUEJACKETS landed at 11.30 this morning immediately taking possession of cable office, post office, telegraph office and customs house, also railroad terminal and yards with rolling-stock. Notwithstanding firing from housetops we are masters situation so far without use heavy guns. Firing all around Consulate several shots having struck building. Steamer *Ypiranga* stopped outside by Admiral Fletcher. Our men now simply defending themselves but may have to use big guns from ships if Mexican troops do not cease firing soon. Some resistance from naval, soon silenced by guns on *Prairie*. At this time reported four our men killed, twenty wounded. American newspaper men and several other Americans in Consulate. Several Americans including some women who refused to go aboard refugee ship now marooned in hotels within firing-line. Trains from Mexico City did not arrive. Am now making efforts reach General Maas, Commandant of Port, requesting him in name of humanity cease firing to prevent necessity our ships bombarding city. This telegram sent at first opportunity.

CANADA

WILLIAM J. BRYAN, Secretary of State, to the Brazilian Ambassador and the Argentine and Chilean Ministers to the United States, April 25, 1914
Foreign Relations of the United States, 1914, p. 489

YOUR EXCELLENCIES:

The Government of the United States is deeply sensible of the friendliness, the good feeling and the generous concern for the peace and welfare of America manifested in the joint note just received from your excellencies tendering the good offices of your Governments to effect, if possible, a settlement of the present difficulties between the Government of the United States and those who now claim to represent our sister Republic of Mexico.

Conscious of the purpose with which the proffer is made, this Government does not feel at liberty to decline it. Its own chief interest is in the peace of America, the cordial intercourse of her republics and their people, and the happiness and prosperity which can spring only out of frank, mutual understandings and the friendship which is created by common purpose. The generous offer of your Governments is, therefore, accepted.

This Government hopes most earnestly that you may find those who speak for the several elements of the Mexican people willing and ready to discuss terms of satisfactory and, therefore, permanent settlement. If you should find them willing, this Government will be glad to take up with you for discussion in the frankest and most conciliatory spirit any proposals that may be authoritatively formulated, and will hope that they may prove feasible and prophetic of a new day of mutual cooperation and confidence in America.

This Government feels bound in candor to say that, its diplomatic relations with Mexico being for the present severed, it is not possible for it to make sure of an uninterrupted opportunity to carry out the plan of intermediation which you propose. It is, of course, possible that some act of aggression on the part of those who control the military forces of Mexico might oblige the United States to act to the upsetting of the hope of immediate peace; but this does not justify us in hesitating to accept your generous suggestion. We shall hope for the best results within a time brief enough to relieve our anxiety lest ill-considered hostile demonstrations should interrupt negotiations and disappoint our hopes of peace.

I take [etc.].   W. J. BRYAN

[The offer of mediation, dated at the Argentine Legation, the same day, reads in translation as follows:

MR. SECRETARY OF STATE:

With the purpose of serving the interests of peace and civilization in our continent and with the earnest desire to prevent any further bloodshed to the prejudice of the cordiality and union, that have always surrounded the relations of the Governments and peoples of America, we the plenipotentiaries of Brazil, Argentina and Chile, duly authorized thereto, have the honor to offer to your excellency's Government our good offices for the peaceful and friendly settlement of the conflict between the United States and Mexico.

This offer puts in due form the suggestions which we have had occasion to make heretofore on the subject to the Secretary, to whom we renew the assurances of our highest and most distinguished consideration.] (*Foreign Relations of the United States*, 1914, p. 488.)

STATEMENT by President Woodrow Wilson, June 2, 1915
Foreign Relations of the United States, 1915, p. 694

FOR MORE than two years revolutionary conditions have existed in Mexico. The purpose of the revolution was to rid Mexico of men who ignored the constitution of the Republic and used their power in contempt of the rights of its people; and with these purposes the people of the United States instinctively and generously sympathized. But the leaders of the revolution, in the very hour of their success, have disagreed and turned their arms against one another. All professing the same objects, they are nevertheless unable or unwilling to cooperate. A central authority at Mexico City is no sooner set up than it is undermined and its authority denied by those who were expected to support it. Mexico is apparently no nearer a solution of her tragical troubles than she was when the revolution was first kindled. And she has been swept by civil war as if by fire. Her crops are destroyed, her fields lie unseeded, her work cattle are confiscated for the use of the armed factions, her people flee to the mountains to escape being drawn into unavailing bloodshed, and no man seems to see or lead the way to peace and settled order. There is no proper protection either for her own citizens or for the citizens of other nations resident and at work within her territory. Mexico is starving and without a government.

In these circumstances the people and Government of the United States cannot stand indifferently by and do nothing to serve their neighbor. They want nothing for themselves in Mexico. Least of all do they desire to settle her affairs for her, or claim any right to do so. But neither do they wish to see utter ruin come upon her, and they deem it their duty as friend and neighbors to lend any aid they properly can to any instrumentality which promises to be effective in bringing about a settlement which will embody the real objects of the revolution—constitutional government and the rights of the people. Patriotic Mexicans are sick at heart and cry out for peace and for every self-sacrifice that may be necessary to procure it. Their people cry out for food and will presently hate as much as they fear every man, in their country or out of it, who stands between them and their daily bread.

It is time, therefore, that the Government of the United States should frankly state the policy which in these extraordinary circumstances it becomes its duty to adopt. It must presently do what it has not hitherto done or felt at liberty to do, lend its active moral support to some man or group of men, if such may be found, who can rally the suffering people of Mexico to their support in an effort to ignore, if they cannot unite, the warring factions of the country, return to the constitution of the Republic so long in abeyance, and set up a government at Mexico City which the great powers of the world can recognize and deal with, a government with whom the program of the revolution will be a business and not merely a platform. I, therefore, publicly and very solemnly, call upon the leaders of faction in Mexico to act, to act together, and to act promptly for the relief and redemption of their prostrate country. I feel it to be my duty to tell them that, if they cannot accommodate their differences and unite for this great purpose within a very short time, this Government will be constrained to decide what means should be employed by the United States in order to help Mexico save herself and serve her people.

WOODROW WILSON

The White House,
Washington, June 2, 1915

ROBERT LANSING, *Secretary of State, to the Secretary of Foreign Relations of the* de facto *Government of Mexico,* June 20, 1916
Foreign Relations of the United States, 1916, p. 581

SIR:

I have read your communication, which was delivered to me on May 22, 1916, under instructions of the Chief Executive of the *de facto* Government of Mexico, on the subject of the presence of American troops in Mexican territory, and I would be wanting in candor if I did not, before making answer to the allegations of fact and the conclusions reached by your Government, express the surprise and regret which have been caused this Government by the discourteous tone and temper of this last communication of the *de facto* Government of Mexico.

The Government of the United States has viewed with deep concern and increasing disappointment the progress of the revolution in Mexico. Continuous bloodshed and disorders have marked its progress. For three years the Mexican Republic has been torn with civil strife; the lives of Americans and other aliens have been sacrificed; vast properties developed by American capital and enterprise have been destroyed or rendered nonproductive; bandits have been permitted to roam at will through the territory contiguous to the United States and to seize, without punishment or without effective attempt at punishment, the property of Americans, while the lives of citizens of the United States who ventured to remain in Mexican territory or to return there to protect their interests, have been taken, and in some cases barbarously taken, and the murderers have neither been apprehended nor brought to justice. It would be difficult to find in the annals of the history of Mexico conditions more deplorable than those which have existed there during these recent years of civil war.

It would be tedious to recount instance after instance, outrage after outrage, atrocity after atrocity, to illustrate the true nature and extent of the widespread conditions of lawlessness and violence which have prevailed. During the past nine months in particular, the frontier of the United States along the lower Rio Grande has been thrown into a state of constant apprehension and turmoil because of frequent and sudden incursions into American territory and depredations and murders on American soil by Mexican bandits, who have taken the lives and destroyed the property of American citizens, sometimes carrying American citizens across the international boundary with the booty seized. American garrisons have been attacked at night, American soldiers killed and their equipment and horses stolen; American ranches have been raided, property stolen and destroyed, and American trains wrecked and plundered. The attacks on Brownsville, Red House Ferry, Progreso Post Office, and Las Peladas, all occurring during September last, are typical. In these attacks on American territory, Carrancista adherents, and even Carrancista soldiers took part in the looting, burning and killing. Not only were these murders characterized by ruthless brutality, but uncivilized acts of mutilation were perpetrated. Representations were made to General Carranza and he was emphatically requested to stop these reprehensible acts in a section which he has long claimed to be under the complete domination of his authority. Notwithstanding these representations and the promise of General Nafarrate to prevent attacks along the international boundary, in the following month of October a passenger train was wrecked by bandits and several persons killed seven miles north of Brownsville, and an attack was made upon United States troops at the same place several days later. Since these attacks leaders of the bandits well known both to Mexican civil and military authorities as well as to American officers have been enjoying with impunity the liberty of the towns of northern Mexico. So far has the indifference of the *de facto* Government to these atrocities gone that some of these leaders, as I am advised, have received not only the protection of that Government, but encouragement and aid as well.

Depredations upon American persons and property within Mexican jurisdiction have been still more numerous. This Government has repeatedly requested in the strongest terms that the *de facto* Government safeguard the lives and homes of American citizens and furnish the protection, which international obligation imposes, to American interests in the Northern States of Tamaulipas, Nuevo Leon, Coahuila, Chihuahua, and Sonora, and also in the States to the South. For example, on January 3 troops were requested to punish the bands of outlaws which looted the Cusi mining property, eighty miles west of Chihuahua, but no effective results came from this request. During the following week the bandit Villa with his band of about 200 men was operating without opposition between Rubio and Santa Ysabel, a fact well known to Carrancista authorities. Meanwhile a party of unfortunate Americans started by train from Chihuahua to visit the Cusi mines, after having received assurances from the Carrancista authorities in the State of Chihuahua that the country was safe, and that a guard on the train was not necessary. The Americans held passports or safe conducts issued by authorities of the *de facto* Government. On January 10 the train was stopped by Villa bandits and eighteen of the American party were stripped of their clothing and shot in cold blood, in what is now known as the Santa Ysabel massacre. General Carranza stated to the agent of the Department of State that he had issued orders for the immediate pursuit, capture, and punishment of those responsible for this atrocious crime, and appealed to this Government and to the American people to consider the difficulties of according protection along the railroad where the massacre occurred. Assurances were also given by Mr. Arredondo, presumably under instructions from the *de facto* Government, that the murderers would be brought to justice, and that steps would also be taken to remedy the lawless conditions existing in the State of Durango. It is true that Villa, Castro and Lopez were publicly declared to be outlaws and subject to apprehension and execution, but so far as known, only a single man personally connected with this massacre has been brought to justice by Mexican authorities. Within a month after this barbarous slaughter of inoffensive Americans it was notorious that Villa was operating within twenty miles of Cusihuiri-achic, and publicly stated that his purpose was to destroy American lives and property. Despite repeated and insistent demands that military protection should be furnished to Americans, Villa openly carried on his operations, constantly approaching closer and closer to the border. He was not intercepted, nor were his movements impeded by troops of the *de facto* Government, and no effectual attempt was made to frustrate his hostile designs against Americans. In fact, as I am informed, while Villa and his band were slowly moving toward the American frontier in the neighborhood of Columbus, New Mexico, not a single Mexican soldier was seen in his vicinity. Yet the Mexican authorities were fully cognizant of his movements, for on March 6, as General Gavira publicly announced, he advised the American military authorities of the outlaw's approach to the border, so that they might be prepared to prevent him from crossing the boundary. Villa's unhindered activities culminated in the unprovoked and cold-blooded attack upon American soldiers and citizens in the town of Columbus on the night of March 9, the details of which do not need repetition here in order to refresh your memory with the heinousness of the crime. After murdering, burning and plundering, Villa and his bandits fleeing south passed within sight of the Carrancista military post at Casas Grandes, and no effort was made to stop him by the officers and garrison of the *de facto* Government stationed there.

In the face of these depredations not only on American lives and property on Mexican soil but on American soldiers, citizens and homes on American territory, the perpetrators of which General Carranza was unable or possibly considered it inadvisable to apprehend and punish, the United States had no recourse other than to employ force to disperse the bands of Mexican outlaws who were with increasing boldness systematically raiding across the international boundary. The marauders engaged in the attack on Columbus were driven back across the border by American cavalry, and subsequently, as soon as a sufficient force to cope with the band could be collected, were pursued into Mexico in an effort to capture or destroy them. Without cooperation or assistance in the field on the part of the *de facto* Government, despite repeated requests by the United States, and without apparent recognition on its part of the desirability of putting an end to these systematic raids, or of punishing the chief perpetrators of the crimes committed, because they menaced the good relations of the two countries, American forces pursued the lawless bands as far as Parral, where the pursuit was halted by the hostility of Mexicans, presumed to be loyal to the *de facto* Government, who arrayed themselves on the side of outlawry and became in effect the protectors of Villa and his band.

In this manner and for these reasons have the American forces entered Mexican territory. Knowing fully the circumstances set forth the *de facto* Government cannot be blind to the necessity which compelled this Government to act and yet it has seen fit to recite groundless sentiments of hostility toward the expedition and to impute to this Government ulterior motives for the continued presence of American troops on Mexican soil. It is charged that these troops crossed the frontier without first obtaining the consent or permission of the *de facto* Government. Obviously, as immediate action alone could avail, there was no opportunity to reach an agreement (other than that of March 10–13 now repudiated by General Carranza) prior to the entrance of such an expedition into Mexico if the expedition was to be effective. Subsequent events and correspondence have demonstrated to the satisfaction of this Government that General Carranza would not have entered into any agreement providing for an effective plan for the capture and destruction of the Villa bands. While the American troops were moving rapidly southward in pursuit of the raiders, it was the form and nature of the agreement that occupied the attention of General Carranza rather than the practical object which it was to attain—the number of limitations that could be imposed upon the American forces to impede their progress rather than the obstacles that could be raised to prevent the escape of the outlaws. It was General Carranza who suspended through your note of April 12 all discussions and negotiations for an agreement along the lines of the Protocols between the United States and Mexico concluded during the period 1882–1896, under which the two countries had so successfully restored peaceful conditions on their common boundary. It may be mentioned here that, notwithstanding the statement in your note that "the American Government gave no answer to the note of the 12th of April," this note was replied to on April 14, when the Department instructed Mr. Rodgers by telegraph to deliver this Government's answer to General Carranza. Shortly after this reply the conferences between Generals Scott, Funston and Obregon began at El Paso, during which they signed on May 2 a project of a memorandum *ad referendum* regarding the withdrawal of American troops. As an indication of the alleged bad faith of the American Government, you state that though General Scott declared in this memorandum that the destruction and dispersion of the Villa band "had been accomplished," yet American forces are not withdrawn from Mexico. It is only necessary to read the memorandum, which is in the English language, to ascertain that this is clearly a misstatement, for the memorandum states that "the American punitive expeditionary forces have destroyed or dispersed many of the lawless elements and bandits, . . . or have driven them far into the interior of the Republic of Mexico," and further, that the United States forces were then "carrying on a vigorous pursuit of such small numbers of bandits or lawless elements as may have escaped." The context of your note gives the impression that the object of the expedition being admittedly accomplished, the United States had agreed in the memorandum to begin the withdrawal of its troops. The memorandum shows, however, that it was not alone on account of partial dispersion of the bandits that it was decided to begin the withdrawal of American forces, but equally on account of the assurances of the Mexican Government that their forces were "at the present time being augmented and strengthened to such an extent that they will be able to prevent any disorders occurring in Mexico that would in any way endanger American territory," and that they would "continue to diligently pursue, capture or destroy any lawless bands of bandits that may still exist or hereafter exist in the northern part of Mexico," and that it would "make a proper distribution of such of its forces as may be necessary to prevent the possibility of invasion of American territory from Mexico." It was because of these assurances and because of General Scott's confidence that they would be carried out that he stated in the memorandum that the American forces would be *gradually* withdrawn." It is to be noted that, while the American Government was willing to ratify this agreement, General Carranza refused to do so, as General Obregon stated, because, among other things, it imposed improper conditions upon the Mexican Government.

Notwithstanding the assurances in the memorandum, it is well known that the forces of the *de facto* Government have not carried on a vigorous pursuit of the remaining bandits and that no proper distribution of forces to prevent the invasion of American territory has been made, as will be shown by the further facts hereinafter set forth. I am reluctant to be forced to the conclusion which might be drawn from these circumstances that the *de facto* Government, in spite of the crimes committed and the sinister designs of Villa and his followers, did not and does not now intend or desire that these outlaws should be captured, destroyed, or dispersed by American troops or, at the request of this Government, by Mexican troops.

While the conferences at El Paso were in progress, and after the American conferees had been assured on May 2 that the Mexican forces in the northern part of the Republic were then being augmented so as to be able to prevent any disorders that would endanger American territory, a band of Mexicans, on the night of May 5, made an attack at Glen Springs, Texas, about twenty miles north of the border, killing American soldiers and civilians, burning and sacking property and carrying off two Americans as prisoners. Subsequent to this event, the Mexican Government, as you state, "gave instructions to General Obregon to notify that of the United States that it would not permit the further passage of American troops into Mexico on this account, and that orders had been given to all military commanders along the frontier not to consent to same." This Government is of course not in a position to dispute the statement that these instructions had been given to General Obregon, but it can decisively assert that General Obregon never gave any such notification to General Scott or General Funston or, so far as known, to any other American official. General Obregon did, however, inquire as to whether American troops had entered Mexico in pursuit of the Glen Springs raiders, and General Funston stated that no orders had been issued to American troops to cross the frontier on account of the raid, but this statement was made before any such orders had been issued, and not afterwards, as the erroneous account of the interview given in your note would appear to indicate. Moreover, no statement was made by the American Generals that "no more American troops would cross into our territory." On the contrary, it was pointed out to General Obregon and to Mr. Juan Amador, who was present at the conference, and pointed out with emphasis, that the bandits de la Rosa and Pedro Vino, who had been instrumental in causing the invasion of Texas above Brownsville, were even then reported to be arranging in the neighborhood of Victoria for another raid across the border, and it was made clear to General Obregon that if the Mexican Government did not take immediate steps to prevent another invasion of the United States by these marauders, who were frequently seen in the company of General Nafarrate, the Constitutionalist commander, Mexico would find in Tamaulipas another punitive expedition similar to that then in Chihuahua. American troops crossed into Mexico on May 10, upon notification to the local military authorities, under the repudiated agreement of March 10–13, or in any event in accordance with the practice adopted over forty years ago, when there was no agreement regarding pursuit of marauders across the international boundary. These troops penetrated 168 miles into Mexican territory in pursuit of the Glen Springs marauders without encountering a detachment of Mexican troops or a single Mexican soldier. Further discussion of this raid, however, is not necessary, because the American forces sent in pursuit of the bandits recrossed into Texas on the morning of May 22, the date of your note under consideration—a further proof of the singleness of purpose of this Government in endeavoring to quell disorder and stamp out lawlessness along the border.

During the continuance of the El Paso conferences, General Scott you assert, did not take into consideration the plan proposed by the Mexican Government for the protection of the frontier by the reciprocal distribution of troops along the boundary. This proposition was made by General Obregon a number of times, but each time conditioned upon the immediate withdrawal of American troops, and the Mexican conferees were invariably informed that *immediate* withdrawal could not take place, and that therefore it was impossible to discuss the project on that basis.

I have noted the fact that your communication is not limited to a discussion of the deplorable conditions existing along the border and their important bearing on the peaceful relations of our Governments, but that an effort is made to connect it with other circumstances in order to support, if possible, a mistaken interpretation of the attitude of the Government of the United States toward Mexico. You state in effect that the American Government has placed every obstacle in the way of attaining the pacification of Mexico, and that this is shown by the volume of diplomatic representations in behalf of American interests which constantly impede efforts to reorganize the political, economical and social conditions of the country; by the decided aid lent at one time to Villa by American officers and by the Department of State; by the aid extended by the American Catholic clergy to that of Mexico; by the constant activity of the American press in favor of intervention and the interests of American business men; by the shelter and supply of rebels and conspirators on American territory; by the detention of shipments of arms and munitions purchased by the Mexican Government; and by the detention of machinery intended for their manufacture.

In reply to this sweeping charge, I can truthfully affirm that the American Government has given every possible encouragement to the *de facto* Government in the pacification and rehabilitation of Mexico. From the moment of its recognition, it has had the undivided support of this Government. An embargo was placed upon arms and ammunition going into Chihuahua, Sonora and Lower California, in order to prevent their falling into the hands of the armed opponents of the *de facto* Government. Permission has been granted from time to time, as requested, for Mexican troops and equipment to traverse American territory from one point to another in Mexico in order that the operations of Mexican troops against Villa and his forces might be facilitated. In view of these friendly acts, I am surprised that the *de facto* Government has construed diplomatic representations in regard to the unjust treatment accorded American interests, private assistance to opponents to the *de facto* Government by sympathizers in a foreign country, and the activity of a foreign press as interference by the United States Government in the domestic politics of Mexico. If a denial is needed that this Government has had ulterior and improper motives in its diplomatic representations, or has countenanced the activities of American sympathizers and the American press opposed to the *de facto* Government, I am glad most emphatically to deny it. It is, however, a matter of common knowledge that the Mexican press has been more active than the press in the United States in endeavoring to inflame the two peoples against each other and to force the two countries into hostilities. With the power of censorship of the Mexican press, so rigorously exercised by the *de facto* Government, the responsibility for this activity cannot, it would seem, be avoided by that Government, and the issue of the appeal of General Carranza himself in the press of March 12th, calling upon the Mexican people to be prepared for any emergency which might arise, and intimating that war with the United States was imminent, evidences the attitude of the *de facto* Government toward these publications. It should not be a matter of surprise that, after such manifestations of hostile feeling, the United States was doubtful of the purpose for which the large amount of ammunition was to be used which the *de facto* Government appeared eager to import from this country. Moreover, the policy of the *de facto* Government in refusing to cooperate and in failing to act independently in destroying the Villa bandits and in otherwise suppressing outlawry in the vicinity of the border so as to remove the danger of war materials, while passing southward through this zone, falling into the hands of the enemies of law and order is, in the opinion of this Government, a sufficient ground, even if there were no other, for the refusal to allow such materials to cross the boundary into the bandit-infested region. To have permitted these shipments without careful scrutiny would, in the circumstances, have been to manifest a sense of security which would have been unjustified.

  Candor compels me to add that the unconcealed hostility of the subordinate military commanders of the *de facto* Government toward the American troops engaged in pursuing the Villa bands and the efforts of the *de facto* Government to compel their withdrawal from Mexican territory by threats and show of military force instead of by aiding in the capture of the outlaws constitute a menace to the safety of the American troops and to the peace of the border. As long as this menace continues and there is any evidence of an intention on the part of the *de facto* Government or its military commanders to use force against the American troops instead of cooperating with them, the Government of the United States will not permit munitions of war or machinery for their manufacture to be exported from this country to Mexico.

As to the shelter and supply of rebels and conspirators on American territory, I can state that vigorous efforts have been and are being made by the agents of the United States to apprehend and bring to justice all persons found to be conspiring to violate the laws of the United States by organizing to oppose with arms the *de facto* Government of Mexico. Political refugees have undoubtedly sought asylum in the United States, but this Government has vigilantly kept them under surveillance and has not hesitated to apprehend them upon proof of their criminal intentions, as the arrest of General Huerta and others fully attests.

Having corrected the erroneous statements of fact to which I have adverted, the real situation stands forth in its true light. It is admitted that American troops have crossed the international boundary in hot pursuit of the Columbus raiders and without notice to or the consent of your Government but the several protestations on the part of this Government by the President, by this Department, and by other American authorities, that the object of the expedition was to capture, destroy or completely disperse the Villa bands of outlaws or to turn this duty over to the Mexican authorities when assured that it would be effectively fulfilled, have been carried out in perfect good faith by the United States. Its efforts, however, have been obstructed at every point; first, by insistence on a palpably useless agreement which you admit was either not to apply to the present expedition or was to contain impracticable restrictions on its organization and operation; then by actual opposition, encouraged and fostered by the *de facto* Government, to the further advance of the expedition into Villa territory, which was followed by the sudden suspension of all negotiations for an arrangement for the pursuit of Villa and his followers and the protection of the frontier; and finally by a demand for the immediate withdrawal of the American troops. Meantime, conditions of anarchy in the border States of Mexico were continually growing worse. Incursions into American territory was plotted and perpetrated; the Glen Springs raid was successfully executed, while no effective efforts were being made by General Carranza to improve the conditions and to protect American territory from constant threat of invasion. In view of this increasing menace, of the inactivity of the Carranza forces, of the lack of cooperation in the apprehension of the Villa bands, and of the known encouragement and aid given to bandit leaders, it is unreasonable to expect the United States to withdraw its forces from Mexican territory or to prevent their entry again when their presence is the only check upon further bandit outrages and the only efficient means of protecting American lives and homes— safeguards which General Carranza, though internationally obligated to supply, is manifestly unable or unwilling to give.

In view of the actual state of affairs as I have outlined it above, I am now in a position to consider the conclusions which you have drawn in your note under acknowledgment from the erroneous statements of fact which you have set forth.

Your Government intimates, if it does not openly charge, that the attitude of the United States is one of insincerity, distrust, and suspicion toward the *de facto* Government of Mexico, and that the intention of the United States in sending its troops into Mexico is to extend its sovereignty over Mexican territory, and not merely for the purpose of pursuing marauders and preventing future raids across the border. The *de facto* Government charges by implication which admits of but one interpretation, that this Government has as its object territorial aggrandizement even at the expense of a war of aggression against a neighbor weakened by years of civil strife. The Government of the United States, if it had had designs upon the territory of Mexico, would have had no difficulty in finding during this period of revolution and disorder many plausible arguments for intervention in Mexican affairs. Hoping, however, that the people of Mexico would through their own efforts restore peace and establish an orderly government, the United States has awaited with patience the consummation of the revolution.

When the superiority of the revolutionary faction led by General Carranza became undoubted, the United States, after conferring with six others of the American Republics, recognized unconditionally the present *de facto* Government. It hoped and expected that that Government would speedily restore order and provide the Mexican people and others, who had given their energy and substance to the development of the great resources of the Republic, opportunity to rebuild in peace and security their shattered fortunes.

This Government has waited month after month for the consummation of its hope and expectation. In spite of increasing discouragements, in spite of repeated provocations to exercise force in the restoration of order in the northern regions of Mexico, where American interests have suffered most seriously from lawlessness, the Government of the United States has refrained from aggressive action and sought by appeals and moderate though explicit demands to impress upon the *de facto* Government the seriousness of the situation and to arouse it to its duty to perform its international obligations toward citizens of the United States who had entered the territory of Mexico or had vested interests within its boundaries.

In the face of constantly renewed evidences of the patience and restraint of this Government in circumstances which only a government imbued with unselfishness and a sincere desire to respect to the full the sovereign rights and national dignity of the Mexican people would have endured, doubts and suspicions as to the motives of the Government of the United States are expressed in your communication of May 22, for which I can imagine no purpose but to impugn the good faith of this Government for I find it hard to believe that such imputations are not universally known to be without the least shadow of justification in fact.

Can the *de facto* Government doubt that, if the United States had turned covetous eyes on Mexican territory, it could have found many pretexts in the past for the gratification of its desire? Can that Government doubt that months ago, when the war between the revolutionary factions was in progress, a much better opportunity than the present was afforded for American intervention, if such has been the purpose of the United States as the *de facto* Government now insinuates? What motive could this Government have had in refraining from taking advantage of such opportunities other than unselfish friendship for the Mexican Republic? I have of course given consideration to your argument that the responsibility for the present situation rests largely upon this Government. In the first place, you state that even the American forces along the border whose attention is undivided by other military operations, "find themselves physically unable to protect effectively the frontier on the American side." Obviously, if there is no means of reaching bands roving on Mexican territory and making sudden dashes at night into American territory it is impossible to prevent such invasions unless the frontier is protected by a cordon of troops. No government could be expected to maintain a force of this strength along the boundary of a nation with which it is at peace for the purpose of resisting the onslaughts of a few bands of lawless men, especially when the neighboring state makes no effort to prevent these attacks. The most effective method of preventing raids of this nature, as past experience has fully demonstrated, is to visit punishment or destruction on the raiders. It is precisely this plan which the United States desires to follow along the border without any intention of infringing upon the sovereign rights of her neighbor, but which, although obviously advantageous to the *de facto* Government, it refuses to allow or even countenance. It is in fact protection to American lives and property about which the United States is solicitous and not the methods or ways in which that protection shall be accomplished. If the Mexican Government is unwilling or unable to give this protection by preventing its territory from being the rendezvous and refuge of murderers and plunderers, that does not relieve this Government from its duty to take all the steps necessary to safeguard American citizens on American soil. The United States Government can not and will not allow bands of lawless men to establish themselves upon its borders with liberty to invade and plunder American territory with impunity and, when pursued, to seek safety across the Rio Grande, relying upon the plea of their Government that the integrity of the soil of the Mexican Republic must not be violated.

The Mexican Government further protests that it has "made every effort on its part to protect the frontier" and that it is doing "all possible to avoid a recurrence of such acts." Attention is again invited to the well-known and unrestricted activity of de la Rosa, Ancieto Piscano, Pedro Vino and others in connection with borders raids and to the fact that, as I am advised, up to June 4 de la Rosa was still collecting troops at Monterey for the openly avowed purpose of making attacks on Texan border towns and that Pedro Vino was recruiting at other places for the same avowed purpose. I have already pointed out the uninterrupted progress of Villa to and from Columbus, and the fact that the American forces in pursuit of the Glen Springs marauders penetrated 168 miles into Mexican territory without encountering a single Carrancista soldier. This does not indicate that the Mexican Government is doing "all possible" to avoid further raids; and if it is doing "all possible," this is not sufficient to prevent border raids, and there is every reason, therefore, why this Government must take such preventive measures as it deems sufficient.

It is suggested that injuries suffered on account of bandit raids are a matter of "pecuniary reparation" but "never the cause for American forces to invade Mexican soil." The precedents which have been established and maintained by the Government of the Mexican Republic for the last half century do not bear out this statement. It has grown to be almost a custom not to settle depredations of bandits by payments of money alone but to quell such disorders and to prevent such crimes by swift and sure punishment.

The *de facto* Government finally argues that "if the frontier were duly protected from incursions from Mexico there would be no reason for the existing difficulty"; thus the *de facto* Government attempts to absolve itself from the first duty of any Government, namely, the protection of life and property. This is the paramount obligation for which governments are instituted, and governments neglecting or failing to perform it are not worthy of the name. This is the duty for which General Carranza, it must be assumed, initiated his revolution in Mexico and organized the present government and for which the United States Government recognized his government as the *de facto* Government of Mexico. Protection of American lives and property, then, in the United States is first the obligation of this Government, and in Mexico is, first, the obligation of Mexico, and second, the obligation of the United States. In securing this protection along the common boundary the United States has a right to expect the co-operation of its neighboring Republic; and yet, instead of taking steps to check or punish the raiders, the *de facto* Government demurs and objects to measures taken by the United States. The Government of the United States does not-wish to believe that the *de facto* Government approves these marauding attacks, yet as they continue to be made, they show that the Mexican Government is unable to repress them. This inability, as this Government has had occasion in the past to say, may excuse the failure to check the outrages complained of, but it only makes stronger the duty of the United States to prevent them, for if the Government of Mexico can not protect the lives and property of Americans, exposed to attack from Mexicans, the Government of the United States is in duty bound, so far as it can, to do so.

In conclusion, the Mexican Government invites the United States to support its "assurances of friendship with real and effective acts" which "can be no other than the immediate withdrawal of the American troops." For the reasons I have herein fully set forth, this request of the *de facto* Government can not now be entertained. The United States has not sought the duty which has been forced upon it of pursuing bandits who under fundamental principles of municipal and international law, ought to be pursued and arrested and punished by Mexican authorities. Whenever Mexico will assume and effectively exercise that responsibility the United States, as it has many times before publicly declared, will be glad to have this obligation fulfilled by the *de facto* Government of Mexico. If, on the contrary, the *de facto* Government is pleased to ignore this obligation and to believe that "in case of a refusal to retire these troops there is no further recourse than to defend its territory by an appeal to arms," the Government of the United States would surely be lacking in sincerity and friendship if it did not frankly impress upon the *de facto* Government that the execution of this threat will lead to the gravest consequences. While this Government would deeply regret such a result, it can not recede from its settled determination to maintain its national rights and to perform its full duty in preventing further invasions of the territory of the United States and in removing the peril which Americans along the international boundary have borne so long with patience and forbearance.

Accept, etc.,   ROBERT LANSING

ROBERT LANSING, Secretary of State, to President Woodrow Wilson, June 21, 1916
Department of State, *The Lansing Papers,* II, 558

MY DEAR MR. PRESIDENT:

As there appears to be an increasing probability that the Mexican situation may develop into a state of war I desire to make a suggestion for your consideration.

It seems to me that we should avoid the use of the word "Intervention" and deny that any invasion of Mexico is for the sake of intervention.

There are several reasons why this appears to me expedient:

First. We have all along denied any purpose to interfere in the internal affairs of Mexico and the St. Louis platform declares against it. Intervention conveys the idea of such interference.

Second. Intervention would be humiliating to many Mexicans whose pride and sense of national honor would not resent severe terms of peace in case of being defeated in a war.

Third. American intervention in Mexico is extremely distasteful to all Latin America and might have a very bad effect upon our Pan-American program.

Fourth. Intervention, which suggests a definite purpose to "clean up" the country, would bind us to certain accomplishments which circumstances might make extremely difficult or inadvisable, and, on the other hand, it would impose conditions which might be found to be serious restraints upon us as the situation develops.

Fifth. Intervention also implies that the war would be made primarily in the interest of the Mexican people, while the fact is it would be a war forced on us by the Mexican Government, and, if we term it intervention, we will have considerable difficulty in explaining why we had not intervened before but waited until attacked.

It seems to me that the real attitude is that the *de facto* Government having attacked our forces engaged in a rightful enterprise or invaded our borders (as the case may be) we had no recourse but to defend ourselves and to do so it has become necessary to prevent future attacks by forcing the Mexican Government to perform its obligations. That is, it is simply a state of international war without purpose on our part other than to end the conditions which menace our national peace and the safety of our citizens, and that it is *not* intervention with all that that word implies.

I offer the foregoing suggestion, because I feel that we should have constantly in view the attitude we intend to take if worse comes to worse, so that we may regulate our present policy and future correspondence with Mexico and other American Republics with that attitude.

In case this suggestion meets with your approval I further suggest that we send to each diplomatic representative of a Latin American Republic in Washington a communication stating briefly our attitude and denying any intention to intervene. I enclose a draft of such a note. If this is to be done at all, it seems to me that it should be done at once, otherwise we will lose the chief benefit, namely, a right understanding by Latin America at the very outset.

Faithfully yours,

ROBERT LANSING

PROTOCOL of Agreement ad Referendum Signed by Commissioners of the United States and of Mexico, November 24, 1916
Foreign Relations of the United States, 1917, p. 926

ARTICLE 1

THE GOVERNMENT of the United States agrees to begin the withdrawal of American troops from Mexican soil as soon as practicable, such withdrawal, subject to the further terms of this agreement, to be completed not later than————; that is to say forty (40) days after the approval of this agreement by both Governments.

ARTICLE 2

The American commander shall determine the manner in which the withdrawal shall be effected, so as to insure the safety of the territory affected by the withdrawal.

ARTICLE 3

The territory evacuated by the American troops shall be occupied and adequately protected by the Constitutionalist forces, and such evacuation shall take place when the Constitutionalist forces have taken position to the south of the American forces so as to make effective such occupation and protection. The Mexican commander shall determine the plan for the occupation and protection of the territory evacuated by the American forces.

ARTICLE 4

The American and Mexican commanders shall deal separately, or wherever practicable, in friendly coöperation, with any obstacles which may arise tending to delay the withdrawal. In case there are any further activities of the forces inimical to the Constitutional Government which threaten the safety of the international border along the northern section of Chihuahua, the withdrawal of American forces shall not be delayed beyond the period strictly necessary to overcome such activities.

ARTICLE 5

The withdrawal of American troops shall be effected by marching to Columbus, or by using the Mexican Northwestern Railroad to El Paso, or by boat routes, as may be deemed most convenient or expedient by the American commander.

ARTICLE 6

Each of the Governments parties to this agreement shall guard its side of the international boundary. This, however, does not preclude such coöperation on the part of the military commanders of both countries, as may be practicable.

ARTICLE 7

This agreement shall take effect immediately upon approval by both Governments. Notification of approval shall be communicated by each Government to the other.

In testimony whereof [etc.]

[Although the Mexican government declined to ratify the agreement, the United States commissioners recommended to the President that the troops be withdrawn, full diplomatic relations re-established, and the border patrolled against further raids.]

Agrarian and Petroleum Claims

CORDELL HULL, Secretary of State, to Francisco Castillo Nájera, Mexican Ambassador to the United States, July 21, 1938

Department of State, *Press Releases,* July 23, 1938, p. 50

EXCELLENCY:

During recent years the Government of the United States has upon repeated occasions made representations to the Government of Mexico with regard to the continuing expropriation by Your Excellency's Government of agrarian properties owned by American citizens, without adequate, effective and prompt compensation being made therefor.

In extenuation of such action, the Mexican Government both in its official correspondence and in its public pronouncements has adverted to the fact that it is earnestly endeavoring to carry forward a program for the social betterment of the masses of its people.

The purposes of this program, however desirable they may be, are entirely unrelated to and apart from the real issue under discussion between our two Governments. The issue is not whether Mexico should pursue social and economic policies designed to improve the standard of living of its people. The issue is whether in pursuing them the property of American nationals may be taken by the Mexican Government without making prompt payment of just compensation to the owner in accordance with the universally recognized rules of law and equity.

My Government has frequently asserted the right of all countries freely to determine their own social, agrarian and industrial problems. This right includes the sovereign right of any government to expropriate private property within its borders in furtherance of public purposes. The Government of the United States has itself been very actively pursuing a program of social betterment. For example it has undertaken to improve the share of the farmer in the national income, to provide better housing, the wider use of electric power at reasonable rates, and security against old age and unemployment, to expand foreign trade through reduction of trade barriers, to prevent exploitation of labor through excessive hours and inadequate pay, to protect debtors from oppression, to curb monopolies; in short it is carrying out the most far-reaching program for the improvement of the general standard of living that this country has ever seen. Under this program it has expropriated from foreigners as well as its own citizens properties of various kinds, such as submarginal and eroded lands to be retired from farming, slums to be cleared for housing projects, land for power dams, lands containing resources to be preserved for government use. In each and every case the Government of the United States has scrupulously observed the universally recognized principle of compensation and has reimbursed promptly and in cash the owners of the properties that have been expropriated.

Since the right of compensation is unquestioned under international law, it cannot be conceived that insistence on it by this Government should impair in any way the warm friendship which exists between the Government of Mexico and our own, and between the people of Mexico and our own. This is particularly true because we have, in fact, pursued a constantly expanding program of financial, economic and moral cooperation. We have been mutually helpful to each other, and this Government is most desirous, in keeping with the good neighbor policy which it has been carrying forward during the last five years, to continue to cooperate with the Mexican Government in every mutually desirable and advantageous way.

One of the greatest services we can render is to pursue, and to urge others to pursue, a policy of fair dealing and fair play based on law and justice. Just as within our own borders we strive to prevent exploitation of debtors by powerful creditors and to protect the common man in making an honest living, so we are justified in accordance with recognized international law in striving to prevent unfair or oppressive treatment of our own people in other countries. It is the experience of this hemisphere, and this Government is convinced, that only by these means can the conditions of the peoples in all countries be soundly and permanently improved. Certainly the destruction of underlying principles of law and equity does not conduce to such improvement.

In its negotiations with the Mexican Government for compensation for the lands of American citizens that have been expropriated, my Government has consistently maintained the principle of compensation. That it has been no party to an unjust or unreasonable use of the doctrine is demonstrated by the following record.

Agrarian expropriations began in Mexico in 1915. Up to August 30, 1927, 161 moderate sized properties of American citizens had been taken. The claims arising therefrom were after much discussion referred to the General Claims Commission established by agreement between the two Governments. It is appropriate to point out, however, that, as yet, and for whatever the reasons may be, not a single claim has been adjusted and none has been paid. The owners of these properties notwithstanding the repeated requests of this Government for settlement, lost their property, its use and proceeds, from eleven years to more than twenty years ago, and are still seeking redress.

Subsequent to 1927, additional properties, chiefly farms of a moderate size, with a value claimed by their owners of $10,132,388, have been expropriated by the Mexican Government. This figure does not include the large land grants frequently mentioned in the press. It refers to the moderate sized holdings which rendered only a modest living. None of them as yet has been paid for. Considering that expropriation was the free act of the Mexican Government and the liability was voluntarily incurred by it, certainly on the basis of the record above stated, the United States Government cannot be accused of being unreasonable or impatient.

This latter group of cases has been in the past few years the subject of frequent representations by my Government. On March 27 of this year, it inquired of your Government what specific action with respect to payment was contemplated. On April 19 the Mexican Government responded, expressing its willingness to make a small monthly payment as settlement for a small number of agrarian claims of American nationals in one locality in Mexico. In response to an inquiry for further information you reiterated to this Department, on May 26 last, substantially what the Government of Mexico had already stated. On June 29 a detailed communication was addressed to you, setting forth the amount of the claims advanced for compensation to American nationals for agrarian properties expropriated, containing suggestions as to how the value of these properties might be determined in a manner satisfactory to both Governments, and requesting that payments be commenced while the determination of value was being reached. On July 15 Your Excellency sent a further communication to this Government in which no reference whatever was made to the suggestions advanced as to the method of determining the amounts owing for compensation, offering no indication that the Government of Mexico is prepared to make payments while the amount of the value of the properties expropriated is being determined, and stating that the Government of Mexico "has not contemplated covering entirely, during the present presidential term, the amount of the properties expropriated; much less has it undertaken, nor can it undertake, to proceed in such manner." In result, the American owners whose properties have been taken, are left not only without present payment, but without assurance that payment will be made within any foreseeable time.

The taking of property without compensation is not expropriation. It is confiscation. It is no less confiscation because there may be an expressed intent to pay at some time in the future.

If it were permissible for a government to take the private property of the citizens of other countries and pay for it as and when, in the judgment of that government, its economic circumstances and its local legislation may perhaps permit, the safeguards which the constitutions of most countries and established international law have sought to provide would be illusory. Governments would be free to take property far beyond their ability or willingness to pay, and the owners thereof would be without recourse. We cannot question the right of a foreign government to treat its own nationals in this fashion if it so desires. This is a matter of domestic concern. But we cannot admit that a foreign government may take the property of American nationals in disregard of the rule of compensation under international law. Nor can we admit that any government unilaterally and through its municipal legislation can, as in this instant case, nullify this universally accepted principle of international law, based as it is on reason, equity and justice.

The representations which this Government has made to the Government of Mexico have been undertaken with entire friendliness and good will, and the Mexican Government has recognized that fact. We are entirely sympathetic to the desires of the Mexican Government for the social betterment of its people. We cannot accept the idea, however, that these plans can be carried forward at the expense of our citizens, any more than we would feel justified in carrying forward our plans for our own social betterment at the expense of citizens of Mexico.

The good neighbor policy can only be based on mutual respect by both governments of the rights of each and of the rights of the citizens of each. President Roosevelt could not have spoken more truly than when he recently stated that the good neighbor policy is "a policy which can never be merely unilateral. In stressing it the American Republics appreciate, I am confident, that it is bilateral and multilateral and that the fair dealing which it implies must be reciprocated." The Government of Mexico from the standpoint of the long run and healthy progress of the Mexican people should be just as vitally interested in maintaining the integrity of the good neighbor policy as any other country. The surest way of breaking up the good neighbor policy would be to allow the impression that it permits the disregard of the just rights of the nationals of one country owning property in another country. In company with the citizens of the other American republics citizens of the United States own properties not only in Mexico, but in practically all countries. The same may be said of the citizens of the great majority of the nations of the world.

The whole structure of friendly intercourse, of international trade and commerce, and many other vital and mutually desirable relations between nations indispensable to their progress rest upon the single and hitherto solid foundation of respect on the part of governments and of peoples for each other's rights under international justice. The right of prompt and just compensation for expropriated property is a part of this structure. It is a principle to which the Government of the United States and most governments of the world have emphatically subscribed and which they have practiced and which must be maintained. It is not a principle which freezes the status quo and denies change in property rights but a principle that permits any country to expropriate private property within its borders in furtherance of public purposes. It enables orderly change without violating the legitimately acquired interests of citizens of other countries.

The Government of Mexico has professed its support of this principle of law. It is the considered judgment, however, of the Government of the United States that the Government of Mexico has not complied therewith in the case of several hundred separate farm or agrarian properties taken from American citizens. This judgment is apparently not admitted by your Government. The Government of the United States therefore proposes that there be submitted to arbitration the question *whether there has been compliance by the Government of Mexico with the rule of compensation as prescribed by international law in the case of the American citizens whose farm and agrarian properties in Mexico have been expropriated by the Mexican Government since August 30, 1927, and if not, the amount of, and terms under which, compensation should be made by the Government of Mexico.* My Government proposes that this arbitration be carried out pursuant to the provisions of the General Treaty of Arbitration signed at Washington January 5, 1929, to which both our countries are parties.

Accept [etc.]

CORDELL HULL

CORDELL HULL, Secretary of State, to Francisco Castillo Nájera, Mexican Ambassador to the United States, April 3, 1940
Department of State Bulletin, April 13, 1940, p. 380

EXCELLENCY:

During the course of the past years there have arisen between the Government of the United States and the Government of Mexico many questions for which no friendly and fair solution, satisfactory to both Governments, has been found. Certain of these problems are of outstanding importance and their equitable solution would redound to the immediate benefit of the peoples of both of our countries.

Animated by the desire to find such an adjustment of all of these pending matters, this Government proposed some two years ago an immediate and comprehensive study by representatives of the Government of the United States and of the Government of Mexico, for the purpose of preparing the way for an expeditious settlement of these controversial questions, the just solution of which would undoubtedly do much to cement the friendly relations between our neighboring peoples.

At that very moment the Government of Mexico by an executive decree expropriated large holdings of oil properties, amounting in value to many millions of dollars and belonging to American nationals, for which no payment has been made and for which there is no present prospect of payment. At various times the Government of Mexico has indicated its ability and readiness to pay. But the fact remains that no payments have been made.

The Government of the United States readily recognizes the right of a sovereign state to expropriate property for public purposes. This view has been stated in a number of communications addressed to your Government during the past two years and in conversations had with you during that same period regarding the expropriation by your Government of property belonging to American nationals. On each occasion, however, it has been stated with equal emphasis that the right to expropriate property is coupled with and conditioned on the obligation to make adequate, effective and prompt compensation. The legality of an expropriation is in fact dependent upon the observance of this requirement.

In my note to you dated July 21, 1938 I stated that the whole structure of friendly intercourse, of international trade and commerce, and many other vital and mutually desirable relations between nations, indispensable to their progress, rest upon respect on the part of governments and of peoples for each other's rights under international law. I stated that the right of prompt and just compensation for expropriated property was a part of this structure; that it was a principle to which the Government of the United States and most governments of the world have emphatically subscribed, and which they have practiced and which must be maintained. The Government of Mexico has professed support of this principle of law.

The Government of Mexico has, however, unfortunately, not carried this principle into practice.

Because of its conviction that until this fundamental question be solved in accordance with the recognized principles of equity and of international law, there could not exist an appropriate or favorable opportunity for the solution of all of the other questions pending between the two Governments, and which my Government had been most desirous of adjusting, the Government of the United States has been prevented from proceeding with the negotiations which it had initiated.

On March 16, 1940 you were good enough to hand to me an informal memorandum pursuant to our earlier discussions of the difficulties arising out of the expropriation by your Government of the oil properties belonging to American nationals. Without undertaking to pass in any way upon the memorandum as a whole, it is important to have clarification of two or three of the points raised therein.

It is stated (a) that "the Mexican Government judges that the right of expropriation is beyond discussion," and (b) that "there exists no divergence of opinion between the Government of the United States and that of Mexico regarding the right of the Mexican State to expropriate any private property by payment of a just compensation, as Mexico is agreeable to paying such indemnity to the expropriated companies."

I am compelled to take exception to the statements that the "right of expropriation is beyond discussion" and that "there exists no divergence of opinion between the Government of the United States and that of Mexico" in this respect.

As above stated, in the opinion of the Government of the United States the legality of an expropriation is contingent upon adequate, effective and prompt compensation.

The difference between our two Governments with respect to this principle lies in the fact that the Government of Mexico has assumed and continues to assume to exercise a right without compliance with the condition necessary to give such exercise a recognizable status of legality.

Expropriation of property by the Mexican Government has been taking place on a large scale since 1915 under the so-called agrarian program. While there are now under way efforts looking to a settlement of agrarian claims arising since August 30, 1927, the large number of such claims which arose prior to that date and which were filed with the General Claims Commission under the Convention of 1923, as well as a very much larger group of general claims, some of which date back over a period of approximately seventy years, remain unadjudicated and not a single dollar has been realized by any of the owners of the properties or by any of the other general claimants.

Accordingly, it is incorrect to state that there is "no divergence of opinion between the Government of the United States and that of Mexico" on the subject of expropriation. As stated in my note to you of July 21, 1938, in which I was discussing the expropriation of agrarian properties, the taking of property without adequate, effective and prompt compensation is not expropriation but is confiscation, and as also stated in that note, it is no less confiscation because there may be an expressed intent to pay at some time in the future.

It is also stated in your memorandum of March 16 that "since the Governments of Mexico and of the United States have not expressed their respective points of view as to what should constitute a prompt, equitable and adequate indemnity to compensate the American oil companies . . . it would be premature to propose the possibility of arbitration," and that the Mexican Government feels that "in order to determine the amount of the indemnity, the decision of the Mexican courts should be awaited."

It is difficult to imagine in what way this Government could have made plainer its point of view as to the compensation owing the American petroleum companies. Our records show that the obligation of the Mexican Government to make compensation has been kept before the Mexican Government constantly since the taking of the property. No stone has been left unturned by this Government to bring about a satisfactory arrangement for compensation. Moreover, the statement of your Government is not in the nature of things an adequate answer to the suggestion that arbitration would be an appropriate method of settling the differences between our two countries; nor is the statement that the decision of the Mexican courts should be awaited by any means reassuring.

You further indicate in your memorandum that your Government would be disposed to accept the good offices of my Government in order to discuss with the companies the question of compensation, or, in the alternative, to join with the United States in the designation of one or more experts to "present and discuss their points of view regarding the calculation of the value of the expropriated properties and regarding the form and guarantee of payment of the indemnity."

My Government has already used its good offices in the promotion of discussions between the American companies and the Mexican Government, and those discussions, as stated in your memorandum, came to naught. I am therefore unable to perceive that there would be any purpose in reverting to a procedure that has already resulted in a complete failure, nor do I perceive how the designation of experts for the purposes stated in the memorandum would promote a satisfactory solution of the problem. The designation of experts merely to "discuss their points of view" and without authority to receive and consider evidence systematically prepared and presented, to hear arguments *pro* and *contra,* and to render decisions of a final and binding character would merely postpone an effective solution which has already been too long delayed.

During the last twenty-five years, one American interest in Mexico after another has suffered at the hands of the Mexican Government. It is recognized that the Mexican Government is making payments on the Special Claims which have to do solely with damages caused by revolutionary disturbances between 1910 and 1920, and has started payments for farm lands expropriated since August 30, 1927. But the Mexican Government has made no compensation for the large number of General Claims of long standing which include an extensive group of claims for the expropriation of farm lands prior to August 30, 1927. It has made no adjustment either of the foreign debt or of the railroad debt both long in default and in both of which American citizens hold important investments. Moreover, the question of the railroad debt was further complicated by the expropriation of the Mexican National Railways on June 23, 1937. Finally, on March 18, 1938, the Mexican Government took over American-owned petroleum property to the value of many millions of dollars, and although two years have elapsed, not one cent of compensation has been paid.

This treatment of American citizens, wholly unjustifiable under any principle of equity or international law, is a matter of grave concern to this Government. These long-standing matters must of necessity be adjusted if the relations between our two countries are to be conducted on a sound and mutually cooperative basis of respect and helpfulness.

As an important step towards placing relations between the two countries on this basis, I suggest resorting to the appropriate, fair and honorable procedure of arbitration. Accordingly, I suggest that the two Governments agree (1) to submit to impartial arbitration all the questions involved in the oil controversy and to clothe a tribunal with authority not only to determine the amount to be paid to American nationals who have been deprived of their properties, but also the means by which its decision shall be executed to make certain that adequate and effective compensation shall promptly be paid, and (2) either to submit to an umpire, as contemplated by the General Claims Protocol of 1934, the unadjudicated claims falling under the Convention of 1923, or proceed immediately to the negotiation of an en bloc settlement in accordance with that Protocol.

There exists at this time a complete solidarity on the part of all the American Republics in upholding the principle that international differences of a justiciable character, which it has not been found possible to adjust by diplomacy, shall be submitted to arbitration. I think that the questions here involved fall within this category. At a period when in other parts of the world there is seemingly a growing disregard for the established principles of international law and orderly processes and an increasing tendency to substitute force for pacific methods of settling controversies, it is all the more desirable that the Governments of Mexico and the United States, firm in their adherence to the enlightened principles advanced and supported by all the American Republics, should signify their willingness to settle the differences between them mentioned in the preceding paragraph in the friendly manner indicated.

With the submission to arbitration of the oil controversy and the adjustment of the General Claims matter, the two Governments would then be in a position to go forward at the same time with the negotiations interrupted by the oil expropriation for a general settlement of all other pending matters. This Government earnestly urges this course, as it has consistently done in the past.

I shall be glad to learn whether your Government is favorably disposed to proceed along these lines.

Accept [etc.]   CORDELL HULL

His Excellency
Señor Dr. Don Francisco Castillo Nájera,
Ambassador of Mexico.

STATEMENT by Cordell Hull, Secretary of State, on Agreements between the United States and Mexico, November 19, 1941

Department of State Bulletin, November 22, 1941, p. 399

THE AGREEMENTS which Mexico and the United States have reached today are of outstanding importance in the relations between the two countries. Not only do they concern most of the principal mutual problems which have long been pending between the two sister republics but they mark a new milestone of great importance in the cause of increasingly closer collaboration and solidarity between the countries of the New World. These agreements constitute a further concrete proof of the fact that problems existing between nations are capable of mutually satisfactory settlement when approached in a reciprocal spirit of good will, tolerance, and a desire to understand each other's points of view.

These agreements have been reached only after months of discussion and negotiation. Some of the questions involved, such as those coming under the heading of General Claims, have defied solution for generations. Others, such as those growing out of the expropriation of petroleum properties owned by nationals of the United States, while of comparatively recent origin, have presented very difficult and complicated issues.

The scope of these agreements is evident from their mention. They cover an adjustment of property claims including the so-called General Claims and the agrarian claims, an agreement covering the expropriation of United States petroleum properties; an agreement in principle to negotiate a reciprocal-trade agreement; an arrangement between the United States Treasury Department and the Mexican Government and the Banco de Mexico for the stabilization of the Mexican peso; an agreement for purchase by the United States Treasury Department of newly mined Mexican silver directly from the Mexican Government; and an agreement between the Export-Import Bank and the Mexican Government for the extension of credits to facilitate the completion of the Inter-American Highway through Mexico. A separate statement regarding the broad outlines of the several agreements has been made available by the Department.

The agreement covering the petroleum expropriations deserves special mention. The petroleum properties were expropriated three and one half years ago. Since that time negotiations have been repeatedly undertaken by the Mexican Government and the affected United States interests. Unfortunately, the negotiations involving the largest United States interests were fruitless. Although this Government was not a direct participant in these negotiations it did what it could to facilitate a solution of the problem through both formal and informal representations to the Mexican Government.

In view of the total absence of any negotiations between the American interests and the Mexican Government during the present calendar year, and because of the importance of advancing the petroleum dispute to a prompt settlement, this Government undertook to canvass the problem with the Mexican Government in the hope that a fair and equitable arrangement might be reached.

This Government believes that the arrangement signed today embodies a practical, efficient, and equitable procedure for promoting a solution of this question. Its central feature is provision for the determination of the value of the expropriated properties, rights, and interests. This information obviously is essential in connection with any settlement. The American interests involved will retain full liberty of action in determining the course they will pursue before, during, and after the valuation proceedings.

Summary of the Agreements

The Governments of the United States and Mexico, desirous of finding practical solutions for a number of problems of mutual interest, have been engaged in a series of conversations and negotiations over a period of months. The Department announces with deep satisfaction that, as a result of these discussions, agreement has been reached with regard to a number of those matters, as follows:

I. EXPROPRIATION OF PETROLEUM PROPERTIES

By an exchange of notes on November 19 between the Mexican Ambassador and the Department of State, provision is made for determining the amount due to the American companies and interests whose properties and rights have been affected to their detriment by acts of the Mexican Government through acts of expropriation or otherwise on March 18, 1938 and subsequent thereto excepting those which have already made separate arrangements with the Mexican Government.

The two Governments will each appoint within the next 30 days an expert whose duty it shall be to determine the just compensation to be paid the American owners for their properties and rights and interests.

If the American and Mexican experts shall agree upon the amount to be paid, they shall render their joint report to the two Governments within five months. If they shall be unable to reach an agreement within that time, each shall submit a separate report to his Government within a further period of 30 days. Upon the receipt of such reports, the two Governments shall seek through diplomatic negotiations to determine the amount of compensation to be paid.

The Mexican Government is at this time making a cash deposit of $9,000,000 on account of the compensation to be paid the affected American companies and interests.

II. CLAIMS

The two Governments have found a means, so long lacking, of adjusting other outstanding property claims, including the so-called General Claims and the agrarian claims.

Under a claims convention signed on November 19, 1941, Mexico agrees to pay to the United States the sum of $40,000,000 in full settlement of these property claims. Mexico will make a payment of $3,000,-000 on account at the time of exchange of ratifications of the convention. Mexico has already made payments amounting to $3,000,000 on account of agrarian claims arising between August 30, 1927 and October 7, 1940.

The balance remaining due to the United States amounting to $34,000,000, after the $3,000,000 payment when ratifications are exchanged, will be liquidated over a period of years through the annual payment by Mexico of $2,500,000, beginning in 1942.

III. TRADE AGREEMENT

The two Governments have decided in principle to negotiate a reciprocal-trade agreement. Formal announcement of intention to negotiate will be made in due course, in accordance with the pertinent provisions of law.

IV. STABILIZATION OF THE MEXICAN PESO—U.S. DOLLAR RATE OF EXCHANGE

The Treasury Department has entered into an agreement for monetary and financial cooperation with the Mexican Government and the Banco de Mexico, which will provide, among other things, for the purchase of Mexican pesos with United States dollars. The U.S. dollars thus acquired by the Mexican authorities will greatly assist them in stabilizing the exchange value of the peso in terms of the dollar, to the mutual benefit and advantage of the two countries.

V. MEXICAN SILVER

The Treasury Department has also indicated its willingness to purchase newly mined Mexican silver direct from the Mexican Government on a basis similar to that under which such purchases were made prior to 1938.

VI. FINANCING OF MEXICAN PROJECTS

The Mexican Government has been engaged for a number of years in an important highway-construction program. It has financed a large part of this construction through the issuance of highway bonds which have been consistently serviced without any delays or difficulties. In order that the Mexican Government may expedite this highway-construction program, it has requested the Export-Import Bank to accept certain of these highway bonds as security for credits. The Export-Import Bank has acceded to this request and has opened a credit on this account.

It will be recalled that the Mexican highway system is a most important part of the Inter-American Highway and that construction work is well advanced in Mexico and a number of the other American republics.

The Export-Import Bank is disposed to consider sympathetically other requests for credits for developments in Mexico, whether they are to be executed by the Mexican Government or are private enterprises guaranteed by that Government, or one of its official agencies.

VII. OTHER PROBLEMS

The two Governments are actively continuing to study all other problems of interest to them. . . .

VI

Interventions in Nicaragua, Haiti, and the Dominican Republic

Nicaragua

MESSAGE from President William H. Taft to the United States Senate, Transmitting a Loan Convention with Nicaragua, June 7, 1911 (extract)

Foreign Relations of the United States, 1912, p. 1072. For various treaties and other agreements relating to United States relations with Nicaragua, Haiti, and the Dominican Republic, see *Appendix, infra,* p. 913 and pp. 916 ff.; see also *supra,* p. 73, regarding Honduras

TO THE SENATE:

In my message of January 26, 1911, transmitting to the Senate the Honduran Loan Convention, I said:

Besides the considerations of propriety, expediency and interest which make the present arrangement with Honduras alike desirable and mutually advantageous, its wisdom as an evolution in the direction of far-sighted international policy is to be borne in mind. Honduras is not alone in financial embarrassment. The continual disturbances of other Central American States put them also, although to a less degree, in the category of prospective borrowers. Within a year past Guatemala has sought the friendly counsel of the United States regarding the terms of a projected foreign loan, and it is announced, as part of the program of national recuperation put forth by the newly installed constitutional Government of Nicaragua, that the aid of the United States will be asked in effecting a readjustment of the debts of that Republic. It needs no profuse argument to show that the financial rehabilitation of the greater part of Central America will work potential good for the stability and peace of all and lead to that development of international resources and expansion of foreign commerce of which they are all capable and of which they all stand in need.

What was then expected with respect to Nicaragua has now become a fact. That Republic, after many years of governmental maladministration, interspersed with internal disturbances and followed by civil war, has at last established a government on a constitutional basis, which finds itself, unfortunately, with a depleted treasury and burdened with an accumulation of debts and claims, both domestic and foreign, which it is unable to meet without outside aid. It has accordingly indicated its desire for assistance on the part of the United

States for the refunding of its debt and the placing of its finances and administration upon a sound and stable basis, with a view to meeting its foreign obligations and to securing the tranquillity, prosperity and progress of the country. Heartily sympathizing with the Government of Nicaragua in its wish to reconstruct the financial and economic situation in that Republic and to further the development of that country, I empowered the Secretary of State to negotiate and conclude with the authorized plenipotentiary of Nicaragua a convention concerning a loan which that country contemplates making with citizens of the United States to provide for the refunding of its debt and the placing of its finances upon a sound and stable basis. This convention, signed at Washington on June 6, 1911, I transmit herewith to the Senate and commend with all earnestness to its favorable consideration, to the end that the advice and consent to ratification required by the Constitution may be given.

The convention with Nicaragua now transmitted is similar in its provisions to that with Honduras already before the Senate, and the weighty considerations of national and international policy which I advanced as counseling the consummation of the convention with Honduras are equally pertinent and applicable to the convention with Nicaragua. I deem it of paramount importance that both conventions should be ratified as contributing to the peace of Central America, for the fostering of which, under the Washington conventions of 1907, a moral obligation at least rests upon the United States.

Not only this, but a further responsibility is thrown upon us by the Monroe doctrine. Much of the debt of Nicaragua is external and held in Europe; and, while it may not be claimed that by the Monroe doctrine we may be called upon to protect an American Republic from the payment of its just foreign claims, still complications might result from the attempted enforced collection of such claims, from the involutions of which this Government might not escape. Hence it should be the policy of this Government, especially with respect to countries in geographical proximity to the Canal Zone, to give to them when requested all proper assistance, within the scope of our limitations, in the promotion of peace, in the development of their resources, and in a sound reorganization of their fiscal systems, thus, by contributing to the removal of conditions of turbulence and instability, enabling them by better established governments to take their rightful places among the law-abiding and progressive countries of the world. Better by far is this beneficial and constructive policy in the neighborhood of the Caribbean Sea, the Panama Canal and the Central American Republics, based as it is on the logic of our geographical position, the development of our commerce in the immediate neighborhood of our shores, our moral responsibilities due to a long-standing policy in the region mentioned, as well as, respecting Central America, arising from our relations to the Washington conventions, than it is with listless indifference to view unconcernedly the whole region in fomentations of turbulence, irresponsibly contracting debts that by their own exertions they would never be able to discharge, or to be required, as in several instances in the past, to land our armed forces for the protection of American citizens and their interests from violence, and for the enforcement of the humane provisions of international law for the observance of which in the region concerned this Government, whether rightfully or wrongfully, is held responsible by the world.

This convention now laid before the Senate, like the loan convention with Honduras, was drawn and signed, and now stands binding upon the Governments of the United States and Nicaragua, when by them ratified, only in respect to a loan contract when one shall have been signed which shall be finally found satisfactory to both Governments and shall consequently be admitted under the protection of the convention.

It is my judgment the part of wisdom and of statesmanship to ratify both the convention with Nicaragua now submitted and that with Honduras transmitted to the Senate on January 26, 1911, and it is my earnest hope that I may early receive the advice and consent of the Senate to their ratification.

Wm. H. Taft

The White House,
Washington, June 7, 1911

Loan Convention between the United States and Nicaragua

The Republic of Nicaragua, being now established on a firm political and constitutional basis, after eleven months of civil war and after seventeen years of administrative abuses resulting in the illegal diversion of public property and revenue, the accumulation of debts and claims in the hands of both natives and foreigners, and the existence of ruinous and disputed concessions in many of which foreigners are beneficiaries, finds the financial and economic situation of the country in urgent need of radical reconstruction;

And believing that this needed reconstruction on account of the circumstances above set forth will be difficult and complicated, especially as it involves the necessity of obtaining a loan adequate in amount yet on terms commensurate with the national resources—

The Republic of Nicaragua has indicated its desire for cooperation on the part of the United States for the refunding of its debt and the placing of its finances and administration upon a sound and stable basis with a view to meeting its foreign obligations, and to securing the tranquillity, prosperity and progress of the country.

And the Government of the United States, animated by a desire to promote the peace and prosperous development of all the Central American countries, and appreciating the wish of Nicaragua to contribute to such development by establishing on a firm footing its own material strength;

And it being recognized as necessary, in view of the present conditions of Nicaraguan finances and resources, that, to afford efficient and legitimate security and to obtain the special benefits sought, the Governments concerned should assume a special relation thereto;

And the two Governments being convinced that some contract should be negotiated and concluded between the Government of Nicaragua and some competent and reliable American banking group, said contract to afford a beneficial, just and equitable accomplishment of the purposes in question, have, with these objects in view, named as their plenipotentiaries:

The President of the United States of America, Philander C. Knox, Secretary of State of the United States; and

The President of Nicaragua, Dr. Salvador Castrillo, junior, Envoy Extraordinary and Minister Plenipotentiary of the Republic of Nicaragua near the Government of the United States;

Who, having communicated to each other their respective full powers, found in good and due form, have agreed upon the following:

ARTICLE I

The Government of Nicaragua undertakes to make and negotiate a contract providing for the refunding of its present internal and external debt and the adjustment and settlement of claims, liquidated and unliquidated; for the placing of its finances upon a sound and stable basis; and for the future development of the natural and economic resources of that country. The Governments of the United States and Nicaragua will take due note of all the provisions of the said contract when made, and will consult, in case of any difficulties, with a view to the faithful execution of the provisions of said contract, in order that all the benefits to Nicaragua and the security of the loan may at the same time be assured.

ARTICLE II

The loan which shall be made by the Government of Nicaragua pursuant to the above undertaking shall be secured upon the customs of Nicaragua, and the Government of Nicaragua agrees not to alter the import or export customs duties, or other charges affecting the entry, exit, or transit of goods, during the existence of the loan under the said contract, without consultation and agreement with the Government of the United States.

ARTICLE III

A full and detailed statement of the operations under this contract shall be submitted by the Fiscal Agent of the loan to the Department of State of the United States and to the Minister of Finance of Nicaragua at the expiration of each twelve months, and at such other times as may be requested by either of the two Governments.

ARTICLE IV

The Government of Nicaragua, so long as the loan exists, will appoint from a list of names to be presented to it by the fiscal agent of the loan and approved by the President of the United States of America a collector general of customs, who need not be a Nicaraguan and who shall administer the customs in accordance with the contract securing said loan, and will give this official full protection in the exercise of his functions. The Government of the United States, should the circumstances require, will in turn afford such protection as it may find requisite.

ARTICLE V

This Convention shall be ratified and the ratifications hereof shall be exchanged at Managua as soon as possible.

In faith whereof, the respective plenipotentiaries have signed the present Convention in the English and Spanish languages and have hereunto affixed their seals.

Done in duplicate, at Washington, this sixth day of June, one thousand nine hundred and eleven.

(seal)   PHILANDER C. KNOX
(seal)   SALVADOR CASTRILLO

PHILANDER C. KNOX, Secretary of State, to President William H. Taft, August 5, 1912

Foreign Relations of the United States, 1913, p. 1032. The letter was returned with the President's notation: "The authority requested herein is hereby given," dated August 5, 1912 (ibid., p. 1033)

DEAR MR. PRESIDENT:

From advices that have reached this Department it appears that one day last week President Adolfo Díaz of Nicaragua demanded the resignation of General Luis Mena, his Secretary of War, whereupon Mena, accompanied by his brother, the Chief of Police of Managua, the entire police force and a number of followers cut the electric light wires in Managua and left in the direction of Masaya, since which time he has openly defied the constituted authorities and is now leading an open rebellion against the Government.

Minister Weitzel now reports from Managua that the American corporation owning the railway which runs from Corinto to Granada and certain steamships on the inland waters of Nicaragua has complained to the Legation that Mena and his followers have seized its property and have used certain of the vessels of the company in bombarding the unfortified town of San Jorge. Minister Weitzel thereupon addressed a communication to the Government of Nicaragua requesting that it give satisfactory assurances that it was willing and able to afford adequate protection to all private property of American citizens in Nicaragua. To this communication the Government of Nicaragua replied to the effect that it was employing every available means to give such protection but that it regretted that, because of the necessity of using forces to put down armed disorders, it was unable for the present to comply with the Legation's request. The note of the Foreign Office closed by saying that,

in consequence, my Government desires that the Government of the United States guarantee with its forces security for the property of American citizens in Nicaragua and that it extend its protection to all the inhabitants of the Republic.

Minister Weitzel then addressed a communication to the Commanding Officer of the U.S.S. *Annapolis* requesting him to take such measures as might be necessary to protect the railroad and to afford security to American citizens and their property.

Minister Weitzel now reports to the Department that a detachment of one hundred men was sent from the *Annapolis* to Managua, where they arrived on August 4th at 3.30 a.m., and that they are now quartered at the Legation. He concludes by recommending the advisability of sending marines from Panama to Corinto by a Pacific Mail steamer, saying that Managua was quiet.

Under date of August 4, 8 p.m., the Minister reports to the Department that quiet continues at Managua and that the effect of the arrival of the bluejackets, according to the unanimous opinion of the Americans, in which he concurs, is thus far favorable. The Minister states that foreigners with whom he has talked are of the same opinion and that the Salvadoran Minister, in his personal capacity and in strict confidence, has informed him that this was the only move that could have prevented complete anarchy and the spread of disorder throughout Central America.

From a telegram received at the Navy Department from the Commander of the *Annapolis*, it appears that the men were sent from

Corinto to the capital in order to protect the lives of American citizens reported to be in imminent danger of attack.

I learn from inquiry at the Navy Department that there are on the Isthmus of Panama three hundred and fifty marines available for this service, and in view of the specific request of the Nicaraguan Government and of the seemingly possible danger of resultant anarchy, I have the honor to request that I be authorized to ask that the Navy Department comply with Minister Weitzel's recommendation.

I have [etc.]

P. C. KNOX

HUNTINGTON WILSON, Acting Secretary of State, to George T. Weitzel, United States Minister to Nicaragua, September 4, 1912 (paraphrase of telegram)

Foreign Relations of the United States, 1912, p. 1043. "In conformity with this pronouncement, 360 United States marines were sent to open the railway communications from Corinto to Managua. A Legation guard at Managua of 100 men had been landed on August 4. The pronouncement sounded the end of the revolution. General Mena, who had fallen ill after the outbreak, soon surrendered. Zeledón, who had taken up a position in the Barranca Fort overlooking Masaya, refused to surrender. United States marines stormed and captured the fort. Shortly afterwards, with the surrender of León, the revolution came to an end. . . . In suppressing the revolution, seven American marines and bluejackets lost their lives. Thenceforth the United States retained at Managua a Legation guard of approximately 130 men." Department of State, The United States and Nicaragua (1932), Latin American Series, No. 6, p. 21

UNLESS a different course appears to you preferable—in which case you will telegraph your suggestions—you may communicate to the Government of Nicaragua the text of the following as the authorized declaration of the policy of the United States in the present disturbances. You may also communicate it unofficially to the rebel leaders, and make it public:

The policy of the Government of the United States in the present Nicaraguan disturbances is to take the necessary measures for an adequate legation guard at Managua, to keep open communications, and to protect American life and property.

In discountenancing Zelaya, whose régime of barbarity and corruption was ended by the Nicaraguan nation after a bloody war, the Government of the United States opposed not only the individual but the system, and this Government could not countenance any movement to restore the same destructive régime. The Government of the United States will, therefore, discountenance any revival of Zelayaism and will lend its strong moral support to the cause of legally constituted good government for the benefit of the people of Nicaragua, whom it has long sought to aid in their just aspiration toward peace and prosperity under constitutional and orderly government.

A group of some 125 American planters residing in one region in Nicaragua have applied for protection. Some two dozen American firms doing business in that country have applied for protection. The American bankers who have made investments in relation to railroads and steamships in Nicaragua, in connection with a plan for the relief of the financial distress of that country, have applied for protection. The American citizens now in the service of the Government of Nicaragua and the Legation itself have been placed in actual jeopardy under fire. Two wounded American citizens are reported to have been ruthlessly slaughtered. Besides the Emery claim due American citizens and the indemnity for the killing of Groce and Cannon in the Zelaya war, there are various American claims and concessionary interests. Under the Washington conventions, the United States has a moral mandate to exert its influence for the preservation of the general peace of Central America, which is seriously menaced by the present uprising, and to this end in the strict enforcement of the Washington conventions and loyal support of their aims and purposes all the Central American Republics will find means of valuable cooperation. These are among the important moral, political, and material interests to be protected.

When the American Minister called upon the Government of Nicaragua to protect American life and property, the Minister for Foreign Affairs replied that the Government troops must be used to put down the rebellion, adding: "In consequence, my Government desires that the Government of the United States guarantee with its forces security for the property of American citizens in Nicaragua, and that they extend this protection to all the inhabitants of the Republic."

In this situation the policy of the Government of the United States will be to protect the life and property of its citizens in the manner indicated and, meanwhile, to contribute its influence in all appropriate ways to the restoration of lawful and orderly government in order that Nicaragua may resume its program of reforms unhampered by the vicious elements who would restore the methods of Zelaya.

The revolt of General Mena in flagrant violation of his solemn promises to his own Government and to the American Minister, and of the Dawson agreement by which he was solemnly bound, and his attempt to overturn the Government of his country for purely selfish purposes and without even the pretense of contending for a principle, make the present rebellion in origin the most inexcusable in the annals of Central America. The nature and methods of the present disturbances, indeed, place them in the category of anarchy rather than ordinary revolution. The reported character of those who promptly joined Mena, together with his uncivilized and savage action in breaking armistices, maltreating messengers, violating his word of honor, torturing peaceable citizens to exact contributions, and, above all, in the ruthless bombardment of the city of Managua, with the deliberate destruction of innocent life and property and the killing of women and children and the sick in hospitals, and the cruel and barbarous slaughter of hundreds reported at Leon, give to the Mena revolt the attributes of the abhorrent and intolerable Zelaya régime.

JOHN E. RAMER, *United States Minister to Nicaragua, to the Nicaraguan Government, November 14, 1923*

Department of State, *The United States and Nicaragua* (1932), Latin American Series, No. 6, p. 47. The Legation guard departed from Nicaragua August 4, 1925 (*ibid.*, p. 54)

I HAVE THE HONOR to inform Your Excellency that my Government desires that the Legation Guard, which has remained in Nicaragua since Your Excellency's Government requested the assistance of the Government of the United States in 1912, in the maintenance of constitutional order, should be withdrawn as soon as practicable. My Government, however, does not desire to make any sudden radical change which would inject a new element into the situation in Central America that might perhaps be a cause for unrest and disturbance.

In this connection I am instructed to state that my Government has noted with gratification and with sympathetic appreciation the steps which have already been taken by the Nicaraguan Government to assure freedom and fairness in the approaching elections. The enactment of the electoral law, drafted by an expert employed by the Nicaraguan Government for this purpose, may be regarded as the first step toward assuring the people of Nicaragua that complete freedom will exist during the electoral period, and my Government is confident that this step will be followed by such effective measures during the electoral period as will assure a free expression of the will of the people and convince all parties that the Government which may result from the elections will have the support of the majority of the people of Nicaragua. Therefore, my Government instructs me to inform Your Excellency that upon the installation in January, 1925, of the government coming into office as the result of the elections to be held in October, 1924, it will feel that there is no further reason to maintain a Legation Guard at Managua and the American Marines will accordingly be withdrawn at that time.

I am further instructed by my Government to state that the American Marines will be retained in Managua during the approaching electoral period only if the Nicaraguan Government considers that their presence will assist the constituted authorities in assuring complete freedom in the presidential elections, and that they remain specifically for the purpose of helping to maintain tranquillity and order during the electoral period.

The electoral law recently voted is as yet unfamiliar alike to the officials charged with its carrying out and enforcement, as to the Nicaraguan electorate which will exercise its rights according to its provisions. Therefore, in order to assist the Nicaraguan Government in the installation of this new electoral system with the least possible amount of confusion, my Government will be glad, should the Nicaraguan Government so desire, to ask Mr. Dodds, the author of the law, or some other qualified technical experts, to come to Nicaragua a few months in advance of the next election in order that he may, by his counsel and advice, assist the Nicaraguan authorities in putting the law into effect. My Government will also be glad to assist the Nicaraguan Government to obtain the services of such additional assistants as may be required to travel throughout Nicaragua to help the local authorities in the installation of the new system and in its proper enforcement, and to report to the authorities at Managua any difficulties that may be encountered throughout the country in the proper enforcement of the law in order that those difficulties may be promptly overcome.

As another evidence of its desire to assist Nicaragua in the orderly and undisturbed conduct of its normal existence, my Government would be glad to assist the Nicaraguan Government in the organization and training of an efficient constabulary which would assure the maintenance of order after the Marines are withdrawn. In establishing a force of this nature, the Nicaraguan Government would be carrying out the terms of Article II of the Convention for the Limitation of Armaments, signed at the recent Conference on Central American Affairs. If the Nicaraguan Government desires, my Government will be glad to suggest the names of persons suitable to act as instructors in the new constabulary, in order that their experience may be made available to Nicaragua.

My Government feels that with the aid of Mr. Dodds and the other assistants in the efficient installation of the new electoral system, free and fair suffrage should be possible in the coming elections so that the government resulting therefrom should have the support of the majority of the Nicaraguan people and would, therefore, need no other assistance in maintaining order than that of the Nicaraguan constabulary, which my Government is ready to assist in training, and that, therefore, upon the installation of that government the Marines may be withdrawn without any noticeable effect upon the normal course of affairs in Nicaragua.

The new government should be in a very strong position indeed, and it is hoped that long before its entry into office the General Treaty of Peace and Amity, signed at Washington on February 7, 1923, by the representatives of the five Central American powers, will have been ratified and put into effect so that any individual or group of individuals who might endeavor to overthrow the constituted authorities will know full well in advance that the other four Central American Governments will not, on account of Article II of that Treaty, recognize any government coming into power contrary to the provisions of that Treaty. In any case, the position and policy of the United States Government with regard to such recognition is and will continue to be that announced by the American Minister to Honduras under instructions from the Department of State of June 30, 1923, which is in complete consonance and accord with the stipulations of Article II of the General Treaty of Peace and Amity, as signed by the delegates of the five Central American Republics at Washington on February 7, last.

MESSAGE from President Calvin Coolidge to the United States Congress, January 10, 1927

Foreign Relations of the United States, 1927, III, 288

TO THE CONGRESS OF THE UNITED STATES:

While conditions in Nicaragua and the action of this Government pertaining thereto have in general been made public, I think the time has arrived for me officially to inform the Congress more in detail of the events leading up to the present disturbances and conditions which seriously threaten American lives and property, endanger the stability of all Central America, and put in jeopardy the rights granted by Nicaragua to the United States for the construction of a canal. It is well known that in 1912 the United States intervened in Nicaragua with a large force and put down a revolution, and that from that time to 1925 a legation guard of American marines was, with the consent of the Nicaraguan Government, kept in Managua to protect American lives and property. In 1923 representatives of the five Central American countries, namely, Costa Rica, Guatemala, Honduras, Nicaragua, and Salvador, at the invitation of the United

States, met in Washington and entered into a series of treaties. These treaties dealt with limitation of armament, a Central American tribunal for arbitration, and the general subject of peace and amity. The treaty last referred to specifically provides in Article II that the Governments of the contracting parties will not recognize any other government which may come into power in any of the five Republics through a *coup d'état* or revolution and disqualifies the leaders of such coup d'état or revolution from assuming the presidency or vice presidency. Article II is as follows:

Desiring to make secure in the Republics of Central America the benefits which are derived from the maintenance of free institutions and to contribute at the same time toward strengthening their stability, and the prestige with which they should be surrounded, they declare that every act, disposition or measure which alters the constitutional organization in any of them is to be deemed a menace to the peace of said Republics, whether it proceed from any public power or from the private citizens.

Consequently, the Governments of the Contracting Parties will not recognize any other Government which may come into power in any of the five Republics through a coup d'etat or a revolution against a recognized Government, so long as the freely elected representatives of the people thereof have not constitutionally reorganized the country. And even in such a case they obligate themselves not to acknowledge the recognition if any of the persons elected as President, Vice-President or Chief of State Designate should fall under any of the following heads:

1) If he should be the leader or one of the leaders of a coup d'etat or revolution, or through blood relationship or marriage, be an ascendent or descendent or brother of such leader or leaders.

2) If he should have been a Secretary of State or should have held some high military command during the accomplishment of the coup d'etat, the revolution, or while the election was being carried on, or if he should have held this office, or command within the six months preceding the coup d'etat, revolution, or the election.

Furthermore, in no case shall recognition be accorded to a government which arises from election to power of a citizen expressly and unquestionably disqualified by the Constitution of his country as eligible to election as President, Vice-President or Chief of State Designate.

The United States was not a party to this treaty, but it was made in Washington under the auspices of the Secretary of State, and this Government has felt a moral obligation to apply its principles in order to encourage the Central American States in their efforts to prevent revolution and disorder. The treaty, it may be noted in passing, was signed on behalf of Nicaragua by Emiliano Chamorro himself, who afterwards assumed the presidency in violation thereof and thereby contributed to the creation of the present difficulty.

In October, 1924, an election was held in Nicaragua for President, Vice President, and members of the Congress. This resulted in the election of a coalition ticket embracing Conservatives and Liberals. Carlos Solorzano, a Conservative Republican, was elected President and Juan B. Sacasa, a Liberal, was elected Vice President. This Government was recognized by the other Central American countries and by the United States. It had been the intention of the United States to withdraw the marines immediately after this election, and notice was given of the intention to withdraw them in January, 1925. At the request of the President of Nicaragua this time was extended to September 1, 1925. Pursuant to this determination and notice, the marines were withdrawn in August, 1925, and it appeared at that time as though tranquility in Nicaragua was assured. Within two months, however, further disturbances broke out between the supporters of General Chamorro and the supporters of the President, culminating in the seizure of the Loma, a fortress dominating the city of Managua. Once in possession of the Loma, General Chamorro dictated an agreement which President Solorzano signed the next day. According to the terms of this agreement the President agreed to substitute supporters of General Chamorro for certain members of his cabinet, to pay General Chamorro $10,000 for the expenses of the uprising, and to grant amnesty to all those who participated in it. Vice President Sacasa thereupon left the country. In the meantime General Chamorro, who, while he had not actually taken over the office of President, was able to dictate his will to the actual Executive, brought about the expulsion from the Congress of 18 members, on the ground that their election had been fraudulent, and caused to be put in their places candidates who had been defeated at the election of 1924. Having thus gained the control of Congress, he caused himself to be appointed by the Congress as designate on January 16, 1926. On January 16, 1926, Solorzano resigned as President and immediately General Chamorro took office. The four Central American countries and the United States refused to recognize him as President. On January 22 the Secretary of State addressed to the Nicaraguan representative in Washington the following letter:

DEAR DOCTOR CASTRILLO:

In your communication of the 19th instant addressed to the Secretary of State you advise that President Solorzano having resigned his office General Emiliano Chamorro took charge of the executive power on January 17.

The hope expressed in your letter that the relations which have been close and cordial for so many years between Nicaragua and the United States will continue and grow stronger has been noted with pleasure. The Government and people of the United States have feelings of sincerest friendship for Nicaragua and the people of Nicaragua and the Government of the United States will of course continue to maintain the most friendly relations with the people of Nicaragua. This Government has felt privileged to be able to be of assistance in the past at their request not only to Nicaragua but to all countries of Central America more especially during the Conference on Central American Affairs which resulted in the signing of a General Treaty of Peace and Amity on February 7, 1923, between the five Republics of Central America. The object of the Central American countries with which the United States was heartily in accord, was to promote constitutional government and orderly procedure in Central America and those Governments agreed upon a joint course of action with regard to the nonrecognition of governments coming into office through *coup d'etat* or revolution. The United States has adopted the principles of that Treaty as its policy in the future recognition of Central American Governments as it feels that by so doing it can best show its friendly disposition towards and its desire to be helpful to the Republics of Central America.

It is therefore with regret that I have to inform you that the Government of the United States has not recognized and will not recognize as the Government of Nicaragua the regime now headed by General Chamorro, as the latter was duly advised on several occasions by the American Minister after General Chamorro had taken charge of the citadel at Managua on October 25th last. This action is, I am happy to learn, in accord with that taken by all the Governments that signed with Nicaragua the Treaty of 1923.

Notwithstanding the refusal of this Government and of the other Central American Governments to recognize him, General Chamorro continued to exercise the functions of President until October 30, 1926. In the meantime, a revolution broke out in May on the east coast in the neighborhood of Bluefields and was speedily suppressed by the troops of General Chamorro. However, it again broke out with considerable more violence. The second attempt was attended with some success and practically all of the east coast of Nicaragua fell into the hands of the revolutionists. Throughout these events Sacasa was at no time in the country, having remained in Mexico and Guatemala during this period.

Repeated requests were made of the United States for protection, especially on the east coast, and, on August 24, 1926, the Secretary of State addressed to the Secretary of the Navy the following communication:

I have the honor to suggest that war vessels of the Special Service Squadron proceed as soon as possible to the Nicaraguan ports of Corinto and Bluefields for the protection of American and foreign lives and property in case that threatened emergencies materialize. The American Chargé d'Affaires at Managua has informed the Department that he considers the presence of war vessels at these ports desirable, and the American Consul at Bluefields has reported that a warship is urgently needed to protect life and property at that port. An attack on The Bluff and Bluefields is expected momentarily.

Accordingly, the Navy Department ordered Admiral Latimer, in command of the special service squadron, to proceed to Bluefields. Upon arriving there he found it necessary for the adequate protection of American lives and property to declare Bluefields a neutral zone. This was done with the consent of both factions, afterwards, on October 26, 1926, reduced to a written agreement, which is still in force. In October [*September*], 1926, the good offices of the United States were sought by both parties for the purpose of effecting a settlement of the conflict. Admiral Latimer, commanding the special service squadron, brought about an armistice to permit of a conference being held between the delegates of the two factions. The armistice was originally for 15 days and was later extended 15 days more. At the request of both parties, marines were landed at Corinto to establish a neutral zone in which the conference could be held. Doctor Sacasa was invited to attend this conference but refrained from doing so and remained in Guatemala City. The United States Government did not participate in the conference except to provide a neutral chairman; it simply offered its good offices to make the conference possible and arranged a neutral zone at Corinto at the request of both parties during the time the conference was held. I understand that at this conference General Chamorro offered to resign and permit the Congress to elect a new designate to assume the Presidency. The conference led to no result, since just at the time when it seemed as though some compromise agreement would be reached the representatives of Doctor Sacasa suddenly broke off negotiations.

According to our reports, the Sacasa delegates on this occasion stated freely that to accept any government other than one presided over by Doctor Sacasa himself would be a breach of faith with their Mexican allies. Hostilities were resumed on October 30, 1926. On the same date General Chamorro formally turned over the executive power to Sebastian Uriza, who had been appointed designate by the Congress controlled by General Chamorro. The United States Government refused to recognize Señor Uriza, on the ground that his assumption of the Presidency had no constitutional basis. Uriza thereupon convoked Congress in extraordinary session, and the entire 18 members who had been expelled during the Chamorro régime were notified to resume their seats. The Congress which met in extraordinary session on November 10 had, therefore, substantially the same membership as when first convened following the election of 1924. This Congress, whose acts may be considered as constitutional, designated Señor Adolfo Diaz as first designate. At this session of Congress 53 members were present out of a total membership of 67, of whom 44 voted for Diaz and 2 for Solorzano. The balance abstained from voting. On November 11 Señor Uriza turned over the executive power to Diaz, who was inaugurated on the 14th.

The Nicaraguan constitution provides in article 106 that in the absence of the President and Vice President the Congress shall designate one of its members to complete the unexpired term of President. As President Solorzano had resigned and was then residing in California, and as the Vice President, Doctor Sacasa, was in Guatemala, having been out of the country since November, 1925, the action of Congress in designating Señor Diaz was perfectly legal and in accordance with the constitution. Therefore the United States Government on November 17 extended recognition to Señor Diaz.

Following his assumption of office, President Diaz, in the following note, dated November 15, 1926, requested the assistance of the United States Government to protect American and foreign lives and property:

Upon assuming the presidency I found the Republic in a very difficult situation because of the attitude, assumed without motive by the Government of Mexico in open hostility to Nicaragua. It must be clear to you that, given the forces which that Government disposes of, its elements of attack are irresistible for this feeble and small Nation. This condition places in imminent risk the sovereignty and independence of Nicaragua, and consequently, the continental equilibrium on which the Pan-Americanism is founded which the United States has fostered with such lofty spirit.

Naturally the emergency resulting from these conditions places in peril the interests of American citizens and other foreigners residing in our territory and renders it impossible for a Government so rudely attacked, to protect them as is its duty and as it desires.

For these reasons and appreciating the friendly disposition of the United States toward weak Republics and the intentions which your Government has always manifested for the protection of the sovereignty and independence of all the countries of America by morally supporting legitimate Governments in order to enable them [to] afford a tranquil field of labor for foreigners which is needed for the stimulation of the growth of the prosperity of these countries, I address myself to you in order that, with the same good will with which you have aided in Nicaraguan reconciliation, you may solicit for my Government and in my name the support of the Department of State in order to reach a solution in the present crisis and avoid further hostilities and invasions on the part of the Government of Mexico.

I desire to manifest to you at the same time that whatever may be the means chosen by the Department of State, they will meet with the approval of my absolute confidence in the high spirit of justice of the Government of the United States.

Immediately following the inauguration of President Diaz and frequently since that date he has appealed to the United States for support, has informed this Government of the aid which Mexico is giving to the revolutionists, and has stated that he is unable solely because of the aid given by Mexico to the revolutionists to protect the lives and property of American citizens and other foreigners. When negotiations leading up to the Corinto conference began, I immediately placed an embargo on the shipment of arms and ammunition to Nicaragua. The Department of State notified the other Central American States, to wit, Costa Rica, Honduras, Salvador, and Guatemala, and they assured the department that they would cooperate in this measure. So far as known, they have done so. The State Department also notified the Mexican Government of this embargo and informally suggested to that Government like action. The Mexican Government did not adopt the suggestion to put on an embargo, but informed the American ambassador at Mexico City that in the absence of manufacturing plants in Mexico for the making of arms and ammunition the matter had little practical importance.

As a matter of fact, I have the most conclusive evidence that arms and munitions in large quantities have been on several occasions since August, 1926, shipped to the revolutionists in Nicaragua. Boats carrying these munitions have been fitted out in Mexican ports, and some of the munitions bear evidence of having belonged to the Mexican Government. It also appears that the ships were fitted out with the full knowledge of and, in some cases, with the encouragement of Mexican officials and were in one instance, at least, commanded by a Mexican naval reserve officer. At the end of November, after spending some time in Mexico City, Doctor Sacasa went back to Nicaragua, landing at Puerto Cabezas, near Bragmans Bluff. He immediately placed himself at the head of the insurrection and declared himself President of Nicaragua. He has never been recognized by any of the Central American Republics nor by any other Government, with the exception of Mexico, which recognized him immediately. As arms and munitions in large quantities were reaching the revolutionists, I deemed it unfair to prevent the recognized Government from purchasing arms abroad, and, accordingly, the Secretary of State has notified the Diaz Government that licenses would be issued for the export of arms and munitions purchased in this country. It would be thoroughly inconsistent for this country not to support the Government recognized by it while the revolutionists were receiving arms and munitions from abroad.

During the last two months the Government of the United States has received repeated requests from various American citizens, both directly and through our consuls and legation, for the protection of their lives and property. The Government of the United States has also received requests from the British Chargé at Managua and from the Italian ambassador at Washington for the protection of their respective nationals. Pursuant to such requests, Admiral Latimer, in charge of the special service squadron, has not only maintained the neutral zone at Bluefields under the agreement of both parties but has landed forces at Puerto Cabezas and Rio Grande, and established neutral zones at these points where considerable numbers of Americans live and are engaged in carrying on various industries. He has also been authorized to establish such other neutral zones as are necessary for the purposes above mentioned.

For many years numerous Americans have been living in Nicaragua developing its industries and carrying on business. At the present time there are large investments in lumbering, mining, coffee growing, banana culture, shipping, and also in general mercantile and other collateral business. All these people and these industries have been encouraged by the Nicaraguan Government. That Government has at all times owed them protection, but the United States has occasionally been obliged to send naval forces for their proper protection. In the present crisis such forces are requested by the Nicaraguan Government, which protests to the United States its inability to protect these interests and states that any measures which the United States deems appropriate for their protection will be satisfactory to the Nicaraguan Government.

In addition to these industries now in existence, the Government of Nicaragua, by a treaty entered into on the 5th day of August, 1914, granted in perpetuity to the United States the exclusive proprietary rights necessary and convenient for the construction, operation, and maintenance of an oceanic canal. . . .

The consideration paid by the United States to Nicaragua was the sum of $3,000,000. At the time of the payment of this money a financial plan was drawn up between the Nicaraguan Government and its creditors which provided for the consolidation of Nicaragua's obligations. At that time the bondholders holding the Nicaraguan external debt consented to a reduction in interest from 6 to 5 per cent, providing the service of this loan was handled through the American collector of customs, and at the same time a series of internal guaranteed customs bonds amounting to $3,744,000 was issued by the Nicaraguan Government to pay off the claims which had arisen against it because of revolutionary disturbances from 1909 to 1912. The other outstanding external bonds, amounting on February 1, 1926, to about £772,000, are held in Great Britain. Of the guaranteed customs bonds, $2,867,000 were on February 1, 1926, still in circulation, and of these about $1,000,000 were held by Nicaraguans, $1,000,000 by American citizens, and the balance by nationals of other countries. The bonds held in the United States are held by the public in general circulation and, so far as the department knows, no American bankers are directly interested in the Nicaraguan indebtedness. This financial plan was adopted by an act of the Congress of Nicaragua on August 31, 1917. The National Bank of Nicaragua was made the depository of all Government revenues. The internal revenues were, as heretofore, to be collected by the Government. Collection of the internal revenue, however, was to be taken over by the collector general of customs, an American citizen appointed by the Nicaraguan Government and approved by the Secretary of State of the United States, if the products should average less than $60,000 a month for three consecutive months. This has never yet been necessary. The proceeds of the customs revenues were to be applied, first, to the payment of such sums as might be agreed upon in the contemplated contracts for the service of the foreign loan, the internal loan, and claims against the Nicaraguan Government. From the balance of the revenue $80,000 a month was to be used for the ordinary budget expenses and an additional $15,000 for extraordinary expenses.

Under this financial plan the finances of Nicaragua have been rehabilitated in a very satisfactory manner. Of the $3,744,000 of internal customs bonds issued in 1917 about $900,000 have been paid. Of the external debt, bonds issued in 1909 amounting to £1,250,000, there now remain only about £770,000. The total public debt of Nicaragua has been reduced from about $22,000,000 in 1917 to $6,625,203 at the beginning of 1926. Furthermore, the country in time of peace has ample revenues for its ordinary budget expenses and a surplus which has been used in extensive public improvements. The Nicaraguan National Bank and the National Railroad, controlling interests in which were formerly owned by American bankers, were repurchased by the Nicaraguan Government in 1920 and 1924, and are now wholly owned by that Government.

There is no question that if the revolution continues American investments and business interests in Nicaragua will be very seriously affected, if not destroyed. The currency, which is now at par, will be inflated. American as well as foreign bondholders will undoubtedly look to the United States for the protection of their interests.

It is true that the United States did not establish the financial plan by any treaty, but it nevertheless did aid through diplomatic channels and advise in the negotiation and establishment of this plan for the financial rehabilitation of Nicaragua.

Manifestly the relation of this Government to the Nicaraguan situation, and its policy in the existing emergency, are determined by the facts which I have described. The proprietary rights of the United States in the Nicaraguan canal route, with the necessary implications growing out of it affecting the Panama Canal, together with the obligations flowing from the investments of all classes of our citizens in Nicaragua, place us in a position of peculiar responsibility. I am sure it is not the desire of the United States to intervene in the internal affairs of Nicaragua or of any other Central American Republic. Nevertheless it must be said that we have a very definite and special interest in the maintenance of order and good government in Nicaragua at the present time, and that the stability, prosperity, and independence of all Central American countries can never be a matter of indifference to us. The United States can not, therefore, fail to view with deep concern any serious threat to stability and constitutional government in Nicaragua tending toward anarchy and jeopardizing American interests, especially if such state of affairs is contributed to or brought about by outside influences or by any foreign power. It has always been and remains the policy of the United States in such circumstances to take the steps that may be necessary for the preservation and protection of the lives, the property, and the interests of its citizens and of this Government itself. In this respect I propose to follow the path of my predecessors.

Consequently, I have deemed it my duty to use the powers committed to me to insure the adequate protection of all American interests in Nicaragua, whether they be endangered by internal strife or by outside interference in the affairs of that Republic.

CALVIN COOLIDGE

The White House,
January 10, 1927

HENRY L. STIMSON, Personal Representative of the President of the United States to Nicaragua, to General José María Moncada, Leader of the Liberal Revolutionary Forces in Nicaragua, May 11, 1927
Department of State, *The United States and Nicaragua* (1932), p. 76

Tipitapa, Nicaragua, May 11, 1927

DEAR GENERAL MONCADA:

I am glad to learn of the authority that has been placed in you by your army to arrange for a general disarmament. I am also glad to make clear to you and to your army the attitude of the President of the United States as to this matter. In seeking to terminate this war, President Coolidge is actuated only by a desire to benefit the people of Nicaragua and to secure for them a free, fair and impartial election. He believes that only by such free and fair elections can permament peace be secured for Nicaragua. To insure this in 1928 he has consented to the request that American representatives selected by him shall supervise the election. He has also consented to assign American officers to train and command a non-partisan national constabulary for Nicaragua which will have the duty of securing such a fair election and of preventing any fraud or intimidation of voters. He is willing also to leave in Nicaragua until after the election a sufficient force of marines to support the work of the constabulary and insure peace and freedom at the election.

As further evidence of the good faith of the American Government and of the present Nicaraguan Government in this matter, I am glad to tell you what has already been done. It will answer the questions contained in the letter of your soldiers which you have shown me. General amnesty has already been granted by the President of Nicaragua. I have recommended to President Diaz that the Supreme Court be reconstituted by the elimination of the illegal judges placed in that court under Sr. Chamorro. President Diaz has already called upon those judges for their resignations and I believe that these resignations will be obtained. I have already advised that the Congress be reconstituted by holding of special elections in these Liberal districts where elections were not held in 1926 under conditions which will insure that the Liberal voters will be amply protected in their rights. I have also recommended that members of the Congress illegally expelled by Sr. Chamorro whose terms have not yet expired be reinstated. I have been assured that this will be done.

I have recommended that Liberal *Jefes Politicos* be appointed in the six Liberal districts of Bluefields, Jinotega, Nueva Segovia, Esteli, Chinandega, and Leon. I have been assured that this will be done.

In short, I have recommended that steps be taken so far as possible to restore the political condition as it existed in Nicaragua before the Chamorro *coup d'etat* and I believe that so far as possible it will be done.

I hope that these steps will assure you and your army of the fairness of the United States Government and its desire to see peace, justice and freedom re-established in Nicaragua without any unfairness or favoritism towards any party but being regardful of the rights of Liberals and Conservatives alike.

Very respectfully yours,

HENRY L. STIMSON

STATEMENT by the Department of State, 1932, Regarding Withdrawal of the United States Marines from Nicaragua
Department of State, *The United States and Nicaragua* (1932), p. 107

ARMED FORCES of the United States were sent to Nicaragua in August, 1926, to protect American lives. At the request of both President Diaz and General Moncada, they facilitated the disarming of both the Government and the revolutionary forces in accordance with the terms of the Tipitapa Agreement. Due to the outbreak of banditry, their number was increased to prevent interference with the 1928 elections, which the United States agreed to supervise also under the terms of the Tipitapa Agreement. In November, 1928, the marine and naval forces totaled 5,480. As the Guardia developed into a fighting force and took over the patrolling of the bandit-infested provinces, the marines were withdrawn, so that by June, 1930, they numbered only 1,248. Beginning in July, 1930, additional forces were sent to assist in the conduct of the elections of that year, bringing the total in November to 1,763.

On February 13, 1931, the Department of State announced its intention of withdrawing from Nicaragua "all of the Marine Brigade who are now on combatant duty probably by June next, leaving in Nicaragua only the Marines who are still engaged in instruction in the Nicaraguan National Guard and an instruction battalion to support such instruction and an aviation section which is being used for the present to carry supplies in the bandit provinces which are entirely without roads." At the same time, it announced that the step contemplated, together with the increase in the Guardia Nacional and the road-building activities, made feasible by the $1,000,000 credit, "have paved the way for the ultimate removal of all of the Marine forces from Nicaragua immediately after the election of 1932."

In February, 1931, the total armed force of the United States in Nicaragua numbered 1,500 men. Despite the Managua earthquake catastrophe and the bandit raid on the east coast in April, 1931, there was little deviation from the withdrawal program, which was effected by June 3, 1931. The aviation force was slightly increased at the time of the outbreak on the Atlantic coast, to make it easier to reinforce the Guardia there. On April 1, 1932, the marine and naval personnel in Nicaragua totalled 753, exclusive of the 205 officers in the Guardia Nacional.

From May 7, 1926, when marines were landed at Bluefields, until January 1, 1932, 30 officers and men have been killed in action and 15 died of wounds received in action.

Haiti

ROBERT LANSING, Secretary of State, to R. B. Davis, United States Chargé d'Affaires at Port-au-Prince, August 10, 1915
Foreign Relations of the United States, 1915, p. 479

IN VIEW OF the fact that the Navy last night informed Admiral Caperton that he might allow election of a President whenever the Haitians wish, and of the impression which exists here that the elections may take place Thursday next, it is desired that you confer with the Admiral to the end that, in some way to be determined between you, the following things be made perfectly clear:

First: Let Congress understand that the Government of the United States intends to uphold it, but that it can not recognize action which does not establish in charge of Haitian affairs those whose abilities and dispositions give assurances of putting an end to factional disorders.

Second. In order that no misunderstanding can possibly occur after election, it should be made perfectly clear to candidates as soon as possible and in advance of their election, that the United States expects to be entrusted with the practical control of the customs, and such financial control over the affairs of the Republic of Haiti as the United States may deem necessary for an efficient administration.

The Government of the United States considers it its duty to support a constitutional government. It means to assist in the establishing of such a government, and to support it as long as necessity may require. It has no design upon the political or territorial integrity of Haiti; on the contrary, what has been done, as well as what will be done, is conceived in an effort to aid the people of Haiti in establishing a stable government and in maintaining domestic peace throughout the Republic.

LANSING

LEMUEL W. LIVINGSTON, United States Consul at Cape Haitien, to Robert Lansing, Secretary of State, August 12, 1915
Foreign Relations of the United States, 1915, p. 480

SIR:

I have the honor to report that, owing to the excitement here following the recent events at Port au Prince, culminating in the death of President Vilbrun Guillaume Sam, the commanding officer of the U.S.S. *Eagle* placed a guard of 20 men at the French Consular Agency where several prominent revolutionists had taken refuge since June 19 when the Government troops retook the town. These men remained at the Consular Agency until August 4, the day following the departure of the principal Government generals. On that day the *Nashville* landed sixty men and those from the *Eagle* remained as a part of the landing party. This reassured the refugees and they left the Consular Agency.

General Blot, commander in chief of the Government forces, left for Monte Christi on a Haitian gunboat during the night of the 3d with his family and the most active of his generals and men. Many of the Government troops voluntarily laid down their arms and took refuge in the yard of the Bishop's residence. Others went aboard the Haitian gunboat *Nord Alexis*, but a good contingent remained with their arms and marched out of town in the direction of Port au Prince. Those remaining here, about 750 in all, were sent to Port au Prince on board the *Nord Alexis*.

The *Jason* arrived from Port au Prince on the 3d instant with a commission composed of Archbishop Conan, ex-President Legitime, Lieutenant Coffee, Flag Secretary of Admiral Caperton, Charles Zamor and Edmond Polynice. The commission returned on the 5th with Dr. R. Bobo and staff, General Bourand who commanded the Government troops at Fort Liberté, Ouanaminthe adjacent territory, and a few other prominent citizens.

The U.S.S. *Connecticut* arrived on the 6th instant and immediately landed about 63 marines. After the departure of the *Eagle* on the 8th, the *Connecticut* landed 108 bluejackets, making a total of about 230 men landed.

Captain Durell of the *Connecticut* and Commander Olmsted of the *Nashville* have taken temporary charge of the administration of affairs in the city. Most of the former Haitian employees have been re-stored to their places, with one American at the custom house and others at the port. They are beginning now to clean up the town so far as the limited means at their disposal will permit. Everything is working smoothly and the people are taking it good-naturedly.

Captain Durell has received instructions to give 100 gourdes to each principal officer and 10 gourdes to each private who comes in and surrenders his arms. Arrangements are being made to carry out these instructions; but word comes this morning from Port au Prince that Dr. Bobo may start a revolt in case he is not elected. One of his emissaries is expected on the steamer that is due here to-day.

Yesterday the accompanying printed translation of the enclosed proclamation by Admiral Caperton was distributed throughout the city and made a good impression.

Commander Olmsted is in charge of the forces ashore.

I have [etc.]

LIVINGSTON

[*Inclosure*]
PROCLAMATION OF THE UNITED STATES
U. S. S. *"Washington,"* FLAGSHIP
Port au Prince, Haiti, August 9, 1915

I am directed by the United States Government to assure the Haitian people that the United States has no object in view except to insure, to establish, and to help maintain Haitian independence and the establishment of a stable and firm government by the Haitian people.

Every assistance will be given to the Haitian people in their attempt to secure these ends. It is the intention to retain the United States forces in Haiti only so long as will be necessary for this purpose.

W. B. CAPERTON,
Rear Admiral, United States Navy,
Commanding U. S. Forces in Haitian Waters

JOSEPHUS DANIELS, *Secretary of the Navy, to Rear Admiral*
W. B. Caperton, November 10, 1915
Foreign Relations of the United States, 1915, p. 458

ARRANGE WITH President Dartiguenave that he call a Cabinet meeting before the session of Senate which will pass upon ratification of treaty and request that you be permitted to appear before that meeting to make a statement to President and to members of Cabinet. On your own authority state the following before these officers:

I have the honor to inform the President of Haiti and the members of his Cabinet that I am personally gratified that public sentiment continues favorable to the treaty, that there is a strong demand from all classes for immediate ratification, and that treaty will be ratified Thursday.

I am sure that you, gentlemen, will understand my sentiment in this matter and I am confident if the treaty fails of ratification that my Government has the intention to retain control in Haiti until the desired end is accomplished and that it will forthwith proceed to the complete pacification of Haiti so as to insure internal tranquility necessary to such development of the country and its industry as will afford relief to the starving populace now unemployed. Meanwhile the present Government will be supported in the effort to secure stable conditions and lasting peace in Haiti whereas those offering opposition can only expect such treatment as their conduct merits.

The United States Government is particularly anxious for immediate ratification by the present Senate of this treaty, which was drawn up with the full intention of employing as many Haitians as possible to aid in giving effect to its provisions, so that suffering may be relieved at the earliest possible date.

Rumors of bribery to defeat the treaty are rife but are not believed. However, should they prove true those who accept or give bribes will be vigorously prosecuted.

It is expected that you will be able to make this sufficiently clear to remove all opposition and to secure immediate ratification.

DANIELS

ROBERT LANSING, Formerly Secretary of State, to Senator Medill McCormick, Chairman of the United States Senate Select Committee on Haiti and Santo Domingo, May 4, 1922

Inquiry into Occupation and Administration of Haiti and the Dominican Republic, 67th Congress, 2d Session, Senate Report No. 794, p. 31. See *supra*, p. 375

Hon. Medill McCormick,
Chairman Select Committee on Haiti and Santo Domingo,
Senate Chamber, Washington, D.C.
MY DEAR SENATOR:

Complying with your request for a statement from me regarding Haiti, I beg to submit the following as embodying the contemporary views of the State Department on the financial and political disorders in Haiti, which caused a critical state of affairs during the last days of July, 1915, and on the attitude of the German Government toward

Haiti, because largely upon those two considerations were based the instructions of the State Department to the United States Legation in Haiti and, through the Navy Department, to the United States naval commander in Haitian waters. The events to which I shall refer in this statement were succeeded by the ratification of the present treaty between the United States and Haiti, which had for its objects the insurance of Haiti's future welfare upon a permanent basis of law and order and the prevention of foreign intervention in the future based on political and financial disorders in Haiti.

On July 30, 1915, the U.S.S. *Connecticut* came into the harbor of Port au Prince just as President Guillaume Sam was being murdered and his body mutilated by an infuriated mob. This was an act of vengeance for the massacre of some scores of prisoners in the prison at Port au Prince who were political opponents of Guillaume Sam's government. The crowds attending the funeral processions of these victims of tyranny turned from them in a frenzy, dragged Guillaume Sam from the asylum which he had sought in the French Legation, killed him, dismembered his body, and paraded through the streets exhibiting the ghastly fragments. Revolutionary forces were at the time in possession of other principal ports of the country and threatened to attack the city of Port au Prince. There was no government to preserve order in the city or in the country. On the contrary, there was anarchy and armed insurrection. Universal fear prevailed, while the lives of Haitians and foreigners alike were imperiled by the conditions which existed. The violation of the extraterritoriality of the French Legation indicated the ruthless lawlessness of the revolutionaries. In the circumstances the forces of the United States were landed as a matter of urgent necessity.

The murders and atrocities perpetrated marked the complete breakdown of Haitian institutions, the culmination of a process of disintegration which had been in progress for a generation or more. It was evident from the state of affairs that there remained no possibility of a civilized government functioning without external assistance. The limit of tolerance for such conditions, which menaced the lives and property of Americans and other foreigners, was finally reached when the French Legation was violated. The restoration of order and government in Haiti was as clearly the duty of the Government of the United States as was the landing of the marines. If the United States had not assumed the responsibility, some other power would. To permit such action by a European power would have been to abandon the principles of the Monroe Doctrine. The United States had no alternative but to act, and to act with vigor.

The process of disintegration above referred to is a matter of common knowledge. It is enough to say that none of the many Haitian Governments immediately preceding that of Guillaume Sam was able to maintain itself against revolution. Those persons who were from time to time in power were irresponsible and arbitrary. The inhabitants were exploited and robbed. So insecure were they in their possessions and so frequently in danger of their lives that industry throughout the country was paralyzed. Foreign lives were not taken, but there was such recurrent apprehension of violence that few years passed without the necessity of United States ships appearing in Haitian waters. Cruisers of foreign powers often came on similar errands, and on occasions European sailors or marines had been landed. These conditions had become chronic, and they had, year after year, grown progressively worse. In June of 1915 a French cruiser had landed a force at Cape Haitien, and these were only withdrawn when American marines were landed to take their place. After the invasion of the French Legation France dispatched a cruiser to Port au Prince and landed a force, which guarded the legation for several weeks without objection on the part of the United States Government. It was manifest that the danger to foreign lives in Haiti, which was constantly increasing, made the possibility of European intervention more and more probable unless the United States acted.

A default in payments to European creditors presented another danger. Haitian foreign loans were held by Germans, French, and English, but not to any great extent by Americans. The foreign loans were secured by the customs revenues—thus a default would have given rise to the desire on the part of European Governments to seize the Haitian customhouses and administer the customs—a situation which, being of indefinite duration, would have caused serious political complications and been a grave menace to the peace of this hemisphere and to the immunity from European interference with American institutions. The finances of Haiti had been growing steadily weaker, and the ability to meet her obligations had ceased. Interest on the public debt of about $20,000,000 had been paid with creditable regularity, but it had become necessary to borrow from the National Bank of Haiti and to make local forced loans elsewhere in order to meet these interest payments, and the limit of the ability to borrow had been reached. Amortization of foreign loans were many years in arrears. Revolutions had greatly increased the internal and floating debt. Fiat paper money was being issued but not used and payment of salaries of public employees was suspended. For this state of affairs no temporary remedy could suffice. This financial situation need hardly be treated here in greater detail.

In this connection, however, there was a more critical state of affairs than has been generally known. I refer to the attitude of the Imperial German Government in connection with the political disorders and financial straits of Haiti and the pretexts for aggression thereby afforded. There was good reason to believe that in the years 1913–14 Germany was ready to go to great lengths to secure the exclusive customs control of Haiti, and also to secure a coaling station at Mole St. Nicholas. It is this feature that I would particularly call to the attention of your committee.

The United States had no wish to obtain a naval coaling station at Mole St. Nicholas. The Navy Department had long since definitely determined that a station there was not desirable, but it was also perfectly clear that a coaling station directly or indirectly controlled by another power would be a menace to the position of the United States in the Caribbean Sea, to the security of the Panama Canal and, consequently, to the peace of this hemisphere. A privately owned coaling station, whether in the hands of Americans or Europeans, would have been a danger if ever a coal supply was allowed to accumulate there greater than necessary for current commercial needs. In case of war the station and coal stored there would have been subject to capture. In view of the possible consequences the policy of the United States was clear. It could not look with favor on a privately owned coaling station at Mole St. Nicholas unless that was subject to its direct control. Though it did not need and it did not want such a station for itself, it could not permit a European Government to secure one. The indications were that Germany intended to obtain one unless she was prevented from doing so by the United States.

Although French is the official language of Haiti and French customs prevail as well as the practice of sending the children of wealthy Haitian families to France for their education there has been, for many years, a strong German influence in the country resulting primarily from the establishment of German commercial houses at Haitian ports and the sending of young Germans to gain their livelihood in those concerns. A considerable number of these German residents have intermarried, so I have been informed, with the Haitians and are closely connected with and more or less active in the political and social life of the country.

During a number of years the Government at Washington was in receipt of various reports to the effect that foreign interests were desirous of obtaining coaling stations at Mole St. Nicholas, and in the year 1911 the Haitian Government at the insistence of the then American minister eliminated from a contract with a German national for a coastwise steamship service the granting of rights for a coaling station in Haiti.

In the year 1912 Hon. George von L. Meyer, then Secretary of the Navy, in reply to a communication from the Department of State in regard to the establishment of a coaling depot in Haiti for the steamship line of a foreign country, replied, referring to a communication made by the Navy Department to the State Department in 1910, to the effect that the Navy Department did not look with favor upon any proposition to establish so many coaling stations within such a limited geographical radius and could not contemplate favorably the prospect of having such stations in the hands of citizens of any of the European nations. The establishment of such stations would actually amount to the maintenance of a very considerable number of coaling stations close to our shores, which could be used by foreign vessels of war in the event of hostilities, and this, the Navy Department believed, should be prevented, if it were in the power of diplomacy to do so.

In the year 1913, and particularly in the year 1914, information was conveyed to the Department of State, through official and unofficial sources to the effect that a German commercial firm was active in an attempt to secure extensive concessions from Haiti containing grants sufficiently broad to permit the building of coaling stations at Mole St. Nicholas, the concessions to be combined with a loan secured by control of the Haitian customs by the concessionaire. It was further stated that the German Government was back of the German commercial firm making the proposal.

On June 1, 1914, the American minister at Port au Prince reported to the Department of State that he was reliably informed that the Haitian Government would entertain a proposition to lease to the United States Mole St. Nicholas on the basis of a cash payment and a yearly rental. It was further stated that the Government of Haiti would most probably require, as an essential provision of such lease, that the United States should pledge itself not to interfere now or at any future time with the collection or administration of the customs of Haiti and would agree to afford protection to Haiti against any other nation or nations which might attempt to secure control of the customs. The minister concluded his telegram with the statement that the German cruiser *Marietta* had arrived the day before at Port au Prince.

As the United States was not interested in obtaining a lease of Mole St. Nicholas, no reply was sent to the minister's telegram.

Meanwhile, during the late winter and spring of 1914, financial conditions in Haiti, as a result of the political chaos existing, had been rapidly becoming more and more involved and foreign interests were increasingly anxious to obtain some form of guaranty from Haiti that that Government would continue to respect its obligations. As in most cases of this nature, suggestions were made relative to the collection and control of the Haitian customs by foreign nationals representing the foreign debtor interests. The foreign interests referred to were the holders of shares in the National Railroad of Haiti and in the National Bank of Haiti, and also the holders of the bonds representing the Haitian external debt. It was also obvious that those interested in the National Bank, which was controlled by French shareholders, were deeply concerned as to the ability of the Haitian Government to continue its existing financial policy on account of its outstanding loans.

Although various plans were discussed in the Department of State, which had as their object the aiding of Haiti and at the same time the protection of the interests of its creditors by means of a regulation of customs collections and their application, no agreement was reached between the Government of the United States and the Government of Haiti. However, under date of July 15, 1914, two weeks before the beginning of the World War, the American consul at Cape Haitien informed the department confidentially that he had learned from reliable source that the German minister at Port au Prince had telegraphed the German consul at Cape Haitien asking whether an American warship had landed its forces and taken possession of the customhouse.

On July 18, 1914, Mr. von Haniel, the chargé d'affaires of the Imperial German Government, spoke with the Third Assistant Secretary of State, Mr. Phillips, in relation to Haitian affairs, and on July 21 Mr. Phillips requested Mr. von Haniel to submit to him a written memorandum of the views of his Government which he had orally expressed. On July 25 Mr. von Haniel wrote to Mr. Phillips:

MY DEAR MR. PHILLIPS:

In reply to your favor of the 21st instant and with reference to our conversation of the 18th instant concerning the participation of the Imperial Government in a customs control in Haiti, in case such a control would be established by the American Government, I beg to say that my Government comprehends that the American Government, probably for reasons of interior politics, does not think it desirable, if the most interested European powers participate in an eventual customs control in Haiti, but the Imperial Government as well has to take into account the public opinion in their country. Considering our economical interests in Haiti and the part of the Banque Nationale which is owned by Germans, people in Germany would not understand, if my Government gave up their claim to participate in such a customs control. In the opinion of the Imperial Government therefore it will be the simplest solution if the status quo is maintained.

I remain, my dear Mr. Phillips,

Very sincerely yours,
E. V. HANIEL.

Shortly following the delivery of the note of the German chargé d'affaires war broke out between Germany and France, and the communication was not replied to until September 16, 1914, when the then Secretary of State, Mr. Bryan, wrote the following note to the German ambassador, Count von Bernstorff:

MY DEAR MR. AMBASSADOR:

Replying to the note of your Government's chargé dated July 25, 1914, regarding the matter of customs control in Haiti, I beg to say that the Government of the United States recognizes the large part which German merchants and German bankers have played in the development of the trade and enterprise of Haiti and wishes to make this correspondence the occasion for expressing the pleasure with which it witnesses the employment of German capital and the activity of German men of affairs in this hemisphere, but represents to the Government of his Imperial Majesty that German interests are not the only interests which have played a conspicuous and highly influential part in the development of the Haitian Republic and that the Government of the United States is well known to have taken for many years and without variation of policy and position that neither foreign influence nor interest proceeding from outside the American hemisphere could with the consent of the United States be so broadened or extended as to constitute a control, either wholly or in part, of the Government or administration of any independent American State.

The Government of the United States can not depart from that policy and feels confident that the Government of his Imperial Majesty will not expect it to do so.

Probably a participation of the Government of his Imperial Majesty in any method which might be agreed upon by which the Government of the Republic of Haiti should be assisted in the orderly, efficient, and economical administration of its customs revenues did not present itself to his Imperial Majesty's Government as a departure from the traditional policy of the Government of the United States when its note of July 25 was drafted. But this Government would regard such a participation as a very serious departure from that policy alike in principle and in practice. The Government of the United States regards it as one of the grave possibilities of certain sorts of concessions granted by governments in America to European financiers and contractors and of certain sorts of contracts entered into by those governments with European banking houses and financiers that the legitimate and natural course of enforcing claims might lead to measures which would imperil the political independence, or, at least, the complete political autonomy of the American States involved, and might issue in results which the Government of the United States has always regarded it as its duty to guard against as the nearest friend and natural champion of those States whenever they should need a friend and champion.

Whatever the Government of the United States might deem it friendly and wise to agree to with the Government of the Republic of Haiti by way of assisting her to make good her obligations and escape the risks of default or disorder to her finances would be done without intending to serve the interest of any citizen of the United States in preference to the interest of the citizens or government of any other country. It would be planned for the benefit of all concerned and upon a basis of absolute neutrality. This Government does not regard its insistence upon an exclusive privilege in matters of this kind, therefore, as a course dictated by selfishness, but, on the contrary, as a course clearly dictated by a desire for peace and the exclusion of all occasion of unfriendliness with any nation of the other hemisphere. It is willing to give any pledges of disinterest and impartiality that may reasonably suggest themselves, but thinks that its best pledge is the course which it has, in fact, invariably pursued in matters and in circumstances of this kind. Its declared purpose in this case, should the Republic of Haiti desire a convention with regard to the administration of her customs revenues, would, as always, be made frankly and without reservation of any kind, and this it would deem the best evidence of its friendship and respect for the Government of Germany and the rights of German citizens wherever American influence may touch them. This is the way of peace and of mutual accommodation.

Accept, Excellency, the renewed assurances of my highest consideration.

W. J. BRYAN

On the eve of the declaration of war between Germany and Russia the U.S.S. *Connecticut* and the German cruiser *Karlsrhue* were both in the harbor of Port au Prince. On July 31, 1914, the *Karlsrhue* changed her position in order to screen the movements of her crew and a number of boatloads of German sailors with small arms and machine guns left the *Karlsrhue* and proceeded to the wharf where they landed. When halfway down the wharf the Germans turned about, returned to their boats, and went back to their ship. This mysterious action took place at dusk. Shortly afterwards the captain of the *Karlsrhue* came aboard the *Connecticut* and told the captain he had received orders to proceed to St. Thomas for coal and asked the captain of the *Connecticut* to protect German interests while he was gone. The *Karlsrhue* then steamed out of the harbor to begin her commerce-destroying cruise. Shortly afterwards the captain of the *Connecticut* was informed by wireless that war between Russia and Germany had been declared.

There is reason to believe that the German landing party was turned back on the wharf by the German minister to Haiti pursuant to cabled orders for the *Karlsrhue* to leave Port au Prince at once. Thus the local situation was, by the outbreak of war, relieved of a conflict of interests, which might have caused serious embarrassment.

In the month of July, 1914, the Secretary of State sent a draft of a proposed agreement between the Government of the United States and the Government of Haiti to the American minister at Port au

Prince. This agreement, which was modeled after the treaty entered into between the United States and the Dominican Republic during the administration of President Roosevelt, embodied the following provisions:

The appointment of a general receiver of customs and his assistants by the President of the United States; the payment of customs duties to the general receiver, and granting him all protection in the performance of his duties; the appointment of the financial adviser to the Government of Haiti; the application of all sums collected to the payment of interest and sinking fund of the public debt of Haiti. That the Republic of Haiti would not increase its public debt, except by previous agreement with the United States. That the United States should have authority to prevent any and all interferences with the receipt, collection, or free course of the customs, or with the free exercise of powers imposed upon the receivership.

However, a short time after the receipt of the proposed agreement by the minister a revolution broke out against the government of President Zamor, which, as usual in Haiti, started at Cape Haitien in the north and proceeded to Port au Prince via the town of St. Mark. It is interesting to observe in connection with the history of revolutions in Haiti that they have uniformly been conceived in or about Cape Haitien and have proceeded along practically the same roads in the direction of the capital, namely, by way of the strategic town of St. Mark. It has been the established belief of most Americans who have been in Haiti, and of American officials who have been cognizant of Haitian affairs during the past decade, that the majority of these revolutions have been financed in the north of Haiti by German merchants, who could expect sufficient financial advantages from the success of the revolution to warrant the initial outlay.

The revolution against the Zamor government was successful, and Davilmar Theodore proclaimed himself President of Haiti. The Government of the United States withheld its recognition of Theodore as President of Haiti pending an investigation of his activities and the incidents in connection with his seizure of the sovereign power. Before any definite policy in this connection was determined a revolution against the Theodore government was started in the usual manner and culminated in the overthrow of Davilmar Theodore and the assumption of the presidency by Guillaume Sam. The United States, consistent with its policy in regard to the recognition of revolutionary governments, refused to recognize the government of Sam, and not long after Sam had installed himself in the presidential palace another revolution, headed by one Dr. Bobo, broke out in the north. The resulting conditions alarmed the French minister, and in June, 1915, a French cruiser occupied Cape Haitien with a landing party, as has already been stated. Before the revolutionary forces had actually reached Port au Prince, the massacre of political prisoners above referred to had taken place and Sam had been butchered.

During the terms of office of these Presidents various attempts were made on the part of the Government of the United States through special missions and through the minister in Port au Prince to obtain from these provisional governments an agreement as to the entrance into some form of convention between the United States and Haiti. The essential provisions of these conventions were, like the Dominican treaty, the guaranty by the United States of Haitian independence and of the stability of the Haitian Government, and the privilege of the United States minister to advise the Haitian Government in its selection of Haitian citizens as officials of the Haitian customs service, as the customs revenue was a prize which attracted revolutionists and their financial supporters.

On account of the state of the country during this period, in which violence and anarchy were rife, the overtures made by the United States, solely out of a sincere desire to aid the Haitian people to establish an orderly and law-enforcing Government, which would restore stable political and economic conditions in the island, were fruitless.

Admiral Caperton, of the United States Navy, who had arrived with his flagship in Port au Prince on the day of the assassination of Sam, landed a naval force of the United States and assumed military control of Port au Prince on July 30, 1915. The admiral and the American chargé immediately took steps to cooperate with the Haitian committee of safety for the protection of life and property in the city and adjacent country.

Various aspirants for election by the Assembly of Haiti for President presented themselves, among whom the most notable were Dr. Bobo and Senator Dartiguenave. The American representatives, under direction of the Government of the United States, discussed with these candidates and with members of the Haitian Congress the conditions upon which the United States would recognize a Government in Haiti. These conditions were as follows:

First. Let Congress understand that the Government of the United States intends to uphold it, but that it can not recognize action which does not establish in charge of Haitian affairs those whose abilities and dispositions give assurances of putting an end to factional disorder.

Second. In order that no misunderstanding can possibly occur after election, it should be made perfectly clear to candidates, as soon as possible and in advance of their election, that the United States expects to be intrusted with the practical control of the customs and such financial control over the affairs of the Republic of Haiti as the United States may deem necessary for efficient administration.

The Government of the United States considers it its duty to support a constitutional government. It means to assist in the establishment of such a government and to support it as long as necessity may require. It has no design upon the political or territorial integrity of Haiti. On the contrary, what has been done, as well as what will be done, is conceived in an effort to aid the people of Haiti in establishing a stable government and maintaining domestic peace throughout the Republic.

Congress elected Senator Dartiguenave President on August 12.

On August 14 the Department of State dispatched to the legation at Port au Prince instructions embodying the terms of a treaty to be negotiated, if possible, with the Government of Haiti.

On August 17 the chargé d'affaires of the United States, complying with the instructions received from the department, submitted to President Dartiguenave a draft of the proposed treaty. Negotiations with President Dartiguenave then proceeded. The President expressed his approval of the terms of the treaty, but for a month was unable to secure agreement on the part of his cabinet.

On September 15 the chargé d'affaires at Port au Prince reported to the department by telegraph that the Haitian Government had forwarded to the legation a copy of a formal protest addressed to it by the German minister, in which he stated that the American occupation and management of customs would be prejudicial to German interests. To this telegram the department replied that it would seem desirable that the Haitian Government should reply to the German minister to the effect that legitimate German interests would be accorded the same equitable and impartial treatment as would be given to all foreigners and foreign interests in Haiti.

On September 16 the treaty was signed, and on February 28, 1916, it was ratified by the Senate of the United States without a dissenting vote and without an amendment being offered. The principal provisions of this treaty were the guaranteeing of the independence of Haiti, the establishment of a native gendarmerie, the appointment of an American financial adviser, and the administration of the customs service by Americans.

It is especially to be noted in connection with those provisions of the treaty that the Government of the United States, although it had received a proposal from Haiti to cede to the United States outright without restriction Mole St. Nicholas, declined to insert such a provision in the treaty and insisted upon the inclusion in the treaty of an article expressly embodying the idea that no Haitian territory was to be ceded to it.

On September 17 President Dartiguenave's Government was accorded recognition by the United States.

The situation which confronted the representatives of the American civil and military forces in Haiti after the revolution, and prior to the recognition of the Dartiguenave Government was briefly as follows:

The customhouses throughout the country had been disorganized by an order of the preceding Government which directed the deposit of funds with private firms instead of with the Banque Nationale, the legal depositary, and also by the threatened seizure of the customhouses by armed insurrectionary groups. The government of President Dartiguenave had not funds available to pay the small number of troops under its orders and these dissatisfied troops were becoming a menace to peace and order. The inhabitants of towns in which customhouses were situated were deprived of their food supply by the hostile armed bands which infested the highways, and even the water system of Cape Haitien was cut by these brigands. Commerce was paralyzed and the city populations were starving, for the authority of the Dartiguenave Government did not extend far beyond the outskirts of Port au Prince.

On August 19, in view of the serious conditions existing, which had been reported to the Government at Washington, Admiral Caperton received instructions to administer the customhouses so that the proceeds therefrom might be used temporarily to provide sustenance for the starving natives by paying them for labor on public works, to establish a gendarmerie to aid the Dartiguenave Government in the pacification of the country, and also to prevent the diversion of the public funds of the Haitian Government into the pockets of unscrupulous persons.

The customhouses were taken over between August 20 and September 2 as rapidly as the American squadron commander could place in charge of them American officers as administrators, and could furnish them adequate protection. The customhouse at Port au Prince was the last to be taken over on September 2. On September 3 the prevailing conditions of anarchy called for the proclamation of martial law. Thereafter, until the treaty was ratified by both countries, the customs were administered by the naval forces of the United States. After ratification the customhouses were taken over by the receiver general, a treaty official.

In October, 1915, attacks were made on parties of United States marines near Cape Haitien, and thereafter a sharp campaign was carried on against the lawless bands operating in the Republic which resulted in the restoration of order throughout the country. Many hundreds of the outlaws surrendered their arms, receiving a small sum for each rifle, and those who did not surrender were dispersed. With the restoration of order and the coming into effect of the treaty this period of the American occupation came to a close.

As may be concluded from the foregoing review of the circumstances leading up to the establishment of treaty relations between the United States and Haiti, the Government of the United States was animated by two dominating ideas:

1. To terminate the appalling conditions of anarchy, savagery, and oppression which had been prevalent in Haiti for decades, and to undertake the establishment of domestic peace in the Republic in order that the great bulk of the population, who had been downtrodden by dictators and the innocent victims of repeated revolutions, should énjoy a prosperity and an economic and industrial development to which every people of an American nation are entitled.

2. A desire to forestall any attempt by a foreign power to obtain a foothold on the territory of an American nation which, if a seizure of customs control by such a power had occurred, or if a grant of a coaling station or naval base had been obtained, would have most certainly been a menace to the peace of the Western Hemisphere, and in flagrant defiance of the Monroe Doctrine.

Very sincerely yours,

ROBERT LANSING

REPORT of the United States Senate Select Committee on Haiti and Santo Domingo, June 26, 1922 (extracts)

Inquiry into Occupation and Administration of Haiti and the Dominican Republic, 67th Congress, 2d Session, Senate Report No. 794, p. 4

HAITIAN HISTORY

No reviewer of the condition of Haiti can be just to its inhabitants which does not recognize existing anomalies and the antecedent historic facts which explain the economic and political backwardness of a people among whom may be found groups whose cultivation, education, and capabilities are comparable with corresponding elements of society in more advanced countries.

At the time of the overthrow of the French government and of the expulsion of their French masters by the Haitians there were among the former slaves to whom the government of the country fell few who were literate and absolutely none who were so trained in public affairs or who were so skilled in tropical agriculture as to make possible either the successful maintenance of civil order or the necessary continued development of the country's agricultural resources. Thus the Haitians labored under insuperable handicaps. There were among them for all practical purposes no trained agriculturists and administrators, no engineers and educators. Haiti had no means of educating her people or of developing men competent to govern. Misgovernment and revolution ensued, and as a consequence Haitian trade, by comparison with that of the other West Indian Islands, diminished. Haiti drifted, as it were, out of the currents of commerce.

During the six score years of Haitian independence there have been a dozen constitutions. The people have lived under self-styled monarchs as well as under military dictators and self-constituted presidents.

Since the Haitians gained control in 1804 there have been one series of revolutions after another. Part have been successful, part unsuccessful. Since 1804 there have been 29 chiefs of state. Otto Schoenrich in his work on Santo Domingo says:

It is to be observed, however, that of the Haitian executives only one completed his term of office and voluntarily retired; of the others, four remained in power until their death from natural causes; 18 were deposed by revolutions, one of them committing suicide, another being executed on the steps of his burning palace, and still another being cut to pieces by the mob; five were assassinated; and one is chief magistrate at the present time.

The disorders to which Haiti has been subject since the achievement of its independence attained such destructive frequency during the last decade before the American intervention in 1915, that in the space of 10 years no less than eight presidents assumed office (it would be a mistake to say that they were elected) for the nominal constitutional term of 7 years each. Three of the eight fled the country; one was blown up in the presidential palace; another died mysteriously, and according to popular belief by poison, while two were murdered. The last Haitian President who held office before the landing of the American forces was Sam, who had caused several scores of political prisoners to be massacred as they huddled in their cells. He himself was dragged from the French Legation by a mob, his head and limbs were torn from his body to be carried aloft on sticks and bayonets, while his bleeding trunk was dragged through the streets of the capital city.

It will not be wondered that under conditions thus indicated the irrigation works and highways built by the French disappeared, fertile sugar plantations vanished, coffee cultivation ceased, and that the country made no progress, material or social, political or economic. The mass of the people—gentle, kindly, generous—their peace and property threatened rather than secured by the so-called authorities, sought such quiet as they might find by hiding in the hills, where they have lived in a condition of primitive poverty and ignorance. Not only did the sugar and coffee plantations disappear, but almost all true agriculture, all organized cultivation of the soil, except as little patches of yams and plantains may be called such, ceased. The coffee crop, which is the principal article of Haitian export, is gathered from the wild trees—sprung from the stock planted by the French over a hundred years ago. The domestic animals include wretched swine, poor cattle, poultry of scrawny tropic strains, and little asses which, as saddle or pack animals, served as the sole means of conveyance or transport in the country until the arrival of the American forces.

NO REPRESENTATIVE GOVERNMENT IN HAITI

In brief, before American intervention there had been no popular representative or stable government in Haiti. The public finances were in disarray, public credit was exhausted, and the public revenues were wasted or stolen. Highways and agriculture had given way to the jungle. The people, most of whom lived in wretched poverty, were illiterate and spoke no other language than the native Creole. The country and its inhabitants have been a prey to chronic revolutionary disorders, banditry, and even during periods of comparative peace to such oppressive and capricious governors that the great mass of the people who, under happier circumstances might have become prosperous peasant farmers, have had neither opportunity nor incentive to labor, to save, or to learn. They had no security for their property and little for their lives. Voodoo practices, of course, were general throughout the territory of the Republic.

This view has been contested by certain Americans who, equally ignorant of the facts and indifferent to them, have given voice to general and unsubstantiable charges which if credited would blacken the good name of the American Navy and impugn the honor of the American Government. It is, however, the view of your committee, and is supported by those informed and impartial investigators of

Haitian conditions, whose opinions have come to the attention of your committee.

HAITIAN OPINION

Lest this summary of Haitian conditions be considered prejudiced or overdrawn, the committee quotes the following from the report of the Haitian Commission of Verification of Documents of the Floating Debt.

But neither the Pressoit-Delbau Commission, nor the successors of Mr. Barjon in the position of paymaster of the Department of the Interior have been able to tell the Secretary of State for Finance what has become of those archives. Only one fact remains, from all the preceding, and it is to be remembered; that is, that the said archives have disappeared, and that they remain unfindable, for a cause which the commission is not in a position to verify nor to comment upon. . . .

This great question of the revolutionary debts—of the revolutionary debt of Davilmar Theodore above all—constitutes the most delicate and certainly the most painful of the work of the commission. Without doubt, we have not the mission, Mr. Secretary of State, to judge the motives, interested or not, which determined and guided the conduct and the acts of such a chief, of such a political group, in the course of the years forever ill-omened before the month of July, 1915. In any case, this mission is not imparted to us, if at least we confine ourselves to considering strictly and narrowly our attributions of commissioners charged to investigate the arrears of the floating debt. . . .

This expression "revolutionary debt" carries in itself its condemnation, by reason of the lugubrious ideas which it awakens in the mind. From the moment that our internal torments had to have as a final consequence the issuance of certificates of indebtedness of the State, to the profit of their authors of all classes, or, which means the same things, the flood of favors to the detriment of the national treasury, a premium was thus created to the profit of Haitian revolutionaryism. And it is thus that we have attended in these recent times this sad pageant marking the pages of our history; the revolution of the day being an appeal to the revolution of to-morrow; insurrection never disarmed, always erect and campaigning, perpetually assailing the supreme power, and never stopping but to divide the spoils of the hour, after the enthronement of the new idol which it was to undermine and overthrow.

In presence of the figures at once scandalous and formidable of the debt called revolutionary and in view of the deplorable conditions in which the different original notes were issued, whether at Ouanaminthe, at Pignor, at St. Michel, at Cape Haitien, at Port-au-Prince, and even at Kingston (Jamaica), finally a little everywhere; some in Haitien gourdes, the others in American gold, pounds sterling, or in francs—the commission thinks it opportune to make without offense or passion the following remarks which it offers for the meditation of the country. . . .

There is no really productive work without the help of capital.

But when the loan is contracted for an unavowable purpose, having for motive the arming of the citizens of a country against their fellows, sustaining a disastrous and debasing war, sowing terror in all the social levels, with a view of satisfying personal ambitions—oh, then the conditions are not longer the same, and we find ourselves here in face of a hidden operation.

Incontestably, wherever civil war has passed it has sowed destruction, disunion, and death; cities devastated, factories destroyed, families reduced to the most frightful misery, the pleasant fields of the north transformed into charnal places three or more years ago; all these horrors worthy of the times of antiquity and of savage hordes have caused and still cause the raising of cries of pain and of indignation, and retell for ages and ages the cruelty of the political leaders who conducted directly or indirectly the bands of madmen and who excited them to carnage in the sole and unique purpose of seizing the power for the purpose of better assaulting the Public Treasury.

The country can not make itself the accomplice of such financial disorder having hidden behind it crime and immorality.

The mass of notes issued, the considerable number of individuals who had or who arrogated to themselves the power of issue, and who unscrupulously, without restraint or the least reserve, thus compromised the future; the colossal figure to which these issues mounted have necessarily given birth in our mind to this question of palpitating interest, In what case can the recognizances issued be considered sincere? In what case are they not sincere? In other terms, when is it that the amounts subscribed have been really paid? When is it that we are found in the presence of fictitious values represented by notes of complaisance? . . .

Revolutions are possible only on the condition that their authors find interested persons to finance these criminal enterprises. Unhappily with us the hard and honest work was always the exception, the revolutionary politics the rule, the great industry which attracted to it and monopolized all—energy, intelligence, and capacity. Therefore, there came a moment when the sole preoccupation for each energy unemployed, each intelligence searching its way, each capacity desirous of exerting itself; it was to clothe himself in revolutionary livery in which a campaign was instituted to gain access to the public treasury.

Testimony taken by the committee shows how the chronic anarchy into which Haiti had fallen, the exhaustion of its credit, the threatened intervention of the German government and the actual landing of the French naval forces, all imperiled the Monroe Doctrine and lead the Government of the United States to take the successive steps set forth in the testimony, to establish order in Haiti to help to institute a government as nearly representative as might be, and to assure the collaboration of the Governments of the United States and Haiti for the future maintenance of peace and the development of the Haitian people.

Your committee believes that doubtless the American representatives might have done better and that they have made mistakes, which in the light of experience they would not make again; that as will presently be indicated in more detail, not only did the treaty fail to take cognizance of certain reforms essential to Haitian progress, but that in the choice of its agents and the determination of their responsibilities, the Government of the United States was not always happy.

THE OCCUPATION AND THE TREATY

The history of the landing of American naval forces in Haiti and of the intervention of the United States to establish a government as representative, stable, and effective as possible, is set forth at length in the public hearings of the committee. The naval forces of the United States landed in July, 1915, when the country and more particularly the capital, after the murder of President Sam, had fallen into a condition of anarchy. The diplomatic representatives and naval forces of the United States made it possible for the Haitian Assembly to sit in security. The American representatives in the opinion of your committee influenced the majority of the Assembly in the choice of a president. Later, they exercised pressure to induce the ratification by Haiti of the convention in September, 1915, precisely as the United States had exercised pressure to induce the incorporation of the Platt Amendment in the Cuban Constitution, thus to assure the tranquillity and prosperity of Cuba. At about the same time representatives of the United States Navy took over temporarily the administration of the Haitian customhouses, which were then answerable to no central control, of which the revenues were disposed of at the discretion of the various local customs officers.

The convention of 1915 provides that a receiver general of customs, a financial advisor, and directors of public works and sanitation shall be nominated by the President of the United States and appointed by the President of the Republic of Haiti. It provides, furthermore, for the organization and discipline of an adequate force of constabulary or gendarmerie under the direction of officers nominated by the President of the United States, but commissioned in the service of the Haitian Government by the President of the Republic of Haiti.

Your committee has sought carefully to measure the benefits accruing to the Haitian people as the result of the convention, and to determine wherein the American Government or its representatives had failed in their duty and to advise as to the correction of mistakes or abuses in order that the maintenance of American forces in Haiti may be terminated as soon as possible.

Peace, sure and undisturbed peace, has been established throughout Haiti for the first time in generations. In former years men who were peasants—countrymen—were never seen upon the trails or in the market towns. They feared to appear lest they be pressed into the wretched and underpaid forces of the Republic or of revolutionary pretenders. Women only were found, driving pack animals or carrying burdens on the trails, and chaffering in the market places. The men were hidden in the hills. To-day, as old travelers will bear witness, for the first time in generations the men have come down freely from their hidden huts to the trails and to the towns.

Conformably with the terms of the treaty, the Haitian customs have been administered by the American receiver efficiently and honestly, whereas in the past, by common confession, the administration of them was characterized by waste, discrimination, if not by peculation. The Minister of Finance has acceded to the disbursement of revenues under American supervision. Finally, although the Haitian Government has declined to employ American experts in the administration of internal revenues, nevertheless, under the insistence of the financial advisor and despite general business depression, the sum of internal revenue collected has increased threefold, although the internal revenue laws are unchanged.

There has been very little criticism of the collection of customs under American supervision or of the American receiver general. The financial advisor has been the object of bitter attack, partly because of his personal relations with Haitian officials, partly because under instruction of the Secretary of State he withheld salaries of the principal Haitian officials as a measure of coercion and partly because he has been more than once, and for long periods, in Washington, absent from his post of duty in Port au Prince. In Justice to the financial advisor, it must be said that he was ordered to Washington by the State Department and has remained in Washington by order of the State Department to further the negotiation of the loan for the refunding of the Haitian debt.

THE HAITIAN DEBT

It has been stated that the Haitian Government had never defaulted on the service of its foreign debts prior to the American occupation. This statement is not exactly correct, but it is undoubtedly true that it had exerted itself to an extraordinary degree to maintain the service of its foreign debts. Your committee is informed that to do this the Haitian Government had, during the three years immediately preceding the occupation, floated internal loans at the rates of 59, 56, and 47, to a gold value of $2,868,131, had defaulted on salaries, pensions, etc., to the extent of $1,111,280, had borrowed from the Bank of Haiti $1,733,000, had issued fiat paper money, and had borrowed to a very large amount from private individuals at enormous discounts on treasury notes. The Haitian Government had, at the time of the American intervention, totally exhausted its credit both at home and abroad. The amortization of the loan of 1875 was in arrears. A great deal has been made of the fact that after the naval forces took over the administration of the customhouses and after the outbreak of the Great War, there was a time when, despite careful administration, both interest and amortization due on the Haitian debt were unpaid. This is true, but the inability of the Haitian Government and its American advisors to pay was due to the state of anarchy into which the country had fallen and to the inestimable injury to Haitian trade with Europe consequent upon the outbreak of the Great War. During the last three years, $5,000,000 of interest and principal have been paid. To-day there is no interest or capital overdue. The foreign debt has been reduced by one third. On the contrary, there is a surplus in the treasury and it is proposed to refund the outstanding debt to the great benefit of the Haitian taxpayer.

The Republic of Haiti owes, largely in France, some $14,000,000, part of which could have been paid when the franc was at a discount of 17 to the dollar and which can now be paid while exchange stands at about 10 francs to the dollar. The Haitian Government has lost something over a million dollars by delaying the refunding of the debt. It is still to the patent advantage of the Haitian Government to refund the debt by borrowing in dollars and paying in francs, when the francs are worth not 5 for a dollar, as formerly, but 10 for a dollar. Apart from this, in the opinion of your committee, it is of primary importance that the proposed loan should be made without delay, partly because it will afford a sum of money necessary to finish certain public works including the highway to Jacmel and that from Las Cahobas to Hinche, but also because under the proposed terms of the loan, the debt will be a general charge upon the revenues of the country and those revenues which are now specifically and irrevocably hypothecated to the service of certain loans will be freed from such rigid hypothecation and the onerous and inequitable revenue system of the country can be revised. There is appended to this report a table showing the contractual charges upon revenues in Haiti. A student of the Haitian financial system will be struck first by the charges upon exports (indirect and direct) and especially by the fact that they bear very heavily upon the poorest element of the population. If the debt be refunded as proposed, the revenue system can be revised and at one and the same time the burden upon the poor can be lightened and the export trade can be freed of uneconomic taxes.

It may be added that the new refunding loan, if consummated, will be made upon better terms than those recently made in the American market by European and South American governments.

As the negotiations for the revision of the charter of the national bank are all but consummated, the committee thinks it unnecessary to dwell upon the matter further than to say that due to the insistence of the American State Department and of the vigilant financial advisor, the terms of the new charter are more advantageous to Haiti than those of the old and that already an end has been put to the fluctuation of the currency, in which foreign merchants and exporters speculated to their own advantage and to the injury of the Haitian peasant. It is because of this last that certain foreign financial interests, that is, interests neither American nor Haitian, have covertly, persistently, and perhaps corruptly, opposed the determination of the new bank charter and the stabilization of the currency.

As was indicated earlier in the report, when the American naval forces were landed in Haiti in 1915 the fine highway system left by the French had disappeared. In 1917 the commander of the occupation, in collaboration with the Haitian Government, invoked the Haitian law requiring the inhabitants to work upon the highways. This was the forced labor or corvee upon the roads. The law requiring the inhabitants to maintain roads was in principle not unlike some of the highway statutes of our own States. It had not been enforced for decades when, at the instance of the American naval command in Haiti, the Haitian Government invoked it in July, 1916. At first this step appears to have met with no opposition from the natives. On the contrary, under the tactful management of the gendarmerie command at that time, encouraged and stimulated by the enthusiasm of the American officers, they were eager to open a highway from the north to the south of the country. It is the almost unbelievable truth that with the decay of the French roads it was impossible for a vehicle to traverse any section of the roadless republic. People worked with great good will upon those sections of the highway near which they dwelt. It was only after a year or more, when the gendarmerie command unwisely compelled natives to leave the neighborhoods in which they lived in order to complete the roads through the mountains, that discontent and dissatisfaction were first manifest. It is impossible to say in what measure the corvee contributed to the armed outbreak in the north. Almost all Haitian revolutions have had their beginning in the broken country lying between Cape Haitien and the Dominican border. Here the Cacos had lived for generations, and hence they marched to make their periodical attacks upon the capital as followers of one or another revolutionary chieftain. At all events, when the road law had been invoked for nearly two years, and when its enforcement had given rise to discontent, for the reasons indicated, Charlemagne Peralte, an escaped prisoner, raised a band of Cacos in the north, which for some 15 or 18 months carried on a formidable guerilla war against the native gendarmerie and the American Marine Corps.

CHARGES OF MILITARY ABUSES

The accusations of cruelty which have been made against members of the Marine Corps have deeply concerned your committee and required its full consideration. If cruelty toward the inhabitants has been countenanced or has escaped the punishment which vigilance could impose, or on the other hand, if false or groundless accusations have been made, if facts have been distorted, the true conditions should be revealed. Your committee has realized the gravity of the charges and the importance of impartial investigation and it has allotted a full portion of its time to the investigation of these complaints made by or on behalf of the Haitians. Examination has been made of the records and methods of investigations conducted by the Navy Department. Many witnesses have been heard in this country and in Haiti, and some scores of affidavits read and considered. So far as time permitted no one was refused a hearing and no limit has so far been placed on the number of written complaints in affidavit form. . . .

A SUMMARY OF THE FACTS

On the evidence before it the committee can now state—

(1) That the accusations of military abuses are limited in point of time to a few months and in location to restricted area.

(2) Very few of the many Americans who have served in Haiti are thus accused. The others have restored order and tranquillity under arduous conditions of service, and generally won the confidence of the inhabitants of the country with whom they came in touch.

(3) That certain Caco prisoners were executed without trial. Two such cases have been judicially determined. The evidence to which reference has been made shows eight more cases with sufficient clearness to allow them to be regarded without much doubt as having occurred. Lack of communications and the type of operations conducted by small patrols not in direct contact with superior authority

in some cases prevented knowledge of such occurrences on the part of higher authority until it was too late for effective investigation. When reported, investigations were held with no apparent desire to shield any guilty party. Such executions were unauthorized and directly contrary to the policy of the brigade commanders.

(4) That tortures of Haitians by Americans has not in any case been established, but that some accusations may have a foundation in excesses committed by hostile natives or members of the gendarmerie without the knowledge of American officers. Mutilations have not been practiced by Americans.

(5) That in the course of the campaign certain inhabitants other than bandits were killed during operations against the outlaws, but that such killings were unavoidable, accidental, and not intentional.

(6) That there was a period of about six months at the beginning of the outbreak when the gendarmerie lost control of the situation and was not itself sufficiently controlled by its higher officers, with the result that subordinate officers in the field were left too much discretion as to methods of patrol and local administration, and that this state of affairs was not investigated promptly enough, but that it was remedied as soon as known to the brigade commander. That the type of operations necessarily required the exercise of much independent discretion by detachment commanders.

(7) That undue severity or reckless treatment of natives was never countenanced by the brigade or gendarmerie commanders and that the investigation by naval authority of charges against members of the Marine Corps displays no desire to shield any individual, but on the contrary an intention to get at the facts.

(8) That the testimony of most native witnesses is highly unreliable and must be closely scrutinized and that many unfounded accusations have been made. It is also felt that in the case of accusations of abuses committed two years ago now made for the first time, the delay has not arisen through any well grounded fear of oppression by military authority, but that many of those accusations in affidavit form, now forthcoming, are produced at this late date because it is thought by those who are agitating for the immediate termination of the occupation that such accusations will create in the United States a sentiment in favor of such termination. In such cases the delay in making the charges and in presenting the evidence weighs heavily against the truth of the charge. All such charges, however, require full investigation. The committee feels certain that the necessary investigation by the Navy Department will be thoroughly conducted, that the rights of those accused will be respected, and that there will be no suppression of facts. When collected the facts so

obtained may be weighed with the facts alleged in the accusation. If, when all such evidence is in, the committee has any reason to change any of its conclusions it will submit with the evidence as printed such revision of this report on the alleged military abuses as may be required.

The committee believes that an important lesson may be learned from a study of the bandit campaign and the subsequent grave charges of misconduct. The lesson is the extreme importance in a campaign of this kind for higher command to require daily operation reports to be prepared by patrol leaders. In the early days of the outbreak such reports were not systematically required. Small patrols would be out of touch with the rest of our forces for days or weeks under distressing conditions of service. There is no complete record of the places they visited or when the visits were made or who was in command. If such reports or records were in existence, innocent individuals could instantly be cleared of unfounded charges, and guilty individuals could be identified with certainty. Such reports would have been a safeguard to the inhabitants and to the reputation of the Americans.

AMERICAN EFFORT TO BLACKEN THE NAME OF THE NAVY

In concluding this portion of the report the committee expresses its chagrin at the improper or criminal conduct of some few members of the Marine Corps and at the same time feels it to be its duty to condemn the process by which biased or interested individuals and committees and propagandists have seized on isolated instances, or have adopted as true any rumor however vile or baseless in an effort to bring into general disrepute the whole American naval force in Haiti. The committee wishes to express its admiration for the manner in which our men accomplished their dangerous and delicate task.

Patrolling still goes on, although the country is peaceful. For the last two years or more daily reports have been required. It is noteworthy that in the last two years or more there have arisen no serious grounds for complaint.

The confidence placed in the Americans by the Haitian peasants and the approval frequently communicated to the committee by those who know and sympathize with the peasants and who are engaged in philanthropic or educational work among them negative the idea of any campaign of terrorism against the inhabitants such as agitators and professional propagandists, Haitian and American, would have appear.

The acceptance of the status quo, the appreciation of the present peace and increasing prosperity of the country, by the mass of the people, is proven by the fact that there are among two and a half million people only twenty-five hundred gendarmes and less than twenty-five hundred marines.

A SUMMARY OF FAILURE AND ACHIEVEMENT

It has been necessary to interrupt the general consideration of the American occupation in Haiti, in order to review at length the incidents of the outbreak of 1918 and 1919. The committee is not prepared to say that the rising of Caco bands in the section of the country, where for a generation revolution habitually originated, was encouraged by the corvee. But it is impossible not to condemn the blunder committed when, under the corvee, laborers were carried beyond their vicinage to work under guard in strange surroundings. This was an error of commission like those of omission arising from failure to develop a definite and constructive policy under the treaty or to centralize in some degree responsibility for the conduct of American officers and officials serving in Haiti under the Government of Haiti or that of the United States. The blunder arose, too, from the failure of the departments in Washington to appreciate the importance of selecting for service in Haiti, whether in civil or military capacities, men who were sympathetic to the Haitians and able to maintain cordial personal and official relations with them.

It may be set down to the credit of the American occupation and the treaty officials that the Haitian cities, once foul and insanitary, are now clean, with well-kept and well-lighted streets. The greater part of an arterial highway system opening up the heart of the country has been built. The currency, which once violently fluctuated under the manipulations of European merchants, has been stabilized, to the great advantage of the Haitian peasant. Arrears of amortization as well as of interest on the public debt have been paid, as also are regularly paid the salaries of the smallest officials. The steamship communications between Haiti and the United States are greatly improved. Trade and revenues are increasing. The revision of the customs and internal taxes, so important to the prosperity of Haiti and especially of its poorest classes, awaits the funding of the debt by a new loan. There is peace and security of property and person throughout the Republic. The peasant in his hovel or on the road to market is safe from molestation by brigand or official authority. A force of 2,500 gendarmes, insufficiently trained to cope with the Caco outbreak in 1918, is now admirably disciplined. As its morale has improved, the force has become at once more considerate and more efficient in the discharge of its duties. It is noteworthy that an increasing proportion of the commissioned officers are native Haitians, those promoted from the ranks to be supplemented by others, graduates of the newly established cadet school. In brief, under the treaty, the peace of the Republic, the solvency of its Government, and the security of its people have been established for the first time in many years.

WHAT MUST BE DONE

Nevertheless your committee submits that the American people will not consider their duty under the treaty discharged if, in addition to what has been accomplished, there are not placed within the reach of the Haitian masses, justice, schools, and agricultural instruction. The treaty itself makes no provision to consummate these things, necessary to be done for progress in Haiti. There ought to be appointed a legal advisor to the High Commissioner. It would be an act of statesmanship and of comity on the part of our Government if it would send to Haiti a commission comprising a commercial advisor, an expert in tropical agriculture, and an educator of the standing and special experience of Doctor Moton of Tuskegee. There ought to be a survey of the need and opportunity for industrial and especially of agricultural instruction and development in a country which depends upon agriculture as its sole source of wealth. Cuba is as exclusively an agricultural country as Haiti. Like Haiti it pays for its imports of manufactures by exports of tropical agricultural products. The per capita foreign trade of Cuba is from twenty to twenty-five times that of Haiti, and the per capita revenue greater in like proportion. Obviously, with continued peace and order, with the further building of highways and trails, with instruction in agriculture, the wealth, trade, and the revenues of Haiti will increase very greatly. Your committee submits that such an increase in wealth, commerce, and revenue is necessary to the social and political progress of the Haitian people. Although at this time a beginning may be made in the establishment of elementary schools throughout the country, primary education can not be made accessible to a majority of the children unless the wealth and revenue of the Republic are very much increased. As wealth and revenues increase, schools, trails, and highways may be extended and as they are extended, in turn, the revenues will be further enhanced and so enable the further development of the public services. At the same time the buying power and the well-being of the people will increase as under American guidance or control they have so marvelously increased in Cuba and Porto Rico during the last generation. It is for this reason that your committee attaches importance to the dispatch of a commission such as suggested.

In this connection your committee believes it to be the duty of the American government to advise the Haitian government against permitting foreign interests to acquire great land holdings in Haiti.

Your committee would point out further that as communications are opened up and as the peasants are secure in their life and their property, and as each is able to earn something regularly from the sale of his little crop, the danger of revolution and banditry will diminish. It will be possible progressively to reduce the force of marines in the territory of the Republic and ultimately to intrust the maintenance of order and peace exclusively to the gendarmes. Your committee believes that a beginning in this direction may be made without further delay and that a concentration of the marine force may be begun and that the aggregate number of marines in the territory of the Republic may be reduced. It holds, however, that drastic reduction of the marine force, or its early withdrawal, would certainly be followed by a recurrence of brigandage and by the organization of revolutionary bands. The committee urges further that in connection with the concentration of the marine force in a limited number of posts, steps should be taken to put an end to the system of military law under which persons are tried in provost courts for offenses by the press against public order, or for attacks upon the military and peace forces within the Republic. These provost courts to-day do not touch the lives of the overwhelming majority of the people. It was doubtless necessary to establish such courts, but it is not consonant with our declared purposes under the treaty to continue them indefinitely. Their abolition is conditioned upon certain precedent steps, among them a reform of the courts of first instance. This last is urgent and important.

Along the lines suggested there can be a rapid development in Haiti, moral, social, political, and economic, provided always that American policy be marked by continuity and by the spirit of service. Not only have certain American officers and officials been chosen for service in Haiti who were unsuited to their task, but men have been transferred from responsible posts before they could very well have learned the duties to which they had been appointed. During the six years of the American occupation in Haiti there have been half a dozen chiefs of the Latin American Bureau, half a dozen commandants of the forces of occupation, half a dozen commanders of the Gendarmerie d'Haiti. The committee holds that the reforms proposed (and heretofore informally suggested to responsible officials) should be energetically carried out.

So much for an American policy of constructive service to be rendered by American officials. On the part of Haitian officials and the literate element of the Haitian people there must be cooperation with the American officials. Haitians must candidly realize the meaning of the unhappy events of the last 20 years and appreciate that in collaboration with America under the treaty Haiti can develop the wealth necessary to progress, provide for the general education of her people, and establish a more truly representative system of government than she has ever known. There are certain elements in Haiti which can balk and perhaps delay the rehabilitation of the country. They can not prevent it. They can do much to further it. The obvious duty of patriotic Haitians is to uphold their own Government in effectively cooperating with that of the United States under the treaty, and so hasten the day when Haiti may stand alone. The alternative to the course herein suggested is the immediate withdrawal of American support and the abandonment of the Haitian people to chronic revolution, anarchy, barbarism, and ruin.

Your committee deems it wise to defer the report upon the Dominican Republic in view of the negotiations happily to begin between the State Department and the Dominican leaders looking to the termination of the military government in Santo Domingo.

MEDILL McCORMICK
TASKER L. ODDIE
ATLEE POMERENE
ANDRIEUS A. JONES

STATEMENT by President Herbert Hoover at a Press Conference, February 4, 1930

William Starr Myers, *The State Papers and Other Public Writings of Herbert Hoover,* p. 209

Now THAT the Senate and House have approved the appropriation for a thorough inquiry into our problems in Haiti, I shall appoint a Commission at once to undertake it. I hope to be able to announce its personnel within a week.

The primary question which is to be investigated is when and how we are to withdraw from Haiti. The second question is what we shall do in the meantime. Certainly we shall withdraw our marines and officials some time. There are some people who wish for us to scuttle overnight. I am informed that every group in Haiti considers that such action would result in disaster to the Haitian people. On the other hand, our Treaty of 1915, under which our forces are present in that country, in the main expires in 1936, or six years hence. We have no mandate to continue the present relationship after that date.

We have an obligation to the people of Haiti, and we need to plan how we will discharge that obligation. There is need to build up a certainty of efficient and stable government, in order that life and property may be protected after we withdraw. We need to know, therefore, what sequent steps should be taken in cooperation with the Haitian people to bring about this result.

The answers to these questions must be worked out in broad vision after careful investigation of the entire subject by men of unbiased minds. It is for this reason that I have proposed to send a Commission to Haiti to determine the facts, to study and survey the whole problem in the light of our experience in the past 15 years and the social and political background of the Haitian people, to confer with all sides, to recommend the sequent and positive steps which will lead to the liquidation of our responsibilities and at the same time assure stable government in Haiti.

As I have stated before, I have no desire for representation of the American Government abroad through our military forces. We entered Haiti in 1915 for reasons arising from chaotic and distressing conditions, the consequence of a long period of civil war and disorganization. We assumed by treaty the obligation to assist the Republic of Haiti in the restoration of order; the organization of an efficient police force; and the rehabilitation of its finances, and the development of its natural resources. We have the implied obligation of assisting in building up of a stable self-government. Peace and order have been restored, finances have been largely rehabilitated, a police force is functioning under the leadership of Marine officers. The economic development of Haiti has shown extraordinary improvement under this regime. It is marked by highway systems, vocational schools, public health measures. General Russell deserves great credit for these accomplishments.

We need now a new and definite policy looking forward to the expiration of our treaties.

REPORT of the President's Commission for the Study and Review of Conditions in the Republic of Haiti (the "Forbes' Commission"), March 26, 1930 (extracts)
Department of State, Latin American Series, No. 2, p. 6

AMERICAN INTERVENTION

THE REASONS which impelled the United States to enter Haiti in 1915 are so well known that they need not be set forth in this report.

Conditions were chaotic; means of communication were largely nonexistent; the peasant class was impoverished; disease was general; property was menaced; and the debt of the government, indeterminate in amount, had risen—at least on paper—to staggering proportions.

Having landed a force of Marines, thus restoring public order and protecting the citizens of the United States and other countries from violence, the United States by treaty obtained control of a variety of governmental agencies with a view to assisting in the reestablishment of a stable government. There was not and there never has been on the part of the United States any desire to impair Haitian sovereignty.

There is no room for doubt that Haiti, under the control of the American Occupation, has made great material progress in the past fifteen years.

Indeed, the greater part of what has been done has been accomplished in the past eight years, because it was not until the disastrous and involved financial situation could be straightened out by the flotation of the loan of 1922 that a constructive policy could be carried out.

Peace and order were restored by the Marines by 1920 and road building was begun under Marine auspices. The essential primary steps for the reform of the administration were taken as soon as peace was secured by the elimination of banditry, but the American officials were working at cross purposes and progress was hampered. It was therefore decided to entrust General Russell, of the United States Marine Corps, who had served in Haiti almost from the beginning of the Occupation, with the duty of coordinating and directing the efforts of the treaty officials. In order that he might also have the highest civilian rank it was decided not to appoint an American Minister, and he was given the title of High Commissioner. As such he is the representative of the United States near the Haitian Government.

The commission desires to record its high praise of General Russell's whole-hearted and single-minded devotion to the interests of Haiti as he conceived them, his unremitting labor, and his patient and painstaking efforts to bring order out of chaos and to reconstruct a governmental machine which had been largely destroyed by years of abuse, incapacity, and anarchy. Since the Occupation the Haitian Government, especially under President Borno, with the guidance and assistance of the American officials in its service, has a fine record of accomplishment. . . .

The commission was disappointed at the evidence it received of the lack of appreciation on the part of the educated and cultured Haitians of the services rendered them by the Occupation and their own Government. Out of many dozen witnesses only one or two made favorable mention of the achievements of their administration. . . .

Under the American Occupation—and with its consent—the legislative chambers were dissolved in 1918, and by an interpretation of a new constitution, adopted under its egis, they have not since been reassembled. The country has been ruled by a President and a Council of State exercising, under the direction of American officials, the legislative authority. Local self-government has also largely disappeared. The important municipalities and communes are ruled by commissioners appointed by the President. The members of the Council of State itself have been appointed and removed by him. The Council of State under the legislative authority vested in it by the 1918 constitution has exercised the powers of a National Assembly in electing the President.

The people of Haiti, since the dissolution of the National Assembly by President Dartiquenave, have had no popularly elected representatives in control of their Government. The American Occupation has accepted—if not indeed encouraged—this state of affairs. Certainly reforms could be instituted and governmental measures carried through more easily in these circumstances, and were.

The acts and attitude of the treaty officials gave your commission the impression that they had been based upon the assumption that the Occupation would continue indefinitely. In other words, their plans and projects did not seem to take into account that their work should be completed by 1936, and the commission was disappointed to find that the preparation for the political and administrative training of Haitians for the responsibilities of government had been inadequate.

The commission is under no delusions as to what may happen in Haiti after the convocation of the elected legislative assembly and, to a greater extent, after the complete withdrawal of the United States forces. The Government of Haiti before American intervention was, so far as the commission could learn, more democratic and representative in name than in fact. The Deputies and Senators were, the commission was informed, more often chosen by the President than elected by the people.

The commission is not convinced that the foundations for democratic and representative government are now broad enough in Haiti. The educated public opinion and literate minority are so small that any government formed in these circumstances is liable to become an oligarchy. The literate few too often look to public office as a means of livelihood. Until the basis of political structure is broadened by education—a matter of years—the Government must necessarily be more or less unstable and in constant danger of political upheavals.

TREATY RELATIONS

The commission is of the opinion that the progressive steps looking toward the withdrawal of the assistance now being given by the American Occupation should be taken on the theory and understanding that the present treaty will remain in force until 1936, it being understood that such modifications as circumstances require and the two Governments agree upon may be made at any time. It is too early to suggest in what form the American Occupation should be liquidated upon the expiration of the treaty or in what form such further aid and assistance as the Haitian Government might desire from the United States should be provided. This can be more wisely decided in the light of the experience of the next few years.

MARINES

The question of the withdrawal of the Marine Brigade, which acts as a stabilizing and supporting force in the preservation of order, is one which the commission has carefully considered. Very little complaint was heard of the presence of the Marines, except as they formed part of the American Occupation. They are not much in evidence. All except about one hundred and fifty are stationed in Port au Prince; the rest are at Cape Haitien. The commission considered the question of removing the Marines from these two centers and putting them in barracks a short distance from these cities, but concluded that this was impracticable and unwise. The commission recommends the gradual reduction of the Marine Brigade if and as, in the judgment of the two Governments, the political situation warrants. . . .

SEQUENT STEPS

Complying with your instructions to suggest sequent steps to be taken with respect to the Haitian situation your commission offers the following:

(1) That the President declare that the United States will approve a policy, the details of which all the United States officials in Haiti are directed to assist in working out, providing for an increasingly rapid Haitianization of the services, with the object of having Haitians experienced in every department of the Government ready to take over full responsibility at the expiration of the existing treaty;

(2) That in retaining officers now in Haitian service, or selecting new Americans for employment therein, the utmost care be taken that only those free from strong racial antipathies should be preferred;

(3) That the United States recognize the temporary President when

elected, provided the election is in accordance with the agreement reached by your commission with President Borno and the leaders representing the opposition;

(4) That the United States recognize the President elected by the new legislature, acting as a National Assembly, provided that neither force nor fraud have been used in the elections;

(5) That at the expiration of General Russell's tour of duty in Haiti, and in any such event not before the inauguration of the permanent President, the office of High Commissioner be abolished and a nonmilitary Minister appointed to take over his duties as well as those of diplomatic representative;

(6) That whether or not a certain loss of efficiency is entailed, the new Minister to Haiti be charged with the duty of carrying out the early Haitianization of the services called for in the Declaration of the President of the United States above recommended;

(7) That, as the commission found the immediate withdrawal of the Marines inadvisable, it recommends their gradual withdrawal in accordance with arrangements to be made in future agreement between the two Governments;

(8) That the United States limit its intervention in Haitian affairs definitely to those activities for which provision is made for American assistance by treaty or by specific agreement between the two Governments;

(9) That the new Minister be charged with the duty of negotiating with the Haitian Government further modifications of the existing treaty and agreements providing for less intervention in Haitian domestic affairs and defining the conditions under which the United States would lend its assistance in the restoration of order or maintenance of credit.

Respectfully submitted,

W. CAMERON FORBES
HENRY P. FLETCHER
ELIE VEZINA
JAMES KERNEY
W. A. WHITE

*STATEMENT by Cordell Hull, Secretary of State, Regarding
the Withdrawal of Marine and Naval Forces from Haiti,
August 15, 1934*
Department of State, *Press Releases*, August 18, 1934, p. 103

TODAY the withdrawal of our marine and naval forces from Haiti is
being completed. Under an agreement between the two Governments
of August 7, 1933, the Haitian Garde, which has been trained and
partly officered by our marines, would be turned over to the complete
command of Haitian officers on October 1, 1934, and our marine
and naval forces would be withdrawn during the month of October.
However, when President Roosevelt visited Cap Haitien July 5, last,
President Vincent requested that, if at all possible, the date for carrying out these movements should be advanced; and President Roosevelt stated that we would advance the date for turning over the
command of the Garde to August 1, instead of October 1, and would
withdraw our forces from Haiti in the following fortnight. In accordance with President Roosevelt's statement, and with a subsequent
exchange of notes between the two Governments, complete command
of the Haitian Garde was formally turned over on August 1, 1934, to
a Haitian officer, designated by the President of Haiti as Commandant
of the Garde. Since that date the withdrawal of our forces has been
taking place, and is being completed today.

Arrangements have also been made whereby President Roosevelt,
acting under authority expressly conferred upon him by Congress,
is making a gift to the Haitian Government of a considerable amount
of material and property belonging to our marine and naval units in
Haiti and which the Haitian Government felt would be valuable and
useful to it.

In the nearly 20 years during which our marine and naval forces
have been stationed in Haiti, they have rendered invaluable, disinterested service to the Haitian Government and people. At this present moment they are withdrawing from the island in an atmosphere
of great friendliness and the best of understanding. We wish for the
Government and people of Haiti stability, progress, and all success.

The Dominican Republic

PRESIDENT THEODORE ROOSEVELT to Joseph B. Bishop, February 23, 1904 (extract)
Joseph B. Bishop, *Theodore Roosevelt and His Time*, I, 431

I HAVE BEEN HOPING and praying for three months that the Santo Domingans would behave so that I would not have to act in any way. I want to do nothing but what a policeman has to do in Santo Domingo. As for annexing the island, I have about the same desire to annex it as a gorged boa constrictor might have to swallow a porcupine wrong-end-to. Is that strong enough? I have asked some of our people to go there because, after having refused for three months to do anything, the attitude of the Santo Domingans has become one of half chaotic war towards us. If I possibly can I want to do nothing to them. If it is absolutely necessary to do something, then I want to do as little as possible. Their government has been bedeviling us to establish some kind of a protectorate over the islands, and take charge of their finances. We have been answering them that we could not possibly go into the subject now at all.

MESSAGE from President Theodore Roosevelt to the United States Senate, February 15, 1905
John Bassett Moore, *A Digest of International Law*, VI, 518. The Senate declined to approve the agreement. For the Convention of 1907, which was ratified, see *infra*, p. 943

I SUBMIT HEREWITH a protocol concluded between the Dominican Republic and the United States.

The conditions in the Republic of Santo Domingo have been growing steadily worse for many years. There have been many disturbances and revolutions, and debts have been contracted beyond the power of the Republic to pay. Some of these debts were properly contracted and are held by those who have a legitimate right to their

money. Others are without question improper or exorbitant, constituting claims which should never be paid in full and perhaps only
to the extent of a very small portion of their nominal value.

Certain foreign countries have long felt themselves aggrieved because of the nonpayment of debts due their citizens. The only way
by which foreign creditors could ever obtain from the Republic itself
any guaranty of payment would be either by the acquisition of territory outright or temporarily, or else by taking possession of the
custom-houses, which would of course in itself, in effect, be taking
possession of a certain amount of territory.

It has for some time been obvious that those who profit by the
Monroe doctrine must accept certain responsibilities along with the
rights which it confers; and that the same statement applies to those
who uphold the doctrine. It can not be too often and too emphatically
asserted that the United States has not the slightest desire for territorial aggrandizement at the expense of any of its southern neighbors,
and will not treat the Monroe doctrine as an excuse for such aggrandizement on its part. We do not propose to take any part of Santo
Domingo, or exercise any other control over the island save what is
necessary to its financial rehabilitation in connection with the collection of revenue, part of which will be turned over to the Government to meet the necessary expense of running it, and part of which
will be distributed pro rata among the creditors of the Republic
upon a basis of absolute equity. The justification for the United
States taking this burden and incurring this responsibility is to be
found in the fact that it is incompatible with international equity for
the United States to refuse to allow other powers to take the only
means at their disposal of satisfying the claims of their creditors and
yet to refuse, itself, to take any such steps.

An aggrieved nation can without interfering with the Monroe doctrine take what action it sees fit in the adjustment of its disputes with
American states, provided that action does not take the shape of
interference with their form of government or of the despoilment of
their territory under any disguise. But, short of this, when the question is one of a money claim, the only way which remains, finally, to
collect it is a blockade, or bombardment, or the seizure of the custom-
houses, and this means, as has been said above, what is in effect a
possession, even though only a temporary possession, of territory. The
United States then becomes a party in interest, because under the
Monroe doctrine it can not see any European power seize and permanently occupy the territory of one of these Republics; and yet such
seizure of territory, disguised or undisguised, may eventually offer

the only way in which the power in question can collect any debts, unless there is interference on the part of the United States.

One of the difficult and increasingly complicated problems, which often arise in Santo Domingo, grows out of the violations of contracts and concessions, sometimes improvidently granted, with valuable privileges and exemptions stipulated for upon grossly inadequate considerations which were burdensome to the state, and which are not infrequently disregarded and violated by the governing authorities. Citizens of the United States and of other governments holding these concessions and contracts appeal to their respective governments for active protection and intervention. Except for arbitrary wrong, done or sanctioned by superior authority, to persons or to vested property rights, the United States Government, following its traditional usage in such cases, aims to go no further than the mere use of its good offices, a measure which frequently proves ineffective. On the other hand, there are governments which do sometimes take energetic action for the protection of their subjects in the enforcement of merely contractual claims, and thereupon American concessionaries, supported by powerful influences, make loud appeal to the United States Government in similar cases for similar action. They complain that in the actual posture of affairs their valuable properties are practically confiscated, that American enterprise is paralyzed, and that unless they are fully protected, even by the enforcement of their merely contractual rights, it means the abandonment to the subjects of other governments of the interests of American trade and commerce through the sacrifice of their investments by excessive taxes imposed in violation of contract, and by other devices, and the sacrifice of the output of their mines and other industries, and even of their railway and shipping interests, which they have established in connection with the exploitation of their concessions. Thus the attempted solution of the complex problem by the ordinary methods of diplomacy reacts injuriously upon the United States Government itself, and in a measure paralyzes the action of the Executive in the direction of a sound and consistent policy. The United States Government is embarrassed in its efforts to foster American enterprise and the growth of our commerce through the cultivation of friendly relations with Santo Domingo, by the irritating effects on those relations, and the consequent injurious influence upon that commerce, of frequent interventions. As a method of solution of the complicated problem arbitration has become nugatory, inasmuch as, in the condition of its finances, an award against the Republic is worthless unless its payment is secured by the pledge of at least some portion of the customs revenues. This pledge is ineffectual without actual delivery over of the custom-houses to secure the appropriation of the pledged revenues to the payment of the award. This situation again reacts injuriously upon the relations of the United States with other nations. For when an award and such security are thus obtained, as in the case of the Santo Domingo Improvement Company, some foreign government complains that the award conflicts with its rights, as a creditor, to some portion of these revenues under an alleged prior pledge; and still other governments complain that an award in any considerable sum, secured by pledges of the customs revenues, is prejudicial to the payment of their equally meritorious claims out of the ordinary revenues; and thus controversies are begotten between the United States and other creditor nations because of the apparent sacrifice of some of their claims, which may be just or may be grossly exaggerated, but which the United States Government can not inquire into without giving grounds of offense to other friendly creditor nations. Still further illustrations might easily be furnished of the hopelessness of the present situation growing out of the social disorders and the bankrupt finances of the Dominican Republic, where for considerable periods during recent years the bonds of civil society have been practically dissolved.

Under the accepted law of nations foreign governments are within their right, if they choose to exercise it, when they actively intervene in support of the contractual claims of their subjects. They sometimes exercise this power, and on account of commercial rivalries there is a growing tendency on the part of other governments more and more to aid diplomatically in the enforcement of the claims of their subjects. In view of the dilemma in which the Government of the United States is thus placed, it must either adhere to its usual attitude of nonintervention in such cases—an attitude proper under normal conditions, but one which in this particular kind of case results to the disadvantage of its citizens in comparison with those of other states— or else it must, in order to be consistent in its policy, actively intervene to protect the contracts and concessions of its citizens engaged in agriculture, commerce, and transportation in competition with the subjects and citizens of other states. This course would render the United States the insurer of all the speculative risks of its citizens in the public securities and franchises of Santo Domingo.

Under the plan in the protocol herewith submitted to the Senate, insuring a faithful collection and application of the revenues to the specified objects, we are well assured that this difficult task can be accomplished with the friendly cooperation and good will of all the parties concerned, and to the great relief of the Dominican Republic.

The conditions in the Dominican Republic not only constitute a menace to our relations with other foreign nations, but they also concern the prosperity of the people of the island, as well as the security of American interests, and they are intimately associated with the interests of the South Atlantic and Gulf States, the normal expansion of whose commerce lies in that direction. At one time, and that only a year ago, three revolutions were in progress in the island at the same time.

It is impossible to state with anything like approximate accuracy the present population of the Dominican Republic. In the report of the Commission appointed by President Grant in 1871, the population was estimated at not over 150,000 souls, but according to the Statesman's Yearbook for 1904 the estimated population in 1888 is given as 610,000. The Bureau of the American Republics considers this the best estimate of the present population of the Republic. As shown by the unanimous report of the Grant Commission the public debt of the Dominican Republic, including claims, was $1,565,-831.59¼. The total revenues were $772,684.75¼. The public indebtedness of the Dominican Republic, not including all claims, was on September 12 last, as the Department of State is advised, $32,-280,000; the estimated revenues under Dominican management of custom-houses were $1,850,000; the proposed budget for current administration was $1,300,000, leaving only $550,000 to pay foreign and liquidated obligations, and payments on these latter will amount during the ensuing year to $1,700,000, besides $900,000 of arrearages of payments overdue, amounting in all to $2,600,000. It is therefore impossible under existing conditions, which are chronic, and with the estimated yearly revenues of the Republic, which during the last decade have averaged approximately $1,600,000, to defray the ordinary expenses of the Government and to meet its obligations.

The Dominican debt owed to European creditors is about $22,-000,000, and of this sum over $18,000,000 is more or less formally recognized. The representatives of European governments have several times approached the Secretary of State setting forth the wrongs and intolerable delays to which they have been subjected at the hands of the successive governments of Santo Domingo in the collection of their just claims, and intimating that unless the Dominican Government should receive some assistance from the United States in the way of regulating its finances, the creditor governments in Europe would be forced to resort to more effective measures of compulsion to secure the satisfaction of their claims.

If the United States Government declines to take action and other foreign governments resort to action to secure payment of their claims, the latter would be entitled, according to the decision of The Hague tribunal in the Venezuelan cases, to the preferential payment of their claims; and this would absorb all the Dominican revenues and would be a virtual sacrifice of American claims and interests in the island. If, moreover, any such action should be taken by them, the only method to enable them to secure the payment of their claims would be to take possession of the custom-houses, and considering the state of the Dominican finances this would mean a definite and very possibly permanent occupation of Dominican territory, for no period could be set to the time which would be necessarily required for the payment of their obligations and unliquidated claims. The United States Government could not interfere to prevent such seizure and occupation of Dominican territory without either itself proposing some feasible alternative in the way of action, or else virtually saying to European governments that they would not be allowed to collect their claims. This would be an unfortunate attitude for the Government of the United States to be forced to maintain at present. It can not with propriety say that it will protect its own citizens and interests, on the one hand, and yet on the other hand refuse to allow other governments to protect their citizens and interests.

The actual situation in the Dominican Republic can not, perhaps, be more forcibly stated than by giving a brief account of the case of the San Domingo Improvement Company.

From 1869 to 1897 the Dominican Government issued successive series of bonds, the majority of which were in the hands of European holders. Successive issues bore interest at rates ranging from 2¾ to 6 per cent, and what with commissions and other deductions and the heavy discount in the market the Government probably did not receive over 50 to 75 per cent of their nominal value. Other portions of the debt were created by loans, for which the Government received only one-half of the amount it was nominally to repay, and these obligations bore interest at the rate of 1 to 2 per cent a month on their face, some of them compounded monthly.

The improvidence of the Government in its financial management was due to its weakness, to its impaired credit, and to its pecuniary needs, occasioned by frequent insurrections and revolutionary changes, and by its inability to collect its revenues.

In 1888 the Government, in order to secure the payment of an issue of bonds, placed the custom-houses and the collection of its customs duties, which are substantially the only revenues of the Republic, in the hands of the Westendorps, bankers of Amsterdam, Holland. But the national debt continued to grow and the Government finally intrusted the collection of its revenues to an American corporation, the San Domingo Improvement Company, which was to take over the bonds of the Westendorps. The Dominican Government finally became dissatisfied with this arrangement, and, in 1901, ousted the improvement company from its custom-houses and took into its own hands the collection of its revenues. The company thereupon appealed to the United States Government to maintain them in their position, but their request was refused. The Dominican Government then sent its minister of foreign affairs to Washington to negotiate a settlement. He admitted that the improvement company had equities which ought not to be disregarded, and the Department of State suggested that the Dominican Government and the improvement company should effect, by private negotiation, a satisfactory settlement between them. They accordingly entered into an arrangement for a settlement, which was mutually satisfactory to the parties. A similar arrangement was likewise made between the Dominican Government and the European bondholders. The latter arrangement was carried into execution by the Dominican Government and payments made toward the liquidation of the bonds held by the European holders. The Dominican Congress refused to ratify the similar arrangement made with the improvement company, and the Government refused to provide for the payment of the American claimants. In this state of the case it was evident that a continuance of this treatment of the American creditors, and its repetition in other cases, would, if allowed to run its course, result in handing over the island to European creditors, and in time would ripen into serious controversies between the United States and other governments, unless the United States should deliberately and finally abandon its interests in the island.

The improvement company and its allied companies held, besides bonds, certain banking and railway interests in the island. The Dominican Government, desirous to own and possess these properties, agreed with the companies that the value of their bonds and properties was $4,500,000, and they submitted to arbitration the question as to the installments in which this sum should be paid and the security that should be given. The Hon. George Gray, judge of the United States circuit court of appeals, and the Hon. Manuel de J. Galvan, both named by the Dominican Republic, and the Hon. John G. Carlisle, named by the United States, were the arbitrators and rendered their award on July 14, 1904. By its terms the Dominican Government was to pay the above-mentioned sum of $4,500,000, with 4 per cent interest per annum, in monthly installments of $37,500 each during two years, and of $41,666.66 each month thereafter, beginning with the month of September, 1904, said award to be secured by the customs revenues and port dues of all the ports on the northern coast of Santo Domingo. The award further provides for the appointment of a financial agent of the United States, who was authorized, in case of failure during any month to receive the sum then due, to enter into possession of the custom-house at Puerto Plata in the first instance and assume charge of the collection of customs duties and port dues and to fix and determine these duties and dues and secure their payment; in case the sums collected at Puerto Plata should at any time be insufficient for the payment of the amounts due under the award, or in case of any other manifest necessity, or in case the Dominican Government should so request, the financial agent of the United States was authorized to have and exercise at any and all of the other ports above described all the rights and powers vested in him by the award in respect of Puerto Plata. Under the award the financial agent could only apply the revenues collected toward its payment after he had first paid the expenses of collection and certain other obligations styled "apartados," which constituted prior charges on the revenues assigned. These prior charges are specified in the award. The Dominican Government defaulted in their payments; and in virtue of the award and the authority conferred by the Dominican Government, and at its request, possession was delivered of the custom-house of Puerto Plata to the fiscal agent appointed by the United States to collect the revenues assigned by the arbitrators for the payment of the award; and in virtue of the same authority possession of the custom-house of Monte Cristi has also been handed over. I submit herewith a report of Mr. John B. Moore, agent of the United States in this case, and a copy of the award of the arbitrators.

During the past two years the European claimants, except the English, whose interests were embraced in those of the American companies, have, with the support of their respective governments, been growing more and more importunate in pressing their unsatisfied demands. The French and the Belgians, in 1901, had entered into a contract with the Dominican Government, but, after a few payments were made on account, it fell into neglect. Other governments also obliged the Dominican Government to enter into arrangements of various kinds by which the revenues of the Republic were in large part sequestrated, and under one of the agreements, which was concluded with Italy in 1903, the minister of that Government was empowered directly to collect from the importers and exporters that portion of the customs revenues assigned to him as security. As the result of chronic disorders, attended with a constant increase of debt, the state of things in Santo Domingo has become hopeless, unless the United States or some other strong government shall interpose to bring order out of the chaos. The custom-houses, with the exception of the two in the possession of the financial agent appointed by the United States, have become unproductive for the discharge of indebtedness, except as to persons making emergency loans to the Government or to its enemies for the purpose of carrying on political contests by force. They have, in fact, become the nuclei of the various revolutions. The first effort of revolutionists is to take possession of a custom-house so as to obtain funds, which are then disposed of at the absolute discretion of those who are collecting them. The chronic disorders prevailing in Santo Domingo have moreover become exceedingly dangerous to the interests of Americans holding property in that country. Constant complaints have been received of the injuries and inconveniences to which they have been subjected. As an evidence of the increasing aggravation of conditions, the fact may be mentioned that about a year ago the American railway, which had previously been exempt from such attacks, was seized, its tracks torn up, and a station destroyed by revolutionary bands.

The ordinary resources of diplomacy and international arbitration are absolutely impotent to deal wisely and effectively with the situation in the Dominican Republic, which can only be met by organizing its finances on a sound basis and by placing the custom-houses beyond the temptation of insurgent chieftains. Either we must abandon our duty under our traditional policy toward the Dominican people, who aspire to a republican form of government while they are actually drifting into a condition of permanent anarchy, in which case we must permit some other government to adopt its own measures in order to safeguard its own interests, or else we must ourselves take seasonable and appropriate action.

Again and again has the Dominican Government invoked on its own behalf the aid of the United States. It has repeatedly done so of recent years. In 1899 it sought to enter into treaty relations by which it would be placed under the protection of the United States Government. The request was refused. Again, in January, 1904, its minister of foreign affairs visited Washington and besought the help of the United States Government to enable it to escape from its financial and social disorders. Compliance with this request was again declined, for this Government has been most reluctant to interfere in any way, and has finally concluded to take action only because it has become evident that failure to do so may result in a situation fraught with grave danger to the cause of international peace.

In 1903 a representative of a foreign government proposed to the United States the joint fiscal control of the Dominican Republic by certain creditor nations, and that the latter should take charge of the custom-houses and revenues and give to the Dominican Government a certain percentage and apply the residue to the payment ratably of claims of foreign creditors. The United States Government declined to approve or to enter into such an arrangement. But it has now become evident that decided action of some kind can not be much longer delayed. In view of our best experience and our knowledge of the actual situation of the Dominican Republic, a definite refusal of the United States Government to take any effective action looking to the relief of the Dominican Republic and to the discharge of its own duty under the Monroe doctrine can only be considered as an acquiescence in some such action by another government.

That most wise measure of international statesmanship, the Platt amendment, has provided a method for preventing such difficulties from arising in the new Republic of Cuba. In accordance with the terms of this amendment the Republic of Cuba can not issue any bonds which can be collected from Cuba, save as a matter of grace, unless with the consent of the United States, which is·at liberty at all times to take measures to prevent the violation of the letter and spirit of the Platt amendment. If a similar plan could now be entered upon by the Dominican Republic, it would undoubtedly be of great advantage to them and to all other peoples, for under such an arrangement no larger debt would be incurred than could be honestly paid, and those who took debts not thus authorized would, by the mere fact of taking them, put themselves in the category of speculators or gamblers, who deserved no consideration and who would be permitted to receive none; so that the honest creditor would on the one hand be safe while on the other hand the Republic would be safe-guarded against molestation in the interest of mere speculators.

But no such plan at present exists; and under existing circumstances, when the condition of affairs becomes such as it has become in Santo Domingo, either we must submit to the likelihood of infringement of the Monroe doctrine or we must ourselves agree to some such arrangement as that herewith submitted to the Senate. In this case, fortunately, the prudent and far-seeing statesmanship of the Dominican Government has relieved us of all trouble. At their request we have entered into the agreement herewith submitted. Under it the custom-houses will be administered peacefully, honestly, and economically, 45 per cent of the proceeds being turned over to the Dominican Government and the remainder being used by the United States to pay what proportion of the debts it is possible to pay on an equitable basis. The Republic will be secured against over-seas aggression. This in reality entails no new obligation upon us, for the Monroe doctrine means precisely such a guarantee on our part.

It is perhaps unnecessary to state that no step of any kind has been taken by the Administration under the terms of the protocol which is herewith submitted.

The Republic of Santo Domingo has by this protocol wisely and patriotically accepted the responsibilities as well as the privileges of liberty, and is showing with evident good faith its purpose to pay all that its resources will permit of its obligations. More than this it can not do, and when it has done this we should not permit it to be molested. We on our part are simply performing in peaceful manner, not only with the cordial acquiescence, but in accordance with the earnest request of the Government concerned, part of that international duty which is necessarily involved in the assertion of the Monroe doctrine. We are bound to show that we perform this duty in good faith and without any intention of aggrandizing ourselves at the expense of our weaker neighbors or of conducting ourselves otherwise than so as to benefit both these weaker neighbors and those European powers which may be brought into contact with them. It is in the highest degree necessary that we should prove by our action that the world may trust in our good faith and may understand that this international duty will be performed by us within our own sphere, in the interest not merely of ourselves, but of all other nations, and with strict justice toward all. If this is done a general acceptance of the Monroe doctrine will in the end surely follow; and this will mean an increase of the sphere in which peaceful measures for the settlement of international difficulties gradually displace those of a warlike character.

We can point with just pride to what we have done in Cuba as a guaranty of our good faith. We stayed in Cuba only so long as to start her aright on the road to self-government, which she has since trod with such marked and distinguished success; and upon leaving the island we exacted no conditions save such as would prevent her from ever becoming the prey of the stranger. Our purpose in Santo Domingo is as beneficent. The good that this country got from its action in Cuba was indirect rather than direct. So it is as regards Santo Domingo. The chief material advantage that will come from the action proposed to be taken will be to Santo Domingo itself and to Santo Domingo's creditors. The advantages that will come to the United States will be indirect, but nevertheless great, for it is supremely to our interest that all the communities immediately south of us should be or become prosperous and stable, and therefore not merely in name but in fact independent and self-governing.

I call attention to the urgent need of prompt action on this matter. We now have a great opportunity to secure peace and stability in the

island, without friction or bloodshed, by acting in accordance with
the cordial invitation of the governmental authorities themselves. It
will be unfortunate from every standpoint if we fail to grasp this
opportunity; for such failure will probably mean increasing revolutionary violence in Santo Domingo, and very possibly embarrassing
foreign complications in addition. This protocol affords a practical test
of the efficiency of the United States Government in maintaining the
Monroe doctrine.

*PLAN of President Woodrow Wilson Handed to John Franklin
Fort and Charles Cogswell Smith, United States Commissioners Proceeding to Santo Domingo, August, 1914*

Foreign Relations of the United States, 1914, p. 247. On August 13, 1914, William
J. Bryan, Secretary of State, telegraphed to the Commission: "You are instructed
to observe and follow out with utmost care plan which has been presented you
by the Secretary of State. No opportunity for argument should be given to any
person or faction. It is desired that you present plan and see that it is complied
with" (*ibid.,* p. 247)

THE GOVERNMENT of the United States desires nothing for itself from
the Dominican Republic and no concessions or advantages for its
citizens which are not accorded citizens of other countries. It desires
only to prove its sincere and disinterested friendship for the republic
and its people and to fulfill its responsibilities as the friend to whom
in such crises as the present all the world looks to guide Santo Domingo
out of its difficulties.

It, therefore, makes the following earnest representations not only
to the existing de facto Government of the Dominican Republic, but
also to all who are in any way responsible for the present posture of
affairs there:

I. It warns everyone concerned that it is absolutely imperative that
the present hostilities should cease and that all who are concerned in
them should disperse to their several homes, disbanding the existing
armed forces and returning to the peaceful occupations upon which
the welfare of the people of the republic depends. This is necessary,
and necessary at once. Nothing can be successfully accomplished until
this is done.

II. It is also necessary that there should be an immediate recon-
stitution of political authority in the republic. To this end the
Government of the United States very solemnly advises all concerned

with the public affairs of the republic to adopt the following plan:

(1) Let all those who have any pretensions to be chosen President of the Republic and who can make any sufficient show of exercising a recognized leadership and having an acknowledged following agree upon some responsible and representative man to act as Provisional President of the Republic, it being understood that Mr. Bordas will relinquish his present position and authority. If these candidates can agree in this matter, the Government of the United States will recognize and support the man of their choice as Provisional President. If they cannot agree, the Government of the United States will itself name a Provisional President, sustain him in the assumption of office, and support him in the exercise of his temporary authority. The Provisional President will not be a candidate for President.

(2) At the earliest feasible date after the establishment and recognition of the Provisional Government thus established let elections for a regular President and Congress be held under the authority and direction of the Provisional President, who will, it must of course be understood, exercise during his tenure of office the full powers of President of the Republic; but let it be understood that the Government of the United States will send representatives of its own choosing to observe the election throughout the republic and that it will expect those observers not only to be accorded a courteous welcome but also to be accorded the freest opportunities to observe the circumstances and processes of the election.

(3) Let it be understood that if the United States Government is satisfied that these elections have been free and fair and carried out under conditions which enable the people of the republic to express their real choice, it will recognize the President and Congress thus chosen as the legitimate and constitutional Government of the Republic and will support them in the exercise of their functions and authority in every way it can. If it should not be satisfied that elections of the right kind have been held, let it be understood that another election will be held at which the mistakes observed will be corrected.

III. A regular and constitutional government having thus been set up, the Government of the United States would feel at liberty thereafter to insist that revolutionary movements cease and that all subsequent changes in the Government of the Republic be effected by the peaceful processes provided in the Dominican Constitution. By no other course can the Government of the United States fulfill its treaty obligations with Santo Domingo or its tacitly conceded obligations as the nearest friend of Santo Domingo in her relations with the rest of the world.

WILLIAM J. BRYAN, Secretary of State, to James M. Sullivan,
United States Minister to the Dominican Republic, January
12, 1915
Foreign Relations of the United States, 1915, p. 279

You MAY SAY to President Jiménes that this Government will support
him to the fullest extent in the suppression of any insurrection against
his Government. The election having been held and a Government
chosen by the people having been established, no more revolutions
will be permitted. You may notify both Horacio Vásquez and Arias
that they will be held personally responsible if they attempt to embarrass the Government. The people of Santo Domingo will be given
an opportunity to develop the resources of their country in peace.
Their revenues will no longer be absorbed by graft or wasted in insurrections. This Government meant what it said when it sent a
commission there with a proposal looking to permanent peace and it
will live up to the promises it has made. Reasonable delay in carrying
out the proposed reforms is not objectionable but the changes advised
are the reforms necessary for the honest and efficient administration of
the Government and the early and proper development of the country. There should be no unnecessary delay therefore in putting them
into operation. Keep us advised. A naval force will be sent whenever
necessary.

BRYAN

WILLIAM J. BRYAN, Secretary of State, to James M. Sullivan,
United States Minister to the Dominican Republic, April 9,
1915
Foreign Relations of the United States, 1915, p. 283

ANSWERING your April 8, 10 a.m. you may say to President Jiménes
and to those connected with the plot that this Government will not
permit any attack to be made upon President Jiménes for acting in
good faith toward the United States. Notify the plotters, as you have
opportunity to do so, that President Jiménes having been chosen
President by the people, is entitled to and will receive from this

Government, any assistance that will be necessary to compel respect for his administration. This support will be given whether the attacks made upon him are direct, or indirect, open or in secret.

BRYAN

WILLIAM W. RUSSELL, United States Minister to the Dominican Republic, to the Dominican Minister for Foreign Affairs, November 19, 1915
Foreign Relations of the United States, 1915, p. 333

American Legation
Santo Domingo, November 19, 1915

MR. MINISTER:

In accordance with instructions I have the honor to say to your excellency that the Government of the United States is anxiously concerned over the present unsettled conditions, both political and financial, in the Dominican Republic. My Government, by reason of the obligations assumed and by virtue of the authority given under the provisions of the convention concluded on February 8, 1907, is particularly interested in the material progress and welfare of the Dominican Republic and to that end is most anxious to secure the early establishment of a permanent peace throughout the country.

The two or three years following the enactment of the Dominican convention in 1907 seem to have passed without a violation on the part of the Dominican Government of clause III of that convention. Since 1910, however, it appears that the exigencies of the conditions in the Republic, have gradually caused first one of its administrations and then another to disregard the provisions of clause III of the solemn covenant entered into between the United States and the Dominican Republic. The Government of the United States, finding the administration of affairs at Santo Domingo in a deplorable condition, towards the close of 1912, was compelled to send delegates from the Departments of State and War, Mr. Doyle representing the former and General McIntyre the latter, to compose the difference of factional leaders. The result of their friendly good offices was that Archbishop Nouel became President.

Before this event the Dominicans have incurred by degrees a relatively large indebtedness entirely without the consent of the United States and in absolute contravention to the terms of the convention.

The Government of the United States finally gave its approval, with reluctance, to an increase of a million and one half dollars of the public debt of Santo Domingo, because it was thought that the Nouel administration could not survive unless it repaid those to whom money was due.

It seems to have been represented that one and one half million dollars would suffice to pay the current debts of the Dominican Republic at that time. This proved to be untrue. The payment of certain accounts, and the ignoring of others resulted in hard feelings on the part of those unpaid and in severe criticism of the Bordas Government, which followed the short-lived administration of Archbishop Nouel.

Again, in 1913, my Government studied the Dominican problem with especial care and deep interest and sympathy. Governor Osborne, First Assistant Secretary of State, was charged with the duty of calling the attention of the administration of José Bordas Valdés to the necessity properly to respect and live within the terms of the convention. To his representations, Governor Osborne received assurances that the Dominicans would accommodate expenditures to revenues, and that they would faithfully observe the terms of the convention.

Within a few months after the visit of Governor Osborne, it became only too apparent that there was general carelessness and improvidence in all financial matters; that the Bordas administration, without obtaining the consent of the United States, was increasing its indebtedness on every hand in an alleged effort to put down a revolution; and that the salaries of Government employees were not being paid, which caused so much discontent as to threaten the stability of the Bordas régime.

Seeking a remedy for these distressing conditions, the United States, after careful consideration, became convinced that a regular payment of salaries to all employees of the Government would go far to remove the odium to which officials of the Bordas Government were being subjected, and thus allay, if not prevent, the armed protest, which starvation and abuse were slowly forcing upon employees of the Government. For this purpose, the United States viewed with favor a suggestion to secure for the Dominican Republic some form of financial control, in the hope that thereby a remedy would result, at least in part, by securing an adjustment of expenditures to revenues. Actuated by the highest motives and in the belief that a competent financial comptroller would be of material assistance, the Department of State conferred freely with Mr. Peynado, the Dominican Minister to the United States, and later with Mr. Soler, who succeeded Mr. Peynado.

These conferences and the many and extended communications passed between the Governments resulted in the appointment of a financial adviser to the Dominican Republic. So keen, however, was the rivalry between the various contending political factions, that no loan plan was approved at that time.

During eight months the financial adviser exercised his functions, to the best of his ability and achieved the saving of considerable sums, in so far as it was possible, to the Government. Due to his active services, Government employees were regularly paid, but this novel condition did not obtain over a period sufficient to demonstrate whether an honest handling of public funds would permanently remove one of the main causes of factional strife.

The continuous state of internal disturbance which existed in the Dominican Republic from the time of the arrival of the financial adviser until the retirement of the Bordas administration (when the Provisional Government of Dr. Báez assumed control of the Dominican Republic), resulted in the failure to confirm or ratify the official recognition of the office of financial adviser.

Prior to the recognition of the Government of President Jiménes, by the United States, President Jiménes and Mr. Federico Velasquez assured my Government that the appointment of the financial adviser would be ratified and, in addition to this, other assurances were given, but not respected.

Even so, the Department of State, anxious to cooperate with Dominicans in every proper way, received the commission which President Jiménes sent to Washington. In view of that body's firm assurances that the Dominicans would live within their revenues, provided the office of financial adviser were abolished, the State Department, in June, 1915, acquiesced in many of the suggestions submitted by the Dominican Executive through the special commission, which visited Washington in that month. Since the departure of that commission the Department of State has confidently expected that the Dominican Government would receive sympathetically, and respect in full, according to agreement, the indications of the receivership, to which by common consent the modified powers of the financial adviser had been transferred.

The Department of State has awaited the receipt of some plan looking to the adjudication and final liquidation of the very considerable current indebtedness which has been accumulating slowly under previous administrations and rapidly under the Jiménes administration, and it has naturally expected to be informed that the daily increase in this indebtedness had ceased.

To its surprise and deep regret, no favorable information has come to hand. From a variety of sources advices have been received that the Government of President Jiménes is increasing the indebtedness of the Dominican Government at the rate of from one to three thousand dollars per day. In addition to this it is alleged that the extreme peculations taking place in the collection of the internal revenues are being used largely to benefit politicians, while the civilian employees of the Government go unsalaried and unfed. So extreme does the struggle for a division of the spoils appear to be, that natural remedies, such as a loan, which, if properly used to defray current indebtedness, would be of very material value in the proper conduct of economic affairs, go unconsidered. It is said that the financial policy now pursued can but result in the Government's inevitable bankruptcy.

The present current indebtedness is variously described at from five to seven million dollars. This staggering statement clearly indicates the existence of some fundamental improprieties in the present Government. If tribute has been paid to prevent those who otherwise would do so, from starting revolutions, or to quell incipient revolutions; if the officers of the Government of President Jiménes are enriching themselves and leaving in want civilian employees of the Government, it can but be manifest that such a state of discontent will soon be reached as will threaten the very existence of the Dominican Republic.

It is, therefore, evident that since 1910 there has been a continuous violation of the provisions of the Convention of 1907, especially in that part which reads:

Until the Dominican Republic has paid the whole amount of the bonds of the debt its public debt shall not be increased except by previous agreement between the Dominican Government and the United States.

In direct contravention of the foregoing solemn undertaking, the Dominican debt has been increased by some seven millions of dollars. Closely associated with this regrettable failure to comply with treaty obligations, there has been a continual internecine struggle to obtain control of the Government and Government funds, which has resulted in a state of revolution so continuous as almost entirely to interrupt all national development in the Republic.

It is not amiss here to recall that in 1907 the indebtedness of the Republic amounted approximately to thirty million dollars, which, through the good offices of the United States, was finally reduced to some seventeen million dollars. Twenty million in new bonds were then issued, which, with the four millions in cash accumulated under the *modus vivendi,* enabled the Dominican Government to pay its adjudicated debt of seventeen million, purchase and extinguish certain onerous concessions at a cost of one and one half million, and provide a handsome surplus for public works necessary to rehabilitate the deplorable condition of the country. Since that time, aside from paying interest, the total of twenty millions has been reduced by some three and one half million; this reduction being accomplished by payments made under the convention, and through earnings thereon.

During this same time, and without achieving the least permanent good, the various administrations in the Dominican Republic have, in direct violation of the convention, increased the total debt of the Republic by about seven million dollars. It is, therefore, self-evident that should this procedure be allowed to continue, the life of the convention may be eternal, and the objects for which it was created and enacted, be defeated.

While my Government has recognized its perfect right to insist that the Dominican Republic should observe all the obligations of the Convention of 1907, especially those regarding the increase of the public debt and the obligation to give full protection to the general receiver, so that the free course of the customs should not be interrupted, it has now, for the first time, determined that further violations of the obligations of the convention, which the Dominican Republic freely assumed, shall cease.

The Department of State maintains that a strict compliance on the part of the Dominican Government, of clause III of the Convention of 1907, in which the Dominican Government is prohibited from making any increase in its public indebtedness without the sanction of the Government of the United States, will constitute a most effective deterrent to all those who might contemplate the instigation of political disorders, to which the Republic has been subject for many years. The creation of a floating indebtedness, directly or indirectly, must certainly be interpreted as contravening the provision of the Convention of 1907. Failure to meet budgetary expenses, the appropriation of sums in excess of probable revenues, the purchase of supplies and materials, no adequate provision for the payment of which has been made, are considered by the Department of State as a contravention of clause III and should be discouraged.

My Government therefore has decided that the American-Dominican Convention of 1907 gives it the right:—

A. To compel the observance of article III by insisting upon the immediate appointment of a financial adviser to the Dominican Republic, who shall be appointed by the President of the Dominican Republic, upon designation of the President of the United States, and who shall be attached to the Ministry of Finance to give effect to whose proposals and labors the Minister will lend all efficient aid. The financial adviser shall render effective the clauses of the Convention of 1907 by aiding the proper officials of the Dominican Government in the adjudication and settlement of all its outstanding indebtedness; devise and inaugurate an adequate system of public accountability; investigate proper means of increasing the public revenues and of so adjusting the public disbursements thereto that deficits may be avoided; inquire into the validity of any and all claims which may be presented against the Dominican Government; countersign all checks, drafts, warrants or orders for the payment of Dominican funds to third parties; enlighten both Governments with reference to any eventual debt and to determine if such debt is or is not in conformity with the Convention of 1907; compose whatever differences may arise between the receivership and the Department of Treasury and Commerce, in which matters not requiring the intervention of both Governments are involved; assist the proper officials of the Dominican Government in the preparation of the annual budget and to aid them in correlating the governmental expenditures thereto; recommend improved methods of obtaining and applying the revenues and make such other recommendations to the minister of finance as may be deemed necessary for the welfare and prosperity of the Dominican Republic; provided, that the authority of the general receiver as described in article I, to collect and apply the customs revenues shall in no way be affected by this interpretation.

B. To provide for the free course of the customs and prevent factional strife and disturbances by the creation of a constabulary, which the Dominican Government obligates itself, for the preservation of domestic peace, security of individual rights and the full observance of the provisions of the Convention, to create without delay and maintain. This constabulary shall be organized and commanded by an American to be appointed, as "Director of Constabulary," by the President of the Dominican Republic, upon nomination of the President of the United States. In like manner there shall be appointed to the constabulary such other American officers as the director of constabulary shall consider requisite; also there shall be appointed by the President of the Dominican Republic, on the nomination of the director of constabulary, such Dominican officers as, in the judgment of the director of constabulary, may be desirable from the standpoint of efficiency. The Dominican Government shall clothe these officers with the proper and necessary authority and uphold them in the performance of their functions. The Dominican Government shall authorize for the constabulary such commissioned officers, and enlisted men (non-commissioned officers and privates) as the director of constabulary may deem necessary for the proper preservation of peace and order, within the Republic, and shall ratify and promulgate such regulations as to pay of personnel, enlistment, appointment and reduction of non-commissioned officers, discharge, discipline, etc., as the director of constabulary may recommend; provided that the President of the United States shall decide any question of regulation affecting the organization upon which the Dominican Government and the director of constabulary may fail to agree, and shall by agreement with the Dominican Republic fix the salary of the director of constabulary.

The constabulary thus provided for, shall, under the direction of the Dominican Government have supervision and control of the arms and ammunition, military supplies and traffic therein, throughout the country.

In regard to the financial adviser I will say to your excellency that my Government would prefer to have this office so established that it would not be in danger of being abolished by future administrations, but, in view of past experiences with the post of financial adviser, is willing to have his rights and duties vested in the receivership, provided that said receivership is properly authorized to exercise full budgetary control, and is given all the powers herein set forth in section "A."

In insisting upon the establishment of the constabulary your excellency can not fail to see that its organization will afford ample protection to the constituted authorities at a minimum of cost, and will be subject to the control of the central Government, thus placing it beyond the domination of provincial administrators; and the maintenance of this constabulary will be less onerous and far more effective than the present system of the army and customs guard, and guardia republicana.

In requesting your excellency to give this matter your serious and immediate consideration,

    I take [etc.]

W. W. RUSSELL

REAR ADMIRAL W. B. CAPERTON, in Command of the United States Forces in the Dominican Republic, to Josephus Daniels, Secretary of the Navy, May 13, 1916
Foreign Relations of the United States, 1916, p. 226

AT 10 A. M., May 13, I called upon the United States Ministei at the Legation, and after discussing the situation with him, arranged to see, at the Haitian Legation in Santo Domingo City, General Aiias and some of the other rebel leaders. There were present at this conference, in addition to the Minister and myself, Commander W. S. Crosley, Lieutenant-Commander William D. Leahy, my Chief of Staff, Mr. Johnson, Secretary of the Legation, General Desiderio Arias, General Mauricio Jiménez, Commandant of the fortress, and Mr. Cesáreo Jiménez. After an extended discussion undertaken with the object of finding an amicable method of supporting the constituted government, I delivered at 11.50 a. m., to General Arias, a written communication signed by the United States Minister and myself, (Inclosure D) which informed him that, if the rebel forces now in the city of Santo Domingo do not disarm and turn over their arms and ammunition to the United States forces by 6 a. m. Monday, May 15, 1916, it is my intention to occupy the city and forcibly disarm the rebels therein. I informed General Arias that my purpose in doing this was only to insure the peaceful performance of the work of the constituted government without fear of armed coercion, and that I would regret very much the necessity for the use of force.

MAY 14, 1916

At 9.20 a. m., I received a radio request from the United States Minister to come ashore and see him, as important developments had occurred during the night. I immediately went ashore, landing through the surf, and was informed by the American Minister that General Arias, with other leaders of the rebel forces, had abandoned Santo Domingo City before daylight today, taking with him the rebel soldiers and a number of released convicts from the prison, with small arms and as much ammunition as they could carry.

The Dominican Republic 689

[Inclosure D]

Minister Russell and Admiral Caperton to General Arias, General Mauricio Jiménez and General Cesáreo Jiménez

GENTLEMEN:

In view of the fact that the armed forces in rebellion against the present constituted authority of the Government of the Dominican Republic are occupying all the military positions of the city of Santo Domingo and are forcibly preventing the constitutional executive representatives of the Dominican Republic from entering the city in safety to take charge of their respective portfolios; and in view of the fact that all efforts to bring about a pacific agreement with those in control of the military power of the city have failed; and in view of the publicly announced policy of the United States of America to support, by force if necessary, the present constituted authority of the Republic;

Therefore, we, the undersigned hereby call upon you to disarm the military force at present in the city of Santo Domingo, to evacuate all fortified positions within the city, and to turn over to the custody of the forces of the United States of America all arms and ammunition now in the city; and we hold each and all of you responsible for the consequences that may result from a refusal to comply with the terms of this communication.

The demands herein made must be complied with at or before the hour of 6 a. m., May 14, 1916, and must be indicated by the hoisting of white flags on the tower of the fortress and of the municipal building and at other fortified places within the city in such a way as to be plainly visible from the sea and from commanding positions outside the city wall; and we hereby formally demand that in case a disarmament is not made, as above specified, you notify all the civilian population, native and foreign, to leave the city within 24 hours after the day and hour above specified, that is 6 a. m. May 14, 1916, at which time, to wit 6 a. m. May 15, 1916, force will be used to disarm the rebel forces in the city of Santo Domingo and to support the constituted government.

Noncombatants leaving the city by water transportation must keep out of the line of fire of the American warships.

Noncombatants must leave the city via Avenida Bolívar (Santa Ana Road) to or beyond the point where it meets the Carretera del Oeste.

A copy of this communication has been delivered to the respresentatives of foreign nations and to the President of the City Council (Ayuntamiento).

WILLIAM W. RUSSELL, *American Minister*
W. B. CAPERTON, *Rear Admiral,*
United States Navy

NOTICE by Rear Admiral W. B. Caperton, in Command of the
United States Forces in the Dominican Republic, to the
People of Santo Domingo, May 13, 1916
Foreign Relations of the United States, 1916, p. 228

1. OWING TO the conditions that have existed in and around this city in consequence of the fact that rebels in arms have taken possession of the city, excluding therefrom the constitutional officials of the Government, and after all means to arrive at a peaceful settlement of the situation had been exhausted, it became necessary to have the city occupied by forces of the United States of America.

2. Notice is hereby given to the citizens of Santo Domingo that the forces of the United States of America have assumed control in this city.

3. All the inhabitants are requested to stay in the city and cooperate with me and my representatives in protecting life and property and maintaining order.

4. All public officials are asked to remain at their posts and cooperate with me and my representatives in maintaining order within and around the city.

5. The sale of all kinds of spirituous beverages to the American troops is strictly forbidden and any infringement of this order shall be immediately punished.

W. B. CAPERTON
Rear Admiral of the American Navy

REAR ADMIRAL W. B. CAPERTON, in Command of the
United States Forces in the Dominican Republic, to Josephus
Daniels, Secretary of the Navy, May 30, 1916
Foreign Relations of the United States, 1916, p. 230

HAVE DIRECTED landing of United States forces at Puerto Plata and Monte Cristi after consulting with American Minister and in agreement with him to preserve peace and maintain constituted government. Have senior officer present to take such military action only as is necessary to protect United States forces ashore, preserve peace, lives, protection and property of American citizens and other foreigners and to constituted authority. Serious opposition to landing not anticipated.

CAPERTON

WILLIAM W. RUSSELL, United States Minister to the Dominican Republic, to Robert Lansing, Secretary of State, June 26, 1916
Foreign Relations of the United States, 1916, p. 231

SIR:

I have the honor to enclose herewith English and Spanish text of the proclamation issued by Rear Admiral Caperton in regard to the advance of our forces on Santiago.

The 4th Regiment of Marines, Colonel J. H. Pendleton, arrived here on the 18th instant, and left on the evening of the 19th for Monte Cristi, and are now on the march to Santiago, where they will arrive in three or four days.

I have [etc.]

WILLIAM W. RUSSELL

[*Inclosure*]

BY THE COMMANDER-IN-CHIEF OF THE FORCES OF THE UNITED STATES OF AMERICA IN SANTO DOMINGO

A PROCLAMATION

WHEREAS, the forces of the United States of America have entered the Dominican Republic for the purpose of supporting the constituted authorities and of putting a stop to revolutions and consequent disorders, impeding the progress and prosperity of the country;

Now, therefore, I, William B. Caperton, Rear-Admiral United States Navy, Commander Cruiser Squadron and Commanding United States Forces in Santo Domingo and Dominican Waters, hereby make it known that it is my purpose to occupy immediately the towns of Santiago, Moca and La Vega, with the above purpose in view, as these towns are now in the possession of, or menaced by, a considerable force of revolutionists against the constituted government.

It is not the intention of the United States Government to acquire by conquest any territory in the Dominican Republic nor to attack its sovereignty, but our troops will remain here until all revolutionary movements have been stamped out and until such reforms as are deemed necessary to insure the future welfare of the country have been initiated and are in effective operation.

It is hoped that all this may be accomplished peacefully and without, bloodshed, and I call upon all true Dominican patriots both in public and private life, to cooperate with me to the fullest extent.

W. B. CAPERTON

PROCLAMATION of Occupation and Military Government, by Captain H. S. Knapp, in Command of the United States Forces in the Dominican Republic, November 29, 1916
Foreign Relations of the United States, 1916, p. 246

WHEREAS, a treaty was concluded between the United States of America and the Republic of Santo Domingo on February 8, 1907, Article III of which reads:

"Until the Dominican Republic has paid the whole amount of the bonds of the debt its public debt shall not be increased except by previous agreement between the Dominican Government and the United States. A like agreement shall be necessary to modify the import duties, it being an indispensable condition for the modification of such duties that the Dominican Executive demonstrate and that the President of the United States recognize that, on the basis of exportations and importations of the like amount and the like character during the two years preceding that in which it is desired to make such modification, the total net customs receipts would at such altered rates of duties have been for each of such two years in excess of the sum of $2,000,000 United States gold"; and

WHEREAS, the Government of Santo Domingo has violated the said Article III on more than one occasion; and

WHEREAS, the Government of Santo Domingo has from time to time explained such violation by the necessity of incurring expenses incident to the repression of revolution; and

WHEREAS, the United States Government, with great forbearance and with a friendly desire to enable Santo Domingo to maintain domestic tranquility and observe the terms of the aforesaid treaty, has urged upon the Government of Santo Domingo certain necessary measures which that Government has been unwilling or unable to adopt; and

WHEREAS, in consequence domestic tranquility has been disturbed and is not now established, nor is the future observance of the treaty by the Government of Santo Domingo assured; and

WHEREAS, the Government of the United States is determined that the time has come to take measures to insure the observance of the provisions of the aforesaid treaty by the Republic of Santo Domingo and to maintain the domestic tranquility in the said Republic of Santo Domingo necessary thereto;

Now, therefore, I, H. S. Knapp, Captain, United States Navy, commanding the Cruiser Force of the United States Atlantic Fleet, and the armed forces of the United States stationed in various places within the territory of the Republic of Santo Domingo, acting under the authority and by the direction of the Government of the United States, declare and announce to all concerned that the Republic of Santo Domingo is hereby placed in a state of Military Occupation by the forces under my command, and is made subject to Military Government and to the exercise of military law applicable to such occupation.

This military occupation is undertaken with no immediate or ulterior object of destroying the sovereignty of the Republic of Santo Domingo, but, on the contrary, is designed to give aid to that country in returning to a condition of internal order that will enable it to observe the terms of the treaty aforesaid, and the obligations resting upon it as one of the family of nations.

Dominican statutes, therefore, will continue in effect in so far as they do not conflict with the objects of the Occupation or necessary regulations established thereunder, and their lawful administration will continue in the hands of such duly authorized Dominican officials as may be necessary, all under the oversight and control of the United States Forces exercising Military Government.

The ordinary administration of justice, both in civil and criminal matters, through the regularly constituted Dominican courts will not be interfered with by the Military Government herein established; but cases to which a member of the United States Forces in Occupation is a party, or in which are involved contempt or defiance of the authority of the Military Government, will be tried by tribunals set up by the Military Government.

All revenue accruing to the Dominican Government, including revenues hitherto accrued and unpaid—whether from customs duties under the terms of the Treaty concluded on February 8, 1907, the Receivership established by which remains in effect, or from internal revenue—shall be paid to the Military Government herein established, which will, in trust for the Republic of Santo Domingo, hold such revenue and will make all the proper legal disbursements there-from necessary for the administration of the Dominican Government, and for the purposes of the Occupation.

I call upon the citizens of, and residents and sojourners in, Santo Domingo to cooperate with the Forces of the United States in Occupation to the end that the purposes thereof may promptly be attained, and that the country may be restored to domestic order and tranquility and to the prosperity that can be attained only under such conditions.

The Forces of the United States in Occupation will act in accordance with military law governing their conduct, with due respect for the personal and property rights of citizens of, and residents and sojourners in, Santo Domingo, upholding Dominican laws in so far as they do not conflict with the purposes for which the Occupation is undertaken.

> H. S. KNAPP
> *Captain United States Navy,*
> *Commander Cruiser Force,*
> *United States Atlantic Fleet*

U.S.S. "OLYMPIA," FLAGSHIP,
SANTO DOMINGO CITY, R.D.
November 29, 1916

A. PÉREZ PERDOMO, Dominican Minister to the United States, to Robert Lansing, Secretary of State, December 4, 1916 (translation)
Foreign Relations of the United States, 1916, p. 244

MR. SECRETARY:

In compliance with instructions received from my Government I have the honor to lay before the Government of the United States of America through your excellency the formal protest by which the legitimate Government of the Dominican Republic finally and irrevocably resists the unexampled act in contempt of the sovereignty of the Dominican people which on the 29th of November, brought to a climax the illegal course of the forces of American intervention in the territory of the Dominican Republic: the act is the proclamation of Captain Knapp, commander of the said forces, by authority of your excellency's Government, in the capacity of Military Governor of the Dominican Republic.

The Dominican Government bases its protest on the following:

1st. The United States has always recognized the international entity of the Dominican Republic and it was in that capacity that the Dominican Republic concluded with the United States of America the Convention of 1907.

2nd. If the American Government considered as is stated in the proclamation which installs Captain Knapp as Military Governor of the Republic "that previous Governments of the Dominican Republic had violated Clause 3 of the said Convention by increasing, *for causes beyond their control,* the internal debt of the Dominican Republic, which interpretation differs from that put on the said Clause 3 by the Dominican Government, the American Government only had the right to sue out against the Dominican State through the proceedings in force for such cases the legal consequences of the fault the latter was supposed to have fallen into, but by no means that of sitting in supreme judgment of the contract and destroying, by way of penalty, the sovereignty of the Dominican people.

3rd. Nor could the Washington Government any more derive that right from the alleged state of domestic unrest which is also invoked in the aforesaid proclamation, since no State has the right to interfere in the domestic questions of another State, and, on the other hand, the sentiments of brotherly friendship which always governed the relations of the two States are not to be understood as affording the Government of this nation, in the face of such an occasion, anything but an opportunity to discharge the imperative duty put upon it by its exceptional situation on this continent and its constant humanitarian promises toward the several autonomous units of America whose evolution, socially or politically, has not yet reached the prodigious development of the exemplary North American Commonwealth. But it is a humane duty whose correlative can be no more than a humane right; such a right as that which in 1912 brought to the Dominican Republic the noble Peace Commission that strengthened the ties of the Dominican family's gratitude to the Northern Republic, again such as that which brought the Lind Commission to the Mexican Capital in 1913, that which gave birth to the idea of the Central American Court of Justice and many other agencies of true American brotherhood which strengthened in the same manner the sentiment of well deserved admiration, profound respect and earned gratitude from the Latin-American peoples for your excellency's Government and country. But never, never, a right which ceases to be one when it goes so far as to smother traditions and demolish attributes that are so inherent in human personality and in the very life of politico-social entities as to place beyond conception any possible finality if that finality is not to begin with cementing its own virtuality with an unequivocal and permanent recognition of those prerogatives, and

4th. A state of war which alone could have justified such a proceeding on the part of the Government of the United States toward the Dominican Republic has never existed between the two nations.

And therefore by acting as it has with the Dominican Republic, your excellency's Government plainly violated in the first place the fundamental principles of public international law which lay down as an invariable rule of public order for the nations the reciprocal respect of the sovereignty of each and every one of the free states of the civilized world, and in the second place the principles which guide the doctrine of Pan Americanism which also hallow the inviolability of American nationalities; principles which may be said to have found their highest authorities in the many official declarations of the learned President of the United States; the Constitutional Government of the Dominican Republic hereby formulates, in addition, the concomitant reservation of its rights which it will vindicate at the proper time.

Saluting [etc.]

A. PÉREZ PERDOMO

CHARLES E. HUGHES, Secretary of State, to Curtis D. Wilbur, Secretary of the Navy, June 4, 1924
Foreign Relations of the United States, 1924, I, 629. See infra, p. 946

SIR:

The final provisions of the Plan for the Evacuation of the Dominican Republic by the American Forces of Occupation are now being carried out. It is probable that all the remaining steps will have been taken before the end of the present month and that the Constitutional President of the Republic will be inaugurated upon some day between July 1st and July 10th. Since the Plan of Evacuation provides that as soon as the Constitutional President has taken office and has signed the Convention and the legislation stipulated in the Plan of Evacuation, the Military Forces of the United States will at once evacuate the territory of the Dominican Republic, I have the honor to request that the necessary instructions be sent to the Military Governor to take all the steps necessary to make possible the immediate evacuation of the Republic after the inauguration of the Constitutional

President. I am informed by the American Commissioner in the Dominican Republic that he is advised by the Military Governor that no instructions have been received by him relative to the evacuation of the Forces of Occupation. The Military Governor has stated that some time will be required to make the necessary arrangements, and in view of the fact that the inauguration of the Constitutional President of the Dominican Republic will take place approximately a month from the present date, I have the honor to request that the Military Governor be instructed to expedite the arrangements for evacuation.

I have [etc.]

CHARLES E. HUGHES

Appendices

Appendix A

CERTAIN AGREEMENTS, RESOLUTIONS, AND CONVENTIONS OF VARIOUS INTER-AMERICAN CONFERENCES

First International Conference of American States, at Washington, October 2, 1889, to April 19, 1890

REPORT of Committee on Customs Regulations Regarding a Bureau of Information

James Brown Scott, *The International Conferences of American States, 1889–1928,* p. 36

AT THE MEETING of the Conference, held March 29, 1890, the following resolution was adopted:

That the Governments here represented shall unite for the establishment of an American International Bureau for the collection, tabulation, and publication in the English, Spanish, and Portuguese languages of information as to the productions and commerce, and as to the customs, laws, and regulations of their respective countries; such Bureau to be maintained in one of the countries for the common benefit and at the common expense, and to furnish to all the other countries such commercial statistics and other useful information as may be contributed to it by any of the American Republics. That the Committee on Customs Regulations be authorized and instructed to furnish to the Conference a plan of organization and a scheme for the practical work of the proposed Bureau.

In accordance with said resolution the committee submits the following recommendations:

1. There shall be formed by the countries represented in this Conference an association under the title of "The International Union of American Republics" for the prompt collection and distribution of commercial information.

2. The International Union shall be represented by a Bureau to be established in the city of Washington, D.C., under the supervision of the Secretary of State of the United States and to be charged with the

care of all translations and publications and with all correspondence pertaining to the International Union.

3. This Bureau shall be called "The Commercial Bureau of the American Republics," and its organ shall be a publication to be entitled "Bulletin of the Commercial Bureau of the American Republics."

4. The Bulletin shall be printed in the English, Spanish, and Portuguese languages.

5. The contents of the Bulletin shall consist of—

(a) The existing customs tariffs of the several countries belonging to the Union and all changes of the same as they occur, with such explanations as may be deemed useful.

(b) All official regulations which affect the entrance and clearance of vessels and the importation and exportation of merchandise in the ports of the represented countries; also all circulars of instruction to customs officials which relate to customs procedure or to the classification of merchandise for duty.

(c) Ample quotations from commercial and parcel-post treaties between any of the American Republics.

(d) Important statistics of external commerce and domestic products and other information of special interest to merchants and shippers of the represented countries.

6. In order to enable the Commercial Bureau to secure the utmost accuracy in the publication of the Bulletin, each country belonging to this Union shall send directly to the Bureau, without delay, two copies each of all official documents which may pertain to matters having relation to the objects of the Union, including customs tariffs, official circulars, international treaties, or agreements, local regulations, and, so far as practical, complete statistics regarding commerce and domestic products and resources.

7. This Bureau shall at all times be available as a medium of communication and correspondence for persons applying for reasonable information in regard to matters pertaining to the customs tariffs and regulations, and to the commerce and navigation of the American Republics.

8. The form and style of the Bulletin shall be determined by the commercial Bureau, and each edition shall consist of at least 1,000 copies. In order that diplomatic representatives, consular agents, boards of trade, and other preferred persons shall be promptly supplied with the Bulletin, each member of the Union may furnish the Bureau with addresses to which copies shall be mailed at its expense.

9. Every country belonging to the International Union shall re-

ceive its quota of each issue of the Bulletin and the quota of each country shall be in proportion to its population.

Copies of the Bulletin may be sold (if there be a surplus) at a price to be fixed by the Bureau.

10. While it shall be required that the utmost possible care be taken to insure absolute accuracy in the publications of the Bureau, the International Union will assume no pecuniary responsibility on account of errors or inaccuracies which may occur therein. A notice to this effect shall be conspicuously printed upon the first page of every successive issue of the Bulletin.

11. The maximum expense to be incurred for establishing the Bureau and for its annual maintenance shall be $36,000, and the following is a detailed estimate of its organization, subject to such changes as may prove desirable:

One director in charge of Bureau, compensation	$5,000
One secretary	3,000
One accountant	2,200
One clerk	1,800
One clerk and type-writer	1,600
One translator (Spanish and English)	2,500
One translator (Spanish and English)	2,000
One translator (Portuguese and English)	2,500
One messenger	800
One porter	600
	22,000

Office Expenses

Rent of apartments, to contain one room for director, one room for secretary, one room for translators, one room for clerks, etc., and one room for library and archives	3,000
Lights, heat, cleaning, etc.	500
	3,500

Publication of Bulletin

Printing, paper, and other expenses	10,000
Postage, express, and miscellaneous expenses	500
	10,500

12. The Government of the United States will advance to the International Union a fund of $36,000, or so much of that amount as may be required for the expenses of the Commercial Bureau during its first year, and a like sum for each subsequent year of the existence of this Union.

13. On the 1st day of July of the year 1891, and of each subsequent year during the continuance of this Union, the director of the Commercial Bureau shall transmit to every Government belonging to the Union a statement in detail of the expenses incurred for the purposes of the Union, not to exceed $36,000, and shall assess upon each of said Governments the same proportion of the total outlay as the populations of the respective countries bear to the total populations of all the countries represented in the Union, and all the Governments so assessed shall promptly remit to the Secretary of State of the United States, in coin or its equivalent, the amounts respectively assessed upon them by the director of the Bureau. In computing the population of any of the countries of this Union, the director of the Bureau shall be authorized to use the latest official statistics in his possession. The first assessment to be made according to the following table:

Table of Assessments for Commercial Bureau

Countries	Population	Tax
Hayti	500,000	$187.50
Nicaragua	400,000	150.00
Peru	2,600,000	975.00
Guatemala	1,400,000	525.00
Uruguay	600,000	225.00
Colombia	3,900,000	1,462.50
Argentina	3,900,000	1,462.50
Costa Rica	200,000	75.00
Paraguay	250,000	93.75
Brazil	14,400,000	5,250.00
Honduras	350,000	131.25
Mexico	10,400,000	3,900.00
Bolivia	1,200,000	450.00
United States	50,150,000	18,806.00
Venezuela	2,200,000	825.00
Chili	2,500,000	937.50
Salvador	650,000	243.75
Ecuador	1,000,000	375.00
Total	96,000,000	36,000.00

14. In order to avoid delay in the establishment of the Union herein described, the delegates assembled in this Conference will promptly communicate to their respective Governments the plan of organization and of practical work adopted by the Conference, and will ask the said Governments to notify the Secretary of State of the United States, through their accredited representatives at this capital or

otherwise, of their adhesion or non-adhesion, as the case may be, to the terms proposed.

15. The Secretary of State of the United States is requested to organize and establish the Commercial Bureau as soon as practicable, after a majority of the countries here represented have officially signified their consent to join the International Union.

16. Amendments and modifications of the plan of this Union may be made, at any time during its continuance, by the vote, officially communicated to the Secretary of State of the United States, of a majority of the members of the Union.

17. This Union shall continue in force during a term of ten years from the date of its organization, and no country becoming a member of the Union shall cease to be a member until the end of said period of ten years. Unless twelve months before the expiration of said period a majority of the members of the Union shall have given to the Secretary of State of the United States official notice of their wish to terminate the Union at the end of its first period, the Union shall continue to be maintained for another period of ten years and thereafter, under the same conditions, for successive periods of ten years each.

(Signatures omitted)

(Adopted April 14, 1890)

[Pursuant to this action, the Commercial Bureau of the American Republics was set up in Washington in 1890. At the Second Conference in 1901–1902, the name was changed to "The International Bureau of the American Republics," and at the Fourth Conference, in 1910, to "The Pan American Union." Important changes broadening the activities of the organization have been made at the various conferences. For the present charter, see *postea,* p. 855.]

PLAN of Arbitration

James Brown Scott, *The International Conferences of American States, 1889–1928,* p. 40

THE DELEGATIONS from North, Central, and South America in Conference assembled:

Believing that war is the most cruel, the most fruitless, and the most dangerous expedient for the settlement of international differences;

Recognizing that the growth of the moral principles which govern political societies has created an earnest desire in favor of the amicable adjustment of such differences;

Animated by the conviction of the great moral and material benefits that peace offers to mankind, and trusting that the existing conditions of the respective nations are especially propitious for the adoption of Arbitration as a substitute for armed struggles;

Convinced by reason of their friendly and cordial meeting in the present Conference, that the American Republics, controlled alike by the principles, duties, and responsibilities of popular Government, and bound together by vast and increasing mutual interests, can, within the sphere of their own action, maintain the peace of the continent, and the good-will of all its inhabitants;

And considering it their duty to lend their assent to the lofty principles of peace which the most enlightened public sentiment of the world approves;

Do solemnly recommend all the Governments by which they are accredited to conclude a uniform treaty of Arbitration in the articles following:

ARTICLE 1

The Republics of North, Central, and South America hereby adopt Arbitration as a principle of American international law for the settlement of the differences, disputes, or controversies that may arise between two or more of them.

ARTICLE 2

Arbitration shall be obligatory in all controversies concerning diplomatic and consular privileges, boundaries, territories, indemnities, the right of navigation, and the validity, construction, and enforcement of treaties.

ARTICLE 3

Arbitration shall be equally obligatory in all cases other than those mentioned in the foregoing article, whatever may be their origin, nature, or object, with the single exception mentioned in the next following article.

ARTICLE 4

The sole questions excepted from the provisions of the preceding articles are those which, in the judgment of any one of the nations involved in the controversy, may imperil its independence. In this event, for such nation, Arbitration shall be optional; but it shall be obligatory upon the adversary power when demanded.

ARTICLE 5

All controversies or differences, whether pending or hereafter arising, shall be submitted to Arbitration, even though they may have originated in occurrences antedating the present treaty.

ARTICLE 6

No question shall be revived by virtue of this treaty concerning which a definite agreement shall already have been reached. In such cases Arbitration shall be resorted to only for the settlement of questions concerning the validity, interpretation, or enforcement of such agreements.

ARTICLE 7

The choice of Arbitrators shall not be limited or confined to American States. Any government may serve in the capacity of Arbitrator which maintains friendly relations with the nation opposed to the one selecting it. The office of Arbitrator may also be intrusted to tribunals of justice, to scientific bodies, to public officials, or to private individuals, whether citizens or not of the States selecting them.

ARTICLE 8

The Court of Arbitration may consist of one or more persons. If of one person, he shall be selected jointly by the nations concerned. If of several persons, their selection may be jointly made by the nations concerned. Should no choice be agreed upon, each nation showing a distinct interest in the question at issue shall have the right to appoint one Arbitrator on its own behalf.

ARTICLE 9

Whenever the court shall consist of an even number of Arbitrators, the nations concerned shall appoint an umpire, who shall decide all questions upon which the Arbitrators may disagree. If the nations interested fail to agree in the selection of an Umpire, such Umpire shall be selected by the Arbitrators already appointed.

ARTICLE 10

The appointment of an Umpire, and his acceptance, shall take place before the Arbitrators enter upon the hearing of the questions in dispute.

ARTICLE 11

The Umpire shall not act as a member of the court, but his duties and powers shall be limited to the decision of questions, whether principal or incidental, upon which the Arbitrators shall be unable to agree.

ARTICLE 12

Should an Arbitrator or an Umpire be prevented from serving by reason of death, resignation, or other cause, such Arbitrator or Umpire shall be replaced by a substitute to be selected in the same manner in which the original Arbitrator or Umpire shall have been chosen.

ARTICLE 13

The court shall hold its sessions at such place as the parties in interest may agree upon, and in case of disagreement or failure to name a place the court itself may determine the location.

ARTICLE 14

When the court shall consist of several Arbitrators, a majority of the whole number may act notwithstanding the absence or withdrawal of the minority. In such case the majority shall continue in the performance of their duties until they shall have reached a final determination of the questions submitted for their consideration.

ARTICLE 15

The decision of a majority of the whole number of Arbitrators shall be final both on the main and incidental issues, unless in the agreement to arbitrate it shall have been expressly provided that unanimity is essential.

ARTICLE 16

The general expenses of arbitration proceedings shall be paid in equal proportions by the governments that are parties thereto; but expenses incurred by either party in the preparation and prosecution of its case shall be defrayed by it individually.

ARTICLE 17

Whenever disputes arise the nations involved shall appoint Courts of Arbitration in accordance with the provisions of the preceding articles. Only by the mutual and free consent of all such nations may those provisions be disregarded, and Courts of Arbitration be appointed under different arrangements.

ARTICLE 18

This Treaty shall remain in force for twenty years from the date of the exchange of ratifications. After the expiration of that period, it shall continue in operation until one of the contracting parties shall have notified all the others of its desire to terminate it. In the event of such notice the treaty shall continue obligatory upon the party giving it for one year thereafter, but the withdrawal of one or more nations shall not invalidate the treaty with respect to the other nations concerned.

ARTICLE 19

This Treaty shall be ratified by all the nations approving it, according to their respective constitutional methods; and the ratifications shall be exchanged in the city of Washington on or before the first day of May, A. D. 1891.

Any other nation may accept this treaty and become a party thereto, by signing a copy thereof and depositing the same with the Government of the United States; whereupon the said Government shall communicate this fact to the other contracting parties.

In testimony whereof the undersigned Plenipotentiaries have hereunto affixed their signatures and seals.

Done in the city of Washington, in ——— copies in English, Spanish, and Portuguese, on this 24th day of the month of April, one thousand eight hundred and ninety.

(Signed by the delegates for: Bolivia, Brazil, Ecuador, Guatemala, Haiti, Honduras, Nicaragua, El Salvador, United States of America)

[The plan was submitted by the Committee on General Welfare and adopted by the Conference in sessions during April 15–18. Following the conference, a treaty with virtually the same language was signed by eleven States, including the United States, but it lapsed owing to the failure of all the signatories to exchange ratifications within the prescribed time.]

RECOMMENDATION Regarding Claims and Diplomatic Intervention

James Brown Scott, *The International Conferences of American States, 1889–1928,* p. 45

THE INTERNATIONAL AMERICAN CONFERENCE recommends to the Governments of the countries therein represented the adoption, as principles of American international law, of the following:

(1) Foreigners are entitled to enjoy all the civil rights enjoyed by natives; and they shall be accorded all the benefits of said rights in all that is essential as well as in the form or procedure, and the legal

remedies incident thereto, absolutely in like manner as said natives.

(2) A nation has not, nor recognizes in favor of foreigners, any other obligations or responsibilities than those which in favor of the natives are established, in like cases, by the constitution and the laws.

(Adopted April 18, 1890)

Second International Conference of American States, at Mexico City, October 22, 1901, to January 31, 1902

PROTOCOL on Adherence to the Conventions of The Hague (translation)

James Brown Scott, *The International Conferences of American States, 1889–1928*, p. 61

WHEREAS: The Delegates to the International Conference of the American States, believing that public sentiment in the Republics represented by them is constantly growing in the direction of heartily favoring the widest application of the principles of arbitration; that the American Republics controlled alike by the principles and responsibilities of popular government and bound together by increasing mutual interests, can, by their own actions, maintain peace in the Continent, and that permanent peace between them will be the forerunner and harbinger of their national development and of the happiness and commercial greatness of their peoples;

They have, therefore, agreed upon the following project:

ARTICLE 1

The American Republics, represented at the International Conference of American States in Mexico, which have not subscribed to the three Conventions signed at The Hague on the 29th. of July, 1899, hereby recognize as a part of Public International American Law the principles set forth therein.

ARTICLE 2

With respect to the Conventions which are of an open character, the adherence thereto will be communicated to the Government of Holland through diplomatic channels by the respective Governments, upon the ratification thereof.

ARTICLE 3

The wide general convenience being so clearly apparent that would be secured by confiding the solution of differences to be submitted to arbitration to the jurisdiction of a tribunal of so high a character as that of the Arbitration Court at The Hague, and, also, that the American Nations, not now signatory to the Convention creating that beneficent institution, can become adherents thereo by virtue of an accepted and recognized right; and, further, taking into consideration the offer of the Government of the United States of America and the United States of Mexico, the Conference hereby confers upon said Governments the authority to negotiate with the other signatory Powers to the Convention for the Peaceful Adjustment of International Differences, for the adherence thereto of the American Nations so requesting and not now signatory to the said Convention.

(Here follow in the Spanish text the names of delegates of the following countries: Guatemala, Mexico, Argentina, Peru, Uruguay, Venezuela (signing *ad referendum* and reserving with respect to Venezuela questions of navigation and other questions relative thereto), Costa Rica, Haiti, Dominican Republic, Paraguay, Bolivia, El Salvador, Colombia, Honduras, Nicaragua, United States of America.)

ARTICLE 4

In order that the widest and most unrestricted application of the principle of just arbitration may be satisfactorily and definitely brought about at the earliest possible day, and, to the end that the most advanced and mutually advantageous form in which the said principle can be expressed in a Convention to be signed between the American Republics may be fully ascertained, the President of Mexico is hereby most respectfully requested to ascertain by careful investigation the views of the different Governments represented in the Conference regarding the most advanced form in which a General Arbitration Convention could be drawn that would meet with the approval and secure the final ratification of all the countries in the Conference, and, after the conclusion of this inquiry, to prepare a plan for such a General Convention as would apparently meet the wishes of all the Republics; and, if possible, arrange for a series of protocols to carry the plan into execution; or, if this should be found to be impracticable, then to present the correspondence with a report to the next Conference.

Mexico, January 15th, 1902.

(Here follow in the Spanish text the names of delegates of the countries listed above under Article 3, with the exception of Venezuela.)

CONVENTION for the Formation of Codes on Public and Private International Law

James Brown Scott, *The International Conferences of American States, 1889–1928,* p. 69. The committee provided for was not appointed as the convention was ratified only by Bolivia, El Salvador, and Guatemala

THEIR EXCELLENCIES the Presidents of the Argentine Republic, Bolivia, Colombia, Costa Rica, Chili, the Dominican Republic, Ecuador, El Salvador, the United States of America, Guatemala, Haiti, Honduras, the United Mexican States, Nicaragua, Paraguay, Peru and Uruguay,

Desiring that their respective countries should be represented at the Second International American Conference, sent thereto duly authorized to approve the recommendations, resolutions, conventions and treaties that they might deem convenient for the interests of America, the following Delegates:

(Here follow the names of the delegates.)

Who, after having communicated to each other their respective full powers and found them to be in due and proper form, excepting those presented by the representatives of Their Excellencies the Presidents of the United States of America, Nicaragua and Paraguay, who act "ad referendum," have agreed to a Convention for the formation of Codes on Public and Private International Law in the following terms:

ARTICLE 1

The Secretary of State of the United States of America and the Ministers of the American Republics accredited in Washington shall appoint a Committee of five American and two European jurists, of acknowledged reputation, to be entrusted with the drafting, during the interval from the present to the next Conference, and in the shortest possible time, of a "Code of Public International Law" and another of "Private International Law" which will govern the relations between the American Nations.

ARTICLE 2

As soon as said Codes have been drafted, the Committee shall cause them to be printed and submit them to the consideration of the respective Governments of the American Nations in order that they may make such suggestions as they may deem advisable.

ARTICLE 3

After said suggestions have been systematically classified, and the Codes have been revised in conformity with them by the Committee which drafted them, they shall be submitted again to the Governments of the American Republics to be adopted by those who desire it, either in the next American International Conference or by means of Treaties negotiated directly.

ARTICLE 4

The Committee in charge of the drafting of the Codes shall conduct its work at such European or American capital as the Diplomatic Corps authorized to appoint it may designate, in conformity with Article 1st.

Such expense as may be incurred by this Convention shall be defrayed by the Signatory Governments in the same form and proportion as those in force with regard to the Bureau of American Republics.

ARTICLE 5

The Governments that may desire to ratify the present Convention may communicate it to the Secretary of State of the United States of America, within one year counted from the closing of this Conference.

In Testimony whereof the Plenipotentiaries and Delegates sign the present Convention and set thereto the Seal of the Second International American Conference;

Made in the City of Mexico on the twenty-seventh day of January nineteen hundred and two, in three copies, written in Spanish, English and French respectively which shall be deposited at the Department of Foreign Relations of the Government of the Mexican United States, so that certified copies thereof may be made, in order to send them through the diplomatic channel to the signatory States.

(Signed by the delegates for: Argentina, Bolivia, Chile, Colombia, Costa Rica, Dominican Republic, Ecuador, Guatemala, Haiti, Honduras, Mexico, Nicaragua, Paraguay, Peru, El Salvador, United States of America, Uruguay.)

RESOLUTION on Future American International Conferences

James Brown Scott, *The International Conferences of American States, 1889–1928*, p. 96

THE UNDERSIGNED, Delegates of the Republics represented in the Second International American Conference, duly authorized by their Governments, have approved the following Resolution:

The Second International American Conference

Resolves:

That the Third International American Conference shall meet within five years, in the place which the Secretary of State of the United States of America and the diplomatic representatives accredited by the American Republics in Washington, may designate for the purpose, and in accordance with what at the meeting of the said representatives may be resolved, regarding the programme and other necessary details, for all of which they are hereby expressly authorized by the present Resolution.

If due to any circumstances it were not possible for the Third Conference to assemble within five years, the Secretary of State of the United States of America and the diplomatic representatives accredited in Washington may designate another date for its reunion.

It is also resolved to recommend to each one of the Governments that they present to the next Conference a complete report of all that has been done by the respective countries in obedience to the recommendations adopted by the First and Second Conferences.

Made and signed in the City of Mexico, on the twenty-ninth day of the month of January, one thousand nine hundred and two, in three copies, in Spanish, English and French, respectively, which shall be deposited in the Department of Foreign Relations of the Government of the United States of Mexico, in order that certified copies thereof be made to transmit them through diplomatic channels to each one of the Signatory States.

(Signed by the delegates for: Argentina, Bolivia, Chile, Colombia, Costa Rica, Dominican Republic, Ecuador, Guatemala, Haiti, Honduras, Mexico, Nicaragua, Paraguay, Peru, El Salvador, United States of America, Uruguay)

TREATY of Arbitration for Pecuniary Claims

James Brown Scott, *The International Conferences of American States, 1889–1928,* p. 104. The treaty was ratified by the President of the United States, January 28, 1905

THEIR EXCELLENCIES the Presidents of the Argentine Republic, Bolivia, Colombia, Costa Rica, Chili, Dominican Republic, Ecuador, El Salvador, the United States of America, Guatemala, Haiti, Honduras, the United Mexican States, Nicaragua, Paraguay, Peru and Uruguay,

Desiring that their respective countries should be represented at the Second International American Conference, sent thereto duly authorized to approve the recommendations, resolutions, conventions and treaties that they might deem convenient for the interests of America, the following Delegates:

(Here follow the names of the delegates.)

Who, after having communicated to each other their respective full powers and found them to be in due and proper form, excepting those presented by the representatives of Their Excellencies the Presidents of the United States of America, Nicaragua and Paraguay, who act "ad referendum," have agreed to celebrate a Treaty to submit to the decision of arbitrators Pecuniary Claims for damages that have not been settled by diplomatic· channel, in the following terms:

ARTICLE 1

The High Contracting Parties agree to submit to arbitration all claims for pecuniary loss or damage which may be presented by their respective citizens, and which cannot be amicably adjusted through diplomatic channels and when said claims are of sufficient importance to warrant the expenses of arbitration.

ARTICLE 2

By virtue of the faculty recognized by Article 26 of the Convention of The Hague for the pacific settlement of international disputes, the High Contracting Parties agree to submit to the decision of the permanent Court of Arbitration established by said Convention, all controversies which are the subject matter of the present Treaty, unless both Parties should prefer that a special jurisdiction be organized, according to Article 21 of the Convention referred to.

If a case is submitted to the Permament Court of The Hague, the High Contracting Parties accept the provisions of the said Convention, in so far as they relate to the organization of the Arbitral Tribunal, and with regard to the procedure to be followed, and to the obligation to comply with the sentence.

ARTICLE 3

The present Treaty shall not be obligatory except upon those States which have subscribed to the Convention for the pacific settlement of international disputes, signed at The Hague, July 29, 1899, and upon those which ratify the Protocol unanimously adopted by the Republics represented in the Second International Conference of American States, for their adherence to the Conventions signed at The Hague, July 29, 1899.

ARTICLE 4

If, for any cause whatever, the Permanent Court of The Hague should not be opened to one or more of the High Contracting Parties, they obligate themselves to stipulate, in a special Treaty, the rules under which the Tribunal shall be established, as well as its form of procedure, which shall take cognizance of the questions referred to in article 1 of the present Treaty.

ARTICLE 5

This Treaty shall be binding on the States ratifying it, from the date on which five signatory governments have ratified the same, and shall be in force for five years. The ratification of this Treaty by the signatory States shall be transmitted to the Government of the United States of Mexico, which shall notify the other Governments of the ratifications it may receive.

In testimony whereof the Plenipotentiaries and Delegates also sign the present Treaty, and affix the seal of the Second International American Conference.

Made in the City of Mexico the thirtieth day of January nineteen hundred and two, in three copies, written in Spanish, English and French, respectively, which shall be deposited with the Secretary of Foreign Relations of the Mexican United States, so that certified copies thereof be made, in order to send them through the diplomatic channel to the signatory States.

(Signed by the delegates for: Argentina, Bolivia, Chile, Colombia, Costa Rica, Dominican Republic, Ecuador, Guatemala, Haiti, Honduras, Mexico. Nicaragua, Paraguay, Peru, El Salvador, United States of American, Uruguay)

Third International Conference of American States, at Rio de Janeiro, July 23 to August 27, 1906

RESOLUTION on Arbitration

James Brown Scott, *The International Conferences of American States, 1889–1928,* p. 124

THE UNDERSIGNED, Delegates of the Republics represented in the Third International American Conference, duly authorized by their Governments, have approved the following Resolution:
    The Third International American Conference
    Resolves:
    To ratify adherence to the principle of arbitration; and to the end that so high a purpose may be rendered practicable, to recommend to the Nations represented at this Conference that instructions be given to their Delegates to the Second Conference to be held at The Hague, to endeavor to secure by the said Assembly, of world-wide character, the celebration of a General Arbitration Convention, so effective and definite that, meriting the approval of the civilized world, it shall be accepted and put in force by every nation.
    Made and signed in the City of Rio de Janeiro, on the seventh day of the month of August nineteen hundred and six, in English, Spanish, Portuguese and French, and deposited in the Department of Foreign Affairs of the Government of the United States of Brazil, in order that certified copies thereof be made, and forwarded through diplomatic channels to each one of the Signatory States.
    (Signed by the delegates for: Argentina, Bolivia, Brazil, Chile, Colombia, Costa Rica, Cuba, Dominican Republic, Ecuador, Guatemala, Honduras, Mexico, Nicaragua, Panama, Paraguay, Peru, El Salvador, United States of America, Uruguay)

RESOLUTION on Public Debts

James Brown Scott, *The International Conferences of American States, 1889–1928,* p. 135

THE UNDERSIGNED, Delegates of the Republics represented in the Third International American Conference, duly authorized by their Governments, have approved the following Resolution:

The Third International American Conference
Resolves:

To recommend to the Governments represented therein that they consider the point of inviting the Second Peace Conference, at The Hague, to examine the question of the compulsory collection of public debts, and, in general, means tending to diminish between Nations conflicts having an exclusively pecuniary origin.

Made and signed in the city of Rio de Janeiro, on the twenty-second day of the month of August, nineteen hundred and six, in English, Portuguese and Spanish, and deposited in the Department of Foreign Affairs of the Government of the United States of Brazil, in order that certified copies thereof be made, and forwarded through diplomatic channels to each one of the Signatory States.

(Signed by the delegates for: Argentina, Bolivia, Brazil, Chile, Colombia, Costa Rica, Cuba, Dominican Republic, Ecuador, Guatemala, Honduras, Mexico, Nicaragua, Panama, Paraguay, Peru, El Salvador, United States of America, Uruguay)

CONVENTION on Pecuniary Claims

James Brown Scott, *The International Conferences of American States, 1889–1928,* p. 132. The convention was ratified by the President of the United States, March 13, 1907

THEIR EXCELLENCIES, the Presidents of Ecuador, Paraguay, Bolivia, Colombia, Honduras, Panamá, Cuba, the Dominican Republic, Peru, El Salvador, Costa Rica, the United States of Mexico, Guatemala, Uruguay, the Argentine Republic, Nicaragua, the United States of Brazil, the United States of America, and Chile;

Desiring that their respective countries should be represented at the Third International American Conference, sent thereto, duly authorized to approve the recommendations, resolutions, conventions and treaties that they might deem convenient for the interests of America, the following Delegates:

(Here follow the names of the delegates.)

Who, after having communicated to each other their respective full powers and found them to be in due and proper form, have agreed to celebrate a Convention extending the Treaty on Pecuniary Claims celebrated in Mexico on the thirtieth of January nineteen hundred and two, in the following terms:

The High Contracting Parties, animated by the desire to extend the term of duration of the Treaty on pecuniary claims, signed at

Mexico, January thirtieth, nineteen hundred and two, and believing that, under present conditions, the reasons underlying the third article of said Treaty have disappeared, have agreed upon the following:

Sole article. The treaty on pecuniary claims, signed at Mexico, January thirtieth, nineteen hundred and two, shall continue in force, with the exception of the third article, which is hereby abolished, until the thirty-first day of December, nineteen hundred and twelve, both for the nations which have already ratified it, and for those which may hereafter ratify it.

In testimony whereof the Plenipotentiaries and Delegates have signed the present Convention, and affixed the Seal of the Third International American Conference.

Made in the city of Rio de Janeiro the thirteenth of August, nineteen hundred and six, in English, Portuguese, and Spanish, and deposited with the Secretary of Foreign Affairs of the United States of Brazil, in order that certified copies thereof be made, and sent through diplomatic channels to the signatory States.

(Signed by the delegates for: Argentina, Bolivia, Brazil, Chile, Colombia, Costa Rica, Cuba, Dominican Republic, Ecuador, Guatemala, Honduras, Mexico, Nicaragua, Panama, Paraguay, Peru, El Salvador, United States of America, Uruguay)

CONVENTION on International Law

James Brown Scott, *The International Conferences of American States, 1889-1928*, p. 144. The convention was ratified by the President of the United States, February 8, 1908

THEIR EXCELLENCIES, the Presidents of Ecuador, Paraguay, Bolivia, Colombia, Honduras, Panama, Cuba, Peru, the Dominican Republic, El Salvador, Costa Rica, the United States of Mexico, Guatemala, Uruguay, the Argentine Republic, Nicaragua, the United States of Brazil, the United States of America, and Chile;

Desiring that their respective countries should be represented at the Third International American Conference, sent, thereto, duly authorized to approve the recommendations, resolutions, conventions and treaties that they might deem convenient for the interests of America, the following Delegates:

(Here follow the names of the delegates.)

Who, after having communicated to each other their respective full powers and found them to be in due and proper form, have agreed to establish an international Commission of Jurists, in the following terms:

ARTICLE 1

There shall be established an international Commission of Jurists, composed of one representative from each of the signatory States, appointed by their respective Governments, which commission shall meet for the purpose of preparing a draft of a Code of Private International Law and one of Public International Law, regulating the relations between the Nations of America. Two or more Governments may appoint a single representative, but such representative shall have but one vote.

ARTICLE 2

Notice of the appointment of the members of the Commission shall be addressed by the Governments adhering to this Convention, to the Government of the United States of Brazil, which shall take the necessary steps for the holding of the first meeting.

Notice of these appointments shall be communicated to the Government of the United States of Brazil before April 1st, 1907.

ARTICLE 3

The first meeting of said Commission shall be held in the City of Rio de Janeiro during the year 1907. The presence of at least twelve of the representatives of the signatory States shall be necessary for the organization of the Commission.

Said Commission shall designate the time and place for subsequent sessions, provided, however, that sufficient time be allowed from the date of the final meeting to permit of the submission to the signatory States of all drafts or all important portions thereof at least one year before the date fixed for the Fourth International American Conference.

ARTICLE 4

Said Commission after having met for the purpose of organization and for the distribution of the work to the members thereof, may divide itself into two distinct committees, one to consider the preparation of a draft of a Code of Private International Law, and the other for the preparation of a Code of Public International Law. In the event of such division being made, the committees must proceed separately until they conclude their duties, or else as provided in the final clause of article three.

In order to expedite and increase the efficiency of this work, both committees may request the Governments to assign experts for the consideration of especial topics. Both committees shall also have the power to determine the period within which such special reports shall be presented.

ARTICLE 5

In order to determine the subjects to be included within the scope of the work of the Commission, the Third International Conference recommends to the Commissions that they give special attention to the subjects and principles which have been agreed upon in existing treaties and conventions, as well as to those which are incorporated in the national laws of the American States, and furthermore recommends to the special attention of the Commission the Treaties of Montevideo of 1889 and the debates relating thereto, as well as the projects of conventions adopted at the Second International Conference of the American States held in Mexico in 1902, and the discussions thereon; also all other questions which give promise of juridical progress, or which tend to eliminate the causes of misunderstanding or conflicts between said States.

ARTICLE 6

The expense incident to the preparation of the drafts, including the compensation for technical studies made pursuant to article four, shall be defrayed by all the signatory States in the proportion and form established for the support of the International Bureau of the American Republics, of Washington, with the exception of the compensation of the members of the Commission, which shall be paid to the representatives by their respective Governments.

ARTICLE 7

The Fourth International Conference of the American States shall embody in one or more treaties, the principles upon which an agreement may be reached, and shall endeavor to secure their adoption and ratification by the Nations of America.

ARTICLE 8

The Governments desiring to ratify this Convention, shall so advise the Government of the United States of Brazil, in order that the said Government may notify the other Governments through diplomatic channels, such action taking the place of an exchange of Notes.

In testimony whereof the Plenipotentiaries and Delegates have signed the present Convention, and affixed the Seal of the Third Internacional American Conference.

Made in the city of Rio de Janeiro the twenty-third day of August, nineteen hundred and six, in English, Portuguese, and Spanish, and deposited with the Secretary of Foreign Affairs of the United States of Brazil, in order that certified copies thereof be made, and sent through diplomatic channels to the signatory States.

(Signed by the delegates for: Argentina, Bolivia, Brazil, Chile, Colombia, Costa Rica, Cuba, Dominican Republic, Ecuador, Guatemala, Honduras, Mexico, Nicaragua, Panama, Paraguay, Peru, El Salvador, United States of America, Uruguay)

Fourth International Conference of American States, at Buenos Aires, July 12 to August 30, 1910

RESOLUTION on the Reorganization of the "Union of American Republics"

James Brown Scott, *The International Conferences of American States, 1889–1928*, p. 172, and footnote, p. 173

THE UNDERSIGNED, Delegates of the Republics represented in the Fourth International American Conference, duly authorized by their respective Governments, have approved the following resolution:
The Fourth International American Conference
Resolves:

ARTICLE 1

To maintain, under the name of "Union of American Republics," the International Union created by the First, and confirmed by the Second and Third Conferences, and under the name of "Pan American Union" the institution serving as its Agent and having its seat in the Building of the American Republics in the City of Washington, D.C.

The purposes of the "Pan American Union" are the following:
1. To compile and distribute commercial information and prepare commercial reports.
2. To compile and classify information respecting the treaties and Conventions between the American Republics, and between these and other States, and their legislation in force.
3. To supply information on educational matters.
4. To prepare reports on questions assigned to it by resolutions of the International American Conferences.

5. To assist in obtaining the ratification of the Resolutions and Conventions adopted by the different Conferences.

6. To carry into effect all resolutions, the execution of which may have been assigned or may hereafter be assigned to it by the International American Conference.

7. To act as a Permanent Committee of the International American Conferences, recommending topics to be included in the programme of the next Conference; such projects must be communicated to the various Governments forming the Union, at least six months before the date of the meeting of the next Conference.

8. To submit within the same period a report to the various Governments on the work of the "Pan American Union" during the term covered since the meeting of the last Conference, and also special reports on any matter which may have been referred to it for report.

9. To keep the records of the International American Conferences.

ARTICLE 2

The control of the "Pan American Union" is vested in a Governing Board consisting of the diplomatic representatives of all the Governments of said Republics accredited to the Government of the United States of America, and the Secretary of State of the United States, on whom the American Republics have conferred the presidency of the Governing Board.

ARTICLE 3

Any diplomatic representative unable to attend the meetings of the Board may transmit his vote, stating his reason therefor in writing. Representation by proxy is prohibited. Any Republic having no representative accredited before the Government of the United States of America may designate a member of the Governing Board to represent it in the "Union of American Republics," and in this case said representative will have a vote for each representation.

ARTICLE 4

The Governing Board shall meet in regular session the first Wednesday of every month, excepting the months of June, July, and August; and in special session at the call of the President issued on his own initiative, or at the request of two members of the Board.

The attendance of five members at any ordinary or special session shall be sufficient to permit the Board to proceed with Business.

ARTICLE 5

In the absence of the Secretary of State of the United States, one of the diplomatic representatives in Washington then present, shall preside according to rank and seniority, with the title of Vice-Chairman.

ARTICLE 6

At the regular session to be held in November the Governing Board shall fix by lot the order of precedence among all the representatives of the American Republics forming the Union in order to create a Supervisory Committee. The first four on this list and the Secretary of the United States of America will constitute the first Supervisory Committee; and the four members of the Committee shall be replaced in turn, one every year, so that the Committee shall be totally renewed in four years. The outgoing members shall always be replaced by those following on the list, the same method being observed in event of resignation. The Secretary of State of the United States of America shall always be the Chairman of the Committee.

The Supervisory Committee shall hold their regular session the first Monday of every month, and three members shall be sufficient to constitute a quorum.

ARTICLE 7

There shall be a General Director [sic] appointed by the Governing Board and an Assistant Director who shall also act as Secretary to the said Board.

ARTICLE 8

The Director General shall have charge of the administration of the "Pan American Union" in accordance with these fundamental rules, the regulations, and the resolutions of the Governing Board.

He shall have charge of the correspondence with the Governments of the Union through their diplomatic representatives in Washington, or directly in the absence of such representatives, and with the Pan-American Committees. He shall attend in an advisory capacity the meetings of the Governing Board, of the Committees, and of International American Conferences, except in the case of resolution to the contrary.

ARTICLE 9

The personnel of the "Pan American Union," the number of employees, their appointment, duties and everything pertaining thereto, shall be determined by the Regulations.

ARTICLE 10

There shall be in the Capital of each of the Republics of this Union a Pan American Commission responsible to the Minister of

Foreign Affairs consisting, if possible, of persons who have been Delegates to some International American Conference, their functions being:

a) To obtain the approval of the resolutions adopted by these Conferences.

b) To furnish accurately and without delay to the "Pan American Union" all the data needed in the preparation of its work.

c) To submit of their own initiative any projects they may deem proper to foster the interest of the Union, and to exercise such further functions as the respective Governments may entrust to them.

These Commissions may correspond with the "Pan American Union" either directly or through the diplomatic representatives in Washington.

The Governments represented shall be entitled to send, at their own cost, to the "Pan American Union" a special agent of the respective Commission, charged with the supplying of such data and information as may be asked from him and at the same time to secure such as may be needed by his Government.

ARTICLE 11

The Director-General of the "Pan American Union" shall submit at the regular meeting in November a detailed budget of the expenses for the following year. This Budget, after approval by the Governing Board shall be transmitted to the various Signatory Governments with a statement of the annual quota which each is to contribute, this quota being fixed in proportion to the population of the country.

ARTICLE 12

The "Pan American Union" shall issue such publications as the Governing Board may determine, and shall publish a Bulletin at least once a month.

All geographical maps published by the "Pan American Union" shall bear a statement thereon that they do not constitute documents approved by the Government of the country to which they apply, nor by the Governments of the countries whose boundaries appear thereon, unless the former and the latter Governments shall have expressly given their approval, which shall in each case also be stated on the map. A similar statement shall be made on the other publications of the Union, save those which are of an official nature.

All these publications, with the exceptions determined by the Governing Board, shall be distributed gratuitously.

ARTICLE 13

In order to assure the greatest possible accuracy in the publications of the "Pan American Union," each of the Signatory States shall transmit directly to the Union two copies of all official documents or publications relating to matters connected with the purposes of the Union; and with the same object they shall also send one copy to each of the Pan American Commissions.

ARTICLE 14

All correspondence and publications of the "Pan American Union" shall be carried free of charge by the mails of the American Republics.

ARTICLE 15

The "Pan American Union" shall be governed by the regulations prepared by the Governing Board in accordance with the Statutes.

ARTICLE 16

The American Republics bind themselves to continue to support the "'Pan American Union" for a term of ten years from this date, and to pay annually into the Treasury of the "Pan American Union" their respective quotas. Any of the Republics may cease to belong to the Union of American Republics upon notice to the Governing Board, two years in advance. The "Pan American Union" shall continue for successive terms of ten years unless twelve months before the expiration of such term a majority of the members of the Union shall express the wish, through the Secretary of State of the United States of America, to withdraw therefrom on the expiration of the term.

ARTICLE 17

All rules contrary to the present Resolution are hereby repealed.

Made and signed in the city of Buenos Aires on the eleventh day of the month of August in the year one thousand nine hundred and ten in the Spanish, English, Portuguese and French languages, and filed in the Ministry of Foreign Affairs of the Argentine Republic, in order that certified copies may be taken to be forwarded through the Diplomatic Channels to each one of the Signatory States.

(Signed by the delegates for: Argentina, Brazil, Chile, Colombia, Costa Rica, Cuba, Dominican Republic, Ecuador, Guatemala, Haiti, Honduras, Mexico, Nicaragua, Panama, Paraguay, Peru, El Salvador, United States of America, Uruguay, Venezuela)

[There is some question as to whether clause 5 belongs in the final text.]

RESOLUTION on the Interchange of Professors and Students
James Brown Scott, *The International Conferences of American States, 1889–1928,* p. 190

THE UNDERSIGNED, Delegates of the Republics represented at the Fourth International American Conference, duly authorized by their respective Governments, have approved the following Resolution:

The Fourth International American Conference, assembled at Buenos Aires,
Resolves:

I

To recommend to the Governments of America in regard to their public Universities and to the Universities recognized by those Governments, that they establish the interchange of professors on the following principles:

First: The above mentioned Universities shall grant facilities for professors sent from one to another for the holding of classes or giving lectures.

Second: Such classes or lectures shall treat chiefly of scientific matters of interest to America, or relating to the conditions of one or more of the American countries, especially that in which the professor is teaching.

Third: Every year the Universities desiring the interchange shall give notice to each other of the matters of which their professors can treat and of those which they desire to be treated of respectively in their classes.

Fourth: The remuneration of a professor shall be paid by the University which has appointed him, unless his services shall have been expressly requested, in which case his remuneration shall be charged to the University which has engaged his services.

Fifth: The Universities shall determine annually the amount, to be taken from their own funds, should they have any, or to be asked from their respective Governments, for the costs incurred in fulfilment of the terms of this Resolution.

Sixth: It is to be desired that the Universities of America should assemble at a Congress to provide for University extension and other means of American intellectual cooperation.

II

The Fourth International American Conference being of opinion, also, that it would be well for the strengthening of the solidarity of the nations of the Continent that there should be an interchange of students between the American Universities, resolves:

1. To recommend that the Universities of America should create scholarships in favor of students of other countries of this same Continent, with or without reciprocal charges, adopting, either directly, or through the Government on which they are dependent, the necessary measures for the practical carrying out of this agreement.

2. Each University which shall have created such scholarship shall appoint a committee to be charged with the care of the students to whom such scholarships have been given, to direct their studies and to lay down the rules necessary to secure due performance of their duties.

3. The Universities so attended by a foreign student shall enter him in his corresponding course in conformity with the plan of studies and the respective regulations.

Done and signed in the city of Buenos Aires, on the eighteenth day of August in the year one thousand nine hundred and ten, in Spanish, Portuguese, English and French, and deposited in the Ministry of Foreign Affairs of the Argentine Republic, in order that certified copies be made for transmission to each one of the Signatory Nations through the appropriate diplomatic channels.

(Signed by the delegates for: Argentina, Brazil, Chile, Colombia, Costa Rica, Cuba, Dominican Republic, Ecuador, Guatemala, Haiti, Honduras, Mexico, Nicaragua, Panama, Paraguay, Peru, El Salvador, United States of America, Uruguay, Venezuela)

CONVENTION on Pecuniary Claims

James Brown Scott, *The International Conferences of American States, 1889–1928*, p. 183. The convention was ratified by the President of the United States, March 21, 1911

THEIR EXCELLENCIES the Presidents of the United States of America, Argentine Republic, Brazil, Chili, Colombia, Costa Rica, Cuba, Dominican Republic, Ecuador, Guatemala, Haiti, Honduras, Mexico, Nicaragua, Panama, Paraguay, Peru, Salvador, Uruguay and Venezuela;

Being desirous that their respective countries may be represented at the Fourth International American Conference have sent thereto the following Delegates, duly authorized to approve the recommendations, resolutions, conventions and treaties which may be advantageous to the interests of America:

(Here follow the names of the delegates.)

Who, after having presented their credentials and the same having been found in due and proper form, have agreed upon the following Convention on Pecuniary Claims.

1st. The High Contracting Parties agree to submit to arbitration all claims for pecuniary loss or damage which may be presented by their respective citizens and which cannot be amicably adjusted through diplomatic channels, when said claims are of sufficient importance to warrant the expense of arbitration.

The decision shall be rendered in accordance with the principles of International Law.

2nd. The High Contracting Parties agree to submit to the decision of the permanent Court of Arbitration of The Hague all controversies which are the subject-matter of the present Treaty, unless both parties agree to constitute a special jurisdiction.

If a case is submitted to the Permanent Court of The Hague, the High Contracting Parties accept the provisions of the treaty relating to the organization of that arbitral Tribunal, to the procedure to be followed and to the obligation to comply with the sentence.

3rd. If it shall be agreed to constitute a special jurisdiction, there shall be prescribed in the convention by which this is determined the rules according to which the tribunal shall proceed, which shall have cognizance of the questions involved in the claims referred to in Article 1st. of the present treaty.

4th. The present Treaty shall come into force immediately after the thirty-first of December 1912, when the treaty on pecuniary claims, signed at Mexico, on January 31, 1902, and extended by the treaty signed at Rio de Janeiro on August 13, 1906, expires.

It shall remain in force indefinitely, as well for the nations which shall then have ratified it as those which shall ratify it subsequently.

The ratifications shall be transmitted to the Government of the Argentine Republic, which shall communicate them to the other Contracting Parties.

5th. Any of the nations ratifying the present Treaty may denounce it, on its own part, by giving two years notice in writing, in advance, of its intention so to do.

This notice shall be transmitted to the Government of the Argentine Republic and through its intermediation, to the other contracting Parties.

6th. The treaty of Mexico shall continue in force after December 31, 1912, as to any claims which may, prior to that date, have been submitted to arbitration under its provisions.

In witness whereof, the Plenipotentiaries and Delegates sign this Convention and affix to it the Seal of the Fourth International American Conference.

Made and signed in the city of Buenos Aires, on the eleventh day of August in the year one thousand nine hundred and ten, in the Spanish, English, Portuguese and French languages, and filed in the Ministry of Foreign Affairs of the Argentine Republic, in order that certified copies may be taken to be forwarded through the appropriate Diplomatic channels to each one of the Signatory Nations.

(Signed by the delegates for: Argentina, Brazil, Chile, Colombia, Costa Rica, Cuba, Dominican Republic, Ecuador, Guatemala, Haiti, Honduras, Mexico, Nicaragua, Panama, Paraguay, Peru, El Salvador, United States of America, Uruguay, Venezuela)

Fifth International Conference of American States, at Santiago, March 25 to May 3, 1923

RESOLUTION on Codification of International Law

James Brown Scott, *The International Conferences of American States, 1889–1928,* p. 245

THE FIFTH International Conference of American States,
Resolves:

1. To request each Government of the American Republics to appoint two Delegates to constitute the Congress of Jurists of Rio de Janeiro;

2. To recommend that the Committees appointed by the Congress of Jurists be reestablished;

3. To request these Committees to undertake and to reconsider their work in the light of the experience of recent years and also in view of the resolutions of the Fifth International Conference of American States;

4. To designate a Committee for the study of the comparative Civil Law of all the nations of America in order to contribute to the formation of Private International Law, so that the results of this study may be utilized at the next meeting of the Congress of Jurists. It is understood that in the term "Civil Law" there are included the following topics: Commercial Law, Mining Law, Law of Procedure, etc. Criminal Law may also be included therein;

5. To convene the International Congress of Jurists at Rio de Janeiro during the year 1925; the precise date to be determined by the Pan American Union after consultation with the Government of Brazil;

6. To recommend to this Congress that in the domain of International Law, the codification should be gradual and progressive, accepting as the basis the project presented to the Fifth International Conference by the Delegate of Chile, Mr. Alejandro Alvarez, entitled "The Codification of American International Law";

7. The names of the Delegates referred to in Clause 1, should be communicated to the Government of Brazil and to the Pan American Union;

8. The resolutions of the Congress of Jurists shall be submitted to the Sixth International Conference of American States, in order that, if approved, they may be communicated to the Governments and incorporated in Conventions;

9. To recommend to the Congress of Jurists that there be prepared an American code of Private International Law, which code shall determine, if deemed advisable, the juridical system or systems which shall be adopted, or what combinations thereof shall be used, in order to avoid conflicts; the Congress shall for this purpose instruct the Committees that may be named for the purpose of formulating the above mentioned code; in these instructions the proposals presented to the Fifth International Conference of American States by the Delegations of Argentina, Brazil and Uruguay shall be taken into account, as well as any others that may be suggested.

This recommendation shall be transmitted immediately to the respective Governments, in order that they may in turn be transmitted to the Delegates who will form part of the Committees on Private International Law.

(Number 30 of the General Report.)

(Adopted at the 8th Session of the Conference, April 26, 1923)

TREATY to Avoid or Prevent Conflicts between the American States

Department of State, Treaty Series, No. 752. The treaty was ratified by the President of the United States April 21, 1924

THE GOVERNMENTS represented at the Fifth International Conference of American States, desiring to strengthen progressively the principles of justice and of mutual respect which inspire the policy observed by them in their reciprocal relations, and to quicken in their peoples sentiments of concord and of loyal friendship which may contribute toward the consolidation of such relations,

Confirm their most sincere desire to maintain an immutable peace, not only between themselves but also with all the other nations of the earth;

Condemn armed peace which increases military and naval forces beyond the necessities of domestic security and the sovereignty and independence of States, and,

With the firm purpose of taking all measures which will avoid or prevent the conflicts which may eventually occur between them, AGREE to the present TREATY, negotiated and concluded by the Plenipotentiary Delegates whose full powers were found to be in good and due form by the Conference:

[*Names of the Plenipotentiaries*]

ARTICLE 1

All controversies which for any cause whatsoever may arise between two or more of the High Contracting Parties and which it has been impossible to settle through diplomatic channels, or to submit to arbitration in accordance with existing treaties, shall be submitted for investigation and report to a Commission to be established in the manner provided for in Article 4. The High Contracting Parties undertake, in case of disputes, not to begin mobilization or concentration of troops on the frontier of the other Party, nor to engage in any hostile acts or preparations for hostilities, from the time steps are taken to convene the Commission until the said Commission has rendered its report or until the expiration of the time provided for in Article 7.

This provision shall not abrogate nor limit the obligations contained in treaties of arbitration in force between two or more of the High Contracting Parties, nor the obligations arising out of them.

It is understood that in disputes arising between Nations which have no general treaties of arbitration, the investigation shall not take place in questions affecting constitutional provisions, nor in questions already settled by other treaties.

ARTICLE 2

The controversies referred to in Article 1 shall be submitted to the Commission of Inquiry whenever it has been impossible to settle them through diplomatic negotiations or procedure or by submission to arbitration, or in cases in which the circumstances of fact render all negotiation impossible and there is imminent danger of an armed conflict between the Parties. Any one of the Governments directly interested in the investigation of the facts giving rise to the controversy may apply for the convocation of the Commission of Inquiry and to this end it shall be necessary only to communicate officially this decision to the other Party and to one of the Permanent Commissions established by Article 3.

ARTICLE 3

Two Commissions to be designated as permanent shall be established with their seats at Washington (United States of America) and at Montevideo (Uruguay). They shall be composed of the three American diplomatic agents longest accredited in said capitals, and at the call of the Foreign Offices of those States they shall organize, appointing their respective chairmen. Their functions shall be limited to receiving from the interested Parties the request for a convocation of the Commission of Inquiry, and to notifying the other Party thereof immediately. The Government requesting the convocation shall appoint at the same time the persons who shall compose the Commission of Inquiry in representation of that Government, and the other Party shall, likewise, as soon as it receives notification, designate its members.

The Party initiating the procedure established by this Treaty may address itself, in doing so, to the Permanent Commission which it considers most efficacious for a rapid organization of the Commission of Inquiry. Once the request for convocation has been received and the Permanent Commission has made the respective notifications the question or controversy existing between the Parties and as to which no agreement has been reached, will *ipso facto* be suspended.

ARTICLE 4

The Commission of Inquiry shall be composed of five members, all nationals of American States, appointed in the following manner: each Government shall appoint two at the time of convocation, only one of whom may be a national of its country. The fifth shall be chosen by common accord by those already appointed and shall perform the duties of President. However, a citizen of a nation already represented on the Commission may not be elected. Any of the Governments may refuse to accept the elected member, for reasons which it may reserve to itself, and in such event a substitute shall be appointed, with the mutual consent of the Parties, within thirty days following the notification of this refusal. In the failure of such agreement, the designation shall be made by the President of an American Republic not interested in the dispute, who shall be selected by lot by the Commissioners already appointed, from a list of not more than six American Presidents to be formed as follows: each Government party to the controversy, or if there are more than two Governments directly interested in the dispute, the Government or Governments on each side of the controversy, shall designate three Presidents of American States which maintain the same friendly relations with all the Parties to the dispute.

Whenever there are more than two Governments directly interested in a controversy, and the interest of two or more of them are identical, the Government or Governments on each side of the controversy shall have the right to increase the number of their Commissioners, as far as it may be necessary, so that both sides in the dispute may always have equal representation on the Commission.

Once the Commission has been thus organized in the capital city, seat of the Permanent Commission which issued the order of convocation, it shall notify the respective Governments of the date of its inauguration, and it may then determine upon the place or places in which it will function, taking into account the greater facilities for investigation.

The Commission of Inquiry shall itself establish its rules of procedure. In this regard there are recommended for incorporation into said rules of procedure the provisions contained in Articles 9, 10, 11, 12 and 13 of the Convention signed in Washington, February, 1923, between the Government of the United States of America and the Governments of the Republics of Guatemala, El Salvador, Honduras, Nicaragua and Costa Rica, which appear in the appendix to this Treaty.

Its decisions and final report shall be agreed to by the majority of its members.

Each Party shall bear its own expenses and a proportionate share of the general expenses of the Commission.

ARTICLE 5

The Parties to the controversy shall furnish the antecedents and data necessary for the investigation. The Commission shall render its report within one year from the date of its inauguration. If it has been impossible to finish the investigation or draft the report within the period agreed upon, it may be extended six months beyond the period established, provided the Parties to the controversy are in agreement upon this point.

ARTICLE 6

The findings of the Commission will be considered as reports upon the disputes, which were the subjects of the investigation, but will not have the value or force of judicial decisions or arbitral awards.

ARTICLE 7

Once the report is in possession of the Governments parties to the dispute, six months' time will be available for renewed negotiations in order to bring about a settlement of the difficulty in view of the findings of said report; and if during this new term they should be unable to reach a friendly arrangement, the Parties in dispute shall recover entire liberty of action to proceed as their interests may dictate in the question dealt with in the investigation.

ARTICLE 8

The present Treaty does not abrogate analogous conventions which may exist or may in the future exist between two or more of the High Contracting Parties; neither does it partially abrogate any of their provisions, although they may provide special circumstances or conditions differing from those herein stipulated.

ARTICLE 9

The present Treaty shall be ratified by the High Contracting Parties, in conformity with their respective constitutional procedures, and the ratifications shall be deposited in the Ministry for Foreign Affairs of the Republic of Chile, which will communicate them through diplomatic channels to the other Signatory Governments, and it shall enter into effect for the Contracting Parties in the order of ratification.

The Treaty shall remain in force indefinitely; any of the High Contracting Parties may denounce it and the denunciation shall take effect as regards the Party denouncing one year after notification thereof has been given.

Notice of the denunciation shall be sent to the Government of Chile, which will transmit it for appropriate action to the other Signatory Governments.

ARTICLE 10

The American States which have not been represented in the Fifth Conference may adhere to the present Treaty, transmitting the official documents setting forth such adherence to the Ministry for Foreign Affairs of Chile, which will communicate it to the other Contracting Parties.

In WITNESS WHEREOF, the Plenipotentiaries and Delegates sign this Convention in Spanish, English, Portuguese and French and affix the seal of the Fifth International Conference of American States, in the city of Santiago, Chile, on the 3rd day of May in the year one thousand nine hundred and twenty three.

This Convention shall be filed in the Ministry for Foreign Affairs of the Republic of Chile in order that certified copies thereof may be forwarded through diplomatic channels to each of the Signatory States.

[*Signatures*]

Appendix

ARTICLE 1

The Signatory Governments grant to all the Commissions which may be constituted the power to summon witnesses, to administer oaths and to receive evidence and testimony.

ARTICLE 2

During the investigation the Parties shall be heard and may have the right to be represented by one or more agents and counsel.

ARTICLE 3

All members of the Commission shall take oath duly and faithfully to discharge their duties before the highest judicial authority of the place where it may meet.

ARTICLE 4

The Inquiry shall be conducted so that both Parties shall be heard. Consequently, the Commission shall notify each Party of the statements of facts submitted by the other, and shall fix periods of time in which to receive evidence.

Once the Parties are notified, the Commission shall proceed to the investigation, even though they fail to appear.

ARTICLE 5

As soon as the Commission of Inquiry is organized, it shall at the request of any of the Parties to the dispute, have the right to fix the status in which the Parties must remain, in order that the situation may not be aggravated and matters may remain in *statu quo* pending the rendering of the report by the Commission.

Sixth International Conference of American States, at Habana, January 16 to February 20, 1928

RESOLUTION on Arbitration and Conciliation Conference

James Brown Scott, *The International Conferences of American States, 1889–1928,* p. 437

THE SIXTH International Conference of American States
Resolves:

WHEREAS: The American Republics desire to express that they condemn war as an instrument of national policy in their mutual relations; and

WHEREAS: The American Republics have the most fervent desire to contribute in every possible manner to the development of international means for the pacific settlement of conflicts between States:

1. That the American Republics adopt obligatory arbitration as the means which they will employ for the pacific solution of their international differences of a juridical character.

2. That the American Republics will meet in Washington within the period of one year in a conference of conciliation and arbitration to give conventional form to the realization of this principle, with the minimum exceptions which they may consider indispensable to safeguard the independence and sovereignty of the States, as well as matters of a domestic concern, and to the exclusion also of matters involving the interest or referring to the action of a State not a party to the convention.

3. That the Governments of the American Republics will send for this end plenipotentiary jurisconsults with instructions regarding the maximum and the minimum which they would accept in the extension of obligatory arbitral jurisdiction.

4. That the convention or conventions of conciliation and arbitration which may be concluded should leave open a protocol for progressive arbitration which would permit the development of this beneficent institution up to its maximum.

5. That the convention or conventions which may be agreed upon, after signature, should be submitted immediately to the respective Governments for their ratification in the shortest possible time.

(February 18, 1928)

RESOLUTION on Future Codification of International Law
James Brown Scott, *The International Conferences of American States, 1889–1928,*
p. 439

THE SIXTH International Conference of American States
Resolves:

First: That the future formulation of international law shall be effected by means of technical preparation, duly organized, with the cooperation of the committees on investigation and international coordination and of the scientific institutes hereinafter mentioned.

Second: That the International Commission of Jurists of Rio de Janeiro shall meet on the dates which may be appointed by the respective governments, for the purpose of undertaking the codification of public and private international law, the Pan American Union being entrusted with furthering the agreement necessary to bring about its meeting.

Third: That three permanent Committees shall be organized, one in Rio de Janeiro, for the work relating to public international law; another at Montevideo, for the work dealing with private international law; and another in Habana, for the study of comparative legislation and uniformity of legislations. Said bodies shall have the following functions:

a) To present to the governments a report or statement of the matters which are ready for codification and legislative uniformity comprising those definitely subject to regulation and formulation, as well as those regarding which international experience and the new principles and aspirations of justice may indicate require prudent juridical development.

This report would be presented for the purpose of having the governments indicate which matters they deem susceptible to study to the end that they may be used as a basis in the formulation of conventional rules or fundamental declarations.

b) To classify, in view of the aforementioned statement and of the answers given by the governments, the matters submitted to discussion, in the following form:

1. Subjects which are in proper condition for codification, because they have been unanimously consented to by the governments;

2. Matters susceptible of being proposed as subject to codification because, although not unanimously endorsed by, they represent a predominant opinion on the part of most Governments;

3. Matters respecting which there is no predominant opinion, in favor of immediate regulation.

c) To present to the governments the foregoing classifications, in order to learn their general views as to the manner in which the juridical problems of codifiable matters could be enunciated and resolved, together with all juridical, legal, political, and diplomatic data and antecedents which may lead to a full clarification of the subject.

d) To solicit and obtain from the National Societies of International Law scientific opinions and general views on the regulation and formulation of the juridical questions entrusted to the Committees.

e) To compile all the aforementioned material for its transmission, together with draft-projects thereon, to the Pan American Union, which shall submit them to the Executive Council of the American Institute of International Law to the end that through a scientific consideration thereof the latter may make a technical study of such draft-projects and present its findings and formulas, in a report on the matter.

Fourth: That the opinion of the Inter American High Commission shall likewise be heard, as that of a technical cooperative body, on those matters of an economic, financial and maritime nature.

Fifth: That after said studies and formulas are presented, they shall be communicated to the governments, which may agree upon the advisability of convening the Commission of Jurists, or else have them incorporated into the program of a forthcoming International Conference.

Sixth: That in order to include in the program of the International Conferences of American States the matters susceptible of codification or uniformity of legislation, and also for their incorporation into the agenda of the Commission of Jurists, whenever agreed upon, it shall be necessary that the governments have the draft-projects and antecedents for study at least one year in advance.

Seventh: That the three aforementioned Committees shall be constituted by the governments with members of the respective National Societies of International Law. Communication with the Governments and with the Executive Council of the Institute shall be conducted through the Pan American Union.

Eighth: That a Commission of Jurists, learned in the civil legislation of the American countries, may be constituted whenever deemed advisable, in order to undertake the study of said legislation and the drafting of a project of uniform civil legislation for the American nations, especially those of Latin America, choosing the proper means to obviate the inconveniences resulting from the diversity of legislations.

Ninth: That the Pan American Union, in so far as its statutes may permit, shall cooperate in the preparatory work to which the foregoing articles refer.

(February 18, 1928)

CONVENTION on Duties and Rights of States in the Event of Civil Strife
Department of State, Treaty Series, No. 814

THE GOVERNMENTS of the Republics represented at the Sixth International Conference of American States, held in the city of Habana, Republic of Cuba, in the year 1928, desirous of reaching an agreement as to the duties and rights of states in the event of civil strife have appointed the following plenipotentiaries:

[*Names of plenipotentiaries*]

Who, after exchanging their respective full powers, which were found to be in good and due form, have agreed upon the following:

ARTICLE 1

The contracting states bind themselves to observe the following rules with regard to civil strife in another one of them:

1. To use all means at their disposal to prevent the inhabitants of their territory, nationals or aliens, from participating in, gathering elements, crossing the boundary or sailing from their territory for the purpose of starting or promoting civil strife.

2. To disarm and intern every rebel force crossing their boundaries, the expenses of internment to be borne by the state where public order may have been disturbed. The arms found in the hands of the rebels may be seized and withdrawn by the government of the country granting asylum, to be returned, once the struggle has ended, to the state in civil strife.

3. To forbid the traffic in arms and war material, except when intended for the government, while the belligerency of the rebels has not been recognized, in which latter case the rules of neutrality shall be applied.

4. To prevent that within their jurisdiction there be equipped, armed or adapted for warlike purposes any vessel intended to operate in favor of the rebellion.

ARTICLE 2

The declaration of piracy against vessels which have risen in arms, emanating from a government, is not binding upon the other states.

The state that may be injured by depredations originating from insurgent vessels is entitled to adopt the following punitive measures against them: Should the authors of the damages be warships, it may capture and return them to the government of the state to which they belong, for their trial; should the damage originate with merchantmen, the injured state may capture and subject them to the appropriate penal laws.

The insurgent vessel, whether a warship or a merchantman, which flies the flag of a foreign country to shield its actions, may also be captured and tried by the state of said flag.

ARTICLE 3

The insurgent vessel, whether a warship or a merchantman, equipped by the rebels, which arrives at a foreign country or seeks refuge therein, shall be delivered by the government of the latter to the constituted government of the state in civil strife, and the members of the crew shall be considered as political refugees.

ARTICLE 4

The present convention does not affect obligations previously undertaken by the contracting parties through international agreements.

ARTICLE 5

After being signed, the present convention shall be submitted to the ratification of the signatory states. The Government of Cuba is charged with transmitting authentic certified copies to the governments for the aforementioned purpose of ratification. The instrument of ratification shall be deposited in the archives of the Pan American Union in Washington, the Union to notify the signatory governments of said deposit. Such notification shall be considered as an exchange of ratifications. This convention shall remain open to the adherence of non-signatory states.

In witness whereof the aforenamed plenipotentiaries sign the present convention in Spanish, English, French, and Portuguese, in the city of Habana, the 20th day of February, 1928.

[*Signatures*]

[Ratified by the President of the United States, May 7, 1930, subject to the understanding that the provisions of Article 3 thereof shall not apply where a state of belligerency has been recognized.]

*International Conference of American States on Concilia-
tion and Arbitration, at Washington, December 10, 1928,
to January 5, 1929*

GENERAL CONVENTION of Inter-American Conciliation

Department of State, Treaty Series, No. 780. The treaty was ratified by the President of the United States, February 26, 1929

THE GOVERNMENTS of Venezuela, Chile, Bolivia, Uruguay, Costa Rica, Perú, Honduras, Guatemala, Haiti, Ecuador, Colombia, Brazil, Panamá, Paraguay, Nicaragua, Mexico, El Salvador, the Dominican Republic, Cuba, and the United States of America, represented at the Conference on Conciliation and Arbitration, assembled at Washington, pursuant to the Resolution adopted on February 18, 1928, by the Sixth International Conference of American States held in the City of Habana:

Desiring to demonstrate that the condemnation of war as an instrument of national policy in their mutual relations, set forth in the above mentioned resolution, constitutes one of the fundamental bases of inter-American relations;

Animated by the purpose of promoting, in every possible way, the development of international methods for the pacific settlement of differences between the States;

Being convinced that the "Treaty to Avoid or Prevent Conflicts between the American States," signed at Santiago de Chile, May 3, 1923, constitutes a notable achievement in inter-American relations, which it is necessary to maintain by giving additional prestige and strength to the action of the commissions established by Articles III and IV of the aforementioned treaty;

Acknowledging the need of giving conventional form to these purposes have agreed to enter into the present Convention, for which purpose they have appointed plenipotentiaries as follows:

[*Names of plenipotentiaries*]

Who, after having deposited their full powers, which were found to be in good and due form by the Conference, have agreed as follows:

ARTICLE 1

The High Contracting Parties agree to submit to the procedure of conciliation established by this convention all controversies of any kind which have arisen or may arise between them for any reason and which it may not have been possible to settle through diplomatic channels.

The Commission of Inquiry to be established pursuant to the provisions of Article IV of the Treaty signed in Santiago de Chile on May 3, 1923, shall likewise have the character of Commission of Conciliation.

The Permanent Commissions which have been established by virtue of Article III of the Treaty of Santiago de Chile of May 3, 1923, shall be bound to exercise conciliatory functions, either on their own motion when it appears that there is a prospect of disturbance of peaceful relations, or at the request of a Party to the dispute, until the Commission referred to in the preceding article is organized.

The conciliatory functions of the Commission described in Article 2 shall be exercised on the occasions hereinafter set forth:

(1) The Commission shall be at liberty to begin its work with an effort to conciliate the differences submitted to its examination with a view to arriving at a settlement between the Parties.

(2) Likewise the same Commission shall be at liberty to endeavor to conciliate the Parties at any time which in the opinion of the Commission may be considered to be favorable in the course of the investigation and within the period of time fixed therefor in Article V of the Treaty of Santiago de Chile of May 3, 1923.

(3) Finally, the Commission shall be bound to carry out its conciliatory function within the period of six months which is referred to in Article VII of the Treaty of Santiago de Chile of May 3, 1923.

The Parties to the controversy may, however, extend this time, if they so agree and notify the Commission in due time.

The present convention does not preclude the High Contracting Parties, or one or more of them, from tendering their good offices or their mediation, jointly or severally, on their own motion or at the request of one or more of the Parties to the controversy; but the High Contracting Parties agree not to make use of those means of pacific settlement from the moment that the Commission described in Article 2 is organized until the final act referred to in Article 11 of this convention is signed.

ARTICLE 6

The function of the Commission, as an organ of conciliation, in all cases specified in Article 2 of this convention, is to procure the conciliation of the differences subject to its examination by endeavoring to effect a settlement between the Parties.

When the Commission finds itself to be within the case foreseen in paragraph 3 of Article 4 of this convention, it shall undertake a conscientious and impartial examination of the questions which are the subject of the controversy, shall set forth in a report the results of its proceedings, and shall propose to the Parties the bases of a settlement for the equitable solution of the controversy.

ARTICLE 7

Except when the Parties agree otherwise, the decisions and recommendations of any Commission of Conciliation shall be made by a majority vote.

ARTICLE 8

The Commission described in Article 2 of this convention shall establish its rules of procedure. In the absence of agreement to the contrary, the procedure indicated in Article IV of the Treaty of Santiago de Chile of May 3, 1923, shall be followed.

Each party shall bear its own expenses and a proportionate share of the general expenses of the Commission.

ARTICLE 9

The report and the recommendations of the Commission, insofar as it may be acting as an organ of conciliation, shall not have the character of a decision nor an arbitral award, and shall not be binding on the Parties either as regards the exposition or interpretation of the facts or as regards questions of law.

ARTICLE 10

As soon as possible after the termination of its labors the Commission shall transmit to the Parties a certified copy of the report and of the bases of settlement which it may propose.

The Commission in transmitting the report and the recommendations to the Parties shall fix a period of time, which shall not exceed six months, within which the Parties shall pass upon the bases of settlement above referred to.

ARTICLE 11

Once the period of time fixed by the Commission for the Parties to make their decisions has expired, the Commission shall set forth in a final act the decision of the Parties, and if the conciliation has been effected, the terms of the settlement.

ARTICLE 12

The obligations set forth in the second sentence of the first paragraph of Article I of the Treaty of Santiago de Chile of May 3, 1923, shall extend to the time when the final act referred to in the preceding article is signed.

ARTICLE 13

Once the procedure of conciliation is under way it shall be interrupted only by a direct settlement between the Parties or by their agreement to accept absolutely the decision *ex aequo et bono* of an American Chief of State or to submit the controversy to arbitration or to an international court.

ARTICLE 14

Whenever for any reason the Treaty of Santiago de Chile of May 3, 1923, does not apply, the Commission referred to in Article 2 of this convention shall be organized to the end that it may exercise the conciliatory functions stipulated in this convention; the Commission shall be organized in the same manner as that prescribed in Article IV of said treaty.

In such cases, the Commission thus organized shall be governed in its operation by the provisions, relative to conciliation, of this convention.

ARTICLE 15

The provisions of the preceding article shall also apply with regard to the Permanent Commissions constituted by the aforementioned Treaty of Santiago de Chile, to the end that said Commissions may exercise the conciliatory functions prescribed in Article 3 of this convention.

ARTICLE 16

The present convention shall be ratified by the High Contracting Parties in conformity with their respective constitutional procedures, provided that they have previously ratified the Treaty of Santiago, Chile, of May 3, 1923.

The original convention and the instruments of ratification shall be deposited in the Ministry for Foreign Affairs of the Republic of Chile which shall give notice of the ratifications through diplomatic channels to the other signatory Governments and the convention shall enter into effect for the High Contracting Parties in the order that they deposit their ratifications.

This convention shall remain in force indefinitely, but it may be denounced by means of notice given one year in advance at the expiration of which it shall cease to be in force as regards the Party denouncing the same, but shall remain in force as regards the other signatories. Notice of the denunciation shall be addressed to the Ministry for Foreign Affairs of the Republic of Chile which will transmit it for appropriate action to the other signatory Governments.

Any American State not a signatory of this convention may adhere to the same by transmitting the official instrument setting forth such adherence, to the Ministry for Foreign Affairs of the Republic of Chile which will notify the other High Contracting Parties thereof in the manner heretofore mentioned.

In witness whereof the above mentioned Plenipotentiaries have signed this convention in English, Spanish, Portuguese and French and hereunto affix their respective seals.

Done at the city of Washington, on this fifth day of January, 1929.

[*Signatures*]

GENERAL TREATY of Inter-American Arbitration and Protocol of Progressive Arbitration

Department of State, Treaty Series, No. 886

THE GOVERNMENTS of Venezuela, Chile, Bolivia, Uruguay, Costa Rica, Perú, Honduras, Guatemala, Haiti, Ecuador, Colombia, Brazil, Panamá, Paraguay, Nicaragua, Mexico, El Salvador, the Dominican Republic, Cuba, and the United States of America, represented at the Conference on Conciliation and Arbitration, assembled at Washington, pursuant to the Resolution adopted on February 18, 1928, by the Sixth International Conference of American States held in the City of Habana;

In accordance with the solemn declarations made at said Conference to the effect that the American Republics condemn war as an instrument of national policy and adopt obligatory arbitration as the means for the settlement of their international differences of a juridical character;

Being convinced that the Republics of the New World, governed by the principles, institutions and practices of democracy and bound furthermore by mutual interests, which are increasing each day, have not only the necessity but also the duty of avoiding the disturbance of continental harmony whenever differences which are susceptible of judicial decision arise among them;

Conscious of the great moral and material benefits which peace offers to humanity and that the sentiment and opinion of America demand, without delay, the organization of an arbitral system which shall strengthen the permanent reign of justice and law;

And animated by the purpose of giving conventional form to these postulates and aspirations with the minimum exceptions which they have considered indispensable to safeguard the independence and sovereignty of the States and in the most ample manner possible under present international conditions, have resolved to effect the present treaty, and for that purpose have designated the Plenipotentiaries hereinafter named:

[*Names of Plenipotentiaries*]

Who, after having deposited their full powers, found in good and due form by the Conference, have agreed upon the following:

ARTICLE 1

The High Contracting Parties bind themselves to submit to arbitration all differences of an international character which have arisen or may arise between them by virtue of a claim of right made by one against the other under treaty or otherwise, which it has not been possible to adjust by diplomacy and which are juridical in their nature by reason of being susceptible of decision by the application of the principles of law.

There shall be considered as included among the questions of juridical character:

(a) The interpretation of a treaty;

(b) Any question of international law;

(c) The existence of any fact which, if established, would constitute a breach of an international obligation;

(d) The nature and extent of the reparation to be made for the breach of an international obligation.

The provisions of this treaty shall not preclude any of the Parties, before resorting to arbitration, from having recourse to procedures of investigation and conciliation established in conventions then in force between them.

ARTICLE 2

There are excepted from the stipulations of this treaty the following controversies:

(a) Those which are within the domestic jurisdiction of any of the Parties to the dispute and are not controlled by international law; and

(b) Those which affect the interest or refer to the action of a State not a Party to this treaty.

ARTICLE 3

The arbitrator or tribunal who shall decide the controversy shall be designated by agreement of the Parties.

In the absence of an agreement the following procedure shall be adopted:

Each Party shall nominate two arbitrators, of whom only one may be a national of said Party or selected from the persons whom said Party has designated as members of the Permanent Court of Arbitration at The Hague. The other member may be of any other American nationality. These arbitrators shall in turn select a fifth arbitrator who shall be the president of the court.

Should the arbitrators be unable to reach an agreement among themselves for the selection of a fifth American arbitrator, or in lieu thereof, of another who is not, each Party shall designate a non-American member of the Permanent Court of Arbitration at The Hague, and the two persons so designated shall select the fifth arbitrator, who may be of any nationality other than that of a Party to the dispute.

ARTICLE 4

The Parties to the dispute shall formulate by common accord, in each case, a special agreement which shall clearly define the particular subject-matter of the controversy, the seat of the court, the rules which will be observed in the proceedings, and the other conditions to which the Parties may agree.

If an accord has not been reached with regard to the agreement within three months reckoned from the date of the installation of the court, the agreement shall be formulated by the court.

ARTICLE 5

In case of death, resignation or incapacity of one or more of the arbitrators the vacancy shall be filled in the same manner as the original appointment.

ARTICLE 6

When there are more than two States directly interested in the same controversy, and the interests of two or more of them are similar, the State or States who are on the same side of the question may increase the number of arbitrators on the court, provided that in all cases the Parties on each side of the controversy shall appoint an equal number of arbitrators. There shall also be a presiding arbitrator selected in the same manner as that provided in the last paragraph of Article 3, the Parties on each side of the controversy being regarded as a single Party for the purpose of making the designation therein described.

ARTICLE 7

The award, duly pronounced and notified to the Parties, settles the dispute definitively and without appeal.

Differentes which arise with regard to its interpretation or execution shall be submitted to the decision of the court which rendered the award.

ARTICLE 8

The reservations made by one of the High Contracting Parties shall have the effect that the other Contracting Parties are not bound with respect to the Party making the reservations except to the same extent as that expressed therein.

ARTICLE 9

The present treaty shall be ratified by the High Contracting Parties in conformity with their respective constitutional procedures.

The original treaty and the instruments of ratification shall be deposited in the Department of State of the United States of America which shall give notice of the ratifications through diplomatic channels to the other signatory Governments and the treaty shall enter into effect for the High Contracting Parties in the order that they deposit their ratifications.

This treaty shall remain in force indefinitely, but it may be denounced by means of one year's previous notice at the expiration of which it shall cease to be in force as regards the Party denouncing the same, but shall remain in force as regards the other signatories. Notice of the denunciation shall be addressed to the Department of State of the United States of America which will transmit it for appropriate action to the other signatory Governments.

Any American State not a signatory of this treaty may adhere to the same by transmitting the official instrument setting forth such adherence to the Department of State of the United States of America which will notify the other High Contracting Parties thereof in the manner heretofore mentioned.

In witness whereof the above mentioned Plenipotentiaries have signed this treaty in English, Spanish, Portuguese, and French and hereunto affix their respective seals.

Done at the city of Washington, on this fifth day of January, 1929.

[*Signatures*]

Protocol of Progressive Arbitration

WHEREAS, a General Treaty of Inter-American Arbitration has this day been signed at Washington by Plenipotentiaries of the Governments of Venezuela, Chile, Bolivia, Uruguay, Costa Rica, Perú, Honduras, Guatemala, Haiti, Ecuador, Colombia, Brazil, Panama, Paraguay, Nicaragua, Mexico, El Salvador, the Dominican Republic, Cuba, and the United States of America;

WHEREAS, that treaty by its terms excepts certain controversies from the stipulations thereof;

WHEREAS, by means of reservations attached to the treaty at the time of signing, ratifying or adhering, certain other controversies have been or may be also excepted from the stipulations of the treaty or reserved from the operation thereof;

WHEREAS, it is deemed desirable to establish a procedure whereby such exceptions or reservations may from time to time be abandoned in whole or in part by the Parties to said treaty, thus progressively extending the field of arbitration;

The Governments named above have agreed as follows:

ARTICLE 1

Any Party to the General Treaty of Inter-American Arbitration signed at Washington the fifth day of January, 1929, may at any time deposit with the Department of State of the United States of America an appropriate instrument evidencing that it has abandoned in whole or in part the exceptions from arbitration stipulated in the said treaty or the reservation or reservations attached by it thereto.

ARTICLE 2

A certified copy of each instrument deposited with the Department of State of the United States of America pursuant to the provisions of Article 1 of this protocol shall be transmitted by the said Department through diplomatic channels to every other Party to the above-mentioned General Treaty of Inter-American Arbitration.

In witness whereof the above-mentioned Plenipotentiaries have signed this protocol in English, Spanish, Portuguese, and French and hereunto affix their respective seals.

Done at the city of Washington, on this fifth day of January, 1929.

[*Signatures*]

[The treaty was ratified by the President of the United States, April 16, 1935, with the understanding "that the special agreement in each case shall be made only by the President, and then only by and with the advice and consent of the Senate, provided two-thirds of the Senators present concur."]

Seventh International Conference of American States, at Montevideo, December 3–26, 1933

RESOLUTION V: Economic, Commercial, and Tariff Policy

Report of the Delegates of the United States of America to the Seventh International Conference of American States, p. 196

WHEREAS, the Governments of the American Republics, convened at the Seventh International Conference of American States,

Are impressed with the disastrous effect of obstructions to international trade upon the full and stable business recovery of individual nations as well as upon general world prosperity;

Are desirous of abandoning economic conflict and of achieving some measure of economic disarmament;

Are confident that through mutually profitable exchange of goods they themselves and the governments of the other nations of the world may reduce unemployment, increase domestic prices, and improve business conditions in their respective countries; and

Recognize that the existing high trade barriers can be effectively reduced only through simultaneous action by the nations of the world;

The Seventh International Conference of American States

Resolves:

That the governments of the American Republics will promptly undertake to promote trade among their respective peoples and other nations and to reduce high trade barriers through the negotiation of comprehensive bilateral reciprocity treaties based upon mutual con cessions; and

That the governments of the American Republics do each subscribe, and call upon other governments of the world to subscribe, to the policy and undertaking, through simultaneous action of the principal nations, of gradually reducing tariffs and other barriers to mutually profitable movements of goods, services, and capital between nations, such policy and undertaking being in words and figures as follows:

That at the earliest practicable date consistent with the exceptions and reservations herein, the subscribing governments, while not neglecting unilateral action, will simultaneously initiate between and among themselves negotiations for the conclusion of bilateral or multilateral agreements for the removal of prohibitions and restrictions and for the reduction of tariff rates to a moderate level. The reservations and exceptions shall apply to the entire undertaking herein and shall expressly include the operation of temporary, emergency, or other extraordinary measures comprising domestic programs, primarily for national economic recovery, now or hereafter in operation in any country party to this undertaking. The object of this undertaking is to assert and maintain the broad economic policy of gradually combining with any existing domestic program a suitable program of international economic cooperation as each nation emerges from serious panic conditions.

The subscribing governments undertake, moreover, that their aim will be substantial reductions of basic trade barriers and liberalization of commercial policy as aforesaid and not merely the removal of temporary and abnormal restrictions and increments imposed for bargaining purposes. They will endeavor in so doing to direct their greatest efforts toward the elimination of those duties and restrictions which retard most severely the normal flow of international trade; for instance, duties or restrictions which completely or almost completely exclude international competition, such as those which restrict the importation of particular commodities to less than three to five per centum of domestic consumption; and also protective duties or restrictions which have been in effect for a considerable period of time without having brought about domestic production equal to fifteen per centum of the total domestic consumption thereof.

As a part of this undertaking they will revive and revise the convention of 1927, or agree upon a new convention, for the abolition of import and export prohibitions and restrictions, together with other general conventions having in view the removal of impediments to commerce, and endeavor to obtain, for all such instruments, acceptance as nearly universal as possible.

The subscribing governments declare that the principle of equality of treatment stands and must continue to stand as the basis of all acceptable commercial policy. Accordingly they undertake that whatever agreements they enter into shall include the most-favored-nation clause in its unconditional and unrestricted form, to be applied to all types of control of international trade, limited only by such exceptions as may be commonly recognized as legitimate, and they undertake that such agreements shall not introduce features which, while possibly providing an immediate advantage for the contracting parties, might react disadvantageously upon world trade as a whole.

The subscribing governments declare further that the most-favored-nation principle enjoins upon states making use of the quota system or other systems for limiting imports, the application of these systems in such a way as to dislocate as little as possible the relative competitive positions naturally enjoyed by the various countries in supplying the articles affected.

With a view to encouraging the development of unified and comprehensive multilateral treaties as a vitally important instrument of trade liberalization, the advantages of which treaties ought not to be open to countries which refuse to confer similar advantages, the subscribing governments declare, and call upon all countries to declare that they will not invoke their right to demand, under the most-favored-nation clause contained in bilateral treaties to which they may be parties, any benefits of multilateral treaties which have as their general purpose the liberalization of international economic relations and which are open to the accession of all countries, provided that such renunciation shall not operate in so far as the country entitled to most-favored-nation treatment in fact reciprocally accords the benefits which it seeks.

For the purpose of carrying out the policy embraced in the foregoing undertaking, the subscribing governments favor the establishment of a permanent international agency which shall closely observe the steps taken by each of them in effecting reductions of trade barriers and which shall upon request furnish information to them regarding the progress made by each in effectuating the aforesaid program.

In consideration of the premises, the governments of the American Republics earnestly call upon the appropriate agencies of the World Monetary and Economic Conference at London, now in recess, promptly to cooperate in bringing this proposal to a favorable conclusion.

(Approved December 16, 1933)

RECOMMENDATION LXXXI: Multilateral Commercial Treaties

Report of the Delegates of the United States of America to the Seventh International Conference of American States, p. 275

THE SEVENTH International Conference of the American States: After deliberating on the proposition of the United States of America relative to multilateral Treaties, which proposition it will deposit with the office of the Pan American Union, and adherence thereto shall be open to all countries,

Recommends:

To the Governments convened in this Conference the study of multilateral commercial treaties and of the possibility of adopting a universal agreement, or at least one which shall be accepted by the nations of greatest economic power. This agreement shall include stipulations by which the States shall be obliged not to invoke the unconditional most-favored-nation clause in bilateral treaties without assuming the corresponding obligations.

The proposition of the Delegation of the United States, to which the recommendation for study refers, is as follows:

The Governments of the Republics convened at the Seventh International Conference of American States, desirous of encouraging the development of economic relations among the peoples of the world by means of multilateral conventions, the benefits of which ought not to inure to countries which refuse to assume their obligations; and desirous also, while reaffirming as a fundamental doctrine the policy of equality of treatment, to develop such policy in a manner harmonious with the development of general economic rapprochement in which every country shall do its part; have decided to enter into an agreement for those purposes, as set forth in the following articles:

ARTICLE 1

The High Contracting Parties, with respect to their relations with one another, will not, except as provided in Article 2 hereof, invoke the obligations of the most-favored-nation clause for the purpose of obtaining advantages enjoyed by the parties to multilateral economic conventions of general applicability, which include a trade area of substantial size, have as their objective the liberalization and promotion of international trade or other international economic intercourse, and are open to adoption by all countries.

ARTICLE 2

Nothwithstanding the stipulations of Article 1, the High Contracting Parties may demand the fulfillment of the most-favored-nation clause in so far as each respectively accords in fact the benefits required by the economic agreement the advantage of which it claims.

ARTICLE 3

The present agreement is operative on the date hereof among those Governments on behalf of which it is signed. Thereafter it shall be open to signature on behalf of any State and shall become operative with respect to each such State on the date of signing thereby. It shall remain operative indefinitely, but any Party may terminate its own obligations hereunder three months after it has given to the Pan American Union notice of such intention.

ARTICLE 4

This agreement is a single document in Spanish, Portuguese, French and English, all of which texts are equally authoritative. It shall be deposited with the Pan American Union, which is charged with the duty of keeping it open for signature or re-signature indefinitely, and with transmitting certified copies, with invitations to become parties, to all of the states of the world. In performing this function, the Pan American Union may invoke the assistance of any of its members signatory hereto.

(Approved December 24, 1933)

RESOLUTION LXXIV: International Responsibility of the State

Report of the Delegates of the United States of America to the Seventh International Conference of American States, p. 270

THE SEVENTH International Conference of American States
Resolves:

1. To recommend that the study of the entire problem relating to the international responsibility of the state, with special reference to responsibility for manifest denial or unmotivated delay of justice be handed over to the agencies of codification instituted by the International Conferences of American States and that their studies be coordinated with the work of codification being done under the auspices of the League of Nations.

2. That, notwithstanding this, it reaffirms once more, as a principle of international law, the civil equality of the foreigner with the national as the maximum limit of protection to which he may aspire in the positive legislations of the states.

3. Reaffirms equally that diplomatic protection cannot be initiated in favor of foreigners unless they exhaust all legal measures established by the laws of the country before which the action is begun. There are excepted those cases of manifest denial or unreasonable delay of justice which shall always be interpreted restrictively, that is, in favor of the sovereignty of the State in which the difference may have arisen. Should no agreement on said difference be reached through diplomatic channels, within a reasonable period of time, the matter shall then be referred to arbitration.

4. The Conference recognizes, at the same time, that these general principles may be the subject of definition or limitations and that the agencies charged with planning the codification shall take into account the necessity of definition and limitations in formulating the rules applicable to the various cases which may be provided for.

(Approved December 24, 1933)

CONVENTION on the Teaching of History

Report of the Delegates of the United States of America to the Seventh International Conference of American States, p. 145

THE GOVERNMENTS represented in the Seventh International Conference of American States, considering:

That it is necessary to complement the political and juridical organization of peace with the moral disarmament of peoples, by means of the revision of text books in use in the several countries;

That the need of effecting this corrective labor has been recognized by the Pan American Scientific Congress of Lima (1924), the National History Congress of Montevideo (1928), the Congress of History of Buenos Aires (1929), the Congress of History of Bogota (1930), the Second National History Congress of Rio de Janeiro (1931), the American University Congress of Montevideo (1931), and by the adoption of measures in this respect by several American Governments, and that, the United States of Brazil, and the Argentine and Uruguayan Republics, evidencing their deep desire for international peace and understanding, have recently subscribed to agreements for the revision of their text books of History and Geography;

Have appointed as their plenipotentiaries:

[Here follow the names of the plenipotentiaries of Honduras, the United States of America, El Salvador, the Dominican Republic, Haiti, Argentina, Venezuela, Uruguay, Paraguay, Mexico, Panama, Bolivia, Guatemala, Brazil, Ecuador, Nicaragua, Colombia, Chile, Peru, and Cuba.]

Who, after having exchanged their Full Powers, which were found in good and proper form, have agreed to the following:

ARTICLE 1

To revise the text books adopted for instruction in their respective countries, with the object of eliminating from them whatever might tend to arouse in the immature mind of youth aversion to any American Country.

ARTICLE 2

To review periodically the text books adopted for instruction on the several subjects, in order to harmonize them with most recent statistical and general information so that they shall convey the most accurate data respecting the wealth and productive capacity of the American Republics.

ARTICLE 3

To found an "Institute for the Teaching of History" of the American Republics, to be located in Buenos Aires, and to be responsible for the coordination and inter-American realization of the purposes described, and whose ends shall be to recommend:

a) That each American Republic foster the teaching of the history of the others,

b) That greater attention be given to the history of Spain, Portugal, Great Britain and France, and of any other non-American country in respect to matters of major interest to the history of America.

c) That the nations endeavor to prevent the inclusion, in educational programs and handbooks on History, of unfriendly references to other countries or of errors that may have been dispelled by historical criticism.

d) That the bellicose emphasis in handbooks on History be lessened and that the study of the culture of the peoples, and the universal development of civilization of each country made by foreigners and by other nations, be urged.

e) That annoying comparisons between national and foreign historical characters, and also belittling and offensive coments [sic] regarding other countries, be deleted from text books.

f) That the narration of victories over other nations shall not be used as the basis for a deprecatory estimate of the defeated people.

g) That facts in the narration of wars and battles whose results may have been adverse, be not appraised with hatred, or distorted.

h) That emphasis be placed upon whatever may contribute constructively to understanding and cooperation among the American countries.

In the fulfillment of the important educational functions committed to it, the "Institute for the Teaching of History" shall maintain close affiliation with the Pan American Institute of Geography and History, established as an organ of cooperation between the Geographic and Historic Institutes of the Americas, of Mexico City, and with other bodies whose ends are similar to its own.

ARTICLE 4

The present Convention shall not affect obligations previously entered into by the High Contracting Parties by virtue of international agreements.

ARTICLE 5

The present Convention shall be ratified by the High Contracting Parties in conformity with their respective constitutional procedures. The Minister of Foreign Affairs of the Republic of Uruguay shall transmit authentic certified copies to the governments for the aforementioned purpose of ratification. The instrument of ratification shall be deposited in the archives of the Pan American Union in Washington, which shall notify the signatory governments of said deposit. Such notification shall be considered as an exchange of ratifications.

ARTICLE 6

The present Convention will enter into force between the High Contracting Parties in the order in which they deposit their respective ratifications.

ARTICLE 7

The present Convention shall remain in force indefinitely but may be denounced by means of one year's notice given to the Pan American Union, which shall transmit it to the other signatory governments. After the expiration of this period the Convention shall cease in its effects as regards the party which denounces but shall remain in effect for the remaining High Contracting Parties.

ARTICLE 8

The present Convention shall be open for the adherence and accession of the States which are not signatories. The corresponding instruments shall be deposited in the archives of the Pan American Union which shall communicate them to the other High Contracting Parties.

It witness whereof, the following Plenipotentiaries have signed this Convention in Spanish, English, Portuguese and French and hereunto affix their respective seals in the city of Montevideo, Republic of Uruguay, this 26th day of December, 1933.

STATEMENT OF THE DELEGATION OF THE UNITED STATES OF AMERICA

The United States heartily applauds this initiative and desires to record its deep sympathy with every measure which tends to encourage the teaching of the history of the American nations, and particularly the purification of the texts of history books, correcting errors, freeing them from bias and prejudice, and eliminating matter which might tend to engender hatred between nations. The Delegation of the United States of America desires to point out, however, that the system of education in the United States, differs from that in other countries of the Americas in that it lies largely outside the sphere of activity of the Federal Government and is supported and administered by the State and Municipal authorities and by private institutions and individuals. The Conference will appreciate, therefore, the constitutional inability of this Delegation to sign the above Convention.

[Signatures]

CONVENTION on Rights and Duties of States

Report of the Delegates of the United States of America to the Seventh International Conference of American States, p. 165. The convention was ratified by the President of the United States June 29, 1934, with the reservation made by the U.S. Delegation

THE GOVERNMENTS represented in the Seventh International Conference of American States:

Wishing to conclude a Convention on Rights and Duties of States, have appointed the following Plenipotentiaries:

(Here follow the names of the plenipotentiaries of Honduras, the United States of America, El Salvador, the Dominican Republic,

Haiti, Argentina, Venezuela, Uruguay, Paraguay, Mexico, Panama, Bolivia, Guatemala, Brazil, Ecuador, Nicaragua, Colombia, Chile, Peru, and Cuba.)

Who, after having exhibited their Full Powers, which were found to be in good and due order, have agreed upon the following:

ARTICLE 1

The state as a person of international law should possess the following qualifications: *a*) a permanent population; *b*) a defined territory; *c*) government; and *d*) capacity to enter into relations with the other States.

ARTICLE 2

The federal state shall constitute a sole person in the eyes of international law.

ARTICLE 3

The political existence of the state is independent of recognition by the other states. Even before recognition the state has the right to defend its integrity and independence, to provide for its conservation and prosperity, and consequently to organize itself as it sees fit, to legislate upon its interests, administer its services, and to define the jurisdiction and competence of its courts.

The exercise of these rights has no other limitation than the exercise of the rights of other states according to international law.

ARTICLE 4

States are juridically equal, enjoy the same rights, and have equal capacity in their exercise. The rights of each one do not depend upon the power which it possesses to assure its exercise, but upon the simple fact of its existence as a person under international law.

ARTICLE 5

The fundamental rights of states are not susceptible of being affected in any manner whatsoever.

ARTICLE 6

The recognition of a state merely signifies that the state which recognizes it accepts the personality of the other with all the rights and duties determined by international law. Recognition is unconditional and irrevocable.

ARTICLE 7

The recognition of a state may be express or tacit. The latter results from any act which implies the intention of recognizing the new state.

ARTICLE 8

No state has the right to intervene in the internal or external affairs of another.

ARTICLE 9

The jurisdiction of states within the limits of national territory applies to all the inhabitants.

Nationals and foreigners are under the same protection of the law and the national authorities and the foreigners may not claim rights other or more extensive than those of the nationals.

ARTICLE 10

The primary interest of states is the conservation of peace. Differences of any nature which arise between them should be settled by recognized pacific methods.

ARTICLE 11

The contracting states definitely establish as the rule of their conduct the precise obligation not to recognize territorial acquisitions or special advantages which have been obtained by force whether this consists in the employment of arms, in threatening diplomatic representations, or in any other effective coercive measure. The territory of a state is inviolable and may not be the object of military occupation nor of other measures of force imposed by another state directly or indirectly or for any motive whatever even temporarily.

ARTICLE 12

The present Convention shall not affect obligations previously entered into by the High Contracting Parties by virtue of international agreements.

ARTICLE 13

The present Convention shall be ratified by the High Contracting Parties in conformity with their respective constitutional procedures. The Minister of Foreign Affairs of the Republic of Uruguay shall transmit authentic certified copies to the governments for the aforementioned purpose of ratification. The instrument of ratification shall be deposited in the archives of the Pan American Union in Washington, which shall notify the signatory governments of said deposit. Such notification shall be considered as an exchange of ratifications.

ARTICLE 14

The present Convention will enter into force between the High' Contracting Parties in the order in which they deposit their respective ratifications.

ARTICLE 15

The present Convention shall remain in force indefinitely but may be denounced by means of one year's notice given to the Pan American Union, which shall transmit it to the other signatory governments. After the expiration of this period the Convention shall cease in its effects as regards the party which denounces but shall remain in effect for the remaining High Contracting Parties.

ARTICLE 16

The present Convention shall be open for the adherence and accession of the States which are not signatories. The corresponding instruments shall be deposited in the archives of the Pan American Union which shall communicate them to the other High Contracting Parties.

In witness whereof, the following Plenipotentiaries have signed this Convention in Spanish, English, Portuguese and French and hereunto affix their respective seals in the city of Montevideo, Republic of Uruguay, this 26th day of December, 1933.

RESERVATIONS

The Delegation of the United States of America, in signing the Convention on the Rights and Duties of States, does so with the express reservation presented to the Plenary Session of the Conference on December 22, 1933, which reservation reads as follows:

The Delegation of the United States, in voting "yes" on the final vote on this committee recommendation and proposal, makes the same reservation to the eleven articles of the project or proposal that the United States Delegation made to the first ten articles during the final vote in the full Commission, which reservation is in words as follows:

The policy and attitude of the United States Government toward every important phase of international relationships in this hemisphere could scarcely be made more clear and definite than they have been made by both word and action especially since March 4. I have no disposition therefore to indulge in any repetition or rehearsal of these acts and utterances and shall not do so. Every observing person must by this time thoroughly understand that under the Roosevelt Administration the United States Government is as much opposed as any other government to interference with the freedom, the sovereignty, or other internal affairs or processes of the governments of other nations.

In addition to numerous acts and utterances in connection with the carrying out of these doctrines and policies, President Roosevelt, during recent weeks, gave out a public statement expressing his disposition to open negotiations with the Cuban Government for the purpose of dealing with the treaty which has existed since 1903. I feel safe in undertaking to say that under our support of the general principle of non-intervention as has been suggested, no government need fear any intervention on the part of the United States under the Roosevelt Administration. I think it unfortunate that during the brief period of this Conference there is apparently not time within which to prepare interpretations and definitions of these fundamental terms that are embraced in the report. Such definitions and interpretations would enable every government to proceed in a uniform way without any difference of opinion or of interpretations. I hope that at the earliest possible date such very important work will be done. In the meantime in case of differences of interpretations and also until they (the proposed doctrines and principles) can be worked out and codified for the common use of every government, I desire to say that the United States Government in all of its international associations and relationships and conduct will follow scrupulously the doctrines and policies which it has pursued since March 4 which are embodied in the different addresses of President Roosevelt since that time and in the recent peace address of myself on the 15th day of December before this Conference and in the law of nations as generally recognized and accepted.

The delegates of Brazil and Peru recorded the following private vote with regard to article 11: "That they accept the doctrine in principle but that they do not consider it codifiable because there are some countries which have not yet signed the Anti-War Pact of Rio de Janeiro of which this doctrine is a part and therefore it does not yet constitute positive international law suitable for codification."

[Signatures]

ADDITIONAL PROTOCOL to the General Convention of Inter-American Conciliation

Report of the Delegates of the United States of America to the Seventh International Conference of American States, p. 162. The protocol was ratified by the President of the United States June 29, 1934

THE HIGH CONTRACTING PARTIES of the General Convention of Inter-American Conciliation of the 5th of January, 1929, convinced of the undeniable advantage of giving a permanent character to the Commissions of Investigation and Conciliation to which Article 2 of said Convention refers, agree to add to the aforementioned Convention the following and additional Protocol.

ARTICLE 1

Each country signatory to the Treaty signed in Santiago, Chile, the 3rd of May, 1923, shall name, as soon as possible, by means of a bilateral agreement which shall be recorded in a simple exchange of notes with each one of the other signatories of the aforementioned Treaty, those members of the various commissions provided for in Article 4 of said Treaty. The commissions so named shall have a permanent character and shall be called Commissions of Investigation and Conciliation.

ARTICLE 2

Any of the contracting parties may replace the members which have been designated, whether they be nationals or foreigners; but, at the same time, the substitute shall be named. In case the substitution is not made, the replacement shall not be effective.

ARTICLE 3

The commissions organized in fulfillment of Article 3 of the aforementioned Treaty of Santiago, Chile, shall be called Permanent Diplomatic Commissions of Investigation and Conciliation.

ARTICLE 4

To secure the immediate organization of the commissions mentioned in the first Article hereof, the High Contracting Parties engage themselves to notify the Pan American Union at the time of the deposit of the ratification of the present Additional Protocol in the Ministry of Foreign Relations of the Republic of Chile, the names of the two members whose designation they are empowered to make by Article 4 of the Convention of Santiago, Chile, and said members, so named, shall constitute the members of the Commissions which are to be organized with bilateral character in accordance with this Protocol.

ARTICLE 5

It shall be left to the Governing Board of the Pan American Union to initiate measures for bringing about the nomination of the fifth member of each Commission of Investigation and Conciliation in accordance with the stipulation established in Article 4 of the Convention of Santiago, Chile.

ARTICLE 6

In view of the character which this Protocol has as an addition to the Convention of Conciliation of Washington, of January 5, 1929, the provision of Article 16 of said Convention shall be applied thereto.

IN WITNESS WHEREOF, the Plenipotentiaries hereinafter indicated, have set their hands and their seals to this Additional Protocol in English, and Spanish, in the city of Montevideo, Republic of Uruguay, this twenty-sixth day of the month of December in the year nineteen hundred and thirty-three.

(Here follow the signatures of plenipotentiaries of the United States of America, Uruguay, Ecuador, and Chile.)

Inter-American Conference for the Maintenance of Peace, at Buenos Aires, December 1–23, 1936

RESOLUTION VI: Codification of International Law

Report of the Delegation of the United States of America to the Inter-American Conference for the Maintenance of Peace, p. 211

CONSIDERING the importance of carrying forward the work of codifying international law and of not permitting the nullification of the beneficial work of the International Commission of American Jurists, as well as that of the Permanent Committees on Codification created by the Sixth International Conference of American States;

Considering the necessity of harmonizing the resolutions on methods of codification adopted at Montevideo and Havana;

Considering that this work, by its very nature, requires constant and continuous preliminary study, and that this can be done only by centralized and permanent agencies;

Considering, that in view of the importance of the Committee of Experts created by the Seventh International Conference of American States, it is more within the scope of that Committee to undertake the work of revision and coordination, but that it is not possible for that Committee to meet for the length of time and as frequently as necessary to carry on the slow work of elaborating preliminary projects of codification,

The Inter-American Conference for the Maintenance of Peace
Resolves:

1. To re-establish the Permanent Committees created by the Sixth

International Conference of American States, in order that they may undertake the preliminary studies for the codification of international law.

2. That these studies shall be made in the following manner, in view of the recommendations of the Sixth and Seventh International Conferences of American States:

(a) The National Committees on Codification of International Law shall, in their respective countries, undertake studies of the doctrine on the various subjects to be codified, and shall transmit the results thereof to the Permanent Committees on Codification.

(b) The Permanent Committees shall prepare draft conventions and resolutions as bases of discussion and preparatory work for the International Commission of American Jurists.

(c) The studies of the Permanent Committees on Codification shall be transmitted, in ample time, to the members of the Committee of Experts, at Washington, who will meet to revise and coordinate them.

(d) Upon completion of the work of general revision of the studies of the Permanent Committees, the Committee of Experts, at Washington, shall transmit all such preparatory studies with a detailed report to the Pan American Union, for transmission to the Governments of the American Republics and ultimate submission for discussion and consideration by the International Commission of American Jurists. The Pan American Union, whenever it is deemed advisable but at least once a year, shall inform the Governments of the American Republics of the progress made in the work of codification. The Pan American Union shall also prepare a report concerning the rules, principles and standards and submit it to the Committee of Experts.

(e) The Committee of Experts may act by a majority of the members present at a meeting, provided, however, that the two great juridical systems of the hemisphere are represented thereat.

(Approved December 16, 1936)

RECOMMENDATION AND RESOLUTION XLVI: Restrictions on International Trade

Report of the Delegates of the United States of America to the Inter-American Conference for the Maintenance of Peace, p. 242

CONSIDERING:

That the development of international trade unquestionably contributes to the progress and well-being of nations;

That closer commercial relationships contribute to drawing peoples together and create bonds of greater solidarity between the countries which maintain them; and that one of the most justifiable desires of the American Republics has always been to strengthen in every way the bonds of peace which unite them;

That the greater the interchange, the greater also will be the possibility for each country to specialize in those collective activities which will assure to it a maximum return with a minimum effort;

That this trade is being impeded by a great number of excessive or unreasonable restrictions and prohibitions, which have considerably diminished its volume;

That such restrictions and prohibitions give rise to discontent and uncertainty as well as to fear and disputes among all countries;

That it is essential, at this time, as a preliminary step toward eliminating and gradually reducing said prohibitions and restrictions, to prevent increase in the obstacles which hinder international trade and render it more difficult; and

Having in mind the recommendations approved in the International Economic Conference held under the auspices of the League of Nations in 1927, and the conclusions of the subsequent Conferences of that organization; especially with respect to the effects of the "clearing" agreements as established by the Economic Committee of Geneva in 1935; and ratifying the declaration of principles approved in the Inter-American Conference of Montevideo in 1933 and the resolution adopted in the Pan American Commercial Conference of Buenos Aires in 1935;

The Inter-American Conference for the Maintenance of Peace
Recommends:

1. That the American States abstain, so far as possible, from raising or augmenting tariff barriers and every other kind of restrictions which directly or indirectly hinder international trade and resulting payments;

2. That immediately, and to the extent that the several national economies permit, a policy of abolishing and gradually reducing the said excessive or unreasonable prohibitions and restrictions upon international commerce be undertaken and carried forward by each of the said States, through the conclusion or revision of bilateral economic or commercial Agreements and Treaties and through unilateral action by each country;

3. That these recommendations become effective as early as possible in order that the Eighth Inter-American Conference to be held soon in Lima, and the Economic Financial Conference, which is to be held in Santiago, Chile, may mark a definite step towards a system of greater freedom in international commerce; and

Resolves:

4. To invite all Governments which do not participate in this Conference to follow the policy proposed in the present recommendation.

(With the reservation by El Salvador to the effect that due to its special geographic and economic situation it cannot comply immediately with the doctrine contained in the above recommendation while the factors obtain which require it to maintain the existing dispositions and organization. See minutes of the Fifth Committee, meeting of December 17, published in the Diario of the Conference December 21, 1936).

(Approved December 21, 1936.)

RECOMMENDATION XLIV: Equality of Treatment in International Trade

Report of the Delegates of the United States of America to the Inter-American Conference for the Maintenance of Peace, p. 240

WHEREAS:

The Governments of the American Republics meeting in Buenos Aires are convinced that the growth of international trade can serve to strengthen greatly the foundations of peace by improving the material welfare and contentment of nations and by drawing them together in mutual understanding and interest; but

Recognize that these important benefits of trade will only be achieved if governmental policies which regulate trade conform to the spirit of equity and neighborliness; and

Recognize that, as a world condition which has affected all countries, discriminatory practices which impair the advantages naturally enjoyed by various countries in international trade tend to give rise to dissatisfaction and ill-will and, thereby, to frustrate the peaceful ends which trade should serve;

The Inter-American Conference for the Maintenance of Peace

Recommends:

That the Governments of the American Republics reaffirm the statement enunciated by the Seventh International Conference of American States that "the principle of equality of treatment stands and must continue to stand as the basis of all acceptable commercial policy";

That each Government declare its determination to bend every effort, having in mind the different national economies, towards the objective of enforcing in all the phases of its general commercial policy the peaceful and equitable principle of equality of treatment, and recommends that the Governments of all countries adopt this principle in their commercial policies, and in accordance therewith suppress as soon as possible all discriminatory practices including those arising in connection with import-license systems, exchange control, and bilateral clearing and compensation agreements.

(With the reservation by El Salvador to the effect that due to its special geographic and economic situation it cannot comply immediately with the doctrine contained in the above recommendation while the factors obtain which require it to maintain the existing dispositions and organization. See minutes of the Fifth Committee, meeting of December 17, published in the Diario of the Conference December 21, 1936).

(Approved December 21, 1936)

RECOMMENDATION XXXV: Pecuniary Claims

Report of the Delegates of the United States of America to the Inter-American Conference for the Maintenance of Peace, p. 232

WHEREAS:

This topic, which has for its object the formulation of principles tending toward the elimination of force and of diplomatic intervention in cases of pecuniary claims, was submitted for study to the Committee on Juridical Problems; and

In spite of repeated efforts made in the Committee, during the course of various sessions devoted to its examination, as well as in the Subcommittee appointed for the same purpose, it was not possible to secure such unanimity of opinion as might serve as the basis for a Convention between the American Republics; and

The Commission devoted earnest attention to the matter of the collection of public or contractual debts and other claims of an exclusively pecuniary character, leaving for another opportunity the study of Diplomatic Protection for nationals and for legal entities, as well as that of the international responsibility of the State; and

The original project of the Argentine Delegation on this subject having set forth the matter in the first article as follows:

"The High Contracting Powers pledge themselves without any reservations, not to employ armed force, or resort to diplomatic intervention for the collection of public or contractual debts or to support claims of an exclusively pecuniary origin"; and

Having heard the respective Subcommittee the Reporter prepared an article which by itself could have been used to give contractual form to the prohibition intended, and which read:

"The High Contracting Parties pledge themselves without any reservations not to employ armed force, nor to resort to other coercive measures, nor to accept them for the collection of public or contractual debts; nor to support claims of exclusively pecuniary origin"; and

The Commission later prepared two articles for the purpose required by the statement of the topic, but proceeding further to the development of the matter in reference to the use of arbitration, making it compulsory in the following form:

"1. The High Contracting Parties pledge themselves, without any reservations, not to use armed force nor to resort to intervention, nor to accept it for the collection of public or contractual debts, nor to support claims of exclusively pecuniary origin.

"2. If after diplomatic negotiations have been exhausted it has not been possible satisfactorily to settle the matter, the debtor may not refuse to submit the case to arbitration," and

The two proposed articles provoked the announcement on the part of some delegations that they would formulate various reservations in case any such Convention should be drawn up;

As became evident during the course of the deliberations, the reservations referred to would tend fundamentally to leave the opinion established that arbitration could not be resorted to except in the case where after having sought and exhausted local jurisdiction a denial of justice was alleged; and

The Committee, convinced of the slight value of a Convention burdened with reservations, has believed it preferable to limit their tasks to the recommendation that the technical organizations at our disposal make a study of coordination, in order that the matter, with such a valuable antecedent, may be submitted to the consideration of the next International Conference of American States;

The Inter-American Conference for the Maintenance of Peace

Recommends:

1.–That in view of the above-mentioned antecedents, and of the Minutes of the Sessions of the Committee on Juridical Problems, a work of coordination and a study of the principles of the subject considered in the said sessions, be undertaken by the Committee of Experts (created by an agreement of the Conference of Montevideo), and that a Project of Convention be submitted to the Eighth International Conference of American States.

2.–That the above-mentioned Conference proceed to the study of the subject which has given rise to this recommendation.

(Approved December 21, 1936)

RESOLUTION XXXIII: Limitation of Armaments

Report of the Delegates of the United States of America to the Inter-American Conference for the Maintenance of Peace, p. 231

RECOGNIZING the evident importance and significance of the limitation of armaments as an effective means of perfecting any international action directed toward the maintenance of peace;

In the certainty that all the American Nations exercise due respect for the sovereignty of other States, repudiate measures of force and violence and base their procedures upon the standards of international justice and law; and

Recognizing the necessity that the organizations and armaments of national defence shall be sufficient only to guarantee the internal security of the States and their effective protection in case of foreign aggression,

The Inter-American Conference for the Maintenance of Peace
Resolves:

To recommend that all Governments, which consider themselves in a position to do so, shall conclude general or bilateral agreements to limit, or to limit further, their armaments to the greatest possible extent, within the requirements of internal order, and the justified defence of their sovereignty.

(The Paraguayan Delegation gives its vote of approval with the following reservation: Paraguay does not accept limitation of armaments beyond that stated in its bilateral agreements. Notice is given at the same time that there is a protocol now in force, signed between Paraguay and Bolivia, in which a limitation of armaments is expressly declared).

(Approved December 21, 1936)

RESOLUTION XXXIV: Humanization of War

Report of the Delegates of the United States of America to the Inter-American Conference for the Maintenance of Peace, p. 232

REAFFIRMING once more the principles on which are based the various instruments of peace recommended by previous Conventions, and interpreting the moral principles and humanitarian sentiments which form the conscience of the peoples of America,

The Inter-American Conference for the Maintenance of Peace
Resolves:

1. To declare the formal repudiation of war as a means to settle differences between States.

2. To proscribe the use of chemical elements whose use in war may cause cruelly unnecessary damage.

3. To exclude civil populations as far as possible from the effects of international conflagrations; and

4. To recommend to the American Governments that in the pacts of limitation of armaments which they may sign they include stipulations of a humanitarian character such as those rejecting the poisoning of water, the dissemination of pathogenic bacteria, the use of poisonous gas, the use of inflammable liquids or substances, etc., in accordance with maximum possibilities calculated by their technical representations.

(Approved December 21, 1936)

DECLARATION XXVII: *Principles of Inter-American Solidarity and Co-operation*

Report of the Delegates of the United States of America to the Inter-American Conference for the Maintenance of Peace, p. 227

THE GOVERNMENTS of the American Republics, having considered:

That they have a common likeness in their democratic form of government and their common ideals of peace and justice, manifested in the several Treaties and Conventions which they have signed for the purpose of constituting a purely American system tending towards the preservation of peace, the proscription of war, the harmonious development of their commerce and of their cultural aspirations in the various fields of political, economic, social, scientific and artistic activities;

That the existence of continental interests obliges them to maintain solidarity of principles as the basis of the life of the relations of each to every other American nation;

That Pan Americanism, as a principle of American International Law, by which is understood a moral union of all of the American Republics in defence of their common interests based upon the most perfect equality and reciprocal respect for their rights of autonomy, independence and free development, requires the proclamation of principles of American International Law; and

That it is necessary to consecrate the principle of American solidarity in all non-continental conflicts, especially since those limited to the American Continent should find a peaceful solution by the means established by the Treaties and Conventions now in force or in the instruments hereafter to be executed,

The Inter-American Conference for the Maintenance of Peace *Declares:*

1. That the American Nations, true to their republican institutions, proclaim their absolute juridical liberty, their unqualified respect for their respective sovereignties and the existence of a common democracy throughout America;

2. That every act susceptible of disturbing the peace of America affects each and every one of them, and justifies the initiation of the procedure of consultation provided for in the Convention for the Maintenance, Preservation and Reestablishment of Peace, signed at this Conference; and

3. That the following principles are accepted by the American community of Nations:

(a) Proscription of territorial conquest and that, in consequence, no acquisition made through violence shall be recognized;

(b) Intervention by one State in the internal or external affairs of another State is condemned;

(c) Forcible collection of pecuniary debts is illegal; and

(d) Any difference or dispute between the American nations, whatever its nature or origin, shall be settled by the methods of conciliation, or unrestricted arbitration, or through operation of international justice.

(Approved December 21, 1936)

TREATY on Good Offices and Mediation

Department of State, Treaty Series, No. 925. The treaty was ratified by the President of the United States, July 15, 1937

THE GOVERNMENTS represented at the Inter-American Conference for the Maintenance of Peace;

Considering that, notwithstanding the pacts which have been concluded between them, it is desirable to facilitate, even more, recourse to peaceful methods for the solution of controversies,

Have resolved to celebrate a treaty of Good Offices and Mediation between the American Countries, and to this end have named the following Plenipotentiaries:

[Names of Plenipotentiaries]

Who, after having deposited their full powers, found to be in good and due form, have agreed as follows:

ARTICLE 1

When a controversy arises between them, that cannot be settled by the usual diplomatic means, the High Contracting Parties may have recourse to the good offices or mediation of an eminent citizen of any of the other American countries, preferably chosen from a general list made up in accordance with the following article.

ARTICLE 2

To prepare the aforementioned list, each Government, as soon as the present treaty is ratified, shall name two citizens selected from among the most eminent by reason of their high character and juridical learning.

The designations shall immediately be communicated to the Pan American Union, which shall prepare the list and shall forward copies thereof to the contracting parties.

ARTICLE 3

According to the hypothesis set forth in Article 1, the countries in controversy shall, by common agreement, select one of the persons named on this list, for the purposes indicated in this treaty.

The person selected shall name the place where, under his chairmanship, one duly authorized representative of each of the parties shall meet in order to seek a peaceful and equitable solution of the difference.

If the parties are unable to agree concerning the selection of the person lending his good offices or mediation, each one shall choose one of those named on the list. The two citizens chosen in this way shall select, from among the names listed, a third person who shall undertake the functions referred to, endeavoring, in so far as possible, to make a choice that shall be acceptable to both parties.

ARTICLE 4

The mediator shall determine a period of time, not to exceed six nor be less than three months for the parties to arrive at some peaceful settlement. Should this period expire before the parties have reached some solution, the controversy shall be submitted to the procedure of conciliation provided for in existing inter-American agreements.

ARTICLE 5

During the procedure established in this Treaty each of the interested parties shall provide for its own expense and shall contribute equally to common costs or honoraria.

ARTICLE 6

The present Treaty shall not affect obligations previously entered into by the High Contracting Parties by virtue of international agreements.

ARTICLE 7

The present Treaty shall be ratified by the High Contracting Parties in conformity with their respective constitutional procedures. The original instrument shall be deposited in the Ministry of Foreign Affairs of the Argentine Republic which shall transmit authentic certified copies to the Governments for the aforementioned purpose of ratification. The instruments of ratification shall be deposited in the archives of the Pan American Union in Washington, which shall notify the signatory governments of said deposit. Such notification shall be considered as an exchange of ratifications.

ARTICLE 8

The present Treaty will come into effect between the High Contracting Parties in the order in which they deposit their respective ratifications.

ARTICLE 9

The present Treaty shall remain in effect indefinitely but may be denounced by means of one year's notice given to the Pan American Union, which shall transmit it to the other signatory Governments. After the expiration of this period the Treaty shall cease in its effects as regards the Party which denounces it, but shall remain in effect for the remaining High Contracting Parties.

In witness whereof, the above mentioned Plenipotentiaries sign the present Treaty in English, Spanish, Portuguese and French, and hereunto affix their respective seals, at the City of Buenos Aires, Capital of the Argentine Republic, on the twenty-third day of the month of December, 1936.

[*Signatures*]

TREATY on the Prevention of Controversies

Department of State, Treaty Series No. 924. The treaty was ratified by the President of the United States, July 15, 1937

THE GOVERNMENTS represented at the Inter-American Conference for the Maintenance of Peace,

In order to adopt, in the interest of the maintenance of international peace so far as may be attainable, a preventive system for the consideration of possible causes of future controversies and their settlement by pacific means; and

Convinced that whatever assures and facilitates compliance with the treaties in force constitutes an effective guarantee of international peace,

Have agreed to conclude a treaty and to this effect have named the following plenipotentiaries:

[*Names of Plenipotentiaries*]

Who, after having deposited their full powers, found to be in good and due form, have agreed as follows:

ARTICLE 1

The High Contracting Parties bind themselves to establish permanent bilateral mixed commissions composed of representatives of the signatory governments which shall in fact be constituted, at the request of any of them, and such party shall give notice of such request to the other signatory governments.

Each Government shall appoint its own representative to the said commission, the meetings of which are to be held, alternatively, in the capital city of one and the other Governments represented in each of them. The first meeting shall be held at the seat of the Government which convokes it.

ARTICLE 2

The duty of the aforementioned commissions shall be to study, with the primary object of eliminating them, as far as possible, the causes of future difficulties or controversies; and to propose additional or detailed lawful measures which it might be convenient to take in order to promote, as far as possible, the due and regular application of treaties in force between the respective parties, and also to promote the development of increasingly good relations in all ways between the two countries dealt with in each case.

ARTICLE 3

After each meeting of any of the said preventive Commissions a minute shall be drawn and signed by its members setting out the considerations and decisions thereof and such minute shall be transmitted to the governments represented in the commissions.

ARTICLE 4

The present treaty shall not affect obligations previously entered into by the High Contracting Parties by virtue of international agreements.

ARTICLE 5

The present Treaty shall be ratified by the High Contracting Parties in conformity with their respective constitutional procedures. The original instrument shall be deposited in the Ministry of Foreign Affairs of the Argentine Republic which shall transmit authentic certified copies to the Governments for the aforementioned purpose of ratification. The instruments of ratification shall be deposited in the archives of the Pan American Union in Washington, which shall notify the signatory Governments of said deposit. Such notification shall be considered as an exchange of ratifications.

ARTICLE 6

The present Treaty will come into effect between the High Contracting Parties in the order in which they deposit their respective ratifications.

ARTICLE 7

The present Treaty shall remain in effect indefinitely but may be denounced by means of one year's notice given to the Pan American Union, which shall transmit it to the other signatory governments. After the expiration of this period the Treaty shall cease in its effects as regards the party which denounces it but shall remain in effect for the remaining High Contracting Parties.

In witness whereof, the above mentioned Plenipotentiaries sign the present Treaty in English, Spanish, Portuguese and French and hereunto affix their respective seals, at the City of Buenos Aires, Capital of the Argentine Republic, on the twenty-third day of the month of December, 1936.

[Signatures]

ADDITIONAL PROTOCOL Relative to Non-Intervention
Department of State, Treaty Series, No. 923. The treaty was ratified by the President of the United States, July 15, 1937

THE GOVERNMENTS represented at the Inter-American Conference for the Maintenance of Peace,

Desiring to assure the benefits of peace in their mutual relations and in their relations with all the nations of the earth, and to abolish the practice of intervention; and

Taking into account that the Convention on Rights and Duties of States, signed at the Seventh International Conference of American States, December 26, 1933, solemnly affirmed the fundamental principle that "no State has the right to intervene in the internal or external affairs of another,"

Have resolved to reaffirm this principle through the negotiation of the following Additional Protocol, and to that end they have appointed the Plenipotentiaries hereafter mentioned:

[*Names of Plenipotentiaries*]

Who, after having deposited their full powers, found to be in good and due form, have agreed as follows:

ARTICLE 1

The High Contracting Parties declare inadmissible the intervention of any one of them, directly or indirectly, and for whatever reason, in the internal or external affairs of any other of the Parties.

The violation of the provisions of this Article shall give rise to mutual consultation, with the object of exchanging views and seeking methods of peaceful adjustment.

ARTICLE 2

It is agreed that every question concerning the interpretation of the present Additional Protocol, which it has not been possible to settle through diplomatic channels, shall be submitted to the procedure of conciliation provided for in the agreements in force, or to arbitration, or to judicial settlement.

ARTICLE 3

The present Additional Protocol shall be ratified by the High Contracting Parties in conformity with their respective constitutional procedures. The original instrument and the instruments of ratification shall be deposited in the Ministry of Foreign Affairs of the Argentine Republic which shall communicate the ratification to the other signatories. The Additional Protocol shall come into effect between the High Contracting Parties in the order in which they shall have deposited their ratifications.

ARTICLE 4

The present Additional Protocol shall remain in effect indefinitely but may be denounced by means of one year's notice after the expiration of which period the Protocol shall cease in its effects as regards the party which denounces it but shall remain in effect for the remaining Signatory States. Denunciations shall be addressed to the Government of the Argentine Republic which shall notify them to the other Contracting States.

In witness whereof, the above mentioned Plenipotentiaries sign the present Additional Protocol in English, Spanish, Portuguese and French and hereunto affix their respective seals, at the City of Buenos Aires, Capital of the Argentine Republic, on the twenty-third day of the month of December, nineteen hundred and thirty-six.

[Signatures]

CONVENTION for the Maintenance, Preservation, and Reestablishment of Peace

Department of State, Treaty Series, No. 922. The convention was ratified by the President of the United States July 15, 1937

THE GOVERNMENTS represented at the Inter-American Conference for the Maintenance of Peace,

Considering:

That according to the statement of Franklin D. Roosevelt, the President of the United States, to whose lofty ideals the meeting of this Conference is due, the measures to be adopted by it "would advance the cause of world peace, inasmuch as the agreements which might be reached would supplement and reinforce the efforts of the League of Nations and of all other existing or future peace agencies in seeking to prevent war";

That every war or threat of war affects directly or indirectly all civilized peoples and endangers the great principles of liberty and justice which constitute the American ideal and the standard of American international policy;

That the Treaty of Paris of 1928 (Kellogg-Briand Pact) has been accepted by almost all the civilized states, whether or not members of other peace organizations, and that the Treaty of Non-Aggression and Conciliation of 1933 (Saavedra Lamas Pact signed at Rio de Janeiro) has the approval of the twenty-one American Republics represented in this Conference,

Have resolved to give contractual form to these purposes by concluding the present Convention, to which end they have appointed the Plenipotentiaries hereafter mentioned:

[Names of Plenipotentiaries]

Who, after having deposited their full powers, found to be in good and due form, have agreed as follows:

ARTICLE 1

In the event that the peace of the American Republics is menaced, and in order to coordinate efforts to prevent war, any of the Governments of the American Republics signatory to the Treaty of Paris of 1928 or to the Treaty of Non-Aggression and Conciliation of 1933, or to both, whether or not a member of other peace organizations, shall consult with the other Governments of the American Republics, which, in such event, shall consult together for the purpose of finding and adopting methods of peaceful cooperation.

ARTICLE 2

In the event of war, or a virtual state of war between American States, the Governments of the American Republics represented at this Conference shall undertake without delay the necessary mutual consultations, in order to exchange views and to seek, within the obligations resulting from the pacts above mentioned and from the standards of international morality, a method of peaceful collaboration; and, in the event of an international war outside America which might menace the peace of the American Republics, such consultation shall also take place to determine the proper time and manner in which the signatory states, if they so desire, may eventually cooperate in some action tending to preserve the peace of the American Continent.

ARTICLE 3

It is agreed that any question regarding the interpretation of the present Convention, which it has not been possible to settle through diplomatic channels, shall be submitted to the procedure of conciliation provided by existing agreements, or to arbitration or to judicial settlement.

ARTICLE 4

The present Convention shall be ratified by the High Contracting Parties in conformity with their respective constitutional procedures. The original convention shall be deposited in the Ministry of Foreign Affairs of the Argentine Republic which shall communicate the ratifications to the other signatories. The Convention shall come into effect between the High Contracting Parties in the order in which they have deposited their ratifications.

ARTICLE 5

The present Convention shall remain in effect indefinitely but may be denounced by means of one year's notice, after the expiration of which period the Convention shall cease in its effects as regards the party which denounces it but shall remain in effect for the remaining signatory States. Denunciations shall be addressed to the Government of the Argentine Republic, which shall transmit them to the other contracting States.

In witness whereof, the above mentioned Plenipotentiaries sign the present Convention in English, Spanish, Portuguese and French and hereunto affix their respective seals, at the City of Buenos Aires, Capital of the Argentine Republic, on the twenty-third day of the month of December, nineteen hundred and thirty-six.

[*Signatures*]

CONVENTION for the Promotion of Inter-American Cultural Relations

Department of State, Treaty Series, No. 928. The convention was ratified by the President of the United States, July 15, 1937

THE GOVERNMENTS represented at the Inter-American Conference for the Maintenance of Peace;

Considering that the purpose for which the Conference was called would be advanced by greater mutual knowledge and understanding of the people and institutions of the countries represented and a more consistent educational solidarity on the American continent; and

That such results would be appreciably promoted by an exchange of professors, teachers and students among the American countries, as well as by the encouragement of a closer relationship between unofficial organizations which exert an influence on the formation of public opinion,

Have resolved to conclude a convention for that purpose and to that effect have designated the following plenipotentiaries:

[*Names of Plenipotentiaries*]

Who, after having deposited their Full Powers, found to be in good and due form, have agreed as follows:

ARTICLE 1

Every year each Government shall award to each of two graduate students or teachers of each other country selected in accordance with the procedure established in Article II hereof, a fellowship for the ensuing scholastic year. The awards shall be made after an exchange between the two Governments concerned of the panels referred to in Article II hereof. Each fellowship shall provide tuition and subsidiary expenses and maintenance at an institution of higher learning to be designated by the country awarding the fellowship, through such agency as may seem to it appropriate, in cooperation with the recipient so far as may be practicable. Traveling expenses to and from the designated institution and other incidental expenses shall be met by the recipient or the nominating Government. Furthermore, each Government agrees to encourage, by appropriate means, the interchange of students and teachers of institutions within its territory and those of the other contracting countries, during the usual vacation periods.

ARTICLE 2

Each Government shall have the privilege of nominating and presenting to each other Government on or before the date fixed at the close of this article a panel of the names of five graduate students or teachers together with such information concerning them as the Government awarding the fellowship shall deem necessary, from which panel the latter Government shall select the names of two persons. The same students shall not be nominated for more than two successive years; and, except under unusual circumstances, for more than one year. There shall be no obligation for any country to give consideration to the panel of any other country not nominated and presented on or before the date fixed at the close of this article, and fellowships for which no panel of names is presented on or before the date specified may be awarded to applicants nominated on the panels of any other country but not receiving fellowships. Unless otherwise agreed upon between the countries concerned, the following dates shall prevail:

Countries of South America, November 30th.
All other countries, March 31st.

ARTICLE 3

If for any reason it becomes necessary that a student be repatriated the Government awarding the fellowship may effect the repatriation, at the expense of the nominating Government.

ARTICLE 4

Each High Contracting Party shall communicate to each of the other High Contracting Parties through diplomatic channels, on the first of January of every alternate year, a complete list of the full professors available for exchange service from the outstanding universities, scientific institutions and technical schools of each country. From this list each one of the other High Contracting Parties shall arrange to select a visiting professor who shall either give lectures in various centers, or conduct regular courses of instruction, or pursue special research in some designated institution and who shall in other appropriate ways promote better understanding between the parties cooperating, it being understood, however, that preference shall be given to teaching rather than to research work. The sending Government shall provide the expenses for travel to and from the capital where the exchange professor resides and the maintenance and local travel expenses while carrying out the duties for which the professor was selected. Salaries of the professors shall be paid by the sending country.

ARTICLE 5

The High Contracting Parties agree that each Government shall designate or create an appropriate agency or appoint a special officer, charged with the responsibility of carrying out in the most efficient way possible the obligations assumed by such Government in this Convention.

ARTICLE 6

Nothing in this convention shall be construed by the High Contracting Parties as obligating any one of them to interfere with the independence of its institutions of learning or with the freedom of academic teaching and administration therein.

ARTICLE 7

Regulations concerning details for which it shall appear advisable to provide, shall be framed, in each of the contracting countries, by such agency as may seem appropriate to its Government, and copies of such regulations shall be promptly furnished, through the diplomatic channel, to the Governments of the other High Contracting Parties.

ARTICLE 8

The present Convention shall not affect obligations previously entered into by the High Contracting Parties by virtue of international agreements.

ARTICLE 9

The present Convention shall be ratified by the High Contracting Parties in conformity with their respective constitutional procedures. The original instrument shall be deposited in the Ministry of Foreign Affairs of the Argentine Republic which shall transmit authentic certified copies to the Governments for the aforementioned purpose of ratification. The instruments of ratification shall be deposited in the archives of the Pan American Union in Washington, which shall notify the signatory Governments of said deposit. Such notification shall be considered as an exchange of ratifications.

ARTICLE 10

The present Convention will come into effect between the High Contracting Parties in the order in which they deposit their respective ratifications.

ARTICLE 11

The present Convention shall remain in effect indefinitely but may be denounced by means of one year's notice given to the Pan American Union, which shall transmit it to the other signatory Governments. After the expiration of this period the Convention shall cease in its effects as regards the party which denounces it but shall remain in effect for the remaining High Contracting Parties.

IN WITNESS WHEREOF, the above mentioned Plenipotentiaries sign the present Convention in English, Spanish, Portuguese and French and hereunto affix their respective seals, at the city of Buenos Aires, Capital of the Argentine Republic, on the twenty-third day of the month of December 1936.

[Signatures]

Eighth International Conference of American States, at Lima, December 9–27, 1938

RESOLUTION II: Reduction of Barriers to International Trade

Report of the Delegation of the United States of America to the Eighth International Conference of American States, p. 109

CONSIDERING:

That the full economic development of nations requires the greatest possible volume of mutually profitable international trade;

That such a volume of trade cannot be developed while excessive barriers exist whether in the form of (*a*) unreasonably high tariffs; (*b*) quotas, licenses, exchange controls, and other types of quantitative restriction; (*c*) methods of administering commercial, exchange and monetary policies which impair the maintenance of complete equality of commercial opportunity as between all foreign suppliers;

That all such obstacles to trade create unemployment, lower standards of living, limit opportunities for economic advancement, obstruct the fulfillment of broad social programs, divert trade into uneconomic channels and tend to create international friction and ill-will; and

That the American Republics have at previous conferences expressed their support of measures intended to halt further increases in, and to bring about the persistent elimination of, unreasonable and excessive barriers of all kinds to international trade,

The Eighth International Conference of American States
Resolves:

1. To reaffirm the declarations of the Seventh International Conference of American States at Montevideo and the Conference for the Maintenance of Peace at Buenos Aires calling upon the American Governments to reduce, to the greatest extent found possible, all existing types of restrictions upon international trade.

2. To endorse the negotiation of trade agreements, embodying the principle of equality of treatment, as the most beneficial and effective method of extending and facilitating international trade; and
Recommends:

1. That the Governments of the American Republics substitute, as rapidly as possible, reasonable tariffs in lieu of other forms of trade

restrictions, inasmuch as experience has shown that such tariffs tend in general to be less restrictive and more susceptible of administration on the basis of most-favored-nation treatment than are any of the other forms of control over trade and payments.

2. That they reduce, by mutual agreement or otherwise, administrative and technical formalities in connection with the importation of goods to the minimum required for the adequate enforcement of the customs laws.

3. That they proceed, as vigorously as possible, with the negotiation of trade agreements, embodying the principle of non-discrimination.

4. That they make every effort, by whatever appropriate means are open to each of them, to encourage other nations to adopt, in the conduct of their commercial policies, the methods and principles recommended above.

(Approved December 16, 1938)

DECLARATION CIX: Principles of the Solidarity of America (the "Declaration of Lima")

Report of the Delegation of the United States of America to the Eighth International Conference of American States, p. 189

THE EIGHTH International Conference of American States
Considering:

That the peoples of America have achieved spiritual unity through the similarity of their republican institutions, their unshakeable will for peace, their profound sentiment of humanity and tolerance, and through their absolute adherence to the principles of international law, of the equal sovereignty of States and of individual liberty without religious or racial prejudices;

That on the basis of such principles and will, they seek and defend the peace of the continent and work together in the cause of universal concord;

That respect for the personality, sovereignty, and independence of each American State constitutes the essence of international order sustained by continental solidarity, which historically has been expressed and sustained by declarations and treaties in force; and

That the Inter-American Conference for the Maintenance of Peace, held at Buenos Aires, approved on December 21, 1936, the Declaration of the Principles of Inter-American Solidarity and Cooperation, and approved, on December 23, 1936, the Protocol of Non-intervention,

The Governments of the American States
Declare:

First. That they reaffirm their continental solidarity and their purpose to collaborate in the maintenance of the principles upon which the said solidarity is based.

Second. That faithful to the above-mentioned principles and to their absolute sovereignty, they reaffirm their decision to maintain them and to defend them against all foreign intervention or activity that may threaten them.

Third. And in case the peace, security or territorial integrity of any American Republic is thus threatened by acts of any nature that may impair them, they proclaim their common concern and their determination to make effective their solidarity, coordinating their respective sovereign wills by means of the procedure of consultation, established by conventions in force and by declarations of the Inter-American Conferences, using the measures which in each case the circumstances may make advisable. It is understood that the Governments of the American Republics will act independently in their individual capacity, recognizing fully their juridical equality as sovereign states.

Fourth. That in order to facilitate the consultations established in this and other American peace instruments, the Ministers for Foreign Affairs of the American Republics, when deemed desirable and at the initiative of any one of them, will meet in their several capitals by rotation and without protocolary character. Each Government may, under special circumstances or for special reasons, designate a representative as a substitute for its Minister for Foreign Affairs.

Fifth. This Declaration shall be known as the "Declaration of Lima."

(Approved December 24, 1938)

DECLARATION CX: *American Principles*

Report of the Delegation of the United States of America to the Eighth International Conference of American States, p. 190

WHEREAS:

The need for keeping alive the fundamental principles of relations among nations was never greater than today; and

Each State is interested in the preservation of world order under law, in peace with justice, and in the social and economic welfare of mankind,

The Governments of the American Republics

Resolve:

To proclaim, support and recommend, once again, the following principles, as essential to the achievement of the aforesaid objectives:

1. The intervention of any State in the internal or external affairs of another is inadmissible.

2. All differences of an international character should be settled by peaceful means.

3. The use of force as an instrument of national or international policy is proscribed.

4. Relations between States should be governed by the precepts of international law.

5. Respect for and the faithful observance of treaties constitute the indispensable rule for the development of peaceful relations between States, and treaties can only be revised by agreement of the contracting parties.

6. Peaceful collaboration between representatives of the various States and the development of intellectual interchange among their peoples are conducive to an understanding by each of the problems of the other as well as of problems common to all, and makes more readily possible the peaceful adjustment of international controversies.

7. Economic reconstruction contributes to national and international well-being, as well as to peace among nations.

8. International cooperation is a necessary condition to the maintenance of the aforementioned principles.

(Approved December 24, 1938)

DECLARATION XXVI: *Non-Recognition of the Acquisition of Territory by Force*

Report of the Delegation of the United States of America to the Eighth International Conference of American States, p. 132

WHEREAS:

The maintenance of peace and the preservation of the juridical order between the nations of America demand the adoption of a common and solidary attitude, already recognized by the Anti-War Treaty of Non-Aggression and Conciliation;

It is necessary to define the scope of the continental doctrine of the non-recognition of the conquest or acquisition of territory by force;

The geographical, historical and political conditions of the American nations preclude, on this continent, all territorial acquisitions by force; and

It is desirable to coordinate, reiterate and strengthen the declarations and statements contained in the treaty of July 15, 1826, signed at the Congress of Panama; and in the treaties adopted at the Inter-American Congresses of Lima of 1847 and 1864; in the resolutions of April 18, 1890, approved at the First International Conference of American States; in the resolutions of February 18, 1928, adopted at the Sixth International Conference of American States; in the declaration of August 3, 1932, signed at Washington; in the Anti-War Pact signed at Rio de Janeiro on October 10, 1933; in the Convention on Rights and Duties of States, signed at Montevideo on December 26, 1933, at the Seventh International Conference of American States; and in the instruments approved on December 23, 1936, at the Inter-American Conference for the Maintenance of Peace, held at Buenos Aires,

The Eighth International Conference of American States
Declares:

That it reiterates, as a fundamental principle of the Public Law of America, that the occupation or acquisition of territory or any other modification or territorial or boundary arrangement obtained through conquest by force or by non-pacific means shall not be valid or have legal effect.

The pledge of non-recognition of situations arising from the foregoing conditions is an obligation which cannot be avoided either unilaterally or collectively.

(Approved December 22, 1938)

First Meeting of the Foreign Ministers of the American Republics, at Panama, September 23 to October 3, 1939

RESOLUTION III: *Economic Cooperation*

Report of the Delegate of the United States of America to the Meeting of the Foreign Ministers of the American Republics, p. 50

THE MEETING of the Foreign Ministers of the American Republics
Resolves:

1. In view of the present circumstances, to declare that today it is more desirable and necessary than ever to establish a close and sincere cooperation between the American republics in order that they may protect their economic and financial structure, maintain their fiscal equilibrium, safeguard the stability of their currencies, promote and expand their industries, intensify their agriculture, and develop their commerce.

2. To create an Inter-American Financial and Economic Advisory Committee consisting of twenty-one (21) experts in economic problems, one for each of the American republics, which shall be installed in Washington, D.C., not later than November 15, 1939, and which shall have the following functions:

(a) To consider any problem of monetary relationships, foreign-exchange management, or balance-of-international-payments situation, which may be presented to it by the government of any of the American republics, and to offer to that government whatever recommendations it deems desirable.

(b) To study the most practical and satisfactory means of obtaining the stability of the monetary and commercial relationships between the American republics.

(c) To provide, with the cooperation of the Pan American Union, the means for the interchange of information between the governments of the American republics with reference to the matters mentioned in the two preceding subparagraphs, as well as for the exchange of production, foreign trade, financial and monetary statistics, custom legislation, and other reports on inter-American commerce.

(d) To study and propose to the governments the most effective measures for mutual cooperation to lessen or offset any dislocations which may arise in the trade of the American republics and to maintain trade among themselves, and, so far as possible, their trade with the rest of the world, which may be affected by the present war, on the basis of those liberal principles of international trade approved at the Seventh and Eighth International Conferences of American States and the Inter-American Conference for the Maintenance of Peace. These principles shall be retained as the goal of their long-term commercial policies in order that the world shall not lack a basis of world-wide international trade in which all may participate after world order and peace may be restored.

(e) To study the possibility of establishing a custom truce, of reducing custom duties on the typical commodities which an American country may offer in the market of another American country, of abolishing or modifying import licenses on such commodities, as well as all the other obstacles which render difficult the interchange of products between the said countries, of adopting a uniform principle of equality of treatment, eliminating all discriminatory measures, and of giving ample facilities to salesmen traveling from one American country to another.

(f) To study the necessity of creating an inter-American institution which may render feasible and insure permanent financial cooperation between the treasuries, the central banks and analogous institutions of the American republics, and propose the manner and conditions under which such an organization should be established and determine the matters with which it should deal.

(g) To study measures which tend to promote the importation and consumption of products of the American republics, especially through the promotion of lower prices and better transportation and credit facilities.

(h) To study the usefulness and feasibility of organizing an Inter-American Commercial Institute to maintain the importers and exporters of the American republics in contact with each other and to supply them with the necessary data for the promotion of inter-American trade.

(i) To study the possibility of establishing new industries and negotiating commercial treaties, especially for the interchange of the raw materials of each country.

(j) To study the possibility that silver be also one of the mediums for international payments.

The Inter-American Economic Advisory Committee shall communicate to the governments the results of the studies made in each case and shall recommend the measures which it considers should be taken.

3. To recommend to the governments of the American republics:

(a) To take measures in accordance with their own respective legislation, with a view to avoiding increases of rates or premiums to an extent not justified by the special expenses and risks incurred because of the present state of war, by shipping companies which maintain transportation services between the countries of the continent, and marine insurance companies operating in their territories.

(b) To promote the negotiation of bilateral or multilateral agreements for the organization and maintenance of regular and connected steamship services between the countries of the continent in order to facilitate the direct traffic of passengers and cargoes. These agreements are to make special provisions for traveling salesmen and commercial samples.

(c) To study the possibility of reducing to a minimum consular fees on manifests of vessels in the above-mentioned services, so as to make possible the shipment of reduced quantities of commodities which require rapid and special transportation.

(d) To study the possibility, in accordance with their legislation, of reducing to a minimum, port, sanitary, and other formalities applied to the traffic of merchandise between the American republics.

4. To recommend to the governments that they do everything possible to abolish obstacles to the free inter-American movement of capital.

5. To recommend to the governments that, when deemed necessary, they negotiate agreements in accordance with the circumstances and legislation of each country, with a view to the establishment of bases that would make feasible and secure the granting of inter-American credits which may serve to intensify the interchange of products as well as for the development of natural resources.

6. To request the governments of the most industrialized countries of the continent to do whatever is possible, within their legal faculties and circumstances, to prevent excessive and unjustified increases in the prices of manufactured articles destined for export.

7. To recommend that the American governments promote the negotiation of arrangements, in accordance with their legislation and within their possibilities, with a view to obtaining ample facilities with regard to the treatment of reembarkation of merchandise sold or acquired by American countries, detained at the present moment on board merchant vessels of countries at war which are unable to transport it to its original destination.

8. To recommend to the respective governments that they preserve in a reciprocal and generous form the legitimate principle of freedom of communications and transit through the ports and territories of the American nations, in accordance with the legislation and international agreements in force.

9. To recommend that countries bordering on each other hold, among themselves, meetings of their Ministers of Foreign Affairs, or of their Ministers of Finance, or of special plenipotentiaries, in the capital of one of them, in order to arrive at agreements for solving common problems of a financial, fiscal, or economic character, in conformity with the relevant general principles of commercial policy approved at recent inter-American conferences.

10. To make every effort in order to complete their respective sections of the Pan American Highway and to recommend to the countries which have ratified the Buenos Aires convention that they designate as soon as possible one or more experts to expedite the fulfilment of the recommendations of the Third Pan American Highway Congress.

(Approved October 3, 1939)

*RESOLUTION AND DECLARATION XIV: Declaration of
Panama*

Report of the Delegate of the United.States of America to the Meeting of the
Foreign Ministers of the American Republics, p. 62

THE GOVERNMENTS of the American republics meeting at Panama,
have solemnly ratified their neutral status in the conflict which is
disrupting the peace of Europe, but the present war may lead to unexpected results which may affect the fundamental interests of
America and there can be no justification for the interests of the
belligerents to prevail over the rights of neutrals causing disturbances
and suffering to nations which by their neutrality in the conflict and
their distance from the scene of events, should not be burdened with
its fatal and painful consequences.

During the World War of 1914–18 the Governments of Argentina,
Brazil, Chile, Colombia, Ecuador and Peru advanced, or supported,
individual proposals providing in principle a declaration by the
American republics that the belligerent nations must refrain from
committing hostile acts within a reasonable distance from their
shores.

The nature of the present conflagration, in spite of its already
lamentable proportions, would not justify any obstruction to inter-
American communications which, engendered by important interests,
call for adequate protection. This fact requires the demarcation of
a zone of security including all the normal maritime routes of communication and trade between the countries of America.

To this end it is essential as a measure of necessity to adopt immediately provisions based on the above-mentioned precedents for
the safeguarding of such interests, in order to avoid a repetition of
the damages and sufferings sustained by the American nations and
by their citizens in the war of 1914–1918.

There is no doubt that the governments of the American republics
must foresee those dangers and as a measure of self-protection insist
that the waters to a reasonable distance from their coasts shall remain
free from the commission of hostile acts or from the undertaking of
belligerent activities by nations engaged in a war in which the said
governments are not involved.

For these reasons the governments of the American republics
Resolve and hereby declare:

1. As a measure of continental self-protection, the American republics, so long as they maintain their neutrality, are as of inherent

right entitled to have those waters adjacent to the American Continent, which they regard as of primary concern and direct utility in their relations, free from the commission of any hostile act by any non-American belligerent nation, whether such hostile act be attempted or made from land, sea, or air.

Such waters shall be defined as follows. All waters comprised within the limits set forth hereafter except the territorial waters of Canada and of the undisputed colonies and possessions of European countries within these limits:

Beginning at the terminus of the United States–Canada boundary in Passamaquoddy Bay, in 44°46′36″ north latitude, and 66°54′11″ west longitude;

Thence due east along the parallel 44°46′36″ to a point 60° west of Greenwich;

Thence due south to a point in 20° north latitude;

Thence by a rhumb line to a point in 5° north latitude, 24° west longitude;

Thence due south to a point in 20° south latitude;

Thence by a rhumb line to a point in 58° south latitude, 57° west longitude;

Thence due west to a point in 80° west longitude;

Thence by a rhumb line to a point on the equator in 97° west longitude;

Thence by a rhumb line to a point in 15° north latitude, 120° west longitude;

Thence by a rhumb line to a point in 48°29′38″ north latitude, 136° west longitude;

Thence due east to the Pacific terminus of the United States–Canada boundary in the Strait of Juan de Fuca.

2. The governments of the American republics agree that they will endeavor, through joint representation to such belligerents as may now or in the future be engaged in hostilities, to secure the compliance by them with the provisions of this declaration, without prejudice to the exercise of the individual rights of each state inherent in their sovereignty.

3. The governments of the American republics further declare that whenever they consider it necessary they will consult together to determine upon the measures which they may individually or collectively undertake in order to secure the observance of the provisions of this declaration.

4. The American republics, during the existence of a state of war in which they themselves are not involved, may undertake, whenever

they may determine that the need therefor exists, to patrol, either individually or collectively, as may be agreed upon by common consent, and in so far as the means and resources of each may permit, the waters adjacent to their coasts within the area above defined.

(Approved October 3, 1939)

RESOLUTION V: General Declaration of Neutrality of the American Republics

Report of the Delegate of the United States of America to the Meeting of the Foreign Ministers of the American Republics, p. 54

WHEREAS:

As proclaimed in the Declaration of Lima, "The peoples of America have achieved'spiritual unity through the similarity of their republican institutions, their unshakable will for peace, their profound sentiment of humanity and tolerance, and through their absolute adherence to the principles of international law, of the equal sovereignty of states and of individual liberty without religious or racial prejudices";

This acknowledged spiritual unity presupposes common and solidary attitudes with reference to situations of force which, as in the case of the present European war, may threaten the security of the sovereign rights of the American republics;

The attitude assumed by the American republics has served to demonstrate that it is their unanimous intention not to become involved in the European conflict; and

It is desirable to state the standards of conduct, which, in conformity with international law and their respective internal legislation, the American republics propose to follow, in order to maintain their status as neutral states and fulfil their neutral duties, as well as require the recognition of the rights inherent in such a status,

The Meeting of the Foreign Ministers of the American Republics *Resolves:*

1. To reaffirm the status of general neutrality of the American republics, it being left to each one of them to regulate in their individual and sovereign capacities the manner in which they are to give it concrete application.

2. To have their rights and status as neutrals fully respected and observed by all belligerents and by all persons who may be acting for or on behalf of or in the interest of the belligerents.

3. To declare that with regard to their status as neutrals, there

exist certain standards recognized by the American republics applicable in these circumstances and that in accordance with them they:

(a) Shall prevent their respective terrestrial, maritime, and aerial territories from being utilized as bases of belligerent operations.

(b) Shall prevent, in accordance with their internal legislations, the inhabitants of their territories from engaging in activities capable of affecting the neutral status of the American republics.

(c) Shall prevent on their respective territories the enlistment of persons to serve in the military, naval, or air forces of the belligerents; the retaining or inducing of persons to go beyond their respective shores for the purpose of taking part in belligerent operations; the setting on foot of any military, naval, or aerial expedition in the interests of the belligerents; the fitting out, arming, or augmenting of the forces or armament of any ship or vessel to be employed in the service of one of the belligerents, to cruise or commit hostilities against another belligerent, or its nationals or property; the establishment by the belligerents or their agents of radio stations in the terrestrial or maritime territory of the American republics, or the utilization of such stations to communicate with the governments or armed forces of the belligerents.

(d) May determine, with regard to belligerent warships, that not more than three at a time be admitted in their own ports or waters and in any case they shall not be allowed to remain for more than 24 hours. Vessels engaged exclusively in scientific, religious, or philanthropic missions may be exempted from this provision, as well as those which arrive in distress.

(e) Shall require all belligerent vessels and aircraft seeking the hospitality of areas under their jurisdiction and control to respect strictly their neutral status and to observe their respective laws and regulations and the rules of international law pertaining to the rights and duties of neutrals and belligerents; and in the event that difficulties are experienced in enforcing the observance of and respect for their rights, the case, if so requested, shall thereupon become a subject of consultation between them.

(f) Shall regard as a contravention of their neutrality any flight by the military aircraft of a belligerent state over their own territory. With respect to non-military aircraft, they shall adopt the following measures: such aircraft shall fly only with the permission of the competent authority; all aircraft, regardless of nationality, shall follow routes determined by the said authorities; their commanders or pilots shall declare the place of departure, the stops to be made and their destination; they shall be allowed to use radiotelegraphy only to determine their route and flying conditions, utilizing for this purpose the national language, without code, only the standard abbreviations being allowed; the competent authorities may require aircraft to carry a co-pilot or a radio operator for purposes of control. Belligerent military aircraft transported on board warships shall not leave these vessels while in the waters of the American republics; belligerent military aircraft landing in the territory of an American republic shall be interned with their crews until the cessation of hostilities, except in cases in which the landing is made because of proven distress. There shall be exempted from the application of these rules cases in which there exist conventions to the contrary.

(g) May submit belligerent merchant vessels, as well as their passengers, documents and cargo, to inspection in their own ports; the respective consular agent shall certify as to the ports of call and destination as well as to the fact that the voyage is undertaken solely for purposes of commercial interchange. They may also supply fuel to such vessels in amounts sufficient for the voyage to a port of supply and call in another American republic, except in the case of a direct voyage to another continent, in which circumstance they may supply the necessary amount of fuel. Should it be proven that these vessels have supplied belligerent warships with fuel, they shall be considered as auxiliary transports.

(h) May concentrate and place a guard on board belligerent merchant vessels which have sought asylum in their waters, and may intern those which have made false declarations as to their destinations, as well as those which have taken an unjustified or excessive time in their voyage, or have adopted the distinctive signs of warships.

(i) Shall consider as lawful the transfer of the flag of a merchant vessel to that of any American republic provided such transfer is made in good faith, without agreement for resale to the vendor, and that it takes place in the waters of an American republic.

(j) Shall not assimilate to warships belligerent armed merchant vessels if they do not carry more than four six-inch guns mounted on the stern, and their lateral decks are not reinforced, and if, in the judgment of the local authorities, there do not exist other circumstances which reveal that the merchant vessels can be used for offensive purposes. They may require of the said vessels, in order to enter their ports, to deposit explosives and munitions in such places as the local authorities may determine.

(k) May exclude belligerent submarines from the waters adjacent to their territories or admit them under the condition that they conform to the regulations which each country may prescribe.

4. In the spirit of this declaration, the governments of the Ameri-

can republics shall maintain close contact with a view to making uniform, so far as possible, the enforcement of their neutrality and to safeguarding it in defense of their fundamental rights.

5. With a view to studying and formulating recommendations with respect to the problems of neutrality, in the light of experience and changing circumstances, there shall be established, for the duration of the European war, an Inter-American Neutrality Committee, composed of seven experts in international law, who shall be designated by the Governing Board of the Pan American Union before November 1, 1939. The recommendations of the committee shall be transmitted, through the Pan American Union, to the governments of the American republics.

(Approved October 3, 1939)

Second Meeting of the Ministers of Foreign Affairs of the American Republics, at Habana, July 21–30, 1940

RESOLUTION XIV: The Peaceful Solution of Conflicts

Second Meeting of the Ministers of Foreign Affairs of the American Republics, Report of the Secretary of State, p. 71

WHEREAS:

In behalf of the closest possible unity of the continent, it is imperative that differences existing between some of the American nations be settled,

The Second Meeting of the Ministers of Foreign Affairs of the American Republics

Resolves:

To recommend to the Governing Board of the Pan American Union that it organize, in the American capital deemed most suitable for the purpose, a committee composed of representatives of five countries, which shall have the duty of keeping constant vigilance to insure that states between which any dispute exists or may arise, of any nature whatsoever, may solve it as quickly as possible, and of suggesting, without detriment to the methods adopted by the parties or to the procedures which they may agree upon, the measures and steps which may be conducive to a settlement.

The committee shall submit a report to each meeting of the ministers of foreign affairs and to each international conference of American states regarding the status of such conflicts and the steps which may have been taken to bring about a solution.

DECLARATION XV: Reciprocal Assistance and Cooperation for the Defense of the Nations of the Americas

Second Meeting of the Ministers of Foreign Affairs of the American Republics, Report of the Secretary of State, p. 71

THE SECOND MEETING of the Ministers of Foreign Affairs of the American Republics
Declares:
That any attempt on the part of a non-American state against the integrity or inviolability of the territory, the sovereignty or the political independence of an American state shall be considered as an act of aggression against the states which sign this declaration.

In case acts of aggression are committed or should there be reason to believe that an act of aggression is being prepared by a non-American nation against the integrity or inviolability of the territory, the sovereignty or the political independence of an American nation, the nations signatory to the present declaration will consult among themselves in order to agree upon the measure it may be advisable to take.

All the signatory nations, or two or more of them, according to circumstances, shall proceed to negotiate the necessary complementary agreements so as to organize cooperation for defense and the assistance that they shall lend each other in the event of aggressions such as those referred to in this declaration.

DECLARATION AND RESOLUTION XX: Act of Habana Concerning the Provisional Administration of European Colonies and Possessions in the Americas

Second Meeting of the Ministers of Foreign Affairs of the American Republics, Report of the Secretary of State, p. 75

WHEREAS:
1. The status of regions in this continent belonging to European powers is a subject of deep concern to all of the governments of the American republics;
2. As a result of the present European war there may be attempts at conquest, which has been repudiated in the international relations

of the American republics, thus placing in danger the essence and pattern of the institutions of America;

3. The doctrine of inter-American solidarity agreed upon at the meetings at Lima and at Panamá requires the adoption of a policy of vigilance and defense so that systems or regimes in conflict with their institutions shall not upset the peaceful life of the American republics, the normal functioning of their institutions, or the rule of law and order;

4. The course of military events in Europe and the changes resulting from them may create the grave danger that European territorial possessions in America may be converted into strategic centers of aggression against nations of the American Continent,

The Second Meeting of the Ministers of Foreign Affairs of the American Republics

Declares:

That when islands or regions in the Americas now under the possession of non-American nations are in danger of becoming the subject of barter of territory or change of sovereignty, the American nations, taking into account the imperative need of continental security and the desires of the inhabitants of the said islands or regions, may set up a regime of provisional administration under the following conditions:

(a) That as soon as the reasons requiring this measure shall cease to exist, and in the event that it would not be prejudicial to the safety of the American republics, such territories shall, in accordance with the principle reaffirmed by this declaration that peoples of this continent have the right freely to determine their own destinies, be organized as autonomous states if it shall appear that they are able to constitute and maintain themselves in such condition, or be restored to their previous status, whichever of these alternatives shall appear the more practicable and just;

(b) That the regions to which this declaration refers shall be placed temporarily under the provisional administration of the American republics, and this administration shall be exercised with the twofold purpose of contributing to the security and defense of the continent, and to the economic, political, and social progress of such regions, and

Resolves:

To create an emergency committee, composed of one representative of each of the American republics, which committee shall be deemed constituted as soon as two thirds of its members shall have been appointed. Such appointments shall be made by the American republics as soon as possible.

The committee shall meet on the request of any signatory of this resolution.

If it becomes necessary, as an imperative emergency measure before the coming into effect of the convention approved by this Consultative Meeting, to apply its provisions in order to safeguard the peace of the continent, taking into account also the desires of the inhabitants of any of the above-mentioned regions, the committee shall assume the administration of the region attacked or threatened, acting in accordance with the provisions of the said convention. As soon as the convention comes into effect, the authority and functions exercised by the committee shall be transferred to the Inter-American Commission for Territorial Administration.

Should the need for emergency action be so urgent that action by the committee cannot be awaited, any of the American republics, individually or jointly with others, shall have the right to act in the manner which its own defense or that of the continent requires. Should this situation arise, the American republic or republics taking action shall place the matter before the committee immediately, in order that it may consider the action taken and adopt appropriate measures.

None of the provisions contained in the present act refers to territories or possessions which are the subject of dispute or claims between European powers and one or more of the republics of the Americas.

CONVENTION on the Provisional Administration of European Colonies and Possessions in the Americas

Second Meeting of the Ministers of Foreign Affairs of the American Republics, Report of the Secretary of State, p. 84. The convention was ratified by the President of the United States October 10, 1940

THE GOVERNMENTS represented at the Second Meeting of Ministers of Foreign Affairs of the American Republics,

Considering:

One. That the American Republics have formulated at the Second Consultative Meeting the Act of Habana with regard to the destiny of colonies of non-American countries located in this hemisphere as well as with respect to the provisional administration of such colonies;

Two. That as a result of the events which are taking place in the

European Continent situations may develop in the territories of the possessions which some of the belligerent nations have in the Americas which may extinguish or materially impair the sovereignty which they exercise over them, or leave their government without a leader, thus creating a state of danger to the peace of the continent and a state of affairs in which the rule of law, order, and respect for life, liberty and the property of inhabitants may disappear;

Three. That the American Republics consider that force cannot constitute the basis of rights, and they condemn all violence whether under the form of conquest, of stipulations which may have been imposed by the belligerents in the clauses of treaty, or by any other process;

Four. That any transfer, or attempted transfer, of the sovereignty, jurisdiction, possession or any interest in or control over any such region to another non-American State, would be regarded by the American Republics as against American sentiments and principles and the rights of American States to maintain their security and political independence;

Five. That no such transfer or attempt to transfer or acquire any interest or right in any such region, directly or indirectly, would be recognized or accepted by the American Republics no matter what form was employed to attain such purpose;

Six. That by virtue of a principle of American international law, recognized by various conferences, the acquisition of territories by force cannot be permitted;

Seven. That the American Republics, through their respective government agencies, reserve the right to judge whether any transfer or attempted transfer of sovereignty, jurisdiction, cession or incorporation of geographic regions in the Americas, possessed by European countries up to September 1, 1939, has the effect of impairing their political independence even though no formal transfer or change in the status of such region or regions shall have taken place;

Eight. That in the cases foreseen, as well as any others which might leave the government of such regions without a leader, it is, therefore, necessary to establish a provisional administrative regime for such regions until such time as their definitive regime is established by the free determination of their people;

Nine. That the American Republics, as an international community which acts strongly and integrally, using as a basis political and juridical principles which they have applied for more than a century, have the unquestionable right, in order to preserve their unity and security, to take such regions under their administration and to deliberate as to their destinies, in accordance with their respective degrees of political and economic development;

Ten. That the provisional and transitory character of the measures agreed to does not imply an oversight or abrogation of the principle of non-intervention which regulates inter-American life, a principle proclaimed by the American Institute, recognized by the meeting of jurists held at Rio de Janeiro and fully reaffirmed at the Seventh International American Conference held at Montevideo;

Eleven. That this community has therefore international juridical capacity to act in this manner;

Twelve. That in this case, the most appropriate regime is that of a provisional administration; and that this system entails no danger because the American Republics do not entertain any purpose whatsoever of territorial aggrandizement;

Thirteen. That the establishment of a special provisional regime in the present convention and in the Act of Habana concerning the provisional administration of European colonies and possessions in the Americas does not eliminate or modify the system of consultation agreed upon at Buenos Aires, confirmed at Lima, and practiced at Panama and Habana;

Fourteen. Being desirous of protecting their peace and safety and of promoting the interests of any of the regions herein referred to which may fall within the purview of the foregoing recitations, have resolved to conclude the following convention:

I

If a non-American State shall directly or indirectly attempt to replace another non-American State in the sovereignty or control which it exercised over any territory located in the Americas, thus threatening the peace of the continent, such territory shall automatically come under the provisions of this convention and shall be submitted to a provisional administrative regime.

II

The administration shall be exercised, as may be considered advisable in each case, by one or more American States, with their previous approval.

III

When the administration shall have been established for any region it shall be exercised in the interest of the security of the Americas and for the benefit of the region under administration, with a view to its welfare and progress, until such time as the region is in a position to govern itself or is restored to its former status, whenever the latter is compatible with the security of the American Republics.

IV

The administration of the region shall be exercised under conditions which shall guarantee freedom of conscience and of worship, subject to the regulations which public order and good habits may demand.

V

The administration shall enforce the local laws coordinating them with the purposes of this convention, but it may furthermore adopt such measures as may be necessary to meet situations in which such laws do not exist.

VI

In all that concerns commerce and industry, the American nations shall enjoy the same situation and benefits, and the administrator is forbidden to establish a privileged position for itself or its nationals or for certain states. Open economic relations shall be maintained with all countries on a reciprocity basis.

VII

Natives of the region shall participate, as citizens, in public administration and in the courts of justice without further qualification than their capacity so to do.

VIII

To the extent that it may be practicable, rights of every sort shall be governed by local law and custom, and vested rights shall be protected in accordance with such law.

IX

Forced labor shall be abolished in the regions where it exists.

X

The administration shall provide facilities for education of all kinds with the two-fold purpose of developing the wealth of the region and improving the living conditions of the population, especially as regards public and individual hygiene and preparation for the exercise of political autonomy as soon as possible.

XI

The natives of a region under administration shall have their own Organic Act which the administration shall establish, consulting the people in whatever manner is possible.

XII

The administration shall submit an annual report to the inter-American organization entrusted with the control of the regions under administration, of the manner in which it has fulfilled its functions, attaching thereto copies of its accounts and of the measures adopted in the region during the year.

XIII

The organization referred to in the preceding article shall be competent to take cognizance of the petitions submitted by inhabitants of the region through the medium of the administration, with reference to the exercise of the provisional administration. The administration shall transmit, with this petition, such observations as it may deem proper.

XIV

The first administration shall be granted for a period of three years; at the end of this period, if necessary, it shall be renewed for successive periods not longer than ten years.

XV

The expenses incurred in the exercise of the administration shall be defrayed with the revenues of the region under administration but in case they are insufficient the deficit shall be met by the State or States which act as administrators.

XVI

A commission to be known as the "Inter-American Commission for Territorial Administration" is hereby established, to be composed of a representative from each one of the States which ratifies this convention; it shall be the international organization to which this convention refers. Once this convention has become effective, any country which ratifies it may convoke the first meeting proposing the city in which it is to be held. The Commission shall elect its chairman, complete its organization and fix its definitive seat. Two-thirds of the members of the Commission shall constitute a quorum and two-thirds of the members present may adopt decisions.

XVII

The Commission is authorized to establish a provisional administration in the regions to which the present convention refers; allow
such administration to be exercised by the number of States which it
may determine in each case, and supervise its exercise under the
terms of the preceding articles.

XVIII

None of the provisions contained in the present convention refers to
territories or possessions which are the subject of dispute or claims
between European powers and one or more of the Republics of the
Americas.

XIX

The present convention is open for signature by the American
Republics at the City of Habana and shall be ratified by the High
Contracting Parties in conformity with their constitutional procedures. The Secretary of State of the Republic of Cuba shall transmit
at the earliest possible date authentic certified copies to the governments for the aforementioned purpose of ratification. The instrument of ratification shall be deposited in the archives of the Pan
American Union in Washington, which shall notify the signatory
governments of said deposit. Such notification shall be considered
as an exchange of ratifications.

The present convention shall enter into force when two-thirds of
the American Republics have deposited their respective instruments
of ratification.

It witness whereof, the undersigned Plenipotentiaries, having deposited their full powers found to be in due and proper form, sign
this convention on behalf of their respective Governments and affix
thereto their seals on the dates appearing opposite their signatures.

[*Signatures*]

Third Meeting of the Ministers of Foreign Affairs of the American Republics, at Rio de Janeiro, January 15–28, 1942

RECOMMENDATION I: Breaking of Diplomatic Relations with Japan, Germany, and Italy
Department of State Bulletin, Vol. VI, No. 137, p. 118

I

THE AMERICAN REPUBLICS reaffirm their declaration to consider any act of aggression on the part of a non-American State against one of them as an act of aggression against all of them, constituting as it does an immediate threat to the liberty and independence of America.

II

The American Republics reaffirm their complete solidarity and their determination to cooperate jointly for their mutual protection until the effects of the present aggression against the Continent have disappeared.

III

The American Republics, in accordance with the procedures established by their own laws and in conformity with the position and circumstances obtaining in each country in the existing continental conflict, recommend the breaking of their diplomatic relations with Japan, Germany and Italy, since the first-mentioned State attacked and the other two declared war on an American country.

IV

Finally, the American Republics declare that, prior to the reestablishment of the relations referred to in the preceding paragraph, they will consult among themselves in order that their action may have a solidary character.

RECOMMENDATION V: Severance of Commercial and Financial Relations
   Department of State Bulletin, Vol. VI, No. 137, p. 124

WHEREAS:
   1. At the Second Meeting of Ministers of Foreign Affairs of the American Republics, held at Habana in July 1940, it was declared that any attempt on the part of a non-American State against the integrity or inviolability of the territory, the sovereignty or the political independence of an American State should be considered as an act of aggression against all of the American States;
   2. As a result of the aggression committed against the Western Hemisphere a state of war exists between American Republics and non-American States, which affects the political and economic interests of the whole Continent and demands the adoption of measures for the defense and security of all of the American Republics;
   3. All of the American Republics have already adopted measures which subject to some control the exportation or re-exportation of merchandise; most of the American Republics have instituted systems of restriction and control of financial and commercial transactions with the nations signatory to the Tripartite Pact and the territories dominated by them, and others have adopted measures to curb other alien economic activities prejudicial to their welfare; and all the American Republics have approved the recommendations of the Inter-American Financial and Economic Advisory Committee regarding the immediate placing into service of the merchant vessels of non-American registry lying immobilized in American ports,
   The Third Meeting of the Ministers of Foreign Affairs of the American Republics
   Recommends:
   1. That the Governments of the American Republics, in a manner consistent with the usual practices and the legislation of the respective countries, adopt immediately:
   (a) Any additional measures necessary to cut off for the duration of the present Hemispheric emergency all commercial and financial intercourse, direct or indirect, between the Western Hemisphere and the nations signatory to the Tripartite Pact and the territories dominated by them;
   (b) Measures to eliminate all other financial and commercial activities prejudicial to the welfare and security of the American Re-

publics, measures which shall have, among others, the following purposes:

(i) To prevent, within the American Republics, all commercial and financial transactions inimical to the security of the Western Hemisphere, which are entered into directly or indirectly, by or for the benefit of the members of the Tripartite Pact, the territories dominated by them, as well as the nationals of any of them, whether real or juridical persons, it being understood that real persons may be excepted if they are resident within an American Republic and on condition that they are controlled according to the following paragraph;

(ii) To supervise and control all commercial and financial transactions within the American Republics by nationals of the states signatory to the Tripartite Pact, or of the territories dominated by them, who are resident within the American Republics, and to prevent all transactions of whatsoever nature which are inimical to the security of the Western Hemisphere.

Whenever a government of an American Republic considers it desirable and in accordance with its national interest and its own legislation, and especially if any of the aforesaid measures, when applied to concrete cases, should be prejudicial to its national economy, the properties, interests, and enterprises of such states and nationals which exist within its jurisdiction, may be placed in trust or subjected to permanent administrative intervention for purposes of control; moreover, such government of an American Republic may resort to sales to its nationals, provided that the proceeds thereof be subject to the same control and to similar regulations as those applicable to the funds of the above-mentioned aliens.

2. That the Governments of the American Republics adopt, severally or jointly, measures to counteract any adverse effects upon their respective economies which may result from the application of this recommendation. Special consideration should be given to measures to avoid the problems of partial or total unemployment which might arise in the American countries as a result of the application of the measures of control and restriction of the activities of aliens.

RESOLUTION XVII: Subversive Activities

Department of State Bulletin, Vol. VI, No. 137, p. 128

WHEREAS:

1. Acts of aggression of the nature contemplated in Resolution XV adopted by the Second Meeting of the Ministers of Foreign Affairs

of the American Republics at Habana have now taken place against the integrity and inviolability of the territory of an American Republic;

2. Acts of aggression of a non-military character, including systematic espionage, sabotage, and subversive propaganda are being committed on this Continent, inspired by and under the direction of member states of the Tripartite Pact and states subservient to them, and the fate of numbers of the formerly free nations of Europe has shown them to be both preliminary to and an integral part of a program of military aggression;

3. The American Republics are determined to maintain their integrity and solidarity, in the emergency created by aggression by non-American States, and to give the fullest cooperation in the establishment and enforcement of extraordinary measures of continental defense;

4. The Second Meeting of the Ministers of Foreign Affairs of the American Republics recommended that the necessary steps be taken to prevent the carrying on of such subversive activities in the resolutions entitled:

"II.   Norms Concerning Diplomatic and Consular Functions."
"III.   Coordination of Police and Judicial Measures for the Defense of Society and Institutions of Each American State."
"V.   Precautionary Measures With Reference to the Issuance of Passports."
"VI.   Activities Directed From Abroad Against Domestic Institutions."
"VII.   Diffusion of Doctrines Tending To Place in Jeopardy the Common Inter-American Democratic Ideal or To Threaten the Security and Neutrality of the American Republics."

5. The gravity of the present emergency requires that the American states, individually and in concert, take additional and more stringent measures to protect themselves against groups and individuals that seek to weaken their defenses from within,

The Third Meeting of the Ministers of Foreign Affairs of the American Republics
Resolves:
1. To reaffirm the determination of the American Republics to prevent individuals or groups within their respective jurisdictions from engaging in activities detrimental to the individual or collective security and welfare of the American Republics as expressed in

Resolutions II, III, V, VI, and VII of the Second Meeting of the Ministers of Foreign Affairs of the American Republics.

2. To recommend to the Governments of the American Republics the adoption of similar legislative measures tending to prevent or punish as crimes, acts against the democratic institutions of the States of the Continent in the same manner as attempts against the integrity, independence or sovereignty of any one of them; and that the Governments of the American Republics maintain and expand their systems of surveillance designed to prevent subversive activities of nationals of non-American countries, as individuals or groups of individuals, that originate in or are directed from a foreign country and are intended to interfere with or limit the efforts of the American Republics individually or collectively to preserve their integrity and independence, and the integrity and solidarity of the American Continent.

3. To recommend to the American Republics that they adopt in conformance with their constitutions and laws, regulatory provisions that are, as far as possible, in keeping with the memorandum which is attached to this Resolution for purposes of information.

4. To recommend, according to Resolution VII of the Habana Meeting on the subject of anti-democratic propaganda, that the Governments of the American Republics control, within their respective national jurisdictions, the existence of organizations directed or supported by elements of non-American States which are now or may in the future be at war with American countries, whose activities are harmful to American security; and proceed to terminate their existence if it is established that they are centers of totalitarian propaganda.

5. That, to study and coordinate the measures recommended in this Resolution, the Governing Board of the Pan American Union shall elect, prior to March 1, 1942, a committee of seven members to be known as "The Emergency Advisory Committee for Political Defense."

6. The Governing Board of the Pan American Union, after consulting the Governments of the American Republics, shall determine the functions of this committee, prepare the regulations which shall govern its activities, and fix its budget of expenditures.

Attachment to Resolution XVII: Memorandum on the Regulation of Subversive Activities

It is recommended to the American Republics that, as far as practicable in view of present conditions and those which may be foreseen, they take comprehensive regulatory measures, that are not in conflict with their respective constitutional provisions, and that these measures include the following, it being recognized that many of them are already in force:

A. To control dangerous aliens by:

1. Requiring that all aliens register and periodically report in person to the proper authorities and exercising a strict supervision over the activities and conduct of all nationals of member states of the Tripartite Pact and states subservient to them; communicating immediately to other American Republics information that may be obtained relative to the presence of foreigners suspect with relation to the peace and security of such other Republics;

2. Establishing procedures whereby such nationals of the aforesaid states as are deemed dangerous to the country of their residence shall during their stay therein remain in detention or be restricted in their freedom of movement;

3. Preventing such nationals from possessing, trading in or making use of aircraft, firearms, explosives, radio transmitting instruments, or other implements of warfare, propaganda, espionage, or sabotage;

4. Limiting internal travel and change of residence of those aliens deemed dangerous in so far as such travel may be incompatible with national security;

5. Forbidding the participation by such nationals in organizations controlled by or acting in the interest of member states of the Tripartite Pact or states subservient to them;

6. Protecting all aliens not deemed dangerous from being deprived of adequate means of livelihood, unfairly discriminated against, or otherwise interfered with in the conduct of their normal social and business activities.

B. To prevent the abuse of citizenship by:

1. Exercising that redoubled vigilance which the circumstances demand in the naturalization of aliens, with particular reference to denying citizenship to those who continue in any way to retain allegiance to, or to recognize citizenship in the member states of the Tripartite Pact or states subservient to them;

2. Causing the status of citizenship and the inherent rights with respect thereto of those citizens of non-American origin who have been granted the privilege of becoming citizens of an American state to be forfeited if, by acts detrimental to the security or independence of that state or otherwise, they demonstrate allegiance to a member state of the Tripartite Pact or any state subservient to them, including

the termination of the status of citizenship of such persons recognizing or attempting to exercise dual rights of citizenship.

C. To regulate transit across national boundaries by:

1. Exercising strict surveillance over all persons seeking to enter or depart from the country, particularly those persons engaged in the interests of member states of the Tripartite Pact or subservient to them, or whose point of departure or destination is such a state, without prejudice, however, to the maintenance of the most liberal practices consistent with local conditions for the granting of safe refuge to those persons who, as victims of aggression, are fleeing from oppression by foreign powers, and by cooperating fully in the exchange of information on the transit of persons from one state to another;

2. Strictly regulating and controlling the entry and departure of all persons as to whom there are well-founded and sufficient grounds to believe that they are engaged in political activities as agents or in the interest of member states of the Tripartite Pact or states subservient to them;

D. To prevent acts of political aggression by:

1. Establishing penalties for acts designed to obstruct the war or defense efforts of the country concerned or its cooperation with other American Republics in matters of mutual defense;

2. Preventing the dissemination by any agent or national of or by any political party organized in any member state of the Tripartite Pact or any state subservient to them, or by any other person or organization acting at the behest or under the direction thereof, of propaganda designed to impair the security of any of the American Republics or the relations between them, to create political or social dissension, to intimidate the nationals of any American Republic, or to influence the policies of any American state;

3. Requiring the registration with an appropriate agency of Government of or otherwise regulating any persons or organizations seeking to act in any way on behalf of, or in the political interest of, any non-American state which is not engaged at war on the side of an American Republic; or of a political party thereof, including clubs, societies and institutions, whether of a social, humanitarian, sporting, educational, technical or charitable nature, which are directed or supported by nationals of any such states; requiring the full and constant public disclosure to the people of the country in which they are carried on, of the identity and nature of all activities of such persons and organizations, and maintaining constant surveillance of all such

persons and members of such organizations, whether citizens or aliens;

4. Punishing acts of sabotage, injury to and destruction of essential defense materials, factories, buildings, areas and utilities for manufacture and storage, public services, means of transportation and communication, and water front areas and facilities; punishing acts of espionage and the collection and communication of vital defense information for hostile purposes; and anticipating and forestalling acts of sabotage and espionage by measures to protect and safeguard vital documents, installations, and operations;

5. Supervising all communications to and from states subservient to or in communication with member states of the Tripartite Pact, in order to censor any information or intelligence of use to any such state in the execution of hostile designs against any of the American Republics, or in activities otherwise detrimental to the security of any or all of the American Republics.

RESOLUTION XXIV: Condemnation of Japanese Aggression
Department of State Bulletin, Vol. VI, No. 137, p. 134

WHEREAS:

1. On December 7, 1941, the armed forces of Japan attacked, without previous warning or without a declaration of war, certain possessions of the United States of America in the Pacific Ocean;

2. These unforeseen and hostile acts were perpetrated by Japan while diplomatic conversations were in progress between the two States looking toward the pacific solution of their international differences;

3. The aforementioned nature and circumstances of these acts characterizes them as armed aggression in flagrant violation of all the standards of international law which proscribe and condemn the use of force in the solution of international controversies, and particularly those of American international law;

4. Several instruments signed by the American Republics at recent international conferences and meetings impose the unlimited duty of solidarity upon the signatory Governments for the defense of their sovereignty, independence, and territorial integrity; and

5. Resolution XV on Reciprocal Assistance and Cooperation for the Defense of the Nations of the Americas, signed at the Second Meeting of the Ministers of Foreign Affairs of the American Republics, held at Habana, established the principle "That any attempt

on the part of a non-American State against the integrity or inviolability of the territory, the sovereignty, or the political independence of an American State shall be considered as an act of aggression against the States which sign this declaration,"

The Third Meeting of the Ministers of Foreign Affairs of the American Republics
Resolves:
1. To make it of record that Japan by perpetrating armed aggression against the United States of America has violated the fundamental principles and standards of international law.
2. To condemn such aggression and protest against it to the civilized world and extend this condemnation and protest to the powers which have associated themselves with Japan.

RECOMMENDATION XL: *Telecommunications*
Department of State Bulletin, Vol. VI, No. 137, p. 140

THE THIRD MEETING of the Ministers of Foreign Affairs of the American Republics
Resolves:
1. To recommend that each American Republic adopt the necessary and immediate measures to close all radiotelephone and radiotelegraph communication between the American Republics and the aggressor States and all territories subservient to them, except in so far as official communications of the American Governments are concerned.
2. To recommend the establishment and maintenance, through a system of licenses, or other adequate means, of an effective control of the transmission and reception of messages whatever might be the telecommunication system used; and that telecommunications which might endanger the security of each American State and of the Continent in general be prohibited.
3. To recommend the adoption of immediate measures to eliminate clandestine telecommunication stations and that bilateral or multilateral agreements be concluded by the interested Governments to facilitate the fulfillment of the technical requirements of this Resolution.

Inter-American Conference on Problems of War and Peace, at Mexico City, February 21 to March 8, 1945

DECLARATION AND RECOMMENDATION VIII: Reciprocal Assistance and American Solidarity (the "Act of Chapultepec")

Report of the Delegation of the United States of America to the Inter-American Conference on Problems of War and Peace, p. 72

WHEREAS:

The peoples of the Americas, animated by a profound love of justice, remain sincerely devoted to the principles of international law;

It is their desire that such principles, notwithstanding the present difficult circumstances, prevail with even greater force in future international relations;

The inter-American conferences have repeatedly proclaimed certain fundamental principles, but these must be reaffirmed at a time when the juridical bases of the community of nations are being reestablished;

The new situation in the world makes more imperative than ever the union and solidarity of the American peoples, for the defense of their rights and the maintenance of international peace;

The American states have been incorporating in their international law, since 1890, by means of conventions, resolutions and declarations, the following principles:

a) The proscription of territorial conquest and the nonrecognition of all acquisitions made by force (First International Conference of American States, 1890);

b) The condemnation of intervention by one State in the internal or external affairs of another (Seventh International Conference of American States, 1933, and Inter-American Conference for the Maintenance of Peace, 1936);

c) The recognition that every war or threat of war affects directly or indirectly all civilized peoples, and endangers the great principles of liberty and justice which constitute the American ideal and the standard of American international policy (Inter-American Conference for the Maintenance of Peace, 1936);

d) The system of mutual consultation in order to find means of peaceful cooperation in the event of war or threat of war between American countries (Inter-American Conference for the Maintenance of Peace, 1936);

e) The recognition that every act susceptible of disturbing the peace of America affects each and every one of the American nations and justifies the initiation of the procedure of consultation (Inter-American Conference for the Maintenance of Peace, 1936);

f) The adoption of conciliation, unrestricted arbitration, or the application of international justice, in the solution of any difference or dispute between American nations, whatever its nature or origin (Inter-American Conference for the Maintenance of Peace, 1936);

g) The recognition that respect for the personality, sovereignty and independence of each American State constitutes the essence of international order sustained by continental solidarity, which historically has been expressed and sustained by declarations and treaties in force (Eighth International Conference of American States, 1938);

h) The affirmation that respect for and the faithful observance of treaties constitute the indispensable rule for the development of peaceful relations between States, and that treaties can only be revised by agreement of the contracting parties (Declaration of American Principles, Eighth International Conference of American States, 1938);

i) The proclamation that, in case the peace, security or territorial integrity of any American republic is threatened by acts of any nature that may impair them, they proclaim their common concern and their determination to make effective their solidarity, coordinating their respective sovereign wills by means of the procedure of consultation, using the measures which in each case the circumstances may make advisable (Declaration of Lima, Eighth International Conference of American States, 1938);

j) The declaration that any attempt on the part of a non-American state against the integrity or inviolability of the territory, the sovereignty or the political independence of an American State shall be considered as an act of aggression against all the American States (Declaration XV of the Second Meeting of the Ministers of Foreign Affairs, Habana, 1940);

The furtherance of these principles, which the American States have constantly practised in order to assure peace and solidarity among the nations of the Continent, constitutes an effective means of contributing to the general system of world security and of facilitating its establishment;

The security and solidarity of the Continent are affected to the same extent by an act of aggression against any of the American

States by a non-American State, as by an act of aggression of an American State against one or more American States;

The Governments Represented at the Inter-American Conference on Problems of War and Peace
Declare:

1. That all sovereign States are juridically equal among themselves.

2. That every State has the right to the respect of its individuality and independence, on the part of the other members of the international community.

3. That every attack of a State against the integrity or the inviolability of the territory, or against the sovereignty or political independence of an American State, shall, conformably to Part III hereof, be considered as an act of aggression against the other States which sign this Act. In any case invasion by armed forces of one State into the territory of another trespassing boundaries established by treaty and demarcated in accordance therewith shall constitute an act of aggression.

4. That in case acts of aggression occur or there are reasons to believe that an aggression is being prepared by any other State against the integrity or inviolability of the territory, or against the sovereignty or political independence of an American State, the States signatory to this Act will consult among themselves in order to agree upon the measures it may be advisable to take.

5. That during the war, and until the treaty recommended in Part II hereof is concluded, the signatories of this Act recognize that such threats and acts of aggression, as indicated in paragraphs 3 and 4 above, constitute an interference with the war effort of the United Nations, calling for such procedures, within the scope of their constitutional powers of a general nature and for war, as may be found necessary, including: recall of chiefs of diplomatic missions; breaking of diplomatic relations; breaking of consular relations; breaking of postal, telegraphic, telephonic, radio-telephonic relations; interruption of economic, commercial and financial relations; use of armed force to prevent or repel aggression.

6. That the principles and procedure contained in this Declaration shall become effective immediately, inasmuch as any act of aggression or threat of aggression during the present state of war interferes with the war effort of the United Nations to obtain victory. Henceforth, and to the end that the principles and procedures herein stipulated shall conform with the constitutional processes of each Republic, the

respective Governments shall take the necessary steps to perfect this instrument in order that it shall be in force at all times.

PART II

The Inter-American Conference on Problems of War and Peace *Recommends:*

That for the purpose of meeting threats or acts of aggression against any American Republic following the establishment of peace, the Governments of the American Republics consider the conclusion, in accordance with their constitutional processes, of a treaty establishing procedures whereby such threats or acts may be met by the use, by all or some of the signatories of said treaty, of any one or more of the following measures: recall of chiefs of diplomatic missions; breaking of diplomatic relations; breaking of consular relations; breaking of postal, telegraphic, telephonic, radio-telephonic relations; interruption of economic, commercial and financial relations; use of armed force to prevent or repel aggression.

PART III

The above Declaration and Recommendation constitute a regional arrangement for dealing with such matters relating to the maintenance of international peace and security as are appropriate for regional action in this Hemisphere. The said arrangement, and the pertinent activities and procedures, shall be consistent with the purposes and principles of the general international organization, when established.

This agreement shall be known as the "ACT OF CHAPULTEPEC." (Approved at the plenary session of March 6, 1945)

DECLARATION XI: Declaration of Mexico

Report of the Delegation of the United States of America to the Inter-American Conference on Problems of War and Peace, p. 80

THE STATES OF AMERICA, through their Plenipotentiary Delegates meeting at the Inter-American Conference on Problems of War and Peace

Declare:

The American community maintains the following essential principles as governing the relations among the States composing it:

1. International Law is the rule of conduct for all States.

2. States are juridically equal.

3. Each State is free and sovereign, and no State may intervene in the internal or external affairs of another.

4. The territory of the American States is inviolable and also immutable, except when changes are made by peaceful agreement.

5. The American States do not recognize the validity of territorial conquests.

6. The mission of the American States is the preservation of peace and the maintenance of the best possible relations with all States.

7. Conflicts between States are to be settled exclusively by peaceful means.

8. War of aggression in any of its forms is outlawed.

9. An aggression against an American State constitutes an aggression against all American States.

10. The American States are united in their aspirations and common interests.

11. The American States reiterate their fervent adherence to democratic principles, which they consider essential for the peace of America.

12. The purpose of the State is the happiness of man in society. The interests of the community should be harmonized with the rights of the individual. The American man cannot conceive of living without justice, just as he cannot conceive of living without liberty.

13. Among the rights of man, the first is equality of opportunity to enjoy all the spiritual and material blessings offered by civilization, through the legitimate exercise of his activity, his industry, and his ingenuity.

14. Education and material well-being are indispensable to the development of democracy.

15. Economic cooperation is essential to the common prosperity of the American Nations. Want among any of their peoples, whether in the form of poverty, malnutrition, or ill health, affects each one of them and consequently all of them jointly.

16. The American States consider as necessary the equitable coordination of all interests to create an economy of abundance in which natural resources and human labor will be utilized to raise the standard of living of all the peoples of the Continent.

17. The inter-American community is dedicated to the ideals of universal cooperation.

(Approved at the plenary session of March 6, 1945)

RESOLUTION LIX: On the Communication Addressed by the Argentine Government to the Pan American Union

Report of the Delegation of the United States of America to the Inter-American Conference on Problems of War and Peace, p. 133

THE INTER-AMERICAN CONFERENCE of Problems of War and Peace,

Having considered the text of the communication addressed by the Argentine Government to the Pan American Union, and

CONSIDERING:

1. That the Conference was called for the purpose of taking measures to intensify the war effort of the American Nations united against Germany and Japan, and to seek the strengthening of their political and economic sovereignty and their co-operation and security, and

2. That the circumstances existing before the meeting have undergone no change that would have justified the Conference in taking steps to reestablish, as it earnestly desires to do, the unity of the twenty-one States in the policy of solidarity that has been strengthened during the deliberations of the Conference,

Resolves:

1. To deplore that the Argentine Nation has up to the present time not found it possible to take the steps that would permit its participation in the Inter-American Conference on Problems of War and Peace, the conclusions of which have consolidated and extended the principle of solidarity of the hemisphere against all types of aggression.

2. To recognize that the unity of the peoples of America is indivisible and that the Argentine Nation is and always has been an integral part of the Union of the American Republics.

3. To express its desire that the Argentine Nation may put itself in a position to express its conformity with and adherence to the principles and declarations resulting from the Conference of Mexico, which enrich the juridical and political heritage of the Continent and enlarge the scope of American public law, to which on so many occasions Argentina itself has made notable contributions.

4. To reiterate that—as proclaimed at Habana, amplified and strengthened by the "Act of Chapultepec," and demonstrated by the action of the American Republics in becoming members of the United Nations—the Conference considers that, in the event of threats or acts of aggression by any State against an American State, complete solidarity and a common policy among the American States are essential to the security and peace of the Continent.

5. To declare that the Conference hopes that the Argentine Nation will cooperate with the other American Nations, identifying itself with the common policy these nations are pursuing, and orienting its own policy so that it may achieve its incorporation into the United Nations as a signatory to the Joint Declaration entered into by them.

6. To declare that the Final Act of this Conference shall be open to adherence by the Argentine Nation, in accordance with the criteria of this resolution, and to authorize His Excellency Dr. Ezequiel Padilla, President of the Conference, to communicate the resolutions of this assembly to the Argentine Government through the Pan American Union.

(Approved at the plenary session of March 7, 1945)

Inter-American Conference for the Maintenance of Continental Peace and Security, at Quitandinha, Brazil, August 15 to September 2, 1947

INTER-AMERICAN TREATY of Reciprocal Assistance

Department of State, *Inter-American Conference for the Maintenance of Continental Peace and Security, Report of the Delegation of the United States of America*, p. 59. The U.S. Senate on December 8, 1947, advised and consented to ratification of the treaty by a vote of 72 to 1; the President ratified on December 12, 1947

IN THE NAME of their Peoples, the Governments represented at the Inter-American Conference for the Maintenance of Continental Peace and Security, desirous of consolidating and strengthening their relations of friendship and good neighborliness, and

CONSIDERING:

That Resolution VIII of the Inter-American Conference on Problems of War and Peace, which met in Mexico City, recommended the conclusion of a treaty to prevent and repel threats and acts of aggression against any of the countries of America;

That the High Contracting Parties reiterate their will to remain united in an inter-American system consistent with the purposes and principles of the United Nations, and reaffirm the existence of the agreement which they have concluded concerning those matters relating to the maintenance of international peace and security which are appropriate for regional action;

That the High Contracting Parties reaffirm their adherence to the principles of inter-American solidarity and cooperation, and especially

to those set forth in the preamble and declarations of the Act of Chapultepec, all of which should be understood to be accepted as standards
of their mutual relations and as the juridical basis of the Inter-
American System;

That the American States propose, in order to improve the procedures for the pacific settlement of their controversies, to conclude
the treaty concerning the "Inter-American Peace System" envisaged
in Resolutions IX and XXXIX of the Inter-American Conference on
Problems of War and Peace,

That the obligation of mutual assistance and common defense of
the American Republics is essentially related to their democratic
ideals and to their will to cooperate permanently in the fulfillment of
the principles and purposes of a policy of peace;

That the American regional community affirms as a manifest truth
that juridical organization is a necessary prerequisite of security and
peace, and that peace is founded on justice and moral order and,
consequently, on the international recognition and protection of
human rights and freedoms, on the indispensable well-being of the
people, and on the effectiveness of democracy for the international
realization of justice and security,

Have resolved, in conformity with the objectives stated above, to
conclude the following Treaty, in order to assure peace, through
adequate means, to provide for effective reciprocal assistance to meet
armed attacks against any American State, and in order to deal with
threats of aggression against any of them:

ARTICLE 1

The High Contracting Parties formally condemn war and undertake in their international relations not to resort to the threat or the
use of force in any manner inconsistent with the provisions of the
Charter of the United Nations or of this Treaty.

ARTICLE 2

As a consequence of the principle set forth in the preceding Article,
the High Contracting Parties undertake to submit every controversy
which may arise between them to methods of peaceful settlement and
to endeavor to settle any such controversy among themselves by means
of the procedures in force in the Inter-American System before referring it to the General Assembly or the Security Council of the
United Nations.

ARTICLE 3

1. The High Contracting Parties agree that an armed attack by
any State against an American State shall be considered as an attack

against all the American States and, consequently, each one of the said Contracting Parties undertakes to assist in meeting the attack in the exercise of the inherent right of individual or collective self-defense recognized by Article 51 of the Charter of the United Nations.

2. On the request of the State or States directly attacked and until the decision of the Organ of Consultation of the Inter-American System, each one of the Contracting Parties may determine the immediate measures which it may individually take in fulfillment of the obligation contained in the preceding paragraph and in accordance with the principle of continental solidarity. The Organ of Consultation shall meet without delay for the purpose of examining those measures and agreeing upon the measures of a collective character that should be taken.

3. The provisions of this Article shall be applied in case of any armed attack which takes place within the region described in Article 4 or within the territory of an American State. When the attack takes place outside of the said areas, the provisions of Article 6 shall be applied.

4. Measures of self-defense provided for under this Article may be taken until the Security Council of the United Nations has taken the measures necessary to maintain international peace and security.

ARTICLE 4

The region to which this Treaty refers is bounded as follows: beginning at the North Pole; thence due south to a point 74 degrees north latitude, 10 degrees west longitude; thence by a rhumb line to a point 47 degrees 30 minutes north latitude, 50 degrees west longitude; thence by a rhumb line to a point 35 degrees north latitude, 60 degrees west longitude; thence due south to a point in 20 degrees north latitude; thence by a rhumb line to a point 5 degrees north latitude, 24 degrees west longitude; thence due south to the South Pole; thence due north to a point 30 degrees south latitude, 90 degrees west longitude; thence by a rhumb line to a point on the Equator at 97 degrees west longitude; thence by a rhumb line to a point 15 degrees north latitude, 120 degrees west longitude; thence by a rhumb line to a point 50 degrees north latitude, 170 degrees east longitude; thence due north to a point in 54 degrees north latitude; thence by a rhumb line to a point 65 degrees 30 minutes north latitude, 168 degrees 58 minutes 5 seconds west longitude; thence due north to the North Pole.

ARTICLE 5

The High Contracting Parties shall immediately send to the Security Council of the United Nations, in conformity with Articles 51 and 54 of the Charter of the United Nations, complete information concerning the activities undertaken or in contemplation in the exercise of the right of self-defense or for the purpose of maintaining inter-American peace and security.

ARTICLE 6

If the inviolability or the integrity of the territory or the sovereignty or political independence of any American State should be affected by an aggression which is not an armed attack or by an extra-continental or intra-continental conflict, or by any other fact or situation that might endanger the peace of America, the Organ of Consultation shall meet immediately in order to agree on the measures which must be taken in case of aggression to assist the victim of the aggression or, in any case, the measures which should be taken for the common defense and for the maintenance of the peace and security of the Continent.

ARTICLE 7

In the case of a conflict between two or more American States, without prejudice to the right of self-defense in conformity with Article 51 of the Charter of the United Nations, the High Contracting Parties, meeting in consultation shall call upon the contending States to suspend hostilities and restore matters to the *statu quo ante bellum,* and shall take in addition all other necessary measures to reestablish or maintain inter-American peace and security and for the solution of the conflict by peaceful means. The rejection of the pacifying action will be considered in the determination of the aggressor and in the application of the measures which the consultative meeting may agree upon.

ARTICLE 8

For the purposes of this Treaty, the measures on which the Organ of Consultation may agree will comprise one or more of the following: recall of chiefs of diplomatic missions; breaking of diplomatic relations; breaking of consular relations; partial or complete interruption of economic relations or of rail, sea, air, postal, telegraphic, telephonic, and radiotelephonic or radiotelegraphic communications; and use of armed force.

ARTICLE 9

In addition to other acts which the Organ of Consultation may characterize as aggression, the following shall be considered as such:

a. Unprovoked armed attack by a State against the territory, the people, or the land, sea, or air forces of another State;

b. Invasion, by the armed forces of a State, of the territory of an American State, through the trespassing of boundaries demarcated in accordance with a treaty, judicial decision, or arbitral award, or, in the absence of frontiers thus demarcated, invasion affecting a region which is under the effective jurisdiction of another State.

ARTICLE 10

None of the provisions of this Treaty shall be construed as impairing the rights and obligations of the High Contracting Parties under the Charter of the United Nations.

ARTICLE 11

The consultations to which this Treaty refers shall be carried out by means of the Meetings of Ministers of Foreign Affairs of the American Republics which have ratified the Treaty, or in the manner or by the organ which in the future may be agreed upon.

ARTICLE 12

The Governing Board of the Pan American Union may act provisionally as an organ of consultation until the meeting of the Organ of Consultation referred to in the preceding Article takes place.

ARTICLE 13

The consultations shall be initiated at the request addressed to the Governing Board of the Pan American Union by any of the Signatory States which has ratified the Treaty.

ARTICLE 14

In the voting referred to in this Treaty only the representatives of the Signatory States which have ratified the Treaty may take part.

ARTICLE 15

The Governing Board of the Pan American Union shall act in all matters concerning this Treaty as an organ of liaison among the Signatory States which have ratified this Treaty and between these States and the United Nations.

ARTICLE 16

The decisions of the Governing Board of the Pan American Union referred to in Articles 13 and 15 above shall be taken by an absolute majority of the Members entitled to vote.

ARTICLE 17

The Organ of Consultation shall take its decisions by a vote of two-thirds of the Signatory States which have ratified the Treaty.

ARTICLE 18

In the case of a situation or dispute between American States, the parties directly interested shall be excluded from the voting referred to in the two preceding Articles.

ARTICLE 19

To constitute a quorum in all the meetings referred to in the previous Articles, it shall be necessary that the number of States represented shall be at least equal to the number of votes necessary for the taking of the decision.

ARTICLE 20

Decisions which require the application of the measures specified in Article 8 shall be binding upon all the Signatory States which have ratified this Treaty, with the sole exception that no State shall be required to use armed force without its consent.

ARTICLE 21

The measures agreed upon by the Organ of Consultation shall be executed through the procedures and agencies now existing or those which may in the future be established.

ARTICLE 22

This Treaty shall come into effect between the States which ratify it as soon as the ratifications of two-thirds of the Signatory States have been deposited.

ARTICLE 23

This Treaty is open for signature by the American States at the city of Rio de Janeiro, and shall be ratified by the Signatory States as soon as possible in accordance with their respective constitutional processes. The ratifications shall be deposited with the Pan American Union, which shall notify the Signatory States of each deposit. Such notification shall be considered as an exchange of ratifications.

ARTICLE 24

The present Treaty shall be registered with the Secretariat of the United Nations through the Pan American Union, when two-thirds of the Signatory States have deposited their ratifications.

ARTICLE 25

This Treaty shall remain in force indefinitely, but may be denounced by any High Contracting Party by a notification in writing to the Pan American Union, which shall inform all the other High Contracting Parties of each notification of denunciation received. After the expiration of two years from the date of the receipt by the Pan American Union of a notification of denunciation by any High Contracting Party, the present Treaty shall cease to be in force with respect to such State, but shall remain in full force and effect with respect to all the other High Contracting Parties.

ARTICLE 26

The principles and fundamental provisions of this Treaty shall be incorporated in the Organic Pact of the Inter-American System.

In witness whereof, the undersigned Plenipotentiaries, having deposited their full powers found to be in due and proper form, sign this Treaty on behalf of their respective Governments, on the dates appearing opposite their signatures.

Done in the city of Rio de Janeiro, in four texts respectively in the English, French, Portuguese and Spanish languages, on the second of September nineteen hundred forty-seven.

[*Signatures*]

PERTINENT PROVISIONS of the United Nations Charter with Respect to the Inter-American Treaty of Reciprocal Assistance

Department of State, *Inter-American Conference for the Maintenance of Continental Peace and Security, Report of the Delegation of the United States of America*, p. 223

Chapter 1. Purposes and Principles

ARTICLE 2

3. All Members shall settle their international disputes by peaceful means in such a manner that international peace and security, and justice, are not endangered.

4. All Members shall refrain in their international relations from the threat or use of force against the territorial integrity or political

independence of any state, or in any other manner inconsistent with the Purposes of the United Nations.

Chapter VI. Pacific Settlement of Disputes

ARTICLE 33

1. The parties to any dispute, the continuance of which is likely to endanger the maintenance of international peace and security, shall, first of all, seek a solution by negotiation, enquiry, mediation, conciliation, arbitration, judicial settlement, resort to regional agencies or arrangements, or other peaceful means of their own choice.

2. The Security Council shall, when it deems necessary, call upon the parties to settle their dispute by such means.

ARTICLE 37

1. Should the parties to a dispute of the nature referred to in Article 33 fail to settle it by the means indicated in that Article, they shall refer it to the Security Council.

2. If the Security Council deems that the continuance of the dispute is in fact likely to endanger the maintenance of international peace and security, it shall decide whether to take action under Article 36 or to recommend such terms of settlement as it may consider appropriate.

Chapter VII. Action with Respect to Threats to the Peace, Breaches of the Peace, and Acts of Aggression

ARTICLE 39

The Security Council shall determine the existence of any threat to the peace, breach of the peace, or act of aggression and shall make recommendations, or decide what measures shall be taken in accordance with Articles 41 and 42, to maintain or restore international peace and security.

ARTICLE 40

In order to prevent an aggravation of the situation, the Security Council may, before making the recommendations or deciding upon the measures provided for in Article 39, call upon the parties concerned to comply with such provisional measures as it deems necessary or desirable. Such provisional measures shall be without prejudice to the rights, claims, or position of the parties concerned. The Security Council shall duly take account of failure to comply with such provisional measures.

ARTICLE 41

The Security Council may decide what measures not involving the use of armed force are to be employed to give effect to its decisions, and it may call upon the Members of the United Nations to apply such measures. These may include complete or partial interruption of economic relations and of rail, sea, air, postal, telegraphic, radio, and other means of communication, and the severance of diplomatic relations.

ARTICLE 42

Should the Security Council consider that measures provided for in Article 41 would be inadequate or have proved to be inadequate, it may take such action by air, sea, or land forces as may be necessary to maintain or restore international peace and security. Such action may include demonstrations, blockade, and other operations by air, sea, or land forces of Members of the United Nations.

ARTICLE 51

Nothing in the present Charter shall impair the inherent right of individual or collective self-defense if an armed attack occurs against a Member of the United Nations, until the Security Council has taken the measures necessary to maintain international peace and security. Measures taken by Members in the exercise of this right of self-defense shall be immediately reported to the Security Council and shall not in any way affect the authority and responsibility of the Security Council under the present Charter to take at any time such action as it deems necessary in order to maintain or restore international peace and security.

Chapter VIII. Regional Arrangements

ARTICLE 52

1. Nothing in the present Charter precludes the existence of regional arrangements or agencies for dealing with such matters relating to the maintenance of international peace and security as are appropriate for regional action, provided that such arrangements or agencies and their activities are consistent with the Purposes and Principles of the United Nations.

2. The Members of the United Nations entering into such arrangements or constituting such agencies shall make every effort to achieve pacific settlement of local disputes through such regional arrange-

ments or by such regional agencies before referring them to the Security Council.

3. The Security Council shall encourage the development of pacific settlement of local disputes through such regional arrangements or by such regional agencies either on the initiative of the states concerned or by reference from the Security Council.

4. This Article in no way impairs the application of Articles 34 and 35.

ARTICLE 53

1. The Security Council shall, where appropriate, utilize such regional arrangements or agencies for enforcement action under its authority. But no enforcement action shall be taken under regional arrangements or by regional agencies without the authorization of the Security Council, with the exception of measures against any enemy state, as defined in paragraph 2 of this Article, provided for pursuant to Article 107 or in regional arrangements directed against renewal of aggressive policy on the part of any such state, until such time as the Organization may, on request of the Governments concerned, be charged with the responsibility for preventing further aggression by such a state.

2. The term enemy state as used in paragraph 1 of this Article applies to any state which during the Second World War has been an enemy of any signatory of the present Charter.

ARTICLE 54

The Security Council shall at all times be kept fully informed of activities undertaken or in contemplation under regional arrangements or by regional agencies for the maintenance of international peace and security.

Ninth International Conference of American States, at Bogotá, March 30 to May 2, 1948

DECLARATION XXX: American Declaration of the Rights and Duties of Man

Department of State press release, May 21, 1948 (No. 400), *Final Act of Bogotá*, p. 39

WHEREAS:

The American nations have acknowledged the dignity of the individual, and their national constitutions recognize that juridical and political institutions, which regulate life in human society, have as their principal aim the protection of the essential rights of man and the creation of circumstances that will permit him to achieve spiritual and material progress, and attain happiness;

The American states have on repeated occasions recognized that the essential rights of man are not derived from the fact of one's being a national of a certain state, but are fundamental attributes of the individual;

The international protection of the rights of man should be the supreme guide of an evolving American law;

Both the American affirmation of essential human rights and the guarantees given by the internal regimes of the respective states establish the initial system of protection considered by the American States as being suited to the present social and juridical conditions, not without recognizing that they should increasingly strengthen that system in the international field as these conditions become more favorable;

The Ninth International Conference of American States agrees to adopt the following

AMERICAN DECLARATION OF THE RIGHTS AND DUTIES OF MAN

Preamble

All men are born free and equal, in dignity and in rights, and, being endowed by nature with reason and conscience, they should conduct themselves as brothers one to another.

The fulfillment of duty by each individual is a prerequisite to the rights of all. Rights and duties are interrelated in every social and political activity of man. While rights exalt individual liberty, duties express the dignity of that liberty.

Duties of a juridical nature presuppose others of a moral nature that support those duties in concept and are the basis therefor.

Inasmuch as the spirit is the supreme aim of human existence and the greatest expression thereof, it is the duty of man to serve that end with all his strength and resources.

Since culture is the maximum social and historical expression of that spirit, it is the duty of man to preserve, practice, and foster culture by every means within his power.

And, since morality and good manners constitute the noblest flowering of culture, it is the duty of every man always to hold them in high respect.

Chapter One: Rights

ARTICLE 1. (RIGHT TO LIFE, LIBERTY, AND PERSONAL SECURITY)

Every human being has the right to life, liberty, and the security of his person.

ARTICLE 2. (RIGHT TO EQUALITY BEFORE THE LAW)

All persons are equal before the law and have the rights and duties established in this Declaration, without distinction as to race, sex, language, creed, or any other factor.

ARTICLE 3. (RIGHT TO RELIGIOUS FREEDOM AND WORSHIP)

Every person has the right freely to profess a religious faith, and to manifest and practice it both in public and in private.

ARTICLE 4. (RIGHT TO FREEDOM OF INVESTIGATION, OPINION, EXPRESSION, AND DISSEMINATION)

Every person has the right to freedom of investigation, of opinion, and of the expression and dissemination of thought, by any medium whatsoever.

ARTICLE 5. (RIGHT TO PROTECTION OF HONOR, PERSONAL REPUTATION, AND PRIVATE AND FAMILY LIFE)

Every person has the right to the protection of the law against abusive attacks upon his honor, his reputation, and his private and family life.

ARTICLE 6. (RIGHT TO A FAMILY AND TO THE PROTECTION THEREOF)

Every person has the right to establish a family, the basic element of society, and to receive protection therefor.

ARTICLE 7. (RIGHT TO PROTECTION FOR MOTHERS AND CHILDREN)

All women, during pregnancy and the nursing period, and all children have the right to special protection, care and aid.

ARTICLE 8. (RIGHT TO RESIDENCE AND MOVEMENT)

Every person has the right to fix his residence within the territory of the state of which he is a national, to move about freely within such territory, and not to leave it except by his own will.

ARTICLE 9. (RIGHT TO INVIOLABILITY OF THE HOME)

Every person has the right to the inviolability of his home.

ARTICLE 10. (RIGHT TO INVIOLABILITY AND CIRCULATION OF CORRESPONDENCE)

Every person has the right to the inviolability and circulation of his correspondence.

ARTICLE 11. (RIGHT TO THE PRESERVATION OF HEALTH AND TO WELL-
BEING)

Every person has the right to the preservation of his health through
sanitary and social measures relating to food, clothing, housing, and
medical care, to the extent permitted by public and community resources.

ARTICLE 12. (RIGHT TO EDUCATION)

Every person has the right to an education, which should be based
on the principles of liberty, ethics, and human solidarity.

Furthermore, every person has the right to an education that will
prepare him to lead a decent life, to raise his standard of living, and
to be a useful member of society.

The right to an education includes the right to equality of opportunity in every case, in accordance with natural talents, merit, and
the desire to utilize the resources that the state or the community is in
a position to provide.

Every person has the right to receive, free, at least a primary education.

ARTICLE 13. (RIGHT TO THE BENEFITS OF CULTURE)

Every person has the right to take part in the cultural life of the
community, to enjoy the arts, and to participate in the benefits that result from intellectual progress, especially scientific discoveries.

He likewise has the right to the protection of his moral and material interests as regards his inventions or any literary, scientific, or
artistic works of which he is the author.

ARTICLE 14. (RIGHT TO WORK AND TO FAIR REMUNERATION)

Every person has the right to work, under proper conditions, and
to follow his vocation freely, in so far as existing conditions of employment permit.

Every person who works has the right to receive such remuneration as will, in proportion to his capacity and skill, assure him a
standard of living suitable for himself and for his family.

ARTICLE 15. (RIGHT TO LEISURE TIME AND TO THE USE THEREOF)

Every person has the right to leisure time, to wholesome recreation,
and to the opportunity for advantageous use of his free time to his
spiritual, cultural and physical benefit.

ARTICLE 16. (RIGHT TO SOCIAL SECURITY)

Every person has the right to social security which will protect
him from the consequences of unemployment, old age, and any

disabilities arising from causes beyond his control that make it physically or mentally impossible for him to earn a living.

ARTICLE 17. (RIGHT TO RECOGNITION OF JURIDICAL PERSONALITY AND OF CIVIL RIGHTS)

Every person has the right to be recognized everywhere as a person having rights and obligations, and to enjoy the basic civil rights.

ARTICLE 18. (RIGHT TO A FAIR TRIAL)

Every person may resort to the courts to ensure respect for his legal rights. There should likewise be available to him a simple, brief procedure whereby justice will protect him from acts of authority that, to his prejudice, violate any fundamental constitutional rights.

ARTICLE 19. (RIGHT TO NATIONALITY)

Every person has the right to the nationality to which he is entitled by law and to change it, if he so wishes, for the nationality of any other country that is willing to grant it to him.

ARTICLE 20. (RIGHT TO VOTE AND TO PARTICIPATE IN GOVERNMENT)

Every person having legal capacity is entitled to participate in the government of his country, directly or through his representative, and to take part in popular elections, which shall be by secret ballot, and shall be genuine, periodic, and free.

ARTICLE 21. (RIGHT OF ASSEMBLY)

Every person has the right to assembly peaceably with others in a formal public meeting or an informal gathering, in connection with matters of common interest of any nature.

ARTICLE 22. (RIGHT OF ASSOCIATION)

Every person has the right to associate with others to promote, exercise, and protect his legitimate interests of a political, economic, religious, social, cultural, professional, trade union, or other nature.

ARTICLE 23. (RIGHT TO PROPERTY)

Every person has a right to own such private property as meets the essential needs of decent living and helps to maintain the dignity of the individual and of the home.

ARTICLE 24. (RIGHT OF PETITION)

Every person has the right to submit respectful petitions to any competent authority, for reasons of either general or private interest, and the right to obtain prompt action thereon.

ARTICLE 25. (RIGHT TO PROTECTION)

No person may be deprived of his liberty except in the cases and according to the procedures established by pre-existing law.

No person may be deprived of liberty for non-fulfillment of obligations of a purely civil character.

Every individual who has been deprived of his liberty has the right to have the legality of the measure ascertained without delay by a court, and the right to be tried without undue delay or, otherwise, to be released. He also has the right to humane treatment during the time he is in custody.

ARTICLE 26. (RIGHT TO DUE PROCESS OF LAW)

Every accused person is presumed to be innocent until proved guilty.

Every person accused of an offense has the right to be given an impartial and public hearing, and to be tried by courts previously established in accordance with pre-existing laws, and not to receive cruel, infamous, or unusual punishment.

ARTICLE 27. (RIGHT OF ASYLUM)

Every person has the right to seek and receive asylum in foreign territory, in case of pursuit not resulting from common law crimes, and in accordance with the laws of each country and with international agreements.

ARTICLE 28. (SCOPE OF THE RIGHTS OF MAN)

The rights of man are limited by the rights of others, by the security of all, and by the just demands of the general welfare and the advancement of democracy.

Chapter Two: Duties

ARTICLE 29. (DUTIES TO SOCIETY)

It is the duty of the individual so to conduct himself in relation to others that each and every one may fully form and develop his personality.

ARTICLE 30. (DUTIES TOWARD CHILDREN AND PARENTS)

It is the duty of every person to aid, support, educate, and protect his minor children, and it is the duty of children to honor their parents always and to aid, support, and protect them when they need it.

ARTICLE 31. (DUTY TO RECEIVE INSTRUCTION)

It is the duty of every person to acquire at least an elementary education.

ARTICLE 32. (DUTY TO VOTE)

It is the duty of every person to vote in the popular elections of the country of which he is a national, when he is legally capable of doing so.

ARTICLE 33. (DUTY TO OBEY THE LAW)

It is the duty of every person to obey the law and other legitimate commands of the authorities of his country and those of the country in which he may be.

ARTICLE 34. (DUTY TO SERVE THE COMMUNITY AND THE NATION)

It is the duty of every able-bodied person to render whatever civil and military service his country may require for its defense and preservation, and in case of public disaster, to render such civil services as may be in his power.

It is likewise his duty to hold any popular elective office that devolves upon him in the state in which he is a national.

ARTICLE 35. (DUTIES WITH RESPECT TO SOCIAL SECURITY AND WELFARE)

It is the duty of every person to cooperate with the state and the community with respect to social security and welfare, in accordance with his ability and with existing circumstances.

ARTICLE 36. (DUTY TO PAY TAXES)

It is the duty of every person to pay the taxes established by law for the support of public services.

ARTICLE 37. (DUTY TO WORK)

It is the duty of every person to work, as far as his capacity and possibilities permit, in order to obtain the means of livelihood or to benefit his community.

ARTICLE 38. (DUTY TO REFRAIN FROM POLITICAL ACTIVITIES IN A FOREIGN COUNTRY)

It is the duty of every person to refrain from taking part in political activities that, according to law, are reserved exclusively to the citizens of the state in which he is an alien.

DECLARATION AND RESOLUTION XXXII: The Preservation and Defense of Democracy in America
Department of State press release, May 21, 1948 (No. 400), *Final Act of Bogotá*, p. 46

WHEREAS:
In order to safeguard peace and maintain mutual respect among states, the present situation of the world demands that urgent measures be taken to proscribe tactics of totalitarian domination that are inconsistent with the tradition of the countries of America, and prevent agents at the service of international communism or of any totalitarian doctrine from seeking to distort the true and the free will of the peoples of this continent;

The Republics Represented at the Ninth International Conference of American States

Declare that by its anti-democratic nature and its interventionist tendency, the political activity of international communism or any totalitarian doctrine is incompatible with the concept of American freedom, which rests upon two undeniable postulates: the dignity of man as an individual and the sovereignty of the nation as a state;

Reiterate the faith that the peoples of the New World have placed in the ideal and in the reality of democracy, under the protection of which they shall achieve social justice, by offering to all increasingly broader opportunities to enjoy the spiritual and material benefits that are the guarantee of civilization and the heritage of humanity;

Condemn in the name of the Law of Nations, interference by any foreign power, or by any political organization serving the interests of a foreign power, in the public life of the nations of the American continent.

And Resolve:

1. To reaffirm their decision to maintain and further an effective social and economic policy for the purpose of raising the standard of living of their peoples; and their conviction that only under a system founded upon a guarantee of the essential freedoms and rights of the individual is it possible to attain this goal.

2. To condemn the methods of every system tending to suppress political and civil rights and liberties, and in particular the action of international communism or any totalitarian doctrine.

3. To adopt, within their respective territories and in accordance with the constitutional provisions of each state, the measures neces-

sary to eradicate and prevent activities directed, assisted, or insti-gated by foreign governments, organizations, or individuals, that tend to overthrow their institutions by violence, to foment disorder in their domestic political life, or to disturb, by means of pressure, subversive propaganda, threats or by any other means, the free and sovereign fight of their peoples to govern themselves in accordance with their democratic aspirations.

4. To proceed with a full exchange of information concerning any of the aforementioned activities that are carried on within their respective jurisdictions.

DECLARATION AND RESOLUTION XXXIII: Regarding Colonies and Occupied Territories in America and Creation of the American Committee on Dependent Territories
Department of State press release, May 21, 1948 (No. 400), *Final Act of Bogotá,* p. 47

WHEREAS:

The historical process of the emancipation of America will not be complete as long as peoples and regions subject to a colonial regime, or territories occupied by non-American countries remain on the continent;

The ideal that inspired the epic of the independence of America will always animate our peoples and governments, united in their moral pledge to strive by all peaceful means within their power to eliminate from the continent any status of dependency, whatever its form—political, economic, or juridical;

Ever since they achieved their independence, the American states have had this common objective, which has lately been defined in precise terms in the Meetings of Consultation of Ministers of Foreign Affairs, held at Habana and Rio de Janeiro, in resolutions condemning colonial regimes in America and reaffirming the right of the peoples of this continent freely to determine their own destinies;

The American States have fixed a zone of continental security to which extra-continental conflicts should not extend, as might occur by reason of the existence on the continent of dependent territories or those occupied by non-American countries;

The principle of pacific settlement of international controversies is part of the juridical heritage of the Organization of American States, and controversies exist between American Republics and

European States over sovereignty rights with respect to certain territories of the continent;

The *de facto* or *de jure* status of colonies and dependent or occupied possessions and territories on the American continent, or within its security zone, varies according to each case, within the framework of their common status, which makes it necessary to carry out studies on each of them in order to find a suitable solution in each case;

The idea of preserving and strengthening the close solidarity of all the democratic nations of both hemispheres exists in the spirit of the countries of America;

The Ninth International Conference of American States

Declares:

That it is a just aspiration of the American republics for colonialism and the occupation of American territories by extra-continental countries to come to an end; and

Resolves:

First: To create an "American Committee on Dependent Territories" to centralize the study of the problem of the existence of dependent and occupied territories, in order to find an adequate solution to that question:

Second: The Committee shall be composed of one representative of each member of the Organization of American States, whose appointment shall, in each case, be communicated to the Council of the Organization before September 1, 1948, if possible. As soon as fourteen have been appointed the Council, by prior agreement with the Government of Cuba, shall convoke the Committee in order that it may be installed and perform its duties in the city of Habana.

Third: The functions of the Committee shall be the following:

a) To centralize all information on any of the above-mentioned problems referred to it by the governments and entities concerned;

b) To study the situation of the colonies, possessions and occupied territories existing in America, and the problems related to such situation, whatever their nature, with a view to seeking pacific means of eliminating both colonialism and the occupation of American territories by extra-continental countries;

c) The Committee shall submit a report on each of such colonies, possessions and territories to the Council of the Organization of American States which shall transmit copies to the member states of the Organization for their information and study; these reports shall be considered at the first Meeting of Consultation of Ministers of Foreign Affairs that is held after their presentation;

d) The Committee shall draw up its own regulations.

Fourth: The creation of this Committee and the performance of its functions shall not exclude or limit the right and action of the interested states directly concerned with the problems to which this Resolution refers, to seek a solution of such problems by themselves through pacific means.

DECLARATION XXXV: On Exercise of the Right to Continuity of Diplomatic Relations

Department of State press release, May 21, 1948 (No. 400), *Final Act of Bogotá*, p. 50

WHEREAS:

The American States have taken countless practical measures to strengthen their cooperation in economic, social, political, cultural, juridical, and military matters;

The Charter of the Organization of American States recognizes the mutual advantages derived from inter-American solidarity, and affords the Organization permanence and continuity;

The development of the activities, and the full benefits, of inter-American cooperation can be realized more effectively if continuous and friendly relations are maintained among the States;

The Ninth International Conference of American States
Declares:

1. That continuity of diplomatic relations among the American States is to be desired;

2. That the right of maintaining, suspending, or renewing diplomatic relations with another government shall not be exercised as a means of individually obtaining unjustified advantages under international law;

3. That the establishment or maintenance of diplomatic relations with a government does not imply an opinion on the domestic policy of that government.

ECONOMIC AGREEMENT of Bogotá, Signed May 2, 1948 (provisional and unofficial English translation)

Department of State press release, May 12, 1948 (No. 367)

WHEREAS:

It is the desire of the American States to maintain, strengthen and develop in the economic field and within the framework of the United Nations the special relations that unite them;

The economic welfare of each state depends in large measure upon the well-being of the others;

At the Inter-American Conference for the Maintenance of Continental Peace and Security, they considered that the economic security indispensable for the progress of all the American peoples is at all times the best guarantee of their political security and of the success of their joint effort in behalf of the maintenance of continental peace;

In the Economic Charter of the Americas they have established the essential principles that should guide their economic and social policy;

They have adopted as their own the economic and social principles and aims of the Charter of the United Nations;

The American States Represented at the Ninth International Conference of American States have resolved:

To authorize their respective representatives, whose Full Powers have been found to be in good and due form, to sign the following articles:

Chapter I: Principles

ARTICLE 1

The American States, represented at the Ninth International Conference of American States and which hereinafter shall be called the States, declare that it is their duty to cooperate toward the solution of their economic problems, and to conduct their international economic relations in the American spirit of good neighborliness.

ARTICLE 2

The purpose of the cooperation to which this Agreement refers and the principles that inspire it are those set forth in the Charter of the United Nations, the Economic Charter of the Americas, and the Charter of the Organization of American States.

ARTICLE 3

The States declare their intention to cooperate individually and collectively and with other nations to carry out the principle of facilitating access, on equal terms, to the trade, products, and means of production, including scientific and technical advances, that are needed for their industrial and general economic development.

At the same time, they reaffirm their resolution that, as a general policy, there should be taken into account the need to compensate for the disparity that is frequently noted between the prices of raw materials and the prices of manufactured products, by establishing the necessary balance between them.

ARTICLE 4

The States agree that encouragement should be given to such bilateral or multilateral agreements as will contribute to their economic welfare and common security, as provided for in this Agreement.

ARTICLE 5

The States reiterate that the productive use of their human and material resources is of interest and benefit to all countries, and that

a) General economic development, including the exploitation of natural resources, the diversification of economies, and technological advancement, will improve employment possibilities, augment the productivity and income of labor, increase demand for goods and services, help balance economies, expand international trade, and raise the level of real income; and

b) Sound industrialization, particularly that of those States which have not succeeded in fully utilizing their natural resources, is indispensable for the achievement of the aims mentioned in the foregoing paragraph.

ARTICLE 6

The extent and character of economic cooperation shall, for each participating country, be determined by its resources, the provisions of its own laws and by its commitments made through international agreements.

ARTICLE 7

The States recognize their common interest in maintaining economic conditions favorable to the development of a balanced and expanding world economy and to a high level of international trade, in such a way as to contribute to the economic strengthening and progress of each State.

ARTICLE 8

No State may apply or encourage coercive measures of an economic and political character in order to force the sovereign will of another State and to obtain from the latter advantages of any nature.

Chapter II: Technical Cooperation

ARTICLE 9

The States undertake through individual and joint action to continue and to expand technical cooperation for carrying out studies;

preparing plans and projects directed toward intensifying their agriculture, cattle raising, and mining; developing their industry; increasing their trade; diversifying their production and generally strengthening their economic structures.

ARTICLE 10

In order to realize the objectives set forth in the preceding Article, the Inter-American Economic and Social Council which, in the text of this Agreement, is hereinafter called the Council, shall within the sphere of its competence be responsible for the development and coordination of the activities necessary to:

a) Make a study of the current economic situation and prepare an inventory of the economic potential of the States, consisting of studies of their natural and human resources and of the possibilities of agriculture, mineral and industrial development, with a view to the full utilization of these resources and the expansion of their economies;

b) Promote such laboratory research and experimental work as it considers necessary;

c) Promote the training of technical and administrative personnel in all economic activities through such means as teacher and student exchange between technical educational institutions in the Americas; the exchange of specialized administrative officials; the exchange of specialists between governmental, technical and economic agencies; the apprenticing of skilled workers, foremen and auxiliary personnel in industrial plants and technical schools; and lectures and seminars;

d) Prepare studies on technical problems in public administration and finance, relating to trade and economic development;

e) Promote measures to increase trade among the States and between them and other countries of the world. Such measures should include the study and promotion of the adoption of sanitary standards with respect to plants and animals, for the purpose of reaching an international understanding to prevent the application of sanitary regulations as an indirect means of imposing barriers to international trade. The said study should be undertaken in cooperation with other appropriate organizations;

f) Place at the disposal of the interested country or countries the statistical data, information, and general plans that it is possible to develop in connection with the above-mentioned program;

g) Study, at the request of the Member States, specific proposals for development or for immigration with a view to giving advice in regard to their practicability and their utility in the sound economic development of the country concerned, and to assist in preparing for their later presentation to private capital, or to governmental or intergovernmental lending agencies for possible financing:

h) Place technical advice at the disposal of countries requesting it and make arrangements for the exchange of technical aid in all fields of economic activity, including social security and welfare.

ARTICLE 11

In order to perform the functions assigned to it in Article 10, the Council shall organize a permanent Technical Staff. This Staff shall be directed by a technical chief, who in matters within his competence shall participate and have a voice in the deliberations of the Council and shall execute the decisions of the latter.

The Council shall absorb existing inter-American organizations having similar functions and shall utilize the services of the Pan American Union.

ARTICLE 12

The Council shall maintain permanent contact with the Economic Commission for Latin America of the United Nations Economic and Social Council, in order to assure close collaboration and a practical division of functions so as to avoid duplication of work and expense.

In carrying out its activities, the Council shall maintain communication and exchange of information with the agencies in each country that are engaged in the study of economic problems or that serve as directing and planning agencies for the national economy, as well as with educational, technical, and scientific institutions, and with private, national and international organizations of production and trade. The Council shall transmit to the governments concerned copies of its correspondence with such entities.

ARTICLE 13

In carrying out its functions the Council may request of the respective governments the assistance which in its judgment it needs. The Governments may decline to give any information they consider to be confidential in character. The Council may perform its functions in the territory of a country only if authorized by that country.

ARTICLE 14

The Member States may request special studies by the Council, which shall determine whether the studies requested are within its competence and which may also indicate whether it would be more appropriate for the respective requests to be directed, in whole or in part, to other national or international institutions or to private entities.

ARTICLE 15

The States, in fixing the budget of the Pan American Union, shall take into account the amounts necessary to cover the increased expenditures of the Council and of its Technical Staff, in order that they may be able to perform the functions set forth in Article 10.

ARTICLE 16

Whenever one or more countries request the preparation of specific projects on economic development or immigration, such projects shall be drawn up by the Council with its own staff or with experts especially engaged for the account and at the cost of the country or countries requesting them, it being left to the Council, in the latter case, to determine the proportion of the costs to be borne by those countries.

Only in cases determined to be exceptional by the Council itself may the costs of specific studies on reconstruction or economic development be chargeable to the general budget.

ARTICLE 17

Nothing in this Chapter shall interfere with other arrangements entered into by the States for the reciprocal granting of technical cooperation in the economic field.

Chapter III: Financial Cooperation

ARTICLE 18

The States, in accordance with Article 6 of this Agreement undertake to grant reciprocal financial cooperation for accelerating their economic development.

Without prejudice to the obligation of each country to take the domestic measures within its power for such development, they may request financial cooperation of other States.

ARTICLE 19

The States reaffirm their purpose to bring about a high level of international trade among themselves and with the rest of the world and to promote general economic and social progress by providing stimulation for the local investment of national savings, and for private foreign capital, and they undertake to continue their efforts toward the realization of this purpose.

The States that are members of the International Monetary Fund reaffirm the aims of the Fund and in normal circumstances will utilize its services to achieve those aims that will facilitate the accomplishment of the objectives mentioned above.

All the States agree, in appropriate cases, to supplement financial cooperation for the aforesaid objectives:

a) By means of non-discriminatory bilateral stabilization agreements on mutually advantageous bases; and

b) By the utilization of whatever institutions it may be desirable to create in the future and of which they may be members.

ARTICLE 20

The States that are members of the International Bank for Reconstruction and Development reaffirm the objectives of the Bank and agree to coordinate their efforts to make it an increasingly effective instrument for the realization of such objectives, especially those concerned with promoting their mutual economic development.

All of the States declare, furthermore, that in appropriate cases they will continue to extend medium and long-term credits to one another through governmental or inter-governmental institutions for economic development and the expansion of international trade, for the purpose of complementing the flow of private investments. Sufficient economic reasons should exist for the particular purposes to be served by such credits, and the projects to be undertaken should be adapted to local conditions and be able to survive without the need of excessive permanent protection or subsidy.

Furthermore, the States agree that with respect to such loans a criterion shall be established whereby it will be possible to grant facilities to debtor countries with respect to conditions and/or currencies in which they should make payment, in cases where such countries suffer an acute shortage of foreign exchange, which prevents them from complying with the terms stipulated in the loan.

ARTICLE 21

The States recognize that the lack of domestic savings, or the ineffective use thereof, has contributed to inflationary practices in many countries of America, which may ultimately endanger the stability of their rates of exchange and the orderly development of their economies.

The States agree, therefore, to stimulate the development of local money markets to provide, from non-inflationary sources, the funds needed to cover investment expenditures in national currency. The States agree that, in general, international financing should not be sought for the purpose of covering expenditures in local currency. However, they recognize that as long as available national savings in local money markets or elsewhere are not sufficient, expenditures in local currency may, in justified circumstances, be considered for the financing referred to in Article 20.

Chapter IV: Private Investments

ARTICLE 22

The States declare that the investment of private capital and the introduction of modern methods and administrative skills from other countries, for productive and economic and socially adequate purposes, are an important factor in their general economic development and the resulting social progress.

They recognize that the international flow of such capital will be stimulated to the extent that nationals of other countries are afforded opportunities for investment and security for existing and future investments.

Foreign capital shall receive equitable treatment. The States therefore agree not to take unjustified, unreasonable or discriminatory measures that would impair the legally acquired rights or interests of nationals of other countries in the enterprises, capital, skills, arts or technology they have established or supplied.

The States shall reciprocally grant appropriate facilities and incentives for the investment and reinvestment of foreign capital, and they shall impose no unjustifiable restrictions upon the transfer of such capital and the earnings thereon.

The States agree not to set up within their respective territories unreasonable or unjustifiable impediments that would prevent other States from obtaining on equitable terms the capital, skills, and technology needed for their economic development.

ARTICLE 23

The States declare that foreign investments should be made with due regard not only for the legitimate profit of the investors, but also with a view to both increasing the national income and accelerating the sound economic development of the country in which the investment is made and to promoting the economic and social welfare of the persons directly dependent upon the enterprise in question.

They further declare that, with respect to employment and the conditions thereof, just and equitable treatment should be accorded to all personnel, national and foreign, and that the development of the technical and administrative training of national personnel should be encouraged.

The States recognize that, for private capital to contribute as much as possible to their development and progress and to the training of their nationals, it is desirable to permit enterprises, without prejudice to the laws of each country, to employ and utilize the services of a reasonable number of technical experts and executive personnel, whatever their nationality may be.

ARTICLE 24

Foreign capital shall be subject to national laws, with the guarantees provided for in this chapter, especially Article 22, and without prejudice to existing or future obligations (acuerdos) between States. The States reaffirm their right to establish, within a system of equity and of effective legal and judicial guarantees:

a) Measures to prevent foreign investments from being utilized directly or indirectly as an instrument for intervening in national politics or for prejudicing the security or fundamental interests of the receiving countries; and

b) Standards with respect to the extent, conditions, and terms upon which they will permit future foreign investments.

ARTICLE 25

The States shall take no discriminatory action against investments by virtue of which foreign enterprises or capital may be deprived of legally acquired property rights, for reasons or under conditions different from those that the Constitution or laws of each country provide for the expropriation of national property. Any expropriation shall be accompanied by payment of a fair price in a prompt, adequate and effective manner.

ARTICLE 26

The States declare their intention to promote sound investment by developing, whenever possible and in accordance with the laws of each country, uniform principles of corporate accounting, and of standards of fair disclosure to private investors.

ARTICLE 27

Each State, in order to stimulate private investment for the purpose of economic development, shall, within the framework of its own institutions, seek to liberalize its tax laws so as progressively to reduce or eliminate double taxation, as regards income from foreign sources and to avoid unduly burdensome and discriminatory taxation, without, however, creating international avenues for tax avoidance.

The States shall also seek to conclude as soon as possible agreements to prevent double taxation.

Chapter V: Cooperation for Industrial and Economic Development

ARTICLE 28

In accordance with Article 5 of this Agreement, the States:

a) Recognize that they have an obligation to cooperate with one another, by all appropriate means, so that their economic development shall not be retarded but rather accelerated as much as possible, and when suitable, to collaborate with inter-governmental agencies to facilitate and promote industrial and economic development in general, including the expansion of agriculture, mining, and the production of other raw materials with which to meet their needs;

b) Shall seek to utilize industries and production in general, of present or potential efficiency, so that they may be able to participate in joint economic plans of interest to the Americas; and

c) Also consider it desirable that progressive development of production be carried forward in accordance with the agricultural and industrial potentialities of each country, in order fully to meet the requirements of consumer nations at prices that are fair to them and that offer the producers reasonable returns.

ARTICLE 29

Progressive industrial and economic development requires, among other things, adequate supplies of capital, materials, raw materials, modern equipment, technology, and technical and administrative skill. Therefore, to promote and assist in supplying such facilities:

a) The States, in accordance with the objectives of economic cooperation of this Agreement, agree in so far as possible, within the limits of their powers, to facilitate the acquisition and exportation, for their mutual benefit, of the capital, machinery, raw materials, services and other elements needed for their economic requirements.

b) The States undertake not to impose unreasonable or unjustifiable obstacles that impede the acquisition from one another, on fair and equitable terms, of the elements, materials and services mentioned in the preceding paragraph;

c) If exceptional circumstances make it necessary to apply restrictions on exports, priorities for purchases and exports, or both, the States shall apply such measures on a fair and equitable basis, taking into account their mutual needs and other appropriate and pertinent factors; and

d) In applying the restrictions mentioned in the preceding paragraph, the States shall seek to make the distribution of and the trade in the restricted products approximate as nearly as possible the amounts that the various countries could have obtained in the absence of such restrictions.

Chapter VI: Economic Security

ARTICLE 30

The States agree to cooperate among themselves and with other producing and consumer nations, for the purpose of concluding intergovernmental agreements to prevent or correct dislocations in international trade in regard to raw materials that are basic and essential for the economies of the producing countries of the Hemisphere, such as tendencies and situations of persistent disequilibrium between production and consumption, of accumulation of excessive stocks, or of sharp fluctuations in prices, without prejudice to the provisions of the second paragraph of Article 3.

ARTICLE 31

States with common boundaries or those belonging within the same economic region, may conclude preferential agreements for purposes of economic development, each State respecting the obligations that it has undertaken by virtue of existing international bilateral agreements or multilateral agreements that have been or may be concluded. The benefits granted in such agreements shall not be extended to other countries by application of the most-favored-nation clause, except in case of a special agreement in that respect.

The development of the principle contained in this Article is assigned to the Specialized Economic Conference to be held during the second half of the present year.

Chapter VII: Social Guarantees

ARTICLE 32

The States, within the economic objectives expressed in this Agreement, agree to cooperate in the most effective manner in the solution of their social problems, and to adopt measures appropriate to their political and social institutions in accordance with what is provided in the Inter-American Charter of Social Guarantees, and leading to:

a) Assuring the effective reign of social justice and good relations between workers and employers;

b) Fostering opportunities for useful and regular employment, at fair wages, for all persons who want and are able to work;

c) Minimizing the disruptive effect of illness, old age, temporary unemployment and occupational hazards on the continuity of earnings;

d) Safeguarding of the health, welfare, and education of the entire population, with special regard to maternal and child health;

e) Providing in each country suitable administrative machinery and personnel to implement these programs;

f) Insuring a legal system of paid annual vacations for all workers, taking into special account the suitable period in the case of minors; and

g) Insuring permanence of tenure to all wage earners, and preventing the possibility of discharge without just cause.

Chapter VIII: Maritime Transportation

ARTICLE 33

The States agree to encourage and coordinate the most effective use of their transportation facilities, including ports and free ports, so as to satisfy their economic needs at the lowest possible cost compatible with reliable and adequate service.

ARTICLE 34

The States agree to encourage the reduction of transportation costs by all means possible, through the improvement of port conditions, regulations affecting the working of ports and vessels, customs requirements, and the lowering of fees and other charges and imposts that unduly restrict inter-American maritime trade.

ARTICLE 35

The States agree to encourage the removal of discriminatory actions and unnecessary restrictions applied by governments affecting shipping engaged in international trade, in order to promote the availability of shipping services to the commerce of the world without discrimination; assistance and encouragement given by a government for the development of its national merchant marine and for purposes of security does not in itself constitute discrimination, provided that such assistance and encouragement are not based on measures designed to restrict the freedom of shipping of all flags to take part in international trade.

Chapter IX: Freedom of Transit

ARTICLE 36

The States consider that, to encourage international trade among them, there should be freedom of transit through their respective territories.

Regional and general agreements shall regulate the application of this principle among the States of the Continent.

Chapter X: Inter-American Travel

ARTICLE 37

The States declare that the development of inter-American travel, including tourist travel, constitutes an important factor in their economic development which contributes to expanding trade, facilitating technical cooperation, and increasing economic harmony. They undertake, therefore, to promote national and international action to reduce restrictions on non-immigrant travelers of the States, without discrimination among visitors because of the object of their visit, whether for pleasure, health, business or education.

The States consider that one of the most effective means to encourage inter-American travel is to reduce the cost of fares.

Chapter XI: Adjustment of Economic Disputes

ARTICLE 38

The States agree, individually and collectively, to resort only to orderly and amicable means in the settling of all economic differences or disputes between them. They agree, when such controversies arise, to enter into consultations through diplomatic channels for the purpose of reaching a mutually satisfactory solution. If such consultations prove ineffective, any State that is a party to the controversy may request the Council to arrange for further discussions sponsored by the Council for the purpose of facilitating an amicable settlement of the controversy between the parties.

If necessary, the States shall submit the solution of economic disputes or controversies to the procedure set forth in the Inter-American Peace System or to other procedures set forth in agreements already in existence or which may be concluded in the future.

Chapter XII: Coordination with Other International Agencies

ARTICLE 39

The Council, in accordance with the provisions of the Charter of the Organization of the American States, shall take all necessary measures to coordinate the activities within its jurisdiction with the activities of other international agencies, in order to eliminate duplication of effort and to establish a basis for effective cooperation in areas of common interest. To this end the Council shall maintain the fullest exchange of information necessary for such cooperation and coordination of efforts, and establish working arrangements with other international agencies regarding the preparation and execution of studies and programs.

Chapter XIII: Ratification, Entry into Force and Amendments

ARTICLE 40

The present Economic Agreement of Bogota shall remain open to signature by the American States, and shall be ratified in accordance with their respective constitutional procedures. The original instrument, whose texts in Spanish, English, Portuguese and French are equally authentic, shall be deposited with the Pan American Union, which shall transmit certified copies to the Governments for purposes of ratification. The instruments of ratification shall be deposited with the Pan American Union, which shall notify the signatory Governments of such deposit. Such notification shall be considered an exchange of ratifications.

ARTICLE 41

The present Agreement shall enter into effect among the ratifying States when two-thirds of the signatory States have deposited their ratifications. The present Agreement shall enter into effect with respect to the remaining States in the order in which they deposit their ratifications.

ARTICLE 42

The present Agreement shall be registered in the Secretariat of the United Nations through the Pan American Union, upon the deposit of the ratifications of two-thirds of the signatory States.

ARTICLE 43

Amendments to the present Agreement should be proposed, with the necessary advance notice through the Council, for consideration, together with the respective reports, if any, of the Council, by an inter-American Conference or a Specialized Conference.

Such amendments shall enter into force as among the States accepting them when, in fulfillment of the provisions of Article 40, two-thirds of the Member States at that time parties to the Agreement, have deposited the document containing their acceptance with the General Secretariat of the Organization of American States, which shall send certified copies of such document to the Governments of all the signatory States.

CHARTER of the Organization of American States, Signed April 30, 1948
Text as published by the Pan American Union, Washington, D.C.

IN THE NAME of Their Peoples, the States Represented at the Ninth International Conference of American States,

Convinced that the historic mission of America is to offer to man a land of liberty, and a favorable environment for the development of his personality and the realization of his just aspirations;

Conscious that that mission has already inspired numerous agreements, whose essential value lies in the desire of the American peoples to live together in peace, and, through their mutual understanding and respect for the sovereignty of each one, to provide for the betterment of all, in independence, in equality and under law;

Confident that the true significance of American solidarity and good neighborliness can only mean the consolidation on this continent, within the framework of democratic institutions, of a system of individual liberty and social justice based on respect for the essential rights of man;

Persuaded that their welfare and their contribution to the progress and the civilization of the world will increasingly require intensive continental cooperation;

Resolved to persevere in the noble undertaking that humanity has conferred upon the United Nations, whose principles and purposes they solemnly reaffirm;

Convinced that juridical organization is a necessary condition for security and peace founded on moral order and on justice; and

In accordance with Resolution IX of the Inter-American Conference on Problems of War and Peace, held at Mexico City, have agreed upon the following

CHARTER OF THE ORGANIZATION OF AMERICAN STATES

PART ONE

Chapter I: Nature and Purposes

ARTICLE 1. The American States establish by this Charter the international organization that they have developed to achieve an order of peace and justice, to promote their solidarity, to strengthen their collaboration, and to defend their sovereignty, their territorial integrity and their independence. Within the United Nations, the Organization of American States is a regional agency.

ARTICLE 2. All American States that ratify the present Charter are Members of the Organization.

ARTICLE 3. Any new political entity that arises from the union of several Member States and that, as such, ratifies the present Charter, shall become a Member of the Organization. The entry of the new political entity into the Organization shall result in the loss of membership of each one of the States which constitute it.

ARTICLE 4. The Organization of American States, in order to put into practice the principles on which it is founded and to fulfill its regional obligations under the Charter of the United Nations, proclaims the following essential purposes:

a) To strengthen the peace and security of the continent;

b) To prevent possible causes of difficulties and to ensure the pacific settlement of disputes that may arise among the Member States;

c) To provide for common action on the part of those States in the event of aggression;

d) To seek the solution of political, juridical and economic problems that may arise among them; and

e) To promote, by cooperative action, their economic, social and cultural development.

Chapter II: Principles

ARTICLE 5. The American States reaffirm the following principles:

a) International law is the standard of conduct of States in their reciprocal relations;

b) International order consists essentially of respect for the personality, sovereignty and independence of States, and the faithful fulfillment of obligations derived from treaties and other sources of international law;

c) Good faith shall govern the relations between States;

d) The solidarity of the American States and the high aims which are sought through it require the political organization of those States on the basis of the effective exercise of representative democracy;

e) The American States condemn war of aggression: victory does not give rights;

f) An act of aggression against one American State is an act of aggression against all the other American States;

g) Controversies of an international character arising between two or more American States shall be settled by peaceful procedures;

h) Social justice and social security are bases of lasting peace;

i) Economic cooperation is essential to the common welfare and prosperity of the peoples of the continent;

j) The American States proclaim the fundamental rights of the individual without distinction as to race, nationality, creed or sex;

k) The spiritual unity of the continent is based on respect for the cultural values of the American countries and requires their close cooperation for the high purposes of civilization;

l) The education of peoples should be directed toward justice, freedom and peace.

Chapter III: Fundamental Rights and Duties of States

ARTICLE 6. States are juridically equal, enjoy equal rights and equal capacity to exercise these rights, and have equal duties. The rights of each State depend not upon its power to ensure the exercise thereof, but upon the mere fact of its existence as a person under international law.

ARTICLE 7. Every American State has the duty to respect the rights enjoyed by every other State in accordance with international law.

ARTICLE 8. The fundamental rights of States may not be impaired in any manner whatsoever.

ARTICLE 9. The political existence of the State is independent of recognition by other States. Even before being recognized, the State has the right to defend its integrity and independence, to provide for its preservation and prosperity, and consequently to organize itself as its sees fit, to legislate concerning its interests, to administer its services, and to determine the jurisdiction and competence of its courts. The exercise of these rights is limited only by the exercise of the rights of other States in accordance with international law.

ARTICLE 10. Recognition implies that the State granting it accepts the personality of the new State, with all the rights and duties that international law prescribes for the two States.

ARTICLE 11. The right of each State to protect itself and to live its own life does not authorize it to commit unjust acts against another State.

ARTICLE 12. The jurisdiction of States within the limits of their national territory is exercised equally over all the inhabitants, whether nationals or aliens.

ARTICLE 13. Each State has the right to develop its cultural, political and economic life freely and naturally. In this free development, the State shall respect the rights of the individual and the principles of universal morality.

ARTICLE 14. Respect for and the faithful observance of treaties constitute standards for the development of peaceful relations among States. International treaties and agreements should be public.

ARTICLE 15. No State or group of States has the right to intervene, directly or indirectly, for any reason whatever, in the internal or external affairs of any other State. The foregoing principle prohibits not only armed force but also any other form of interference or attempted threat against the personality of the State or against its political, economic and cultural elements.

ARTICLE 16. No State may use or encourage the use of coercive measures of an economic or political character in order to force the sovereign will of another State and obtain from it advantages of any kind.

ARTICLE 17. The territory of a State is inviolable; it may not be the object, even temporarily, of military occupation or of other measures of force taken by another State, directly or indirectly, on any grounds whatever. No territorial acquisitions or special advantages obtained either by force or by other means of coercion shall be recognized.

ARTICLE 18. The American States bind themselves in their international relations not to have recourse to the use of force, except in the case of self-defense in accordance with existing treaties or in fulfillment thereof.

ARTICLE 19. Measures adopted for the maintenance of peace and security in accordance with existing treaties do not constitute a violation of the principles set forth in Articles 15 and 17.

Chapter IV: Pacific Settlement of Disputes

ARTICLE 20. All international disputes that may arise between American States shall be submitted to the peaceful procedures set forth in this Charter, before being referred to the Security Council of the United Nations.

ARTICLE 21. The following are peaceful procedures: direct negotiation, good offices, mediation, investigation and conciliation, judicial settlement, arbitration, and those which the parties to the dispute may especially agree upon at any time.

ARTICLE 22. In the event that a dispute arises between two or more American States which, in the opinion of one of them, cannot be settled through the usual diplomatic channels, the Parties shall agree on some other peaceful procedure that will enable them to reach a solution.

ARTICLE 23. A special treaty will establish adequate procedures for the pacific settlement of disputes and will determine the appropriate means for their application, so that no dispute between American States shall fail of definitive settlement within a reasonable period.

Chapter V: Collective Security

ARTICLE 24. Every act of aggression by a State against the territorial integrity or the inviolability of the territory or against the sovereignty or political independence of an American State shall be considered an act of aggression against the other American States.

ARTICLE 25. If the inviolability or the integrity of the territory or the sovereignty or political independence of any American State should be affected by an armed attack or by an act of aggression that is not an armed attack, or by an extra-continental conflict, or by a conflict between two or more American States, or by any other fact or situation that might endanger the peace of America, the American States, in furtherance of the principles of continental solidarity or collective self-defense, shall apply the measures and procedures established in the special treaties on the subject.

Chapter VI: Economic Standards

ARTICLE 26. The Member States agree to cooperate with one another, as far as their resources may permit and their laws may provide, in the broadest spirit of good neighborliness, in order to strengthen their economic structure, develop their agriculture and mining, promote their industry and increase their trade.

ARTICLE 27. If the economy of an American State is affected by serious conditions that cannot be satisfactorily remedied by its own unaided effort, such State may place its economic problems before the Inter-American Economic and Social Council to seek through consultation the most appropriate solution for such problems.

Chapter VII: Social Standards

ARTICLE 28. The Member States agree to cooperate with one another to achieve just and decent living conditions for their entire populations.

ARTICLE 29. The Member States agree upon the desirability of developing their social legislation on the following bases:

a) All human beings, without distinction as to race, nationality, sex, creed or social condition, have the right to attain material well-being and spiritual growth under circumstances of liberty, dignity, equality of opportunity and economic security;

b) Work is a right and a social duty; it shall not be considered as an article of commerce; it demands respect for freedom of association and for the dignity of the worker; and it is to be performed under conditions that ensure life, health and a decent standard of living, both during the working years and during old age, or when any circumstance deprives the individual of the possibility of working.

Chapter VIII: Cultural Standards

ARTICLE 30. The Member States agree to promote, in accordance with their constitutional provisions and their material resources, the exercise of the right to education, on the following bases:

a) Elementary education shall be compulsory and, when provided by the State, shall be without cost;

b) Higher education shall be available to all, without distinction as to race, nationality, sex, language, creed or social condition.

ARTICLE 31. With due consideration for the national character of each State, the Member States undertake to facilitate free cultural interchange by every medium of expression.

PART TWO

Chapter IX: The Organs

ARTICLE 32. The Organization of American States accomplishes its purposes by means of:

a) The Inter-American Conference;

b) The Meeting of Consultation of Ministers of Foreign Affairs;

c) The Council;

d) The Pan American Union;

e) The Specialized Conferences; and

f) The Specialized Organizations.

Chapter X: The Inter-American Conference

ARTICLE 33. The Inter-American Conference is the supreme organ of the Organization of American States. It decides the general action and policy of the Organization and determines the structure and functions of its Organs, and has the authority to consider any matter relating to friendly relations among the American States. These functions shall be carried out in accordance with the provisions of this Charter and of other inter-American treaties.

ARTICLE 34. All Member States have the right to be represented at the Inter-American Conference. Each State has the right to one vote.

ARTICLE 35. The Conference shall convene every five years at the time fixed by the Council of the Organization, after consultation with the government of the country where the Conference is to be held.

ARTICLE 36. In special circumstances and with the approval of two-thirds of the American Governments, a special Inter-American Conference may be held, or the date of the next regular Conference may be changed.

ARTICLE 37. Each Inter-American Conference shall designate the place of meeting of the next Conference. If for any unforeseen reason the Conference cannot be held at the place designated, the Council of the Organization shall designate a new place.

ARTICLE 38. The program and regulations of the Inter-American Conference shall be prepared by the Council of the Organization and submitted to the Member States for consideration.

Chapter XI: The Meeting of Consultation of Ministers of Foreign Affairs

ARTICLE 39. The Meeting of Consultation of Ministers of Foreign Affairs shall be held in order to consider problems of an urgent nature and of common interest to the American States, and to serve as the Organ of Consultation.

ARTICLE 40. Any Member State may request that a Meeting of Consultation be called. The request shall be addressed to the Council of the Organization, which shall decide by an absolute majority whether a meeting should be held.

ARTICLE 41. The program and regulations of the Meeting of Consultation shall be prepared by the Council of the Organization and submitted to the Member States for consideration.

ARTICLE 42. If, for exceptional reasons, a Minister of Foreign Affairs is unable to attend the meeting, he shall be represented by a special delegate.

ARTICLE 43. In case of an armed attack within the territory of an American State or within the region of security delimited by treaties in force, a Meeting of Consultation shall be held without delay. Such Meeting shall be called immediately by the Chairman of the Council of the Organization, who shall at the same time call a meeting of the Council itself.

ARTICLE 44. An Advisory Defense Committee shall be established to advise the Organ of Consultation on problems of military cooperation that may arise in connection with the application of existing special treaties on collective security.

ARTICLE 45. The Advisory Defense Committee shall be composed of the highest military authorities of the American States participating in the Meeting of Consultation. Under exceptional circumstances the Governments may appoint substitutes. Each State shall be entitled to one vote.

ARTICLE 46. The Advisory Defense Committee shall be convoked under the same conditions as the Organ of Consultation, when the latter deals with matters relating to defense against aggression.

ARTICLE 47. The Committee shall also meet when the Conference or the Meeting of Consultation or the Governments, by a two-thirds majority of the Member States, assign to it technical studies or reports on specific subjects.

Chapter XII: The Council

ARTICLE 48. The Council of the Organization of American States is composed of one Representative of each Member State of the Organization, especially appointed by the respective Government, with the rank of Ambassador. The appointment may be given to the diplomatic representative accredited to the Government of the country in which the Council has its seat. During the absence of the titular Representative, the Government may appoint an interim Representative.

ARTICLE 49. The Council shall elect a Chairman and a Vice Chairman, who shall serve for one year and shall not be eligible for reelection to either of those positions for the term immediately following.

ARTICLE 50. The Council takes cognizance, within the limits of the present Charter and of inter-American treaties and agreements, of any matter referred to it by the Inter-American Conference or the Meeting of Consultation of Ministers of Foreign Affairs.

ARTICLE 51. The Council shall be responsible for the proper discharge by the Pan American Union of the duties assigned to it.

ARTICLE 52. The Council shall serve provisionally as the Organ of Consultation when the circumstances contemplated in Article 43 of this Charter arise.

ARTICLE 53. It is also the duty of the Council:

a) To draft and submit to the Governments and to the Inter-American Conference proposals for the creation of new Specialized Organizations or for the combination, adaptation or elimination of existing ones, including matters relating to the financing and support thereof;

b) To draft recommendations to the Governments, the Inter-American Conference, the Specialized Conferences or the Specialized Organizations, for the coordination of the activities and programs of such organizations, after consultation with them;

c) To conclude agreements with the Inter-American Specialized Organizations to determine the relations that shall exist between the respective agency and the Organization;

d) To conclude agreements or special arrangements for cooperation with other American organizations of recognized international standing;

e) To promote and facilitate collaboration between the Organization of American States and the United Nations, as well as between Inter-American Specialized Organizations and similar international agencies;

f) To adopt resolutions that will enable the Secretary General to perform the duties envisaged in Article 84;

g) To perform the other duties assigned to it by the present Charter.

ARTICLE 54. The Council shall establish the bases for fixing the quota that each Government is to contribute to the maintenance of the Pan American Union, taking into account the ability to pay of the respective countries and their determination to contribute in an equitable manner. The budget, after approval by the Council, shall be transmitted to the Governments at least six months before the first day of the fiscal year, with a statement of the annual quota of each country. Decisions on budgetary matters require the approval of two-thirds of the members of the Council.

ARTICLE 55. The Council shall formulate its own regulations.

ARTICLE 56. The Council shall function at the seat of the Pan American Union.

ARTICLE 57. The following are organs of the Council of the Organization of American States:

a) The Inter-American Economic and Social Council;

b) The Inter-American Council of Jurists; and

c) The Inter-American Cultural Council.

ARTICLE 58. The organs referred to in the preceding article shall have technical autonomy within the limits of this Charter; but their decisions shall not encroach upon the sphere of action of the Council of the Organization.

ARTICLE 59. The organs of the Council of the Organization are composed of representatives of all the Member States of the Organization.

ARTICLE 60. The organs of the Council of the Organization shall, as far as possible, render to the Governments such technical services as the latter may request; and they shall advise the Council of the Organization on matters within their jurisdiction.

ARTICLE 61. The organs of the Council of the Organization shall, in agreement with the Council, establish cooperative relations with the corresponding organs of the United Nations and with the national or international agencies that function within their respective spheres of action.

ARTICLE 62. The Council of the Organization, with the advice of the appropriate bodies and after consultation with the Governments, shall formulate the statutes of its organs in accordance with and in the execution of the provisions of this Charter. The organs shall formulate their own regulations.

A. THE INTER-AMERICAN ECONOMIC AND SOCIAL COUNCIL

ARTICLE 63. The Inter-American Economic and Social Council has for its principal purpose the promotion of the economic and social welfare of the American nations through effective cooperation for the better utilization of their natural resources, the development of their agriculture and industry and the raising of the standards of living of their peoples.

ARTICLE 64. To accomplish this purpose the Council shall:

a) Propose the means by which the American nations may give each other technical assistance in making studies and formulating and executing plans to carry out the purposes referred to in Article 26 and to develop and improve their social services;

b) Act as coordinating agency for all official inter-American activities of an economic and social nature;

c) Undertake studies on its own initiative or at the request of any Member State;

d) Assemble and prepare reports on economic and social matters for the use of the Member States;

e) Suggest to the Council of the Organization the advisability of holding Specialized Conferences on economic and social matters;

f) Carry on such other activities as may be assigned to it by the Inter-American Conference, the Meeting of Consultation of Ministers of Foreign Affairs, or the Council of the Organization.

ARTICLE 65. The Inter-American Economic and Social Council, composed of technical delegates appointed by each Member State, shall meet on its own initiative or on that of the Council of the Organization.

ARTICLE 66. The Inter-American Economic and Social Council shall function at the seat of the Pan American Union, but it may hold meetings in any American city by a majority decision of the Member States.

B. THE INTER-AMERICAN COUNCIL OF JURISTS

ARTICLE 67. The purpose of the Inter-American Council of Jurists is to serve as an advisory body on juridical matters; to promote the development and codification of public and private international law; and to study the possibility of attaining uniformity in the legislation of the various American countries, insofar as it may appear desirable.

ARTICLE 68. The Inter-American Juridical Committee of Rio de Janeiro shall be the permanent committee of the Inter-American Council of Jurists.

ARTICLE 69. The Juridical Committee shall be composed of jurists of the nine countries selected by the Inter-American Conference. The selection of the jurists shall be made by the Inter-American Council of Jurists from a panel submitted by each country chosen by the Conference. The members of the Juridical Committee represent all Member States of the Organization. The Council of the Organization is empowered to fill any vacancies that occur during the intervals between Inter-American Conferences and between meetings of the Inter-American Council of Jurists.

ARTICLE 70. The Juridical Committee shall undertake such studies and preparatory work as are assigned to it by the Inter-American Council of Jurists, the Inter-American Conference, the Meeting of Consultation of Ministers of Foreign Affairs, or the Council of the Organization. It may also undertake those studies and projects which, on its own initiative, it considers advisable.

ARTICLE 71. The Inter-American Council of Jurists and the Juridical Committee should seek the cooperation of national committees for the codification of international law, of institutes of international and comparative law, and of other specialized agencies.

ARTICLE 72. The Inter-American Council of Jurists shall meet when convened by the Council of the Organization, at the place determined by the Council of Jurists at its previous meeting.

C. THE INTER-AMERICAN CULTURAL COUNCIL

ARTICLE 73. The purpose of the Inter-American Cultural Council is to promote friendly relations and mutual understanding among the American peoples, in order to strengthen the peaceful sentiments that have characterized the evolution of America, through the promotion of educational, scientific and cultural exchange.

ARTICLE 74. To this end the principal functions of the Council shall be:

a) To sponsor inter-American cultural activities;

b) To collect and supply information on cultural activities carried on in and among the American States by private and official agencies both national and international in character;

c) To promote the adoption of basic educational programs adapted to the needs of all population groups in the American countries;

d) To promote, in addition, the adoption of special programs of training, education and culture for the indigenous groups of the American countries;

e) To cooperate in the protection, preservation and increase of the cultural heritage of the continent;

f) To promote cooperation among the American nations in the fields of education, science and culture, by means of the exchange of materials for research and study, as well as the exchange of teachers, students, specialists and, in general, such other persons and materials as are useful for the realization of these ends;

g) To encourage the education of the peoples for harmonious international relations;

h) To carry on such other activities as may be assigned to it by the Inter-American Conference, the Meeting of Consultation of Ministers of Foreign Affairs, or the Council of the Organization.

ARTICLE 75. The Inter-American Cultural Council shall determine the place of its next meeting and shall be convened by the Council of the Organization on the date chosen by the latter in agreement with the Government of the country selected as the seat of the meeting.

ARTICLE 76. There shall be a Committee for Cultural Action of which five States, chosen at each Inter-American Conference, shall be members. The individuals composing the Committee for Cultural Action shall be selected by the Inter-American Cultural Council from a panel submitted by each country chosen by the Conference, and they shall be specialists in education or cultural matters. When the Inter-American Cultural Council and the Inter-American Conference are not in session, the Council of the Organization may fill vacancies that arise and replace those countries that find it necessary to discontinue their cooperation.

ARTICLE 77. The Committee for Cultural Action shall function as the permanent committee of the Inter-American Cultural Council, for the purpose of preparing any studies that the latter may assign to it. With respect to these studies the Council shall have the final decision.

Chapter XIII: The Pan American Union

ARTICLE 78. The Pan American Union is the central and permanent organ of the Organization of American States and the General Secretariat of the Organization. It shall perform the duties assigned to it in this Charter and such other duties as may be assigned to it in other inter-American treaties and agreements.

ARTICLE 79. There shall be a Secretary General of the Organization, who shall be elected by the Council for a ten-year term and who may not be reelected or be succeeded by a person of the same nationality. In the event of a vacancy in the office of the Secretary General, the Council shall, within the next ninety days, elect a successor to fill the office for the remainder of the term, who may be reelected if the vacancy occurs during the second half of the term.

ARTICLE 80. The Secretary General shall direct the Pan American Union and be the legal representative thereof.

ARTICLE 81. The Secretary General shall participate with voice, but without vote, in the deliberations of the Inter-American Conference, the Meeting of Consultation of Ministers of Foreign Affairs, the Specialized Conferences, and the Council and its organs.

ARTICLE 82. The Pan American Union, through its technical and information offices, shall, under the direction of the Council, promote economic, social, juridical and cultural relations among all the Member States of the Organization.

ARTICLE 83. The Pan American Union shall also perform the following functions:

a) Transmit *ex officio* to Member States the convocation to the Inter-American Conference, the Meeting of Consultation of Ministers of Foreign Affairs, and the Specialized Conferences;

b) Advise the Council and its organs in the preparation of programs and regulations of the Inter-American Conference, the Meeting of Consultation of Ministers of Foreign Affairs, and the Specialized Conferences;

c) Place, to the extent of its ability, at the disposal of the Government of the country where a conference is to be held, the technical aid and personnel which such Government may request;

d) Serve as custodian of the documents and archives of the Inter-American Conference, of the Meeting of Consultation of Ministers of Foreign Affairs, and, insofar as possible, of the Specialized Conferences;

e) Serve as depository of the instruments of ratification of inter-American agreements;

f) Perform the functions entrusted to it by the Inter-American Conference, and the Meeting of Consultation of Ministers of Foreign Affairs;

g) Submit to the Council an annual report on the activities of the Organization;

h) Submit to the Inter-American Conference a report on the work accomplished by the Organs of the Organization since the previous Conference.

ARTICLE 84. It is the duty of the Secretary General:

a) To establish, with the approval of the Council, such technical and administrative offices of the Pan American Union as are necessary to accomplish its purposes;

b) To determine the number of department heads, officers and employees of the Pan American Union; to appoint them, regulate their powers and duties, and fix their compensation, in accordance with general standards established by the Council.

ARTICLE 85. There shall be an Assistant Secretary General, elected by the Council for a term of ten years and eligible for reelection. In the event of a vacancy in the office of Assistant Secretary General, the Council shall, within the next ninety days, elect a successor to fill such office for the remainder of the term.

ARTICLE 86. The Assistant Secretary General shall be the Secretary of the Council. He shall perform the duties of the Secretary General during the temporary absence or disability of the latter, or during the ninety-day vacancy referred to in Article 79. He shall also serve as advisory officer to the Secretary General, with the power to act as his delegate in all matters that the Secretary General may entrust to him.

ARTICLE 87. The Council, by a two-thirds vote of its members, may remove the Secretary General or the Assistant Secretary General whenever the proper functioning of the Organization so demands.

ARTICLE 88. The heads of the respective departments of the Pan American Union, appointed by the Secretary General, shall be the Executive Secretaries of the Inter-American Economic and Social Council, the Council of Jurists and the Cultural Council.

ARTICLE 89. In the performance of their duties the personnel shall not seek or receive instructions from any government or from any other authority outside the Pan American Union. They shall refrain from any action that might reflect upon their position as international officials responsible only to the Union.

ARTICLE 90. Every Member of the Organization of American States pledges itself to respect the exclusively international character of the responsibilities of the Secretary General and the personnel, and not to seek to influence them in the discharge of their duties.

ARTICLE 91. In selecting its personnel the Pan American Union shall give first consideration to efficiency, competence and integrity; but at the same time importance shall be given to the necessity of recruiting personnel on as broad a geographical basis as possible.

ARTICLE 92. The seat of the Pan American Union is the City of Washington.

Chapter XIV: The Specialized Conferences

ARTICLE 93. The Specialized Conferences shall meet to deal with special technical matters or to develop specific aspects of inter-

American cooperation, when it is so decided by the Inter-American Conference or the Meeting of Consultation of Ministers of Foreign Affairs; when inter-American agreements so provide; or when the Council of the Organization considers it necessary, either on its own initiative or at the request of one of its organs or of one of the Specialized Organizations.

ARTICLE 94. The program and regulations of the Specialized Conferences shall be prepared by the organs of the Council of the Organization or by the Specialized Organizations concerned; they shall be submitted to the Member Governments for consideration and transmitted to the Council for its information.

Chapter XV: The Specialized Organizations

ARTICLE 95. For the purposes of the present Charter, Inter-American Specialized Organizations are the inter-governmental organizations established by multilateral agreements and having specific functions with respect to technical matters of common interest to the American States.

ARTICLE 96. The Council shall, for the purposes stated in Article 53, maintain a register of the Organizations that fulfill the conditions set forth in the foregoing Article.

ARTICLE 97. The Specialized Organizations shall enjoy the fullest technical autonomy and shall take into account the recommendations of the Council, in conformity with the provisions of the present Charter.

ARTICLE 98. The Specialized Organizations shall submit to the Council periodic reports on the progress of their work and on their annual budgets and expenses.

ARTICLE 99. Agreements between the Council and the Specialized Organizations contemplated in paragraph c) of Article 53 may provide that such Organizations transmit their budgets to the Council for approval. Arrangements may also be made for the Pan American Union to receive the quotas of the contributing countries and distribute them in accordance with the said agreements.

ARTICLE 100. The Specialized Organizations shall establish cooperative relations with world agencies of the same character in order to coordinate their activities. In concluding agreements with international agencies of a world-wide character, the Inter-American Specialized Organizations shall preserve their identity and their status as integral parts of the Organization of American States, even when they perform regional functions of international agencies.

ARTICLE 101. In determining the geographic location of the Spe-

cialized Organizations the interests of all the American States shall
be taken into account.

PART THREE

Chapter XVI: The United Nations

ARTICLE 102. None of the provisions of this Charter shall be construed as impairing the rights and obligations of the Member States
under the Charter of the United Nations.

Chapter XVII: Miscellaneous Provisions

ARTICLE 103. The Organization of American States shall enjoy
in the territory of each Member such legal capacity, privileges and
immunities as are necessary for the exercise of its functions and the
accomplishment of its purposes.

ARTICLE 104. The Representatives of the Governments on the
Council of the Organization, the representatives on the organs of
the Council, the personnel of their delegations, as well as the Secretary General and the Assistant Secretary General of the Organization,
shall enjoy the privileges and immunities necessary for the independent performance of their duties.

ARTICLE 105. The juridical status of the Inter-American Specialized
Organizations and the privileges and immunities that should be
granted to them and to their personnel, as well as to the officials of the
Pan American Union, shall be determined in each case through
agreements between the respective organizations and the Governments concerned.

ARTICLE 106. Correspondence of the Organization of American
States, including printed matter and parcels, bearing the frank thereof,
shall be carried free of charge in the mails of the Member States.

ARTICLE 107. The Organization of American States does not recognize any restriction on the eligibility of men and women to participate in the activities of the various Organs and to hold positions
therein.

Chapter XVIII: Ratification and Entry into Force

ARTICLE 108. The present Charter shall remain open for signature
by the American States and shall be ratified in accordance with their
respective constitutional procedures. The original instrument, the
Spanish, English, Portuguese and French texts of which are equally
authentic, shall be deposited with the Pan American Union, which
shall transmit certified copies thereof to the Governments for pur-

poses of ratification. The instruments of ratification shall be deposited with the Pan American Union, which shall notify the signatory States of such deposit.

ARTICLE 109. The present Charter shall enter into force among the ratifying States when two-thirds of the signatory States have deposited their ratifications. It shall enter into force with respect to the remaining States in the order in which they deposit their ratifications.

ARTICLE 110. The present Charter shall be registered with the Secretariat of the United Nations through the Pan American Union.

ARTICLE 111. Amendments to the present Charter may be adopted only at an Inter-American Conference convened for that purpose. Amendments shall enter into force in accordance with the terms and the procedure set forth in Article 109.

ARTICLE 112. The present Charter shall remain in force indefinitely, but may be denounced by any Member State upon written notification to the Pan American Union, which shall communicate to all the others each notice of denunciation received. After two years from the date on which the Pan American Union receives a notice of denunciation, the present Charter shall cease to be in force with respect to the denouncing State, which shall cease to belong to the Organization after it has fulfilled the obligations arising from the present Charter.

IN WITNESS WHEREOF the undersigned Plenipotentiaries, whose full powers have been presented and found to be in good and due form, sign the present Charter at the city of Bogotá, Colombia, on the dates that appear opposite their respective signatures.

[Signatures]

DIAGRAM *of the Organization of American States as Established by the Charter Signed at Bogotá, April 30, 1948*

Organization of American States, *The Results of Bogotá*, Appendix

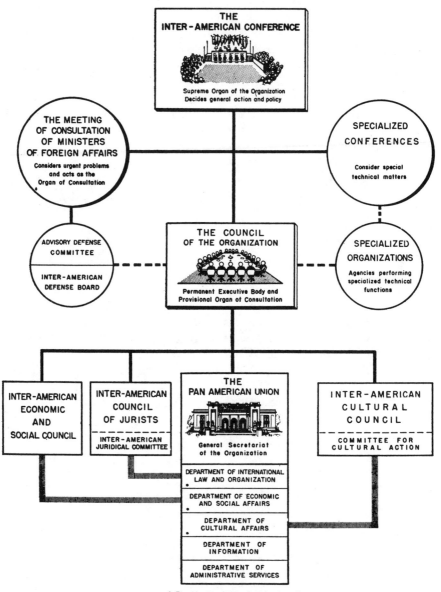

Appendix B

TREATY SIGNED BY ARGENTINA, BRAZIL, CHILE, MEXICO, PARAGUAY, AND URUGUAY

ANTI-WAR TREATY of Nonaggression and Conciliation, Signed at Rio de Janeiro, October 10, 1933 (translation)

Department of State, Treaty Series No. 906. The treaty is often referred to as the "Saavedra Lamas Pact"

THE STATES designated below, in the desire to contribute to the consolidation of peace, and to express their adherence to the efforts made by all civilized nations to promote the spirit of universal harmony;

To the end of condemning wars of aggression and territorial acquisitions that may be obtained by armed conquest, making them impossible and establishing their invalidity through the positive provisions of this treaty, and in order to replace them with pacific solutions based on lofty concepts of justice and equity;

Convinced that one of the most effective means of assuring the moral and material benefits which peace offers to the world, is the organization of a permanent system of conciliation for international disputes, to be applied immediately on the violation of the principles mentioned;

Have decided to put these aims of nonaggression and concord in conventional form by concluding the present treaty, to which end they have appointed the undersigned plenipotentiaries, who, having exhibited their respective full powers, found to be in good and due form, have agreed upon the following:

ARTICLE 1

The high contracting parties solemnly declare that they condemn wars of aggression in their mutual relations or in those with other states, and that the settlement of disputes or controversies of any kind that may arise among them shall be effected only by the pacific means which have the sanction of international law.

They declare that as between the high contracting parties territorial questions must not be settled by violence, and that they will not recognize any territorial arrangement which is not obtained by pacific means, nor the validity of the occupation or acquisition of territories that may be brought about by force of arms.

ARTICLE 3

In case of noncompliance, by any state engaged in a dispute, with the obligations contained in the foregoing articles, the contracting states undertake to make every effort for the maintenance of peace. To that end they will adopt in their character as neutrals a common and solidary attitude; they will exercise the political, juridical, or economic means authorized by international law; they will bring the influence of public opinion to bear, but will in no case resort to intervention, either diplomatic or armed; subject to the attitude that may be incumbent on them by virtue of other collective treaties to which such states are signatories.

ARTICLE 4

The high contracting parties obligate themselves to submit to the conciliation procedure established by this treaty the disputes specially mentioned and any others that may arise in their reciprocal relations, without further limitations than those enumerated in the following article, in all controversies which it has not been possible to settle by diplomatic means within a reasonable period of time.

ARTICLE 5

The high contracting parties and the states which may in the future adhere to this treaty may not formulate, at the time of signature, ratification, or adherence, other limitations to the conciliation procedure than those which are indicated below:

(a) Differences for the solution of which treaties, conventions, pacts, or pacific agreements of any kind whatever may have been concluded, which in no case shall be considered as annulled by this agreement, but supplemented thereby insofar as they tend to assure peace; as well as the questions or matters settled by previous treaties;

(b) Disputes which the parties prefer to solve by direct settlement or submit by common agreement to an arbitral or judicial solution;

(c) Questions which international law leaves to the exclusive competence of each state, under its constitutional system, for which reason the parties may object to their being submitted to the conciliation procedure before the national or local jurisdiction has decided definitively; except in the case of manifest denial or delay of justice, in which case the conciliation procedure shall be initiated within a year at the latest;

(d) Matters which affect constitutional precepts of the parties to the controversy. In case of doubt, each party shall obtain the reasoned opinion of its respective tribunal or supreme court of justice, if the latter should be invested with such powers.

The high contracting parties may communicate, at any time and in the manner provided for by Article 15, an instrument stating that they have abandoned wholly or in part the limitations established by them in the conciliation procedure.

The effect of the limitations formulated by one of the contracting parties shall be that the other parties shall not consider themselves obligated in regard to that party save in the measure of the exceptions established.

ARTICLE 6

In the absence of a permanent conciliation commission or of some other international organization charged with this mission by virtue of previous treaties in effect, the high contracting parties undertake to submit their differences to the examination and investigation of a conciliation commission which shall be formed as follows, unless there is an agreement to the contrary of the parties in each case;

The conciliation commission shall consist of five members. Each party to the controversy shall designate a member, who may be chosen by it from among its own nationals. The three remaining members shall be designated by common agreement by the parties from among the nationals of third powers, who must be of different nationalities, must not have their customary residence in the territory of the interested parties, nor be in the service of any of them. The parties shall choose the president of the conciliation commission from among the said three members.

If they cannot arrive at an agreement with regard to such designations, they may entrust the selection thereof to a third power or to some other existing international organism. If the candidates so designated are rejected by the parties or by any one of them, each party shall present a list of candidates equal in number to that of the members to be selected, and the names of those to sit on the conciliation commission shall be determined by lot.

ARTICLE 7

The tribunals or supreme courts of justice which, in accordance with the domestic legislation of each state, may be competent to interpret, in the last or the sole instance and in matters under their respective jurisdiction, the constitution, treaties, or the general principles of the law of nations, may be designated preferentially by the high contracting parties to discharge the duties entrusted by the present treaty to the conciliation commission. In this case the tribunal or court may function as a whole or may designate some of its members to proceed alone or by forming a mixed commission with members of other courts or tribunals, as may be agreed upon by common accord between the parties to the dispute.

ARTICLE 8

The conciliation commission shall establish its own rules of procedure, which shall provide in all cases for hearing both sides.

The parties to the controversy may furnish, and the commission may require from them, all the antecedents and information necessary. The parties may have themselves represented by delegates and assisted by advisers or experts, and also present evidence of all kinds.

ARTICLE 9

The labors and deliberations of the conciliation commission shall not be made public except by a decision of its own to that effect, with the assent of the parties.

In the absence of stipulation to the contrary, the decisions of the commission shall be made by a majority vote, but the commission may not pronounce judgment on the substance of the case except in the presence of all its members.

ARTICLE 10

It is the duty of the commission to secure the conciliatory settlement of the disputes submitted to its consideration.

After an impartial study of the questions in dispute, it shall set forth in a report the outcome of its work and shall propose to the parties bases of settlement by means of a just and equitable solution.

The report of the commission shall in no case have the character of a final decision or arbitral award either with respect to the exposition or interpretation of the facts, or with regard to the considerations or conclusions of law.

ARTICLE 11

The conciliation commission must present its report within 1 year, counting from its first meeting, unless the parties should decide by common agreement to shorten or extend this period.

The conciliation procedure, having been once begun, may be interrupted only by a direct settlement between the parties or by their subsequent decision to submit the dispute by common accord to arbitration or to international justice.

ARTICLE 12

In communicating its report to the parties, the conciliation commission shall fix for them a period, which shall not exceed 6 months, within which they must decide as to the bases of the settlement it has proposed. On the expiration of this term, the commission shall record in a final act the decision of the parties.

This period having expired without acceptance of the settlement by the parties, or the adoption by common accord of another friendly solution, the parties to the dispute shall regain their freedom of action to proceed as they may see fit within the limitations flowing from Articles 1 and 2 of this treaty.

ARTICLE 13

From the initiation of the conciliatory procedure until the expiration of the period fixed by the commission for the parties to make a decision, they must abstain from any measure prejudicial to the execution of the agreement that may be proposed by the commission and, in general, from any act capable of aggravating or prolonging the controversy.

ARTICLE 14

During the conciliation procedure the members of the commission shall receive honoraria the amount of which shall be established by common agreement by the parties to the controversy. Each of them shall bear its own expenses and a moiety of the joint expenses or honoraria.

ARTICLE 15

The present treaty shall be ratified by the high contracting parties as soon as possible, in accordance with their respective constitutional procedures.

The original treaty and the instruments of ratification shall be deposited in the Ministry of Foreign Relations and Worship of the Argentine Republic, which shall communicate the ratifications to the other signatory states. The treaty shall go into effect between the high contracting parties 30 days after the deposit of the respective ratifications, and in the order in which they are effected.

ARTICLE 16

This treaty shall remain open to the adherence of all states.

Adherence shall be effected by the deposit of the respective instrument in the Ministry of Foreign Relations and Worship of the Argentine Republic, which shall give notice thereof to the other interested states.

ARTICLE 17

The present treaty is concluded for an indefinite time, but may be denounced by 1 year's notice, on the expiration of which the effects thereof shall cease for the denouncing state, and remain in force for the other states which are parties thereto, by signature or adherence.

The denunciation shall be addressed to the Ministry of Foreign Relations and Worship of the Argentine Republic, which shall transmit it to the other interested states.

In witness whereof, the respective plenipotentiaries sign the present treaty in one copy, in the Spanish and Portuguese languages, and affix their seals thereto, at Rio de Janeiro, D.F., on the tenth day of the month of October nineteen hundred and thirty-three.

[Signatures]

[The treaty was adhered to by the United States, subject to ratification, April 27, 1934, and ratified by the President on June 27, 1934, subject to the reservation that "In adhering to this Treaty the United States does not thereby waive any rights it may have under other treaties or conventions or under international law."]

Appendix C

CERTAIN UNITED STATES AGREEMENTS REGARDING THE INTER-OCEANIC CANALS

TREATY OF PEACE, Amity, Navigation, and Commerce between the United States and New Granada (Colombia), Signed at Bogotá, December 12, 1846 (extract)

William M. Malloy, *Treaties, Conventions, International Acts* . . . , I, 302, 312. The treaty was ratified by the President of the United States June 10, 1848, and ratifications were exchanged the same day. It is sometimes referred to as the "Bidlack Treaty"

ARTICLE 35

THE UNITED STATES of America and the Republic of New Granada, desiring to make as durable as possible the relations which are to be established between the two parties by virtue of this treaty, have declared solemnly, and do agree to the following points:

1st. For the better understanding of the preceding articles, it is and has been stipulated between the high contracting parties, that the citizens, vessels and merchandise of the United States shall enjoy in the ports of New Granada, including those of the part of the Granadian territory generally denominated Isthmus of Panama, from its southernmost extremity until the boundary of Costa Rica, all the exemptions, privileges and immunities concerning commerce and navigation, which are now or may hereafter be enjoyed by Granadian citizens, their vessels and merchandise; and that this equality of favors shall be made to extend to the passengers, correspondence and merchandise of the United States, in their transit across the said territory from one sea to the other. The Government of New Granada guarantees to the Government of the United States that the right of way or transit across the Isthmus of Panama upon any modes of communication that now exist, or that may be hereafter constructed, shall be open and free to the Government and citizens of the United States, and for the transportation of any articles of produce, manufactures or merchandise, of lawful commerce, belonging to the citizens of the

United States; that no other tolls or charges shall be levied or collected upon the citizens of the United States, or their said merchandise thus passing over any road or canal that may be made by the Government of New Granada, or by the authority of the same, than is, under like circumstances, levied upon and collected from the Granadian citizens; that any lawful produce, manufactures or merchandise, belonging to citizens of the United States, thus passing from one sea to the other, in either direction, for the purpose of exportation to any other foreign country, shall not be liable to any import-duties whatever; or, having paid such duties, they shall be entitled to drawback upon their exportation; nor shall the citizens of the United States be liable to any duties, tolls or charges of any kind, to which native citizens are not subjected for thus passing the said Isthmus. And, in order to secure to themselves the tranquil and constant enjoyment of these advantages, and as an especial compensation for the said advantages, and for the favors they have acquired by the 4th, 5th, and 6th articles of this treaty, the United States guarantee, positively and efficaciously, to New Granada, by the present stipulation, the perfect neutrality of the before-mentioned Isthmus, with the view that the free transit from the one to the other sea may not be interrupted or embarrassed in any future time while this treaty exists; and, in consequence, the United States also guarantee, in the same manner, the rights of sovereignty and property which New Granada has and possesses over the said territory.

THE "CLAYTON-BULWER" TREATY between the United States and Great Britain, Signed at Washington, April 19, 1850

William M. Malloy, *Treaties, Conventions. International Acts* . . . , I, 659. The treaty was ratified by the President of the United States May 23, 1850, and ratifications were exchanged July 4, 1850

THE UNITED STATES of America and Her Britannic Majesty, being desirous of consolidating the relations of amity which so happily subsist between them by setting forth and fixing in a convention their views and intentions with reference to any means of communication by ship-canal which may be constructed between the Atlantic and Pacific Oceans by the way of the river San Juan de Nicaragua, and either or both of the lakes of Nicaragua or Managua, to any port or place on the Pacific Ocean, the President of the United States has conferred full powers on John M. Clayton, Secretary of State of the United States, and Her Britannic Majesty on the Right Honourable Sir Henry Lytton Bulwer, a member of Her Majesty's Most Honourable Privy Council, Knight Commander of the Most Honourable Order of the Bath, and Envoy Extraordinary and Minister Plenipotentiary of Her Britannic Majesty to the United States, for the aforesaid purpose; and the said Plenipotentiaries, having exchanged their full powers, which were found to be in proper form, have agreed to the following articles:

ARTICLE 1

The Governments of the United States and Great Britain hereby declare that neither the one nor the other will ever obtain or maintain for itself any exclusive control over the said ship-canal: agreeing that neither will ever erect or maintain any fortifications commanding the same, or in the vicinity thereof, or occupy, or fortify, or colonize, or assume or exercise any dominion over Nicaragua, Costa Rica, the Mosquito coast, or any part of Central America; nor will either make use of any protection which either affords or may afford, or any alliance which either has or may have to or with any State or people for the purpose of erecting or maintaining any such fortifications, or of occupying, fortifying, or colonizing Nicaragua, Costa Rica, the Mosquito coast, or any part of Central America, or of assuming or exercising dominion over the same; nor will the United States or Great Britain take advantage of any intimacy, or use any alliance, connection, or influence that either may possess, with any State or Government through whose territory the said canal may pass, for the purpose of acquiring or holding, directly or indirectly, for the citizens or subjects of the one any rights or advantages in regard to commerce or navigation through the said canal which shall not be offered on the same terms to the citizens or subjects of the other.

ARTICLE 2

Vessels of the United States or Great Britain traversing the said canal shall, in case of war between the contracting parties, be exempted from blockade, detention, or capture by either of the belligerents; and this provision shall extend to such a distance from the two ends of the said canal as may hereafter be found expedient to establish.

ARTICLE 3

In order to secure the construction of the said canal, the contracting parties engage that, if any such canal shall be undertaken upon fair and equitable terms by any parties having the authority of the local government or governments through whose territory the same may pass, then the persons employed in making the said canal, and their property used or to be used for that object, shall be protected, from the commencement of the said canal to its completion, by the Governments of the United States and Great Britain, from unjust detention, confiscation, seizure, or any violence whatsoever.

ARTICLE 4

The contracting parties will use whatever influence they respectively exercise with any State, States, or Governments possessing or claiming to possess, any jurisdiction or right over the territory which the said canal shall traverse, or which shall be near the waters applicable thereto, in order to induce such States or Governments to facilitate the construction of the said canal by every means in their power; and, furthermore, the United States and Great Britain agree to use their good offices, wherever or however it may be most expedient, in order to procure the establishment of two free ports, one at each end of the said canal.

ARTICLE 5

The contracting parties further engage that when the said canal shall have been completed they will protect it from interruption, seizure, or unjust confiscation, and that they will guarantee the neutrality thereof, so that the said canal may forever be open and free, and the capital invested therein secure. Nevertheless, the Governments of the United States and Great Britain, in according their protection to the construction of the said canal, and guaranteeing its neutrality and security when completed, always understand that this protection and guarantee are granted conditionally, and may be withdrawn by both Governments, or either Government, if both Governments or either Government should deem that the persons or company undertaking or managing the same adopt or establish such regulations concerning the traffic thereupon as are contrary to the spirit and intention of this convention, either by making unfair discriminations in favor of the commerce of one of the contracting parties over the commerce of the other, or by imposing oppressive exactions or unreasonable tolls upon passengers, vessels, goods, wares, merchandise, or other articles. Neither party, however, shall withdraw the aforesaid protection and guarantee without first giving six months' notice to the other.

ARTICLE 6

The contracting parties in this convention engage to invite every State with which both or either have friendly intercourse to enter into stipulations with them similar to those which they have entered into with each other, to the end that all other States may share in the honor and advantage of having contributed to a work of such general interest and importance as the canal herein contemplated. And the contracting parties likewise agree that each shall enter into treaty stipulations with such of the Central American States as they may deem advisable for the purpose of more effectually carrying out the great design of this convention, namely, that of constructing and maintaining the said canal as a ship communication between the two oceans, for the benefit of mankind, on equal terms to all, and of protecting the same; and they also agree that the good offices of either shall be employed, when requested by the other, in aiding and assisting the negotiation of such treaty stipulations; and should any differences arise as to right or property over the territory through which the said canal shall pass, between the States or Governments of Central America, and such differences should in any way impede or obstruct the execution of the said canal, the Governments of the United States and Great Britain will use their good offices to settle such differences in the manner best suited to promote the interests of the said canal, and to strengthen the bonds of friendship and alliance which exist between the contracting parties.

ARTICLE 7

It being desirable that no time should be unnecessarily lost in commencing and constructing the said canal, the Governments of the United States and Great Britain determine to give their support and encouragement to such persons or company as may first offer to commence the same, with the necessary capital, the consent of the local authorities, and on such principles as accord with the spirit and intention of this convention; and if any persons or company should already have, with any State through which the proposed ship-canal may pass, a contract for the construction of such a canal as that specified in this convention, to the stipulations of which contract neither of the contracting parties in this convention have any just cause to object, and the said persons or company shall, moreover, have made preparations and expended time, money, and trouble on the faith of such contract, it is hereby agreed that such persons or company shall have a priority of claim over every other person, persons, or company to the protection of the Governments of the United States and Great Britain, and be allowed a year from the date of the exchange of the ratifications of this convention for concluding their arrangements and presenting evidence of sufficient capital subscribed to accomplish the contemplated undertaking; it being understood that if, at the expiration of the aforesaid period, such persons or company be not able to commence and carry out the proposed enterprize, then the Governments of the United States and Great Britain shall be free to afford their protection to any other persons or company that shall be prepared to commence and proceed with the construction of the canal in question.

ARTICLE 8

The Governments of the United States and Great Britain having not only desired, in entering into this convention, to accomplish a particular object, but also to establish a general principle, they hereby agree to extend their protection, by treaty stipulations, to any other practicable communications, whether by canal or railway, across the isthmus which connects North and South America, and especially to the interoceanic communications, should the same prove to be practicable, whether by canal or railway, which are now proposed to be established by the way of Tehuantepec or Panama. In granting, however, their joint protection to any such canals or railways as are by this article specified, it is always understood by the United States and Great Britain that the parties constructing or owning the same shall impose no other charges or conditions of traffic thereupon than the aforesaid Governments shall approve of as just and equitable; and that the same canals or railways, being open to the citizens and subjects of the United States and Great Britain on equal terms, shall also be open on like terms to the citizens and subjects of every other State which is willing to grant thereto such protection as the United States and Great Britain engage to afford.

ARTICLE 9

The ratifications of this convention shall be exchanged at Washington within six months from this day, or sooner if possible.

In faith whereof we, the respective Plenipotentiaries, have signed this convention, and have hereunto affixed our seals.

Done at Washington the nineteenth day of April, anno Domini one thousand eight hundred and fifty.

[SEAL]   JOHN M. CLAYTON

[SEAL]   HENRY LYTTON BULWER

THE SECOND "HAY–PAUNCEFOTE" TREATY between the United States and Great Britain, Signed at Washington, November 18, 1901

Diplomatic History of the Panama Canal, 63d Congress, 2d Session, Senate Document No. 474, p. 292. The treaty was ratified by the President of the United States December 26, 1901, and ratifications were exchanged February 21, 1902. An earlier Hay-Pauncefote Treaty was approved by the U.S. Senate only on conditions that were unacceptable to the British Government

THE UNITED STATES of America and His Majesty Edward the Seventh, of the United Kingdom of Great Britain and Ireland, and of the British Dominions beyond the Seas, King, and Emperor of India, being desirous to facilitate the construction of a ship canal to connect the Atlantic and Pacific Oceans, by whatever route may be considered expedient, and to that end to remove any objection which may arise out of the Convention of the 19th April, 1850, commonly called the Clayton-Bulwer Treaty, to the construction of such canal under the auspices of the Government of the United States, without impairing the "general principle" of neutralization established in Article 8 of that Convention, have for that purpose appointed as their Plenipotentiaries:

The President of the United States, John Hay, Secretary of State of the United States of America;

And His Majesty Edward the Seventh, of the United Kingdom of Great Britain and Ireland, and of the British Dominions beyond the Seas, King, and Emperor of India, the Right Honourable Lord Pauncefote, G.C.B., G.C.M.G., His Majesty's Ambassador Extraordinary and Plenipotentiary to the United States;

Who, having communicated to each other their full powers which were found to be in due and proper form, have agreed upon the following Articles:

ARTICLE 1

The High Contracting Parties agree that the present Treaty shall supersede the afore-mentioned Convention of the 19th April, 1850.

ARTICLE 2

It is agreed that the canal may be constructed under the auspices of the Government of the United States, either directly at its own cost, or by gift or loan of money to individuals or Corporations, or through subscription to or purchase of stock or shares, and that, subject to the provisions of the present Treaty, the said Government shall have and enjoy all the rights incident to such construction, as well as the exclusive right of providing for the regulation and management of the canal.

The United States adopts, as the basis of the neutralization of such ship canal, the following Rules, substantially as embodied in the Convention of Constantinople, signed the 28th October, 1888, for the free navigation of the Suez Canal, that is to say:

1. The canal shall be free and open to the vessels of commerce and of war of all nations observing these Rules, on terms of entire equality, so that there shall be no discrimination against any such nation, or its citizens or subjects, in respect of the conditions or charges of traffic, or otherwise. Such conditions and charges of traffic shall be just and equitable.

2. The canal shall never be blockaded, nor shall any right of war be exercised nor any act of hostility be committed within it. The United States, however, shall be at liberty to maintain such military police along the canal as may be necessary to protect it against lawlessness and disorder.

3. Vessels of war of a belligerent shall not revictual nor take any stores in the canal except so far as may be strictly necessary; and the transit of such vessels through the canal shall be effected with the least possible delay in accordance with the Regulations in force, and with only such intermission as may result from the necessities of the service.

Prizes shall be in all respects subject to the same Rules as vessels of war of the belligerents.

4. No belligerent shall embark or disembark troops, munitions of war, or warlike materials in the canal, except in case of accidental hindrance of the transit, and in such case the transit shall be resumed with all possible dispatch.

5. The provisions of this Article shall apply to waters adjacent to the canal, within 3 marine miles of either end. Vessels of war of a belligerent shall not remain in such waters longer than twenty-four hours at any one time, except in case of distress, and in such case shall depart as soon as possible; but a vessel of war of one belligerent shall not depart within twenty-four hours from the departure of a vessel of war of the other belligerent.

6. The plant, establishments, buildings, and all works necessary to the construction, maintenance, and operation of the canal shall be deemed to be part thereof, for the purposes of this Treaty, and

in time of war, as in time of peace, shall enjoy complete immunity from attack or injury by belligerents, and from acts calculated to impair their usefulness as part of the canal.

ARTICLE 4

It is agreed that no change of territorial sovereignty or of the international relations of the country or countries traversed by the before-mentioned canal shall affect the general principle of neutralization or the obligation of the High Contracting Parties under the present Treaty.

ARTICLE 5

The present Treaty shall be ratified by the President of the United States, by and with the advice and consent of the Senate thereof, and by His Britannic Majesty; and the ratifications shall be exchanged at Washington or at London at the earliest possible time within six months from the date hereof.

IN FAITH WHEREOF the respective Plenipotentiaries have signed this Treaty and thereunto affixed their seals.

DONE in duplicate at Washington, the 18th day of November, in the year of Our Lord one thousand nine hundred and one.

JOHN HAY [SEAL]
PAUNCEFOTE [SEAL]

THE "HAY–HERRÁN" TREATY between the United States and Colombia, Signed at Washington, January 22, 1903

Diplomatic History of the Panama Canal, 63d Congress, 2d Session, Senate Document No. 474, p. 277. Although promptly ratified by the United States, the treaty was rejected by the Colombian Congress

THE UNITED STATES of America and the Republic of Colombia, being desirous to assure the construction of a ship canal to connect the Atlantic and Pacific Oceans and the Congress of the United States of America having passed an Act approved June 28, 1902, in furtherance of that object, a copy of which is hereunto annexed, the high contracting parties have resolved, for that purpose, to conclude a Convention and have accordingly appointed as their plenipotentiaries,

The President of the United States of America, John Hay, Secretary of State, and

The President of the Republic of Colombia, Thomas Herran, Chargé d'Affaires, thereunto specially empowered by said government, who, after communicating to each other their respective full powers, found in good and due form, have agreed upon and concluded the following Articles:

ARTICLE 1

The Government of Colombia authorizes the New Panama Canal Company to sell and transfer to the United States its rights, privileges, properties, and concessions, as well as the Panama Railroad and all the shares or part of the shares of that company; but the public lands situated outside of the zone hereinafter specified, now corresponding to the concessions of both said enterprises shall revert to the Republic of Colombia, except any property now owned by or in the possession of the said companies within Panama or Colon, or the ports and terminals thereof.

But it is understood that Colombia reserves all its rights to the special shares in the capital of the New Panama Canal Company to which reference is made in Article 4 of the contract of December 10, 1890, which shares shall be paid their full nominal value at least; but as such right of Colombia exists solely in its character of stockholder in said Company, no obligation under this provision is imposed upon or assumed by the United States.

The Railroad Company (and the United States as owner of the enterprise) shall be free from the obligations imposed by the railroad concession, excepting as to the payment at maturity by the Railroad Company of the outstanding bonds issued by said Railroad Company.

ARTICLE 2

The United States shall have the exclusive right for the term of one hundred years, renewable at the sole and absolute option of the United States, for periods of similar duration so long as the United States may desire, to excavate, construct, maintain, operate, control, and protect the Maritime Canal with or without locks from the Atlantic to the Pacific Ocean, to and across the territory of Colombia, such canal to be of sufficient depth and capacity for vessels of the largest tonnage and greatest draft now engaged in commerce, and such as may be reasonably anticipated, and also the same rights for the construction, maintenance, operation, control, and protection of the Panama Railroad and of railway, telegraph and telephone lines, canals, dikes, dams and reservoirs, and such other auxiliary works as may be necessary and convenient for the construction, maintenance, protection and operation of the canal and railroads.

To enable the United States to exercise the rights and privileges granted by this Treaty the Republic of Colombia grants to that Government the use and control for the term of one hundred years, renewable at the sole and absolute option of the United States, for periods of similar duration so long as the United States may desire, of a zone of territory along the route of the canal to be constructed five kilometers in width on either side thereof measured from its center line including therein the necessary auxiliary canals not exceeding in any case fifteen miles from the main canal and other works, together with ten fathoms of water in the Bay of Limon in extension of the canal, and at least three marine miles from mean low water mark from each terminus of the canal into the Caribbean Sea and the Pacific Ocean respectively. So far as necessary for the construction, maintenance and operation of the canal, the United States shall have the use and occupation of the group of small islands in the Bay of Panama named Perico, Naos, Culebra and Flamenco, but the same shall not be construed as being within the zone herein defined or governed by the special provisions applicable to the same.

This grant shall in no manner invalidate the titles or rights of private land holders in the said zone of territory, nor shall it interfere with the rights of way over the public roads of the Department; provided, however, that nothing herein contained shall operate to diminish, impair or restrict the rights elsewhere herein granted to the United States.

This grant shall not include the cities of Panama and Colon, except so far as lands and other property therein are now owned by or in possession of the said Canal Company or the said Railroad Company; but all the stipulations contained in Article 35 of the Treaty of 1846–48 between the contracting parties shall continue and apply in full force to the cities of Panama and Colon and to the accessory community lands and other property within the said zone, and the territory thereon shall be neutral territory, and the United States shall continue to guarantee the neutrality thereof and the sovereignty of Colombia thereover, in conformity with the above mentioned Article 35 of said Treaty.

In furtherance of this last provision there shall be created a Joint Commission by the Governments of Colombia and the United States that shall establish and enforce sanitary and police regulations.

ARTICLE 4

The rights and privileges granted to the United States by the terms of this convention shall not affect the sovereignty of the Republic of

Colombia over the territory within whose boundaries such rights and privileges are to be exercised.

The United States freely acknowledges and recognizes this sovereignty and disavows any intention to impair it in any way whatever or to increase its territory at the expense of Colombia or of any of the sister republics in Central or South America, but on the contrary, it desires to strengthen the power of the republics on this continent, and to promote, develop and maintain their prosperity and independence.

ARTICLE 5

The Republic of Colombia authorizes the United States to construct and maintain at each entrance and terminus of the proposed canal a port for vessels using the same, with suitable light houses and other aids to navigation, and the United States is authorized to use and occupy within the limits of the zone fixed by this convention, such parts of the coast line and of the lands and islands adjacent thereto as are necessary for this purpose, including the construction and maintenance of breakwaters, dikes, jetties, embankments, coaling stations, docks and other appropriate works, and the United States undertakes the construction and maintenance of such works and will bear all the expense thereof. The ports when established are declared free, and their demarcations shall be clearly and definitely defined.

To give effect to this Article, the United States will give special attention and care to the maintenance of works for drainage, sanitary and healthful purposes along the line of the canal, and its dependencies, in order to prevent the invasion of epidemics or of securing their prompt suppression should they appear. With this end in view the United States will organize hospitals along the line of the canal, and will suitably supply or cause to be supplied the towns of Panama and Colon with the necessary aqueducts and drainage works, in order to prevent their becoming centers of infection on account of their proximity to the canal.

The Government of Colombia will secure for the United States or its nominees the lands and rights that may be required in the towns of Panama and Colon to effect the improvements above referred to, and the Government of the United States or its nominees shall be authorized to impose and collect equitable water rates, during fifty years for the service rendered; but on the expiration of said term the use of the water shall be free for the inhabitants of Panama and Colon, except to the extent that may be necessary for the operation and maintenance of said water system, including reservoirs, aqueducts, hydrants, supply service, drainage and other works.

ARTICLE 6

The Republic of Colombia agrees that it will not cede or lease to any foreign Government any of its islands or harbors within or adjacent to the Bay of Panama, nor on the Atlantic Coast of Colombia, between the Atrato River and the western boundary of the Department of Panama, for the purpose of establishing fortifications, naval or coaling stations, military posts, docks or other works that might interfere with the construction, maintenance, operation, protection, safety, and free use of the canal and auxiliary works. In order to enable Colombia to comply with this stipulation, the Government of the United States agrees to give Colombia the material support that may be required in order to prevent the occupation of said islands and ports, guaranteeing there the sovereignty, independence and integrity of Colombia.

ARTICLE 7

The Republic of Colombia includes in the foregoing grant the right without obstacle, cost, or impediment, to such control, consumption and general utilization in any manner found necessary by the United States to the exercise by it of the grants to, and rights conferred upon it by this Treaty, the waters of the Chagres River and other streams, lakes and lagoons, of all non-navigable waters, natural and artificial, and also to navigate all rivers, streams, lakes and other navigable water-ways, within the jurisdiction and under the domain of the Republic of Colombia, in the Department of Panama, within or without said zone, as may be necessary or desirable for the construction, maintenance and operation of the canal and its auxiliary canals and other works, and without tolls or charges of any kind; and to raise and lower the levels of the waters, and to deflect them, and to impound any such waters, and to overflow any lands necessary for the due exercise of such grants and rights to the United States; and to rectify, construct and improve the navigation of any such rivers, streams, lakes and lagoons at the sole cost of the United States; but any such water-ways so made by the United States may be used by citizens of Colombia free of tolls or other charges. And the United States shall have the right to use without cost, any water, stone, clay, earth or other minerals belonging to Colombia on the public domain that may be needed by it.

All damages caused to private land owners by inundation or by the deviation of water courses, or in other ways, arising out of the construction or operation of the canal, shall in each case be appraised and settled by a joint commission appointed by the Governments of the United States and Colombia, but the cost of the indemnities so agreed upon shall be borne solely by the United States.

ARTICLE 8

The Government of Colombia declares free for all time the ports at either entrance of the Canal, including Panama and Colon and the waters thereof in such manner that there shall not be collected by the Government of Colombia custom house tolls, tonnage, anchorage, light-house, wharf, pilot, or quarantine dues, nor any other charges or taxes of any kind shall be levied or imposed by the Government of Colombia upon any vessel using or passing through the Canal or belonging to or employed by the United States, directly or indirectly, in connection with the construction, maintenance and operation of the main work or its auxiliaries, or upon the cargo, officers, crew, or passengers of any such vessels; it being the intent of this convention that all vessels and their cargoes, crews, and passengers, shall be permitted to use and pass through the Canal and the ports leading thereto, subject to no other demands or impositions than such tolls and charges as may be imposed by the United States for the use of the Canal and other works. It being understood that such tolls and charges shall be governed by the provisions of Article 16.

The ports leading to the Canal, including Panama and Colon, also shall be free to the commerce of the world, and no duties or taxes shall be imposed, except upon merchandise destined to be introduced for the consumption of the rest of the Republic of Colombia, or the Department of Panama, and upon vessels touching at the ports of Colon and Panama and which do not cross the Canal.

Though the said ports shall be free and open to all, the Government of Colombia may establish in them such custom houses and guards as Colombia may deem necessary to collect duties on importations destined to other portions of Colombia and to prevent contraband trade. The United States shall have the right to make use of the ports at the two extremities of the Canal including Panama and Colon as places of anchorage, in order to make repairs for loading, unloading, depositing, or transshipping cargoes either in transit or destined for the service of the Canal and other works.

Any concessions or privileges granted by Colombia for the operation of light houses at Colon and Panama shall be subject to expropriation, indemnification and payment in the same manner as is provided by Article 14 in respect to the property therein mentioned; but Colombia shall make no additional grant of any such privilege nor change the status of any existing concession.

ARTICLE 9

There shall not be imposed any taxes, national, municipal, departmental, or of any other class, upon the canal, the vessels that may use it, tugs and other vessels employed in the service of the canal, the railways and auxiliary works, store houses, work shops, offices, quarters for laborers, factories of all kinds, warehouses, wharves, machinery and other works, property, and effects appertaining to the canal or railroad or that may be necessary for the service of the canal or railroad and their dependencies, whether situated within the cities of Panama and Colon, or any other place authorized by the provisions of this convention.

Nor shall there be imposed contributions or charges of a personal character of whatever species upon officers, employees, laborers, and other individuals in the service of the canal and its dependencies.

ARTICLE 10

It is agreed that telegraph and telephone lines, when established for canal purposes, may also, under suitable regulations, be used for public and private business in connection with the systems of Colombia and the other American Republics and with the lines of cable companies authorized to enter the ports and territories of these Republics; but the official dispatches of the Government of Colombia and the authorities of the Department of Panama shall not pay for such service higher tolls than those required from the officials in the service of the United States.

ARTICLE 11

The Government of Colombia shall permit the immigration and free access to the lands and workshops of the canal and its dependencies of all employees and workmen of whatever nationality under contract to work upon or seeking employment or in any wise connected with the said canal and its dependencies, with their respective families, and all such persons shall be free and exempt from the military service of the Republic of Colombia.

ARTICLE 12

The United States may import at any time into the said zone, free of customs duties, imposts, taxes, or other charges, and without any restriction, any and all vessels, dredges, engines, cars, machinery, tools, explosives, materials, supplies, and other articles necessary and convenient in the construction, maintenance and operation of the canal and auxiliary works, also all provisions, medicines, clothing, supplies and other things necessary and convenient for the officers, employees, workmen and laborers in the service and employ of the United States and for their families. If any such articles are disposed of for use without the zone excepting Panama and Colon and within the territory of the Republic, they shall be subject to the same import or other duties as like articles under the laws of Colombia or the ordinances of the Department of Panama.

ARTICLE 13

The United States shall have authority to protect and make secure the canal, as well as railways and other auxiliary works and dependencies, and to preserve order and discipline among the laborers and other persons who may congregate in that region, and to make and enforce such police and sanitary regulations as it may deem necessary to preserve order and public health thereon, and to protect navigation and commerce through and over said canal, railways and other works and dependencies from interruption or damage.

I. The Republic of Colombia may establish judicial tribunals within said zone, for the determination, according to its laws and judicial procedure, of certain controversies hereinafter mentioned.

Such judicial tribunal or tribunals so established by the Republic of Colombia shall have exclusive jurisdiction in said zone of all controversies between citizens of the Republic of Colombia, or between citizens of the Republic of Colombia and citizens of any foreign nation other than the United States.

II. Subject to the general sovereignty of Colombia over said zone, the United States may establish judicial tribunals thereon, which shall have jurisdiction of certain controversies hereinafter mentioned to be determined according to the laws and judicial procedure of the United States.

Such judicial tribunal or tribunals so established by the United States shall have exclusive jurisdiction in said zone of all controversies between citizens of the United States, and between citizens of the United States and citizens of any foreign nation other than the Republic of Colombia; and of all controversies in any wise growing out of or relating to the construction, maintenance or operation of the canal, railway and other properties and works.

III. The United States and Colombia engage jointly to establish and maintain upon said zone, judicial tribunals having civil, criminal and admiralty jurisdiction, and to be composed of jurists appointed by the Governments of the United States and Colombia in a manner hereafter to be agreed upon between said Governments, and which tribunals shall have jurisdiction of certain controversies hereinafter mentioned, and of all crimes, felonies and misdemeanors committed within said zone, and of all cases arising in admiralty, according to such laws and procedure as shall be hereafter agreed upon and declared by the two Governments.

Such joint judicial tribunal shall have exclusive jurisdiction in said zone of all controversies between citizens of the United States and citizens of Colombia, and between citizens of nations other than Colombia or the United States; and also of all crimes, felonies and misdemeanors committed within said zone, and of all questions of admiralty arising therein.

IV. The two Governments hereafter, and from time to time as occasion arises, shall agree upon and establish the laws and procedures which shall govern such joint judicial tribunal and which shall be applicable to the persons and cases over which such tribunal shall have jurisdiction, and also shall likewise create the requisite officers and employees of such court and establish their powers and duties; and further shall make adequate provision by like agreement for the pursuit, capture, imprisonment, detention and delivery within said zone of persons charged with the commitment of crimes, felonies or misdemeanors without said zone; and for the pursuit, capture, imprisonment, detention and delivery without said zone of persons charged with the commitment of crimes, felonies and misdemeanors within said zone.

ARTICLE 14

The works of the canal, the railways and their auxiliaries are declared of public utility, and in consequence all areas of land and water necessary for the construction, maintenance, and operation of the canal and other specified works may be expropriated in conformity with the laws of Colombia, except that the indemnity shall be conclusively determined without appeal, by a joint commission appointed by the Governments of Colombia and the United States.

The indemnities awarded by the Commission for such expropriation shall be borne by the United States, but the appraisal of said lands and the assessment of damages shall be based upon their value before the commencement of the work upon the canal.

ARTICLE 15

The Republic of Colombia grants to the United States the use of all the ports of the Republic open to commerce as places of refuge for any vessels employed in the canal enterprise, and for all vessels in distress having the right to pass through the canal and wishing to anchor in said ports. Such vessels shall be exempt from anchorage and tonnage dues on the part of Colombia.

ARTICLE 16

The canal, when constructed, and the entrance thereto shall be neutral in perpetuity, and shall be opened upon the terms provided for by Section I of Article three of, and in conformity with all the stipulations of, the treaty entered into by the Governments of the United States and Great Britain on November 18, 1901.

ARTICLE 17

The Government of Colombia shall have the right to transport over the canal its vessels, troops, and munitions of war at all times without paying charges of any kind. This exemption is to be extended to the auxiliary railway for the transportation of persons in the service of the Republic of Colombia or of the Department of Panama, or of the police force charged with the preservation of public order outside of said zone, as well as to their baggage, munitions of war and supplies.

ARTICLE 18

The United States shall have full power and authority to establish and enforce regulations for the use of the canal, railways, and the entering ports and auxiliary works, and to fix rates of tolls and charges thereof, subject to the limitations stated in Article 16.

ARTICLE 19

The rights and privileges granted to the United States by this convention shall not affect the sovereignty of the Republic of Colombia over the real estate that may be acquired by the United States by reason of the transfer of the rights of the New Panama Canal Company and the Panama Railroad Company lying outside of the said canal zone.

ARTICLE 20

If by virtue of any existing treaty between the Republic of Colombia and any third power, there may be any privilege or concession relative to an interoceanic means of communication which especially favors such third power, and which in any of its terms may be incompatible with the terms of the present convention, the Republic of Colombia agrees to cancel or modify such treaty in due form, for which purpose it shall give to the said third power the requisite notification within the term of four months from the date of the present convention, and in case the existing treaty contains no clause permitting its modification or annulment, the Republic of Colombia agrees to procure its modification or annulment in such form that there shall not exist any conflict with the stipulations of the present convention.

ARTICLE 21

The rights and privileges granted by the Republic of Colombia to the United States in the preceding Articles are understood to be free of all anterior concessions or privileges to other Governments, corporations, syndicates or individuals, and consequently, if there should arise any claims on account of the present concessions and privileges or otherwise, the claimants shall resort to the Government of Colombia and not to the United States for any indemnity or compromise which may be required.

ARTICLE 22

The Republic of Colombia renounces and grants to the United States the participation to which it might be entitled in the future earnings of the canal under Article 15 of the concessionary contract with Lucien N. B. Wyse now owned by the New Panama Canal Company and any and all other rights or claims of a pecuniary nature arising under or relating to said concession, or arising under or relating to the concessions to the Panama Railroad Company or any extension or modification thereof; and it likewise renounces, confirms and grants to the United States, now and hereafter, all the rights and property reserved in the said concessions which otherwise would belong to Colombia at or before the expiration of the terms of ninety-nine years of the concessions granted to or held by the above mentioned party and companies, and all right, title and interest which it now has or may hereafter have, in and to the lands, canal, works, property and rights held by the said companies under said concessions or otherwise, and acquired or to be acquired by the United States from or through the New Panama Canal Company, including any property and rights which might or may in the future either by lapse of time, forfeiture or otherwise, revert to the Republic of Colombia under any contracts of concessions, with said Wyse, the Universal Panama Canal Company, the Panama Railroad Company and the New Panama Canal Company.

The aforesaid rights and property shall be and are free and released from any present or reversionary interest in or claims of Colombia and the title of the United States thereto upon consummation of the contemplated purchase by the United States from the New

Panama Canal Company, shall be absolute, so far as concerns the Republic of Colombia, excepting always the rights of Colombia specifically secured under this treaty.

If it should become necessary at any time to employ armed forces for the safety or protection of the canal, or of the ships that make use of the same, or the railways and other works, the Republic of Colombia agrees to provide the forces necessary for such purpose, according to the circumstances of the case, but if the Government of Colombia cannot effectively comply with this obligation, then, with the consent of or at the request of Colombia, or of her Minister at Washington, or of the local authorities, civil or military, the United States shall employ such force as may be necessary for that sole purpose; and as soon as the necessity shall have ceased will withdraw the forces so employed. Under exceptional circumstances, however, on account of unforeseen or imminent danger to said canal, railways and other works, or to the lives and property of the persons employed upon the canal, railways, and other works, the Government of the United States is authorized to act in the interest of their protection, without the necessity of obtaining the consent beforehand of the Government of Colombia; and it shall give immediate advice of the measures adopted for the purpose stated; and as soon as sufficient Colombian forces shall arrive to attend to the indicated purpose, those of the United States shall retire.

The Government of the United States agrees to complete the construction of the preliminary works necessary, together with all the auxiliary works, in the shortest time possible; and within two years from the date of the exchange of ratification of this convention the main works of the canal proper shall be commenced, and it shall be opened to the traffic between the two oceans within twelve years after such period of two years. In case, however, that any difficulties or obstacles should arise in the construction of the canal which are at present impossible to foresee, in consideration of the good faith with which the Government of the United States shall have proceeded, and the large amount of money expended so far on the works and the nature of the difficulties which may have arisen, the Government of Colombia will prolong the terms stipulated in this Article up to twelve years more for the completion of the work of the canal.

But in case the United States should, at any time, determine to make such canal practically a sea level canal, then such period shall be extended for ten years further.

ARTICLE 25

As the price or compensation for the right to use the zone granted in this convention by Colombia to the United States for the construction of a canal, together with the proprietary right over the Panama Railroad, and for the annuity of two hundred and fifty thousand dollars gold, which Colombia ceases to receive from the said railroad, as well as in compensation for other rights, privileges and exemptions granted to the United States, and in consideration of the increase in the administrative expenses of the Department of Panama consequent upon the construction of the said canal, the Government of the United States binds itself to pay Colombia the sum of ten million dollars in gold coin of the United States on the exchange of the ratification of this convention after its approval according to the laws of the respective countries, and also an annual payment during the life of this convention of two hundred and fifty thousand dollars in like gold coin, beginning nine years after the date aforesaid.

The provisions of this Article shall be in addition to all other benefits assured to Colombia under this convention.

But no delay nor difference of opinion under this Article shall affect nor interrupt the full operation and effect of this convention in all other respects:

ARTICLE 26

No change either in the Government or in the laws and treaties of Columbia, shall, without the consent of the United States, affect any right of the United States under the present convention, or under any treaty stipulation between the two countries (that now exist or may hereafter exist) touching the subject matter of this convention.

If Colombia shall hereafter enter as a constituent into any other Government or into any union or confederation of States so as to merge her sovereignty or independence in such Government, union, or confederation, the rights of the United States under this convention shall not be in any respect lessened or impaired.

ARTICLE 27

The joint commission referred to in Articles 3, 7, and 14 shall be established as follows:

The President of the United States shall nominate two persons and the President of Colombia shall nominate two persons and they shall proceed to a decision; but in case of disagreement of the Commission (by reason of their being equally divided in conclusion) an umpire shall be appointed by the two Governments, who shall render the decision. In the event of death, absence or incapacity of any Commissioner or umpire, or of his omitting, declining or ceasing to act, his place shall be filled by the appointment of another person in the manner above indicated. All decisions by a majority of the Commission or by the umpire shall be final.

ARTICLE 28

This convention when signed by the contracting parties, shall be ratified according to the laws of the respective countries and shall be exchanged at Washington within a term of eight months from this date, or earlier if possible.

In faith whereof, the respective plenipotentiaries have signed the present convention in duplicate and have hereunto affixed their respective seals.

Done at the City of Washington, the 22d day of January in the year of our Lord nineteen hundred and three.

(Signed)   JOHN HAY   [SEAL]

(Signed)   TOMÁS HERRÁN   [SEAL]

THE "HAY–BUNAU-VARILLA CONVENTION" between *the United States and Panama, Signed at Washington, November 18, 1903*

Department of State, Treaty Series, No. 431. The treaty was ratified by the President of the United States, February 25, 1904, and ratifications exchanged February 26, 1904

ISTHMIAN CANAL CONVENTION

THE UNITED STATES of America and the Republic of Panama being desirous to insure the construction of a ship canal across the Isthmus of Panama to connect the Atlantic and Pacific oceans, and the Congress of the United States of America having passed an act approved June 28, 1902, in furtherance of that object, by which the President of the United States is authorized to acquire within a reasonable time the control of the necessary territory of the Republic of Colombia, and the sovereignty of such territory being actually vested in the Republic of Panama, the high contracting parties have resolved for that purpose to conclude a convention and have accordingly appointed as their plenipotentiaries,—

The President of the United States of America, JOHN HAY, Secretary of State, and

The Government of the Republic of Panama, PHILIPPE BUNAU-VARILLA, Envoy Extraordinary and Minister Plenipotentiary of the Republic of Panama, thereunto specially empowered by said government, who after communicating with each other their respective full powers, found to be in good and due form, have agreed upon and concluded the following articles:

ARTICLE 1

The United States guarantees and will maintain the independence of the Republic of Panama.

ARTICLE 2

The Republic of Panama grants to the United States in perpetuity the use, occupation and control of a zone of land and land under water for the construction, maintenance, operation, sanitation and protection of said Canal of the width of ten miles extending to the distance of five miles on each side of the center line of the route of the Canal to be constructed; the said zone beginning in the Caribbean Sea three marine miles from mean low water mark and extending to and across the Isthmus of Panama into the Pacific ocean to a distance of three marine miles from mean low water mark with the proviso that the cities of Panama and Colon and the harbors adjacent to said cities, which are included within the boundaries of the zone above described, shall not be included within this grant. The Republic of Panama further grants to the United States in perpetuity the use, occupation and control of any other lands and waters outside of the zone above described which may be necessary and convenient for the construction, maintenance, operations, sanitation and protection of the said Canal or of any auxiliary canals or other works necessary and convenient for the construction, maintenance, operation, sanitation and protection of the said enterprise.

The Republic of Panama further grants in like manner to the United States in perpetuity all islands within the limits of the zone above described and in addition thereto the group of small islands in the Bay of Panama, named Perico, Naos, Culebra and Flamenco.

ARTICLE 3

The Republic of Panama grants to the United States all the rights, power and authority within the zone mentioned and described in

Article 2 of this agreement and within the limits of all auxiliary lands and waters mentioned and described in said Article 2 which the United States would possess and exercise if it were the sovereign of the territory within which said lands and waters are located to the entire exclusion of the exercise by the Republic of Panama of any such sovereign rights, power or authority.

ARTICLE 4

As rights subsidiary to the above grants the Republic of Panama grants in perpetuity to the United States the right to use the rivers, streams, lakes and other bodies of water within its limits for navigation, the supply of water or water-power or other purposes, so far as the use of said rivers, streams, lakes and bodies of water and the waters thereof may be necessary and convenient for the construction, maintenance, operation, sanitation and protection of the said Canal.

ARTICLE 5

The Republic of Panama grants to the United States in perpetuity a monopoly for the construction, maintenance and operation of any system of communication by means of canal or railroad across its territory between the Caribbean Sea and the Pacific ocean.

ARTICLE 6

The grants herein contained shall in no manner invalidate the titles or rights of private land holders or owners of private property in the said zone or in or to any of the lands or waters granted to the United States by the provisions of any Article of this treaty, nor shall they interfere with the rights of way over the public roads passing through the said zone or over any of the said lands or waters unless said rights of way or private rights shall conflict with rights herein granted to the United States in which case the rights of the United States shall be superior. All damages caused to the owners of private lands or private property of any kind by reason of the grants contained in this treaty or by reason of the operations of the United States, its agents or employees, or by reason of the construction, maintenance, operation, sanitation and protection of the said Canal or of the works of sanitation and protection herein provided for, shall be appraised and settled by a joint Commission appointed by the Governments of the United States and the Republic of Panama, whose decisions as to such damages shall be final and whose awards as to such damages shall be paid solely by the United States. No part of the work on said Canal or the Panama railroad or on any auxiliary works relating thereto and authorized by the terms of this treaty shall be prevented, delayed or impeded by or pending such proceedings to ascertain such damages. The appraisal of said private lands and private property and the assessment of damages to them shall be based upon their value before the date of this convention.

ARTICLE 7

The Republic of Panama grants to the United States within the limits of the cities of Panama and Colon and their adjacent harbors and within the territory adjacent thereto the right to acquire by purchase or by the exercise of the right of eminent domain, any lands, buildings, water rights or other properties necessary and convenient for the construction, maintenance, operation and protection of the Canal and of any works of sanitation, such as the collection and disposition of sewage and the distribution of water in the said cities of Panama and Colon, which, in the discretion of the United States may be necessary and convenient for the construction, maintenance, operation, sanitation and protection of the said Canal and railroad. All such works of sanitation, collection and disposition of sewage and distribution of water in the cities of Panama and Colon shall be made at the expense of the United States, and the Government of the United States, its agents or nominees shall be authorized to impose and collect water rates and sewerage rates which shall be sufficient to provide for the payment of interest and the amortization of the principal of the cost of said works within a period of fifty years and upon the expiration of said term of fifty years the system of sewers and water works shall revert to and become the properties of the cities of Panama and Colon respectively, and the use of the water shall be free to the inhabitants of Panama and Colon, except to the extent that water rates may be necessary for the operation and maintenance of said system of sewers and water.

The Republic of Panama agrees that the cities of Panama and Colon shall comply in perpetuity with the sanitary ordinances whether of a preventive or curative character prescribed by the United States and in case the Government of Panama is unable or fails in its duty to enforce this compliance by the cities of Panama and Colon with the sanitary ordinances of the United States the Republic of Panama grants to the United States the right and authority to enforce the same.

The same right and authority are granted to the United States for the maintenance of public order in the cities of Panama and Colon and the territories and harbors adjacent thereto in case the Republic of Panama should not be, in the judgment of the United States, able to maintain such order.

ARTICLE 8

The Republic of Panama grants to the United States all rights which it now has or hereafter may acquire to the property of the New Panama Canal Company and the Panama Railroad Company as a result of the transfer of sovereignty from the Republic of Colombia to the Republic of Panama over the Isthmus of Panama and authorizes the New Panama Canal Company to sell and transfer to the United States its rights, privileges, properties and concessions as well as the Panama Railroad and all the shares or part of the shares of that company; but the public lands situated outside of the zone described in Article 2 of this treaty now included in the concessions to both said enterprises and not required in the construction or operation of the Canal shall revert to the Republic of Panama except any property now owned by or in the possession of said companies within Panama or Colon or the ports or terminals thereof.

ARTICLE 9

The United States agrees that the ports at either entrance of the Canal and the waters thereof, and the Republic of Panama agrees that the towns of Panama and Colon shall be free for all time so that there shall not be imposed or collected custom house tolls, tonnage, anchorage, lighthouse, wharf, pilot, or quarantine dues or any other charges or taxes of any kind upon any vessel using or passing through the Canal or belonging to or employed by the United States, directly or indirectly, in connection with the construction, maintenance, operation, sanitation and protection of the main Canal, or auxiliary works, or upon the cargo, officers, crew, or passengers of any such vessels, except such tolls and charges as may be imposed by the United States for the use of the Canal and other works, and except tolls and charges imposed by the Republic of Panama upon merchandise destined to be introduced for the consumption of the rest of the Republic of Panama, and upon vessels touching at the ports of Colon and Panama and which do not cross the Canal.

The Government of the Republic of Panama shall have the right to establish in such ports and in the towns of Panama and Colon such houses and guards as it may deem necessary to collect duties on importations destined to other portions of Panama and to prevent contraband trade. The United States shall have the right to make use of the towns and harbors of Panama and Colon as places of anchorage, and for making repairs, for loading, unloading, depositing, or transshipping cargoes either in transit or destined for the service of the Canal and for other works pertaining to the Canal.

ARTICLE 10

The Republic of Panama agrees that there shall not be imposed any taxes, national, municipal, departmental, or of any other class, upon the Canal, the railways and auxiliary works, tugs and other vessels employed in the service of the Canal, store houses, work shops, offices, quarters for laborers, factories of all kinds, warehouses, wharves, machinery and other works, property, and effects appertaining to the Canal or railroad and auxiliary works, or their officers or employees, situated within the cities of Panama and Colon, and that there shall not be imposed contributions or charges of a personal character of any kind upon officers, employees, laborers, and other individuals in the service of the Canal and railroad and auxiliary works.

ARTICLE 11

The United States agrees that the official dispatches of the Government of the Republic of Panama shall be transmitted over any telegraph and telephone lines established for canal purposes and used for public and private business at rates not higher than those required from officials in the service of the United States.

ARTICLE 12

The Government of the Republic of Panama shall permit the immigration and free access to the lands and workshops of the Canal and its auxiliary works of all employees and workmen of whatever nationality under contract to work upon or seeking employment upon or in any wise connected with the said Canal and its auxiliary works, with their respective families, and all such persons shall be free and exempt from the military service of the Republic of Panama.

ARTICLE 13

The United States may import at any time into the said zone and auxiliary lands, free of custom duties, imposts, taxes, or other charges, and without any restrictions, any and all vessels, dredges, engines, cars, machinery, tools, explosives, materials, supplies, and other articles necessary and convenient in the construction, maintenance, operation, sanitation and protection of the Canal and auxiliary works, and all provisions, medicines, clothing, supplies and other things necessary and convenient for the officers, employees, workmen and laborers in the service and employ of the United States and for their families. If any such articles are disposed of for use outside of the zone and auxiliary lands granted to the United States and within the territory of the Republic, they shall be subject to the same import or other duties as like articles imported under the laws of the Republic of Panama.

ARTICLE 14

As the price or compensation for the rights, powers and privileges granted in this convention by the Republic of Panama to the United States, the Government of the United States agrees to pay to the Republic of Panama the sum of ten million dollars ($10,000,000) in gold coin of the United States on the exchange of the ratification of this convention and also an annual payment during the life of this convention of two hundred and fifty thousand dollars ($250,000) in like gold coin, beginning nine years after the date aforesaid.

The provisions of this Article shall be in addition to all other benefits assured to the Republic of Panama under this convention.

But no delay or difference of opinion under this Article or any other provisions of this treaty shall affect or interrupt the full operation and effect of this convention in all other respects.

ARTICLE 15

The joint commission referred to in Article 6 shall be established as follows:

The President of the United States shall nominate two persons and the President of the Republic of Panama shall nominate two persons and they shall proceed to a decision; but in case of disagreement of the Commission (by reason of their being equally divided in conclusion) an umpire shall be appointed by the two Governments who shall render the decision. In the event of the death, absence, or incapacity of a Commissioner or Umpire, or of his omitting, declining or ceasing to act, his place shall be filled by the appointment of another person in the manner above indicated. All decisions by a majority of the Commission or by the umpire shall be final.

ARTICLE 16

The two Governments shall make adequate provision by future agreement for the pursuit, capture, imprisonment, detention and delivery within said zone and auxiliary lands to the authorities of the Republic of Panama of persons charged with the commitment of crimes, felonies or misdemeanors without said zone and for the pursuit, capture, imprisonment, detention and delivery without said zone to the authorities of the United States of persons charged with the commitment of crimes, felonies and misdemeanors within said zone and auxiliary lands.

ARTICLE 17

The Republic of Panama grants to the United States the use of all the ports of the Republic open to commerce as places of refuge for any vessels employed in the Canal enterprise, and for all vessels passing or bound to pass through the Canal which may be in distress and be driven to seek refuge in said ports. Such vessels shall be exempt from anchorage and tonnage dues on the part of the Republic of Panama.

ARTICLE 18

The Canal, when constructed, and the entrances thereto shall be neutral in perpetuity, and shall be opened upon the terms provided for by Section I of Article three of, and in conformity with all the stipulations of, the treaty entered into by the Governments of the United States and Great Britain on November 18, 1901.

ARTICLE 19

The Government of the Republic of Panama shall have the right to transport over the Canal its vessels and its troops and munitions of war in such vessels at all times without paying charges of any kind. The exemption is to be extended to the auxiliary railway for the transportation of persons in the service of the Republic of Panama, or of the police force charged with the preservation of public order outside of said zone, as well as to their baggage, munitions of war and supplies.

ARTICLE 20

If by virtue of any existing treaty in relation to the territory of the Isthmus of Panama, whereof the obligations shall descend or be assumed by the Republic of Panama, there may be any privilege or concession in favor of the Government or the citizens and subjects of a third power relative to an interoceanic means of communication which in any of its terms may be incompatible with the terms of the present convention, the Republic of Panama agrees to cancel or modify such treaty in due form, for which purpose it shall give to the said third power the requisite notification within the term of four months from the date of the present convention, and in case the existing treaty contains no clause permitting its modifications or annulment, the Republic of Panama agrees to procure its modification or annulment in such form that there shall not exist any conflict with the stipulations of the present convention.

ARTICLE 21

The rights and privileges granted by the Republic of Panama to the United States in the preceding Articles are understood to be free of all anterior debts, liens, trusts, or liabilities, or concessions or privileges to other Governments, corporations, syndicates or individuals, and consequently, if there should arise any claims on account of the present concessions and privileges or otherwise, the claimants shall resort to the Government of the Republic of Panama and not to the United States for any indemnity or compromise which may be required.

ARTICLE 22

The Republic of Panama renounces and grants to the United States the participation to which it might be entitled in the future earnings of the Canal under Article 15 of the concessionary contract with Lucien N. B. Wyse now owned by the New Panama Canal Company and any and all other rights or claims of a pecuniary nature arising under or relating to said concession, or arising under or relating to the concessions to the Panama Railroad Company or any extension or modification thereof; and it likewise renounces, confirms and grants to the United States, now and hereafter, all the rights and property reserved in the said concessions which otherwise would belong to Panama at or before the expiration of the terms of ninety-nine years of the concessions granted to or held by the above mentioned party and companies, and all right, title and interest which it now has or may hereafter have, in and to the lands, canal, works, property and rights held by the said companies under said concessions or otherwise, and acquired or to be acquired by the United States from or through the New Panama Canal Company, including any property and rights which might or may in the future either by lapse of time, forfeiture or otherwise, revert to the Republic of Panama under any contracts or concessions, with said Wyse, the Universal Panama Canal Company, the Panama Railroad Company and the New Panama Canal Company.

The aforesaid rights and property shall be and are free and released from any present or reversionary interest in or claims of Panama and the title of the United States thereto upon consummation of the contemplated purchase by the United States from the New Panama Canal Company, shall be absolute, so far as concerns the Republic of Panama, excepting always the rights of the Republic specifically secured under this treaty.

ARTICLE 23

If it should become necessary at any time to employ armed forces for the safety or protection of the Canal, or of the ships that make use of the same, or the railways and auxiliary works, the United States shall have the right, at all times and in its discretion, to use its police and its land and naval forces or to establish fortifications for these purposes.

ARTICLE 24

No change either in the Government or in the laws and treaties of the Republic of Panama shall, without the consent of the United States, affect any right of the United States under the present convention, or under any treaty stipulation between the two countries that now exists or may hereafter exist touching the subject matter of this convention.

If the Republic of Panama shall hereafter enter as a constituent into any other Government or into any union or confederation of states, so as to merge her sovereignty or independence in such Government, union or confederation, the rights of the United States under this convention shall not be in any respect lessened or impaired.

ARTICLE 25

For the better performance of the engagements of this convention and to the end of the efficient protection of the Canal and the preservation of its neutrality, the Government of the Republic of Panama will sell or lease to the United States lands adequate and necessary for naval or coaling stations on the Pacific coast and on the western Caribbean coast of the Republic at certain points to be agreed upon with the President of the United States.

ARTICLE 26

This convention when signed by the Plenipotentiaries of the Contracting Parties shall be ratified by the respective Governments and the ratifications shall be exchanged at Washington at the earliest date possible.

In faith whereof the respective Plenipotentiaries have signed the present convention in duplicate and have hereunto affixed their respective seals.

Done at the City of Washington the 18th day of November in the year of our Lord nineteen hundred and three.

JOHN HAY [SEAL]
P. BUNAU VARILLA [SEAL]

TREATY between the United States and Colombia, Signed at Bogotá, April 6, 1914

Department of State, Treaty Series, No. 661; as amended by the United States Senate

TREATY between the United States of America and the Republic of Colombia for the settlement of their differences arising out of the events which took place on the Isthmus of Panama in November 1903.

The United States of America and the Republic of Colombia, being desirous to remove all the misunderstandings growing out of the political events in Panama in November 1903; to restore the cordial friendship that formerly characterized the relations between the two countries, and also to define and regulate their rights and interests in respect of the interoceanic canal which the Government of the United States has constructed across the Isthmus of Panama, have resolved for this purpose to conclude a Treaty and have accordingly appointed as their Plenipotentiaries:

His Excellency the President of the United States of America, Thaddeus Austin Thomson, Envoy Extraordinary and Minister Plenipotentiary of the United States of America to the Government of the Republic of Colombia; and

His Excellency the President of the Republic of Colombia, Francisco José Urrutia, Minister for Foreign Affairs; Marco Fidel Suárez, First Designate to exercise the Executive Power; Nicolás Esguerra, Ex-Minister of State; José María González Valencia, Senator; Rafael Uribe Uribe, Senator; and Antonio José Uribe, President of the House of Representatives;

Who, after communicating to each other their respective full powers, which were found to be in due and proper form, have agreed upon the following:

ARTICLE 1

The Republic of Colombia shall enjoy the following rights in respect to the interoceanic Canal and the Panama Railway, the title to which is now vested entirely and absolutely in the United States of America, without any incumbrances or indemnities whatever.

1. The Republic of Colombia shall be at liberty at all times to transport through the interoceanic Canal its troops, materials of war and ships of war, without paying any charges to the United States.

2. The products of the soil and industry of Colombia passing through the Canal, as well as the Colombian mails, shall be exempt from any charge or duty other than those to which the products and mails of the United States may be subject. The products of the soil and industry of Colombia, such as cattle, salt and provisions, shall be admitted to entry in the Canal Zone, and likewise in the islands and mainland occupied or which may be occupied by the United States as auxiliary and accessory thereto, without paying other duties or charges than those payable by similar products of the United States.

3. Colombian citizens crossing the Canal Zone shall, upon production of proper proof of their nationality, be exempt from every toll, tax or duty to which citizens of the United States are not subject.

4. Whenever traffic by the Canal is interrupted or whenever it shall be necessary for any other reason to use the railway, the troops, materials of war, products and mails of the Republic of Colombia, as above mentioned, shall, be transported on the Railway between Ancon and Cristobal or on any other Railway substituted therefor, paying only the same charges and duties as are imposed upon the troops, materials of war, products and mails of the United States. The officers, agents and employees of the Government of Colombia shall, upon production of proper proof of their official character or their employment, also be entitled to passage on the said Railway on the same terms as officers, agents and employees of the Government of the United States.

5. Coal, petroleum and sea salt, being the products of Colombia, for Colombian consumption passing from the Atlantic coast of Colombia to any Colombian port on the Pacific coast, and vice-versa, shall, whenever traffic by the Canal is interrupted, be transported over the aforesaid Railway free of any charge except the actual cost of handling and transportation, which shall not in any case exceed one half of the ordinary freight charges levied upon similar products of the United States passing over the Railway and in transit from one port to another of the United States.

ARTICLE 2

The Government of the United States of America agrees to pay at the City of Washington to the Republic of Colombia the sum of twenty-five million dollars, gold, United States money, as follows: The sum of five million dollars shall be paid within six months after the exchange of ratifications of the present treaty, and reckoning from the date of that payment, the remaining twenty million dollars shall be paid in four annual installments of five million dollars each.

ARTICLE 3

The Republic of Colombia recognizes Panama as an independent nation and taking as a basis the Colombian Law of June 9, 1855, agrees that the boundary shall be the following: From Cape Tiburón to the headwaters of the Rio de la Miel and following the mountain chain by the ridge of Gandi to the Sierra de Chugargun and that of Mali going down by the ridges of Nigue to the heights of Aspave and from thence to a point on the Pacific half way between Cocalito and La Ardita.

In consideration of this recognition, the Government of the United States will, immediately after the exchange of the ratifications of the present Treaty, take the necessary steps in order to obtain from the Government of Panama the despatch of a duly accredited agent to negotiate and conclude with the Government of Colombia a Treaty of Peace and Friendship, with a view to bring about both the establishment of regular diplomatic relations between Colombia and Panama and the adjustment of all questions of pecuniary liability as between the two countries, in accordance with recognized principles of law and precedents.

ARTICLE 4

The present Treaty shall be approved and ratified by the High Contracting Parties in conformity with their respective laws, and the ratifications thereof shall be exchanged in the city of Bogotá, as soon as may be possible.

In faith whereof, the said Plenipotentiaries have signed the present Treaty in duplicate and have hereunto affixed their respective seals.

Done at the city of Bogotá, the sixth day of April in the year of our Lord nineteen hundred and fourteen.

[Signatures]

[The treaty was ratified by the President of the United States, January 11, 1922, with the "understanding, to be made a part of such treaty and ratification, that the provisions of section 1 of Article I of the treaty granting to the Republic of Colombia free passage through the Panama Canal for its troops, materials of war and ships of war, shall not apply in case of war between the Republic of Colombia and any other country." Ratifications were exchanged, March 1, 1922.]

CONVENTION between the United States and Nicaragua, Signed at Washington, August 5, 1914

Department of State, Treaty Series, No. 624; as amended by the United States Senate

THE GOVERNMENT of the United States of America and the Government of Nicaragua being animated by the desire to strengthen their ancient and cordial friendship by the most sincere cooperation for all purposes of their mutual advantage and interest and to provide for the possible future construction of an interoceanic ship canal by way of the San Juan River and the great Lake of Nicaragua, or by any route over Nicaraguan territory, whenever the construction of such canal shall be deemed by the Government of the United States conducive to the interests of both countries, and the Government of Nicaragua wishing to facilitate in every way possible the successful maintenance and operation of the Panama Canal, the two Governments have resolved to conclude a Convention to these ends, and have accordingly appointed as their plenipotentiaries:

The President of the United States, the Honorable William Jennings Bryan, Secretary of State; and

The President of Nicaragua, Señor General Don Emiliano Chamorro, Envoy Extraordinary and Minister Plenipotentiary of Nicaragua to the United States;

Who, having exhibited to each other their respective full powers, found to be in good and due form, have agreed upon and concluded the following articles:

ARTICLE 1

The Government of Nicaragua grants in perpetuity to the Government of the United States, forever free from all taxation or other public charge, the exclusive proprietary rights necessary and convenient for the construction, operation and maintenance of an interoceanic canal by way of the San Juan River and the great Lake of Nicaragua or by way of any route over Nicaraguan territory, the details of the terms upon which such canal shall be constructed, operated and maintained to be agreed to by the two governments whenever the Government of the United States shall notify the Government of Nicaragua of its desire or intention to construct such canal.

ARTICLE 2

To enable the Government of the United States to protect the Panama Canal and the proprietary rights granted to the Government of the United States by the foregoing article, and also to enable the Government of the United States to take any measure necessary to the ends contemplated herein, the Government of Nicaragua hereby leases for a term of ninety-nine years to the Government of the United States the islands in the Caribbean Sea known as Great Corn Island and Little Corn Island; and the Government of Nicaragua further grants to the Government of the United States for a like period of ninety-nine years the right to establish, operate and maintain a naval base at such place on the territory of Nicaragua bordering upon the Gulf of Fonseca as the Government of the United States may select. The Government of the United States shall have the option of renewing for a further term of ninety-nine years the above leases and grants upon the expiration of their respective terms, it being expressly agreed that the territory hereby leased and the naval base which may be maintained under the grant aforesaid shall be subject exclusively to the laws and sovereign authority of the United States during the terms of such lease and grant and of any renewal or renewals thereof.

ARTICLE 3

In consideration of the foregoing stipulations and for the purposes contemplated by this Convention and for the purpose of reducing the present indebtedness of Nicaragua, the Government of the United States shall, upon the date of the exchange of ratification of this Convention, pay for the benefit of the Republic of Nicaragua the sum of three million dollars United States gold coin, of the present weight and fineness, to be deposited to the order of the Government of Nicaragua in such bank or banks or with such banking corporation as the Government of the United States may determine, to be applied by Nicaragua upon its indebtedness or other public purposes for the advancement of the welfare of Nicaragua in a manner to be determined by the two High Contracting Parties, all such disbursements to be made by orders drawn by the Minister of Finance of the Republic of Nicaragua and approved by the Secretary of State of the United States or by such person as he may designate.

ARTICLE 4

This Convention shall be ratified by the High Contracting Parties in accordance with their respective laws, and the ratifications thereof shall be exchanged at Washington as soon as possible.

It witness whereof the respective plenipotentiaries have signed the present treaty and have affixed thereunto their seals.

Done at Washington, in duplicate, in the English and Spanish languages, on the 5th day of August, in the year nineteen hundred and fourteen.

WILLIAM JENNINGS BRYAN [SEAL]
EMILIANO CHAMORRO   [SEAL]

[The convention was ratified by the President of the United States, June 19, 1916, with the proviso: "Provided, That, whereas, Costa Rica, Salvador and Honduras have protested against the ratification of the said Convention in the fear or belief that said Convention might in some respect impair existing rights of said States; therefore, it is declared by the Senate that in advising and consenting to the ratification of the said Convention as amended such advice and consent are given with the understanding, to be expressed as a part of the instrument of ratification, that nothing in said Convention is intended to affect any existing right of any of the said named States." Ratifications were exchanged, June 22, 1916.]

Appendix D

CERTAIN TREATIES AND AGREEMENTS WITH HAITI AND THE DOMINICAN REPUBLIC

Haiti

TREATY between the United States and Haiti Concerning the Finances, Economic Development, and Tranquillity of Haiti, Signed September 16, 1915

Foreign Relations of the United States, 1915, p. 449. Ratifications were exchanged May 3, 1916

Preamble

THE UNITED STATES and the Republic of Haiti desiring to confirm and strengthen the amity existing between them by the most cordial coöperation in measures for their common advantage;

And the Republic of Haiti desiring to remedy the present condition of its revenues and finances, to maintain the tranquillity of the Republic, to carry out plans for the economic development and prosperity of the Republic and its people;

And the United States being in full sympathy with all of these aims and objects and desiring to contribute in all proper ways to their accomplishment;

The United States and the Republic of Haiti have resolved to conclude a Convention with these objects in view, and have appointed for that purpose, Plenipotentiaries,

The President of the United States, Robert Beale Davis, Junior, Chargé d'Affaires of the United States;

And the President of the Republic of Haiti, Louis Borno, Secretary of State for Foreign Affairs and Public Instruction, who, having exhibited to each other their respective powers, which are seen to be in full and good and true form, have agreed as follows:

ARTICLE 1

The Government of the United States will, by its good offices, aid the Haitian Government in the proper and efficient development of its agricultural, mineral and commercial resources and in the establishment of the finances of Haiti on a firm and solid basis.

ARTICLE 2

The President of Haiti shall appoint, upon nomination by the President of the United States, a General Receiver and such aids and employees as may be necessary, who shall collect, receive and apply all customs duties on imports and exports accruing at the several custom houses and ports of entry of the Republic of Haiti.

The President of Haiti shall appoint, upon nomination by the President of the United States, a Financial Adviser, who shall be an officer attached to the Ministry of Finance, to give effect to whose proposals and labors the Minister will lend efficient aid. The Financial Adviser shall devise an adequate system of public accounting, aid in increasing the revenues and adjusting them to the expenses, inquire into the validity of the debts of the Republic, enlighten both Governments with reference to all eventual debts, recommend improved methods of collecting and applying the revenues, and make such other recommendations to the Minister of Finance as mav be deemed necessary for the welfare and prosperity of Haiti.

ARTICLE 3

The Government of the Republic of Haiti will provide by law or appropriate decrees for the payment of all customs duties to the General Receiver, and will extend to the Receivership, and to the Financial Adviser, all needful aid and full protection in the execution of the powers conferred and duties imposed herein; and the United States on its part will extend like aid and protection.

ARTICLE 4

Upon the appointment of the Financial Adviser, the Government of the Republic of Haiti, in coöperation with the Financial Adviser, shall collate, classify, arrange and make full statement of all the debts of the Republic, the amounts, character, maturity and condition thereof, and the interest accruing and the sinking fund requisite to their final discharge.

ARTICLE 5

All sums collected and received by the General Receiver shall be applied, first, to the payment of the salaries and allowances of the

General Receiver, his assistants and employees and expenses of the Receivership, including the salary and expenses of the Financial Adviser, which salaries will be determined by previous agreement; second, to the interest and sinking fund of the public debt of the Republic of Haiti; and, third, to the maintenance of the constabulary referred to in Article 10 and then the remainder to the Haitian Government for purposes of current expenses.

In making these applications the General Receiver will proceed to pay salaries and allowances monthly and expenses as they arise, and on the first of each calendar month, will set aside in a separate fund the quantum of the collection and receipts of the previous month.

ARTICLE 6

The expenses of the Receivership, including salaries and allowances of the General Receiver, his assistants and employees, and the salary and expenses of the Financial Adviser, shall not exceed five per centum of the collections and receipts from customs duties, unless by agreement by the two Governments.

ARTICLE 7

The General Receiver shall make monthly reports of all collections, receipts and disbursements to the appropriate officer of the Republic of Haiti and to the Department of State of the United States, which reports shall be open to inspection and verification at all times by the appropriate authorities of each of the said Governments.

ARTICLE 8

The Republic of Haiti shall not increase its public debt except by previous agreement with the President of the United States, and shall not contract any debt or assume any financial obligation unless the ordinary revenues of the Republic available for that purpose, after defraying the expenses of the Government, shall be adequate to pay the interest and provide a sinking fund for the final discharge of such debt.

ARTICLE 9

The Republic of Haiti will not without a previous agreement with the President of the United States, modify the customs duties in a manner to reduce the revenues therefrom; and in order that the revenues of the Republic may be adequate to meet the public debt and the expenses of the Government, to preserve tranquillity and to promote material prosperity, the Republic of Haiti will coöperate with the Financial Adviser in his recommendations for improvement in the methods of collecting and disbursing the revenues and for new sources of needed income.

ARTICLE 10

The Haitian Government obligates itself, for the preservation of domestic peace, the security of individual rights and full observance of the provisions of this treaty, to create without delay an efficient constabulary, urban and rural, composed of native Haitians. This constabulary shall be organized and officered by Americans, appointed by the President of Haiti, upon nomination by the President of the United States. The Haitian Government shall clothe these officers with the proper and necessary authority and uphold them in the performance of their functions. These officers will be replaced by Haitians as they, by examination, conducted under the direction of a board to be selected by the senior American officer of this constabulary and in the presence of a representative of the Haitian Government, are found to be qualified to assume such duties. The constabulary herein provided for, shall, under the direction of the Haitian Government, have supervision and control of arms and ammunition, military supplies, and traffic therein, throughout the country. The high contracting parties agree that the stipulations in this Article are necessary to prevent factional strife and disturbances.

HAITIANIZATION AGREEMENT between the United States and Haiti, Signed at Port-au-Prince, August 5, 1931

Department of State, Executive Agreement Series, No. 22

THE UNDERSIGNED plenipotentiaries duly authorized by their respective governments have agreed upon the following Accord:

ARTICLE 1

The services of the Engineers provided for by Article 13 of the Treaty of September 16, 1915, for the sanitation and public improvement of the Republic, and by the Accord of July 17, 1923, regarding the Service Technique d'Agriculture, as well as their foreign aids and employees, shall definitely cease on September 30, 1931, except as provided below in Articles 3 and 4.

ARTICLE 2

Accordingly, on October 1, 1931, the Government of Haiti will assume rightfully and definitely the administration and control of the Direction Generale des Travaux Publics, of the Service d'Hygiene, and of the Service Technique d'Agriculture, and the President of the Republic will deliver, in conformity with the Constitution and the laws, commissions to the Haitian engineers, physicians, and employees deemed necessary for the functioning of the above mentioned Services.

ARTICLE 3

In that which concerns the Service Nationale d'Hygiene, it is understood that in conformity with the laws in force it will have, under the direction of the Secretary of State for the Interior, throughout the Republic, the administration, inspection, and supervision of all of the public services of hygiene, sanitation and quarantine of the hospitals, rural dispensaries, poor relief, insane asylums and sanitary garages, of the Medical School, the Health Center, the laboratories, etc.

Nevertheless, in the cities of Port-au-Prince and Cape Haitian, and their immediate environs (that is within a radius of two miles of the cities proper but including also Petionville) where, pending other arrangements and until the conclusion of a protocol for their evacuation, American troops are stationed, an American scientific mission shall be especially charged in accord with the laws and regulations now in force with the control of sanitation and chlorination of water.

The Service Nationale d'Hygiene will be entitled, if it so requests, to receive the advice and recommendations of the above mentioned scientific mission within the restricted field of sanitation.

The Government agrees to leave to the Mission the sanitary garages at Port-au-Prince and Cape Haitian and the motor equipment strictly necessary for its activities but the Service Nationale d'Hygiene may always requisition the material thus loaned by agreement with the Mission if the need therefor should arise.

The Government of Haiti agrees that in case of epidemic or grave danger menacing the public health within the above mentioned cities of Cape Haitian and Port-au-Prince the Mission will cooperate with the National Public Health Service to combat the danger and for this purpose shall be authorized to make all necessary recommendations, and to make use of all the facilities and all of the organizations of the above mentioned Service; and the Haitian Government, under such circumstances, will take the necessary measures and provide the necessary credits.

ARTICLE 4

The Mission provided for in the preceding article will comprise three American medical officers nominated by the Government of the United States and appointed by the President of Haiti. Their status will be assimilated so far as the salary that they receive from the public treasury is concerned to that of Public Health Officers first class provided for by the law of August 8, 1926. The Mission may also include, in addition, as a maximum six hospital corpsmen of the United States Navy who will be paid in conformity with a budget approved by the Minister of Interior upon the basis of the law of December 5, 1924.

The Mission will have the right to suitable offices at Cape Haitian and Port-au-Prince.

The funds necessary for the payment of the Haitian personnel and for the functioning of the sanitary services in the cities of Cape Haitian and Port-au-Prince will be provided for in a budget which shall be approved in advance by the Minister of Interior.

ARTICLE 5

The Accord of August 24, 1918, regarding the communication of projects of Haitian laws to the Legation of the United States of America at Port-au-Prince, is and remains abrogated from this date.

If, nevertheless, the Government of the United States should deem a given law to be seriously inconsistent with any rights arising from provisions of agreements still in force, it will present its views to the Haitian Government through diplomatic channels for all proper purposes.

ARTICLE 6

The Accord of December 3, 1918, relating to the visa of the Financial Adviser on orders of payment issued by the Secretary of State for Finance, on the Receiver-General of Customs, or on the National Bank of the Republic of Haiti, is and remains abrogated. The Minister of Finance shall reach an agreement with the Financial Adviser on the procedure governing the service of payments.

The abrogation of the visa implies an obligation on the part of the Government of Haiti until the liquidation of the services of the Financial Adviser-General Receiver to make its expenditures within the limits of laws and credits voted or decreed with the accord of the Financial Adviser. The Haitian Government will reach agreements with the Financial Adviser regarding the measures affecting sources of revenue pending the liquidation of the services of the Financial Adviser-General Receiver.

ARTICLE 7

The land title registry office (Bureau d'Enregistrement) shall be entirely detached from the Office of the Financial Adviser-General

Receiver and will pass under the complete control of the Secretary of Finance upon the signature of this Accord.

ARTICLE 8

In view of the difficulties which have arisen with regard to the Law of May 26, 1931, it is understood that the travelling or representation allowances of the Legislative Body as provided for in the above mentioned law, will be paid without delay, starting from April 6, 1931, and up to September 30, 1931, from the general funds of the Treasury. After September 30, 1931, these allowances will be paid in accordance with a balanced budget.

ARTICLE 9

Since the Government of the United States believes that the discharge of the civilian officials and employees in the Services mentioned above in Articles 1 and 2 of the present Accord, will be unduly precipitate and has requested an indemnity for them, the Secretary of State for Finance in accord with the Financial Adviser is authorized to indemnify them upon an equitable basis from the general funds of the Treasury.

Specialists in the Service Technique who, upon the express request of the Government of Haiti, shall desire to remain in their former positions and sign the necessary contracts for this purpose with the Secretary of State for Agriculture shall not have the right to any indemnity by virtue of the liquidation of the Treaty Services.

ARTICLE 10

The two Governments agree to continue their discussions regarding the other problems arising from the Treaty.

ARTICLE 11

While awaiting the settlement of the question of the Garde, the two Governments agree to maintain the "status quo" established by existing laws and agreements and to respect said laws and agreements.

Signed at Port-au-Prince in duplicate in the English and French languages, this fifth day of August, 1931.

DANA G. MUNRO
A. N. LEGER

TREATY OF FRIENDSHIP between the United States and Haiti, with Accompanying Protocols, Signed at Port-au-Prince, September 3, 1932

Department of State, *Press Releases,* September 10, 1932. The treaty was rejected by Haitian legislation, September 15, 1932

THE UNITED STATES of America and the Republic of Haiti, desirous of strengthening the bonds of amity which happily prevail between them and of giving a satisfactory solution to certain questions which have arisen in connection with the treaty of September 16, 1915, have resolved to conclude a treaty for that purpose and have appointed as their plenipotentiaries [et cetera].

ARTICLE 1

In view of the substantial accomplishment of the purposes of the Treaty of September 16, 1915, the two Governments have agreed to terminate as soon as practicable and in an orderly manner the special situation created thereunder and for this purpose have agreed upon the following program:

(1) Articles 4, 12, and 13 of the Treaty are declared to have been fully executed and are hereby abrogated.

(2) Article 10 will be abrogated upon the complete Haitianization of the Garde, as provided for in Protocol A attached to this Treaty.

(3) Articles 2, 3, and 5–9 inclusive will be abrogated on December 31, 1934, upon which date the two Governments will put into effect the provisions of Protocol B attached to this treaty.

ARTICLE 2

The present treaty shall be ratified by each party in conformity with the respective constitutions of the two countries and ratifications shall be exchanged in the city of Port-au-Prince as soon as possible.

Protocol A

ARTICLE 1

The American officers now serving with the Garde d'Haiti will be replaced as rapidly as possible by Haitian officers, in such a manner that by December 31, 1934, the Garde shall be completely commanded by Haitian officers.

ARTICLE 2

By December 31, 1934, the Garde, under complete command of Haitian officers, will be turned over to a Colonel of the Garde in active service whom the President of the Republic shall designate as Commandant.

ARTICLE 3

In order to carry out the above program intensive training of Haitian officers will be carried on from the date of the present agreement.

ARTICLE 4

The department of the South will be completely Haitianized at the latest on December 31, 1932; the Department of the North at the latest December 31, 1933; and the Department of Port-au-Prince at the latest on December 31, 1934.

ARTICLE 5

The promotions to be effected during the course of the Haitianization of the Garde will be made after examinations held in the presence of the representative of the Government of Haiti in conformity with Article 10 of the Treaty of September 16, 1915.

ARTICLE 6

Since it is considered desirable to employ the services of a Military Mission to complete the instruction, training and discipline of the Garde, the President of the United States agrees to designate such a mission. The details of the organization of this mission and the powers to be conferred upon it will be the subject of a separate agreement.

ARTICLE 7

The Marine Brigade of the United States and the American Scientific Mission established by the accord of August 5, 1931, will be withdrawn from Haitian territory as soon as may prove practicable, and in any event withdrawal will begin not later than the time when complete Haitianization of the Garde is effected.

ARTICLE 8

The Government of Haiti, in order to maintain the public order and peace necessary for the regular collection of the revenues pledged for the service of the bonds issued in accord with the Protocol of October 3, 1919, assumes the obligation of maintaining direct discipline in the Garde and of applying, until all of the bonds are amortized or redeemed, the present regulations of the Garde d'Haiti. It will enact a statute which will fix the conditions of appointments, promotions and retirement in the Garde.

Protocol B

I

Until the total retirement or refunding of all bonds issued in accord with the Protocol of October 3, 1919, a Fiscal Representative and a deputy Fiscal Representative, appointed by the President of Haiti upon the nomination of the President of the United States, shall exercise the powers hereinafter conferred in order adequately to insure the interest and amortization of the said loan.

II

The Fiscal Representative shall administer the tariff and shall collect all duties and other charges on imports and exports accruing at the several custom houses and ports of entry of the Republic of Haiti under the customs tariff and laws now or hereafter in force. He shall have for this purpose and for the necessary audit and accounting services such assistants and employees as may appear necessary. The expenses of the customs service, however, including the amounts upon which the two Governments may agree as the salary of the Fiscal Representative, and the Deputy Fiscal Representative, may not exceed five per centum of the receipts from the customs duties, unless by agreement of the two Governments, and these expenses will constitute a second charge upon the customs receipts next in order after the payment of the service of the bonds issued in accord with the Protocol of October 3, 1919.

The President of Haiti will issue commissions to employees occupying positions of authority and trust in the Customs Service upon the recommendation of the Fiscal Representative. The form of these commissions will be agreed upon by the Minister of Finance and the Fiscal Representative. If the services of a commissioned employee should not be satisfactory or if his removal should be deemed necessary for other reasons, the Fiscal Representative may terminate his services and may at the same time recommend such action as he considers advisable regarding his replacement, making a temporary appointment if necessary until a new commission is issued.

The Fiscal Representative will make every effort to train Haitian personnel for all positions in the Customs Service. At least two years before the complete amortization of the outstanding bonds, he shall select Haitian employees for special training as Receiver General and Deputy Receiver General of Customs in order that the Service, efficiently organized and fully Haitianized, may be turned over to their direction when complete amortization takes place.

III

The Internal Revenue Service with its present organization shall be placed under a Haitian Director and with an exclusively Haitian personnel, unless the Haitian Government should express its desire to retain the services of one or more foreign technical employees. The Director of Internal Revenue shall have full administrative authority over the Service, under the high direction of the Minister of Finance, but the Fiscal Representative shall have the power and the duty to inspect all activities of the Internal Revenue Service and to make any appropriate recommendations regarding the conduct of the service or the efficiency of individual employees.

The Fiscal Representative, for this inspection service, shall employ such American and Haitian inspectors and assistants as may appear necessary, providing, however, that the total amount allocated annually for this service shall not exceed 5 per cent of the total amount of the internal revenue collections, except by previous agreement between the two governments. This allocation shall be made by means of funds established, as set forth in Article 5 hereof.

If the Fiscal Representative should notify the Minister of Finance that there is reason to suppose that the conduct of any officer or employee of the Internal Revenue Service is incorrect or inefficient, such employee will be suspended and will not be reinstated until the charges against him have been disproved to the satisfaction of the Minister of Finance and of the Fiscal Representative.

The Fiscal Representative shall present to the Minister of Finance such suggestions as may appear helpful regarding the improvement of existing internal revenue legislation.

The revenues collected by the Internal Revenue Service shall be deposited in the National Bank as provided in Article 8 hereof.

A law regarding the organization of the Internal Revenue Service will govern the appointment, promotion, and retirement of the personnel of this Service.

IV

If for any reason the internal revenues should decline so that the amount collected falls below 3,000,000 gourdes during the six months from October to March inclusive, or below 2,000,000 gourdes during the six months from April to September inclusive, the Fiscal Representative shall call the situation to the attention of the Minister of Finance and shall make such recommendations as he may deem appropriate for restoring collections to their proper level; and the Haitian Government will put these recommendations into effect.

V

The expenses of the Internal Revenue Service shall be paid out of the amounts collected, in accord with a schedule of payments agreed upon between the Fiscal Representative and the Minister of Finance. These expenses shall not exceed 12 per cent of the total amount of internal revenue collections, except by agreement between the Minister of Finance and the Fiscal Representative. An additional amount not exceeding 5 per cent of the total amount of the internal revenue collections shall be included in the same schedule to cover the salaries and expenses of the inspectors who shall be attached to the office of the Fiscal Representative for the inspection of the Internal Revenue Service.

VI

The expenses of the Internal Revenue Service, including the expenses of the inspectors attached to the office of the Fiscal Representative, shall constitute a second charge upon the internal revenues, next in order after the payment of the service of the bonds issued in accord with the Protocol of October 3, 1919.

VII

All authorities of the Haitian Government will extend full protection and all proper assistance to the Customs Service and to the Internal Revenue Service in order to assure their proper operation and the enforcement of the tax laws.

VIII

All monies received by the Haitian Government shall be deposited in the National Bank to the credit of the Haitian Government with the exception of the amounts needed for payment of the debt service as required by the loan contracts and 5 per cent of the customs collections, which amounts shall be retained by the fiscal representative from the customs duties and charges collected and received by him. The bank shall set aside preferentially each month to the credit of the Fiscal Representative before permitting the withdrawal of any funds belonging to the Government the amount required for the expenses of the internal revenue collection and of the internal revenue inspection service, in addition to any amount which might be required in any month to cover a deficit in the sum needed for the service of the loans resulting from failure of the customs collections to aggregate that sum.

All payments of government funds shall continue to be made by checks prepared by the Service of Payments. The existing arrangement, as agreed upon between the two governments on August 5, 1931, shall continue to govern this Service, except that checks for the payment of the debt service and the expenses of revenue collection, shall be signed by the Fiscal Representative and checks for other governmental expenses shall bear the signature of the Minister of Finance.

IX

Until the complete amortization of the bonds issued in accord with the Protocol of October 3, 1919, or the retirement of these bonds before their due date, the Government of Haiti undertakes:

1. To balance its budget each year and not to authorize any extraordinary or supplemental appropriations in excess of budgetary items unless unobligated funds are available to cover such extraordinary or supplemental appropriations after setting up such reserves as may be necessary to assure the payment of the debt service and other budgetary expenses during those months of the fiscal year when receipts are normally reduced.

2. Not to permit any department of the Government to exceed its monthly allocation (*douzième*) except in case of demonstrated necessity.

3. Not to reduce the customs tariff nor to modify the internal taxes in such a way as to reduce the total yield of the internal revenues.

4. Not to contract any debt nor assume any financial obligation unless the ordinary revenues of the Republic available for that purpose after defraying the expenses of the Government shall be adequate to pay the interest and provide a sinking fund for the final discharge of such debt; and not to grant any subsidy for a period of more than one year, except with the accord of the Fiscal Representative.

5. To include annually in the budget of the Republic the amounts necessary for the regular service of the public debt and other contractual obligations, as well as lump sums representing the customs 5 per cent and the internal revenue 12 per cent and inspection service funds. If the revenues received in any month should be insufficient to meet the full debt service and expenses of collection, the Minister of Finance will pay to the Fiscal Representative from his reserves the amount required to make up the deficit.

In everything relating to the matters dealt with in this article, the

Haitian Government will proceed in accord with the Fiscal Representative.

The Government of Haiti will reach an accord with the Government of the United States regarding the issue of any new series of the loan authorized by the law of June 26, 1922.

X

If it should appear during the course of a fiscal year that the revenues will be substantially less than the estimates used in preparing the budget, the Haitian Government, acting in accord with the Fiscal Representative, will adopt adequate means to meet the deficit, either by reducing expenditures or by providing new sources of revenue.

The Government will not sell the securities held in the investment account, or other public property, except with the prior accord of the Fiscal Representative.

XI

The system of financial administration of the Republic of Haiti shall be governed by a special law of finance the project of which has been submitted to the Legislative Body.

XII

In order to assure the maintenance of public order, the monthly allocation for the Garde d'Haiti will be set aside preferentially by the National Bank from the funds remaining after deduction of any amounts which may be necessary to cover the service of the foreign debt and the expenses of the internal revenue collection, including the internal revenue inspection service, and the sums thus set aside shall not be subject to withdrawal for any other purpose than the necessary expenses of the Garde. Any unexpended balance at the end of the fiscal year shall revert to the general fund of the treasury.

XIII

The Fiscal Representative shall maintain adequate records of all receipts and disbursements, which records shall be open to inspection and verification by the appropriate authorities. Monthly reports of his operations shall be submitted to the Secretary of State for Finance of Haiti and the Secretary of State of the United States.

XIV

The Haitian Government reserves the right to retire the bonds issued in accord with the Protocol of October 3, 1919, in advance of their due date; and the Government of the United States will not invoke the provisions of Article 6 of the Protocol as an obstacle to such retirement before the expiration of the period of fifteen years fixed therein, provided that the Haitian Government is able to make an arrangement for this purpose satisfactory to the holders of the outstanding bonds.

In this case the provisions of this protocol shall automatically become null and void and of no effect upon the completion of the refunding operation.

AGREEMENT Regarding Withdrawal of Forces and Haitian Finances, Signed at Port-au-Prince, August 7, 1933
Department of State, Executive Agreement Series, No. 46

Section 1: Haitianization of the Garde d'Haiti and Withdrawal of Military Forces from Haiti

THE UNDERSIGNED plenipotentiaries, duly authorized by their respective governments, have agreed upon the following Accord:

ARTICLE 1

The American officers now serving with the Garde d'Haiti will be replaced in such a manner that by October 1, 1934, the Garde shall be completely commanded by Haitian officers.

ARTICLE 2

On October 1, 1934, the Garde, under complete command of Haitian officers, will be turned over to a Colonel in active service whom the President of the Republic shall designate as Commandant.

ARTICLE 3

The promotions to be effected until the complete Haitianization of the Garde will be made after examinations held in the presence of the representative of the Government of Haiti in conformity with Article 10 of the Treaty of September 16, 1915.

ARTICLE 4

To complete the instruction, training and discipline of the Garde the President of Haiti, may, if he consider it desirable, request the President of the United States to designate a Military Mission of not more than seven members among the American officers who have served in Haiti. The powers to be granted to this Mission will be determined by a decree of the President of Haiti. The services of this Mission shall terminate at the request of either party to the agreement upon sixty days notice given by either party.

ARTICLE 5

The withdrawal of the Marine Brigade of the United States and the American Scientific Mission established by the Accord of August 5, 1931, shall commence on October 1, 1934, and shall be completed within thirty days.

ARTICLE 6

The Government of Haiti, in order to preserve public order, assumes the obligation of maintaining strict discipline in the Garde and of applying for this purpose the present regulations of the Garde d'Haiti.

It will enact a statute which will fix the conditions of appointment, promotion and retirement in the Garde. It will also take all legislative measures recognized as necessary to guarantee public peace and security.

Section II. Financial Arrangement. Adjustment of financial guarantees stipulated in the Protocol of 1919 and the loan contract of 1922

ARTICLE 7

Beginning January 1, 1934, the services of the Financial Adviser-General Receiver and of the Deputy General Receiver shall be carried on, in fulfillment of the obligations and guarantees undertaken in order to obtain the loan issued in accord with the Protocol of October 3, 1919, by a Fiscal Representative and a Deputy Fiscal Representative, appointed by the President of the Republic upon nomination of the President of the United States, who shall exercise the powers hereinafter set forth.

ARTICLE 8

As the Customs Revenues constitute the principal pledge to the holders of the bonds of the 1922 loan, the Fiscal Representative will have under his direction, until the complete amortization or the prior refunding of the loan under reference, the Customs Service and the application of the laws relative thereto. In addition he shall inspect the activities of the Internal Revenue Service and make appropriate recommendations for its proper operation; he shall be in charge of the existing Service of Payments, reserve being made of the provisions of Article 12 hereafter; he shall maintain adequate records of receipts and disbursements which records shall be open to inspection and verification by the appropriate authorities; and he shall submit monthly reports of his activities to the Secretary of State for Finance and the Secretary of State of the United States.

In order properly to carry out his duties, the Fiscal Representative shall have such employees and assistants as may appear necessary. The number of Americans so employed shall not exceed eighteen. The President of Haiti, upon the presentation which will be made to him by the Secretary of State for Finance, will commission as of January 1, 1934, the employees occupying positions of authority and trust under the Fiscal Representative and recommended by the latter. Thereafter, any position which may become vacant among the commissioned employees shall be filled by examination, the form and procedure of which shall be determined by an accord between the Secretary of State for Finance and the Fiscal Representative. The successful competitor in such examination shall be recommended for the vacancy and will be commissioned by the President of Haiti. Such commissioned employees may be suspended without pay by the Fiscal Representative, on charges filed with the Secretary of State for Finance and such employee or assistant shall not be reinstated unless the charges shall have been disproved to the satisfaction of the Secretary of State for Finance, and of the Fiscal Representative. Pending the hearing of the charges made, the Fiscal Representative, after a report to the Secretary of State for Finance, may fill the vacancy provisionally, if necessary, until the charges have been disproved or a new commission issued.

ARTICLE 9

The salaries of the Fiscal Representative and of the Deputy Fiscal Representative shall be made the subject of an accord between the two Governments. These salaries, together with the expenses of the activities of the Fiscal Representative, but excluding the expenses of the Internal Revenue Inspection Service, may not exceed five per centum of customs receipts except by agreement between the two Governments.

ARTICLE 10

The Internal Revenue Service, the personnel of which shall be exclusively Haitian, shall be placed in charge of a Haitian Director under the Secretary of State for Finance.

Nevertheless, if the Fiscal Representative should notify the Secretary of State for Finance and the Director General of Internal Revenue in writing that there is reason to suppose any officer or employee of the Internal Revenue Service is inefficient, or that his action is not correct, such officer or employee shall be suspended, and not reinstated unless the charges shall have been disproved to the satisfaction of the Secretary of State for Finance.

The expenses of the Internal Revenue Service shall be paid from the funds set aside for this purpose by the National Bank of the Republic of Haiti in accordance with schedules of payments agreed upon between the Secretary of State for Finance and the Fiscal Representative. These expenses shall not exceed ten per centum of internal revenue receipts, and the expenses of the Internal Revenue Inspection Service shall not exceed five per centum of internal revenue receipts. Any sums not required by the Internal Revenue Inspection Service within this allowance shall be made available to the Internal Revenue Service.

ARTICLE 11

On and after January 1, 1934, all monies received by or for the Haitian Government shall be deposited in the National Bank of the Republic of Haiti to the credit of the Haitian Government with the exception of the five per centum of customs revenues foreseen in Article 9 above and the amounts needed for payments connected with execution of the loan contracts, which amounts shall be credited to the Fiscal Representative. The National Bank of the Republic of Haiti also shall set aside preferentially each month to the credit of the Fiscal Representative the amounts provided in Article 10 above for the expenses of the Internal Revenue Service and of the Internal Revenue Inspection Service.

In order to assure the maintenance of public order, the monthly allocation for the Garde d'Haiti will be set aside preferentially by the National Bank of the Republic of Haiti for the exclusive use of the Garde from the funds thereafter remaining.

ARTICLE 12

All payments of Government funds shall continue to be made by checks prepared by the Service of Payments. The existing arrangement, as agreed upon between the two Governments on August 5, 1931, shall continue to govern this service except that all checks henceforth will be signed by the Secretary of State for Finance, or his delegate, reserve being made in the case of those checks drawn against the funds deposited at the National Bank of the Republic of Haiti to the credit of the Fiscal Representative, which checks shall be signed only by the latter, or his delegate.

ARTICLE 13

Each year, by January 31st at the latest, the Fiscal Representative shall present a detailed estimate of receipts for the following fiscal year. Except by special agreement, the budget of the Republic shall not exceed the amount of probable ways and means which the Secretary of State for Finance and the Fiscal Representative shall have agreed upon.

ARTICLE 14

The Haitian Government may authorize any appropriations whatsoever if unobligated funds are available, or derivable at an early date from the ordinary revenues, to cover such appropriations after setting up such reserves as may appear to the Secretary of State for Finance and the Fiscal Representative to be necessary.

ARTICLE 15

In case of a probable budgetary deficit, expenditures must be brought to the level of ways and means, either by reducing expenditures or by the creation of new receipts. In every case, it will not be possible without the accord of the Fiscal Representative to cover a deficit by calling upon the reserve funds of the Government.

ARTICLE 16

There shall be included annually in the budget of the Republic the amounts necessary for the regular service of the funded debt and other contractual obligations, as well as two lump sums representing five per centum of customs and five per centum of internal revenues, respectively, for the payment of the expenses of the Fiscal Representative, and those of the Internal Revenue Inspection Service, and finally a lump sum representing ten per centum of internal revenue receipts for the payment of the expenses of the Internal Revenue Service. The balance may be apportioned by the Haitian Government between the budgets of the various departments as it may see fit. If the revenues received in any month shall be insufficient to meet the full debt service and expenses of collection, the Government will make available the amount required to make up the difference.

ARTICLE 17

Without the accord of the Fiscal Representative no new financial obligation will be assumed unless the ordinary revenues of the Republic, after defraying the expenses of the Government, shall be adequate to assure the final discharge of such obligation.

ARTICLE 18

The Government will not dispose of its investments except with the accord of the Fiscal Representative.

ARTICLE 19

The present finance law shall be the organic act of the Republic so far as concerns the administration of government finances.

ARTICLE 20

The Government of Haiti agrees not to reduce the tariff nor to modify the taxes and internal revenues in such a manner as to reduce the total amount thereof without the accord of the Fiscal Representative.

ARTICLE 21

The Custom Houses of the Republic will have an exclusively Haitian personnel and the title of Director shall be reestablished in lieu of that of Collector. However, inspectors of the Customs Service may be assigned, either temporarily or permanently, to oversee the operation and the strict application of the customs laws.

ARTICLE 22

In case of payment under protest of customs duties or internal revenue taxes, and where restitution of such payment is requested, a written claim shall be presented to the competent service within a time limit of thirty working days beginning with the date on which the duties or taxes were paid. If the decision is not accepted, the matter shall be presented to a commission composed of a representative of the Secretary of State for Finance and a representative of the Fiscal Representative.

If there should still be failure to reach an agreement, the claim for restitution shall be decided by legal proceedings, but the State may not be liable for any compensatory or punitive damages.

ARTICLE 23

In view of the fact that under normal conditions the operation of the sinking fund will result in retirement of the outstanding series of the loan authorized by the law of June 26, 1922, approximately by the year 1944, and inasmuch as any further issue of the loan would necessarily extend the operation of this agreement, to a period beyond that year, which extension is contrary to their desire, it is hereby agreed by both Governments that the loan shall be considered closed and that no additional series shall be issued thereunder.

ARTICLE 24

In case there should appear to be occasion for judicial proceedings against the Fiscal Representative or his American assistants, the two Governments, in order to avoid possible misunderstanding, agree to examine each case impartially and to agree upon the legal action which might be appropriate.

ARTICLE 25

The Haitian Government, upon the signature of the present agreement, will issue irrevocable instructions to the National Bank of the Republic of Haiti in order that there may be full and complete execution of the clauses herein respecting the deposit and disbursement of the funds of the Government.

ARTICLE 26

The Haitian Government reserves the right to retire the bonds issued in accord with the Protocol of October 3, 1919, in advance of their due date; and the Government of the United States will not invoke the provisions of Article 6 of the Protocol as an obstacle to such retirement before the expiration of the period of fifteen years fixed therein, provided that the Haitian Government is able to make an arrangement for this purpose satisfactory to the holders of the outstanding bonds.

In this case the provisions of this accord shall automatically become null and void and of no effect upon the completion of the funding operation. The Haitian Government in order to hasten the retirement of the loan of 1922 may continue as rapidly as its resources will permit, to buy on the open market bonds of the several series of the said loan.

ARTICLE 27

Any controversy which may arise between the two Governments on the subject of the clauses of the present accord shall be submitted to arbitration in case it cannot be settled through diplomatic channels, in accordance with the Arbitration Treaty of January 7, 1909 between the two countries.

Signed at Port-au-Prince in duplicate in the English and French languages, this seventh day of August, 1933.

[SEAL]
[SEAL]

NORMAN ARMOUR
A. BLANCHET

AGREEMENT *to Replace the Agreement of August 7, 1933, Signed at Port-au-Prince, September 13, 1941*
Department of State, Executive Agreement Series, No. 220

WHEREAS the Government of the United States of America and the Government of the Republic of Haiti are both desirous of maintaining the friendly relations existing between the two countries and to that end of concluding an agreement establishing those relations upon a firm basis of mutual understanding and cooperation, the undersigned Plenipotentiaries, duly authorized by their respective Governments, have agreed upon the following Articles:

ARTICLE 1

On the date on which the present agreement enters into effect, the offices of Fiscal Representative and Deputy Fiscal Representative, as provided for in Article 7 of the Accord of August 7, 1933 shall be abolished.

All property and funds belonging to or in the custody of the Fiscal Representative or Deputy Fiscal Representative shall on that day be transferred to the National Bank of the Republic of Haiti as depository for the Government of the Republic of Haiti.

No claims shall be advanced by either Government against the other Government on account of any act of the Fiscal Representative, the Deputy Fiscal Representative or any of their employees.

ARTICLE 2

The National Bank of the Republic of Haiti shall have fiscal functions as defined in this agreement, as well as the usual commercial operations of a national bank, and shall be the sole depository of all revenues and public funds of whatsoever nature of the Government of Haiti. These funds shall consist of revenues, customs, duties, excises, fees, fines, imposts, charges, levies or any other kind of income, receipts or funds which belong to and are under the control of the National Government of the Republic of Haiti. It is understood that these revenues and public funds will include funds under the control of the Government of Haiti, which, under existing laws, and those which may be made in future, are collected or expended on behalf of the Haitian communes; a separate account of revenues and expenditures shall be kept for each commune by the National Bank of the Republic of Haiti.

The assets of the National Bank of the Republic of Haiti shall not be alienated nor shall its investments be disposed of except with the approval of the Board of Directors.

The Bank shall have all administrative powers necessary to carry out its functions under this agreement.

The National Bank of the Republic of Haiti shall be reorganized with a Board of Directors consisting of an Honorary President and six voting members. The Haitian Minister of Finance or, in his absence, the Acting Minister of Finance, shall be ex officio the Honorary President. Three of the voting members are always to be citizens of the Republic of Haiti. The other three voting members are always to be citizens of the United States of America. Decisions of the Board of Directors shall require a majority vote of the voting members of the Board. The President of the Republic of Haiti shall appoint the Haitian members of the Board of Directors; the citizens of the United States of America who are members of the Board shall be chosen by mutual agreement of the two Governments. All of the voting members of the Board shall hold office for a period of five years and shall not be removed except for cause. Vacancies on the Board of Directors shall be filled in the same manner as the original appointments.

There shall be two co-Presidents of the Board of Directors of the Bank. One of these, the Haitian Minister of Finance, shall act as Honorary President, as indicated above, and shall preside over the meetings of the Board of Directors, and may be one of the three Haitian voting members. The other co-President shall be one of the three citizens of the United States of America. It shall be his duty to represent the holders of the bonds of 1922 and 1923 and to coordinate and direct the functions and activities of the two Vice Presidents, who shall be elected by the Board of Directors of the Bank, and who may be members of the Board. One of the Vice Presidents shall be charged with supervising and carrying out the commercial operations of the Bank, and the other shall be charged with supervising and carrying out the fiscal functions of the Bank, under the immediate direction of the President who shall be responsible for such work.

Any voting member of the Board of Directors of the Bank who is unable to attend a meeting of the Board may give a proxy to any other member of the Board of Directors.

The Board of Directors shall exercise with respect to the fiscal functions of the Bank the powers hereinafter set forth. The fiscal functions of the Bank shall be undertaken by a Fiscal Department to be operated in accordance with the regulations issued by the Board of Directors pursuant to such powers.

The Board of Directors shall continue to exercise with respect to all other functions of the Bank the powers set forth in the charter and by-laws of the Bank.

ARTICLE 4

The Board of Directors of the National Bank of the Republic of Haiti shall be charged with the responsibility for:

(a) the formulation of the Haitian budget in the manner described in Article 5 of this agreement, and in accordance with the existing budgetary laws of the Republic of Haiti, which are to remain in effect except so far as they are modified to conform with this agreement;

(b) the accounting for and disbursing of the funds of the Government of Haiti;

(c) the collection of all customs revenues;

(d) the supervision and inspection of the collection of all revenues as defined in Article 2 other than customs revenues;

(e) establishing the regulations and the administration, under such legislation as may be necessary, for the handling of the revenues of the various communes. These regulations or laws shall authorize the collection of communal revenues by the regular internal revenue collectors; disbursements on behalf of the communes shall be made by the National Bank of the Republic of Haiti; the budgets of revenues and expenditures of the communes shall be prepared and approved by the Government of the Republic of Haiti in agreement with the National Bank of the Republic of Haiti; the municipal services performed by, or in behalf of the communes, shall be paid, so far as it is possible, from the communal revenues.

ARTICLE 5

Each year, as soon after January 1 as may be practicable but not later than March 1, the Haitian budget of income and expenditures shall be presented to the Legislature of the Republic by the Government of the Republic. Such budget shall be prepared cooperatively by the Government of the Republic and by the National Bank of the Republic of Haiti as follows:

(a) the Board of Directors of the National Bank shall estimate the expected revenues; shall estimate the global expenditures which can be anticipated to be made within the revenues available; shall suggest limits within which the various ministries, including the

Garde d'Haiti, shall operate, and shall fix by agreement with the Government of Haiti the expenditures which are necessary for the operation of the Bank in its fiscal functions; and

(b) the Government of the Republic shall estimate in detail the expenditures envisaged for each of the various ministries, including the Garde d'Haiti, within the limits suggested by the Board of Directors of the National Bank.

ARTICLE 6

The National Bank of the Republic of Haiti, as the sole depository of all revenues as defined in Article 2, shall have the power and duty of receiving in the first instance all the receipts of the Government and all payments made in favor thereof, and to set aside in preference to any other expenses the sums necessary for the service of the 1922 and 1923 bonds, and, as the duly constituted agent of the Government, to make all the payments required by the loan contracts.

During the first ten days of each calendar month the representative of the holders of the bonds of 1922 and 1923 who shall be, in accordance with Article 3, a member of the Board of Directors of the National Bank of the Republic of Haiti, shall receive from the said Bank the sums necessary to cover monthly payments as follows:

(1) The payment of $\frac{1}{12}$ of the annual interest charges of all the outstanding bonds of the external debt of 1922 and 1923;

(2) The payment of $\frac{1}{12}$ of the annual amounts designated for the amortization of said bonds, including the interest of all the bonds which are or may be retained in the sinking fund.

The annual interest charges and the amounts of amortization shall be computed and effected in accordance with the loan contracts dated October 6, 1922, and May 26, 1925, with the National City Company and the National City Bank of New York, authorized by the Haitian Law of June 26, 1922, as modified by the Accord signed at Port-au-Prince by the representatives of the Governments of the United States of America and the Republic of Haiti on August 7, 1933, and as further modified by the agreements signed on January 13, 1938, July 1, 1938, July 8, 1939, September 27, 1940 and February 13, 1941.

No disbursement of funds of the Government of Haiti shall be made by the National Bank of the Republic of Haiti until an allotment has been made to satisfy the above provisions and, in addition, to make the payment of $\frac{1}{12}$ of the annual amount agreed upon between the Government of Haiti and the National Bank of the Republic of Haiti as compensation for the services of the said Bank, or in the absence of any such agreement, $\frac{1}{12}$ of the annual amount last agreed upon. After setting aside those funds which are considered necessary by the Board of Directors of the National Bank of the Republic of Haiti to establish appropriate reserves during a given fiscal year in anticipation of seasonal variations in revenues and expenditures, to make the payments envisaged in Articles 6 and 8 hereof, and for other similar purposes, any surplus funds will be held at the disposal of the Government of Haiti for necessary public expenditures in accordance with the approved budget.

ARTICLE 7

The Government of the Republic of Haiti declares that the interest and amortization service of the bonds of the external debt of 1922 and 1923 constitute an irrevocable first lien upon all its revenues as defined in Article 2. It is understood that the communal revenues specified in Article 2 shall not be included in the provision of this clause.

Until the complete amortization of the whole amount of the bonds of the external debt of 1922 and 1923 of the Government of Haiti, the public debt of the Republic of Haiti shall not be increased except by previous agreement between the Governments of the United States of America and the Republic of Haiti.

ARTICLE 8

In case the total collections of all the revenues as defined in Article 2, exclusive of communal revenues, should in any fiscal year exceed the equivalent of $7,000,000 in currency of the United States of America, there shall be applied to the sinking fund for the redemption of bonds of the external debt of 1922 and 1923, 10 percent of the excess above $7,000,000 but less than $8,000,000 and in addition 5 percent of all sums exceeding $8,000,000.

ARTICLE 9

The system of deposit and disbursing of all revenues, as defined in Article 2, of the Government of Haiti shall be carried out in accordance with Haitian laws relating to accounting methods and financial regulations now governing such matters which shall not be modified during the life of this agreement without the previous consent of both Governments.

The Government of Haiti agrees to enact and to maintain in effect the legislation and executive and administrative regulations necessary to put this and other articles of the present agreement into effect.

ARTICLE 10

Any controversy which may arise between the Government of the United States of America and the Government of Haiti in relation to the interpretation or execution of the provisions of the present agreement shall, if possible, be settled through diplomatic channels. Upon notification by either the Government of the United States of America or the Government of Haiti that, in its opinion, possibilities of settlement by this means have been exhausted, such controversies shall be settled in accordance with the procedure stipulated in the Inter-American Arbitration Convention signed at Washington January 5, 1929, notwithstanding the provisions of Article 2 (a) thereof.

ARTICLE 11

The Accord signed by representatives of the Governments of the United States of America and the Republic of Haiti on August 7, 1933, shall cease to have effect when the present agreement shall enter into force, provided, however, that the Accord of August 7, 1933 shall continue in full force and effect until the two Governments agree that there have been adopted and put into operation the measures necessary for the execution of the present agreement.

The present agreement shall continue in full force and effect during the existence of the outstanding external bonds of 1922 and 1923. After the redemption of the said bonds, the provisions of this agreement shall automatically cease to have effect.

It witness whereof the respective Plenipotentiaries have signed at Port-au-Prince the present agreement in duplicate in the English and French languages, both texts being equally authoritative, and have hereunto affixed their seals.

Done in the City of Port-au-Prince the 13th day of September nineteen hundred and forty-one.

For the Government of the United States of America:
[SEAL]   J. C. WHITE
Envoy Extraordinary and Minister
Plenipotentiary of the United States
of America to the Republic of Haiti.

For the Government of the Republic of Haiti:
FOMBRUN
Minister of Foreign Relations
of the Republic of Haiti

[SEAL]

The Dominican Republic

CONVENTION *between the United States and the Dominican Republic Regarding Assistance in the Collection and Application of the Dominican Customs Revenues, Signed at Santo Domingo, February 8, 1907*

Department of State, Treaty Series, No. 465. The convention was ratified by the President of the United States June 22, 1907, and ratifications were exchanged July 8, 1907

WHEREAS during disturbed political conditions in the Dominican Republic debts and claims have been created, some by regular and some by revolutionary governments, many of doubtful validity in whole or in part, and amounting in all to over $30,000,000 nominal or face value;

And WHEREAS the same conditions have prevented the peaceable and continuous collection and application of National revenues for payment of interest or principal of such debts or for liquidation and settlement of such claims; and the said debts and claims continually increase by accretion of interest and are a grievous burden upon the people of the Dominican Republic and a barrier to their improvement and prosperity;

And WHEREAS the Dominican Government has now effected a conditional adjustment and settlement of said debts and claims under which all its foreign creditors have agreed to accept about $12,407,000 for debts and claims amounting to about $21,184,000 of nominal or face value, and the holders of internal debts or claims of about $2,028,-258 nominal or face value have agreed to accept about $645,827 therefor, and the remaining holders of internal debts or claims on the same basis as the assents already given will receive about $2,400,000 therefor, which sum the Dominican Government has fixed and determined as the amount which it will pay to such remaining internal debt holders; making the total payments under such adjustment and settlement, including interest as adjusted and claims not yet liquidated, amount to not more than about $17,000,000.

And WHEREAS a part of such plan of settlement is the issue and sale of bonds of the Dominican Republic to the amount of $20,000,000 bearing five per cent interest payable in fifty years and redeemable after ten years at 102½ and requiring payment of at least one per cent per annum for amortization, the proceeds of said bonds, together with such funds as are now deposited for the benefit of creditors from customs revenues of the Dominican Republic heretofore received, after payment of the expenses of such adjustment, to be applied first to the payment of said debts and claims as adjusted and second out of the balance remaining to the retirement and extinction of certain concessions and harbor monopolies which are a burden and hindrance to the commerce of the country and third the entire balance still remaining to the construction of certain railroads and bridges and other public improvements necessary to the industrial development of the country;

And WHEREAS the whole of said plan is conditioned and dependent upon the assistance of the United States in the collection of customs revenues of the Dominican Republic and the application thereof so far as necessary to the interest upon and the amortization and redemption of said bonds, and the Dominican Republic has requested the United States to give and the United States is willing to give such assistance:

The Dominican Government, represented by its Minister of State for Foreign Relations, Emiliano Tejera, and its Minister of State for Finance and Commerce, Federico Velasquez H., and the United States Government, represented by Thomas C. Dawson, Minister Resident and Consul General of the United States to the Dominican Republic, have agreed:

I. That the President of the United States shall appoint, a General Receiver of Dominican Customs, who, with such Assistant Receivers and other employees of the Receivership as shall be appointed by the President of the United States in his discretion, shall collect all the customs duties accruing at the several customs houses of the Dominican Republic until the payment or retirement of any and all bonds issued by the Dominican Government in accordance with the plan and under the limitations as to terms and amounts hereinbefore recited; and said General Receiver shall apply the sums so collected, as follows:

First, to paying the expenses of the receivership; second, to the payment of interest upon said bonds; third, to the payment of the annual sums provided for amortization of said bonds including interest upon all bonds held in sinking fund; fourth, to the purchase and cancellation or the retirement and cancellation pursuant to the terms thereof of any of said bonds as may be directed by the Dominican

Government; fifth, the remainder to be paid to the Dominican Government.

The method of distributing the current collections of revenue in order to accomplish the application thereof as hereinbefore provided shall be as follows:

The expenses of the receivership shall be paid by the Receiver as they arise. The allowances to the General Receiver and his assistants for the expenses of collecting the revenues shall not exceed five per cent unless by agreement between the two Governments.

On the first day of each calendar month the sum of $100,000 shall be paid over by the Receiver to the Fiscal Agent of the loan, and the remaining collection of the last preceding month shall be paid over to the Dominican Government, or applied to the sinking fund for the purchase or redemption of bonds, as the Dominican Government shall direct.

Provided, that in case the customs revenues collected by the General Receiver shall in any year exceed the sum of $3,000,000, one half of the surplus above such sum of $3,000,000 shall be applied to the sinking fund for the redemption of bonds.

II. The Dominican Government will provide by law for the payment of all customs duties to the General Receiver and his assistants, and will give to them all needful aid and assistance and full protection to the extent of its powers. The Government of the United States will give to the General Receiver and his assistants such protection as it may find to be requisite for the performance of their duties.

III. Until the Dominican Republic has paid the whole amount of the bonds of the debt its public debt shall not be increased except by previous agreement between the Dominican Government and the United States. A like agreement shall be necessary to modify the import duties, it being an indispensable condition for the modification of such duties that the Dominican Executive demonstrate and that the President of the United States recognize that, on the basis of exportations and importations to the like amount and the like character during the two years preceding that in which it is desired to make such modification, the total net customs receipts would at such altered rates of duties have been for each of such two years in excess of the sum of $2,000,000 United States gold.

IV. The accounts of the General Receiver shall be rendered monthly to the Contaduria General of the Dominican Republic and to the State Department of the United States and shall be subject to examination and verification by the appropriate officers of the Dominican and the United States Governments.

V. This agreement shall take effect after its approval by the Senate of the United States and the Congress of the Dominican Republic.

Done in four originals, two being in the English language, and two in the Spanish, and the representatives of the high contracting parties signing them in the City of Santo Domingo this 8th day of February, in the Year of our Lord 1907.

THOMAS C. DAWSON
EMILIANO TEJERA
FEDERICO VELÁZQUEZ H.

MEMORANDUM of the Plan of June 30, 1922, for the Withdrawal of the Military Government, as Amended and Signed at Santo Domingo, September 18, 1922
Foreign Relations of the United States, 1922, II, 54

1. ANNOUNCEMENT by the Military Government that a Provisional Government will be set up for the purpose of promulgating legislation to regulate the holding of elections, and to provide for the reorganization of the provincial and municipal governments, and to enable the Dominican people to make such amendments to the Constitution as they may deem appropriate and hold general elections without the intervention of the Military Government. At the same time, the Military Government will announce that the Provisional Government will assume from the date of its installation, administrative powers to carry out freely the aforesaid purposes; and the said Provisional Government, from that date, will alone be responsible for its acts.

2. The selection of a Provisional President and Cabinet by majority vote of the members of a Commission composed of General Horacio Vasquez, Don Federico Velasquez, Don Elias Brache, Don Francisco Peynado, and of Monseñor Dr. Adolfo Nouel, upon the inclusion of whom the four above named representatives have agreed. The Commission, in determining upon the members of the Provisional Government, will determine the conditions placed upon the exercise of that Government and the said Commission, by a majority vote, will fill the vacancies that may occur in that Government on

account of death, resignation, or disability, of any of its members. Upon the inauguration of the Provisional Government, the Executive Departments of the Dominican Republic shall be turned over to the members of the Cabinet thus designated. There shall be no change in the personnel of these Departments, except for duly proved cause; the judges and other officials of the Judiciary cannot be removed except for the same reason. Officials in charge of the Executive Departments of the Military Government will lend their assistance to the respective Secretaries of State of the Provisional Government whenever such assistance may be requested. There shall be no payment made by the Department of Finance except in accordance with the budget in force, nor will any payment be made otherwise than as customary. Any necessary item of expenditure not provided for in the budget will be appropriated by the Provisional Government in accord with the Military Governor. Immediately upon the installation of the Provisional Government, the Military Government will deliver to that Government the National Palace, and, at the same time, the Military Forces of the United States in the Dominican Republic will be concentrated at one, two, or three places, as may be determined by the Military Governor. From that date, peace and order will be maintained by the Dominican National Police under the Orders of the Provisional Government, except in the case of serious disturbances, which in the opinion of the Provisional Government and of the Military Governor, cannot be suppressed by the Forces of the Dominican Police.

3. The Provisional President will promulgate the legislation above referred to concerning the holding of elections and the reorganization of the Government of the Provinces and Communes.

4. The Provisional President will convene the Primary Assemblies in accordance with the provisions of the new election law and those Assemblies will elect the electors as provided by Article 84 of the present Constitution and the public functionaries whose election is prescribed in the laws regulating the organization of the Provinces and Communes.

5. The Electoral Colleges so elected by the Primary Assemblies will elect the members of the Senate and of the Chamber of Deputies and will prepare the lists of the members of the Judiciary to be submitted to the National Senate.

6. The Congress will vote the necessary amendments to the Constitution and will issue the call for the election of the Constituent Assembly, to which the proposed amendments will be submitted.

7. The Provisional President will designate plenipotentiaries to negotiate a Convention of Ratification reading as follows:

I. The Dominican Government hereby recognizes the validity of all the Executive Orders, promulgated by the Military Government and published in the *Official Gazette,* which may have levied taxes, authorized expenditures, or established rights on behalf of third persons, and the administrative regulations issued, and contracts which may have been entered into, in accordance with those Orders or with any law of the Republic. These Orders, administrative regulations and contracts are those listed below:

[Here follows a list of Executive orders, departmental resolutions, municipal resolutions, water contracts, etc.]

The Dominican Government likewise agrees that those Executive Orders, those resolutions, those administrative regulations, and those contracts shall remain in full force and effect unless and until they are abrogated by those bodies which, in accordance with the Dominican Constitution, can legislate. But, this ratification, in so far as concerns those of the above mentioned Executive Orders, resolutions, administrative regulations, and contracts, which have been modified or abrogated by other Executive Orders, resolutions, or administrative regulations of the Military Government, only refers to the legal effects which they created while they were in force.

The Dominican Government further agrees that neither the subsequent abrogation of those Executive Orders, resolutions, administrative regulations, or contracts, or any other law, Executive Order, or other official act of the Dominican Government, shall affect the validity or security of rights acquired in accordance with those orders, those resolutions, those administrative regulations and those contracts of the Military Government; the controversies which may arise related with those rights acquired will be determined solely by the Dominican Courts, subject, however, in accordance with the generally accepted rules and principles of international law, to the right of diplomatic intervention if those courts should be responsible for cases of notorious injustice or denial of justice. The determination of such cases in which the interests of the United States and the Dominican Republic only are concerned shall, should the two Governments disagree, be by arbitration. In the carrying out of this agreement, in each individual case, the High Contracting Parties, once the necessity of arbitration is determined, shall conclude a special agreement defining clearly the scope of the dispute, the scope of the powers of the arbitrators, and the periods to be fixed for the formation of the arbitral tribunal and the several stages of the procedure. It is understood that on the part of the United States, such special agreements will be made by the President of the United States, by and with the advice and consent of the Senate thereto, and on the part of the Dominican Republic shall be subject to the procedure required by the Constitution and laws thereof.

II. The Dominican Government, in accordance with the Provisions of Article 1, specifically recognizes the bond issue of 1918 and the twenty-year five and one-half percent Customs Administration Sinking Fund Gold

Bond Issue authorized in 1922, as legal, binding, and irrevocable obligations of the Republic, and pledges its full faith and credit to the maintenance of the service of those bond issues. With reference to the stipulation contained in Article 10 of the Executive Order No. 735, in accordance with which the loan of five and one-half percent authorized in 1922 was issued, which provides:—

> "that the present customs tariff will not be changed during the life of this loan without previous agreement between the Dominican Government and the Government of the United States";

the two Governments concerned agree in interpreting this stipulation in the sense that, in accordance with Article 3 of the Convention of 1907, a previous agreement between the Dominican Government and the United States shall be necessary to modify the import duties, it being an indispensable condition before the modification of such duties that the Dominican Executive demonstrate and that the President of the United States recognize, that on the basis of exportations and importations to the like amount and the like character during the two years preceding that in which it is desired to make such modification, the total net customs receipts would at such altered rates of duties have been, for each of such two years, in excess of the sum of $2,000,000 United States gold.

III. The Dominican Government and the Government of the United States agree that the Convention signed on February 8, 1907, between the United States and the Dominican Republic, shall remain in force so long as any bonds of the issues of 1918 and 1922 shall remain unpaid, and that the duties of the General Receiver of Dominican Customs appointed in accordance with that Convention shall be extended to include the application of the revenues pledged for the service of those bond issues in accordance with the terms of the Executive Orders and of the contracts under which the bonds were issued.

IV. This arrangement shall take effect after its approval by the Senate of the United States and the Congress of the Dominican Republic.

This Convention will be referred to the Congress for its approval. The Congress will, in addition, pass the law recognizing independently of the Convention of Ratification the validity of the Executive Orders referred to in the said Convention.

8. The members of the Judicial Power will be elected in accordance with the Constitution.

9. After all the steps specified in the foregoing articles have been taken and after the Convention mentioned in Article 7 has been approved and the law referred to in the same article has gone into effect, the members of the Executive Power will be elected in accordance with the Constitution. Immediately upon taking possession of his office, the President will sign the law ratifying the Executive Orders

and the Convention, and the Military Forces of the United States will thereupon leave the territory of the Dominican Republic.

ADOLFO A.BIZPO DE STO DOMINGO
FED^{co} VELASQUEZ
HORACIO VASQUEZ
FRAN^{co} J. PEYNADO
E. BRACHE, HIJO
SUMNER WELLES, *American Commissioner*
WILLIAM W. RUSSELL, *American Minister*

CONVENTION of Ratification between the United States and the Dominican Republic, Signed at Santo Domingo, June 12, 1924 (extracts)

Department of State, Treaty Series, No. 729. The convention was ratified by the President of the United States June 1, 1925, and ratifications were exchanged December 4, 1925

WHEREAS, in the month of May, 1916, the territory of the Dominican Republic was occupied by the forces of the United States of America, during which occupation there was established, in substitution of the Dominican Government, a Military Government which issued governmental regulations under the name of Executive Orders and Resolutions and Administrative Regulations, and also celebrated several contracts by virtue of said Executive Orders or by virtue of some existing laws of the Republic;

WHEREAS, the Dominican Republic has always maintained its right to self-government, the disoccupation of its territory and the integrity of its sovereignty and independence; and the Government of the United States has declared that, on occupying the territory of the Dominican Republic, it never had, nor has at present, the purpose of attacking the sovereignty and independence of the Dominican Nation; and these rights and declarations gave rise to a Plan or *Modus Operandi* of Evacuation signed on June 30, 1922, by Monseñor A. Nouel, General Horacio Vasquez, Don Federico Valesquez y H., Don Elías Brache, hijo, and Don Francisco J. Peynado, and the Department of State, represented by the Honorable William W. Russell, Envoy Extraordinary and Minister Plenipotentiary of the United States in the Dominican Republic, and the Honorable Sumner Welles, Commissioner of the President of the United States, which met with the approval of the Dominican people, and which approval was confirmed at the elections that took place on March 15, of the present year;

WHEREAS, although the Dominican Republic has never delegated authority to any foreign power to legislate for it, still, it understands that the internal interests of the Republic require the validation or ratification of several of the Executive Orders and Resolutions, published in the Official Gazette, as well as the Administrative Regulations and Contracts of the Military Government celebrated by virtue of said Orders or of any Law of the Republic; and, on its part, the United States considers that it is also to its interest that said acts be validated or ratified; for these reasons one of the stipulations in the above-mentioned Plan of Evacuation provides for the celebration of a Treaty or Convention of Ratification or Validation of said Orders, Resolutions, Regulations and Contracts;

Therefore, the United States of America and the Dominican Republic, desirous of celebrating the above-mentioned Treaty or Convention, have named for this purpose their Plenipotentiaries as follows:

The President of the United States, William W. Russell, Envoy Extraordinary and Minister Plenipotentiary of the United States in Santo Domingo, and,

The Provisional President of the Dominican Republic, Don Horacio Vasquez, Don Federico Velasquez y H., and Don Francisco J. Peynado.

who, after having exchanged their full powers, and after having found them in due and proper form, have agreed upon the following:

I. The Dominican Government hereby recognizes the validity of all the Executive Orders and Resolutions, promulgated by the Military Government and published in the Official Gazette, which may have levied taxes, authorized expenditures, or established rights on behalf of third persons, and the administrative regulations issued, and contracts which may have been entered into, in accordance with those Orders or with any law of the Republic. Those Executive Orders and Resolutions, Administrative Regulations and Contracts are those listed below:

[*List omitted*]

The Dominican Government likewise agrees that those Executive Orders, those resolutions, those administrative regulations, and those contracts shall remain in full force and effect unless and until they are abrogated by those bodies which, in accordance with the Dominican Constitution, can legislate. But, this ratification, in so far as concerns those of the above mentioned Executive Orders, resolutions, administrative regulations, and contracts, which have been modified or abrogated by other Executive Orders, resolutions, or administrative regulations of the Military Government, only refers to the legal effects which they created while they were in force.

The Dominican Government further agrees that neither the subsequent abrogation of those Executive Orders, resolutions, administrative regulations, or contracts, or any other law, Executive Order, or other official act of the Dominican Government, shall affect the validity or security of rights acquired in accordance with those orders, those resolutions, those administrative regulations and those contracts of the Military Government; the controversies which may arise related with those rights acquired will be determined solely by the Dominican Courts, subject, however, in accordance with the generally accepted rules and principles of international law, to the right of diplomatic intervention if those Courts should be responsible for cases of notorious injustice or denial of justice. The determination of such cases in which the interests of the United States and the Dominican Republic only are concerned shall, should the two Governments disagree, be by arbitration. In the carrying out of this agreement, in each individual case, the High Contracting Parties, once the necessity of arbitration is determined, shall conclude a special agreement defining clearly the scope of the dispute, the scope of the powers of the arbitrators, and the periods to be fixed for the formation of the arbitral tribunal and the several stages of the procedure. It is understood that on the part of the United States, such special agreements will be made by the President of the United States, by and with the advice and consent of the Senate thereto, and on the part of the Dominican Republic shall be subject to the procedure required by the Constitution and laws thereof.

II. The Dominican Government, in accordance with the provisions of Article 1, specifically recognizes the bond issue of 1918 and the twenty-year five and one-half percent Customs Administration Sinking Fund Gold Bond Issue authorized in 1922, as legal, binding, and irrevocable obligations of the Republic, and pledges its full faith and credit to the maintenance of the service of those bond issues. With reference to the stipulation contained in Article 10 of the Executive Order No. 735, in accordance with which the loan of five and one-half percent authorized in 1922 was issued, which provides:—

"That the present customs tariff will not be changed during the life of this loan without previous agreement between the Dominican Government and the Government of the United States";

the two Governments concerned agree in interpreting this stipulation in the sense that, in accordance with Article 3 of the Convention of 1907, a previous agreement between the Dominican Government and the United States shall be necessary to modify the import duties of the Dominican Republic, it being an indispensable condition for the modification of such duties that the Dominican Executive demonstrate and that the President of the United States recognize that, on the basis of exportations and importations to the like amount and the like character during the two years preceding that in which it is desired to make such modification, the total net customs receipts would at such altered rates of duties have been, for each of such two years, in excess of the sum of $2,000,000 United States gold.

III. The Dominican Government and the Government of the United States agree that the Convention signed on February 8, 1907, between the United States and the Dominican Republic, shall remain in force so long as any bonds of the issues of 1918 and 1922 shall remain unpaid, and that the duties of the General Receiver of Dominican Customs appointed in accordance with that Convention shall be extended to include the application of the revenues pledged for the service of those bond issues in accordance with the terms of the Executive Orders and of the contracts under which the bonds were issued.

IV. This arrangement shall take effect after its approval by the Senate of the United States and the Congress of the Dominican Republic.

Done in four originals, two in the English language, and two in the Spanish, and the representatives of the High Contracting Powers signing them in the City of Santo Domingo, this twelfth day of June, nineteen hundred and twenty-four.

[SEAL]
[SEAL]
[SEAL]
[SEAL]

WILLIAM W. RUSSELL
HORACIO VASQUEZ
FED^{co} VELÁSQUEZ Y H.
FRAN^c J. PEYNADO

CONVENTION between the United States and the Dominican Republic Regarding the Collection and Application of the Dominican Customs Revenues, Signed at Washington, September 24, 1940

Department of State, Treaty Series, No. 965. The U.S. Senate advised and consented to ratification February 14, 1941, and ratifications were exchanged March 10, 1941. For the convention of December 27, 1924, replacing the convention of February 8, 1907, see William M. Malloy, *Treaties, Conventions, International Acts* . . . , IV, 4091

WHEREAS at the City of Washington, D.C. on the twenty-seventh day of December of 1924 a Convention was concluded and signed between the Plenipotentiaries of the United States of America and the Dominican Republic, providing for the assistance of the United States of America in the collection and application of the customs revenues of the Dominican Republic; and

WHEREAS the Government of the United States of America and the Government of the Dominican Republic have performed their obligations under the said Convention of 1924 in a manner satisfactory to both parties; and

WHEREAS the Government of the United States of America and the Government of the Dominican Republic are both desirous of modifying the said Convention to the advantage of both parties and at the same time safeguarding the rights of the holders of the bonds of the issues of 1922 and 1926;

The President of the United States of America, represented by Cordell Hull, Secretary of State of the United States of America, and

The President of the Dominican Republic, represented by Generalissimo Rafael Leonidas Trujillo Molina, Benefactor of the Country, Ambassador Extraordinary on Special Mission,

Who, having communicated to each other their respective full powers, found to be in good and due form, have agreed upon the following Articles:

ARTICLE 1

The Government of the Dominican Republic shall collect through its appropriate national officials the customs revenues of the Dominican Republic and all revenues pertaining to the customs duties. The General Receivership of the Dominican Customs provided for in the Convention of December 27, 1924, shall cease to operate on the day on which the Dominican Government undertakes the collection of customs revenues.

All property and funds of the General Receivership shall be turned over on that day to the Government of the Dominican Republic.

No claim shall be advanced by either Government against the other on account of any act of the General Receivership.

ARTICLE 2

The Government of the United States of America and the Government of the Dominican Republic, in common accord, shall designate a Bank, with establishment in the Dominican Republic, as sole depository of all revenues and public funds of whatsoever nature of the Dominican Government. They likewise shall designate, by common accord, an official who shall act in the said Bank as representative of the holders of the bonds of the external debt of 1922 and 1926, in all matters that concern the service of the said external debt. If at any time the Bank so designated ceases for any reason to function in this capacity or if either Government shall deem a change advisable, a successor shall be designated under the procedure stipulated above. If the representative of the holders of the bonds of the external debt of 1922 and 1926 shall, for any reason, be unable to continue in that capacity, or if either Government shall deem a change advisable, his successor shall be designated in accordance with the same procedure established for the original designation. In the event that it should become necessary to designate a successor to either the Bank or the official representing the holders of the bonds of the external debt of 1922 and 1926, and in the further event that the two Governments should be unable to reach mutual accord on such designation within a period of three months, the Foreign Bondholders Protective Council, Incorporated, shall be requested to nominate said successor, and in the event of its failure to make such nomination the President or a Vice President of the American Bankers Association, or his duly authorized representative, shall be requested to make the nomination; provided, however, that neither a Bank nor a person previously rejected by either Government may be so nominated. In the event that a Bank or person is nominated in accordance with this procedure, the two Governments shall designate such nominee.

The official representing the holders of the bonds of the external debt of 1922 and 1926 shall, with the approval of the two Governments, designate a deputy to serve in his stead in the event of his temporary absence or incapacity.

ARTICLE 3

During the first ten days of each calendar month the representative of the holders of the bonds of the external debt of 1922 and 1926 or his deputy shall receive, by endorsement and orders of payment which shall be issued to the Depository Bank by the Dominican Government through the intermediary of the Secretary of State for Treasury and Commerce, the sum necessary to cover monthly payments as follows:

(1) the payment of one-twelfth of the annual interest charges of all of the outstanding bonds of the external debt of 1922 and 1926;

(2) the payment of one-twelfth of the annual amounts designated for the amortization of the said bonds, including the interest of all the bonds which are or may be retained in the sinking fund. The said amortization shall be computed and effected in accordance with the loan contracts as modified by the agreement between the Dominican

Republic and the Foreign Bondholders Protective Council, Incorporated, concluded on August 16, 1934, and by the provisions of Article 5 of the present Convention;

(3) the payment of one-twelfth of the annual cost of the services rendered by the representative of the holders of the bonds of the external debt of 1922 and 1926, or his deputy, who shall receive salaries which are the subject of an exchange of notes attached hereto, which shall be given full force and effect as integral parts of this Convention, and a reasonable amount for expenses incurred in the performance of their duties, and the payment of one-twelfth of the annual amount agreed upon between the Dominican Government and the Depository Bank as the compensation for the services of the said Bank.

No disbursements of funds of the Dominican Government shall be made by the Depository Bank until the payments provided for in this Article shall have been made.

The sums received by the above-mentioned representative for the service of the bonds shall be immediately transmitted by him to the Fiscal Agent or Agents of the loans.

ARTICLE 4

The Government of the Dominican Republic declares that the interest and amortization service of the bonds of the external debt of 1922 and 1926 as well as the payments stipulated in the third numbered paragraph of Article 3 of the present Convention, constitute an irrevocable first lien upon all of its revenues of whatsoever nature.

ARTICLE 5

In case the total collections from all the revenues of whatsoever nature of the Dominican Government should in any calendar year exceed twelve million five hundred thousand dollars ($12,500,000) there shall be applied to the sinking fund for the redemption of bonds of the external debt of 1922 and 1926 which may be outstanding, ten percent (10%) of the excess above twelve million five hundred thousand dollars ($12,500,000) but less than thirteen million five hundred thousand dollars ($13,500,000), and in addition five percent (5%) of all sums exceeding thirteen million five hundred thousand dollars ($13,-500,000).

ARTICLE 6

The representative of the holders of the bonds of the external debt of 1922 and 1926 shall have complete access to all records and books of the Depository Bank relating to the public revenues.

The Secretary of State for Treasury and Commerce of the Dominican Government shall supply monthly to the representative of the holders of the bonds of the loans of 1922 and 1926 complete and detailed reports, duly certified, of all the revenues and disbursements and other fiscal operations of the Dominican Government.

ARTICLE 7

The system of deposit of all revenues of the Dominican Republic shall be carried out in accordance with the Dominican laws of accounting and of the Treasury now governing such matters, and these laws as well as the powers conferred by this Convention upon the representative of the holders of the bonds of the loans of 1922 and 1926, shall not be modified by the Dominican Government during the life of this Convention without the previous consent of both Governments.

ARTICLE 8

Any controversy which may arise between the Government of the United States of America and the Government of the Dominican Republic in relation to the execution of the provisions of the present Convention shall, if possible, be settled through diplomatic channels. Upon notification by either the Government of the United States of America or the Government of the Dominican Republic that, in its opinion, possibilities of settlement by this means have been exhausted, such controversies shall be settled in accordance with the procedure stipulated in the Inter-American Arbitration Convention signed at Washington, January 5, 1929, notwithstanding the provisions of Article 2 (a) thereof.

ARTICLE 9

The Convention signed by the United States of America and the Dominican Republic on December 27, 1924, shall cease to have effect, and the present Convention shall enter into force upon the exchange of ratifications which shall take place in the City of Washington within thirty days following ratification by the Government which ratifies the later in point of time; provided, however, that Articles 1, 2, and 5 of the said Convention of December 27, 1924 shall continue in full force and effect until the two Governments agree that there have been adopted and put into operation all the measures necessary for the execution of the present Convention.

The present Convention shall continue in full force and effect during the existence of the outstanding external bonds of 1922 and 1926. After the redemption or cancellation of the said bonds, the provisions of this Convention shall automatically cease to have effect.

IN WITNESS WHEREOF the respective Plenipotentiaries have signed the present Convention in duplicate in the English and Spanish languages, both texts being equally authoritative, and have hereunto affixed their seals.

Done in the City of Washington this twenty-fourth day of September, 1940.

[SEAL]   CORDELL HULL

[SEAL]   RAFAEL L. TRUJILLO

Index

Dec. 23, 1903, *re* grievances of Colombia against U.S., 504-17; Hay's reply, Jan. 5, 1904, 517-33; statement by Theodore Roosevelt on, 534-40; Harding's message, March 9, 1921, 541

Panama Canal Zone, sanitation in, 90; Hay-Bunau-Varilla Convention, 900

Panama Railroad Company, 507, 511, 521, 524

Pan American Commercial Conference, Fourth, address by Hoover, 153

Pan American Commission, 724

Pan American Conference, Habana, 1928; treaty *re* rights and duties in event of civil strife, 136, 139

Pan American Conference of Arbitration and Conciliation, 151

Pan American conferences, the general, and the special dealing with specific problems, 114 f.; *see also entries under* Inter-American, *and* International, conferences

Pan American Day addresses, *see* Pan American Union

Pan American Institute of Geography and History, 147

Pan-Americanism, peace the essential basis of co-operation, 112, 114; a basic doctrine: its essence and fundamental charter, 150; basis in principles of the Farewell Address: Monroe Doctrine does not stand in way of, 398

Pan American organization, birth of, 49-58; *see also* International American Conference

Pan American Society, 140; Armour's address, Dec. 9, 1947, 268 ff.

Pan American treaty, 112; draft articles for, 100; correspondence of Wilson, Lansing, House, and Fletcher, 1915–17, 100-107

Pan American Union, 705; purposes, control, etc., 114, 722 ff.; importance as a cultural agency, 148; convention on, 150; addresses before: by Hoover, Apr. 14, 1931, 139 ff.; White, Nov. 11, 1931, 155; Roosevelt, Apr. 12, 1933, 159; Apr. 15, 1940, 202 ff.; May 27, 1941, 221 ff.; Hull, Apr. 14, 1944, 244 ff.; Acheson, Apr. 14, 1949, 293 ff.; resolution of Inter-American Conference on Problems of War and Peace on Communication addressed by Argentina, 821

Paraguay, meeting between delegates of Bolivia and, to discuss a nonaggression pact, 155 f.; Anti-War Treaty of Non-aggression and Conciliation, Oct. 10, 1933, 873-78

Paredes, Victoriano de Diego, from C. M. Conrad, Oct. 5, 1852, *re* Flores' expedition against Ecuador, 503

Pauncefote, Julian, *see* Hay-Pauncefote treaty

Payne, John Barton, 118

Peace Congress, proposed: opposing views of Blaine and Frelinghuysen, 49, 67 f., *see also* International Conference of American States, First

Peace, Taft's message to Congress, Dec. 3, 1912, *re* U.S. efforts in the promotion of, 85 ff.; Bryan's statement to U.S. diplomatic officers, July 7, 1913, *re* Wilson's peace proposal, 95; Wilson's message to Congress, Dec. 2, 1913, 99; the essential basis of Pan-American co-operation, 112, 114; Hoover's Inaugural Address, March 4, 1929, 123 ff.; efforts of the Roosevelt administration, to establish and maintain, among American republics, 1933–35, 159-247 *passim;* Hull's co-operation with proposals of Saavedra Lamas, Dec. 15, 1933, 161 ff.; address by Welles on foreign policy and, Oct. 19, 1936, 172; Hull's enumeration and discussion of principles and proposals for a comprehensive peace structure and program, 179 ff., 194 ff.; the five treaties to safeguard nations against use of force: Draft Convention Coordinating the. . . Treaties . . . , 183; why Monroe Doctrine one of the most effective instruments for, 362; U.S. efforts to promote: in Western Hemisphere, 399; in international affairs, 400; *see also* Central American Peace Conference; Inter-American Conference for the Maintenance of Peace; Inter-American Conference on Problems of War and Peace

Peace conference, 1870, Spain and allied republics, 47

Peace Conference at The Hague, *see* International Peace Conference

Pecuniary claims, treaty of arbitration for, 715; conventions on, 718, 728 ff.; recommendation of Inter-American Conference for the Maintenance of Peace, 769

Pelletier claim against Haiti resisted, 346

Pendleton, J. H., 691

Pérez Perdomo, A., to Lansing, Dec. 4, 1916, protesting military occupation of Dominican Republic, 694